ARCHIVES

OF

RUSSIA

Volume 2

Part G – Indexes

Archives of Russia is an updated and much expanded English-language version of the Russian edition published by "Arkheograficheskii tsentr" (Moscow, 1997):

ARKHIVY ROSSII:
Moskva i Sankt-Peterburg.
Spravochnik-obozrenie i bibliograficheskii ukazatel´.

Editors: Vladimir Petrovich Kozlov and Patricia Kennedy Grimsted
Compiler-in-Chief: Lada Vladimirovna Repulo

Both editions are based on the ArcheoBiblioBase data files maintained at the Federal Archival Service of Russia (Rosarkhiv).

Compilers: Patricia Kennedy Grimsted, Lada Vladimirovna Repulo, and Irina Vladimirovna Tunkina.

Technical assistants: Marianna Ivanovna Afanas´eva, Valentina Evgen´evna Antonets, Natal´ia Iur´evna Kostenko, Natal´ia Aleksandrovna Maslova, Vladimir Georgievich Zabavskii, with participation of the staff of the Rosarkhiv Division of Information and Automated Technology.

Editorial Board: Mikhail Dmitrievich Afanas´ev, Patricia Kennedy Grimsted, Vladimir Petrovich Kozlov, and Vladimir Semenovich Sobolev.

ArcheoBiblioBase Programmer: Iurii Alekseevich Liamin.

Support for the preparation of ArcheoBiblioBase was provided by:
The International Research & Exchanges Board
The National Endowment for the Humanities
The Eurasia Foundation
The International Institute for Social History (Amsterdam)
The Open Society Institute (Moscow)
The Smith-Richardson Foundation, and other sources.

Federal Archival Service of Russia (Rosarkhiv)
Historico-Archival Institute of the Russian State University for the Humanities (IAI RGGU)
State Public Historical Library of the Russian Federation (GPIB)
Archive of the Russian Academy of Sciences - St. Petersburg Branch (PFA RAN)

ARCHIVES OF RUSSIA

A Directory and Bibliographic Guide to Holdings in Moscow and St. Petersburg

English-language Edition

Edited by

Patricia Kennedy Grimsted

Compiled by Patricia Kennedy Grimsted,
Lada Vladimirovna Repulo, and Irina Vladimirovna Tunkina

With an Introduction by Vladimir Petrovich Kozlov,
Chairman of Rosarkhiv and Chief Archivist of Russia

M.E. Sharpe
Armonk, New York
London, England

Library of Congress Cataloging-in-Publication Data

Arkhivy Rossii.
    Archives of Russia : a directory and bibliographic guide to
holdings in Moscow and St. Petersburg / edited by Patricia Kennedy Grimsted [et al.].
        p. cm.
    Includes bibliographical references and index.
        Contents : v.1. Introduction–Part F—v. 2. Part G–Indexes
    ISBN 0-7656-0034-X (set, alk. paper)
    1. Archives—Russia (Federation)—Moscow—Directories.
    2. Archives—Russia (Federation)—Saint Petersburg—Directories.
    3. Russia—Archival resources—Directories.   4. Russia (Federation)—
Archival resources—Directories.
    CD1710.A76   1997
    027'.002547'31—dc21   96-47237
                                                                    CIP

Summary Table of Contents

Table of Contents
VOLUME 2

PART G

Archives and Manuscript Holdings in Libraries

Moscow

Rossiiskaia gosudarstvennaia biblioteka (RGB)
[Russian State Library]

Agency: Ministerstvo kul'tury RF (Minkul'tury Rossii)
[Ministry of Culture]

Address:	101000, Moscow, ul. Vozdvizhenka (*formerly* prosp. Kalinina), 3/5
Telephone:	202-57-90; *Fax:* (7-095) 290-60-62; 913-69-33
E-mail:	irgb@glasnet.ru; mbs@rsl.ru
Website:	(Russian): http://www.rsl.ru
Transport:	metro: Biblioteka im. Lenina, Aleksandrovskii sad, Borovitskaia, Arbatskaia
Hours:	MSa 9:00–21:00

Director: Viktor Vasil'evich Fedorov (*tel.* 222-85-51)
Deputy Director for Scientific Work: Vadim Borisovich Churbanov (*tel.* 203-78-93)
Deputy Director for International Relations: Tat'iana Viktorovna Ershova
   (*tel.* 203-77-56)
Deputy Director for Library Affairs: Nina Ivanovna Khakhaleva (*tel.* 202-78-93)
Scientific Secretary: Tat'iana Vasil'evna Vlasenko (*tel/fax* 203-77-56)

HISTORY:

Moskovskii Publichnyi muzeum i Rumiantsevskii muzeum
   [Moscow Public Museum and Rumiantsev Museum] (1862–1872)
Moskovskii Publichnyi i Rumiantsevskii muzei
   [Moscow Public and Rumiantsev Museum] (1872–1918)
Gosudarstvennyi Rumiantsevskii muzei i biblioteka
   [Rumiantsev State Museum and Library] (1918–1921)
Gosudarstvennaia Rumiantsevskaia biblioteka
   [Rumiantsev State Library] (1921–1924)
Vserossiiskaia publichnaia biblioteka
   [All-Russian Public Library] (1924–1925)
Publichnaia biblioteka im. V. I. Lenina
   [V. I. Lenin Public Library] (1925–1945)
Gosudarstvennaia biblioteka SSSR im. V. I. Lenina (GBL)
   [V. I. Lenin State Library] (1945–1992)

The library, together with its manuscript holdings, was founded in 1862 as part of the Moscow Public and Rumiantsev Museum, on the basis of the large library, manuscript collection, and family archive (starting with the 17th c.) of Nikolai Petrovich Rumiantsev, which was left to the public on his death in 1826. Initially set up in St. Petersburg as the Rumiantsev Museum, it was transferred to Moscow in 1862 and installed in the imposing late eighteenth-century Pashkov Palace (*Dom Pashkóva*) facing the Kremlin. The library and manuscript holdings were expanded in the course of the late nineteenth century to become one of the largest and most prestigious collections in prerevolutionary Russia.

During its first half-century it acquired many important collections of manuscript books and significant institutional and personal archives. Among the notable manuscript collections were those of the bibliographer and archivist V. M. Undol'skii (1,350 manuscripts); the Slavicists F. F.

669

Bol'shakov, V. I. Grigorovich, and N. S. Tikhonravov; the specialist on the Church Schism (*Raskol*) and Old Believers, N. I. Popov, and the traveller and Oriental specialist P. I. Sevast'ianov, to name only a few. It also acquired extensive collections from other parts of the Russian Empire, including the rich collections of I. Ia. Lukashevich and M. A. Markevych (N. A. Markevich) from what is now Ukraine.

Nationalized in 1918, the library was reorganized as the State Rumiantsev Museum and Library, and in 1921 it was officially named the State Rumiantsev Library. After the Rumiantsev Museum was made independent, the library came under the control of the People's Commissariat of Education and in 1924 was renamed the Lenin Public Library.

After the Revolution, the library was significantly enriched by the accession of nationalized collections from religious institutions and private organizations. It also started acquiring major family and estate papers from prerevolutionary gentry families, along with additional important manuscript collections, as well as literary and other archives. The library also received many important literary archives from the State Historical Museum, as well as other archival materials from various liquidated institutions and organizations. Already in 1919, the rich library and manuscript collections of the Moscow Theological Academy (*Moskovskaia Dukhovnaia Akademiia*—MDA), then held in the Holy Trinity-St. Sergius Monastery (*Sviato-Troitse-Sergieva Lavra*) in Sergiev-Posad were organized as the Sergiev Branch of the Library, which remained active there for the next ten years (it was finally liquidated in 1937). First amalgamated with the library holdings after the closing of the Rumiantsev Museum in 1924, the manuscript collections and archival holdings were then reorganized as the separate Division of Manuscripts. When the large new building was completed for the library, the Manuscript Division remained in the Pashkov Palace. The Museum of the Book was founded in 1918, and subsequently became the separate Division of Rare Books.

Several other branches and subsidiary museums were organized during the 1920s. A subordinate Literary Museum was organized in 1921 as a gathering depository for many of the collected literary archival materials and memorabilia that had been nationalized after the Revolution, or otherwise acquired or donated to the library. In 1925, the L. N. Tolstoi Cabinet (*Kabinet L. N. Tolstogo*) was organized as a subsidiary museum, as was the A. P. Chekhov Museum, which had already been established in Moscow in 1921, along with a separate Chekhov Museum in the Crimea, and the F. M. Dostoevskii Museum (*Muzei F. M. Dostoevskogo*). In 1934 the Literary Museum became part of the newly formed separate State Literary Museum (see H–33), and the other three literary memorial museums became branches of that museum.

Following the Nazi invasion in the summer of 1941, some of the most valuable library holdings, including manuscript and rare book collections, were evacuated to the East—some by barge, first to Gor'kii (now Nizhnii Novgorod) and then to Perm. A branch was established in Perm during the wartime years, although the library itself continued to function in Moscow. In 1945 the library was given the official name of the Lenin State Library.

In the aftermath of World War II, the library's collections, including the Division of Manuscripts, were significantly enriched by a large number of "trophy" books and manuscripts brought to Moscow from Germany and Eastern Europe, most of which were put in the "special collection" (*spetskhran*), which was opened to the public only in 1992. The extensive manuscript materials received from Dresden were subsequently returned to East Germany in the late 1950s. Many of the "trophy" archival materials that came with the book collections, such as the records of the Turgenev Library in Paris were subsequently transferred to central state archives under the NKVD/MVD, and most of the transferred archival collections ended up in what is now GA RF. The extent of trophy manuscript books and archival materials acquired by the Manuscript Division has yet to be documented.

The Archive was separated from the administrative department in 1932, when a government resolution gave the library the right to the permanent retention of its own records.

670

In addition to the separate divisions listed below, the library has a large collection of *samizdat* and independent press from the pre-1992 period.

The library was reorganized and renamed the Russian State Library in 1992, and at the same time it was added to the register of the most valuable monuments of the cultural heritage of the peoples of the Russian Federation. During the recent decade, the library has been in the process of major building renovation and modernization, but funding has been seriously inadequate. In the fall of 1994, for example, renovation was halted completely, while the library was trying to raise money to continue, but by 1997, the exterior renovation of the Pashkov Palace was completed. As of 1998, funding still remains indefinite, while modernization and computerization move slowly.

Access: A passport and visa-size photograph are required to obtain a reader's ticket to the library, which also entitles researchers to work in the Division of Rare Books (Museum of the Book) and most other divisions of the library. For access to materials in the Division of Manuscripts and the Archive, an official letter stating the subject and purpose of research should be addressed to the division head or to the RGB director, who will in turn provide the appropriate endorsement.

Working Conditions: Total reconstruction of the Pashkov Palace (started in the 1980s) and major renovation of other parts of the library complex have forced several divisions into temporary quarters with some curtailment of facilities. Budget deficiences have further affected library services and acquisition possibilities. When the renovation is completed, plans call for the entire Division of Manuscripts and the RGB Archive to be returned to their former location in the Pashkov House.

Library Facilities: See the RGB website for additional information. See also PKG *Handbook* (1989), Chapter 7 for information about other bibliographies and collections in RGB.

Otdel rukopisei (OR)
[Division of Manuscripts]

Telephone: 222-03-58; *RdngRm:* 222-83-38; Branch (Korpus T): 222-85-10
Hours: M–Th 10:00–16:00; (Korpus T): TuW 10:00–16:00
Head: Viktor Fedorovich Molchanov (*tel.* 202-98-47)
Deputy Head: Nikolai Nikolaevich Pavlikov

HOLDINGS: 834 (40 fonds unarranged) fonds, 478,594 units, 6th–20th cc.
Slavic-Cyrillic MS collections—91 fonds; Western MS collections—3 fonds;
Oriental MS collections—10 fonds; institutional and society fonds—46 fonds;
personal papers—529 fonds; family and estate papers —50 fonds;
collections of Russian historical and literary documents—18 fonds;
collection of graphic materials—1 fond

The Division of Manuscripts, like the library itself, owes its beginnings to the large collection of early Russian and Slavic manuscripts accumulated in the late eighteenth and early nineteenth centuries by N. P. Rumiantsev. The division now contains a vast number of collections of manuscript books, literary and other manuscripts; personal, family and estate archives; and records from a number of state institutions and public organizations; as well as iconographic material on Russian history and culture.

The collections of manuscript books in the early Slavonic tradition represent one of the most important components of the Manuscript Division, with more than 100 collections acquired both from official sources and from private individuals. Largest and most valuable is what is known as the Museum Collection (*Muzeinoe sobranie*) (fond no. 178), consisting of acquisitions brought together between 1862 and 1947 by the Rumiantsev Museum and the Manuscript Division itself. These include copies of early Russian, Ukrainian, and other chronicles dating back to the twelfth century, as well as annals, legends, tales, cosmographies, and descriptions of guberniias, uezds, cities, towns, and monasteries. Among its special riches, this collection has the Glagolitic eleventh-century Codex Marianus of the Gospels from Mount Athos (*Mariinskoe Evangelie*) and the Archangel Gospel (*Arkhangel'skoe Evangelie*) of 1092—one of the oldest dated Early Rus' manuscripts. The Museum Collection also includes numerous memoirs, diaries, and biographical materials, educational and medical literature from Early Rus', and music manuscripts with early non-linear, neumatic notation.

Individual accessions made after 1947 were put into a special fond known as the Manuscript Division Collection (*Sobranie Otdela rukopisei*) (fond 218). Individual accessions of manuscripts in the early Slavonic tradition (mostly pre–nineteenth-century) received after 1977 comprise the "Collection of Early Books of the Old Tradition" (*Sobranie knig drevnikh i drevnei traditsii*) (fond 722).

The division also holds collections of Slavonic-Rus' manuscript books acquired from church institutions, including monasteries and ecclesiastical academies, and from private collectors. The most important of these acquisitions include collections from the library and archives of the Trinity-St. Sergius (*Troitse-Sergiev*) Monastery, the Joseph of Volokolamsk (*Iosifo-Volokolamskii*) Monastery, the Vvedenskaia Opta Hermitage (*Vvedenskaia Optina pustyn'*), the Moscow Theological Academy (MDA), and part of the collection from the Moscow Eparchial Library (*Moskovskaia eparkhial'naia biblioteka*).

Private manuscript collections acquired by the library include those of V. I. Grigorovich, N. S. Tikhonravov, V. M. Undol'skii, E. E. Egorov, I. Ia. Lukashevich, and M. A. Markevych. Several important local collections of early manuscripts came from oblast libraries in Arkhangel'sk, Kostroma, and Vologda, and from the Crimean (Simferopol) Pedagogical Institute.

A number of collections represent Old Believer traditions. Of particular interest, the collection of the Rogozhskoe Cemetery Community represents mainly the Belokrinitsa faction; the manuscript book collection from the merchant E. E. Egorov once belonged to the Preobrazhenie (Transfiguration) Community; the archive of the Mel'nikov family Old Believer activities (documents from 1850–1915) includes materials relating to the Moscow Old Believer Congress of 1905–1906; and a large collection of manuscripts from the Old Believer merchant P. A. Ovchinnikov includes the earliest copy of the seventeenth-century map of Russia known as *Kniga Bol'shomu chertezhu*, the original of which no longer exists.

The division has significant collections of manuscript books in Greek and Latin and other Western European languages. The collection of Greek manuscripts contains the earliest written text to be found in the Manuscript Division, namely a fragment from a sixth-century Greek Books of the Apostles. Among the early Latin manuscripts from Western Europe is the text "Jewish Antiquities" of Josephus Flavius and the Mass for St. Willigis, Archbishop of Mainz (12th c.).

Manuscript collections in Oriental languages includes manuscripts in Chinese, Arabic, Persian, Turkic, and ancient Hebrew languages. The collection of the Sinologist K. A. Skachkov includes Chinese xylographs (wood engravings) and manuscripts which date back to the Ming Dynasty, as well as albums of drawings, maps, and historical and geographical descriptions. The world-famous Hebraic collection of the Orientalist Baron D. G. Gintsburg (Günzburg), accumulated before the Revolution, contains close to 2,000 texts (9th-18th cc.). There are some inscribed books from the former Hassidic Community in Liubavichi (now in Smolensk Oblast), headed by the Rabbi Schneersohn. Among "trophy" receipts not yet publicly described are an estimated 300 Hebrew manuscripts from various European Jewish communities.

The Manuscript Division retains a number of rich separate fonds from several state institutions, such as the Trading Quarter of Prince Shuiskii (*Shuiskii posad*), the Law Codification Commission (*Komissiia ob ulozhenii*) of Catherine the Great (1767), the Library of the General Staff, and the Moscow Ecclesiastical Censorship Committee (*Moskovskii komitet dukhovnoi tsenzury*); from social organizations and editorial offices, such as those of the journals *Russkaia mysl'* (Russian Thought—

1880–1918) and *Russkoe slovo* (Russian Word—1894–1918), which was published by I. D. Sytin. There are also the fonds of a number of Russian academic societies, such as the Society for Russian History and Antiquities (*Obshchestvo istorii i drevnostei rossiiskikh*), the Society of Friends of Russian Philology (*Obshchestvo liubitelei rossiiskoi slovesnosti*), the Society of Russian Doctors (*Obshchestvo russkikh vrachei*), the Society for Early Russian Art (*Obshchestvo drevnerusskogo iskusstva*), and the Society of Friends of Spiritual Enlightenment (*Obshchestvo liubitelei dukhovnogo prosveshcheniia*).

There are several collections of Masonic manuscripts and documents (some written in German and French) from Masonic lodges in Russia. These include materials of V. S. Arsen'ev and D. I. Popov, the high-ranking government official S. S. Lanskoi, and the historian S. V. Eshevskii.

The division has family and estate archives from a number of high-ranking Russian gentry—the Apraksin, Bariatinskii, Kamenskii, Korsakov, Orlov-Davydov, Rumiantsev, Samarin, Sheremetev, Venevitinov, and Vorontsov-Dashkov families. There are also family archives of several industrial dynasties, such as the Chizhov and the Riabushinskii families, and estate archives of land-owning gentry such as the Gnidin, Kublitskii, Nasonov, Pavlov, Pazukhin, Rebinder, and Volynskii families.

Personal papers of people who made themselves known in the social and revolutionary movement include major collections of papers of some of the Decembrists, and of A. I. Hertzen, N. P. Ogarev, and P. A. Kropotkin. There are papers of a number of important political and public figures of prerevolutionary Russia like A. D. Menshikov, A. N. Murav'ev, A. S. Norov, P. D. Kiselev, M. I. Kutuzov, D. A. Miliutin, K. P. Pobedonostsev, and N. P. Rumiantsev. There are personal papers of Church leaders such as Fotii (P. N. Spasskii), Leonid (L. V. Krasnopevkov), Filaret (V. M. Drozdov), Leonid (L. A. Kavelin), Nikon (N. I. Rozhdestvenskii), and Platon (P. G. Levshin); and those of famous Russian historians such as N. M. Karamzin, M. P. Pogodin, T. N. Granovskii, Ia. D. Barskov, V. O. Kliuchevskii, and S. M. Solov'ev.

The division also holds the personal papers of many important political and intellectual figures of the Soviet period—for example, V. D. Bonch-Bruevich, M. N. Liadov (*pseud. of* Mandel'shtam), and V. I. Nevskii (*pseud. of* Krivobokov). The fields of history, philology, and philosophy during the Soviet period are represented by the papers of such scholars as N. K. Gudzii, B. P. Koz'min, M. K. Liubavskii, A. Z. Manfred, B. F. Porshnev, I. N. Rozanov, P. N. Sakulin, G. G. Shpet, and B. V. Tomashevskii, among others.

Major fonds of personal papers of Russian classical literary and cultural figures include those of A. P. Chekhov, G. R. Derzhavin, F. M. Dostoevskii, N. V. Gogol', A. A. Fet (Shenshin), M. Iu. Lermontov, N. A. Nekrasov, A. N. Ostrovskii, V. V. Rozanov, I. S. Turgenev, F. I. Tiutchev, and V. A. Zhukovskii. There are also personal archives of a number of Soviet writers and poets—among them I. E. Babel', A. A. Blok, M. A. Bulgakov, K. I. Chukovskii, S. A. Esenin (Yesenin), D. A. Furmanov, A. Ia. Iashin (*pseud. of* Popov), V. V. Ivanov, V. Ia. Shishkov.

Apart from acquired fonds and collections, the Manuscript Division has itself formed several "Territorial Collections" (*territorial'nye sobraniia*), which contain manuscript books and documents of government bodies and services, monasteries and churches, families and individual persons. The most significant of these are the Gor'kii, Smolensk, Guslitsy, and the Riazan Collections.

There are important collections of autographs of world-famous people from past centuries. Of particular interest is the Museum Collection of Foreign Autographs, which includes documents of French kings and statesmen (a collection which once belonged to Thomas Münzer), of Germans who were prominent during the Reformation, of Italian revolutionaries, such as Giuseppe Mazzini; of social philosophers Jean Le Rond d'Alembert and Louis Blanc, of scientists such as Nicolaus Copernicus; and of the composers Giuseppe Verdi and Richard Wagner, to name only a few.

An extensive collection of microfilms, which were acquired from repositories abroad, includes copies of early manuscript books, as well as more recent manuscripts and archival documents—for example, from the archives of Goethe and Schiller in Weimar, and from the archive of the historian Theodor Mommsen.

Working Conditions: Reconstruction of the library building has forced the Division of Manuscripts to move to temporary quarters and temporarily reduced the number of places available in the reading room. At present there are two reading rooms: one for archival materials on the third floor of the main library building (room 312), and second for early manuscript books (korpus "T"—entrance behind the Pashkov Palace), the latter with considerably reduced hours and space for readers.

Reference Facilities: There is no comprehensive guide to the holdings of the Division of Manuscripts. The extensive reference system of the division as of 1962 was first described in an article by G. I. Dovgallo (g-1.1).

For the early Slavonic-Rus' manuscript books, only the first three volumes of the planned six-volume directory (g-2) have been published (1983–1996). Earlier printed catalogues or manuscript descriptions have been prepared for many of the earlier integral collections. Typewritten descriptions of the most important collections of manuscript books supplement published reference literature. Many of the collections are still found as originally described, but some of them have been reorganized and renumerated on acquisition. There is a chronological catalogue listing manuscripts by date from the sixteenth through the twentieth century. There are separate card catalogues covering titles and incipits (Russian and foreign), and several auxiliary catalogues, but these do not cover all of the collections.

For archival materials in the division, there are card catalogues listing all fonds. More detailed card catalogues, covering approximately two-thirds of the archival fonds, include an alphabetic catalogue of personal names (Russian and foreign) for authors of manuscripts and authors and recipients of letters, a composite catalogue of personal names (including reference within texts and letters), and a subject catalogue. The alphabetic catalogues of titles and incipits, in addition to manuscript books of the early Slavonic-Rus' tradition, also cover literary, historical, and other types of more recent manuscripts. There is also a special catalogue of genealogical tables.

There are inventory books which cover some of the collections and archival fonds.

In 1992 a computerized catalogue was established for the Gintsburg Collection of Hebraic manuscripts in a cooperative project with the Jewish National and University Library (Jerusalem) (see a-243.1). Work is currently underway to establish computerized description of all manuscript books in the division.

Library Facilities: The Division of Manuscripts has its own separate reference library (*podsobnaia biblioteka*), a large part on open shelves, apart from the main library holdings and special reference facilities of the Central Reference Library (*Tsentral'naia spravochnaia biblioteka—TsSB*), which are open to the public in the main building. During the renovation period, parts of the division's separate reference library are not accessible to researchers. Earlier, when the Manuscript Division was housed in the Pashkov Palace, researchers could order books to the division from the main library, and presumably that system will be reinstated when the division returns to its earlier home.

Copying: Xerox and photographic copies, microfilms, and microfiche may be obtained in accordance with printed library regulations.

Nauchno-issledovatel'skii otdel redkikh knig (Muzei knigi)
[Scientific Research Division of Rare Books (Museum of the Book)]

Telephone: 222-85-30; 222-86-71; *RdngRm:* 222-86-79
Website: (Museum of the Book)
http://moscow.lvl.ru/culture/museum/knigi/knigi.html
Hours: MF 9:00–17:00; W 12:00–20:00;
Museum of the Book: M–F 10:00–17:00
Head: Aleksandra Alekseevna Guseva (*tel.* 222-86-66)

HOLDINGS: ca. 8,000 units, 15th–20th cc.
autographs—ca. 8,000 units

The Division of Rare Books has a number of materials that should be considered of archival importance. Most particularly there are books with dedicatory autographs, inscriptions and marginal notations made not only by prominent public figures, scientists, scholars and writers, but also by unknown persons. Many of these entries have historical importance in relation to the history of the book—for example, an entry recording the date of acquisition and price paid for a particular book. There are also copies of special numbered editions and publications that have been specially inscribed, presented, or hand-painted by artists.

Working Conditions: There is a special division reading room. Rare editions that are held under special conditions of storage may only be examined with the permission of the division head, but copies can be viewed on microfilm.

Reference Facilities: The division holdings are included in the general and subject RGB catalogues with the special notation "MK" (*Muzei knigi*). There are also separate catalogues in the division itself—alphabetical catalogues of Russian/Soviet and foreign publications and a thematic card catalogue of books with dedicatory autographs. There is also an electronic catalogue of autographed books. Work is currently underway to produce an electronic catalogue with graphic reproductions of autographs.

Copying: Bona fide researchers may order copies of documents, but xerox copies and microfilms are not permitted from particularly valuable publications (such as those with miniatures and ornamentation or folio editions). Photographic and videotape reproductions in the reading room may be produced only with the permission of the division head on the basis of an official letter from the reader's sponsoring institution stating the purpose and intended use of the copies to be made.

Otdel izoizdanii
[Division of Graphic Imprints]

Telephone: 222-84-35
Hours: MW 10:00–18:00; TuThF 10:00–17:00; Sa 11:00–17:00
Head: Svetlana Nikolaevna Artamonova (*tel.* 222-86-02)

HOLDINGS: 1,400,000 units, 16th–to present

photographs—38,174 units (mid-19th c.–1960s); posters—372,442 units (1863–1986); leaflets—9,663 units (17th c.–1923); *lubok*—33,797 units (17th–early 20th cc.); engravings—87,224 units (16th c.–1980s)

The Division of Graphic Imprints retains printed productions issued from the sixteenth century to the present. These include posters, prints, brochures, reproductions, engravings, popular prints (*lubok*), photographs, and other graphic materials. The holdings include the personal collections of artists, graphic artists, and photographers, including collections of engravings by A. S. Petrovskii, bookplates and book markings by S. P. Fortinskii, ex libris by S. A. Vule, book dust-covers by K. Burov, and photographs by S. Strunnikov and V. P. Grebnev.

There are also albums of eighteenth-century engravings by M. I. Makhaev and Gérard Delabart, albums of O. Kadol', A. E. Martynov, and André Durand, and a series of nineteenth-century lithographs by the Daziaro publishers. The Soviet period is represented by albums of engravings by I. N. Pavlov, M. A. Matorin, and E. B. Bernshtein.

The division has collectors' albums and photographic albums containing unique pictures of Moscow and its individual architectural complexes and buildings. Of particular interest are the albums from the collection made by E. Gauthier Dufaillet with some 500 pictures of Moscow between 1912 and 1914.

Working Conditions: Materials from the fourteenth level of the stacks are currently accessible only on Tuesdays (10:00–17:00).

Copying: Photographic facilities are available.

Arkhiv
[Archive]

Address: 103009, Moscow, ul. Mokhovaia, 16
Hours: MF 10:00–17:00
Transport: metro: Biblioteka im. Lenina, Arbatskaia, Borovitskaia,
                Aleksandrovskii sad
Head: Marina Vasil'evna Volkova (*tel.* 202-67-30)

Holdings: 1 fond, ca 53,000 units, 1862–to present (some of documents—1857)
personnel files—30,000 units; photographs—3,800 units (1879–to present); negatives—2,000 units; films—11 units

The RGB Archive (or *Otdel khraneniia i ispol'zovaniia dokumentov*) contains the official records of the library, providing rich sources for the development of culture and library affairs in Russia and the Soviet Union.

There are documents preserved regarding the work of the Rumiantsev Museum and library in the prerevolutionary period. These include decrees on the organization of the museum, the Statute and Charter (*Polozhenie i Ustav*) of 1869, official documents from the Ministry of Education (*Ministerstvo prosveshcheniia*), internal regulations for readers, and reports on the holdings. There are also newspaper clippings on the work of the Rumiantsev Museum and its library covering the years 1867 to 1883 from a collection made by N. Iu. Ul'ianinskii.

Documentation for the postrevolutionary period relates to the various administrative bodies in the library (the Director's Office, the Secretariat, the Academic Council) and their correspondence with higher agencies such as the Ministry of Culture, and with readers. There are copies of the library staff announcements and wall newspapers starting from the 1920s.

The archive also contains documents from a number of academic societies, organizations, and institutions that at one time or another were attached to the library. These include the Association of Scientific Libraries (*Assotsiatsiia nauchnykh bibliotek*) (1928–1937), the Russian Library for People's Education (*Rossiiskaia biblioteka po narodnomu obrazovaniiu*) (1923–1927), the Institute of Library Science (*Institut bibliotekovedeniia*) (1930–, now the Moscow State University of Culture [*Moskovskii gosudarstvennyi universitet kul'tury*]), the Literary Museum (*Literaturnyi muzei*) (1921–1931), the F. M. Dostoevskii Museum (1925–1938), the Chekhov Museums in Yalta and in Moscow (1923–1936), and the Tiutchev Estate-Museum in Muranovo. On the whole these files consist of correspondence, descriptions of exhibitions, and various legal documents.

There are photographs and negatives held in the archive showing the work of the library since its organization and featuring individual items from the holdings. The earliest photographs of the Rumiantsev Museum (1879–1880) are to be found in an album by the photographer Mitreiter.

The archives has 35 mm. films on the history and work of the library at various periods.

N.B. Records of the various divisions of the former Rumiantsev Museum (pictorial materials, graphics, etc.) have been dispersed among several different library divisions and other repositories, since they were transferred together with the collections.

Working Conditions: The Archive has recently moved into the building across Mokhovaia from the main library building (Korpus "K"). Researchers work in the storage areas since there is no special reading room.

Reference Facilities: There are inventories, a card catalogue of personnel files, and a subject catalogue with auxiliary card catalogues.

Library Facilities: There is a reference library, which is open to researchers.

Copying: Photographic and xerox copies can be prepared, as well as microfilms. Copying is done at the RGB laboratory, on the basis of special application to the Scientific Secretary.

FINDING AIDS — PUBLISHED — GENERAL:

Biblioteki: Putevoditel' (1996), pp. 19–26; *Lit. arkhivy* (1996), pp. 20–21, 29–32; *GAF Spravochnik* (1991), pp. 8–14; PKG *M&L* (1972), pp. 263–74; Sup. 1 (1976), pp. 87–100; G&K *Spravochnik* (1983), pp. 118–38 and 381–86.

There is no general guide or published description of the archival materials in the various divisions of the library.

For a more complete description and bibliography of related literature about the Rare Book Division, see *Fondy red. izd.* (1991), pp. 10–20.

Division of Manuscripts

The first volume of a guide to the archival materials in the Manuscript Division is being prepared for publication.

General Surveys and Bibliography

g-1. Safronova, Galina Fedorovna. "Fondy i deiatel'nost' Otdela rukopisei Gosudarstvennoi biblioteki SSSR im. V. I. Lenina: Bibliografiia 1836–1962." *Zapiski OR* 25 (1962): 487– 520. (Lib: DLC; IU; MH) [IDC-in R-10,287]

> Provides an alphabetical index for the collections of early manuscript books (pp. 513–15) and for the archival fonds (pp. 515–19), with reference to current fond numbers and bibliographic information on published descriptions of individual fonds and collections. Gives a bibliographic survey of reference and other literature on the Manuscript Division. Includes analysis of *Zapiski OR* from 1938 to 1961. Unfortunately this survey has not been superseded, although the information provided is obviously outdated.

g-1.1. Dovgallo, Galina Ivanovna. "Spravochnyi apparat Otdela rukopisei." *Zapiski OR* 25 (1962): 464–86. (Lib: DLC; IU; MH) [IDC-in R-10,287]

Early Slavonic-Rus' Manuscript Collections

g-2. *Rukopisnye sobraniia Gosudarstvennoi biblioteki SSSR im. V. I. Lenina: Ukazatel'.* Edited by L. V. Tiganova, N. B. Tikhomirov, Iu. D. Rykov, et al. Moscow, 1983–. [GBL] (Lib: DDO; DLC; IU; MH)

> Vol. 1, pt. 1: *(1862–1916).* M., 1983. 254 p.; pt. 2: *(1917–1947).* M., 1986. 381 p.; pt. 3: *(1948–1979).* M., 1996. 511 p.

> > The first part of volume 1 contains brief information on the collections of early Slavonic and Rus' manuscripts acquired by the Rumiantsev Public Museum and subsequently the Manuscript Division between 1862 and 1979. The second part of volume 1 contains historical information on the collections of manuscript books accessioned between 1917 and 1947, while the third part covers collections accessioned from 1948 through 1979. In all cases, data are provided on the history of the collections, their creating agencies, and the general content and present arrangement of the collections themselves. Provides full bibliography of surveys, earlier catalogues, and manuscript descriptions and related reference or scholarly literature. Three further volumes of the directory are planned for publication together with auxiliary reference apparatus to volume 1.

Archival Materials

g-3. *Kratkii ukazatel' arkhivnykh fondov Otdela rukopisei.* Compiled by E. N. Konshina and N. K. Shvabe. Edited by P. A. Zaionchkovskii and E. N. Konshina. Moscow: GBL, 1948. 253 p. (Lib: DLC; IU; MH) [IDC-R-11,007]

> Includes information on the fonds accessioned up to the year 1945, arranged alphabetically according to the creating agency. Since the Index used the old system of alphabetical cataloging, there is no information on the fond numbers which are currently in use.

g-4. *Vospominaniia i dnevniki XVIII–XX vv.: Ukazatel' rukopisei.* Edited by
S. V. Zhitomirskaia. Moscow: "Kniga," 1976. 621 p. (Lib: DLC; IU; MH)
> The directory covers memoir sources from the eighteenth to the twentieth centuries, including the Soviet period, with auxiliary indexes. See also the earlier 1951 guide (g-5). A new index of the manuscript fonds, which were not included in previous editions (g-4 and g-5), is being prepared for publication.

g-5. *Ukazatel' vospominanii, dnevnikov i putevykh zapisok XVIII–XIX vv. (iz fondov Otdela rukopisei).* Compiled by S. V. Zhitomirskaia et al. Edited by P. A. Zaionchkovskii and E. N. Konshina. Moscow: GBL, 1951. 224 p. (Lib: DLC; IU; MH) [IDC-R-11,008]
> There is a copy of this guide with corrections in the reading room of the Manuscript Division. See also the corrected and supplemented edition (g-4).

g-6. Zhitomirskaia, Sarra Vladimirovna. "Zapadnoe srednevekov'e v rukopisiakh Gosudarstvennoi biblioteki SSSR im. V. I. Lenina." *Srednie veka* 10 (1957): 285–305. (Lib: DLC; IU; MH)

Manuscript Division Serial

g-7. *Zapiski Otdela rukopisei [GBL]. (Zapiski OR)* Moscow, 1938–. 50 vols. through 1995. Irregular. [GBL] (Lib: DLC; IU; MH) [IDC-R-10,287(v.1-36)]
> Individual volumes contain surveys of manuscript collections and archival materials held by the division, as well as documentary publications. An analysis of contents of previous volumes through 1962 is included in the article by Safronova (g-1).

GBL and Earlier Manuscript Division Serials

g-8. *Trudy Publichnoi biblioteki SSSR im. V. I. Lenina.* 4 vols. Moscow, 1928–1939. [GBL] (Lib: DLC; IU; MH) [IDC-R-11,044]
> INDEX: Articles in this series relating to the MS Division, are listed in g-1.
>> Before publication of the series *Zapiski Otdela rukopisei* (from 1939—see g-7), this series contained some descriptions of the manuscripts and information on the publications of the Manuscript Division. The postwar continuation of the series predominantly covers other divisions of the library.

g-9. *Trudy Gosudarstvennogo Rumiantsevskogo muzeia.* 5 vols. Moscow/Petrograd, 1923–1924. (Lib: IU; MH) [IDC-R-11,042]
> This series predominantly consists of publications of literary manuscripts and correspondence then held by the Rumiantsev Museum, including Pushkin's diary and the correspondence of K. P. Pobedonostsev and V. O. Kliuchevskii.

g-10. *Otchet Moskovskogo Publichnogo i Rumiantsevskogo muzeev za 1864 god–[—. . . za 1915 god].* St. Petersburg/Moscow, 1864–1917. 34 vols. Irregular. Titles vary. (Lib: IU; MH) [IDC-R-11,043]
> "Otchet Rumiantsevskogo muzeia za 1916–1922 gg." 173 p. Typescript.
> INDEX: For a survey of the contents, see g-1.
>> The first two issues (through 1865) were published in St. Petersburg. From 1870 to 1894 volumes came out three times a year; from 1895 to 1915 it was published annually. The volumes contain lengthy descriptions of the manuscript holdings, and in some cases catalogues and published texts. The last issue, covering the years 1916–1922, preserved only in typescript form, lists manuscript receipts for those years.

History of RGB/ GBL

g-11. *Istoriia Gosudarstvennoi Ordena Lenina biblioteki SSSR im. V. I. Lenina za 100 let, 1862–1962.* Edited by F. S. Abrikosova, K. R. Kamenetskaia, and E. V. Seglin. Moscow: Izd. "Biblioteki Moskvy," 1962. 279 p. (Lib: DLC; IU; MH)

This jubilee edition contains an exceptionally helpful chapter devoted to the Manuscript Division by V. G. Zimina, "Otdel rukopisei za 100 let" (pp. 246–71); footnote citations provide a basic bibliography of the division's publications, including earlier published catalogues and inventories. Coverage of the development of other library divisions is included in the general historical text.

g-12. *Piatidesiatiletie Rumiantsevskogo muzeia v Moskve, 1862–1912: Istoricheskii ocherk.* Moscow: T-vo skoropechatni A. A. Levenson, 1913. 40, xliii, 41–194 p. + plates. (Lib: MH-F) [IDC-R-11,124]

> An elaborately published anniversary folio edition with plates reproducing pages from illuminated manuscripts and title pages of early books. See the lengthy section devoted to the history of the Manuscript Division by G. P. Georgievskii, "Otdelenie rukopisei Imperatorskogo Moskovskogo i Rumiantsevskogo muzeia" (pp. 41–78), with mention of published catalogues for some of the important collections.

g-13. *Gosudarstvennyi Rumiantsevskii muzei: Putevoditel'.* 2 vols. Moscow/Petrograd, 1923. Vol. 1: *Biblioteka.* M., 1923, 237 p. [IDC-R-11,123]

> The lengthy section devoted to the Manuscript Division (pp. 159–237) surveys its prerevolutionary development, with mention of published catalogues for some of the important collections. See also the extensive list of manuscript receipts during the 1916–1922 period by G. P. Georgievskii in the final issue of the prerevolutionary series of reports (g-10) available in typescript in the manuscript division reading room.

g-14. Kozlov, Vladimir Petrovich. "K istorii komplektovaniia Rumiantsevskogo sobraniia russkikh i slavianskikh rukopisei." *Zapiski OR* 41 (1980): 4–29. (Lib: DLC; IU; MH)

> Provides a history of the original holdings of the prerevolutionary manuscript collection brought together by Nikolai Petrovich Rumiantsev (1754–1826). See also the Vostokov catalogue of this collection published while it was held in St. Petersburg (g-24).

g-15. *Golos proshlogo: Gosudarstvennaia Ordena Lenina biblioteka SSSR im. V. I. Lenina v gody Velikoi Otechestvennoi voiny.* Compiled by L. M. Koval', M. V. Volkova, L. M. Illarionova, et al. Edited by A. Ia. Cherniak. Moscow: GBL, 1991. 135 p. [GBL; Muzei knigi; Muzei istorii GBL] (Lib: DLC; MH)

> Includes an article by M. V. Volkova, "Iz Arkhiva Gosudarstvennoi biblioteki SSSR im. V. I. Lenina: Obzor materialov Arkhiva Gosudarstvennoi biblioteki SSSR im. V. I. Lenina o rabote Biblioteki v gody Velikoi Otechestvennoi voiny," pp. 89–121.

Division of Graphic Imprints

g-16. Klepikov, Sokrat Aleksandrovich. "Obzor fondov izobrazitel'nykh materialov Gosudarstvennoi biblioteki im. V. I. Lenina." *Trudy GBL* n.s. 5 (1981): 230–68. (Lib: DLC; IU; MH)

> A survey of holdings in the GBL Graphics Division.

GBL/ RGB Bibliography

g-17. *Gosudarstvennaia Ordena Lenina Biblioteka SSSR im. V. I. Lenina: Bibliograficheskii ukazatel'.* Compiled by M. A. Ermolaeva, M. E. Ekshtein, and M. S. Starshinova. Edited by T. E. Ksenzova. 2 vols. Moscow, 1986. [GBL] (Lib: DLC; MH)

> Pt. 1: *Literatura o Biblioteke (1862–1985 gg.).* 324 p.
> Pt. 2: *Izdaniia Biblioteki (1962–1985 gg.).* 190 p.
>> A comprehensive bibliography of library publications, including articles with separate rubrics devoted to reference literature and other publications regarding various divisions. Only covers publications by library staff.

FINDING AIDS — GENERAL — UNPUBLISHED:

Division of Manuscripts

g-18. "Sobraniia Otdela rukopisei (kratkie obzory)." Compiled by G. I. Dovgallo, I. M.
Kudriavtsev, and M. N. Kuz'minskaia. Moscow, 1958. 284 p. Typescript. [GBL]
> Contains brief surveys of 48 collections of Slavic manuscripts acquired up to the year 1958, with
> data regarding published catalogues, descriptions, and unpublished inventories. A large part of the
> coverage has been updated in the published directory of manuscript collections (g-2). Available in
> the reading room.

g-19. Pozdneev, A. "Rukopisnye sborniki pesen v sobraniiakh Otdela rukopisei." Moscow,
n. d. 49 p. Typescript. [GBL]
> A detailed scholarly description of 25 choral convolutes from eight collections and from the fonds of
> the Manuscript Division of the Russian State Library (including the Museum Collection and the
> Undol'skii Collection). Available in the reading room.

g-20. Zhitomirskaia, Sarra Vladimirovna. "Sobranie rukopisei na inostrannykh iazykakh."
Moscow, n. d. 50 p. Typescript.
> A survey of the collection of manuscripts in foreign languages from individual acquisitions (except
> Oriental and Greek manuscripts, which are assigned to separate collections). Available in the
> reading room.

g-21. "Kratkii ukazatel' arkhivnykh fondov Otdela rukopisei: A–Ia." Moscow, n. d. 9 folders.
> A series of xerox copies of published information on archival materials held in the division, assembled
> from various sources (but mainly from the *Zapiski OR*), arranged alphabetically, and varied in
> volume and content. Available in the reading room.

g-22. "Ukazatel' fondov lichnogo proiskhozhdeniia po vidam deiatel'nosti
fondoobrazovatelei." Moscow, n. d. 10 folders.
> A series of xerox copies of published information on personal papers held in the Manuscript
> Division. Assembled from various sources (mainly from *Zapiski OR*), and varied in volume,
> quality, and content, it is arranged according to the type of activity of the creating individual.
> Available in the reading room.

FINDING AIDS — SPECIALIZED:

A full list of specialized finding aids is not possible here. More of the pre-1976 specialized finding
aids for the Manuscript Division that have been reproduced on IDC microfiche are listed in PKG
M&L Sup. 1 (1976), pp. 87–100 and 160.

Division of Manuscripts

Slavonic-Rus' Manuscripts

Many of the prerevolutionary catalogues of early Slavonic-Rus' manuscripts in RGB have been
reproduced on IDC microfiche, as listed in PKG *M&L* Sup. 1 (1976), pp. 87–100 and 160. For
earlier bibliographic coverage see Begunov, *Sprav.-ukaz.* (1963), pp. 124–43. Only a few of the
more recent ones are listed here. Typescript catalogues for many of the individual collections are
available in the reading room. For a survey of the collection from the Rogozhskaia Old Believer
community, see g-79, vol.2.

g-23. *Muzeinoe sobranie rukopisei: Opisanie.* Edited by I. M. Kudriavtsev et al. Moscow,
1961–. [GBL] (Lib: DLC; MH)
> Vol. 1: *No. 1–3005.* M., 1961. 524 p. [IDC-R-10,340]
> Vol. 2: *No. 3006–4500.* M., 1997. 496 p. + plates.

Vol. 3: "No. 4501–6500." Typescript.
Vol. 4: "No. 6501–8461." Typescript.
Vol. 5: "No. 8462–9500." Typescript.
Vol. 6: "No. 9501–10659." Typescript.
Vol. 7: "No. 10660–11092." Typescript.

> The first two published volumes provide scholarly descriptions of Slavonic-Rus' manuscripts received by the Rumiantsev Museum and Library through 1922, arranged and numbered by year of acccession. The manuscripts described are all catalogued as part of the Museum Collection (fond 178). Note the additional volumes 3–7 that are available in typescript form in the division.

g-24. Vostokov, Aleksandr Khristoforovich. *Opisanie russkikh i slovenskikh rukopisei Rumiantsevskogo muzeuma.* St. Petersburg: V tip. Imp. Akademii nauk, 1842. iii, 899, 3 p. (Lib: DDO; MH) [IDC-R-5928]

> An initial published description of 473 predominantly early Slavonic-Rus' manuscripts and historical documentation from the original collection of Count Nikolai Petrovich Rumiantsev (1754–1826), acquired by the Rumiantsev Museum when it was still in St. Petersburg (now fond 256). See also the history of the formation of the Rumiantsev collection by V. P. Kozlov (g-14).

g-25. *Sobraniia D. V. Razumovskogo i V. F. Odoevskogo. Arkhiv A. V. Razumovskogo: Opisaniia.* Edited by I. M. Kudriavtsev. Moscow: GBL, 1960. 261 p. (Lib: DLC; MH) [IDC-R-11,004]

> A description of manuscript materials collected by the musicologists Dmitrii Vasil'evich Razumovskii (1818–1889) and Prince Vladimir Fedorovich Odoevskii (1803–1869), along with Razumovskii's own archive acquired by the Rumiantsev Museum (now fond 380).

g-26. *Sobranie I. Ia. Lukashevicha i N. A. Markevicha: Opisanie.* Compiled by Ia. N. Shchapov. Edited by I. M. Kudriavtsev. Moscow: GBL, 1959. 144 p. (Lib: DLC; MH) [IDC-R-11,005]

> A description of manuscripts collected by the gentry historian and Slavic specialist Ivan Iakolevich Lukashevich (1811–1860) and the historian and ethnographer Mykola Andriiovych Markevych (N. A. Markevih) (1804–1860) both acquired from Ukraine.

g-27. *Otkrovenie sv. Ioanna Bogoslova v mirovoi knizhnioi traditsii: Vystavka/ The Revelation of St. John the Theologian in the World Book Tradition: Exhibition.* Compiled by T. A. Dolgodrova, A. A. Guseva, T. V. Anisimova, et al. Edited by A. A. Turilov. Moscow: "Indrik," 1995. 199 p. [Posol'stvo Gretsii v Moskve; RGB]

> A scholarly catalogue describing apocryphal manuscripts and early printed books in a special exhibition, sponsored by the Greek Embassy in Moscow, centering around the Biblical Book of Revelations of St. John the Apostle. The elaborately printed catalogue gives scholarly descriptions of 13 Greek and Latin manuscripts, 63 manuscripts in the Slavonic-Rus' and Old Believer traditions, 25 incunabula and early printed books, and 12 later manuscript commentaries (18th–19th cc.). Of special interest, several especially notable German "trophy" manuscripts and early books were exhibited and described for the first time, including the 1454/1455 Gutenberg Bible acquired in 1945 from the Leipzig Museum of the Book and Printing.

Greek Manuscripts

For an updated annotated bibliography covering Greek manuscripts, see the 1995 edition of Richard (a-210). A copy of the unpublished catalogue prepared by A. P. Kazhdan is available in the Institut de recherche et l'histoire des textes in Paris.

Hebrew Manuscripts

For updated descriptive cataloguing of Hebrew manuscripts in RGB, see the electronic catalogue prepared by the Institute of Microfilmed Hebrew Manuscripts (IMHM) in Jerusalem, available on the IMHM website (a-243.1).

g-28. *Catalog of the Baron Guenzburg Collection of Hebrew Manuscripts in the Russian State Library in Moscow Based on Records in the Jewish National and University Library Online Catalog.* (Preliminary Edition) 2 vols. Jerusalem, 1997. [IMHM] (Lib: MH)
> Vol. 1: *Inventory Listing by Manuscript Number.*
> Vol. 2: *Author Index, Title Index, and Reel Concordance.*
>> A scholarly catalogue covering the collection of 1,913 manuscripts brought together in the nineteenth century by Baron David G. Gintsburg (Guenzburg or Ginzburg) and his family, on 235 reels of microfilm, prepared by the IMHM, based on the cataloguing records produced in the Jerusalem library. The present printed catalogue covers approximately three-fourths of the collection. Cataloguing of the remainder of the collection is still underway, but present plans call for availability only in electronic form (see a-243.1). Those manuscripts not yet covered are, however, included in the "Tentative Handlist" (g-29).

g-29. *Tentative Handlist of the Baron Guenzburg Collection of Manuscripts in the Russian State Library in Moscow.* Typescript. [Jerusalem: IMHM, n.d.] (Lib: MH)
>> A tentative list with authors and titles covering the collection of 1,913 manuscripts on 235 reels of microfilm, prepared by IMHM in the Jerusalem library. The first part of the handlist (nos. 1–830) is based on the brief hectographed handwritten list prepared in the late nineteenth century by Senior Sachs (Shn'eur Zaks), a copy of which (lacking title page) is available in RGB, along with a typewritten Russian version: "Opisanie sobraniia rukopisei D. Ginzburga, no. 71 (No. 1–830)" (Moscow, 1957; 255 p.). The second part (Nos. 831–1513) was never published and remains only in manuscript. See the more complete scholarly catalogue, three-quarters of which is available in print (g-28). See also the electronic version of the catalogue available on the IMHM website (a-243.1).

Chinese Manuscripts

g-30. Melnalksnis, Arnold Ivanovich. *Opisanie kitaiskikh rukopisnykh knig i kart iz sobraniia K. A. Skachkova.* Moscow: Glavnaia redaktsiia vostochnoi literatury, 1974. 278 p. (Lib: MH) [IDC-R-9814]
>> A scholarly catalogue covering 333 numbered manuscript items in the collection of Chinese manuscripts brought together by Konstantin Andreevich Skachkov (1821–1883) acquired by the Rumiantsev Museum in 1873 (now fond 274). An introduction provides details about the history of the collection. Appendices include name, title, and geographic indexes, and correlation tables for earlier numbering systems.

Archival Materials

For documentation relating to theater and music, see *Teatr i muzyka* (a-455), pp. 72–90. For coverage of Jewish-related holdings, see *Dok. ist. evreev* (1997), pp. 383–92.

g-31. *Katalog masonskikh rukopisei Moskovskogo Publichnogo i Rumiantsevskogo muzeev.* Compiled by I. D. Berdnikov. Moscow: Pechatnia A. I. Snegirevoi, 1900. 51 p. [IDC-R-9816] Originally published as a supplement to *Otchet Moskovskogo Publichnogo i Rumiantsevskogo muzeev za 1899 god* (Moscow, 1900). [in R-11,043 mf. 32-34].
>> A list of 433 miscellaneous items in the manuscript collection of the prerevolutionary Rumiantsev Museum relating to Free Masons in Russia (mostly late 18th–early 19th cc.). Includes name and subject indexes.

Personal Papers

Only separate, pre-1976 book-length publications are included below, specifically those available in special microfiche editions. Many additional pre-1976 article-length surveys and catalogues are listed in PKG *M&L* (1972), pp. 270–74, and various supplemental bibliographies. Many additional ones have been published since in subsequent volumes of *Zapiski OR GBL* and other scholarly journals. For Andrei Belyi papers, see a-128; for A. A. Blok papers, see a-129–a-130; for F. I. Buslaev papers, see a-134; for Dostoevskii papers in RGB, see a-136; for M. V. Lomonosov, see a-145. Fonds of recently-declassified personal papers of Russian émigrés are listed in *Rus. Zarubezh'e* (1998), pp. 332–39.

g-32. *Rukopisi i perepiska V. G. Belinskogo: Katalog.* Compiled by R. P. Matorina. Edited by N. L. Brodskii. Moscow: GBL, 1948. 42 p. (Lib: DLC; MH) [IDC-R-11,009]
> A catalogue of manuscripts and correspondence of the Russian writer and social critic Vissarion Grigor'evich Belinskii (1811–1848), found in RGB.

g-33. *Rukopisi A. P. Chekhova: Opisanie.* Compiled by E. E. Leitnekker. Moscow: Gos. sotsial'no-ekonomicheskoe izd-vo, 1938. 124 p. (Lib: DLC; MH) [IDC-R-11,011]
> A catalogue of manuscripts of the Russian dramatist Anton Pavlovich Chekhov (1860–1904) in RNB.

g-34. *Arkhiv A. P. Chekhova: Annotirovannoe opisanie pisem k A. P. Chekhovu.* Compiled by E. E. Leitnekker. Edited by N. L. Meshcheriakova. 2 vols. Moscow/Leningrad, 1939–1941. (Lib: DLC; MH) [IDC-R-11,010]
> Vol. 1: M.: Gos. sotsial'no-ekonomicheskoe izd-vo, 1939. 115 p.
> Vol. 2: L.: Ogiz., Gospolitizdat, 1941. 95 p.
> A catalogue of letters to the Russian dramatist Anton Pavlovich Chekhov (1860–1904), found in RGB.

g-35. *Rukopisi N. V. Gogolia: Katalog.* Compiled by A. A. Romodanovskaia and G. P. Georgievskii. Moscow: Sotsekgiz, 1940. 127 p. (Lib: DLC; MH) [IDC-R-11,012]
> A catalogue of manuscripts of the Russian writer Nikolai Vasil'evich Gogol' (1809–1852), found in RGB. A supplement appeared in *Zapiski OR GBL* 19 (1957): 37–46.

g-36. *Opisanie rukopisei A. I. Gertsena.* Compiled by A. V. Askar'iants and Z. V. Kemenova. Edited by B. P. Koz'min. 2d ed. Moscow: GBL, 1950. 159 p. (Lib: DLC) [IDC-R-10,833]
> A catalogue of manuscripts of the Russian publicist and social philosopher Aleksandr Ivanovich Herzen (Gertsen) (1812–1870), found in RGB. For the fate of the Herzen papers, especially those that were dispersed abroad, see a-137. For additional papers of Herzen received by GBL after World War II from Prague (RZIA) and Sofia, see a-138.

g-37. *Opisanie rukopisei V. G. Korolenko.* Moscow: GBL, 1950–1961. [GBL] (Lib: DLC; MH)
> [Vol. 1]: *Khudozhestvennye proizvedeniia, literaturno-kriticheskie stat'i, istoricheskie i etnograficheskie raboty, zapisnye knizhki, materialy k proizvedeniiam.* Compiled by R. P. Matorina. M., 1950. 223 p. [IDC-R-11,013]
> Vol. 2: *Opisanie pisem V. G. Korolenko.* Compiled by V. M. Fedorova. Edited by S. V. Zhitomirskaia. M., 1961. 659 p. [IDC-R-11,014].
> A catalogue of papers of the Russian writer Vladimir Galaktionovich Korolenko (1853–1921), found in his personal papers in RNB.

g-38. *Rukopisi N. A. Nekrasova: Katalog.* Compiled by R. P. Matorina. Moscow: Sotsial'no-ekonomicheskoe izd-vo, 1939. 79 p. (Lib: DLC; MH) [IDC-R-11,015]
> A catalogue of manuscripts of the Russian writer Nikolai Alekseevich Nekrasov (1821–1877) in RGB.

g-39. *Opisanie rukopisei N. P. Ogareva.* Compiled by A. V. Askar'iants. Edited by Ia. Z. Cherniak. Moscow: GBL, 1952. 206 p. (Lib: DLC; MH[mf]) [IDC-R-11,016]
> A catalogue of manuscripts of the Russian publicist and social philosopher Nikolai Platonovich Oragev (1813–1877), found in RGB. For the fate of the Ogarev papers, especially those that were dispersed abroad, see a-137.

g-40. *Rukopisi A. N. Ostrovskogo: Katalog.* Compiled by N. P. Kashin. Moscow: Gos. sotsial'no-ekonomicheskoe izd-vo, 1939. 51 p. (Lib: DLC; MH) [IDC-R-11,017]

> A catalogue of manuscripts of the Russian playwright Aleksandr Nikolaevich Ostrovskii (1823–1886) in RGB.

g-41. Matorina, Raisa Pavlovna. "Opisanie avtografov I. S. Turgeneva." In *I. S. Turgenev: Sbornik,* edited by N. L. Brodskii, pp. 171–219. Moscow, 1940. (Lib: MH) [IDC-R-10,834]

> Describes autograph manuscripts of Ivan Sergeevich Turgenev (1818–1883) held in RGB.

Division of Rare Books

g-42. *Avtografy poetov serebrianogo veka: Darstvennye nadpisi na knigakh.* Compiled by T. V. Avetisova, I. V. Gabova, E. A. Barysheva, et al. Edited by L. A. Morsina, Z. A. Pokrovskaia, and E. I. Iatsunok. Moscow: "Kniga," 1995. 496 p. (Lib: IU; MH)

> A scholarly presentation with facsimiles of close to 400 autographs of 20 poets from books held by the division.

Division of Graphic Imprints

g-43. Onopko-Baburina, Nina Ivanovna. "Russkii i sovetskii khudozhestvennyi knigotorgovyi plakat (po materialam sobraniia Gosudarstvennoi biblioteki SSSR im. V. I. Lenina)." In *Kniga: Issledovaniia i materialy,* pp. 49–92. M., 1960. (Lib: DLC; IU; MH)

g-44. *Graviury i kollektsii A. S. Petrovskogo: Katalog.* Compiled by E. I. Kuzishchina. Moscow, 1980. 116 p.

> A scholarly description of the A. S. Petrovskii collection of early and recent engravings, which was acquired in 1968 (2,271 folios). The largest part of the collection comprises foreign engravings from various nations (15th–20th cc.).

g-45. Onopko-Baburina, Nina Ivanovna. "Sovetskii kinoplakat dvadtsatykh godov." *Trudy GBL* 2 (1958): 252–80. (Lib: DLC; IU; MH) [IDC-in R-10,287]

Special Trophy Collection

g-46. Borodin, Oleg; and Dolgodrova, Tat'iana. "Kollektsiia Nemetskogo muzeia knigi i shrifta v sobranii Rossiiskoi gosudarstvennoi biblioteki." *Nashe nasledie,* no. 32 (1994): 97–106. (Lib: DLC; IU; MH)

> The first published account of the collection of approximately 600 units of manuscripts, incunabula, and early imprints from the Leipzig Museum of the Book and Printing that was brought to Moscow from Germany in 1945–1947. Kept in secret for almost half a century, of special interest among one of the most important German "trophy" library collections now in Moscow is the illuminated 1452–1456 Gutenberg Bible on parchment. RGB is now preparing a full catalogue of the Leipzig collection and other trophy materials from Germany.

Nauchnaia biblioteka im. A. M. Gor'kogo Moskovskogo gosudarstvennogo universiteta im. M. V. Lomonosova (NB MGU)

[A. M. Gor'kii Scientific Library of M. V. Lomonosov Moscow State University]

Agency: Ministerstvo obshchego i professional'nogo obrazovaniia RF
(Minobrazoraniia Rossii)
[Ministry of General and Professional Education]

Address: 119899, Moscow, Universitetskii prosp., 1, MGU
Telephone: 939-22-41; 939-34-61; *Fax:* (095) 202-94-04; 938-01-83
E-mail: inf@lib.msu.su
Website: http://www.lib.msu.su
Transport: metro: Universitet
Hours: vary for different sectors

Director: Viacheslav Viktorovich Mosiagin (*tel.* 939-22-41; 939-24-01)
Deputy Director: Anna Fedorovna Panza (*tel.* 939-13-58)
Deputy Director: Larisa Orazovna Shikhmuradova (*tel.* 203-71-96)
Scientific Secretary: Oksana Vital'evna Krykina (*tel.* 939-44-26)

HISTORY:

Biblioteka Imperatorskogo Moskovskogo universiteta
[Library of Imperial Moscow University] (1755–1917)
Biblioteka Moskovskogo gosudarstvennogo universiteta (Biblioteka MGU)
[Library of Moscow State University] (1917–1932)
Biblioteka im. A. M. Gor'kogo Moskovskogo gosudarstvennogo universiteta
[A. M. Gor'kii Library of Moscow State University] (1932–1933)

The library, one of the oldest in the country, was founded together with the University itself in 1755, on the basis of a project of M. V. Lomonosov. Almost all the manuscripts held by the library before 1812 were lost in the Moscow fire, because they had not been evacuated to Nizhnii Novgorod along with the University. But the new library that was formed subsequently acquired a large number of private libraries, many of which had been preserved intact. Unlike the MGU archive (see E–50), which now only retains documents from the postrevolutionary period, the manuscript fonds of the A. M. Gor'kii Library were never transferred to state archives.

To mark the fortieth anniversary of the literary and public career of A. M. Gor'kii in 1932, the MGU library was renamed in honor of the writer. The following year it received the status of a "scientific library."

The organization of a special fond of rare books and manuscripts began in 1946, when the most valuable materials, including manuscripts, were removed from the general book collections and put into a separate Division of Rare Books and Manuscripts. In the aftermath of World War II, the library's collections were enriched by a large number of "trophy" books brought to Moscow from Germany and Eastern Europe, although most of the materials received from Dresden were subsequently returned to East Germany in the late 1950s.

Access: Manuscript materials in the library are all open for research. Researchers should present an official letter from their sponsoring organization stating the subject and aim of their research.

Otdel redkikh knig i rukopisei (ORKiR)
[Division of Rare Books and Manuscripts]

Address: 103009, Moscow, ul. Mokhovaia, 9
Telephone: 203-26-56; *Fax:* 938-01-83; *RdngRm:* 203-66-45
E-mail: inf@lib.msu.su
Hours: M–F 9:00–17:00 (August—closed)
Transport: metro: Aleksandrovskii sad; Biblioteka im. Lenina
Head: Irina Leonidovna Velikodnaia (*tel.* 203-26-56)

HOLDINGS: 49 fonds, 7 collections, 6,000 units, 10th–20th cc. (some documents 1649–1650)
Slavic MSS—2,315 units; Russian MS books—ca. 800 units (13th–20th cc.);
Oriental MSS—455 units (16th–19th cc.); Greek and Latin MSS—11 units (10th–15th cc.);
personal fonds—48; posters—1,817 units; Western European MSS—100 units (15th–19th cc.);
sound recordings—ca. 1,000 units

The Division of Rare Books and Manuscripts, in terms of archival materials, has extensive collections of manuscript books (over 2,000 units) in Greek, Latin, French, and German, in addition to Slavic languages; major collections of personal papers and libraries of professors and others associated with the university; a collection of documents relating to the history of the University; and major graphic collections.

The important collections of Slavonic-Rus' manuscript books (14th–18th cc.), include many that were collected in the course of MGU archeographic expeditions throughout the former Soviet Union. Notable examples include an early thirteenth-century Gospel from Rostov the Great; a fourteenth-century Galician-Volhynian parchment Gospel-Aprakos imitating the text and miniatures of the Ostromir Gospel; lives of saints; annals and chronicles; a feudal military register book (*razriadnaia kniga*) (1500–1646) containing a chronicle of the "Moldavian Lands" (1509); and a seventeenth-century codex on the establishment of the patriarchate in Russia. The Moldavian and Ukrainian Collection contains early manuscripts of Moldavian origin. Among other manuscripts of ecclesiastic provenance are cadastral (*pistsovye*) and registration (*zapisnye*) books from the Bezhetsk Armenian Enclave (*Bezhetskaia piatina*) of the Beloozero region, economic documents from monasteries, and the founding charter of the Polotsk Brotherhood. There are also manuscripts from secular sources of a later period, which include letters of Peter the Great, an investigative report into the case of the Tsarevich Aleksei (1718), and materials relating to the history of Poland (1767–1792).

The division has seventeen territorial collections and collections of Old Believer religious manuscript books, which were also acquired on MGU archeographic expeditions, such as those to the early villages of Vetka (Homel Oblast), Starodub (Briansk Oblast), Vereshchagin (Perm Oblast), and Samodurovka (now Belogorno). Of particular importance in extent and significance are the territorial collections from Vetka-Starodub, Kareliia, and Perm.

MGU also holds a number of theological, historical, juridical, and literary manuscripts, incunabula, and paleotypes in Greek and Latin. These include a Greek chronicle of the Byzantinist Peter of Alexandria (10th c.), a Greek Gospel dated 1072, and a fifteenth-century manuscript convolute of the speeches of Attic orators. Latin manuscripts include a thirteenth-century illuminated Bible on parchment from France. The earliest incunabulum is the parchment fragments of the fourth-century Latin grammarian, Aelius Donatus, printed by Johannes Gutenberg between 1445 and 1450 in Mainz. There are a number of later manuscripts of West European origin in French and German, among other languages.

Among the forty-one Oriental manuscripts in the division (from several different collections), there are the works of Chinese philosophers, Chinese phrasebooks, and Manchu, Mongolian, and Tibetan dictionaries. A fifteenth-century Arabic dictionary by Firuzabadi is among the most valuable Arabic manuscripts. Persian manuscripts include accounts of pilgrimages to Mecca in the sixteenth and eighteenth centuries. There are also literary and juridical works in Turkic, Tatar, and Arabic languages.

The collection of documents devoted to the history of the University contains the first manuscript charter of the Imperial Moscow University and the charter of confirmation (*Utverditel'naia gramota*) (1804). It also includes a collection of university and secondary school course and study prospectuses, dissertations, and official speeches. Archival documents saved from the fire in 1812 include fifteen volumes of the minutes (protocols) of the university Conference (*Konferentsiia* [academic council]) during the eighteenth century.

Then there are collections of more than fifty private libraries spanning the nineteenth and twentieth centuries that formerly belonged to professors and staff of the University and to persons prominent in the world of culture. These include the libraries of several members of the Dmitriev, Murav'ev, and Turgenev families, among other important holdings from the late eighteenth and early nineteenth centuries. Some of these collections contain literary manuscripts that were acquired by the library after the fire of 1812. There are also originals and copies of eighteenth- and nineteenth-century literary works, including the "Satire" of A. Kantemir, poetry of G. S. Skovoroda, 14 manuscript volumes by I. M. Dolgorukov, forbidden compositions of A. N. Radishchev, A. S. Griboedov, and K. F. Ryleev, and a manuscript of "A Hunter's Sketches" by I. S. Turgenev with the censor's corrections. Many of these were acquired from the censor's office of the University press. Also of particular archival importance, these personal libraries contain many volumes with dedicatory autographs, inscriptions, and marginalia.

Among the personal fonds of former university faculty are the papers of the logician A. S. Akhmanov; the linguistics specialist F. I. Buslaev; the philologist F. E. Korsh; the historians T. N. Granovskii, N. K. Gudzii, M. M. Kovalevskii, and F. F. Veselago; and the Kharusin brothers, who were ethnographers. The archive of the historian and university bibliographer E. I. Sokolov is rich in documents relating to the nineteenth-century Society for History and Antiquities. There are also the personal papers and manuscript collections of P. N. and M. N. Krechetnikov, who were active in government in the eighteenth century, and the literary figures D. Ia. and E. Ia. Kolbasin.

The division holds significant cartographic and iconographic materials. These include a complete collection of the portraits of the Decembrists and an extensive collection of engravings and lithographs (3,123 units) brought together by F. F. Vigel', also known for his memoirs and other writings. The graphic materials in the division also include collections of posters from World War I, the Civil War, the War of Foreign Intervention, and World War II.

During the 1990s the division acquired a collection of sound recordings collected by the faculty, staff, and students of the Moscow State University. These include recordings of the speeches made by the professors and lecturers of the University, by important Soviet scholars and scientists, and by persons prominent in the world of literature and the arts (including V. V. Maiakovskii).

N.B. Manuscripts and archival materials are also held in the MGU Archive (see E–50).

Working Conditions: Manuscripts can be consulted in a special reading room within a day after they are ordered. Advance orders can be made by telephone or personal visit.

Reference Facilities: For manuscripts and archival materials, there are inventory registers, inventory books for different fonds in the division, and *opisi* of the archival fonds. There are subject and topograhic catalogues. A separate catalogue covers books with inscriptions and dedicatory autographs, and there are separate catalogues for several of the private libraries held by the division, including those of the Murav'ev and Turgenev families, and of the Vigel' collection. There is also a separate catalogue covering the Slavonic-Rus' manuscript books, and a database is being compiled (in adapted MARC format) with descriptions of the manuscript books.

Library Facilities: There is a specialized reference library available to researchers, and readers may order books from the main university library collections.

Copying: Photographic and xerox copies can be prepared.

FINDING AIDS — PUBLISHED — GENERAL:

Biblioteki: Putevoditel' (1996), pp. 182–84; G&K *Spravochnik* (1983), pp. 227–29 and 420–22; PKG *M&L* (1972), pp. 275–76; Sup. 1 (1976), p. 101.

There is no published guide to the archival materials in the library. For a general description of the division with a list of private libraries held there, together with bibliography of finding aids, see *Fondy red. izd.* (1991), pp. 150–54. See also the short description of the division on the MGU library website.

General Guides and Surveys

g-66. *Redkie knigi i rukopisi biblioteki Moskovskogo universiteta: Putevoditel' po fondam otdela redkikh knig i rukopisei.* Compiled by N. V. Maslova. Edited by V. V. Mosiagin. Munich: Verlag Otto Sagner, 1991. 22 p. + 7 plates. [MGU] (Lib: MH)

> A short brochure giving a brief history of the formation of the division and a survey of its fonds. Of particular value is the bibliography on research work based on the holdings (pp. 21–22).

g-68. Mel'nikova, Natal'ia Nikolaevna. "Rukopisi i redkie knigi v fondakh Nauchnoi biblioteki." *Opyt raboty Nauchnoi biblioteki MGU* 1 (1955): 35–47. [IDC-in R-10,835]

> A general survey of the division holdings.

g-69. *Redkie knigi i rukopisi Nauchnoi biblioteki Moskovskogo universiteta: Putevoditel' po vystavke.* Compiled by E. S. Karpova and N. I. Safonova. Edited by N. S. Avalova. Moscow: Izd-vo MGU, 1980. 106 p. + 16 ill. (Lib: MH)

> An exhibit catalogue presenting many examples of the MGU holdings of rare books and manuscripts.

Slavonic-Rus' Manuscripts

g-70. *Slaviano-russkie rukopisi XIII–XVII vv. v fondakh Nauchnoi biblioteki im. A. M. Gor'kogo Moskovskogo gosudarstvennogo universiteta: Opisanie.* Compiled by E. I. Koniukhova. Edited by A. M. Sakharov. Translated by A. I. Rogov. Moscow: Izd-vo MGU, 1964. 103 p. (Lib: DLC; IU; MH) [IDC-R-11,019]

> A scholarly catalogue with a detailed description of each manuscript including incipits. Includes a chronological index.

g-71. *Slaviano-russkie rukopisi XV–XVI vekov Nauchnoi biblioteki Moskovskogo universiteta: (Postupleniia 1964–1978 godov).* Compiled by N. A. Kobiak and I. V. Pozdeeva. Moscow: Izd-vo MGU, 1981. 224 p. (Lib: DLC; IU; MH)

> A scholarly description of 54 fifteenth- and sixteenth-century manuscripts, most of which were gathered on MGU archeographic expeditions. Each description provides information on watermarks, decorations, miniatures, and on the condition of the text.

g-72. *Slaviano-russkie rukopisi XIV–XVII vekov Nauchnoi biblioteki Moskovskogo universiteta: (Postupleniia 1964–1984 godov).* Compiled by N. A. Kobiak and I. V. Pozdeeva. Moscow: Izd-vo MGU, 1986. 136 p. (Lib: DDO; DLC; IU; MH)

> Provides scholarly descriptions of 40 manuscripts (14th–17th cc.), most of which were found on archeographic expeditions. The appended folder contains watermark and decorative drawings together with chronological and geographic indexes.

g-73. Peretts, Vladimir Nikolaevich. *Rukopisi biblioteki Moskovskogo universiteta, samarskikh bibliotek i muzeia i minskikh sobranii.* Leningrad: Izd-vo AN SSSR, 1934. 193 p. "Opisanie rukopisnykh sobranii," vol. 3. (Lib: DLC; IU; MH) [IDC-R-10,349]

> Describes early Slavic manuscript books held by MGU before World War II (pp. 13–29).

Collected Surveys of Fonds

g-74. *Rukopisnaia i pechatnaia kniga v fondakh Nauchnoi biblioteki Moskovskogo universiteta: (Sbornik statei).* Moscow: Izd-vo MGU, 1973. 128 p. (Lib: DLC; IU; MH) [IDC-R-11,097]

> A collection of articles, some describing several individual manuscripts, and others surveying personal libraries and dedicatory autographs from the libraries of I. I. Dmitriev and F. I. Buslaev.

g-75. *Iz istorii fondov nauchnoi biblioteki Moskovskogo universiteta.* Edited by E. S. Karpova. Moscow: Izd-vo MGU, 1978. 167 p. + 16 plates. (Lib: DLC; IU; MH)

> The collection of articles includes a survey of the manuscripts of I. S. Turgenev (pp. 72–77), a survey of graphic materials held in the library (pp. 101–108), and a brief description of 64 manuscripts found in 1973 on an archeographic expedition to Moldavia and Odessa Oblast (pp. 152–58), among other contributions.

g-76. *Iz kollektsii redkikh knig i rukopisei Nauchnoi biblioteki Moskovskogo universiteta.* Edited by E. S. Karpova. Moscow: Izd-vo MGU, 1981. 111 p. + 16 plates. (Lib: DLC; IU; MH)

> Different articles include surveys of the engravings of James Walker from the F. F. Vigel' Collection (pp. 81–89), and the retrieval of a document on A. P. Gannibal and his family (pp. 72–80). There is also a description of the marginalia by the Decembrist N. M. Murav'ev on one of the books by N. M. Karamzin (pp. 48–71).

g-77. *Russkie pis'mennye i ustnye traditsii i dukhovnaia kul'tura (po materialam arkheograficheskikh ekspeditsii MGU 1966–1980 gg.).* Edited by I. V. Pozdeeva and I. D. Koval'chenko. Moscow: MGU, 1982. 317 p. (Lib: DLC; IU; MH)

> Includes a detailed report on manuscript and early printed books found on archeographic expeditions, and more specialized analyses of specific materials.

g-78. *Iz fonda redkikh knig i rukopisei Nauchnoi biblioteki Moskovskogo universiteta: Sbornik statei.* Edited by E. S. Karpova. Moscow: Izd-vo MGU, 1987. 156 p. + 18 plates. (Lib: DLC; IU; MH)

> Articles devoted both to individual manuscripts and selected collections in the library include surveys of the personal libraries and archives of such prominent Russian scholars as T. N. Granovskii, S. M. Solov'ev, and N. K. Gudzii. There is also a survey of the manuscripts and early printed books acquired by MGU during the 1980s.

g-79. *Mir staroobriadchestva.* Edited by E. B. Smilianskaia and I. V. Pozdeeva. 2 vols. Moscow/St. Petersburg, 1992–1995. (Lib: DLC; IU; MH)

> Vol. 1: *Lichnost', kniga, traditsiia.* Edited by E. B. Smilianskaia and I. V. Pozdeeva. M./SPb.: "Khronograf," 1992. 139 p.

> Vol. 2: *Moskva staroobriadcheskaia.* Edited by I. V. Pozdeeva. M.: Rossiiskoe universitetskoe izd-vo, 1995. 221 p.

> The first volume comprises papers from the conference "Traditional Book Culture and Culture of Russian Old Believers: 25 years of MGU Field Research" (Moscow, 25–26 January 1992). Of particular importance is the comprehensive bibliography of related publications during that period (pp. 127–37). The second volume includes several general studies, including a survey of Moscow Old Believer necropolises and the materials on the history of the Rogozhskaia Old Believer community in the RGB Manuscript Division (G–1, fond 246).

g-80. *Iz fonda redkikh knig i rukopisei Nauchnoi biblioteki Moskovskogo universiteta: Sbornik statei.* Edited by S. O. Shmidt. Moscow: Izd-vo MGU, 1993. 256 p. (Lib: DLC; MH)

> Articles include survey descriptions of the library collections of T. N. Granovskii, O. M. Bodianskii, and V. V. Velichko; the collection of Old Believer manuscripts and early imprints from the village of Samodurovka (now Belogorno); the archives of E. I. Sokolov and P. N. Kudriavtsev; and an inventory of seventeenth- and eighteenth-century documents from the archive of the Ievlev family. A special section summarizes library accessions during the years 1984–1989.

g-81. *Rukopisi. Redkie izdaniia. Arkhivy: Iz fondov biblioteki Moskovskogo universiteta.*
Edited by G. A. Kosmolinskaia. Moscow: "Arkheograficheskii tsentr," 1997. 316 p. +
plates. [Rossiiskii Gumanitarnyi Nauchnyi Fond] (Lib: MH)

> In addition to several research articles and documentary publication, the collection includes scholarly
> descriptions by N. A. Kobiak of 72 Old Believer manuscripts (16th–20th cc.) from the Nizhnii
> Novgorod region held by MGU (pp. 268–304) and a survey of acquisitions from recent MGU
> archeographic expeditions (1990–1994).

Early Cyrillic Imprints

g-82. Lerenman, Maiia Mikhailovna; Pozdeeva, Irina Vasil'evna; and Kashkarova,
Inna Danilovna. *Katalog knig kirillicheskoi pechati XV–XVII vekov Nauchnoi biblioteki
Moskovskogo universiteta.* Moscow: Izd-vo MGU, 1980. 360 p. (Lib: DLC; IU; MH)

> A scholarly catalogue (in original orthography) of the unique collection of Cyrillic printed books, which
> includes imprints from all the famous printing houses of the fifteenth, sixteenth, and seventeenth centuries.

Oriental Manuscripts

g-83. Kleinman, Galina Aleksandrovna. "Vostochnye fondy Nauchnoi biblioteki im. A. M.
Gor'kogo Moskovskogo Gosudarstvennogo universiteta im. M. V. Lomonosova." In
Vostokovednye fondy krupneishikh bibliotek Sovetskogo Soiuza, pp. 202–18. Moscow,
1963. (Lib: DLC; IU; MH) [IDC-in R-10, 664]

> The main part of the article is devoted to published books and other materials. For a review of the
> Oriental manuscripts, see pp. 212–16.

MGU Library History

g-84. Penchko, Nina Aleksandrovna. *Biblioteka Moskovskogo universiteta s osnovaniia do
1812 goda.* Moscow: Izd-vo MGU, 1969. 162 p. "Istoriia biblioteki Moskovskogo
universiteta 1755–1967." (Lib: MH)

> A scholarly study of the early history of the library with considerable bibliography and with mention
> of many of the collections lost in 1812.

g-85. Sorokin, Viktor Vasil'evich. *Istoriia biblioteki Moskovskogo universiteta (1800–
1917 gg.).* Moscow: Izd-vo MGU, 1980. 254 p. (Lib: MH)

> A scholarly study of the history of the library with mention of many of the major collections acquired
> after the 1812 fire.

g-86. Khar'kova, A. M; and Lesokhina, E. I. *Istoriia biblioteki Moskovskogo universiteta,
1917–1949.* Edited by V. I. Zlobin. Moscow: Izd-vo MGU, 1981. 129 p. (Lib: DLC; MH)

> A scholarly study of the history of the library with mention of many of the major collections acquired
> after 1917.

g-87. Penchko, Nina Aleksandrovna. "Rabota Biblioteki nad rukopisiami po istorii
Moskovskogo universiteta." *Opyt raboty Nauchnoi biblioteki MGU* 1 (1955): 19–34.
(Lib: IU) [IDC-in R-10,835]

> A survey of archival materials on the history of Moscow State University held in the library fonds.

FINDING AIDS — SPECIALIZED:

g-88. "Ancient Slavic Manuscripts from the Moscow State University Library." New York:
Norman Ross Publishing, 1998–. Microfiche edition. With printed guide.

> A microfiche collection of selected Slavic manuscripts. The initial offering includes 21 manuscripts
> (13th–16th cc.). The printed guide provides minimal descriptive data in chronological listings with
> entries in Russian and English.

g-89. Fonkich, Boris L'vovich. "Grecheskie rukopisi Biblioteki Moskovskogo universiteta." *Vestnik drevnei istorii*, 1967, no. 4, pp. 95–103. (Lib: DLC; IU)

A scholarly description of four Greek manuscripts.

g-90. Mokretsova, Inna Pavlovna. "Rukopisnaia Bibliia XIII v. iz Nauchnoi biblioteki Moskovskogo universiteta." *Pamiatniki kul'tury. Novye otkrytiia: Ezhegodnik za 1974 god* (1975): 354–68. (Lib: DLC; IU; MH) [IDC-in R-14,784]

Describes a thirteenth-century Latin Bible of French provenance on parchment, with elaborate illuminations.

g-91. *Rukopisi Verkhokam'ia XV–XX vv. v sobranii MGU.* Compiled by T. A. Kruglova, E. A. Ageeva, N. A. Kobiak, and E. B. Smilianskaia. Moscow: Tsimeliia, 1994. 459 p. Introduction by I. V. Pozdeeva. (Lib: DLC; MH)

A scholarly catalogue with descriptions of more than 350 Old Believer manuscripts.

g-92. Pashaeva, N. M. "Slavianskaia biblioteka O. M. Bodianskogo." *Sovetskoe slavianovedenie*, 1982, no. 1, pp. 94–103. (Lib: DLC; IU; MH)

A survey of the library collection of the Slavonic philologist, O. M. Bodianskii, collected during his travels abroad in the late 1830s and early 1840s (2,349 volumes). Some of the books have dedicatory autographs and owner inscriptions.

g-93. Kuibysheva, Ksana Semenovna; and Safonova, Natal'ia Ivanovna. *Akvareli dekabrista Petra Ivanovicha Borisova.* Moscow: "Iskusstvo," 1986. 552 p. + plates. (Lib: DLC; IU; MH)

g-94. Saprykina, Natal'ia Gansovna. *Kollektsiia portretov sobraniia F. F. Vigelia: Graviura i litografiia XVIII–pervoi poloviny XIX veka: Annotirovannyi katalog.* Edited by E. S. Karpova. Moscow: Izd-vo MGU, 1980. 192 p. + 41 ill. (Lib: IU)

A catalogue of portrait engravings (17th to early 19th c.) and lithographs (mid-19th c.) from the collection of F. F. Vigel' (1786–1856), who served in the Moscow Archive of the Ministry of Foreign Affairs (MGAMID), including rare (some unique) works by Russian and foreign masters, as well as portraits of state and public figures in eighteenth- and early nineteenth-century Russia.

Gosudarstvennaia publichnaia istoricheskaia biblioteka Rossii (GPIB)
[State Public Historical Library of Russia]

Agency: Ministerstvo kul'tury RF (Minkul'tury Rossii) [Ministry of Culture]
Rossiiskaia Akademiia nauk
[Russian Academy of Sciences]

Address:	101000, Moscow, Starosadskii per., 9
Telephone:	928-02-84; 925-65-14; *Fax:* (095) 928-43-32; 928-02-84
E-mail:	galina@shpl.ru; zgm@shpl.msk.ru
Website:	http://www.shpl.ru
Transport:	metro: Kitai-gorod
Hours:	M–Sa 9:00–20:00

Director: Mikhail Dmitrievich Afanas'ev (*tel.* 928-02-84; *e-mail:* maf@shpl.ru)

Deputy Director for Library Affairs: Elena Arturovna Iastrzhembskaia (*tel.* 925-71-39; *e-mail:* elena@shpl.ru)

HISTORY:

Gosudarstvennaia publichnaia istoricheskaia biblioteka RSFSR (GPIB RSFSR)
[State Public Historical Library of the RSFSR] (1938–1991)

The Historical Library dates its origin to the Moscow City Chertkov Public Library, which was opened to the public in 1863 on the basis of the personal library of Aleksandr Dmitrievich Chertkov (1789–1858), the historian, archeologist, and chairman of the Society of Russian History and Antiquities (*Obshchestvo istorii i drevnostei rossiiskikh*). During his lifetime, Chertkov had assembled what was recognized as the richest library on Russian history at the time. The library came under the auspices of the Moscow City Duma in 1871 and subsequently became the basis of the library of the Historical Museum (now GIM—H–1). During the late nineteenth century the library acquired a number of important private libraries and historical collections, including those of M. D. Khmyrov, A. N. Golitsyn, and I. E. Zabelin, the Slavicist D. M. Shchepkin, A. P. Bakhrushin, and the bibliophile General Field-Marshal A. I. Bariatinskii, among others. After the Revolution, the library of the Historical Museum acquired the library holdings of many abolished institutions and organizations as well as nationalized collections from religious and private sources. In several cases, the library acquired the books from major private collectors, whose manuscript books and museum and documentary collections went to other divisions of the Historical Museum, such as those of the historian and archeologist A. A. Bobrinskii, A. S. Uvarov, and the genealogist L. M. Savelov.

In 1922, the library holdings were reorganized with the status of the State Historical Library under what was then called the Russian Historical Museum—after 1929, the State Historical Museum (GIM). In 1938, the State Public Historical Library of the RSFSR (GPIB) was established as a separate institution, consolidating the bulk of the library holdings of the State Historical Museum, and the library of the abolished Institute of Red Professors (*Institut Krasnoi professury*), which was formed on the basis of the library of the Moscow Pedagogical Assembly (*Moskovskoe pedagogicheskoe sobranie*), together with the collections of several smaller libraries oriented to the humanities. During the 1930s and 1940s GPIB received a vast complex of library materials which had been confiscated by state security organs (OGPU and NKVD, and later KGB). After

World War II the library also received a significant number of "trophy" books brought to Moscow from Germany and Eastern Europe. Since 1991, the library is known by its present name of the State Public Historical Library of Russia.

The Division (now Fond) of Rare Books was established in 1976.

The Sector for Nontraditional Imprints was created as a separate unit in 1996, on the basis of a large special collection of nontraditional press started in 1989, within the library Division of Basic Holdings. In 1997 GPIB acquired the important collection of the former private Library of Unpublished Manuscripts (*Biblioteka neizdannykh rukopisei*—BNR), thus further enriching this sector.

Some archival materials are also found within the separate Russia Abroad Collection, including scattered historical documentation remaining from collection of the émigré White Army officer Ia. M. Lisovoi donated to the library, although most of the archival materials from that collection were unforunately scattered among several state archives.

Access: A passport and visa-size photograph are required to obtain a reader's ticket to the library, which also entitles research access to the Fond of Rare Books and the GPIB archive.

Library Facilities: GPIB library holdings total more than 3,000,000 domestic (Russian/Soviet) and foreign publications relating to history and associated disciplines in Russian and many foreign languages.

Copying: Xerox and microfiche facilities are available in the library.

Fond redkoi knigi
[Fond of Rare Books]

Telephone: 928-13-93
Hours: M–Sa 10:00–18:00
Head: Liubov' Borisovna Shitskova (*tel.* 928-13-93)

HOLDINGS: MS books—330 (mid-16th c.–1910s)

The GPIB Fond of Rare Books holds a small collection of early Slavonic and Russian manuscript books, including original and translated liturgical works, lives of saints, tales and other secular texts, Old Believer and Masonic manuscripts, and various seventeenth- and eighteenth-century codices including compilations (*sborniki*).

The fond also retains a few personal papers of the historian V. O. Kliuchevskii (including one of his notebooks and two lectures transcribed by his niece), and the papers of the lawyer, E. I. Baranovskii, who was active in the Russian government.

There are several late eighteenth-century manuscript maps of Russia.

Among rare books, there are a number of incunabula and other early Cyrillic imprints. There are also some autographed books, but most of the latter are shelved with the general collection of the fond.

Reference Facilities: There is a separate card catalogue for the manuscript books.

Copying: Xerox copying of rare and manuscript books is not permitted; in some cases, limited photographic copies can be arranged.

Osnovnoi fond
[Basic Holdings]

Hours: M–Sa 9:00–20:00

HOLDINGS:

There are several groups of archival materials within the basic library holdings. Within the Periodical Division is the M. D. Khmyrov Collection, which consists of 1,734 bound volumes of newspaper, journal, and book clippings, together with unpublished documents (1755–1865) relating to Russian and world history, and biographies of noted people.

Unpublished materials are also found in the A. S. Uvarov and A. P. Bakhrushin Collections, including contemporary materials presented by authors together with memoirs and historical monographs.

The Russia Abroad Collection contains some archival materials, including a few of the historical documents from the Ia. M. Lisovoi Collection.

The library's collection of nontraditional press now constitutes a special sector (see below).

Reference Facilities: Materials of the Khmyrov Collection, along with other archival documentation, are not separated into special fonds, but are rather described in the main library card catalogues, which are accessible in the Periodical Division.

Sektor netraditsionnoi pechati
[Sector of Nontraditional Imprints]

Telephone: 928-56-82
Fax: (095) 928-65-14
E-mail: stru@shpl.ru
Hours: by appointment
Head: Elena Nikolaevna Strukova

HOLDINGS: books—1,300 (1976–1996); newspapers—1,300 (1976–1996); journals—500 (1976–1996); posters and leaflets—ca. 10,000 (1980–1997);

In 1989 the library started a special collection of nontraditional press, which includes a small number of rare *samizdat* from the 1950s, 60s, and 70s; informal and alternative press of the period of *perestroika*; and an extensive collection of materials from the years 1989 onwards.

Pre-1976 holdings include approximately 15–20 titles (a total of 150–200 items). More regular receipts start in 1989, and are increasingly complete starting in 1993. These include programs of political parties, documents of social and religious movements, handbills, election materials, and posters.

The collected posters and leaflets are still being processed (ca. 10,000 documents, 1989–1997). There is an especially large collection from the 1993 elections.

In the summer of 1997, the sector acquired the rich *samizdat* collection of the former Library of Unpublished Manuscripts (*Biblioteka neizdannykh rukopisei*—BNR), which had earlier been under the Pushkin Humanitarian Fond), consisting of an additional 70 books and 210 journal issues from the period prior to 1993, including many extremely rare, or even unique materials.

Reference Facilities: A special database (in Procite) covers the nontraditional press collection, with annotated entries for articles from periodical publications (i.e. those not recorded in *Letopis' periodicheskoi pechati*), for which a system of thematic search has been developed. A CD-ROM production of scanned images of documents and articles from the period 1989–1993 is being prepared with an appropriate reference system for the materials covered.

Arkhiv
[Archive]

Hours: MW 9:00–17:00
Head: Alevtina Nikolaevna Gorbacheva

HOLDINGS: 1 fond, 341 units, 1966–1985 (scattered documents from 1938)

Documentation remaining in the library consists of a part of the GPIB administrative records and files relating to the GPIB trade-union organization (the latter covers the entire period since the foundation of the library in 1938).

N.B. Part of the GPIB library records (426 units), was earlier transferred to the former Central State Archive of the RSFSR (TsGA RSFSR), now part of the State Archive of the Russian Federation (GA RF) (fond 513; 1938–1985).

Reference Facilities: Reference catalogues are arranged according to types of documents, file unit numbers, and years.

FINDING AIDS — PUBLISHED — GENERAL:

Biblioteki: Putevoditel' (1996), pp. 33–35; *GAF Spravochnik (1991)*, p. 78; G&K *Spravochnik* (1983), pp. 217–21 and 416–17; PKG *M&L* (1972), p. 298.

There is no complete published guide to the manuscript books and archival materials in the library. For a general description of the Division of Rare Books with a list of private libraries held there, together with a bibliography of finding aids, see *Fondy red. izd.* (1991), pp. 168–71.

g-100. *Katalog rukopisnykh knig [GPIB, Otdel redkikh knig].* Compiled by Z. V. Fedotova and N. F. Chernysheva. Moscow, 1976. 14 p. [GPIB] (Lib: DLC; IU; MH)
   A list with minimal descriptive data covering 185 manuscripts (16th–20th cc.), including 6 religious texts.

g-101. Malyshev, Vladimir Ivanovich. "Rukopisi Gosudarstvennoi publichnoi istoricheskoi biblioteki." *Voprosy istorii*, 1953, no. 2, pp. 125–27. (Lib: DLC; IU; MH)
   A brief survey of early manuscript books in the Division of Rare Books.

g-102. *Katalog russkikh knig kirillovskoi pechati XVI–XVIII vv.* Compiled by N. F. Chernysheva. Moscow, 1972. 37 p. [GPIB] (Lib: DLC; MH)
   Lists the early Cyrillic imprints held by the library some of which have important marginalia and inscriptions.

g-103. *Katalog kollektsii avtorskikh nadpisei: (Izdaniia XVIII–XIX vv.).* Compiled by L. B. Shitskova. Moscow, 1994. 73 p. [GPIB; Otdel redkikh knig] (Lib: DLC; IU; MH)

FINDING AIDS — SPECIALIZED:

See the description of the GPIB *samizdat* and nontraditional press collections in a-417 and a-418, including those there described as earlier held by the Library of Unpublished Manuscripts (BNR); those volumes also provide complete listings for the GPIB holdings as part of the ongoing union catalogue of Moscow and St. Petersburg collections. GPIB is in the process of preparing a complete computerized catalogue of its holdings in this category.

g-104. Afanas'ev, Mikhail Dmitrievich. "M. D. Khmyrov i ego kollektsiia." *Otechestvennye arkhivy*, 1996, no. 3, pp. 30–35. (Lib: DLC; IU; MH)
   Surveys the collection of the well-known Russian collector Mikhail Dmitrievich Khmyrov (1830–1872) in terms of the archival materials contained within. Along with Khmyrov's own writings and notes about various phases of Russian history, there are copies of original documentation, bibliographic data, and 1,723 volumes of newspaper and journal clippings, arranged under subject rubrics.

g-105. *Kollektsiia Ia. M. Lisovogo: Opyt rekonstruktsii.* Compiled by S. V. Glinnikova, N. G. Kirillova, A. S. Kruchinin, et al. Edited by T. K. Mishchenko. Moscow: GPIB, 1997. 145 p. (Also listed as a-143A).
   A detailed scholarly reconstruction of the library, documentary, and film collection of the Russian imperial and White Army officer Iakov Markovich Lisovoi (1882–1966), which was donated to the State Public Historical Library after his death in emigration. Most of the archival materials, including the photographic collection, were divided among several Moscow archives (see full listing under a-143A), but the library remained in GPIB, held in classified collections until 1991. The library (1,049

books and 10 periodicals) is now open in GPIB as part of the Russia Abroad Collection, and each item is listed appropriately in the published catalogue. Scattered original historical archival materials also remain in GPIB.

g-106. *Listovki Belogo Doma: Moskovskie letuchie izdaniia 22 sentiabria–4 oktiabria 1993 g.: Iz fondov GPIB Rossii i biblioteki NIPTs "Memorial."* Compiled by B. I. Belenkin and E. N. Strukova. Moscow, 1993. 264 p. (Lib: DLC; IU)

Most of the volume is devoted to the publication of leaflets held in GPIB and the collections of Memorial (see F–5), but also describes the collection. Lacks reference apparatus with precise identification of the location of the materials.

g-107. "Forbidden Books from the Library of A. I. Ostroglazov from the State Historical Library in Moscow." New York: Norman Ross Publishing, 1998–1999. A microfilm edition.

The book collection assembled by one of the Moscow censors at the turn of the century, Andrei Ivanovich Ostroglazov (1872–1908), with imprints predominantly between 1905–1907, now available in microform. This special collection comprises a copy Ostroglazov kept of each book that was supposed to be destroyed with markings on each one as to why, from whom, and when the publication was confiscated, and if a court order for its destruction existed.

Vserossiiskaia gosudarstvennaia biblioteka inostrannoi literatury im. M. I. Rudomino (VGBIL)

[M. I. Rudomino All-Russian State Library for Foreign Literature]

Agency: Ministerstvo kul'tury RF (Minkul'tury Rossii)
[Ministry of Culture]

Address: 109189, Moscow, ul. Nikoloiamskaia (*formerly* Ul'ianovskaia), 1
Telephone: 915-36-21; *Fax:* (095) 915-36-37
E-mail: vgbil@libfl.ru; root@libfl.ru
Website: http://www.libfl.ru
Transport: metro: Novokuznetskaia + tram A, 39; metro: Kitai-gorod + trol. 45, 63; metro: Taganskaia + trol. 63
Hours: W–F 9:00–20:00, SaSu 10:00–20:00 (closed Su—July and August)

General Director: Ekaterina Iur'evna Genieva (*tel.* 297-28-39;
   e-mail: genieva@libfl.ru)
Deputy Director for International and Administrative Affairs:
   Evgeniia Mikhailovna Rosinskaia (*tel.* 915-36-19)
Deputy Director for Library Work: Galina Alexandrovna Kislovskaia (*tel.* 915-55-19)

HISTORY:

Neofilologicheskaia biblioteka Akademicheskogo tsentra Narkomprosa RSFSR
   [Neophilological Library of the Academic Center of the People's Commissariat for Education of the RSFSR] (1921–1924)
Biblioteka inostrannoi literatury
   [Library for Foreign Literature] (1924–1927)
Gosudarstvennaia biblioteka inostrannoi literatury
   [State Library for Foreign Literature] (1927–1932)
Gosudarstvennaia tsentral'naia biblioteka inostrannoi literatury
   [State Central Library for Foreign Literature] (1932–1948)
Vsesoiuznaia gosudarstvennaia biblioteka inostrannoi literatury (VGBIL)
   [All-Union State Library for Foreign Literature] (1948–1990)
Vsesoiuznaia gosudarstvennaia biblioteka inostrannoi literatury im. M. I. Rudomino (VGBIL)
   [M. I. Rudomino All-Union State Library for Foreign Literature] (30.VIII.1990–1991)

The All-Russian State Library for Foreign Literature was formed in 1921 as the Neophilological Library of the Department of Pedagogical Education (*Otdel pedagogicheskogo obrazovaniia*) of the Main Administration for Professional Training (*Glavnoe upravlenie professional'nogo obrazovaniia—Glavprofobr*), which was under the authority of the People's Commissariat of Education (Narkompros) of the RSFSR. It subsequently came under the control of the Academic Center of the commissariat. In 1924 it was renamed the State Library for Foreign Literature; in 1927 the State Library for Foreign Literature; and in 1932 the State Central Library for Foreign Literature, still remaining under Narkompros RSFSR.

   In the aftermath of World War II, the library's collections were significantly enriched by a large number of "trophy" books brought to Moscow from Germany and Eastern Europe. In 1948 it received All-Union status and its name was changed accordingly, and from then until 1957 it was under the authority of the State Foreign Languages Publishing House (*Gosudarstvennoe izdatel'stvo innostrannoi literatury*), which itself was under the control of the Council of Ministers of the USSR. In September 1957, the library was transferred to the control of the Ministry of Culture of the USSR. In 1973 it was given the status of a scientific research institute, and in 1990 it was renamed in honor of its founder and long-time director, Margarita Ivanovna Rudomino.

The archive was organized in 1950.

Access: A passport and two visa-size photographs are required to obtain a reader's ticket, which entitles the researcher to use all divisions of the library.

Nauchno-issledovatel'skii otdel redkikh knig
[Scientific Research Division of Rare Books]

Hours: Tu–Th 10:00–17:00
Head: Karina Aleksandrovna Dmitrieva (*tel.* 915-57-28)

HOLDINGS: 140 units, 16th–20th cc.

The division holds a number of manuscript books dating from sixteenth through nineteenth centuries, especially on linguistics and jurisprudence in German and Latin. There is also a rich collection of early printed books, many of which were brought from Germany and other European countries after the Second World War.

There are a number of personal archives on deposit here, including the personal papers of the library founder M. I. Rudomino (except for part of the archive that remains in family custody). The division also holds the personal papers of V. V. Ivasheva, a literary specialist on the staff of the library, whose correspondence includes letters from such British writers as William Golding, John Le Carré (*pseud. of* David Cornwall), and C. P. Snow. There are also autographs of A. A. Fet (Shenshin), K. D. Bal'mont, A. A. Blok, and a number of foreign cultural luminaries from the eighteenth to the twentieth centuries. The division holds the personal archive of Father Aleksandr Men' (some of his documents and his conversation and lecture notes are to be found in the People's Archive [*Narodnyi arkhiv*]—see F–3).

A collection entitled "Resistance" (*Soprotivlenie*), which was donated to the library in 1962 by the French Communist Georges Roman contains documents relating to the Second World War, such as leaflets, posters, and photographs, and forms the basis of the library's special Cabinet-Museum of French Anti-Fascist Resistance Literature (*Kabinet-muzei literatury frantsuzskogo antifashistskogo soprotivleniia*).

Reference Facilities: There are inventory *opisi.*

Arkhiv
[Archive]

Hours: M–F 11:00–18:00
Archivist: Igor' Anatol'evich Bordachenkov (*tel.* 915-36-08)

HOLDINGS: ca. 15,000 units, 1921–present

Most of the material in the archive is composed of the administrative records of the library itself, which has been preserved since its foundation in 1921. The archives consist of several fonds divided into various sections according to library divisions. The "Director's Office" (*Direktsiia*) holds documents starting with 1921. The divisional fond 6 entitled "Personnel Division" (*Otdel kadrov*) holds personnel files of the staff starting with the 1930s. Starting with 1954 there are records of the International Book Exchange and the Scientific Bibliographic Divisions. Fond 8 comprises the Photograph Archive (*Fotoarkhiv*) with photographs and negatives dating back to the 1920s. These include photographs of well-known persons in the cultural world of the Soviet Union and foreign countries who have visited the library. There are also photographic chronicles illustrating the work of the library and some photograph albums.

The archive holds the collection of the famous religious philosopher N. M. Zernov, which was formed in the library from materials bequeathed by his relatives. Of particular interest in this collection are the photograph albums that illustrate the life and work of N. M. Zernov and his family.

N.B. A large number of the files in the Archive were destroyed in 1979, including the files under conditions of permanent storage. A small number of documents (mainly relating to the first years of the library's existence) are housed in GA RF (see B–1) as part of the records of the Main Administration for Vocational Training (*Glavprofobr*) of the RSFSR, while the VGBIL Archive holds copies.

Reference Facilities: There are inventory *opisi*, part of which have an auxiliary reference system. Part of the files have still not been properly arranged.

Copying: Xerox copies can be made and microfilming is possible.

Uchebno-lingvisticheskii tsentr
[Linguistic Training Center]

Hours: M–F 9:00–20:00
Head: Liudmila Gennad'evna Levykina (*tel.* 915-00-67)

HOLDINGS: ca. 40 units, 1960s–1994
   photographs—9 units (1920s–1980s); films—3 units; video- and sound recordings—33 units (1972–1986)

The Center retains films recording speeches and performances at the library by famous personages in the Soviet and foreign cultural world together with photograph albums and photographs of special events in the history of the library. There are also original recordings of readings made by foreign literary and cultural representatives, such as the Chilean poet Pablo Neruda (*pseud. of* N. R. R. Basualto), the Hindi poet Rahman Shamsur, the German writer Heinrich Böll, the French historical novelist Maurice Druon, the Australian novelist Dymphna Cusack, the Danish graphic artist and cartoonist Herluf Bidstrup, the American poet Robert Frost, novelists John Cheever and Irving Stone, and civil rights activist Angela Davis.

Reference Facilities: There are inventory *opisi*.

FINDING AIDS — PUBLISHED — GENERAL:

   Biblioteki: Putevoditel' (1996), pp. 35–36; *GAF Spravochnik* (1991), pp. 14–16; G&K *Spravochnik* (1983), pp. 209–10 and 412–13.

There is no published guide to the manuscript books and other archival materials in the library. For a general description of the Division of Rare Books, see *Fondy red. izd.* (1991), pp. 23–25.

FINDING AIDS — GENERAL — UNPUBLISHED:

g-115. Bordachenkov, Igor' Anatol'evich. "Organizatsiia raboty arkhiva Vserossiiskoi Gosudarstvennoi biblioteki inostrannoi literatury na sovremennom etape: Diplomnaia rabota." Moscow: RGGU, 1994. 93 p. Typescript.

> A senior thesis provides a brief history of the library and its archive. Available in the RGGU library (G–5).

Biblioteka Rossiiskogo gosudarstvennogo gumanitarnogo universiteta (Biblioteka RGGU)

[Library of the Russian State University for the Humanities]

Agency: Ministerstvo obshchego i professional'nogo obrazovaniia RF
(Minobrazovaniia Rossi)
[Ministry of General and Professional Education]

Address: 125267, Moscow, Miusskaia pl., 6, korpus 7, kab. 214
Telephone: 250-61-18; 250-67-00; *Fax:* (095) 973-42-84, 250-67-87;
RdngRm: 250-65-82
E-mail: rshulib@rsuh.ru
Website: http://www.rsuh.ru/eng/library.html
Transport: metro: Novoslobodskaia, Mendeleevskaia
Hours: M–Sa 9:00–20:00

Director: Vera Zakharovna Grigor'eva (*tel.* 251-34-36; 250-67-87)
Deputy Director: Irina Nikolaevna Martynova (*tel.* 250-65-86)
Deputy Director: Marina Vadimovna Reshetnikova (*tel.* 250-66-65)

HISTORY:

Biblioteka Moskovskogo narodnogo universiteta im. A. L. Shaniavskogo
[Library of the A. L. Shaniavskii Moscow People's University] (1908–1918)
Biblioteka Instituta arkhivovedeniia
[Library of the Institute of Archival Affairs] (1930–1932)
Biblioteka Moskovskogo gosudarstvennogo istoriko-arkhivnogo instituta (Biblioteka MGIAI)
[Library of the Moscow State Historico-Archival Institute] (1933–1991)
Biblioteka Vysshei partiinoi shkoly pri TsK KPSS (Biblioteka VPSh)
[Library of the Higher Party School under the CC CPSU] (1939–1991)

The Russian State University for the Humanities was founded in 1991 on the basis of the Moscow State Historico-Archival Institute (MGIAI—see also E–52) and the former Higher Party School (*Vysshaia partiinaia shkola*—VPSh) under the CC CPSU. The former MGIAI library became part of the new RGGU library, although some of the MGIAI holdings are still kept in the original MGIAI building (ul. Nikol'skaia, 15). Acquired as part of the library of the Higher Party School were collections from the former A. L. Shaniavskii Moscow People's University (1908–1918).

The basic holdings of the library consist of over 1,500,000 volumes with some 10,000 rare editions (18th–19th cc.). These include collections from several important prerevolutionary libraries, along with the private collection of the well-known scholars E. E. Golubinskii, S. D. Sheremetev, and others. There are also candidate and doctoral dissertations defended at MGIAI and RGGU, many of which contain important reference materials for archives and manuscript collections. Presently the library is processing collections from the Shaniavskii People's University.

The Division of Rare Books was established in 1993.

N.B. For the Center for Archival Research under IAI RGGU, see E–52.

HOLDINGS:

The library and archival holdings are currently in a state of formation.

Some important archival materials that remained in the MGIAI library collections have now been taken over by the RGGU library, but most of these are being processed in the Division of Rare Books.

N.B. Among materials acquired by the RGGU library were documents and books from the archive of N. A. Troitskii, but these were subsequently transferred to the State Archive of the Russian Federation (GA RF—B–1).

Access: Faculty and students of RGGU with a university library card are permitted to work with archival materials. For researchers unaffiliated with RGGU, an official letter addressed to the director of the library or an official personal letter of application is required.

Working Conditions: The archives are currently being arranged and hence many of the materials are not available to researchers.

Otdel redkikh knig
[Division of Rare Books]

Address:	103012, Moscow, ul. Nikol'skaia, 15
Hours:	M–Sa 12:00–17:00
Transport:	metro: Ploshchad' Revoliutsii, Teatral'naia, Okhotnyi Riad, Lubianka
Head:	Tat'iana Nikolaevna Rybina (*tel.* 924–06–33)

HOLDINGS: MS books—7 units (late 15th–19th cc.)

The Rare Book Division, which is still being organized, already contains over 20,000 imprints (18th–19th cc.). The most valuable parts of its holdings are several manuscript books from the holdings of the MGIAI library, predominantly of religious contents, including a fifteenth-century service prayer book (*mineia*), a book of hours (*chasoslov*) (16th c.), a *kanonnik* (with 17th c. additions), an *oktoikh* (a 17th c. book of canticles for eight voices), and a hermologion with neumatic notation (mid-18th c.), among others.

Archival materials from the MGIAI library are being transferred to the division, including the entire collection of manuscript dissertations and student senior theses (*diplomnaia rabota*), some of which comprise descriptions of archival fonds and manuscript collections, or studies of archival materials. Another complex includes archival materials collected by former MGIAI faculty and unpublished works by several archivists in the Soviet system (Tsentrarkhiv and Glavarkhiv). There are copies of lectures by M. K. Liubavskii, scholarly articles and methodological materials prepared for MGIAI courses by V. A. Dombrovskii, N. A. Fomin, I. V. Puzino, N. V. Rusinov, and others.

Starting in 1994, the division has been actively collecting materials of personal origin within the interests of RGGU, and has acquired the personal papers of the Russian ethnographer Iu. V. Bromlei (1921–1990).

Working Conditions: The archival materials are still being processed and are not yet available for researchers.

Reference Facilities: The manuscript books are covered by a card catalogue.

Copying: Xerox facilities are available.

Comment: A questionnaire was not returned to Rosarkhiv by the library.

FINDING AIDS — PUBLISHED — GENERAL:

Lit. russkogo zarubezh'ia (1993), pp. 34–37.

There is no published description of the archival materials in the library. For candidate and doctoral dissertations defended at MGIAI/RGGU, see the bibliographies a-834 and a-835.

g-120. Paskal', A. D. "Slaviano-russkie rukopisnye knigi biblioteki MGIAI." *Sovetskie arkhivy,* 1986, no. 1, pp. 31–33. (Lib: DLC; IU; MH)

> A scholarly description of the manuscript books now held in the Rare Book Division of the RGGU library.

Rossiiskaia gosudarstvennaia biblioteka po iskusstvu (RGBI)
[Russian State Library for the Arts]

Agency: Ministerstvo kul'tury RF (Minkul'tury Rossii)
[Ministry of Culture]

Address:	103031, Moscow, ul. Bol'shaia Dmitrovka (*formerly* Pushkinskaia), 8/1
Telephone:	292-67-04; 292-09-84; 292-48-92; *Fax:* (095) 292-06-53
E-mail:	admin@artlib.ru; mabis@artlib.ru
Website:	http://www.artlib.ru
Transport:	metro: Okhotnyi riad, Teatral'naia
Hours:	M–F 11:00–18:45; Sa 11:00–17:45; (July or August—closed)

Director: Tamara Iosifovna Silina (*tel.* 292-06-53; *e-mail:* silina@artlib.ru)
Deputy Director: Ada Aronovna Kolganova (*tel.* 292-65-20)
Scientific Secretary: Tat'iana Anatol'evna Glazunova (*tel.* 292-06-53)

HISTORY:

Gosudarstvennaia tsentral'naia teatral'naia biblioteka (GTsTB)
[State Central Theater Library] (1922–1992)

The library was founded in 1922 as the State Central Theater Library, on the initiative of professor of literature and dean of the theater school of the Malyi Theater, A. A. Fomin, who served as its first director. From the start it was closely connected with the Malyi Theater, whose premises it occupied, and the associated Higher Theater Workshop. By 1925, it started to serve other theaters as well, and its holdings were considerably expanded. Among the early acquisitions was the library of the Society of Russian Dramatic Writers, books from the Theater Department of the State Academy of Arts, the library of E. S. Rassokhina, the collection of the actor A. P. Lenskii (*pseud. of* Vervitsiotti), and a large collection of lithographed and manuscript plays.

In 1948 the library moved into the building it occupies today, which had been built in 1793 on the design of the Russian architect M. F. Kazakov. While owned by the Moscow deputy governor, N. E. Miasoedov, it housed a serf theater, and later in the nineteenth century, it housed a theater school.

Starting in the 1960s the library acquired a number of important collections from the theater world of producers, actors, and theater historians and critics, including those of M. N. and A. P. Gaziev, S. S. Ignatov, S. S. Mokul'skii, Iu. I. Slonimskii, and N. D. Volkov. As the library grew, its holdings extended to a broad range of holdings in the humanities and the arts, totalling over 1,670,000 units. In 1992 it was renamed the Russian State Library for the Arts.

Most particularly, the library holds extensive documentary and visual materials on the history of the theater, opera, ballet, the circus, and other performing arts in Russia and abroad. There are archival materials and manuscript music as part in the Sector of Rare Books, which is administratively part of the Division for Storage of Library Fonds—(*Otdel khraneniia bibliotechnykh fondov*), and significant archival materials in the Division of Graphic Imprints. The library also collects videocassettes of theater performances.

Access: Access is granted on the basis of an official letter from the researcher's sponsoring organization. Materials that have not been fully arranged and described (the Engravings Fond and part of the Original Photograph Fond) are not issued to readers.

Library Facilities: There is an auxiliary library in the reference and information division, which is accessible to researchers through the bibliographer on duty.

Sector redkoi knigi
[Sector of Rare Books]

Telephone: 292-09-84, ext. 4
Hours: M–F 10:00–20:45; Sa 10:00–19:45
Head: Tat'iana Petrovna Solov'eva

HOLDINGS: 2 fonds, ca. 2,500 units unarranged, 9,546 units, 1880–1992
  fond of manuscript plays—4,546 units (1800–1945)

Of particular interest in the Sector of Rare Books is a collection of original manuscripts and copies of dramatic works in Russian and in translation from other languages. The sector has a collection of over 5,000 manuscript and lithograph plays, including significant prerevolutionary drama. Some of these came from the libraries of E. S. Rassokhina, M. A. Sokolova-Zhamson, S. I. Napoikin, and many were prepared or issued by private theatrical agencies. Among them are many working copies and promptbooks of various authors, stage managers, and actors—often with handwritten notes and commentaries of actors and stage managers concerning staging, properties, lighting, and textual changes.

There are also rare materials from the early postrevolutionary stage, including fragmentary, limited-edition publications, along with collections of newpaper and magazine clippings.

As an example of the riches in the library, the collection of S. S. Mokul'skii (1896–1960) which contains over 5,000 volumes, was collected during the first half of the twentieth century and consists of books on the history of the theater, belles-lettres, and literature on art and history in Russian and a number of foreign languages. Over 1,000 books from this collection in the sector have dedicatory autographs by such prominent persons in the theater and literary world as I. A. Bunin, V. V. Veresaev, V. E. Meyerhold (Meierkhol'd), L. V. Sobinov, A. Ia. Tairov, and A. P. Chekhov, among others. The Mokul'skii Collection also includes many manuscript materials relating to the theater.

Working Conditions: Documents requested from the division are issued in the general reading room through the librarian on duty.

Reference Facilities: The Sector of Rare Books has alphabetical catalogues and card catalogues (of personal names and titles of plays), an inventory acquisition register, a separate card catalogue of the Mokul'skii Collection, and a card catalogue of autographs.

Copying: Manuscripts can be xeroxed, but the permission of the director of the library is required.

Otdel izoizdanii
[Division of Graphic Imprints]

Telephone: 292-35-08; 292-09-84
Hours: M–W, FSa 12:00–20:45, Th 14:00–20:45
Head: Natal'ia Alekseevna Ezdina (*tel.* 292-35-08)

HOLDINGS: 3 fonds, 250,000 units, late 18th c.–1992
  photographs—73,859 units (1890s–1986)

Iconographic materials held by the library were started with the collection of Professor P. P. Pashkov, and augmented by collections of S. S. Mokul'skii, A. V. Tunkel', L. A. Ureklian, and M. B. Zagorskii. Illustrative materials include sketches, engravings, lithographs, photographs, postcards, as well as billboard posters, and other graphic materials.

There are many original sketches for theater stage design, scenery, and costumes, including those by A. N. Benois (Benua), I. Ia. Bilibin, B. R. Erdman, V. N. Khodasevich, and K. I. Korovin.

The library has a large collection of photographs on the history of the theater, ballet, and opera in Russia and abroad, as well as photographs of actors, directors, and designers. These include signed photographs of the directors K. S. Stanislavskii and V. I. Nemirovich-Danchenko, who created the Moscow Arts Theater, as well as the signed photographs of many of the performers in the Bolshoi Theater. There are also photographs of the costumes worn by members of the various social classes in nineteenth- and early twentieth-century Russia, which are arranged in a separate fond for photographs of daily life. Another separate fond retains negatives depicting scenes from plays performed in the country's principal theaters—particularly the Bolshoi and Mariinskii (Imperial Maria) Theaters, the State Academic Malyi Theater, and the Moscow Operetta Theater.

There are also collections of postcards (1849–1992), collectors' albums with pictures of Russia, Europe, and Asia, sketches of ordinary life, and a photographic chronicle of events in Moscow for the years 1950–1970.

The Engravings Fond (late 18th–early 19th cc.) contains engravings and lithographs with views of architectural monuments, costume designs, rural views, and portraits of theater performers.

Working Conditions: Requests for materials from the division should be made to the consultant in the division reading room.

Reference Facilities: There is a subject catalogue for iconographic materials of different types, a numbered catalogue of engravings, and a card catalogue of photographs of plays (listed under the name of the play).

Copying: Selected materials may be xerox-copied.

FINDING AIDS — PUBLISHED — GENERAL:
Biblioteki: Putevoditel' (1996), pp. 40–41; GAF *Spravochnik* (1991), pp. 16–17.

There is no published guide to the archival materials in the library. For a general description of the Sector of Rare Books, see *Fondy red. izd.* (1991), pp. 173–74. See also the brief description of the archival holdings on the library website.

FINDING AIDS — GENERAL — UNPUBLISHED:

g-125. "Rossiiskaia gosudarstvennaia biblioteka po iskusstvu: K 70-letiiu sozdaniia." Moscow, [1993]. 10 p. Typescript.

> Includes an essay on the history of the library, part of which has also been reproduced for the library's website.

Nauchnaia muzykal'naia biblioteka im. S. I. Taneeva Moskovskoi gosudarstvennoi konservatorii im. P. I. Chaikovskogo (NMB MGK)
[S. I. Taneev Scientific Music Library of the P. I. Tchaikovsky Moscow State Conservatory]

Agency: Ministerstvo kul'tury RF (Minkul'tury Rossii)
[Ministry of Culture]

Address: 103871, Moscow, ul. Bol'shaia Nikitskaia (*formerly* ul. Gertsena), 13
Telephone: 229-78-00; *Fax:* (095) 229-96-59
E-mail: bibuu@bibconsv.msu.ru
Transport: metro: Biblioteka im. Lenina, Arbatskaia, Tverskaia
Hours: M–F 9:00–18:00 (August—closed)

Director: Emma Borisovna Rassina (*tel.* 229-60-62)
Head, Division of International Relations: Svetlana Iur'evna Sigida (*tel.* 229-97-36)

HISTORY:
Biblioteka Muzykal'nykh klassov Moskovskogo otdeleniia Russkogo muzykal'nogo obshchestva
    [Library of Music Classes of the Moscow Division of the Russian Music Society] (1860–1872)
Biblioteka Moskovskoi konservatorii
    [Library of the Moscow Conservatory] (1872–1918)
Muzykal'naia biblioteka Moskovskoi gosudarstvennoi konservatorii
    [Music Library of the Moscow State Conservatory] (1918–1944)
Nauchnaia muzykal'naia biblioteka Moskovskoi gosudarstvennoi konservatorii (NMB MGK)
    [Scientific Music Library of the Moscow State Conservatory] (1944–1956)

The Moscow Conservatory was opened in 1866 on the basis of music classes of the Moscow Branch of the Russian Music Society under the initiative of N. G. Rubinstein (Rubinshtein), who served as its first director from 1866 to 1881. The library was founded on the basis of Rubinstein's private collection of books, sheet music, and manuscript music scores, which he had presented to the music classes in 1860. The library collection, together with the music classes, formally came under the authority of the Conservatory in 1872, but the library only became a properly organized book repository in 1893, when I. P. Shoning took over the duties of librarian.

In 1924 the library acquired the holdings of the Library of Music Theory (*Muzykal'no-teoreticheskaia biblioteka*) under the Russian Academy of Art Studies (*Rossiiskaia akademiia khudozhestvennykh nauk*—RAKhN), and in the same year also took over part of the fonds of the disbanded Choral Academy (*Khorovaia akademiia*), which was formerly the Synodal Secondary School (*Sinodal'noe uchilishche*). In 1934 part of the fonds of the Music Division of the Library of the Academy of Sciences (BAN—G–16) were also transferred to the library.

During the 1930s the conservatory library amassed a huge collection of original manuscripts of numerous composers and a series of archives formerly belonging to various institutions and private individuals. But in 1943 all of these materials were transferred to the Central Museum of Musical Culture (*Tsentral'nyi muzei muzykal'noi kul'tury*—H–45).

In 1956, to mark the centenary of the birth of the Russian composer Sergei Ivanovich Taneev (1856–1915), who had been a professor at the Conservatory, the Music Library of the Moscow Conservatory was renamed in his honor.

N.B. For the Scientific Archive and the N. G. Rubinstein Museum of the Conservatory, see E–53.

Otdel redkikh izdanii i rukopisei
[Division of Rare Editions and Manuscripts]

Telephone: 229-50-56
Hours: by appointment
Head: Irina Viacheslavovna Brezhneva

HOLDINGS: publications and manuscripts—15,300 units (late 15th–early 20th cc.); church music manuscripts—ca. 50 units; music scores—ca. 20 units

The basis of the holdings in this division came from the private collections of V. F. Odoevskii, A. Ia. Scriabin (Skriabin), A. V. Panaeva-Kartseva, and S. I. Taneev.

The Taneev Collection includes numerous autographs of the composer's contemporaries, friends, colleagues, students, and publishers, with dedicatory inscriptions by such fellow-composers as P. I. Tchaikovsky, N. A. Rimskii-Korsakov, S. V. Rakhmaninov, A. S. Arenskii, N. D. Kashkin, and E. A. Kuper, among others.

Many books in the Odoevskii Collection are inscribed with autographs and have bookplates. The music scores contain handwritten notes by their owners and numerous pencil corrections. The rarities in this collection include a transcription of the Joseph Haydn oratorio, "The Creation," by A. E. Müller, published by Breitkopf in German and Italian with a Russian translation written below in various hands. There is also a manuscript of "Scipio in Spain" by Baldassare Galuppi (1745) and copies of scores with the autograph of Franz Liszt.

The division has manuscript scores of early Russian church music (15th–18th cc.), most of which came from the collection of the musicologist N. F. Findeizen. Many of these manuscripts have notes made by, among others, Professor S. V. Smolenskii of the Moscow Conservatory, who was a specialist on early Russian music. Here there are manuscript codices of music written in early Russian non-linear neumatic notation, the most interesting of which are a late fifteenth-century compilation of antiphonic melodies, an early seventeenth-century compilation in neumatic notation, and an eighteenth-century linear score of the "All-Night Vigil" of a Kyivan eighteenth-century melody. There is also a manuscript containing rules for singing to non-linear neumatic notation (*obikhod znamennyi*); a complete late seventeenth-century *oktoikh* (i.e. a book of canticles composed for eight voices, containing verses from the Gospels set to music); and a manuscript copy dated 1743 of Nikolai Diletskii's "The Grammar of Music" (*Musikiiskaia grammatika*) (1670).

The division also holds manuscript scores of operatic and vocal works by Russian and foreign composers. These include works written by the director of the Court Capella, A. F. L'vov (1798–1870), the manuscript score of an unknown opera by L. V. Maurer (1798–1878), and a copy of the cantata composed by A. D. Kastal'skii (1856–1926), among others.

The division has the manuscript volumes of the works of the composer A. N. Verstovskii (the so-called Verstovskii Library) and manuscript copies of musical compositions from the collection made by A. Ia. Skariatin, secretary of the Russian Embassy in Rome. There is also the manuscript biobibliographical card catalogue of Russian musicians compiled by N. F. Findeizen.

There are manuscript collections of Russian folk songs, including those written down by the well-known collector of folklore, N. E. Pal'chikov (1839–1888), and four notebooks of Russian folk songs collected by the writer and musician M. A. Stakhovich (1819–1858), many with autographs.

There is also a manuscript written by M. I. Medvedeva, a former director of the library, containing information on the history of the library since its founding.

N.B. Some of the music scores and books from the S. I. Taneev Collection are to be found in the P. I. Tchaikovsky State House-Museum in Klin (H–48).

Working Conditions: Normally, manuscripts are available in the reading room the day they are ordered.

Reference Facilities: Opisi have been compiled for only part of the manuscript materials. Many of them are covered by the general catalogues of the division. A full catalogue of the manuscripts is in process.

FINDING AIDS — PUBLISHED — GENERAL:

There is no published guide to the archival materials in the Conservatory.

g-130. *Nauchnaia muzykal'naia biblioteka im. S. I. Taneeva: Ocherk.* Compiled by
E. S. Bulgakova, O. V. Grigorova, I. A. Adamov, et al. Edited by E. N. Artem'eva and
N. N. Grigorovich. Moscow: "Muzyka," 1966. 234 p. [MGK] (Lib: DLC; IU; MH)
> Contains a detailed account of the history of the library and a description of its fonds and collections, including the manuscript materials (pp. 202–11).

FINDING AIDS — SPECIALIZED:

Pre-1850 manuscript scores held by the library are now being entered in the RISM database (see a-463; URL: http://RISM.harvard.edu/RISM DB.html); 116 entries had been recorded by the end of 1997.

g-131. *Kollektsiia S. I. Taneeva. Knigi i noty: Katalog.* Compiled and edited by
I. V. Brezhneva. Moscow, 1991–1993. (Lib: DLC; MH)
> Vol. 1: *Knigi.* 127 p.
> Vol. 2, bk. 1: *Noty (A–L).* 170 p. bk. 2: *Noty (M–Ia).* 162 p.
>> The first volume describes printed book editions in the S. I. Taneev Collection (16th–early 20th c.) containing manuscript notes by Taneev himself and his contemporaries. The second volume (in 2 books) provides scholarly descriptions of 1,500 printed and manuscript music scores. Includes an index of personal names.

g-132. *Sergei Ivanovich Taneev: Lichnost', tvorchestvo, dokumenty ego zhizni.* Moscow/
Leningrad: Gosizdat, Muzsektor, 1925. 213 p. "Trudy Gosudarstvennogo instituta muzykal'noi nauki, Istoriia russkoi muzyki v issledovaniiakh i materialakh," vol. 2.
(Lib: MH)
> Includes a survey of the S. I. Taneev Collection (pp. 187–205).

Tsentral'naia nauchnaia biblioteka
Soiuza teatral'nykh deiatelei RF (TsNB STD RF)
[Central Scientific Library of the Union of Theater Workers]

Agency: Soiuz teatral'nykh deiatelei RF (STD Rossii)
[Union of Theater Workers]

Address: 107031, Moscow, Strastnoi bul'var, 10/34
Telephone: 229-09-13 (reference-bibliographic division); *RdngRm:* 200-38-34
Fax: (095) 959-22-58
Transport: metro: Chekovskaia, Pushkinskaia, Tverskaia
Hours: M–F 11:00–20:00; July–August 11:00–18:00

Director: Viacheslav Petrovich Nechaev (*tel.* 229-39-96)
Deputy Director: Vladimir Mikhailovich Kraev (*tel.* 229-10-56)

HISTORY:

Biblioteka Moskovskogo teatral'no-statisticheskogo biuro Russkogo teatral'nogo obshchestva
  [Library of the Moscow Theater-Statistical Office of the Russian Theater Society] (1896–1916)
Teatral'naia biblioteka Russkogo teatral'nogo obshchestva (Biblioteka RTO)
  [Theater Library of the Russian Theater Society] (1916–1921)
Nauchnaia teatral'naia biblioteka Russkogo teatral'nogo obshchestva (Biblioteka RTO)
  [Scientific Theater Library of the Russian Theater Society] (1921–1932)
Nauchnaia biblioteka Vserossiiskogo teatral'nogo obshchestva (Biblioteka VTO)
  [Scientific Library of the All-Russian Theater Society] (1932–1946)
Tsentral'naia nauchnaia biblioteka Vserossiiskogo teatral'nogo obshchestva (TsNB VTO)
  [Central Scientific Library of the All-Russian Theater Society] (1947–1986)
Tsentral'naia nauchnaia biblioteka Soiuza teatral'nykh deiatelei RSFSR (TsNB STD)
  [Central Scientific Library of the Union of Theater Workers of the RSFSR] (1986–1991)

The library was founded in 1896, at the same time as the establishment of the Moscow Theater-Statistical Office of the Russian Theater Society (RTO). When the presidium of the RTO was moved from St. Petersburg to Moscow in 1916, the library was reorganized as the Theater Library of the Russian Theater Society (RTO). In 1932, the RTO was transformed into the All-Russian Theater Society (VTO—*Vserossiiskoe teatral'noe obshchestvo*) and became the major professional union for actors, directors, theater designers, and other specialists in the realm of theater. The library was renamed accordingly. When in 1947 a network of theater libraries was organized with the Moscow library at its center, the name accordingly was changed to "Central." When in 1987, the VTO was renamed the Union of Theater Workers of the RSFSR (*Soiuz teatral'nykh deiatelei RSFSR*), the name of the library changed again. Since the collapse of the Soviet Union, the library remains the center of the library network of the Union of Theater Workers of the Russian Federation (*Soiuz teatral'nykh deiatelei RF*).

From the outset the library collected materials relating to the theatrical repertory. The personal libraries of many personalities of the theater world were acquired by the library, although in many cases their archival materials were transferred to TsGALI (now RGALI—B–7). Among more recent receipts, for example, TsNB STD received the library and collected reference materials of the theater critic, translator, literary historian, Professor A. A. Anikst, who had served on the library's governing board, as well as the library collections of the theater critics and historians E. V. Azernikova, A. K. Dzhivelegov, N. I. El'iash, and A. Ia. Shneer.

The library's Manuscript Division has developed an important collection of archival materials relating to the theater. The VTO established a theatrical memoirs collection in the 1930s, some of which were edited for publication. Starting in 1967, the memoir collection was transferred to the library, and at the same time the library started actively collecting autobiographies of luminaries in the theater world. More recently, the library has started to acquire and/or purchase personal papers and documentary collections of theater personalities.

The library also has a special Reference-Bibliographic Division, with extensive card catalogues, handling over 12,000 inquiries a year. The relatively recently organized Iconographic Division specializes in illustrative materials. The Apartment of People's Artists B. M. Tenin and L. P. Sukharevskaia (*Kvartira narodnykh artistov SSSR B. M. Tenina i L. P. Sukharevskoi*), with its family collections, is administered as a branch (see below).

N.B. Major records of the RTO and VTO itself, including some documentation about the library, were transferred to the Central State Archive of Literature and Art of the USSR (TsGALI SSSR), now RGALI (B–7—fond 641, 1889–1918; fond 970, 1917–).

Access: Research access requires a letter of application addressed to the library director. Access to materials held in the branch apartment of B. M. Tenin and L. P. Sukharevskaia should be arranged through the library itself.

Reference Facilities: The library Reference-Bibliographic Division has special card catalogues covering entries for prerevolutionary Russian, Soviet, and foreign theater; for theater personalia, including playwrights, composers, and theater designers (starting with the late 17th c.).

Copying: Xerox copies can be prepared at established rates, which are the same for Russian citizens and foreigners.

Rukopisnyi otdel (RO)
[Manuscript Division]

Hours: M–F 11:00–20:00; July–August, 11:00–18:00
Head: Natal'ia Robertovna Balatova (*tel.* 200-13-57)

HOLDINGS: 115 fonds and personal collections (30 fonds unarranged) fonds, ca. 10,000 units, 19th–20th cc.

The Manuscript Division has extensive materials relating to the nineteenth- and twentieth-century theater in Russia and the Soviet Union. There are many original manuscripts pertaining to the history of the theater, including manuscript plays, promptbooks, correspondence, theater programs, theater clippings, and scores/libretti. Of special interest is the collection of theatrical memoirs and autobiographies brought together since the 1930s by the VTO/STD.

While the library does not collect institutional or organizational records, there is considerable documentation of the RTO/VTO itself, and the archive of the library. There is also the collected archive of theater veterans associated with the M. G. Savina Leningrad Home of Stage Veterans.

Of particular importance are many fonds of personal papers of theater personalities, such as K. S. Stanislavskii (175 units), V. E. Meyerhold (Meierkhol'd) (ca. 120 units), and the actor and leader of the Jewish theater S. M. Mikhoels (ca. 100 units). There are also collected papers of the Russian actors M. I. Tsarev and M. M. Shtraukh, and the theater director A. Ia. Tairov and his wife, the actress A. G. Koonen.

There are also a significant number of fonds of personal papers of Russian émigrés, some of which contain copies of materials held abroad. The papers of the actor and director M. A. (Mikhail Aleksandrovich) Chekhov (1891–1955), who is buried in Hollywood, include copies of his letters, the originals of which remain abroad. There are also fonds for the ballet master and dancer M. M. (Mikhail Mikhailovich) Mordkin (1990–1955), active in Lithuania and then New York, and some papers of the historian and political activist A. A. Kizevetter (1866–1933), who in emigration was a professor in Prague.

There is a very extensive collection of photographs, with a negative archive of over 50,000. This includes the recently acquired photographic archive of the actor Andrei (A. A.) Mironov.

Working Conditions: Some of the recently received and émigré fonds have not been arranged, and hence are not readily accessible.

Reference Facilities: Opisi (inventories) are available for processed fonds.

Otdel ikonografii
[Iconography Division]

Hours: M–F 11:00–20:00; July–August, 11:00–18:00
Head: Ol'ga Konstantinovna Basolova (*tel.* 200-13-57)

HOLDINGS:

The separate Iconography Division has amassed considerable theater graphics, including many illustrative publications. Graphic materials include stage and costume designs, along with many illustrative materials from Soviet theaters. Of relatively recent acquisition is the collection of iconographic materials on the history of theater costumes, which were donated by the artist and costume designer N. B. Glinskii. There are photographs and albums made by the French theater photographer Serge Lido, including a collection of ballet photographs from France and other countries, which was donated by his widow Irina Lidova.

Reference Facilities: An annotated card catalogue has been prepared with over 400,000 cards.

Kvartira narodnykh artistov SSSR B. M. Tenina i
L. P. Sukharevskoi—Sobranie lichnykh kollektsii
[Apartment of People's Artists B. M. Tenin and L. P. Sukharevskaia—
Collected Personal Collections]

Address: Moscow, Bol'shaia Nikitskaia, 49
Telephone: 202-48-61
Hours: by appointment

HOLDINGS:

The memorial apartment, which is administratively a branch of the library, houses the personal library of this theater family, centering on the careers of Boris Mikhailovich Tenin (1905–1990) and his wife, the stage and film actress Lidiia Pavlovna Sukharevskaia (1909–1991). Holdings of an archival interest include their personal archives, a collection of ex libris from Moscow theater personalities, a collection of theatrical caricatures, and also films and videotapes of performances.

Working Conditions: Research arrangements are made through the main library, since the apartment has no facilities of its own.

FINDING AIDS — PUBLISHED — GENERAL:

There are no published descriptions of the archival materials in the library.

FINDING AIDS — SPECIALIZED:

Fonds of personal papers of Russian émigrés held by TsNB STD RF, most of which have been declassifed recently, are listed in *Russ. Zarubezh'e* (1998), pp. 352–56 (a-372A).

Rossiiskaia gosudarstvennaia detskaia biblioteka (RGDB)
[Russian State Children's Library]

Agency: Ministerstvo kul'tury RF (Minkul'tury Rossii)
[Ministry of Culture]

Address: 117049, Moscow, Kaluzhskaia (*formerly* Oktiabr'skaia) pl., 1
Telephone: 238-96-55; *Fax:* (095) 956-35-28
Transport: metro: Oktiabr'skaia; trol.: 33, 4, 62, 7; bus: 111
Hours: M–F 10:00–19:00; SaSu 10:00–18:00

Director: Lidiia Mikhailovna Zharkova (*tel.* 959-06-49)
Deputy Director for Scientific Work: Elena Ivanovna Golubeva (*tel.* 959-18-49)

HISTORY:
Gosudarstvennaia respublikanskaia detskaia biblioteka RSFSR (GRDB)
    [State Republican Children's Library of the RSFSR] (1969–1992)
Gosudarstvennaia respublikanskaia detskaia biblioteka Rossii (GRDBR)
    [Russian State Republican Children's Library] (1992–1993)

The Library was founded by order of the Ministry of Culture of the RSFSR in December, 1969. Since 1987, it has been specially collecting rare books and archival materials for its museum exhibitions on the children's book.

HOLDINGS: 1 fond, 309 units, 1957–1986
    photographs—78 units (1957–1986); sound recordings—9 units (1978–1985)

The library fond holds books with dedicatory autographs of well-known Soviet and foreign writers of literature for children, often in artistic and poetic form. These books include those written by the founder of the pioneer movement in the Soviet Union, N. V. Bogdanov, and authors such as S. Alekseev, V. D. Berestov, K. Bulychev, N. Iu. Durova, Iu. Koval', and E. N. Uspenskii. There are also works by foreign writers, such as Astryd Lindgren (Sweden) and Asen Bosev (Bulgaria), and books with autographs of artistic illustrators such as as N. Ustinov, L. Tokmakov, L. Vladimirskii, A. Eliseev, and E. Monin. The library has a Bible autographed by Patriarch Aleksii II.

    The manuscript journals held in the library illustrate the work of children's literary studios and the film club "Literary Heroes on the Screen" (*Geroi knigi na ekrane*).

    The library holds albums and folders containing photographs of writers meeting with their readers and a video film of a meeting with the children's writer Thomas Brezina.

    There are sound recordings of the stories of the book illustrator V. I. Tauber, and gramophone records of children's songs by such famous song writers as A. B. Zhurbin, E. P. Krylatov, and M. S. Pliatskovskii.

    The archive holds documents relating to the founding and development of the library.

Access: An official letter from the sponsoring organization stating the subject of research and the presentation of a passport are required for access to materials.

Working Conditions: The library has no special subdivision for archival materials. Matters relating to research work with the documents are handled by the inspector of the Personnel Division (*Inspektor otdela kadrov*).

Reference Facilities: There are inventories of the files.

Copying: Xerox copies can be prepared.

FINDING AIDS — PUBLISHED — GENERAL:
Biblioteki: Putevoditel' (1996), pp. 38–39; *GAF Spravochnik* (1991), pp. 79–80.

There is no published guide to the archival materials in the library.

Sinodal'naia biblioteka Moskovskoi patriarkhii
[Synodal Library of the Moscow Patriarchate]

Agency: Moskovskaia Patriarkhiia
[Moscow Patriarchate]

Address: 117334, Moscow, Andreevskaia nab., 2
Telephone: 135-81-15
Transport: metro: Leninskii prospekt
Hours: M–F 12:00–17:00

Head: Father (*sviashchennik*) Boris (Boris Olegovich Danilenko) (*tel.* 135-81-15)

HISTORY:

The library was reestablished in 1987. The remaining holdings of its prerevolutionary predecessor were all nationalized after 1917.

HOLDINGS: ca. 30 manuscript units, 15th–20th cc.

The archival section of the library has several Cyrillic manuscript books. Among several personal fonds, the richest is the archive of Archbishop Mikhail (Chub).

Access: Access is by personal letter of request with the presentation of a passport or other official identity document.

Reference Facilities: An inventory and catalogue are being compiled.

FINDING AIDS — PUBLISHED — GENERAL:
Biblioteki: Putevoditel' (1996), p. 219.

There is no published guide for the manuscript books and archival materials in the library.

Moskovskaia Dukhovnaia Akademiia (MDA)
[Moscow Theological Academy]

Agency: Moskovskaia Patriarkhiia
[Moscow Patriarchate]

Address: 141300, Moskovskaia oblast', Sergiev Posad, Troitse-Sergieva Lavra
Telephone: (254) 543–52
Transport: suburban train from Iaroslavl station to Sergiev Posad

Rector: Bishop Evgenii Vereiskii (Valerii Germanovich Reshetnikov)
  (*tel.* [254] 453–46 [reception])
Scientific Secretary: Archimandrite Platon (Igumnov) (*tel.* [254] 453-43; 453-44)

HISTORY:

Ellino-grecheskaia akademiia
  [Hellenic Greek Academy] (1685–1701)
Slaviano-latinskaia akademiia
  [Slavonic-Latin Academy] (1701–1775)
Slaviano-greko-latinskaia akademiia
  [Slavonic, Greek, and Latin Academy] (1775–1814)
Moskovskaia Dukhovnaia Akademiia
  [Moscow Theological Academy] (1814–1917)
Pravoslavnyi dukhovnyi institut
  [Orthodox Theological Institute] (1944–1945)
Moskovskii bogoslovskii institut
  [Moscow Theological Institute] (1945–1946)

The Moscow Theological Academy, together with its library, was founded in 1685 as the Hellenic Greek Academy on the basis of the school at the Monastery of the Epiphany (*Bogoiavlenskii monastyr'*). In 1701 it became the Slavonic-Latin Academy, and in 1775 the Slavonic, Greek, and Latin Academy. In 1814 it was given its present name and moved to the Holy Trinity-St. Sergius Monastery (*Sviato-Troitse-Sergieva Lavra*) in Sergiev Posad. In the course of the nineteenth century, the Academy developed an extensive library, which by 1917 totaled over 300,000 printed editions and over 1,600 manuscript books with manuscript collections from a number of other Russian religious institutions, including part of the collection from the Joseph of Volokolamsk (*Iosifo-Volokolamskii*) Monastery.

After the October Revolution, when the Theological Academy was closed down, the library was nationalized, and in October 1919 officially transferred to the control of the administration of the Rumiantsev Museum and Library (after 1924, the Lenin Public Library—G–1). Reorganized as the Sergiev Branch of the latter library, in 1920 it acquired the library with extensive manuscript holdings of the Vifan Theological Seminary (*Vifanskaia Dukhovnaia Seminariia*) and also formally accessioned the library holdings and archive of the Trinity-St. Sergius Monastery itself. During the next ten years, the Sergiev Branch continued to operate and expand its valuable collections of manuscripts. Between 1930 and 1934, however, the manuscript collections, together with most of the archives were all transferred to Moscow and incorporated into the Manuscript Division of the Lenin Library itself, although the branch in Sergiev Posad (after 1930, renamed Zagorsk) retained some of its printed library collections.

The Academy was opened again in 1944 as the Orthodox Theological Institute, in the Lopukhin corpus of the Novodevichii Convent. Briefly named the Moscow Theological Institute (*Moskovskii bogoslovskii institut*), it was subsequently renamed the Moscow Theological Academy, and in 1947 it was returned to the Trinity-St. Sergius Monastery in Zagorsk. The library as presently constituted was started anew on the basis of private gifts (including the personal library of Patriarch Aleksii) and accessions from various educational establishments.

In 1944, the archive was reinstated as a repository for documentary materials of the Academy.

The Church-Archeological Cabinet (*Tserkovno-arkheologicheskii kabinet*) was founded in 1950 within the Subdepartment (*kafedra*) of Church Archeology.

Access: By letter of permission from the rector.

Working Conditions: There is a reading room in the library.

Biblioteka
[Library]

Librarian: Hegumen Feofilakt (Moiseev)

HOLDINGS: no statistics are available on the archival holdings
   books—ca. 160,000 units

The library collections currently comprise holdings brought together after World War II. These include 4,514 books on theology received in 1954 from the Iaroslavl Pedagogical Institute (which previously belonged to the Iaroslavl Theological Seminary). Other accessions include collections from the libraries of the Saratov, Stavropol, and Minsk Theological Academies, the Scientific Library of the University of Tartu, and from the former Theological Mission of the Russian Orthodox Church in Beijing.

Tserkovno-arkheologicheskii kabinet
[Church-Archeological Cabinet]

HOLDINGS: no statistics available

The Cabinet (study room) holds a separate collection of early printed books and manuscripts, dating from the sixteenth through the eighteenth century. Early printed books include the works of the first Russian printer, Ivan Fedorov—a copy of the Moscow Books of the Apostles (*Moskovskii Apostol*) of 1564, which has a hand-engraved frontispiece, the L'viv Books of the Apostles of 1574, and a copy of the first printed Slavonic Bible (1581), known as the Ostrog Bible.

Arkhiv
[Archive]

HOLDINGS: no statistics available

The Archive has the journal of meetings of the Scholarly Council of the Academy and the Moscow Theological Seminary, journals of the general meetings of the Council of the Orthodox Theological Institute and the Orthodox Pastoral Courses (1944–1946), together with annual reports of the Academy and Seminary starting in 1944. There are also some unpublished writings of the faculty.

N.B. Documentation from the prerevolutionary archive of MDA is divided between TsIAM (D–2) and RGB (G–1).

FINDING AIDS — PUBLISHED — GENERAL:

There is no published description of the manuscript materials in the library.

g-137. *Moskovskaia Dukhovnaia Akademiia—300 let (1685–1985): Bogoslovskie trudy:*
Iubileinyi sbornik. Moscow: Izd. Moskovskoi Patriarkhii, 1986. 336 p. + plates. (Lib: IU)
    A collection of articles by Moscow Theological Academy faculty includes information about
    the history of the Academy and its library (pp. 247–69), and the Church-Archeological Cabinet
    (pp. 160–61).

g-138. *Moskovskaia Dukhovnaia Akademiia i sobranie Tserkovno-arkheologicheskogo*
kabineta. Moscow: Izd. Moskovskoi Patriarkhii, 1986. 48 p. + plates. (Lib: DLC; IU; MH)
    Provides brief information on the manuscript books in the Church-Archeological Cabinet.

FINDING AIDS — GENERAL — UNPUBLISHED:

g-139. Ostapov, A. D. (Archpriest). "K 20-letiiu Tserkovno-arkheologicheskogo kabineta."
Moscow, [n.d.]. Typescript. "Sochineniia," vol. 15. [MDA]

Archives and Manuscript Holdings in Libraries

St. Petersburg

Rossiiskaia natsional'naia biblioteka (RNB)
[Russian National Library]

Agency: Ministerstvo kul'tury RF (Minkul'tury Rossii)
[Ministry of Culture]

Address: 191069, St. Petersburg, ul. Sadovaia, 18
Telephone: 310-71-37; *Fax:* (812) 310-61-48
E-mail: office@nlr.ru (inquiries); ref.reader@nlr.ru
Website: http://www.nlr.ru
Transport: metro: Gostinyi Dvor, Nevskii prospekt; bus: 14, 22; trol.: 1, 5, 7, 10, 14, 22; tram: 2, 5, 14, 54

Director: Vladimir Nikolaevich Zaitsev (*tel.* 310-28-56)
Deputy Director for Foreign Relations and Marketing:
   Elena Vladimirovna Nebogatikova (*tel.* 310-56-72)
Deputy Director for Scientific Work: Vladimir Rufinovich Firsov (*tel.* 310-86-29)
Deputy Director for Library Work and Automation: Irina Borisovna Tsvetkova
   (*tel.* 110-57-62)
Scientific Secretary: Vladimir Anatol'evich Kolobkov (*tel.* 310-98-50)

HISTORY:

Imperatorskaia Publichnaia biblioteka (IPB)
   [Imperial Public Library] (1795–1917)
Rossiiskaia Publichnaia biblioteka (RPB)
   [Russian Public Library] (1918–1932)
Rossiiskaia Publichnaia biblioteka im. M. E. Saltykova-Shchedrina (RPB)
   [M. E. Saltykov-Shchedrin Russian Public Library] (1932–1937)
Gosudarstvennaia Publichnaia biblioteka im. M. E. Saltykova-Shchedrina (GPB)
   [M. E. Saltykov-Shchedrin State Public Library] (1937–III.1992)

The library, established by order of Catherine II in 1795, and opened as the Imperial Public Library in 1814, had the status of a national library and legal depository for all books published in Russia (since 1811). After the Revolution, in 1918 it was renamed the Russian Public Library. In 1932 its name was ammended to honor M. E. Saltykov-Shchedrin, and in 1937 it became the M. E. Saltykov-Shchedrin State Public Library. One of the richest libraries in the world (with over 30,000,000 volumes), it was given its present name as the Russian National Library by presidential decree in March 1992, which also named it to the register of the most valuable cultural monuments of the people of the Russian Federation.

A large, modern building for the library has recently been completed for the main library reading rooms and stacks across from the "Park Pobeda" metro station at the southern edge of the city (Moskovskii prosp., 165). Some of the holdings have already been transferred and, as of fall 1998, others are in transit. However, the Division of Manuscripts, the Division of Prints and Engravings, and the Sector of Rare Books, will remain in the old building at the corner of Nevskii Prospekt and ul. Sadovaia, and other divisions of the library described below will most probably remain in their present locations.

The Division of Manuscripts was first established as the Depot of Manuscripts in 1805 on the basis of the P. P. Dubrovskii (Dubrowski) collection of manuscripts and historical documents, mostly gathered in France and other European countries in the course of thirty years by the Russian diplomat, and significantly increased during the upheavals of the French Revolution, and the library of the Załuski brothers that had been brought from Warsaw to St. Petersburg in 1795 by Catherine II to become one of the founding collections of the new library. (Most of the Załuski collection was returned to Poland after the Treaty of Riga in 1921 and perished in World War II.) The manuscript holdings were expanded with the accession of many private collections during the nineteenth century, such as those of P. K. Frolov (1817), F. A. Tolstoi (1830), and the Repository of Antiquities (*Drevlekhranilishche*) of M. P. Pogodin (1852), and a major part of the library from the Imperial Hermitage (1852–1861). It acquired the collection of Western European books and documents of General P. K. Sukhtelen (Suchtelen), and the collections of Oriental manuscripts of A. S. Firkovich and Archimandrite Porfirii (K. A. Uspenskii), to name only a few. By 1917 it ranked second to the Bibliothèque Nationale in Paris among world libraries in terms of the extent and value of its manuscript holdings.

With the nationalization of imperial, religious, and private collections after the October Revolution, the Division of Manuscripts was expanded extensively. It acquired an additional part of the library from the Imperial Hermitage (1920s) and manuscript materials from a number of other imperial and high gentry palace collections. It received the extensive manuscript collections from the libraries of the Petersburg Theological Academy (along with part of the archive), the Novgorod Theological Seminary and the Cathedral of St. Sophia in Novgorod, the Alexander-Nevskii Lavra, and the Kirillo-Belozerskii and Solovetskii Monasteries (1928). Among secular organizations, it acquired the collection of the Society of Friends of Early Written Texts (*Obshchestvo liubitelei drevnei pis'mennosti*) (1932), part of the manuscript book collection from the Russian Archeological Society, the editorial records of a number of prerevolutionary journals, and other nationalized and donated private collections, archives from other institutions, and personal papers and manuscript collections of a number of important families and individuals.

Plekhanov House, which was founded in 1928 and has the status of a branch of the Division of Manuscripts, houses the personal archive and library of the noted Russian revolutionary, parts of which were transferred from abroad by his heirs, together with documentation of his entourage.

From 1970 to 1988, the Division of Manuscripts was combined with the Division of Rare Books, but now the Scientific Research Sector of Rare Books and Bibliology (*Nauchno-issledovatel'skii sektor redkikh knig i knigovedeniia*) is administratively separate within the Division of Fonds and Services (*Otdel fondov i obsluzhivaniia*—OFO). The Division of Prints and Engravings (*Otdel estampov*) is likewise separate, as is the Division of Music Scores and Sound Recordings.

In addition to specific archival holdings mentioned below, it should be noted that RNB has collected extensive *samizdat* and unofficial periodicals from the pre-1991 period.

Access: A reader's ticket for the library itself is obtained by first obtaining a temporary control slip at the main entrance and presenting a passport and two visa-size photographs at the service desk on the second floor. For access to archival material in the Rare Books Sector, the Prints Division, and the RNB Archive, reseachers should present an official letter to the Director of the Library. Access to the Division of Manuscripts requires an official letter of application to the head of the division, indicating the researcher's position, subject, and aim of research. Foreign researchers not on official exchange programs are advised to send a letter of inquiry in advance of arrival, explaining the time and purpose of their research.

Library Facilities: See the RNB website and PKG *Handbook* (1989), Ch. 7, for information about other bibliographies and collections in RNB, some of which are already moved or in transit to the new building. During the transitional period of transfers to the new building, some chronological segments of the library holdings may be temporarily unavailable.

Otdel rukopisei (OR)
[Division of Manuscripts]

Address:	pl. Ostrovskogo, 1/3
Telephone:	312-28-63
E-mail:	manuscripts@nlr.ru
Hours:	MWF 13:00–21:00; TuTh 9:00–21:00; SaSu 11:00–19:00;
	(July, August: MW 13:00–21:00; TuTh–Sa 9:00–17:00)

Head: Liudmila Igorevna Buchina (*tel.* 312-28-63)
Head of Reading Room: Natal'ia Borisovna Rogova

HOLDINGS: 1,249 (71 unarranged) fonds, 375,263 units, 5th c.–1994
(some documents 10th c. B.C.–5th c.)
early Slavic MS books—30,000 units; early Russian charters—18,000 units;
Russian archival fonds—over 220,000 units (18th–20th cc.); Western MSS—ca. 80,000 units;
Oriental MSS—ca. 20,700 units

The Division of Manuscripts houses one of the world's richest collections of Slavic, Western, and Oriental manuscripts, together with over 1,000 modern institutional and personal archival fonds.

The Slavonic-Rus' manuscript tradition is represented in the Basic Collection of Manuscript Books (*Osnovnoe sobranie rukopisnoi knigi—OSRK*), which was formed in the division from individual acquisitions from prerevolutionary collectors and scholars—Archimandrite Amfilokhii (P. I. Sergievskii), A. I. Artem'ev, P. D. Bogdanov, F. I. Buslaev, P. K. Frolov, the historian N. M. Karamzin, Bishop Porfirii (K. A. Uspenskii), the archeologist P. I. Savvaitov, and E. V. Trekhletov, to name only a few. A corresponding New Collection of Manuscript Books (*Novoe sobranie rukopisnoi knigi—NSRK*) includes manuscripts collected by the Manuscript Division after 1917.

Many other manuscript books remain part of major private collections received by the library, some in the early nineteenth century—such as the collections of F. A. Tolstoi (1830—with over 1,300 manuscripts and early historical documents) and the so-called Repository of Antiquities (*Drevlekhranilishche*) of M. P. Pogodin (1852), which also included the Arkhangel'sk library of D. M. Golitsyn and part of the P. M. Stroev collection. The part of the Hermitage Collection transferred to the Public Library in the 1850s and 1860s also included part of the collection of M. M. Shcherbatov. Among the many other collections acquired later were those of Ivan Berchich, A. F. Gil'ferding, Iu. A. Iavors'kyi (Iavorskii—especially rich in materials from Ukrainian lands), and A. A. Titov (1902), which was the largest private manuscript collection in prerevolutionary Russia (ca. 5,000 units).

Among Slavonic manuscript treasures are the earliest dated Church Slavonic manuscript, the illuminated "Ostromir Gospel" (1056–1057); the so-called *Izbornik Sviatoslava* (1076); the Laurentian Chronicle (*Lavrent'evskaia letopis'*) of 1377, which is the oldest part of the so-called Russian (Rus') Primary Chronicle; the Kyivan (Kievan) Psalter (*Kievskaia Psaltir'*) (1397); the illuminated Four Gospels (1508); and the earliest text of the Rus' law code, "*Russkaia pravda.*" There are many other famous legal, historical, and literary manuscripts of all types, as well as materials on the history of the Church and the Schism (*Raskol*), diplomatic documents, and genealogical books, in original and copies.

Among important Slavic holdings from outside of Russia, is a collection of Bulgarian and Serbo-Croatian manuscripts (11th–16th cc.), among which are Cyrillic and Glagolitic texts, including an eleventh-century Gospel from Mount Athos. There are a number of Czech materials, and the A. F. Gil'ferding collection includes some 100 manuscripts (13th–18th cc.) from Serbia, Bosnia, and Herzegovina. There are a number of later manuscript materials from Poland, including some from the P. P. Dubrovskii (Dubrowski) and other collections, along with some important materials from the Radziwiłł family archive from Nesvizh (Pol. Nieśwież).

Early Rus' and Moscovite charters (*akty* and *gramoty*) dating from the thirteenth through seventeenth centuries form a Basic Collection of Documents and Charters (*Osnovnoe sobranie aktov i gramot*—OSAG), which combines materials from many individual collections. There are also separate territorial collections of charters from Tavrensk, Ust'-Sysol'sk (Syktyvkar), and Iarensk, and several named collections, including those of I. K. Zinchenko, A. S. Orlov, and P. N. Tikhanov, among others. These include original grand ducal and tsarist charters, petitions, interrogations, mercantile agreements, and testaments, among other types of early official documents.

Russian fonds from the eighteenth through twentieth centuries contain documents on social-economic, political, and military history, the history of science, culture, and the fine arts. Among fonds and subject-oriented collections are those from the Commission of the Imperial Public Library director Baron M. A. Korf for collecting materials relating to the reign of Nicholas I, documents on the elections to the First State Duma, collected on the instructions of the then Prime Minister S. Iu. Witte (Vitte) (1905–1906, 15 vols.), a collection on finance in Russia (1900–1908), and a collection of censorship materials, among others.

A significant number of sources for the history of Russian domestic and foreign policy are to be found among hundreds of personal fonds of government and society leaders of the eighteenth to twentieth centuries—A. D. Menshikov, chancellery secretary of Peter I A. V. Makarov, and Prince G. A. Potemkin-Tavricheskii; the ministers and high officials A. A. Arakcheev, M. M. Speranskii (with drafts and papers on administrative and legal reform), head of the St. Petersburg Censorship Committee V. A. Tsei (with extensive materials on censorship and the prison system), and Minister of Internal Affairs V. K. Pleve; diplomat D. P. Tatishchev, diplomat and minister N. P. Ignat'ev, and ambassador to Japan and the USA, R. R. Rozen; military commanders General A. V. Suvorov, Admirals S. K. and A. S. Greig, and World War I front Commander D. V. Balanin, to name only a few. Here also is a collection of autographs of representatives of the Romanov family, including original letters and documents of Peter I and Catherine II. Gentry estate and family fonds and collections include papers of the Mansyrov family (with 175 charters, 1572–1809), the Novgorod landowners Koshkarev and Elagin, the Riazan and Kashira landowners Protasov, the Polovtsev family archive (with materials on the inspection [*reviziia*] by Senator A. A. Polovtsev of Kyiv and Chernihiv guberniias in 1880–1881), and the family archive of Princes P. G. and A. P. Ol'denburg.

The entire spectrum of nineteenth-century social and political thought is represented—from manuscripts of the Slavophile I. S. Aksakov to the populist A. A. Sleptsov, to the Cadet Party leader P. N. Miliukov, the economist, and politician P. B. Struve, and the populist A. V. Peshekhonov, among others.

The documentary record of science and culture is represented by institutional collections from the Free Economic Society, the Russian Archeological Society, the Committee of the Society for Aid to Needy Men of Letters and Scholars (in part), and editorial offices of journals such as *Novoe vremia, Russkoe slovo, Russkii bibliofil*, among others.

Among fonds and collections of personal origin, many with unpublished writings, mention should be made of papers of the historians K. F. Kalaidovich, N. I. Kostomarov (with extensive correspondence), A. I. Mikhailovskii-Danilevskii (with many of his diaries and journals), A. N. Olenin, P. P. Pekarskii (with extensive materials on the eighteenth century), S. F. Platonov (with 12,000 letters from 2,400 correspondents), S. N. Shubinskii (with 20,000 letters and parts of the archive of the journals *Drevniaia i novaia Rossiia* and *Istoricheskii vestnik*), and N. K. Shil'der (Schilder) (with extensive notes and original documents from state and family archives). There are also fonds of the jurist A. F. Koni; the director of the Archeological Institute, N. V. Pokrovskii; and the specialist on church history, A. A. Dmitrievskii, among others. Among papers of Slavicists are those of I. I. Sreznevskii, A. N. Pypin, and A. A. Shakhmatov.

Most of the great Russian writers of the eighteenth, nineteenth, and early twentieth centuries are represented by a significant number of literary manuscripts in well-known collections, and some with more extensive personal fonds. These include many materials of M. Iu. Lermontov, I. A. Goncharov, D. S. Merezhkovskii, and Z. N. Gippius, A. Belyi, V. V. Khlebnikov, and A. M. Remizov. Manuscript materials range from holographs of I. A. Krylov's *Fables*, to the manuscripts of N. V. Gogol''s *Dead Souls* and I. S. Turgenev's *Fathers and Sons*, to 207 autograph manuscripts of A. A. Blok, and samples of A. A. Akhmatova and S. A. Esenin (Yesenin), to give only a few examples. Among rich fonds of literary and artistic critics are those of V. G. Belinskii and the extensive documentary collections of N. A. Dobroliubov and V. V. Stasov. (Many of these are described in printed catalogues.)

The library is one of the richest in Russia for musicology. It holds especially important manuscript materials for the Russian composers A. P. Borodin, A. K. Glazunov, M. I. Glinka, César Cui (Ts. A. Kiui), M. P. Musorgskii, S. S. Prokof'ev, and N. A. Rimskii-Korsakov. There are many letters and scores of many famous foreign composers from the seventeenth through nineteenth century. In 1938 it received many of the manuscript materials collected by the Leningrad Philharmonic after the Revolution (G–20), some that have been retained with specific collections, such as the V. V. Stasov collection, others arranged within individual fonds.

Other fields of culture and the arts are likewise well represented. For example, the papers of the theater director V. I. Nemirovich-Danchenko, the architects N. L. Benois (Benua) and A. S. Nikol'skii, and those of many famous Russian artists, including B. M. Kustodiev, G. S. Vereiskii, and A. P. Ostroumova-Lebedeva. Aside from personal papers there are other archival collections including those for theater plays, drawings and other documents of Leningrad artists, documents for the biobibliography of Soviet writers, and letters of Soviet scholars relating to bibliography.

The most important collection of Greek manuscripts in the country—and one of the most important outside Greece (over 1,000)—includes, for example, the collections of the Leipzig professor Constantin von Tischendorf and the German archeographer Christian Friedrich von Matthaei (another part of the Matthaei collection is in RGADA—B–2); the collection of Bishop Porfirii (K. A. Uspenskii), who for eighteen years headed the Orthodox mission in Palestine and brought back close to 290 Greek manuscripts, including 34 on parchment (the earliest from the 9th c.); those of Archimandrite Antonin (A. V. Kapustin) and the historian-Byzantinist A. P. Papadopulo-Keramevs; several manuscripts from the library of the Byzantine emperors (4th–13th cc.); and manuscripts from the Nizhyn Greek Brotherhood (17th–18th cc. from the collection of A. A. Dmitrievskii). Most important among Greek manuscripts are early papyruses (2d–4th cc. A.D.) and religious texts, including fragments of the sixth-century "Codex Sinaiticus," the Porfiry Gospel (835) and Psalter (862), and the tenth-century "Gospel of Trebizond." There are also legal texts, dictionaries, copies of ancient and Byzantine authors dating from the fourth to the nineteenth centuries, including some important palimpsests, and a large collection of photographic copies of illuminated manuscripts from many repositories. Several Greek manuscripts are of Moldavian and Wallachian provenance.

Almost a thousand Latin manuscripts, many of which are illuminated, represent monuments of medieval religious and lay literature, annals and chronicles, and legal codices, including a number in Gothic script (11th–17th cc.). Some of the most notable early manuscripts include texts of Cicero, a fifth-century parchment codex of writings of Saint Augustine, and an early text of Bede's *Historia ecclesiastica* (746). Historical documents from the Middle Ages and Italian Renaissance include papal bulls and municipal charters. There are charters of French kings, humanists, scholars, and writers.

In terms of Western European manuscripts (6,000 codices of the 15th–20th cc. and over 70,000 documents) of particular importance is the collection of the diplomat P. P. Dubrovskii (Dubrowski), which includes documents of provenance in French monastic and royal libraries and other archives in France and other countries of Western Europe. Many of them were gathered in France during the revolutionary period, with a major segment from the archive of the Bastille (400 documents), and materials from the monasteries of St. Germain des Près and St. Antoine des Champs.

Many significant Western European manuscripts were acquired from the Hermitage, such as a famous French chronicle from the fifteenth century, "Grands chroniques de France." Others came directly from the imperial family, such as the collection of Diderot's personal papers, including manuscript writings with the author's corrections, that was purchased for Catherine II. The collections of P. K. Sukhtelen (Suchtelen), P. L. Vaksel', and A. Ia. Lobanov-Rostovskii, are also especially rich in foreign autographs, along with many letters of statesmen, scholars, and literary figures and important texts from England, Germany, the Netherlands, Spain, Portugal, and Italy—in addition to France. Famous autographs from all over Europe include those of Richelieu, Mazarin, Mary Stuart, Napoleon, Bismarck, Simon Bolivar, Honoré de Balzac, Goethe, and Charles Dickens. The American presidents George Washington and Abraham Lincoln are also represented. Closer to home, there are charters from gentry on the Island of Ösel, and letters of French officers during the Crimean War.

The collection of the Russian military engineer and diplomat P. K. Sukhtelen (Suchtelen) is particularly rich in materials from Scandinavia, in addition to 30,000 autographs (16th–mid-19th cc.). Historical materials in that collection especially relate to the Swedish involvement in the Baltic from the seventeenth through the nineteenth centuries, to the 30 Years War, the Great Northern War, reports from the Swedish governors-general in Finland, diplomatic relations with Russia, official decrees of King Charles XII of Sweden, papers of eight Danish kings, and documents of many Scandinavian scholars.

Oriental holdings in the Division of Manuscripts are among the richest in Russia. Ancient Egyptian papyruses from the Libyan Era of the tenth and ninth centuries B.C. are among its oldest manuscripts. There are Indian Buddhist texts in the Pali language on palm leaves, fifth-century Syriac manuscripts, and early inscriptions on stone and leather. Oriental holdings include religious, historical, legal, scientific, and literary texts—from the "Church History" of Eusebius of Caesaria (462), a manuscript life of Judas Iscariot (6th c.), the second earliest known copy (1332–1333) of the "Shakh Name" of the Persian epic poet Firdawsi, to a collection of documents from the field chancery of the Turkish commanding forces under Ali Pasha from the period of the Crimean War (1853–1856).

Most of the Oriental holdings are arranged in collections by language groups, but some have been retained in the collections of their provenance, such as the Bakhchisarai collections, or those of their individual collector, such as those of Archimandrite Antonin (A. I. Kapustin), the Arabist I. Iu. Krachkovskii, and the Orientalist N. V. Khanykov. The A. S. Firkovich (Firkowitsch) collection is particularly rich in early Hebrew, Hebrew-Arabic, and Samaritan manuscripts, including biblical and Talmud texts, many of which were acquired from the Cairo Geniza. It includes the earliest known copy of the Pentateuch in Hebrew (1010). Another important group of Hebrew manuscripts was transferred to the library in the nineteenth century from the Odessa Society for History and Antiquities.

The largest number of manuscripts in any language group are those in Persian (ca. 1,000), followed by Arabic (ca. 800), Turkic languages (ca. 400), and Chinese manuscripts and xylographs (ca. 250). There are also representative early manuscripts in the Coptic and Chaldean languages, and some in Armenian, Georgian, Mongolian, Manchu, and Japanese, which indicates the extent, richness, and variety of the Oriental holdings. The archives of the Khanates of Khiva and Kokand that were earlier held and catalogued in the Division of Manuscripts were returned to Tashkent, although microfilms remain.

Cartographic materials include maps of the fifteenth through twentieth centuries, including economic and topographic descriptions of Russia and other countries. There is a collection of architectural drawings which provide rich sources for construction projects and city planning in Russian cities, and include drawings and blueprints of Antonio Rinaldi, I. E. Starov, and Carlo (K. I.) Rossi, among others.

Working Conditions: Manuscript materials are delivered to the reading room the day after order (except for Friday and Saturday orders).

Reference Facilities: There are typewritten or manuscript *opisi* of all processed fonds and a card catalogue of existing *opisi*.

There is a short card catalogue listing all fonds in the division. There is a more extensive card catalogue of names for many of the processed manuscript fonds in Russian and foreign languages. For those institutional fonds and personal papers included (the catalogue is far from complete or comprehensive), there are cross-references to correspondents whose letters may be found in various fonds.

There are separate catalogues for manuscript music scores (alphabetically by composer), graphic materials, and preservation microfilms, as well as for Russian-related microfilms received from abroad.

The Manuscript Division has issued many limited pressrun in-house published finding aids, including catalogues, manuscript descriptions, surveys, and other indexes, some oriented to individual fonds or collections, others oriented by subject or type of materials. These are all listed in the latest Manuscript Division bibliography (g-156) and in a catalogue in the reading room, where copies of most of them are housed on open shelves. In addition there are many additional internal catalogues available in typescript form, such as a two-volume guide to memoir literature in the MS Division. There is also a card catalogue of printed catalogues and directories, and a name index to the published library reports.

Library Facilities: Researchers have open access to the extensive reference collection, which is covered by a card catalogue, and most of which is on open shelves in the reading room.

Copying: Microfilms and photographic copies can be ordered in extremely limited quantities—the current limit is 20 folios. Xeroxing is not normally permitted from manuscript materials. In recent years the library has been charging high license or "right to copy" fees for copies from unique manuscripts. Foreigners can often negotiate barter arrangements for foreign manuscript materials of which the library may want copies, but the net cost per frame is exceedingly high.

Nauchno-issledovatel'skii sektor redkikh knig i knigovedeniia
[Scientific Research Sector of Rare Books and Bibliology]

Telephone:　310-83-36
Hours:　　 M–F 9:00–17:00
Head: Nikolai Aleksandrovich Kopanev

HOLDINGS: ca. 57,000 units, 15th–20th cc.

Among its other extensive holdings, the Rare Books Sector retains approximately 7,000 volumes (16th–18th cc.) of the library of Voltaire that were presented to Catherine II in 1779. At least 2,000 of these have marginalia and other readers' notes, and include 141 thematic archival selections and 20 volumes of related manuscript writings. Among them are 5 volumes of materials on the history of Russia in the Petrine epoch, drafts and copies of letters, and manuscript copies of illegal books, among other documents. The sector also has a collection of imprints from the period of the Paris Commune (newspapers, leaflets, and handbills).

N.B. As part of the general fond of the Division of Fonds and Services (OFO), is a collection entitled "Free Russian Press," consisting of illegal and censored publications from the early nineteenth century through 1916, and a collection of leaflets and handbills from the early years of Soviet rule, among other materials of interest.

Working Conditions: Readers are accommodated in the reading room of the Manuscript Division, since there is no separate reading room for the sector.

Reference Facilities: There are published catalogues of the Voltaire library (see g-261–g-264) and the publications from the period of the Paris Commune (g-265).

Library Facilities: The sector has its own reference collection, which is open to readers.

Copying: Photographic copies and microfilms can be prepared.

Otdel estampov
[Division of Prints and Engravings]

Telephone: 312-34-59
E-mail: manuscripts@nlr.ru
Hours: M–F 9:00–21:00; SaSu 11:00–19:00 (Summer: MW 13:00–21:00; TuTh–Sa 9:00–17:00)
Head: Elena Valentinovna Barkhatova (*tel.* 110-58-33)

HOLDINGS: ca. 240,000 units, late 17th–20th cc.
    photographs—ca. 10,000 units (1860–1900); engravings—ca. 85,000 units (18th–20th c.); posters and other printed graphics—ca. 150,000 units (1850–1917)

The Prints and Engravings Division houses an extensive collection of Russian and Western European prints and engravings, lithographs, wood-block prints (*lubok*), posters (including advertising posters) and handbills, commercial graphics, ex libris, postcards, reproductions, portrait and landscape photographs, and various albums. Graphic art materials from the collections of M. P. Pogodin, V. Ia. Adariukov, G. Laddei, N. K. Siniagin, I. I. Rybakov, I. I. Alekseev, N. G. Churakov, and others, constitute valuable historical sources.

Drawings and engravings depict views of cities and towns, historical events, and everyday life in Russia during the nineteenth century. There are also albums of literary life with notes and drawings (18th–early 20th cc.). There are thematic collections "Russian Engraved Portraits of the 17th–19th centuries," "A Gallery of Portraits of Peter the Great," "Views of Russian Cities (late 18th–mid-19th cc.)," "Views of Petersburg and its Environs," and a collection of foreign portraits (over 40,000) that were bequeathed in 1895 by D. A. Rovinskii. Among the rarities of the Division are copper engravings of the "Crucifixion (*Raspiatie*)" (1460–1470), a complete collection of etchings of the Italian architect and painter Giovanni Battista Piranesi, and folios of the work of Albrecht Dürer, Marcantonio Raimondi, Jacques Callot, and Rembrandt and their students.

Impressive holdings of Russian *lubok* (late 17th–mid-19th c.) came from the collections of M. P. Pogodin, A. V, Olsuf'ev, V. I. Dal', and others, supplemented by copies that came to the library from censorship committees and those acquired as obligatory deposit copies.

The division has an exceptionally rich collection of photographs from early photography in Russia in the nineteenth century through major Soviet photographers, as well as the work of many foreign photographers. These include individual photographs, as well as photo albums and photo postcards, with views of cities and towns, the countryside and daily life, and historical events (including the revolutionary and Civil War period, as well as the two world wars).

There is also an extensive representative collection of printed graphics—approximately 1,200,000 examples of the work of contemporary artists. These include originals and rare examples of the production of the "Windows of ROSTA"—"Okna ROSTA" (1919–1921) and a complete collection of posters from the period of World War II. There are advertising and theater posters from the prerevolutionary period, as well as many political and film posters from the Soviet period. The collection is annually accessioning materials of contemporary graphic artists.

Working Conditions: The division reading room is shared with the Manuscript Division.

Reference Facilities: There are alphabetical and subject catalogues, and a catalogue of printed leaflets and handbills and albums.

Library Facilities: There is a reference collection in the division that is accessible to readers. Of special interest is the large collection of exhibition catalogues (especially since 1956).

Copying: Microfilm, xerox, and photographic copies can be prepared.

Dom Plekhanova
[Plekhanov House]

Address: 198005, St. Petersburg, ul. 4-ia Krasnoarmeiskaia, 1/33
Telephone: 316-77-74; 316-74-11
Hours: M–F 9:00–17:00
Transport: metro: Tekhnologicheskii institut; tram: 16, 28, 34
Head: Tat'iana Ivanovna Filimonova

HOLDINGS: ca. 14,900 units, 1832–1994
     personal papers—26 fonds

The Plekhanov House, administratively a branch of the MS Division, holds a major collection of documentation on the history of the Russian and European social and revolutionary movements, including 26 personal fonds of social and revolutionary leaders. It was founded on the basis of the archive and library of G. V. Plekhanov, which—transferred from abroad by his heirs in 1928—includes manuscripts of his writings and related materials which had been prepared for publication, biographical documents, and correspondence, including materials prepared for the unpublished "Marxist Encyclopedia." The Plekhanov library includes more than 8,000 books and periodicals in 18 languages, with extensive illegal press.

Other personal fonds comprise the papers of Plekhanov's wife R. M. Bograd (including her extensive memoirs), personal papers of the revolutionary group "Liberation of Labor" ("Osvobozhdenie truda"), V. I. Zasulich (including documentation on the First International), L. G. Deich (including his writings, memoirs, and other materials relating to the history of the revolutionary movement), and the Social-Democrats A. I. Liubimov (including documentation on the history of the RSDRP), A. F. Bur'ianov, and N. V. Vasil'ev, among other revolutionaries. There are also personal papers of the Cadet P. N. Miliukov, the economists P. P. Maslov and P. B. Struve, and other political leaders.

Working Conditions: There is a separate reading room.

Reference Facilities: There are typewritten *opisi* for all fonds of political-revolutionary activists. There are separate catalogues for the G. V. Plekhanov fond (no. 1093)—name, systematic, subject, and chronological; also a chronology of his life and biobibliography of all Plekhanov's own writings and publications about him ("Plekhanoviana"). A contemporary computerized information-retrieval system for the archival fonds is being established.

Library Facilities: The reference library is intended for staff use.

Copying: Photographs, xerox copies, and microfilms can be prepared through the RNB Division of External Service.

Otdel notnykh izdanii i zvukozapisei (ONIZ)
[Division of Music Scores and Sound Recordings]

Address: 191069, St. Petersburg, nab. Fontanki, 36
Telephone: 272-47-40, 272-47-41
Hours: M–Su 12:00–21:00
Head: Irina Fedotovna Bezuglova (*tel.* 272-61-28)

HOLDINGS: sound recordings—29,500 units (early 20th c.–1994)

In terms of archival materials, the division retains phonograph records, compact disks, and cassettes of musical compositions of Russian and foreign composers, and folk music.

N.B. Manuscript music scores and other archival materials relating to music are held in the Manuscript Division.

Working Conditions: Materials are delivered to the well-equipped reading room the day they are ordered.

Reference Facilities: There are alphabetical and systematic catalogues for researchers, as well as those for staff use.

Copying: Reproduction facilities are available.

Arkhiv
[Archive]

Address: Fonds of the 19th c. (ul. Sadovaia, 18);
                Fonds of the 20th c. (Obvodnoi kanal, 11)
Telephone: 110-58-68
Hours: Fonds of the 19th c.: Tu 21:00–17:00, WF 10:00–15:00;
                Fonds of the 20th c.: Th 10:00–15:00

Head: *Aleksandr Sergeevich Antonov (tel. 110-58-68)*

HOLDINGS: 14 (4 unarranged) fonds, ca. 250,000 units, 1795–1994

The RNB Archive holds manuscript and photographic, phonographic, and film documentation relating to the history of the library and its structural subdivisions. The GPB archive from the prerevolutionary period is retained here, with complete descriptions and catalogues of books in the library from the time of its establishment, unpublished scholarly works of its staff, work plans and reports, documents of personal provenance, and personnel records, museum materials, and personal papers of various members of the staff—such as V. S. Liublinskii, D. D. Blagoi, and others.

N.B. Part of the GPB administrative records for the years 1918–1973 are held in TsGALI SPb (D– 15, fond 97).

Working Conditions: There is no formal reading room. Files are delivered to researchers the following day after orders are placed.

Reference Facilities: A multivolume dictionary of the RNB staff is in preparation (see g-148), and a guide to the archive is being planned, of which the recent two-part survey article is a helpful start (g-273). There are reference catalogues, inventories, and card files. A computer database is being established to describe files designated for permanent preservation.

Library Facilities: There is a reference collection within the archive, which is available to researchers.

Copying: Xerox copies can be prepared.

FINDING AIDS — PUBLISHED — GENERAL:

GAF Spravochnik (1991), pp. 71–78; G&K *Spravochnik* (1983), pp. 137–59; PKG *M&L* (1972), pp. 305–27; Sup. 1 (1976), pp. 117–40; Myl'nikov (1970), pp. 15–17, 68–91; Begunov, *Sprav.-ukaz.* (1963), pp. 90–99; *Muzykal'nyi Leningrad* (1958), pp. 351–55; *Biblioteki SPb* (1993), pp. 7–10; *Biblioteki: Putevoditel'* (1996), pp. 26–33.

There is no general guide or current survey of the archival holdings in RNB, nor in the Manuscript Division itself, although several recent publications and bibliographies provide important orientation. The most complete survey description and bibliography of finding aids for the Manuscript Division remains that in the G&K *Spravochnik* (1983), pp. 137–59. For a survey description of the rare book holdings, with bibliography of catalogues of incunabula and other rare books, see *Fondy red. izd.* (1990), pp. 20–23. The library's website provides a comprehensive bibliography of recent RNB publications, and surveys of holdings of the specialized divisions are in preparation.

General RNB History

g-145. *Rossiiskaia natsional'naia biblioteka. 1795–1995.* Edited by E. V. Barkhatova,
V. N. Zaitsev, et al. St. Petersburg: "Liki Rossii," 1995. 245 p. [RNB] (Lib: DLC; MH)
> An elaborately illustrated popular history of the library with a good survey of the various collections.
> Also issued in English translation (g-145.1).

g-145.1. *The National Library in Russia.* Edited by V. N. Zaitsev, E. V. Barkhatova, et al.
Translated by Paul Williams. St. Petersburg: "Liki Rossii," 1995. 245 p. [RNB]
(Lib: DLC; MH)
> An English translation of g-145.

g-146. *Istoriia Gosudarstvennoi Ordena Trudovogo Krasnogo Znameni Publichnoi biblioteki im.
M. E. Saltykova-Shchedrina.* Edited by V. M. Barashenkov, Iu. S. Afanas'ev, A. S. Myl'nikov,
et al. Leningrad: Lenizdat, 1963. 435 p. (Lib: DLC; IU; MH) [IDC-R-10,841]

g-147. *Imperatorskaia Publichnaia biblioteka za sto let: 1814–1914.* Edited by D. F. Kobeko.
St. Petersburg: Tip. V. F. Kirshbauma, 1914. 481 p. xxvi + 30 plates. (Lib: DLC; IU; MH)
[IDC-R-4619]

g-148. *Sotrudniki Rossiiskoi natsional'noi biblioteki—deiateli nauki i kul'tury: Biograficheskii
slovar'.* Edited by Ts. I. Grin, L. A. Shilov et al.. St. Petersburg: RNB, 1995–. (Lib: DLC;
IU; MH)
> Vol. 1: *Imperatorskaia Publichnaia biblioteka, 1795–1917.* 688 p.
> An important biographical reference work covering the library staff, many of whose papers are held
> in the library.

General RNB Series

g-149. *Otchet Imperatorskoi Publichnoi biblioteki za 1850 g.– [—za 1913 g.].* St. Petersburg,
1851–1917. (Lib: DLC; IU; MH) [IDC-R-10,847]
> Reports of the library issued from 1851 through 1917 (the final volume covers the year 1913)
> included many descriptions of archival fonds and manuscript collections. Many issues had
> supplemental volumes containing inventories of specific fonds and collections.

g-150. *Sbornik Gosudarstvennoi Publichnoi biblioteki im. M. E. Saltykova-Shchedrina.
(Sbornik GPB)* 3 vols. Leningrad, 1953–1955. (Lib: DLC; IU; MH) [IDC-R-10,848]
> A short-lived general serial publication of the library, superseded by *Trudy* (g-151).

g-151. *Trudy Gosudarstvennoi Publichnoi biblioteki im. M. E. Saltykova-Shchedrina. (Trudy GPB).*
12 vols. (nos. 1–12[4–15]). Leningrad, 1957–1964. (Lib: DLC; IU; MH) [IDC-R-10,849]

g-152. *Gosudarstvennaia Publichnaia biblioteka im. M. E. Saltykova-Shchedrina v 1954 g.*
Leningrad, 1955. (Lib: DLC; IU; MH) [IDC-R-10,850]
> ——*v 1961.* 1962. ——*v 1962–1963.* 1964. ——*v 1964–1968.* 1969.

General RNB Bibliography

g-153. *Izdaniia Gosudarstvennoi Publichnoi biblioteki im. M. E. Saltykova-Shchedrina za 25
let (1957–1982 gg.).* Compiled by I. E. Krylova. Edited by L. A. Shilov and N. A. Efimova.
Leningrad: GPB, 1983. 406 p. (Lib: DLC; IU; MH)
> Lists reference publications issued by various divisions of GPB, including those covering holdings
> in the Manuscript Division and archival materials in other parts of the library, continuing the coverage
> in g-153.1.

g-153.1. *Izdaniia Rossiiskoi natsional'noi biblioteki (Gosudarstvennoi Publichnoi biblioteki im. M. E. Saltykova-Shchedrina) za 1983–1994 gg.: Bibliograficheskii ukazatel'.* Compiled by E. V. Tikhonova and E. L. Kokorina. Edited by G. V. Mikheeva. St. Petersburg: Izd-vo RNB, 1996. 228 p. [RNB] (Lib: DLC; IU; MH)

> A ten-year compendium of GPB/RNB publications, covering those for different divisions of the library. Of particular importance is the section for the Manuscript Fonds (pp. 17–28) which includes analytics for the series of collected articles about the division holdings (g-161).

g-153.2. Morachevskii, Nikolai Iakovlevich; and Ivkov, Iu. P. "Obzor bibliograficheskikh izdanii Gosudarstvennoi Publichnoi biblioteki za 1917–1957 gg." *Trudy GPB* 4 (7) (1957): 177–274. (Lib: DLC; IU; MH) [IDC-R-10,840]

> Lists reference publications issued by various divisions of GPB, including those covering holdings in the Manuscript Division and archival materials in other parts of the library. Updated for 1957–1994 imprints by g-153 and g-153.1.

g-154. *Gosudarstvennaia Publichnaia biblioteka im. M. E. Saltykova-Shchedrina: Bibliograficheskii ukazatel': Literatura o Publichnoi biblioteke, izdannaia do Velikoi Oktiabr'skoi sotsialisticheskoi revoliutsii.* Compiled by L. M. Dvorkina et al. Edited by Ts. I. Grin, L. A. Shilov, et al. Leningrad, 1989. 314 p. [GPB] (Lib: DLC; MH)

> A retrospective compendium of books and articles relating to the library, covering those for different divisions of the library. A lengthy section covers surveys and catalogues of the manuscript holdings (pp. 150–95), while other sections cover graphic materials and other aspects of library history.

g-154.1. *Gosudarstvennaia Publichnaia biblioteka im. M. E. Saltykova-Shchedrina (1814–1986): Bibliograficheskii ukazatel': Literatura o Publichnoi biblioteke, izdannaia posle Velikoi Oktiabr'skoi sotsialisticheskoi revoliutsii.* Compiled by D. G. Korolev, I. E. Krylova, O. V. Zvegintseva, et al. Edited by Ts. I. Grin, L. A. Shilov, et al. 2 vols. Leningrad, 1987–1988. 293 p., 187 p. [GPB] (Lib: DLC; MH)

> A retrospective compendium of books and articles relating to the library published since 1917, continuing the prerevolutionary coverage in g-154. See the extensive literature covering the manuscript holdings (vol. 1, pp. 239–76, and vol. 2, pp. 72–77).

g-154.2. *Rossiiskaia natsional'naia biblioteka (Gosudarstvennaia Publichnaia biblioteka im. M. E. Saltykova-Shchedrina): Ukazatel' literatury o biblioteke za 1987–1994 gg.* Compiled by V. D. Chursin and N. A. Khmelevskaia. Edited by L. A. Shilov. St. Petersburg: Izd-vo RNB, 1996. 255 p. [GPB] (Lib: DLC; MH)

> Supplements the listing of publications relating to the library in g-154 and g-154.1. See especially the section covering manuscript holdings (pp. 121–49).

g-155. *Katalogi i kartoteki Gosudarstvennoi Publichnoi biblioteki im. M. E. Saltykova-Shchedrina: Annotirovannyi ukazatel'.* Compiled by E. L. Viaz'menskaia, S. I. Demenok, O. N. Kulish, et al. Edited by O. N. Kulish and V. L. Pariiskii. Leningrad: GPB, 1987. 64 p. (Lib: IU)

> A very helpful annotated guide to specialized catalogues in different divisions of the library. Since that publication, however, many more previous restricted catalogues have been opened to the public.

Division of Manuscripts

g-156. *Rukopisnye fondy Publichnoi biblioteki: Pechatnye katalogi, obzory, istoriko-metodicheskie materialy.* Compiled by N. A. Zubkova. Edited by V. D. Chursin. 2d ed. Leningrad: GPB, 1990. 222 p. (Lib: DLC; IU; MH)

> Updates the earlier 1971 edition, providing a comprehensive retrospective bibliography of publications by and about the division, including analysis of series and collective volumes.

g-156.1. *Rukopisnye fondy Publichnoi biblioteki: Pechatnye katalogi i obzory.* Compiled by N. A. Zubkova. Edited by A. S. Myl'nikov. Leningrad: GPB, 1971. 118 p. (Lib: IU; MH[mf]) [IDC-R-11,099]

> Updated by the 1990 edition (g-156).

g-157. Stetskevich, Mirra Iakovlevna. "Spravochnye i metodicheskie posobiia Otdela rukopisei i redkikh knig Gosudarstvennoi Publichnoi biblioteki im. M. E. Saltykova-Shchedrina (Annotirovannyi spisok)." *AE za 1975 god* (1976): 324–35. (Lib: DLC; IU; MH)

> An annotated list of catalogues, manuscript descriptions, surveys, and methodological literature published by the Manuscript Division starting in 1960, most of them issued in limited pressrun *rotaprint* editions (50–200 copies). Includes separate rubrics for history, literature, fine arts, history of the book, and information and methodological subjects.

New Accessions

g-158. *Kratkii otchet Rukopisnogo otdela za 1914–1938 gg. so vstupitel'nym istoricheskim ocherkom.* Edited by T. K. Ukhmylova and V. G. Geiman. Leningrad: GPB, 1940. 302 p. (Lib: DLC; IU; MH) [IDC-R-10,842]

> *Kratkii otchet o novykh postupleniiakh za 1939–1946 gg.* L., 1951. 162 p. [IDC-R-10,843]
> ——*za 1947–1949 gg.* L., 1952. 131 p. [IDC-R-10,844]
> ——*za 1950–1951 gg.* L., 1953. 142 p. [IDC-R-10,845]
> *Novye postupleniia v Otdel rukopisei (1952–1966): Kratkii otchet.* Edited by R. B. Zarubova, A. S. Myl'nikov. M.: "Kniga," 1968. 200 p. [IDC-R-10,846]
> "Kratkii otchet o novykh postupleniiakh v Otdel rukopisei za 1967–1968 gg." In *Gosudarstvennaia Publichnaia biblioteka im. M. E. Saltykova-Shchedrina v 1964–1968 gg.*, pp. 154–208. [in IDC-R-10,850]
> *Kratkii otchet o novykh postupleniiakh rukopisei v biblioteku (1969–1973).* Compiled by A. N. Mikhaleva. L.: GPB, 1974. 152 p. [IDC-R-11,325]
> *Novye postupleniia v Otdel rukopisei i redkikh knig GPB (1974–1978): Katalog.* L., 1980. 220 p.
> *Novye postupleniia . . . (1979–1983): Katalog.* L., 1985. 220 p.
> *Novye postupleniia . . . (1984–1988): Katalog.* Compiled by L. S. Georgieva and P. A. Medvedev. L., 1991. 200 p.
> *Novye postupleniia v Otdel rukopisei RNB . . . (1989–1993).* Compiled by L. S. Georgieva and P. A. Medvedev. SPb.: RNB, 1998. 148 p. (Lib: MH).

> The initial volume, although now considerably dated, with an extensive history of the MS Division to 1938 provides a relatively comprehensive survey of fonds acquired between 1917 and 1938. The first part—covering medieval Slavic manuscripts—briefly describes 8 major collections from prerevolutionary religious institutions and antiquarian societies, 13 private collections, and several other special collections. The second part—covering archival fonds—briefly describes archival materials acquired from 13 societies and organizations, 5 literary organizations, and 120 individuals. Other sections cover Greek, Western, and Oriental manuscripts. A complete index covers proper names of individuals and organizations. See also the survey article covering accessions during the years 1917–1941 in *Trudy GPB* 8(11) (1960): 267–87. Supplemental coverage of new accessions is provided in later reports as indicated.

Series of Collected Surveys, Studies, and Publications

g-159. *Rukopisnye pamiatniki.* St. Petersburg: RNB, 1995/1996–. Some volumes have separate titles. Editors and compilers vary. [RNB] (Lib: DLC; MH)

> Vol. 1: *Publikatsii i issledovaniia.* Edited by L. I. Buchina, M. Iu. Liubimova, V. N. Zaitsev, and N. R. Bochkareva. 1996. 245 p.

Vol. 2: *Slovesnyi voevodskii sud: Issledovanie i istochniki.* Compiled by G. P. Enin. 1995. 148 p.

Vol. 3 (in 2 parts): *Rukopisnoe nasledie Evgeniia Ivanovicha Zamiatina.* Compiled by L. I. Buchina and M. Iu. Liubimova. 1997. 568 p. (pagination continuous).

Vol. 4: *Publikatsii i issledovaniia.* Compiled by G. P. Enin. Edited by G. P. Enin, N. V. Ramazanova, and N. R. Bochkareva. 1997. 226 p.

> A new series devoted to surveys, studies, and publications of texts of RNB manuscript holdings. The initial issue includes a complete analysis of contents, i.e. a list of the authors and titles of articles contained in the previous series of volumes of collective articles issued by the division (g-160–g-161).

g-160. *Knigi. Arkhivy. Avtografy: Obzory, soobshcheniia, publikatsii.* Edited by T. P. Voronova, R. B. Zaborova, G. I. Kostygova, A. S. Myl'nikov, and N. N. Rozov. Moscow: "Kniga," 1973. 284 p. (Lib: DLC; IU; MH) [IDC-R-11,100]

> The first in an irregular series of volumes with collected articles providing surveys, studies, and publications of division holdings. The initial volume includes descriptions of major archival collections and some individual personal fonds, as well as specialized surveys of medieval Slavic and Oriental manuscripts. A summary of the contents of the entire series is provided in the cumulative bibliographies mentioned above (g-153, g-154, g-156) and in the first issue of *Rukopisnye pamiatniki* (g-159), pp. 225–32.

g-160.1. *Problemy istochnikovedcheskogo izucheniia rukopisnykh i staropechatnykh fondov: Sbornik nauchnykh trudov.* Edited by I. N. Kurbatova and M. A. Tarasov. 2 vols. Leningrad, 1979–1980. 200 p., 218 p. [GPB] (Lib: DLC; IU; MH)

g-160.2. *Iz istorii rukopisnykh i staropechatnykh sobranii: Sbornik nauchnykh trudov.* Edited by L. L. Al'bina, I. N. Kurbatova, and M. Ia. Stetskevich. Leningrad, 1979. 188 p. [GPB] (Lib: DLC; IU; MH)

g-160.3. *Istochniki po istorii otechestvennoi kul'tury v sobraniiakh i arkhivakh Otdela rukopisei i redkikh knig: Sbornik nauchnykh trudov.* Edited by G. P. Enin. Leningrad, 1983. 173 p. [GPB] (Lib: DLC; IU; MH)

g-160.4. *Istochnikovedcheskoe izuchenie pamiatnikov pis'mennoi kul'tury: Sbornik nauchnykh trudov.* Edited by G. P. Enin and N. A. Efimova. Leningrad, 1984. 179 p. [GPB] (Lib: DLC; IU; MH)

g-160.5. *Issledovanie pamiatnikov pis'mennoi kul'tury v sobraniiakh i arkhivakh Otdela rukopisei i redkikh knig: Sbornik nauchnykh trudov.* Edited by N. A. Efimova and G. P. Enin. 3 vols. Leningrad, 1985, 1987, 1988. 154 p., 159 p., 218 p. [GPB] (Lib: DLC; IU; MH)

g-160.6. *Problemy istochnikovedcheskogo izucheniia istorii russkoi i sovetskoi literatury: Sbornik nauchnykh statei.* Edited by V. N. Sazhin. Leningrad, 1989. 203 p. [GPB] (Lib: DLC; IU; MH)

g-160.7. *Istochnikovedcheskoe izuchenie pamiatnikov pis'mennoi kul'tury: Sbornik nauchnykh trudov.* Edited by L. I. Buchina, A. Kh. Gorfunkel', G. P. Enin, and N. A. Efimova. Leningrad, 1990. 183 p. [GPB] (Lib: DLC; IU; MH)

g-160.8. *Istochnikovedcheskoe izuchenie pamiatnikov pis'mennoi kul'tury v sobraniiakh i arkhivakh GPB. Istoriia Rossii XIX–XX vekov: Sbornik nauchnykh trudov.* Edited by V. N. Sazhnin. Leningrad, 1991. 216 p. [GPB] (Lib: DLC; IU; MH)

g-160.9. *Istochnikovedcheskoe izuchenie pamiatnikov pis'mennoi kul'tury. Poetika drevnerusskogo pevcheskogo iskusstva: Sbornik nauchnykh trudov.* Edited by N. A. Efimova, A. N. Kruchinina, and N. V. Ramazanova. St. Petersburg, 1992. 217 p. (Lib: DLC; IU; MH)

g-160.10. *Istochnikovedcheskoe izuchenie pamiatnikov pis'mennoi kul'tury: Sbornik nauchnykh trudov.* Compiled by L. I. Buchina and M. Iu. Liubimova. Edited by N. A. Efimova and I. G. Kravtsova. St. Petersburg, 1994. 145 p. [RNB] (Lib: DLC; IU; MH)

> The last in a series of 14 volumes with surveys, publications, and commentaries based on materials in the division (g-160–g-160.9). The tables of contents of all volumes appear in *Rukopisnye pamiatniki*, vol. 1.

g-161. *Kollektsii. Knigi. Avtografy: Sbornik nauchnykh trudov.* Edited by L. L. Al'bina, T. A. Afanas'eva, and A. Kh. Gorfunkel'. 2 vols. Leningrad: GPB, 1989–1991. 130 p., 180 p. (Lib: DLC; IU; MH)

> Different articles describe a number of private library collections, both with dedicatory autographs, and related materials, although predominantly devoted to printed materials.

Russian Archival Materials

g-162. *Annotirovannyi ukazatel' rukopisnykh fondov GPB im. M. E. Saltykova-Shchedrina: Fondy russkikh deiatelei XVIII–XX vv.* Compiled by R. B. Zaborova et al. Edited by V. I. Afanas'ev. 4 vols. Leningrad: GPB, 1981–1985. (Lib: DLC; IU; MH)
REPRINT ED.: New York: Norman Ross Publishers, 1994.
Pt. 1: *Abaza–Viazemskii.* 1981.
Pt. 2: *Gabaev–Kiui.* 1982.
Pt. 3: *Lavrov–Rybakov.* 1983.
Pt. 4: *Savvaitov–Iastrebtsev.* 1985.

> A basic guide with essential annotations of approximately 1,000 fonds of personal papers and other collections of archival materials acquired by the library through 1975, representing individuals active in Russian political, social, scientific, and cultural life from the eighteenth through twentieth centuries. Presentation is organized alphabetically by name of the creator of the fond, with basic data about its extent, content, and published descriptions. Unfortunately, the 1994 reprint is a facsimile of the original with no updated coverage.

Oriental Manuscripts

g-163. Lebedev, Viktor Vladimirovich; and Vasil'eva, Ol'ga Valentinovna. "Vostochnye rukopisnye fondy Gosudarstvennoi Publichnoi biblioteki im. M. E. Saltykova-Shchedrina." In *Materialy Vsesoiuznogo rabochego soveshchaniia po problemam vostochnoi arkheografii (Leningrad, 1–4 marta 1988 g.)/ Archaeographia Orientalis* (a-232), pp. 93–119. Moscow, 1990. (Lib: CU; PU)

> The most recent general survey of the Oriental holdings in the division, listing 45 different collections (numbered fonds) with brief data including published descriptive literature about each.

g-163.1. Lebedev, Viktor Vladimirovich; and Vasil'eva, Ol'ga Valentinovna. "Iz istorii formirovaniia vostochnykh rukopisnykh fondov GPB. Prilozhenie: Alfavitnyi spisok kollektsii, lits i uchrezhdenii, ot kotorykh postupili vostochnye rukopisi, ksilografy i risunki v Publichnuiu biblioteku." *Vostochnyi sbornik* 5 (1993): 10–31. (Lib: DLC; IU; MH) [IDC-R-11,101(v. 1-3)]

> Supplements the general description (g-163), with emphasis on the formation of the Oriental holdings, includes a list of collections and references to major published descriptions.

g-163A. Vasil'eva, Ol'ga Valentinovna. "Oriental Manuscripts in the National Library of Russia." *Manuscripta Orientalia* 2:2 (1996): 36–43. (Lib: MH)

> A brief general description with emphasis on the historical formation of the Oriental holdings, with references to major published descriptions.

g-164. Demidova, M. I.; and Kostygova, G. I. "Fondy rukopisei i pechatnykh izdanii na iazykakh narodov Vostoka v Gosudarstvennoi Publichnoi biblioteke im. M. E. Saltykova-Shchedrina." In *Vostokovednye fondy krupneishikh bibliotek Sovetskogo Soiuza: Stat'i i soobshcheniia,* pp. 156–71. Moscow: Izd-vo vostochnoi literatury, 1963. (Lib: DLC; IU; MH) [IDC-in R-10,664]
> A survey of the holdings of Oriental printed books and manuscripts. The manuscript coverage (pp. 163–71) notes different language groups with a starting bibliography of published descriptions.

g-165. Dorn, Boris Andreevich. *Catalogue des manuscripts et xylographes orientaux de la Bibliothèque Impériale publique de St. Pétersbourg.* St. Petersburg: Imprimérie de l'Académie Impériale des sciences, 1852. 719 p. (Lib: DLC; MH) [IDC-R-10,875]
> REPRINT ED.: Munich: K. G. Saur, 1978.
>> This monumental catalogue has never been superseded by a more comprehensive, up-to-date version, although it describes, to be sure, only the earliest accessions of the Oriental holdings. Unfortunately, the 1978 reprint adds neither introductory explanation nor updated coverage. See also the later Dorn catalogue (g-258) covering the Nikolai Khanykov collection of Arabic, Persian, and Turkic manuscripts acquired by the library in 1864.

g-166. *Vostochnyi sbornik.* Leningrad/St. Petersburg/Moscow, 1926–. Irregular. 5 vols. through 1993. Vol. 1: 1926; vol. 2: 1957; vol. 3: 1972; vol. 4: 1990; vol. 5: 1993. [GPB/RNB] (Lib: DLC; IU; MH) [IDC-R-11,101(v. 1-3)]
> The series contains many surveys of manuscripts in different Oriental languages and historical data about the formation of collections. The fourth volume (1990) lists the table of contents of earlier issues.

Division of Prints and Engravings

g-167. *Putevoditel' po fondam Otdela estampov.* Compiled by A. V. Chistiakova. Leningrad: GPB, 1961. 112 p. [Minkul't RSFSR; GPB]
> A new edition is promised, but a summary version will probably first appear at the RNB website.

FINDING AIDS — SPECIALIZED:

No attempt has been made here to list all of the specialized finding aids for the RNB Manuscript Division, particularly since most of them are listed in the 1990 GPB bibliography (g-156) and the general RNB bibliographies (g-154–g-154.2). Only a selected few are listed below, particularly more recent book-length editions, earlier imprints available in separate microfiche editions, and especially those covering foreign holdings. Many others published before 1970, in both book and article form, were listed with annotations in PKG *M&L* (a-16), pp. 305–27, and the 1976 *Bibliographical Addenda,* pp. 117–40; most of those listings have been issued in IDC microfiche reprint editions in connection with the publication of that 1976 Supplement, which provides a correlation table for the microfiche order numbers (pp. 162–63). The initial 1972 edition and the 1976 supplement provide more detailed annotations and references to many article-length finding aids that are also available on microfiche.

For notes on *samizdat* and pre-1991 unofficial press holdings see a-417, pp. 32–33. For lists of Jewish-related fonds, see *Jewish Doc.* (1996), pp. 50–51; and *Dok. ist. evreev* (1994), pp. 89–90. See other subject-oriented references in Part A.

Division of Manuscripts

Early Charters

g-168. *Katalog drevnerusskikh gramot, khraniashchikhsia v Otdele rukopisei Gosudarstvennoi Publichnoi biblioteki im. M. E. Saltykova-Shchedrina v Leningrade.* Compiled by A. I. Andreev, V. G. Geiman, E. E. Granstrem, et al. 11 vols. Petrograd/Leningrad: GPB, 1923–1991. Compilers and editors vary. (Lib: DLC; IU; MH) [IDC-R-10,854 (pts. 1–5)]

2d ED. (vols. 1 and 2): ——*1269–1612 gg.* Compiled by G. P. Enin. Edited by V. I. Afanas'ev. SPb., 1992. 261 p. (Lib: MH).

> A detailed catalogue of early Russian charters in the Manuscript Division special collection (OSAG—fond 532), published serially in 11 parts, some as separate *rotaprint* imprints, others in serial publications of the library. The complete series (with marginal corrections) can be consulted in the MS Division reading room. The second edition of volumes 1 and 2 contains corrections and additions.

g-169. *Pskovskie akty sobraniia A. F. Bychkova, 1623–1698: Katalog.* Compiled by G. P. Enin. St. Petersburg: RNB, 1997. 216 p.

> A scholarly catalogue of 563 seventeenth-century charters and related documents from the archives of administrative agencies, namely the *prikaznaia izba* and *palata* in the land of Pskov. These are now held as part of the collection of the late nineteenth-century Public Library director, Afanasii Fedorovich Bychkov (fond 120, *opis'* 2). Includes indexes of personal and geographic names.

Medieval Slavonic Manuscripts

Almost all of the prerevolutionary catalogues and descriptions of Slavic manuscript books have been issued in IDC microfiche edition, but those listings are not repeated here. See PKG *M&L* (1972), and Sup. 1 (1976), pp. 117–40. Only a few most recent publications are listed below. For a comprehensive bibliography of earlier manuscript descriptions for early Slavic manuscript books, see Begunov, *Sprav.-ukaz.* (1963), pp. 90–99, and later GPB/RNB bibliographies listed above.

g-170. *Opisanie dokumentov XIV–XVII vv. v kopiinykh knigakh Kirillo-Belozerskogo monastyria, khraniashchikhsia v Otdele rukopisei Rossiiskoi natsional'noi biblioteki.* Compiled by G. P. Enin. Edited by V. I. Afanas'ev. St. Petersburg: RNB, 1994. 452 p. (Lib: DLC; IU; MH)

> Describes copies of 2,002 fourteenth- and fifteenth-century documents in two manuscript copy books, one from the first half of the sixteenth century and the other dating from 1620–1621.

g-171. *Opis' stroenii i imushchestva Kirillo-Belozerskogo monastyria, 1601 goda: Kommentirovannoe izdanie.* Compiled by Z. V. Dmitrieva and M. N. Sharomazov. St. Petersburg: "Peterburgskoe Vostokovedenie," 1998. 380 p. "Slavica Petropolitana." [SPbF IRI RAN; RNB; Kirillo-Belozerskii istoriko-arkhitekturnyi i khudozhestvennyi muzei-zapovednik] (Lib: MH)

> A scholarly edition of a 1601 inventory of the Kirillo-Belozerskii Monastery from a manuscript copy in RNB. Of particular importance in an archival context, commentaries include an appended catalogue/correlation table providing present locations (if extant) and descriptive data for 160 manuscript books then included in the monastic library, 14 choral manuscripts, and 120 documents from the monastic archive—many of which are now scattered in several different archives, including SPbF IRI RAN and RGADA, as well as the collection from the Belozerskii Monastery itself in RNB.

g-172. *Opisanie russkikh i slavianskikh pergamennykh rukopisei. Rukopisi russkie, bolgarskie, moldavskie, serbskie.* Compiled by E. E. Granstrem. Edited by D. S. Likhachev. Leningrad: GPB, 1953. 129 p. (Lib: DDO; MH) [IDC-R-10,853]

> Describes 471 medieval Slavic parchment manuscripts.

g-173. *Rukopisnye knigi sobraniia M. P. Pogodina: Katalog.* Edited by O. V. Tvorogov and V. M. Zagrebin. 2 vols. Leningrad/St. Petersburg: GPB/RNB, 1988–1992. 342 p., 305 p. (Lib: DLC; IU; MH)

> A scholarly description of manuscript books in the collection of Mikhail Petrovich Pogodin (1808–1875) (fond 588) which was acquired by the library in 1852. The first volume includes a history of the collection (pp. 6–12) and covers MSS nos. 1–368. The second volume covers MSS nos. 369–636. Includes detailed indexes. Updates the prerevolutionary catalogues (available on microfiche).

Hermitage Collection

See additional historical coverage of the Hermitage Library in h-575 and h-581A–h-588. For the Diderot manuscripts from the Hermitage Collection, see g-227 and g-228.

g-174. Al'shits, Daniil Natanovich. *Istoricheskaia kollektsiia Ermitazhnogo sobraniia rukopisei. Pamiatniki XI–XVII vv.: Opisanie.* Edited by A. S. Myl'nikov. Moscow: "Kniga," 1968. 158 p. (Lib: DLC; MH) [IDC-R-10,851]
> A description of 434 manuscripts that came to the Public Library from the Hermitage, part in the nineteenth century and part after 1917, with emphasis on the earliest part of the collection.

g-174.1. Al'shits, Daniil Natanovich; and Shapot, Elena Georgievna. *Katalog russkikh rukopisei Ermitazhnogo sobraniia.* Leningrad: Izd. GPB, 1960. 381 p. (Lib: MH) [IDC-R-10,852]
> Describes 816 manuscripts (mostly 18th–19th cc.) that came to the Public Library from the Hermitage, part in the nineteenth century and part after 1917.

g-175. Afferica, Joan. "Considerations on the Formation of the Hermitage Collection of Russian Manuscripts." *Forschungen zur osteuropäischen Geschichte*, 1976. (Lib: MH) [IDC-R-9899]
> An analysis of the provenance and migration of the Russian section of the Hermitage Collection, with emphasis on the contributions of Catherine II and M. M. Shcherbatov. Includes charts of the collection and facsimiles of two eighteenth-century catalogues.

Russian Archival Materials—Modern Russian History

g-176. Bychkov, Afanasii Fedorovich. *Pis'ma Petra Velikogo, khraniashchiesia v Imperatorskoi Publichnoi biblioteke, i opisanie nakhodiashchikhsia v nei rukopisei, soderzhashchikh materialy dlia istorii ego tsarstvovaniia.* St. Petersburg: Tip. A. Transhelia, 1872. xx, 180 p. (Lib: DLC; MH[mf]; NN) [IDC-R-5880]
> A description with extensive excerpts from letters of Peter I held in RNB.

g-177. *Katalog rukopisnykh materialov o voine 1812 goda.* Compiled by T. P. Voronova, L. A. Mandrykina, and S. O. Vialova. Edited by V. G. Geiman. Leningrad: GPB, 1961. 168 p. [Minkul't; GPB] (Lib: MH) [IDC-R-10,886]

g-178. Fedoseeva, Elizaveta Petrovna. *Opisanie rukopisnykh materialov po istorii dvizheniia dekabristov.* Edited by S. B. Okun'. Leningrad, 1954. 77 p. [Minkul't; GPB] (Lib: DLC; MH) [IDC-R-10,887]

g-179. Stetskevich, Mirra Iakovlevna. *Katalog fonda revizii senatora A. A. Polovtsova Kievskoi i Chernigovskoi gubernii, 1880–1881 gg.* Leningrad: GPB, 1960. 376 p. [Minkul't; GPB] (Lib: DLC; MH) [IDC-R-10,887]
> Describes archival materials relating to the inspection of Kyiv and Chernihiv Guberniias by Senator A. A. Polovtsov (Polovtsev) (1832–1918).

g-180. Stetskevich, Mirra Iakovlevna. *Katalog rukopisnykh materialov po sotsial'no-ekonomicheskoi istorii imperializma v Rossii.* Leningrad: GPB, 1960. 60 p. [Minkul't; GPB] (Lib: MH) [IDC-R-10,888]

g-180.1. Stetskevich, Mirra Iakovlevna. "Materialy po sotsial'no-ekonomicheskoi istorii Rossii v 1890–1917 gg. v Otdele rukopisei Gosudarstvennoi Publichnoi biblioteki im. M. E. Saltykova-Shchedrina." In *Iz istorii imperializma v Rossii,* edited by M. P. Viatkin, pp. 434–44. Moscow/Leningrad: Izd-vo AN SSSR, 1959. (Lib: MH) [IDC-R-11,110]
> A brief survey of archival materials on socio-economic history (1890–1917), mostly found in personal papers in RNB, but also mentions some other fonds, collections, and individual manuscripts. A condensed version of g-180.

g-181. *Istoriia Leningrada: Katalog rukopisei.* Compiled by V. I. Pishvanova and T. P. Glushkov. Edited by A. I. Andreev. Leningrad: GPB, 1954. 124 p. (Lib: MH[mf]) [IDC-R-10,889]

Autograph Collections

g-182. Dvoretskaia, Nadezhda Aleksandrovna. *Katalog sobraniia avrografov M. P. Pogodina.* Leningrad: GPB, 1988–1992. 127 p. (Lib: MH[mf]) [IDC-R-10,874]

> A catalogue of the autographs in the collection of Mikhail Petrovich Pogodin (1808–1875).

Russian Archival Materials—Personal Papers

See additional coverage of personal papers in the sections for theater and music and art and architecture below.

g-183. Zaborova, R. B. *Rukopisi V. G. Belinskogo: Opisanie.* Edited by N. Ia. Morachevskii. Leningrad, 1952. 31 p. (Lib: MH[mf]) [IDC-R-10,897]

> A catalogue of manuscripts of the Russian writer and social critic Vissarion Grigor'evich Belinskii (1811–1848) in RNB.

g-184. Zaborova, R. B. *Rukopisi A. A. Bloka: Katalog.* Leningrad: GPB, 1970. 59 folios. (Lib: MH[mf]) [IDC-R-11,112]

> A catalogue of manuscripts of the Russian poet Aleksandr Aleksandrovich Blok (1880–1921).

g-185. Naidich, Erik Erozovich. *Arkhiv N. A. Dobroliubova: Opis'.* Edited by N. Ia. Morachevskii. Leningrad: GPB, 1952. 35 p. (Lib: DLC; MH) [IDC-R-11,899]

> A catalogue of the papers of the Russian social critic Nikolai Aleksandrovich Dobroliubov (1836–1861) in RNB.

g-186. Zaborova, R. B. *Rukopisi F. M. Dostoevskogo: Katalog.* Leningrad: GPB, 1963. vii, 65 p. (Lib: MH) [IDC-R-10,900]

> A catalogue of manuscripts of the Russian writer Feodor Mikhailovich Dostoevskii (1821–1881). See also the comprehensive catalogue of Dostoevskii manuscripts (a-136).

g-187. Zaborova, R. B. *Rukopisi S. A. Esenina: Katalog.* Leningrad, 1970. 18 p. (Lib: MH[mf]) [IDC-R-11,115]

> A catalogue of manuscripts of the Russian poet Sergei Aleksandrovich Esenin (Yesenin) (1895–1925).

g-188. Zaborova, R. B. *Rukopisi N. V. Gogolia: Opisanie.* Edited by N. Ia. Morachevskii. Leningrad, 1952. 58 p. (Lib: MH[mf]) [IDC-R-10,903]

> A catalogue of manuscripts of the Russian writer Nikolai Vasil'evich Gogol' (1809–1852).

g-189. Ravkina, Berta Izrailevna. *Rukopisi I. A. Goncharova: Katalog s prilozheniem neopublikovannoi stat'i.* Vol. 1. Edited by S. D. Balukhatyi. Leningrad: GPB, 1940. 44 p. (Lib: DLC; MH[mf]; NN) [IDC-R-10,905]

> A catalogue of manuscripts of the Russian writer Ivan Aleksandrovich Goncharov (1812–1891).

g-190. Konopleva, Irina Aleksandrovna. *Rukopisi A. I. Gertsena: Katalog.* Edited by R. B. Zaborova. Leningrad: GPB, 1966. 41 p. Cover title: *Katalog rukopisei A. I. Gertsena.* [Minkul't; GPB] (Lib: MH) [IDC-R-10,905]

> A catalogue of manuscripts of the Russian publicist and social philosopher Aleksandr Ivanovich Herzen (Gertsen) (1812–1870) in RNB.

g-191. Bychkov, Ivan Afans'evich. *Bumagi A. A. Kraevskogo: Opis' ikh sobraniia, postupivshego v 1889 godu v Imperatorskuiu Publichnuiu biblioteku.* St. Petersburg: [Tip. V. S. Balasheva], 1893. 169 p. (Lib: NN) [IDC-R-11,221]

SERIAL ED.: In *Otchet Imperatorskoi Publichnoi biblioteki za 1889 g.*, pp. 35–78, and supplements, pp. 1–14, pp. 1–109. (Lib: DLC; MH) [IDC-in R-10,847].
> A catalogue of the papers of the Russian publicist and literary critic Andrei Aleksandrovich Kraevskii (1810–1889), who was the influential editor of *Otechestvennyia zapiski*.

g-192. Mikhailov, Anatolii Nikolaevich. *Rukopisi M. Iu. Lermontova: Opisanie.* Edited by B. M. Eikhenbaum. Leningrad, 1941. 74 p. + plates. Added title page in French. "Trudy Gosudarstvennoi Publichnoi biblioteki im. M. E. Saltykova-Shchedrina," vol. 2. (Lib: MH) [IDC-R-10,906]
> A catalogue of manuscripts of the Russian writer Mikhail Iur'evich Lermontov (1814–1841) in RNB. See also the additional coverage of Lermontov papers in a-141 and a-142.

g-193. Sazhnin, Valerii Nikolaevich. *N. S. Leskov: Rukopisnoe nasledie: Katalog.* Edited by N. A. Efimova. Leningrad: GPB, 1991. 63 p. (Lib: DLC; IU; MH)
> A catalogue of the manuscript legacy of Nikolai Semenovich Leskov (1831–1895) in RNB, including a few literary manuscripts, 163 letters, 15 dedicatory autographs, and some photographs.

g-194. Mikhailov, Anatolii Nikolaevich. *Rukopisi N. A. Nekrasova: Katalog.* Edited by N. K. Piksanova. Leningrad: GPB, 1940. 58 p. (Lib: MH[mf]) [IDC-R-10,906]
> A catalogue of manuscripts of the Russian writer Nikolai Alekseevich Nekrasov (1821–1877).

g-195. *Arkhiv akademika S. F. Platonova v Otdele rukopisei Rossiiskoi natsional'noi biblioteki: Katalog.* Vol. 1. Compiled by V. A. Kolobkov. Edited by V. I. Afanas'ev. St. Petersburg: RNB, 1994. 423 p. (Lib: DLC; MH)
> Describes the papers of the historian Sergei Fedorovich Platonov (1860–1933) held in RNB.

g-196. Zaborova, R. B.; and Petrova, V. F. *Katalog fonda A. N. Pypina.* Leningrad: GPB, 1962. 244, 14 p. (Lib: MH) [IDC-R-10,910]
> Describes the papers of Aleksandr Nikolaevich Pypin (1833–1904) held in RNB.

g-197. Maikov, Vladimir Vladimirovich. *Opis' bumag N. K. Shil'dera, postupivshikh v 1903 godu v Imperatorskuiu Publichnuiu biblioteku.* St. Petersburg: V. F. Kirshbaum, 1910. 196 p. Published as a supplement to *Otchet Imperatorskoi Publichnoi biblioteki* (SPb., 1910). (Lib: MH) [IDC-in R-10,847 mf. 212-17]
> Inventories the papers of the German-born historian Nikolai Karlovich Shil'der (Schilder) (1842–1902) held in RNB, with particularly rich notes and copies of documents from many archives gathered for his lengthy histories of the reigns of Alexander I and Nicholas I, among others.

g-198. Stetskevich, Mirra Iakovlevna. *Katalog fonda M. M. Speranskogo (no. 731).* Leningrad: GPB, 1962. 422 p. (Lib: MH[mf]) [IDC-R-10,889]
> Describes the papers of Russian statesman and legal reformer Mikhail Mikhailovich Speranskii (1772–1839) held in RNB.

g-199. Mandrykina, Liudmila Alekseevna. *Opisanie sobraniia rukopisnykh materialov A. V. Suvorova.* Edited by S. N. Valk. Leningrad, 1955. 301 p. (Lib: DLC; MH) [IDC-R-10,914]
> Describes the manuscript legacy in RNB of the Russian General Aleksandr Vasil'evich Suvorov (1730–1800).

g-200. Zaborova, R. B. *Rukopisnye materialy, otnosiashchiesia k L. N. Tolstomu: Katalog.* Leningrad: GPB, 1966. 64 folios. (Lib: MH[mf]) [IDC-R-10,915]
> Describes manuscript materials relating to the Russian writer Lev Nikolaevich Tolstoi (1828–1910) held in RNB.

g-201. Zaborova, R. B. *Rukopisi I. S. Turgeneva: Opisanie.* Edited by M. P. Alekseev. Leningrad, 1953. 141 p. (Lib: DLC; MH) [IDC-R-10,916]
> Describes manuscripts of the Russian writer Ivan Sergeevich Turgenev (1818–1883) held in RNB.

Theater and Music Manuscripts

See the survey of theater materials in *Teatr i muzyka* (1963) (a-455), pp. 55–71; see also g-216.

g-202. Petrova, Valentina Fedorovna. *Materialy k istorii teatral'noi kul'tury Rossii XVII–XX vv.: Annotirovannyi katalog.* Edited by I. A. Konopleva and V. I. Afanas'ev. 3 vols. Leningrad/St. Petersburg, 1980–1992. (Lib: DLC; IU; MH)

> Vol. 1: *Obshchie voprosy istorii i teorii teatra. Teatr dorevoliutsionnoi Rossii. Sovetskii teatr.* 1980. 296 p.

> Vol. 2 (in 2 books): *P'esy. Libretto. Notnye materialy.* 1984. 586 p. (pagination continuous): Bk. 1: *Materialy XVII–1917 g.* Bk. 2: *Sovetskii period.*

> Vol. 3 (in 2 books): *Personaliia.* 1992. 569 p. (pagination continuous): Bk. 1: *A–K.* Bk. 2: *L–Ia. Ukazateli.*

g-203. *Muzykal'nye sokrovishcha rukopisnogo otdeleniia Gosudarstvennoi Publichnoi biblioteki im. M. E. Saltykova-Shchedrina: (Obzor muzykal'nykh rukopisnykh fondov).* Compiled by A. N. Rimskii-Korsakov. Leningrad: GPB, 1938. 111 p. (Lib: DLC) [IDC-R-10,892]

g-204. Liapunova, Anastasiia Sergeevna. *Tvorcheskoe nasledie M. A. Balakireva: Katalog proizvedenii.* 3 vols. Leningrad: GPB, 1960. 198 p.; 164 p.; 312 p. (Lib: MH) [IDC-R-10,896]

> Describes manuscripts and personal papers of the Russian composer Milii Alekseevich Balakirev (1837–1910) held in the library.

g-205. Liapunova, Anastasiia Sergeevna. *Rukopisi M. I. Glinki: Katalog.* Edited by V. M. Bogdanov-Berezovskii. Leningrad: GPB, 1950. 98 p. An introduction by V. M. Bogdanov-Berezovskii. (Lib: MH) [IDC-R-10,901]

> Describes manuscripts and personal papers of the Russian composer Mikhail Ivanovich Glinka (1804–1857) held in the library. Updates the 1898 catalogue of Glinka manuscripts by N. F. Findeizen.

g-205.1. Liapunova, Anastasiia Sergeevna. "Opis' arkhiva M. I. Glinki." *Sbornik GPB* 2 (1954): 187–234. (Lib: MH) [IDC-in R-10,848 mf. 7-12]

g-206. *Vladimir Vasil'evich Stasov. Materialy k bibliografii: Opisanie rukopisei.* Compiled by S.M. Babintsev, E. N. Viner, M. V. Kal'fa, et al. Moscow: Gos. izd-vo kul'turno-prosvetitel'noi literatury, 1956. 283 p. (Lib: DLC; MH) [IDC-R-10,913]

> Describes manuscripts and personal papers of the Russian music and art critic Vladimir Vasil'evich Stasov (1824–1906) held in the library.

g-207. Stasov, Vladimir Vasil'evich. "Avtografy muzykantov v Imperatorskoi Publichnoi biblioteke." In *Sobranie sochinenii V. V. Stasova, 1847–1886,* vol. 3, pp. 17–86. St. Petersburg: Tip. I. N. Skorokhodova, 1894. (Lib: MH) [IDC-R-9894]

> Describes autograph manuscripts of 24 well-known foreign composers and musicians (17th–19th cc.) with lengthy extracts and texts of some letters.

g-208. Konopleva, I. A. *Katalog fonda M. N. Zagoskina.* Leningrad: GPB, 1960. 28 p. (Lib: MH) [IDC-R-10,917]

> Describes manuscripts and personal papers of the Russian dramatist Mikhail Nikolaevich Zagoskin (1789–1852) held in the library.

g-209. Ramazanova, Natal'ia Vasil'evna. *Rukopisnye knigi sobraniia Pridvornoi pevcheskoi kapelly: Katalog.* Edited by V. M. Zagrebin and N. A. Efimova. St. Petersburg: RNB, 1994. 260 p. (Lib: DLC; IU; MH)

> Describes 105 manuscript books (17th–20th cc.) from the collection of the Imperial Court Capella.

Art and Architectural Manuscripts

g-210. Fedoseeva, Elizaveta Petrovna. *Katalog materialov po arkhitekture SSSR*. Edited by G. G. Grimm. 3 vols. Leningrad: GPB, 1960. 273 p.; 171 p.; 95 p. (Lib: DLC) [IDC-R-10,895]

g-211. Fedoseeva, Elizaveta Petrovna. *Opisanie arkhitekturnykh materialov: Moskva i Moskovskaia oblast'*. Edited by G. G. Grimm. Leningrad: GPB, 1938. 88p. + 21 plates. (Lib: DLC; MH) [IDC-R-10,893]

g-212. Fedoseeva, Elizaveta Petrovna. *Opisanie arkhitekturnykh materialov: Leningrad i prigorody*. Edited by G. G. Grimm. Leningrad: GPB, 1953. 144 p. (Lib: DLC) [IDC-R-10,894]

g-213. Fedoseeva, Elizaveta Petrovna. *Katalog arkhitekturnykh materialov iz arkhiva N. L. Benua*. Edited by R. B. Zaborova and Z. I. Fomicheva. Leningrad: GPB, 1965. 135 p. + 5 plates. (Lib: MH[mf]) [IDC-R-10,898]
> Describes the architectural drawings and other papers of the French-born Russian architect Nicholas Benois (N. L. Benua) (1813–1898) held with his papers in RNB. See also the survey of the Benois papers in *Trudy GPB* 12(15) (1964): 215–18.

g-214. Fedoseeva, Elizaveta Petrovna. *Leningradskie khudozhniki: Katalog akvarelei i risunkov iz lichnykh fondov, khraniashchikhsia v Otdele rukopisei i redkikh knig Gosudarstvennoi Publichnoi biblioteki im. M. E. Saltykova-Shchedrina*. Edited by A. V. Povelikhina and V. I. Afanas'ev. Leningrad: GPB, 1982. 370 p. (Lib: DLC; MH-F)

Greek Manuscripts

See the updated descriptions of Greek manuscripts by Granstrem in a-216–a-218. Some of the Greek manuscripts acquired by the library before 1917 are described in published catalogues of many of the major manuscript collections with which they were acquired. See the helpful annotated bibliography of catalogues and manuscript descriptions in the 1995 edition of Richard (a-210), pp. 717–28.

g-215. *Catalogue des manuscrits grecs de la Bibliothèque Impériale publique*. Compiled by Eduard de Muralt. St. Petersburg: Imprimerie de l'Académie Impériale des Sciences, 1864. iv, 100 p. + [12] plates. (Lib: DDO; DLC; MH) [IDC-R-10,855]
> The original catalogue of 179 Greek manuscripts and fragments, many from the collection of Constantin von Tischendorf (1815–1874).

g-216. Gertsman, Evgenii Vladimirovich. *Grecheskie muzykal'nye rukopisi Peterburga: Katalog*. Vol. 1: *Rossiiskaia natsional'naia biblioteka/ Ellenika mousika cheirografa the Petroupoleos: Katalogos*. Vol. 1: *Ethnike bibliotheke Rossias*. St. Petersburg: "Glagol'," 1996. 706 p. + 29 plates. Text in Greek with Russian resumés. (Lib: MH)
> An illustrated scholarly catalogue describing Greek music manuscripts held in RNB.

Latin Manuscripts

g-217. *Latinskie rukopisi V–XII vekov Gosudarstvennoi Publichnoi biblioteki im. M. E. Saltykova-Shchedrina: Kratkoe opisanie dlia Svodnogo kataloga rukopisei, khraniashchikhsia v SSSR*. Compiled by E. V. Bernadskaia, T. P. Voronova, and S. O. Vialova. Edited by S. O. Shmidt. Leningrad: BAN, 1983. 83 p. [AK AN SSSR; BAN SSSR; GPB] (Lib: DDO; DLC; IU; MH)
> A short description of 257 manuscripts (157 codices and 100 fragments) arranged chronologically. Includes alphabetical and geographic name indexes and a list of illuminated manuscripts.

g-218. Dobiash-Rozhdestvenskaia, Ol'ga Antonovna (Dobiaš-Roždestvenska, Olga A.); and Bakhtin, Vsevolod V. (Bakhtine, Wsevolod W.) *Les anciens manuscrits latins de la Bibliothèque publique Saltykov-Ščedrin de Leningrad, VIIIè–début IXè siècle.* Translated by Xénia Grichine. Paris: Centre nationale de la recherche scientifique, 1991. 126 p. + 8 plates. [Institut de recherche et d'histoire des textes] (Lib: DLC; MH)

> Part 1: *Les anciens manuscrits latins ..., V–VII siècle.* Leningrad, 1929. "Srednevekov'e v rukopisiakh Publichnoi biblioteki"/ "Analecta Medii Aevi," vol. 3. [IDC-R-9812]
>
> ORIGINAL RUSSIAN ED. (Part 2): *Drevneishie latinskie rukopisi Publichnoi biblioteki: Katalog.* Part 2: *Rukopisi VIII–nach. IX vv.* Edited by A. D. Liublinskaia. Leningrad: GPB, 1965. 153 p. (Lib: MH) [IDC-R-9812]
>
>> The second part of the scholarly description of medieval Latin manuscripts from the Abbey of Corbie, which were acquired in the late eighteenth century by P. P. Dubrovskii (Dubrowski) from the Abbey of Saint-Germain des Près, prepared by the Russian medievalist O. A. Dobiash-Rozhdestvenskaia before her death in 1940. Includes indexes of authors, incipits, libraries, and other subjects. The first part of the catalogue covering earlier manuscripts (5th–7th cc.) appeared in French and is included with the earlier Russian edition of the second part in the microfiche edition [IDC-R-9812].

g-219. Dobiash-Rozhdestvenskaia, Ol'ga Antonovna (Dobiaš-Roždestvenskaïa, Olga). *Histoire de l'atelier graphique de Corbie de 651 à 830 reflétée dans les manuscrits de Léningrad.* Leningrad: Publié par L'Académie des Sciences de l'URSS, 1934. 173 p. + album of 98 plates. Added Latin and Russian titles: *Codices Corbeienses Leninopolitani/ Istoriia korbiiskoi masterskoi pis'ma v gody 651–830 po leningradskim kodeksam.* Leningrad: Izd-vo AN SSSR, 1934. "Trudy Instituta istorii nauki i tekhniki," ser. II, no. 3. (Lib: DLC; MH) [IDC-R-11,104]

> A scholarly description of 36 manuscripts from the scriptorium of the Abbey of Corbie, together with a history of the monastic library and related bibliography. The copy in Widener Library at Harvard Univesity includes a hand-prepared album of 98 photographic plates prepared by the author (included in the microfiche edition).

g-220. Voronova, Tamara Pavlovna; and Sterligov, Aleksandr. *Western European Illuminated Manuscripts of the 8th to the 16th Centuries in the National Library of Russia, St. Petersburg: France, Spain, England, Germany, Italy, The Netherlands.* Translated by M. Faure. Bournemouth: Parkstone Press/St. Petersburg: Aurora, 1997. 287 p. + colored plates. (Lib: MH-F)

> An exquisitely printed album of illustrations from 69 manuscripts from the Dubrovskii (Dubrowski), Suchtelen, Hermitage, and Stroganov collections, among others. A preface by Voronova (pp. 29–37) provides a history of the collections acquired by RNB, and one by Sterligov surveys the tradition of illuminated manuscripts represented. There is a technical description of each manuscript, a summary of its history and contents, and references to earlier published descriptions.

g-221. Laborde, Alexandre de. *Les principaux manuscrits à peintures conservés dans l'ancienne Bibliothèque Impériale publique de Saint-Pétersbourg.* 2 vols. Paris: Pour les membres de la Société française de reproductions de manuscrits à peintures, 1936–1938. 196 p. unbound + 86 plates. (Lib: DDO; MH-F) [IDC-R-10,860]

> REPRINT ED.: Hildesheim, GDR/ New York: Georg Olms, 1976.
>
>> A catalogue prepared before World War I, but not all of the illuminated manuscripts covered remain in RNB. Unfortunately, the reprint edition does not update the coverage, nor indicate missing numbers.

g-222. Staerk, Dom Antonio. *Les manuscrits latins du Ve au XIIIe siècle conservés à la Bibliothèque Impériale de Saint-Pétersbourg: Description, textes inédits, reproductions autotypiques.* 2 vols. St. Petersburg: Imprimerie artistique Franz Krais, 1910. 320 p. + 142 plates. (Lib: DLC; MH-F) [IDC-R-10,857]

> REPRINT ED.: Hildesheim, GDR/ New York: Georg Olms, 1976.
>
>> Many of the manuscripts described are from the Dubrovskii (Dubrowski) and Załuski collections. Most of the latter were returned to Warsaw after 1918 and perished in World War II. The second volume consists of facsimiles.

French Manuscripts and Archival Materials

See the section above for medieval Latin manuscripts, many of which are from France.

g-223. Bertrand, Jean Edouard Gustave. *Catalogue des manuscrits français de la Bibliothèque de Saint-Pétersbourg.* Paris: Imprimerie nationale, 1874. 227 p. [IDC-R-10,864]
SERIAL ED.: In *Revue des sociétés savantes,* 5th series, 6 (1873): 373–599. (Lib: MH)
SUPPLEMENT: "Catalogue de la collection des autographes au département des manuscrits de la Bibliothèque de Saint-Pétersbourg. Relevé sommaire de ce qui intéresse l'histoire de France." *Revue des sociétés savantes,* 5th series, 4 (1872): 448–57. (Lib: MH).
> A catalogue of manuscripts from several different collections, including those of Dubrovskii (Dubrowski) and Załuski, arranged by subject. Many of the manuscripts from the Załuski collection were returned to Warsaw after 1918 and perished in World War II. The documents (autographs) listed in the 1872 article are not included in the 1874 catalogue.

g-224. Bernadskaia, Elena Viktorovna. *Gramoty abbatstva Sent-Antuan XIII–XVIII vv.: Katalog.* Edited by V. I. Mazhuga. Leningrad: GPB, 1979. 78 p. (Lib: DLC; MH)
> Describes historical documents including charters from the Abbey of Saint-Antoine-les-Champs near Paris, acquired as part of the Dubrovskii (Dubrowski) collection.

g-225. Voronova, Tamara Pavlovna; and Luizova, T. V. *Sbornik dokumentov kollektsii P. P. Dubrovskogo: Katalog.* Leningrad: GPB, 1979. 131 p. (Lib: MH)

g-226. Voronova, Tamara Pavlovna. *Katalog pisem gosudarstvennykh i politicheskikh deiatelei Frantsii XV veka iz sobraniia P. P. Dubrovskogo.* Edited by Iu. P. Malinin and N. A. Efimova. St. Petersburg: RNB, 1993. 93 p. (Lib: IU; MH)
> Describes 232 documents (166 descriptions) from the collections of charters and autographs of P. P. Dubrovskii (Dubrowski). Includes indexes of names and places.

g-227. Voronova, Tamara Pavlovna; and Bernadskaia, Elena Viktorovna. *Katalog pisem i drugikh materialov zapadnoevropeiskikh uchenykh i pisatelei XVI–XVIII vv. iz sobraniia P. P. Dubrovskogo/ Catalogue of Letters and Other Papers of European Scientists and Writers of XVI–XVIII Centuries Desposited in P. Dubrovsky's Collection.* Edited by M. P. Alekseev. Leningrad: GPB, 1963. 105 p. Added title page, summary, and table of contents in English, French, and German. (Lib: DLC; MH) [IDC-R-10,856]
> Describes 308 documents from France, Germany, Italy, and the Netherlands in the collection of charters and autographs of P. P. Dubrovskii (Dubrowski).

g-228. Tourneux, Maurice. *Les manuscrits de Diderot conservés en Russie, catalogue dressé.* Geneva: Slatkine Reprints, 1967. 42 p. (Lib: MH)
ORIGINAL SERIAL ED.: Tourneux, Maurice. "Les manuscrits de Diderot conservés en Russie: Catalogue." *Archives des missions scientifiques,* 3d series, 12 (Paris, 1885): 439–74. (Lib: DLC; MH) [IDC-R-10,869].
> Describes the 32 volumes of manuscripts of Diderot's works, from the Imperial Hermitage Collection transferred to the Public Library in the 1860s. See the separate analysis of the earlier missing vol. 17 (g-229).

g-229. Johansson, Johan Viktor. *Études sur Denis Diderot: Recherches sur un volume-manuscrit conservé à la Bibliothèque Publique de l'état à Léningrad.* Goteborg: Wettergren & Kerbers/ Paris: Champion, [1927]. ix, 209 p. + plates. Translated from the Swedish by M. Ransson. (Lib: MH) [IDC-R-10,870]
> Analyzes volume 17 of the Diderot manuscripts from the Imperial Hermitage Collection, which was missing at the time of the Tourneux catalogue (g-228).

g-230. Liublinskaia, Aleksandra Dmitrievna. *Bastil'skii arkhiv v Leningrade: Annotirovannyi katalog.* Edited by T. P. Voronova. Leningrad: GPB, 1988. 185 p. [Minkul't RSFSR; GPB] (Lib: DLC; IU; MH)

> EARLIER ED.: *Dokumenty iz bastil'skogo arkhiva: Annotirovannyi katalog.* Leningrad: GPB, 1960. 327 p. (Lib: MH) [IDC-R-10,865]

g-231. Voronova, Tamara Pavlovna. *Dokumenty epokhi Velikoi frantsuzskoi revoliutsii XVIII veka v sobranii P. K. Sukhtelena: Annotirovannyi katalog.* Edited by S. N. Iskiul'. Leningrad: GPB, 1992. 78 p. (Lib: DLC; MH)

> A catalogue of 225 documents (1789–1804) from the collection of the Russian military engineer and diplomat Petr Kornil'evich Sukhtelen (Suchtelen) (1751–1836), which was acquired by the library in 1836. An appendix describes an additional 44 documents from the same period from the archive of Jean-François-Marie, Baron de Bongars (1758–1833). Includes a list of French documents from the same period in other fonds in the division and an index of names of correspondents and addresses.

German Manuscripts

See also g-227.

g-232. Minzloff, Rudolf. *Die altdeutschen Handschriften der kaiserlichen Öffentlichen Bibliothek zu St. Petersburg.* St. Petersburg: Buchdrückerei der Kaiserlichen Akademie der Wissenschaften/ Berlin: Verlag bei E. S. Mittler, 1853. 128 p. (Lib: DLC; MH) [IDC-R-11,212]

> A scholarly description of 21 manuscripts (14th–15th cc.) with extensive extracts.

Italian Manuscripts and Archival Materials

g-233. Bernadskaia, Elena Viktorovna. *Ital'ianskie gumanisty v sobranii rukopisei Gosudarstvennoi Publichnoi biblioteki im. M. E. Saltykova-Shchedrina: Katalog.* Leningrad: GPB, 1981. xiv, 134 p. (Lib: DLC; MH)

g-233.1. Bernadskaia, Elena Viktorovna. "Ital'ianskie gumanisticheskie rukopisi v sobranii rukopisei Gosudarstvennoi Publichnoi biblioteki im. M. E. Saltykova-Shchedrina." *Srednie veka* 47 (1984): 185–214, and 48 (1985): 270–99. (Lib: DLC; IU; MH)

g-234. De Michelis, C. "L'epistolario di Angelo Calogerà." *Studi veneziani Firenze* 10 (1968): 621–704. (Lib: DLC; MH) [IDC-R-11,105]

> A catalogue of correspondence of the Abbot Angelo Calogerà (1696–1755), arranged alphabetically by author, with index. Now part of fond 975 in RNB.

Manuscripts from the Netherlands

g-235. Welter, Willem Leonard. *Lijst der Nederlandsche handschriften in de Rus-Keizerlijke Bibliotheek te St. Petersburg.* [Leiden: s.n., 1856]. 16 p. (Lib: MH[mf]) [IDC-R-9896]

> Lists 98 manuscripts (15th–18th cc.) from the Netherlands found in RNB in the nineteenth century.

g-236. Van Bleeck van Rijsewijk, F. G. B. "Catalogus van Nederlandsche Handschriften, welke berusten in de Keizerlijke Bibliotheek te St. Petersburg." *Berigten van het Historisch Gezelschap te Utrecht* 2 (1848): 46–79. (Lib: MH[mf])

> Lists 19 manuscripts (14th–18th cc.) from the Netherlands found in RNB in the nineteenth century.

Scandinavian Documents

For documentation in the Sukhtelen (Suchtelen) collection, see the article in *Istoricheskie sviazi Skandinavii i Rossii* (a-624), pp. 356–66, and g-231.

Manuscripts from Poland

g-237. Korzeniowski, Józef. *Zapiski z rękopisów Cesarskiej Biblioteki Publicznej w Petersburgu i innych bibliotek peterburskich: Sprawozdanie z podrózy naukowych odbytych w 1891–1892 i w 1907 r.* Cracow: Nakładem Akademii Umiejętności, 1910. xli, 408 p. "Archiwum do dziejów literatury i oświaty w Polsce," vol. 11: *Zapiski i wyciągi z rękopisów bibliotek polskich i obcych, do Polski się odnoszących. I. Cesarska Biblioteka Publiczna w Petersburgu.* (Lib: DLC; MH[mf]) [IDC-R-11,103]

REVIEW AND SUPPLEMENT: A. C. Croiset van der Kop, in *Archiv für slavische Philologie* 35 (1913): 226–52.

> A catalogue of 491 codices, including manuscript books and collections of documents, mostly relating to Poland, retained before World War I in the Imperial Public Library. Also includes 35 manuscripts in the library of the General Staff and 10 in the library of the Roman Catholic Seminary in St. Petersburg. Manuscripts from the Załuski collection and some others were returned to Poland in the 1920s, a large portion of which perished during World War II. See the continuation by Kozłowska-Studnicka (g-238).

g-238. Kozłowska-Studnicka, Janina. *Katalog rękopisów polskich (poezyj), wywiezionych niegdyś do Cesarskiej Biblioteki Publicznej w Petersburgu, znajdujących się obecnie w Bibliotece Uniwersyteckiej w Warszawie.* Cracow: Nakładem Polskiej Akademii Umiejętności; skł. gł. w księg. Gebethnera i Wolffa, 1929. 132 p. [Biblioteka Uniwersytecka w Warszawie] (Lib: MH) [IDC-R-9813]

> A continuation of the Korzeniowski catalogue (g-237), describing 194 manuscripts of Polish poetry and collections of documents, mostly relating to Poland (the catalogue was prepared in 1913). All but 7 items (Pol. Q.XIV 85, 111, 126, 132; Pol. Q.XIV 8, 22, 23) were returned to Poland in the 1920s and housed in the University Library in Warsaw; but most of them perished in World War II (according to a later Polish account Pol. Q.XIV 126 and 132 were also returned to Poland, but that was apparently not the case). See further details about the fate of the manuscripts in g-239 below.

g-239. *Sigla codicum manuscriptorum que olim in Bibliotheca Publica Leninopolitana exstantes nunc in Bibliotheca Universitatis Varsoviensis asservantur.* Cracow: [Drukarnia W. L. Anczyca i spolki], 1928. 75 p. [Edita cura Delegationis polonicae in Mixta polono-sovietica commissione peculiari Moscoviae/ Delegacja w Mieszanej polsko-sowieckiej komisji specjalnej w Moskwie]. "Prace biblioteczne Krakowskiego Kola Związku bibliotekarzy polskich," vol. 4. (Lib: MH) [IDC-R-11,205]

SUPPLEMENT: *Supplementum ad sigla codicum manuscriptorum que olim in Bibliotheca Publica Leninopolitana exstantes nunc in Bibliotheca Universitatis Varsoviensis asservantur.* [Compiled by Edward Kuntzy]. Cracow, 1937. 7 p. [IDC-in R-11,205].

> A list of approximately 13,200 manuscripts returned to Poland from Leningrad in the 1920s (according to revindication agreements of the Treaty of Riga). The supplement lists (by code number) additional manuscripts returned subsequently, or which had been omitted from the initial catalogue. These lists provide correlation for earlier catalogues of the Załuski collection and other materials relating to Poland covered by the prerevolutionary catalogues in RNB. Regarding the destruction of these manuscripts in Warsaw during World War II, see *Straty bibliotek i archiwów warszawskich w zakresie rękopismiennych źródeł historycznych,* vol. 3: *Biblioteki* (Warsaw: Państwowe Wydawnictwo Naukowe, 1955; 395 p.).

Czech Manuscripts

g-240. Flajšhans, Václav. *Knihy české v knihovnách švédských a ruských.* Prague: Nákladem České akademie cisaře Františka Josefa pro vědy, slovesnost a uměni, 1897. 72 p. "Sbirka pramenuv ku poznáni literárniho života v Čechách, na Moravě a v Slezsku," Section 3: "Prace bibliograficke," vol. 2. (Lib: MH) [IDC-R-11,211]

Describes 51 Czech manuscripts (1419–1815), including some Latin codices, held by the Public Library in the late nineteenth century, some of which were revindicated to Poland after World War I. See also the later survey by A. S. Myl'nikov in *Trudy GPB* 5(8) (1958): 119–36, but that coverage provides no correlation with those described by Flajšhans.

Manuscripts from Ukrainian Lands

g-241. Fetisov, I. I. "Ukrains'ki rukopysy zbirky Iu. A. Iavors'koho." *Naukovyi zbirnyk Leninhrads'koho tovarystva doslidnykiv ukrains'koi istorii, pys'menstva ta movy* 3 (Kyiv, 1931): 17–31. (Lib: MH) [IDC-R-11,209]

Describes 62 manuscripts in the collection of Iulian Andriiovych Iavors'kyi (Iu. A. Iavorskii) (1873–1937) (fond 893) acquired by the Public Library in 1917, including 2 Latin, 27 Russian, and 33 Galician and Carpatho-Ruthenian manuscript codices, and an additional 5 charters.

Hebrew and Related Manuscripts

See the scholarly cataloguing data for many of the Hebrew manuscripts in RNB prepared by the Institute for Microfilmed Hebrew Manuscripts (IMHM) in Jerusalem soon to be available electronically on the Internet (a-243.1).

g-242. Starkova, Klavdiia Borisovna. "Rukopisi kollektsii Firkovicha Gosudarstvennoi Publichnoi biblioteki im. M. E. Saltykova-Shchedrina." *Pis'mennye pamiatniki Vostoka. 1970* 3 (1974): 165–92. (Lib: DLC; IU; MH)

FRENCH ED.: "Les manuscrits de la collection Firkovič conservés à la Bibliothèque publique d'État Saltykov-Ščedrin." in *Revue des Études Juives*, 134:3-4 (July–December 1975): 101–17. (Lib: DLC; IU; MH)

A general survey of the history and contents of the first and second collections of Abraham ben Samuel Firkovich (A. S. Firkowitsch) (1786–1874), with extensive updated references to relevant scholarly literature.

g-243. *Samaritianskie dokumenty Gosudarstvennoi Publichnoi biblioteki im. M. E. Saltykova-Shchedrina: Katalog.* Compiled by L. Kh. Vil'sker. Edited by V. V. Lebedev. St. Petersburg: RNB, 1992. 105 p. [Minkul't RSFSR; GPB] (Lib: DLC; IU; MH)

Provides a full scholarly description of documents from the Samaritan community in Nablus (Palestine) from the A. S. Firkovich (Firkowitsch) collection. The 98 documents described (16th–19th cc.) are in the Samaritan (Aramaic) and Arabic languages.

g-244. *Reshimat kitve-yad be-'Arvit-Yehudit be-Leningrad: Reshimah ara'it shel kitve-yad be'Arvit-Yehudit be-osfe Firḳovits/ A Handlist of Judeo-Arabic Manuscripts in Leningrad: A Tentative Handlist of Judeo-Arabic Manuscripts in the Firkovič Collections/ Spisok arabsko-evreiskikh rukopisei v Leningrade: Nepolnyi spisok iz kollektsii Firkovicha po katalogam Publichnoi biblioteki.* Compiled by Paul B. Fenton. Jerusalem, 1991. xvi, 152 p. [Mekhon Ben-Tsevi, Yad Yitshak Ben-Tseyiveha-Universiṭah ha-'Ivrit /Ben-Zvi Institute and the Hebrew University (Jerusalem); GPB] Based on the card catalogue of the State Public Library prepared and updated by A. A. Garkavi (Harkavy), R. Kokovtsov, R. Ravrebe, A. Vasil'ev, and V. V. Lebedev. Introduction and table of contents also in English. (Lib: DLC)

An updated listing in Hebrew of Judeo-Arabic manuscripts (Arabic texts written in Hebrew characters) in the A. S. Firkovich second collection. The introduction provides a summary history of the collection and cites earlier literature and existing catalogues that served as a basis for the handlist. Appendices provide a list of Judeo-Arabic items in the first Firkovich collection, and a selective list of the philosophical, ethical, and medical manuscripts in the Judeo-Arabic first series, as well as indexes. Updates the coverage in the 1987 Lebedev catalogue (g-245).

g-245. Lebedev, Viktor Vladimirovich. *Arabskie sochineniia v evreiskoi grafike: Katalog rukopisei*. Leningrad: GPB, 1987. 122 p. [GPB] (Lib: MH)

An inventory of Judeo-Arabic manuscripts in the Firkovich collection.

g-246. *Kitve ha-yad be-'Arvit-Yehudit be-osfe Firḳoyitsh: ḥibure Yosef Albatsir: ḳaṭalog le-dugma: meḳorot u-meḥḳarim; David Sḳler; be-hishtatfut, Ḥagai Ben-Shamai/ Judaeo-Arabic Manuscripts in the Firkovitch Collections: The Works of Yusuf al-Basir*. Jerusalem, 1997. 139 p. "Mifal le-ḥeḳer ha-tarbut ha-Arvit-ha-Yehudit ve-sifrutah." [Mekhon Ben-Tsevi, le-ḥeḳer ḳehilot Yisrael ba-Mizraḥ (Jerusalem); RNB] (Lib: MH)

A catalogue of eleventh-century manuscripts by Basir, Joseph ben Abraham from the A. S. Firkovich (Firkowitsch) collection.

g-247. Harkavy (Garkavi), Albert [Abraham]; and Strack, Hermann Leberecht. *Catalog der hebräischen und samaritanischen Handschriften der Kaiserlichen Öffentlichen Bibliothek in St. Petersburg*. 2 vols. St. Petersburg, 1874–1875. (Lib: DLC; MH)

Vol. 1: *Catalog der hebräischen Bibelhandschriften*. SPb: C. Ricker/ Leipzig, J. C. Hinrichs, 1875. xxxiii, 297 p. [IDC-R-10,878]

Vol. 2: *Opisanie rukopisei samaritanskogo piatiknizhiia, khraniashchikhsia v Imperatorskoi Publichnoi biblioteke*. 2 vols. SPb: Tip. Imp. AN, 1874–1875. 536 p. (pagination continuous). Added title page in German: *Die samaritanischen Pentateuchhandschriften*. [IDC-R-7103]

The initial published catalogues covering the Firkovich collection. The first volume describes the Torah scrolls (nos. 1–47) and codices (nos. 48–146) from the first Firkovich collection; and also the Torah scrolls (nos. 1–35) and codices (nos. 1–19) from the collection transferred to the Imperial Public Library from Odessa, and earlier described by Pinner (see g-248).

The second volume describes manuscripts of the Samaritan Pentateuch from the first Firkovich collection.

g-248. Pinner, Moses. *Prospectus der Odessaer Gesellschaft für Geschichte und Altherthümer gehörenden ältesten hebräischen und rabbinischen Manuscripte*. Odessa, 1845. 92 p. + 3 plates. Added title: *Reshimat ve-tokhen kitve yad . . ..* (Lib: MH) [IDC-R-11,214]

RUSSIAN SUMMARY: Mikhnevich, I. "O evreiskikh rukopisiakh, khraniashchikhsia v Muzeume Odesskogo obshchestva istorii i drevnostei." *Zapiski Odesskogo obshchestva istorii i drevnostei*, 1848, pp. 47–77. [IDC-in R-1439]

Describes the collection of Hebrew manuscripts formerly held by the Society for History and Antiquities in Odessa, subsequently transferred to the Imperial Public Library. Most of them were later described by Harkavy (g-247).

g-249. Gurland, Jonah (Jonas) Hayyim. *Kurze Beschreibung der mathematischen, astronomischen und astrologischen hebräischen Handschriften der Firkowitsch'schen Sammlung in der Kaiserlichen Öffentlichen Bibliothek zu St. Petersburg*. St. Petersburg: Buchdrückerei der Kaiserlichen Akademie der Wissenschaften, 1866. 57 p. Added title page in Hebrew. "Neue Denkmaler der judischen Litteratur in St. Petersburg," vol. 2. (Lib: DLC; MH[mf]) [IDC-R-10,880]

RUSSIAN ED.: Gurliand, Iona. *Kratkoe opisanie matematicheskikh, astronomicheskikh i astrologicheskikh evreiskikh rukopisei iz kollektsii Firkovichei, khraniashchikhsia v Imperatorskoi Publichnoi biblioteke v S.-Peterburge*. SPb.: Tip. Imp. AN, 1866. 59 p. "Novye pamiatniki evreiskoi literatury v S.-Peterburge," vol. 2. [IDC-R-11,231] Also published in *Trudy Vostochnogo otdeleniia Imperatorskogo Russkogo arkheologicheskogo obshchestva* 14 (1869): 163-221.

Describes manuscripts in the first Firkovich collection.

g-250. Katsh, Abraham Isaac. *The Antonin Genizah in the Saltykov-Shchedrin Public Library in Leningrad*. New York: Institute of Hebrew Studies, New York University, 1963 [c1962]. 17 p. Cover title: "Reprinted, with corrections, from the Leo Jung Jubilee Volume, 1962."

EARLIER ED.: *The Leo Jung Jubilee Volume: Essays in his honor on the occasion of his seventieth birthday 5722/1962.* Edited by M. M. Kasher, N. Lamm, and L. Rosenfeld, pp. 115–31. New York, 1962. (DLC; MH)

> Describes part of the collection of Hebrew manuscripts made by Archimandrite Antonin, listing documents acquired from the Cairo Geniza. The list is based on the card catalogue in GPB prepared by Harkavy in the nineteenth century.

g-251. Vartanov, Iurii P. *Evreiskie paleotipy Rossiiskoi natsional'noi biblioteki: Nauchnoe opisanie.* St. Petersburg: RNB, 1996. 166 p. Added English title page: *Hebrew Paleotypes in the National Library of Russia: Detailed Description.* [RNB] (Lib: DLC; MH)

> A scholarly description of 101 early sixteenth-century imprints, which should be considered of archival interest by virtue of their uniqueness and inscriptions.

Coptic Manuscripts

For Ethiopic manuscripts see a-239–a-241.

g-252. Elanskaia, Alla Ivanovna. *Koptskie rukopisi Gosudarstvennoi Publichnoi biblioteki im. M. E. Saltykova-Shchedrina.* Leningrad: "Nauka," 1969. 151 p. "Palestinskii sbornik," vol. 20(83). (Lib: DLC; MH) [IDC-R-10,876]

Kurdish Manuscripts

g-253. Rudenko, Margarita Borisovna. *Opisanie kurdskikh rukopisei leningradskikh sobranii.* Moscow: Izd-vo vostochnoi literatury, 1961. 125 p. [AN SSSR; INA] (Lib: DLC; MH) [IDC-R-10,877] (Also listed as e-101).

> Covers manuscripts in the A. D. Jaba (Zhaba) Collection in RNB as well as a few manuscripts in SPbF IV. See also the author's earlier article "Kollektsiia A. D. Zhaba (Kurdskie rukopisi)," in *Trudy GPB* 2(5) (1957): 165–84.

Chinese and Manchu Manuscripts

g-254. *Manchzhurskie rukopisi i ksilografy Gosudarstvennoi Publichnoi biblioteki im. M. E. Saltykova-Shchedrina: Sistematicheskii katalog.* Compiled by K. S. Iakhontov. Edited by O. V. Vasil'eva. Leningrad: GPB, 1991. 115 p. [Minkul't RSFSR; GPB] (Lib: DLC; IU; MH)

> Provides a full scholarly description of 91 Manchu manuscripts and xylographs, Dagur manuscripts, bi- and multilingual editions of the Ching dynasty (1644–1911), and also manuscript materials of well-known Russian Manchu specialists. See corrections and supplemental notes in g-255.

g-255. *Kitaiskie rukopisi i ksilografy Publichnoi biblioteki: Sistematicheskii katalog.* Compiled by K. S. Iakhontov. Edited by Iu. L. Krol'. St. Petersburg: RNB, 1993. 311 p. (Lib: DLC; IU; MH)

> Describes 364 Chinese manuscripts and xylographs (16th–19th cc.), which constitute almost all of the Chinese materials in the MS Division, and also the manuscripts and xylographs in the Division of Literature of Countries of Asia and Africa, and the collection of New Year's woodprints in the Prints and Engravings Division. Includes corrections and supplemental notes for g-254.

Indian Manuscripts

g-256. Mironov, N. D. *Katalog indiiskikh rukopisei Rossiiskoi Publichnoi biblioteki: Sobranie I. P. Minaeva i nekotorye drugie.* Petrograd: Izd. Rossiiskoi AN, 1918. 360 p. [IDC-R-10,885] (Lib: DLC)

> A scholarly description of manuscripts in Sanskrit and other Indian languages held by the library before World War I. See also the later survey coverage by V. M. Beskrovnyi in *Sbornik GPB* 3 (1955): 157–70.

Arabic, Persian (and Tadzhik), and Turkic Manuscripts

For Syriac manuscripts, see a-256/e-113, which also covers manuscripts in SPbF IV RAN. Note that the archives of the Khanates of Khiva and Kokand, catalogues for the manuscripts from which were prepared in GPB, are now held in the Historical Archive of the Uzbek Republic in Tashkent, although microfilms remain in RNB.

g-257. Kostygova, G. I. *Persidskie i tadzhikskie rukopisi Gosudarstvennoi Publichnoi biblioteki im. M. E. Saltykova-Shchedrina: Alfavitnyi katalog.* Edited by A. N. Boldyrev. 2 vols. Leningrad: GPB, 1988–1989. (Lib: DLC; MH)

> Vol. 1: *Alif-sin.* Vol. 2: *Shin-ya.*

> EARLIER ED.: *Persidskie i tadzhikskie rukopisi "Novoi serii" Gosudarstvennoi Publichnoi biblioteki im. M. E. Saltykova-Shchedrina: Alfavitnyi katalog.* Leningrad, 1973. 349 p. [GPB] [IDC-R-11,108] (Lib: MH).

> > A scholarly description of approximately 1,400 manuscripts (14th–20th cc.). Updates the coverage in the 1973 catalogue, which described 777 manuscripts acquired by the division since 1852, and not covered by Dorn (g-165 and g-258).

g-258. Dorn, Boris Andreevich. *Die Sammlung von morgenländischen Handschriften, welche die Kaiserliche Öffentliche Bibliothek zu St. Petersburg im Jahre 1864 von Hrn. v. Chanykov erworben hat.* St. Petersburg: Buchdrückerei der Kaiserlichen Akademie der Wissenschaften, 1865. 93 p. *Nachträge.* 1865. 43 p. [IDC-R-10,884]

> SERIAL ED.: in *Bulletin de l'Académie impériale des sciences de Saint-Pétersbourg* 8 (1865): cols. 245–309; 9 (1866): cols. 202–31.

> > Describes Arabic, Persian, and Turkic manuscripts in the collection of Nikolai Khanykov (1819–1878) acquired by the library in 1864. Supplements Dorn's earlier coverage of Oriental manuscripts in the library (g-165).

g-259. Lebedev, Viktor Vladimirovich. *Arabskie dokumenty IX–X vv.: Katalog.* Edited by O. G. Bol'shakov. Leningrad: GPB, 1978. 105 p. (Lib: DLC; MH)

g-259A. Iastrebova, Ol'ga M. "Reconstruction and Description of Mirza Muhammad Muquim's Collection of Manuscripts in the National Library of Russia." *Manuscripta Orientalia* 3 (1997, no. 3): 24–38. (Lib: MH)

> Describes 23 Persian manuscripts in the nineteenth-century collection of Mirza Muhammad Muquim b. Muhammad Amin-jan Kishi (1819-1878), which had presumably been in the Palace of *bek* in Shahrisabz (*earlier* Kish) in the Bukhara emirate, when it was captured by Russian troops. Most of the manuscripts were acquired by the library with the collection of K. P. von Kaufman, the governor-general of Turkestan.

g-260. Vasil'eva, Ol'ga Valentinovna. "Krymsko-tatarskie rukopisnye materialy v Otdele rukopisei Publichnoi biblioteki." *Vostochnyi sbornik* 5 (1993): 37–45. (Lib: DLC; MH)

Rare Books Sector

g-261. *Biblioteka Vol'tera: Katalog knig/ Biblilothèque de Voltaire: Catalogue des livres.* Edited by M. P. Alekseev and T. N. Kopreeva. Moscow/Leningrad: Izd-vo AN SSSR, 1961. 1171 p. [AN SSSR; IRLI (PD); GPB] (Lib: DLC; IU; MH) [IDC-R-10,867]

> > Provides a comprehensive scholarly description of books, periodicals, and manuscripts from the personal library of Voltaire, which is now held in the Rare Book Sector of RNB. Includes indications of marginalia and other notations by Voltaire.

g-262. *Corpus des notes marginales de Voltaire/ Korpus der Marginalien Voltaires/ Korpus chitatel'skikh pomet Vol'tera.* Edited by O. D. Golubeva (O. Golubiéva), T. P. Voronova,

S. M. Manevich (S. Manevitch), et al. Berlin: Akademie Verlag, 1979–. 5 vols. published through 1994 (vol. 5: L–M.). (Lib: DLC; MH)

> A scholarly edition reproducing and copiously indexing the marginalia in the Voltaire library in RNB.

g-263. Caussy, Fernan. *Inventaire des manuscrits de la Bibliothèque de Voltaire conservés à la Bibliothèque Impériale de Saint-Pétersbourg.* Paris: Imprimerie nationale, 1913. 96 p. "Nouvelles Archives des missions scientifiques et litteraires," vol. 7.

> REPRINT ED.: Geneva: Slatkine Reprints, 1970. 96 p. (Lib: DLC; MH)

> Provides a detailed inventory of 13 volumes of correspondence, 5 volumes of notes and manuscripts for Voltaire's *Histoire de Russie sous Pierre le Grand*, a volume of memoranda, and a volume of copies of his letters to Madame d'Epinay, which are held with his library, along with related documents from other RNB collections.

g-264. Liublinskii, Vladimir Sergeevich. "Nasledie Vol'tera v SSSR." *Literaturnoe nasledstvo* 29/30 (1937): 3–200. (Lib: DLC; IU; MH) [IDC-R-10,868 and in 1174]

> See especially the section "Vol'terovskie materialy v sovetskikh sobraniiakh" (pp. 162–200), with most of the materials discussed are in RNB, although a few documents held elsewhere are also listed.

g-265. *Frantsuzskie izdaniia perioda Parizhskoi kommuny 1871 g.: Annotirovannyi katalog kollektsii Gosudarstvennoi Publichnoi biblioteki im. M. E. Saltykova-Shchedrina.* Compiled by M. N. Alekseeva, S. M. Manevich, and E. M. Teper. 3 vols. Leningrad: GPB, 1961.

g-266. *Listovki pervykh let Sovetskoi vlasti (25 oktiabria [7 noiabria] 1917–1927 gg.): Katalog kollektsii Gosudarstvennoi Publichnoi biblioteki im. M. E. Saltykova-Shchedrina.* Compiled by Iu. S. Afanas'ev, A. F. Shevtsova, I. I. Krylova, et al. Edited by M. A. Aref'eva, A. F. Shevtsova, S. F. Varlamova, et al. 2 vols. Moscow: "Kniga," 1967–1970. 373 p., 813 p. (Lib: DLC; IU; MH)

> Vol. 2: *Listovki mestnykh partiinykh, sovetskikh, voennykh, profsoiuznykh, komsomol'skikh i drugikh organizatsii.*

> The first volume includes leaflets of central Party, Soviet, trade-union, and Komsomol organs, as well as Moscow and Petrograd (Leningrad) and Army CP organizations. The second volume covers those of similar organizations on a local level. Both volumes are organized systematically by structural and geographic principles.

Division of Prints and Engravings

See the survey of the prerevolutionary photograph collections in a-516.

g-267. *Gravirovannye i litografirovannye vidy Peterburga-Leningrada v sobranii Gosudarstvennoi Publichnoi biblioteki im. M. E. Saltykova-Shchedrina: Katalog.* Compiled by L. K. Kashkarova. Leningrad: GPB, 1965. 432 p. [Minkul't RSFSR; GPB]

g-268. *Prigorody i okrestnosti Peterburga-Leningrada XVIII–XX vv.: Katalog graviur i litografii v sobranii Gosudarstvennoi Publichnoi biblioteki im. M. E. Saltykova-Shchedrina.* Compiled by L. K. Kashkarova. Leningrad: GPB, 1968. 313 p. [Minkul't RSFSR; GPB] (Lib: IU)

g-269. *Fond graviur kak istochnik izucheniia arkhitektury russkikh gorodov: Sbornik trudov.* Edited by O. S. Ostroi. Leningrad: GPB, 1978. 167 p. [Minkul't RSFSR; GPB; Otdel estampov] (Lib: DLC; MH-F; NN)

g-270. *Petrogradskie "Okna ROSTA": Svodnyi katalog.* Compiled by A. V. Chistiakova. Leningrad: GPB, 1964. 169 p. [Minkul't RSFSR; GPB] (Lib: MH[mf])

g-271. *Russkii sovetskii lubok v sobranii Gosudarstvennoi Publichnoi biblioteki im. M. E. Saltykova-Shchedrina. 1921–1945: Katalog.* Compiled by L. M. Mel'nikova. Leningrad: GPB, 1962. 165 p. [Minkul't RSFSR; GPB]

g-272. *Katalog plakatov Ispanskoi respubliki (1936–1937 gg.).* Compiled by E. M. Teper. Leningrad: GPB, 1967. 136 p. [Minkul't RSFSR; GPB]

RNB Archive

g-273. Vakhtina, P. L.; and Vol'ftsun, L. B. "Istoriia arkhiva Rossiiskoi Natsional'noi biblioteki." *AE za 1995 god* (1997): 120–26; *AE za 1996 god* (1998): 130–37. (Lib: DLC; IU; MH)

> The first segment presents a survey history of the RNB Archive. The second part provides a substantive survey of holdings, with brief descriptions of the 16 fonds. Of particular note, fond 1 (with 6 *opisi*) includes the prerevolutionary records (1795–1917), while fond 2 covers the main library records for the period 1918–1992. In the 1970s, a large part of the GPB records designated for permanent preservation (1918–1973) were transferred to what is now TsGALI SPb (fond 97).

Biblioteka Akademii nauk Rossii (BAN)
[Library of the Russian Academy of Sciences]

Agency: Rossiiskaia Akademiia nauk (RAN)
[Russian Academy of Sciences]

Address: 199034, St. Petersburg, Birzhevaia liniia, 1
Telephone: 328-35-92; *Fax:* (812) 328-74-36
E-mail: po@ban.pu.ru; ban@info.rasl.spb.ru
Website: http://www.ban.pu.ru
Transport: metro: Vasileostrovskaia, Sportivnaia, Nevskii prospekt, Gostinyi Dvor; trol.: 1, 7, 9, 10; tram: 31; bus: 10
Hours: M–Sa 9:00–20:00; Su 9:00–18:00

Director: Valerii Pavlovich Leonov (*tel.* 328-35-92)
Deputy Director: Irina Mikhailovna Beliaeva (*tel.* 328-40-92)
Scientific Secretary: Natal'ia Vladimirovna Kolpakova (*tel.* 328-40-91)

HISTORY:

Biblioteka Imperatorskoi Akademii nauk
[Library of the Imperial Academy of Sciences] (1725–1917)
Biblioteka Rossiiskoi Akademii nauk
[Library of the Russian Academy of Sciences] (1917–1925)
Biblioteka Akademii nauk SSSR (BAN)
[Library of the Academy of Sciences of the USSR] (1925–1992)

The initial predecessor of BAN was established in 1714 by Peter the Great as the first publicly accessible library in Russia, initially connected to the Kunstkammer, and in 1725 it came under the Imperial Petersburg Academy of Sciences. The basis of the library fonds and manuscripts were the books from the Kremlin Tsar's Library in Moscow, from the Apothecary *prikaz*, the Library of the Duchy of Holstein-Gottorp, the Mitava Library of the Duchy of Courland, the personal collection of Peter I from the Summer Palace, and the book and manuscript collections of several members of the Emperor's entourage—Jacob Daniel Bruce (Ia. V. Brius), Feofan Prokopovich, J. W. Pause (I. V. Pauze), Andreus (A. A.) Vinius, Robert Areskin (Erskine), the disgraced great noble (*vel'mozha*) Count Andrejs Ostermann (A. I. Osterman), and Burchard Christoph Münnich (B. K. Minikh).

As the most important library of the Russian Academy of Sciences, BAN now ranks among the richest libraries in the world (over 19 million titles). In addition to the holdings in its main building, BAN also has specialized divisions or sectors in over forty Academy institutes or other institutions under the St. Petersburg Scientific Center of RAN. (Many of these are mentioned under Academy institutes in Part E [E–20—E–33]).

Starting in the eighteenth century, many manuscript books were also acquired from institutional sources, especially the Russian Academy, the Archeographic Commission, and the Archeological Institute. A separate Manuscript Division was founded in 1901, which was subsequently augmented by these and a number of private collections—including those of the Novgorod gentry landowner P. N. Krekshin, the historian V. N. Tatishchev, Professor Nordquist (Nordkvist) (with Slavic manuscripts from the Finnish Senate), the Slavicists A. I. Iatsimirskii and I. I. Sreznevskii, the merchants F. M. Pliushkin and N. Ia. Kolobov, the Slavicists and Old Believer researcher V. G. Druzhinin, and many others. After 1901, on the initiative of V. I. Sreznevskii, a series of archeographic expeditions started gathering manuscripts and early printed books from throughout Russia, greatly augmenting the manuscript fonds of BAN.

After the Revolution, in 1924, a Cabinet of Incunabula, Foreign Rare and Early Printed Books, Manuscripts, and Prints was established, to which was transferred foreign manuscripts that had earlier been held (since the 18th c.) in the Second Division of the library. In 1931, foreign manuscript materials were transferred to the Manuscript Division, which previously had only housed Russian and Slavic manuscript books.

In connection with the archival reform and reorganization within the Academy of Sciences (1931), the library was required to transfer many of its archival fonds from the Manuscript Division to state archives (including LOTsIA, now RGIA), to the Public Library (now RNB), and to archives and institutes of the Academy of Sciences. Among those transferred were archives of the Department of Police and other government organs, especially documentation on the history of social and cultural movements, including archives and illegal publications of political parties, as well as personal papers of revolutionaries, writers, and scholars. (For example, many fonds relating to literature, folklore, and social thought were transferred to Pushkinskii Dom—E–28.) Since that time, the Manuscript Division (OR) became an Academy-wide special depository for manuscript books in Russian, Slavonic, Greek, and Latin languages from the earliest times to the early twentieth century. It was renamed the Division of Manuscripts and Rare Books—ORRK (*Otdel rukopisei i redkoi knigi*) in 1952. In 1993, as a result of the consolidation of three sectors, the division became known as the Division of Manuscripts, Rare Books, and Cartography—ORRKK (often, ORRKiK—*Otdel rukopisei, redkoi knigi i kartografii*). Further reorganization in 1996 has left those three sectors again separate, with the collections of manuscript books now constituting the Scientific Research Division of Manuscripts (NIOR).

A devastating fire ravaged the library in February 1988, and approximately 400,000 volumes were lost beyond repair and over 3,600,000 damaged by water, steam, and moisture, but the holdings of the Manuscript and Rare Book Division were fortunately spared. Losses were most severe in the obligatory depository sections of the basic holdings, in the K. M. Baer collection (foreign books to 1930), in holdings of foreign serials, and in the Newspaper Division (approximately one third), especially the Soviet-period holdings.

The current Sector for Museum Exhibition and Archival Work was established in 1990.

In addition to other archival holdings described below, it should also be noted that BAN has been actively collecting *samizdat* and unofficial periodicals from the pre-1991 period. The library recently purchased the rich collection brought together by the St. Petersburg Independent Public Library (*Sankt-Peterburgskaia nezavisimaia obshchestvennaia biblioteka*), which had been founded in 1989, specifically to collect underground and unofficial materials of socio-political interest and those relating to current political parties and social movements.

Access: Access to manuscript books in NIOR requires an official application or personal letter addressed to the head of NIOR, indicating the subject of research. Applications for foreign scholars must obtain permission through the BAN director's office. Materials in the Division of Museum Exhibition and Archival Work are not open to foreign researchers, although specialists in the sector will reply to written inquiries from institutions and individuals.

Nauchno-issledovatel'skii otdel rukopisei (NIOR)
[Scientific Research Division of Manuscripts]

Telephone:	328-08-81
Hours:	MWF 12:00–18:00; TuTh 9:30–18:00 (August—closed)
Head:	Vladimir Semenovich Sobolev

HOLDINGS: 80 fonds, ca. 20,920 units, 5th–20th cc.

Greek MSS—287 units (5th–20th cc.); Latin MSS—ca. 1,500 units (10th–20th cc.); maps and drawings—ca. 1,400 units (18th–20th cc.); Slavonic-Rus' parchment MSS—195 units (11th–16th cc.)

Originally based on the personal library of Peter the Great and his family, the Manuscript Division has developed into one of the most valuable manuscript collections in Russia with over 16,000 medieval manuscript books. In addition to those in Slavic languages, there are many Greek and Latin manuscript books and others of Western origin, as well as a variety of other prerevolutionary manuscript materials, along with a very rich geographic section.

The core of the Manuscript Division is a Basic Collection which includes several sections— materials acquired before 1900, a "New Collection" (*Novoe sobranie*) of materials acquired between 1900–1934, a Northern Collection (manuscripts acquired by V. I. Sreznevskii, 1901–1915, from the Northern Region of Russia), the Collection of Current Accessions (acquired after 1935), and also several collections acquired in the nineteenth and twentieth centuries that retain the names of their collectors—F. A. Tolstoi, the Vorontsov family, I. N. Zhdanov, F. A. Vitberg, N. E. Onchukov, P. A. Syrku, A. I. Iatsimirskii, N. P. Likhachev (part of his collection), G. D. Filimonov, A. L. Petrov, A. S. Petrushevich, I. I. Sreznevskii, S. G. Stroganov, A. A. Dmitrievskii, N. F. Romanchenko, M. I. Uspenskii, and others. A separate group consists of manuscripts that were collected by various institutions—the journal *Russkaia starina*, the Arkhangel'sk Repository of Antiquities (*Drevlekhranilishche*), the Arkhangel'sk Theological Seminary (*Arkhangel'skoe sobranie*), the Archeographic Commission, the Petersburg Archeological Institute, the community of Old Believers of the Pomor'e Accord in St. Petersburg, the cathedral church of Velikii Ustiug (*Ustiuzhskoe sobranie*), the Old Believer (*Edinovercheskaia*) Church in St. Petersburg, and the Aleksandro-Svirskii, Solovetskii, and Tikhvinskii Uspenskii Monasteries.

Represented in the Basic Collection are various types of Slavonic-Rus' manuscripts—chronicles, including several unique fifteenth-century chronicle texts—the Ipat'ev, the Radziwiłł, and two Novgorod I and IV (fragmentary) chronicles, several volumes of the "Litsevoi svod" that was compiled under Ivan IV; annals, chronologies and chronological codices—"Paleia Tolkovaia," the "Vremennik" of George Amartol (Georgios Amartolos), the "Ellinskii letopisets" (the Hellenistic Chronicler), the Chronograph of Ioann Zonaras, and others; genealogical registry books (*stepennye, rodoslovnye* and *razriadnye knigi*); codices of historical collections; juridical documentary registers; literary compositions of all genres (originals and translations from Byzantine authors); bilingual and multilingual dictionaries, alphabet primers, phrase books, grammars, and others. Included are Bulgarian, Serbian, and Cyrillic Moldavian-Wallachian manuscripts.

Of particular note is the Petrine Collection from the library of Peter I and his family, especially his son Aleksei Petrovich, with manuscript books of the seventeenth century of historical and hagiographical content by well-known writers. There are also manuscripts of the eighteenth century on history, military arts, geometry, fortifications, architecture, shipbuilding, and navigation that were compiled by order of the emperor, many with his autographs and handwritten notes. These have been joined by manuscripts from the collections of his entourage and contemporaries—Jacob Bruce (Ia. V. Brius), J. W. Pause (I. V. Pauze), Feofan Prokopovich, Andrejs Ostermann (A. I. Osterman), V. N. Tatishchev, and others.

Within the Collection of Current Accessions it is worth mentioning several important manuscripts of a documentary character from the eighteenth and nineteenth centuries, describing events of Russian and world history, writings of foreigners about Russia, artistic and scientific works by A. D. Kantemir, M. V. Lomonosov, A. P. Sumarokov, Molière, Jean-Jacques Rousseau, and others, and also manuscripts of medical content.

The collection of the archeologist and art scholar G. D. Filimonov also contains some exquisite watercolor drawings of Russian cities, churches, and monasteries of the eighteenth and early nineteenth century. Graphic materials are also represented with albums of engravings and drawings of Dutch and Flemish artists of the seventeenth century, sketches of Petersburg in the epoch of Peter I drawn by the architect Christophorus Marselius, and others.

Materials gathered during archeographic expeditions are arranged in collections by territorial principle—Kargopol, Viatka, and Belokrinitsa, and the Dvina, Neman, and Kuban regions, among others. These contain manuscript books, manuscripts, engravings from the fifteenth to twentieth centuries, and also Old Believer archives. The collection of V. G. Druzhinin has some unique autographs of elders of Old Believer communities, and also the seventeenth "Life" of Avvakum composed in the stockade of Pustozersk.

Manuscript cartographic materials (more than 1,400 units) include maps and atlases of Russia and foreign countries, and plans of cities and fortifications. There are also drawings of buildings, palaces, gardens, and ships, including architectural sketches of Domenico Andrea Trezzini, Jean-Baptiste Le Blond, Carlo Bartolomeo Rastrelli, A. K. Nartov, and others.

Foreign collections have been formed on the basis of the manuscript books of the Cabinet of Incunabula of BAN (1924–1931), which acquired part of the library of the Petersburg Roman Catholic Theological Academy, and the collections of F. A. Tolstoi, S. G. Stroganov, and others. There are representative examples of Latin-alphabet manuscripts (10th–20th cc.) of religious, literary, and scientific content, including many on parchment and often illuminated, and many with autographs and marginalia by well-known scholars and historical figures. These include a wealth of materials for the history of many countries of Europe in the medieval and modern periods. There are religious service books (missals, psalters, antiphonaries, breviaries, and books of hours), historical and juridical sources (law codes, statutes, notarial documents, charters, and calendars), scientific works, artistic compositions, memoirs and biographical literature, and letters. There are compositions of ancient and medieval authors such as Archimedes, Cicero, Titus Livy, Pliny the Elder, Virgil, Ovid, Boethius, Saint Gregory the Great, Petrarch, Tycho de Brahe, and others. Within the collection are entomological drawings of the seventeenth-century Swiss artist Maria Sibylla Merian once owned by Peter the Great's doctor-in-ordinary Robert Areskin (Erskine) and earlier held in the Kunstkammer. A significant part of the collection consists of manuscripts of foreigners who served in Russia from the sixteenth to the nineteenth centuries, with materials they collected on history, geography, economics, culture, and everyday life.

Greek manuscripts (5th–20th cc.) come principally from the collections of the Russian Archeological Institute in Constantinople and the collection of A. A. Dmitrievskii. Among them are literary and religious writings (gospels, *mineia*, canonicals, psalters, and lives of saints, among others), dictionaries, grammar books, texts of historical and scientific content, and music scores (15th–19th cc.).

The division has a collection of ex libris of E. A. Rozenbladt and several collections of Russian *lubok* (wood prints) (late 17th–19th cc.). There are watermark collections gathered by P. N. Kartavov (18th–19th cc.), S. A. Klepikov, and G. A. Ensh (J. Jenšs) (15th–20th cc.), including tracings and reproductions from manuscripts from various repositories.

Working Conditions: Manuscripts are delivered to the reading room immediately after they are ordered.

Reference Facilities: Inventories and scholarly manuscript descriptions for many of the manuscripts in BAN have been published, and are hence readily available for researchers. Manuscripts are listed in accession registers, in inventory and dated registers, and in card files, but these are usually not available to readers. There are *opisi* of collections, systematic readers' and staff card catalogues (subject and alphabetical). There are selected indices to codices of varied contents and systematic cardfiles of watermarks from the albums of N. P. Likhachev and K. Ia. Tromonin. The card file of N. K. Nikol'skii (174,000 cards in envelopes) contains data on several tens of thousands of early Rus' manuscript books (11th–17th cc.); it was compiled for a dictionary of scribes, translators, and owners of manuscripts, based on de visu examination of manuscripts and bibliographic data on them (see g-314).

Library Facilities: Limited specialized reference materials are available in NIOR; others can be ordered from the main library collections.

Copying: Microfilms and photographic copies can be ordered through the LAFOKI RAN (E–34). Xerographic copies are not prepared from manuscript books. Foreign scholars can order microfilms of manuscripts through inter-library exchanges.

Sektor muzeino-vystavochnoi i arkhivnoi raboty
[Sector of Museum-Exhibition and Archival Work]

Telephone: 328-55-11
Hours: M–F 10:00–17:00
Head: Valentina Iosifovna Kapusta
Head of Scientific Archive: Anna Nikolaevna Nesler
Editor of the Museum and Exhibition Group: Ol'ga Vital'evna Kliukanova

HOLDINGS: 1,970 units, 1955–1989 (some documents 1920s–1940s)

The sector holds a collection of archival materials about the history of BAN and its component divisions, which includes memoirs of scholars and librarians, letters, photographs, and other documents.

The Scientific Archive holds the administrative records of BAN (1955–1989) that are designated for permanent and long-term preservation. These include plans, reports, protocols (minutes) of meetings of the directors, the Learned Council, and councils of different divisions; organizational-administrative documents, scientific-methodological materials from library divisions, documentation on international relations and book exchange, and materials on conferences and symposia; financial, budgetary, and accounting records; and personnel files.

N.B. Records of BAN from 1714 through 1955 are held in the St. Petersburg Branch of the Archive of RAN—PFA RAN (E–20), fond 158.

Working Conditions: There is no formal reading room. Files in the Scientific Archive which have not been processed are not open to researchers.

Reference Facilities: The museum and exhibit holdings have been described and registered according to museum rules. Files in the Scientific Archive are currently being processed, and reference facilities are being compiled.

Copying: Microfilm, xerographic, and photographic copies can be ordered.

FINDING AIDS — PUBLISHED — GENERAL:

GAF *Spravochnik* (1991), pp. 418–20; Begunov, *Sprav.-ukaz.* (1963), pp. 71–77; PKG *M&L* (1972), pp. 209–12; Sup. 1 (1976), pp. 62–73; G&K *Spravochnik* (1983), pp. 159–67; *Muzykal'nyi Leningrad*, p. 373; *Biblioteki SPb* (1993), pp. 10–14; *Biblioteki: Putevoditel'* (1996), pp. 134–38.

Division of Manuscripts

g-290. Kukushkina, Margarita Vladimirovna. *Rukopisnye fondy Biblioteki Akademii nauk SSSR.* Edited by V. A. Filov. Leningrad: "Nauka," 1988. 68 p. [AN SSSR; BAN] (Lib: DLC; IU; MH)

A survey of BAN history and manuscript holdings from the time of its establishment.

g-291. *Istoricheskii ocherk i obzor fondov Rukopisnogo otdela Biblioteki Akademii nauk.* Edited by V. P. Adrianova-Peretts. Moscow/Leningrad: Izd-vo AN SSSR, 1956–1961. (Lib: DLC; IU; MH) [IDC-R-3535]

Pt. 1: *XVIII vek.* 483 p.
Pt. 2: *XIX–XX veka.* 398 p.
[Pt. 3]: *Karty, plany, chertezhi, risunki, graviury sobraniia Petra I.* 289 p.

The first volume surveys the history of the formation of the manuscript holdings in BAN through the eighteenth century, including the library and manuscript collection of Peter I and Tsarevich Aleksei Petrovich, with appended inventories of those libraries, as well as the collection of V. N. Tatishchev. Separate articles describe the foreign manuscript books in those collections and later eighteenth-century acquisitions. The second volume continues the history of the manuscript holdings in the nineteenth and twentieth centuries, with separate surveys of 47 major institutional collections (pp. 77–204), foreign manuscripts (pp. 205–71), and Greek manuscripts (pp. 272–84). A final section surveys the A. P. Kartavov collection of watermarks. A supplemental volume provides a detailed description and inventory of maps and other graphic manuscripts in the collection of Peter I, with indexes.

Manuscript Catalogues

g-292. *Opisanie Rukopisnogo otdeleniia Biblioteki Imperatorskoi Akademii nauk.* Edited by V. I. Sreznevskii and F. I. Pokrovskii. 2 vols. St. Petersburg/Petrograd: Tip. Imp. AN, 1910–1915. (Lib: DLC; IU; MH) [IDC-R-10,953]

Vol. 1: *Rukopisi.* I. *Knigi Sviashchennogo pisaniia*; II. *Knigi bogosluzhebnye.* 525 p.
Vol. 2: III. *Tvoreniia ottsov i uchitelei tserkvi*; IV. *Bogoslovie dogmaticheskoe i polemicheskoe*; V. *Bogoslovie uchitel'noe.* 629 p.

g-293. *Opisanie Rukopisnogo otdela Biblioteki Akademii nauk SSSR.* 8 vols. Moscow/Leningrad, 1959–1989. (Lib: DLC; IU; MH) [IDC-R-10,954 (vols. 3-5)]

g-293.1. *Khronografy, letopisi, stepennye, rodoslovnye, razriadnye knigi.* Compiled by V. F. Pokrovskaia, A. I. Kopanev, M. V. Kukushkina, et al. Edited by A. I. Andreev. 2d ed. Moscow/Leningrad: Izd-vo AN SSSR, 1959. 708 p. "Opisanie Rukopisnogo otdela BAN," vol. 3, pt. 1. (Lib: DLC; IU; MH) [IDC-R-10,954]

1st ED.: L., 1930. [IDC-R-10,955]

Describes 253 historical manuscripts, with supplemental descriptions of 100 new acquisitions since the 1930 edition.

g-293.2. *Istoricheskie sborniki XV–XVII vv.* Compiled by A. I. Kopanev, M. V. Kukushkina, and V. F. Pokrovskaia. Edited by V. A. Petrov. Moscow/Leningrad: "Nauka," 1965. 362 p. "Opisanie Rukopisnogo otdela BAN," vol. 3, pt. 2. (Lib: DLC; IU; MH) [IDC-R-10,954]

Describes 146 historical codices (15th–17th cc.), with various chronicle texts.

g-293.3. *Istoricheskie sborniki XVIII–XIX vv.* Compiled by N. Iu. Bubnov, A. I. Kopanev, M. V. Kukushkina, and O. P. Likhacheva. Edited by A. I. Kopanev. Leningrad: "Nauka," 1971. 420 p. "Opisanie Rukopisnogo otdela BAN," vol. 3, pt. 3. (Lib: DLC; IU; MH) [IDC-R-10,954]

Describes 166 historical codices from the eighteenth and nineteenth centuries, which include later copies of earlier chronicles, 175 historical-literary codices with descriptions of cities, monasteries, and other historical events, along with 65 codices from the seventeenth century and other earlier documentary materials.

g-293.4. *Povesti, romany, skazaniia, skazki, rasskazy.* Edited by A. P. Konusov and V. F. Pokrovskaia. Moscow/Leningrad: Izd-vo AN SSSR, 1951. 598 p. "Opisanie Rukopisnogo otdela BAN," vol. 4, pt. 1. (Lib: DLC; IU; MH) [IDC-R-10,954]

g-293.5. *Stikhotvoreniia, romansy, poemy i dramaticheskie sochineniia XVII–pervoi treti XIX v.* Compiled by I. F. Martynov. Edited by A. M. Panchenko. Leningrad: "Nauka," 1980. 349 p. "Opisanie Rukopisnogo otdela BAN," vol. 4, pt. 2. (Lib: DLC; IU; MH)

Describes over 200 Russian and foreign texts (late 17th–early 19th cc.).

g-293.6. *Grecheskie rukopisi.* Compiled by I. N. Lebedeva. Edited by E. E. Granstrem. Leningrad: "Nauka," 1973. 242 p. "Opisanie Rukopisnogo otdela BAN," vol. 5. (Lib: DLC; IU; MH) [IDC-R-10,954]

Describes 293 Greek manuscripts (5th–20th cc.), 75 of which are on parchment.

g-293.7. *Rukopisi latinskogo alfavita XVI–XVII vv.* Compiled by I. N. Lebedeva. Edited by T. P. Voronova. Leningrad: "Nauka," 1979. 287 p. "Opisanie Rukopisnogo otdela BAN," vol. 6. (Lib: DLC; IU; MH)

Describes ca. 200 manuscript books in ten European languages—on history, law, science, and other subjects.

g-293.8. *Sochineniia pisatelei-staroobriadtsev XVII v.* Compiled by N. Iu. Bubnov. Edited by A. I. Kopanev. Leningrad: "Nauka," 1984. 316 p. "Opisanie Rukopisnogo otdela BAN," vol. 7, pt. 1. (Lib: DLC; IU; MH)

> Describes 133 manuscripts with writings of Old Believer authors (17th–early 20th cc.).

g-293.9. *Rukopisi Arkhangel'skogo sobraniia.* Compiled by A. A. Amosov, L. V. Belova, and M. V. Kukushkina. Edited by M. V. Kukushkina. Leningrad: "Nauka," 1989. 326 p. "Opisanie Rukopisnogo otdela BAN," vol. 8, pt. 1. (Lib: DLC; IU; MH)

> Describes 189 manuscript books of an historical and literary character, some on parchment, arranged in order of the inventory numbers.

g-294. *Pergamennye rukopisi Biblioteki Akademii nauk SSSR: Opisanie russkikh i slavianskikh rukopisei XI–XVI vv.* Compiled by N. Iu. Bubnov, O. P. Likhacheva, and V. F. Pokrovskaia. Edited by V. F. Pokrovskaia. Leningrad: "Nauka," 1976. 235 p. (Lib: DDO; DLC; IU; MH)

> Describes 195 parchment books and fragments in Russian, Bulgarian, and Serbian, consisting of the earliest and most valuable manuscripts in BAN.

g-295. *Latinskie rukopisi Biblioteki Akademii nauk SSSR: Opisanie rukopisei latinskogo alfavita X–XV vv.* Compiled by L. I. Kiseleva. Edited by A. D. Liublinskaia. Leningrad: "Nauka," 1978. 319 p. (Lib: DLC; IU; MH)

> Describes 196 Latin-alphabet manuscripts and fragments in various European languages—German, early Flemish, French, Italian, Polish, and Czech, in addition to Latin—on history, law, theology, medicine, astronomy, and other subjects.

ORRK Series

g-297. *Materialy i soobshcheniia po fondam Otdela rukopisnoi i redkoi knigi Biblioteki Akademii nauk SSSR.* Edited by M. V. Kukushkina and A. I. Kopanev. 3 vols. Leningrad/ Moscow: "Nauka," 1966–1987. [AN SSSR; BAN] (Lib: DLC; IU; MH)

> Vol. 1: M./L., 1966. 207 p. [IDC-R-10,956]
> Vol. 2: L., 1978. 352 p. Vol. 3: *1985.* L., 1987. 286 p.

> A series of volumes of collected archives with several of importance for the manuscript holdings. In terms of manuscript holdings, the 1966 volume describes the Petrine collection—"Sobranie Petrovskoi galerei." The 1978 volume surveys Russian and other Slavic parchment manuscripts, Masonic manuscripts, Western European manuscripts, *lubok* holdings, and new acquisitions between 1955 and 1976. The 1987 volume describes new acquisitions between 1977 and 1985, and a bibliography of surveys and other publications regarding manuscript holdings during the period 1979–1987.

g-298. *Rukopisnye i redkie pechatnye knigi v fondakh Biblioteki AN SSSR: Sbornik nauchnykh trudov.* Edited by S. P. Luppov and A. A. Moiseeva. Leningrad: BAN, 1976. 159 p. (Lib: DLC; IU; MH)

> Includes an article by I. N. Lebedeva *"Obzor rukopisnykh knig Kurliandskogo sobraniia Biblioteki AN SSSR"* (pp. 5–26).

g-299. *Sbornik statei i materialov Biblioteki AN SSSR po knigovedeniiu.* 3 vols. Leningrad: "Nauka," 1965–1973. (Lib: DLC; IU; MH) [IDC-R-11,089]

> Vol. 1: 1965. 339 p. + plates. Vol. 2: 1970. 341 p. + plates.
> Vol. 3: (added subtitle): *K 400–letiiu russkogo knigopechataniia.* 1973. 495 p. + plates.

> A series of volumes of collected articles covering different aspects of library developments, including descriptions of manuscript collections—such as Greek manuscripts from Mount Athos (vol. 2, pp. 183–92), Italian manuscripts (vol. 3, pp. 423–41), reports on archeographic expeditions (e.g., vol. 2, pp. 307–36, and vol. 3, pp. 443–84), and new acquisitions in BAN.

BAN History

g-300. Luppov, Sergei Pavlovich; Kukushkina, Margarita Vladimirovna; Kopanev, Aleksandr Il'ich, et al. *Istoriia Biblioteki Akademii nauk SSSR: 1714–1964.* Edited by M. S. Filippov. Moscow/Leningrad: "Nauka," 1964. 599 p. [AN SSSR; BAN] (Lib: DLC; IU; MH) [IDC-R-11,306]

> An extensive history honoring the 250th anniversary of BAN, with considerable attention to development of the holdings with background information about many of the manuscript collections.

g-301. Liutova, Kseniia Vladimirovna. *Biblioteka Akademii nauk SSSR: K 275-letiiu pervoi gosudarstvennoi nauchnoi biblioteki Rossii.* Compiled by N. P. Kopaneva. Leningrad: BAN, 1990. 114 p. [BAN] (Lib: DLC; IU; MH)

> A popular survey history of the library and its holdings and activities.

g-302. *275 let Biblioteke Akademii nauk: Sbornik dokladov iubileinoi nauchnoi konferentsii.* Edited by V. P. Leonov, L. M. Ravich, and M. A. Shaparneva. St. Petersburg: BAN, 1991. 318 p. [RAN; Biblioteka RAN] (Lib: DLC; IU)

> A collection of materials from a conference honoring the anniversary of BAN, including reports on restoration efforts after the 1988 fire. See especially the article by L. I. Kiseleva, "Problemy sokhrannosti i ispol'zovaniia rukopisnykh i redkikh knig BAN" (pp. 67–76) and A. A. Amosov, "Populiarizatsiia pamiatnikov pis'mennosti BAN" (pp. 98–105).

BAN Bibliography

g-303. *Biblioteka Akademii nauk SSSR, 1714–1964: Bibliograficheskii ukazatel'.* Compiled by E. P. Faidel' et al. Edited by M. S. Filippov. Leningrad: BAN, 1964. 308 p. (Lib: DLC; IU; MH) [IDC-R-10,951]

> SUPPLEMENT:
>
> —*Ukazatel' literatury za 1964–1974 gg.* Compiled by G. V. Sergienko. L., 1981. 173 p.
> —*za 1964–1974 g.* Compiled by N. A. Laskeev and O. N. Peskova. L., 1986. 168 p.
>
> Presents a comprehensive bibliography of books and articles published by and about the library and its various divisions. See the coverage of prerevolutionary publications describing the manuscript holding (pp. 106–40), and those published since, 1917–1963 (pp. 215–36). The supplements continue the coverage and are expanded by g-304 and g-305.

g-304. *Biblioteka Akademii nauk SSSR: Ukazatel' literatury za 1964–1988 gg.* Compiled by N. A. Laskeev. Edited by M. V. Petrovskaia. Leningrad, 1989. 345 p. (Lib: IU; MH)

> Supplements g-303.

g-305. Amosov, Aleksandr Aleksandrovich; and Bubnov, Nikolai Iur'evich. "Bibliografiia rabot sotrudnikov Otdela rukopisnoi i redkoi knigi Biblioteki Akademii nauk SSSR (1945–1984)." *Polata k"nigopis'naia/ Polata knigopisnaia* 13 (December 1985): 2–28. (Lib: DLC; MH)

FINDING AIDS — SPECIALIZED:

For additional prerevolutionary descriptions of Slavic manuscript materials in BAN, see the bibliographies cited above (g-303–g-304), and for pre-1963 publications, the extensive coverage by Begunov, *Spravochnik-ukazatel'* (1963), pp. 71–77, and the additional listings in PKG *M&L* (1972), pp. 209–12. The *M&L* Sup. 1 (1976), pp. 71–77, continues the bibliography for prerevolutionary descriptions of Slavic manuscripts and provides indications of IDC microfiche editions available for all of those listed. For manuscripts from the collections of the Archeographic Commission, many of which are held by SPbF IRI, see e-131–e-135.

Regarding the collection of the St. Petersburg Independent Public Library (*Sankt-Petersburgskaia nezavisimaia obshchestvennaia biblioteka*), see a-417, p. 31.

g-306. *Korpus zapisei na staropechatnykh knigakh.* Compiled by L. I. Kiseleva. Edited by
A. I. Kopanev. St. Petersburg: BAN, 1992–. [BAN] (Lib: DLC; IU; MH)
   Vol. 1: *Zapisi na knigakh kirillicheskogo shrifta, napechatannykh v Moskve v XVI–XVII
vv.* 218 p.

> The first volume in a planned series describing inscriptions in early printed books, including scholarly
> description of textual inscriptions, library marks, stamps, and ex libris, monograms, and other
> markings on books printed in Moscow, the Aleksandrovskaia *sloboda*, and Iverskii Monastery
> (with over 900 descriptions).

g-307. Waugh, Daniel Clarke. *Slavianskie rukopisi sobraniia F. A. Tolstogo: Materialy k istorii
sobraniia i ukazateli starykh i novykh shifrov.* Edited by M. V. Kukushkina and
D. S. Likhachev. Leningrad: BAN SSSR, 1980. 135 p. + plates. (Lib: MH)
   EARLIER MICROFICHE ED.: *The F. A. Tolstoi collection: The Slavic Manuscripts in
the Collection of Count F. A. Tolstoi: Materials on the History of the Collection and
Indexes of Former and Current Code Numbers/ Slavianskie rukopisi sobraniia grafa F. A.
Tolstogo: Materialy k istorii sobraniia i ukazateli starykh i novykh shifrov.* Zug: Inter
Documentation Company AG, 1976. 122 p. An original IDC "Micro-Book" publication
with printed introduction and table of contents. [IDC-R-9898].

> A guide to the formation and present locations of Slavic manuscripts from the collection of Count
> Fedor Andreevich Tolstoi (1758–1849). Most of the collection is now in BAN, but some manuscripts
> are in RNB (G–15) and SPbF IRI (E–25).

g-308. *Mir rukopisnoi knigi: Avtografy Petra I.* Compiled by A. A. Amosov et al. St.
Petersburg: BAN, 1994. 21 p. [Mezhdunarodnaia assotsiatsiia bibliofilov; BAN]
(Lib: DLC; MH) Parallel texts in Russian, English, and French.

g-309. *Biblioteka Ia. V. Briusa: Katalog.* Compiled by E. A. Savel'eva. Edited by A. I.
Kopanev. St. Petersburg: BAN, 1989. 410 p. [BAN] (Lib: MH)

> An extensive scholarly reconstruction, describing 25 manuscripts and 797 printed books from the
> personal library of Jacob Bruce (1669–1735), of Scottish descent, who came to Russia to serve as an
> advisor of Peter I. The original library of approximately 1,500 volumes was acquired by BAN in
> 1737 but not kept together as an integral collection. Includes indexes of names, titles, geographical
> names, notes and autographs by Bruce, and books by language.

g-310. *Rukopisnoe nasledie baronov Budbergov v fondakh biblioteki Rossiiskoi Akademii
nauk.* Compiled by O. N. Bleskina. Edited by L. I. Kiseleva. St. Petersburg: BAN, 1996.
76 p. + plates. [BAN]

> A detailed description of 18 manuscripts, predominantly diaries and travelogues by different members
> of the Budberg family (18th–19th cc.). Includes a history of the family with reference to specific
> manuscripts from their library and archive (pp. 10–31). Extensive indexes.

g-311. *Rukopisnaia illiustrirovannaia kniga Biblioteki AN SSSR: Katalog vystavki
illiustrirovannykh rukopisei XI–XIX vv., napisannykh latinskim alfavitom.* Compiled by
O. N. Bleskina. Edited by L. I. Kiseleva. Leningrad: BAN, 1991. 56 p. + 19 plates.
(Lib: DLC; IU; MH)

> An exhibition catalogue which describes 43 illuminated manuscripts of Italian, French, Swiss,
> German, Dutch, Dalmatian, and Russian provenance.

g-312. *Pevcheskie rukopisi v sobranii Biblioteki Rossiiskoi Akademii nauk: Katalog vystavki.*
Compiled by F. V. Panchenko. Edited by A. A. Amosov. St. Petersburg: BAN, 1994. 52 p.
+ plates. (Lib: DLC; IU; MH)

> An exhibition catalogue describing 52 choral manuscripts (11th–20th cc.), including those with early
> Rus' neumatic notation, Old Believer chants, and linear notations.

g-313. Aleksandrov, B. V. "Opisanie rukopisnykh kart XVIII v., khraniashchikhsia v Otdele rukopisnoi knigi Biblioteki Akademii nauk SSSR." In *Geograficheskii departament Akademii nauk XVIII veka,* Sup. 2, edited by V. F. Gnucheva, pp. 267–412. Moscow/ Leningrad: Izd-vo AN SSSR, 1946. "Trudy Arkhiva AN SSSR," vol. 6. (Lib: DLC; IU; MH) [IDC-in R-10,949]

g-314. Pokrovskaia, Vera Fedorovna. "Kartoteka akademika N. K. Nikol'skogo." In *Trudy Biblioteki Akademii nauk,* vol. 1, pp. 143–51. Moscow, 1948. (Lib: DLC; IU; MH)
Describes the card catalogue held in BAN, prepared by the Slavicist N. K. Nikol'skii for his extensive reference work on early Slavic manuscripts, including a biographical index of scribes, translators, manuscript collectors, etc., with detailed references to other published catalogues and locations of related materials. Only the first part of the series, *Rukopisnaia knizhnost' drevnerusskikh bibliotek (XI–XVII vv.),* covering entries "A–V" (the first three letters of the Russian alphabet) was published in 1914, but has now been updated by a new series (see a-192).

Nauchnaia biblioteka im. M. Gor'kogo Sankt-Peterburgskogo gosudarstvennogo universiteta (NB SPbGU)
[M. Gor'kii Scientific Library of St. Petersburg State University]

Agency: Ministerstvo obshchego i professional'nogo obrazovaniia RF
(Minobrazovaniia Rossii)
[Ministry of General and Professional Education]

Address: 199034, St. Petersburg, Universitetskaia nab., 7/9
Telephone: 328-95-46; *Fax:* (812) 328-27-41; 328-13-46
E-mail: marina@lib.pu.ru
Website: http://www.lib.pu.ru; http://www.spbu.ru
Transport: metro: Gostinyi Dvor, Nevskii prospekt, Vasileostrovskaia, Sportivnaia; trol.: 1, 7, 9, 10; bus: 10
Hours: M–Sa 10:00–20:00

Director: Natal'ia Andreevna Sheshina (*tel.* /*fax* 328-27-41)
Deputy Director for Scientific Work: Tat'iana Anatol'evna Ligun (*tel.* 328-95-46;
 e-mail: ligun@lib.pu.ru)
Scientific Secretary: Galina Grigor'evna Shilova (*tel.* 328-95-46)

HISTORY:

Biblioteka Uchitel'skoi seminarii
 [Library of the Teachers' Seminary] (1783–1803)
Biblioteka Uchitel'skoi gimnazii
 [Library of the Teachers' Gymnasium] (1803–1804)
Biblioteka Pedagogicheskogo instituta
 [Library of the Pedagogical Institute] (1804–1816)
Biblioteka Glavnogo pedagogicheskogo instituta
 [Library of the Main Pedagogical Institute] (1816–1819)
Biblioteka Imperatorskogo Sankt-Peterburgskogo universiteta
 [Library of Imperial St. Petersburg University] (1819–1914)
Biblioteka Petrogradskogo universiteta
 [Library of Petrograd University] (1914–1924)
Biblioteka Leningradskogo gosudarstvennogo universiteta
 [Library of Leningrad State University] (1924–1932, 1937–1948)
Nauchnaia biblioteka im. M. Gor'kogo Leningradskogo gosudarstvennogo universiteta (NB LGU)
 [M. Gor'kii Scientific Library of Leningrad State University] (1932–1933)
Nauchnaia biblioteka im. M. Gor'kogo Leningradskogo gosudarstvennogo universiteta im. A. S. Bubnova (NB LGU)
 [M. Gor'kii Scientific Library of A. S. Bubnov Leningrad State University] (1933–1937)
Nauchnaia biblioteka im. M. Gor'kogo Leningradskogo gosudarstvennogo universiteta im. A. A. Zhdanova (NB LGU)
 [M. Gor'kii Scientific Library of A. A. Zhdanov Leningrad State University] (1948–1988)

Established in 1783 as a library of the Teachers' Seminary in St. Petersburg under the Main People's Higher School, in 1819 it became the Library of the Imperial St. Petersburg University, which was founded on the basis of the Main Pedagogical Institute. It acquired the book collections of various institutions and university professors, and also books and manuscripts that were acquired or given as gifts by scholars, writers, teachers, university graduates, and students. Its most important book collections are those of P. F. Zhukov, P. B. Inokhodtsev, P. I. Preis, N. N. Strakhov, and M. I. Rostovtsev, among many others. It also acquired the library and archive of the Free Society of Friends of Russian Philology, Science, and Art (*Vol'noe obshchestvo liubitelei rossiiskoi slovesnosti, nauk i khudozhestv*), and the libraries of the Petersburg Censorship Committee, the Committee of Foreign Censorship, and the Higher (Bestuzhev) Courses for Women, among other institutional collections. Its holdings today, total approximately 6,400,000 volumes, including 145,000 rare publications and manuscripts. Dissertations defended at the University from the end of the 1940s to the present are held within the main library collection.

In the mid-1920s a Cabinet of Rarities (*Kabinet redkostei*) was organized, which in 1944 was reorganized as the Division of Rare Books and Manuscripts; later suspended, it was recreated in 1956. Since 1963 the division has been conducting archeographic expeditions together with Pushkinskii Dom in the northeastern regions of Russia.

Access: Access to manuscript holdings requires an official letter to the director of the library indicating the subject and aim of research.

Otdel redkikh knig i rukopisei (ORKR)
[Division of Rare Books and Manuscripts]

Telephone: 328-27-51; *RdngRm:* 328-27-51
E-mail: alex@lib.pu.ru; audrey@lib.pu.ru
Hours: M–F 10:00–20:00
Head: Nikolai Ivanovich Nikolaev (*tel.* ex. 338)
Chief Librarian: Andrei Vladimirovich Voznesenskii
Head of Sector: Aleksei Aleksandrovich Savel'ev

HOLDINGS: 1,038 units, 11th–early 20th c.

Slavonic-Rus' MSS—234 units (14th–20th cc.); Greek MSS—18 units (13th, 17th–19th cc.); institutional fonds—2 fonds (742 units) (1801–1944); personal fonds—14 (18th–20th cc.)

The Division of Rare Books and Manuscripts holds a small but valuable group of early manuscript books and other documents dating from the eleventh to the twentieth centuries, in ancient Greek, Latin, Church Slavonic, Russian, German, French, and Polish languages. The division also holds incunabula, paleotypes, and early printed Cyrillic books (16th–17th cc.).

Among early manuscript receipts, with the library of the Leipzig University professor of jurisprudence Karl Friedrich Christian Wenck (acquired in 1830), came five medieval Latin judicial texts (11th–14th cc.). Most of the manuscript books are in the Slavonic-Rus' manuscript tradition, including copies of literary and historical monuments of the fourteenth to twentieth centuries, such as the "Aleksandriia" and "Sudebnik" (1550) of Ivan IV, the "Ulozhenie" (1649) of Tsar Aleksei Mikhailovich. Along with other historical manuscripts and documents from the eighteenth to early twentieth centuries, these came from the collections of the Petersburg merchant V. A. Pivovarov, the gymnasium director A. A. Gofman, and the historian L. N. Tselepi, among others. Some of the holdings were collected since 1963 on archeographic expeditions undertaken in conjunction with IRLI (Pushkinskii Dom).

The most valuable single institutional fond is the rich archive of the early nineteenth-century Free Society of Friends of Russian Philology, Science, and Art (*Vol'noe obshchestvo liubitelei slovesnosti, nauk i khudozhestv*) (222 items; 1801–1826), which was presented to the library by the Minister of Public Education in 1833. The division holds the archive of the university library (521 units, 1819–1944), including manuscript catalogues of libraries acquired during the eighteenth and nineteenth centuries.

There are 14 personal fonds and collections of personal origin (1,098 units) (11th–20th cc.), predominantly papers of university professors and teachers, including scattered technical manuscripts and copies of university lectures—Prince A. D. Menshikov (1673–1729), Hofmeister D. P. Volkonskii (1805–1859), the educator and organizer of Higher Women's Courses A. N. Strannoliubskii (1839–1903), the mining engineer and collector N. N. Klimkovskii, the collector V. A. Ivanov, the Byzantinists S. Iu. Destunis and V. N. Beneshevich, the Mongolist O. M. Kovalevskii, the Slavicist V. I. Lamanskii, the theology professor V. G. Rozhdestvenskii, the literary historian V. V. Sipovskii, the historian and regional studies specialist V. A. Shakhmatov, the chemist N. A. Menshutkin, and the biochemist S. P. Kostychev.

There is a large collection of illegal and restricted publications of the nineteenth and early twentieth century. These include the book collections of the Committee for Foreign Censorship (1811–1860—ca. 9,000 books), and of the St. Petersburg Censorship Committee (1801–1862—ca. 10,000 books), many of which bear censorship stamps and other markings; as well as a collection from the Ministry of Public Education with official censorship copies of publications in Russia (1856–1862—ca. 11,000 books), including those in languages of subject peoples.

Many of the rare books in the division from personal library collections have important autographs and marginalia, some of which are described in published catalogues.

Working Conditions: Researchers are accommodated in the general library reading room, since there is no special reading room for the division. Archival materials are delivered the same day they are ordered.

Reference Facilities: *Opisi* are available for processed fonds. Division holdings are included in the general alphabetical and subject catalogues of the university library. The manuscript holdings are covered in an inventory register. Work is underway on a separate alphabetical and chronological catalogue for the division, but only part of the holdings are covered. There is an unpublished survey of the manuscripts.

Copying: Microfilms and photographic copies can be prepared.

Vostochnyi otdel
[Oriental Division]

Address:	St. Petersburg, Universitetskaia nab., 11
Telephone:	328-95-45
Hours:	Tu–F 10:00–16:00
Head:	Amaliia Stanislavovna Zhukovskaia (*tel.* 328-95-49)
Chief Librarian:	Tamara Petrovna Deriagina

HOLDINGS: ca. 55,000 units, 11th–19th cc.

The Oriental Division—administratively a subdivision of the Scientific Library—is housed in the University's Oriental Faculty. Its holdings, the first of which were acquired in the early nineteenth century, now include Oriental manuscripts and xylographs with texts of philology, literature, history, geography, and religion. During the mid- to late nineteenth century the library acquired a collection of Oriental manuscripts from Kazan University, the First Kazan Gymnasium, the Richelieu Lyceum in Odessa, and also personal collections of Oriental scholars including the professors A. K. Kazembek (1871), I. P. Minaev (1887–1892), Antoni Muchliński (A. O Mukhlinskii), and V. P. Vasil'ev, who were members of the University's noted Oriental Faculty.

The Chinese and Japanese collections are the largest. The Chinese collection, consisting of encyclopedias, dynastic histories, literary anthologies, collected sources, and other manuscripts, includes the collection from the Russian Ecclesiastical Mission in Beijing, and collections of the Orientalists P. I. Zakharov, P. S. Popov, V. M. Uspenskii, A. E. Liubimov, and others; there is also a selection of historical maps of China collected by V. P. Vasil'ev. Significant East Asian manuscript holdings include those in Manchu, Tibetan, Mongolian, and Korean languages, with representative

Buddhist texts, among other materials. The earliest manuscripts in ancient Indian languages come mostly from the collection of I. P. Minaev, including the earliest eleventh-century text on palm leaves. The division has over 800 Arabic and close to 600 Persian and Tadzhik manuscripts, many important texts in Turkic languages, and a few manuscripts in Georgian and Armenian languages. The division also holds personal fonds of several Orientalists—with personal papers and collected documents—including the Iranist and Kurdic scholar, archeologist, and archeographer P. I. Lerkh, the Iranist A. A. Romaskevich, and professors V. A. Ivanov, A. L. Kun, and P. I. Melioranskii.

Reference Facilities: There are topographic and alphabetical card catalogues of all manuscripts and xylographs in Oriental languages. The personal fonds of scholars have not been processed.

Copying: Facilities are available for photographic copies and microfilm.

FINDING AIDS — PUBLISHED — GENERAL:

Biblioteki: Putevoditel' (1996), pp. 184–86; *Fondy red. izd.* (1991), pp. 146–50; G&K *Spravochnik* (1983), pp. 225–26; *Biblioteki SPb* (1993), p. 14; PKG *M&L* (1972), pp. 228–30; *Peterburg* (1992), p. 420; Myl'nikov (1970), pp. 26–27.

General

g-330. *Putevoditel' po Nauchnoi biblioteke im. M. Gor'kogo pri LGU.* Compiled by
A. Kh. Gorfunkel', A. A. Kononova, and I. A. Frantsuzova. Edited by K. M. Romanovskaia.
Leningrad: Izd-vo Leningradskogo un-ta, 1982. 72 p. [LGU] (Lib: IU; MH)
> The guide briefly surveys the history, structure and functions of the library, its divisions and catalogues, the holdings of the Division of Rare Books and Manuscripts (pp. 33–39) and the Oriental Division (pp. 59–64).

g-331. Gorfunkel', Aleksandr Khaimovich; and Nikolaev, Nikolai Ivanovich. *Neotchuzhdaemaia tsennost': Rasskazy o knizhnykh redkostiakh universitetskoi biblioteki.* Leningrad: Izd-vo Leningradskogo un-ta, 1984. 176 p. [LGU; NB im. M. Gor'kogo] (Lib: DLC; IU; MH)
> The collection contains a general survey of book and manuscript collections in the Division of Rare Books, and the history and formation of its fonds, beginning with the eighteenth century. A supplemental list of book collections includes information on manuscript collections and archives (pp. 161–175), with indications of previous owners, date of acquisition, and related reference literature, including citations to archival sources.

g-332. *Putevoditel' po katalogam Nauchnoi biblioteki im. M. Gor'kogo pri LGU.* Leningrad, 1956. 15 p. [NB LGU]

Slavonic-Rus' Manuscripts

g-333. Shustorovich, E. M. "Slaviano-russkie rukopisi Biblioteki im. A. M. Gor'kogo Leningradskogo gosudarstvennogo universiteta." *Vestnik Leningradskogo gosudarstvennogo universiteta* 14:3 (1963): 110–15. "Seriia istorii, iazyka i literatury," no. 3. (Lib: DLC; IU; MH) [IDC-R-10,918]
> A general survey of medieval Slavonic-Rus' manuscripts.

Greek Manuscripts

g-334. Tonberg, M. F. "Grecheskie rukopisi Biblioteki im. A. M. Gor'kogo Leningradskogo Ordena Lenina Gosudarstvennogo universiteta im. A. A. Zhdanova." *Vizantiiskii vremennik* 31 (1971): 128–31. (Lib: DLC; IU; MH)
> Describes 18 Greek manuscripts held by the division, one dating from the thirteenth century, the others from the seventeenth to the nineteenth centuries.

Oriental Manuscripts

g-335. Abramov, A. T. "Vostochnyi otdel Nauchnoi biblioteki im. A. M. Gor'kogo Leningradskogo Ordena Lenina gosudarstvennogo universiteta im. A. A. Zhdanova." In *Vostokovednye fondy krupneishikh bibliotek Sovetskogo Soiuza: Stat'i i soobshcheniia,* pp. 218–28. Moscow: Izd-vo vostochnoi literatury, 1963. (Lib: DLC; IU; MH) [IDC-in R-10,664]
   Surveys the Oriental book and manuscript holdings in the library.

g-336. Abramov, A. T. "Biblioteka Vostochnogo fakul'teta." *Uchenye zapiski Leningradskogo gosudarstvennogo universiteta: Seriia vostokovedcheskikh nauk* 296:13 (1960): 177–88. (Lib: DLC; IU; MH)

g-336A. *Knizhnoe sobraniie Peterburgskogo universiteta. I: Bibliofil'skie kollektsii. II: Vostochnye knigi.* Edited by T. P. Deriagina, N. I. Nikolaev, A. A. Savel'ev. St. Petersburg: BAN, 1994. 27 p.
   The second section of this exhibition catalogue provides brief annotated descriptions (in Russian, pp. 18–22; and in French, pp. 23–27) of 20 manuscripts held by Oriental Division of the library—3 Arabic, 8 Persian, 1 South Indian on palm leaves, 2 Japanese xylographs, 3 Chinese xylographs, 1 Japanese and Chinese xylograph, and 2 Mongol manuscripts. The first part of the catalogue describes 30 incunabula and early printed books (15th–18th cc.) from Western Europe in Latin and other languages, which are covered more thoroughly in earlier printed catalogues.

g-337. Zaleman, Karl Germanovich (Salemann, C.); and Rozen, Victor Romanovich. "Spisok persidskikh, turetsko-tatarskikh i arabskikh rukopisei Biblioteki Imperatorskogo S.-Peterburgskogo universiteta." *Zapiski Vostochnogo otdeleniia Imperatorskogo Russkogo arkheologicheskogo obshchestva* 2–3 (1887–1888): 2:241–62; 3:197–222. (Lib: DLC; IU; MH) Also issued separately: SPb., 1888. 50 p.

g-338. Romaskevich, Aleksandr Aleksandrovich. "Spisok persidskikh, turetsko-tatarskikh i arabskikh rukopisei biblioteki Petrogradskogo universiteta: Prodolzhenie spiska K. G. Zalemana i V. R. Rozena." In *Zapiski Kollegii vostokovedov,* vol. 1, pp. 353–71. Leningrad: Izd-vo Rossiiskoi AN, 1925. (Lib: DLC; IU; MH) [IDC-R-10,920]
   A supplement to the Zaleman and Rozen 1887/1888 lists.

g-339. Tagirdzhanov, Aburkhaman Tagirovich (Tahirjanov, Gabdrakhman). *Opisanie tadzhikskikh i persidskikh rukopisei Vostochnogo otdela biblioteki LGU.* Vol. 1: *Istoriia, biografii, geografiia.* Edited by A. N. Boldyrev. Leningrad: Izd-vo LGU, 1962. 513 p. (Lib: DLC; IU; MH) [IDC-R-10,923]

g-340. Tagirdzhanov, Aburkhaman Tagirovich (Tahirjanov, Gabdrakhman). *Spisok tadzhikskikh, persidskikh i tiurkskikh rukopisei Vostochnogo otdela Biblioteki LGU: Prodolzhenie spiskov K. G. Zalemana i A. A. Romaskevicha.* Edited by A. N. Boldyrev. Moscow: "Nauka," 1967. 19 p. [LGU] (Lib: DDO; DLC; IU; MH) [IDC-R-10,924]
   Lists 177 Tadzhik and Persian manuscripts and 76 manuscripts in Turkic languages supplementing g-337–g-339.

g-341. Beliaev, Viktor Ivanovich; and Bulgakov, Pavel Georgievich. "Arabskie rukopisi sobraniia Leningradskogo gosudarstvennogo universiteta." In *Pamiati akademika Ignatiia Iulianovicha Krachkovskogo: Sbornik statei,* pp. 21–35. Leningrad: Izd-vo LGU, 1958. (Lib: DLC; IU; MH) [IDC-R-10,921]

g-341A. Frolova, Olga Borisovna. "Izuchenie arabskikh rukopisnykh sochinenii, khraniashchikhsia v vostochnom otdele nauchnoi biblioteki im. M. Gor'kogo v Leningradskom universitete." In *Materialy Vsesoiuznogo rabochego soveshchaniia po problemam vostochnoi arkheografii (Leningrad, 1–4 marta 1988 g.)/ Archaeographia Orientalis* (a-232), pp. 147–52. Moscow, 1990. (Lib: CU; PU)
   A survey of Arabic manuscript holdings and previous descriptive and publication work.

g-341A.1. Frolova, Olga Borisovna. "Some Notes on the Arabic Manuscripts and Collections in the Library of the Oriental Faculty of the St. Petersburg University." *Manuscripta Orientalia* 2:2 (1996): 36–43. (Lib: MH)

> A brief survey of Arabic manuscript holdings and comprehensive bibliography of previous descriptive and publication work.

FINDING AIDS — GENERAL — UNPUBLISHED:

g-342. "Opisanie rukopisei biblioteki LGU, sostavlennoe slushateliami seminariia akademika V. N. Perettsa pod ego rukovodstvom." Leningrad, 1924. 148 p. Typescript.

g-343. "Katalog knig na man'chzhurskom iazyke, khraniashchikhsia v fondakh biblioteki Vostochnogo fakul'teta Leningradskogo universiteta." Compiled by K. S. Iakhontov. 2 vols. Leningrad, 1986. 295 p. Typescript.

> See also Iakhontov's brief published notes about the SPbGU Manchu manuscripts in *Materialy Vsesoiuznogo rabochego soveshchaniia po problemam vostochnoi arkheografii (Leningrad, 1–4 marta 1988 g.)/ Archaeographia Orientalis* (a-232), pp. 172–73. Moscow, 1990.

FINDING AIDS — SPECIALIZED:

P. F. Zhukov Collection

g-344. Gorfunkel', Aleksandr Khaimovich; and Nikolaev, Nikolai Ivanovich. *Nachalo universitetskoi biblioteki (1783 g.): Sobranie P. F. Zhukova—pamiatnik russkoi kul'tury XVIII v.: Katalog.* Leningrad: Izd-vo LGU, 1980. 88 p. [LGU; NB im. M. Gor'kogo] (Lib: DLC; IU; MH)

> A scholarly catalogue of the collection of Petr Fedorovich Zhukov (1736–1782), the most important founding collection in the division.

Latin Manuscripts

g-345. Mur'ianov, M. F. "Piat' rukopisei Korpusa Iustiniana v sobranii Leningradskogo universiteta." *Vizantiiskii vremennik* 27 (1967): 306–09. (Lib: DDO; DLC; IU; MH)

> Description of the Latin codex of civil law of Emperor Justinian (11th–14th cc.), from the Leipzig collection of Professor Karl Friedrich Christian Wenck.

g-346. Mur'ianov, M. F. "Drevneishii pergamen Leningradskogo universiteta." *Vestnik Leningradskogo gosudarstvennogo universiteta. Seriia istorii, iazyka i literatury* 20:4 (1964): 151–54. (Lib: DLC; IU)

> Description and analysis of a fragment of an eleventh-century Latin religious text on parchment from Northern France.

Oriental Manuscripts

g-347. *Katalog peterburgskogo rukopisnogo "Gandzhura."* Compiled by Z. K. Kas'ianenko. Moscow: "Nauka," izd. firma "Vostochnaia literatura," 1993. 380 p. "Bibliotheca Buddhica," vol. 39. "Pamiatniki pis'mennosti Vostoka," vol. 102. (Lib: DLC; MH)

> A scholarly description of the Buddhist canon "Gandzhur" (Kanjur) from the first half of the seventeenth century in Mongolian, held in the collection in SPbGU. The publication includes facsimile fragments from the manuscript, which consists of 113 volumes in 100 parts.

g-348. Deriagina (Deryagina), Tamara P.; and Frolova, Olga Borisovna. "Antoni Muchliński and His Collection of Arabic Manuscripts in the St. Petersburg University Library." *Manuscripta Orientalia* 3:4 (1997): 45–51. (Lib: MH)

> A brief biography of the Polish Orientalist, diplomat, and professor at St. Petersburg University Antoni Muchliński (A. O. Mukhlinskii) (1808–1877), with a description of 18 Arabic manuscripts in the collection he left to the University.

Nauchnaia biblioteka Rossiiskoi Akademii khudozhestv (NB RAKh)

[Scientific Library of the Russian Academy of Arts]

Agency: Rossiiskaia Akademiia khudozhestv (RAKh)
[Russian Academy of Arts]

Address: 199034, St. Petersburg, Universitetskaia nab., 17
Telephone: 323-71-78
Transport: metro: Vasileostrovskaia, Sportivnaia
Hours: M–F 9:30–21:00, Sa 10:30–19:00

Director: Kira Nikolaevna Odar-Boiarskaia (*tel.* 323-65-29)
Deputy Director: Tamara Nikolaevna Lukashina (*tel.* 323-65-29)

HISTORY:

Biblioteka Akademii trekh znatneishikh khudozhestv—zhivopisi, skul'ptury i arkhitektury
  [Academy of the Three Distinguished Arts—Painting, Sculpture, and Architecture] (1757–1764)
Biblioteka Imperatorskoi Akademii khudozhestv (Biblioteka IAKh)
  [Library of the Imperial Academy of Arts] (1764–1917)
Biblioteka Akademii khudozhestv
  [Library of the Academy of Arts] (1917–1918)
Biblioteka Petrogradskikh gosudarstvennykh svobodnykh khudozhestvenno-uchebnykh masterskikh
  [Library of the Petrograd State Free Art Training Studios] (1918–1921)
Biblioteka Vysshikh khudozhestvenno-tekhnicheskikh masterskikh (Biblioteka VKhUTEMAS)
  [Library of the Higher Technical Art Studios] (1921–1922)
Biblioteka Vysshego khudozhestvenno-tekhnicheskogo instituta (Biblioteka VKhUTEINa)
  [Library of the Higher Technical Art Institute] (1922–1930)
Biblioteka Instituta proletarskikh izobrazitel'nykh iskusstv (Biblioteka INPII)
  [Library of the Institute of Proletarian Fine Arts] (1930–1932)
Biblioteka Leningradskogo instituta zhivopisi, skul'ptury i arkhitektury (Biblioteka LINZhAS)
  [Library of the Leningrad Institute of Painting, Sculpture, and Architecture] (1932–1933)
Nauchnaia biblioteka Vserossiiskoi Akademii khudozhestv (NB VAKh)
  [Scientific Library of the All-Russian Academy of Arts] (1933–1947)
Nauchnaia biblioteka Akademii khudozhestv SSSR (NB AKh SSSR)
  [Scientific Library of the Academy of the Arts of the USSR] (1947–1991)

One of the oldest public libraries of St. Petersburg, the library was established in 1757 together with the Imperial Academy of Arts. Before 1917, the library had acquired an extensive collection of graphic materials, including over 16,000 original drawings; 44,000 engravings, etchings, and lithographs; and 18,000 photographs and negatives. Transferred to the authority of the People's Commissariat of Education in 1918, its collections were partly scattered among various museums in Petrograd and other cities of the Soviet Union. In 1924 by order of Glavnauka, the majority of original drawings and xylographs that remained were transferred to the Russian Museum and the Hermitage—in exchange for which the Hermitage provided some luxury editions on architecture, and the Russian Museum provided architectural drawings from the S. Gagarin collection.

After the All-Russian Academy of Arts (VAKh) was reestablished in 1933, as primarily an educational institution, the library was in a subordinate posititon. In 1947 it became the independent research library of the Academy of Arts of the USSR (AKh SSSR)—since 1991, of the Russian Academy of Arts (RAKh).

The library has a branch in Moscow under the RAKh Presidium.

N.B. See more details about the history of RAKh, its archival records and its Scientific Bibliographic Archive and Archive of Negatives and Photo-Reproductions under E–45. For a description of the archival materials held by museums under RAKh, see H–90–H–93 and H–156.

HOLDINGS: ca. 20,000 units, 17th–20th c.

> MS books—10 units (17th–19th cc.); photographs—ca. 3,500 (late 19th–20th cc.); ex libris—ca. 2,500 units (18th–20th cc.); prints, lithographs—ca. 14,000 units (18th–20th cc.)

The library, founded as part of the Academy, specializes in literature relating to fine arts, decorative and applied art, architecture, and the history of art. The basic holdings (ca. 510,000 units) include the former private libraries of I. I. Betskoi, S. G. Gasilov, G. G. Grimm, August Ricard de Monferrand, A. N. Olenin, D. A. Rovinskii, I. I. Shuvalov, A. S. Stroganov, and G. S. Vereiskii, among others. Many of the rare holdings include autographs and other inscriptions.

In addition to printed materials, the library has significant manuscript books and archival materials, as well as collections of engravings, prints, lithographs, ex libris, posters, reproductions, and photographs.

Ten manuscript books of religious content (17th–19th cc.) include an illuminated codex of religious morality, primers, an illuminated Apocalypse with glosses by St. Andreas, Archbishop of Crete, an iconic original from Mount Athos, texts relating to Christian iconography, and reproductions of Byzantine miniatures (10th–12th cc.).

The collection of engravings includes the works of Russian painters from the eighteenth to twentieth centuries, such as E. P. Chemesov, I. V. Cheskii, M. I. Makhaev, I. I. Skorodumov, and N. I. Utkin, as well as the works of foreign masters. Among those are a series of volumes from the collection of prints from the cabinet of Louis XIV, which was transferred to the Academy by Count I. I. Shuvalov in 1760, and albums of engravings by Giambattista Piranesi and William Hogarth.

Ex libris from 18th–20th cc. include the collection of Baron Armin de Fölkersam (A. E. Fel'kerzam), who prepared ex libris for the imperial palace libraries. There are works of teachers and students of the All-Russian Academy of Arts from the 1930s, and works of modern painters who were affiliated with the Academy, such as P. A. Shillingovskii, K. I. Rudakov, and I. N. Pavlov, among others. There are prints and engravings by P. P. Belousov, G. S. Vereiskii, V. A. Vetrogonskii, V. V. Voinov, and M. S. Taranov, among others.

Photographs (19th–20th cc.) are represented by the original work of photographic artists such as I. F. Barshchevskii, I. V. Boldyrev, M. P. Dmitriev, and A. O. Karelin, among others. There are also albums of landscape photographs from different countries; pictures of ethnographic subjects; many photographs of architectural monuments and interiors of buildings of St. Petersburg, and of works of art; and portraits of statesmen, scientists, painters, architects, and art collectors. There are also commemorative albums of students and teachers of the Academy who were killed in World War II, as well as photographic records of the Telegraph Agency of the Soviet Union (TASS) from the 1930s through 1960s.

Exhibitions of the Academy over the last two centuries are reflected in collections of posters, leaflets, and invitations. The library holds reports beginning with the 1960s of conferences and memorial meetings dedicated to painters that were held on its premises, starting in the 1960s.

Access: A fee is charged for access to the library for foreigners. Access to manuscripts and other materials in the library for foreigners requires an official letter addressed to the director of the library.

Working Conditions: Manuscript materials are consulted in the general library reading room.

Reference Facilities: There are inventory *opisi*, a topographic catalogue, and catalogues of engravings and ex libris (by author and owner).

Copying: Photographs of graphic materials can be prepared, but require prior presentation of an institutional letter guaranteeing payment.

FINDING AIDS — PUBLISHED — GENERAL:

Biblioteki: Putevoditel' (1996), pp. 181–82; *Biblioteki SPb* (1993), pp. 71–72; *Peterburg* (1992), p. 86; *Putsko* (1970), p. 345.

There is no published guide to the archival materials in the library.

g-350. Odar-Boiarskaia, Kira Nikolaevna. "Biblioteka Akademii khudozhestv za 225 let i ee rol' v khudozhestvennom obrazovanii khudozhnikov." *Voprosy khudozhestvennogo obrazovaniia* 23 (1983): 20–29.

> A brief history of the library in honor of its 225th anniversary with a survey of its then current activities.

g-351. Vittenburg, E. P. "K istorii biblioteki 'Akademii trekh znatneishikh khudozhestv'." In *Nauka i kul'tura Rossii XVIII v,* edited by E. P. Karpeev, pp. 89–112. Leningrad, 1984. (Lib: DLC)

> Describes the founding of the RAKh predecessor library in the eighteenth-century.

g-352. Alekhnovich, Iu. P. *Biblioteka Akademii khudozhestv: Kratkii ocherk.* Leningrad: Izd-vo VAKh, 1940. 32 p.

g-353. *Akademiia khudozhestv SSSR. Nauchnaia biblioteka: Raboty i materialy.* 7 vols. Leningrad, 1955–1972. [AKh SSSR; Nauchnaia biblioteka] (Lib: IU; MH[mf])

Vols. 8–9 remain in typescript: Beloutova, Natal'ia Evgen'evna. "Knigi XVIII veka v fonde Nauchnoi biblioteki Akademii khudozhestv SSSR: Annotirovannyi katalog." Edited by N. V. Sultanova. 2 vols. L., 1963–1967. (The first volume covers Russian imprints; the second covers those from abroad).

The series continued as *Trudy Akademii khudozhestv SSSR.* 5 vols. Irregular. M.: Izobrazitel'noe iskusstvo, 1983–1987.

> Individual volumes listed provide an annotated catalogue of early books held by the library (15th–18th cc.). Other volumes in the catalogue series cover more specific types of literature. The fifth volume provides a full bibliography of Academy publications and literature about the history of RAKh (see g-353.3/e-274). A prerevolutionary series of catalogues of the library holdings was published in the 1870s and 1880s, but they are not listed here, since many of the library holdings were dispersed after the Revolution, and it has not been possible to coordinate them with present holdings.

g-353.1. Beloutova, Natal'ia Evgen'evna. *Knigi XV–XVI vekov v fonde Nauchnoi biblioteki Akademii khudozhestv SSSR: Kratkii annotirovannyi katalog.* Leningrad, 1955. "Akademiia khudozhestv SSSR. Nauchnaia biblioteka: Raboty i materialy," vol. 2. (Lib: IU)

g-353.2. Beloutova, Natal'ia Evgen'evna. *Knigi XVII veka v fonde Nauchnoi biblioteki Akademii khudozhestv SSSR: Annotirovannyi katalog.* Edited by S. S. Bronshtein. Leningrad, 1962. 420 p. "Akademiia khudozhestv SSSR. Nauchnaia biblioteka: Raboty i materialy," vol. 7. (Lib: IU)

g-353.3. *Materialy k bibliografii po istorii Akademii khudozhestv, 1757–1957.* Compiled by N. E. Beloutova, O. F. Beliaeva et. al. Edited by O. F. Beliaeva, L. L. Rakov et. al. Leningrad: Tip. VMOLA im. K. E. Voroshilova, 1957. 210 p. "Akademiia khudozhestv SSSR. Nauchnaia biblioteka: Raboty i materialy," vol. 5. (Lib: IU; MH) (Also listed as e-274).

FINDING AIDS — GENERAL — UNPUBLISHED:

g-354. Beloutova, Natal'ia Evgen'evna. "Sobranie graviur Dzhovanni-Battista i Franchesko Piranezi v fondakh Nauchnoi biblioteki Akademii khudozhestv SSSR: Annotirovannyi katalog." Leningrad, 1967. 37 p. Typescript.

Describes the collection of engravings by Giambattista and Francesco Piranesi.

Nauchno-muzykal'naia biblioteka Sankt-Peterburgskoi gosudarstvennoi konservatorii im. N. A. Rimskogo-Korsakova (NMB SPbGK)

[Scientific Music Library of the N. A. Rimskii-Korsakov
St. Petersburg State Conservatory]

Agency: Ministerstvo kul'tury RF (Minkul'tury Rossii)
[Ministry of Culture]

Address: 190000, St. Petersburg, Teatral'naia pl., 3
Telephone: 312-21-29 (reception); *Fax:* (812) 311-62-78, 311-63-89
E-mail: root@colibry.nit.spb.su
Website: http://www.csa.ru:81/Colibry/index.html
Transport: metro: Nevskii prospekt, Gostinyi Dvor; bus: 22, 27; tram: 1
Hours: M–F 11:00–18:00

Library Director: Elena Vladimirovna Nekrasova (*tel.* 311-32-23;
   e-mail: evn@hm.csa.ru)
Rector of the Conservatory: Vladislav Aleksandrovich Chernushenko (*tel.* 312-21-29)
Pro Rector for Scientific Work: Aleksandr Sergeevich Belonenko (*tel.* 311-73-19)

HISTORY:

Biblioteka Russkogo muzykal'nogo obshchestva (Biblioteka RMO)
   [Library of the Russian Music Society] (1859–1862)
Biblioteka Muzykal'nykh klassov Russkogo muzykal'nogo obshchestva
   [Library of the Music Classes of the Russian Music Society] (1862–1866)
Biblioteka Sankt-Peterburgskoi konservatorii
   [Library of the St. Petersburg Conservatory] (1866–1914)
Biblioteka Petrogradskoi konservatorii Russkogo muzykal'nogo obshchestva
   [Library of the Petrograd Conservatory of the Russian Music Society] (1914–1918)
Muzykal'naia biblioteka Petrogradskoi gosudarstvennoi konservatorii
   [Music Library of the Petrograd State Conservatory] (1918–1924)
Muzykal'naia biblioteka Leningradskoi gosudarstvennoi konservatorii
   [Music Library of the Leningrad State Conservatory] (1924–1944)
Nauchno-muzykal'naia biblioteka Leningradskoi gosudarstvennoi konservatorii im. N. A. Rimskogo-Korsakova (NMB LGK)
   [Scientific Music Library of the N. A. Rimskii-Korsakov Leningrad State Conservatory] (1944–1991)

The library was established in 1859 by the members of the Russian Music Society (after 1869, the Imperial Russian Music Society). In 1862, still under the society, it became the library of the so-called Music Classes. The Conservatory itself was founded in 1866 and took over the earlier library collections as the basis for its library.

The library's manuscript holdings started in 1870, when the music collector M. P. Azanchevskii donated to the Conservatory his library and collection of autographs, which contained the valuable library collection of G. E. Anders, the Curator of the Music Division of St. Geneviève Library, which Azanchevskii had purchased in Paris. In 1872 the library acquired a collection of manuscripts of A. S. Dargomyzhskii, as part of the library collection of the conservatory inspector, A. Demidov. In 1896 it received the manuscripts that had belonged to the composer, violinist, and teacher N. Ia.

Afanas'ev. During the late nineteenth and early twentieth centuries, the library acquired the libraries and archives of a series of other well-known Russian composers, musicians, and teachers—the book and music score collection of the Russian Music Society and the libraries of Anton Rubinstein (A. G. Rubinshtein), A. K. Glazunov, F. I. Stravinskii, N. A. Rimskii-Korsakov, and V. V. Stasov, among others, as well as the archives of A. N. Serov and M. Iu. Viel'gorskii.

In 1918 the Conservatory was transferred to the jurisdiction of the People's Commissariat of Education (Narkompros) RSFSR and became part of the state network of higher educational institutions. During World War II, part of the library fonds together with the conservatory staff were evacuated to Tashkent (1941–1944).

In general the library collects literature on music and musicology (ca. 500,000 volumes) and has been enriched over the years by a number of private collections. Dissertations that have been defended in the Conservatory, starting in the late 1920s, are shelved in the reading room.

The Manuscript Division was established in 1937 and later became a separate sector of the library.

In 1969, in honor of the 125th anniversary of the birth of N. A. Rimskii-Korsakov, a Museum of the History of the N. A. Rimskii-Korsakov St. Petersburg Conservatory was opened in the building of the Conservatory, to which was transferred some of the archival and manuscript materials held by the Conservatory for display purposes.

N.B. The archive of the Conservatory for the period 1917–1979 is retained in TsGALI SPb (D–15, fond no. 298).

Access: Research access requires an official letter addressed to the director of the library, indicating the subject and aim of research. Access to the dissertation collection requires an additional special written request, with an endorsement by the Pro-Rector for Scientific Work.

Reference Facilities: An extensive card catalogue covers the entire library, including the Sector for Manuscripts, Rare Books, and Music Scores. It has recently been prepared in a microfiche edition and can be purchased from Norman Ross Publishers (New York) (g-360).

Copying: Xerox and photographic copies can be ordered.

Sektor rukopisei, redkikh knig i not
[Sector of Manuscripts, Rare Books, and Music Scores]

RdngRm: 311-64-89
Hours: M–F 10:00–17:00; Sa 10:00–16:00
Head: Tamara Zakirovna Skvirskaia (*tel.* 311-99-31; *e-mail* tamara@colibry.nit.spb.su)

HOLDINGS: 4 fonds, ca. 9,000 units, early 18th–20th cc. (some documents 15th–17th cc.)
music scores—ca. 1,500 units (15th–20th cc.); personal papers, letters—ca. 5,000 units; photographs, postcards—ca. 2,500 units (mid 19th–20th cc.)

The sector houses autograph music scores, documents relating to the life and activities of Russian and Western European musicians, including correspondence and photographs, a collection of manuscript choral scores, in ordinary and neumatic notation (15th–20th cc.).

Part of the choral collection belonged to the famous researcher on early choral music, S. V. Smolenskii. Among them there are collections of music scores for church services, written in traditional and neumatic notation (*irmologii, oktoikhi, trezvony prazdnikov, obikhody*, and others), music primers, a collection of music scores with Russian poetry of the eighteenth century, and a collection of Catholic hymns in Latin (15th–16th cc.) from the collection of the Grand Duke Michael (Mikhail) Pavlovich.

There are also materials from the collection of the Russian Music Society and from the libraries of Anton Rubinstein (A. G. Rubinshtein), A. K. Glazunov, A. S. Dargomyzhskii, F. I. Stravinskii,

N. A. Rimskii-Korsakov, V. V. Stasov, and the archives of A. N. Serov and M. Iu. Viel'gorskii, although most of the materials have not been catalogued according to the collection of their provenance.

There are individual scores of composers of the late eighteenth and early nineteenth centuries, including A. A. Aliab'ev, D. S. Bortnians'kyi (Bortnianskii), A. E. Varlamov, M. Iu. Viel'gorskii, S. A. Degtiarev, and O. A. Kozlovskii. The main part of the holdings consists of scores of Russian composers of the late nineteenth century to the twentieth. Among these are compositions of M. I. Glinka, A. S. Dargomyzhskii, M. P. Musorgskii, A. P. Borodin, N. A. Rimskii-Korsakov, and P. I. Tchaikovsky (Chaikovskii), autograph scores of M. A. Balakirev, A. N. Serov, César Cui (Ts. A. Kiui), and A. G. Rubinstein, among others, including fragments and scores of the operas "A Life for the Tsar" by Glinka, "Prince Igor'" by Borodin, and "May Night," "Sadko," and "The Tsar's Bride" by Rimskii-Korsakov. Most complete is the collection of the compositions of A. K. Glazunov (ca. 100 autograph scores).

The division holds copies of manuscript librettos and scores for orchestration of operas performed in Russia in the eighteenth century, as well as works of Western European composers, such as Francesco Araia, Baldassare Galuppi, and others.

The extensive epistolary legacy of Russian and foreign composers, performers and musical figures (about 5,000 units) is arranged as a separate collection. The division also retains organizational correspondence of the late nineteenth-century Patronage Council for the Encouragement of Russian Composers and Musicians (*Popechitel'nyi sovet dlia pooshchreniia russkikh kompozitorov i muzykantov*), and of the employees of the M. P. Beliaev Publishing House in Leipzig (*Beliaevskii arkhiv*). The collection of letters includes those of Borodin, Glazunov, A. K. Liadov, Serov, Rubinstein, and others. There are also letters signed by Johannes Brahms, Carl Maria von Weber, Charles Gounod, Franz Liszt, Camille Saint-Saëns, Richard Wagner, Felix Mendelssohn, and others, as well as two letters signed by Ludwig van Beethoven and drafts of the adagio movement of his string quartet (op. 18, no. 6). Among the treasures from the M. P. Azanchevskii library there is an album with the autographs of Wolfgang Amadeus Mozart, Carl Philipp Emanuel Bach, Luigi Cherubini, François Adrien Boieldieu, Gasparo Spontini, Robert Schumann, Carl Maria von Weber, Felix Mendelssohn, Gaetano Donizetti.

The iconographic fond includes collections of original photographs (many with autographs) and postcards, dating from the second half of the nineteenth and early twentieth centuries. There are portraits of teachers and students of the Conservatory (1860s–1880s), such as A. G. Rubinstein, A. N. Esipova, A. K. Glazunov, and K. Iu. Davydov, and of Russian and foreign composers and opera singers, such as F. I. Chaliapin (Shaliapin), Angelo Masini, and Antonio Cotogni, among others, and photographs of the reconstruction of the Conservatory building in 1891–1896.

Working Conditions: Materials are delivered to the library reading room the day they are ordered.

Reference Facilities: There are card catalogues and inventory registers for all materials in the manuscript sector. The general card catalogue of the library also covers the Sector for Manuscripts, Rare Books, and Music Scores, with a separate section for manuscripts; it has recently been prepared in a microfiche edition which can be purchased from Norman Ross Publishers (New York) (g-360). A separate catalogue of the manuscript materials is in preparation, including the collection of M. P. Azanchevskii.

Copying: Facilities are available for xerox and photographic copies.

Kabinet zvukozapisei
[Cabinet of Sound Recordings]

Head: Nelli Ivanovna Kuznetsova (*tel.* 314-99-97)

HOLDINGS: statistics not available

The Conservatory has a collection of sound recordings on manufactured phonograph records, compact disks, and magnetic tapes, retained in the Cabinet of Sound Recordings. The core of the holdings came from the collection of the Music History Cabinet of the Institute of Theater and Music, which was transferred to the Conservatory in 1935. The holdings include many compositions by classical Russian and foreign composers, as well as some folk music, recorded by past masters and the best contemporary performers.

Reference Facilities: The fonds are described in inventory books, and there are also alphabetical and systematic catalogues.

Muzei istorii Sankt-Peterburgskoi gosudarstvennoi konservatorii im. N. A. Rimskogo-Korsakova (Muzei istorii SPbGK)
[Museum of the History of the N. A. Rimskii-Korsakov St. Petersburg Conservatory]

Telephone: 311-66-10
Hours: by appointment

HOLDINGS:

Since the opening of a Museum of the History of the Petersburg Conservatory in 1969, a few materials from the Conservatory collections have been used there for display purposes, namely those relating to well-known Russian musicians who were associated with the Conservatory. These include manuscript music scores, correspondence and memoir materials, as well as newspaper clippings, iconographic, photographic, and other documentary materials. Archival materials include personal documentation and memorabilia of A. G. Rubinstein, P. I. Tchaikovsky, and A. K. Glazunov, among others.

FINDING AIDS — PUBLISHED — GENERAL:
Biblioteki SPb (1993), p. 74; *Peterburg* (1992), pp. 280–281; PKG *M&L* (1972), p. 338; Putsko (1970), p. 346; Myl'nikov (1970), p. 21; *Muzykal'nyi Leningrad* (1958), pp. 359–65.

There is no published guide to the manuscript holdings, although a catalogue is in preparation. See the brief survey by the current head of the Manuscript Sector, T. Z. Skvirskaia, in the recent collective volume, *Petersburgskii muzykal'nyi arkhiv* (a-454), which also includes several other accounts of specific Conservatory manuscript holdings.

g-360. *Card Catalog of the Music Library of the St. Petersburg Conservatory (Rimsky-Korsakov) on microfiche.* New York: Norman Ross Publishing, 1994–. 312 microfiches. (Lib: MH)
> A microfiche edition of the general card catalogue of the library which also covers the Sector of Manuscripts, Rare Books, and Music Scores.

g-361. *100 let Leningradskoi konservatorii, 1862–1962: Istoricheskii ocherk.* Compiled by E. F. Bronfin, V. N. Aleksandrova, M. A. Ganina, et al. Leningrad: "Muzyka," 1962. 303 p. [LGK] (Lib: DLC; IU)
> A historical survey. Includes a bibliography of published literature (pp. 286–302).

g-362. *Leningradskaia konservatoriia v vospominaniiakh: [Sbornik].* Edited by G. G. Tigranov et al. 2 vols. 2d ed. Leningrad: "Muzyka," 1987–1988. 253 p., 273 p. (Lib: DLC; IU; MH)
> 1st ED.: *Leningradskaia konservatoriia v vospominaniiakh, 1862–1962.* L.: Muzgiz, 1962. 415 p. (Lib: MH)

Muzykal'naia biblioteka Sankt-Peterburgskoi filarmonii im. D. D. Shostakovicha (MB SPbF)

[Music Library of the D. D. Shostakovich St. Petersburg Philharmonic]

Agency: Ministerstvo kul'tury RF (Minkul'tury Rossii)
[Ministry of Culture]

Address: 191011, St. Petersburg, ul. Mikhailovskaia, 2
Telephone: 311-73-81; *Fax:* (812) 311-21-26; *RdngRm:* 110-49-28
Transport: metro: Gostinyi Dvor, Nevskii prospekt
Hours: Tu–F 13:30–19:30

Director of the St. Petersburg Philharmonic: Boris Mikhailovich Skvortsov
(*tel.* 110-49-27)
Head of the Library: Galina Leonidovna Petrovskaia (*tel.* 110-49-28)

HISTORY:

Biblioteka Pridvornogo orkestra
[Library of the Court Orchestra] (1882–1917)
Biblioteka Petrogradskogo gosudarstvennogo simfonicheskogo orkestra
[Library of the Petrograd State Symphonic Orchestra] (1917–1921)
Biblioteka Petrogradskoi gosudarstvennoi filarmonii
[Library of the Petrograd State Philharmonic] (1921–1922)
Biblioteka Petrogradskoi gosudarstvennoi akademicheskoi filarmonii
[Library of the Petrograd State Academic Philharmonic] (1922–1924)
Biblioteka Leningradskoi akademicheskoi gosudarstvennoi filarmonii
[Library of the Leningrad Academic State Philharmonic] (1924–1975)
Muzykal'naia biblioteka Leningradskoi akademicheskoi gosudarstvennoi filarmonii im. D. D. Shostakovicha
[Music Library of the D. D. Shostakovich Leningrad Academic State Philharmonic] (1975–1991)

The Music Library was founded in 1882 at the same time as the Court Orchestra (*Pridvornyi orkestr*), the music scores of which formed the foundation of the library collections. The orchestra came under state control in 1917 was reorganized as the Petrograd State Philharmonic in 1921, and in 1924 was renamed the Leningrad Philharmonic. It was renamed in honor of D. D. Shostakovich in 1975.

After the October Revolution the library acquired a number of important music holdings from state and public organizations as well as private collections, including the libraries of the orchestra of Count A. D. Sheremetev and the Pavlovsk Railroad Station Orchestra, and part of the library of the A. I. Ziloti Orchestra, along with fonds of the St. Petersburg "Singakademie" Choral Society, the music division of the People's Commissariat of Education (*Narkompros*), and the Division for Furniture and Interior Decoration of the City Museum, among others. Later, the library acquired a collection of music scores for symphonic orchestra from the State People's Home (*Gosnardom*), the library of the conductor K. I. Eliasberg, the collection of scores for orchestra gathered by the conductor G. N. Rozhdestvenskii, and the book collection of the musicologist A. M. Stupel'. Part of the library's manuscript holdings were transferred to the Music Division of the Hermitage in 1932, and in 1936 a collection of music scores for brass bands was transferred from the library to the Ministry of Defense and the State Brass Band (which was subsequently disbanded). The remaining manuscript materials were transferred to the State Public Library (now the Russian National Library—G–15) in 1938.

N.B. The archive of the Philharmonic Orchestra for the period 1921–1970 is now retained in TsGALI SPb (D–15).

HOLDINGS: ca. 17,000 units, 1896–1990s
   graphic materials—ca. 17,000 units

Most of the archival materials earlier held by the library have been transferred to other institutions as described above; nevertheless, significant materials of importance remain.

Most extensive in terms of archival holdings in the library are graphic materials, which include historical materials relating to the Court Orchestra and the St. Petersburg Philharmonic. Among these is a collection of programs of concerts of the Russian Music Society, the Philharmonic, and the Pavlovsk Railroad Station Orchestra, among others. There are also various albums, prints and engravings, Philharmonic billboard posters, reproductions of pictures, postcards, photographs, and portraits of music personalities, as well as a collection of press clippings relating to the history of Russian music and to individual composers and musicians.

Access: There are no limitations on access to the library holdings.

Working Conditions: Materials are delivered in the general reading room the same day that they are ordered.

Reference Facilities: There are auxiliary reference card catalogues including a chronicle of the musical life of the Philharmonic since 1921.

Copying: Xerox copies can be ordered.

FINDING AIDS — PUBLISHED — GENERAL:

Biblioteki SPb (1993), pp. 74–75; *Peterburg* (1992), pp. 86, 64; *Muzykal'nyi Leningrad* (1958), pp. 368–70.

There is no published guide or general description of the archival holdings remaining in the library.

g-365. *Leningradskaia gosudarstvennaia Ordena Trudovogo Krasnogo Znameni filarmoniia: Stat'i. Vospominaniia. Materialy: [Sbornik].* Edited by B. A. Arapov, O. S. Sarkisov, and V. Fomin. Leningrad: "Muzyka," 1972. 376 p. + plates. [Leningradskaia gos. filarmoniia] (Lib: DLC; IU; MH)
    Provides historical data about the Philharmonic Orchestra with documents and reminiscences.

Sankt-Peterburgskaia gosudarstvennaia teatral'naia biblioteka (SPbGTB)

[St. Petersburg State Theater Library]

Agency: Ministerstvo kul'tury RF (Minkul'tury Rossii)
[Ministry of Culture]
Komitet po kul'ture Administratsii Sankt-Peterburga
[Committee on Culture of the Administration of St. Petersburg]

Address: 191011, St. Petersburg, ul. Zodchego Rossi (pl. Ostrovskogo), 2
Telephone: 312-03-11; 311-61-04; 311-08-45; *Fax:* (812) 314-47-76;
RdngRm: 311-61-04
E-mail: apavlova@spt1.org
Website: http://www.sptl.org
Transport: metro: Gostinyi Dvor, Nevskii prospekt
Hours: M–Sa 11:00–19:00

Acting Director: Anastasiia Grigor'evna Pavlova (*tel./fax* 312-03-11;
e-mail: apalova@spt1.org)
Deputy Director for Library Affairs: Elena Grigor'evna Pogosova (*tel.* 315-66-47)

HISTORY:

Biblioteka Rossiiskogo pridvornogo teatra
[Library of the Russian Court Theater] (1756–1832)
Biblioteka Aleksandrinskogo teatra
[Library of the Aleksandrinskii Theater] (1832–1889)
Tsentral'naia biblioteka Imperatorskikh teatrov
[Central Library of the Imperial Theaters] (1889–1917)
Tsentral'naia biblioteka russkoi dramy
[Central Library of Russian Drama] (1917–1930)
Tsentral'naia biblioteka russkoi dramy pri Gosudarstvennom
Akademicheskom teatre dramy im. A. S. Pushkina (TsBRD)
[Central Library of Russian Drama of the A. S. Pushkin State Academic Theater of Drama] (1931–1934)
Leningradskaia gosudarstvennaia teatral'naia biblioteka im. A. V. Lunacharskogo (LGTB)
[A. V. Lunacharskii Leningrad State Theater Library] (1934–V.1992)
Sankt-Peterburgskaia gosudarstvennaia teatral'naia biblioteka im. A. V. Lunacharskogo (SPbGTB)
[A. V. Lunacharskii St. Petersburg State Theater Library] (VI.1992–1995)

Established in 1756 as the Repertory Library of the Court Theater (renamed the Aleksandrinskii [Imperial Alexandra] Theater in 1832, and the Academic Theater in 1919), the library was reorganized as the Central Library of the Imperial Theaters in 1889. From the Direction of Imperial Theaters it acquired the collected materials pertaining to French drama of the St. Petersburg State French Troupe (the so-called Mikhailovskii Theater) and the theater library of Prince A. Ia. Lobanov-Rostovskii, who had assembled one of the largest existing collections of original French plays (16th–early 19th cc.). Before 1917 the library served as an official depository that received copies of all plays staged in state theaters in St. Petersburg.

It was reorganized after 1917 as the Central Library of Russian Drama under the Division of State Theaters of the People's Commissariat of Education (Narkompros). In 1919 the library acquired the complete collection of plays submitted to the censorship office from the archive of the Main Department for Affairs of the Press, which now forms the so-called "Censorship Fond" (1865–1917). Most of the additional manuscript materials were acquired during the 1920s and 1930s. These include the collection of Grand Duke Paul (Pavel) Aleksandrovich from the library of the Palei Palace in Tsarskoe Selo, the so-called Northern Theater Library of K. P. Larin, as well as private collections of A. E. Molchanov, M. G. Savina, N. N. Khodotov, V. V. Protopopov, and L. D. Blok, among others.

In 1931 the library came under the administration of the A. S. Pushkin State Academic Drama Theater (the former Aleksandrinskii Theater had been named in honor of Pushkin in 1920). It was administratively separated from the theater in 1934 and was renamed the A. V. Lunacharskii Leningrad State Theater Library. In 1955 the library came under the jurisdiction of the Main Administration of Theaters and Music Institutions of the Ministry of Culture of the USSR. In 1955 it was shifted to the jurisdiction of the Ministry of Culture of the Russian Federation, and in 1958 to the Administration of Culture of the Executive Committee of the Leningrad City Soviet. The library's present name dates from 1995, when it dropped the honorific name of Lunacharskii.

The Division of Manuscript and Rare Fonds, Archival and Graphic Materials as presently organized dates from 1991.

Access: Access requires an official or personal application with indication of the subject and aim of research.

Otdel rukopisnykh i redkikh fondov, arkhivnykh i izomaterialov
[Division of Manuscript and Rare Fonds, Archival and Graphic Materials]

Telephone: 311-61-04
Hours: M–Sa 11:00–19:00
Head: Marina Igorevna Tsapovetskaia

HOLDINGS: 19 (7 unarranged) fonds, ca. 153,000 units, 18th–20th cc. (scattered from 16th–17th cc.) manuscript fond—65,526 units; sketches—87,392 units

The library's extensive manuscript collections are particularly rich in materials pertaining to the history of the prerevolutionary Russian theater. They are subdivided into several principal sections or fonds.

The "Russian Fond" contains all plays (and in many cases promptbooks) in the repertory of Russian dramatic troupes, dating from the mid-eighteenth to the early twentieth centuries, the imperial collection of plays from the theater section of the Palei Palace library (18th–19th cc.), and the theater library of K. P. Larin (late 19th–early 20th cc.), including manuscript, typescript, and lithographic copies of plays. The "French Fond" includes plays in French and Italian from the repertory of the St. Petersburg State French Troupe (19th–early 20th cc.), and also the collection of Prince A. Ia. Lobanov-Rostovskii (16th–19th cc.). There are also plays in other foreign languages, including English, Bulgarian, and modern Greek, among others. The "Repertory Library of the Former German Capital (*stolichnaia*) Troupe" includes plays in German, and a collection of librettos for opera and ballet (19th–early 20th cc.).

The "Censorship Fond" (42,000 units; 1865–1917) consists of copies of all submitted plays with censor's marks "Permitted" or "Banned." In addition to plays in Russian, there are also plays in Ukrainian, Belorussian, and languages of other nationalities of the Russian Empire, including Armenian, Georgian, Tatar, Yiddish, Estonian, and Latvian, among others. Considered unique in terms of its completeness and historical significance, the fond includes autograph manuscript texts, stage versions, adaptations, promptbooks, and stage-directors' copies of plays by A. S. Pushkin, A. S. Griboedov, N. V. Gogol', A. N. Ostrovskii, A. V. Sukhovo-Kobylin, I. S. Turgenev, M. E.

Saltykov-Shchedrin, L. N Tolstoi, A. P. Chekhov, A. M. Gor'kii, and others. The fond is intensively used for the preparation of academic collections of classic Russian literary works.

The Artistic Production Division contains the collection of the Imperial Theater Production (*montirovochnaia*) Library, consisting of authentic set and costume designs, furniture, and other props relating to theater productions (17th c.–1917), together with various graphic materials on theater architecture and interiors. There are drawings and production sketches of the most distinguished stage designers from the eighteenth to the twentieth centuries, such as Pietro Gottardo di Gonzaga, Alfred (A. A.) Roller, K. A. Korovin, A. Ia. Golovin, Léon Bakst (*pseud. of* L. S. Rozenberg), A. N. Benois (Benua), and B. I. Anisfel'd (Anisfeldt), among others.

Documentary materials of the Manuscript Division include the editorial records of the journal *Biriuch Petrogradskikh gosudarstvennykh teatrov* (Herald of Petrograd State Theaters). Personal papers of theater personalities from the nineteenth and twentieth centuries include those of N. F. Sazonov, P. V. Samoilov, and E. I. Time, along with the private collection of the distinguished twentieth-century ballet-master M. M. Fokin (Michel Fokine), donated to the library by his son.

The "Epistolary" section includes approximately 3,000 personal letters of literary and theater personalities of the eighteenth through twentieth centuries, such as Voltaire, Maria Taglioni, Ernesto Rossi, M. S. Shchepkin, P. S. Mochalov, N. A. Nekrasov, A. N. Ostrovskii, L. N. Tolstoi, Eleonora Duse, Enrico Caruso, I. E. Repin, F. I. Chaliapin (Shaliapin), V. F. Komissarzhevskaia, M. N. Ermolova, and M. G. Savina, among others.

Since 1934 the library has collected press clippings relating to theaters throughout the former USSR.

Working Conditions: Usually materials are delivered to the special reading room the day they are ordered.

Reference Facilities: Reference and bibliography facilities consist of system of catalogues and card files, some limited for staff use and others for readers. The manuscript materials are recorded in the official staff general alphabetical catalogue. There are separate alphabetical catalogues covering the Censorship Fond, Russian plays, librettos of operas, musical comedies, and ballets. Additional card catalogues provide names of plays in Russian and foreign languages. There are alphabetical and systematic subject catalogues of the Artistic Production Division and of the Manuscript Fond, and a catalogue of the K. P. Larin library.

Copying: Xerox facilities are available.

FINDING AIDS — PUBLISHED — GENERAL:

PKG *M&L* (1972), p. 332; Myl'nikov (1970), pp. 18–19; *Teatr i muzyka* (1963), pp. 174–76; *Biblioteki SPb* (1993), pp. 78–79; *Peterburg* (1992), p. 610.

There is no published guide to the archival and manuscript holdings. The new library website has a brief survey of the history of the library, the manuscript holdings, and other information about library services and exhibits.

g-366. Nelidov, Iu. A. "Leningardskaia teatral'naia biblioteka im. A. V. Lunacharskogo." In *Teatral'noe nasledie: Sbornik pervyi,* pp. 9–44. Leningrad: Gosudarstvennyi Akademicheskii teatr dramy, 1934. (Lib: DLC; MH) [IDC-in R-10,926] Also available as a separate offprint (36 p.).

> A general survey of the library holdings with description of separate library and manuscript collections. Other parts of the volume cover additional library holdings, such as the article covering rare editions of plays and promptbooks by A. N. Ostrovskii.

g-367. *Informatsionnye materialy k 200-letiiu Gosudarstvennogo akademicheskogo Ordena Trudovogo Krasnogo Znameni teatra dramy im. A. S. Pushkina i Gosudarstvennoi teatral'noi biblioteki im. A. V. Lunacharskogo (1750–1950).* Leningrad, 1957. 73 p.

Tsentral'naia muzykal'naia biblioteka Gosudarstvennogo akademicheskogo Mariinskogo teatra

[Central Music Library of the State Academic Mariinskii Theater]

Agency: Ministerstvo kul'tury RF (Minkul'tury Rossii)
[Ministry of Culture]

Address: 191002, St. Petersburg, ul. Zodchego Rossi (pl. Ostrovskogo), 2
Telephone: 312-35-73
Transport: metro: Nevskii prospekt, Gostinyi Dvor
Hours: Tu–Su 11:00–15:00

Director of the Theater: Iurii Alekseevich Shvartskopf (*tel.* 114-59-24)
Director of the Library: Natal'ia Ivanovna Morozova (*tel.* 114–73-16)
Head of the Fonds Division: Tat'iana Mikhailovna Kuznetsova (*tel.* 114-73-16)

HISTORY:

Notnaia kontora Imperatorskikh teatrov
    [Music Score Office of the Imperial Theaters] (early 18th c.)
Notnaia biblioteka Imperatorskikh teatrov
    [Music Score Library of the Imperial Theaters]
Tsentral'naia muzykal'naia biblioteka Gosudarstvennogo akademicheskogo teatra opery i baleta
    im. S. M. Kirova
    [Central Music Library of the S. M. Kirov State Academic Theater] (1935–1992)

What is now one of the most important music libraries in Russia was originally founded in the first half of eighteenth century as the Music Score Office (later—the Music Score Library) of the Imperial Theaters. After the Revolution the library came under the Administration of Academic Theaters. In 1934, half of those library holdings were given to what had been the Mariinskii (Imperial Maria) Theater and the other half to the A. V. Lunacharskii Theater Library (G–21) and the Theater Museum (H–102). The following year, the Mariinskii Theater was renamed in honor of the slain CP leader S. M. Kirov, and its library was reorganized as the Central Music Library of the Kirov State Academic Theater, with holdings considerably broader than those of the theater itself. Before World War II, it acquired the holdings of the Music Score Library of the State People's Home (*Gosnardom*), and later it acquired the collection of the Leningrad Conservatory Professor S. V. El'tsin and the music collection of the Military Medical Academy.

    The basic holdings of the library (ca. 500,000 volumes) include literature on music, musicology, and theater studies. Almost the entire music score collection consists of rare editions.

    The archival materials of the theater are held as part of the Division of Fonds and the Literary Division. As well as administrative records, these include collections of photographs, theater designs, posters, theater programs, and other materials relating to the theater productions (tel. 114-41-64).

N.B. The archive of the theater for the period 1917–1981 is retained in TsGALI SPb (D–15, fond 337).

HOLDINGS: ca 350,000 units, 18th c. to present

The library holds one of the largest collections of autograph manuscript music scores of Russian and foreign composers of the eighteenth to twentieth centuries, especially of opera and ballet, but also scores for orchestra and piano, and for vaudeville, presented at the imperial theaters—including the Mariinskii (from 1935–1992—the S. M. Kirov State Academic Theater of Opera and Ballet), and also a rich iconographic collection relating to music and musicians. The holdings have been arranged according to major subject categories, rather than the collection from whence they came.

Most significant among the library holdings is the fond of the Division of Russian Music, which consists of manuscripts of Russian and foreign composers who worked in St. Petersburg. Among these are manuscript music scores of the first operas staged in Russia, particularly on the St. Petersburg stage, including the score of the opera by Francesco Araia "Power of Love and Hatred" (1734) with the libretto translated by V. K. Trediakovskii. There are more than 100 manuscript scores for orchestra, opera, and ballet. There is also a unique collection of scores of Russian vaudeville composed during the 1812 Napoleonic invasion of Russia, including the very first A. A. Shakhovskoi's "The Cossack Poet" ("Kazak-stikhotvorets"), with music by K. A. Kavos.

The Autograph Division includes manuscript scores, letters, and various biographical documents relating to Russian, Soviet, and foreign composers, musicians, and other celebrities of the music stage from the eighteenth through twentieth centuries. These include autograph music scores of P. I. Tchaikovsky's operas "The Queen of Spades," "The Oprichnik," and for the ballet "Sleeping Beauty"; N. A. Rimskii-Korsakov's "May Night" and "The Maid of Pskov"; M. P. Musorgskii's "Boris Godunov"; A. S. Dargomyzhskii's "The Stone Guest" and "Bacchic Exultation" ("Torzhestvo Vakkha"); and A. P. Borodin's "Valiant Knights" ("Bogatyri"). Many other musicians are represented—with significant documents relating to A. A. Aliab'ev, César Cui (Ts. A. Kiui), M. I. Glinka, A. K. Glazunov, A. I. Khachaturian, S. S. Prokofiev, and D. D. Shostakovich, to name only a few. Among other autographs is the unique inscription of A. S. Pushkin addressed to P. A. Viazemskii, written on the reverse side of the music score of the A. N. Verstovskii song "Staryi muzh, groznyi muzh" (Old Husband, Dreadful Husband) (1825). There are also manuscript materials of a number of Western European composers dating from the seventeenth through nineteenth centuries, including Wolfgang Amadeus Mozart, Ludwig van Beethoven, Hector Berlioz, Camille Saint-Saëns, Riccardo Drigo, Léo Delibes, and Richard Wagner, among many others.

The "Foreign Fond" has an extensive collection of music scores, including eighteenth-century Italian operas and French operas and ballets from the eighteenth and nineteenth centuries, some of which represent the only surviving copy. Among these is the opera "Antigone" by the Italian composer Tommazo Traetta, staged in St. Petersburg in 1772.

Access: Permission for research in the library and use of manuscript collections is by application to the director of the theater on the basis of an official letter from the researcher or an official letter from the sponsoring institution with indication of the subject and aim of the research. As of the 1998–1999 season, the library is closed for major renovation.

Working Conditions: There is a general reading room for the library. Manuscript materials are ordered similarly to other printed materials, and are delivered the same day they are ordered.

Reference Facilities: Manuscript materials are not separated from printed library materials within the catalogues, which include information on letters, autographs, and also music scores and librettos, including both manuscript and printed materials. There is a separate catalogue for the autograph section. There are also catalogues of music scores, orchestrations, and librettos (both printed and manuscript materials).

Copying: Xerox copies can be ordered.

FINDING AIDS — PUBLISHED — GENERAL:

PKG *M&L* (1972), p. 337; Myl'nikov, (1970), p. 30; *Teatr i muzyka* (1963), pp. 10–11, 21–22; *Muzykal'nyi Leningrad* (1958), pp. 366–68; *Biblioteki SPb* (1993), pp. 75–76; *Peterburg* (1992), pp. 609–10.

There is no guide to the archival materials in the library.

g-368. *Gosudarstvennyi Ordena Lenina Leningradskii akademicheskii teatr opery i baleta im. S. M. Kirova: [Kniga-al'bom].* Compiled by A. P. Konnov and I. V. Tupnikov. Leningrad: "Muzyka," 1976. 159 p. (Lib: DLC; MH)

Includes information about the history of the theater and its collections.

g-369. Bogdanov-Berezovskii, Valerian Mikhailovich. *Leningradskii gosudarstvennyi akademicheskii Ordena Lenina teatr opery i baleta im. S. M. Kirova.* Leningrad/Moscow: "Iskusstvo," 1959. 342 p. (Lib: IU; MH)

Provides a detailed history of the theater with illustrations from the V. S. Gil' collection on the history of music theaters.

Biblioteka Sankt-Peterburgskogo otdeleniia
Soiuza teatral'nykh deiatelei RF (Biblioteka SPbO STD RF)
[Library of St. Petersburg Division of the Union of Theater Workers]

Agency: Soiuz teatral'nykh deiatelei RF (STD Rossii)
[Union of Theater Workers]

Address: 191025, St. Petersburg, Nevskii prospekt, 86
Telephone: 279-42-81
Transport: metro: Maiakovskaia
Hours: M–F 14:00–18:00; (closed July and August)

Director: Marina Iuzefovna Komarova

HISTORY:

Biblioteka Leningradskogo otdeleniia Vserossiiskogo teatral'nogo obshchestva (Biblioteka LO VTO)
[Library of the Leningrad Division of the All-Russian Theater Society] (1936–1959)
Biblioteka Dvortsa rabotnikov iskusstv im. K. S. Stanislavskogo (Biblioteka Doma aktera)
[Library of the K. S. Stanislavskii Palace for Workers in the Arts] (1959–1991)

The Library of the Leningrad Division of the All-Russian Theater Society was established in 1936. Merged with the Library of the Palace for Workers in the Arts in 1959, it was renamed for K. S. Stanislavskii. It was then under the Leningrad Branch of the All-Russian Theater Society, and later in the 1980s to 1991, under the Leningrad organization of the Union of Theater Workers of the RSFSR, as part of the so-called House of Actors (*Dom aktera*). Since 1991, the library serves the St. Petersburg Division of the Union of Theater Workers of the Russian Federation. The manuscript holdings were first organized in 1946.

N.B. Collections of photographic materials, sound recordings, and other archival documentation have been transferred to the Museum of Theater and Musical Arts (H–102) in St. Petersburg. For the Moscow Central Scientific Library of the Union of Theater Workers, see G–8.

Access: Research access requires an official letter with indication of the subject and aim of research.

Rukopisnyi otdel
[Manuscript Division]

Hours: M–F 14:00–18:00; (closed July–August)
Head: Vera Mikhailovna Mironova

HOLDINGS: ca. 1,500 units, 1930s–1990s

The library retains some of the documentary materials of the Leningrad Division of the All-Russian Theater Society, which was reestablished in 1935. These include minutes and stenograms of the meetings, conferences, and discussion held by the Society, as well as performances by G. A. Tovstonogov, N. K. Cherkasov, and N. P. Akimov, among others. There are also factual dossiers about St. Petersburg theaters and theater productions, theater programs, and biographical materials relating to distinguished actors and stage directors of St. Peterburg theaters, among other materials.

Documentary collections have been formed of press-clippings by the most prominent theater critics of St. Petersburg, such as M. O. Iankovskii, S. L. Tsimbal, and V. A. Sakhnovskii.

Working Conditions: Materials are delivered to the reading room the same day they are ordered.

Reference Facilities: There are reference card catalogues of theater premieres, "Theater Life in St. Petersburg," "Honorary Titles," names of theater personalities, and other materials.

Copying: Limited xerox copies can be ordered.

FINDING AIDS — PUBLISHED — GENERAL:

Biblioteki SPb (1993), p. 79; *Peterburg* (1992), p. 528; PKG *M&L* (1972), p. 336; Myl'nikov (1970), p. 13.

There is no published description of the archival materials in the library.

Nauchno-tekhnicheskaia biblioteka Sankt-Peterburgskogo gosudarstvennogo universiteta putei soobshcheniia (NTB PGUPS)
[Scientific-Technical Library of the
St. Petersburg State University of Transportation]

Agency: Ministerstvo putei soobshcheniia RF (MPS Rossii)
[Ministry of Transportation]

Address: 190031, St. Petersburg, Moskovskii prospekt, 9
Telephone: 168-86-11; *Fax (University):* (812) 315-20-21; 315-26-21;
   E-mail: fforeign@pgups.nw.ru
Website: http://www.ruslan.ru:8001/spb/univer/univer_ups.html
Transport: metro: Sennaia ploshchad', Sadovaia; tram: 2, 5, 14, 54

Rector of the University: Valerii Ivanovich Koralev (*tel.* 168-81-29; 310-25-21;
   e-mail: rectorat@pgus.nw.ru)
Director of the Library: Liudmila Mikhailovna Rodionova (*tel.* 168-82-52)
Deputy Director of the Library: Nonna Vladimirovna Trepetina (*tel.* 168-87-00)

HISTORY:
Biblioteka Instituta korpusa inzhenerov vodianykh i sukhoputnykh soobshchenii
   [Library of the Institute of the Corps of Engineers of Water and Land Communication] (1809–1810)
Biblioteka Instituta korpusa inzhenerov putei soobshcheniia
   [Library of the Institute of the Corps of Transportation Engineers] (1810–1864)
Biblioteka Instituta inzhenerov putei soobshcheniia
   [Library of the Institute of Transportation Engineers] (1864–1877)
Biblioteka Instituta inzhenerov putei soobshcheniia Imperatora Aleksandra I
   [Library of the Emperor Alexander I Institute of Transportation Engineers] (1877–1882, 1890–1917)
Biblioteka Vysshei akademii inzhenernogo dela
   [Library of the Higher Academy of Engineering] (1882–1890)
Biblioteka Petrogradskogo (Leningradskogo) instituta inzhenerov putei soobshcheniia (Biblioteka PIIPS)
   [Library of the Petrograd (Leningrad) Institute of Transportation Engineers] (1917–1931)
Biblioteka Leningradskogo instituta inzhenerov zheleznodorozhnogo transporta (Biblioteka LIIZhT)
   [Library of the Leningrad Institute of Railroad Transport Engineers] (1931–1932, 1937–1949)
Biblioteka Leningradskogo instituta inzhenerov zheleznodorozhnogo transporta im. Ia. E. Rudzutaka
   (Biblioteka LIIZhT)
   [Library of the Ia. E. Rudzutak Leningrad Institute of Railroad Transport Engineers] (1932–1937)
Biblioteka Leningradskogo instituta inzhenerov zheleznodorozhnogo transporta im. akad. V. N. Obraztsova
   (Biblioteka LIIZhT)
   [Library of the V. N. Obraztsov Leningrad Institute of Railroad Transport Engineers] (1949–1992)
Biblioteka Peterburgskogo instituta inzhenerov zheleznodorozhnogo transporta (Biblioteka PIIT)
   [Library of the St. Petersburg Institute of Railroad Transport Engineers] (1992–1993)

The library was established in 1809 together with the Institute of the Corps of Transportation Engineers under the Main Administration of Transportation and Public Buildings, and later, the Ministry of Transportation (or literally, Means of Communication). The first rector of the Institute, who had been instrumental in its foundation, was the civil engineer, Lieutenant-General Augustin de Betancourt Béthencourt (A. A. Betankur). Previously in service to the Spanish government, he arranged academic relations with the French School of Bridges and Highways (*École des ponts et chaussés*) and brought other faculty from France. One of the first technical engineering schools in the country, the Institute trained engineers for the development of the major railroads, canals, and highways of the Russian Empire, although before 1864, it had a predominantly military orientation. The name and administrative affiliation of the Institute has changed many times in the course of its long history.

During the Soviet period (1931–1991), while the name of the Institute suggested its orientation for railroad engineering, its faculty and graduates were also involved in electrification, hydroelectric projects, and other major construction enterprises. In 1949, the Institute took the honorific name of the Soviet transportation engineer Vladimir Nikolaevich Obraztsov (1874–1949), which it dropped in 1992. The Institute was raised to the status of a university in 1993, at which time it received its present name, sometimes translated as the St. Petersburg State University of Means of Communication.

Before 1917, the library acquired holdings from the private libraries of Minister of Transportation K. N. Pos'et, the architect Auguste Ricard de Montferrand, and the engineer N. A. Beleliubskii, as well as manuscript materials from the Main Administration of Transportation and other state institutions, construction agencies, archives, and libraries. In 1918 the library ceased being only an agency depository.

The library developed considerably during the Soviet period. With the change of the Institute to university status in 1993, the library acquired its present name and status as a scientific university library. Current library holdings (ca. 1,300,000 volumes) comprise literature on civil and electrical engineering, railroad transportation, manufacturing, automation and computer technology, and include dissertations defended at the Institute.

Most of the manuscript holdings—now part of the Fond of Manuscripts and Rare Books—are connected with prominent engineers and architects who were teachers or students of the Institute and who donated their personal documentary collections or writings to the library during their lifetime or by will.

N.B. Considerable documentation from LIIZhT and specialists connected with that Institute is now held by the Central Museum of Railroad Transport—TsMZhT (H–111), which is currently under the administration of the University, as it was after its foundation in the nineteenth century and during parts of the Soviet period.

Access: Research access requires a letter addressed to the director or personal application with indication of the subject and aim of the research.

Fond rukopisei i redkikh knig
[Fond of Manuscripts and Rare Books]

Telephone: 168-86-11
Hours: M–F 10:40–18:00
Head: Irina Georgievna Tokareva

HOLDINGS: ca. 1,000 units, 18th c. to present

Documentary holdings of the fond include manuscript materials relating to the history of the administration of transportation and public buildings, as well as an extensive collection of architectural drawings and plans for engineering construction in Russia. Documentation of the Main Administration of Transportation, earlier held in the St. Petersburg Main Archive of the Ministry of Foreign Affairs (1811–1813), includes materials on the design and construction of the most important canals and highways in Russia, as well as of the first Russian railroads. For example, there are technical notes and other documents relating to the construction of the Ladoga and Obvodnoi Canals, bridges and embankments in St. Petersburg, the Georgian Military Highway, St. Petersburg flood prevention projects (1792–1842), registers with measurements and descriptions of rivers, technical manuals, and expense records. Among other materials, there is a "Report on the Present Situation, Prospects, and Suggestions Regarding the Inland Water Transportation in Russia" (1782) by General Ia. E. Sivers, Director of Water Transportation; a file from the Chancellery of the Main Administration of Transportation relating to railroad construction in Russia submitted by the Czech engineer Franz Anton von Gerstner (1835–1836), which documents plans for the construction of the first Russian railroad connecting St. Petersburg and Tsarskoe Selo; and a collection of comprehensive manuscript supplements to the I. F. Stuckenberg (Shtukenberg)'s "Hydrographie des Russischen Reiches" (Hydrography in Russia) (1855).

Most extensive is a collection of materials relating to the Institute of the Corps of Transportation Engineers itself, which includes the original reports of the Institute's inspector and first director, Lieutenant-General Augustin de Betancourt (Béthencourt; A. A. Betankur), rescripts of Alexander I (1813–1819), journals of Institute conferences (1836–1842), resolutions of the Ministry, lists of professors and students, documents relating to the Institute buildings and workshops, and reports of expeditions undertaken by Institute teachers throughout Russia, Western Europe, and America, including data on hydrography, ports, communications, and transportation construction.

A complex of documentation on construction and architecture includes the manuscript version of an "Elementary Course in Architecture" (1763) from August Ricard de Montferrand's library and a collection of the architectural drawings of St. Petersburg historical monuments (1810s). It also includes technical notes and projects relating to construction in St. Petersburg, Moscow, Mykolaiv, Sevastopol, and Novgorod, and other cities in the Russian Empire, including plans by Pierre Dominique Bazaine, Betancourt, Jean-François Thomas de Thomon, M. O. Mikeshin, and A. A. Mikhailov, among others. Of considerable significance is the file of the Commission for the Construction of St. Isaac Cathedral (1821–1826) in St. Petersburg acquired from office papers of Alexander I, which includes the original plans by Bazaine, V. V. Stasov, A. A. Mikhailov, V. I. and A. V. Beretti, A. I. Mel'nikov, and Montferrand, along with sixteen folders of drawings relating to the Montferrand construction plan (1818–1868) approved by the Emperor, and sketches of the Cathedral interior (1843–1852) by F. P. Briullov, V. K. Shebuev, and Giovanni Battista (I. K.) Scotti, among others. There are also plans and drawings by Charles Cameron (1764), Carlo (K. I.) Rossi, Scotti, Montferrand, and others, for the interior decoration of palaces.

There is a large collection of plans of Russian cities, including plans for water-supply, sewers, and heating systems, as well as maps of krais and oblasts, railroads and highways, and atlases, along with plans of rivers and canals and sea and river ports.

A collection of biographical materials includes, for example, autobiographical notes of General F. P. Devolan Sainte (de Wollant), Chief Director of Transportation (1787–1815) and his letters to K. I. von Liphardt, Director of the Mariinskii Canal (1806–1815); the original signed register of I. P. Kulibin's inventions (1807), letters of M. G. Destrem (1845), and the memoirs of A. I. Shtuckenberg (Stukenberg) (1836–1861), as well as correspondence of Minister of Transportation Admiral K. N. Pos'et (1874–1875) and the civil engineer N. A. Beleliubskii (1892–1901), who specialized in bridge-building.

Working Conditions: Files are delivered to the reading room on the day after orders are placed.

Reference Facilities: There is an alphabetical card catalogue; manuscript materials also are reflected in a systematic catalogue.

Copying: Xerox and photographic copies can be ordered.

FINDING AIDS — PUBLISHED — GENERAL:

Biblioteki SPb (1993), p. 170; *Peterburg* (1992), pp. 236–37; PKG *M&L* (1972), p. 348; Myl'nikov, (1970), p. 24.

g-370. *Rukopisnyi fond biblioteki LIIZhTa: Katalog.* Compiled by I. V. Shkliar. Leningrad: LIIZhT, 1969. 223 p. (Lib: IU; MH) [IDC-R-10,931]

> A detailed catalogue of the manuscript holdings of the library organized thematically—natural science and technology (pp. 10–14), transportation (pp. 15–101), construction design and architecture (pp. 102–46), and historico-biographical materials (in alphabetical order by name, pp. 147–49). Includes indexes of family and geographic names.

g-371. *Leningradskii Ordena Lenina institut inzhenerov zheleznodorozhnogo transporta im. akademika V. N. Obraztsova: 1809–1959.* Compiled by I. V. Veviorovskii, M. I. Voronin, M. M. Uzdin, et al. Edited by I. V. Veviorovskii et al. Leningrad: Transzheldorizdat, 1960. 388 p. [LIIZhT] (Lib: MH)

> A history of the development and activities of the Institute in honor of its 150th anniversary. Includes a section on the library before 1917 (pp. 181–84) and during the Soviet period (pp. 376–79).

g-372. Zhitkov, S. M. *Institut inzhenerov putei soobshcheniia imp. Aleksandra I: Istoricheskii ocherk.* St. Petersburg: Tip. Min-va putei soobshcheniia, 1899. vi, 500 p. [Min-vo putei soobshcheniia] (Lib: MH)

> A history of the Institute during the nineteenth century, providing considerable background for the documentation held in the library, with references to government regulations about the Institute.

Fundamental'naia biblioteka Voenno-meditsinskoi akademii (Biblioteka VMedA)
[Fundamental Library of the Military Medical Academy]

Agency: Ministerstvo oborony RF (Minoborony Rossii)
[Ministry of Defense]

Address: 195009, St. Petersburg, Pirogovskaia nab., 3; (postal): 195009, St. Petersburg, K-9, a/ia (box) 921
Telephone: 542-32-75
Transport: metro: Ploshchad' Lenina

Chief of the Academy: Iurii Leonidovich Shevchenko
Head of the Library: Vladimir Aleksandrovich Smirnov (*tel.* 248-33-10)

HISTORY:

Meditsinskaia biblioteka pri Meditsinskoi kantseliarii Senata
[Medical Library of the Medical Chancellery of the Senate] (1756–1798)
Biblioteka pri Admiralteiskom gospitale
[Library of the Admiralty Hospital] (1796–1798)
Biblioteka Mediko-khirurgicheskoi akademii
[Library of the Medico-Surgical Academy] (1798–1881)
Biblioteka Voenno-meditsinskoi akademii
[Library of the Military Medical Academy] (1881–1935)
Biblioteka Voenno-meditsinskoi akademii im. S. M. Kirova
[S. M. Kirov Library of the Military Medical Academy] (1935–1956)
Fundamental'naia biblioteka Voenno-meditsinskoi akademii im. S. M. Kirova (Biblioteka VMedA)
[Fundamental Library of the S. M. Kirov Military Medical Academy] (1956–1991)

The first Russian medical library was opened in 1756 under the Medical Chancellery by a Senate decree following the application of the physician-in-ordinary P. Z. Kondoidi. In 1796 the director of the Medical Board A. I. Vasil'ev organized a library attached to the Admiralty Hospital, which was used by teachers and students of the medical school. When in 1798 the Library of the Medico-Surgical Academy was established, it absorbed the libraries of the Medical Chancellery and the Admiralty Hospital. In 1881 it was reorganized as the Library of the Military Medical Academy.

The library holdings were enlarged in the nineteenth and twentieth centuries with the acquisition of various library and archival collections of professors and teachers at the Academy, and its status as a depository library for medical-related publications. In 1935 it was renamed the Fundamental Library at the same time the Academy took the honorific name of the Leningrad Communist leader S. M. Kirov. That honorific name was dropped in 1991. Current holdings (ca. 2,000,000) consist of literature on medicine and the natural sciences.

The Division of Manuscripts and Rare Books was established in 1958.

Access: Access requires an official letter of application addressed to the director of the library with indication of the subject and aim of research.

Otdel rukopisei i redkoi knigi (ORRK)
[Division of Manuscripts and Rare Books]

Address: 198013, St. Petersburg, Zagorodnyi prosp., 47
Telephone: 542-32-75, 259-52-36
Hours: M–F 10:00–17:00
Head: Galina Mikhailovna Rosolik

HOLDINGS: 20 fonds, 2,540 units, 1710–1967

The manuscript collection consists of the fonds of institutions and individuals affiliated with the Academy. It contains materials on the history of medicine, medical education, and medical press in Russia and several foreign countries. Among eighteenth- and nineteenth-century holdings are fonds of the Military Medical Academy, the Medico-Surgical Institute, the Society of Russian Physicians in St. Petersburg, the N. I. Pirogov Russian Surgical Society, and the Russian Society of the Red Cross.

There are personal papers of Russian physicians of the eighteenth and nineteenth centuries, such as N. I. Pirogov, N. F. Zdekauer, S. P. Botkin, Hermann Boerhaave, A. P. Dianov, A. S. Zalmanov. Archival collections include scientific manuscripts, biographical records, and correspondence of N. A. Vil'iaminov, Ia. A. Chistovich, S. P. Fedorov, G. I. Turner, V. V. Oppel', M. I. Arinkin. Among the papers of A. A. Tatarinov, a member of the Russian Mission in China, are nineteenth-century manuscripts on Chinese medicine and the use of Chinese drugs. The collection contains materials relating to consultations by physicians of the Medico-Surgical Academy to members of the imperial family, including Peter the Great, Peter II, and Alexander III, as well as illnesses of other prominent figures of Russian history, such as Prince A. D. Menshikov.

N.B. The general fond of the library holds reports on academic research and dissertations defended at the Academy since the middle of the eighteenth century.

Working Conditions: Materials are delivered to the reading room the day they are ordered.

Reference Facilities: Opisi have been compiled for all fonds with indexes of authors, subjects, and autographs.

Copying: Xerox copying facilities are available.

FINDING AIDS — PUBLISHED — GENERAL:

Biblioteki: Putevoditel' (1996), pp. 177–78; *Biblioteki SPb* (1993), p. 187; *Peterburg* (1992), pp. 119–20; PKG *M&L* (1972), p. 354; Myl'nikov (1970), p. 14.

There is no published guide to the archival materials in the library.

g-373. *Sistematicheskii katalog biblioteki Imperatorskoi Mediko-khirurgicheskoi akademii.* 2 parts. (in 6 vols). St. Petersburg: Izd. Mediko-khirurgicheskoi akademii, 1871–1884. (Lib: DLC; MH) [IDC-R-7258(inc)]

Part I (in 2 vols.): *Katalog knig, broshiur i dissertatsii.* SPb., 1871. viii, 658 p.; 636 p.
Part II (in 4 vols.): *Glavneishie stat'i zhurnalov, gazet, i sborniki.* SPb., 1873–1884. xi, 1124 p.; xii, 1136, iv p.; 1014, xxxii p.; 416 p.

The first part, organized systematically by subject, includes some unpublished, or semi-published, materials. The second provides analytics of periodicals and collective volumes held by the library. The first volume includes a brief history noting major acquisitions by the library.

g-374. *Sistematicheskii knizhnyi katalog biblioteki Imperatorskoi Voenno-meditsinskoi akademii.* 4 vols. St. Petersburg, 1901–1903. [IDC-R-7264]

Updates the coverage in g-373. The library also issued separate lists covering dissertations defended at the Academy before 1914.

Biblioteka Sankt-Peterburgskoi Pravoslavnoi Dukhovnoi Akademii i Seminarii (Biblioteka SPbDAiS)

[Library of the St. Petersburg Orthodox Theological Academy and Seminary]

Agency: Sankt-Peterburgskoe eparkhial'noe upravlenie
Moskovskogo Patriarkhata
[St. Petersburg Eparchial Administration of the Moscow Patriarchate]

Address: 193167, St. Petersburg, nab. Obvodnogo kanala, 17
Telephone: 277-35-67
Transport: metro: Ploshchad' Aleksandra Nevskogo
Hours: M–Sa 9:00–17:00; Reading Room: M–Su 10:00–21:00

Rector: Bishop Konstantin (Gorianov) (*tel.* 277-16-73)
Director of Library: Hieromonk (Ieromonakh) Stefan (Sado) (*tel.* 227-16-73)
Head of Reading Room: Tatiana Veniaminovna Ambartsumova

HISTORY:

Biblioteka Slaviano-Greko-Latinskoi seminarii
    [Library of the Slavonic-Greek-Latin Seminary] (1788–1797)
Biblioteka Aleksandro-Nevskoi Akademii
    [Library of the Alexander Nevskii Academy] (1797–1809)
Biblioteka Sankt-Peterburgskoi Dukhovnoi Akademii (Biblioteka SPbDA)
    [Library of the St. Petersburg Theological Academy] (1809–1918)
Biblioteka Leningradskoi Dukhovnoi Akademii (Biblioteka LDA)
    [Library of the Leningrad Theological Academy] (1946–1991)
Biblioteka Sankt-Peterburgskoi Dukhovnoi Akademii i Seminarii (Biblioteka SPbDAiS)
    [Library of the St. Petersburg Theological Academy and Seminary] (VIII.1991–IV.1992)

The precursors of the St. Petersburg Theological Academy and Seminary were the Seminary on the Karpovka River (established in 1716) and the School in the Alexander Nevskii Lavra (Monastery). The latter was renamed the Slavonic-Greek-Latin Seminary in 1726 and in 1788 became the principal religious educational institution in Russia. In 1797 the Seminary was renamed the Alexander Nevskii Academy, which in 1809, after the 1808 reform of religious educational institutions in Russia, was divided into the St. Petersburg Theological Academy, the Seminary, and the School (*uchilishche*).

When the Academy and Seminary were closed in 1918, the Academy manuscript collection was nationalized by the state, and it is now housed in the Manuscript Division of the Russian National Library (G–15). The Academy and Seminary were reopened in 1946, as was the library. Among other accessions are the book collections of the Byzantinist V. N. Beneshevich, the historians and ethnographers A. I. and M. I. Uspenskii, and Vasilii (V. Krivoshin), Archbishop of Brussels, the later received from emigration. The present collection of manuscripts and manuscript books in the library was formed during the postwar years through private contributions.

N.B. For the Archive of the St. Petersburg Metropolitanate, see F–20.

HOLDINGS: ca. 850 units, 16th–20th cc.
    dissertations—ca. 700 units (1946–1994); MS books and manuscripts—ca. 150 (16th–20th cc.)

The library retains manuscript books and manuscripts, including illuminated ones, relating to theology and liturgy, as well as compositions on historical and other subjects.

Lives of saints and educational literature dating from the sixteenth through the nineteenth centuries are represented by Russian, as well as translated lives, legends, and tales, as well as collections of essays, exhortations, and descriptions of religious ceremonies. Among these are the "Tale of Cyrill of Turov (Kirill Turovskii)," "Tale of Gregory of Sinai (Gregorius Sinaita)," "About the Pilgrimage of Antony-the-Roman to Tsar′grad (Constantinople)," a copy of the "Izmaragd" (a book of religious exaltations), Revelations with an exegesis by St. Andreas, Archbishop of Crete, and a collection of exhortations attributed to St. Cyprianus, bishop of Carthage. There are also apocryphal works dating from the eighteenth and the nineteenth centuries, such as "The Passion of Christ," "The Epistle of Apostle Varnavva," and various biblical stories based on the New Testament, among others. There are Russian Orthodox iconographic materials dating from the nineteenth century, such as an iconographic original, an illuminated history of fine arts, and codices with textual copies of manuscripts. Among other texts of an historico-literary character are a description of Asia and China (1686), a chronicle (to 1630), stories about Patriarch Nikon (18th c.), and materials on the history of the town of Trubchevsk (19th c.).

Liturgical literature is represented by materials dating from the sixteenth through the nineteenth centuries, including a prayer-book (*molitvennik*), Psalters, *mineia* (service book), along with services for Our Lady, saints, and martyrs; and services for the icons of Our Lady of Vladimir, Kazan, Kostroma, and Smolensk, as well as liturgical and other codices (*sborniki*).

Old Believer literature from the eighteenth to the early twentieth centuries is represented by the rules of the Pomor′e Old Believer marriage ceremony (*brachnyi chin pomorskogo soglasiia*), the illuminated manuscript "About the Most Needed Events of the Very Last Century" (*O samykh nuzhneishikh sluchaiakh poslednego veka sego*) (18th c.), and the nineteenth-century manuscript "A Brief Analysis of the Church of Unitarian Belief" (*edinovercheskaia tserkov′*), among others.

Manuscripts of sacred choral music from the seventeenth to the nineteenth centuries include *oktoikh* (book of eight tones), *obikhody* (rules of church singing), hirmologia (*irmologii*), triodions, liturgies, feast services, and other liturgical books.

There is also a small collection of student compositions from the Academy and Seminary (18th–20th cc.), most of which relate to the history of the Russian Church, beginning with the Petrine period. Writings on other subjects include "Moral Ideals of Dostoevskii and their Christian Moral Evaluation" by V. Iartsev (1902) and "Religious and Philosophic Outlook of A. S. Khomiakov" by V. Novitskii (1916), among others. There is a collection of *kandidat*, master's, and doctoral dissertations defended at the Academy from the 1940s to the present.

There are some manuscripts in Greek, including a nineteenth-century copy of the letter from the brothers of the Savva Osviashchennyi Monastery to Ivan IV and his son Fedor.

Personal papers of scholars and administrators related to the Academy include those of the Byzantinist A. I. Ivanov and the Academy inspector L. N. Parieiskii, among others.

Access: For access to the library, an application should be addressed to the director of the library.

Working Conditions: Materials are delivered to the reading room the same day they are ordered.

Reference Facilities: There are alphabetical and subject-thematic catalogues. There is also a catalogue of dissertations by Academy graduates. There is a card catalogue on the "History of the Eparchy" and on "Churches and Monasteries," among others.

Copying: There are no copying facilities.

FINDING AIDS — PUBLISHED — GENERAL:

Biblioteki: Putevoditel' (1996), p. 177; *Biblioteki SPb* (1993), pp. 54–55; *Peterburg* (1992), p. 199; PKG *M&L* (1972), p. 355; Putsko (1970), pp. 346–48.

There is no published guide to the manuscript holdings.

g-375. *Bogoslovskie trudy: Iubileinyi sbornik, posviashchennyi 175-letiiu Leningradskoi Dukhovnoi Akademii.* Moscow: Izd-vo Moskovskoi Patriarkhii, 1986. 350 p. "Bogoslovskie trudy," vol. 27. (Lib: DDO; DLC; IU; MH)

> Includes a survey history of the Theological Academy during different periods (1809–1984). Extensive references provide citations to related documents in various archives.

PART H

Archives and Manuscript Holdings of Museums

Moscow

Historical Museums

H-1

Gosudarstvennyi Istoricheskii muzei (GIM)
[State Historical Museum]

Agency: Ministerstvo kul'tury RF (Minkul'tury Rossii)
[Ministry of Culture]

Address: 103012, Moscow, Krasnaia pl., 1/2
Telephone: 921-43-11; *Fax:* (095) 925-95-27
Transport: metro: Okhotnyi riad, Teatral'naia, Ploshchad' Revoliutsii
Hours: MW–F 10:00–18:00

Director: Aleksandr Ivanovich Shkurko (*tel.* 924-45-29)
Deputy Director for Scientific Work: Vadim Leonidovich Egorov (*tel.* 924-89-08)
Deputy Director for Fonds: Tat'iana Timofeevna Ivanova (*tel.* 921-47-91)
Scientific Secretary: Aleksandr Aleksandrovich Smirnov (*tel.* 921-43-11)

HISTORY:

Imperatorskii Rossiiskii Istoricheskii muzei
[Imperial Russian Historical Museum] (1881–1917)
Rossiiskii Istoricheskii muzei
[Russian Historical Museum] (1917–1929)
Gosudarstvennyi Istoricheskii muzei (GIM)
[State Historical Museum] (1929–1990)
Ob"edinenie "Gosudarstvennyi Istoricheskii muzei" (OGIM)
[Consolidated State Historical Museum] (1990–1994)

A commission to establish the museum was founded in 1872, and there were several different names proposed before its official opening. The museum was given its imperial name in 1881 (and in some cases also used the name of Emperor Alexander III), and placed under the jurisdiction of the Ministry of Public Education. It was opened to the public in 1883 in the building specially constructed for it in Red Square, designed by the architect V. O. Shervud (Sherwood) and the engineer A. A. Semenov. The initial museum collection came from the Sevastopol Division of the Polytechnic Exhibition which was held in Moscow in 1872 by the Society of Friends of Natural Science, Anthropology, and Ethnography (*Obshchestvo liubitelei estestvoznaniia, antropologii i etnografii*) to mark the bicentennial of the birth of Peter the Great. Later the museum holdings were augmented by the collections of P. I. Shchukin, I. E. Zabelin, D. Ia. Samokvasov, A. P. Bakhrushin, A. D. Chertkov, and other well-known Russian collectors.

Many private library holdings were acquired with the major prerevolutionary collections. The museum's library from the beginning included the rich prerevolutionary holdings from the Moscow City Chertkov Public Library, which had been opened to the public in 1863 but was taken over by the Moscow City Duma in 1871 and became the basis for the library of the Historical Museum. The library was likewise enriched by other prerevolutionary acquisitions.

From 1917 to 1929 the museum was called the Russian Historical Museum, but was subsequently renamed the State Historical Museum (GIM). After the Revolution, its holdings were significantly augmented by nationalized collections, including many from Russian Orthodox Church sources, such as the rich manuscript collection from the Synodal Library. The rich Museum of Old Moscow (*Muzei "Staraia Moskva"*), established in 1918, was affiliated with GIM through the early 1920s, but when that museum was closed down in 1926, its collections were taken over by GIM. The museum library was likewise enriched by holdings from nationalized private and religious collections were also acquired by the Historical Museum, and in 1922 they were reorganized as the State Historical Library. Remaining part of the museum until 1938, it was then transformed into the newly established separate State Public Historical Library of the RSFSR (GPIB) (see G–3). GIM itself was enriched by many "trophy" acquisitions in the aftermath of World War II. Starting in 1983, the museum was closed down completely for major renovation.

In 1990 GIM was reorganized as the Consolidated State Historical Museum, but in 1994 resumed its previous name. Already in December 1991, GIM was added to the federal register of the most valuable monuments of the cultural heritage of the peoples of the Russian Federation. When the neighboring Central Lenin Museum was abolished as a separate institution in 1993, its holdings and building were transferred to GIM (except for its archival holdings which were transferred to RTsKhIDNI—B–12, now RGASPI). The building had been constructed in 1890–1892 for the Moscow City Council (*Gorodskaia duma*), designed by the architect D. N. Chichagov. After the Revolution, however, it was taken over by the Lenin Museum, which opened in 1924. That building now houses the Division of Manuscripts, and some museum exhibits are planned there, including some from the Lenin Museum itself. After a long hiatus, several of the newly renovated GIM exhibition rooms opened in September 1997, honoring the Moscow 850-year anniversary celebration, but renovation of other parts of the buildings and exhibits continue.

Based on extensive prerevolutionary acquisitions, the Division of Manuscripts and Early Printed Books was founded in 1912, together with the Museum Archive, the latter of which in 1938 was reorganized into the Division of Written Sources (OPI). When the State Literary Museum (GLM) was founded in the 1930s, some of the literary manuscript holdings were transferred there. And after the establishment of the Central State Literary Archive of the USSR (now RGALI—see B–7) in 1941, additional literary materials that had been collected in that division were transferred to the new archive. OPI is now located in the GIM branch in the Izmailovo Estate. The Division of Pictorial Materials (sometimes translated Graphic Materials) was also formed in 1912 and the Division of Cartography in 1923.

The museum has seven affiliated branches; several of those containing archival materials of particular interest are described separately below:

(1) The Izmailovo Estate-Museum (*Muzei-usad'ba "Izmailovo"*) is situated in a large architectural ensemble dating from the mid-seventeenth to the mid-nineteenth century, some parts of which were built for the Romanov family. The GIM branch now embraces only the former Nicholas Military Alms House (*Nikolaevskaia voennaia bogadel'nia*), built in the 1840s by the architect K. A. Ton, and the 1671 Tower-Bridge (*Mostovaia bashnia*), which had been part of the estate of Tsar Alexis (Aleksei) Mikhailovich. The Pokrovskii Cathedral (*sobor*) was restored to the Orthodox Church in 1996, but the northern building of the cathedral is still part of the GIM branch. It now houses the Division of Written Sources and the Division of the Countryside. The surrounding park was raised to the status of the Izmailovo Nature-Historical Park (*Izmailovskii prirodno-istoricheskii park*) in March 1997. (105037, Moscow, gorodok im. N. E. Baumana, Izmailovskii ostrov, 1A; tel. 367-56-61, 367-55-79).

(2) Krutitskii Town House (*Muzei "Krutitskoe Podvor'e"*), an architectural ensemble dating from the seventeenth century, was originally under the jurisdiction of the Moscow Patriarchate. (109044, Moscow, Krutitskii val, 11; tel. 276-92-56, 298-33-04).

(3) Novodevichii Monastery [Convent] (*Novodevichii monastyr'*) (H–2).

(4) Pokrovskii (St. Basil's) Cathedral Museum (*Muzei "Pokrovskii sobor" [Khram Vasiliia Blazhennogo]*) (H–3).

(5) The Palaces in Zariad'e—Home of the Romanov Boyars (*Palaty v Zariad'e—"Dom boiar Romanovykh"—Istoriko-arkhitekturnyi pamiatnik kontsa XV–XVII vv.*), an architectural

monument of the fifteenth to seventeenth centuries, established as a museum in 1859, with displays of cultural materials from the sixteenth to eighteenth centuries. (103012, Moscow, ul. Varvarka, 10; tel. 298-32-35, 298-37-86; website: http://moscow.lvl.ru/culture/ museum/zar/zar.html).

(6) Church of the Trinity in Nikitniki (*Tserkov' "Troitsy v Nikitnikakh"*), constructed in 1628–1653 with subsidy from the Nikitnikov merchants. (102012, Moscow, Nikitnikov per., 3; tel. 298-34-51, 298-50-18).

(7) Museum of V. I. Lenin (*Muzei V. I. Lenina*), scaled down from the Central Museum of V. I. Lenin (founded in 1924), was abolished as a separate museum in 1993. The museum has exhibits of Leniniana, although most of the archival materials from the former Lenin Museum have been transferred to RGASPI (B–12). (103073, Moscow, ul. Nikol'skaia, 1/5; tel. 928-49-05, 925-14-43).

The Museum of the Decembrists (*Muzei dekabristov*) was founded as a branch of GIM in 1987, housed in the main building of the Moscow city estate that had belonged to the Murav'ev-Apostol family, and where several Decembrists had gathered. But when GIM could not raise the funds needed for repair and reconstruction of the building, the branch museum was closed down in 1997. The archival and other materials from GIM displayed there relating to the Decembrists, and the collection of books made by the Decembrist scholar Academician N. M. Druzhinin, have been transferred to the main GIM facility.

From 1917 to 1925 the Borodino Museum was a branch of the Historical Museum but was subsequently made independent (see H–12). Before 1926 the Kolomenskoe Museum Estate was also a branch of GIM, but has since been under separate administration (see H–20).

Access: For access to documentary materials in all divisions, a researcher must submit an official letter addressed to the museum director and obtain his official endorsement of approval.

As of 1999, the Division of Manuscripts and Early Printed Books is still in the process of reorganization, following its move to new quarters in the building of the former Lenin Museum; hence, advance arrangements are necessary for access to specific manuscripts. Researchers wishing to work in the Division of Written Sources (which is housed in the GIM Izmailovo Estate-Museum Branch) must first obtain permission from the Deputy Director or Scientific Secretary in the main building.

Library Facilities: As explained above, most of the library holdings before 1938 were transformed into the State Public Historical Library of the RSFSR (GPIB), which was established as a separate library that year (see G–3). GIM has subsequently developed considerable reference library holdings, and auxiliary specialized reference libraries are located in several different GIM divisions.

Otdel rukopisei i staropechatnykh knig (OR/RO GIM)
[Division of Manuscripts and Early Printed Books]

Hours: TuWTh (by prior appointment)
Head: Elena Ivanovna Serebriakova (*tel.* 292-11-70)

HOLDINGS: 28,827 units, 8th–19th cc. (scattered documents from the 6th c.)
MS books—27 collections (20,323 units) (8th–19th cc.); early printed books—8 collections (7,264 units); birchbark documents—236 units

The Division of Manuscripts and Early Printed Books contains an extensive collection of early Slavonic-Rus' and other manuscript books and manuscripts dating from the eighth to the nineteenth centuries. The division was considerably augmented after the Revolution with the transfer of archives and manuscript collections from many of the most important religious institutions of the Russian Orthodox Church, such as the holdings of the Moscow Administration of the Synod. Many extensive private collections of early manuscript books were also transferred to GIM.

The Synodal (or Patriarchal) Collection, as it is still known in GIM, consists of manuscripts originating from the the library of the metropolitans and patriarchs of All Russia, including some manuscripts from the seventeenth-century Tsar's Library, along with manuscripts from many cathedrals and monasteries in the Moscow region and the second largest collection of Greek manuscripts in Russia. There are manuscript books from collections of the Cathedral of St. Michael the Archangel (*Arkhangel'skii*) and the Cathedral of the Dormition (*Uspenskii*) in the Kremlin, and of the Chudov, Voskresenskii, Donskoi, and Simonov Monasteries, which had been acquired by the Synodal Library before 1917 (subsidiary collections within the Synodal Collection are retained separately in their integrity). The Synodal Collection includes part of the former Library of the Moscow Eparchy, which was transferred to the Synodal Library earlier as the Eparchial (*Eparkhial'noe*) Collection. That component consists of manuscripts from the Joseph of Volokolamsk (*Iosifo-Volokolamskii*), Andronikov (Spaso-Andronievskii), Novodevichii, Borovskii-Pafnutiev (Kaluga Oblast), Solovetskii, Voskresenskii (Novoierusalimskii, or New Jerusalem), and other Russian monasteries. (Another part of the Eparchial Collection is in RGB—G–1).

Among the world-wide renowned manuscripts in the Synodal Collection are the Anthology of Sviatoslav (*Izbornik Sviatoslava*) (1073), the Mstislav Gospels (12th c.), Metropolitan Makarii's Great Lives of Saints (*Velikie Chet'i- Minei*) (16th c.), and other early copies of ecclesiastical manuscripts. The most important historical manuscripts in the Synodal Collection include the mid-thirteenth to early fourteenth-century copy of the First Novgorod Chronicle (*Pervaia Novgorodskaia letopis'*), the 1544 copy of the Fourth Novgorod Chronicle (*Chetvertaia Novgorodskaia letopis'*), and the Illuminated Chronicle Codex (*Litsevoi letopisnyi svod*) of the sixteenth century. Juridical manuscripts in the Synodal Collection include the twelfth-century Efremov Nomocanon (*Efremovskaia kormchaia*) and the Kliment Nomocanon (*Klimentovskaia kormchaia*) of 1281, which include the earliest copies of the medieval Rus' Code of Laws (*Pravda Russkaia*). The division contains a separate Synodal choral collection, which includes early manuscript liturgical music scores.

Among the Greek manuscripts in the Synodal Collection are books that were brought back from Mount Athos by A. Sukhanov and individual acquisitions from other collections. These include folios from a sixth-century Greek parchment Book of the Apostles (i.e. Acts of the Apostles and the Epistles), eleventh- to twelfth-century Gospels, and secular manuscripts on literary, juridical, and medical subjects. There are also a number of South Slavic manuscripts.

The Synodal Collection contains a large number of scrolls. Apart from documents of a doctrinal, administrative, and economic nature, are twelve scrolls relating to the legal disputes of Patriarch Nikon, as well as documents relating to the schism (*raskol*), to the Solovetskii Uprising (1656–1657), and correspondence of the Orthodox hierarchy in Ukraine and Belarus and between Ukrainian hetmen and the Moscow Patriarchate.

The particularly rich Museum Collection (consisting mostly of GIM individual acquisitions) includes a number of illuminated manuscripts, among them the first volume of the Illuminated Chronicle Codex (*Litsevoi letopisnyi svod*) of the sixteenth century and the Onega Psalter of 1395. It also has Old Believer manuscripts illustrated with miniatures, fifteenth-century chronicles, seventeenth- and eighteenth-century chronicles, and sixteenth-century codes of laws. In 1983 a Second Museum Collection (*Muzeiskoe 2-e sobranie*) was started, together with the Museum Collection of Early Printed Books.

The division has a large number of printed books, manuscripts, and documents from Old Believer monasteries and communities. Many of these are found in the collection of the Moscow Eparchial Library and the Nikolskii Old Believer Monastery (*Nikol'skii edinovercheskii monastyr'*), and include books on monastic rules, Old Believer religious polemics, and choral manuscripts (17th–19th cc.).

Private collections have significantly augmented the division holdings. The first such acquisition was the collection of manuscript books and manuscripts from the Chertkov family in the late nineteenth century. Then came the collection of Field Marshal A. I. Bariatinskii, followed by the collections of P. I. Shchukin and I. A. Vakhrameev (1,075 manuscripts), the historian A. P. Bakhrushin, and I. E. Zabelin, one of the founders of the museum. Among the most significant postrevolutionary acquisitions from private sources were the collections of A. I. Khludov, A. S. Uvarov, and N. P. Vostriakov (part of the Khludov collection is held in the Russian State Library (RGB—G–1).

A collection of birchbark documents from the eleventh to the fifteenth centuries was formed in 1952, and has been continually augmented by many archeological excavations in Novgorod and other areas.

N.B. Many of the private collections acquired by GIM both before and after 1917 have been divided between the Division of Written Sources and the Division of Manuscripts and Early Printed Books.

Working Conditions: Long closed in connection with the GIM renovation, the division reopened in 1997 in the building of the former Lenin Museum. Advance arrangements are essential since some manuscripts may be temporarily unavailable with the recent move.

Reference Facilities: There are brief scholarly descriptions of all manuscripts and early printed books in an alphabetical and chronological card catalogue. Of particular importance, card files (with many entries based on earlier published descriptions), contain references to individual works (many entries with incipits) within codices held by the division. There are also inventories of each major collection and specialized thematic card catalogues for miniatures, inscriptions on manuscripts and early printed books, music manuscripts, and birchbark charters, among others.

Library Facilities: There is an auxiliary library (ca. 5,000 volumes) located in the Division of Manuscripts and Early Printed Books, which is accessible to researchers. It is covered by a reference card catalogue available through the reading room.

Copying: Copying arrangements are subject to negotiation.

Otdel pis'mennykh istochnikov (OPI)
[Division of Written Sources]

Address:	105037, Moscow, gorodok im. Baumana, Severnyi korpus, stroenie 3
Telephone:	166-22-09; *RdngRm:* 166-21-54
Hours:	TuWTh 10:00–17:00
Transport:	metro: Izmailovskii park
Comment:	Located in the north building of the Pokrovskii sobor; fourth floor

Head: Andrei Dmitrievich Ianovskii (*tel.* 166-22-09)

HOLDINGS: 509 fonds (95 unarranged), 62,865 units (12,663 unarranged), 15th c.–1991
institutional fonds—1; personal fonds—365; charters and decrees—6 fonds; collections—94; autograph collections—3 fonds

The division holds especially important archival materials relating to literature, science, and culture starting with late seventeenth-century Russia.

There are fonds of a series of state, church and public organizations and institutions of the prerevolutionary and Soviet periods. These include records of the Sarskaia and Podonskaia Eparchy from the seventeenth and eighteenth centuries; of scholarly societies such as the Moscow Numismatic Society and the Moscow Archeological Society; and of tutelary institutions like the Moscow Foundling Home (*Moskovskii vospitatel'nyi dom*). The postrevolutionary period is represented here by the records of the Museum Division of the Main Scientific Administration of the People's Commissariat of Education RSFSR (*Muzeinyi otdel Glavnauki Narkomprosa RSFSR*) (1918–1944) and a collection of documents from the Moscow Section of the State Academy of the History of Material Culture (GAIMK, 1919–1937).

By far the most significant holdings in this division are the extensive fonds of personal papers. Recently declassified is an extensive collection of documents of the Romanov family, with materials from all the Russian emperors and many members of the imperial family starting with Peter I; of particular interest is the original imperial documentation from the museum in Belgrade honoring Nicholas II, which was brought to Moscow after World War II. There are documents and papers from many of the well-known gentry families who played an important part in the political, economic, and cultural life of prerevolutionary Russia, including a very large group of family landed-estate records from the eighteenth and nineteenth centuries and personal papers of some of the richest land and mine owners in Russia. The Vorontsov, Golitsyn, Demidov, Kurakin, Lazarev, and Sheremetev families are all represented here, as are some of the lesser landed gentry in Russia, Ukraine, and Belarus, like A. T. Bolotov and D. I. Maslov, along with the Bereznikov, Mukhanov, Makerovskii, and Oshanin families. There are papers of representative rich industrial and commercial bourgeoisie, such as the Botkin, Guchkov, Shishkin, and Zhuravlev families, along with those of P. A. Buryshkin and K. V. Prokhorov, among others.

This division also holds the personal papers of some of the highest ranking civil servants and other persons who were prominent in government, politics, and the military in prerevolutionary Russia, such as F. I. Soimonov, A. I. and D. G. Bibikov, P. A. and V. A. Zubov, A. A. Arakcheev, N. N. Novosil'tsev, and V. A. Maklakov, among others. The Maklakov papers are among those enriched by RZIA holdings acquired from Prague after World War II, and include documentation from the Liberal Beseda Circle (1899-1905).

Personal papers of major public figures and members of the cultural elite are also widely represented. These include materials of the Decembrists (D. I. Zavalishin, N. I. and A. I. Turgenev, and M. I. Murav'ev-Apostol); the Slavophiles (A. S. Khomiakov and M. D. Raevskii); and historians such as V. N. Tatishchev, M. M. Shcherbatov, T. N. Granovskii, and D. I. Ilovaiskii.

The division also contains several large private collections of historical sources and autographs collected during the nineteenth century with documents of varied provenance. These include documentation of Russian central and provincial institutions and church authorities; collections on the history of the army, navy, and foreign policy; a collection from many sources on the Napoleonic Invasion of 1812 (Patriotic War), with original documents of Napoleon and his entourage; Masonic manuscripts; documents pertaining to the history of the theater, literature, and architecture; along with correspondence and autographs of numerous famous people. Many of these collections were separated out of the major named collections that were acquired by the division together with the personal papers of their collectors. Among such collections that were broken up were those of A. I. Bariatinskii, E. V. Barsov, P. I. Shchukin, I. A. Vakhrameev, and I. E. Zabelin, along with those of the Chertkov and Uvarov families.

Thematic collections formed in the division are extremely varied, including collections of charters of privilege (or letters patent—*zhalovannye gramoty*), appointment certificates to particular bureaucratic ranks (*patenty na chin*), resignation documents, decrees and warrants (*ukazy* and *reskripty*), autographs of prominent figures, codices of particularly types, and diaries and memoirs. Some of the thematic collections preserved in the division were collected by other museums—the Museum of Old Moscow, the Military History Museum, the Museum of the 1840s, the Solovetskii Museum, fourteenth-century materials from the Opta Hermitage (*Optina pustyn'*) Museum, and a variety of materials from the former State Academy of the History of Material Culture (GAIMK). Others were collected on special historical daily-life expeditions organized by the Historical Museum since 1925.

There are several collections of documents from the Soviet period. The October Revolution Collection includes documents issued by the Soviets (until mid-October 1918), local Bolshevik organizations, Red Guard and local revolutionary committees, as well as letters from private citizens and notes and memoirs of participants in the October Revolution. There are also official documents from the Provisional Government, materials from the various political parties and social organizations, and personal documents of G. E. L'vov.

Documents pertaining to the Second World War form a special collection, which includes materials from military commissariats, military units and formations on active service, the home guard, and documents from some plants and factories in the capital during the Battle of Moscow. Here too are to be found the archives of the frontline press and military correspondents, as well as personal papers and memoirs of participants in the war.

Documents relating to the postwar period, which were gathered on historical expeditions to factories in Moscow, St. Petersburg, Ivanovo-Voznesensk, Kolomna, Sormovo, and in Siberia, as well as in former Soviet Baltic republics and Central Asia, include personal papers of exemplary workers together with their awards, photographs, placards, and posters.

Reference Facilities: Surveys are available for all the fonds in the Division of Written Sources that have been systematically arranged, or, if the fond is small, there is an historical report with a survey of the documents contained therein. *Opisi* are available for all fonds. There are also name, geographic, subject, thematic, and inventory card catalogues. A database is being developed for description of seventeenth-century documents.

Library Facilities: There is a reference library with open access located in the reading room.

Copying: There are no photographic or xerox copying facilities.

Otdel izobrazitel'nykh materialov
[Division of Pictorial Materials]

Telephone: 292-14-80
Head: Elena Igorevna Itkina

HOLDINGS: 444,531 units, 18th–20th cc.
Russian advertising posters—28,000 units (late 19th c.–1990); architectural graphics—139,500 units (late 19th–early 20th cc.); *lubok* wood prints—258,500 units (late 17th–early 20th cc.); photographs—133,284 (mid-19th c.–1990)

This division holds documentary photographic material (negatives, daguerreotypes, slides, and photographs), original and printed graphics (engravings, lithographs, and lubok), and architectural drawings. Iconographic sources have been taken from various major collections or have been acquired as separate historical pictorial art collections.

Documentary photographic materials illustrate the life and customs of the peoples of Russia. Many of these result from historical daily-life expeditions between 1860 and 1917, and from similar expeditions after the Revolution (the Magadan and Vladivostok Expedition of 1966, the Novosibirsk Expedition of 1970, and the Baltic Expedition of 1972, among others). These materials form a separate fond of expedition photographs.

Another separate collection contains photographs of early Russian architectural monuments in Moscow and annotated photographs of streets, localities, and buildings of historical interest in the city, which were referred to in the excursions around Moscow conducted by the prominent historians P. N. Miller and M. I. Aleksandrovskii. The division also has collections of negatives taken by Z. Z. Vinogradov, A. A. Gubarev, and John Hopwood on various subjects (Moscow architecture and life, European Russia, the Crimea, the Volga Region, and Central Asia). Other collections have pictures taken by E. S. Bialyi, V. P. Grebnev, O. A. Lander, and S. Strunnikov (events of the Second World War from the Battle of Moscow to the Battle of Stalingrad).

There is a collection of photographic material from the former Artillery History Museum on the history of the Armed Forces of the USSR and international relations from 1917 to the 1950s, taken by the Soiuzfoto and TASS agencies.

Architectural drawings and sketches form a separate complex. Spanning the mid-eighteenth to the early twentieth centuries, they illustrate the work of such well-known Russian architects as O. I. Bove, A. L. Vitberg, M. F. Kazakov, Domenico Gilardi (D. I. Zhiliardi), V. P. Stasov, and A. V. Shchusev. They include the drawings and plans of buildings restored after the fire of 1812; drawings and plans of Moscow buildings erected between 1860 and 1890; ensembles and individual buildings in Russia and abroad that illustrate the use of different architectural techniques; and drawings by R. M. Gabe showing the dwellings and domestic implements used by peasants in the north of Russia (1921–1939).

There is also a collection of printed engravings. Most prominent here is the collection of P. Ia. Dashkov containing more than 39,000 plates, and the thematic collection of I. Kh. Kolodeev devoted to the Napoleonic War of 1812.

The division has a collection of original Russian graphics and a collection of posters, which includes prerevolutionary advertising posters and trade marks from the late nineteenth and early twentieth centuries, as well as Soviet posters and Second World War posters from the windows of TASS.

Reference Facilities: There are alphabetical card catalogues, which include name, geographic, and several thematic files. There are two registration card files—by acquisition register numbers and by inventory registers.

Otdel kartografii
[Division of Cartography]

Telephone: 925-88-44
Head: Aleksei Konstantinovich Zaitsev (*tel.* 925-88-44)

HOLDINGS: 41,541 (200 unarranged) units, 16th–20th cc.
atlases, maps and plans—41,523 units; globes—18 units

This division contains manuscript and printed maps of both Russian and foreign origin and includes atlases, globes, and plans done on various media (such as paper and silk), and using different techniques. Many of these were acquired as part of private collections (P. Ia. Dashkov, I. E. Zabelin, and A. P. Bakhrushin) or from institutions such as the Military History Museum. The collection includes a 1556 edition of the Map of Muscovy, which was prepared by Sigmund von Herberstein in 1549; a Willem Barents' Map engraved in 1598; the first academic "Atlas of Russia consisting of Nineteen Special Maps" (1745) with handwritten notes by its owner (1750s–1760s) on towns and cities, factories and roads, and the defense lines of fortresses; and cartographic materials from the General Land Survey of Russia, such as the manuscript "Atlas of Tver Namestnichestvo" (1783–1793).

Of particular interest from the postrevolutionary period are cartographic sources from the first years of Soviet rule, showing environmental and social phenomena, including historical, administrative, and demographic maps, as well as economic, scientific, and cultural maps.

The division also has maps of seas and rivers, and maps and globes of the heavens.

Reference Facilities: There are two inventory card indexes—to acquisition register numbers and to inventory registers—and also a systematic card catalogue.

FINDING AIDS — PUBLISHED — GENERAL:

GAF *Spravochnik* (1991), pp. 81–95; G&K *Spravochnik* (1983), pp. 234–44 and 425–31; PKG *M&L* (1972), pp. 277–81; Sup. 1 (1976), pp. 102–11; Begunov, *Sprav.-ukaz.* (1963), pp. 143–61; *Muzei Moskvy* (1997), pp. 18–21.

h-1. *Istoricheskii muzei—entsiklopediia otechestvennoi istorii i kul'tury (Zabelinskie nauchnye chteniia 1993 goda).* Edited by V. L. Egorov. Moscow, 1995. 464 p. + plates. "Trudy GIM," vol. 87. (Lib: MH)

A large collection of articles covering selected aspects of the history of GIM and its collections. Includes surveys and source analyses of materials in the Division of Manuscripts and Early Printed Books, the Division of Written Sources, and the Division of Pictorial Materials.

Manuscript and Rare Book Division

h-2. Protas'eva, Tat'iana Nikolaevna; and Shchepkina, Marfa Viacheslavovna. *Sokrovishcha drevnei pis'mennosti i staroi pechati: Obzor rukopisei russkikh, slavianskikh, grecheskikh, a takzhe knig staroi pechati Gosudarstvennogo Istoricheskogo muzeia.* Edited by T. V. Dianova. 2d ed. Moscow, 1995. 104 p. (Lib: IU)

    1st ED.: Edited by M. N. Tikhomirov. M.: "Sovetskaia Rossiia," 1958. 87 p. "Trudy GIM: Pamiatniki kul'tury," vol. 30. [IDC-R-11,018] (Lib: DLC; IU; MH).

        The 1978 edition surveys 27 collections of medieval manuscripts and 7 collections of early printed books. The second edition (1995) reprints and updates the surveys, and adds a comprehensive bibliography of published literature, including earlier catalogues of manuscript descriptions and related reference literature.

h-3. "Otdelu rukopisei i staropechatnykh knig Gosudarstvennogo Istoricheskogo muzeia—75 let." In *Russkaia knizhnost' XV–XIX vv,* edited by T. V. Dianova, pp. 3–24. Moscow, 1989. "Trudy GIM," vol. 71. [GIM] (Lib: DLC; IU; MH)

        Commemorating the 75th anniversary of GIM, recounts the history of the founding, accession of collections, and scholarly work in the division.

h-4. Levochkin, Ivan Vasil'evich. "Opisaniia rukopisei Gosudarstvennogo Istoricheskogo muzeia: XIX–nach. XX vv." In *Problemy nauchnogo opisaniia rukopisei i faksimil'nogo izdaniia pamiatnikov pis'mennosti: Materialy Vsesoiuznoi konferentsii,* edited by M. V. Kukushkina et al., pp. 151–160. Leningrad: "Nauka," Leningradskoe otdelenie, 1981. [AN SSSR; BAN; AK] (Lib: DLC; IU; MH) [IDC-R-14,774]

        A detailed bibliographic review of available scholarly descriptions covering manuscript collections in GIM, together with related reference materials.

Division of Written Sources

h-5. *Pis'mennye istochniki v sobranii Gosudarstvennogo Istoricheskogo muzeia.* Vol. 1. Compiled by S. I. Sakovich. Edited by S. Margolin. Moscow, 1958. 110 p. (Lib: DLC; IU; MH) [IDC-R-11,021]

        A detailed survey of archival fonds in the Division of Written Sources, including feudal estate records; collections of seventeenth-century charters; personal papers of scholars and cultural leaders (18th–19th cc.); nineteenth-century private collections of historical sources; and documents relating to the history of the revolutionary movement in Russia. An appendix lists personal papers.

h-5.1. *Pis'mennye istochniki v sobranii GIM.* Vol. 2: *Materialy po istorii kul'tury i nauki v Rossii.* Edited by A. K. Afanas'ev. Moscow, 1993. 152 p. "Trudy GIM," vol. 84. (Lib: DLC; MH)

        A collection of survey articles on the history of science and culture in Russia (17th–20th cc.), including surveys of fonds from the Solovetskii Museum, the Opta Hermitage (*Optina pustyn'*) (14th c.), and the State Academy of the History of Material Culture (GAIMK); sources relating to the history of Moscow University from the personal papers of P. A. Bessonov; the collection of documents of the architect-restorer M. V. D'iakonova; and materials from the P. I. Shchukin documentary collection relating to Russian cultural history (17th–early 20th cc.).

h-5.2. *Pis'mennye istochniki v sobranii GIM.* Vol. 3: *Materialy po voennoi istorii Rossii.* Edited by A. K. Afanas'ev. Moscow, 1997. 183 p. "Trudy GIM," vol. 92. (Lib: MH)

        A collection of articles surveying materials relating to military history, including a detailed survey (with appended chart and name index) of the extensive documentary collection from the former

Military History Museum (fond 137), the GIM collections on the history of the army, navy, and foreign policy (17th–early 20th cc.—fonds 155 and 264), materials from various fonds relating to the Napoleonic Invasion of 1812 (Patriotic War), materials from the archive of N. N. Murav'ev-Karskii (1794–1866) (fond 254), and materials from the papers of N. M. Iolshin (1860–1914?) (fond 225–late 19th–early 20th cc.), including documents relating to the Russo-Japanese War.

h-6. *Putevoditel' po fondam lichnogo proiskhozhdeniia Otdela pis'mennykh istochnikov Gosudarstvennogo Istoricheskogo muzeia.* Compiled by E. I. Bakst et al. Edited by I. S. Kalantyrskaia and V. G. Verzhbitskii. Moscow: "Sovetskaia Rossiia," 1967. 388 p. (Lib: DLC; IU; MH) [IDC-R-11,022]

> An annotated guide to the personal papers of prominent prerevolutionary Russians that are held in the division, covering approximately 95% of the fonds with detailed indexes.

Cartographic Division

h-7. Navrot, M. I. "Katalog gravirovannykh kart Rossii XVI–XVIII vv. i reproduktsii s nikh, khraniashchikhsia v Otdele istoricheskoi geografii i kartografii Gosudarstvennogo Istoricheskogo muzeia." *Istoriia geograficheskikh znanii i istoricheskaia geografiia. Etnografiia* 4 (1970): 39–43. (Lib: DLC; IU; MH) [IDC-in R-11,023]

> A short description of engraved maps in the GIM collections.

h-8. Navrot, M. I. "Katalog rukopisnykh istoricheskikh kart XVIII–XX vv., khraniashchikhsia v fondakh Gosudarstvennogo Istoricheskogo muzeia." *Istoriia geograficheskikh znanii i istoricheskaia geografiia. Etnografiia* 2 (1967): 17–19. (Lib: DLC; IU; MH) [IDC-in R-11,023]

> A short description of manuscript maps in GIM collections, and the reference system for them.

GIM Series

h-9. *Otchet Imperatorskogo Rossiiskogo Istoricheskogo muzeia imeni Imperatora Aleksandra III v Moskve za 1905 god . . . –[. . . za 1914 god].* 11 vols. Moscow, 1906–1926. Final vol.: *Otchet Gosudarstvennogo Istoricheskogo muzeia za 1916–1925 gg.* (Lib: MH) [IDC-R-11,191]

> Reports issued by the prerevolutionary Historical Museum containing significant information about the manuscript holdings. The final volume reports acquisitions through 1925.

h-10. *Trudy Gosudarstvennogo Istoricheskogo muzeia. (Trudy GIM)* Moscow, 1926–. 92 vols. through 1997. Includes several subseries, including h-11. (Lib: DLC; IU; MH)

h-11. *Pamiatniki kul'tury.* 35 vols. Moscow: "Sovetskaia Rossiia," 1949–1969. Irregular. Many volumes numbered as a subseries of *Trudy GIM.* (Lib: DLC; IU; MH)

h-12. *Ezhegodnik Gosudarstvennogo Istoricheskogo muzeia. (Ezhegodnik GIM)* 6 vols. Moscow, 1958–1964. Irregular. (Lib: IU)

GIM History

h-12A. "Gosudarstvennomu Istoricheskomu muzeiu—125 let." *AE za 1997 god* (1998): 7–39. (Lib: DLC; IU; MH)

> Includes several reports and memoirs about the Historical Museum, with historical surveys of the Manuscript Division—OR (pp. 25–33) and the Division of Written Sources—OPI (1987–1996, pp. 34–39), and an article about the original Sevastopol collection.

h-13. Lebedinskaia, O. M. "Istochniki po istorii Rossiiskogo Istoricheskogo muzeia (1872–1917 gg.)." *Vestnik Moskovskogo universiteta. Istoriia,* 1992, no. 2, pp. 75–79. (Lib: DLC; IU; MH)

Izmailovo Estate-Museum

h-13A. Korobko, M. Iu.; Rysin, L. P.; and Avilova, K. V. *Izmailovo.* Moscow, 1997. 45 p. "Prirodnoe i kul'turnoe nasledie Moskvy." [Sovet po izucheniiu i okhrane kul'turnogo i prirodnogo naslediia pri Prezidiume RAN] (Lib: MH)

> A brief historical and descriptive survey of the Izmailovo Estate-Museum and its natural surroundings that were established as a Nature-Historical Park in 1997.

FINDING AIDS — SPECIALIZED:

Special effort has been made here to list published specialized finding aids, because there is no comprehensive bibliography of finding aids covering GIM collections. Although hardly comprehensive, the list below emphasizes the most recent publications, and includes all pre-1976 imprints that are available in microfiche reprint editions. Some additional earlier editions and more detailed annotations for some entries are to be found in the PKG 1976 *M & L Supplement* (a-16), pp. 102–11. For more detailed coverage of earlier descriptions of Greek manuscripts, see the 1995 edition of Richard (a-210), pp. 554–60.

For coverage of Jewish-related holdings, see *Dok. ist. evreev* (1997), pp. 393–94, and *Jewish Doc.* (1996), p. 23.

Manuscript and Rare Book Division

Parchment Manuscripts

h-14. Shchepkina, Marfa Viacheslavovna; Protas'eva, Tat'iana Nikolaevna; Kostiukhina, L. M., et al. "Opisanie pergamentnykh rukopisei Gosudarstvennogo Istoricheskogo muzeia." 2 parts. Moscow, 1966–1967. (Lib: DLC; IU; MH) [IDC-R-10,379; and in R-10,754]

> Part 1: "Russkie rukopisi." *AE za 1964 god* (1966): 135–234;
> Part 2: "Rukopisi bolgarskie, serbskie, moldavskie." *AE za 1965 god* (1967): 273–309.

Synodal Collection

h-15. *Opisanie slavianskikh rukopisei Moskovskoi Sinodal'noi (Patriarshei) biblioteki.* Compiled by A. V. Gorskii and K. I. Nevostruev. 3 parts, 6 vols. Moscow: Sinodal'naia tip., 1855–1917. (Lib: IU; MH) [IDC-R-10,324]

> REPRINT ED.: Wiesbaden: Otto Harrassowitz, 1964. "Monumenta linquae slavicae dialecti veteris," vol. 2.
> INDEX: See h-16.
> SUPPLEMENT: See h-17.

>> Provides scholarly descriptions of Slavonic manuscripts (up to no. 576) from the Library of the Holy Synod that were transferred to the Historical Museum after 1917.

h-16. Vitoshinskii, E. M. *Ukazatel' imennoi i predmetnyi k trudu A. V. Gorskogo i K. I. Nevostrueva "Opisanie slavianskikh rukopisei Moskovskoi Sinodal'noi biblioteki."* Warsaw, 1915. vi, 316 p. (Lib: DDO; IU; MH; NN) [IDC-R-11,195]

> REPRINT ED.: Wiesbaden: Otto Harrassowitz, 1964. "Monumenta linquae slavicae dialecti veteris," vol. 6.

>> Provides alphabetic and subject indexes and an index of proper names to the first four volumes of Gorskii and Nevostruev's catalogue of Slavonic manuscripts (h-15). Not complete, even for volumes covered.

h-17. Protas'eva, Tat'iana Nikolaevna. *Opisanie rukopisei Sinodal'nogo sobraniia (ne voshedshikh v opisanie A. V. Gorskogo i K. I. Nevostrueva).* Edited by M. Shchepkina. 2 vols. Moscow, 1970–1973. xxv, 211 p. + 19 plates; 164 p. (Lib: DLC; MH) [IDC-R-11,098]

> Continues the scholarly description of Slavonic manuscripts from the Synodal Library (nos. 577 to 1051), which were not included in the prerevolutionary catalogue (h-15). Provides detailed bibliography of previous descriptions of each manuscript, name and subject indexes, and a correlation table for earlier manuscript catalogue numbers.

h-18. Popov, Nikolai Petrovich. *Rukopisi Moskovskoi Sinodal'noi (Patriarshei) biblioteki.* 2 vols. Moscow, 1905–1910. (Lib: DLC; IU; MH) [IDC-R-7319]

> Vol. 1: *Novospasskoe sobranie.* Moscow: Tip. O. O. Gerbeka, 1905. viii, 189 p. + 3 plates.

> Vol. 2: *Sobranie rukopisei Moskovskogo Simonova monastyria.* Moscow, 1910. viii, 214 p. Originally published in *ChOIDR* 233 (1910, no. 2): i-vii, 1–214.

> The first two volumes of a larger projected catalogue covering manuscripts from religious institutions in the Moscow area that were acquired by the Synodal Library and are now held in GIM. Vol. 1 describes 18 manuscripts from the Novospasskii Monastery and vol. 2 describes 70 manuscripts from the Simonov Monastery.

h-18A. Savva, Archbishop of Tver and Kashin (Archimandrite). *Ukazatel' dlia obozreniia Moskovskoi Patriarshei (nyne Sinodal'noi) riznitsy i biblioteki.* 3d ed. Moscow: Universitetskaia tip., 1859. iii, iii, 126, viii, 292, 40, iv, 2 p. (Lib: MH-F) [IDC-R-7324]

> 2d ED.: *Ukazatel' dlia obozreniia Moskovskoi patriarshei (nynie sinodal'noi) biblioteki: s prilozheniem poiasnitel'nago slovaria neudobopon iatnykh slov i nazvanii predmetov, vstrechaiushchikhsia v knige.* Moscow: V Universitetskoi tip., 1858. viii, 292, 40, iv, 2 p. (Lib: DLC)

> *Ukazatel' dlia obozreniia Moskovskoi patriarshei (nynie sinodal'noi) riznitsy: s prilozheniem . . ..* Moscow: V Universitetskoi tip., 1858. ii, 126 p, 33, iv, ii p. (Lib: DLC)

> 1st ED.: Moscow, 1855.

> An early survey and descriptions of the manuscripts in the Synodal Library now held in GIM. The code numbers cited by Savva are correlated to current ones in the more recent supplementary catalogues listed above (h-15–h-17). The third edition contains a reprint of the earlier separate 1858 description of the ecclesiastical holdings in the sacristy (*riznitsa*) as well as the descriptions of the manuscripts in the library as its two component parts, and is the last one that covers manuscripts in the Synodal Library. There are fourth (1863) and fifth (1883) editions of the description of holdings in the sacristy, but these do not include any manuscripts.

Synodal Collection—Greek Manuscripts

h-19. Vladimir, Archimandrite (Filantropov, Vasilii). *Sistematicheskoe opisanie rukopisei Moskovskoi Sinodal'noi (Patriarshei) biblioteki.* Pt. 1: *Rukopisi grecheskie.* Moscow, 1894. 885 p. (Lib: DDO; IU; MH) [IDC-R-7043]

> GREEK VERSION: *Moskovskaia sinodal'naia biblioteka rukopisei: Ocherk kataloga nakhodiashchikhsia v Kremle grecheskikh rukopisei/ He en Moscha Synodike Vivliotheke ton cheirographon.* Compiled by Archimandrite Iakov Vatopedskii. Moscow: Tip. E. Lissnera i Iu. Romana, 1896. 71 p. Added title page and text in Greek.

> Provides scholarly descriptions of Greek manuscripts from the Synodal Library that are now held in GIM. For additional descriptions and updated bibliography, see h-20.

h-20. Fonkich, Boris L'vovich; and Poliakov, Fedor B. (Poljakov, Fjodor B.) *Grecheskie rukopisi Moskovskoi Sinodal'noi biblioteki: Paleograficheskie, kodikologicheskie i bibliograficheskie dopolneniia k katalogu arkhimandrita Vladimira (Filantropova).* Moscow: Sinodal'naia biblioteka, 1993. 239 p. (Lib: DDO; DLC; MH)

> Provides additional descriptions and updated scholarly reference covering Greek manuscripts from the Synodal Library.

Chudov Collection

h-21. Protas'eva, Tat'iana Nikolaevna. *Opisanie rukopisei Chudovskogo sobraniia.* Edited by N. Pokrovskii. Novosibirsk: "Nauka," 1986. 232 p. [AN SSSR, Sibirskoe otdelenie; Institut istorii, filologii i filosofii; Minkul't RSFSR; GIM] (Lib: DLC; IU; MH)

> A scholarly description of 372 manuscripts from the Chudov Monastery in the Kremlin, which became part of the Synodal Library and were subsequently transferred to GIM. Includes an extensive bibliography, geographic, subject, and proper-name indexes. For an earlier survey of this collection, see N. P. Petrov, "Knigokhranilishche Chudova monastyria," in *Pamiatniki drevnei pis'mennosti* 5 (1897, no. 4): 141–99. [IDC-R-11,193]

Synodal Collection—Eparchial Library

h-22. Amfilokhii, Archimandrite (Sergievskii, Pavel Ivanovich). *Opisanie Voskresenskoi Ierusalimskoi biblioteki . . . s prilozheniem snimkov so vsekh pergamennykh rukopisei i nekotorykh pisannykh na bumage.* Moscow: Sinodal'naia tip., 1875. 9, ii, 216 p. + 18 ill. (Lib: IU; MH) [IDC-R-11,198]

> A description of 242 manuscripts from the library of the Voskresenskii (Novoierusalimskii) Monastery, 33 of which are on parchment. See also the later description by Stroev (h-23).

h-23. Stroev, Pavel Mikhailovich. *Opisanie rukopisei monastyrei Volokolamskogo, Novyi-Ierusalim, Savvina-Storozhevskogo i Pafnutieva-Borovskogo.* St. Petersburg, 1891. xviii, 343 p. "Obshchestvo liubitelei drevnei pis'mennosti [Izdanie]," vol. 98. (Lib: DDO; IU; MH) [IDC-R-7337; 1030 mf. 399-405]

> Describes 141 manuscript books from the Voskresenskii (Novoierusalimskii) Monastery, the majority of which are part of the Eparchial Collection in GIM and were earlier held in the Synodal Library. Also describes 690 manuscript books from the Joseph of Volokolamsk Monastery, before the collection was split; those that were transferred to the Moscow Eparchial Library are now in GIM (others are in RGB). There are also descriptions of 47 manuscript books from the Borovskii Pafnut'ev Monastery in Kaluga Oblast, some of which are to be found in GIM (although that collection was later dispersed).

Joseph of Volokolamsk Monastery Collection

h-24. *Knizhnye tsentry Drevnei Rusi XI–XVI vv.: Iosifo-Volokolamskii monastyr' kak tsentr knizhnosti.* Edited by D. S. Likhachev and R. P. Dmitrieva. Leningrad: "Nauka," Leningradskoe otdelenie, 1991. 366 p. [PD; GIM] (Lib: DLC; IU; MH)

> Articles describe sixteenth-century manuscripts from the Joseph of Volokolamsk (*Iosifo-Volokolamskii*) Monastery, approximately 430 of which were transferred to the Moscow Eparchial Library in 1863, and which were subsequently acquired by GIM (pp. 122–414) (other parts of the Volokolamsk/Eparchial Collection are now in RGB).

Museum Collection

h-25. "Katalog rukopisei Muzeiskogo sobraniia Otdela rukopisei GIM." In *Voprosy istochnikovedeniia i paleografii,* edited by T. V. Dianova, vol. 78, pp. 6–131. Moscow, 1993. "Trudy GIM," vol. 78. (Lib: DLC; IU; MH)

> Describes the first 400 manuscripts (by inventory numbers) of the 4,061 manuscripts in the Museum Collection brought together from various acquisitions by the Manuscript Division.

Vakhrameev Collection

h-26. Titov, Andrei Aleksandrovich. *Rukopisi slavianskie i russkie, prinadlezhashchie . . .*
I. A. Vakhrameevu. 6 vols. Moscow/Sergiev Posad: Tip. E. Lissnera i Iu. Romanova, 1888–
1907. (Lib: DDO [vol. 1]; DLC; MH [vols. 2–5]) [IDC-R-7290]

> Describes 1,132 manuscripts from the I. A. Vakhrameev Collection, 1,075 of which are held in GIM.

Uvarov Collection

h-27. Leonid, Archimandrite (Kavelin, Lev Aleksandrovich). *Sistematicheskoe opisanie slaviano-*
russkikh rukopisei sobraniia grafa A. S. Uvarova. 4 vols. Moscow: Tip. A. I. Mamontova,
1893–1894. 695 p. + plates; 578 p. + plates; 364 p.; 564 p. (Lib: DLC; IU; MH) [IDC-R-7296]

> CORRELATION TABLE: Druzhinin, Vasilii Grigor'evich. "Tablitsy dlia otyskaniia
> rukopisei sobraniia A. S. Uvarova v opisanii etogo sobraniia, sostavlennom arkhim.
> Leonidom i izdannom v 4 tomakh v Moskve v 1893–1894 gg." *Izvestiia Otdeleniia*
> *russkogo iazyka i slovesnosti Imperatorskoi Akademii nauk* 28 (1923, no. 1): 259–72.
> (Lib: DLC; IU; MH) [IDC-in R-7296].

> Provides a scholarly description of 2,243 Slavonic manuscripts that once belonged to A. S. Uvarov,
> including those earlier belonging to I. N. Tsarskii (see h-28).

h-28. Stroev, Pavel Mikhailovich. *Rukopisi slavianskie i rossiiskie, prinadlezhashchie . . . Ivanu*
Nikitichu Tsarskomu. Moscow: Tip. V. Got'e, 1848. 918 p. (Lib: DLC; IU; MH) [IDC-R-7338]

> A description of 749 Slavonic manuscripts and 194 historical documents that once belonged to I. N.
> Tsarskii, were acquired by A. S. Uvarov in 1853, and are now held in GIM as part of the Uvarov
> Collection. These descriptions were subsequently included in Archimandrite Leonid's work (see h-27).

h-29. [Sakharov, Ivan Petrovich]. *Slaviano-russkie rukopisi: Otdelenie pervoe.* St. Petersburg:
Tip. Sakharova, 1839. 32 p. Variant edition: St. Petersburg, 1842. 40 p. (Lib: IU; MH)
[IDC-R-11,150]

> Describes 46 manuscripts that were part of the Sakharov Collection, but were subsequently acquired
> by Uvarov. They are currently held in GIM, although part are in RGB (fond 550).

h-30. Kataev, I. M.; and Kabanov, A. K. *Opisanie aktov sobraniia grafa A. S. Uvarova: Akty*
istoricheskie. Edited by M. Dovnar-Zapol'skii. Moscow: Tip. G. Lessnera i D. Sobko, 1905.
vii, 666 p. (Lib: MH) [IDC-R-11,202]

> An indexed description of 995 charters, legal acts, and other historical documents (15th–18th cc.)
> that are now part of the Uvarov collection.

Khludov Collection

h-31. Popov, Andrei Nikolaevich. *Opisanie rukopisei i katalog knig tserkovnoi pechati biblioteki*
A. I. Khludova. Moscow: Sinodal'naia tip., 1872. x, 664, 54 p. (Lib: MH) [IDC-R-7318]

> SUPPLEMENT: *Pervoe pribavlenie k opisaniiu rukopisei i katalogu knig tserkovnoi*
> *pechati biblioteki A. I. Khludova.* M.: Sinodal'naia tip., 1875. iii, 94 p. [IDC-in R-7318]

> Describes 361 Slavonic manuscripts from the A. I. Khludov library currently held in GIM. The
> supplemental section in the initial volume (pp. 1–54) covers Slavonic printed books. Part of the
> Khludov Collection is held in RGB (G–1).

Chertkov Collection

h-32. *Opisanie rukopisei sobraniia Chertkova.* Compiled by E. V. Shul'gina and M. M. Chernilovskaia. Edited by E. K. Romodanovskaia and N. N. Pokrovskii. Novosibirsk: "Nauka," Sibirskoe otd., 1986. 134 p. [AN SSSR; Institut istorii, filologii i filosofii; S.-Peterburgskoe otdelenie AK; Minkul't SSSR; GIM] (Lib: DLC; IU; MH)

> A scholarly description of the A. D. Chertkov Collection held in GIM, with details about marginal inscriptions and decorative work. Provides extensive bibliography, together with geographic, subject, and proper-name indexes.

Shchukin Collection

h-33. Iatsimirskii, Aleksandr Ivanovich. *Opis' starinnykh slavianskikh i russkikh rukopisei sobraniia P. I. Shchukina.* 2 vols. Moscow: Izd. P. I. Shchukina, 1896–1897. 369 p.; 278 p. (Lib: DLC) [IDC-R-7287]

> A description of 488 Slavonic manuscripts from the P. I. Shchukin Collection held in GIM.

Novgorod Birchbark Documents

h-34. Artsikhovskii, Artemii Vladimirovich; Tikhomirov, Mikhail Nikolaevich; and Borkovskii, V. I. *Novgorodskie gramoty na bereste (iz raskopok 1951 g.)* through —— *[...(iz raskopok 1983 g.)].* Unnumbered series [8] vols. Moscow: Izd-vo AN SSSR/ "Nauka," 1953–1989. Authors vary for individual volumes. (Lib: DLC; IU; MH) [IDC-R-10,110; R-10,113; R-11,197; R-11,200(inc)]

> A series of detailed analyses with transcribed texts of the birchbark documents found in archeological excavations in Novgorod between the years 1951 and 1989. The eighth volume contains commentaries and a word index to the documents found between 1951 and 1983.

h-34.1. Ianin, Valentin Lavrent'evich; and Zalizniak, Andrei Anatol'evich. *Novgorodskie gramoty na bereste (iz raskopok 1984–1989 gg.).* Moscow: "Nauka," 1993. 349 p. (Lib: DLC; MH)

> The last issued volume in the series includes full bibliography and updates of the earlier coverage.

h-35. Ianin, Valentin Lavrent'evich. *Novgorodskie akty, XII–XV vv.: Khronologicheskii kommentarii.* Moscow: "Nauka," 1991. 383 p. (Lib: DLC; IU; MH)

> A detailed catalogue with commentary on the series of birchbark documents.

Division of Written Sources (OPI)

h-37. *Obzor fonda "Muzei Staraia Moskva."* Compiled by F. A. Petrov. Moscow, 1991. 199 p. [Minkul't RSFSR; AN SSSR; NII kul'tury] (Lib: MH)

> Surveys the history of the Museum of Old Moscow (*Muzei "Staraia Moskva"*), its holdings and archival records (fond 402), representing one of the largest museums in Moscow between the years 1919 and 1926, whose unique collections are now in GIM, spanning a period of 300 years (1630–1930). Includes an index of proper names, together with subject and topographical indexes of Moscow and the Moscow Region (*Podmoskov'e*).

h-38. Kalantyrskaia, I. S. "Materialy po istorii russkogo teatra XVIII–XX vv. v OPI GIM v Moskve." In *Teatr i muzyka: Dokumenty i materialy,* edited by I. Petrovskaia et al., pp. 91–104. Moscow/Leningrad: Izd-vo AN SSSR, 1963. (Lib: DLC; IU; MH) [IDC-in R-10,753]

h-38A. Falaleeva, M. B. "Fond Romanovykh v sobranii OPI GIM." *AE za 1996 god* (1998): 270–81. (Lib: DLC; IU; MH)

> Surveys documentary materials of the imperial family in the recently opened special collection in GIM (fond 180, 395 units with 1677 documents), including documentation from almost all Russian emperors since Peter I and many members of the imperial family. Of special interest is the large collection of materials transferred to GIM in 1947 that came from the Belgrade museum honoring Nicholas II (see pp. 279–81).

h-39. Kalantyrskaia, I. S. "Avtografy M. Iu. Lermontova i materialy o M. Iu. Lermontove v Otdele pis'mennykh istochnikov GIM i ispol'zovanie etikh materialov v literaturovedcheskikh trudakh." In *Ezhegodnik GIM,* vol. 1963–1964, pp. 168–89. 1966. (Lib: IU)

h-40. Samgina, E. I. "Obzor fonda Saltykovykh v Gosudarstvennom Istoricheskom muzee." *AE za 1970 god* (1971): 294–99. (Lib: DLC; IU; MH) [IDC-R-10,754 mf. 114–20]
Surveys documents from the Saltykov family archive (1616–1757).

h-40A. Riumina, T. D. "Arkhiv moskvoveda P. N. Millera v OPI GIM." *AE za 1971 god* (1972): 344–46. (Lib: DLC; IU; MH) [IDC-R-10,754 mf. 121–28]
Surveys the historian of local Moscow history, Petr Nikolaevich Miller (1859–1943) held in GIM (fond 134). Additional Miller papers are held in the Museum of the History of the City of Moscow (H–5, fond 8169).

h-41. Filimonov, Sergei Borisovich. "Obzor arkhiva M. I. Smirnova." *AE za 1971 god* (1972): 318–24. (Lib: DLC; IU; MH) [IDC-R-10,754 mf. 121–28]
Surveys the papers of the Soviet historian of local history, M. I. Smirnov (1866–1949) held in GIM (fond 191). Additional Smirnov papers are held in the State Archive of Iaroslavl Oblast. Includes a complete bibliography of Smirnov's publications.

h-42. Krasavin, A. S. "Obzor dokumental'nykh materialov kruzhka "Beseda" v fonde V. A. Maklakova." *AE za 1968 god* (1969): 352–59. (Lib: DLC; IU; MH) [IDC-R-10,754 mf. 98-106]
A detailed survey of documents relating to the liberal Beseda literary circle (1899–1905), part of which were acquired from the Russian Foreign Historical Archive (RZIA) in Prague. Includes a list of members of the circle. See also the review of these materials by Terence Emmons, "The Beseda Circle 1899–1905," *Slavic Review* 32 (Sept. 1973): 461–90.

h-43. Zents, E. M. "Materialy I. E. Grabaria i A. M. Vasnetsova v sobranii Otdela pis'mennykh istochnikov Gosudarstvennogo Istoricheskogo muzeia." In *Vsesoiuznaia konferentsiia-seminar "Arkhivnye fondy khudozhestvennykh muzeev SSSR,"* vol. 1, pp. 113–34. Moscow, 1981.

h-43A. Ianovskii, A. D.; and Petrov, F. A. "Napoleon. Ego sem'ia. Ego spodvizhniki: (Avtografy iz sobraniia Gosudarstvennogo Istoricheskogo muzeia)." *AE za 1992 god* (1994): 224–36; *AE za 1993 god* (1995): 246–69. (Lib: DLC; IU; MH)
Surveys the collection of more than 2,500 Napoleonic documents in the Division of Written Sources (OPI), including 30 letters and documents in Napoleon's own hand or bearing his signature, 100 documents written or signed by Napoleon's family members, and over 2,400 documents from his political and military entourage.

h-43A.1. "Napoléon. Sa Famille. Son entourage. Autographes de la collection du Musée Historique National (Autographs of the State Historical Museum in Moscow)." Compiled by A. D. Ianovskii and F. A. Petrov. Moscow, 1997. 20 reels of microfilm, including catalogue in French. Distributed by Norman Ross Publishers (New York).
A collection of more than 2,500 Napoleonic documents in the Division of Written Sources (OPI), including 30 letters and documents in Napeolon's own hand or bearing his signature, 100 documents written or signed by Napoleon's family members, and over 2,400 documents from his political and military entourage.

Cartographic Division

h-44. Navrot, M. I. "Katalog gravirovannykh i rukopisnykh kart Sibiri XVI–XVII vv., khraniashchikhsia v sektore kartografii Istoricheskogo muzeia." *Istoriia geograficheskikh znanii i istoricheskaia geografiia. Etnografiia* 5 (1971): 34–38. (Lib: DLC; IU; MH) [IDC-in R-11,023]

> A short description of sixteenth and seventeenth century maps of Siberia held in the State Historical Museum.

Graphic/Pictorial Materials

See also the survey of the GIM prerevolutionary photograph collections in a-516 and a-516.1.

h-45. Skorniakova, Natal'ia Nikolaevna. *Staraia Moskva: Graviury i litografii XVI–XIX vekov iz sobraniia Gosudarstvennogo Istoricheskogo muzeia/ Old Moscow: Sixteenth–Nineteenth-Century Engravings and Lithographs from the Collection of the State Historical Museum in Moscow.* Moscow: "Galart," 1996. 310 p. + plates. Added title page, preface, and list of illustrations in English. (Lib: MH)

> An elaborate edition of over 200 reproductions of historic engravings and lithograghs with city plans and views of prerevolutionary Moscow from the museum graphic and cartographic collections. Provides names of attributed artists and/or engravers with appended summary biographical data and a list of illustrations.

h-46. Saburova, T. G. "Katalog: Portrety dekabristov: Dagerrotipy i fotografii iz sobraniia GIM." In *Dekabristy i ikh vremia,* edited by V. M. Bokova, pp. 175–285. Moscow, 1995. "Trudy GIM," vol. 88. (Lib: MH)

> A detailed catalogue describing 119 pictures with reproductions of some of them.

FINDING AIDS — SPECIALIZED — UNPUBLISHED:

h-47. "Materialy po istorii dvizheniia dekabristov v OPI GIM: Podokumental'nyi ukazatel'." Compiled by I. S. Kalantyrskaia. Moscow. ca. 250 p.

> An extended thematic survey of documents relating to the Decembrist movement prepared for publication, but presently accessible only in the reading room of the Division of Written Sources.

Muzei "Novodevichii monastyr'"—
Filial Gosudarstvennogo Istoricheskogo muzeia
[Novodevichii Monastery Museum—Branch of the State Historical Museum]

Agency: Ministerstvo kul'tury RF (Minkul'tury Rossii)
[Ministry of Culture]

Address: 119435, Moscow, Novodevichii proezd, 1
Telephone: 246-22-01
Website: http://moscow.lvl.ru/culture/museum/novdev/novdev.html
Transport: metro: Sportivnaia; bus: 64, 132; trol.: 5, 15
Hours: MW–F 10:00–17:00

Head of Branch: Irina Gavrilovna Borisenko (*tel.* 246-22-01)

HISTORY:

Muzei tsarevny Soph'i i strel'tsov
[Museum of Princess Sophia and the Streltsy] (1922–1925)
Istoriko-bytovoi muzei
[Historical Daily-Life Museum] (1925–1930)
Muzei raskreposhcheniia zhenshchin
[Museum of the Emancipation of Women] (1930–1934)

The museum is located on the grounds of the Novodevichii (Bogoroditse-Smolenskii) Monastery (Convent) (sometimes known in English as the Convent of the Maidens). A spectacular architectural ensemble of the sixteenth and seventeenth centuries, the monastery was founded by Grand Prince Vasilii III in 1524 to commemorate the union of Smolensk with Muscovy. During the sixteenth and seventeenth centuries, many women from the families of the tsars and high boyar elite took the veil and spent their lives there. After the October Revolution in 1917 the monastery was closed, and in 1922, its buildings reopened as the Museum of Princess Sophia and the Strel'tsy. In 1926 it became the Historical Daily-Life Museum, and in 1934 was reorganized as a branch of the State Historical Museum (H–1). The adjoining Novodevichii Cemetery is one of the most famous in Moscow for the many well-known people and high government elite who are buried there.

HOLDINGS: 3,949 units, 17th–20th cc.

archival documents—1,622 (17th–20th cc.); MS books—160; monastery library—2,167 units

The museum has significant archival materials and an important collection of manuscript books, namely part of the monastery archive and library, all of which are officially considered part of the Scientific Fond Division (*Nauchno-fondovyi otdel*).

The archive contains documentation of all aspects of convent life from the eighteenth to the twentieth century: the estates, exiles to the convent, edicts of the Moscow Ecclesiastical Consistory, files on monastic staff, income and expenditure accounts, architectural plans and drafts, rental agreements, cemetery records and burial receipts, inventories of churches, church property, and museum fonds, and documents relating to renovation and restoration work in the monastery. The archive also holds a collection of similar documents from the Zachat'evskii Monastery (Convent) (founded in Moscow in the sixteenth century on the grounds of Belyi Gorod).

The monastic library contains many theological works, early printed books, and additional materials of archival interest. The manuscript book collection consists of seventeenth- and eighteenth-century illustrated books of parables and legends and readings for the deceased (*sinodiki*), lives of saints, anthologies of liturgical and choral music, psalms and canticles (*irmologii*), and other religious manuscripts, such as florilegia (*tsvetniki*). Some of the music and hagiographic manuscripts were produced in the artistic workshops of the convent during the 1660s. These are ornamented with miniatures and illuminations, and through these the decorative motifs of the early printed books can be traced. There is also an early printed Bible (1663) with a plan of Moscow. In a purely secular vein, there are donation and income registers of Novodevichii and Kutainskii Monasteries, which technically would be considered part of the archive. Cemetery register books have particular importance for genealogical research, given its status as a burial place for the elite.

Access: For access to documentary materials, researchers must present an official letter from their sponsoring institution addressed to the director of the State Historical Museum (GIM) and obtain an endorsement from the Deputy Director for Fonds (see H–1).

Reference Facilities: There are inventory registers and card catalogues.

Library Facilities: The museum has an auxiliary reference library.

Copying: Xerox copies can be prepared.

FINDING AIDS — PUBLISHED — GENERAL:

GAF Spravochnik (1991), p. 95; *Muzei Moskvy* (1997), pp. 25–28.

There is no published guide to the archival and manuscript materials in the museum.

h-49. Shvedova, M. M.; and Trutneva, Nadezhda Fedorovna. *Novodevichii monastyr': Filial Gosudarstvennogo Istoricheskogo muzeia: Putevoditel'.* Moscow: "Sovetskaia Rossiia," 1988. 111 p. Parallel texts in Russian and English. (Lib: DLC)
   A brief history of the monastery and the founding of the museum with references to the manuscripts held there.

FINDING AIDS — SPECIALIZED:

h-50. Borisenko, Irina Gavrilovna. "Stolbtsy XVII–XVIII vv. iz arkhiva Novodevich'ego monastyria kak istoricheskii istochnik." In *Istoricheskii muzei—entsiklopediia otechestvennoi istorii i kul'tury (Zabelinskie nauchnye chteniia 1993 goda),* edited by V. L. Egorov, pp. 157–160 + plates. Moscow, 1995. "Trudy GIM," vol. 87.
   Describes documentation from the estate archive of the monastery (1623–1703), which was discovered during restoration work in 1959.

h-51. Trutneva, Nadezhda Fedorovna. "Arkhiv Novodevich'ego monastyria kak istochnik po genealogii rossiiskogo dvorianstva (XVIII–XX vv.)." In *Kul'turnoe nasledie rossiiskoi emigratsii. 1917–1940-e gg.: Materialy mezhdunarodnoi nauchnoi konferentsii (Moskva, 8–12 sentiabria 1993 g.),* edited by E. P. Chelyshev et al., vol. 1, pp. 487-88. Moscow: "Nasledie," 1994. (Lib: MH)
   Describes the Novodevichii Cemetery records held in the archive and related necropolis materials of importance for genealogical research.

Muzei "Pokrovskii sobor" (Khram Vasiliia Blazhennogo)— Filial Gosudarstvennogo Istoricheskogo muzeia

[Pokrovskii (St. Basil's) Cathedral Museum—
Branch of the State Historical Museum]

Agency: Ministerstvo kul'tury RF (Minkul'tury Rossii)
[Ministry of Culture]

Address:	103012, Moscow, Krasnaia ploshchad'
Telephone:	298-33-04
Website:	http://moscow.lvl.ru/culture/museum/pokrov/epokrov.html
Transport:	metro: Ploshchad' Revoliutsii, Okhotnyi riad, Kitai-gorod
Hours:	MW–F 10:00–16:30; November–April: 11:00–16:00
	(research—by appointment)

Director: Gennadii Viacheslavovich Sharygin (*tel.* 298-58-80)
Chief Curator: Liubov' Sergeevna Uspenskaia (*tel.* 298-33-04)

HISTORY:

Muzei "Pokrovskii sobor"
[Pokrovskii Cathedral Museum] (1923–1931)

The Pokrovskii Cathedral Museum was founded in 1923 in the Pokrovskii (St. Basil's) Cathedral, the well-known architectural monument (often also known in English as the Cathedral of the Intercession), which lies on the south side of Red Square and which was built between 1555 and 1561 by the architects Barma and Postnik to commemorate the Russian victory over Kazan. In 1931 it became a branch of the State Historical Museum (GIM) (H–1).

HOLDINGS: 4 fonds, 1640s–1923

MS and early printed books—819 units (1640s–1923);
archive of former "Pokrovskii sobor"—ca. 5,000 folios of documents

The museum holds a collection of manuscripts and early printed books mainly of a theological nature, including an Altar Gospel written in the 1540s for Metropolitan Ioasaf Skripitsin, the Books of the Apostles with an inscription dated 1591, the Life of Nikolai Chudotvorets (1671), and a seventeenth-century service Gospel in the Georgian language.

Also found here are the archives of the former Pokrovskii Cathedral (including income and expenditure account books and edicts of the Ecclesiastical Consistory). The museum also retains the restoration archive, and the administrative records of the Pokrovskii Cathedral Museum.

N.B. Much of the archive of the former Pokrovskii Cathedral was destroyed after the October Revolution in 1917, though there is no precise information on the size of the loss.

Access: For access to documentary materials, researchers must present an official letter from their sponsoring institution addressed to the director of the State Historical Museum (GIM) and obtain an endorsement from the Deputy Director for Fonds (see H–1).

Reference Facilities: There are inventory registers of the manuscript and early printed book collections, as well as inventories (*opisi*) of the archives of the Pokrovskii Cathedral and the museum.

FINDING AIDS — PUBLISHED — GENERAL:
GAF Spravochnik (1991), p. 95; *Muzei Moskvy* (1997), pp. 32–35.

There is no published guide to the archival and manuscript materials in the museum.

h-52. *Muzei-sobor Vasiliia Blazhennogo: Ocherk, sostavlennyi sotrudnikami muzeia.*
Leningrad: Academia, 1928. 38 p. [Upr. muzeiami-usad'bami i muzeiami-monastyriami Glavnauki Narkomprosa]

> A detailed history of the cathedral and its reconstruction at various times, with a brief survey of the manuscript holdings held there in the 1920s (pp. 33–34).

Gosudarstvennyi tsentral'nyi muzei sovremennoi istorii Rossii (GTsMSIR)

[State Central Museum of the Contemporary History of Russia]

Agency: Ministerstvo kul'tury RF (Minkul'tury Rossii)
[Ministry of Culture]

Address:	103050, Moscow, ul. Tverskaia, 21
Telephone:	299-52-17; *Fax:* (095) 299-85-15
E-mail:	0955.g23@g23.relcom.ru
Website:	http://moscow.lvl.ru/culture/museum/revolut/erevol.html
Transport:	metro: Pushkinskaia; Tverskaia; Chekhovskaia; trol.: 1, 12, 20, 15, 31
Hours:	TuTh–Su 10:00–18:00; W 11:00–19:00

Director: Tamara Grigor'evna Shumnaia (*tel.* 229-52-17)
Deputy Director for Scientific Work: Larisa Aleksandrovna Shatsillo (tel. 299-44-82)
Deputy Director for Scientific Enlightenment Work and Exhibitions:
      Irina Antol'evna Prokhorova (*tel.* 299-61-76)
Deputy Director for Scientific Fonds: Irina Vasil'evna Orlova (*tel.* 299-22-96)

HISTORY:

Moskovskii istoriko-revoliutsionnyi muzei
      [Moscow Historico-Revolutionary Museum] (1923–1924)
Muzei revoliutsii Soiuza SSR
      [Museum of Revolution of the USSR] (1924–1947)
Gosudarstvennyi muzei revoliutsii SSSR (GMR SSSR)
      [State Museum of Revolution of the USSR] (1947–1968)
Tsentral'nyi muzei revoliutsii SSSR (TsMR SSSR)
      [Central Museum of Revolution of the USSR] (1968–1992)
Muzei revoliutsii (MR)
      [Museum of Revolution] (1992–1998)

The museum was founded in 1924 on the basis of the Moscow Historico-Revolutionary Museum, which had itself been formed in 1923 as a continuation of the so-called Red Moscow Exhibition. This latter had been prepared in 1922 by the Society of the Museum of Revolution (*Obshchestvo Muzeia Revoliutsii*), under the Executive Committee of Social Organizations in Moscow (*Ispolnitel'nyi komitet moskovskikh obshchestvennykh organizatsii*) (from 1917). In 1924 the museum was officially named the Museum of Revolution of the USSR, and was transferred to the authority of the Presidium of the Central Executive Committee of the USSR. During the 1930s the museum was under the control of the Museums and Regional Studies Division of the People's Commissariat of Education of the RSFSR.

In 1947 control of the museum was transferred to the Committee for Cultural and Educational Establishments (*Komitet po delam kul'turno-prosvetitel'nykh uchrezhdenii*) of the Council of Ministers of the RSFSR and was renamed the State Museum of Revolution of the USSR. When the museum was transferred to the jurisdiction of the Ministry of Culture of the USSR in 1968, it was renamed the Central Museum of Revolution of the USSR. In 1992 it was renamed the Museum of Revolution, but in 1998 was given its present name of the State Central Museum of the Contemporary

History of Russia. The museum remains located in the building of the former Kheraskov Palace (1780), a monument of eighteenth-century architecture, which from 1831 to 1917 housed the English Club.

The museum archival repository, originally known as the Archive and Library Division, and later called the Division for Preservation of Scientific Fonds, was reorganized in 1969 into the Documentary Sector of the Division of Scientific Fonds, which also includes the Photograph Archive.

The museum now has four branches:

(1) The branch "Seeking Freedom," as now organized, takes its name from an exhibition on the political history of Russia starting in 1985, which opened on the 75th anniversary of the 1917 February "bourgeois" Revolution in February 1992. The branch occupies part of the historic eighteenth-century building that belonged to the Osterman-Tolstoi family, near Sukharevskaia Square, which also houses the All-Russian Museum of Decorative, Applied, and Folk Art (H–31). That branch is heir to the the former M. I. Kalinin Museum, honoring the prominent Communist leader, that became a Branch of the Museum of Revolution in 1990. Initially located across from the Lenin Library on what is now ul. Mokhovaia, the Kalinin exhibits were closed down, and the museum was reorganized as a branch of the Museum of Revolution on Mokhovaia, before it moved to its present location. The extensive archival materials relating to Kalinin were transferred to the Museum of Revolution itself, and the branch now does not hold any archival materials, except for those actually used for its exhibits; its most important exhibits now portray social and political changes in the final four decades of the Soviet regime, starting with the XXth Congress of the CPSU (1956). (103473, Moscow, ul. Delegatskaia, 3; tel. 924-34-81, 299-22-96).

(2) The Krasnaia Presnia (Red Presnia) Museum (*Muzei "Krasnaia Presnia"*) was founded in 1924, in what had been a prerevolutionary labor suburb known for its role in revolutionary events. From 1940 it was a branch of the Museum of Revolution, originally memorializing the barricades of the Revolution of 1905 with the diarama "Heroic Presnia, 1905." It now also presents a number of other exhibits with photographs and documentary materials, including one on the history of the Prokhorov textile mills. (123022, Moscow, Bol'shoi Predtechenskii per., 4; tel. 252-30-35, 252-29-00; fax: 299-85-15; webpage: http://moscow.lvl.ru/culture/museum/kraspres/kraspr.html).

(3) The G. M. Krzhizhanovskii Memorial Apartment-Museum (*Memorial'nyi muzei-kvartira G. M. Krzhizhanovskogo*), founded in 1924, occupies the apartment where Lenin's friend and prominent electrical engineer Gleb Maximilianovich Krzhizhanovskii (1872–1959) lived from 1919 until his death. One of the founders of the Social Democratic Workers' Party (SDRP), Krzhizhanovskii, as head the Kommission for the Electrification of Russia, starting in 1920, developed the plan for the electrification of the USSR (GOELRO). (113035, Moscow, ul. Sadovnicheskaia [*formerly* Osipenko], 30; tel. 220-21-12, 953-06-40).

(4) The Museum of the Underground Press 1905–1906 gg. (*Muzei "Podpol'naia tipografiia 1905–1906"*), founded in 1924, memorializes the site of one of the most important revolutionary presses, which prepared leaflets and handbills for the 1905 Revolution and printed the socialist newspaper *Rabochii*. There is considerable original documentation and a reconstruction of the historical printing operations. (103055, Moscow, ul. Lesnaia, 55; tel. 250-30-74, 251-25-93; fax: [095] 299-85-15; webpage: http://moscow.lvl.ru/culture/museum/podtip/podtip.html).

During the years 1955 through 1991, the State Museum of the Great October Socialist Revolution in Leningrad (*Gosudarstvennyi muzei Velikoi Oktiabr'skoi sotsialisticheskoi revoliutsii—GMVOSR*), which opened in Petrograd in 1919, was also a branch, but it is now the separate State Museum of the Political History of Russia (GMPIR) (H–66).

Access: Research access requires a written application with an endorsement of permission from the director or her deputy.

Library Facilities: There is a scientific reference library available for researchers (tel. 299-25-06).

Dokumental'nyi sektor
[Documentary Sector]

Hours: WTh 15:00–18:00
Chief Curator: Irina Vasil'evna Orlova (*tel.* 299-22-94)
Head of Documentary Sector: Irina Iur'evna Margulova (*tel.* 299-70-01)
Scientific Worker (Photograph Archive): Galina Pavlovna Davniaia (*tel.* 299-66-93)

HOLDINGS: 467 fonds, 520,856 units, mid-19th c.–1993
        photographs—173,785 units

The Documentary Sector within the so-called Division of Scientific Fonds (*Otdel nauchnykh fondov*) contains extensive and varied manuscript and graphic materials relating to the history of the revolutionary movement in Russia, as well as copies of documents from other archives. The documents are grouped chronologically in two complexes or fonds: the first covers the period from the beginning of the workers' movement and the spread of Marxism in Russia (1883–1894) to the revolution of February 1917; the second extends from the October Revolution to the present. The extensive Photograph Archive is administratively part of the sector.

The first section contains a collection of documents relating to the history of the workers' and democratic movement in Russia (dating back to the 1880s). Here there are documents from the pre-October period from all over the country, such as deeds attesting to the sale, purchase, or division of land, and loan receipts and promissory notes signed by peasants (1883–1906).

There is rich documentation on the 1905 Revolution, including the original petition presented by the workers of St. Petersburg to the Emperor in January 1905 and manuscripts of participants in the uprising (N. V. Sineva, F. K. Golovanov and A. V. Ukhtomskii). The museum has a collection of photographs from the revolutionary years of 1905–1907, which include photographic portraits of prominent figures in the Russian Social Democratic Workers' Party (RSDRP) and other members of the revolutionary movement together with scenes from the period. Another collection of documents relating to the mutiny of sailors on the battleship "Potemkin" in June 1905 was acquired from the Romanian doctor, Rolle Arbor.

The first section also contains personal papers and individual documents from the archives of a number of professional revolutionaries, such as R. S. Zemliachka (*pseud. of* Samoilova), F. I. Makharadze, and S. I. Mickiewicz. Among the papers of E. V. Baranzin and N. N. Panin there are letters written from prison by P. A. Moiseenko and N. E. Bauman and manuscript writings of V. K. Kurnatovskii.

The museum has amassed a considerable collection of broadsheets and leaflets issued by the Central Committee of the RSDRP, the Bureau of the Majority Committee (*Biuro Komiteta Bol'shinstva*), and by committees and other organizations in St. Petersburg, Kazan, Nizhnii Novgorod, Voronezh, and Odessa. By far the largest and most complete of these is the collection of leaflets issued by the Moscow RSDRP Committee during the 1905 Revolution.

The documentary fond for the period of the October Revolution, foreign military intervention, and the Civil War (1917–1920) is one of the largest, containing some 80,000 units. It is arranged thematically and chronologically into four sections: the preparation and carrying out of the October Revolution throughout the country, the establishment and consolidation of Soviet rule, the fight against internal counterrevolution, and the Civil War and foreign intervention. This fond contains photographs taken by such well-known photographers of the day as V. K. Bulla, Ia. V. Shteinberg, and M. I. Abrosimov, as well as photographic chronicles of political life in a number of cities in European Russia, Siberia, and Ukraine. The museum possesses a large collection of documentation relating to the work of the factory committees and the trade unions, which includes leaflets, documents, and photographs.

The museum also retains personal papers of various revolutionaries and prominent party and state officials, such as A. A. Andreev, N. E. Bauman, K. E. Voroshilov, F. E. Dzerzhinskii, N. K. Krupskaia, G. K. Ordzhonikidze, and Ia. M. Sverdlov.

Of particular note in this connection are the documentary materials taken over from the former M. I. Kalinin Museum, honoring the prominent Communist leader, Mikhail Ivanovich Kalinin (1875–1946), which became a branch of the Museum of Revolution in 1990, but was then closed down. The fond of Kalinin's personal papers contains materials relating to his official activities, biographical documents, correspondence with family and friends, and documents relating to various anniversary celebrations. There are also a number of newsreels, other documentary films, sound recordings, and an extensive collection of photographs (close to 8,000, 1889–1983).

The period from 1921 to 1941 in the history of Soviet society is largely reflected in documentation relating to the building of factories, plants, and collective farms, as well as scientific, cultural, and educational establishments. As a rule, the personal papers of those who managed the economy, as well as of prominent individuals from the realms of science and culture, and those who distinguished themselves as leading workers during this period, are arranged in thematic collections.

Another very large collection in the museum is devoted to the history of the Second World War. This collection contains letters from frontline soldiers and from those who worked behind the lines editing newspapers and magazines. There are also operational documents relating to troop movements on various fronts, partisan operations in the Minsk and Polessia Oblasts, as well as memoirs of war veterans, directors of firms and enterprises, concentration camp inmates, and Soviet citizens who fought in the Resistance in various European countries. There is also a collection of manuscripts and publications of the Soviet Information Bureau (*Sovinformbiuro*), which were prepared for the foreign press together with the photograph archives of the All-Union Society for Cultural Relations Abroad—VOKS (*Vsesoiuznoe obshchestvo kul'turnoi sviazi s zagranitsei*) and the Telegraphic Agency of the Soviet Union—TASS (*Telegrafnoe agentstvo Sovetskogo Soiuza*).

The postwar period is represented by a large number of documents on the work of labor heroes, leading exemplary workers, and winners of various prizes. Collections have also been developed on Soviet cosmonauts, outstanding scientists and scholars, and representatives of the literary and cultural intelligentsia.

The museum has a considerable amount of documentation on the international workers' and national liberation movements arranged in several collections. These include leaflets, newspapers, brochures, photographs, and other documents on revolutionary events from 1917 to the present day in countries such as Hungary, Germany, Italy, Spain, Cuba, and Yugoslavia.

The division also retains a large collection of posters, which includes the work of D. S. Moor (*pseud. of* D. S. Orlov), V. N. Deni (*pseud. of* V. N. Denisov), and the Kukryniksy (*pseud. of* P. N. Krylov, M. V. Kupriianov, and N. A. Sokolov).

Working Conditions: Researchers work in the sector workroom, since there is no reading room. The Photograph Archive is part of the Documentary Sector.

Reference Facilities: There is a systematic catalogue with proper names, subject, thematic, and geographic entries, as well as inventories (*opisi*) of collections.

Copying: Photographic copies can be prepared for researchers, and xerox copies can also be ordered.

FINDING AIDS — PUBLISHED — GENERAL:

GAF Spravochnik (1991), pp. 21–32; *G&K Spravochnik* (1983), p. 243 and 264–68; PKG *M&L* (1972), p. 296; *Muzei Moskvy* (1997), pp. 38–42.

There is no published guide to the archival materials held by the museum.

h-60. [Tsentral'nyi muzei revoliutsii SSSR]. *Nauchnye fondy muzeia.* Edited by S. N. Manevich, L. I. Arapova, and Z. I. Kostrikina. Moscow, 1975. 254 p. [Minkul't SSSR; TsMR SSSR]

The collection includes several surveys of documents and sound recordings in the museum.

h-61. *Muzeinye kollektsii kak istochnik izucheniia i propagandy istorii Velikoi Oktiabr'skoi sotsialisticheskoi revoliutsii: Sbornik nauchnykh trudov.* Edited by E. V. Vedernikova et al. Moscow, 1987. 153 p. + plates. "Trudy Tsentral'nogo muzeia revoliutsii SSSR." [Minkul'tury SSSR; TsMR SSSR] (Lib: MH)

Individual articles discuss the history and formation of museum holdings and specific groups of materials.

h-62. **Tsentral'nyi muzei revoliutsii SSSR.* Compiled by A. I. Tolstikhina et al. Moscow: "Reklama," 1972. 287 p. + plates. [Minkul't SSSR; TsMR SSSR]

A popularized museum guide with some coverage of the documentary holdings.

h-62.1. Berezov, Pavel Ivanovich. *Muzei revoliutsii SSSR.* Edited by A. I. Tolstikhina. 3d ed. Moscow: "Moskovskii rabochii," 1958. 202 p. + plates. "Po muzeiam i vystavkam Moskvy i Podmoskov'ia." (Lib: MH)

2d ED.: M., 1955. 244 p.

1st ED.: M., 1952. 202 p. (Lib: DLC; MH).

A separate chapter in the popularized museum guide surveys documentary holdings.

h-63. Vedernikova, Galina Ivanovna. *Istoriia formirovaniia dokumental'nogo fonda Tsentral'nogo muzeia revoliutsii SSSR (1923–1937 gg.): Avtoreferat dissertatsii na soiskanie uchenoi stepeni kandidata istoricheskikh nauk.* Moscow: MGIAI, 1985. 29 p. [MGIAI; Minvuz RSFSR]

The dissertation discusses the early history of the documentary materials in the museum. The full dissertation is available in the RGGU library.

h-63.1. Vedernikova, Galina Ivanovna. "Formirovanie fondov Tsentral'nogo muzeia revoliutsii SSSR v 1923–1937 gg." In *Muzeinye kollektsii kak istochnik izucheniia i propagandy istorii Velikoi Oktiabr'skoi sotsialisticheskoi revoliutsii: Sbornik nauchnykh trudov,* edited by E. V. Vedernikova et al., pp. 7–9 + plates. Moscow, 1987. "Trudy Tsentral'nogo muzeia revoliutsii SSSR." [Minkul'tury SSSR; TsMR SSSR] (Lib: MH)

A published article based on the author's dissertation.

h-64. Shumnaia, Tamara Grigor'evna. "Tsentral'nyi muzei revoliutsii SSSR." *Voenno-istoricheskii zhurnal,* 1987, no. 11, pp. 29–33. (Lib: DLC; IU; MH)

A brief survey of the history, acquisitions, exhibitions, and publication work of the museum.

h-65. *Trudy Tsentral'nogo muzeia revoliutsii SSSR.* Moscow, 1972–. Irregular. 23 vols. through 1992. Some volumes in the 1980s lack numbers. Some vols. have added subtitle or form subseries. [Minkul't SSSR; TsMR SSSR] (Lib: MH[inc])

New title from vol. 12: *Nauchnye trudy...*

Some volumes have the subtitle *Sbornik nauchnykh trudov.*

h-65.1. *Golosa istorii: Muzeinye materialy kak istochnik poznaniia proshlogo.* Edited by G. I. Vedernikova et al. 2 vols. Moscow, 1990–1992. "Sbornik nauchnykh trudov Tsentral'nogo muzeia revoliutsii SSSR," vols. 22, bk. 1, and 23, bk. 2. Added subtitle for vol. 2: *Redkie materialy v fondakh Muzeia revoliutsii.*

The volumes publish selected revealing documents from the museum holdings relating to the revolutionary movement and Soviet repression with introductory notes describing their provenance and related materials in the museum collections.

h-66. *Izdaniia Tsentral'nogo muzeia revoliutsii SSSR, 1926–1978 gg.: Bibliograficheskii ukazatel'*. Compiled by N. G. Novikova. Moscow, 1980. 159 p. [Minkul't SSSR; TsMR SSSR] (Lib: DLC; MH)

———, *1979 g.–fevral' 1984 g.: Bibliograficheskii ukazatel'*. Compiled by L. A. Bruskina, A. A. Golomysova, and N. G. Novikova. Moscow, 1985. 67 p.

> The initial bibliography lists 211 publications on the theory, methodology, and work in the museum. Includes analyzed entries from the RM *Trudy*, and catalogues of several fonds.

FINDING AIDS — SPECIALIZED:

h-67. *Relikvii Velikogo Oktiabria. Iz fondov Tsentral'nogo gosudarstvennogo muzeia revoliutsii SSSR i gosudarstvennogo muzeia Velikoi Oktiabr'skoi sotsialisticheskoi revoliutsii: Katalog*. Compiled by I. S. Rozental', O. M. Kormil'tseva, V. A. Bessonov, et al. Edited by T. G. Shumnaia, E. G. Artemov, L. I. Arapova, et al. Moscow, 1987. 231 p. + plates. [TsMR SSSR; GMVOSR] (Lib: MH) (Also listed as h-420).

> A detailed catalogue covering Leniniana, documentary materials, brochures, photographs, and other graphic art relating to the October Revolution, as well as more traditional museum exhibits from the collections of the two museums, the second of which—now GMPIR—is covered below (see H–66).

h-68. *Arkhiv "Zemli i voli" i "Narodnoi voli."* Compiled by N. L. Pivovarskaia and V. R. Leikina[-Svirskaia]. Moscow: Izd-vo politkatorzhan, 1932. 454 p. Edited with a preface by S. N. Valk. Introduction by A. P. Korba-Pribyleva, N. A. Morozov, M. F. Frolenko, A. V. Iakimova. "Istoriko-revoliutsionnaia biblioteka," vol. 11–12. [GMR] (Lib: MH)

> Primarily a publication of documents from the archives of the revolutionary groups "Land and Freedom" and the "People's Will." Includes an introductory article by Nikolai Morozov about the archive (pp. 32–38), a preface by S. N. Valk (pp. 5–31), and a list of documents that are not included.

h-69. Nitoburg, E. "Dokumenty po istorii osvoboditel'nogo dvizheniia na Kube. (Obzor kollektsii dokumentov Gosudarstvennogo muzeia revoliutsii SSSR)." *Novaia i noveishaia istoriia*, 1966, no. 2, pp. 83–94. (Lib: DLC; IU; MH)

> Describes part of the collection of foreign materials in the museum, including original documents on the history of the workers' and liberation movements in Latin America and the United States in the interwar period.

h-70. Shatsillo, Larisa Aleksandrovna. "Fond G. M. Krzhizhanovskogo v Tsentral'nom muzee revoliutsii SSSR." *AE za 1985 god* (1986): 240–46. (Lib: DLC; IU; MH)

> A survey of part of the personal papers of the prominent Soviet CP leader and electrical engineer G. M. Krzhizhanovskii (1872–1959) that are held in the museum.

h-71. *Katalog postuplenii 1959 goda*. Compiled by I. S. Il'inskaia, Iu. K. Poloshchuk, and M. A. Nilova. Edited by A. I. Tolstikhina. Moscow, 1960. [Minkul't RSFSR; GMR]

Vol. 1: *Dokumenty i materialy perioda s kontsa XIX veka do 1920 g.*

Vol. 2: *Dokumenty i materialy za 1921–1941 gg.*

> Provides titles and other information on newly acquired materials.

h-72. Lupalo, I. G. "Po sledam voiny: Sobiranie materialov Muzeem revoliutsii SSSR." *AE za 1975 god* (1976): 159–62. (Lib: DLC; IU; MH) [IDC-in R-10,754]

> Discusses the acquisition of materials relating to World War II.

h-73. **Listovki iz sobraniia Tsentral'nogo muzeia revoliutsii SSSR: 90-e gg. XIX v.–1904 g.: Katalog*. Compiled by I. S. Rozental'. Edited by T. G. Shumnaia and I. S. Rozental'. Moscow, 1984.

h-73.1. *Listovki 1905–1907 gg.: Katalog.* Compiled by V. A. Bessonov, G. I. Vedernikova, I. S. Il'inskaia, and I. S. Rozental'. Edited by T. G. Shumnaia and I. S. Rozental'. Moscow, 1986. 311 p. Cover title: *Listovki 1905–1907 gg. iz sobraniia Tsentral'nogo muzeia revoliutsii SSSR.* (Lib: DLC; MH)
    Continues h-73.

h-74. *Bol'shevistskie listovki pervoi russkoi revoliutsii: Katalog (iz kollektsii Tsentral'nogo muzeia revoliutsii SSSR).* Compiled by I. S. Il'inskaia and R. I. Pikovskaia. Moscow: TsMR, 1977. 272 p. Cover title: *Bol'shevistskie listovki, 1905–1907 gg.* (Lib: DLC; MH)

h-75. *Listovki, 1907 (iiun')–1917 (mart).* Compiled by I. S. Il'inskaia and V. A. Bessonov. Edited by I. S. Rozental'. Moscow, 1989. 222 p. Cover title: *Listovki, 1907–1917 gg.: Katalog.* [TsMR] (Lib: MH)

h-76. *Listovki Velikogo Oktiabria: Katalog Tsentral'nogo muzeia revoliutsii SSSR.* Compiled by I. M. Zaichenko. Edited by G. I. Vedernikova and I. S. Rozental'. Moscow, 1988. 306 p. Cover title: *Listovki Velikogo Oktiabria: Iz sobraniia Tsentral'nogo muzeia revoliutsii SSSR: Katalog.* [TsMR] (Lib: MH)

h-76.1. *Listovki Velikogo Oktiabria: Mart 1917–iiun' 1918 g.: (Iz kollektsii Muzeia revoliutsii SSSR): Katalog.* Compiled by R. I. Pikovskaia, Iu. K. Poloshchuk, and L. I. Arapova. Moscow: "Moskovskii rabochii," 1975. 191 p. (Lib: MH)

h-77. *Listovki perioda inostrannoi voennoi interventsii i grazhdanskoi voiny, 1918–1920 gg. Iz kollektsii Tsentral'nogo muzeia revoliutsii SSSR: Katalog.* Compiled by I. M. Zaichenko. Moscow, 1989. 536 p. (Lib: MH)

h-78. *Listovki, 1921–1941. Iz fondov Tsentral'nogo muzeia revoliutsii SSSR: Katalog.* Compiled by S. I. Zaslavskaia, T. V. Klimanova, I. V. Kashkina, et al. Edited by T. G. Shumnaia. Moscow, 1989. 270 p. (Lib: MH)

h-79. **Listovki Velikoi Otechestvennoi voiny 1941–1945 gg.: Katalog Tsentral'nogo muzeia revoliutsii SSSR.* Compiled by T. S. Borodina and O. I. Iaroslavtseva. Edited by T. G. Shumnaia. Moscow, 1985.

h-80. *Listovki 1961–1980. Iz fondov Tsentral'nogo muzeia revoliutsii SSSR: Katalog.* Compiled by A. S. Balakirev. Edited by T. G. Shumnaia. Moscow, 1990. 181 p. (Lib: MH)

h-81. **Plakaty, vypushchennye k godovshchine Velikoi Oktiabr'skoi sotsialisticheskoi revoliutsii v Sovetskom Soiuze i za rubezhom: (Po fondam Gosudarstvennogo muzeia revoliutsii SSSR): Katalog.* Compiled by E. V. Litvinenko. Moscow, 1958.

h-82. *Partiinye i komsomol'skie bilety: Iz sobraniia Tsentral'nogo muzeia revoliutsii SSSR: Katalog.* Compiled by N. A. Danchenko, L. V. Kudina, and G. B. Urvacheva. Edited by T. G. Shumnaia and M. E. Kucherenko. Moscow, 1988. 87 p. (Lib: MH)
    Describes museum collections of 130 Communist Party cards (1906, 1916–1974) and 188 Komsomol cards (1917–1976) from different parts of the USSR. The two sections are arranged chronologically with the full name and date of birth of the individual, the place of work, and dates of membership in the Party. Includes name indexes.

Muzei istorii g. Moskvy (MIgM)
[Museum of the History of the City of Moscow]

Agency: Komitet po kul'ture Pravitel'stva Moskvy
[Committee on Culture of the Government of Moscow]

Address:	103012, Moscow, Novaia pl., 12
Telephone:	925-58-25; *Fax:* (095) 924-31-45; *RdngRm:* 923-85-88
Website:	http://www.museum.ru/moscow
Transport:	metro: Kitai-gorod, Lubianka
Hours:	TuThSa 10:00–18:00; WF 11:00–19:00

Director: Galina Ivanovna Vedernikova (*tel.* 925-46-60)

HISTORY:

Muzei moskovskogo gorodskogo khoziaistva
[Museum of the Moscow Urban Economy] (1896–1920)
Muzei kommunal'nogo khoziaistva Moskvy
[Museum of the Communal Economy of Moscow] (1920–1935)
Muzei istorii i rekonstruktsii Moskvy (MIRM)
[Museum of the History and Reconstruction of Moscow] (1935–1985)

The museum was founded by the City Duma in 1896 as the Museum of the Moscow Urban Economy, on the basis of a collection taken from the City Duma pavilions and exhibited at the All-Russian Arts and Industrial Fair in Nizhnii Novgorod. In 1920 the museum was renamed the Museum of the Communal Economy of Moscow, and in 1935 renamed again by the Moscow City Soviet as the Museum of the History and Reconstruction of Moscow. The museum was given its present name in 1985. Since 1935 the museum has been housed in the former Church of St. John the Evangelist (*Tserkov' Ioanna Bogoslova "Chto pod Viazom"*), which was built between 1825 and 1850 and is registered as an architectural monument of the period.

The museum now has one affiliated branch:

The Old English Courtyard Museum (*Muzei "Staryi Angliiskii dvor"*) was opened in May 1995. (103012, Moscow, ul. Varvarka, 4a; tel. 298-39-61, 298-39-52).

Earlier, the museum had three affiliated branches, all of which are now under different or independent administration.

(1) The A. M. Vasnetsov Memorial Apartment-Museum (*Memorial'nyi muzei-kvartira akademika zhivopisi A. M. Vasnetsova*), which is now a branch of the Tret'iakov Gallery (H–23).

(2) The Memorial House-Museum of the Artist V. M. Vasnetsov (*Memorial'nyi dom-muzei khudozhnika V. M. Vasnetsova*), which is now a branch of the Tret'iakov Gallery (see H–25).

(3) The A. N. Skriabin State Memorial Apartment-Museum (*Gosudarstvennyi memorial'nyi muzei-kvartira A. N. Skriabina*), which has been a separate museum (see H–49) since 1991.

Access: A letter from a sponsoring scholarly organization must be presented for access to archival materials.

Library Facilities: The museum has an extensive library totalling 60,000 books and 50,000 issues of newspapers and journals. There is a comprehensive collection of city guides and related literature and city plans, including many rare early editions. There are extensive publications of many municipal organizations and institutions, including those from the prerevolutionary period. The library is open to researchers.

Fondovyi otdel
[Fonds Division]

Hours: W 12:00–17:00
Main Curator: Pavel Fedorovich Nikolaev (*tel.* 923-85-88)

HOLDINGS: 5 fonds, 260,000 units, 17th c.–1990s
documents—131,000 units (late 17th c.–1990); books, newspapers, journals—24,000 units
(late 19th c.–1990); posters—5,000 (late 19th c.–1990); photographs and negatives—100,000
(mid-19th c.–1990)

All of the archival materials held in the museum are directly connected with the political, economic, and cultural life of the city of Moscow and, to a certain extent, Moscow Oblast. All are held as part of the general Division of Fonds (*Fondovyi otdel*).

The earliest documents come from the seventeenth-century patrimonial archive of the Artem'ev-Khlyzov clan of free peasants living in the Pomor'e region. Other documents relating to the pre-Soviet period have been arranged in thematic collections. Official documents include those issued by the city governor (*gradonachal'nik*), organs of city administration, and verdicts and sentences passed by Moscow courts.

There are documents originating from some of the large Moscow enterprises and trading companies such as the Prokhorov and Izmailov Textile Mills, the Danilov Sugar Refinery, and the "Kooperatsiia" Consumer Society. Thematic arrangement is also given to documents from insurance companies, savings and merchant banks, and documents on the history of the fire-brigade.

The history of education, science, culture, and the arts is reflected in documentation from higher educational establishments, such as the Imperial Technical Secondary School (*Imperatorskoe Tekhnicheskoe uchilishche*), the Higher Educational Courses for Women (*Vysshie zhenskie kursy*), the Moscow Archeological Institute, and Moscow Imperial University, as well as from secondary schools (*litsei, gimnazii, uchilishcha*), social organizations, scientific institutions, and clubs, such as the Moscow Technical Society and the Russian Theater Society.

The museum contains the plans and facade drawings of a number of famous buildings in Moscow that were constructed from the eighteenth to twentieth centuries, together with documents issued by a number of city-planning organizations like the Moscow Building Commission (*Komissiia dlia stroenii v gorode Moskve*) and the Commission for the Restoration of the Kitai-Gorod Wall (1815–1840).

There is an extensive collection of proclamations, leaflets, and handbills issued by various parties and unions that were active during the three Russian revolutions at the beginning of the century.

The postrevolutionary period is represented by documentation from such Moscow plants and factories as the "Kotloapparat" (*formerly* Dangauer & Kaiser), "Manometr," "Dinamo," Hammer and Sickle ("*Serp i Molot*"—see also H–180), and "Borets." These collections include the memoirs and recollections of various workers.

The museum has a large collection of materials relating to the period of the Second World War. There are documents showing the formation and military operations of the various home-guard divisions during the Battle of Moscow, together with the written memoirs and recollections of the men who fought in the home guard and some of their personal possessions and documents.

There are documents in the museum which reveal, albeit in a fragmentary fashion, the work of those engaged in public education and the teaching of culture and sport. These include documents from the Russian Bibliophile Society (*Russkoe obshchestvo druzei knigi*), the Commission under the Old Moscow Museum (*Komissiia pri muzee "Staraia Moskva"*), and the Society for the Study of Moscow Guberniia (*Obshchestvo izucheniia Moskovskoi gubernii*) (1921–1934).

Of particular importance are the personal archives of a number of historians who specialized in the study of Moscow antiquities, such as P. V. Sytin, B. S. Zemenkov, P. N. Miller, and N. P. Chulkov.

There are also personal papers of the Syreishchikov and Bakhrushin merchant families, the historians Veber, and the Volkonskii and Egor'ev-Svarichevskii families. In addition, considerable space in the archives is devoted to the personal documentation of people who were repressed under the Stalin regime, people who became heroes or who fought in World War II (the Great Patriotic War), war photo-correspondents, Moscow City Soviet deputies, scientists and scholars, and those who worked in the construction of the city and the underground metro.

There are a number of early manuscript books. Graphic materials include many posters.

Working Conditions: Archival documents are held in the general Division of Fonds and can be consulted by researchers as required in museum offices.

Reference Facilities: There are inventories and reference card catalogues.

Copying: Photographic copies can be made upon request.

Fototeka
[Photograph Archive]

Hours: W 12:00–18:00
Head: Vadim Pavlovich Panfilov (*tel.* 923-58-25)

HOLDINGS: 70,000 units, 1844–to present
daguerreotypes—3 units (1844)

The Photograph Archive contains the work of such famous Moscow photographers as I. D'iagovchenko, M. Konarskii, B. Nabholz (B. I. Nabgol'ts), F. Opitz (F. P. Opitts), and O. Renart, who photographed the architectural monuments in the Kremlin, the sights of Moscow, and historical events in the capital during the years 1905 and 1917 and the Second World War. There are also contemporary photographs of the city and its environs and photograph albums with portraits of the Imperial family and noted theater performers, among others.

Reference Facilities: There is a thematic card catalogue of negatives.

Copying: A charge is made for copying photographs. Negatives may be rented for publication or other use.

FINDING AIDS — PUBLISHED — GENERAL:

Muzei Moskvy (1997), pp. 50–54; G&K *Spravochnik* (1983), pp. 250–51; PKG *M&L* (1972), p. 295.

There is no published guide to the archival materials in the museum.

h-85. Shegal, M. M. "Muzei Moskvy." In *Muzeinoe delo v SSSR*, edited by I. G. Lupalo et al., vol. 5, pp. 167–70. Moscow: "Sovetskaia Rossiia," 1973. [Minkul't SSSR]
A popular account of the history and holdings of the museum.

FINDING AIDS — SPECIALIZED:

h-86. Voskoboinikova, Natal'ia Petrovna. "Rodovoi arkhiv krest'ianskoi sem'i Artem'evykh-Khlyzovykh." *AE za 1966 god* (1968): 384–406. (Lib: DLC; IU; MH) [in IDC-R-10, 754]
A publication of documents with a two-and-a-half page introduction describing the archive.

h-87. Shokarev, S. Iu. "Fond N. P. Chulkova v Muzee istorii goroda Moskvy." *AE za 1996 god* (1998): 299–309.

Describes the personal papers of Nikolai Petrovich Chulkov (1870–1940), an historian-archivist who worked in the Moscow Archive of the Ministry of Justice (MAMiu) and after the Revolution in the subsequent predecessors of RGADA. Chulkov's papers include a number of unpublished works and working notebooks relating to the history of Moscow, genealogy, bibliology, and ancillary historical disciplines.

h-88. *Oblik staroi Moskvy XVII—nachalo XX veka.* Edited by G. I. Vederinikova et al. Moscow: "Izobratel'noe iskusstvo," 1997. 335 p. + plates. [MIgM] Added English title and captions: *Old Moscow Image: the XVII–early XX centuries.*

A beautifully illustrated display album honoring the 850th anniversary of the city with reproductions of engravings, photographs, postcards, and other graphic works from the museum collections. Indexes with identification of artists, photographers, and engravers.

Military and Military History Museums

❋❙ H–6 ❙❋

Tsentral'nyi muzei Vooruzhennykh Sil (TsMVS)
[Central Museum of the Armed Forces]

Agency: Ministerstvo oborony RF (Minoborony Rossii)
[Ministry of Defense]

Address: 129110, Moscow, a/ia 125, ul. Sovetskoi Armii, 2
Telephone: 281-18-80, 281-48-77; *Fax:* (095) 281-77-35; *RdngRm:* 284-30-28
Transport: metro: Novoslobodskaia, Tsvetnoi bul'var + trol. 13, 69;
Prospekt Mira + tram 50
Hours: W–Su 10:00–16:30

Chief: Aleksandr Konstantinovich Nikonov (*tel.* 293-57-93)
Head of Library: Liudmila Nikolaevna Eremina
Scientific Secretary: Nikolai Nikolaevich Kashuta (*tel.* 281-23-33)

HISTORY:
Muzei Krasnoi Armii i Flota
[Museum of the Red Army and Navy] (1921–1946)
Tsentral'nyi muzei Sovetskoi Armii
[Central Museum of the Soviet Army] (1946–1964)
Tsentral'nyi muzei Vooruzhennykh Sil SSSR (TsMVS SSSR)
[Central Museum of the Armed Forces of the USSR] (1964–1992)

The museum was established in 1921 on the basis of a permanent exhibition entitled "Life in the Red Army and Navy" (*"Zhizn' Krasnoi Armii i Flota"*), which had been in existence since 1919. After the Second World War it was renamed the Central Museum of the Soviet Army, and in 1964, the Central Museum of the Armed Forces of the USSR. Its present name dates from 1992.

N.B.: The administrative records of the museum through 1934 are held in RGVA (B–8).

Access: A letter to the museum director is required stating the subject and purpose of research.

Working Conditions: There is a common reading room for all divisions of the museum.

Library Facilities: There is a specialized library for research work. Conditions for access to the library are the same as for access to documentary materials.

Copying: There are xerox copying facilities, a photographic laboratory, and a room for sound recordings.

Dokumental'nyi fond
[Documentary Fond]

Hours: Tu–F 10:00–12:00, 14:00–16:30
Head: Irina Dmitrievna Baranova (*tel.* 284-45-52)

HOLDINGS: over 200,000 units, 1918–1991 (scattered documents from 1905–1907, 1914–1918)
personal fonds—897; collections—380

The museum holds a wide range of documents on military operations and on the history of the Soviet Army, including the personal papers of commanding officers. Most of the documentation relates to the Second World War (1941–1945), but there are also materials from the Russo-Japanese War (1904–1905) and the First World War (1914–1918), and scattered documents relating to 1992 and 1993.

The Documentary Fond was built up with various accessions from units and formations of the Soviet Army and Navy, from military institutions, military registration and enlistment offices (*voenkomaty*), military schools and academies, and private individuals (soldiers, veterans of the Armed Forces, participants in revolutionary events and wars, and their families). Documentation has also been acquired from social organizations, such as the Central Committee of the Voluntary Society for Aid to the Army, Air Force, and Navy (*Dobrovol'noye obshchestvo sodeistviia armii, aviatsii i flotu*), the Soviet Committee for the Defense of Peace (*Sovetskii komitet zashchity mira*), and Councils for Veterans of War and Labor (*Sovety veteranov voiny i truda*).

From the period of the Civil War and foreign military intervention there are documents from Red Army international brigades and their commanding officers (A. Shipek and P. Borevich) together with written descriptions of military operations by those who took part in them.

Almost half of the Documentary Fond is comprised of handbills and leaflets. These include appeals issued by the Central Headquarters of the Partisan Movement (*Tsentral'nyi shtab partizanskogo dvizheniia*), the Chief Political Directorate (*Glavnoe politicheskoe upravlenie*), the Central Committees of the Communist Parties of Ukraine and Belarus, military councils of fronts and armies, and various underground organizations and partisan brigades. There are also collections of documents relating to all periods in the history of the Armed Forces, some of which have been arranged thematically, such as those relating to major battles of the Second World War (the Battles of Moscow and Stalingrad, etc.). The collection includes Party and Komsomol cards, personal identification cards, warrants, reports, letters from the front, and topographic maps and diagrams.

Among the many collections of personal papers, most important are those of leading Soviet military commanders, such as T. M. and M. V. Frunze, K. E. Voroshilov, S. S. Kamenev, Ia. F. Fabritsius, G. K. Zhukov, P. S. Rybalko, F. I. Tolbukhin, V. I. Chapaev, and I. D. Cherniakhovskii.

The museum also has a collection of military posters, the work of D. S. Moor (*pseud. of* D. S. Orlov), V. N. Deni (*pseud. of* V. N. Denisov), and V. V. Maiakovskii.

Reference Facilities: There is a central card catalogue, which includes personal and thematic card files. There is also a computerized database for registration of documents on temporary loan.

Fotofond
[Photograph Fond]

Hours: W 13:00–17:00; F 10:00–13:00
Head: Ol'ga Sergeevna Tolstova (*tel.* 284-51-97)

HOLDINGS: 107,726 units, 1918–1992

The Photograph Fond holds collections made by such frontline correspondents as G. M. Vail', O. A. Lander, B. E. Vdovenko, and E. A. Khaldei. There are also photograph albums and pictures of such famous military commanders as M. V. Frunze, K. E. Voroshilov, S. M. Kirov, A. A. Ignat'ev, K. K. Rokossovskii, and M. N. Tukhachevskii.

Reference Facilities: Materials in the Photograph Fond are reflected in the composite catalogue of the Division of Fonds.

Fond negativov
[Fond of Negatives]

Hours: Tu–F 10:00–12:00, 14:00–16:30
Head: Natal'ia Vladimirovna Lavrenko (*tel.* 284-44-50)

HOLDINGS: ca. 150,000 units, 1920s–1994

The fond contains negatives (both on glass and on film), motion-picture films, gramophone records, and magnetic tape recordings, all of which are thematically connected with the Second World War.

Reference Facilities: There is a special card catalogue for the Fond of Negatives.

FINDING AIDS — PUBLISHED — GENERAL:

G&K *Spravochnik* (1983), pp. 269–70; PKG *M&L* (1972), p. 297; *Muzei Moskvy* (1997), pp. 59–61.

There is no published guide to the archival materials in the museum.

h-90. **Tsentral'nyi muzei Vooruzhennykh Sil SSSR: Putevoditel'.* Edited by V. I. Shelekasov and V. I. Krasnov. Moscow: Voenizdat, 1969. 238 p.
> A popularized guide to the museum with mention of the documentary and graphic holdings.

h-90.1. *USSR Armed Forces Central Museum: A Guide.* Compiled by N. G. Alekseeva et al. Edited by A. V. Buianovskaia and Iu.V. Semionov. Translated by T. Gorshunova and Iu. V. Semionov. Moscow: Raduga, 1983. 222 p. + plates. (Lib: MH)
> A translation from a later version of h-90.

h-90.2. *Tsentral'nyi muzei Vooruzhennykh Sil SSSR: Putevoditel'.* Compiled by A. A. Bolotin. Edited by N. G. Nemirov, V. I. Shelekasov, et al. Moscow: Voennoe izd-vo Minoborony SSSR, 1965. 215 p. (Lib: IU; MH)
> A popularized guide to the museum exhibits with a brief note about documentary and graphic holdings (pp. 210–11).

h-91. Kuznetsov, A. *Muzei Sovetskoi Armii.* Moscow: "Moskovskii rabochii," 1958. 211 p.
> A guide to the museum exhibits. The manuscripts are not systematically described, but there are many references and quotations from documents held in the museum.

h-92. *Soobshcheniia i materialy Tsentral'nogo muzeia Sovetskoi Armii.* Compiled by N. G. Nemirov. Edited by G. S. Azarov, V. G. Verzhbitskii, et al. 2 vols. Moscow, 1959–1962.
> The first two volumes of the museum publication series include surveys of some of the documentary materials in the museum (see vol. 1, pp. 104–14; vol. 2, pp. 105–57 and 191–205) as well as other scholarly articles.

h-93. Rafienko, E. N. "Stanovlenie muzeia Krasnoi Armii v Moskve." *Voprosy istorii,* 1986, no. 2, pp. 182–85. (Lib: DLC; IU; MH)

h-93.1. Krasnov, V. I. "Tsentral'nyi muzei Vooruzhennykh Sil SSSR." In *Bol'shaia Sovetskaia Entsiklopediia,* vol. 28, p. 517. 1978. (Lib: DLC; IU; MH)
> Provides brief information on the history of the museum and its holdings.

h-94. *Stranitsy geroicheskoi istorii. Izobrazitel'noe iskusstvo v Tsentral'nom muzee Vooruzhennykh Sil SSSR: [Albom].* Compiled by A. F. Shvechkov, V. T. Pasechnikov, L. N. Balashova, and M. P. Lazarev. Moscow: "Sov. khudozhnik," 1988. 175 p. [TsMVS SSSR] (Lib: MH)

> A large-format album of illustrations of paintings, graphic arts (including posters), and documentary materials in the museum collections.

FINDING AIDS — SPECIALIZED:

h-95. Kozhin, S. V. "Komplektovanie dokumental'nogo fonda Tsentral'nogo muzeia Vooruzhennykh Sil materialami po istorii Velikoi Otechestvennoi voiny." *AE za 1989 god* (1990): 99–109. (Lib: DLC; IU; MH)

> A detailed description of the formation of the Documentary Fond relating to World War II.

h-96. *Listovki Velikoi Otechestvennoi voiny, 1941–1945: Katalog kollektsii muzeia.* Compiled by E. G. Ushakova and I. D. Baranova. 2 vols. Moscow: TsMVS SSSR, 1989. 110 p., 183 p. (Lib: DLC; MH)

h-97. *Frontovoi risunok: Katalog.* Compiled by L. N. Balashova and G. Z. Tambieva. Moscow: TsMVS SSSR, 1974. 128 p.

> An illustrated catalogue, with coverage of graphic works by military artists from the M. B. Grekov Studio, which was established during the Second World War.

Muzei Voenno-vozdushnykh sil (Muzei VVS)
[Museum of the Military Air Force]

Agency: Voenno-vozdushnaia akademiia im. Iu. A. Gagarina
[Iu. A. Gagarin Military Air Force Academy]
Ministerstvo oborony RF
[Ministry of Defense]

Address: 141170, Moskovskaia oblast', Shchelkovskii raion, g. Monino
Telephone: 526-33-27; *Fax:* (095) 526-33-51
Website: http://www.infoart.ru/avia/company/monino/index.htm
http://www.ritmpress.ru/avia/company/monino/index.htm
Transport: suburban train from Iaroslavl Station to Monino
Hours: TuWFSa 9:30–13:00, 14:15–17:00, Su 9:30–14:00

Director: Aleksandr Iur'evich Iablonskikh (*tel:* 584-21-80, 747-39-28)
Deputy Director: Sergei Vladimirovich Gapeev (*tel:* 584-21-80)

HISTORY:

The museum was opened in 1960 (founded in 1958) under the auspices of the Iu. A. Gagarin Military Air Force Academy in the village of Monino (Moscow Oblast—38 km. out, Gor'kovskoe shosse). Now under the jurisdiction of the Ministry of Defense, it has become one of the largest and richest aviation museums in the country, specializing in the history of the air force, as well as military and civil aviation.

HOLDINGS: negatives—15,000; documentary films—125; graphic materials—550 units

In addition to its technical exhibits, the museum has brought together significant original documentation regarding the development of aviation, including technical plans and drawings, photographs, and published materials. Audiovisual materials include 125 documentary films on the development of aviation and aerotechnology.

Access: Researchers should present a letter addressed to the director of the museum or to the Academy. Special advance permission is required for foreigners to visit the museum premises, because of its high-security location.

Working condition: Researchers can be accomodated in the library.

Library: The museum has a library relating to its collections, which is also used for the Air Force Academy.

Reference Facilties: There is an extensive card catalogue regarding airplanes, based on the museum holdings.

FINDING AIDS — PUBLISHED — GENERAL:

Nauchno-tekhn. muzei (1992), p. 31; *Pamiatniki nauki i tekhniki v muzeiakh* 2 (1996).

h-99. *Muzei Voenno-vozdushnykh sil: Putevoditel'.* Compiled by V. P. Zaitsev, S. V. Savel'ev, S. Ia. Fedorov, et al. Edited by S. Ia. Fedorov. 2d ed. Moscow: Voennoe izd-vo, 1988. 76 p. (Lib: MH)

Tsentral'nyi muzei Velikoi Otechestvennoi voiny 1941–1945 gg.
[Central Museum of the Great Patriotic War (1941–1945)]

Agency: Ministerstvo kul'tury RF (Minkul'tury Rossii)
[Ministry of Culture]

Address:	121293, Moscow, ul. Brat'ev Fonchenko, 11 (Park Pobedy)
Telephone:	148-91-72, 148-07-15, 148-55-50; *Fax:* (095) 145-55-58
Transport:	metro: Kievskaia + trol. 2, 7, 39; Kutuzovskii prospekt;
	bus: 6, 45, 91, 157, 505
Hours:	Tu–F 10:00–17:00

Director: Viacheslav Ivanovich Bragin (*tel.* 148-55-50)
Deputy Director and Chief Curator, Division of Fonds:
Tat'iana Ivanovna Chesnykh (*tel.* 148-07-13)
Scientific Secretary: Alla Andreevna Prussakova (*tel.* 148-07-15)

HISTORY:

Officially established 4 March 1986, the museum was opened to the public in May 1995 in a new building specially constructed for it, to mark the fiftieth anniversary of victory in the Great Patriotic War, as the Soviet Front of World War II is known in Russia. Since its foundation, the museum has been collecting extensive materials relating to the war. In the process of expanding its exhibition and research functions, the museum has developed significant archival holdings of various types, part of which are held in the so-called Division of Fonds, and some in the Division of Scientific Reference Service.

In addition to other holdings of its own, the museum also houses the "Sud'ba" (Fate) Scientific Information Center, comprising the memorial database recording information about all Soviet citizens who perished in the war or were missing in action from World War II. The center was established in 1991 by the International Association of Fonds for Peace (*Mezhdunarodnaia assotsiatsiia fondov mira*—MAFM), in cooperation with the All-Union (now All-Russian) Scientific Research Institute for Documentation and Archival Affairs (VNIIDAD), to continue and expand the extensive, computized Memorial Book Central Database (*TsBD "Kniga pamiati"*), which was started at VNIIDAD in 1989.

Library Facilities: The museum library (4,500 volumes) includes a small quantity of unpublished typescript memoirs of participants in the war and some manuscript diaries from the wartime period, all of which are open for consultation in the reading room. (Library tel.: 142-08-67).

Otdel fondov
[Division of Fonds]

Telephone:	148-07-13
Head:	Tat'iana Ivanovna Chesnykh (*tel.* 148-07-13)

HOLDINGS: 27,750 units, 1930s–to present
photographs—3,467 units

The basic collection in the Division of Fonds comprises documents from personal collections of war veterans, either donated to or purchased by the museum. There are also documents on the history of the war received from exchange fonds from other museums.

The division comprises several sectors: the Manuscript-Document Sector, the Pictorial Sector (*Sektor IZO*), and the Photograph Sector, among others. The Manuscript-Document Sector retains documents from personal collections of war veterans, letters from the front, books, and other documents (many in xerox copy), as well as handbills and leaflets (both Soviet partisans and Germans), military maps, and other materials.

The Pictorial Sector collects paintings and graphic materials, including some frontline drawings of E. A. Afanas'ev, A. V. Kokorin, and others, as well as many wartime posters.

Photographs and negatives are held in the Photograph Sector.

Access: As of the end of 1998, the documentation in the Division of Fonds is not sufficiently processed for public access.

Reference Facilities: There is an ongoing database covering documents in the Manuscript-Document Sector, and a separate card catalogue of "Letters from the Front."

Otdel nauchno-informatsionnoi sluzhby
[Division of Scientific Reference Service]

Telephone: 142-05-74
Head: Nina Nikolaevna Borisova (*tel.* 142-05-74)

HOLDINGS:

The Division of Scientific Reference Service, while first organized as an auxiliary unit, now has brought together significant archival materials acquired by the museum during the 1990s, most of which have not been fully processed. There are three important collections of note.

One collection of documents relates to war heroes who were awarded the honor of "Hero of the Soviet Union," collected by Vladimir Nikolaevich Kirpichnikov in 1953. It includes newspaper clippings, correspondence of Kirpichnikov with those who received the awards, copies of their certificates of award, and other documentation. A collection entitled "Children of the War," brought together by the journalist Sof'iia Urlanis, already numbers between 8,000 and 9,000 units, including newspaper clippings, photographs, and copies of documents. The museum also holds part of the collection of the Council of Veterans (*Sovet veteranov*), including some of the administrative documentation of the Council itself, along with over 500 photograph albums regarding the burial of those who perished during the war.

The personal papers of the composer and musicologist Viktor Evgen'evich Biriukov (ca. 1,500 units) include documentary materials he gathered for his television series in the 1980s entitled "Songs of the Great Patriotic War."

Access: Access to documentation in the museum requires a formal letter of request addressed to the director of the museum.

Reference Facilities: The division has a card catalogue for the "Heroes of the Soviet Union" collection. A computer reference system is being planned for the division holdings.

Nauchno-informatsionnyi tsentr "Sud'ba" (NITs "Sud'ba")
["Sud'ba" (Fate) Scientific Information Center]

Postal address: 103012, Moscow, Bol'shoi Cherkasskii per., 5/2/6
Telephone: 142-32-79, 923-17-69 (VNIIDAD, secretary)
Director: Nadezhda Aleksandrovna Pivovarova (*tel.* 142-08-65)

HOLDINGS:

The "Sud'ba" Database gathers and records information from official documents received from the three major archives of the Ministry of Defense: the Central Archive of the Ministry of Defense—

TsAMO (C–4) in Podol'sk, The Central Naval Archive—TsVMA (C–5) in Gatchina, and the Archive of Military Medical Records in the Military Medical Museum—VMM (H–75) in St. Petersburg, with additional verification from reports of military commissariats. The database retains precise references to specific documents, and currently it is being augmented and edited with reference to documents received from other archives throughout the former Soviet Union, such as archives of the Registry of Vital Statistics (ZAGS), local oblast archives, and other sources. Copies of the referenced documents as well as official answers to individual inquiries are retained in the Center.

The "Sud'ba" Database now has entries for over 19 million Soviet citizens who perished or were missing during the war. Thanks to the materials collected, it has been possible to establish the fate of many thousands of citizens who had been missing since the war. On the basis of the documentation plans called for the publication of 760 "Memorial Books." Due to a shortfall of funding, however, so far only some more limited individual subject-oriented, regional, and republic-level "Memorial Books" have been issued, including those for the Ministry (Commissariat) of Internal Affairs (MVD), for Kirghistan and Turkmenistan, and for "Jews Who Perished During World War II," and several others.

Access: The published "Memorial Books" and the personal name catalogue from the "Sud'ba" Database are accessible in the museum. The Center responds to queries from citizens regarding the fate of those who perished or were missing during the war. Inquiries should be addressed in writing to the address for the database indicated above.

FINDING AIDS — PUBLISHED — GENERAL:

Muzei Moskvy (1997), pp. 56–58.

There is no published description of the archival materials in the museum.

FINDING AIDS — SPECIALIZED:

h-100. Chernin, E. A. "Avtomatizirovannyi bank dannykh 'Kniga pamiati'." *Otechestvennye arkhivy*, 1995, no. 3, pp. 100–101. (Lib: DLC; IU; MH)

> Describes the database for the "Memorial Books," started and developed under VNIIDAD, covering Soviet citizens who perished during the war.

Gosudarstvennyi muzei oborony Moskvy (GMOM)
[State Museum of the Defense of Moscow]

Agency: Komitet po kul'ture Pravitel'stva Moskvy
[Committee on Culture of the Government of Moscow]

Address:	117602, Olimpiiskaia derevnia, Michurinskii prosp., 3 (ul. Pel'she)
Telephone:	430-05-49; *Fax:* (095) 437-60-74
Transport:	metro: Iugo-Zapadnaia + bus 227, 667;
	Prospekt Vernadskogo + bus 793, 810
Hours:	Tu–Sa 10:00–17:00

Director: Alla Stepanovna Lukicheva (*tel.* 437-60-66)
Custodian: Irina Aleksandrovna Pavlova (*tel.* 430-79-67)

HISTORY:

The museum was founded in 1979 to mark the fortieth anniversary of the Battle of Moscow during the World War II (1941–1942). It was opened to the public in 1981. In 1994 the museum exhibition halls were reconstructed and new exhibitions were organized. The museum was reopened to the public and to researchers in 1995.

HOLDINGS: 3 fonds, 14,959 units, 1914–1991
 sound recordings—14; manuscripts—9,154 units; photographs—4,153

Manuscript collections in the museum contain documentation on the defense of Moscow and the defeat of the German armies outside Moscow in 1941–1942. They include personal documents of those who took part in the defense of Moscow and their relatives, comprising memoirs, diaries, letters, photographs, and maps. Among the personal papers, for example, are personal documents and memoirs of the army doctor M. K. Kuz'min; the writer and editor of the army newspaper *Unichtozhim vraga*, T. S. Grits; a head of one of the medical units, M. I. Potemkina; and a commissar in the 17th Artillery Division, I. S. Kuvshinov. There is also a general collection of documents, "Participants of the Battle of Moscow," with miscellaneous documents, memoirs, and lists of veterans.
 The museum archive contains newspapers from the wartime period acquired from collectors.

Access: Access for researchers to materials in the basic fond of the museum requires a letter from their sponsoring institution. Access to the scientific auxiliary fond requires the permission of the museum director. In certain circumstances, permission from the Moscow Committee on Culture may also be required.

Reference Facilities: There are inventories of collections and an inventory book of acquisitions, as well as subject, chronological, name and thematic card catalogues.

Library Facilities: The museum has a reference library, access to which is possible with permission of the museum director.

Copying: There are no facilities for copying documents.

FINDING AIDS — PUBLISHED — GENERAL:

 GAF Spravochnik (1991), pp. 111–13; *Muzei Moskvy* (1997), pp. 61–63.

There is no published guide to the archival materials in the museum.

Memorial'nyi muzei nemetskikh antifashistov v g. Krasnogorske (MMNA)

[Memorial Museum of German Anti-Fascists in Krasnogorsk]

Agency: Ministerstvo kul'tury RF (Minkul'tury Rossii)
[Ministry of Culture]

Address: 143400, Moskovskaia oblast', g. Krasnogorsk, ul. Narodnogo Opolcheniia, 15
Telephone: 563-86-27
Transport: metro: Tushinskaia + bus 542

Director: Arkadii Anisimovich Krupennikov (*tel.* 563-72-12)

HISTORY:

The museum was founded in 1985 in the town of Krasnogorsk, west of Moscow, where, starting in 1942, there was a prisoner-of-war camp for German soldiers and, starting in 1943, the Central Anti-Fascist School (*Tsentral'naia shkola antifashistov*).

Access: For access to documents, a letter is required addressed to the museum director. All of the fonds are open for researchers.

Rukopisno-dokumental'nyi fond
[Manuscript-Documentary Fond]

Hours: M–F 9:00–17:00
Head: Irina Petrovna Kuz'micheva (*tel.* 563-32-95)

HOLDINGS: 17,729 units, 1898–1991
manuscripts—1,290 units; leaflets—3,000 units; photographs—3,545; sound recordings—53; films (including video recordings)—25

Within its general Division of Fonds (*Otdel fondov*), the Manuscript-Documentary Fond holds documents on the history of the anti-fascist movement in Germany, with emphasis on pro-Communist German anti-fascists. There are separate documents regarding the activities of such renowned opponents of the Nazi regime as Friedrich Wolf, Richard Sorge, Wilhelm Pieck, and Ernst Thälmann.

 The documents are arranged thematically into several collections. The collection devoted to the 1918 November revolution in Germany emphasizes the establishment of the Communist Party in Germany with related documentation and contains personal documents of a number of internationalists, including documents relating to Ernst Thälmann.

 The collection of documents from the early period of the Nazi dictatorship (1933–1939) emphasizes activities of German Communists, and contains the personal documents of those who fought in the international brigades in Spain as well as appeals and addresses calling for solidarity with those fighting against fascist terror.

 Documents in the collection entitled "The Beginning of the Second World War and Anti-Fascist Forces in Germany (1939–1941)" deal with the formation and the activities of the anti-Nazi groups in Germany, such as the vocal groups the Red Choir (*Rote Kapelle*) and the White Rose.

For the period 1941–1945 there are documents from the Central Anti-Fascist School in Krasnogorsk, which include programs and study plans, student course summaries, and lectures given by the instructors.

A separate collection has documents on the changes that took place in East Germany between the years 1945 and 1949, which include orders from the Soviet Military Administration in Germany (SVAG) and ration cards for the German population.

The museum has a large collection of leaflets and handbills, with appeals and addresses related to its main theme.

The photographic, film, and video materials held by the museum were mainly acquired from the Russian State Archive of Documentary Films and Photographs (RGAKFD—B–11) and from private archives. These include photographs of street rioting in Berlin in 1918, pictures of those attending the school for German prisoners of war, and photographs of Germans who fought in the international brigades during the Spanish Civil War.

Reference Facilities: There are thematic, subject and personal-name card catalogues.

Library Facilities: There is a reference library with more than 7,000 volumes.

Copying: Xerox copies can be prepared.

FINDING AIDS — PUBLISHED — GENERAL:

GAF Spravochnik (1991), pp. 36–37.

There is no published guide to the archival materials in the museum.

Muzei-panorama "Borodinskaia bitva"
[Battle of Borodino Panorama-Museum]

Agency: Komitet po kul'ture Pravitel'stva Moskvy
[Committee on Culture of the Government of Moscow]

Address: 121170, Moscow, Kutuzovskii prosp., 38
Telephone: 148-19-65; 148-66-63, 148-56-76; *Fax:* (095) 148-19-67
E-mail: borodina@microdin.ru
Website: http://www.museum.ru/borodino/;
http://moscow.lvl.ru/culture/museum/borpan/eborpan
Transport: metro: Kutuzovskaia
Hours: M–Th, SaSu 10:00–18:00

Director: Irina Alekseevna Nikolaeva (*tel.* 148-94-89 [also fax])
Curator of Written Sources: Tamara Timofeevna Aliavdina (*tel.* 148-79-84)

HISTORY:

The museum was founded in 1962 to mark the 150th anniversary of the Russian victory in the 1812 War against the Napoleonic invasion of Russia. It houses the impressive battle panorama by the Odessa-born painter F. A. Rubo (Roubaud), son of an immigrant French merchant. The reconstructed peasant hut used during the battle by General Mikhail Illarionovich Kutuzov (*Kutuzovskaia izba*) remains part of the museum complex. The collection of archival documents was begun in April 1984. In the early 1990s, the museum underwent major renovation and has since been reopened.

HOLDINGS: 23 fonds, 1,189 units, 1765–1914

films—5 (1960s); photographs—364 (1913–1986); sound recordings—7 (1960–1985); personal fonds—9

The museum retains documents relating to Russian social history during the first quarter of the nineteenth century, the history of the 1812 War against Napoleon (known in Russia as the Patriotic War—*Otechestvennaia voina*), and on the foreign campaigns of the Russian Army in 1813 and 1814. There is also documentation on celebrations held to mark the anniversary of victory.

The museum holdings are divided into three thematic sections. The first contains documents on the Romanov dynasty, highest state institutions of the Russian Empire, and the supreme command of the Russian Army during the years 1806 to 1815. There are signed edicts and manifestos of Alexander I, dispatches and reports from army commanders, communiqués, and a record of military operations during the Patriotic War and subsequent foreign campaigns covering the period from October 1812 to September 1813. The most significant component in this section is the fond entitled "Communiqués from the Patriotic War Era, the Foreign Campaigns of the Russian Army, and the Russo-Persian Campaigns of 1804–1813" with printed excerpts and copies of documents printed by the field printing press under the control of military headquarters.

There is a separate fond consisting of documents about the French imperial family and the government of France during the years 1812 to 1815.

The second section is comprised of a group of fonds consisting of documents attesting to promotions in rank and title covering the period from 1765 to 1857. These include personnel service-record files (*formuliarnye spiski*) of officers who fought in the 1812 Napoleonic War, officers' demobilization documents, and diplomas issued with military decorations. The earliest document in this section records the promotion of M. I. Golenishchev-Kutuzov to the rank of Premier Major in 1765 and is signed by Catherine the Great.

The third section contains materials relating to the centennial celebrations of the victory in the 1812 War (late-19th c.–1914). There are the records of the Special Committee formed to set up an 1812 museum in Moscow (1910–1912), of the Circle of Those Dedicated to Preserve the Memory of the Patriotic War (1913–1914), and of the Society for the Preservation of Memorials (1913–1914). There is a separate fond for monuments to the Battle of Borodino.

The museum holds the personal papers of those who fought in the Napoleonic War of 1812 and took part in the foreign campaigns (the documentation covers the period from 1810 to 1850). These include papers of the Alekseev Brothers, A. A. Bistrom, M. S. Vorontsov, A. A. Protasov, N. P. Antropov, S. A. Figner, and A. I. Shmakov. There is a separate fond relating to the life and work of the famous battle painter, F. A. Rubo (Roubaud) (documents covering the period from 1903 to 1912), which includes original letters sent by the artist from Munich to P. A. Vorontsov-Vel'iaminov. The museum also has a collection of documents on the life and work of F. A. Rubo, which were collected by M. I. Anin and donated to the museum, as well as the personal papers of A. P. Vereshchagin, who created the monuments on the field of Borodino.

Access: Despite the continuing renovation which has involved closing the museum exhibits to the public, research access can be arranged. Researchers should present an official letter from their sponsoring institution indicating the subject and aim of their research. A fee is charged for research.

Reference Facilities: There are inventory registers and author, subject, inventory, and card catalogues.

Library Facilities: There is a reference library. Access is granted on the same conditions as access to the archival documents.

Copying: No copying facilities are available.

FINDING AIDS — PUBLISHED — GENERAL:

GAF Spravochnik (1991), pp. 110–11; *Muzei Moskvy* (1997), pp. 64–66; *Khudozh. muzei* (1996), p. 47.

There is no published guide to the archival materials in the museum.

h-130. *Borodinskaia panorama: Sbornik statei.* Edited by N. A. Kolosov and
  G. A. Boguslavskii. Moscow: "Moskovskii rabochii," 1966. 128 p.
> Different articles cover the history of the museum and its development, and reference documents on the history of the Battle of Borodino that are held by the museum (p. 25 ff.).

h-131. *Borodinskaia panorama: Putevoditel'.* Compiled by T. D. Shuvalova, I. Ia. Kraivanova,
  L. V. Efremova, and O. P. Andreev. Edited by Iu. Aleksandrov. 4th ed. Moscow:
  "Moskovskii rabochii," 1985. 157 p. + plates.
  *3d ED. M., 1979. 160 p.
  2d ED. M., 1976. 157 p. (Lib: MH)
  *1st ED. M., 1973. 144 p.
> A tourist guide to the museum describing the exhibits and providing data on various military figures and the artists displayed.

h-132. *1812 god—Borodinskaia panorama: Iz sobraniia Muzeia-panoramy "Borodinskaia bitva."* Compiled by I. A. Nikolaeva, N. A. Kolosov, and P. M. Volodin. 4th ed. Moscow: "Izobrazitel'noe iskusstvo," 1989. [136] p. mostly plates.

> *3d ED.: M., 1985. [136] p.
> *2d ED.: M., 1984. [136] p.
> 1st ED.: M., 1982. [136] p. (Lib: MH).
>
> A volume of reproductions from the museum panorama and other collections with a six-page introduction about the history of the museum and appended data about the Russian and foreign artists represented.

FINDING AIDS — SPECIALIZED:

h-133. Afanas'ev, Mikhail Dmitrievich; Afanas'ev, Dmitrii Nikolaevich; and Sapozhnikov, Sergei Alekseevich. "K voprosu o sozdanii genealogicheskogo fonda uchastnikov Otechestvennoi voiny 1812 g." In *Genealogicheskie issledovaniia: Sbornik nauchnykh trudov,* edited by V. A. Murav'ev et al., pp. 227–34. Moscow: RGGU, 1994. (Lib: DLC; IU; MH) (In a-555)

> An analysis of the scholarly work underway to establish a collection of genealogical materials relating to participants in the Napoleonic War of 1812.

Gosudarstvennyi Borodinskii voenno-istoricheskii muzei-zapovednik

[Borodino State Military History Museum-Preserve]

Agency: Ministerstvo kul'tury RF (Minkul'tury Rossii)
[Ministry of Culture]

Address: 143240, Moskovskaia oblast', Mozhaiskii raion, selo Borodino
Telephone: (8-238) 5-15-46
Transport: suburban train from Belorussian Station to Borodino

Director: Alisa Dmitrievna Kachalova (*tel.* [8-238] 5-10-57)

HISTORY:

Vystavka-memorial na Borodinskom pole
  [Memorial Exhibition in Borodino Field] (1839–1903)
Muzei Otechestvennoi voiny 1812 g. na stantsii Borodino
  [Museum of the Patriotic War of 1812 in Borodino Station] (1903–1917)
Borodinskii muzei—Filial Rossiiskogo Istoricheskogo muzeia
  [Borodino Museum—Branch of the Russian Historical Museum] (1917–1925)
Gosudarstvennyi Borodinskii voenno-istoricheskii muzei
  [Borodino State Military History Museum] (1925–1962)

The museum was founded in 1839 as a memorial and exhibition by veterans of the 1812 War against the Napoleonic invasion of Russia (often known in Russia as the Patriotic War), who lived in a stone lodge at the spot where General N. N. Raevskii maintained his stubborn defense in the Battle of Borodino. This lodge served as the prototype for the museum. In August 1903 the exhibits were transferred to the Borodino railroad station and the Museum of the Patriotic War of 1912 was officially opened. To mark the centennial of the Battle of Borodino in 1912 a new building was erected in place of the old lodge and shortly afterwards exhibits were transferred there from the Borodino railroad station, the Spaso-Borodinskii Monastery (Convent), and the imperial palace in the village of Borodino (built in 1839).

After 1917 the museum became a branch of the Russian Historical Museum. In 1925 the museum was made independent and was given a new name—the Borodino State Museum of Military History. It then came under the authority of the Moscow Department of Public Education (*Moskovskii otdel narodnogo obrazovaniia*). In 1962 it was renamed the Borodino State Military History Museum-Preserve.

In 1995 the museum was entered in the federal register of the most valuable monuments of the cultural heritage of the peoples of the Russian Federation.

Access: For access to archival materials a letter is required from the researcher's sponsoring organization together with the permission of the museum director.

Library Facilities: There is a library in the reference and information division. (Hours: M–F 10:00–16:00).

Dokumental'nyi fond
[Documentary Fond]

Hours: WTh 10:00–16:00
Chief Curator: Galina Nikolaevna Nevskaia (*tel.* [8-238] 5-10-57)
Curator: Ol'ga Viktorovna Kravchenkova

HOLDINGS: 52 fonds, 2,644 units, 1769–1991

The museum holds a collection of materials on the history of the Napoleonic (Patriotic) War of 1812, which includes documents on the domestic and foreign policy of the government of the Russian Empire from the end of the eighteenth century to 1825 and materials relating to those who fought in the war (service records [*formuliarnye spiski*], letters, and decorations and medals) and their families, relatives and descendants (including the diplomas issued with the decorations awarded to 1812 heroes the brothers N. A. and A. A. Tuchkov, and V. and P. Kokhius).

There are maps and plans of the Battles of Smolensk, Borodino, and Tarutino, and other documentation on military operations around Moscow in the summer and fall of 1812.

There are also documents relating to the founding of the Spaso-Borodinskii Monastery on the former battlefield.

A separate collection of documents pertains to the Second World War and includes the papers of men who fought in the Fifth Army at Borodino in 1941 and 1942, and newspapers and magazines of the war period. There are copies of documentary films and photographs from state archives, particularly the Russian State Archive of Documentary Films and Photographs (RGAKFD—B–11) on the liberation of Mozhaisk and Borodino from the Germans and on the arrival of Soviet troops in Boleslavets (*formerly* Bunzlau).

A separate fond contains documents on the founding and activities of the museum.

Working Conditions: There is no reading room.

Reference Facilities: There are inventories and card catalogues. A computerized database has been set up providing information from the service records of officers who fought at the Battle of Borodino, which includes data from the museum fonds and from the Russian State Military History Archive (RGVIA—B–4).

FINDING AIDS — PUBLISHED — GENERAL:

GAF *Spravochnik* (1991), pp. 107–09.

There is no published guide to the archival materials in the museum.

h-136. *Borodino: Gosudarstvennyi Borodinskii voenno-istoricheskii muzei-zapovednik: Fotoputevoditel'.* Compiled by E. V. Vinokurova. Moscow: "Planeta," 1991. 191 p. Photographs by V. Tsoffka. (Lib: MH)
> A highly illustrated small-format tourist description of the museum exhibits with samples of documentary, graphic, and other archival materials.

h-137. Sviridov, N. G. "Dokumenty gosudarstvennykh arkhivov v ekspozitsii Borodinskogo muzeia." *Sovetskie arkhivy*, 1969, no. 6, pp. 104–07. (Lib: DLC; IU; MH) [in IDC-R-10, 756]
> Briefly surveys documents which are exhibited in the museum, including those from TsAMO, RGAKFD, and RGVIA.

FINDING AIDS — GENERAL — UNPUBLISHED:

h-138. Tomchina, O. V. "Obzor dokumentov, khraniashchikhsia v fondakh Gosudarstvennogo Borodinskogo voenno-istoricheskogo muzeia-zapovednika: Diplomnaia rabota." Moscow: MGIAI, 1989. 97 p. Typescript.
> A survey prepared as a senior thesis at MGIAI, which is available in the IAI RGGU reading room and in the museum.

Tsentral'nyi muzei Ministerstva vnutrennikh del RF
[Central Museum of the Ministry of Internal Affairs]

Agency: Ministerstvo vnutrennikh del RF (MVD Rossii)
[Ministry of Internal Affairs]

Address:	103030, Moscow, ul. Seleznevskaia, 11
Telephone:	978-78-15; 258-06-59; 258-01-35
Transport:	metro: Novoslobodskaia
Hours:	Tu–Sa 10:00–18:00

Director: Vladimir Aleksandrovich Evdokimov (*tel.* 978-33-10)
Head of Division of Fonds: Galina Dmitrievna Ozerova (*tel.* 978-78-20)

HISTORY:

The museum was established in 1970 as the Central Museum of the Ministry of Internal Affairs of the USSR (MVD SSSR), and was opened to broader public access in November 1991. The present name of the museum dates from its reorganization in late 1991. It serves as the main museum for materials relating to various subordinate organs, agencies, and units (troops) of the MVD throughout the former USSR.

The museum is housed in the administrative building of the former Sushchevo fire and police brigade (*Sushchevskaia chast'*), an architectural monument of the late eighteenth and early nineteenth century.

HOLDINGS: statistics not available

Museum exhibits illustrate the history and activities of the NKVD/MVD (and predecessor) agencies from their beginnings to the present. Museum holdings include rare printed materials, photographs, and original documents (partially in copy) of the history of various operational agencies and troops of the NKVD/MVD SSSR.

Access: Research use of documentary materials requires a letter to the museum director stating the subject and purpose of research.

Comment: A completed questionnaire from the museum was not returned to Rosarkhiv.

FINDING AIDS — PUBLISHED — GENERAL:

Muzei Moskvy (1997), p. 67.

There is no published description of the archival materials in the museum.

h-140. Poikhalo, V. "Tsentral'nyi muzei MVD." *Sovetskii voin*, 1980, no. 22, pp. 34–35. (Lib: DLC; IU; MH)
>   Provides brief popular information on the formation of the museum.

Tsentral'nyi muzei vnutrennikh voisk MVD Rossii
[Central Museum of the Internal Troops]

Agency: Ministerstvo vnutrennikh del RF (MVD Rossii)
[Ministry of Internal Affairs]

Address:	111250, Moscow, ul. Krasnokazarmennaia, 9a
Telephone:	361-85-87; 361-81-77
Transport:	metro: Krasnye vorota + trol. 24; metro: Aviamotornaia + tram. 24, 37, 50
Hours:	M–F 9:00–18:00

Head: Anatolii Petrovich Belash (*tel.* 361-81-77)

HISTORY:
Tsentral'nyi muzei vnutrennikh voisk MVD SSSR
[Central Museum of the Internal Troops of the MVD SSSR] (1968–1991)

The museum was established in 1968 under the Political Administration of the Internal Troops of the Ministry of Internal Affairs of the USSR (MVD SSSR). It was reorganized under Russian federal administration at the end of 1991.

HOLDINGS: statistics not available

The museum has a collection of CPSU, Komsomol, and military documents, as well as posters and photographic materials.

Access: A letter to the museum head is required stating the subject and purpose of research.

Working Conditions: Researchers are received in working offices of the museum.

Comment: A completed questionnaire from the museum was not returned to Rosarkhiv.

FINDING AIDS — PUBLISHED — GENERAL:
Muzei Moskvy (1997), pp. 68–69.

There is no published description of the archival materials in the museum.

Tsentral'nyi muzei Federal'noi pogranichnoi sluzhby RF
[Central Museum of the Federal Border Service]

Agency: Federal'naia pogranichnaia sluzhba RF (FPS Rossii)
[Federal Border Service]

Address: 109028, Moscow, Iauzskii bul'var, 13
Telephone: 917-96-68, 917-31-04
Transport: metro: Kitai-gorod + trol. 45, 63; Taganskaia + trol. 63
Hours: M–F 9:00–17:00

Director of the FPS: Andrei Ivanovich Nikolaev
Chief of the Museum: Vasilii Dmitrievich Murzabaev (*tel.* 917-96-68)
Chief of the Groups of Fonds: Aleksei Nikolaevich Gur'ianov (*tel.* 917-31-04)

HISTORY:
Muzei pogranichnykh voisk NKVD SSSR
[Museum of the Border Guards of the NKVD USSR] (1932–1943)
Muzei voisk NKVD/MVD SSSR
[Museum of the Guards of the NKVD/MVD USSR] (1943–1957)
Muzei pogranvoisk KGB SSSR
[Museum of the Border Guards of the KGB USSR] (1957–1977)
Tsentral'nyi muzei pogranichnykh voisk KGB SSSR
[Central Museum of the Border Guards of the KGB USSR] (1977–1991)
Tsentral'nyi muzei pogranichnykh voisk
[Central Museum of the Border Guards] (1991–1997)

An earlier museum under the staff of one of the units of border guards was founded in St. Petersburg in 1914, but only lasted for several months. The present museum was established in 1932 under the Chief Political Directorate (or Main Political Administration) of the Border Guards (literally Frontier Troops) under the OGPU/NKVD, and then in May 1935 was transferred to the administration of the Higher Border Guards School under the NKVD USSR. Starting in September 1935 it was under the authority of the F. Dzerzhinskii Special Motorized Artillery Division Special Forces (*Osobaia motostrelkovaia diviziia osobogo naznacheniia im. F. Dzerzhinskogo*—OMSDON). In 1939 it was transformed into the Chief Directorate of Border Guards (*Glavnoe upravlenie pogranvoisk*) under the NKVD USSR.

During the Second World War, the museum was evacuated to Tashkent, and after its return to Moscow in June 1943, it was reorganized as the Museum of the Guards of the NKVD (later MVD) USSR. In March 1957, it became the Museum of the Border Guards under the KGB USSR, and in 1977, it acquired the status of the Central Museum of the Border Guards. After the reform of the structure of the former KGB, following the attempted coup in August 1991, the Border Guards became a separate federal service. The museum was reorganized accordingly and, following a new federal decree regarding the agency, the museum was also renamed.

HOLDINGS: statistics not available

The museum has a collection of documentary and photographic materials relating to the history of the Border Guards under the Cheka (VChK)–GPU–OGPU–NKVD–MVD–KGB. There are materials relating to F. E. Dzerzhinskii as first chief of the Cheka and his deputy and later successor under the OGPU (1926–1934), V. R. Menzhinskii.

There are collected photocopied documents regarding the organization and development of the Border Guards in the USSR since 1918. There are maps and diagrams of various border posts of the USSR.

Access: Research access requires an official letter of application stating the subject and aim of research.

Comment: A completed questionnaire was not returned to Rosarkhiv.

FINDING AIDS — PUBLISHED — GENERAL:

Muzei Moskvy (1997), pp. 69–71.

There is no guide to the archival materials held in the museum.

h-141. *Tsentral'nyi muzei pogranichnykh voisk SSSR: Putevoditel'.* Compiled by
    S. E. Liubimov, V. T. Kukin, and A. V. Nesterov. Edited by L. A. Volkov and A. P. Glukhov.
    Moscow: Voennoe izd-vo MO SSSR, 1982. 79 p. [Politicheskoe upravlenie
    pogrannichnykh voisk KGB SSSR]
        This guide to museum exhibits mentions documents and photographs on display and provides a
        history of the museum.

Muzei zheleznodorozhnykh voisk
[Museum of the Railroad Guards]

Agency: Federal'naia sluzhba zheleznodorozhnykh voisk RF (FSZhV Rossii)
[Federal Service of Railroad Guards]

Address: 141100, Moskovskaia oblast', g. Shchelkovo, v/ch 12672
Transport: suburban train from Iaroslavl Station
Hours: by appointment

Director: Oleg Makarovich Lebedev

HISTORY:

The museum was founded in 1976.

HOLDINGS: statistics not available

The museum holdings contain rare documents, photographs, and works of graphic art.

There are copies of orders and leaflets issued by the Petrograd Military Revolutionary Committee for Railroad Troops (*zheleznodorozhnye voiska*) (1917) and copies of resolutions passed at soldiers' rallies. There is also a photocopy of a document entitled "Statute on the Organization of Military Units among Railroad Workers Through Conscription of Railroad Staff" (1918) together with various resolutions to mobilize the railroad workers as an armed force and reports from military commanders, like M. V. Frunze, and military commissars, like A. G. Kniazev.

The collections include a manuscript album compiled by E. F. Veligonova (the wife of the chief of staff of the 65th Railroad Battalion) containing recollections of the defense of Odessa and photographs of the soldiers of the Adzhimushkai Garrison.

The museum has collected photographs and documents illustrating the life and military training of the Special Corps of Railroad Guards, which was attached in 1932 to the Workers' and Peasants' Red Army. These include photographs of the first commander of the Corps, Jānis Lācis (Ia. Ia. Latsis), and the chief of staff, N. I. Trubetskoi, and pictures of reconstructed sections of railroad in the regions of Sverdlovsk, Perm, and Ussuriisk. There are photographs showing military operations by the Railroad Corps to support Soviet troops fighting around the lake of Khasan (Hassan) in Manchuria (1938), the Khalkhin-Gol (Halhin-Gol) River on the Mongolian border (1939), in the occupation of Western Ukraine and Belarus (1939), and in the Soviet-Finnish War (1939).

The period of the Second World War is represented in the museum by documents attesting the awards of Hero of the Soviet Union and broadsheets describing heroic deeds at the front. There are also documents relating to the defenders of Leningrad and to those who built the railroad along the banks of Lake Ladoga.

The museum has a collection of newsreels from the Second World War showing the operations of the Railroad Corps in the defense of such towns as Przemyśl (Ukr. Peremyshl), Odessa, and Sevastopol. There is also lengthy documentary film chronicling the building of the Baikal-Amur Railroad and a number of films shot by amateurs.

Access: Access to documentation in the museum is open. An official letter is required from the researcher's sponsoring orginizations stating the subject and purpose of research. A similar official letter from an unaffiliated individual is also accepted, with verification of the identity of the applicant.

Reference Facilities: There is a card catalogue of personal documents and a chronological card catalogue of acquisitions.

Library Facilities: The library fond of the museum has a number of books presented and inscribed by Marshals A. M. Vasilevskii, A. A. Grechko, and I. Kh. Bagramian.

Comment: A completed questionnaire was not returned to Rosarkhiv.

FINDING AIDS — PUBLISHED — GENERAL:

There is no published guide to the archival materials in the museum.

h-142. *Muzei zheleznodorozhnykh voisk: Putevoditel'.* Compiled by A. M. Filimonov, A. Iu. Iurchenko, S. I. Pozdyshev, et al. Edited by V. E. Serbin. Moscow: Voen. izd-vo MO SSSR, 1980. 62 p.
> This guide includes a brief history of the museum and describes its holdings.

❋❘ ❘❋ H–17 ❋❘ ❘❋

Gosudarstvennyi istoriko-kul′turnyi muzei-zapovednik "Moskovskii Kreml′"
[Moscow Kremlin State Historico-Cultural Museum-Preserve]

Agency: Ministerstvo kul′tury RF (Minkul′tury Rossii)
[Ministry of Culture]

Address: 103073, Moscow, Kreml′
Telephone: 924-55-03; *Fax:* (095) 921-63-23
E-mail: head@kremlin.museum.ru
Website: http://www.kremlin.museum.ru
Transport: metro: Aleksandrovskii sad, Borovitskaia, Biblioteka im. Lenina, Arbatskaia, Okhotnyi riad, Teatral′naia, Ploshchad′ revoliutsii
Hours: M–W, F–Su 10:00–17:30

Director: Irina Aleksandrovna Rodimtseva (*tel.* 924-55-03)

HISTORY:

Masterskaia i Oruzheinaia palata
  [Workshop and Armory] (1806–1831)
Moskovskaia Oruzheinaia palata
  [Moscow Armory] (1831–1918)
Gosudarstvennaia Oruzheinaia palata
  [State Armory] (1918–1922; 1929–1947)
Gosudarstvennyi muzei dekorativnogo iskusstva "Oruzheinaia palata"
  [Armory State Museum of Decorative Arts] (1922–1924)
Ob″edinennyi muzei dekorativnogo iskusstva
  [Consolidated Museum of Decorative Arts] (1924–1929)
Gosudarstvennye muzei Moskovskogo Kremlia
  [Moscow Kremlin State Museums] (1960–1991)

The forerunner of the present museum was the Workshop and Armory, which had existed as a museum since 1806 under the control of the Moscow Building Department (*Ekspeditsiia Moskovskogo stroeniia*). In 1831 the Moscow Armory became an independent organization, under the Moscow Court Office of the Ministry of the Imperial Court, and a new building was constructed between 1849–1851. In 1858 the post of Keeper (*arkhivarius*) of the Armory Archive was created, but in 1869 the earliest records together with the documents of other Kremlin institutions were combined into the Moscow Palace Archive (*Moskovskii dvortsovyi arkhiv*). After a number of subsequent reorganizations and changes of name, these materials were transferred to state archival custody and are now held in the Russian State Archive of Early Acts—RGADA (B–2).

After the October Revolution in 1917 the museum was taken over by the People's Commissariat of Education (Narkompros RSFSR) and was called the State Armory. Subsequently the Kremlin cathedrals—the Cathedral of St. Michael the Archangel (*Arkhangel'skii*), the Cathedral of the Annunciation (*Blagoveshchenskii*), and the Cathedral of the Dormition (or the Assumption)

(*Uspenskii*)—together with a number of churches, the former Boyars' Palace, the Terems (Towers) Palace, and the Patriarchial Palace came under the control of the museum. The museum received part of the archives and libraries of these buildings, as well as those of a number of nationalized historical monuments like the Patriarchial Sacristy (Vestry) (*Patriarshaia riznitsa*), and various monasteries and churches. It also received private collections. At the same time various museum exhibits were transferred from the Armory to the State Valuables Repository (*Gosudarstvennoe khranilishche tsennostei*).

In 1922 the State Armory and the Kremlin cathedrals, which from 1923 onwards functioned as museums, together with the seventeenth-century Boyar Museum, were brought together to form the Armory State Museum of Decorative Arts. In 1924 the museum was renamed the Consolidated Museum of Decorative Arts. It comprised the Furniture Museum (*Muzei mebeli*) (1918–1928), the Porcelain Museum (*Muzei farfora*) (1918–1931, see H–21), and the Toy Museum (*Muzei igrushki*). After the breakup of the Consolidated Museum in 1929, the State Armory went back to its former name, and in 1932 was transferred to the control of the Committee for Supervision of Academic and Educational Establishments (*Komitet po zavedyvaniiu uchenymi i uchebnymi uchrezhdeniiami TsIK SSSR*).

In 1938 the museum was transferred to the control of the Moscow Kremlin Commandant's Administration (*Upravlenie komendatury Moskovskogo Kremlia*) and for all intents and purposes lost its independence as a cultural institution. This situation became a fact in 1947 when the museum was reduced to the status of one of the departments of the Moscow Kremlin Commandant's Administration.

Independent status was restored to the museum in April 1960, when on the basis of its fonds and the Kremlin cathedral museums a new amalgamation was formed—the Moscow Kremlin State Museums, which came under the Ministry of Culture of the USSR. After reconstruction of a number of architectural monuments in the Kremlin that formed part of the museum complex, the Museum of Applied Arts and Seventeenth-Century Russian Life (*Muzei prikladnogo iskusstva i byta Rossii XVII v.*) was opened in 1962 as a branch within the museum complex.

The museum complex received its present name in 1991, when it was reorganized and transferred to the control of the Ministry of Culture of the Russian Federation. In December 1991 the museum was added to the federal register of the most valuable monuments of the cultural heritage of the peoples of the Russian Federation.

The Scientific Archive of the Kremlin Museums has existed since 1960, when all the documents connected with the Armory and the Kremlin cathedrals were transferred from the Moscow Kremlin Commandant's Administration to the museum. In 1975 the fonds of the Scientific Archive and the Library formed the basis of the Division of Manuscript, Printed, and Graphic Art Fonds. There is a separate Division of Photographs and Slides.

Access: For access to archival materials, a letter should be presented from the researcher's sponsoring organization or a written application from the researcher together with a passport or other proof of identity.

Copying: Facilities for making copies of documents are extremely limited.

Otdel rukopisnykh, pechatnykh i graficheskikh fondov
[Division of Manuscript, Printed, and Graphic Art Fonds]

Telephone: 202-12-58
Hours: TuWF 10:00–17:00
Head: Alla Viktorovna Petukhova (*tel.* 202-12-58)

HOLDINGS: 44 fonds (3 fonds and 1 collection unarranged), 27,114 units
MS museum collection—1,653 units (1491, 1539–1995); photographs—7,285 (19th–20th cc.); collection from the Museum of Gifts—874 units (1950s–1990s)

The division comprises the Sector of Manuscript and Documentary Fonds (*Sektor rukopisnykh i dokumental'nykh fondov*), Fond of Graphic Arts (*Fond grafiki*), and the Book Fonds (*Sektor knizhnogo fonda*).

The Sector of Manuscript and Documentary Fonds comprises the earliest, rarest, and most valuable manuscript books and manuscripts held by the division, most of which came from the monasteries and cathedrals of the Kremlin. There are also charters (1491–1707) and manuscript books (16th–18th cc.) from the Sacristy Collection of the Solovetskii Monastery.

There is a thirteenth-century Greek Gospel on parchment, seventeenth- and eighteenth-century Church Slavonic Gospels, and a number of seventeenth- and eighteenth-century manuscript books, like the "Spiritual Healing" (*Lekarstvo dushevnoe*), the Godunov Illuminated Psalter (*Godunovskaia litsevaia Psaltir'*), and the Primer (*Bukvar'*) of Karion Istomin. All are richly illustrated with miniatures, illuminations, initials, and enclosed in rich binding cases. Also here is a unique example of late seventeenth-century book art—the "Book on the Election of the Tsar" (*Kniga ob izbranii na tsarstvo*, 1672–1673).

The sector holds a number of archival fonds from the Voznesenskii (Ascension) and Chudov (Miracles) Monasteries; from the Cathedral of St. Michael the Archangel (*Arkhangel'skii*), the Cathedral of the Annunciation (*Blagoveshchenskii*), the Nikolo-Gostunskii Cathedral, and the Cathedral of the Twelve Apostles in the Kremlin; and from a number of churches, including the Church of Ioann Lestvichnik, the Church of the Annunciation in the Granary (*tserkov' Blagoveshcheniia na Zhitnom dvore*), and the Church of the Deposition of the Virgin's Robe (*tserkov' Rizopolozheniia*). These fonds contain eighteenth- and nineteenth-century property inventories, decrees of the Moscow Ecclesiastical Consistory, income and expenditure books, parish registers, and correspondence relating to repair, restoration, and administrative matters.

Records of the Armory (1812–1959), the Moscow Palace Administration, and the Commission for Restoration of the Cathedral of the Dormition (*Uspenskii*) are found in separate fonds, with documentation relating to property and economic matters, inventories, and income and expenditure books. These reflect the formation of the museum collections, including decorative and applied art and icons and the restoration and repair of Kremlin monuments. The fond of the Moscow Palace Administration also contains property inventories from the Great Kremlin Palace, and a schedule of inscriptions for St. George's Hall (19th c.).

There is a separate fond with records of the State Museums of the Moscow Kremlin (1960–1991). There is also documentation from several museums that formed part of the Armory Museum and subsequently became independent, such as the Ceramics Museum (1918–1932, see H–21) and the Toy Museum.

The sector holds the personal papers of a number of prominent figures in the world of culture, who were on the staff or served as consultants to the museum, such as the historian and ethnographer D. I. Uspenskii, the art experts F. Ia. Mishukov, T. N. Nikolaeva, V. K. Klein, M. N. Levinson-Nechaeva, T. N. Gol'dberg, N. N. Zakharov, and N. V. Gordeev.

The sector continually collects unpublished scholarly work on matters relating to the Armory and the cathedrals together with documents from contemporary jewelers, whose work is exhibited in the museum fonds.

The photograph collection includes views of the architectural monuments of the Kremlin in the nineteenth and early twentieth century, interior decoration of the palaces and halls, and photographs of various works of art and *objets d'art* held in the Kremlin museums.

The Fond of Graphic Arts contains architectural and pictorial graphic materials that are thematically connected to the monuments and antiquities in the Moscow Kremlin.

The vast range of material in the sector is largely made up of scientific-technical documentation, including technical drawings in the basic and auxiliary fonds. There are plans of the Moscow Kremlin, facades, plans and sectional views of the Kremlin buildings and of the walls and towers of the Kremlin, and projects for restoration work from the 1640s to the twentieth century. Many of the technical drawings are the work of famous architects like V. I. Bazhenov, P. A. Gerasimov, F. F. Rikhter, V. P. Stasov, D. V. Ukhtomskii, and K. A. Ton (Thon), among others.

The scientific auxiliary fond of the sector contains architectural measurements, field sketches, and technical drawings (1940s–1960s) made of the Kremlin monuments.

There are engravings, drawings, and watercolors by Russian nineteenth- and early twentieth-century artists of the monuments in the Moscow Kremlin and the interiors of the Kremlin buildings, as well as drawings of the exhibits in the Kremlin museums done by Academician F. G. Solntsev and other artists.

N.B. A large part of the archival records, including documents from the Armory Archive prior to 1813, is held in the Russian State Archive of Early Acts (RGADA—B–2), while another part is held in the State Historical Museum (GIM—H–1).

Working Conditions: There is a small reading room located next to the storage area, and all documents are delivered immediately after request. Inventories (*opisi*) are kept in the reading room.

Reference Facilities: The Sector of Manuscript and Documentary Fonds has inventory *opisi* and card catalogues for the museum collection. *Opisi* are available for all of the documentary fonds, together with subject, thematic, and personal-name card catalogues. The Fond of Graphic Art has inventory *opisi*, subject, author, and registration card catalogues, and inventories of the collections of albums and congratulatory addresses.

Library Facilities: A reference library is located in the reading room, which is part of the Sector of Book Fonds. The library has over 34,000 books and albums. These include a collection of early printed books (16th–18th cc.) on liturgy and art, together with a wide range of literature on art and history, as well as basic prerevolutionary publications along with reference and bibliographic literature.

There is a special alphabetic and chronological card catalogue for the early printed books.

Copying: Photographic copies can be made by special order in another museum division.

Otdel fotodokumentov i slaidov
[Division of Photographs and Slides]

Hours: Tu–Th 10:00–17:00
Head: Aleksandra Vasil'evna Dement'eva (*tel.* 202-02-17)

HOLDINGS: negatives—25,000 units; slides—1,400 units; films—27; microfilms—9; magnetic tape—2 units

This division holds negatives, slides, and motion-picture films on Russian and foreign art of the twentieth-century, and photographs of the architectural monuments in the Kremlin.

Reference Facilities: There is a photograph library and a slide library, together with inventories of negatives and slides.

FINDING AIDS — PUBLISHED — GENERAL:

Muzei Moskvy (1997), pp. 6–17; *Khudozh. muzei* (1996), p. 51; *GAF Spravochnik* (1991), pp. 17–21.

There is no published guide to archival materials held in the museum.

h-151. Zakharov, N. N. "Iz istorii Gosudarstvennykh muzeev Moskovskogo Kremlia." In *Gosudarstvennye muzei Moskovskogo Kremlia: Materialy i issledovaniia,* vol. 1, pp. 9–33. Moscow, 1973.

    A survey of the Kremlin museums after 1917 and their collections. Includes bibliography.

h-152. *Gosudarstvennaia Oruzheinaia palata Moskovskogo Kremlia: Sbornik nauchnykh trudov po materialam Gosudarstvennoi Oruzheinoi palaty.* Edited by G. A. Novitskii and S. K. Bogoiavlenskii. Moscow: "Iskusstvo," 1954. vii, 578 p. + 38 plates. (Lib: DDO; DLC; IU)

> The collection includes an article by G. A. Malitskii on the history of the Armory, "K istorii Oruzheinoi palaty Moskovskogo Kremlia" (pp. 507–60), and another by N. E. Mnevaia on the icon painters who worked in the Armory and on the ornamentation of manuscripts and manuscript books (pp. 217–46).

h-153. Smirnova, E. I. "Oruzheinaia palata posle Oktiabria (1917–1924 gg.)." In *Kuranty: Istoriko-kul'turnyi al'manakh,* pp. 280–86. Moscow: "Moskovskii rabochii," 1983. (Lib: DLC; MH)

> A history of the organization of the museum and its fonds after 1917.

h-154. Zaks, A. B. "K istorii Gosudarstvennoi Oruzheinoi palaty (1917–1956 gg.)." In *Ocherki po istorii muzeinogo dela v SSSR,* edited by D. A. Ravikovich et al., vol. 6, pp. 171–89. Moscow, 1968. [Minkul't SSSR; NII muzeevedeniia i okhrany pamiatnikov]

> Written on the basis of archival sources, the article is largely devoted to the history of the founding of the museum and the reorganization of its exhibits, but there is also information on the formation of the collections, and a detailed bibliography.

h-155. Vysotskii, N. G. *Iz istorii Oruzheinoi palaty: (Russkii arkhiv 1915 goda).* Moscow: Sinodal'naia tip., 1916. 28 p.

> The early development of the Armory as a museum is revealed from documents in the archive of the Senate.

h-156. Arsen'ev, Iu. "Istoricheskii ocherk Moskovskoi Oruzheinoi palaty." *Khudozhestvennye sokrovishcha Rossii,* 1902, no. 9–10, pp. 211–17. (Lib: DLC; IU)

> The entire issue of the journal is devoted to the history and exhibits of the Armory.

h-157. Boguslavskii, Gustav Aleksandrovich. "Iz istorii arkhiva Oruzheinoi palaty." *Istoricheskii arkhiv,* 1959, no. 2, pp. 215–25. (Lib: DLC; IU; MH) [in IDC-R-11, 050]

> Describes the history of the Armory archive now in RGADA (B–2) with extensive bibliography.

h-158. Bogatskaia, Irina Andreevna. *Moskovskii Kreml' i ego okrestnosti: Istoriia, drevnosti, relikvii: Akvareli i litografii XIX stoletiia.* Paris: Izd-vo Alen de Gurkiuf, 1994. 153 p. + plates. Preface by I. A. Rodimtseva.

> An album with reproductions of prerevolutionary watercolors and engravings drawn from the museum collections.

h-159. *Moskovskii Kreml': Ukazatel' literatury (1723–1987).* Compiled by O. A. Semianovskaia, O. A. Tsapina, T. B. Vlasov, et al. Edited by N. S. Vladimirskaia, A. A. Klimenko, E. S. Krasovskaia, et al. Moscow: Tip. VASKhNIL, 1989. 143 p. + 6 plates. [Minkul't SSSR; Gosudarstvennye muzei Moskovskogo Kremlia; Tsentral'naia gorodskaia publichnaia biblioteka im. N. A. Nekrasova] (Lib: DDO)

> An extensive bibliography, including prerevolutionary literature, about the Kremlin and its collections. The first part covers imprints regarding the Kremlin as a whole, while the second part lists coverage of separate monuments and museum collections. Includes many related archival inventories and documentary publications.

FINDING AIDS — SPECIALIZED:

h-160. Tutova, Tat'iana Alekseevna. "Iz istorii arkhiva Solovetskogo monastyria." *AE za 1983 god* (1985): 58–67. Part 2: *AE za 1984 god* (1986): 116–27. (Lib: DLC; IU; MH)

h-161. Tutova, Tat'iana Alekseevna. "Kollektsiia gramot iz riznitsy Solovetskogo monastyria: K istorii dokumental'nogo kompleksa." In *Rossiia v X–XVIII vv.: Problemy istorii i istochnikovedeniia: Tezisy dokladov,* vol. 2, pp. 596–600. 1995. (Lib: DLC; MH)

h-162. Popov, Gennadii Viktorovich. "Ornamentatsiia rukopisi 1499 g. iz Moskovskogo Uspenskogo sobora." In *Drevnerusskoe iskusstvo. Rukopisnaia kniga: Sbornik statei,* edited by O. I. Podobedova et al., vol. [1], pp. 226–45. Moscow: "Nauka," 1972. [AN SSSR; IIMK; AK] (Lib: DLC; IU; MH)
Describes the ornamentation on the Gospel of Metropolitan Simon from the State Armory.

h-163. Pisarskaia, Liudmila Vasil'evna; and Ukhova, T. *Litsevaia rukopis' Uspenskogo sobora: Evangelie nachala XV v. iz Uspenskogo sobora Moskovskogo Kremlia/ Manuscript from the Dormition Cathedral: Early 15th century Gospel from the Dormition Cathedral in the Moscow Kremlin.* Leningrad: "Avrora," 1969. 40 p. + plates. "Publikatsiia odnogo pamiatnika," vol. 2. (Lib: DDO; DLC; IU; MH) Text in Russian with English summary.
The album describes the early fifteenth-century illuminated Morozov Gospel from the Kremlin Cathedral of the Dormition, with its particularly valuable framed binding.

h-164. Protas'eva, Tat'iana Nikolaevna; and Postnikova-Loseva, M. M. "Litsevoe Evangelie Uspenskogo sobora kak pamiatnik drevnerusskogo iskusstva pervoi treti XV v." In *Drevnerusskoe iskusstvo XV–nachala XVI vv,* edited by V. N. Lazarev et al., vol. 1, pp. 133–72. Moscow: Izd-vo AN SSSR, 1963. [AN SSSR; In-t istorii iskusstv; Minkul't SSSR] (Lib: IU; MH)
A description of the Morozov Gospel.

h-165. Pavlovich, M. K. "Fond D. I. Uspenskogo v Otdele rukopisnykh, pechatnykh i graficheskikh fondov Muzeev Kremlia." In *Problemy izucheniia pamiatnikov dukhovnoi i material'noi kul'tury: Materialy nauchnoi konferentsii (Moskva, 1989 g.),* vol. 1, pp. 151–58. Moscow, 1992.

h-166. Belanskaia, K. P. "Dvortsovye muzei i khranilishcha XVIII–pervoi poloviny XIX vv." In *Ocherki istorii muzeinogo dela v SSSR,* edited by A. B. Zaks et al., vol. 3, pp. 300–64. Moscow: "Sovetskaia Rossiia," 1961. [Minkul't RSFSR; NII muzeevedeniia]
Recounts the early history of three major museum collections—the Hermitage, the Tsarskoe Selo Arsenal, and the Armory.

Sergievo-Posadskii gosudarstvennyi
istoriko-khudozhestvennyi muzei-zapovednik
[Sergiev Posad State Historico-Art Museum-Preserve]

Agency: Ministerstvo kul'tury RF (Minkul'tury Rossii)
[Ministry of Culture]

Address: 141300, Moskovskaia oblast', g. Sergiev-Posad, Lavra
Telephone: (8-254) 4-13-58; 4-53-50
Transport: suburban train from Iaroslavl Station to Sergiev Posad

Director: Konstantin Vasil'evich Bobkov
Deputy Director for Scientific Work: Tat'iana Nikolaevna Manushina
   (*tel.* [8-254] 4-53-55)

HISTORY:

Sergievskii gosudarstvennyi istoriko-khudozhestvennyi muzei
   [Sergiev State Historico-Art Museum] (1920–1928)
Sergievskii kraevedcheskii muzei
   [Sergiev Regional Studies Museum] (1928–1930)
Muzei narodnykh khudozhestvennykh remesel
   [Museum of Folk Art and Handicrafts] (1939–1941)
Zagorskii istoriko-khudozhestvennyi i antireligioznyi muzei
   [Zagorsk Historico-Art and Antireligious Museum] (1929–1930)
Zagorskii istoriko-khudozhestvennyi muzei
   [Zagorsk Historico-Art Museum] (1930–1940)
Zagorskii gosudarstvennyi istoriko-khudozhestvennyi muzei-zapovednik
   [Zagorsk State Historico-Art Museum-Preserve] (1940–1991)

In April 1920 the Sergiev Historico-Art Museum was established within the territory and compound encompassing the buildings of the Holy Trinity-St. Sergius Monastery (*Sviato-Troitse-Sergieva Lavra*)—the richest monastery in Russia, which was founded in 1345. Initially all of the Lavra collections were nationalized and became part of the museum. In 1919 the rich sacristy collection of the Lavra, with its approximately 2,000 manuscripts (12th–17th cc.), together with the library and other manuscript materials within the territory of the Lavra, including the collections of the Moscow Theological Academy (*Moskovskaia Dukhovnaia Akademiia*—MDA), was organized as the Sergiev Branch of the State Rumiantsev Library and Museum (now RGB—G–1). That arrangement continued for the next decade, and until 1929, some of the manuscripts and books of the Lavra formed a special exhibit within the Sergiev Museum. During 1929–1931, most of the manuscript and archival materials from the Lavra and MDA were transferred to Moscow—many of the manuscript books to what was then the Lenin Library (now RGB—G–1), and the monastery archive to what is now RGADA (B–2).

A Regional Studies Museum, founded in 1929 on the basis of some of the monastic collections and other early native handicrafts, in 1939 was reorganized as a Museum of Folk Art and Handicrafts.

In 1930, Sergiev-Posad was renamed Zagorsk, honoring the Russian revolutionary leader V. M. Zagorskii (1893–1919), and the monastery compound was reorganized as an Historico-Art and Antireligious Museum, after 1930 known simply as the Zagorsk Historico-Art Museum. It was renamed in 1940 the Zagorsk State Historico-Art Museum-Preserve.

In 1991, after the historic name of Sergiev-Posad was restored, the museum-preserve took its present name. Recently, more of the monastery compound has been restored to the Church and MDA, which in earlier decades had only been operating in limited facilities. In 1993, the Trinity-St. Sergius Monastery ensemble was named to the international register of historical sites under UNESCO.

HOLDINGS: full statistics not available
inventories of Church property—9 units (1641–1908)

The museum collections are based on the treasures of the Trinity-St. Sergius Monastery (*Troitse-Sergieva Lavra*), although the largest part of the holdings was removed in the 1920s and early 1930s.

Particularly important among the archival remains are a series of inventories of monastic property from the mid-seventeenth to the early twentieth century, including property endowment registers (*vkladnye knigi*), revenue books (*kormovye knigi*), and descriptive inventories of monastery properties. The earliest existing text is an inventory of all the buildings and properties of the Trinity Monastery in 1641. There are two copies of a 1673 property endowment register, containing information regarding the unique collection of early Russian art (late 14th–mid-17th cc.). There is also a 1735 inventory of property of the churches and sacristy treasury—"Rospisnye knigi ili opis' imushchestva tserkvei i riznoi kazny"—and another 1842 treasury inventory—"Glavnaia riznichnaia opis' sv. Troitskiia Sergieva Lavra ili opisanie tserkovnykh utvarei, oblachenii i drugikh predmetov." There is also a 1908 inventory of the transfer of Church valuables from the sacristy to the custody of the Commission for the Preservation of Monuments of Art and Antiquity of the former Trinity Lavra.

The museum retains a small collection of manuscript books of a religious character. Most important among them are illuminated manuscripts of the sixteenth century, including two Gospels of Deacon Iona Zui and Archimandrite of the Trinity Merkurii Dmitrovets, and also a Book of the Apostles of Moscow Metropolitan Ioasaf. There is also a late fifteenth-century Gospel from the Nikolo-Pesnoshskii Monastery, a 1674 *sinodik* from the Trinity Monastery, and a 1680 monastery *sinodik*, which was copied from a 1575 *sinodik* by order of the boyar B. M. Khitrovo.

A number of documents remain (either in original or copy) that were used for exhibition purposes during the Soviet period, especially for the anti-religious exhibits of the monastery. These include a few charters of privilege addressed to the monastery, including those from as early as the fifteenth century regarding proprietory rights to saltworks and fish products, scattered documents relating to the juridical and economic affairs of the monastery (16th–17th cc.), official extracts from income-expense registers (*prikhodo-raskhodnye knigi*) of the Joseph of Volokolamsk (*Iosifo-Volokolamskii*) Monastery from 1594 regarding peasant disturbances, various eighteenth-century charters of petition involving protests, documents relating to usurious activities of monks and loans to peasants and traders, and petitions to the troops of Stepan Razin. There are some collected materials of Old Believer origin, including an 1884 polemical "History of the Russian Church" and tales of the Murom cycle.

The museum retains some materials collected during expeditions in the 1950s to study popular handicrafts in Central Russia (Vologda, Kostroma, Gor'kii, Tula, and other oblasts), and also conferences appraising the results of those expeditions. There are some materials from expeditions through Moscow Oblast to appraise early centers of ceramic production (1978–1985).

Among graphic materials are original architectural drawings and plans for various buildings within the monastery, along with plans and projects for restoration in various periods. There is a special collection of graphic representations (engravings and lithographs) of the Moscow Kremlin and local life of the people by the Italian artist Francesco Camporesi.

860

The museum photograph archive includes negative and positive prints of photographs of its collections.

Access: Research access requires an official letter from the researcher's sponsoring organization stating the subject and aim of research.

Reference Facilities: There is a catalogue covering the early Rus' manuscript books.

FINDING AIDS — PUBLISHED — GENERAL:

G&K *Spravochnik* (1983), p. 251.

There is no published guide to the archival materials in the museum.

h-169. *Zagorskii muzei-zapovednik: Putevoditel'.* Compiled by T. N. Manushina. Moscow: "Moskovskii rabochii," 1990. 286 p.
>   EARLIER ED.: M., 1968. 168 p. + plates. "Muzei i vystavki Moskvy i Podmoskov'ia." (Lib: MH).

>   The latest in a series of popular guides to the history and collections of the museum, with expanded coverage of the architectural ensemble of the monastery, and artistic treasures retained there, including paintings, graphic works, and decorative arts. But there is no mention of the archival holdings.

h-170. *Gosudarstvennyi istoriko-khudozhestvennyi i bytovoi muzei v g. Sergieve (byvsh. Troitskaia Lavra): K 10-oi godovshchine Oktiabria [Obzor raboty].* Compiled by A. Svirin. Sergiev: Tip. Ivanova, [1927]. 11 p.

>   Provides a chronological description of the development of the museum during the first decade of Soviet power. Includes brief coverage of the monastery collections.

h-171. Popesku, Tamara Aleksandrovna. "Arkhivnye opisi Zagorskogo muzeia-zapovednika kak istochnik po istorii biblioteki Troitse-Sergieva monastyria." In *Vsesoiuznaia konferentsiia-seminar "Arkhivnye fondy khudozhestvennykh muzeev SSSR,"* vol. 1, pp. 146–58. Moscow, 1981.

>   An analysis of inventories of Church property (1641–1908) remaining in the museum.

h-172. Nikolaeva, Tat'iana Vasil'evna. "Sobranie drevnikh rukopisei." In *Troitse-Sergieva Lavra: Khudozhestvennye pamiatniki,* edited by V. V. Kostochkin et al., pp. 167–75. Moscow, 1968. "Pamiatniki drevnego iskusstva." (Lib: DLC; IU; MH)

>   Provides a detailed historical survey of the manuscripts from the Lavra, most of which are now held in the Manuscript Division of RGB (see G–1), with information about those manuscripts that remain in the museum itself (pp. 170–75).

h-173. Klitina, Evgeniia Nikolaevna. "Vkladnye knigi Troitse-Sergieva monastyria." *TODRL* 26 (1971): 287–93. (Lib: DLC; IU; MH) [IDC-in R-11,164]

h-173.1. *Vkladnaia kniga Troitse-Sergieva monastyria.* Edited by T. V. Nikolaeva, T. N. Manushina, and E. N. Klitina. Moscow: "Nauka," 1987. 439 p. (Lib: MH)

>   The scholarly edition of the 1639 and 1673 property donation registers includes a brief introductory description of the texts.

h-174. Klitina, Evgeniia Nikolaevna. "Novye rukopisnye priobreteniia Zagorskogo muzeia-zapovednika." *TODRL* 30 (1976): 339–42. (Lib: DLC; IU; MH) [IDC-R-11, 164]

h-175. *Soobshcheniia Zagorskogo gosudarstvennogo istoriko-khudozhestvennogo muzeia-zapovednika.* [Zagorsk], 1955–1960; 1990–. Irregular. 5 vols. issued through 1995. Compilers and editors vary with each issue. (Lib: DLC; IU; MH[inc])

Vol . 1: *Kratkoe soobshchenie.* Compiled by I. I. Bureichenko, O. A. Beloborodova, L. N. Boiklava, et al. 1955. 27 p.

Vol. 2: *Soobshchenie.* 1958. 119 p. + plates.

Vol. 3: *Posv. pamiati A. Rubleva v sviazi s 600-letiem ego rozhdeniia.* 1960. 231 p. + 110 plates.

[Vol. 4]: *Drevnerusskoe i narodnoe iskusstvo.* Edited by E. S. Smirnova. M.: "Nauka," 1990. 144 p. + plates.

[Vol. 5]: *Sergievo-Posadskii muzei zapovednik.* Compiled and edited by T. N. Manushina. M.: Pik, 1995. 309 p.

> The basic scholarly series issued by the museum. In terms of archival coverage: The first issue contains a detailed history of the museum and its activities based on inventories of the collections. The second issue contains a description of architectural drawings from 1839 (pp. 113–14). The third issue includes an historical survey of the monastery. The fourth issue includes an article on the history of the museum (pp. 3–7), a scholarly description of the 1641 inventory held by the museum, and a survey of sixteenth-century illuminated manuscripts from the museum collections (pp. 83–96). The fifth issue includes a scholarly description of the charters of petition under Tsar Mikhail Fedorovich (1616) and a survey of the autograph documents and compositions by Simon Azar'in (from RGB and GIM).

Gosudarstvennyi istoriko-khudozhestvennyi i literaturnyi muzei-zapovednik "Abramtsevo"
[Abramtsevo State Historico-Art and Literary Museum-Preserve]

Agency: Ministerstvo kul'tury RF (Minkul'tury Rossii)
[Ministry of Culture]

Address: 141352, Moskovskaia oblast', Sergievo-Posadskii raion, platforma Abramtsevo
Telephone: (8-254) 3-06-68
Transport: suburban train from Iaroslavl Station to Abramtsevo

Director: Ivan Alekseevich Rybakov (*tel.* [8-254] 3-02-78)

HISTORY:

The museum was founded in 1918 on the nationalized estate, which until 1870 had belonged to S. T. Aksakov and his family, and later to the well-known Russian patron of the arts, S. I. Mamontov. During the 1950s and 1960s the museum was under the jurisdiction of the Institute of the History of Art of the Academy of Sciences of the USSR.

HOLDINGS: 3 fonds, 1,605 units, 1768–1950s
photographs—3,381 (1860–1950s)

The manuscript materials of the museum contain documents from the Aksakov family, including personal papers of the Russian writer, S. T. Aksakov (1791–1859) and his sons, K. S. Aksakov (1817–1860) and I. S. Aksakov (1823–1886), who were well-known Slavophiles and public figures. The Aksakov family documents form what is called the Aksakov Fond. Here also are records of the activities of the Abramtsevo Art Circle (*Abramtsevskii khudozhestvennyi kruzhok*).

There is also a special Mamontov Collection which reflects the activities of the Mamontov Art Circle, the Russian Private Opera Theater—"*Russkaia chastnaia opera*" (1885–1904), and the Abramtsevo Carpenter's Workshop (from 1882), which was run by E. D. Polenova. The Mamontov Collection also contains the texts of Mamontov's plays and his correspondence with his wife and such famous artists of the time as M. M. Antokol'skii, V. M. Vasnetsov, M. A. Vrubel', K. A. Korovin, and I. E. Repin.

The collection devoted to the history of the Abramtsevo Estate contains the earliest document, namely a land-survey register (*Mezhevaia kniga*) of the village of Abramtsevo (1768), as well as documentation regarding the proprietors and the plans of the estate.

The museum photographic collection includes portraits of the Aksakov, Mamontov, and Pakhov families, and their relatives and close friends. There are also photographs of performers in the Russian Private Opera Theater, artists of the Abramtsevo Circle, and scenes from the plays and theater productions of the Mamontov Circle and domestic theaters.

The museum archive contains administrative records of the museum from the time of its founding.

Access: A letter from the researcher's sponsoring organization is required.

Comment: No response to the Rosarkhiv questionnaire was received.

FINDING AIDS — PUBLISHED — GENERAL:

GAF Spravochnik (1991), pp. 128–29.

There is no published guide to the archival materials in the museum.

h-176. Nikolaev, A. "Dve zhizni starogo doma." *Smena*, 1977, no. 5, pp. 12–17. (Lib: DLC; IU; MH)

>A popular essay with historical information about the museum.

Gosudarstvennyi khudozhestvennyi istoriko-arkhitekturnyi i prirodno-landshaftnyi muzei-zapovednik "Kolomenskoe" (Muzei-zapovednik "Kolomenskoe")
[Kolomenskoe State Art Historico-Architectural and Natural Landscape Museum-Preserve]

Agency: Ministerstvo kul'tury RF (Minkul'tury Rossii)
[Ministry of Culture]
Komitet po kul'ture Pravitel'stva Moskvy
[Committee on Culture of the Government of Moscow]

Address:	115487, Moscow, prosp. Iu. V. Andropova, 39
Telephone:	112-52-28, 112-21-79; *Fax:* (095) 112-04-14, 112-21-79
E-mail:	kolomen@museum.ru
Website:	http://www.museum.ru/kolomen
Transport:	metro: Kolomenskaia
Hours:	Tu–Th 9:30–18:00

Director: Liudmila Petrovna Kolesnikova (*tel.* 112-52-17, 112-54-74)
Head Curator: Vladimir Egorovich Suzdalev (*tel.* 112-52-28)

HISTORY:

Usad'ba Kolomenskoe—Filial Rossiiskogo Istoricheskogo muzeia
[Kolomenskoe Estate—Branch of the Russian Historical Museum] (1923–1926)
Muzei arkhitekturnykh pamiatnikov Kolomenskogo
[Museum of Kolomenskoe Architectural Monuments] (1926–1966)
Gosudarstvennyi muzei-zapovednik "Kolomenskoe"—Filial Gosudarstvennogo Istoricheskogo muzeia
[Kolomenskoe State Museum-Preserve—Branch of the State Historical Museum] (1966–1971)
Gosudarstvennyi muzei-zapovednik "Kolomenskoe"
[Kolomenskoe State Museum-Preserve] (1971–1974)
Istoriko-arkhitekturnyi gosudarstvennyi muzei-zapovednik "Kolomenskoe"
[Kolomenskoe State Historico-Architectural Museum-Preserve] (1974–1987)

The museum is located on the grounds of the seventeenth-century tsarist palace, overlooking the Moscow River in the village of D'iakovo, which had been the patrimony of Muscovite princes and tsars since the fourteenth century. It was opened in 1923 as a branch of the Historical Museum (H–1), and until 1924 was part of a group of museums controlled by the Pokrovskii (St. Basil's) Cathedral Museum (H–3). In 1926 it became independent and was renamed the Museum of Kolomenskoe Architectural Monuments. In 1928 it was again taken over by the State Historical Museum (GIM), first as a division and subsequently as a branch. In 1966 it was reorganized as the Kolomenskoe State Museum-Preserve (*Gosudarstvennyi muzei-zapovednik "Kolomenskoe"*), but remained a branch of GIM. In 1971 it was again given independent status, and in 1974 when the Kolomenskoe estate was declared a state historico-architectural preserve, the museum was renamed the Kolomenskoe State Historico-Architectural Museum-Preserve (*Istoriko-arkhitekturnyi gosudarstvennyi muzei-zapovednik "Kolomenskoe"*). The present name dates from 1987.

Access: A letter from the researcher's sponsoring organization is required for research access.

Working Conditions: Researchers are received in museum offices.

Copying: Copies may be made on receipt of a guaranteeing letter from the sponsoring organization or on the personal application of the researcher.

Fond redkoi, staropechatnoi i rukopisnoi knigi
[Fond of Rare, Early Printed, and Manuscript Books]

Telephone: 112-11-35
Head: Elena Aleksandrovna Verkhovskaia (*tel.* 115-72-83)

HOLDINGS: ca. 2,000 (ca. 1,000 units unarranged) units, 1615–1924

The museum fond, which was formed in 1924, contains rare early printed and manuscript books, including illustrated *sinodiki* (17th–19th cc.), parish registers, marriage certificates (*brachnye obyski*), and church circulars about parishioners.

The museum holds documentation from several monasteries, including the Nikolo-Ugreshskii Monastery and Nikolo-Perervinskii Monastery, and from village churches. The earliest documents in the collection are early seventeenth-century scrolls recording economic activities in the villages of Kolomenskoe and D'iakovo.

Reference Facilities: There are inventories of the archival materials and a card catalogue.

Nauchnaia biblioteka i arkhiv
[Scientific Library and Archive]

Head: Vladislav Isaevich Stupaev (*tel.* 112-11-35)
Head of Archive: Irina Nikolaevna Sharikova (*tel.* 112-80-74)

HOLDINGS: 778 units, 1921–1991

The museum archive contains documentation on the establishment of the museum and on the organization and content of its collections. There are materials relating to the monuments and exhibits and to archeological surveys on the grounds of the museum, and excerpts from archival documents.

Reference Facilities: There are inventory *opisi* covering the archival documents.

Fototeka
[Photograph Archive]

Head: Liubov' Petrovna Savost'ianova (*tel.* 112-80-74)

HOLDINGS: 14,746 units, 1930–1990

Photographs from 1930 through the 1950s illustrate the acquisition of museum collections, and include pictures of practically all of the museum exhibits.

Photographs taken in recent years show the restoration work carried out on the grounds of the museum-preserve and the museum exhibits.

FINDING AIDS — PUBLISHED — GENERAL:

Muzei Moskvy (1997), pp. 175–79; *GAF Spravochnik* (1991), pp. 129–30.

There is no published guide to the archival materials in the museum.

h-176A. *Zapovednoe Kolomenskoe.* Compiled by M. N, Il'ina et al. Edited by V. E. Sokolov et al. Moscow, 1996. 41 p. [Sovet po izucheniiu i okhrane kul'turnogo i prirodnogo naslediia pri Prezidiume RAN] (Lib: MH)

> A brief tourist pamphlet with details about history and natural setting of the estate and a brief bibliography.

h-176B. Gra, Margarita Armanovna; and Zhiromskii, Boris Borisovich. *Kolomenskoe. Kolomenskoye. Kolomenskoie. Kolomenskoje: Kratkii ocherk.* Moscow: "Iskusstvo," 1971. 159 p. + plates. Photographs by D. Belous. Title, summaries, and lists of illustrations also in English, French, and German. (Lib: DDO; MH)

h-176B.1. Gra, Margarita Armanovna. *Kolomenskoe.* [Moscow]: "Moskovskii rabochii," 1963. 88 p. "Po muzeiam i vystavkam Moskvy i Podmoskov'ia." (Lib: MH)

> A popular, illustrated tourist guide about the estate and museum.

h-176C. *Kolomenskoye: Museum of History, Art and Architecture.* Compiled by Henrietta Gamaleya. Edited by Iulia Cheniakovskaia. Photographs by Roman Boniaminson. Translated by Liudmila (Ludmilla) Lezhneva. Leningrad: Aurora, 1986. 32 p. + plates. (Lib: MH)

> An English-language history of the estate and description of the museum exhibits. Includes an appended biographical summary of craftsmen working in Kolomenskoe in the seventeenth century.

h-176D. *Kolomenskoe: Materialy i issledovaniia.* Moscow, 1991–. 6 issues through 1996.

> A serial with scholarly articles about the estate and its history, many of them based on the museum collections.

Gosudarstvennyi muzei keramiki i "Usad'ba Kuskovo XVIII veka" (GMK i "Usad'ba Kuskovo XVIII veka")

[State Museum of Ceramics and the Kuskovo Estate of the Eighteenth Century]

Agency: Komitet po kul'ture Pravitel'stva Moskvy
[Committee on Culture of the Government of Moscow]

Address: 111402, Moscow, ul. Iunosti, 2
Telephone: 370-01-50; *Fax:* (095) 918-65-40
Transport: metro: Riazanskii prosp.; bus: 133, 208
Hours: W–Sa 10:00–16:00; April–October: 10:00–18:00
(research—by appointment)

Director: Elena Sergeevna Eritsian (*tel.* 370-01-50)
Scientific Secretary: Liudmila Petrovna Sinel'nikova (*tel.* 370-01-01)
Head Curator: Irina Vladimirovna Polozova (*tel.* 374-80-91)
Head of "Estate" Division: Liudmila Venad'evna Siagaeva (*tel.* 370-01-10)
Curator of the Fond of Rare Books and Rare Documents: Tat'iana Rashidovna Panova
(*tel.* 374-80-91)

HISTORY:

Muzei-usad'ba "Kuskovo"
[Kuskovo Estate Museum] (1918–1938)
Muzei farfora
[Porcelain Museum] (1918–1932)

The museum was founded in 1918 on a country estate, which had belonged to the Counts Sheremetev since the beginning of the seventeenth century and which was nationalized in 1917. The palace was built between 1740 and 1770 by the serf architects F. S. Argunov and M. F. Mironov and others. In 1932 the Ceramics Museum, which had been founded as part of the Kremlin museum complex in 1918 on the basis of nationalized private collections (those of A. V. Morozov and I. K. Zubalov, among others), was transferred there from Moscow and the two museums were combined. The present name of the museum dates from 1938.

In 1979 within the Estate Division of the museum, a fond of rare documents was formed, which was later renamed the Fond of Rare Books and Rare Documents (*Fond redkikh knig i redkikh dokumentov*).

HOLDINGS: 2,027 units, 1712–1990s

rare books—1,464 (1712–1913); rare documents—248 units (1712–1917);
scientific archive—248 units (1930s–1990s)

Archival holdings come under the Estate Division of the museum and form part of the Fond of Rare Books and Rare Documents (*Fond redkikh knig i redkikh dokumentov*). The documentary fond has been formed largely from collections built up by the owners of the Kuskovo Estate—Prince M. M. Golitsyn, Prince A. M. Cherkasskii, and the Counts Sheremetev, and by the estate administration. These include records of the owners and reports of the estate managers, inventories of the property, letters, and receipts. A separate group of documents comprises inventories of the Kuskovo estate compiled in the 1770s and again in 1810 and 1814.

The museum holds a collection of technical drawings, including plans of the estate and its neighboring areas and technical drawings of the facades of the different buildings and palaces. There is also an album of photographs showing the estate as it looked in the nineteenth century.

The rare book fond contains genealogical inscriptions and armorials dating from the end of the eighteenth and early nineteenth centuries, albums, reference books, and other architectural publications (early 19th c.), and works of Russian writers like N. M. Karamzin, M. M. Shcherbatov, and M. V. Lomonosov, and the published writings of Count S. D. Sheremetev (early 20th c.).

The scientific archive of the museum contains research work carried out by its staff and includes methodological studies, texts of lectures and excursions, restoration documents, and photograph albums (1930–1990).

Access: For research access, an official letter is required, to be approved by the museum director and the chief curator.

Reference Facilities: There are *opisi*, as well as inventory and thematic card catalogues.

Library Facilities: The museum has a library for its staff. Conditions of access for researchers are the same as for access to the museum fonds.

FINDING AIDS — PUBLISHED — GENERAL:

Muzei Moskvy (1997), pp. 101–103; *Khudozh. muzei* (1996), pp. 47–48; *GAF Spravochnik* (1991), pp. 120–21.

There is no published guide to the archival materials in the museum.

h-177. Sametskaia, E. B.; and Kleiman, L. G. "Nauchnyi arkhiv muzeia i ego ispol'zovanie v nauchno-issledovatel'skoi i restavratsionnoi rabote." In *Vsesoiuznaia konferentsiia-seminar "Arkhivnye fondy khudozhestvennykh muzeev SSSR,"* vol. 1, pp. 55–74. Moscow, 1981.

> Includes information about the history of the museum as well as a survey of documents in the archive and their acquisition.

Moskovskii muzei-usad'ba "Ostankino"
[Moscow Ostankino Estate Museum]

Agency: Komitet po kul'ture Pravitel'stva Moskvy
[Committee on Culture of the Government of Moscow]

Address: 129515, Moscow, ul. 1-ia Ostankinskaia, 5
Telephone: 283-09-29, 283-46-95; *Fax:* (095) 286-02-88
Website: http://moscow.lvl.ru/culture/museum/ostank/ostank.html
Transport: metro: VDNKh + tram 11or trol. 36, 73; bus: 803
Hours: May–September: W–Su 10:00–17:00

Director: Gennadii Dmitrievich Vdovin (*tel.* 286-02-88)
Chief Curator: Varvara Aleksandrovna Rakina (*tel.* 283-08-35)

HISTORY:

Ostankinskii dvorets-muzei tvorchestva krepostnykh
[Ostankino Palace-Museum of Serf Art] (1918–1991)

The late eighteenth-century architectural ensemble, which was part of the former suburban Moscow estate of the Counts Sheremetev, was established as a museum in 1918. The Fond of Written Sources was given independent status in 1978.

Until 1990 the museum had an affiliated branch—the V. A. Tropinin Museum, but that is now under separate administration (see H–30).

Access: A letter of application from the researcher's sponsoring organization is required for research access.

Library Facilities: There is a library, which is open to researchers who have permission to work in the museum fonds.

Fond pis'mennykh istochnikov
[Fond of Written Sources]

Hours: M–F 11:00–16:00
Head: Liia Aleksandrovna Lepskaia (*tel.* 286-11-47)

HOLDINGS: 1 fond, 2,680 units, 1776–1917
photographs—153; scientific-technical documentation—15,276 units (1860–1930)

This division holds the records of the Estate Office (*votchinnaia kontora*) of the Ostankino estate, which was owned by the Counts Sheremetev, the archive of the Barsukov family, and a collection of graphic materials relating to the Sheremetev estates.

The fond of the Ostankino Estate Office is of particular interest. Among property and household records of the Sheremetev estates are materials relating to the villages of Ostankino and Nikol'skoe and to the villages of Mar'ino and Zakharkovo. There are also documents about preparations for the reception of Emperor Alexander II in 1856, together with police reports and instructions. Documents relating to the property and activities of the Ostankino and Trinity (*Troitskaia*) Churches occupy a considerable part of the fond. These include inventories of church property (from 1776), parish registers, and marriage certificates (*brachnye obyski*). The architectural appearance and decor of the

Ostankino Palace Theater and the changes that took place in its original appearance are recorded in nineteenth-century inventories of movable property and real estate, which are also held in this fond.

The Barsukov family fond includes documents from the years 1886–1917, i.e., for the period in which the eight-volume work entitled "The Sheremetev Family" by N. P. Barsukov was being prepared for publication.

Graphic materials include photographs and architectural drawings of various buildings on the Ostankino estate and of other palace and park ensembles in the environs of Moscow and in Leningrad Oblast. Photographs in the museum largely consist of pictures of the Sheremetevs properties—the Ostankino Palace (1863), the Ostankino Church, the palace on the Fontanka (*Fontannyi dom*) in St. Petersburg, and the villages of Mikhailovskoe and Astaf'evo, as well as portraits of S. D. and A. D. Sheremetev.

Architectural drawings are preserved of the Ostankino Palace and its surroundings, the Trinity Church, and other properties of the Counts Sheremetev (18th–19th cc.). There are also drawings of various buildings on the estates and in other park-palace preserves such as Arkhangel'skoe, Peterhof, Pavlovsk, and Astaf'evo, together with plans of Moscow for the years 1786 and 1796.

Working Conditions: Researchers are accomodated in one of the museum offices.

Reference Facilities: There are inventories and thematic card catalogues.

Copying: The museum does not produce copies of its documents, because it has exclusive rights to their use. But in exceptional circumstances researchers may use their own equipment, for which advance permission from the museum director is required.

FINDING AIDS — PUBLISHED — GENERAL:

Muzei Moskvy (1997), pp. 155–59; Khudozh. muzei (1996), pp. 48–49; GAF Spravochnik (1991), pp. 121–23.

There is no published guide to the archival materials in the museum.

h-178. *Novye materialy po istorii russkoi kul'tury: Sbornik trudov.* Edited by
G. D. Kropivnitskaia. Moscow, 1987. 223 p. [Minkul't SSSR; GTsTM im. A. A.
Bakhrushina; Ostankinskii dvorets-muzei tvorchestva krepostnykh] (Lib: DLC; IU; MH)
> A collection of scholarly articles about the Ostankino Palace-Museum, including coverage of the history of the building, the theater, and collections, together with related bibliography.

h-179. *Ostankino.* Moscow, 1996. 44 p. [Sovet po izucheniiu i okhrane kul'turnogo i prirodnogo naslediia pri Prezidiume RAN]. "Prirodnoe i kul'turnoe nasledie Moskvy." (Lib: MH-F)
> The most recent tourist brochure on the Ostankino Palace-Museum, including coverage of the history of the estate, the theater, and collections.

h-180. *Ostankinskii dvorets-muzei tvorchestva krepostnykh.* Compiled by L. A. Lepskaia et al. Photographs by E. K. Dmitrieva. Leningrad: "Khudozhnik RSFSR," 1982. 184 p. + plates. Added title page and summary in English: *The Ostankino Palace-Museum.* (Lib: MH-F)
> A nicely illustrated tourist album on the Ostankino Palace-Museum, with a brief historical introduction.

h-181. Semionova, Irina. *Ostankino: Eighteenth-Century Country Estate.* Compiled by Irina Semionova. Translated from the Russian by Vladimir Friedman. Photography by Alexei Alexandrov and Eduard Steinert. Leningrad: Aurora Art Publishers, 1981. [16] p. + [128] plates. "Art museums in the environs of Moscow." (Lib: MH-F)
> A beautifully illustrated short English-language album on the Ostankino Palace-Museum, with a brief historical introduction.

Art Museums

✦ H–23 ✦

Gosudarstvennaia Tret'iakovskaia galereia (GTG)
[State Tret'iakov Gallery]

Agency: Ministerstvo kul'tury RF (Minkul'tury Rossii)
[Ministry of Culture]

Address: 109017, Moscow, Lavrushinskii per., 10
Telephone: 953-14-16, 231-36-66; *Fax:* (095) 953-10-51
Website: http://www.tretyakov.ru;
http://moscow.lvl.ru/culture/museum/tretyak/etretyak.html;
http://sunsite.cs.msu.su/moscow/tretyakov/tretyakov.html
Transport: metro: Tret'iakovskaia, Novokuznetskaia, Polianka
Hours: Tu–F 10:00–19:00

Director: Valentin Alekseevich Rodionov (*tel.* 953-14-16)
Deputy Director for Scientific Work: Lidiia Ivanovna Iovleva (*tel.* 959-97-05)
Scientific Secretary: Vitol'd Mikhailovich Petiushenko (*tel.* 231-87-64)

HISTORY:
Moskovskaia gorodskaia khudozhestvennaia galereia P. M. i S. M. Tret'iakovykh
[P. M. and S. M. Tret'iakov Moscow Municipal Art Gallery] (1892–1918)
Gosudarstvennaia Tret'iakovskaia galereia
[State Tret'iakov Gallery] (1918–1986)
Vsesoiuznoe muzeinoe ob"edinenie "Gosudarstvennaia Tret'iakovskaia galereia"
[All-Union State Tret'iakov Gallery Museum Association] (1986–1992)
Vserossiiskoe muzeinoe ob"edinenie "Gosudarstvennaia Tret'iakovskaia galereia"
[All-Russian State Tret'iakov Gallery Museum Association] (1992)

The gallery was formed in 1856 from the private collection of Pavel Mikhailovich Tret'iakov (1832–1899) (often in English, Tretyakov). Together with the collections made by his brother, Sergei Mikhailovich, the gallery was donated to the City of Moscow in 1892 and, until nationalization in 1918, was called the P. M. and S. M. Tret'iakov Moscow Municipal Art Gallery (*Moskovskaia gorodskaia khudozhestvennaia galereia P. M. i S. M. Tret'iakovykh*). It was housed in the restructured Tret'iakov House and in a number of adjacent buildings of the same period. The main facade was built in 1902 according to a design by the artist V. M. Vasnetsov.

Most recently in the process of major reconstruction of the museum corpus (1985–1994), the premises on Lavrushinskii pereulok have been significantly enlarged and modernized with a new building on the corner of Kadashevskaia Embankment. The additional buildings on Krymskii Val are still in the process of reconstruction, and hence some of the divisions described below may be subject to transfer to different addresses. Although usually known as the State Tret'iakov Gallery, for some official purposes, since 1986 it has also been known as the All-Union, and since 1992, the All-Russian State Tret'iakov Gallery Museum Association (*Vserossiiskoe muzeinoe ob"edinenie "Gosudarstvennaia Tret'iakovskaia galereia"*). In 1991 the museum was added to the federal register of the most valuable monuments of the cultural heritage of the peoples of the Russian Federation.

The library was donated to the Gallery Council after Tret'iakov's death in 1899. The photograph archive was begun in 1913, when I. E. Grabar' laid the foundations for scholarly work, making the gallery function as a museum.

Some years after the museum collections had been nationalized, the manuscript documents, consisting largely of original letters from Pavel Mikhailovich Tret'iakov, were assigned to a separate Archive Division (1922). This Archive Division also received manuscript materials from numerous private collections. In 1941 more than 33,000 archival units that had been acquired by this division were transferred to the newly formed Central State Literary Archive—TsGLA, which is now known as the Russian State Archive of Literature and Art—RGALI (B–7). Those that remained, together with others acquired later from other sources, now comprise the Manuscript Division.

The Drawings Division (now the Division of Graphic Arts) was formed in 1924 at the initiative of the art specialist A. V. Bakushanskii. After the Second World War it was closed down but later reconstituted during the 1950s.

The museum has five affiliated branches honoring individual artists, which are administered as part of the Division for the Study of Creative Work (*Otdel po issledovaniiu tvorchestva*), each bearing the name of the individual honored. All of them hold some archival documents, including photographs. (Basic coordinates about all of the branches are given on the main GTG website— http://www.tretyakov.ru).

(1) The Studio-Museum of the Sculptress A. S. Golubkina (H–24).

(2) The House-Museum of the Artist V. M. Vasnetsov (H–25).

(3) The Memorial Apartment-Museum of the Painter A. M. Vasnetsov (*Memorial'nyi muzei-kvartira akademika zhivopisi A. M. Vasnetsova*), founded in 1965 as a branch of the Museum of the History of Moscow (see H–5), is located in the house where Apollinarii Mikhailovich Vasnetsov (1856–1933) lived from 1903 until his death. After renovation and expansion, it reopened in 1984, and is now a branch of the Tret'iakov Gallery, with some documentation (including copies) relating to Vasnetsov's artistic and scholarly activities. (103064, Moscow, Furmannyi per., 6, kv. 22; tel. 917-51-35).

(4) The Apartment-Museum of the Artist P. D. Korin (*Muzei-kvartira khudozhnika P. D. Korina*) opened in 1968 in a building where the Russian painter Pavel Dmitrievich Korin (1892–1967) lived and worked for many years. There are many photographs and some correspondence, but the latter has not yet been processed. (119435, Moscow, ul. Malaia Pirogovskaia, 16, fligel' 2; tel. 245-11-90).

(5) The N. S. Goncharova and M. F. Larionov Apartment-Museum (*Muzei-kvartira N. S. Goncharovoi i M. F. Larionova*), honoring the Russian artists Nataliia Sergeevna Goncharova (1861–1962) and Mikhail Fedorovich Larionov (1881–1964), is being organized in the apartment where they lived before their emigration to France. The museum, which possesses numerous archival materials, is expected to open later in 1999. (Moscow, Trekhprudnyi per., 2a, stroenie 2, kv. 3; tel. 209-92-79).

N.B. A large part of the records of the Tret'iakov Gallery itself have been systematically transferred to the Central State Archive of Literature and Art (TsGALI), now RGALI (B–7; fond 343, 1883–1917; fond 990, 1918–).

Access: Access to archival materials requires a letter from the researcher's sponsoring organization, which must be endorsed by the Deputy Director for Scientific Work and the Scientific Secretary. Documents may be temporarily unobtainable, if the museum is conducting research connected with the materials.

Library Facilities: There is a small reference library, as described under "Nauchnaia biblioteka" below.

Copying: Xerox and photographic copying facilities are available.

Otdel rukopisei (OR)
[Division of Manuscripts]

Address: 109017, Moscow, Lavrushinskii per., 4, stroenie 1
Hours: TuTh 10:00–17:00
Transport: metro: Tret'iakovskaia, Novokuznetskaia
Head: Tamara Isakovna Kaftanova (*tel.* 953-28-98)

HOLDINGS: 190 (17 fonds unarranged) fonds, 114,967 units, 1793–1992
  photographs—ca. 9,000

The Division of Manuscripts retains the museum documentary collections, part of the museum archive, and the fonds of various artistic societies. The pre-Soviet period is represented by the fonds of the "Peredvizhniki," or Association of Itinerant Art Exhibitions (*Tovarishchestvo peredvizhnykh khudozhestvennykh vystavok*) (1869–1897), the *Sreda* Arts Society, and the Union of Russian Artists (*Soiuz russkikh khudozhnikov*).

Postrevolutionary fonds include records from the Association of Artists of Revolutionary Russia (*Assotsiatsiia khudozhnikov revoliutsionnoi Rossii*—AKhRR) (1922–1932), the Society of Realist Painters (*Obshchestvo khudozhnikov-realistov*), and the Moscow Union of Soviet Artists (*Moskovskii soiuz sovetskikh khudozhnikov*).

The museum has built up a number of important fonds of personal papers from both prerevolutionary and Soviet artists, as well as from art collectors and art specialists. One of the most significant is the fond of the Gallery founder, Pavel Mikhailovich Tret'iakov, which was purchased in 1937 from A. P. Botkina, and which contains a large amount of correspondence relating to the acquisition of the museum art collections. Many famous artists corresponded with Tret'iakov, as did such famous personages of Russian nineteenth-century literature and the arts as F. M. Dostoevskii, P. I. Tchaikovsky (Chaikovskii), and V. V. Stasov. There are also the fonds of the collectors A. P. Botkina-Tret'iakova, A. P. Langovoi, and M. P. Riabushinskii.

Personal papers of Russian artists are for the most part represented by documents relating to artists of the *peredvizhniki* movement (A. M. and V. M. Vasnetsov, I. I. Levitan, M. V. Nesterov, V. D. Polenov, I. E. Repin, V. A. Serov, K. A. Savitskii, V. I. Surikov, and N. A. Iaroshenko, among others) and to members of the Abramtsevo Circle (M. A. Vrubel' and K. A. Korovin). There are also personal papers of such Soviet artists as I. E. Grabar', P. N. Filonov, and K. F. Iuon, as well as of art specialists, directors, and staff of the State Tret'iakov Gallery (V. N. Vlasov, N. G. Mashkovtsev, and P. I. Neradovskii).

The division holds a collection of autographs of Russian artists collected by I. A. Polonskii (1890–1895).

There is a special fond for documentation relating to the State Tret'iakov Gallery, containing documents from the years 1893–1918. The later administrative documentation of the museum is arranged as a separate fond. It includes a large collection of questionnaires with biographical data on artists (1923–1953), which was begun by A. V. Grigor'ev.

The Manuscript Division also contains photographic portraits of artists, collectors, and other persons prominent in the world of national culture, together with photographs of paintings and other works of art, but most of the photographic documents have been assigned to the separate Photograph Archive (see below).

Reference Facilities: There are inventory *opisi*, to each of which is attached a survey description of the documents in the fond, which was prepared for a still unpublished guide to the Manuscript Division (see h-190). There are also catalogues of personal names.

Otdel grafiki
[Division of Graphic Arts]

Address: 117049, Moscow, ul. Krymskii val., 10
Telephone: 959-77-66
Hours: by appointment
Head: Natal'ia L'vovna Adavkina (*tel.* 959-77-66)

HOLDINGS: over 40,000 units, 18th c.–to present

The Division of Graphic Arts is the largest section, quantitatively speaking, of the entire GTG collections, containing drawings in pencil, charcoal, various types of ink, as well as watercolors, pastels, and engravings. Of particular importance is the collection of portrait miniatures, some on parchment, others on pasteboard. There is also a small collection of posters and ex libris. Strictly speaking, most of the holdings of this division are considered art, rather than archival materials, and hence a survey is not provided here.

Reference Facilities: There are reference card catalogues.

Fototeka
[Photograph Archive]

Address: 117049, Moscow, ul. Krymskii val, 10
Telephone: 223-22-74
Hours: TuTh 10:00–17:00
Transport: metro: Oktiabr'skaia, Park Kul'tury
Head: Nadezhda Vladimirovna Okurenkova (*tel.* 233-22-74)

HOLDINGS: photographs and negatives—427,000 (late 19th–early 20th cc.)

This division holds photographs, negatives, photograph albums, and slides of Russian and foreign pictorial art. The systematic photographing of works in the gallery collections was done by Moscow's finest photographers—A. V. Liadov, Iu. I. Lepkovskii, and I. N. Aleksandrov. The collection has been supplemented through the acquisition of negatives from institutions and private individuals. Thus the collection includes photographs of the work of more than 1,000 Russian and more than 2,000 Soviet painters and graphic artists, covering all of the collections in the museum as well as others.

There is a special group of photographs devoted to the history of the gallery, making it possible to recreate fully the appearance of the halls and their exhibits during various periods.

Some of the photographs represent holdings in other major art collections, like those of the former Rumiantsev Museum, the I. S. Ostroukhov Gallery (Museum of Painting and Icon Painting), and the Tsvetkov Gallery.

An important section of the Photograph Archive is devoted to photographs of buildings and houses of architectural interest in Moscow, St. Petersburg, and other cities and towns in Russia, taken between 1900 and 1917.

Working Conditions: Researchers are accommodated in working offices.

Reference Facilities: There are inventories of accessions and a card catalogue of negatives.

Copying: Photographic copies from negatives may be ordered in the photographic laboratory.

Nauchnaia biblioteka
[Scientific Library]

Address: 113184, Moscow, 1-i Kadashevskii per., 14
Telephone: 953-44-33
Hours: MTuTh 10:00–16:30, F 10:00–15:00
Transport: metro: Tret'iakovskaia, Novokuznetskaia
Head: Zoia Pavlovna Shergina (*tel.* 953-41-85)

HOLDINGS: MS books—12 units (late 11th–19th cc.)

The basic collection of rare books and manuscripts in the library came from P. M. Tret'iakov's personal library. These include early manuscripts of a mainly religious character—Gospels, liturgical books, and Psalters (13th–19th cc.), most of them with miniatures and illuminations. One unique exhibit is a choral manuscript with musical notation, known as the "Tipografskii ustav" (late 11th–early 12th cc.), with marginal drawings from daily life.

The library also has an extensive collection (over 1,000 volumes) of printed books on prerevolutionary Russian, Soviet, and foreign art with dedicatory inscriptions by the artists and art experts who presented them.

Working Conditions: Researchers working with manuscripts are accommodated in staff work rooms.

Reference Facilities: There are no scholarly descriptions of the manuscript books; they are described only according to library standards. The introduction of a computerized reference system is planned.

Copying: In exceptional circumstances manuscripts may be photographed, but only without flash or auxiliary lighting.

FINDING AIDS — PUBLISHED — GENERAL:

Muzei Moskvy (1997), pp. 81–84; *Khudozh. muzei* (1996), pp. 50–51; *GAF Spravochnik* (1991), pp. 41–47; *PKG M&L* (1972), p. 292.

h-185. *Gosudarstvennaia Tret'iakovskaia galereia: Istoriia i kollektsii.* Edited by Ia. V. Bruk et al. 4th ed. Moscow: "Iskusstvo," 1989. 447 p.

> 3d ED.: M., 1988. 445 p. (Lib: IU)
> 2d ED.: M., 1987. 444 p. (Lib: DLC)
> 1st ED.: M., 1986. 448 p. (Lib: MH)
>> A beautifully illustrated collection of articles including a history of the gallery (pp. 30–61) with extensive bibliography (pp. 444–45). The Manuscript Division is described by N. L. Priimak (pp. 422–25). There is a survey of the library by A. I. Bolotova (pp. 426–42) and an article on the Photograph Archive by N. V. Okurenkova (pp. 423–33). Several facsimile editions of this work have appeared.

h-186. *Sto let Tret'iakovskoi galerei: Sbornik statei.* Edited by P. I. Lebedev. Moscow: "Iskusstvo," 1959. 340 p. (Lib: DLC; IU; MH)
> This collection includes a short historical account of the Tret'iakov Gallery (pp. 9–47); a survey of the Scientific Library, 1899–1956 (pp. 252–62); a detailed description of the Manuscript Division (pp. 299–334) (see h-186.1) and the Photograph Archive (pp. 335–39); and a bibliographic survey (pp. 263–98).

h-186.1. Galkina, L. G.; and Grigor'eva, M. N. "Otdel rukopisei Tret'iakovskoi galerei: Kratkii ocherk." In *Sto let Tret'iakovskoi galerei: Sbornik statei,* edited by P. I. Lebedev, pp. 299–334. Moscow: "Iskusstvo," 1959. (Lib: DLC; IU; MH)
> Provides brief data on 100 of the archival fonds in the Manuscript Division, indicating the fond number, the quantity of storage units, the inclusive dates of documents, and a brief annotation of the composition and content of the documents and related finding aids.

h-188. *Gosudarstvennaia Tret'iakovskaia galereia: Ocherki istorii, 1856–1917. K 125-letiiu osnovaniia Tret'iakovskoi galerei.* Edited by Ia. V. Bruk. Leningrad: "Khudozhnik RSFSR," 1981. 351 p. (Lib: DLC; IU; MH)

> Published to mark the 125th anniversary of the founding of the Tret'iakov Gallery, the book is entirely devoted to the prerevolutionary history of the gallery, prefaced with a survey of art collecting in Russia before P. M. Tret'iakov.

h-188A. Nenarokomova, Irina Sergeevna. *Pavel Tret'iakov i ego galereia.* Moscow: Galart, 1994. 287 p. + plates. (Lib: MH)

> A study of the founder of the Tret'iakov Gallery, Pavel Mikhailovich Tret'iakov (1832–1899), and his art collecting.

h-189. Priimak, Natal'ia L'vovna. *Dokumenty po istorii otechestvennogo izobrazitel'nogo iskusstva v sobranii Otdela rukopisei Gosudarstvennoi Tret'iakovskoi galerei. (Istoriia sobraniia: Problemy komplektovaniia i ispol'zovaniia), 1918–1985 gg.: Avtoreferat dissertatsii na soiskanie uchenoi stepeni kandidata istoricheskikh nauk.* Moscow: MGIAI, 1986. 25 p. [Minvuz RSFSR; MGIAI]

> The dissertation discusses the work of the Manuscript Division, which before the formation of the Central State Literary Archive—TsGLA (now RGALI—B–7) in 1941, was the leading archive in the country for documentary materials on the history of Russian art and culture. The dissertation itself is available in the Historico-Archival Institute (IAI) of RGGU.

FINDING AIDS — GENERAL — UNPUBLISHED:

h-190. ***"Putevoditel' po Otdelu rukopisei Gosudarstvennoi Tret'iakovskoi galerei." Moscow, 1987. Typescript.

> Prepared for publication as a continuation and expansion of the 1959 directory (see h-186.1), the guide is not yet available for researchers. Annotations of individual fonds prepared for this guide, however, are attached to *opisi* in the Manuscript Division.

FINDING AIDS — SPECIALIZED:

> For coverage of Jewish-related holdings, see *Jewish Doc.* (1996), pp. 11–12, and *Dok. ist. evreev* (1997), p. 414. Fonds of personal papers of Russian émigrés held by GTG, most of which have been declassified recently, are listed in *Rus. Zarubezh'e* (1998), pp. 346–47.

h-191. *Sovetskaia grafika.* Edited by E. B. Loginova. Moscow: "Sovetskii khudozhnik," 1973. 152 p. (Lib: IU)

> A catalogue of the works of Soviet graphic art (1920s–1950s) that are held in the gallery.

Muzei-masterskaia skul'ptora A. S. Golubkinoi—
Filial Gosudarstvennoi Tret'iakovskoi galerei (MMG)
[Studio-Museum of the Sculptress A. S. Golubkina—
Branch of the State Tret'iakov Gallery]

Agency: Ministerstvo kul'tury RF (Minkul'tury Rossii)
[Ministry of Culture]

Address: 119094, Moscow, Bol'shoi Levshinskii per. (*formerly* ul. Shchukina), 12
(entrance through the courtyard)
Telephone: 201-56-82; 201-25-64
Website: http://moscow.lvl.ru/culture/museum/mmgolubk/mmgolub.html
Transport: metro: Smolenskaia, Park kul'tury; trol.: 10, B
Hours: WF 12:00–18:00; SaSu 10:00–17:00
(by appointment with Curator of Fonds)

Director: Nelli Aleksandrovna Korovich (*tel.* 201-24-17; 202-13-54)
Curator of Fonds, Division of the Custodian of Fonds: Ninel' Vil'ianovna Ivanova
(*tel.* 201-56-82)

HISTORY:

Memorial'nyi muzei-masterskaia skul'ptora A. S. Golubkinoi
[Memorial Studio-Museum of the Sculptress A. S. Golubkina] (1932–1952)
Muzei-masterskaia skul'ptora A. S. Golubkinoi
[Studio-Museum of the Sculptress A. S. Golubkina] (1976–1988)

The museum was founded in 1932 in what had once been the studio of the eminent Russian sculptress Anna Semenovna Golubkina (1864–1927). The museum holdings consist of the works of the sculptress which were donated to the state by her family. In 1952 the museum was closed and not reopened until 1976, although some of the original collections had by then been transferred to other museums. In 1988 the Studio-Museum became a branch of the State Tret'iakov Gallery (H–23).

HOLDINGS: 2 fonds, 558 units, 1880s–1927

The memorial fond of the sculptress Anna Semenovna Golubkina consists of four sections: letters written by Golubkina; letters written to her; personal papers and official documents; and photographs.

Most of the first section consists of letters from the sculptress to her elder sister and mother written while she was studying in Paris in the studio of the artist and architect Filippo Colarossi and in the workshop of Auguste Rodin. There are also letters from Moscow and Zaraisk to her friend and teacher A. N. Glagolev and his wife, and letters and notes to G. I. Chulkov, I. S. Efimov, and other friends and relatives.

Apart from family correspondence the second section includes letters from people who were prominent in the Russian art world—V. G. Chertkov, I. E. Efimov, and K. S. Shokhor-Trotskii, as well as letters from various organizations and museums, including the L. N. Tolstoi Museum, the Tret'iakov Gallery, and the Board of the Moscow Salon Society of Artists (*Pravlenie obshchestva khudozhnikov "Moskovskii salon"*).

The third section comprises Golubkina's personal documents and recollections (originals and copies) by such people as I. I. Bedniakov, E. M. Glagoleva, M. I. Romm, N. V. Khlebnikova, and V. F. Em.

There are rare photographs of Golubkina in various periods of her life, as well as pictures of her family and friends.

The museum also contains pictorial material illustrating Golubkina's work (portraits, studies, and sketches for sculptures).

Access: Access to archival materials requires a letter from the researcher's sponsoring organization, which must be endorsed by the Deputy Academic Director and the Scientific Secretary of the State Tret'iakov Gallery (H–23).

Reference Facilities: There are various thematic card catalogues.

Library Facilities: The division has a library, the conditions of access to which are the same as for the archival materials.

Copying: Photographic and xerox copies can be ordered through the laboratory at the State Tret'iakov Gallery.

FINDING AIDS — PUBLISHED — GENERAL:

Muzei Moskvy (1997), p. 87; *GAF Spravochnik* (1991), p. 49.

There is no published guide to the archival materials in the museum.

h-200. *Muzei-masterskaia skul'ptora A. S. Golubkinoi (Putevoditel').* Compiled by N. Ia. Zaiger. Moscow: "Sovetskii khudozhnik," 1983. 47 p.

> A short guide to the museum exhibitions, which include original documents and photographs (esp. pp. 44–46).

h-201. *Anna Semenovna Golubkina: (1864–1927).* Edited by O. M. Slavinskii. Moscow: Vserokhudozhnik, 1935. 38 p. + plates. Added title page in French. [Gos. muzei-masterskaia skul'ptora A. S. Golubkinoi] (Lib: MH)

> Provides a chronological list of Golubkina's works which were held in the museum in the 1930s (pp. 19–37).

Dom-muzei khudozhnika V. M. Vasnetsova— Filial Gosudarstvennoi Tret'iakovskoi galerei

[V. M. Vasnetsov House-Museum—Branch of the State Tret'iakov Gallery]

Agency: Ministerstvo kul'tury RF (Minkul'tury Rossii)
[Ministry of Culture]

Address:	129090, Moscow, per. Vasnetsova, 13
Telephone:	281-13-29 *Fax:* (095) 873-28-72
Transport:	metro: Sukharevskaia
Hours:	W–Su 10:00–17:00; by appointment *(for the Fond Depository)*

Head of the Branch: Nina Aleksandrovna Iaroslavtseva (*tel.* 971-28-72)
Head of the Fond Depository: Liudmila Vasil'evna Fedorova (*tel.* 971-28-72)

HISTORY:

The museum was founded in 1953 in the house where the well-known realist painter Viktor Mikhailovich Vasnetsov lived from 1894 to 1926. Initially, the museum was a Branch of the Museum of the History and Reconstruction of Moscow (see H–5), but subsequently became a Branch of the Tret'iakov Gallery. The building was designed by the artist, a member of the "*Peredvizhniki,*" the Association of Itinerant Art Exhibitions (*Tovarishchestvo peredvizhnykh khudozhestvennykh vystavok*).

HOLDINGS: 4,816 units, 1875–1960
photographs—1,246 (1875–1960s)

Archival materials in the museum are held as part of the so-called Fond Depository (*Fondokhranilishche*). Documentary materials include many of Vasnetsov's personal papers and other documentation relating to his life and work. Most of his preserved correspondence was with officials, painters, prominent figures in the arts world, and relatives.

Documentary photographs include pictures of Vasnetsov, members of his family, and some of his works.

The museum also retains its own administrative records, which contain documentation on the organization and administration of the museum since its founding. There are also documents pertaining to the building of the house in which the museum is situated.

Access: A letter is required from the researcher's sponsoring organization, which must be endorsed by the head of the Branch Museum and the director of the State Tret'iakov Gallery (H–23).

Working Conditions: Researchers are received in working offices of the museum.

Reference Facilities: There are archival inventories and card catalogues.

Copying: There are no copying facilities.

FINDING AIDS — PUBLISHED — GENERAL:

Muzei Moskvy (1997), pp. 86; *GAF Spravochnik* (1991), p. 48.

There is no published guide to the archival materials in the museum.

h-205. Chebotareva, N. N. "Dom-muzei V. M. Vasnetsova." In *Khudozhestvennye sokrovishcha muzeev Moskvy,* pp. [9–10], 104–15. Moscow: "Sovetskii khudozhnik," 1978. (Lib: DLC; MH)

> A brief description of the museum, with selected illustrations, but containing no information on the manuscript fond.

Gosudarstvennyi muzei izobrazitel'nykh iskusstv
im. A. S. Pushkina (GMII)

[A. S. Pushkin State Museum of Fine Arts]

Agency: Ministerstvo kul'tury RF (Minkul'tury Rossii)
[Ministry of Culture]

Address: 121019, Moscow, ul. Volkhonka, 12
Telephone: 203-93-76; 263-95-78; *Fax:* (7-095) 203-46-74
E-mail: no@russia.agama.com
Website: http://www.global-one.ru/culture/pushkin;
                http://www.museum.ru/gmii
Transport: metro: Kropotkinskaia
Hours: Tu–F 10:00–18:00

Director: Irina Aleksandrovna Antonova (*tel.* 203-69-74)
Deputy Director for Scientific Work: Irina Evgen'evna Danilova (*tel.* 203-69-07)
Chief Curator: Tat'iana Vladimirovna Potapova (*tel.* 203-92-96)

HISTORY:

Muzei iziashchnykh iskusstv im. Imperatora Aleksandra III pri Moskovskom universitete
     [Emperor Alexander III Museum of Fine Arts at Moscow University] (1912–1917)
Muzei iziashchnykh iskusstv pri Moskovskom universitete
     [Museum of Fine Arts at Moscow University] (1917–1923)
Gosudarstvennyi muzei iziashchnykh iskusstv
     [State Museum of Fine Arts] (1923–1932)
Gosudarstvennyi muzei izobrazitel'nykh iskusstv
     [State Museum of Fine Arts] (1932–1937)

The predecessor of the museum in the mid-nineteenth century was the collection gathered by the Coin Cabinet (*Mintskabinet*, from the German, *Münzkabinett*), which also served as a Fine Arts Exhibit, or Cabinet (*Kabinet iziashchnykh iskusstv*) of Moscow University. The organization of a Museum of Fine Arts and the public fund-raising required was first undertaken by Moscow University Professor I. V. Tsvetaev in the early 1890s and subsequently by the Committee to Found a Museum of Fine Arts (*Komitet po sozdaniiu Muzeia iziashchnykh iskusstv*) (1898–1912). In 1912 the Museum of Fine Arts was opened at Moscow University and given imperial patronage under the name of the Emperor Alexander III Museum of Fine Arts. It was housed in a building specially designed for the museum by the architect R. I. Klein. In the same year the museum library was also founded. An Oriental Division was formed in 1912 on the basis of a collection made by the Egyptologist V. S. Golenishchev, which was acquired as state property in 1909.

In 1917 the imperial name was dropped and the museum holdings were enriched by the nationalized private collections of D. I. Shchukin and the Museum of Antiquities (*Muzei stariny*) of the French perfume manufacturer Henri Brocart (G. I. Brokar) in Moscow, among others, and by collections acquired from the reorganized Rumiantsev Museum, the Hermitage, and various palaces and museums in Petrograd. In 1932 the museum was renamed, and since 1937 it has been known by its present name, honoring Aleksandr Sergeevich Pushkin. In December 1991 it was added to the federal register of the most valuable monuments of the cultural heritage of the peoples of the Russian Federation.

The Division of Graphic Arts dates back to 1862, when an Engraving Office (*Graviurnyi kabinet*), as it was called, was opened in the Rumiantsev Museum on the basis of duplicate fonds taken from the Hermitage. This collection was turned over to the Museum of Fine Arts in 1924.

During the Second World War most of the museum collection was evacuated, and the building suffered bomb damage. At the end of the war the collection of the Dresden Gallery, together with many other "trophy" collections which had been seized by the Soviet Army, including the "Trojan Gold" from Berlin were deposited in the museum. Most of the Dresden collection was returned to the German Democratic Republic in 1955, but some Dresden paintings remain, along with treasures from other museums, such as a large part of the Koenigs Collection from the Netherlands.

In 1948 the chronological extent of the museum collections was significantly broadened with the accession of part of the collection from the Museum of Modern Western Art (*Muzei novogo zapadnogo iskusstva*), which since 1925 had been a branch of the museum.

The Archive and the Reproduction Office were established in 1945.

Access: For research access a letter is required from the researcher's sponsoring organization, together with the permission of the museum directors. Certain materials are closed for various periods of time, according to the wishes of those who established the fonds and the present fond holders.

Library Facilities: There is a library, with the same access rules which pertain to the archival materials. The library holds books on art with dedicatory inscriptions by I. V. Tsvetaev, by art specialists, museum staff, and by other authors.

Copying: Photographic and xerox copies may be ordered with the permission of the museum director. Permission from the museum directors must be obtained, if photocopies are to be published.

Sektor Vostoka
[Oriental Sector]

Telephone: 203-74-93
Head: Svetlana Izmailovna Khodzhash (*tel.* 203-74-93)
Head of Art and Ancient Archeology Division:
   Vladimir Petrovich Tolstikov (*tel.* 203-35-08)

HOLDINGS: 2,785 units, 20th c. B.C.–11th c. A.D.

Earliest among the museum archival holdings are the manuscripts held by the Oriental Sector, which is officially a subdivision of the Division of Art and Archeology of the Ancient World (*podrazdelenie Otdela iskusstv i arkheologii Drevnego mira*). This sector has manuscript texts from Mesopotamia and Ancient Egypt, which include documents from Sumer, Accad, Assyria, Babylon, and Cappadocia. Manuscripts range widely in subject matter from diplomatic correspondence to economic documentation, and there are many religious and literary works in different ancient languages written on papyrus or clay tablets.

The whole collection can be divided according to language groups and types of writing. The first and largest group consists of ancient Egyptian papyri (20th c. B.C.–9th c. A.D.), written in hieratic (the abridged form of hieroglyphics used by priests in their records), semi-hieroglyphics and demotic (cursive writing used from the 4th century B.C.). The earliest ancient Egyptian hieratic manuscripts relate to the period of the Middle Kingdom. A few of the papyri have inscriptions written in Aramaic and ancient Hebrew. A large part of the Egyptian holdings come from the collection of the Russian Egyptologist V. S. Golenishchev.

The second group consists of Coptic texts (3d–7th cc. A.D.), ranging from juridical mansucrits to economic documents, from personal letters to religious and historical texts, some with elaborate miniatures. A third group consists of Hellenistic and Roman papyri with fragments of Greek texts.

A fourth group of Arabic texts (9th–17th cc.) also includes juridical and economic documents, along with medical and religious manuscripts. A fifth group consists of Pahlavi papyri, predominantly of an economic content.

Reference Facilities: There is an inventory register. Part of the manscript collection has been published.

Sektor antichnogo iskusstva i arkheologii
[Sector of Ancient Art and Archeology]

Telephone: 203-35-08
Hours: by appointment
Head: Liudmila Ivanovna Akimova (*tel.* 203-50-53)

HOLDINGS:

The Sector of Ancient Art and Archeology, also part of the Division of Art and Archeology of the Ancient World, retains unpublished field reports and inventories of finds made on archeological expeditions organized by the State Museum of Fine Arts from the 1930s to the present. Expeditions and excavations particularly covered a number of ancient settlements on the Black Sea coast— Charax, Neapolis (Scythia), Panticapaeum, Tiritaka, Phanagoria, and Hermonassa. Expeditions were led by various scholars, including L. P. Kharko, P. N. Shul'ts, V. D. Blavatskii, N. M. Loseva, Iu. E. Chistiakov, N. A. Sidorova, I. D. Marchenko, A. K. Korovina, V. P. Tolstikov, L. I. Akimova, S. I. Finogenov, E. A. Savostina, and O. V. Tugusheva.

N.B. In 1993 part of the material collected by these expeditions was transferred to the museum archive (see below).

Working Conditions: Preliminary arrangements for research must be made with the curator responsible for materials relating to a particular expedition.

Reference Facilities: Materials are arranged by subject and geographically, and many are grouped under the names of leaders of the various expeditions or their successors.

Otdel rukopisei
[Division of Manuscripts]

Hours: TuTh 10:00–16:00
Head: Margarita Borisovna Aksenenko (*tel.* 203-46-42)

HOLDINGS: 61 (6 unarranged) fonds, 37 collections, ca. 60,000 units, 1816–1980s
personal papers—48 fonds; photographs—6,463 (1894–1985); sound recordings—47 (1970s–1980s)

The museum archive, officially a subdivision of the Division of Information (*podrazdelenie Otdela informatsii*) retains the records of a number of state institutions, some private collections, and the personal papers of many important individuals and families in the world of art and culture in both the prerevolutionary and Soviet periods.

There is documentation from other state museums whose holdings were transferred to the museum, such as the Fine Arts Division of the Public Rumiantsev Museum (*Otdelenie iziashchnykh iskusstv Publichnogo Rumiantsevskogo muzeia*) and the State Museum of Modern Western Art (*Gosudarstvennyi muzei novogo zapadnogo iskusstva*), and from the organizations and institutions that founded the museum, namely the Museum Development Committee (*Komitet po ustroistvu Muzeia*) and the Building Commission (*Stroitel'naia komissiia*).

The administrative records of the museum itself are also retained here, with numerous documents relating to the history, development, and activities of the museum, its acquisition of nationalized

884

collections, and its international relations (1912–1990). Another group of documents results from various events held in the museum, such as the fond of the International Chess Tournament, which was held there in 1935. In 1993 part of the documents from the Ancient Art and Archeology Division were transferred to the archive, including field reports and the inventoried finds from archeological expeditions organized by the museum since the 1930s.

Personal papers are a large and important component of the museum archive. These include, for example, the fond of the Tsvetaev family (1870–1985), with the papers of the museum's first director I. V. Tsvetaev, and those of the architect R. I. Klein, which contain his correspondence with Tsvetaev. Also from the prerevolutionary period are the personal papers of the art collectors N. S. Mosolov, S. P. Vinogradov, and N. I. Vishniakov, among others, whose collections now form part of the museum.

The archive holds the personal papers of successive museum directors, including V. K. Mal'mberg and N. I. Romanov, and B. N. Ternov, who directed the State Museum of Modern Western Art. Personal papers are retained of important specialists on the museum staff, including such art critics as V. Ia. Adariukov, A. D. Chegodaev, and B. R. Vipper. The extensive fond of art critic and collector P. D. Ettinger (1888–1948) includes correspondence with many Russian and Soviet artists and writers.

There are personal papers of a number of Russian and Soviet artists of various schools and trends, including D. D. Burliuk, D. N. Mitrokhin, and A. I. Troianovskii. The archive also has papers of the French artist Ferdinand Léger and the American graphic artist Rockwell Kent. Among other documentation of foreign artists are materials of the French artist Henri Matisse (among the papers of his private secretary L. N. Delektorskaia), and letters of Pablo Picasso and Marc Chagall, among many others.

The archive retains extensive photograph collections, dating from as early as the 1890s. These include personal and family photographs, which came with the various groups of personal papers, and pictures illustrating the history, exhibits, and activities of the museum in various periods, which supplement the institutional records of the museum and those of the predecessor museum and collections it now holds. There are also some sound recordings from museum events and conferences in the 1970s and 1980s.

Reference Facilities: There are *opisi*, as well as name and subject card catalogues.

Kabinet reproduktsii
[Cabinet of Reproductions]

Telephone: 203-58-07
Hours: TuTh 10:00–16:00
Head: Ol'ga Borisovna Malenkovskaia (*tel.* 203-58-07)

HOLDINGS: 357,980 units, 19th–1986
 negatives—ca. 130,000 units; fond of reproductions—140,000 units; slides—100,000 units; fond of printing slides—ca. 500 units; fond of books and albums—over 10,000 units; fond of prints with negatives—ca. 50,000 units

The Cabinet of Reproductions, or Reproductions Office, administratively a subdivision of the Information Division (*podrazdelenie Otdela informatsii*), contains reproductions of works of art from throughout the world (architecture, painting, sculpture, graphics) executed in various media. It maintains security reproductions of all works of art in the museum.

Reference Facilities: There is a catalogue of negatives and a database for the fonds of negatives, polygraphic slides, and reproductions.

Otdel grafiki
[Division of Graphic Arts]

Address:	121019, Moscow, ul. Marshala Shaposhnikova, 4
Telephone:	203-93-76
Hours:	Th 10:00–16:00 (by appointment with the curator)
Transport:	metro: Kropotkinskaia

Head: Marina Ivanovna Maiskaia (*tel.* 203-30-07)

HOLDINGS: 1 collection, 13th–20th cc.

The Division of Graphic Arts possesses a rich collection of drawings and other graphic material by West European, Oriental, and American artists, and a similar collection of Russian and Soviet graphics. The original basis of its holdings, as mentioned above, came from the Engravings Office (*Graviurnyi kabinet*) of the prerevolutionary Rumianstev Museum. Most of its holdings would not technically be considered archival materials, and hence a survey is not provided here.

Working Conditions: Advance arrangements must be made with the curator of the fond regarding research.

Reference Facilities: There are alphabetic and systematic catalogues, and card catalogues for some of the holdings.

FINDING AIDS — PUBLISHED — GENERAL:

Muzei Moskvy (1997), pp. 89–93; *Khudozh. muzei* (1996), p. 50; *GAF Spravochnik* (1991), pp. 50–55; PKG *M&L* (1972), p. 293.

A guide to personal papers in the archive and a catalogue of the Egyptian papyri are being prepared for publication.

h-209. *Gosudarstvennomu muzeiu izobrazitel'nykh iskusstv im. A. S. Pushkina—100 let: 1898– 1998.* Edited by T. P. Vladimirskaia. Moscow: "Galart," 1998. 420 p. + plates.

A richly illustrated jubilee edition. Includes articles on the history of the museum, and its current situation and activities, the organization and activities of separate divisions, and its holdings of art and archival materials.

h-210. Aleksandrov, Aleksei A. "Iz istorii arkhiva Gosudarstvennogo muzeia izobrazitel'nykh iskusstv im. A. S. Pushkina." In *40 let nauchnomu studencheskomu kruzhku istochnikovedeniia istorii SSSR: Sbornik nauchnykh studencheskikh statei,* edited by S. E. Kniaz'kov et al., pp. 5–11. Moscow: MGIAI, 1990. [Goskomvuz SSSR; MGIAI] (Lib: MH)

A history of the organization of archival materials in the museum and a brief survey of the holdings.

h-211. *50 let Gosudarstvennomu muzeiu izobrazitel'nykh iskusstv im. A. S. Pushkina: Sbornik statei.* Edited by B. R. Vipper. Moscow: Izd-vo Akademii khudozhestv, 1962. 352 p. (Lib: DLC; IU; MH) [IDC-R-11,030]

An anniversary collection of articles about the museum. Of particular relevance here are the following:

R. I. Rubinshtein, "Sobranie rukopisei Otdela drevnego Vostoka GMII im. A. S. Pushkina" (pp. 52–58), which provides a detailed history of the formation of the collections in the Oriental Sector, a large part of which were collected by V. S. Golenishchev; footnotes cite earlier literature on many of the manuscripts.

N. N. Vodo, "Stoletie Graviurnogo kabineta" (pp. 14–30), which provides a detailed history of the formation and development of the Engravings Office in the prerevolutionary Rumiantsev Museum, the holdings from which are a basic part of the Division of Graphic Arts.

h-212. *70 let Gosudarstvennomu muzeiu izobrazitel'nykh iskusstv im. A. S. Pushkina.* Edited by I. I. Pruss. Moscow: "Sovetskii khudozhnik," 1982. 255 p. + plates. "Muzei: Khudozhestvennye sobraniia SSSR," vol. 3. (Lib: MH)

> The entire issue of the museum serial consists of a collection of articles in honor of the seventieth anniversary of the museum, with articles about the history, holdings, and activities of the museum. In contrast to the fiftieth-anniversary volume (h-211), there is no new survey of the archival holdings, although a short section by A. A. Demskaia, "Istoriia kollektsii po arkhivnym dokumentam" (pp. 196–214) presents excerpts of documents from the museum archive. A report by A. K. Korovina summarizes the archeological expeditions undertaken by the museum over the past 50 years (pp. 115–21), and there is a bibliography of museum publications (1939–1981) (pp. 136–38). It also includes a short illustrated article about the fate of the Dresden Gallery by N. E. Eliasberg, "Kartiny Drezdenskoi galerei v GMII (1945–1955)" (pp. 233–35).

h-212A. Sedova, T. "Muzeiu sem'desiat let." *Khudozhnik*, 1982, no. 6, pp. 42–63. (Lib: DLC; IU; MH)

> Provides a short history of the museum and its collections.

h-213. Demskaia, Aleksandra Andreevna. "Muzei v pervye gody Sovetskoi vlasti." *Soobshcheniia Gosudarstvennogo muzeia izobrazitel'nykh iskusstv im. A. S. Pushkina* 5 (1975): 117–25.

h-214. Kuznetsova, I. A. "Muzei v gody Velikoi Otechestvennoi voiny." *Muzei*, 1982, no. 3, pp. 226–30. (Lib: IU; MH)

h-215. Demskaia, Aleksandra Andreevna. *Gosudarstvennyi muzei izobrazitel'nykh iskusstv im. A. S. Pushkina.* Moscow: "Iskusstvo," 1979. 239 p. + 10 plates. "Goroda i muzei mira." (Lib: MH)

> A detailed tourist guide to the museum with a lengthy introductory history (pp. 7–69).

h-215A. *Gosudarstvennyi muzei izobrazitel'nykh iskusstv im. Pushkina: Al'bom.* Compiled by A. N. Zamiatina. Moscow: "Izobrazitel'noe iskusstvo," 1975. 11 p. + 106 plates. (Lib: DLC; MH)

> A large-format display album with reproductions from the museum collections. Includes a brief introductory history of the museum.

h-216. Levitin, E. S. "Otdel graviury i risunka." *Muzei*, 1982, no. 3, pp. 54–65. (Lib: IU; MH)

> Provides a general survey of the Division of Graphic Art, but without reference to the trophy collections acquired from Germany after World War II.

FINDING AIDS — SPECIALIZED:

h-217. Korostovtsev, Mikhail Aleksandrovich. *Ieraticheskii papirus 127 iz sobraniia GMII im. A. S. Pushkina.* Edited by V. V. Struve. Moscow: Izd-vo vostochnoi literatury, 1961. 71 p. [AN SSSR; INA; GMII im. A. S. Pushkina] (Lib: DDO; MH)

> A scholarly description of the Egyptian hieratic manuscript from the collection of Vladimir Semenovich Golenishchev (1856–1947), together with a facsimile of the text and Russian translation.

h-218. Struve, Vasilii Vasil'evich (Struve, V.). *Znachenie nekotorykh iz demoticheskikh papirusov Gosudarstvennogo muzeia izobrazitel'nykh iskusstv im. A. S. Pushkina dlia istorii i kul'tury Ptolemeevskogo Egipta/ The Significance of Certain Demotic Papyri of the State Museum of Fine Arts named after A. S. Pushkin for the History and Culture of Ptolemaic Egypt.* Moscow: Izd-vo AN SSSR, 1955. 56 p. (Lib: DLC; MH)

> A paper presented at the Tenth International Congress of Historians in Rome. Surveys selected Egyptian papyri from the Golenishchev Collection.

h-219. *Vydaiushchiisia russkii vostokoved V. S. Golenishchev i istoriia priobreteniia ego kollektsii v Muzee iziashchnykh iskusstv (1908–1912).* Compiled by A. A. Demskaia et al. Moscow: "Sovetskii khudozhnik," 1987. 343 p. "Iz arkhiva GMII," vol. 3. (Lib: DLC; MH)

> Describes the collection brought together by the Russian Egyptologist Vladimir Semenovich Golenishchev (1856–1947), which was acquired by the museum in 1909. Includes a scholarly description and extracts of documents in the collection, related correspondence, and remembrances about Golenishchev.

h-220. *The Literary Coptic Manuscripts in the A. S. Pushkin State Fine Arts Museum in Moscow.* Edited by A. I. Elanskaia. Leiden/New York: E. J. Brill, 1994. vii, 527 p. "Philosophia Patrum, Texts and Studies of Early Christian Life and Language." Supplement to the series "Vigiliae Christianae," vol. 18. (Lib: DDO; DLC; IU; MH)

> The introduction describes the history of the collection and indicates contiguous fragments found in other collections. Includes facsimiles of the original manuscripts, translations, and commentary.

h-221. Ernshtedt, Petr Viktorovich. *Koptskie teksty Gosudarstvennogo muzeia izobrazitel'nykh iskusstv im. A. S. Pushkina.* Edited by V. V. Struve. Leningrad/Moscow: Izd-vo AN SSSR, 1959. 215 p. [AN SSSR, Otdelenie iazyka i literatury] (Lib: DDO; DLC; IU; MH)

> A scholarly study of the Coptic collection.

h-222. Borisovskaia, Natal'ia. *Starinnye gravirovannye karty i plany XV–XVII vv.: Kosmografii, karty zemnye i nebesnye, plany, veduty, batalii: [Al'bom]/ Early Printed Maps and Plans 15th–18th Centuries: Cosmographies, Terrestrial and Celestial Maps, Plans, Vedutes, Battles.* Translated by V. Iu. Traskin and E. Ia. Bessmertnyi. Moscow: Galaktika, 1992. 272 p. + plates. "Karty i plany iz sobraniia GMII." (Lib: DLC; IU; MH)

> A beautifully illustrated album describing early engraved maps in the museum graphic collections, with indexes of artists, engravers, publishers, and authors. Includes an English summary.

Tsentral'nyi muzei drevnerusskoi kul'tury i iskusstva im. Andreia Rubleva (TsMiAR)
[Andrei Rublev Central Museum of Early Russian Culture and Art]

Agency: Ministerstvo kul'tury RF (Minkul'tury Rossii)
[Ministry of Culture]

Address: 107120, Moscow, Andron'evskaia pl. (*formerly* pl. Priamikova), 10
Telephone: 278-14-67; *Fax:* (095) 278-50-55
Website: http://moscow.lvl.ru/culture/museum/rublev/rublev.html;
http://sunsite.cs.msu.su/moscow/rublev/rublev.html
Transport: metro: Ploshchad' Il'icha; bus: 40, 125; trol. 45, 53
Hours: MTuTh–Su 11:00–18:00

Director: Gennadii Viktorovich Popov (*tel.* 278-14-89)
Deputy Director for Scientific Work: Ol'ga Evgen'evna Pavlovskaia (*tel.* 278-98-03)
Chief Curator: Liudmila Petrovna Tarasenko (*tel.* 278-14-89)

HISTORY:
Istoriko-kul'turnyi zapovednik im. A. Rubleva
[A. Rublev Historico-Cultural Preserve] (1947–1983)
Muzei drevnerusskogo iskusstva im. A. Rubleva
[A. Rublev Museum of Early Russian Art] (1983–1987)

The museum was founded in 1947 as a historical and architectural preserve in the grounds of the former Spaso-Andronievskii (Andronikov) Monastery. In 1960, to mark the 600th anniversary of the birth of the famous medieval Russian painter, Andrei Rublev (1360–1430), the preserve was reorganized into the Rublev Museum of Early Russian Art. In 1987, it was reorganized as the Rublev Central Museum of Early Russian Culture and Art. In 1991 it was entered in the federal register of the most valuable monuments of the cultural heritage of the peoples of the Russian Federation.

The museum has a branch—The Church of the Protection of the Virgin in Fili (*"Tserkov' Pokrova v Filiakh"*) (121087, Moscow, ul. Novozavodskaia, 6; tel. 148-45-52).

The museum archives were first organized in 1967 to retain administrative documentation of the museum and its branch.

Access: Permission of the museum director is required for research access.

Reference Facilities: A database is being created for description of the early manuscript books.

Library Facilities: The museum has a library, access to which for researchers requires permission of the museum director.

Otdel staropechatnoi knigi i rukopisei
[Division of Early Printed Books and Manuscripts]

Head: Larisa Ivanovna Alekhina (*tel.* 278-14-29)

HOLDINGS: ca. 120 units, early 15th c.–1985
films—5 units (1950s–1980s); photographs—over 16,000 units (1951–1990)

The museum holds a collection of theological and liturgical manuscripts in the Slavonic and Early Rus' languages, which includes manuscript convolutes of Old Believer texts and several early manuscripts from the Joseph of Volokolamsk (*Iosifo-Volokolamskii*) Monastery.

The earliest manuscript in the museum is a Western Slavic text copied in the fifteenth century—"On Fasting" ("O postnichestve"), attributed to Basil the Great. Among sixteenth-century manuscripts are two Gospels (*Evangeliia-tetr*), the 1510 *Lestvitsa* from the Joseph of Volokolamsk Monastery, an inspirational religious compilation known as *Izmaragd*, a festal Menaion (*Minei*) for the commemoration of saints, a book of hymns with verses from the Scripture (*Stikhiry*) in neumatic notation, compositions of Maksim Grek (Mikhail Trivolis), and other compiled codices with texts of liturgical and canonical content.

Most noteworthy among seventeenth-century manuscripts is the *sinodik* (book of readings for the deceased) in memory of the Monastery of Ioann Zlatoust (Moscow). There is also an *Izmaragd* and Chronography of 1642 from the Fedorovskii Monastery (Kazan), illuminated with interpretations of the Apocalypse.

A large number of manuscripts from the late seventeenth to twentieth centuries comprise monuments of Old Believer book culture. There are Old Believer codices with extracts from books of dogma, eschatology, and morality; codices with lives of saints; and tales of miracles and miracle workers. Among music manuscripts there are texts with neumatic notation, as well as five-line notation with square and Italian notes.

The museum also has some documentary films showing the restoration of some of the works of such early Rus' painters as Karp Zolotarev and Andrei Rublev, and the restoration of works from the Spaso-Andronievskii (Andronikov) Monastery, as well as other documentary films with historical themes.

The icon collection has a security fond of photographic negatives, and there are many photographs of other works of early Rus' art.

Copying: There are facilities for xerox copying.

FINDING AIDS — PUBLISHED — GENERAL:

Muzei Moskvy (1997), pp. 126–28; *Khudozh. muzei* (1996), pp. 49–50; *GAF Spravochnik* (1991), pp. 119–20.

There is no guide to the archival materials and manuscript collections in the museum.

h-228. Saltykov, Aleksandr Aleksandrovich. *Muzei drevnerusskogo iskusstva im. Andreia Rubleva.* 2d ed. Leningrad: "Khudozhnik RSFSR," 1989. 262 p. + plates. Added titles, summaries, and lists of illustrations in English, French, and German. (Lib: MH)

   1st ED.: L., 1981. 263 p. + plates. (Lib: MH).

   A popular, illustrated guide to the museum, with mention of some documentary holdings and bibliography of other publications about the museum.

h-229. Gal'chenko, M. G. "O drevneishei rukopisi iz sobraniia Tsentral'nogo muzeia drevnerusskoi kul'tury i iskusstva im. Andreia Rubleva." *AE za 1992 god* (1994): 77–84. (Lib: DLC; IU; MH)

   Surveys the earliest part of the manuscript collection.

h-230. Pavlenko, A. A. "Obzor dokumental'nykh materialov filiala Muzeia im. A. Rubleva—'Tserkov' Pokrova v Filiakh': Tezisy." In *Vsesoiuznaia konferentsiia-seminar "Arkhivnye fondy khudozhestvennykh muzeev SSSR,"* vol. 1, pp. 36–45. Moscow, 1981.

   Surveys documentation from the current archive of the museum branch (300 units), which was formed as a result of the restoration of the church, opening of new exhibitions, and the process of acquiring collections.

h-231. Longinova, A. S. "Muzei drevnerusskogo iskusstva im. Andreia Rubleva." In *Khudozhestvennye sokrovishcha muzeev Moskvy*, pp. [5–6], 21–33. Moscow: "Sovetskii khudozhnik," 1978. (Lib: DLC; MH)

   A brief description of the museum, with a mention of the documentary holdings and a few illustrations.

Gosudarstvennyi nauchno-issledovatel'skii muzei arkhitektury im. A. V. Shchuseva (GNIMA)
[A. V. Shchusev State Scientific Research Museum of Architecture]

Agency: Gosudarstvennyi komitet RF po stroitel'noi, arkhitekturnoi i zhilishchnoi politike (Gosstroi Rossii)
[State Committee for Construction, Architecture and Housing Policies]

Address: 121019, Moscow, ul. Vozdvizhenka (*formerly* prosp. Kalinina), 5
Telephone: 291-21-89; *Fax:* (095) 291-21-09
Website: http://moscow.lvl.ru/culture/museum/arhitek/arhitek.html
Transport: metro: Biblioteka im. Lenina, Aleksandrovskii sad, Borovitskaia, Arbatskaia
Hours: Tu–Su 10:00–18:00

Director: Vladimir Aleksandrovich Rezvin (*tel.* 291-21-09)

HISTORY:

Nauchno-issledovatel'skii muzei arkhitektury pri Akademii stroitel'stva i arkhitektury SSSR
[Scientific Research Museum of Architecture under the Academy of Construction and Architecture of the USSR] (1934–1964)
Gosudarstvennyi muzei russkoi arkhitektury im. A. V. Shchuseva
[A. V. Shchusev State Museum of Russian Architecture] (1945–1964)

The museum was founded in 1964 by the State Committee for Construction (sometimes translated Civil Engineering) (*Gosudarstvennyi komitet po delam stroitel'stva*—Gosstroi SSSR) as the result of the consolidation of the Scientific Research Museum of Architecture under the Academy of Construction and Architecture of the USSR with the A. V. Shchusev State Museum of Russian Architecture, which was founded in 1945.

Since the merger the museum had a branch in the Donskoi Monastery (founded in 1591 by Tsar Fedor Ioannovich), where most of the manuscript materials (acquired with the Gosstroi) were held. In 1993, after the monastery was returned to the Church, the museum branch there was closed, and the manuscript collections were moved to the main building.

In 1995 the museum was entered in the federal register of the most valuable monuments of the cultural heritage of the peoples of the Russian Federation.

Access: A letter requesting research access must be addressed to the museum director.

Working Conditions: Researchers are received in working offices of the museum.

Copying: A charge is made for xerox copying of documents and, in the case of organizations, a letter is required guaranteeing payment for services.

Razdel "Arkhiv"
[Archive Section]

Head: Nataliia Viktorovna Egorova

HOLDINGS: over 30 fonds (part not arranged)
institutional fonds—3 fonds; collection of drawings and lithographs—ca. 20,000 folios; architectural graphics—over 25,000 units (18th–20th cc.)

The museum has one of the largest collections of documents and graphic materials relating to architecture and city planning in Russia. They comprise the Archive Section of the Division of Scientific Fonds (*Otdel nauchnykh fondov*).

A large part of the documentary holdings is comprised of technical drawings, sketches, studies, paintings, lithographs, and technical measurements of architectural monuments, many of which were acquired from the State Tret'iakov Gallery, the State Historical Museum, and the State Hermitage. Architectural graphics represent the work of such great masters of Russian classicism as V. I. Bazhenov, O. I. Bove, M. F. Kazakov, Giacomo Quarenghi, A. N. Voronikhin, and Domenico Gilardi (D. I. Zhiliardi). The section on Soviet architecture includes the graphics of major Soviet architects like K. S. Alabian, A. V. Shchusev, I. A. Fomin, I. V. Zholtovskii, F. O. Shekhtel', and V. A. Shchuko, as well as the works of contemporary architects. The personal papers of a number of prominent architects are also held in the museum—the Vesnin Brothers, M. A. Minkus, F. A. Bronnikov, and I. S. Kuznetsov. In 1995 the museum received from the FSK (now FSB) some documents from the personal archive of the well-known art historian A. D. Nekrasov, who had been repressed in the 1930s.

A separate fond is comprised of so-called "passport" or registration data for architectural monuments prepared during the 1940s, which were received from the Main Administration for the Protection of Monuments (*Glavnoe upravlenie okhrany pamiatnikov*) under the Committee for Architecture. This collection is known as the Measurement Fond (*Obmernyi fond*). There are also technical drawings to scale of Russian architectural monuments done by the Moscow Archeological Society (late 19th–early 20th cc.), by the Central State Restoration Studios (*Tsentral'nye gosudarstvennye restavratsionnye masterskie*) (1917–1934); by the Institute of the Academy of Construction and Architecture of the USSR, and by the museum itself up to 1941.

The museum has a large collection of engravings and lithographs by Russian and foreign artists, dating from the sixteenth through nineteenth centuries. These include plans, maps, and town plans. Of particular interest here are the Godunov Drawing (*Godunov chertezh*) (1594–1605), a plan by Matthaeus Merian (1643), the Sigismund plan (1610), and a plan of Moscow by the architect I. F. Michurin (1734–1737). There are engravings and lithographs showing panoramic views of Moscow from different vantage points, general views of building ensembles and streets, views of the largest and most imposing buildings and views of ordinary dwellings. Included here are the drawings of M. I. Makhaev, Gérard Delabart, and Michel-François Damame-Demartrais.

Reference Facilities: Inventories have been compiled for only part of the manuscript material.

Otdel nauchnoi fototeki
[Scientific Photograph Archive Division]

Hours:　　Tu 11:00–17:00
Head: Ol'ga Anatol'evna Smoliakova

HOLDINGS: over 500,000 units, late 19th c.–to present

The Photograph Archive contains one of the largest collections in the country of photographic material pertaining to architecture and city planning, including negatives and photographic prints prepared by well-known architects and architectural researchers. The collection includes the unique glass negatives (2,717 images) that were made in the late nineteenth century (1882–1886) for the Moscow Archeological Society by one of the first Russian photographers, I. F. Barshchevskii. The archive also possesses the work of two other famous photographers—B. I. Dunaev and N. I. Ushakov.

Of particular value are the prints and negatives taken from environmental studies and technical surveys of monuments prepared during museum expeditions in the North, the Moscow region and the Volga region. These include photographs of the Trinity-St. Makarius Monastery in Kaliazin, which now lies under water after the building of the Moscow Reservoir. The museum continually prepares special photographic records (*fiksatsionnaia s"emka*) of architectural monuments throughout the country, such as those in the process of construction, reconstruction, or restoration.

The museum possesses a collection of photograph albums with pictures of architectural monuments acquired from various sources.

Working Conditions: Materials from the photographic print collection and photograph albums should be requested on call slips submitted to the photographic catalogue consultant on duty.

Reference Facilities: There is a subject catalogue of photographs, containing cards with sample photographic prints affixed. The Barshchevskii Collection is available on a separate indexed CD-ROM (h-243).

FINDING AIDS — PUBLISHED — GENERAL:

Muzei Moskvy (1997), pp. 184–86; PKG *M&L* (1972), p. 294.

There is no published guide to the archival materials in the museum.

h-235. Aruin, M. I.; Baldin, V. I.; Geidor, T. I., et al. *Gosudarstvennyi nauchno-issledovatel'skii muzei arkhitektury im. A. V. Shchuseva: Kratkii putevoditel'.* Compiled by T. D. Bozhutina. Moscow: "Moskovskii rabochii," 1988. 157 p.
> The introduction to the guide gives a brief account of the history and holdings of the museum (pp. 3–11).

h-236. *Fotograficheskii fond muzeia: Kratkii putevoditel'.* Compiled by S. E. Zorina and M. G. Rogozina. Edited by V. G. Mironov. Moscow, 1988. 15 p. [Gosstroi SSSR; GNIMA]
> Surveys the collections of negatives in the Photograph Archive and gives a brief description of the most important of them.

h-237. *Goroda RSFSR v graviurakh i litografiiakh: (Katalog iz sobraniia muzeia).* Compiled by B. S. Gluskina and I. V. Miroshnichenko. Moscow, 1982. 189 p. [Gosstroi SSSR; GNIMA]
> Describes over 600 engravings and lithographs from the museum fonds. Listings are arranged geographically with reference to museum catalogue numbers. Includes various indexes.

FINDING AIDS — SPECIALIZED:

h-238. *Ot Aleksandra Briullova do Ivana Fomina: Proekty i risunki russkikh arkhitektorov serediny XIX–nachala XX veka: Katalog vystavki.* Compiled by V. G. Lisovskii, N. V. Golubkova, and T. N. Nikitina. Leningrad: "Iskusstvo," 1981. 53 p. + plates. [NIM AKh SSSR; GNIMA] (Lib: MH)
> An exhibition catalogue describing projects done by famous Russian architects of the period that are held in the museum.

h-239. *Architectural Drawings of the Russian Avant-Garde.* Compiled by Catherine Cooke. New York: Museum of Modern Art (distributed by H. N. Abrams), 1990. 143 p. + plates. "Published on the occasion of the exhibition. . . June 21–September 4, 1990". (Lib: MH)
> An exhibition catalogue with an introductory essay and reproductions of designs and projects of early Soviet architects from the GNIMA exhibited in the Museum of Modern Art, with appended biographical data on the architects. Includes a brief essay on the history of the Shchusev Museum by the then director Igor A. Kazus' (pp. 218–30).

h-239.1. *Architectural Drawings of the Russian Avant-Garde: 1917–1935; Soviet Avant-Garde Publications: 19 June to 8 September 1991.* Compiled by Emily Kies-Folpe and Irena Zantovska-Murray. Montreal: Centre canadien d'architecture / Canadian Centre for Architecture, 1991. 27 p. + plates. (Lib: MH)

> An exhibition catalogue with introductory essays and reproductions of designs and projects of early Soviet architects from the GNIMA exhibited in Montreal.

h-240. *Vesnin L. A. (1880–1933), Vesnin V. A. (1882–1950), Vesnin A. A. (1883–1959): Katalog-putevoditel' po fondam muzeia.* Compiled by E. V. Vasiutinskaia, G. V. Verkhoturova, O. M. Ziuskevich, et al. Edited by K. I. Murashev. Moscow, 1981. 158 p. [Gosstroi SSSR; GNIMA]

> Includes the architectural projects and landscape planning that was done by the Vesnin Brothers, but there is no coverage of their personal papers that are held by the museum.

h-241. Bozhutina, T. D. "O tvorcheskom arkhive I. S. Kuznetsova." In *F. O. Shekhtel' i problemy istorii russkoi arkhitektury kontsa XIX–nachala XX vv.*, pp. 107–10. Moscow, 1988. [Gosstroi SSSR; TsNIPI po gradostroitel'stvu]

> A brief survey of the papers of the architect I. S. Kuznetsov (1867–1942), which were acquired by the museum in 1975.

h-242. *Vladimir Fedorovich Krinskii (1890–1971): Kratkii putevoditel' po fondam muzeia.* Compiled by N. F. Miliushina, D. A. Tiurina, and N. A. Luk'ianov. Edited by I. A. Kazus'. Moscow, 1987. 134 p. [Gosstroi SSSR; GNIMA] (Lib: MH)

> A short catalogue of the personal papers of the architect V. F. Krinskii, with documents from the years 1906–1970 (over 200 units), which were acquired by the museum from the Moscow Institute of Architecture.

h-243. *I. F. Barshchevsky, Photographer of the Imperial Archaeological Society: Complete Collection of Photographs (1882–1896) from the Moscow Museum of Architecture.* CD-ROM ed.—5 computer optical discs. [1996?]. [Leiden: Distributed by IDC; US distributor: Wilmington, DE : Russian Images, Inc.; Tokyo, Japan: Distributed by START Lab.]

> A single CD provides the entire collection of photographs by Ivan Fedorovich Barshchevskii (1851–1948) of Russian art and architecture in a single database with Barshevskii's original descriptions in Russian and English—2,754 thumbnail and medium resolution images, along with historical maps of Russia and plans of several cities. The collection is also available in high-resolution images in a separate series of four CDs, capturing all details from the original 18x24 cm. glass negatives. The maps are keyed to the geographic location of each image, including general views of Russian cities and towns; monasteries, churches, and other religious buildings; liturgical items; clothing and embroideries, furniture and tableware; weapons, armor, and equestrian gear in Russian collections. Also includes some Moslem and other Oriental art.

Gosudarstvennyi muzei Vostoka (GMV)
[State Museum of the Orient]

Agency: Ministerstvo kul'tury RF (Minkul'tury Rossii)
[Ministry of Culture]

Address: 121019, Moscow, Nikitskii (*formerly* Suvorovskii) bul'var, 12a
Telephone: 202-45-55
Transport: metro: Tverskaia, Pushkinskaia, Chekhovskaia, Arbatskaia; trol.: 15, 31
Hours: Tu–Su 11:00–20:00

General Director: Vladimir Aleksandrovich Nabatchikov (*tel.* 291-03-41–secretary)
Deputy Director for Scientific Work: Tat'iana Khristoforovna Metaksa (*tel.* 202-45-55)
Main Curator: Vladimir Efimovich Voitov (*tel.* 202-48-53)
Head of Sector of the Near and Middle East: Natal'ia Iur'evna Sazonova
(*tel.* 291-14-40)

HISTORY:
Ars Asiatica
[Ars Asiatica] (1918–1925)
Gosudarstvennyi muzei vostochnykh kul'tur
[State Museum of Oriental Cultures] (1925–1962)
Gosudarstvennyi muzei iskusstva narodov Vostoka (GMINV)
[State Museum of the Art of Peoples of the Orient] (1962–1991)

The museum was formed in 1918 under the name "Ars Asiatica," mainly from the extensive private collections of P. I. Shchukin, K. F. Nekrasov, and the Soviet diplomat and collector, V. G. Tardov. At the end of 1924 the museum was made a branch of the Museum of Fine Arts (H–26), but in 1925 it became independent and was renamed the State Museum of Oriental Cultures. In 1962 it was renamed again—the State Museum of the Art of Peoples of the Orient (GMINV), but since 1991 has been known by its present name.

In the early 1980s the museum was given the classic Moscow building which had been the home of the Decembrist M. S. Lunin, and which had been designed by the architect Domenico Gilardi (D. I. Zhiliardi) in 1818–1823. Before it reopened there (1984), the museum was plagued by numerous disasters, particularly fires, the worst of which occurred in 1976. At present part of the holdings are still housed in the old building (ul. Obukha, 16), the reconstructed Church of Elijah the Prophet (*tserkov' Il'i Proroka*). In 1991 the museum was added to the federal register of the most valuable monuments of the cultural heritage of the peoples of the Russian Federation.

The Archive of the museum was established in 1977.

HOLDINGS: 61 units, 9th–early 20th c.

The museum holds manuscripts in Arabic, Persian, Turkish, and other Oriental languages. They are not arranged in a separate fond, but are kept as exhibits in several regional specialized exhibition fonds. The largest number of manuscripts are found in the Near and Middle East Sector and in the Central Asian Division. Almost all of them are in fact works of art, given their extensive illuminations. On the whole the manuscripts are of literary or theological content. They include anthologies of the works of the Persian poets Arifi, Jami, Nizami (Ganjavi), Rumi, and Sadi, as well as copies of the

895

classical Oriental poems "Laila and Mejnun," "Kalilah and Dimnah," and others. Among the theological manuscripts there are fragments of the Koran (folios from the 9th–10th cc.) and copies of prayers (18th–early 19th cc.).

There is a unique collection of colored Japanese engravings from the eighteenth and nineteenth centuries, as well as albums and picturesque scrolls from the nineteenth and twentieth centuries, but most of these would also be considered works of art, rather than archival materials. The Japanese masters represented here include Utamaro, Kuniyoshi, Honkei, Sadamasu, and Yoshikuni.

Among the examples of Chinese calligraphy there is a unique horizontal sixteenth-century scroll by the painter Chou Ying, known as the "Poem about the Deserted Wife," and a seventeenth-century scroll "Zou Yuandao" by the painter Yun Shouping.

The collections also include Indian and Mongolian miniatures in the form of illustrations for manuscript books, and folios of the Persian translation of the "Book of Babur" (Babur-Name).

Access: A letter requesting research access should be addressed to the museum director.

Working Conditions: Researchers are accommodated in the storage area.

Reference Facilities: All the manuscripts have been registered in inventory books. For the benefit of researchers there is a special report on the museum holdings, which also gives information on the manuscript collection.

Library Facilities: The museum's Scientific Library is located at ul. Obukha, 16 (tel. 916-34-29).

Copying: Photographic copies can be prepared.

Arkhiv
[Archive]

Head: Vera Evgen'evna Strelkova (*tel.* 202-45-55)

HOLDINGS: 1 fond, 1,425 units, 1918–1985
photographs—48 units (1918–1985)

The museum archive, under the Division of Information, Publicity, and Exhibition Work (*Otdel informatsionno-reklamno-vystavochnoi raboty*) contains organizational and administrative documentation of the museum since 1918, including personnel files (from the 1920s), inventories of acquisitions, the records of the Academic Secretary and the Academic Council of the museum, reports on research trips undertaken by the staff, and correspondence with museums and academic organizations abroad. There are also unpublished manuscripts of scholarly works by a number of famous Orientalists, such as B. P. Denike and O. N. Glukhareva.

Photographic documents include early daguerrotypes of museum exhibits, albums with photographs of the first exhibitions, and displays from the N. A. Narimanov Cabinet of the History of the Revolutionary and National Liberation Movement in the East (*Kabinet istorii revoliutsionnogo i natsional'no-osvoboditel'nogo dvizheniia na Vostoke im. N. N. Narimanova*), exhibited between 1925 and 1932.

The archive also has a slide file and a fond of posters, booklets, and invitations.

N.B. A large part of the museum documentation has been lost since the war as the result of several disasters, and particularly the 1976 fire. The archive is still largely unarranged. Part of the records for the years 1918–1930 remain under the control of the Registration and Acquisitions Department (*Otdel ucheta i komplektovaniia*) (ul. Obukha, 16).

Reference Facilities: There are subject catalogues.

FINDING AIDS — PUBLISHED — GENERAL:

Muzei Moskvy (1997), pp. 98–100; *Khudozh. muzei* (1996), pp. 52; *GAF Spravochnik* (1991), pp. 55–56.

There is no published guide to the archival materials in the museum.

h-246. Ryzhnikova, I. I. "K istorii Gosudarstvennogo muzeia iskusstva narodov Vostoka: (Dokumenty TsGA RSFSR)." *Gosudarstvennyi muzei iskusstva narodov Vostoka: Nauchnye soobshcheniia* 19 (1988): 193–204.

h-247. Shadrina, I. O. "Iz istorii Gosudarstvennogo muzeia iskusstva narodov Vostoka (Po materialam arkhiva muzeia)." *Vestnik muzeinoi komissii*, 1990, no. 1, pp. 80–89.

h-248. Rumiantseva, Ol'ga Vladimirovna. *Gosudarstvennyi muzei Vostoka: Kratkii obzor kollektsii.* Edited by A. I. Voeikov. Moscow: "Izobrazitel'noe iskusstvo," 1993. 224 p. + 120 plates. (Lib: MH)

    1st ED.: Rumiantseva, Ol'ga Vladimirovna. *Gosudarstvennyi muzei iskusstva narodov Vostoka: Kratkii obzor kollektsii.* M., 1982. 220 p. + 12 plates. (Lib: MH).

    EARLIER VERSION: *Gosudarstvennyi muzei iskusstva narodov Vostoka: Putevoditel'.* Compiled by O. V. Rumiantseva. Edited by T. Kostenko. M.: "Reklama," 1970. 48 p.

    A heavily illustrated tourist guide, surveying the museum collections, with separate sections for the Soviet Caucasus and Central Asia, as well as foreign countries in Asia and Africa. Mentions some of the illuminated Oriental manuscripts, but only those actually on exhibit. A special chapter covers the Roerich (Rerikh) collection and memorial cabinet.

h-249. *Gosudarstvennyi muzei iskusstva narodov Vostoka, Moskva: [Al'bom].* Compiled by N. A. Kanevskaia, N. P. Chuikina, M. B. Miasina, et al. Leningrad: "Avrora," 1988. 232 p. Introduction by N. S. Sycheva. (Lib: IU; MH)

    An elaborate, large-format album of illustrations from the museum collections. A brief introduction (pp. 6–27) provides an essay on Oriental studies in the USSR and the formation of the museum collections. Annotations for many of the reproductions indicate the source of acquisition.

h-249.1. *The Museum of Oriental Art, Moscow.* Compiled by Evelina Ganevskaia, Natal'ia P. Chuikina, et al. Translated by Ashkhen Mikoian. Leningrad: "Avrora," 1988. 230 p. Introduction by Natalia Sycheva. (Lib: MH)

    An English translation of h-249.

h-250. Iampol'skaia, N. M. "50 let Gosudarstvennomu muzeiu iskusstva narodov Vostoka." *Narody Azii i Afriki*, 1968, no. 6, pp. 219–22. (Lib: DLC; IU; MH)

FINDING AIDS — GENERAL — UNPUBLISHED:

h-251. Strelkova, Vera Evgen'evna. "Istoriia sozdaniia Gosudarstvennogo muzeia Vostoka: Zhizn' muzeia v 1918–1941 gg.: Diplomnaia rabota." Moscow: RGGU, 1994. 123 p. Typescript.

    A senior thesis at IAI RGGU, available for consultation in the RGGU library.

h-252. Ryzhnikova, I. I. "Obzor-putevoditel' dokumentov fonda GMINV (1919–1985 gg.): Diplomnaia rabota." Moscow, 1988. 115 p. Typescript. [MGIAI]

    A survey done as a senior thesis at MGIAI (now IAI RGGU), available in the RGGU library.

FINDING AIDS — SPECIALIZED:

h-253. Shadrina, I. O. "Dokumenty arkhiva GMINV po istorii muzeia za 1919–1924 gg." *Gosudarstvennyi muzei iskusstva narodov Vostoka: Nauchnye soobshcheniia* 18 (1987): 147–64. (Lib: DLC)

    Surveys the nature and content of the archival documents on the history of the museum.

Muzei V. A. Tropinina
i moskovskikh khudozhnikov ego vremeni
[Museum of V. A. Tropinin and Moscow Artists of His Period]

Agency: Komitet po kul'ture Pravitel'stva Moskvy
[Committee on Culture of the Government of Moscow]

Address: 113095, Moscow, Shchetininskii per., 10, stroenie 1
Telephone: 231-17-99; 231-78-57
Transport: metro: Polianka, Dobryninskaia;
               trol.: 1, 8, 25 (to stop "Magazin Vanda")
Hours: TuW 12:00–17:00 (by appointment)

Director: Galina Davydovna Kropivnitskaia (*tel.* 231-24-59)
Head of Library: Elena Arkad'evna Riakhina (*tel.* 231-78-57)

HISTORY:

Muzei V. A. Tropinina i moskovskikh khudozhnikov ego vremeni—
   Filial Ostankinskogo dvortsa-muzeia tvorchestva krepostnykh
   [Museum of V. A. Tropinin and Moscow Artists of His Period—
   Branch of Ostankino Palace-Museum of Serf Art] (1969–1990)

The museum was opened in 1969. Its basic collection came as a gift from the Moscow collector, F. E. Vishnevskii (1902–1978), including his detached house. Until 1990 it was a branch of the Ostankino Palace-Museum (H–22).

HOLDINGS: 13 fonds, 321 (ca. 900 units unarranged) units, 1823–1993

Documentary materials in this museum consist mainly of the correspondence of the Russian artist Vasilii Andreevich Tropinin (1776–1857) with the Academy of Arts, various Moscow arts societies, and his family (wife and son), friends, and acquaintances. The earliest letters date back to 1823.

Access: Researchers need to make preliminary arrangements, stating the subject and purpose of research, in order to obtain the director's permission.

Working Conditions: Because there is no reading room and because the museum has been undergoing major renovation since 1993, researchers must make advance arrangements.

Reference Facilities: There are inventory and auxiliary card catalogues.

Library Facilities: There is a library for staff use.

Copying: No copying facilities are available.

FINDING AIDS — PUBLISHED — GENERAL:

Muzei Moskvy (1997), pp. 124–25; *Khudozh. muzei* (1996), p. 49; *GAF Spravochnik* (1991), pp. 123–24.

There is no published guide to the archival materials in the museum.

h-256. *Muzei V. A. Tropinina i moskovskikh khudozhnikov ego vremeni: [Al'bom]/ Museum of Works by Vasily Tropinin and Moscow Artists of His Day.* Compiled by

G. D. Kropivnitskaia. Leningrad: Khudozhnik RSFSR, 1987. 216 p. "Khudozhestvennye muzei Rossiiskoi Federatsii." (Lib: DLC; IU; MH)

EARLIER ED.: *Muzei V. A. Tropinina i moskovskikh khudozhnikov ego vremeni: Katalog.* Compiled with an introduction by G. D. Kropivnitskaia with the participation of F. E. Vishnevskii. M.: "Sovetskii khudozhnik," 1975. 238 p. (Lib: MH).

An album of illustrations, which serves as a partial catalogue of the museum collections, including the engravings and drawings done by Russian artists. The introductory article recounts the history of the museum.

h-257. Nikologorskaia, O. "Muzei V. A. Tropinina." *Kul'tura i zhizn'*, 1976, no. 8, pp. 16–17. (Lib: DLC; IU; MH)

Describes the founding and reconstruction of the museum.

h-258. Bernaskoni, L. "Vozvrashchennye shedevry." *Voprosy i otvety*, 1978, no. 8, pp. 56–59. (Lib: IU)

Describes the history of the museum and its collections.

Vserossiskii muzei dekorativno-prikladnogo i narodnogo iskusstva

[All-Russian Museum of Decorative, Applied, and Folk Arts]

Agency: Ministerstvo kul'tury RF (Minkul'tury Rossii)
[Ministry of Culture]

Address: 103473, Moscow, ul. Delegatskaia, 3
Telephone: 921-01-39; 923-17-41 (inquiries); *Fax:* (095) 923-06-20
Website: http://moscow.lvl.ru/culture/museum/decprikl/edecprik
Transport: metro: Novoslobodskaia + trol. 47; Tsvetnoi bul'var;
Sukharevskaia + trol. B, 10
Hours: M–Th 10:00–18:00

Director: Vladimir Andreevich Guliaev (*tel.* 923-77-25)
Chief Curator: Ol'ga Mikhailovna Milovanova (*tel.* 928-14-43)
Head of the Scientific Archive: Tamara Aleksandrovna Popesku (*tel.* 973-32-28)
Chief, Division of Photographic Materials: Ol'ga Vladimirovna Vlasova
(*tel.* 923-99-00)

HISTORY:

The museum was established in 1981. It is housed in an historic eighteenth-century building that belonged to the Osterman-Tolstoi family before 1917, which also houses the "Seeking Freedom" Museum (see H–4).

HOLDINGS: negative and positive photographs—4,987 units; archive—12,264 units

The Scientific Archive (*Nauchnyi arkhiv*) retains the administrative records of the museum itself, together with personal papers of folklore scholars and other folk-art specialists associated with the museum. Of particular interest are the records of its expeditions to various regions of Russia and the former USSR, in connection with its acquisitions of folk art.

In the auxiliary fond of the museum—the Division of Photographic Materials (*Otdel fotoizobrazitel'nykh materialov*) are many photographs and negatives covering the museum exhibits and their acquisition, as well as museum expeditions.

Access: Research access requires an official letter addressed to the director indicating the subject and aim of research.

Working Conditions: Researchers are accommodated in a separate room.

Reference Facilities: There are *opisi* for the archival materials and a reference card catalogue for the photographic materials.

Copying: Facilities are available for limited xerox copies.

Comment: A completed questionnaire from the museum was not returned to Rosarkhiv.

FINDING AIDS — PUBLISHED — GENERAL:

Muzei Moskvy (1997), pp. 94–97; *Khudozh. muzei* (1996), pp. 46–47.

There is no published description of the archival materials in the museum.

Muzei fotografii
[Museum of Photography]

Agency: Soiuz fotokhudozhnikov RF
[Union of Photograph Artists]

Address:	121019, Moscow, Semenovskaia nab., 3/1, kv. 1;
	(postal): 121019, Moscow, a/ia (box) 95
E-mail:	vdfunion@cityline.ru
Transport:	metro: Elektrozavodskaia
Hours:	by appointment

Director and Chairman of the Union of Photographic Artists:
Andrei Ivanovich Baskakov (*tel.* 360-55-01)

HISTORY:

The museum was founded in 1959 based on the personal collection of photographer and journalist E. S. Belyi, and constituted one of the first museums of photography in the country. In 1993 the collection was given to the Union of Photographic Artists of the Russian Federation by Belyi's widow, L. B. Bliumkina. The museum still lacks a permanent building and appropriate exhibition area.

HOLDINGS: photographs—7,500 units (mid-19th–20th cc.); written sources—1,200 units

The museum collects documents on the history of photography, including technological developments, as well as changes in styles and techniques. There are examples of the work of well-known photographers from throughout the world and documentation about them.

The museum has a rich collection of negatives and original proofs, representing practically all stages of the evolution of domestic photographic art. There are some extremely rare examples of daguerreotypes from the mid-1850s. Among photographs from the second half of the nineteenth and early twentieth century, a special place is occupied by such leading photographers as P. P. Pavlov, M. P. Dmitriev, S. M. Prokudin-Gorskii, and others. There is a separate complex of materials and photographs connected with the Russian Photographic Society (1894–1928), including the work of a number of its members—N. I. Babir, Ia. Bulgak, P. K. Novitskii, B. I. Pashkevich, and A. I. Trapani.

Original photographer's prints from the 1920s and 1930s include those of masters of various types—Iu. P. Eremin, A. V. Khlebnikov, P. V. Klepikov, M. S. Nappel'baum, and A. M. Rodchenko, among others. They reflect many different styles, manners, and tendencies, from photojournalism to traditional portraits and lyrical landscapes.

The collection also has samples of author's prints or reproductions of the work of photographers from Germany, Belgium, France, U.S.A., and Czechoslovakia, from 1900 to the late 1980s. These include pictures by Rudolph Dürkoop, Hugo Erfurt, Nicolas Perscheid, and others.

The museum has a collection of contemporary photographs, again representing a wide spectrum of artistic tendencies and directions in Russian photographic art.

The museum has additional unique documents, such as awards and certificates received by Russian and Soviet photographers in prestigious exhibitions in Russia and abroad.

Access: There are no limitations on access.

Working Conditions: The museum does not have a permanent location, and hence working arrangements depend on an available location. An appointment is required.

Library Facilities: The museum has a special collection of literature on the history of world and Soviet photography and photojournalism. There are many photo albums, catalogues, handbooks, and textbooks published in the nineteeenth and twentieth centuries in Russia, Germany, and other countries. There are complete runs of the magazines and journals *Povesti Russkogo Fotograficheskogo obshchestva*, *Vestnik fotografii*, *Fotograf*, *Proletarskoe foto*, and *Sovetskoe foto*.

FINDING AIDS — PUBLISHED — GENERAL:
Nauchno-tekh. muzei (1992), p. 29.

There is no published guide to the archival materials in the museum.

Literary Museums

✳ H–33 ✳

Gosudarstvennyi literaturnyi muzei (GLM)
[State Literary Museum]

Agency: Ministerstvo kul'tury RF (Minkul'tury Rossii)
[Ministry of Culture]

Address: 103051, Moscow, ul. Petrovka, 28
Telephone: 921-38-57, 921-73-95; *Fax:* 923-41-75
Website: http://moscow.lvl.ru/culture/museum/goslit/goslit.html
Transport: metro: Pushkinskaia, Chekhovskaia, Tverskaia; trol.: 5, 15, 31
Hours: WF 14:00–19:00; ThSaSu 11:00–17:00

Director: Natal'ia Vladimirovna Shakhalova (*tel.* 923-30-22)
Chief Curator: Veronika Vartanovna Akopdzhanova (*tel.* 924-60-24)

HISTORY:

Literaturnyi muzei pri Biblioteke im. V. I. Lenina
[Literary Museum under the V. I. Lenin Public Library] (1921–1933)
Tsentral'nyi muzei khudozhestvennoi literatury, kritiki i publitsistiki
[Central Museum of Literature, Criticism, and Publicistic Writings] (1933–1934)

The museum began its acquisition activities with a 1931 decree establishing a Commission to Prepare and Organize the Central Literary Museum, under the direction of the Bolshevik intellectual leader, Vladimir D. Bonch-Bruevich. The Central Museum of Literature, Criticism, and Publicistic Writings was established in 1933. In 1934 that museum was combined with the collections of the former Literary Museum under the Lenin Public Library (and its predecessors, now RGB, see G–1)—a special auxiliary library used for the collection of literary manuscripts and personal papers—to form the State Literary Museum (GLM). The combined museum was then housed in a building opposite the Lenin Library, which was later the Kalinin Museum (and later a branch of the Museum of Revolution—H–4). Continuing under the direction of Bonch-Bruevich, during the 1930s, GLM became one of the largest and best stocked repositories of literary manuscript materials in the Soviet Union, with its unique collections of materials relating to Russian and foreign literature, including many originals and copies of archival Rossica from abroad—totalling some 3,000,000 archival documents, 100,000 units of graphic materials, and over 130,000 books. And at the same time, the museum became a major center of scholarly research, with several important series of archival publications and catalogues.

With the formation of the Central State Literary Archive—TsGLA (now RGALI—B–7) in 1941, however, virtually all of the GLM archival holdings were transferred to state archival custody to form the new repository. The personal papers of A. M. Gor'kii had previously been transferred to the Gor'kii Archive in the Institute of World Literature (IMLI AN SSSR—E–9), the Pushkin archival materials had been transferred to Pushkinskii Dom in Leningrad (IRLI— E–28), and the Tolstoi materials to the State Tolstoi Museum (H–35). Thus, by the outbreak of the Second World War, GLM was left with only its graphic materials and book holdings, while its official status and staff in subsequent years remained on uncertain ground.

Nevertheless, during the war and especially the postwar years, the Literary Museum, still under the direction of Bonch-Bruevich, started replenishing its manuscript holdings with an active collecting program. Among other early postwar receipts of particular significance, in 1951 the museum received approximately 5,000 literary manuscripts and related documents from internal security sources, namely some of those seized from repressed writers and other literary figures. Continuing during the 1950s and 1960s, GLM again came into prominence for significant literary manuscripts and documentary materials, but these never reached the magnitude of its prewar collections. By the 1970s, the museum was spread out in some seventeen different buildings in Moscow, which by 1995 had grown to twenty. Its main exhibits for Russian literature of the eighteenth and nineteenth centuries are now housed in the Naryshkin Palace of the Vysoko-Petrovskii Monastery, which also houses the administrative offices of the museum. The exhibits of Soviet-period literature are concentrated in the house of the former Ostroukhov Gallery (see no. 13 below).

In addition to the Manuscript Division, which existed since the 1930s (during the period after 1941, it had the status of a sector), a Photograph Sector (now Fototeka) was formed in 1944, and a Sound Recordings Division in 1970. The separate Folklore Archive had been established in 1932, but became a sector when it lost most of its holdings in 1941.

The museum now has twelve branches—with the formal status of divisions (*otdely*) of the museum. Many of them have some original documents, including photographic materials, on display among their exhibits, but archival materials are held only in the specially designated GLM divisions described below. Brief webpages have been launched for all of these branch museums (on the same "moscow.lvl.ru" server as GLM itself):

(1) The A. P. Chekhov House-Museum (*Dom-muzei A. P. Chekhova*), founded in 1954, in the house where the writer Anton Pavlovich Chekhov (1860–1904) lived from 1886 to 1890. (103000, Moscow, ul. Sadovo-Kudrinskaia, 6; tel. 291-61-54, 291-38-37; webpage: http://moscow.lvl.ru/culture/museum/chekov/chekhov.html).

(2) The A. I. Herzen Museum (*Muzei A. I. Gertsena*), founded in 1976, in the house where the socialist thinker and publicist Aleksandr Ivanovich Herzen (Gertsen) (1812–1870) lived from 1843 to 1846, and which has recently been designated an architectural landmark of the early nineteenth century. (121002, Moscow, per. Sivtsev Vrazhek, 27; tel. 241-58-59; webpage: http://moscow.lvl.ru/culture/museum/gercen/gercen.html).

(3) The M. Iu. Lermontov House-Museum (*Dom-muzei M. Iu. Lermontova*), founded in 1981, in the house where the poet and novelist Mikhail Iur'evich Lermontov (1814–1841) lived from 1829 to 1832. (121069, Moscow, ul. Malaia Molchanovka, 2; tel. 291-18-60; webpage: http://moscow.lvl.ru/culture/museum/lermont/lermont.html).

(4) The M. M. Prishvin House-Museum (*Dom-muzei M. M. Prishvina*), founded in 1980, where the writer and naturalist Mikhail Mikhailovich Prishvin (1873–1954) lived. (143091, Moskovskaia oblast', Odintsovskii raion, pos. Dunino, dom 2; tel. 419-17-28; webpage: http://moscow.lvl.ru/culture/museum/prishv/prishv.html).

(5) The F. M. Dostoevskii Apartment-Museum (*Muzei-kvartira F. M. Dostoevskogo*), founded in 1928, in the house where the writer Fedor Mikhailovich Dostoevskii (1822–1881) was born and lived until the age of sixteen, also preserves part of the family library. (103030, Moscow, ul. Dostoevskogo, 2; tel. 281-10-85; webpage: http://moscow.lvl.ru/culture/museum/dostoev/dostoev.html).

(6) The A. V. Lunacharskii Cabinet (*Kabinet A. V. Lunacharskogo*), opened in 1964, in the house in which the Bolshevik literary critic and first Commissar of Education, Anatolii Vasil'evich Lunacharskii (1873–1933) lived during the last period of his life (1923–1933). The small museum preserves Lunacharskii's working study and has other memorial exhibits with documents, pictures, and memorabilia. (121002, Moscow, ul. Vesnina, 9/6; tel. 241-08-77; webpage: http://moscow.lvl.ru/culture/museum/lunachr/lunachr.html).

(7) The A. N. Tolstoi Apartment-Museum (*Muzei-kvartira A. N. Tolstogo*), opened in 1987, in the house in which the writer Aleksei Nikolaevich Tolstoi (1883–1945) lived during the last period of his life. The museum exhibits documents and memorabilia and also preserves part of Tolstoi's library. The building, designed by the architect F. O. Shekhtel' (1903), has been designated an architectural landmark. (121069, Moscow, ul. Spiridonovka [*formerly* Alekseia Tolstogo], 2/6; tel. 290-09-56; webpage: http://moscow.lvl.ru/culture/museum/mktolst/mktolst.html).

(8) The B. L. Pasternak House-Museum (*Dom-muzei B. L. Pasternaka*), founded in 1990 in the dacha where the writer Boris Leonidovich Pasternak (1890–1960) lived, has memorial exhibits reflecting the time of Pasternak's life there. (142783, Moskovskaia oblast', pos. Peredelkino, ul. Treneva, 6; tel. 934-51-75; webpage: http://moscow.lvl.ru/culture/museum/pastern/pastern.html).

(9) The K. I. Chukovskii Memorial Museum (*Memorial'nyi muzei K. I. Chukovskogo*), founded in 1995 in the dacha of the writer Kornei Ivanovich Chukovskii (1882–1969), portrays the author's life there from 1939–1969. (142783, Moskovskaia oblast', pos. Peredelkino, ul. Serafimovicha, 3; tel. 593-26-70; webpage: http://moscow.lvl.ru/culture/museum/chukovs/chukovs.html).

(10) The Naryshkin Palace—Division of Russian Nineteenth-Century Classical Literature (*Otdel russkoi klassicheskoi literatury XIX veka*), in the the former Vysoko-Petrovskii Monastery, where the main administration of the museum is located, houses different exhibitions. Started in 1996, "The World of Dostoevskii" exhibit is drawn from manuscript and graphic collections in the museum. (103051, Moscow, ul. Petrovka, 28/2; tel. 923-41-75).

(11) The Aksakov House (*Dom Aksakovykh*), the house where Sergei Timofeevich Aksakov (1791–1859) lived, houses a permanent exhibition of "Almanacs of Literary Life of the 1840s–1880s" (*"Al'manakh literaturnoi zhizni 1840–1880 gg."*). (121002, Moscow, per. Sivtsev Vrazhek, 30; tel. 241-17-10; webpage: http://moscow.lvl.ru/culture/museum/aksak/aksak.html).

(12) The Museum of Silver-Age Literature (*Muzei literatury "Serebrianogo veka"*), preserves the memorial study of Valerii Iakovlevich Briusov (1873–1924) and part of his library. The museum was earlier a branch of the V. V. Maiakovskii Museum (H–36). As of fall of 1998, it is under renovation. (129010, Moscow, prosp. Mira [*formerly* 1-ia Meshchanskaia ul., 30; tel. 280-85-70; webpage: http://moscow.lvl.ru/culture/museum/servek/servek.html).

(13) The Museum of Twentieth-Century Literature (*Muzei literatury XX veka*), located in the historic home of the painter and collector Il'ia Semenovich Ostroukhov (1858–1929), which formerly housed the Ostroukhov Gallery, came under the jurisdiction of GLM in 1983 and is used for various exhibits. (103051, Moscow, Trubnikovskii per., 17; tel. 202-46-18, 202-59-38; webpage: http://moscow.lvl.ru/culture/museum/ruslit/ruslit.html).

Access: Access to archival materials in the various divisions requires an official letter of application endorsed by the director of the museum. The researcher should accordingly first apply to the main administrative office of the museum before proceeding to any of the divisions.

Library Facilities: The museum library collections (ca. 460,000 vols.), dating from early imprints of the sixteenth century to the present, are held in the Book Fond, which is located in the former apartment of the proletarian poet, bibliophile, and collector Dem'ian Bednyi (*pseud. of* E. A. Pridvorov), whose rich library constitutes part of the holdings. There are many books with dedicatory autographs and first editions. For example, the museum retains part of the library of A. I. Herzen and his family, including books with dedicatory autographs by A. I. Herzen, N. P. Ogarev, N. G. Chernyshevskii, and N. I. Turgenev. (Address: Rozhdestvenskii bul'var, 16; tel. 928-77-34; open Thursdays)

Otdel rukopisnykh fondov (OR)
[Division of Manuscript Fonds]

Address: 121002, Moscow, ul. Vesnina, 9/5, kv. 1
Telephone: 241-08-77
Hours: MTh 10:00–16:00
Transport: metro: Smolenskaia; trol.: 10, B
Head: Aleksandra Andreevna Shiriaeva (*tel.* 241-08-77)

HOLDINGS: 410 fonds, 422 collections (over 6,000 items), ca. 50,000 units, mid-15th c.–1990s
folklore collection—150,000 units

The Manuscript Division (located in the same building that houses the A. V. Lunacharskii Study) contains an important collection of literary manuscripts, correspondence, and other personal papers of many Russian classical authors and prominent nineteenth- and twentieth-century writers. There are also a few fonds of literary organizations that functioned during the prerevolutionary and Soviet periods, collections of handwritten albums, folklore collections, and numerous scattered documents dating from the eighteenth through the twentieth centuries pertaining to the development of Russian literature and culture.

The oldest materials, which are found in the collection of manuscript books in the early Slavonic-Rus' tradition, comprise theological works, literary manuscripts, and writings on history and natural science. Among these, the earliest include a liturgical menaion (early 15th c.), a Gospel dated 1464, a codex of saints' lives and homilies (*Sbornik zhitii i pouchenii*) (late 15th–early 16th c.), and a codex with chronological-astronomical tables from the first third of the sixteenth century from the Joseph of Volokolamsk (*Iosifo-Volokolamskii*) Monastery. Among historical texts are annals and chronicles. There are several illuminated manuscripts, including an Old Believer eighteenth-century text of saints' lives with 187 miniatures.

From the eighteenth century there are copies of works of M. V. Lomonosov, G. R. Derzhavin, and N. M. Karamzin, among others, and 49 manuscripts from the eighteenth-century collection of Ia. Ia. Mordvinov.

Literary organizations and associations represented in the archives are the Society of Friends of Russian Philology (*Obshchestvo liubitelei rossiiskoi slovesnosti*) (1811–1830, 1837–1857); the Society of Russian Dramatic Writers (*Obshchestvo russkikh dramaticheskikh pisatelei*) (1870–1930); the cooperative publishing association of Moscow writers (*"Knigoizdatel'stvo pisatelei v Moskve"*) (1912–1925); the All-Russian Union of Poets (*Vserossiiskii soiuz poetov*) (1918–1929); the *"Nikitinskie subbotniki"* Literary Association (1914–1931); the Moscow Writers' Council (*Moskovskii gorodskoi sovet pisatelei*), with documents from the 1930s.

A large fond of the editor of the journal *Byloe*, V. Ia. Bogucharskii (*pseud. of* Ia. V. Iakovlev, 1861–1915), includes over 400 correspondents. There is also the editorial correspondence of a number of magazines and journals, including Milky Way (*Mlechnyi put'*) (1914–1918); Red Army Man (*Krasnoarmeets*); Red Navy Man (*Krasnoflotets*); and Land (*Zemlia*) (1908–1923). There are also some fragments from the archive of the museum's own series *Zven'ia* (1932–1951), including an unpublished report (other parts of those records were transferred to *Literaturnoe nasledstvo* in 1951).

Personal papers (all of which have been acquired since World War II), arranged into fonds for individuals from various accessions, include materials from members of the literary intelligentsia in the prerevolutionary period—V. G. Belinskii, F. M. Dostoevskii, I. S. Turgenev, A. P. Chekhov, and V. G. Korolenko. Herzen materials include original correspondence between Herzen and N. P. Ogarev from the archive of T. A. Astrakova. Another group of personal papers comes from the Orlov family archive (1811–1899), and there are others from archives of the Repnin, Raevskii, Krivtsov, and Volkonskii families, all of which contain documents on the history of Russian culture and life in the nineteenth century.

For the postrevolutionary period there are manuscript materials of A. A. Blok (with at least 85 manuscript poems), S. A. Esenin (Yesenin), M. V. Isakovskii, A. V. Lunacharskii, S. V. Mikhalkov, K. M. Simonov, and many others. Among the 5,000 documents received from MVD sources in 1951 were manuscripts of A. A. Akhmatova, V. Ia. Briusov, S. M. Gorodetskii, and O. E. Mandel'shtam; and letters of N. S. Leskov, V. V. Rozanov, M. A. Bulgakov, and B. L. Pasternak, most of which have been arranged in fonds according to their authors.

There is a collection of original literary autographs of prerevolutionary and Soviet writers; a collection of the manuscript copies of nineteenth-century literary works; and a collection of genre albums and albums containing autographs of famous personages in the Russian cultural world of the nineteenth and twentieth centuries.

The large folklore collection (19th–20th cc.) contains recordings of traditional folklore in the prerevolutionary and postrevolutionary periods, as well as folklore texts on Soviet themes. There is a rich collection of materials from the period of the Second World War. There are also extensive materials and data gathered by ethnographic expeditions to the central regions of Russia, and the personal papers and documents of such scholars of folklore as F. I. Buslaev, E. N. Eleonskaia, and E. V. Pomerantseva.

Working Conditions: Researchers work in a small reading room adjacent to the museum division office and storage area.

Reference Facilities: There are archival inventories of the personal papers and an alphabetic catalogue of personal names. Annotations for a directory of personal fonds in preparation are available, part typewritten and part still in manuscript.

Copying: There are no copying facilities.

Fototeka
[Photograph Archive]

Address:	103001, Moscow, Vspol'nyi per., 14
Telephone:	290-26-71
Hours:	WF 11:00–17:00
Transport:	metro: Krasnopresnenskaia, Barrikadnaia; trol.: 10, B
Head:	Nadezhda Aleksandrovna Vysokolova (*tel.* 291-39-57)

HOLDINGS: 7,017 units, 1882–1986

This sector holds negatives of pictures taken of Russian, Soviet, and foreign nineteenth- and twentieth-century writers and poets, together with portraits of their families, friends, and associates. There are also photographs of places connected with the lives of the writers or described by them in their works. The sector holds the negatives of photographs taken on museum expeditions to places with literary associations.

Reference Facilities: There is a card catalogue of control prints and negatives.

Copying: Photographic copies may be ordered from the negatives and the control prints. Researchers may use their own equipment.

Otdel zvukozapisei
[Division of Sound Recordings]

Address: 103001, Moscow, Vspol'nyi per., 14
Telephone: 290-33-38
Hours: by appointment
Transport: metro: Krasnopresnenskaia, Barrikadnaia; trol.: 10, B
Head: Lev Alekseevich Shilov

HOLDINGS: 2,340 units, 1910–1980s

This division contains gramophone records, tape recordings, cassette recordings, and videotapes of performances given by Russian and foreign writers. The recordings include poetry readings, readings of short stories, and speeches by writers on current affairs.

Copying: Recordings can be copied at commercial rates.

Izobrazitel'nye fondy
[Pictorial Fonds]

Izofond XVII–XIX vv.
[Pictorial Fond of the 17th–19th Centuries]

Address: Moscow, ul. Prechistenka, 12
Telephone: 201-55-66, 291-39-57
Hours: F 10:00–17:00
Transport: metro: Kropotkinskaia
Head: Nonna Aleksandrovna Marchenko

Izofond XX v.
[Pictorial Fond of the 20th Century]

Address: 103001, Moscow, Vspol'nyi per., 14
Telephone: 290-26-71
Hours: F 10:00–17:00
Transport: metro: Krasnopresnenskaia, Barrikadnaia; trol.: B, 10
Head: Galina Nikiforovna Kartasheva

HOLDINGS: 452,773 units, 17th–20th cc.

The exceedingly rich Pictorial Fonds include many painted, graphic, sculptural, and photographic portraits of writers. There are also other graphic materials related to their life and creative work—views of places associated with writers, illustrations, posters for literary and poetry readings, and other assorted memorabilia. There are special collections of graphic materials for many individual authors, especially those for which separate exhibitions or museum branches have been established. For example, in the case of A. I. Herzen (Gertsen), there is Herzen's own collection of portraits of the Decembrists, some of which are on display in the A. I. Herzen Museum.

Reference Facilities: There are working card catalogues for the collections.

FINDING AIDS — PUBLISHED — GENERAL:

Muzei Moskvy (1997), pp. 187–88; *Lit. arkhivy* (1996), pp. 41–44; *GAF Spravochnik* (1991), pp. 140–44; PKG *M&L* (1972), pp. 282–83; Begunov, *Sprav.-ukaz.* (1963), p. 161.

A guide to the manuscript holdings in the museum is in preparation.

Most of the literary manuscript materials covered by the earlier series of inventories *Biulleteni GLM*, vols. 1–5 (1935–1940) and *Katalogi GLM*, vols. 6–8 (1941–1949) are now held in RGALI (B–7, b-189). The L. N. Tolstoi manuscripts (vol. 2), however, are now held in the Tolstoi Museum (H–35, h-284), and the Pushkin materials (vol. 7) are held in Pushkinskii Dom (E–28, e-231.1).

Manuscript Materials

h-260. Shiriaeva, Aleksandra Andreevna. "Rukopisnye fondy Gosudarstvennogo literaturnogo muzeia." In *Novye materialy po istorii russkoi literatury: Sbornik nauchnykh trudov,* edited by N. V. Shakhalova, pp. 6–29. Moscow, 1994. (Lib: IU; MH)

> An up-to-date survey of the history and holdings of the Manuscript Division.

Folklore Materials

h-261. Mints, S. I. "Fol'klornyi arkhiv Gosudarstvennogo literaturnogo muzeia (Moskva)." *Sovetskaia etnografiia*, 1963, no. 3, pp. 148–53. (Lib: DLC; IU; MH) [IDC-in R-2312]

> A detailed survey of the folklore holdings, including collections of folklore brought together by various individuals.

History of GLM

h-262. Shumikhin, Sergei Viktorovich. *Obrazovanie, komplektovanie i ispol'zovanie arkhivnogo sobraniia Gosudarstvennogo literaturnogo muzeia: Avtoreferat dissertatsii na soiskanie zvaniia kandidata istoricheskikh nauk.* Moscow: MGIAI, 1988. 29 p.

> An account of the history and the work of the State Literary Museum from 1931 to 1941, when the director was V. D. Bonch-Bruevich. Provides considerable information on the acquisition and composition of the manuscript fonds, which were subsequently moved to the State Literary Archive (now RGALI). The complete dissertation is available in the RGGU library.

h-263. Mezhova, K. G. *Istochniki po arkhivno-sobiratel'skoi deiatel'nosti V. D. Bonch-Bruevicha (1931–1941): Avtoreferat dissertatsii na soiskanie zvaniia kandidata istoricheskikh nauk.* Moscow, 1974.

> An account of the activities of V. D. Bonch-Bruevich in developing the manuscript collections of the State Literary Museum (1931–1941), which were subsequently moved to the State Literary Archive (now RGALI). See also the author's article "Deiatel'nost' V. D. Bonch-Bruevicha po sobiraniiu dokumentov lichnogo proiskhozhdeniia," *Sovetskie arkhivy*, 1973, no. 3, pp. 37–42.

h-264. Vinogradova, K. M. "Gosudarstvennyi literaturnyi muzei (1921–1960 gg.)." In *Voprosy raboty muzeev literaturnogo profilia,* pp. 51–93. Moscow, 1961. "Trudy Nauchno-issledovatel'skogo instituta muzeevedeniia i okhrany pamiatnikov istorii i kul'tury," vol. 6. (Lib: IU; MH)

> A brief account of the history of the museum and its holdings up to the year 1960.

GLM Series

h-265. *Novye materialy po istorii russkoi i sovetskoi literatury: Sbornik nauchnykh trudov.*
Edited by N. V. Shakhalova. Moscow, 1983. 261 p. [Minkul't RSFSR; GLM] (Lib: DLC;
MH)

> *Novye materialy po istorii russkoi literatury: Sbornik nauchnykh trudov.* Edited by
> N. V. Shakhalova. M.: GLM, 1994. 197 p. [Minkul'tury Rossii; GLM]. (Lib: DLC; MH).

> These two volumes in the unnumbered series issued by GLM contain important descriptions of
> manuscript and other archival materials in addition to many publications of documents from the
> collections. See also the volume devoted to the publication of materials relating to Chekhov—*A. P.*
> *Chekhov i izdatel'stvo "Posrednik" : Sbornik nauchnykh trudov* (Moscow, 1992).

h-266. *Zven'ia: Sborniki materialov i dokumentov po istorii literatury, iskusstva i*
obshchestvennoi mysli XIX v. 9 vols. Moscow/Leningrad: Gos. izd-vo kul't.-prosvet. lit-ry,
1932–1951. Edited by V. D. Bonch-Bruevich, and A. V. Lunacharskii. [GLM] (Lib: MH)

FINDING AIDS — SPECIALIZED:

For Jewish-related holdings, see *Jewish Doc.* (1996), p. 23. Fonds of personal papers of Russian
émigrés held by GLM, most of which have been declassifed recently, are listed in *Rus. Zarubezh'e*
(1998), pp. 347–52.

h-267. *Zven'ia: A. S. Pushkin, A. I. Gertsen, I. S. Turgenev, N. A. Nekrasov, A. N. Ostrovskii,*
M. E. Saltykov-Shchedrin, N. G. Chernyshevskii. Edited by V. D. Bonch-Bruevich.
Moscow: Gos. izd-vo kul't.-prosvet. literatury, 1950. 864 p. "Zven'ia: Sborniki materialov
i dokumentov po istorii literatury, iskusstva i obshchestvennoi mysli XIX v.," vol. 8.
[GLM] (Lib: IU; MH)

> The eighth volume of the important GLM publication series includes a series of surveys of individual
> fonds held by the museum, namely those devoted to N. P. Ogarev (pp. 801–13; from the M. O.
> Gershenzon collection), N. A. Nekrasov (pp. 814–21), N. G. Chernyshevskii (pp. 821–24), D. A.
> Furmanov (pp. 825–27), and letters of the French writer Henri Barbusse (pp. 827–29). Other
> volumes of the series, edited by Bonch-Bruevich, contain documentary publications rather than
> archival descriptions, but those covered by the first six volumes were all transferred to TsGLA (now
> RGALI) in 1941.

h-268. *A. I. Gertsen, N. P. Ogarev i ikh okruzhenie: Knigi. Rukopisi. Izobrazitel'nye materialy.*
Pamiatnye veshchi: Materialy iz sobraniia Gosudarstvennogo Literaturnogo muzeia:
Katalog. Compiled by A. I. Zhelvakova, E. G. Narskaia, and I. M. Rudoi. Edited by
I. G. Ptushkina. Moscow, 1992. 221 p. + plates. [GLM] (Lib: MH)

> A recent catalogue of materials relating to Herzen and Ogarev held in GLM, covering a total of 761
> items. Manuscript and documentary materials (nos. 219–252), including 24 recently accessioned
> letters from the T. A. Astrakova collection. A large part of the catalogue covers books (13 with
> dedicatory autographs) and pictorial materials, including Herzen's collection of portraits of the
> Decembrists (nos. 318–359). Note that all of the Herzen and Ogarev materials covered by the 1940
> GLM catalogue (*Biulleteni GLM*, vol. 5) are now held in RGALI (see B–7, b-189.4).

h-269. Ovcharova, P. I. "Obshchestvo russkikh dramaticheskikh pisatelei: Obzor rukopisnogo
fonda." In *Novye materialy po istorii russkoi literatury: Sbornik nauchnykh trudov,* edited
by N. V. Shakhalova, pp. 131–52. Moscow, 1994. (Lib: DLC; IU; MH)

> A survey of records of the society (1870–1930), started in 1870 on the initiative of A. N. Ostrovskii
> and V. I. Rodislavskii, whose aim was to promote better relations between dramatists and private
> theaters—now fond 151 in the Manuscript Division (other parts of the records are held in RGALI).

h-270. Sokolova, Tat'iana Viktorovna. "Iz arkhiva Pavlovykh." In *Novye materialy po istorii russkoi i sovetskoi literatury: Sbornik nauchnykh trudov,* edited by N. V. Shakhalova, pp. 51–67. Moscow, 1983. [Minkul't RSFSR; GLM] (Lib: DLC; IU; MH)

> A survey and characterization of the archival materials collected by the Moscow University physics professor Mikhail Grigor'evich Pavlov (1793–1840), who was active in literary circles in the early nineteenth century.

h-271. Svetlov, A. P. "Knigi s avtografami v adres D. Bednogo v kollektsii Gosudarstvennogo Literaturnogo muzeia." In *Novye materialy po istorii russkoi i sovetskoi literatury: Sbornik nauchnykh trudov,* edited by N. V. Shakhalova, pp. 162–95. Moscow, 1983. [Minkul't RSFSR; GLM] (Lib: DLC; IU; MH)

> Describes the many books with dedicatory autographs found in the library collection of the Soviet poet and bibliophile, Dem'ian Bednyi (*pseud.* of E. A. Pridvorov). Other articles in the same collection describe dedicatory autographs of writers from different republics of the USSR in the libraries of A. A. Fadeev (pp. 196–205) and M. M. Prishvin (pp. 120–43), and autographs of K. A. Fedin found in the GLM book collections (pp. 207–21).

h-272. Kaidalova, Natal'ia Arkad'evna. *Katalog izobrazitel'nogo fonda A. A. Bloka.* Moscow, 1985. [GLM] "Katalogi Gosudarstvennogo literaturnogo muzeia." (Lib: MH)

> A detailed, scholarly catalogue with item-level descriptions of the 401 units of collected pictorial materials in the fond of the Russian symbolist poet Aleksandr Aleksandrovich Blok (1880–1921). The collection, which was acquired by the museum at different times (1934–1982) includes portraits, photographs, drawings, and other graphic materials. There are many illustrations, an index of Blok's works cited, and an index of personal names.

Gosudarstvennyi muzei A. S. Pushkina (GMP)

[A. S. Pushkin State Museum]

Agency: Komitet po kul'ture Pravitel'stva Moskvy
[Committee on Culture of the Government of Moscow]

Address:	119034, Moscow, ul. Prechistenka, 12/2
Telephone:	201-32-56
E-mail:	internet@museum.ru
Website:	http://www.museum.ru/pushkin
Transport:	metro: Kropotkinskaia; trol.: 5, 15, 16, 31
Hours:	W–F 11:00–18:00 (reception for the Manuscript Cabinet F 10:00–18:00 and by appointment)

Director: Evgenii Anatol'evich Bogatyrev (*tel.* 202-23-21)
Deputy Director for Scientific Research: Natal'ia Ivanovna Mikhailova (*tel.* 202-21-52)
Chief Curator: Nina Sergeevna Nechaeva (*tel.* 201-56-74)

HISTORY:

The museum honoring the Russian poet Aleksandr Sergeevich Pushkin (1799–1837) was founded in 1957, and opened to the public in 1961. It occupies an early nineteenth-century detached house that is a designated architectural landmark—the Khrushchev-Seleznev Estate (*"Usad'ba Khrushchevykh-Seleznevykh"*), which was built in 1814–1817 on the design of A. Grigor'ev.

Archival materials in the museum are held in a number of different divisions or sectors.

The museum has two affiliated branches:

(1) The Pushkin Memorial Apartment on the Arbat (*Memorial'naia kvartira Pushkina na Arbate*), which is located in the House of N. N. Khitrovo, where Pushkin lived from February to May 1831 after his marriage, and which opened as a memorial museum in 1986. (112002, Moscow, ul. Arbat, 53; tel.: 241-92-95; fax: (095) 241-42-12; e-mail: sdm@museum.ru). The Photograph Archive is located there (see below).

(2) The Andrei Belyi Memorial Apartment on the Arbat (*Memorial'naia kvartira Andreia Belogo na Arbate*) (see below).

N.B. The museum underwent major renovation in preparation for the bicentennial of Pushkin's birth in 1999. Note that other Pushkin materials collected in Moscow had been transferred to Leningrad in 1947 and are now held either in Pushkinskii Dom (IRLI—E–28) or in the All-Russian A. S. Pushkin Museum (H–95).

Access: Research access to the museum archival holdings requires a letter from the sponsoring organization addressed to the Deputy Director for Scientific Research or to the Chief Curator.

Working Conditions: There is one reading room for all divisions of the museum. Research hours are limited, but researchers visiting from out of town may, by way of an exception, request additional appointments on special days to work with manuscript materials.

Library Facilities: There is a reference library with a reading room, in which Pushkin memorabilia are displayed. There are scattered publications on the history of Russia, literary criticism, and reference books.

Copying: There is a xerox photocopier, but it is mainly used for internal purposes. Materials selected for copying must be approved by the Deputy Director for Scientific Research and the Head of the Division of Fonds. Reproductions from the Photograph Archive can be ordered through an outside vendor.

Rukopisnyi kabinet
[Manuscript Cabinet]

Hours: WThF 10:00–18:00
Head: Alla Izrailevna Frumkina (*tel.* 201-56-74)
Deputy Head: Elena Arlenovna Ponomareva (*tel.* 201-56-74)

HOLDINGS: 12,689 units, 18th–20th cc.
   photographic fond of Pushkin's manuscripts—11,000 units; manuscript materials, main fond—574 units (1769–1991); manuscript materials, auxiliary fond—1,115 units

Many of the manuscript holdings in the museum are held in the Manuscript Cabinet, which is administratively part of the Division of Fonds. There is considerable documentation (in original and copy) on the life and work of A. S. Pushkin (1799–1837), including manuscript materials of and relating to many of his contemporaries.

Of special interest is the poet's autograph book register (*Registr k knigam gospodina A. S. Pushkina*). The collection entitled "Albums and Manuscript Collections of the Late Eighteenth and Nineteenth Centuries" contains manuscript copies of Pushkin's poetry as well as copies of the verses of contemporary poets like D. V. Davydov, K. N. Batiushkov, and V. A. Zhukovskii.

In the collection of documents entitled "Pushkin's Contemporaries," there are a number of letters from Pushkin's friends and relatives—M. N. Volkonskaia, P. A. Viazemskii, O. S. Pavlishcheva, A. S. Griboedov, the Goncharov family, and others.

There is a separate collection of account books from landed estates together with deeds of purchase, documents issued by the Church hierarchy, and other official documents from the late eighteenth and early nineteenth centuries.

The collection entitled "Pushkin and the Present" (*A. S. Pushkin i sovremennost'*) includes original, handwritten verses by A. A. Blok and B. L. Pasternak, documents relating to the Pushkin anniversaries, articles by Pushkin scholars, and original pieces by modern literary figures relating to Pushkin.

Since most of the Pushkin manuscript materials have been centralized in Pushkinskii Dom (IRLI— E–28) in St. Petersburg, the museum has a special fond known as the "Cabinet of Pushkin Manuscripts" (*Kabinet pushkinskikh rukopisei*) consisting of high quality full-size photographic copies of all the Pushkin manuscripts held in Pushkinskii Dom, which can be used by researchers in Moscow.

Working Conditions: A small reading room is available.

Reference Facilities: There are archival inventories, a card catalogue of the albums, and a card catalogue of Pushkin's drawings.

Sektor genealogii
[Sector of Genealogy]

Hours: F 10:00–18:00
Head: Ol'ga Vladimirovna Rykova (*tel.* 202-91-57)

HOLDINGS: 15,882 units, 18th–20th cc.
   iconographic materials—13,646 units

The Genealogy Sector of the museum's Book Division (*Otdel knizhnykh fondov*) contains the nineteenth-century genealogical collection (including photographs) made by the famous Moscow genealogist Iu. B. Shmarov. The collections include genealogical tables and lists together with excerpts from published and archival sources, and original documents from the eighteenth to the twentieth century taken from family archives.

The iconographic part of the collection consists chiefly of photographs attached to identification documents, the reverse side of which contains the biographical details of the person photographed.

Reference Facilities: The documents in the sector are in the process of being arranged.

Sektor redkoi knigi
[Sector of Rare Books]

Hours:　　F 10:00–18:00
Head: Iuliia Iur'evna Grechikhova (*tel.* 291-95-80)

HOLDINGS: I. N. Rozanov library of Russian poetry—10,000 units (18th c.–1950s); library of S. N. Golubov—ca. 3,000 units

The Rare Books Sector, administratively part of the Book Division (*Otdel knizhnykh fondov*) also holds some materials of archival interest. Many of the books (17th–20th cc.) have dedicatory autographs by their authors.

This fond includes the "I. N. Rozanov Library of Russian Poetry," which contains first editions of Russian poets from the eighteenth century to the 1950s; and the library of S. N. Golubov, which has editions of Russian memoirs, genealogical tables, and reference books on Russian history.

Reference Facilities: There are alphabetic and subject catalogues, and a card catalogue of autographed books. Each collection also has its own inventory, but the Rozanov Library has a printed catalogue, a subject catalogue, and a card catalogue of authors.

Otdel izofondov—Sektor original'noi tekhniki
[Division of Pictorial Fonds—Sector of Original Techniques]

Hours:　　F 10:00–18:00
Head: Lidiia Aleksandrovna Karnaukhova (*tel.* 290-10-25)

HOLDINGS: original drawings, main fond—4,282 units (17th–20th cc.)

In addition to paintings, graphic materials, and watercolors, this sector has a special collection of the works of contemporary Russian painters with Pushkin as their subject. There are many illustrations for Pushkin's works by twentieth-century artists like T. A. Mavrina, N. B. Kuz'min, and D. A. Shmarinov.

Reference Facilities: There are card catalogues, some arranged by subject.

Otdel izofondov—Sektor estampa
[Division of Pictorial Fonds—Sector of Prints and Engravings]

Hours:　　F 10:00–18:00
Head: Lidiia Leonidovna Ivchenko (*tel.* 290-10-25)

HOLDINGS: prints and lithographs, main fond—14,664 units (18th–20th cc.)

The Prints and Engravings Sector, which includes all types of engraving, holds iconographic representations of Pushkin and his contemporaries (E. A. Baratynskii, P. A. Viazemskii, D. V. Venevitinov, N. V. Gogol', and A. S. Griboedov); portraits of Russian and European writers (M. V.

Lomonosov, A. Kantemir, Ovid, Horace, Dante, Byron, Voltaire, Goethe and others); portraits of heroes from the Napoleonic invasion (Patriotic War) of 1812; scenes from Russian and European history; views of towns and gardens; genre scenes; and illustrations for the works of Pushkin, the earliest of which were made during his lifetime.

The sector also holds the iconographic collections of Ia. G. Zak (4,040 plates) and P. V. Gubar which are housed separately in the museum. These include not only iconographic material, but books and *objets d'art.*

Reference Facilities: There are inventory card catalogues and card catalogues describing museum exhibits, as well as subject and author catalogues.

Fototeka
[Photograph Archive]

Address: 121002, Moscow, ul. Arbat, 53
Hours: F 10:00–18:00
Transport: metro: Smolenskaia, Arbatskaia
Head: Elena Aleksandrovna Usova (*tel.* 291-41-92)

HOLDINGS: ca. 300 units, 1850s–early 20th c.

photographs, main fond—160 units; photographs of museum objects—9,000 units; slides—2,000 units

The Photograph Archive constitutes a division of the museum, located in the GMP branch—the Pushkin Memorial Apartment on the Arbat. The historical section has photographs of Pushkin's descendants from the late nineteenth to the early twentieth century and a daguerreotype of his contemporary, S. G. Volkonskii. The photographic documentary section includes photographs of places connected with Pushkin, Pushkin festivals, theater productions, and portraits of Pushkin scholars. The largest part of the archive consists of negatives and prints of items in the museum.

Reference Facilities: There are subject card catalogues.

Memorial'naia kvartira Andreia Belogo na Arbate
[Andrei Belyi Memorial Apartment on the Arbat]

Address: 112002, Moscow, ul. Arbat, 55
Telephone: 241-77-02
Hours: W–Sa 11:00–17:00
Transport: metro: Smolenskaia
Head: Nikolai Dmitrievich Aleksandrov (*tel.* 241-77-02)

HOLDINGS:

The museum was opened in 1993 in the apartment of Andrei Belyi (*pseud.* of Boris Nikolaevich Bugaev) (1880–1934). Among archival holdings are the personal papers of Belyi's first wife A. A. Turgeneva, received from Switzerland in 1994, and those of K. N. Bugaeva (second wife).

FINDING AIDS — PUBLISHED — GENERAL:

Muzei Moskvy (1997), pp. 204–207; *GAF Spravochnik* (1991), pp. 147–48.

There is no published guide to the archival materials in the museum.

h-275. Krein, Aleksandr Zinov'evich. *Rozhdenie muzeia.* Moscow: "Sovetskaia Rossiia," 1969. 208 p. (Lib: DLC; IU; MH)

> A popularized history of the Pushkin Museum in Moscow and its activity during the first years of its existence. Although there is no special description of the manuscript fonds, there is useful information on individual documents (especially pp. 37–66).

h-276. Krein, Aleksandr Zinov'evich. *Zhizn' muzeia.* Moscow: "Sovetskaia Rossiia," 1979. 256 p. (Lib: DLC; IU; MH)

> Continues and supplements the 1969 publication (h-275), with special sections describing the Manuscript Division, the Photograph Archive (pp. 56–60), and the pictorial fonds (pp. 40–46).

FINDING AIDS — SPECIALIZED:

h-277. *Biblioteka russkoi poezii I. N. Rozanova: Bibliograficheskoe opisanie.* Compiled by V. V. Gol'dberg, M. I. Kostrova, K. A. Martsishevskaia, et al. Moscow: "Kniga," 1975. 480 p. (Lib: DLC; IU; MH)

> A detailed catalogue of the I. N. Rozanov Library, listing 6,000 titles of books on Russian poetry with notes on autographs and inscriptions. The catalogue lacks annotations, but occasionally the footnotes provide brief information on authors and publishers.

h-278. *Velikii grad Petra.* Compiled by E. V. Muza. Moscow: "Sovetskaia Rossiia," 1977. 54 p. + plates. (Lib: DLC; MH)

> A catalogue of the engravings and lithographs in the museum collection that are devoted to St. Petersburg and connected with the name of Pushkin.

h-279. *Avtografy sovremennikov Pushkina na knigakh iz sobraniia Gosudarstvennogo muzeia A. S. Pushkina: Annotirovannyi katalog.* Compiled by O. V. Asnina and Iu. Iu. Grechikhova. Edited by S. N. Tikhomirova. Moscow: "Kniga," 1988. 271 p. (Lib: DLC)

> The catalogue includes the autographs of 160 of Pushkin's contemporaries (friends and acquaintances, teachers, literary associates, and older poets) in 386 imprints held in the museum. References are arranged alphabetically and indexed.

h-280. *Moskva i okrestnosti v litografiiakh firmy Dzhuzeppe Datsiaro: Iz sobraniia Gosudarstvennogo muzeia A. S. Pushkina.* Compiled by G. A. Miroliubova and G. Z. Kaganov. Translated by N. V. Tokareva. Moscow: "Iskusstvo," 1996. 190 p. + plates. Introduction by N. S. Nechaeva. (Lib: MH-F)

> An elaborate catalogue with colored reproductions of lithographs of Moscow and its environs from the Moscow firm of Guiseppe Daziaro (Iosif *or* Osip Khristoforovich Datsiaro) (1806–1865), associated with his Paris outlet, most of which were prepared by the French printer Lemercier. Includes a glossary of artists and engravers (pp. 84–91).

Gosudarstvennyi muzei L. N. Tolstogo (GMT)
[L. N. Tolstoi State Museum]

Agency: Ministerstvo kul'tury RF (Minkul'tury Rossii)
[Ministry of Culture]

Address: 119034, Moscow, ul. Prechistenka, 11
Telephone: 201-58-11; 201-77-60; *Fax:* (095) 202-93-38; *RdngRm:* 201-75-18
Website: http://moscow.lvl.ru/culture/museum/tolst/tolst.html
Transport: metro: Kropotkinskaia; trol.: 5, 15
Hours: Tu–Su 11:00–17:00

Director: Lidiia Mikhailovna Liubimova (*tel.* 202-93-38)

HISTORY:

Tolstovskii muzei
[Tolstoi Museum] (1912–1920)
Gosudarstvennyi Tolstovskii muzei
[State Tolstoi Museum] (1920–1979)

The Tolstoi Museum was founded in 1912 at the initiative of the Tolstoi Society (*Tolstovskoe obshchestvo*) on the basis of private funding in memory of the Russian novelist Lev Nikolaevich Tolstoi (1825–1910) (often Leo Tolstoy in English). It was nationalized after the Revolution and in 1920 came under the control of the People's Commissariat for Education of the RSFSR as the State Tolstoi Museum. From 1939 to 1953 the museum was under the authority of the Academy of Sciences of the USSR, during which time its academic status was heightened and manuscript holdings extended. The museum was subsequently transferred to the jurisdiction of the Ministry of Culture, but its present name has been preserved since 1920. After the museum was awarded the "Order of the Red Banner of Labor" (*Orden Trudovogo Krasnogo Znameni*) in 1979, that award became part of its official name. In April 1997 the museum was registered as one of the most valuable monuments of the cultural heritage of the peoples of the Russian Federation.

The Manuscript Division has been part of the museum since its founding. Its organization and scope were substantially enlarged after the museum came under the Academy of Sciences in 1939, when the museum was designated as the centralized repository for all Tolstoi manuscripts, personal papers, and biographical materials relating to Lev Tolstoi and his family, with the aim of preparing a definitive edition of his complete literary works. Later it acquired all of the Tolstoi manuscripts and related documentation that had been collected in the Manuscript Division of the Lenin Library (h-283) and similarly the manuscript materials that had been collected by the State Literary Museum (h-284). Its central role has continued to the present. The division is currently housed, as it has been for many years, in a separate building a block away from the museum (ul. Prechistenka, 11).

The museum has three affiliated branches:

(1) The L. N. Tolstoi Khamovniki Estate Museum (*Muzei-usad'ba L. N. Tolstogo "Khamovniki"*) in Moscow has scattered archival materials on display, particularly from the years 1893–1895 when Tolstoi lived in the house. (119021, Moscow, ul. L'va Tolstogo, 21; tel. 246-94-44).

(2) The exhibition "L. N. Tolstoi during the 1850s and 1860s in Moscow" (*"L. N. Tolstoi v 1850–1860 gody v Moskve"*) has a number of original manuscript and illustrative materials on display. (113035, Moscow, ul. Piatnitskaia, 12; tel. 231-74-02; 231-64-40).

(3) The L. N. Tolstoi Literary-Memorial Museum (*Memorial'nyi muzei L. N. Tolstogo*) in Lipetsk Oblast (over 200 km. southeast of Moscow) at Lev Tolstoi Station has documents, books, and illustrative materials from the fonds of the main museum. (399600, Lipetskaia oblast', st. Lev Tolstoi; tel. [8-07464] 2-34-21).

N.B. A large part of the Tolstoi library, including books with dedicatory autographs, and also additional documentary materials (especially relating to the estate), are held in the Tolstoi Iasnaia Poliana Estate Museum (often Yasnaya Polyana in English)—(*Gosudarstvennyi memorial'nyi i prirodnyi zapovednik "Muzei-usad'ba L. N. Tolstogo 'Iasnaia Poliana'"*), south of Tula. (301214, Tul'skaia oblast', Shchekinskii raion, p/o Iasnaia Poliana; tel. [8-0872] 25-64-37, 21-13-12; fax: [8-0872] 33-26-10; website: http://sunsite.unc.edu/sergei/exs/YasnayaPoliana/yp1.html, as well as other local websites).

Access: Research access remains limited as a result of an exclusive publication agreement between the museum and the Institute of World Literature (IMLI RAN—E–9), involving the preparation of an academic edition of the complete works of Tolstoi. Accordingly, researchers (particularly foreign researchers) will not be given permission to examine papers and documents which are, or potentially could be, under consideration for publication. Inventories and other finding aids for manuscript materials are also not normally available to outside researchers. Furthermore, some fonds or parts of fonds have been closed at the wishes of the creators or donors, and researchers are not given access to materials which could be used to the detriment of the Tolstoi family. All decisions regarding the granting or refusal of access are made by the Academic Council of the museum.

Library Facilities: The museum has an extensive library which is part of the Division of Book Fonds.

Otdel rukopisei
[Manuscript Division]

Hours:　　TuWF 10:00–18:00
Head: Natal'ia Alekseevna Kalinina (*tel.* 201-75-18)

HOLDINGS: 72 fonds (5 fonds are being processed), 291,857 units, late 18th–20th institutional fonds—4; L. N. Tolstoi fond—71,272 units; photographs—22,169

The Manuscript Division is the central repository for all Tolstoi's literary manuscripts, his personal papers, and other materials relating to him and his family. The division is the center for all research and publication work on documents pertaining to L. N. Tolstoi. The writer's fond contains works of both a literary and theoretical nature together with diaries, notebooks, drawings, posters, sheet music, and numerous inscriptions and dedications in the writer's own hand on separate sheets, on photographs, on postcards and in books and magazines. There are also books containing marginal notes written by Tolstoi and various materials relating to his biography and his daily life. A large part of the fond consists of letters written by Tolstoi to Russians and foreigners (approximately 9,000) and letters to Tolstoi in twenty-six languages (approximately 50,000). The fond also contains police and censorship material from various official departments.

There are also personal fonds of members of Tolstoi's family (his wife S. A. Tolstaia; children S. L. Tolstoi, T. L. Sukhotina, I. L. Tolstoi, and L. L. Tolstoi); relatives (T. A. Kuz'minskaia, A. I. Tolstaia-Popova, and S. A. Tolstaia-Esenina); friends and acquaintances (V. G. Chertkov, N. N. Gusev, V. F. Bulgakov, and D. P. Makovitskii); followers of Tolstoi's teaching (R. A. Butkevich, V. A. Molochnikov, and L. D. Semenov-Tian-Shanskii); members of Tolstoi's agricultural communes; and literary critics (N. N. Ardens, V. A. Zhdanov, and E. E. Zaidenshnur). There is also a special family fond containing documents relating to Tolstoi's ancestors, parents, brothers, and sisters.

The museum holds books containing marginal notes or annotations written by Tolstoi, and books and photographs autographed by him, or with dedicatory inscriptions. There are also drawings by Tolstoi, manuscripts by various writers with his editorial corrections, and recollections of Tolstoi by his contemporaries.

There are a number of the fonds of official and public organizations that are connected with the writer. These include records of the Moscow Tolstoi Society (*Tolstovskoe obshchestvo v Moskve*), the editors of the complete works of Tolstoi in ninety volumes (Jubilee Edition), the former Tolstoi Museum in St. Petersburg. Also held here are the administrative records of the museum from the time of its establishment.

Photographs housed in the museum show the writer at different stages of his life, together with various other prominent figures from his cultural circle, such as I. S. Turgenev, A. P. Chekhov, and V. G. Chertkov, and with the peasants at Iasnaia Poliana.

Working Conditions: Researchers in the reading room of the museum are normally permitted to use only photocopies of Tolstoi manuscripts. Inventories and other finding aids for manuscript materials are not normally available to researchers who are not involved with publication projects of the museum.

Reference Facilities: The internal reference system maintains a general alphabetic catalogue of all fonds. There are also individual alphabetic catalogues for each fond, subject catalogues for the L. N. Tolstoi fond (arranged systematically according to subject, chronology, topography, and genre of literary production, and with a separate catalogue covering Tolstoi's diaries and notebooks); catalogues of the writer's letters (arranged alphabetically and chronologically); catalogues of the letters written to Tolstoi (arranged alphabetically, according to Russian and foreign correspondents, and chronologically); an alphabetic catalogue of the letters written on Tolstoi's instructions; catalogues of memoirs and recollections of the writer and documents relating to his life and work (arranged geographically and also by memorial dates [1908, 1910] and so forth); and also inventory registers and *opisi* of documents.

Copying: Xerox copies can be ordered, but restrictions apply, particularly to otherwise unpublished materials.

FINDING AIDS — PUBLISHED — GENERAL:

Muzei Moskvy (1997), pp. 210–14; *GAF Spravochnik* (1991), pp. 148–51; G&K *Spravochnik* (1983), p. 59; PKG *M&L* (1972), pp. 285–86; Sup. 1 (1976), p. 113.

There is no comprehensive published guide or general description to the archival materials in the museum, although there are published catalogues of many parts of the holdings.

h-281. *Opisanie rukopisei khudozhestvennykh proizvedenii L. N. Tolstogo.* Compiled by V. A. Zhdanov, E. E. Zaidenshnur, and E. S. Serebrovskaia. Edited by V. A. Zhdanov. Moscow: Izd-vo AN SSSR, 1955. 634 p. [GMT] (Lib: DLC; IU; MH) [IDC-R-11,025]
    Covers the literary manuscripts in the Tolstoi Museum arranged in chronological order.

h-282. *Opisanie rukopisei statei L. N. Tolstogo: Literatura, iskusstvo, nauka, pedagogika.* Compiled by E. E. Zaidenshnur and E. S. Serebrovskaia. Edited by V. A. Zhdanov. Moscow: "Sovetskaia Rossiia," 1961. 279 p. [GMT] (Lib: DLC; IU; MH) [IDC-R-11,026]
    A scholarly description of Tolstoi's manuscript articles on art, literature, science, and pedagogy, including Tolstoi's prefaces and postscripts to works of other writers. In addition to Tolstoi's own works, descriptions are provided for various other manuscript materials that are related to Tolstoi's school and his activities as a teacher.

h-283. *Rukopisi L. N. Tolstogo: Katalog.* Compiled by F. V. Buslaev. Edited by I. K. Luppol. 2 vols. Moscow: Sotsegiz, 1937. (Lib: DLC; MH) [IDC-R-11,121]
    Vol. 1: *Proizvedeniia.* 151 p. Vol. 2: *Pis'ma.* 152 p.
    This two-volume catalogue of Tolstoi's literary manuscripts and letters was prepared when they were still held in the Manuscript Division of the Lenin Library (now RGB—G–1). They were subsequently transferred to the Tolstoi Museum.

h-284. *L. N. Tolstoi: Rukopisi, perepiska i dokumenty.* Compiled by A. V. Askar'iants et al. Edited by N. N. Gusev. Moscow: Zhurnal'no-gazetnoe ob"edinenie, 1937. 236 p. "Biulleteni Gosudarstvennogo literaturnogo muzeia," vol. 2. (Lib: DLC; IU; MH[mf]) [IDC-R-10,837]

> This catalogue was prepared when the Tolstoi manuscripts were still held in the State Literary Museum, but they were subsequently transferred to the Tolstoi Museum.

h-285. *Korrespondenty L. N. Tolstogo: (Annotirovannyi katalog).* Compiled by F. V. Buslaev. Edited by N. N. Gusev. Moscow: Sotsegiz, 1940. 223 p. (Lib: DLC; IU; MH) [IDC-R-11,122]

> This catalogue of Tolstoi's correspondence was prepared when the materials involved were still held in the Lenin Library (now RGB—G–1), before their transfer to the Tolstoi Museum.

FINDING AIDS — SPECIALIZED — UNPUBLISHED:

h-287. *Kalinina, Natal'ia Alekseevna. "Obzor fonda sem'i Tolstykh." Moscow. Typescript.

> A typewritten copy of this unpublished survey of the Tolstoi family fond is available in the museum reading room.

h-288. *Lobziakova, V. V. "Obzor fonda L. L. Tolstogo." Moscow. Typescript.

> A typewritten copy of this unpublished survey of the personal papers of Tolstoi's son is available in the museum reading room.

h-289. *Shumova B. M. "Obzor fonda V. P. Botkina." Moscow. Typescript.

> An unpublished copy of this survey of personal papers of the publicist and literary critic V. P. Botkin, who was associated with Tolstoi, is available in the museum reading room.

Gosudarstvennyi muzei V. V. Maiakovskogo (GMM)
[V. V. Maiakovskii State Museum]

Agency: Komitet po kul'ture Pravitel'stva Moskvy
[Committee on Culture of the Government of Moscow]

Address: 101000, Moscow, Lubianskii proezd, 3/6 (per. Maiakovskogo, 15/13)
Telephone: 921-93-87
Website: http://www.museum.ru/majakovskiy
Transport: metro: Lubianka, Kitai-gorod
Hours: M 12:00–18:00; Tu–F 10:00–18:00; Th 13:00–21:00

Director: Svetlana Efimovna Strizhneva (*tel.* 921-37-28)

HISTORY:

Gosudarstvennaia biblioteka-muzei Maiakovskogo (BMM)
[Maiakovskii State Library-Museum] (1937–1967)

The museum was founded in 1937 as the Maiakovskii State Library-Museum in the house near Taganka Square, where the Soviet Russian poet Vladimir Vladimirovich Maiakovskii (1893–1930) lived for most of the time from 1926 to 1930. (That street was before 1936 known as Gendrikov pereulok, was in that year renamed, per. Maiakovskogo, 15/13). In 1967 the museum holdings were transferred to the building on what is now Lubianskii proezd (*formerly* proezd Serova), which had previously housed the poet's memorial apartment, and which from 1919 to the end of his life had been Maiakovskii's permanent residence in Moscow. The original home of the museum on Taganka was initially retained as a museum (formally a branch), but is now no longer part of the museum. In 1974 the renamed Maiakovskii State Museum was opened in its new home.

In 1969 the museum was reorganized into sectors, including the now separate Manuscript-Documentary Fond, although the sector containing the Maiakovskii family archives was not formed until 1976. The photograph and pictorial fond was formed as a separate subdivision in 1968, and in 1990, it was divided into two separate fonds.

The museum has a branch in the Maiakovskii family apartment, which is not presently open as a museum, but which houses the library and family archive sector. (123376, Moscow, Studenetskii per., 22; tel. 255-01-86).

N.B. A major part of the Maiakovskii papers are held in the Russian State Archive of Literature and Art (RGALI—B–7) and some are found in other repositories (see h-291/a-147).

Access: Research access to the documentary materials requires a letter from the researcher's sponsoring organization or a personal application.

Library Facilities: The museum has a book fond (ca. 250,000 vols.), including extensive holdings regarding the Russian avant-garde, but the library facilities are only partially accessible at present due to lack of funds. The rare book fond, with over 4,000 titles, including editions of Maiakovskii's writings published during the poet's lifetime, has restricted access, but the index to these editions is available. The library is currently located in the former Maiakovskii family apartment (Studenetskii per., 22).

Rukopisno-dokumental'nyi fond
[Manuscript-Documentary Fond]

Telephone: 921-03-42
Hours: MTu 10:00–17:00
Head: Elena Iosifovna Pogorel'skaia (*tel.* 921-03-42)

HOLDINGS: 23 fonds, 14,447 units, late 19th c.–1983

The Manuscript-Documentary Fond, formally a sector of the museum, comprises personal papers and archival materials relating to Vladimir Maiakovskii. Here are found many of his literary manuscripts and personal papers, including 68 of his notebooks. The fond includes his correspondence with friends and relatives, with prominent personages in the world of literature and the arts, with readers and budding poets, and with organizations and institutions.

The fond contains materials and documents relating to the study and publicizing of Maiakovskii's works, as well as the memoirs and recollections of his contemporaries.

The Manuscript Fond also holds the personal papers of some of Maiakovskii's contemporaries—S. P. Bobrov, S. M. Gorodetskii, N. F. Denisovskii, V. E. Meyerhold (Meierkhol'd), P. V. Neznamov (*pseud. of* Lezhankin), S. Ia. Sen'kin, P. I. Chagin, V. F. Shekhtel' (*née* Tonkova). These papers contain documents and original literary manuscripts by many of the prominent figures in the Russian and Soviet art world during the first half of the twentieth century—D. D. Burliuk, V. I. Gnedov, V. A. Kaverin, B. L. Pasternak, K. A. Fedin, V. V. Khlebnikov, V. B. Shklovskii, and others.

Reference Facilities: There are subject card catalogues, but inventories have been compiled for only part of the material.

Sektor arkhiva sem'i Maiakovskikh
[Maiakovskii Family Archive Sector]

Hours: by appointment
Head: Valentina Vladimirovna Nesterova (*tel.* 921-64-89)

HOLDINGS: 1 fond, 11,925 units, 1822–1972

The Maiakovskii family archives constitute a separate sector and include manuscripts written by the poet's mother, A. A. Maiakovskaia, and by his sisters. The fond includes correspondence with institutions, organizations and relatives, documents relating to Maiakovskii's public work and service, and documents on the Maiakovskii family (articles, recollections and letters from various persons, documents relating to the publication of his works and to evenings given in honor of his memory etc.).

The materials in this sector are actually housed in the Maiakovskii family apartment (Studenetskii per., 22).

Reference Facilities: There are subject catalogues and card catalogues.

Izofond
[Pictorial Fond]

Hours: by appointment
Head: Liubov' Vasil'evna Rodnova (*tel.* 921-85-69)

HOLDINGS: 1 fond, 6,000 units, 1883–1990s

The Pictorial Fond contains Maiakovskii's artistic work (drawings, graphics and paintings) and that of a number of early twentieth-century avant-garde artists who were Maiakovskii's contemporaries—N. S. Goncharova, M. F. Larionov, A. Bard, F. O. Shekhtel', V. V. Kandinskii, and others. There is also an extensive collection of Maiakovskii's satirical posters done on stencils for the Russian Telegraphic Agency—the so-called Windows of ROSTA (*Okna ROSTA*), and for the Telegraphic Agency of the Soviet Union (*Okna TASS*).

Reference Facilities: There is a card catalogue of inventoried items as well as alphabetic and subject catalogues.

Fotonegativnyi fond
[Photograph and Negative Fond]

HOLDINGS: ca. 5,000 units, late 19th c.–1993

This fond contains photographs of Maiakovskii and his family, friends, and acquaintances. There are prints of the public performances of his plays and their rehearsals both on the Russian stage and abroad, and montages done by famous photographers like A. M. Rodchenko, Gustav Klucis (G. G. Klutsis), and El' Lisitskii (*pseud. of* Lazar' Lisitskii).

Comment: A completed questionnaire from the museum was not received by Rosarkhiv.

FINDING AIDS — PUBLISHED — GENERAL:

Muzei Moskvy (1997), pp. 224–26; *GAF Spravochnik* (1991), pp. 153–55; G&K *Spravochnik* (1983), p. 59; PKG *M&L* (1972), p. 284; Sup. 1 (1976), p. 112.

There is no complete published guide to the archival materials in the museum.

h-290. Makarov, Vladimir; and Zakharov, Aleksandr. "The Maiakovsky Museum." *Soviet Literature*, 1973, no. 7, pp. 145–55. (Lib: DLC; IU; MH)
> A short popularized description of the Maiakovskii Museum, with details of the transfer of the holdings from earlier exhibition points in Moscow.

h-290A. Shilov, Lev Alekseevich. *Zdes' zhil Maiakovskii.* Moscow: "Moskovskii rabochii," 1959. 104 p. "Po muzeiam i vystavkam Moskvy i Podmoskov'ia." (Lib: MH)
> A short popularized description of the Maiakovskii Museum, with details about some of the manuscript, pictorial, and library holdings, including data about Maiakovskii-related materials in other archives.

h-291. *V. V. Maiakovskii: Opisanie dokumental'nykh materialov.* 2 vols. Moscow, 1964–1965. 303 p. (Also listed as a-147). [GAU SSSR; TsGALI; BMM] (Lib: DLC; MH) [IDC-R-10,659]
> Vol. 1: *"Okna" ROSTA i Glavpolitprosveta 1919–1922 gg.* Compiled by K. N. Suvorova. Edited by V. D. Duvakina. 287 p.
>
> Vol. 2: *Rukopisi. Zapisnye knizhki. Zhivopis'. Risunki. Afishi. Programmy. Zapisi golosa.* Compiled by V. A. Arutcheva et al. Edited by N. V. Reformatskaia. 303 p.
>> Describes Maiakovskii manuscripts and other archival materials in the museum, but also covers the large collection in RGALI (*formerly* TsGALI). Includes correlations with published editions.

Gosudarstvennyi muzei–gumanitarnyi tsentr "Preodolenie" im. N. A. Ostrovskogo (GM–GTsPO)

[N. A. Ostrovskii State Museum and "Overcoming" Humanitarian Center]

Agency: Komitet po kul'ture Pravitel'stva Moskvy
[Committee on Culture of the Government of Moscow]

Address:	103009, Moscow, ul. Tverskaia (*formerly* Gor'kogo), 14
Telephone:	229-85-52; 229-31-34; 229-49-20
Website:	http://moscow.lvl.ru/culture/museum/ostrovs/ostrov.html
Transport:	metro: Pushkinskaia, Tverskaia, Chekhovskaia; trol.: 1, 12, 15, 20, 31
Hours:	Tu–Su 11:00–18:30 (Division of Fonds—TuTh 10:00–13:00; WF 14:00–17:00)

Director: Galina Ivanovna Khrabrovitskaia (*tel.* 209-12-22)
Chief Curator (Division of Fonds): Natal'ia Vasil'evna Fitigarova (*tel.* 229-37-00)
Scientific Worker (Scientific Archive): Ol'ga Sergeevna Kolesnikova (*tel.* 209-37-90)

HISTORY:

Gosudarstvennyi muzei N. A. Ostrovskogo—Filial Gosudarstvennogo literaturnogo muzeia
[N. A. Ostrovskii State Museum—Branch of State Literary Museum] (1940–1941)
Gosudarstvennyi muzei N. A. Ostrovskogo
[N. A. Ostrovskii State Museum] (1941–1992)

The museum was founded in 1940 as a branch of the State Literary Museum (H–33), to honor the memory of the Soviet Russian writer, Nikolai Aleksandrovich Ostrovskii (1904–1936). In June 1941, it became administratively independent. In 1992, it was renamed the N. A. Ostrovskii State Museum and Humanitarian Center with the thematic epithet "Overcoming" (or "Surmounting" [*"Preodolenie"*]).

The considerable archival documentation is held as part of the general museum collections (*Otdel fondov*).

HOLDINGS: 3 fonds, 14,733 units, 9 collections, early 20th c.–to present

photographs—3,837 (1905–1990s); graphic materials—230 units; motion pictures—22 (1928–1990s); sound recordings—196 units (1935–1986)

The museum contains documents relating to Ostrovskii (1904–1936), his family and co-workers. The major part of the holdings consists of the Ostrovskii Memorial Fond (*Memorial'nyi fond N. A. Ostrovskogo*) (1,300 units), which contains the writer's personal papers and those of his wife, brothers, sisters and nephews. These papers include their correspondence with such well-known Soviet and foreign writers as Mate Zalka, A. A. Karavaeva, M. E. Kol'tsov, Romain Rolland, L. N. Seifullina, A. S. Serafimovich, A. A. Fadeev, and M. A. Sholokhov.

The museum has also acquired the personal papers of a number of people who knew Ostrovskii. These include memoirs and recollections about him, letters and photographs.

There are a number of collections of documents on the Civil War and the Second World War with the personal papers of those who took part in these events, and with photographs, letters, leaflets, and appeals. The museum has several thematic collections including that of the museum's epithet "Overcoming," containing documents about people whose lives were similar to that of Pavel Korchagin, the hero of Ostrovskii's most famous novel, *How the Steel was Tempered* (*Kak zakalialas' stal'*). The thematic collection entitled "Ostrovskii and Art" contains material on the theater productions and screening of his novel. There is also a thematic collection entitled "The Korchagin Movement in Production Collectives and Educational Institutions" (*Korchaginskoe dvizhenie v proizvodstvennykh kollektivakh i uchebnykh zavedeniiakh*), which includes documents on propaganda and educational work in factories, building sites, and collective and state farms. Each collection includes both manuscripts and documentary photographs.

The museum has collected graphic work devoted to Ostrovskii together with illustrations by Soviet and foreign artists for his novels and works by handicapped artists.

There are also documentary films about Ostrovskii and the Korchagin Movement, and the screenplay for the film "How the Steel was Tempered" (1935).

The sound recordings archive contains recordings of Ostrovskii's speeches, recollections by relatives and close friends, and productions thematically connected with his novels.

The Scientific Archive (*Nauchnyi arkhiv*) contains the administrative (including financial) records of the museum and reflect the academic and educational activities of its staff. There are photographs of special events held in the museum.

Access: Access to the document materials requires a letter of application from the researcher's sponsoring organization, stating the aims and purposes of the research, with the written endorsement of the museum director and presentation of a passport.

Working Conditions: An appointment to work with documents must be made in advance with the Chief Curator. Researchers are received in the museum offices.

Reference Facilities: There are surveys of various fonds of personal papers, photographs in the Ostrovskii Memorial Fond, illustrations for the writer's novels, materials on the subject of the "Great Patriotic War," and part of the collection on the theme "Overcoming." There are subject catalogues and card catalogues of the people who knew Ostrovskii.

The Scientific Archive of the museum itself has not yet been fully arranged and described.

Library Facilities: The museum has a library, access to which requires permission from the museum director. The book fond consists of Ostrovskii's personal library, collections of his own writings, separate autographed editions of his novels, publications on Ostrovskii, and works by writers awarded the Ostrovskii Prize.

Copying: Photographic copying facilities are available.

FINDING AIDS — PUBLISHED — GENERAL:

Muzei Moskvy (1997), pp. 226–28; *GAF Spravochnik* (1991), pp. 156–57.

There is no published guide to the archival materials in the museum.

h-292. *Muzei Nikolaia Ostrovskogo v Moskve.* 2d ed. Compiled by R. P. Ostrovskaia and D. E. Sokolova. Moscow: "Moskovskii rabochii," 1964. 140 p. "Po muzeiam i vystavkam Moskvy i Podmoskov'ia." (Lib: MH)

   EARLIER ED.: Compiled by R. P. Ostrovskaia, D. E. Sokolova, and M. G. Nazarova. Moscow: "Moskovskii rabochii," 1960. 120 p. "Po muzeiam i vystavkam Moskvy i Podmoskov'ia." (Lib: MH)

   A short popularized description of the museum, with mention of some of the manuscript, pictorial, and library holdings.

Gosudarstvennyi kul'turnyi tsentr-muzei V. S. Vysotskogo (Dom Vysotskogo na Taganke)

[V. S. Vysotskii State Cultural Center-Museum (Vysotskii House on Taganka)]

Agency: Ministerstvo kul'tury RF (Minkul'tury Rossii)
[Ministry of Culture]
Komitet po kul'ture Pravitel'stva Moskvy
[Committee on Culture of the Government of Moscow]

Address:　109004, Moscow, Nizhnii Taganskii tupik, 3
Telephone:　915-75-78, 915-29-79; *Fax:* (095) 915-29-79
E-mail:　root@visotsky.dnttm.rssi.ru; visotsky@cea.ru
Website:　http://www.visotsky.cea.ru; http://www.openweb.ru/windows/taganka/;
or http://www.openweb.ru/koi8/taganka/
Transport:　metro: Taganskaia-kol'tsevaia
Hours:　Tu–Sa 11:00–17:30; *Research Reading Room:* WThF 10:30–17:30

Director: Nikita Vladimirovich Vysotskii (*tel.* 272-06-00)
Deputy Director: Nataliia Sergeevna Matveeva (*tel.* 272-06-00)
Director-Curator: Mark Davidovich Fil'shchinskii

HISTORY:

The museum was founded in 1990 and opened in 1992 to honor the well-known Russian poet, singer, composer, and actor at the Taganka Theater, Vladimir Semenovich Vysotskii (1938–1980). Most of the holdings were donated by Vysotskii's second wife, L. V. Abramova.

HOLDINGS: photographs—1,524 units; documents—226 units

The museum contains documentation from the life and work of Vladimir Vysotskii (1938–1980), including the poet's manuscripts, letters, and production scripts. There are also *samizdat* editions of collections of his verses and songs, and part of his library.

　　The museum possesses a large video library of all the films in which Vysotskii starred (including those for which he wrote his own music and verses).

　　There are also sound recordings, photographs, and films of Vysotskii donated to the museum by various people.

Access: Access to archival materials requires a formal letter addressed to the director of the museum from the researcher's sponsoring institution, although in some cases, a personal letter of application is acceptable. There are no restrictions on access to archival materials.

Working Conditions: An advance appointment is advised. There is a special reading room for researchers.

Reference Facilities: The entire registration and reference system of the museum has been computerized in a database, which enables retrieval on the level of individual documents.

Copying: Xerographic facilities are available.

FINDING AIDS — PUBLISHED — GENERAL:

Muzei Moskvy (1997), p. 145.

h-293. *Mir Vysotskogo: Issledovanie i materialy.* Moscow, 1997–. 2 vols. available through 1998. [Gos. kul'turnyi tsentr-muzei V. S. Vysotskogo]

A scholarly publication series issued by the museum includes descriptions of the museum holdings, Vysotskii papers in other repositories, studies about Vysotskii, and related museum developments.

The first volume (1997) includes a survey of manuscripts in the archive (pp. 415–16), a catalogue of 436 books from Vysotskii's library (pp. 456–76), and a survey of the library of his son.

The second volume (1998) includes coverage of senior theses (*diplomnaia rabota*) held in the museum (pp. 493–503), some Vysotskii manuscript materials held elsewhere, and a bibliography of writings about Vysotskii: "Vladimir Semenovich Vysotskii: Chto? Gde? Kogda? (1993–1994)" (pp. 557–609), supplementing an earlier bibliography with the same title covering imprints from 1960–1993, published in Kharkiv in 1993.

Muzei-usad'ba "Muranovo" im. F. I. Tiutcheva
[F. I. Tiutchev Muranovo Estate-Museum]

Agency: Komitet po kul'ture i turizmu Administratsii Moskovskoi oblasti
[Committee on Culture and Tourism of the Administration of Moscow Oblast]

Address:	141281, Moskovskaia oblast', Pushkinskii raion, p/o Lugovskoe, d. Muranovo
Telephone:	584-59-47; *Fax:* (095) 402-77-79
Website:	http://moscow.lvl.ru/culture/museum/muranova/muran.html
Transport:	suburban train from Iaroslavl station to Ashukinskaia + bus 34
Hours:	10:00–17:00 (by appointment)

Director: Vladimir Vladimirovich Patsukov
Chief Curator: Svetlana Andreevna Dolgopolova

HISTORY:

Gosudarstvennyi istoriko-kul'turnyi i prirodno-landshaftnyi muzei "Muranovo"
[Muranovo State Historico-Cultural and Natural-Landscape Museum] (1994–1997)

The museum was founded in 1920 to honor the Russian poet Fedor Ivanovich Tiutchev (1803–1873). The F. I. Tiutchev Muranovo Estate-Museum is located on the former estate of the Tiutchev family, which had been associated with a wide range of cultural luminaries in the nineteenth century. The main house on the estate was constructed in 1841–1842, according to a design by the poet E. A. Baratynskii, on the ancestral lands of the Engel'gardt family.

During the period 1994–1997, the name for the museum was changed to the Muranovo State Historico-Cultural and Natural-Landscape Museum, but subsequently, it reverted to its original name.

HOLDINGS: statistics not available

The museum has been collecting archival materials relating to the life and literary creation of Russian poets and specialists on Russian literature of the eighteenth and nineteenth century who were associated with the estate and the Tiutchev family. In addition to those of F. I. Tiutchev, there are documents and literary manuscripts relating to Tiutchev's associates E. A. Baratynskii, L. N. Engel'gardt, S. T. Aksakov, his son, I. S. Aksakov, N. V. Putiata, and N. V. Sushkov, among others.

There is a photograph archive (*fototeka*), with extensive photographs, with many daguerreotypes, and there are some additional graphic materials.

N.B. Major parts of the Tiutchev papers are held in RGALI (B–7, fond 505).

Reference Facilities: There is a registration inventory of the museum holdings and a catalogue of the manuscript materials.

Library Facilities: The book collection in the museum (over 8,000 vols.) features books from the personal libraries of L. N. Engel'gardt, N. V. Putiata, F. I. Tiutchev, and others, many of which have dedicatory autographs. There is considerable literature associated with Tiutchev, including collections of his poetry in various editions. There is an extensive card catalogue.

Comment: A completed questionnaire about the archival holdings in the museum was not returned to Rosarkhiv.

FINDING AIDS — PUBLISHED — GENERAL:

There is no published guide to the archival materials in the museum.

h-294. Gramolina, Natal′ia Nikolaevna. *Dom poetov Muranovo.* Moscow: "Sovetskaia
 Rossiia," 1972. [19] p. + plates. (Lib: MH)
   A brief illustrated tourist pamphlet about the museum.

Gosudarstvennyi literaturno-memorial'nyi muzei-zapovednik A. P. Chekhova

[A. P. Chekhov State Literary-Memorial Museum-Preserve]

Agency: Komitet po kul'ture i turizmu Administratsii Moskovskoi oblasti
[Committee on Culture and Tourism of the Administration of Moscow Oblast]

Address: 142326, Moskovskaia oblast', Chekhovskii raion, p/o Vas'kino,
s. Melikhovo
Telephone: 546-16-01 (ext. 23-09); (8–272) 6-25-45
Transport: suburban train from Kursk Station to Lopasnia

Director: Iurii Konstantinovich Avdeev (*tel.* [8–272] 2–36–10)

HISTORY:

Muzei A. P. Chekhova—Filial Serpukhovskogo kraevedcheskogo muzeia
[A. P. Chekhov Museum—Branch of the Serpukhov Regional Studies Museum] (1940–1944)
Literaturno-memorial'nyi muzei A. P. Chekhova
[A. P. Chekhov Literary-Memorial Museum] (1944–1960)
Literaturno-memorial'nyi muzei-zapovednik A. P. Chekhova
[A. P. Chekhov Literary-Memorial Museum-Preserve] (1960–1967)

The museum was established in 1940 to honor the leading Russian playwright Anton Pavlovich Chekhov (1860–1904). Initially a branch of the Serpukhov Regional Studies Museum, in 1940, in connection with the fortieth anniversary of Chekhov's death, the museum was given separate status, and in 1960, it was reorganized as a Museum-Preserve.

The museum has a branch—the Museum of the Postal Division in Lopasnia (*Muzei "Pochtovoe otdelenie v Lopasne"*). (142300, Moskovskaia oblast', g. Chekhov, ul. Chekhova, 40).

HOLDINGS: complete statistics not available

photographs—over 300 units

The museum has been collecting archival materials of and relating to Chekhov for memorial exhibitions. There are a few original autograph documents, along with some drawings and other graphic materials, particularly works by his artistic relatives—his brother N. P. Chekhov, sister M. P. Chekhova, and nephew S. M. Chekhov, among others.

There is an extensive photograph archive (*fototeka*).

N.B. Major parts of the Chekhov papers are held in the Russian State Archive of Literature and Art (RGALI—B–7).

Reference Facilities: There is an inventory register of the museum holdings and a catalogue of the manuscript materials. There are card catalogues of all museum holdings which include pictures of individual items.

Library Facilities: There is a small book collection associated with the museum.

Comment: A questionnaire about the archival holdings in the museum was not returned to Rosarkhiv.

FINDING AIDS — PUBLISHED — GENERAL:

There is no complete published guide to the archival materials in the museum.

Gosudarstvennyi istoriko-literaturnyi i prirodnyi muzei-zapovednik A. A. Bloka
[A. A. Blok State Historico-Literary and Nature Museum-Preserve]

Agency: Komitet po kul'ture i turizmu Administratsii Moskovskoi oblasti
[Committee on Culture and Tourism of the Administration of Moscow Oblast]

Address:	141500, Moskovskaia oblast', Solnechnogorsk, ul. Naberezhnaia, 11 (temporary museum exhibits in Tarakanovo)
Telephone:	539-72-67
Website:	http://shakchmatovo.amr-museum.ru/index_e.htm
Transport:	surburban train from Leningrad Station to Podsolnechnaia + bus 24 to Tarakanovo
Hours:	Tu–F 9:00–17:00

Director: Valentin Pavlovich Arzamastsev
Chief Curator: Svetlana Mikhailovna Misochnik

HISTORY:

The museum was established in 1984 on the former family estate, Shakhmatovo. The house where the Russian poet Aleksandr Aleksandrovich Blok (1880–1921) lived is currently being reconstructed as a memorial museum. A temporary exhibition is open in the neighboring village of Tarakanovo, with personal memorabilia and some library and archival materials.

HOLDINGS: over 5,000 units

The museum has been collecting archival materials pertaining to Aleksandr Blok, namely, manuscripts, documents, photographs, and other graphic materials. The museum has received the personal archive of the head of the publishing house "Alkonost" (1918–1923), Samuil Mironovich Alianskii, with materials relating to Blok, including books with autographs and albums. There are also some personal papers of the well-known literary specialist Sergei Mikhailovich Solov'ev (1942–1992), with some Blok autographs, and additional autograph materials received from A. A. Polonskaia.

There is an extensive photograph archive (*fototeka*).

N.B. Major parts of the Blok papers are held in Pushkinskii Dom (E–28), the Russian State Library (G–1), and RGALI (B–7). See also the description of A. A. Blok Apartment-Museum in St. Petersburg (H–99), and its manuscript holdings.

Reference Facilities: There is a registration inventory of the museum holdings and a catalogue of the manuscript materials. There are card catalogues of all museum holdings which include pictures of individual items.

Library Facilities: There is a small book collection in the museum, including many autographed books by Blok and his contemporaries, as well as related reference literature. Most of the personal library of Blok, however, is held in Pushkinskii Dom (E–28).

Comment: A questionnaire about the archival holdings in the museum was not returned to Rosarkhiv.

FINDING AIDS — PUBLISHED — GENERAL:

h-295. Saf'ianova, N. V.; and Misochnik, Svetlana Mikhailovna. "Iz sobraniia Gosudarstvennogo istoriko-literaturnogo i prirodnogo muzeia-zapovednika A. A. Bloka: Katalog," part 1: "Rukopisi, knigi s avtografami, pamiatnye veshchi." Edited with a preface by V. P. Arzamastsev. In *Shakhmatovskii vestnik* 6 (1996): 21–146. [Gos. istoriko-literaturnyi i prirodnyi muzei-zapovednik A. A. Bloka] (Lib: MH)

> An item-by-item catalogue of the archival holdings in the museum, covering documentary materials (autographs of Blok and his contemporaries and albums from the archive of S. M. Alianskii) and books with dedicatory autographs, as well as personal memorabilia of Blok, his relatives, and contemporaries, with many reproductions of documents and dedicatory autographs.

h-296. *Shakhmatovskii vestnik: Neperiodicheskoe izdanie Gosudarstvennogo istoriko-literaturnogo i prirodnogo muzeia-zapovednika A. A. Bloka.* Moscow, 1991–. Irregular. 6 issues through 1996. [Gos. istoriko-literaturnyi i prirodnyi muzei-zapovednik A. A. Bloka] (Lib: MH)

> The irregular serial issued by the museum includes scholarly descriptions of the museum holdings and related museum developments. The second issue (1992) is dedicated to the memory of Sergei Mikhailovich Solov'ev (1942–1992) with mention of manuscript materials (pp. 43–48). The third issue (1993) includes a survey of the personal archive of S. M. Alianskii (pp. 42–46). The fourth issue (1994) describes the temporary exhibits and mentions personal memorabilia and some of the archival materials held by the museum. The fifth issue (1995), resulting from a 1995 conference held by the museum, includes an annual report on the museum for 1994, a description of current exhibits, and a survey of pictorial materials held by the museum. The sixth issue (1996) contains a summary of the annual report for 1995, including data on new acquisitions, and the initial segment on an item-level catalogue of the museum holdings (h-295).

Museums of Theater, Music, and Motion Pictures

&– H–42 *–&*

Gosudarstvennyi tsentral'nyi teatral'nyi muzei im. A. A. Bakhrushina (GTsTM)
[A. A. Bakhrushin State Central Theater Museum]

Agency: Ministerstvo kul'tury RF (Minkul'tury Rossii)
[Ministry of Culture]

Address: 113054, Moscow, ul. Bakhrushina, 31/12
Telephone: 953-44-70, 953-53-90; *Fax:* (095) 233-54-48
Website: http://moscow.lvl.ru/culture/museum/teatral/eteatral.html
Transport: metro: Paveletskaia
Hours: MWSa 12:00–18:00; WF 13:00–19:00

Director: Valerii Vladimirovich Gubin (*tel.* 953-48-48)
Scientific Secretary: Svetlana Viktorovna Semikolenova (*tel.* 953-39-77)
Main Curator: Nina Timofeevna Vydrina (*tel.* 953-47-20)

HISTORY:

Literaturno-teatral'nyi muzei Alekseia Bakhrushina
[Literary-Theater Museum of Aleksei Bakhrushin] (1894–1913)
Literaturno-teatral'nyi muzei im. A. A. Bakhrushina
[A. A. Bakhrushin Literary-Theater Museum] (1913–1919)
Gosudarstvennyi teatral'nyi muzei im. A. A. Bakhrushina
[A. A. Bakhrushin State Theater Museum] (1919–1941)

The museum was founded in 1894 by the well-known industrialist and philanthropist, Aleksei Aleksandrovich Bakhrushin (1865–1929), on the basis of his personal collection of theater art and manuscript materials gathered in the late nineteenth century. Known as the Literary-Theater Museum of Aleksei Bakhrushin, the museum was donated to the city of Moscow in 1913 by the Russian Imperial Academy of Sciences. Subsequently renamed in honor of its founder, A. A. Bakhrushin, it remained under Academy of Sciences' jurisdiction through 1917.

In 1918 the museum came under state jurisdiction, subordinate to the People's Commissariat of Education of the RSFSR (Narkompros RSFSR)—at first as a subsidiary of the Theater Society. It continued to bear the name of its life-long director, A. A. Bakhrushin, and in 1919 was renamed the A. A. Bakhrushin State Theater Museum. It took its present name as the state "central" theater museum in 1941, and its archival holdings rank among the most significant for the history of the theater in Russia, the Soviet Union, and foreign countries. In April 1997 the museum was entered in the federal register of the most valuable monuments of the cultural heritage of the peoples of the Russian Federation.

The Manuscript Division, first organized in 1935, is now known as the Archive-Manuscript Division. In addition, separate divisions retain theater posters and programs, photographs and negatives, audiovisual materials, and theater decorations (including stage designs, engravings, and other graphic materials).

933

The museum has six affiliated branches, all of which have on exhibit a few related manuscript and photographic materials from the museum collections. Most of them have webpages on the same server as the museum itself:

(1) The M. N. Ermolova House-Museum (*Dom-muzei M. N. Ermolovoi*), founded in 1970, occupies an eighteenth-century building where the actress Maria Nikolaevna Ermolova (1853–1928) lived for forty years. The museum displays considerable archival materials relating to Ermolova's career, especially in the Malyi Theater. (103104, Moscow, Tverskoi bul'var, 11; tel. 290-49-01, 290-02-15; webpage: http://moscow.lvl.ru/culture/museum/ermolov/ermolov.html).

(2) The A. N. Ostrovskii Estate-Museum (*Muzei-usad'ba A. N. Ostrovskogo*), opened in 1984, is located in the house where the Russian playwright Aleksandr Nikolaevich Ostrovskii (1823–1886) was born and lived his first three years. This branch has some documentary materials of actors from the Malyi Theater who played roles in Ostrovskii's plays. (109017, Moscow, ul. Malaia Ordynka [*formerly* Ostrovskogo], 9; tel. 953-86-84).

(3) The M. S. Shchepkin House-Museum (*Dom-muzei M. S. Shchepkina*), honoring the famous actor (born a serf) Mikhail Semenovich Shchepkin (1788–1863), is in the process of reorganization in the house where Shchepkin spent the last years of his life (1859–1863). As of the end of 1998 renovation is still in progress. (129110, Moscow, ul. Shchepkina, 47, stroenie 2; tel. 288-58-53).

(4) The Theater Salon on Tver Boulevard (*Teatral'nyi salon na Tverskom bul'vare*) is primarily used for temporary exhibits. (102104, Moscow, Tverskoi bul'var, 11, korpus 2; tel. 290-42-89).

(5) The V. E. Meyerhold Apartment-Museum (*Muzei-kvartira V. E. Meierkhol'da*), honors the theater director Vsevolod Emil'evich Meyerhold (Meierhold) (1874–1942). (Briusov per. [*formerly* ul. Nezhdanovoi], 12, kv. 11–11a; tel. 229-53-22).

(6) The Theater Gallery on Ordynka (*Teatral'naia galereia na Ordynke*), founded in 1997, in the same building as the Ostrovskii Estate-Museum, is used as a special exhibition area, displaying various manuscript and graphic archival materials from different divisions of GTsTM. (109017, Moscow, ul. Malaia Ordynka [*formerly* Ostrovskogo], 9; tel. 953-86-84).

Access: Access to archival materials requires a letter from the researcher's sponsoring institution stating the subject and purpose of research. There are restrictions for access to some materials whose creators are still living. There are also restrictions in the case of documents earmarked by the museum or other research institutes for their current planned research, publication, or for the preparation of exhibitions.

Working Conditions: Researchers are usually accomodated in working office areas.

Library Facilities: The museum has an extensive library, which has the status of a separate fond division (the book fond). Access requires the same type of application as is required for archival materials. (Hours: W 10:00–17:00).

Arkhivno-rukopisnyi otdel
[Archive-Manuscript Division]

Telephone: 231-71-11
Hours: W 10:00–18:00 (additional hours by arrangement)
Head: Inesa Sergeevna Preobrazhenskaia (*tel.* 231-71-11)

HOLDINGS: 625 fonds, 172,024 units, 18th c.–to present

The museum holds documents on the history of the dramatic and musical theater in Russia, the Soviet Union, and abroad. The Archival-Manuscript Division has some 400 fonds of personal papers of people who were prominent in the theater world—theater managers, directors, playwrights, theater critics, composers, actors, choreographers, theater historians, and collectors. To name only a few examples, there are separate fonds with papers of the playwrights A. P. Chekhov, A. S. Griboedov, and A. N. Ostrovskii; the theater director V. I. Nemirovich-Danchenko; the actors M. N. Ermolova, P. S. Mochalov, and M. S. Shchepkin; the opera singers F. I. Chaliapin (Shaliapin) and L. V. Sobinov; and the ballet masters A. A. Gorskii and K. Ia. Goleizovskii. These include original manuscripts of plays and articles, directors' copies of scripts and promptbooks, texts for various roles with notes made by the actors who played them, rehearsal notifications, letters, memoirs, and diaries. There are also some personal papers of stage and costume designers, including Léon Bakst (*pseud. of* L. S. Rozenberg), Alexandre Benois (A. N. Benua), A. Ia. Golovin, Pietro di Gottardo Gonzaga, P. V. Vil'iams, and M. A. Vrubel' (although their actual sketches and stage designs are held in the separate Division of Theater Decoration). Prominent among the collections is the fond of the museum founder, A. A. Bakhrushin (1865–1929) and his son, the ballet historian, Iu. A. Bakhrushin.

There are also a number of collections of theater-related documents, including some pertaining to the first actors F. G. and G. G. Volkov, who founded the Russian professional theater in the eighteenth century.

Fonds of a more administrative nature include original documents from the records of the Office of Imperial Theaters (*Kontora imperatorskikh teatrov*), as well as documents originating from various state and private repertory companies in Moscow, St. Petersburg, and the provinces. There is also documentation from theater troupes and theater journals.

Documentation from the postrevolutionary period reflects the development of the dramatic arts in the Soviet Union. The museum holds, for example, personal papers of important personages in the Soviet theater world, such as E. B. Vakhtangov, F. N. Kaverin, K. S. Stanislavskii, and A. Ia. Tairov (*pseud. of* Kornblit). The papers of V. E. Meyerhold (Meierkhol'd) include documentation about his theater and director's copies of plays performed.

World War II is represented in the division by a collection of documents on the theaters and theater brigades that entertained the troops on various fronts. The museum has also collected and preserved the private papers of many contemporary theater figures in the postwar period.

The museum has also established collections of materials on many individual theaters and also collections of memoirs and diaries, letters and autographs, literary autobiographies and professional questionnaires from many of the people in the theater world.

Reference Facilities: There are general alphabetic and subject catalogues, archival *opisi* of all fonds, a card catalogue covering the fonds, and a list of fonds.

Copying: Photographic and xerox copies can be prepared.

Otdel teatral'nykh dekoratsii
[Division of Theater Decoration]

Telephone: 959-20-40
Hours: W 10:00–17:00
Head: Irina Naumovna Duksina (*tel.* 959-20-40)

HOLDINGS:

This division specializes in graphic materials relating to theater decor, among which are many sketches and drawings for stage and costume designs. Many of the materials came from Bakhrushin's own collection. There are sketches and stage designs of such well-known theater artists and designers as Léon Bakst, Alexandre Benois, Aleksandra Ekster (*pseud. of* A. A. Grigorovich), Pietro di Gottardo Gonzaga, B. M. Kustodiev, and M. A. Vrubel', and others whose personal papers remain in the Archive-Manuscript Division.

Nauchno-fondovyi otdel afish i programm
[Scientific Fond Division of Posters and Programs]

Address: 113054, Moscow, ul. Bakhrushina, 29
Hours: W 10:00–18:00
Transport: metro: Paveletskaia
Head: Tat'iana Sergeevna Nebesnaia (*tel.* 235-14-94)

HOLDINGS: 588,402 units, 1795–1992

This division contains only theater posters and programs. It includes programs from the Imperial Theaters of Moscow and St. Petersburg; from Russian and foreign private theaters, such as the V. F. Komissarzhevskaia Theater, the Zimin Opera, and the Korsh Theater; and from private prerevolutionary repertory companies that performed in provincial Russia in the late nineteenth and early twentieth centuries. Materials from the Soviet period come from theaters in Moscow and Leningrad, as well as those in other regions of Russia and the former Soviet republics. This division contains programs designed by such famous artists as A. M. Vasnetsov, A. Ia. Golovin, K. A. Somov, and F. O. Shekhtel'.

Reference Facilities: There is a subject-thematic catalogue for posters by theaters and plays; a catalogue for materials from the period of the Second World War (currently being updated); and a catalogue of materials from prerevolutionary Russian provincial theaters compiled on a geographic basis with an index of repertory companies, benefit performances, and classical repertoires.

Work began in 1991 on a guide to fonds of the Russian provincial theater (over 300,000 units described). Description of a significant part of the materials was completed by 1994, which is already included in a separate card catalogue.

Copying: Xerox copies can be prepared of documents no larger than European standard paper size (A4); photographic copies can be prepared for posters.

Foto-negativnyi otdel (arkhivnyi)
[Photograph-Negative Division (Archival)]

Hours: W 10:00–18:00
Head: Evgeniia Iur'evna Nedzvetskaia (*tel.* 953-49-65)

HOLDINGS: 12 fonds, 415,958 units, 19th c.–to present
photographs—9 fonds; negatives—3 fonds

This division contains documents relating to various theater personalities, or actors' "personalia," as they are often called in Russian. There are also similar fonds for the theater directors and designers. Materials illustrate the history of various repertory companies through the medium of photographs of the actors and actresses performing different roles, and scenes from plays on stage.

The division contains photographic records dating back to the first theater photographs of the 1860s, which were in the form of postcards and known as *vizitki*, *kabinetki*, and *buduarnye* postcards. There are also some glass daguerreotypes covering the period from 1850 to the 1890s, and several relating to the museum founder, A. A. Bakhrushin.

There are albums from famous collectors like A. Ia. Ketcher and V. V. Makarov with photographs of theater performers, and collections of photographs that belonged to M. N. Ermolova, V. F. Komissarzhevskaia, A. G. Koonen, A. P. Pavlova, L. V. Sobinov, and F. I. Chaliapin (Shaliapin).

Photographs portray the history of the theater during the early years of Soviet rule with its mass theater productions and plays performed by the political "Blue Blouse" (*Siniaia bluza*) Theaters, the Proletkul't, and other studio theaters of the 1920s.

The division collects photographs illustrating the development of the modern dramatic and music theaters in Moscow and St. Petersburg, and the formation of new studio theaters and workshops.

Reference Facilities: There are card catalogues of theaters, playwrights, actors, composers, choreographers, and other people who worked in the theater. There is a scholarly inventory book, which provides detailed descriptions of the fonds. A card catalogue registering new acquisitions is being established.

Copying: Photographic copies can be prepared.

Otdel video-, kinofonodokumentov
[Division of Video, Film, and Sound Recordings]

Hours: W 10:00–18:00
Head: Evgeniia Mikhailovna Studenikina (*tel.* 953-33-74)

HOLDINGS: 5 fonds, 16,400 units, 20th c.–to present

This division contains recordings of Russian and foreign operas, church music, canticles, romances, jazz, and music-hall songs. There are also excerpts from plays and literary works performed by some of the finest actors on the Russian stage.

The cinema-document fond contains documentary films, excerpts from plays and rehearsals, complete recordings of plays, and feature films. There are also documentaries on the life and work of directors, actors, and other persons involved in the Russian dramatic and music theaters.

Reference Facilities: There are *opisi* of the fonds, inventories of the main gramophone record fond, a registration card catalogue, and an alphabetic-subject catalogue. In addition to the completed, but still unpublished guide to the Archive-Manuscript Division mentioned below (h-300), work has been progressing since 1991 on a guide to materials relating to the Russian provincial theater.

Copying: Copies of video and sound recordings can be made in conformity with the general rules for all museums upon cash payment or a letter of guarantee from an organization.

FINDING AIDS — PUBLISHED — GENERAL:

Muzei Moskvy (1997), pp. 131–34; *GAF Spravochnik* (1991), pp. 133–38; PKG *M&L* (1972), pp. 289–90.

h-300. **Putevoditel' po fondam Rukopisnogo otdela GTsTM im. A. Bakhrushina.* Moscow, forthcoming.

> A guide to the Archive-Manuscript Division in the museum has been prepared, but publication arrangements have not been completed.

h-301. *Po stranitsam rukopisnykh fondov GTsTM: Iz fondov Teatral'nogo muzeia im. A. A. Bakhrushina: Publikatsii, obzory, nauchnye stat'i, soobshcheniia.* Compiled by N. S. Gozdina and M. V. Shchedrovitskaia. Edited by N. S. Gozdina and M. V. Shchedrovitskaia. Moscow, 1988. 165 p. [Minkul't RSFSR; GTsTM im. A. A. Bakhrushina] (Lib: DLC; MH)

> The collective volume contains a brief survey of the Manuscript Division (pp. 5–10), a survey of the theater collections of A. A. Bakhrushin (pp. 15–40), a survey of correspondence of dramatists connected with the Malyi Theater (pp. 71–89), and a short bibliography of publications prepared on the basis of holdings in the division 1917–1987 (pp. 150–64).

h-302. Miasnikova, E. S. "Mesto rukopisnykh fondov v deiatel'nosti teatral'nogo muzeia." In *Teatral'nye muzei v SSSR,* edited by N. V. Mints, pp. 108–23. Moscow, 1969. "Trudy Nauchno-issledovatel'skogo instituta muzeevedeniia i okhrany pamiatnikov istorii i kul'tury," vol. 23. (Lib: DLC[mf]; IU; MH) [IDC-R-10,748]

> Includes a description of the manuscript materials in the Bakhrushin museum.

h-302A. Filippov, Vladimir Aleksandrovich; and Medvedev, Boris L'vovich. *Teatral'nogo muzeia im. A. A. Bakhrushina*. Moscow: "Moskovskii rabochii," 1955. 268 p. + plates. "Po muzeiam i vystavkam Moskvy i Podmoskov'ia." (Lib: MH)

> A basic guide to the museum and its exhibits, with some description of the archival collections.

h-303. *Trudy Gosudarstvennogo tsentral'nogo teatral'nogo muzeia im. A. A. Bakhrushina*. Edited by E. M. Kolosova and V. A. Filippov. Moscow/Leningrad: "Iskusstvo," 1941. 315 p. (Lib: MH) [IDC-R-10,839]

> The fourth volume in the museum series contains the most detailed available survey of the manuscript holdings: A. Fridenberg, "Rukopisnye materialy, khraniashchiesia v GTsTM" (pp. 175–307), with emphasis on theater memorabilia and autographs (with an index). Other articles in the volume deal with archival materials relating to the actor Pavel Vasil'evich Vasil'ev II, war-front theater during the Civil War, and a detailed catalogue of documentation, including graphic materials, relating to the famous actor Mikhail Semenovich Shchepkin (1788–1863).
>
> Other volumes in the museum *Trudy* series have separate titles (see h-303.1), and most of them are unnumbered.

FINDING AIDS — SPECIALIZED:

Fonds of personal papers of Russian émigrés held by GTsTM, most of which have been declassifed recently, are listed in *Rus. Zarubezh'e* (1998), pp. 339–42.

h-303.1. *A. N. Ostrovskii: Dnevniki i pis'ma. Teatr Ostrovskogo*. Compiled by N. P. Kashin and V. A. Filippov. Moscow/Leningrad: Academia, 1937. vii, 429 p. + plates. "Trudy Gosudarstvennogo tsentral'nogo teatral'nogo muzeia im A. A. Bakhrushina," vol. [3]. (Lib: MH)

> Provides a survey of some of the Aleksandr Nikolaevich Ostrovskii (1823–1886) papers and related materials held by the museum, together with extensive published texts, and a catalogue of graphic materials. Several earlier volumes issued by the museum (Moscow, 1923, 1932, and 1937) also contain previously unpublished letters to Ostrovskii found in his papers, but include no significant commentary about the papers themselves.

h-304. *Aleksandra Ekster: Eskizy dekoratsii i kostiumov iz sobraniia GTsTM im. A. A. Bakhrushina: Katalog*. Compiled by E. P. Tomilovskaia. Edited by V. V. Gubin. Moscow, 1986. 90 p. + plates. [Minkul't RSFSR] (Lib: MH)

> An illustrated catalogue of theater costume designs and stage decorations produced by the avant-garde theater designer Aleksandra Ekster (*pseud. of* A. A. Grigorovich) (1882–1949), which are now held in the museum.

h-305. *Kustodiev v teatre: Teatral'nye eskizy i portrety v sobranii Gosudarstvennogo tsentral'nogo teatral'nogo muzeia im. A. A. Bakhrushina: Nauchnyi katalog fonda*. Compiled by A. K. Robinova-Konenkova, M. V. Petrova, and N. P. Makarova. Moscow: "Sovetskii khudozhnik," 1979. 104 p. [Minkul't RSFSR] (Lib: MH)

> An illustrated catalogue of the stage designs for many productions (1914–1937) and portraits of theater personalities by Boris Mikhailovich Kustodiev (1878–1927), which are now held in the museum. Includes introductory essays and bibliography.

h-305A. *Teater i Revolution: Det ryska avantgardet pa scen 1913–1930*. Edited by Peter Hogan et al. Stockholm: Dansmuseet, 1993. 197 p. + plates. "Dansmusei skrifter," no 30. Text in English and Swedish.

> An illustrated catalogue with introductory text covering exhibits of avant-garde stage designs and related materials from the Bakhrushin State Central Theater Museum. Issued for an exhibition organized by the Dance Museum in Stockholm in collaboration with the Fine Arts Museum in San Francisco.

FINDING AIDS — SPECIALIZED — UNPUBLISHED:

h-306. Shchedrin, Vasilii Al'bertovich. "Istoriia Gosudarstvennogo evreiskogo teatra na idish (GOSET) v Moskve, 1919–1948: Dokumental'nye istochniki po istorii GOSETa v moskovskikh arkhivokhranilishchakh." Moscow, 1994. 26 p. Typescript brochure.

A typescript survey, based on the author's dissertation, with emphasis on sources relating to the Jewish theater held in the museum. See also the brief coverage of the Jewish theater collection (GOSET) in *Dok. ist. evreev* (1997), pp. 404–405.

Muzei Moskovskogo Khudozhestvennogo Akademicheskogo teatra (Muzei MKhAT)

[Museum of the Moscow Academic Art Theater]

Agency: Ministerstvo kul'tury RF (Minkul'tury Rossii)
[Ministry of Culture]

Address: 103009, Moscow, Kamergerskii per. (*formerly* proezd Khudozhestvennogo teatra), 3a
Telephone: 229-00-80; *Fax:* (095) 229-20-87; *RdngRm:* 229-00-80
Website: http://moscow.lvl.ru/culture/museum/mhat/mhat.html
Transport: metro: Okhotnyi riad, Teatral'naia
Hours: Tu–Sa 10:00–17:30

Director: Vladlen Semenovich Davydov (*tel.* 229-20-87)
Chief Curator: Valentina Iakovlevna Kuzina

HISTORY:

Muzei Moskovskogo Khudozhestvennogo Akademicheskogo teatra (Muzei MKhAT)
[Museum of the Moscow Academic Art Theater] (1923–1932)
Muzei Moskovskogo Khudozhestvennogo Akademicheskogo teatra im. M. Gor'kogo (Muzei MKhAT)
[Museum of the A. M. Gorkii Moscow Academic Art Theater] (1932–1943)
Muzei Moskovskogo Khudozhestvennogo Akademicheskogo teatra Soiuza SSR im. A. M. Gor'kogo (Muzei MKhAT)
[Museum of the A. M. Gorkii Moscow Academic Art Theater of the USSR] (1943–1990)

The museum was founded in 1923 on the basis of the archive and museum division of the theater, which itself had been formed in 1922. The exhibits opened in 1925 in the historical building of MKhAT, but in 1939 the museum received separate premises in the four-story building next to the theater. In 1943 it was given nationwide recognition (*soiuznoe znachenie*) and received the name of the Museum of the A. M. Gorkii Moscow Academic Art Theater of the USSR. Since January, 1949, the museum has operated independently of the theater. Its various divisions were organized in 1969, including the Divisions for Archival Fonds and Pictorial Fonds. The present name of the museum dates from December 1990.

The museum has two affiliated branches honoring the cofounders of the theater, neither of which retain significant archival materials, since most documentation is housed in the main museum building. There are, nevertheless, some documents displayed and some books there with dedicatory inscriptions, as well as some correspondence and photographs:

(1) The K. S. Stanislavskii House-Museum (*Dom-muzei K. S. Stanislavskogo*) was opened in 1948 to honor the actor and theater director Konstantin Sergeevich Stanislavskii (*pseud. of* Alekseev, 1863–1938). The museum displays many original archival materials and memorabilia relating to the life and theatrical career of Stanislavskii, including graphic materials and part of his library with many autographed books. (103009, Moscow, ul. Stanislavskogo, 6; tel. 229-28-55; 229-24-42; webpage: http://moscow.lvl.ru/culture/museum/stanisl/stan.html).

(2) The Nemirovich-Danchenko Apartment-Museum (*Muzei-kvartira V. I. Nemirovicha-Danchenko*) was founded in 1943 to honor the playwright and director Vladimir Ivanovich Nemirovich-Danchenko (1858–1943) in the apartment where he lived from 1938–1943. The museum houses many original documents, letters, photographs, and autographed books.

(103009, Moscow, ul. Nemirovicha-Danchenko, 5/7, kv. 52; tel. 209-53-91; webpage: http://moscow.lvl.ru/culture/museum/nem-dan/nem-dan.html).

Access: Research access requires special application by the researcher's sponsoring organization and the permission of the museum director. Documents from MKhAT dating from 1970 to the present are not available for research, nor are certain personal papers (in accordance with the instructions of their owners).

Library Facilities: The library holdings (book fond) on the history of art and the theater are located in the museum reading room, where they are openly available for research. There are many autographed books and rare first editions, and collections of press clippings (from 1898) about MKhAT.

Otdel arkhivnykh fondov
[Division of Archival Fonds]

Telephone: 229-84-79
Hours: W–F 10:30–16:30; Sa 10:30–15:30
Head: Marfa Nikolaevna Bubnova (*tel.* 229-84-79)

HOLDINGS: 430 fonds (176 unarranged), 291,718 units, 1860s–1992

This division contains documents on the history of the theater since its founding in 1898, and on the work of its founders and the actors, directors and staff who worked in the theater. Here are the records of the Moscow Academic Art Theater and its studios (since 1898); the Chekhov Academic Art Theater (*MKhAT im. Chekhova*); the Gor'kii Academic Art Theater (*Moskovskii Khudozhestvennyi Akademicheskii Teatr im. Gor'kogo*); and the Nemirovich-Danchenko Studio School (*Shkola-studiia im. V. I. Nemirovicha-Danchenko pri MKhAT im. Chekhova*). There are separate fonds with documents pertaining to successive MKhAT seasons (*Sezony MKhAT*) (starting in 1897) and the MKhAT Performances Fond (*Fond spektaklei MKhAT*), which document new productions, along with plays that have formed part of the MKhAT repertory since it was opened in 1898. These include many authors', directors', actors', and censors' copies of scripts and promptbooks.

A large part of the archival materials contained in this division is made up of collections of personal papers. These include the fonds of MKhAT founders K. S. Stanislavskii and V. I. Nemirovich-Danchenko, the majority of whose personal papers are located here. There are also extensive personal papers of a number of actors and actresses like V. I. Kachalov (*pseud. of Shverubovich*), O. L. Knipper-Chekhova, A. P. Ktorov, B. N. Livanov, and I. M. Moskvin, as well as other persons who took a prominent part in the work of MKhAT. There are personal papers of the director and actor V. E. Meyerhold (Meierkhol'd), the writer, M. A. Bulgakov, and the artists M. V. Dobuzhinskii and V. A. Simov.

Reference Facilities: There are inventories for all fonds that have been arranged, as well as card inventories, card catalogues, and a catalogue of personal names for part of the fonds of personal papers. There are card catalogues covering MKhAT productions and the actors, directors, and other theater workers back to 1898. Separate card catalogues are being prepared covering MKhAT productions and rehearsals, copies of the scripts and promptbooks of plays held in the archive, and for the theater tours.

Otdel izofondov
[Division of Pictorial Fonds]

Hours: W–F 11:00–16:30; Sa 9:00–15:30
Head: Mariia Fedorovna Polkanova (*tel.* 229-00-80)

HOLDINGS: 2 fonds, over 9,000 units, 1865–1994
    photographs—over 7,500 (1865–1992); graphic documents—900 units (1898–1986)

This division contains a collection of theater art including sketches for sets and costumes, drawings, drafts, layouts, and stage set models prepared by well-known Russian and Soviet designers.

The division has a collection of photographs (1865–present) and a collection of negatives (1898–present) showing plays performed at MKhAT since 1898. There are also photographs of the theater activities of Stanislavskii and Nemirovich-Danchenko before the founding of MKhAT, as well as photographs of tour productions, jubilees, and meetings with actors.

The museum has a collection of posters and programs for MKhAT productions from 1898 to the present.

Sektor ekskursionno-lektsionnoi raboty
[Excursion and Lecture Sector]

Hours:　　　W–F 11:00–16:30; Sa 9:00–15:30
Head: Galina Georgievna Shneiter (*tel.* 229-24-42)

HOLDINGS: films—93 (1912–1992); sound recordings—311 units (1950s–1993)

The division retains audiovisual recordings of the founders of MKhAT, including scenes from plays, rehearsals, tours, and the public life of the theater and its anniversary celebrations.

FINDING AIDS — PUBLISHED — GENERAL:

Muzei Moskvy (1997), pp. 147–50; *GAF Spravochnik* (1991), pp. 57–61; PKG *M&L* (1972), p. 291.

There is no published guide to the archival materials in the museum, although there are many volumes of documentary publications and illustrations about MKhAT, drawing on materials in the museum.

h-307. Mikhal'skii, Fedor Nikolaevich. "Rukopisnye fondy muzeia Moskovskogo Khudozhestvennogo teatra." In *Teatral'nye muzei v SSSR,* edited by N. V. Mints, pp. 124–38. Moscow, 1969. "Trudy Nauchno-issledovatel'skogo instituta muzeevedeniia i okhrany pamiatnikov istorii i kul'tury," vol. 23. (Lib: DLC[mf]; IU; MH) [IDC-R-10,748]
　　Supplements the earlier survey by V. M. Novoselova (h-308).

h-308. Novoselova, V. M. "Dokumental'nye materialy po istorii Khudozhestvennogo teatra v arkhive MKhAT." *Trudy MGIAI,* 1957, no. 10, pp. 199–213. (Lib: DLC; IU; MH) [IDC-in R-10,757]
　　Largely updated by F. N. Mikhal'skii (h-307).

FINDING AIDS — SPECIALIZED:

h-309. Mikhal'skii, Fedor Nikolaevich. *Muzei Moskovskogo Khudozhestvennogo teatra: [Putevoditel'].* Moscow: "Moskovskii rabochii," 1958. 288 p. + plates. "Po muzeiam i vystavkam Moskvy i Podmoskov'ia." (Lib: MH)
　　The most detailed general guide to the museum with considerable reference to archival holdings.

h-310. Mikhal'skii, Fedor Nikolaevich. "Novye materialy muzeia MKhAT." 1960, no. 5, p. 158. (Lib: DLC; IU)
　　Describes a letter sent by A. P. Chekhov to N. M. Kozhin, Secretary to the Board of the Society of Art and Literature (1890) and little known photographs of Chekhov.

Gosudarstvennyi muzei detskikh teatrov (GMDT)
[State Museum of Children's Theaters]

Agency: Ministerstvo kul'tury RF (Minkul'tury Rossii)
[Ministry of Culture]

Address: 129272, Moscow, ul. Sovetskoi Armii, 12, stroenie 2
(*projected future address:* Perunovskii per., 6)
Telephone: 289-15-54
Transport: metro: Rizhskaia + bus 84, trol. 18, 42; metro: Tsvetnoi bul'var + trol. 13
Hours: M–F 10:00–18:00

Director: Nadezhda Nikolaevna Polosina (*tel.* 289-15-54)
Main Curator of Division of Fonds: Irina Il'inichna Rutsinskaia (*tel.* 289-15-54)

HISTORY:

The museum was founded in 1981 as a cultural, educational and research institution, and as a repository for memorabilia, works of art, and archival documents on the history of children's theater in Russia and the republics of the former Soviet Union.

Since 1997 the museum has been preparing to move to a new location. However, the projected new premises are still under construction.

HOLDINGS: 18,057 units (6,500 unarranged), 1918–1994 (scattered documents from late 17th c.)
manuscript-documentary materials—9,765 (1918–1980s);
films, photographs, and sound recordings (with negatives)—8,578 (1920–1980s)

The manuscript holdings are part of the "Division of Fonds," rather than a separate division or sector of the museum. There is documentation on the history of children's theaters, including the Young Audience Theaters (*Teatry iunogo zritelia*—TIuZ), from throughout the Russian Federation and former USSR.

The holdings include materials from leading repertory companies in the former USSR, such as the Erevan Tumanian State Puppet Theater (*Erevanskii gosudarstvennyi teatr kukol im. Tumaniana*), the Leningrad, Moscow, Saratov and Novosibirsk Young Audience Theaters, the State Youth Theater of the Lithuanian SSR (*Gosudarstvennyi teatr molodezhi Litovskoi SSR*), and the State Young Audience Theater of the Latvian SSR. Of particular note are the archival materials (documents, photographs, and sketches) from the first Young Audience Theater in Ukraine.

There are manuscript and typed copies of plays performed at children's theaters; preparatory materials for productions; scripts and promptbooks of directors, and actors; drafts, plans, and drawings by artists and stage designers; and manuscript music scores.

Among the collection of personal papers are those of N. I. Sats, the director and founder of the Central Children's Theater, and of theater performers like V. A. Sperantova, K. P. Koreneva, and Z. A. Sazhin.

The fonds contain photographs and negatives of the various actors and actresses, directors and designers, and pictures of scenes from puppet theater productions.

Access: Research access requires a formal letter from the researcher's sponsoring organization. As of the end of 1998 the fonds are closed in preparation for transfer to a new location.

Working Conditions: Researchers are received in working offices of the Division of Fonds.

Reference Facilities: There are subject, personal-name, and topographic catalogues, inventories, and card catalogues. Work is currently in progress to set up a computerized database for the fonds.

Library Facilities: A library is on the premises.

Copying: There are no facilities for copying documents.

FINDING AIDS — PUBLISHED — GENERAL:

Muzei Moskvy (1997), pp. 146; *GAF Spravochnik* (1991), pp. 56–57.

There is no published guide to the archival materials in the museum.

h-315. *Gosudarstvennyi muzei detskikh teatrov: Al'bom.* Moscow, 1990. 32 p. + plates. [Minkul't SSSR]

> An album of reproductions of graphic materials (posters, theater sketches, etc.) indicative of holdings in the museum.

Gosudarstvennyi tsentral'nyi muzei muzykal'noi kul'tury im. M. I. Glinki (GTsMMK)

[M. I. Glinka State Central Museum of Musical Culture]

Agency: Ministerstvo kul'tury RF (Minkul'tury Rossii)
[Ministry of Culture]

Address:	125047, Moscow, ul. Fadeeva, 4
Telephone:	251-31-43; 972-32-37; *Fax:* (095) 972-32-55; *RdngRm:* 250-44-18
Website:	http://www.museum.ru/glinka;
	http://moscow.lvl.ru/culture/museum/musglink/emusglin.html
Transport:	metro: Maiakovskaia, Novoslobodskaia; trol.: B, 1, 10, 12, 20, 47
Hours:	Tu–F 11:00–19:00

Director: Anatolii Dmitrievich Paniushkin (*tel.* 251-31-43)
Deputy Director for Science: Irina Andreevna Medvedeva (*tel.* 251-06-77)
Scientific Secretary: Marina Pavlovna Rakhmanova (*tel./fax:* 972-32-23)
Scholarly Secretary: Margarita Pavlovna Prianishnikova
Main Curator: Karina Sergeevna Balasanian (*tel.* 250-41-12)

HISTORY:

Muzei im. N. G. Rubinshteina pri Moskovskoi konservatorii im. P. I. Chaikovskogo
[N. G. Rubinstein Museum under the P. I. Tchaikovsky Moscow Conservatory] (1912–1943)
Tsentral'nyi muzei muzykal'noi kul'tury
[Central Museum of Musical Culture] (1943–1954)

The museum was founded in 1943 on the basis of the holdings of the N. G. Rubinstein Memorial Museum (*Memorial'nyi muzei N. G. Rubinshteina*) (1912), which was part of the Moscow Conservatory (see E–53), and until 1964 the museum remained housed in the Conservatory complex. The museum was given the name of the Russian composer M. I. Glinka in 1954. In 1985 it moved to a new contemporary building specially constructed for the museum. In 1995 the museum was entered in the register of the most valuable monuments of the cultural heritage of the peoples of the Russian Federation.

When the museum opened, most of the manuscript materials were stored in the library of the Moscow Conservatory, but during the 1960s they were transferred to the museum when it moved out of the Conservatory.

The museum has three affiliated branches, the first two of which retain important archival materials:

(1) The N. S. Golovanov Apartment-Museum (*Muzei-kvartira N. S. Golovanova*) (H–46).

(2) The A. B. Gol'denveizer Apartment-Museum (*Muzei-kvartira A. B. Gol'denveizera*) (H–47).

(3) The F. I. Chaliapin House-Museum (*Dom-muzei F. I. Shaliapina*), honoring the celebrated opera singer Fedor Ivanovich Chaliapin (Shaliapin) (1873–1938), came under the jurisdiction of the museum in 1978 and opened in 1988 after it had been restored as it was when Chaliapin lived there. The museum houses considerable documentation, including photographs of, and drawings by, Chaliapin, and playbills of operas in which he sang. (123242,

Moscow, Novinskii bul'var, 25–27; tel. 205-62-36; 252-25-30; webpage: http://moscow.lvl.ru/culture/museum/chaliap/eshal.html).

Access: Access to the fonds requires a letter from the researcher's official sponsoring institution or organization stating the research subject.

Library Facilities: There is a reference library (over 200,000 items), which holds sheet music, journals, posters, programs, and newspaper clippings, including many autograph music scores. The library is open to researchers (tel. 251-24-17).

Otdel arkhivno-rukopisnykh materialov
[Division of Archival and Manuscript Materials]

Hours: MF 10:00–16:00, W 13:00–19:00
Head: Natal'ia Iur'evna Tartakovskaia (*tel.* 250-44-18)

HOLDINGS: 462 fonds, 404,791 units, 13th–20th cc.

The museum serves as the central repository for manuscript materials relating to the world of music and undoubtedly holds one of the largest and most extensive collections of its kind in Russia. The composition and content of the archival fonds are linked with the musical profile of the museum and therefore include all types of archival materials that pertain to music in Russia and abroad.

The earliest documents are the early Russian thirteenth- to fifteenth-century choral manuscripts in both linear and non-linear, neumatic notation, and also musical primers (*azbuki*).

Among institutional records, the fonds of music schools include documentation from the Moscow Conservatory (from 1866) and its various divisions or departments (opera studios, the music library, and the research division, among others); the State Institute of Musicology (*Gosudarstvennyi institut muzykal'noi nauki*); the State Academy of Arts (*Gosudarstvennaia Akademiia khudozhestvennykh nauk*); and the Central Music-Pedagogical Institute for External Students (*Tsentral'nyi zaochnyi muzykal'no-pedagogicheskii institut*).

Fonds from social organizations are represented by documents from the Russian Music Society (*Russkoe muzykal'noe obshchestvo*—RMO) (1859–1917), its Moscow branch (1860–1917), and its provincial branches; and the Ethnographic Music Commission (*Muzykal'no-etnograficheskaia komissiia*).

A large part of the materials consists of documents from various repertory and production companies like the Russian Opera in Paris and the Moscow State Jewish Theater (*Moskovskii gosudarstvennyi evreiskii teatr*), and numerous symphonic orchestras and ensembles.

There are also records of such music publishing houses as P. I. Iurgenson, Iu. G. Zimmerman, and M. P. Beliaev, and several specialist musicology journals, such as "Musical Education" (*Muzykal'noe obrazovanie*) and "Soviet Music Dictionary" (*Sovetskii muzykal'nyi slovar'*).

The division holds the personal archives of composers, performers, teachers, and music critics, which contain manuscript scores, personal papers, and other biographical materials. Most important are those of A. A. Aliab'ev, P. I. Tchaikovsky (Chaikovskii), M. M. Ippolitov-Ivanov, S. S. Prokof'ev, S. V. Rakhmaninov, and S. N. Vasilenko. The postrevolutionary period is represented by personal papers of A. A. Babadzhanian, A. F. Gedike, R. M. Glier, D. B. Kabalevskii, D. F. Oistrakh, D. D. Shostakovich, G. V. Sviridov, R. K. Shchedrin, and many others.

There are also collections of autographs and original music scores of M. A. Balakirev, A. P. Borodin, and P. I. Tchaikovsky, A. K. Glazunov, M. I. Glinka, and N. A. Rimskii-Korsakov, to name only a few. Among foreign composers there are collections of manuscripts and autographs of Ludwig van Beethoven, Ferenz (Franz) Liszt, and Richard Wagner.

The division possesses several special collections of music manuscripts, most important being the collection of religious music manuscripts acquired from the A. A. Bakhrushin State Central Theater Museum, which includes the religious works of Guiseppe Sarti, and of the Ukrainian composers M. S. Berezovs'kyi (*Rus.* Berezovskii) and D. S. Bortnians'kyi (*Rus.* Bortnianskii), along with the collection of manuscripts from the library of the Vorontsov Museum in Alupka in the Crimea (18th–20th cc.).

A special separate collection is devoted to documents pertaining to international music competitions such as the Tchaikovsky Piano Competition, the Glinka Vocal Competition, and the Chopin Piano Competition in Warsaw.

The "Album Collection" contains albums of the recordings of piano and vocal works written in the 1830s and 1840s together with the original works of various Russian and foreign composers from the late nineteenth and early twentieth centuries.

Reference Facilities: There are inventories and bound or card catalogues covering all of the holdings, which are arranged in fonds according to archival principles.

Copying: Both photographic and xerox copying facilities are available.

Otdel izobrazitel'nykh materialov
[Division of Pictorial Materials]

Hours: MF 10:00–16:00, W 13:00–19:00
Head: Ol'ga Vsevolodovna Rozhnova (*tel.* 972-32-41)

HOLDINGS: photographs—92,421 units (1870–1990)

The division contains negatives and photographic prints of Russian and Soviet composers, conductors, music critics, and teachers. There are photographic portraits of composers such as S. V. Rakhmaninov, S. I. Taneev, and D. D. Shostakovich. Many of the photographs depict scenes in major theaters from productions featuring such prominent singers and soloists as L. V. Sobinov and F. I. Chaliapin (Shaliapin). There are also photographs of students and teachers from the Moscow Conservatory.

Otdel muzykal'nykh instrumentov i gramplastinok
[Division of Musical Instruments and Phonograph Records]

Hours: MF 10:00–16:00, W 13:00–19:00
Head: Nina Vladimirovna Mileshina (*tel.* 251-30-45)

HOLDINGS: photographs—over 19,000 (1898–1990)

The division holds gramophone records and compact disks of musical works written by Russian and foreign composers. They include recordings made by F. I. Chaliapin (Shaliapin) (1898) and N. I. Zabela-Vrubel', and recordings of the M. E. Piatnitskii Peasant Choir.

Recorded works for piano represent practically all famous Russian composers—M. I. Glinka, A. S. Dargomyzhskii, M. P. Musorgskii (Mussorgsky), A. P. Borodin, M. A. Balakirev, and A. K. Glazunov, among others. There are also recordings of piano works performed by the composers themselves, including Edvard Grieg, Claude Debussy, Charles Saint-Saëns, A. N. Scriabin (Skriabin), and Maurice Ravel.

Choral singing is represented by recordings of the concerts of D. S. Bortnians'kyi and the quartets of I. V. Laskovskii.

Contemporary music can be heard in the works of I. F. Stravinskii (Igor Stravinsky), K. A. Erdeli, E. V. Obraztsova, A. G. Shnitke, E. V. Denisov, R. K. Shchedrin, and many other composers and performers.

Working Conditions: There are no facilities for listening to phonograph records. When necessary, researchers may obtain a cassette tape copy, which can be listened to in the acoustical recording work area.

Reference Facilities: There are card catalogues of performers and composers.

Copying: There are facilities for making copies of music only from magnetic tapes.

Otdel audiovizual'nykh sredstv i zvukozapisi
[Division of Audiovisual Materials and Sound Recordings]

Hours: MF 10:00–16:00, W 13:00–19:00
Head: Aleksandr Ivanovich Kosov (*tel.* 251-01-17)

HOLDINGS:

The division holds tape recordings of the musical works retained in the Division of Musical Instruments and Phonograph Records.

Copying: Musical works can be copied for researchers.

FINDING AIDS — PUBLISHED — GENERAL:

Muzei Moskvy (1997), pp. 159–60; *GAF Spravochnik* (1991), pp. 61–66; PKG *M&L* (1972), p. 287.

h-316. *Putevoditel' po fondam: Otdel arkhivno-rukopisnykh materialov.* Compiled and edited by T. G. Keldysh. Moscow, 1997. 253 p. [GTsMMK im. M. I. Glinki]

> The first part of an extensive new guide includes annotations for 67 fonds (nos. 1–70), with rubrics within each fond as appropriate covering music scores, literary manuscripts, letters (with lists of correspondents), documents, printed materials, programs and posters, photographs, and memorabilia. Although most of the fonds covered consist of personal papers of composers and other musicians, there are a number of institutional fonds of sections of the Moscow Conservatory and also a large collection of albums (1830–1976). A second part is in preparation.

h-317. *Annotirovannyi ukazatel' k fondam Otdela arkhivno-rukopisnykh materialov GTsMMK im. M. I. Glinki.* Compiled by F. A. Krasinskaia. Edited by A. B. Bykov. Moscow, 1974. 48 p. [Minkul't SSSR; GTsMMK im. M. I. Glinki] (Lib: GBL)

> The directory surveys fonds acquired before 1972. The first section covers the personal papers of composers, performers, musicians, teachers, and other persons involved in the music world. The second section surveys the fonds of music institutions and organizations. The third covers music scores and literary manuscripts, letters, and memoirs. Manuscript materials held in the affiliated branches of the museum are not included.

h-318. [Gosudarstvennyi tsentral'nyi muzei muzykal'noi kul'tury im. M. I. Glinki]. *Pamiatka.* Edited by V. A. Kiselev. Moscow: Gos. muzykal'noe izd-vo, 1957. 29 p. + 4 plates. [Minkul't SSSR; GTsMMK im. M. I. Glinki] (Lib: MH)

> A now dated survey of the museum with a bibliography of its publications (pp. 23–33).

FINDING AIDS — SPECIALIZED:

For Jewish-related holdings, see also *Dok. ist. evreev* (1997), pp. 397–403, *Jewish doc.* (1996), pp. 23–24. Fonds of personal papers of Russian émigrés held by GTsMMK, most of which have been declassified recently, are listed in *Rus. Zarubezh'e* (1998), pp. 342–46.

h-319. *Avtografy M. A. Balakireva i materialy, sviazannye s ego deiatel'nost'iu, v fondakh Gosudarstvennogo tsentral'nogo muzeia muzykal'noi kul'tury im. M. I. Glinki: Katalog-spravochnik.* Compiled by V. A. Kiselev. Edited by E. E. Bortnikova. Moscow, 1959. 62 p. [Minkul't SSSR; GTsMMK im. M. I. Glinki] (Lib: MH)

> A scholarly catalogue of the music scores and other personal papers of the Russian composer Milii Alekseevich Balakirev (1836–1910) in the museum.

h-320. *Avtografy L. Betkhovena v khranilishchakh SSSR: Spravochnik.* Compiled by N. L. Fishman. Moscow, 1959. 13 p. [Minkul't SSSR; GTsMMK im. M. I. Glinki] (Lib: MH)

> A scholarly catalogue prepared by the museum of the music scores, letters, and other personal papers of Ludwig van Beethoven (1770–1827) held throughout the Soviet Union. Most of those described are held in GTsMMK, but a few are held in IRLI, RGADA, and RNB.

h-321. *Avtografy A. P. Borodina v fondakh Gosudarstvennogo tsentral'nogo muzeia muzykal'noi kul'tury im. M. I. Glinki: Katalog-spravochnik.* Compiled by E. K. Morozova. Edited by V. A. Kiselev. Moscow: "Muzyka," 1970. 55 p. [Minkul't SSSR; GTsMMK im. M. I. Glinki] (Lib: MH)

> A scholarly catalogue of the music scores and other personal papers of the Russian composer Aleksandr Porfir'evich Borodin (1833–1887) in the museum.

h-322. *Avtografy P. I. Chaikovskogo v fondakh Gosudarstvennogo tsentral'nogo muzeia muzykal'noi kul'tury im. M. I. Glinki: Katalog-spravochnik.* Compiled by B. V. Dobrokhotov and V. A. Kiselev. Edited by V. A. Kiselev. 2d ed. [Moscow], 1956. 78 p. [Minkul't SSSR; GTsMMK im. M. I. Glinki] (Lib: MH)
> 1st ED.: M., 1955.

> A brief catalogue with annotated description of all the original music scores, letters, and other autograph papers of Petr Il'ich Tchaikovsky (Chaikovskii) (1840–1893) held by the museum in various fonds.

h-323. *Pamiati N. M. Danilina: Pis'ma, vospominaniia, dokumenty.* Compiled and edited by A. A. Naumov. Moscow: "Sovetskii kompozitor," 1987. 311 p. + 8 plates. [Minkul't SSSR; GTsMMK im. M. I. Glinki] (Lib: MH)

> A scholarly and memorial edition of selected letters, reminiscences, and other documents relating to the Russian conductor, choir master, and Conservatory professor Nikolai Mikhailovich Danilin (1878–1945) in the museum. Commentary describes and identifies archival locations of Danilin's papers and photographs.

h-324. *Avtografy A. K. Glazunova v fondakh Gosudarstvennogo tsentral'nogo muzeia muzykal'noi kul'tury im. M. I. Glinki: Katalog-spravochnik.* Compiled by E. K. Antipova. Edited by V. A. Kiselev. Moscow: "Sovetskii kompozitor," 1968. 74 p. [Minkul't SSSR; GTsMMK im. M. I. Glinki] (Lib: DLC; MH)

> A briefly annotated description of all the music scores and literary manuscripts, letters, and other original compositions by the Russian composer Aleksandr Konstantinovich Glazunov (1865–1936) held by the museum.

h-325. *Avtografy A. K. Liadova i materialy, sviazannye s ego deiatel'nost'iu, v fondakh Gosudarstvennogo tsentral'nogo muzeia muzykal'noi kul'tury im. M. I. Glinki: Katalog-spravochnik.* Compiled by E. K. Antipova. Edited by V. A. Kiselev. Moscow: Gosmuzizdat, 1963. 15 p. [Minkul't SSSR; GTsMMK im. M. I. Glinki] (Lib: DLC; MH)

> A brief catalogue of all the music scores, letters, and other original papers of the Russian composer Anatolii Konstantinovich Liadov (1855–1914) held by the museum.

h-326. *Avtografy M. P. Musorgskogo i materialy, sviazannye s ego deiatel'nost'iu, v fondakh Gosudarstvennogo tsentral'nogo muzeia muzykal'noi kul'tury im. M. I. Glinki: Katalog-spravochnik.* Compiled by E. K. Antipova. Edited by V. A. Kiselev. Moscow: Gosmuzizdat, 1962. 23 p. [Minkul't SSSR; GTsMMK im. M. I. Glinki] (Lib: DLC; MH)

> A brief catalogue of the music scores, letters, and other original papers of the Russian composer Modest Petrovich Musorgskii (Mussorgsky) (1839–1881) held by the museum.

h-327. *Avtografy S. S. Prokof'eva v fondakh Gosudarstvennogo tsentral'nogo muzeia muzykal'noi kul'tury im. M. I. Glinki: Spravochnik.* Compiled by M. K. Starodubtseva and F. A. Krasinskaia. Moscow: "Sovetskii kompozitor," 1977. 136 p. [Minkul't SSSR; GTsMMK im. M. I. Glinki] (Lib: IU; MH)

> A systematic and briefly annotated description of all the music scores, letters, and other original compositions by Sergei Sergeevich Prokof'ev (1891–1953) found in the museum fonds. There is an appended list of other institutions also holding the composer's original works.

h-328. *Avtografy S. V. Rakhmaninova v fondakh Gosudarstvennogo tsentral'nogo muzeia muzykal'noi kul'tury im. M. I. Glinki: Katalog-spravochnik.* Compiled by E. E. Bortnikova, F. A. Krasinskaia, and M. G. Rytsareva. Edited by M. G. Rytsareva. Moscow: "Sovetskii kompozitor," 1980. 136 p. [Minkul't SSSR; GTsMMK im. M. I. Glinki] (Lib: DLC; IU)

> A systematic and briefly annotated description of the autograph music scores and other documents held in the museum of the Russian composer Sergei Vasil'evich Rakhmaninov (1873–1943).

h-329. *Avtografy N. A. Rimskogo-Korsakova v fondakh Gosudarstvennogo tsentral'nogo muzeia muzykal'noi kul'tury im. M. I. Glinki: Katalog-spravochnik.* Compiled by V. A. Kiselev. Edited by E. E. Bortnikova. Moscow, 1958. 66 p. + 7 plates. [Minkul't SSSR; GTsMMK im. M. I. Glinki] (Lib: DLC; IU; MH)

> A brief catalogue covering all the original music scores and other documents of the Russian composer Nikolai Andreevich Rimskii-Korsakov (1844–1908) held in the museum.

h-330. Sokolov, N. N. *Memorial House of Fyodor Shalyapin: Guide-Book.* Moscow, 1993. 32 p. [Glinka Museum of Musical Culture]

> A brief illustrated, room-by-room tourist description of the F. I. Chaliapin (Shaliapin) Memorial House-Museum, a branch of GTsMMK, with mention of many of the documents, photographs, sketches, and playbills exhibited.

Muzei-kvartira N. S. Golovanova—Filial Gosudarstvennogo tsentral'nogo muzeia muzykal'noi kul'tury im. M. I. Glinki
[N. S. Golovanov Apartment-Museum—
Branch of M. I. Glinka State Central Museum of Musical Culture]

Agency: Ministerstvo kul'tury RF (Minkul'tury Rossii)
[Ministry of Culture]

Address: 103009, Moscow, Briusov per. (*formerly* ul. Nezhdanovoi), 7, kv. 10
Telephone: 229-70-83
Website: http://moscow.lvl.ru/culture/museum/golovan/golov.html
Transport: metro: Okhotnyi riad, Pushkinskaia, Tverskaia; trol.: 1, 12
Hours: W 14:00–19:00; F 10:00–16:00

Director: Vladimir Ivanovich Rudenko (*tel.* 229-70-83)

HISTORY:

The museum was founded in 1969 in the house where the Soviet conductor, composer, and pianist, Nikolai Semenovich Golovanov (1891–1953) lived from 1935 to 1953. It is administratively an affiliated branch of the M. I. Glinka State Central Museum of Musical Culture (GTsMMK) (H–45). Having had the status of N. S. Golovanov conductor's workshop and studio (*Tvorcheskaia laboratoriia dirizherskogo masterstva*), it has brought together many of his papers and recordings.

HOLDINGS: 1 fond, 6,542 units, 1811–1983
photographs—1,014 (1900–1966)

The museum contains documents relating to the life and work of Golovanov, who was made a People's Artist of the USSR in 1948. As well as his own personal documents (such as his diploma from the Conservatory), manuscript music scores of his works (including his written transposition of the Cantata "Princess Iurata" done as part of his graduation thesis), and his correspondence, the collection contains memoirs and recollections of contemporaries.

Also found here are many official files from the Bolshoi Theater (1919–1953) as well as documentation from the Society of Friends of the Stanislavskii Opera Studio (*Obshchestvo druzei Opernoi studii K. S. Stanislavskogo*).

The museum possesses photographs of Golovanov, his friends and relatives, and representatives of the arts world at home and abroad. These include pictures of first year students at the Synodal Secondary School, where Golovanov was himself both student and lecturer, and photographs of a number of professors of the Moscow Conservatory (1914), A. V. Nezhdanova (1915), A. K. Glazunov (1922), A. V. Lunacharskii (1924), K. S. Stanislavskii, V. I. Kachalov (*pseud. of* Shverubovich), and G. G. Neigauz, among others. There is also a collection of photographs autographed by such noted persons as F. I. Chaliapin (Shaliapin), L. V. Sobinov, N. A. Obukhova, and M. P. Maksakova.

The museum also holds posters and programs for operas in which Golovanov performed.

There are numerous gramophone records and tape recordings, one of which is a radio interview with Golovanov, entitled "On the Role of the Conductor."

Access: For research access, a letter is required from the researcher's sponsoring organization stating the purpose of research.

Working Conditions: Researchers are received in museum offices.

Library Facilities: There is a small library which includes Golovanov's collection of music scores.

Copying: Documents can be xeroxed, but researchers are required to sign a written guarantee not to publish the documents without prior agreement from the museum.

Comment: A completed questionnaire from the museum was not returned to Rosarkhiv.

FINDING AIDS — PUBLISHED — GENERAL:

Muzei Moskvy (1997), p. 161; *GAF Spravochnik* (1991), pp. 66–67.

There is no published guide to the archival materials in the museum.

h-331. *Muzei-kvartira Nikolaia Semenovicha Golovanova: Putevoditel'.* Compiled by V. E. Matveeva, V. Rudenko, and O. I. Zakharova. Moscow: VRIB "Soiuzreklamkul'tura," 1990. 30 p. [GTsMMK im. M. I. Glinki; Otdel istorii dirizherskogo iskusstva]

> Provides a brief history of the museum, a biography of Golovanov, and survey of documents held in the museum.

h-332. Pribegina, Galina A. *Nikolai Semenovich Golovanov.* Moscow: "Muzyka," 1990. 141 p. + 96 plates. [GTsMMK im. M. I. Glinki; Otdel istorii dirizherskogo iskusstva]

> An appreciative biography of Golovanov with extensive illustrations from the photograph collection in the museum. A final chapter describes the museum and its holdings.

Muzei-kvartira A. B. Gol'denveizera—Filial Gosudarstvennogo tsentral'nogo muzeia muzykal'noi kul'tury im. M. I. Glinki (Filial GTsMMK im. M. I. Glinki)

[A. B. Gol'denveizer Apartment-Museum—
Branch of M. I. Glinka State Central Museum of Musical Culture]

Agency: Ministerstvo kul'tury RF (Minkul'tury Rossii)
[Ministry of Culture]

Address: 103009, Moscow, ul. Tverskaia, 17, kv. 109–110
Telephone: 229-29-29
Transport: metro: Pushkinskaia, Tverskaia
Hours: WF 11:00–18:00; Th 14:00–17:30

Director: Elena Ivanovna Gol'denveizer (*tel.* 229-29-29)

HISTORY:

The museum was founded in 1955 as a branch of the Glinka Central Museum of Musical Culture (H–45) and as a repository for many culturally valuable items collected by the celebrated pianist and composer, Aleksandr Borisovich Gol'denveizer (1875–1961), and subsequently donated to the state. The museum was later reorganized as the Division for the History of Piano Art within GTsMMK (*Otdel istorii fortepiannogo iskusstva GTsMMK im. M. I. Glinki*), but in 1995 its status as an affiliated branch was restored.

HOLDINGS: 1 fond, 26,166 units, 1865–1961

photographs—2,667 (1876–1961); letters—13,534 units (1867–1961);
documents—2,220 units (1865–1961); concert and theater programs—7,459 units (1867–1961);
rare books—214 (1751–1920s); autographs—72 units (1823–1961)

The archival holdings consist of several collections: original autograph copies of works, concert and theater programs, and collections of rare books. The basis of the fond is made up of personal papers and documents connected with the work of Gol'denveizer as professor and director of the Moscow Conservatory and Chairman of the Moscow Music Council (*Moskovskii muzykal'nyi sovet*). It includes manuscripts of musical compositions by Gol'denveizer, and articles and memoirs written by and about him. There are also forty manuscript notebooks of his diaries (1889–1961), as well as his correspondence with Lev Tolstoi and members of Tolstoi's family, S. V. Rakhmaninov, N. K. Metner, G. L. Katuar, R. M. Glier, and D. D. Shostakovich, among others.

The photograph archive contains autographed photographs of N. A. Rimskii-Korsakov, A. K. Glazunov, S. I. Taneev, S. V. Rakhmaninov, M. A. Chekhov, and K. S. Stanislavskii. There are also pictures taken at Iasnaia Poliana during L. N. Tolstoi's lifetime.

The collection of concert and theater programs reflects the musical world of Moscow from 1886 to the 1960s, although there are a few documents relating to an earlier period (from 1867). Some of the programs contain notes written by Gol'denveizer.

The museum contains a collection of rare books, some of them autographed by A. I. Odoevskii, V. A. Zhukovskii, and E. A. Baratynskii. One of the rarities is an album that formerly belonged to

Princess Golitsyna containing original handwritten pieces by A. S. Pushkin, F. I. Tiutchev, Gioacchino Rossini, and Giacomo Meyerbeer.

Access: There are no restrictions on admission to the archive. As of Winter 1999 the holdings are closed for inventory.

Reference Facilities: There are inventories arranged under the headings of letters, documents, theater and concert programs, photographs, and autographs. There are reference card catalogues of letters, persons named in letters, and performers.

Library Facilities: There is a library of books and music scores based on the books and sheet music collected by Gol'denveizer. Most of the books have marginal notes. A passport or other identity document is required for access to the library.

Copying: Copies of documents can be ordered through the GTsMMK laboratory (see H–45).

FINDING AIDS — PUBLISHED — GENERAL:

Muzei Moskvy (1997), pp. 162–63; *GAF Spravochnik* (1991), pp. 67–68.

There is no published guide to the archival materials in the museum.

h-333. *A. B. Gol'denveizer: Stat'i, materialy, vospominaniia.* Edited by D. D. Blagoi et al. Moscow: "Sov. kompozitor," 1969. 447 p. + 96 plates. [GTsMMK im. M. I. Glinki] (Lib: MH)

> An appreciative collection of biographical and analytic articles about Gol'denveizer and reminiscences about him, with extensive illustrations from the photographic collection in the museum and indications of other documentation held there.

Gosudarstvennyi dom-muzei P. I. Chaikovskogo
[P. I. Tchaikovsky State House-Museum]

Agency: Komitet po kul'ture i turizmu Administratsii Moskovskoi oblasti
[Committee on Culture and Tourism of the Administration of Moscow Oblast]

Address: 141600, Moskovskaia oblast', g. Klin, ul. Chaikovskogo, 48
Telephone: 159-81-96
Transport: suburban train from Leningrad Station to Klin, then bus 5, 13
Hours: MTuTh–Su 10:00–18:00

Director: Galina Ivanovna Belonovich (*tel.* 539-81-96)
Head of Archive: Polina Efimovna Vaidman (*tel.* 539-81-96)

HISTORY:

Dom-muzei P. I. Chaikovskogo
   [P. I. Tchaikovsky House-Museum] (1894–1921)

The museum was founded in 1894 in the house where the Russian composer Petr Il'ich Tchaikovsky (Chaikovskii) (1840–1893) lived from 1885. Immediately after the death of the composer, the house was purchased from its owner and later, in 1916, was bequeathed by the composer's brother, Modest Il'ich Tchaikovsky, to the Russian Music Society (*Russkoe muzykal'noe obshchestvo*), which undertook to preserve it as a museum.

In August 1921 the museum was nationalized. A decade later, in 1931, it was transferred to the jurisdiction of the Bol'shoi Theater, and then after 1937 it was under the administration of the All-Union Committee on Art.

In 1941 the house was in the Nazi zone of occupation and was badly damaged, although many of the materials were evacuated to Udmurtia (Votkinsk). The museum holdings were returned to Klin in 1944.

HOLDINGS: letters by Tchaikovsky—over 4,000; letters to Tchaikovsky—over 7,000

The museum holds the largest single collection of Tchaikovsky's personal papers and music scores, although many of his manuscripts and documents have found their way into other repositories. Among the most interesting documents are the rough copies, studies and drafts for a number of works; several final copies; eighteen notebooks; and all of his remaining diaries (in ten copy-books). The museum holds the greatest part of the originals of Tchaikovsky's correspondence—letters both written by Tchaikovsky and addressed to him.

The museum also contains the archive of his brother, M. I. Tchaikovsky and parts of the archives of a number of other persons who were prominent in the Russian music world during the late nineteenth and early twentieth centuries, including S. I. Taneev, A. S. Arenskii, G. A. Larosh, N. D. Kashkin, A. A. Brandukov, and E. F. Napravnik.

There are many photographs and some additional documentation of relatives, classmates, friends, and musical colleagues, including his father, I. P. Tchaikovsky (Chaikovskii) (1795–1880); his brothers, Nikolai Il'ich (1838–1911), Anatolii Il'ich (1850–1915), Ippolit Il'ich (1843–1927), and Modest Il'ich (1850–1916); his nephew V. L. Davydov (1871–1906); his closest friend, N. F. von Mekk; and students and professors at the Moscow Conservatory.

N.B. A significant part of the literary production and correspondence of the composer was published in the complete collected works of Tchaikovsky, *Polnoe sobranie sochinenii* (Moscow: Gos.

muzykal'noe izd-vo, 1953–), which was based on materials in the museum. Some of the volumes appear in the series of *Trudy Gosudarstvennogo doma-muzeia P. I. Chaikovskogo.*

Access: In connection with the publication (starting in 1991) of a new edition of the collected works of Tchaikovsky, some of the materials may be temporarily closed to outside researchers.

Library Facilities: The museum retains the book and music library of Petr I. Tchaikovsky and his brother, Modest I. Tchaikovsky. The books in Russian and foreign languages (over 2,000 vols.) include ancient classical literature, philosophical works, studies of the history of art, books on history, psychology, logic, and linguistics, and domestic and foreign journals on art.

The music library consists of a basic collection of domestic and foreign composers, and especially piano duet arrangements. There are copies with dedicatory signatures by A. K. Glazunov, E. F. Napravnik, and other cultural leaders.

Comment: A completed questionnaire was not returned to Rosarkhiv from the museum.

FINDING AIDS — PUBLISHED — GENERAL:

PKG *M&L* (1972), p. 288.

For more detailed information on the manuscript legacy of Tchaikovsky, with citations to original music scores in Klin, see the 1958 catalogue (a-135).

h-335. *Dom-muzei P. I. Chaikovskogo v Klinu.* Compiled by G. I. Belonovich. Moscow: RPTs "Vneshtorgizdat," 1994. 211 p. Parallel text in Russian and English. [K-t po kul'ture i turizmu Moskovskoi oblasti] (Lib: IU)

h-336. *Dom-muzei P. I. Chaikovskogo v Klinu: Putevoditel'-spravochnik po memorial'noi ekspozitsii.* Compiled by G. I. Belonovich and P. E. Vaidman. Moscow: "Mir i kul'tura," 1992. 64 p. (Lib: IU; MH)

> A survey of the museum exhibits, including manuscripts and photographs. Includes a history of the founding and development of the museum (pp. 8–12).

h-337. *Gosudarstvennyi dom-muzei P. I. Chaikovskogo v Klinu: Putevoditel'.* Compiled by K. Iu. Davydova, S. S. Kotomina, I. Iu. Sokolinskaia, et al. Edited by G. A. Shamkin. 4th ed. Moscow: "Muzyka," 1980. 95 p. [Minkul't SSSR; Upravlenie kul'tury Mosoblsoveta]

> EARLIER ED.: M.: Gos. muzykal'noe izd-vo, 1953. 60 p. (Lib: MH).

> This guide to the House-Museum contains a brief history and a summary of the contents of the Tchaikovsky archive (pp. 19–21). There is also a bibliography of works written on the basis of the archival materials (pp. 89–91).

h-337.1. *Chaikovsky Home-Museum in Klin: A Short Guide.* Moscow: Foreign Languages Pub. House, 1959. 67 p. + plates. (Lib: MH)

h-338. *Avtografy P. I. Chaikovskogo v arkhive Doma-Muzeia v Klinu: Spravochnik.* Compiled by G. R. Freindling, E. M. Orlova, and K. Iu. Davydova. Edited by E. V. Korotkova-Leviton. 2 vols. Moscow/Leningrad: Gosudarstvennoe muzykal'noe izd-vo, 1950–1952. 96 p., 332 p. (Lib: DLC; IU; MH) [IDC-R-11,028]

> The first volume contains a brief description of the composer's archive and its subdivisions for (1) manuscript music scores and (2) diaries and memoirs. The second volume covers his manuscript correspondence and other writings.

h-339. Kholodovskii, Vladimir. *Dom v Klinu.* 5th ed. Moscow: "Moskovskii rabochii," 1975. 340 p. + plates. (Lib: IU)

> 3d ED.: M., 1962. 338 p. (Lib: MH)

> EARLIER ED.: M., 1959. 334 p. + plates. (Lib: MH).

> A popularized account of the history of the museum and of Tchaikovsky's life, with fragmentary information on the manuscript holdings.

Gosudarstvennyi memorial'nyi muzei A. N. Skriabina

[A. N. Scriabin State Memorial Museum]

Agency: Ministerstvo kul'tury RF (Minkul'tury Rossii)
[Ministry of Culture]
Komitet po kul'ture Pravitel'stva Moskvy
[Committee on Culture of the Government of Moscow]

Address: 121002, Moscow, Bol'shoi Nikolo-Peskovskii per.
(*formerly* ul. Vakhtangova), 11
Telephone: 241-19-01; *Fax:* (095) 377-66-48
Website: http://moscow.lvl.ru/culture/museum/skrjabin/eskrjab.html
Transport: metro: Arbatskaia, Smolenskaia
Hours: WF 12:00–18:00; Th 10:00–16:00 (research—by appointment)

Director: Tamara Viktorovna Rybakova (*tel.* 241-19-01)
Scientific Secretary: Iraida Ivanovna Trapezina (*tel.* 241-19-00)
Deputy Director for Scientific Work: Ol'ga Mikhailovna Tompakova (*tel.* 241-14-10)
Chief Curator: Mira Mikhailovna Petrova (*tel.* 241-14-10)

HISTORY:

Muzei-kvartira A. N. Skriabina—Filial Muzeia istorii g. Moskvy
[A. N. Scriabin Apartment-Museum—Branch of Museum of the History of Moscow] (1922–1991)

In 1918 a cultural protection plaque was placed on the house where the composer and pianist Aleksandr Nikolaevich Scriabin (Skriabin) (1872–1915) lived from 1912 to 1915. In 1922 the Apartment-Museum was officially opened. It subsequently became an affiliated branch of the Museum of the History of Moscow (H–5). During the 1970s it was temporarily closed, but was reopened to the public in 1988. Since 1991 the museum has had independent status under its present name.

HOLDINGS: 6,651 units, 1872–1915

sound recordings—over 700 units (1910–1990)

The museum holds documents relating to the life and work of the Russian composer and professor of the Moscow Conservatory, Aleksandr Nikolaevich Scriabin (Skriabin). These include sheet music and scores for musical works, like his "Poem of Ecstasy" (*Poema ekstaza*) and his symphonic poem "Prometheus." There are also the manuscripts of his original philosophical works and correspondence with his friends and relatives. Among the personal papers there are drawings by B. M. Kustodiev, L. O. Pasternak, and N. P. Ul'ianov.

The museum retains the composer's library, which includes books with dedicatory autographs by G. V. Plekhanov and by the poets K. D. Bal'mont and V. I. Ivanov.

There is a collection of programs and posters that are thematically linked with Scriabin's work.

The Sound Recordings Archive retains recordings of the composer's work played by himself; by such famous pianists as G. G. Neigauz, V. V. Sofronitskii, and S. E. Meinberg; and by orchestras conducted by N. S. Golovanov and Lorin Maazel, among others.

Access: A letter is required from the researcher's sponsoring organization.

Working Conditions: Researchers are accommodated in museum offices.

Reference Facilities: There are subject reference card catalogues.

Library Facilities: The museum retains Scriabin's personal library with books containing his personal notes. Some books have autographs of other contempory musicians (including S. I. Taneev) and the poet K. D. Bal'mont.

Copying: There are facilities for xerox copying.

FINDING AIDS — PUBLISHED — GENERAL:

Muzei Moskvy (1997), pp. 168–70; *GAF Spravochnik* (1991), p. 140.

There is no published guide to the archival materials in the museum.

h-342. Al'shvang, Arnol'd A. *A. N. Skriabin: [Zhizn' i tvorchestvo].* Moscow/Leningrad: Izd-vo i tipolit. Muzgiza v Moskve, 1945. 52 p. (Lib: IU)

> EARLIER ED.: M.: Muzgiz, 1940. 62 p. (Lib: MH).
> > An appendix lists 22 manuscripts held in the museum—"Spisok rukopisei, khraniashchikhsia v muzee A. N. Skriabina v Moskve" (pp. 51–52).

h-343. *Aleksandr Nikolaevich Skriabin i ego muzei: [Sbornik statei].* Edited by D. G. Pershin. Moscow: MONO, 7-ia tip. "Iskra revoliutsii" Mospoligrafa, 1930. 37 p. + plates.

> In an introductory essay the editor provides information about the establishment of the museum (pp. 21–37).

h-344. **Nauchnaia sessiia, posviashchennaia tvorchestvu A. N. Skriabina (Moskva, 1941 g.): Materialy dokladov.* Moscow, 1941.

Muzei kino
[Museum of Cinema]

Agency: [Independent social organization]

Address: 123242, Moscow, ul. Druzhinnikovskaia, 15
Telephone: 255-90-95 (Administrator); *Fax:* (095) 255-90-96
Transport: metro: Krasnopresnenskaia, Barrikadnaia; tram: 5, 35b; bus: 6, 39, 64, 116
Hours: M–F 10:00–17:00

Director: Naum Ikhil'evich Kleiman (*tel.* 255-91-89)
Deputy Director: Mikhail Nikolaevich Bocharov
Main Curator: Nadezhda Aleksandrovna Tarkhova (*tel.* 255-93-04)

HISTORY:

Tsentral'nyi muzei kino
[Central Museum of Cinema] (1989–1992)

The museum was founded in 1992 on the basis of the collection from the Central Museum of Cinema (*Tsentral'nyi muzei kino*), which itself had only been set up three years earlier in 1989. It is located in the motion-picture center known as the House of Cinema (*Dom kino*), which also has several special film presentation theaters and smaller viewing rooms. The building also houses the offices and library (see below) of the Union of Russian Cinematographers (*Soiuz kinematografistov Rossii*). That Union along with other organizations—the State Committee of Cinematographers, the Ministry of Culture, and the Confederation of Unions of Cinematographers (*Konfederatsiia soiuza kinematografistov*)—have supported the founding and contributed to the development of the museum collections.

The Scientific-Memorial Cabinet of Sergei Mikhailovich Eisenstein (Eizenshtein) (1898–1948), founded as a museum in 1967 under the Union of Cinematographers, is housed in the apartment of Eisenstein's wife R. M. Atasheva and, since 1992, is a branch of the Museum of Cinema (see below).

Access: For research access, a letter is required from the researcher's sponsoring organization, or a personal application from the researcher, who must obtain permission of the curator of the section concerned.

Working Conditions: Researchers are accommodated in working offices or the storage area.

Library Facilities: The museum itself has a specialized library.

In addition, within the same building complex is located the Scientific-Technical Library of the Union of Russian Cinematographers (*Nauchno-tekhnicheskaia biblioteka Soiuza kinematografistov Rossii*) (tel. 255-91-15), which has extensive holdings of literature on the history of cinema, theater, and related arts. There is a very strong collection of reference literature, including relatively complete runs of film catalogues from the Soviet period. There are card indexes to films and film personalities, as well as a collection of albums with early photographs and press clippings.

Rukopisnyi fond
[Manuscript Fond]

Telephone: 255-93-04
Hours: by appointment
Deputy Head: Marina Markovna Karaseva (*tel.* 255-93-04)

HOLDINGS: 46 fonds, 1,500 (500 units unarranged) units, 1890–to present

The Manuscript Fond of the museum contains the personal papers of various film directors, film stars, cameramen, animators, and others who have worked in the film industry. The largest collections of personal papers are the fonds of two directors, A. I. Medvedkov and G. F. Shpalikov, and include materials relating to their creative work, biographical documents, and their vast correspondence with friends, relatives, and official institutions.

The fond also holds documents originating from public and state organizations connected with the film industry. For example, there is a part of the archive of the Central Studio for Documentary Films (TsSDF) that relates to the work of cameramen in frontline action during World War II.

The museum retains manuscript scenarios for a number of films.

Reference Facilities: There are card catalogues and inventories, but not for all the documents.

Copying: There are no copying facilities.

Izofond
[Pictorial Fond]

Hours: by appointment
Head: Viktor Alekseevich Voevodin (*tel.* 255-96-81)

HOLDINGS: 1,639 (3,000 unarranged) units, 1950–1994
posters—4,536

The Pictorial Fond holds paintings and graphic studies for films done by such famous artists as V. E. Egorov, E. E. Enei, P. S. Galadzhev, V. P. Kaplunovskii, and V. P. Utkin. There are also outtakes from films, placards, and posters.

Reference Facilities: For some of the documents there are inventories and subject card catalogues. Much of the documentation is still in the process of being arranged.

Fotofond
[Photograph Fond]

Telephone: 255-90-98
Hours: by appointment
Head: Elena Anatol'evna Misalaidi (*tel.* 255-90-98)

HOLDINGS: (ca. 1,000,000 units unarranged), ca. 1,000 units, late 19th c.–to present

The Photograph Fond contains photographs of actors, directors, and cameramen as well as shots taken from various films. There is also a portrait gallery of well-known people in the film world, together with a collection of photographs termed "Characters of the Era" ("*Tipazhi epokhi*"). The fond contains postcards and advertising material connected with the cinema, which includes a collection of photographs of the Russian early twentieth-century film studios in Yalta.

Reference Facilities: Detailed information has been prepared for the museum exhibits in the main fond which may be used for the purposes of reference. But the greater part of the Photograph Fond (some 1,000,000 units) remains undescribed.

Copying: Documents from the auxiliary fond can be copied, but copying photographs from the main fond is not permitted.

Nauchno-memorial'nyi kabinet S.M. Eizenshteina—Filial Muzeia kino
[S. M. Eisenstein Scientific-Memorial Cabinet—Branch of the Museum of Cinema]

Address:	121099, Moscow, ul. Smolenskaia, 10
Telephone:	241-80-30
Hours:	SaSu (by appointment)
Head:	Naum Ikhil'evich Kleiman (*tel.* 255-91-89; 241-80-30)

HOLDINGS:

The museum, honoring the world-renowned Russian film director Sergei Mikhailovich Eisenstein (Eizenshtein) (1898–1948) and housed in the former apartment of Eisenstein's wife, R. M. Atasheva, has been administered by the Museum of Cinema since 1992. The so-called Scientific-Memorial Cabinet, which includes Eisenstein's working study, exhibits many of Eisenstein's personal effects and memorabilia, along with copies of photographs, drawings, and other documents. Of particular importance in terms of archival quality materials is Eisenstein's personal library, with over 4,000 books in four languages, which include significant marginalia and inserted manuscript notes and enclosures prepared by Eisenstein himself.

N.B. Most of Eisenstein's personal papers are now held by RGALI (B–7), but archival copies of his films and related archival materials are held by Gosfil'mofond (C–16).

Comment: A questionnaire was not returned to Rosarkhiv by the museum.

FINDING AIDS — PUBLISHED — GENERAL:

Muzei Moskvy (1997), pp. 171–74.

There is no published guide or other description of the archival materials in the museum.

Museums of Education

✵ H–51 ✵

Muzei A. S. Makarenko
[A. S. Makarenko Museum]

Agency: Zapadnoe okruzhnoe upravlenie Departamenta obrazovaniia g. Moskvy
[West District Administration of the Moscow Department of Education]
Tsentr vneshkol'noi raboty im. A. S. Makarenko
[A. S. Makarenko Center for Outside-School Work]

Address:	121293, Moscow, ul. Poklonnaia, 16
Telephone:	148-08-35
Transport:	metro: Kutuzovskaia; trol.: 2, 39; bus: 77, 91, 505 (to "Ploshchad' Pobedy")
Hours:	M–F 10:00–18:00

Director: Vladimir Vasil'evich Morozov (*tel.* 148-08-35)
Head of Museum: Svetlana Sergeevna Nevskaia (*tel.* 148-08-35)
Deputy Head of Museum: Fania Natanovna Mer

HISTORY:
Muzei A. S. Makarenko
[A. S. Makarenko Museum] (1983–1992)

The A. S. Makarenko Museum was organized as a public organization in 1982 on the basis of collections made by the Moscow Pedagogical Society (*Moskovskoe pedagogicheskoe obshchestvo*), to honor the life and work of the Soviet Ukrainian teacher and educator, Anton Semenovich Makarenko (1888–1939). In 1992 the museum became subordinated to the A. S. Makarenko Center for Outside-School Work (*Tsentr vneshkol'noi raboty im. A. S. Makarenko*), which was then organized under the Western District Administration of the Moscow Department of Education.

HOLDINGS: 36 fonds, 720 units, 1916–1993

The museum, which is now a subdivision of the Makarenko Center, retains some manuscript materials from the collection of the Russian Pedagogical Society (*Rossiiskoe pedagogicheskoe obshchestvo*), particularly relating to the life and work of Makarenko, including Makarenko's letters, unpublished writings, and recollections and studies of his students.

N.B. Most of Makarenko's papers (1,388 units) are held in the Russian State Archive of Literature and Art (RGALI—B–7), and there is some additional materials in the Makarenko Memorial Museum (*Memorial'no-pedagogicheskii muzei A. S. Makarenko*) in Kremenchug (Poltava Oblast), Ukraine (see PKG, *Ukraine* [1988], p. 795).

Access: For access to archival materials, a passport or other identification is required.

Reference Facilities: There are *opisi* and subject card catalogues.

Library Facilities: The center has a library which mainly contains Makarenko's books, literature about him, and general literature on matters connected with education. Access is unrestricted.

Copying: No copying services are available.

FINDING AIDS — PUBLISHED — GENERAL:

There is no published description of the museum manuscript holdings.

Museums of Science and Agriculture

⊛⊷ H–52 ⊶⊛

Gosudarstvennyi biologicheskii muzei im. K. A. Timiriazeva (GBMT)
[K. A. Timiriazev State Biological Museum]

Agency: Ministerstvo kul'tury RF (Minkul'tury Rossii)
[Ministry of Culture]
Komitet po kul'ture Pravitel'stva Moskvy
[Committee on Culture of the Government of Moscow]

Address:	123242, Moscow, ul. Malaia Gruzinskaia, 15
Telephone:	252-36-81; *Fax:* (095) 255-63-21
Website:	http://www.museum.ru/timiryazev/
Transport:	metro: Krasnopresnenskaia, Barrikadnaia, Ulitsa 1905 goda
Hours:	Tu–Su 10:00–18:00; WF 12:00–19:00

Director: Irina Vasil'evna Polikarpova (*tel.* 252-55-42)
Scientific Secretary: Nina Maksimovna Ivannikova (*tel.* 252-39-44)

HISTORY:
Biologicheskii muzei im. K. A. Timiriazeva
[K. A. Timir'iazev Biological Museum] (1920–1945)

The museum was founded in 1920 as part of the Faculty of Biology at the Ia. M. Sverdlov Communist University (*Kommunisticheskii universitet im. Ia. M. Sverdlova*) on the basis of parts of the collections held by the A. L. Shaniavskii People's University (*Narodnyi universitet im. A. L. Shaniavskogo*). It was reorganized and opened to the public in 1922 on the initiative of the scientist B. M. Zavadovskii, who became the first director. In 1932 the museum became independent under the authority of the Academic Committee of the Central Executive Committee of the USSR (*Uchenyi komitet Tsentral'nogo ispolnitel'nogo komiteta SSSR*). In 1938 it was transferred to the control of the People's Commissariat of Education of the RSFSR. Since 1945 it has been under the authority of the Ministry of Culture of the RSFSR (now the Russian Federation), although from 1944 to 1953 it was responsible to the Committee of Cultural and Educational Establishments. Its present name dates from 1945.

The museum occupies the building originally constructed in the late nineteenth century for the art collections of P. I. Shchukin, and which in 1918–1926 housed the Museum of Old Moscow (*Muzei "Staraia Moskva"*). The museum has exhibitions related to the origins and evolution of life on Earth and the origins of the human species, as well as genetics and the physical development of animals.

Access: An official letter is required to obtain the permission of the museum director for access to the archive.

Library Facilities: The museum has a scientific library.

Arkhiv
[Archive]

Hours: by appointment
Scholary Secretary: Nina Maksimovna Ivannikova (*tel.* 252-39-44)

HOLDINGS: 3 fonds, 432 units, 1922–1992
scientific council and conference documents—12 units; scientific methodological materials—20 units; thematic exhibition plans—113 units; texts of lectures and excursions—174 units; personal papers—1 fond; posters—374 (1932–1993); museum publications—46 units

The museum archive consists of three fonds: the administrative fond, the academic and educational fond, and the fond of documentary photographs. The administrative fond contains records of the work of all the subdivisions of the museum since 1922. The academic and educational fond contains the plans of exhibitions and displays, posters, records of the Academic Council, and texts of lectures and excursions. The documentary photograph fond provides a visual record of the history of the museum.

Also retained here are the personal papers of the museum's founder and first director, Academician B. M. Zavadovskii.

The slide collection of Moscow University Professor N. N. Kaden contains photographs of rare plants from Moscow Oblast, nature reserves, and African flora.

The basic main fond of the museum collections contains paintings and drawings done by the animal painters V. A. Vatagin, A. Komarov, and K. Flerov.

Working Conditions: The papers of Academician B. M. Zavadovskii and the photographic collection are still in the process of arrangement and hence not available for researchers.

Reference Facilities: There are subject and auxiliary card catalogues, and inventories for part of the fonds.

Copying: There are no photographic copying facilities.

FINDING AIDS — PUBLISHED — GENERAL:

Muzei Moskvy (1997), pp. 247–49; *GAF Spravochnik* (1991), pp. 159–60.

There is no published description of the archival materials in the museum.

h-350. *Gosudarstvennyi biologicheskii muzei im. K. A. Timiriazeva: Putevoditel'.* Edited by I. P. Kriazhin. Moscow: "Sovetskaia Rossiia," 1960. 109 p. [Minkul't RSFSR]
The preface gives a brief history of the museum.

h-351. *Osnovnye zadachi i printsipy organizatsii Biologicheskogo muzeia im. K. A. Timiriazeva pri Kommunisticheskom universitete im. Ia. M. Sverdlova: Opyt organizatsii biologicheskikh muzeev i ugolkov zhivoi prirody.* Edited by B. M. Zavadovskii. Moscow: Izd-vo Kommunisticheskogo universiteta im. Ia. M. Sverdlova, 1927. 262 p.
Describes the early history of the organization of the museum and its collections (pp. 13–16).

Gosudarstvennyi Darvinovskii muzei (GDM)
[State Darwin Museum]

Agency: Komitet po kul'ture Pravitel'stva Moskvy
[Committee on Culture of the Government of Moscow]

Address:	117292, Moscow, ul. Vavilova, 57
Telephone:	135-33-82, 135-33-84; *Fax:* (095) 135-33-85; 135-33-86
E-mail:	darwin@museum.ru
Website:	http://www.darwin.museum.ru
Transport:	metro: Akademicheskaia; tram: 14, 39; bus: 57, 119

Director: Anna Iosifovna Kliukina (*tel.* 135-33-76)
Scientific Secretary: Iuliia Vadimovna Shubina (*tel.* 135-33-86)

HISTORY:

Muzei evoliutsionnoi istorii
[Museum of the History of Evolution] (1907–1939)
Darvinovskii muzei
[Darwin Museum] (1939–[1946])

The museum was founded in 1907 as the Museum of the History of Evolution. Its original holdings came from the personal collection of the biologist A. F. Kots (1880–1964), which had been donated to the Moscow Higher Education Courses for Women (*Vysshie zhenskie kursy v Moskve*) of Professor V. I. Ger'e. In 1922 it became an independent institution, and in 1939 was renamed the Darwin Museum. In 1995 the museum was moved to a new building specially constructed for it.

Access: For research access, an official letter or a personal application to the museum director is required.

Copying: Facilities are available for xerox copies.

Sector redkoi knigi i pis'mennykh istochnikov. Arkhiv
[Sector of Rare Books and Written Sources. Archive]

Hours: by appointment
Head: Tat'iana Fedorovna Andreeva (*tel.* 135-19-91)

HOLDINGS: 15,000 units, mid-19th c.–1992
photographs—5,000 (1890s–1986); films—435 (1930s–1986)

This sector of the museum contains the personal papers of the biologists A. F. Kots, N. N. Ladygina-Kots, A. A. Paramonov, and P. P. Smolin. They include scientific works on animal psychology, Darwinism, and the study and administration of museums, as well as correspondence with leading scholars throughout the world. There are also photographic copies of letters written by the Russian biologist V. O. Kovalevskii to Charles Darwin, and letters written by Darwin and his relatives.

Photographs illustrate the history of the museum with pictures of various exhibitions that have been held since its founding. There are many photographs of biological species and pictures taken of animals in their natural habitat. There are also photographs of, and those collected by, the biologists V. A. Vagner, Thomas Huxley, N. K. Kol'tsov, and Konrad Lorenz.

The museum has films on the behaviour of anthropoid apes and their study by the American biologist Roberta Yorks.

Working Conditions: There is a special reading room for researchers.

Reference Facilities: There are card catalogues covering the archival materials and the photographs.

Copying: Facilities are available for xerox copies.

FINDING AIDS — PUBLISHED — GENERAL:

Muzei Moskvy (1997), pp. 251–53; *GAF Spravochnik* (1991), pp. 160–61.

There is no published guide to the archival materials in the museum.

h-360. *Gosudarstvennyi Darvinovskii muzei: Stranitsy istorii. Osnovateli muzeia.* Mozhaisk: Mozhaiskii poligraficheskii kombinat, 1993. 144 p. + plates.

> This collection includes articles by A. F. Kots and N. N. Ladygina-Kots on the history of the foundation of the Darwin Museum and its work from 1907 to 1940.

Memorial'nyi dom-muzei I. V. Kurchatova
[I. V. Kurchatov Memorial House-Museum]

Agency: Rossiiskii nauchnyi tsentr "Kurchatovskii institut"
[Kurchatov Institute Russian Scientific Center]

Address:	123182, Moscow, pl. Kurchatova, 1
Telephone:	196-91-25
E-mail:	web-admin@www.kiae.ru
Website:	http://www.kiae.ru/rus/dmk/bdma.htm
Transport:	metro: Oktiabr'skoe pole + bus 100, 253, 800
Hours:	TuTh 10:00–14:00

Chairman of the Board, Kurchatov Institute: Evgenii Petrovich Velikhov
    (*tel.* 196-92-41, 206-38-52; *fax:* 943-00-23; *e-mail:* epv@epv.kiae.su)
Director, Kurchatov Institute Scientific Center: Aleksandr Iurevich Rumiantsev
    (*tel.* 196-91-25; *fax:* 196-18-70; *e-mail:* ray@www.kiae.ru)
Museum Director: Raisa Viktorovna Kuznetsova (*tel.* 196-92-26)

HISTORY:

The museum was founded in 1970 on the grounds of the Institute of Atomic Energy, which is now the independent Kurchatov Institute (see E–41). The museum is located in the house where the Soviet Russian nuclear physicist Igor Vasil'evich Kurchatov (1903–1960) lived.

N.B. See the main entry for the Kurchatov Institute (E–41) for further information about its history, archival holdings, and photo-video archive.

HOLDINGS: 1 fond, over 25,000 units, 4 collections, 1903–1960 (scattered documents—1880–1995)

The museum has collected documents relating to the life, work and public activity of the nuclear physicist Igor Vasil'evich Kurchatov.

The documentation pertaining to his work as a nuclear physicist consists of his own scientific writings, reviews, and work notes recorded in diaries and correspondence. There are documents showing his connections with various academic organizations and illustrating his activities as a member of the Presidium of the Academy of Sciences of the USSR and as a deputy to the Supreme Soviet of the USSR. Documents highlight his duties as a deputy and as organizer and participant in international conferences on problems of nuclear physics, including test-ban conferences. There is extensive scientific and personal correspondence of Kurchatov with scientists abroad, with academic and ministerial institutes in the Soviet Union, and with publishers and editors.

The museum retains biographical documentation on Kurchatov and his relatives, including his personnel questionnaires and application forms, his autobiography, and other personal documents.

Documents relating to Kurchatov include articles, memoirs and recollections about him, and material written to perpetuate his memory. These include contributions by Academicians A. P. Aleksandrov, G. N. Flerov, I. K. Kikoin, Iu. B. Khariton, and N. S. Khlopkin, V. I. Mostovoi, and Ia. B. Zel'dovich; by Minister of Medium Machine Building E. P. Slavskii, and Minister of Armaments B. L. Vannikov; as well as by his wife, his relatives, scientific colleagues and associates, and one of his personal security guards, D. S. Pereverzev, who during the 1970s was the museum curator.

There are separate collections of documents relating to his brother, B. V. Kurchatov, his wife, M. D. Kurchatova, to the scientists A. P. Aleksandrov, E. K. Zavoiskii, I. K. Kikoin, and the director of atomic affairs in the 1940s through 1980s, E. P. Slavskii. There are also documents relating to the management of the house in which Kurchatov lived in Moscow and his dacha in the Crimea.

The museum has a large photograph archive. This comprises rare photographs taken at the end of the nineteenth century and negatives of a more recent period showing Kurchatov's personal life—pictures of his friends and colleagues, and of his daily surroundings and workplace. Other rare photographs show the first instruments and equipment that he and other scientists like K. D. Sinel'nikov built themselves for experimental work during the 1930s. There are collected photographs of many atomic scientists.

The museum has film footage and newsreels of Kurchatov taken at work, at rest, and on his travels around the country and to England. Many reminiscences about Kurchatov have been recorded by the museum staff on videocassettes, including his assistants and colleagues A. P. Aleksandrov, I. N. Golovin, V. V. Goncharov, Iu. B. Khariton, and E. P. Slavskii, among many others.

The sound collection contains recordings of prominent scientists and recollections of contemporaries. There are synchronic recordings of Kurchatov's speeches at Party Congresses and sessions of the USSR Supreme Soviet.

N.B. Many of the Kurchatov papers and other documentation related to the Kurchatov Institute are held in the Institute itself (see E–41).

Access: The archival materials of the museum are closed to researchers, although copies of documents can be requested on the basis of subject-oriented (thematic) searches by the staff.

Working Conditions: The museum conducts subject-oriented searches for documents, including photographs, film, and videocassettes, on a fee-for-service basis (on occasion including the preparation of copies).

Reference Facilities: *Opisi* are being prepared.

Copying: Depending on the materials involved, copies can be prepared at commercial rates, with additional search fees.

FINDING AIDS — PUBLISHED — GENERAL:

There is no published guide to the archival materials in the museum. A partial survey is in preparation by R. V. Kuznetsova on the basis of her dissertation (see a-139).

Muzei zemlevedeniia
[Museum of Earth Sciences]

Agency: Moskovskii gosudarstvennyi universitet (MGU)
[Moscow State University]

Address:	119899, Moscow, Vorob'evy (*formerly* Leninskie) gory, Universitetskaia pl., 1
Telephone:	939-18-23
Website:	http://moscow.lvl.ru/culture/museum/zemmgu/ezemmgu.html
Transport:	metro: Universitet; bus: 1, 111, 113, 119, 661
Hours:	M–F 9:00–17:00

Head: Sergei Aleksandrovich Ushakov (*tel.* 939-14-15)
Chief of the Methodological Sector: Vitol'd Geliodorovich Khodetskii (*tel.* 939-29-76)

HISTORY:

The museum was established in 1950 on the initiative of professors and teachers in several MGU faculties as a scientific and educational museum of geology and geography. It was opened in 1955 in honor of the bicentennial of the University. With its present name dating from 1964, it is considered one of the principal museums for the history of science in Russia.

HOLDINGS: statistics not available

The museum retains considerable documentation relating to its collections, as well as scientific drawings and other graphic materials, maps, geological survey drawings, aerial photographs, and pictures of scholars. There are also photocopies of documents from the Archive of the Russian Academy of Sciences, GIM, and other repositories. Some of the graphic materials, such as landscape drawings, as well as pictures of scholars, appear in the museum exhibits.

Working Conditions: Researchers are accommodated in working offices.

Comment: A completed questionnaire from the museum was not returned to Rosarkhiv.

FINDING AIDS — PUBLISHED — GENERAL:

Muzei Moskvy (1997), pp. 272–76.

There is no published description of the archival materials in the museum.

h-361. *Putevoditel' po Muzeiu zemlevedeniia Moskovskogo gosudarstvennogo universiteta.* Edited by B. A. Savel'ev, N. E. Dik, Iu. K. Efremov, et al. 3d ed. Moscow: Izd-vo MGU, 1967. 168 p. (Lib: DLC; IU)
   1st ED.: M., 1957. 2d ED.: M., 1961.
      Provides information on the history of the museum (pp. 3–19).

h-362. *Zhizn' Zemli: Sbornik Muzeia zemlevedeniia MGU.* Moscow: Izd-vo MGU, 1982. 176 p. Vol. 17 in series. (Lib: DLC; IU)
      The seventeenth volume (1982) in the series of irregular publications issued by the museum includes a history of the museum and describes the preparations for its opening (1953–1955).

Muzei konevodstva
[Museum of Horse Breeding]

Agency: Moscovskaia sel'skokhoziaistvennaia akademiia im. K. A. Timiriazeva
[K. A. Timiriazev Moscow Academy of Agriculture]

Address:	127550, Moscow, ul. Timiriazevskaia, 44
Telephone:	976-10-03
Website:	http://www.deol.ru/culture/museum/koni.htm;
	http://moscow.lvl.ru/culture/museum/konevod/konevod.html
Transport:	metro: Dmitrovskaia, Voikovskaia + tram: 27; metro: Timiriazevskaia + bus 72
Hours:	M–Th 10:00–17:00; F 10:00–15:00

Director: David Iakovlevich Gurevich (*tel.* 976-10-03)

HISTORY:

Gosudarstvennyi muzei konnozavodstva i konevodstva
[State Museum of Stud Farming and Horse Breeding] (1929–1940)

The museum was founded on the basis of the private collection of Ia. I. Butovich, who had been the owner of the Prilepsk Stud Farm in Tula Gubernia. In 1918 the Butovich collection was nationalized and in January 1929, the State Museum of Stud Farming and Horse Breeding was opened under the authority of the All-Union Scientific Research Institute of Horse Breeding (*Vsesoiuznyi nauchno-issledovatel'skii institut konevodstva—VNIIK*). In 1940 the museum was transferred to the control of the K. A. Timiriazev Academy of Agriculture and was given its present name.

HOLDINGS: over 3,000 units, 19th c.–to present
negatives—over 55,000

The collection has more than 3,000 pictures (including watercolors and graphics) of different breeds of horses done by such famous artists as M. A. Vrubel', P. O. Kovalevskii, B. D. Polenov, N. G. Sverchkov, V. A. Serov, and R. F. Frents. The museum also holds manuscripts of Ia. I. Butovich (descriptions of his collections and memoirs) and other materials pertaining to horse breeding.

There is a large photograph collection, videocassettes, stamps, postcards, and other graphic materials, predominantly depicting horses.

Access: For research access, a letter is required from the researcher's sponsoring organization.

Reference Facilities: Reference materials for the documents is still in preparation. The photograph collection has subject and geographic catalogues.

Library Facilities: The library contains over 12,000 books and journals, including many unique folio albums (16th–18th cc.).

Copying: There are no facilities for photographic copying.

Comment: A completed questionnaire was not returned to Rosarkhiv.

FINDING AIDS — PUBLISHED — GENERAL:

Muzei Moskvy (1997), pp. 292–94.

There is no published guide to the archival materials in the museum.

h-364. *Muzei konevodstva: (Putevoditel').* Compiled by A. S. Krasnikov. Moscow, 1974. 39 p. [Minsel'khoz SSSR; Mosk. sel'skokhoziaistvennaia akademiia im. K. A. Timiriazeva]
EARLIER ED.: *Muzei konevodstva: Putevoditel'.* M., 1968. 36 p.
Provides brief information on the history of the museum and the formation of its collections.

h-365. *Moskovskaia Sel'skokhoziaistvennaia akademiia im. K. A. Timiriazeva (1865–1990): Bibliograficheskii ukazatel' literatury.* Moscow: Izd-vo MSKhA, 1991. 12 p. [MSKhA; Tsentral'naia nauchnaia biblioteka im. N. I. Zheleznova]
The bibliography covers writings about the most significant events in the life of the Academy over the last 125 years, including the Horse-Breeding Museum (p. 11) and the V. R. Vil'iams Soil and Agronomy Museum in St. Petersburg.

Museums of Technology and Space Exploration

✤⊶ H–57 ⊷✤

Gosudarstvennyi Politekhnicheskii muzei (GPM)
[State Polytechnic Museum]

Agency: Ministerstvo kul'tury RF (Minkul'tury Rossii)
[Ministry of Culture]

Address: 101000, Moscow, Novaia ploshchad', 3/4, pod"ezd 1
Telephone: 923-07-56; *Fax:* (095) 925-12-90
Website: http://www.deol.ru/culture/museum/politeh/politeh.htm;
http://uchcom.botik.ru/~msh/pol–r
Transport: metro: Kitai-gorod, Lubianka
Hours: Tu–F 10:00–18:00

Director: Giurgen Grigor'evich Grigorian (*tel.* 925-06-14)
Head of Scientific Research for the Division of Fonds:
Liudmila Nikolaevna Agureeva (*tel.* 928-63-16)

HISTORY:
Muzei prikladnykh znanii
[Museum of Applied Knowledge] (1872–1918)
Tsentral'nyi institut politekhnicheskikh znanii
[Central Institute of Polytechnic Knowledge] (1918–1922)
Russkii gosudarstvennyi Politekhnicheskii muzei
[Russian State Polytechnic Museum] (1922–1947)
Politekhnicheskii muzei
[Polytechnic Museum] (1947–1992)

The museum was founded by the Society of Friends of Natural Science, Anthropology, and Ethnography (*Obshchestvo liubitelei estestvoznaniia, antropologii i etnografii*) on the basis of materials from the Polytechnic Exhibition which was held in Moscow in 1872 to mark the bicentennial of the birth of Peter the Great. The museum was opened to the public in December of the same year on ul. Prechistenka under the name of the Museum of Applied Knowlege (*Muzei prikladnykh znanii*). The present building was specially constructed for the museum—the central corpus in 1877, on the plan of Ippolito (I. A.) Monigetti, was one of the first museum buildings in Russia. The side wings were added later in the 1890s and early years of the twentieth century.

In 1918 the museum was transferred to the jurisdiction of the People's Commissariat of Education (Narkompros RSFSR) and reorganized as the Central Institute of Polytechnic Knowledge. Starting in 1922, it came under the Main Administration for Scientific, Museum, and Scientific-Art Institutions (Glavnauka) and renamed as the Russian State Polytechnic Museum. It was known as the Polytechnic Museum from 1947 until 1992, when it became the State Polytechnic Museum. In December 1991 the museum was added to the federal register of the most valuable monuments of the cultural heritage of the peoples of the Russian Federation.

Since 1994, the museum has been administratively combined with the Central Polytechnic Library (*Tsentral'naia Politekhnicheskaia biblioteka*—TsPB), which was originally founded in 1864 by the same society that founded the museum, and later occupied a part of the same building that was specially contructed for the museum.

HOLDINGS: documents—21,766 units; photographs—1,075; negatives—over 41,000

The museum's so-called Written Fond (*Pis'mennyi fond*) includes over 21,000 units of basic holdings. The documentary part of the fond includes a large part of the administrative records of the museum, with many documents about the foundation and development of the museum, the organization of special exhibits, relations with scientists, advertisements, and correspondence with factories and scientific institutions. There is an extensive collection of documents relating to inventions from the eighteenth through the twentieth centuries, including imperial privileges, patents, inventors' plans and attestations. One collection of special interest comprises the fond relating to the Polytechnic Exhibition of 1872 and the foundation of the museum. There are also a number of documents relating to the activities of well-known Russian and foreign scientists, scholars, engineers, and inventors.

There are several fonds of personal papers, including the papers of P. P. Petrov, a specialist in chemical technology, who was the first director of the museum; the scientist and inventor K. E. Tsiolkovskii; and A. A. Petrovskii, a radio-electronic engineer, among many others.

Graphic materials in the basic museum fond total over 5,500 units, many of which had been used for or related to early museum exhibits. There are several auxiliary collections of photographs and negatives, including a collection of diapositives on glass produced by the museum itself (1872–1922) and a collection of reproductions of past exhibits going back to the nineteenth century. There are extensive collections of engravings, photographs, and postcards, relating to workshops, machinery, trade guilds, and other developments in plants, factories, and cottage industries. There are graphic materials relating the first electric power stations, automobiles, and other technological developments. One auxiliary fond consists of photographic negatives (ca. 41,000 units) reproducing published materials relating to science and technology, exhibitions in this museum and others, individual items from museum exhibits, and portraits of scientists and scholars.

The Written Fond also includes 4,748 rare books on the history of science and technology, including many prerevolutionary guides and catalogues to Russian and foreign trade and manufacturing firms.

Library Facilities: The Central Polytechnic Library (TsPB), which since 1994, has been administratively combined with the museum, now holds over three million volumes. Included are books, periodicals, and normative-technical documentation, and dissertation abstracts in many areas of science and technology, as well as in economics, manufacturing, architecture, applied arts, museum affairs, and bibliography. The library has many rare editions and many books with dedicatory autographs. (*Library address:* 101000, Moscow, Politekhnicheskii proezd, 2, pod"ezd 10; tel: 928-64-65, 921-45-85; Website: http://www.deol.ru/culture.museum/ polybib.htm).

Comment: A completed questionnaire from the museum was not returned to Rosarkhiv.

FINDING AIDS — PUBLISHED — GENERAL:

Muzei Moskvy (1997), pp. 237–39; *Pamiatniki nauki v muzeiakh* (1996).

There is no published guide to the archival materials in the museum.

h-366. *Sbornik trudov Gosudarstvennogo Politekhnicheskogo muzeia: K 120-letiiu.* Moscow: "Znanie," 1992. 128 p., 32 p. + plates.

A collection of articles about the museum honoring its 120th anniversary. Of particular relevance here are the following articles by the current director and other museum specialists that describe the museum's history and survey its archival and library materials:

Grigorian, Gurgen Grigor'evich, "Gosudarstvennyi Politekhnicheskii muzei: Ot muzeia prikladnykh znanii do golovnogo muzeia istorii nauki i tekhniki" (pp. 3–9).

Grigorian, Gurgen Grigor'evich; Zabotina, Ol'ga Vladimirovna; Ivanova, Tamara Stepanovna; and Uvarova, Lidiia Borisovna, "O muzeinom sobranii Gosudarstvennogo Politekhnicheskogo muzeia" (pp. 10–27).

Other articles describe other parts of the museum collections and outline the museum's functions, exhibits, organizational work, and scholarly activities. Includes a bibliography of other descriptive publications. The series with the same general title continues in subsequent years with other publications relating to the museum holdings and activities.

h-367. *Po zalam Politekhnicheskogo muzeia: Putevoditel'.* Compiled by Ia. D. Barskii. Moscow: "Znanie," 1990. 96 p. + 16 plates.

EARLIER ED.: *Politekhnicheskii muzei: Putevoditel'.* Compiled by Ia. D. Barskii. M.: "Znanie," 1984. 78 p.

A short popular illustrated guide to the museum exhibits with a brief history of the museum and its holdings, although with no mention of the archival materials.

h-368. Vlček, V. "110 let Polytechnickeho muzea v Moskvě." *Muzejni a vlastivědna práce,* 1982, no. 1, pp. 23–26. (Lib: DLC)

h-369. *Mir chudes [100 let Politekhnicheskomu muzeiu].* Compiled by A. G. Presniakov. Edited by I. I. Artobolevskii. Moscow: "Znanie," 1973. 198 p. + plates. [GPM] (Lib: DLC; MH)

h-370. Volkova, I. "Istorik S. M. Solov'ev i sozdanie Muzeia prikladnykh znanii v Moskve." In *Problemy istorii SSSR,* vol. 13, pp. 203–16. Moscow, 1983. (Lib: DLC; IU)

Recounts the organization of the Polytechnic Exhibition in Moscow in May 1872, on the basis of which the Museum of Applied Knowlege (now the Polytechnic Museum) was founded.

Tsentral'nyi Dom aviatsii i kosmonavtiki (TsDAiK)
[Central House of Aviation and Space Exploration]

Agency: Rossiiskaia oboronnoe sportivno-tekhnicheskoe obshchestvo
(ROSTO)
[Russian Defensive Technical-Sports Society]

Address: 125167, Moscow, ul. Krasnoarmeiskaia, 4
Telephone: 212-54-61; *Fax:* (095) 212-73-01; *RdngRm:* 214-56-80
Website: http://www.infoart.ru/avia/company/dak/dak/index.htm
Transport: metro: Dinamo + bus 110 (to ul. Pilota Nesterova); tram: 23, 27;
trol.: 12, 70 (to "Aerovoksal")
Hours: Tu–F 10:00–17:00

Director: Petr Fedorovich Vialikov (*tel.* 212-73-01 [also fax])
Scientific Secretary: Vitalii Sergeevich Perminov (*tel.* 214-41-68)

HISTORY:

Tsentral'nyi aeromuzei
[Central Museum of Aviation] (1924–1925)
Tsentral'nyi aerokhimicheskii muzei im. M. V. Frunze
[M. V. Frunze Central Aero-Chemical Museum] (1925–1941)
Dom aviatsii, protivovozdushnoi i khimicheskoi oborony im. M. V. Frunze (DAPVKhO)
[M. V. Frunze House of Aviation, Anti-Aircraft, and Chemical Defense] (1941–1948)
Tsentral'nyi Dom aviatsii, protivovozdushnoi i khimicheskoi oborony im. M. V. Frunze (TsDAPVKhO)
[M. V. Frunze Central House of Aviation, Anti-Aircraft, and Chemical Defense] (1948–1963)
Tsentral'nyi Dom aviatsii i kosmonavtiki im. M. V. Frunze
[M. V. Frunze Central House of Aviation and Space Exploration] (1963–1992)

The museum was founded in 1924 at the All-Union Conference of the Society of Friends of the Air
Force and, with the personal support of M. V. Frunze, became the Central Museum of Aviation. In
1925 it was renamed the Frunze Central Museum of the Aviation and Chemical Industries, and in
1927 it was transferred to the Society for Aiding Defense and Promoting Aviation and Chemical
Development in the USSR (*Obshchestro sodeistviia oborone i aviatsionno-khimicheskomu
stroitel'stvu SSSR*—Osoaviakhim). The museum once more received a new name in 1941—the
House of Aviation, Anti-Aircraft, and Chemical Defense. After its sponsoring organization
(Osoaviakhim) was reorganized into the Voluntary Society for Collaboration with the Army, Air
Force and Navy (*Dobrovol'noe obshchestvo sodeistviia armii, aviatsii i flotu*—DOSAAF SSSR) in
1948, the museum was renamed once more the Central House of Aviation, Anti-Aircraft, and
Chemical Defense. In 1963 it was renamed in honor of Frunze.

In 1992 the Russian Defensive Technical-Sports Society (*Rossiiskoe oboronnoe sportivno-
tekhnicheskoe obshchestvo*—ROSTO) became the successor organization to DOSAAF SSSR. Under
its patronage the museum assumed its present name and was registered as an organization with
cultural and historico-scientific functions, as well as a museum.

HOLDINGS: 47,000 units, 1902–1992
manuscripts—100 units (1914–1974); photographs—3,000 (1909–1991);
photoalbums—225 (1909–1984); negatives—27,500 (1910–1991); films—57 (1941–1975)

The museum contains documents relating to the history of aviation, individual Russian pilots, flying clubs, and aviation exhibitions. Most of the documentation found here was acquired from scientific research institutes like the Experimental Design Bureau (*Opytno-konstruktorskoe biuro—OKB*) and the Institute of Aviation Testing (*Letno-ispytatel'nyi institut*), both under the Ministry of the Aviation Industry, the Air Force Research Institute, the higher educational institutes of the Iu. A. Gagarin Air Force Academy, the N. E. Zhukovskii Air Force Engineering Academy (*Voenno-Vozdushnaia inzhenernaia akademiia im. prof. N. E. Zhukovskogo*), the Iu. A. Gagarin Cosmonaut Training Center, and various public organizations of a military nature such as Osoaviakhim, DOSAAF, and ROSTO.

The manuscript fond contains the personal archives of those who were in charge of technological developments for military aircraft and aeronautics in Russia during the years 1914–1915; documents on the organization of aerial communications; draft projects and explanatory information for a number of aircraft designs; and the minutes of conventions held for aviation and aeronautics specialists.

There is an enormous collection of photographs (many of them autographed) showing various types of aircraft and famous pilots and events in the world of aviation. There are also photograph albums devoted to the earliest Russian aircraft; the life and work of pilots from the various aviation and aeronautic schools in Russia; the life and work of aircraft designers; pilots in World War I and the Civil War; aviation operations during the World War II; and the history of aviation schools in Russia and the Soviet Union.

The museum also possesses documentary films on the history of aviation and space exploration.

Access: Researchers should make a prior appointment with the director or the curator.

Reference Facilities: There are inventories and also catalogues of the photographs and negatives.

Library Facilities: A library containing specialist literature on the history of aeronautics, aviation, and space exploration (over 15,000 volumes—1909–1992) is freely open to researchers.

Copying: Xerox facilities are available.

FINDING AIDS — PUBLISHED — GENERAL:

There is no published guide to the archival materials in the museum.

h-372. *Tsentral'nyi dom aviatsii i kosmonavtiki im. M. V. Frunze: Spravochnik-putevoditel'.*
Compiled by N. N. Semenkevich. Edited by V. F. Bashkirov. Moscow: Izd-vo DOSAAF, 1974. 72 p. [DOSAAF SSSR]
Describes themes of the museum exhibitions and the library holdings.

Memorial'nyi muzei kosmonavtiki (MMK)
[Memorial Museum of Space Exploration]

Agency: Ministerstvo kul'tury RF (Minkul'tury Rossii)
[Ministry of Culture]
Komitet po kul'ture Pravitel'stva Moskvy
[Committee on Culture of the Government of Moscow]

Address:	129515, Moscow, ul. 1-ia Ostankinskaia, 41/9 (administration); 129336, Moscow, prosp. Mira, 111 (museum)
Telephone:	283-18-37; 283-37-71; (museum): 283-79-14; *Fax:* (095) 282-82-12; *RdngRm:* 286-79-41
Website:	http://www.infoart.ru/avia/company/mmk/e_mmk/index.htm; http://www.museum.ru/kosmonav; http://moscow.lvl.ru/culture/museum/astron/eastro.html
Transport:	metro: VDNKh
Hours:	Tu–Su 10:00–19:00; *Division of Fonds*—M–F 9:00–17:00

Director: Iurii Mikhailovich Solomko (*tel.* 283-18-37)
Deputy Director: Mikhail Ivanovich Lisun (*tel.* 283-37-71)
Head of Division of Fonds: Ol'ga Nikolaevna Anisimova (*tel.* 283-08-18)

HISTORY:

The museum was opened in 1981 in the stylobate of the monument erected in November, 1964, in honor of the launching of the world's first artificial Earth satellite. The museum has an affiliated branch, namely the S. P. Korolev House-Museum (H–60).

HOLDINGS: 1 fond, 51,527 units, 1929–to present
films and photographs—12,683; documents—3,049

The museum holds documentation relating to the main stages and directions of space research. There are official documents, autographs, manuscripts, photographs, films, and other materials.

The museum holds the personal papers of a number of famous scientists in the field of rocketry, including those of the founder of space exploration, Academician S. P. Korolev (1906–1966), and V. V. Razumov (1890–1967), Chairman of the Leningrad Jet Propulsion Study Group (Lengird). There are also documents of and relating to the Soviet Russian space scientist K. E. Tsiolkovskii (1857–1935). Also included are the writings of some Soviet space scientists and cosmonauts.

Most of the documentary photographs and films in the museum were received from other state repositories, particularly the former RNITsKD (now part of B–9). There are also recordings made by those who took part in launching the first space ship in 1961, as well as biographical material on Iurii Gagarin and his own recollections together with recordings of the speeches of S. P. Korolev.

Access: A letter is required from the researcher's sponsoring organization or a personal application, which must be approved by the museum director.

Reference Facilities: There are thematic and subject card catalogues.

Copying: Copying facilities are available.

FINDING AIDS — PUBLISHED — GENERAL:

Muzei Moskvy (1997), pp. 240–43; *GAF Spravochnik* (1991), pp. 162–64.

There is no published guide to the archival materials in the museum.

Memorial'nyi dom-muzei akademika S. P. Koroleva— Filial Memorial'nogo muzeia kosmonavtiki
[S. P. Korolev Memorial House-Museum—Branch of the Memorial Museum of Space Exploration]

Agency: Ministerstvo kul'tury RF (Minkul'tury Rossii)
[Ministry of Culture]
Komitet po kul'ture Pravitel'stva Moskvy
[Committee on Culture of the Government of Moscow]

Address: 129515, Moscow, 6-i Ostankinskii per., 2/28
Telephone: 286-01-81, 283-81-97; *Fax:* (095) 282-82-12
Website: http://www.infoart.ru/avia/company/mmk/e_mmk/muskorlv.htm;
http://www.museum.ru/kosmonav;
http://moscow.lvl.ru/culture/museum/korolev/korol.html
Transport: metro: VDNKh; trol.: 9; tram: 11, 17
Hours: W–Su 11:00–17:00

Director: Larisa Aleksandrovna Silina
Head of the Division of Fonds: Ol'ga Nikolaevna Anisinova (*tel.* 283-08-18)

HISTORY

The museum was founded in 1972. It is located in the detached house that was specially built by the government for Academician Sergei Pavlovich Korolev (1906–1966) in tribute to his outstanding services in the field of Soviet rocketry and space exploration. Since 1981, the museum has been administered as a branch of the Memorial Museum of Space Exploration (H–59).

HOLDINGS: documents—3,288 units; photographs—211

The museum holds documents connected with the life, work, and public activity of Sergei Pavlovich Korolev (1906–1966), who was a full member of the Academy of Sciences of the USSR (from 1958) and chief designer of the Soviet rocket program.

The earliest documents in the museum archive are dated 1936. These relate to the testing of the experimental glider, RP-318-1, and include official documents, protocols, and other materials. There is also a brief survey of work done on winged missiles.

In April 1970 the Scientific Production Group "Energiia" (*Nauchno-proizvodstvennoe ob"edinenie "Energiia"*) transferred documents (280 units) to the musuem relating to Korolev's work during the war. This was for the most part scientific and technological documentation for the eyars 1940–1946—technical drawings, sketches, and other graphic material, as well as research reports compiled by Korolev himself. Another batch of material consists of documents collected by Korolev for scientific purposes (selections from scientific periodicals, bulletins, abstracts, and notes). These relate to the period when he was the chief designer of rocket systems. The museum also holds documents pertaining to Korolev's public life.

The museum has xerox copies of part of the documentation relating to Korolev's work from 1946 to 1966, which were received from the Scientific Production Group "Energiia," the government agency where the originals are held.

There are photographs of S. P. Korolev and his family and a documentary film entitled "Academician S. P. Korolev," which was produced for the museum by the Central Studio for Documentary Films (Tsentrnauchfil'm).

N.B. Documentation and personal papers resulting from the scientific work of S. P. Korolev during the years 1927–1936, were donated after his death (at the request of his wife, N. I. Koroleva) to the archive of the N. E. Zhukovskii Scientific-Memorial Museum (*Nauchno-memorial'nyi muzei N. E. Zhukovskogo*) (H–175)

Part of the documentation was also transferred to the Archive of the Academy of Sciences of the USSR (now ARAN—E–1) on instructions from the State Commission for Studying the Documentary Heritage of Academician Korolev.

Access: An official letter is required together with the permission of the director of the Memorial Museum of Space Exploration (H–59). Documents for which inventories have not yet been prepared are not available to researchers.

Reference Facilities: The manuscripts are in the process of being arranged and inventories are being prepared.

Library Facilities: The basis of the museum library (ca. 2,000 vols.) is the collection of scientific books, brochures, and periodicals made by S. P. Korolev.

Comment: A completed questionnaire was not returned to Rosarkhiv.

FINDING AIDS—PUBLISHED—GENERAL:
Muzei Moskvy (1997), P. 244.

There is no published guide to the archival materials in the museum.

h-373. Zlobin, G. N. "Memorial'nyi Dom-muzei S. P. Koroleva." *Zemlia i vselennaia*, 1997, no. 2, pp. 62–64. (Lib: DLC; IU)

h-374. "Memorial'nyi Dom-muzei S. P. Koroleva v Ostankine." Otchizna, 1986, no. 1, pp. 18–24. (Lib: DLC)

FINDING AIDS—GENERAL—UNPUBLISHED

h-375. Semenova, S. V. "Nauchnaia kontseptsiia biograficheskoi ekspozitsii v Memorail'nom Dome-muzee S. P. Koroleva: Diplomnaia rabota." Moscow: MGIAI, 1990. 78 p. Typescript. (Lib: RGGU)

> A senior thesis (diploma work), prepared in the *Kafedra* of Museum Studies, includes a survey of the documentary fond of S. P. Korolev held in ARAN Archive (E–1) and in the museum (pp. 40–49).

Archives and Manuscript Holdings of Museums

St. Petersburg

Historical Museums

✸—✸ H–65 ✸—✸

Istoriko-kul'turnyi muzei-zapovednik "Petropavlovskaia krepost'"— Gosudarstvennyi muzei istorii Sankt-Peterburga (GMISPb)
[Peter-Paul Fortress Historico-Cultural Museum-Preserve—
State Museum of the History of St. Petersburg]

Agency: Komitet po kul'ture Administratsii Sankt-Peterburga
[Committee on Culture of the Administration of St. Petersburg]

Address:	197046, St. Petersburg, Petropavlovskaia krepost', 3
Telephone:	238-45-11; 238-42-43; *Fax:* (812) 233-03-60; 238-42-43
E-mail:	direct@ppk.spb.su; lion@mail.lanck.net
Website:	http://www.museum.ru/museum/qmispb
Transport:	metro: Gor'kovskaia, Sportivnaia, bus: 25, 46, 134
Hours:	MTh–Su 11:00–18:00; Tu 11:00–17:00

Director: Boris Serafimovich Arakcheev (*tel.* 238-45-11)
Deputy Director for Scientific Work: Boris Mikhailovich Kirikov (*tel.* 238-45-18)
Deputy Director for Curatorial Affairs: Boris Ivanovich Nazartsev (*tel.* 238-45-57)
Scientific Secretary: Galina Faridovna Urusova (*tel.* 238-46-58)

HISTORY:

Muzei goroda
    [Museum of the City] (1918–1928)
Muzei sotsialisticheskoi rekonstruktsii goroda; Muzei gorodskogo khoziaistva
    [Museum of Socialist Reconstruction of the City; Museum of Municipal Economy] (1928–1938)
Muzei istorii i razvitiia Leningrada
    [Museum of the History and Development of Leningrad] (1938–1951)
Muzei arkhitektury Leningrada
    [Museum of the Architecture of Leningrad] (1951–1953)
Gosudarstvennyi muzei istorii Leningrada (GMIL)
    [State Museum of the History of Leningrad] (1953–1992)
Gosudarstvennyi muzei istorii Sankt-Peterburga
    [State Museum of the History of St. Petersburg] (1992–1993)

The museum was founded in 1918 on the basis of the Museum of the City Administration (*Muzei Gorodskoi upravy*) and the nationalized art collections of the Anichkov Palace (Nevskii prospekt, 39) and the private residence of Duchess N. F. Karlova (nab. reki Fontanka, 46), while those palaces themselves were transferred to the museum and housed its exhibitions for the next decade. Additional collections acquired were those of Duke Georg Alexander (G. G.) Mecklenburg-Strelitskii, as well as materials from the Dresden (1911) and All-Russian (1913) Sanitation-Hygiene Exhibitions, among others. In December 1918, the museum took over the collections of the Museum of Old St. Petersburg (*Muzei "Staryi Peterburg"*), founded in 1907 by the Society of Architects and Artists (*Obshchestvo arkhitektorov-khudozhnikov*), whose first director was Alexandre Benois (A. N. Benua); that museum brought with it impressive collections of architectural and artistic graphics, including rare photographs and drawings of the architecture of early Petersburg. Under increased political and ideological pressures in the late 1920s, most of those exhibits were closed down, and many artistic treasures from the museum were given over to the All-Union Antiquarian Company (*Vsesoiuznoe obshchestvo "Antikvariat"*), or the so-called Export Fund, for sale abroad at auction and within the country for foreign currency.

During the Soviet period the museum was reorganized and renamed a number of times. Between 1952 and 1954 the museum holdings were enlarged with materials from the Museum of the Defense of Leningrad (*Muzei oborony Leningrada*), which was closed down following the arrest of leading Party officials in the city in what became known as the Leningrad Affair (1949–1952). In 1953 it was reorganized as the State Museum of the History of Leningrad (GMIL)—and in 1992, of St. Petersburg (GMISPb).

In 1993, the museum was reorganized and given the status of a historico-cultural preserve. The museum is now based in the formerly separately administered Peter and Paul Fortress-State Museum-Preserve (*Muzei-zapovednik "Petropavlovskaia krepost'"*), which had originally been established as a museum in 1924. The museum also includes the earlier separately administered Gas Dynamics Laboratory of Rocketry and Space Exploration (*Gazodinamicheskaia laboratoriia raketostroeniia i kosmonavtiki*), located within the Peter and Paul Fortress compound. Founded in 1973 as the first museum of the history of Soviet rocket construction, it has many documents and photographs relating to space exploration. (tel. 238-46-64).

The museum administratively encompasses several exhibitions in other locations:

The exposition "Leningrad During Soviet Rule" (*"Leningrad za gody Sovetskoi vlasti"*) is housed in the former city palace of Count N. P. Rumiantsev, which had housed the Rumiantsev Museum in St. Petersburg (1831–1861), before its transfer to Moscow. The building came under the State Museum of the History of St. Petersburg in 1939. (Angliiskaia [*formerly* Krasnogo Flota] nab., 44; tel. 315-51-23).

The Shlissel'burg (Shlüsselburg in German) Fortress (*Shlissel'burgskaia krepost'*), on Lake Ladoga at the mouth of the Neva River, also known as the Little Nut (*Oreshek*, the original pre-1611 name of the town; known in Swedish as Nöteborg before 1711]), a well-known prison for political offenders before 1917, was established as a museum in 1928. (The town with its fortress was known as Petrokrepost' after 1944). Initially a branch of the Museum of the October Revolution in Leningrad (*Muzei Oktiabr'skoi revoliutsii v Leningrade*—see H–66), in 1965 it was made a branch of the State Museum of the History of Leningrad (GMIL). In 1993 it was reorganized as one of the permanent exhibitions of GMISPb. The archival documentation relating to the fortress, however, remains as a separate division at the main administrative headquarters of GMISPb—the Scientific-Technical Archive of Schlissel'burg Fortress (see below). (188691, Leningradskaia oblast', Kirovskii raion, g. Shlissel'burg, krepost' "Oreshek"; tel. 238-46-58).

In addition to those permanent exhibitions GMISPb now also has four branches in other locations:

(1) The Museum of St. Petersburg Printing (*Muzei istorii pechati S.-Peterburga*) was established in 1984 and functioned until October 1991 as the Memorial Museum of V. I. Lenin and the Newspaper Pravda (Memorial'nyi muzei "V. I. Lenin i gazeta 'Pravda' "). The newspaper *Pravda* had been printed in the building starting in March 1917, but currently new exhibitions are being organized there on the basis of GMISPb materials. (191186, St. Petersburg, nab. Reki Moiki, 32/2; tel. 311-02-70; 312-09-77).

(2) The A. A. Blok Apartment-Museum (*Muzei-kvartira A. A. Bloka*) was opened in 1980 and was enriched with the archival materials of the A. A. Blok Fond, which were acquired in 1978 from N. P. Il'in (see H–99).

(3) The S. M. Kirov Museum (*Muzei S. M. Kirova*) was founded in 1938 as an independent museum, but more recently became a branch of GMISPb. The museum is housed in the building where Sergei Mironovich Kirov (*pseud.* of Kostrikov, 1886–1934) lived from 1926–1934, as head of the Leningrad Oblast Party Committee. The holdings include his library, part of his papers (letters, memoirs, and other documents), and photographs of and relating to Kirov.

(197101, St. Petersburg, Kamennostrovskii prosp., 26/28; tel. 346-02-17).

(4) The Monument to the Heroic Defenders of Leningrad (*Pamiatnik geroicheskim zashchitnikam Leningrada*), inaugurated in 1975. (196066, St. Petersburg, pl. Pobedy; tel. 293-65-63).

The Museum of the History of the Town of Pushkin (Tsarskoe Selo) (*Muzei istorii goroda Pushkina*) (H–70), earlier a branch of GMISPb, became a separate museum in the summer of 1996, and was renamed the Regional Studies Museum of the Town of Pushkin.

The Museum of the History of the Town of Lomonosov (*Muzei istorii goroda Lomonosova*) (H–69), also earlier a branch of GMISPb, has been a separate museum since 1994.

The Isaac Cathedral Museum (H–86) was also a branch from 1963 to 1969, but since 1969 it has been under separate administration.

Archival materials are held in a number of different divisions and separate "fonds" within the museum. In 1918 the Scientific Archive and the Fond of Graphic Art and Painting on the History of the City were formed, and in 1932 the Fond of Negatives. In recent decades several independent fonds were created comprising other parts of the holdings: the Manuscript-Documentary Fond (*Rukopisno-dokumental'nyi fond*) (1976) and the Fond of Printed Graphic Art (*Fond tirazhirovannoi grafiki*) (1981). The Fond of Painting and Graphic Art of Cities of Russia and the World (*Fond zhivopisi i grafiki gorodov mira i Rossii*) was organized in 1979, but in 1994, the Fond of Architectural Graphics and Cartography of Cities of Russia and the World (*Fond arkhitekturnoi grafiki i kartografii gorodov mira i Rossii*) was separated out to become a new division, in addition to the already existing Fond of Architectural Graphics of the Soviet Period (*Fond arkhitekturnoi grafiki sovetskogo perioda*). Separate "fonds" or subdivisions within the museum also remain for photographs and negatives, and for the administrative records of the museum itself, which now comprises the Scientific Archive.

Access: Access to the archival holdings and the reference card catalogues requires an official letter from the researcher's sponsoring organization or a personal application addressed to the director stating the subject and aim of the proposed research. Fees are charged for research in archival materials, reference card catalogues, and other reference materials in all divisions and branches of the museum.

Working Conditions: There are no formal reading rooms for the archival and reference materials in museum collections, so researchers are accommodated in working areas. As a rule materials are available the day they are ordered.

Library Facilities: The library (ca. 120,000 vols.), which was started in 1907 as the book collection of the Museum of Old St. Petersburg, contains books, periodicals, maps, and audiovisual material on history and local culture.

Copying: Facilities are available for xerox and photographic copying.

Otdel istorii goroda
[Division of the History of the City]

Hours: M–F 10:00–17:00 (by appointment)
Head: Natal'ia Kirillovna Gerasimova (*tel.* 238-46-65)
Chief, Sector for Socio-Political History: Zinaida Petrovna Solov'eva (*tel.* 238-46-13)
Chief, Sector for the History of Economics and Population: Georgii Georgievich Priamurskii (*tel.* 238-46-82)
Chief, Military History Sector: Vladimir Borisovich Porodin (*tel.* 238-47-75)
Chief, Sector for the History of Architecture: Mariia Leonidovna Makogonova (*tel.* 238-45-89)
Chief, Sector for the History of Streets: Galina Iur'evna Nikitenko (*tel.* 238-45-89)

HOLDINGS:

Research work on St. Petersburg history done by the staff of the Division for History of the City has produced significant reference materials on the basis of a wide range of archival and published

985

sources in five subject areas, which comprise separate sectors of the division: social and political history; economic and demographic history; military history; architectural history; and the history of the city streets.

Each sector retains its own card files and other unpublished scholarly reference material, which are available for use at the request of institutions and individual researchers on a fee basis.

The Sector for the Socio-Political History of St. Petersburg, on the basis of research in archival documents, has produced three card catalogues: "The Revolutionary Movement in St. Petersburg from the Mid-Eighteenth Century to October 1917," "Prisoners in the Peter and Paul Fortress" (arranged both alphabetically and chronologically), and "Major Political Trials of the Nineteenth Century."

The Sector for Economics and Population has card catalogues on the estates, classes and social strata of the population of St. Petersburg (personalia); the establishment of industrial, trade, and transportation enterprises, their names and renaming; and on urban topography (18th–20th cc.) (with associated indexes).

The Military History Sector is continuing a card catalogue with a chronology of events in the city during the Second World War and the Siege of Leningrad, and of industrial enterprises and the transportation system.

The Sector for the History of Architecture has compiled personalia files on architects, engineers, and builders of St. Petersburg (18th–20th cc.), with an index of their projects and construction work; and a topographical card catalogue entitled "The Building of St. Petersburg from the Eighteenth to the Twentieth Centuries," with systematic references to materials from federal (RGIA) and local archives, and textual data copied from plans, drawings, and photographs.

The sector devoted to the history of the city streets possesses a card catalogue entitled "The History of the Streets of St. Petersburg" (late 17th c.–1990s), which contains information on the layout and building of streets; on notable addresses connected with eminent public and political figures representing science, culture, and business; on places of historical interest; and on monuments and memorial plaques. There is also a card catalogue entitled "The Toponymy of St. Petersburg," which serves as a database for the City Commission on the Naming of Streets, with information on the present and previous names of all streets, rivers, canals, bridges, and districts, and on the chronology and boundary changes involved in renaming. All the card catalogues have been compiled on the basis of detailed study of the archival documents and cartographic materials, as well as of the periodical press, city directories, memoir sources, and scholarly literature.

Working Conditions: Card catalogues may be used only in the presence of the division staff.

Rukopisno-dokumental'nyi fond   (RDF)
[Manuscript-Documentary Fond]

Address: Petrovskaia kurtina Petropavlovskoi kreposti (right side)
Telephone: 238-42-93
Hours: Tu 10:00–18:00
Curator: Liudmila Pavlovna Baklan

HOLDINGS: ca. 45,000 units, 1700–1993

The fond retains documents on the history of St. Petersburg from the time of Peter the Great to the present. Materials dating from the eighteenth through the early twentieth century include a petition from foreign sailors to Peter the Great asking for payment for their service to Russia (1700); documents from the papers of the architect Carlo (K. I.) Rossi, including a letter sent to him by the President of the Academy of Arts, A. N. Olenin; and a collection of documents from members of the Russian revolutionary movement who were imprisoned in the Peter and Paul Fortress (N. M. Astyrev, N. P. Vladimirov, P. N. Lepeshinskii, and V. P. Nogin, among others). Among materials from the St. Petersburg Office of Decency (*S.-Peterburgskaia uprava blagochiniia*) there are documents on the apportionment of plots of land for building purposes.

986

Documents from the Soviet period, which have been arranged in subject-related collections, include documentary materials of well-known citizens, such as the scholars G. O. Graftio, S. V. Lebedev, and L. A. Orbeli; and the writers V. B. Azarov, A. A. Prokof'ev, M. L. Slonimskii, and V. V. Vishnevskii. The collection on the history of World War II contains documents pertaining to the defense and siege of Leningrad, including a notebook written during the siege by an eleven-year-old schoolgirl, Tania Savicheva; letters from frontline defenders of the city to their families; documents relating to the partisan movement in Leningrad Oblast; and awards of military decorations. The fond includes documents on the blockade that had been gathered for exhibits in the Museum of the Defense of Leningrad (abolished in 1952).

Reference Facilities: Work is underway to compile a subject catalogue.

Fond grafiki i zhivopisi istorii goroda
[Fond of Graphic Art and Painting of the History of the City]

Telephone: 238-45-71
E-mail: galina@cronver.spb.su
Hours: Tu 11:00–17:00
Curator: Galina Borisovna Vasil'eva

HOLDINGS: ca. 21,000 units, early 18th c.–1917

The fond holds various kinds of iconographic material on the history of St. Petersburg from the founding of the city until 1917. There is a collection of drawings mainly devoted to views and landscapes of St. Petersburg done by such artists as F. G. Bagants, the brothers Albert and Alexandre Benois (Benua), Luigi Premazzi, V. Sadovnikov, Joseph Charlemagne (I. I. Sharleman'), and M. Vorob'ev. Of particular value is the technical drawing collection containing the work of such famous architects as Auguste Ricard de Monferrand, A. A. Ol' (Ohl), Giacomo Quarenghi, Bartolomeo Rastrelli, Antonio Rinaldi, Carlo (K. I.) Rossi, A. I. Shtakenshneider (Stakenschneider), A. N. Voronikhin, and A. Zakharov. There are engravings of portraits, genre scenes, and typical city dwellers.

The lithograph collection contains the early lithograph editions of the Society for Encouragement of Art (*Obshchestvo pooshchreniia khudozhestv*), albums by Adolph Pluchart (A. A. Pliushar) showing views of St. Petersburg and genre scenes, publications by the Fel'ten (Feldten) and the Daziaro publishers, panoramic views of Nevskii Prospekt based on the drawings of V. Sadovnikov, and pictures of the Ekaterinhof Pleasure Gardens. There is also a collection of manuscript plans and maps of the city (18th–20th cc.).

Fond zhivopisi i grafiki gorodov mira i Rossii
[Fond of Painting and Graphic Art of Cities of Russia and the World]

Telephone: 238-46-71
Hours: Tu 10:00–17:00
Curator: Marina Anatol'evna Kondrashova

HOLDINGS: ca. 30,000 units, mid-17th c.–late 19th c.

The basis of the fond was formed from collections assembled by the Museum of the City (1918–1938) and consists of materials on the iconography of cities of the world, particularly those in Europe and Russia. These are arranged in sections for visual and thematic graphics—created with the use of engraving techniques, lithographs, and drawings. The main principle of arrangement is geographic, although there are exceptions for series of works (in groups or individually) by such masters as Giambattista Piranesi, Gérard Delabart, P. A. Briullov, A. P. Briullov, and L. F. Lagorio.

Fond arkhitekturnoi grafiki i kartografii gorodov mira i Rossii
[Fond of Architectural Graphics and Cartography of Cities of Russia and the World]

Telephone: 238-46-71
Hours: Tu 10:00–17:00
Curator: Ol'ga Nikolaevna Egorova

HOLDINGS: over 16,000 units, mid-18th c.–1920s

The basis of the fond was formed from collections assembled by the Museum of the City (1918–1938), but in 1994 this new division was formed to deal exclusively with architectural drawings, together with lithographed and engraved city plans, maps, and other cartographic materials. Materials are arranged geographically.

Fond arkhitekturnoi grafiki sovetskogo perioda
[Fond of Architectural Graphics of the Soviet Period]

Telephone: 238-45-62
Hours: Tu 10:00–17:00, Th 10:00–13:00
Curator: Tat'iana Vasil'evna Lobanova

HOLDINGS: ca. 6,500 units, 1917–1990s

The fond contains graphic materials on the architecture and city planning of St. Petersburg and Leningrad Oblast from 1917 to the present. Most impressive here is the collection of documents on the architecture of St. Petersburg in the 1920s and 1930s, which includes collections of technical drawings by such architects as A. S. Nikol'skii, N. A. Trotskii, and I. G. Langbard.

Fond tirazhirovannoi grafiki (FTG)
[Fond of Printed Graphic Art]

Telephone: 238-45-22
Hours: Tu 10:00–17:00
Curator: *Elena Alekseevna Korzhevskaia*

HOLDINGS: ca. 40,000 units, mid-19th c.–1990s

The holdings of this fond consist of collections of posters, bills, placards, programs, invitations, calendars, labels, and brand names. Its basis are the collections of the Museum of Old Petersburg and the exhibits from the Museum of the Defense of Leningrad. The rarities include a unique collection of late nineteenth- and early twentieth-century advertisements from St. Petersburg and a complete collection of the posters from the Blockade of Leningrad.

Fond fotografii
[Fond of Photographs]

Telephone: 238-47-58
Hours: Tu 10:00–13:00, 14:00–17:00
Curator: Liudmila Georgievna Miasnikova

HOLDINGS: ca. 88,000 units, 1850s–1990s
general fond—ca. 70,000 units; auxiliary fond—ca. 18,000 units

The Fond of Photographs retains pictures relating to the history of the city and oblast. Prerevolutionary material includes pictures illustrating various aspects of life in the capital taken between the mid-nineteenth and early twentieth centuries by St. Petersburg master photographers and features the work of L. G. Andreevskii, Charles (Karl K.) Bergamasco, German-born Karl Bulla and his Russian-born sons A. K. and V. K. Bulla, Giuseppe Bianchi (I. Bianki), A. Iasvoin, E. L. Mrozovskaia, Ia. V. Shteinberg, A. Smirnov, G. Wesenberg (Vesenberg), and I. M. Zubkov. There is also a collection of photographic portraits of state, political, and public figures, scientists and scholars, teachers and lecturers at the St. Petersburg higher educational establishments and secondary schools, writers, artists, architects, and performers at the imperial theaters, as well as pictures of architectural monuments, typical inhabitants of the city, and genre scenes.

The collections of the photojournalists, G. Chertov, V. Fedoseev, V. Kapustin, Ia. Khalin, and B. Kudoiarov contain documentary photographs of the events of the postrevolutionary years, the Second World War, and the Siege of Leningrad.

The collection made by the photographer V. P. Samoilov contains photographs of the city and its suburbs taken from a helicopter. The photographs in the collection made by L. L. Zivert show architectural monuments, city streets and squares, and the environs of Leningrad, as well as providing a chronology of events in the city from the 1940s through the 1960s. Also of interest is the collection of the photographer and artist, A. F. Shuvalov (over 3,000 units), including photographs of the condition of all the churches in the city. In recent years the holdings have been enlarged by documentary photographs taken by A. A. Kitaev of the life of St. Petersburg during the *perestroika* period and the years that have followed. There is also a collection of photographs of the interiors of the palaces taken by G. F. Prikhod'ko, and photographic portraits taken by the noted news correspondent, A. L. Medvednikov.

Fond negativov
[Fond of Negatives]

Telephone: 238-47-58; 238-47-56
Hours: Tu 10:00–13:00, 14:00–17:00
Curator: Natal'ia Vasil'evna Tepliakova

HOLDINGS: 18,718 units, 1890s–1990s

The fond holds negatives showing the history of St. Petersburg. The collection was begun with the photographic materials of two prerevolutionary museums—the City Museum (*Gorodskoi muzei*), which was under the control of the City Duma, and the Museum of Old Petersburg (*Muzei "Staryi Peterburg"*). Later the holdings were enlarged by negatives illustrating the life of the city during the early postrevolutionary decades. Between 1932 and 1938 a fairly large number of documentary photographs were collected reflecting the economic life of the city. These included photographs of the building and reconstruction of streets and squares, the erection of new buildings, and the laying of water supplies and sewage systems. The 1930s are also reflected in the photographs taken of buildings on the main streets, as well as in the separate collections of city life made by two photographers, G. I. Lugovoi and Laptev.

Military operations during the Second World War and the events of the Siege of Leningrad were recorded in the negatives of such war correspondents and photographers as B. Kudoiarov, M. Kashe, B. Utkin, and D. Trakhtenberg.

The postwar period is represented by the collections taken during the 1960s by L. I. Korovin and B. S. Losin, who were members of the Union of Journalists; by the photographs of L. L. Zivert; and by the pictures of architectural ensembles in Leningrad and its suburbs taken from a helicopter by V. P. Samoilov. There is also a collection of negatives devoted to theatrical life in the city of Leningrad between the 1950s and the 1970s. In recent years the holdings have been enlarged by negatives showing the political and business life of contemporary St. Petersburg.

Nauchnyi arkhiv
[Scientific Archive]

Telephone: 238-42-69
Hours: TuTh 14:00–18:00
Curator: El'vina Nikolaevna Shavel'

HOLDINGS: ca. 50,000 units, 1918–1993

The archive retains the administrative records and other materials of the State Museum of the History of St. Petersburg. These include organizational and administrative records, and documents relating to the scholarly, educational, and exhibition functions of the museum and its acquisition work. A whole complex of documents is devoted to the restoration work of the Peter and Paul Fortress during the Soviet period. This complex contains planning and design documentation, including architectural measurements and technical drawings; photographs of the progress of the restoration work during the 1950s; and photocopies of the plans of the Peter and Paul Fortress dating back to 1703 and of contemporary restoration projects. The exhibition functions of the museum are represented by a collection of artistically designed exhibition projects.

Material on city planning at various periods can be found in a collection of plans and scaled projections of architecture and landscape gardening techniques practiced in ancient Egypt, Babylon, Russia, France, and other countries.

The archive also holds materials from the defunct Museum of the Defense and Blockade of Leningrad, administrative documentation, and documents on the work of industrial enterprises in the city during the years of the siege, including decodings of broadcasts made by factory radio stations. The collection of memoirs and recollections contains documents of personal origin and papers recounting the most important events in the life of St. Petersburg during the twentieth century, as well as material on the history of individual families. There is a collection of the personal files of soldiers who were awarded the honor of Heroes of the Soviet Union and of the officers and men who fought on the Leningrad Front, in the home guard divisions, sailors of the Baltic Fleet, and among the partisans of the Leningrad Oblast. The "Chronicle of the Siege" (*"Blokadnaia khronika"*) tells the story of each of the 900 days of the Siege of Leningrad.

N.B. Part of the museum records for the years 1918–1929 is held in TsGALI SPb (D–15, fond 72).

Nauchno-tekhnicheskii arkhiv Shlissel'burgskoi kreposti ("Oreshek")
[Scientific-Technical Archive of Shlissel'burg Fortress (Oreshek [Little Nut])]

Telephone: 238-46-79
Hours: by appointment
Head: Galina Petrovna Ignat'eva

HOLDINGS: ca. 5,000 units, 17th–20th cc.

The Shlissel'burg (*Ger.* Schlüsselburg) Fortress ("Oreshek"—or Little Nut), located at the mouth of the Neva River on Lake Ladoga (Leningrad Oblast, g. Shlissel'burg, see above), is now administratively considered an Exhibition of GMISPb, but its Scientific-Technical Archive is held in the main administrative center of GMISPb, separately from the other parts of the main museum archive. There is considerable documentation on the history of the fortress, its role in military and political history, including the period it was held by Sweden as Nöteborg, 1611–1702, and its use as a political prison from the eighteenth century to 1917. There are many graphic materials relating to the building of the fortress and its restoration from the fourteenth to the twentieth centuries.

There are also photographs, technical drawings, sketches, and copies of plans held in other repositories, such as RGADA (B–2), RGVIA (B–4), the Manuscript Division of BAN (G–16), and the Royal Archives (Riksarkivet) in Stockholm.

The archive retains manuscripts of writings by the museum staff, reports on architectural and archeological work, materials relating to the general plan for restoration of the fortress, and documents showing designs for the restoration of the walls, towers, bastions, historic buildings, and engineering installations within the fortress.

Reference Facilities: There are inventories of photographs and other pictorial materials.

FINDING AIDS — PUBLISHED — GENERAL:

Muzei SPb (1994), pp. 109–20; *GAF Spravochnik* (1991), pp. 102–105; *Peterburg* (1992), pp. 400, 666–67; *Biblioteki SPb* (1993), p. 58; *Muzei Leningrada* (1989), pp. 58–72; *Muzei Leningrada* (1982), pp. 26–36.

There is no published guide to the archival materials in the museum.

Guides, Surveys, and Museum History

h-400. "Muzei i gorod." St. Petersburg: AO "Arsis," 1993, no. 2, p. 112. (Lib: MH)

    A special issue of the journal honoring the 75th anniversary of GMISPb, with articles about the history of the museum and its predecessors and survey articles about several groups of holdings.

h-401. Shpiller, Rita Il'inichna. "Gosudarstvennyi muzei istorii Leningrada (1918–1985)." In *Muzei i vlast': Iz zhizni muzeev: Sbornik nauchnykh trudov,* vol. 2, pp. 150–72. Moscow, 1991. [Minkul'tury RF; RAN; NII kul'tury] (Lib: DLC; IU; MH)

    Describes the various stages in the history and changing profile of the museum from its establishment to the 1980s, as a reflection of changes in state cultural policies and ideology regarding the aims and functions of the museum.

h-402. Gendrikov, V. B.; and Kirikov, Boris Mikhailovich. *Petropavlovskaia (Sankt-Peterburgskaia) krepost'.* [St. Petersburg]: Vneshtorgizdat, 1993. 93 p. (Editions in Russian, English, and German). [GMISPb]

    A popularized brochure about the fortress and exhibitions of GMISPb.

h-403. Bastareva, Liudmila Ivanovna; and Sidorova, Valentina Ivanovna. *Petropavlovskaia krepost': Putevoditel'.* 6th ed. Leningrad: Lenizdat, 1986. 112 p. "Turistu o Leningrade." (Lib: IU)

    2d ED.: L., 1972. 152 p. (Lib: MH).

    A popularized guide to the museum exhibits within the grounds of the Peter and Paul Fortress, with an account of the history of the fortress from the eighteenth century.

h-403A. *Popova, G. A. *Muzei goroda v Anichkovom dvortse.* St. Petersburg, 1998.

Museum Series

h-404. *Kraevedcheskie zapiski: Issledovaniia i materialy.* St. Petersburg, 1993–. 5 vols. published through 1997. [GMISPb] (Lib: DLC; MH)

    The new basic publication series of the museum, with articles relating to its history and collections.

h-404A. *Trudy Gosudarstvennogo muzeia istorii Sankt-Peterburga: Issledovaniia i materialy.* St. Petersburg, 1996–. 3 vols. published through 1997. [GMISPb] (Lib: MH)

    Vol. 1: *Muzei, shkola, sem'ia.* 1996.

    Vol. 2: *Ot muzeia starogo Peterburga k gosudarstvennomu muzeiu istorii Sankt-Peterburga.* 1997.

    Vol. 3: *Peterburzhets puteshestvuet (materialy konferentsii 1997 goda).* 1998.

    A new series based on the history and collections of the museum. The first issue focuses on the educational work of the museum, including an article characterizing the history of changing ideological conceptions for excursions and exhibits. The second issue focuses on the ninetieth anniversary of the Museum of Old Petersburg, including some photographic materials. The third presents reports from a 1997 conference.

FINDING AIDS — SPECIALIZED:

Gas Dynamics Exhibition

h-405. Aleksandrova, Lidiia Mikhailovna; and Ovchinnikov, Leonid Alekseevich. *Muzei "Gazodinamicheskaia laboratoriia" : Putevoditel'.* Leningrad: Lenizdat, 1987. 78 p. (Lib: DLC; MH)

> A guide to the exhibition opened in 1973 in the Ioann Ravelin in the Peter and Paul Fortress, where the country's first experimental Gas Dynamics Laboratory for developing jet engines was housed.

World War II

h-406. *Leningrad v period Velikoi Otechestvennoi voiny 1941–1945 gg.* Leningrad, 1969. 46 p. [GMIL; Upravlenie kul'tury Ispolkoma Lengorsoveta]

> A guide to the exhibition in the former house of Count N. P. Rumiantsev, which is now a special exhibition hall of GMISPb.

h-407. *Nikto ne zabyt i nichto ne zabyto! Katalog otkrytok, izdannykh v Leningrade v gody Velikoi Otechestvennoi voiny 1941–1945 gg.* Leningrad: "Sovetskii khudozhnik," 1970. 175 p. [GMIL; Leningradskoe oblastnoe otdelenie Vsesoiuznogo obshchestva filatelistov; Sektsiia filokartistov] (Lib: DLC; IU)

> A catalogue of propaganda postcards from the years of the war held in GMISPb.

S. M. Kirov Museum

h-408. Nikitin, Semen Erofeevich; and Vikhrov, Aleksandr K. *Muzei S. M. Kirova v Leningrade: Kratkii putevoditel'.* Leningrad, 1967. 92 p. (Lib: DLC; MH)

> A guide to the Kirov Museum, which was founded in 1934 and is now a branch of GMISPb, with mention of the documents on display.

Gosudarstvennyi muzei politicheskoi istorii Rossii (GMPIR)
[State Museum of the Political History of Russia]

Agency: Ministerstvo kul'tury RF (Minkul'tury Rossii)
[Ministry of Culture]

Address: 197046, St. Petersburg, ul. Kuibysheva, 4
Telephone: 233-72-89; 233-73-11; 233-73-22
E-mail: ter@atc.rfntr.neva.ru
Transport: metro: Gor'kovskaia, bus: 25, 46, 134
Hours: M–WF 10:00–17:00

Director: Marta Petrovna Potiforova (*tel.* 233-70-48)
Deputy Director for Scientific Work: Evgenii Grigor'evich Artemov
Scientific Secretary: Alevtina Aleksandrovna Chizhova (*tel.* 233-73-22)
Chief Curator of the Division of Fonds: Liudmila L'vovna Nikolaeva (*tel.* 233-73-11)

HISTORY:

Gosudarstvennyi muzei revoliutsii
[State Museum of Revolution] (1919–1955)
Gosudarstvennyi muzei Velikoi Oktiabr'skoi sotsialisticheskoi revoliutsii—
Filial Tsentral'nogo muzeia revoliutsii SSSR (GMVOSR)
[State Museum of the Great October Socialist Revolution—
Branch of the Central Museum of Revolution of the USSR] (1955–1991)

The museum was founded in 1919 and opened in January 1920 in the Winter Palace, as the first museum in the country devoted to the revolutionary movement. In 1955 it became administratively a branch of the State Museum (after 1968 Central Museum) of Revolution of the USSR in Moscow (now the State Central Museum of the Contemporary History of Russia—see H–4). Since 1957 the museum has occupied the palace which had formerly belonged to the ballerina Matilde Kshesinskaia (a favorite of Emperor Nicholas II), built in 1904–1906 by the architect A. I. Goren. The building had been a meeting place for the Petrograd Bolshevik Party Committee starting in February 1917. The museum also occupies the neighboring building where M. I. Kalinin lived in 1918. Its present name dates from 1991.

The museum has a branch "Gorokhovaia, 2" with exhibits on the history of the political police in Russia (see H–67).

HOLDINGS: 160,000 units, 1826–1990s

fond of documentary materials—ca. 100,000 units (early 19th c.–1990s);
biographical fond—2,584 units (early 19th c.–1990s); prints—ca. 55,000 (19th–20th cc.);
photographs—ca. 60,000 (1878–1990s)

The rich archival collections of the museum, constituting part of the Division of Fonds, contain materials relating to the social and revolutionary movement in Russia during the nineteenth and twentieth centuries. There are documents (originals and/or copies) from the Third Department of His Imperial Majesty's Personal Chancery for Surveillance (*Tret'e Otdelenie Sobstvennoi Ego Imp. Velichestva Kantseliarii po nadzoru*) (the imperial secret police until 1880); court records of political trials; documents on the activity of the "Liberation of Labor" (*"Osvobozhdenie truda"*)

Group led by G. V. Plekhanov; various writings and artistic works by revolutionaries; financial accounts of the Russian Social Democratic Workers' Party (RSDSP) committees, letters written by revolutionaries including A. M. Kollontai, V. P. Nogin, and N. I. Podvoiskii; resolutions passed at conferences of the food commissars (*prodkomissary*); and lists of those who worked in the food requisition brigades (*prodotriady*).

There are the personal papers of some of the people who took part in the revolutionary movement, such as N. E. Burenin (with letters of Maksim Gor'kii, 1925–1927), A. V. Panaeva-Kartseva, and K. M. Ots, together with the archive of the Fine Arts Society (*Obshchestvo iziashchnykh iskusstv*). Among archival collections are letters written during the blockade and from the front line during World War II and letters and telegrams sent to the Presidium of the Twenty-Second Congress of the CPSU.

The fond of biographical materials includes autobiographies, biographies, employment references, questionnaires, testimonials, party cards, identity cards for delegates, credentials issued to those attending Party Congresses and Conferences, and archive information reports. There are also memoirs (including sound recordings) from participants in the "People's Will" (*Narodnaia Volia*) Movement; political prisoners sentenced to labor camps; participants in the revolutionary movement, the Civil War, and the Second World War; Party and Young Communist League (*Komsomol*) veterans; prominent Soviet and foreign Party leaders, state and public figures; and ordinary workers.

Photographs include portraits of revolutionaries; pictures of the events of the February and October Revolutions in Petrograd; group photographs of military commanders, officers and soldiers in the Red Army; newsreels of the postwar period; and photographs of socio-political events.

Access: Access for research purposes to the archival materials and the library of the museum requires an official application to the director stating the subject and aim of the proposed research.

Reference Facilities: There are subject catalogues to the fond of documentary materials and inventories of the larger archive collections and fonds of personal papers.

Library Facilities: The museum library (ca. 248,000 vols.) includes literature on the history of Russia and world history. There are a number of books from the libraries of the suburban imperial palaces (18th–20th cc.) (tel. 233-71-57).

FINDING AIDS — PUBLISHED — GENERAL:

Muzei SPb (1994), pp. 125–27; *Biblioteki SPb* (1993), p. 59; *Peterburg* (1992), pp. 398–99; *GAF Spravochnik* (1991), pp. 32–36; *Muzei Leningrada* (1989), pp. 45–55; *G&K Spravochnik* (1983), p. 268; *Muzei Leningrada* (1982), pp. 18–22; *PKG M&L* (1972), p. 343; *Myl'nikov* (1970), p. 34.

There is no published guide to the archival materials in the museum.

h-415. Grigor'eva, L. Ia.; Emel'ianova, T. M.; Kruglova, A. M., et al. *Muzei Velikoi Oktiabr'skoi sotsialisticheskoi revoliutsii: Putevoditel'.* Leningrad: Lenizdat, 1965. 287 p. [GMVOSR] (Lib: IU)

h-416. Dubinin, Leonid Alekseevich. *Muzei Velikogo Oktiabria.* Leningrad: Lenizdat, 1965. 74 p. "Turistu o Leningrade." (Lib: DLC; MH)

h-417. Potiforova, Mariia Petrovna; Kulegin, A. M.; and Evstigneev, A. A. *Muzei Oktiabr'skoi revoliutsii: [Al'bom].* Leningrad: Lenizdat, 1987. 47 p. + plates.

h-418. *Pervyi istoriko-revoliutsionnyi: Materialy konferentsii, posviashchennoi 70-letiiu muzeia [Velikoi Oktiabr'skoi sotsialisticheskoi revoliutsii].* Compiled by E. E. Molchanova and V. N. Agapitov. Leningrad, 1989. 184 p. [Minkul't SSSR; TsMR SSSR] (Lib: DLC; MH)

h-419. *Zhivoe dykhanie revoliutsii: Gazety o muzee v iubileinom godu.* Compiled by
V. P. Boiarinov. Leningrad, 1979. 92 p. [GMVOSR]

> A collection of newspaper publications devoted to the 60th anniversary of the founding of the first historical-revolutionary museum.

h-420. *Relikvii Velikogo Oktiabria. Iz fondov Tsentral'nogo gosudarstvennogo muzeia revoliutsii SSSR i gosudarstvennogo muzeia Velikogo Oktiabr'skoi sotsialisticheskoi revoliutsii: Katalog.* Compiled by V. A. Bessonov, O. M. Kormil'tseva, I. S. Rozental', et al. Edited by L. I. Arapova, E. G. Artemov, T. G. Shumnaia, et al. Moscow, 1987. 231 p. + plates. [TsMR SSSR; GMVOSR] (Lib: MH) (Also listed as h-67).

> A detailed catalogue covering Leniniana, documentary materials, brochures, photographs, and other graphic materials, as well as more traditional museum exhibits from the collections of the two museums.

FINDING AIDS — SPECIALIZED:

h-421. *Uchastniki Oktiabr'skoi revoliutsii: Katalog.* Leningrad, 1984. 108 p. [GMVOSR]
Includes documents in the museum.

h-422. *Fotoletopis' Krasnoi gvardii: Katalog.* Compiled by A. V. Smirnov. Edited by
I. V. Gavrish. Leningrad, 1984. 99 p. [GMVOSR] (Lib: DLC; MH)

> Lists manuscript documents, photographs, and negatives on the history of the Red Guards.

h-423. Kulegin, A. M. "Listovki 1917 goda v kollektsii Gosudarstvennogo muzeia politicheskoi istorii Rossii." *Otechestvennye arkhivy*, 1993, no. 2, pp. 90–98. (Lib: DLC; IU; MH)

> Discusses the large collection of revolutionary handbills in GMPIR (ca. 10,000), with mention of the removal of some of them in the late 1940s and early 1950s.

h-424. *Na sluzhbe pobedivshei revoliutsii: Katalog sovetskogo politicheskogo plakata, 1918–1921 gg.* Compiled by N. Ia. Suliaeva and L. P. Tugova. Leningrad, 1987. 130 p. [GMVOSR] (Lib: DLC)

> Includes an index of the places where the posters were issued (pp. 123–25).

h-425. *Velikii podvig na fronte truda: Katalog dokumental'nykh materialov perioda chetvertoi i piatoi piatiletok.* Compiled by M. V. Ushakova. Edited by V. N. Agapitov. Leningrad, 1983. 117 p. [GMVOSR]

Muzei "Gorokhovaia, 2"—
Filial Gosudarstvennogo muzeia politicheskoi istorii Rossii ("Gorokhovaia, 2")

["Gorokhovaia, 2" Museum—
Branch of the State Museum of the Political History of Russia]

Agency: Ministerstvo kul'tury RF (Minkul'tury Rossii)
[Ministry of Culture]

Address: 191065, St. Petersburg, Admiralteiskii prosp., 6/2, komn. 303–305a
Telephone: 312-27-42
Transport: metro: Nevskii prospekt, Gostinyi Dvor; trol.: 1, 5, 10, 14, 17, 22; bus: 10; tram: 31
Hours: W–F 11:00–17:00

Head: Liudmila Vasil'evna Mikhailova

HISTORY:

Memorial'nyi muzei-kabinet F. E. Dzerzhinskogo
[Memorial Cabinet-Museum of F. E. Dzerzhinskii] (1974–1992)

The museum, the first devoted to the history of the political police in Russia, was founded by public funding in 1974 as the Memorial Cabinet-Museum in honor of Feliks Edmundovich Dzerzhinskii (*Polish,* Dzierżyński), the Polish revolutionary leader who became the first head of the Bolshevik security services after the October Revolution. It is located in the house where the All-Russian Extraordinary Commission for Combatting Counter-Revolution and Sabotage (*Vserossiiskaia Chrezvychainaia komissiia po bor'be s kontrrevoliutsiei i sabotazhem*—VChK), known as the Cheka, ran its operations from December 1917 through March 1918. In 1975 the museum became a branch of the State Museum of the Great October Socialist Revolution (GMVOSR). It now remains a branch of the successor State Museum of the Political History of Russia (GMPIR—H–66), with its present name dating from 1992.

Access: For research access to archival materials, a letter indicating the subject and purpose of research should be addressed to the director of the State Museum of the Political History of Russia (H–66).

Otdel fondov Gosudarstvennogo muzeia politicheskoi istorii Rossii
[Division of Fonds of the State Museum of Political History of Russia]

Address: 197046, St. Petersburg, ul. Kuibysheva, 4
Telephone: 233-73-20
Hours: MWF 10:00–17:00
Transport: metro: Gor'kovskaia
Chief Curator: Liudmila L'vovna Nikolaeva (*tel.* 233-73-11)

HOLDINGS: ca. 650 units, 1860s–1930s

Archival materials collected for the branch museum on the history of the investigation of political crimes in Russia (1826–1930s) are actually part of the Division of Fonds of GMPIR (H–66), only some of which are on exhibition in the branch museum itself.

There are rare originals and copies of documents and photographs, folders, drawings and postcards showing the work of the Third Department of His Imperial Majesty's Personal Chancery (*Tret'e Otdelenie Sobstvennoi Ego Imp. Velichestva Kantseliarii*) and the Police Department (*Departament politsii*) in prerevolutionary Russia, and the punitive organs of the Soviet state—the Cheka, the Petrograd Cheka, and the Petrograd Division of the Consolidated State Political Administration (*Ob"edinennoe gosudarstvennoe politicheskoe upravlenie*—OGPU). There is documentation relating to political repression from the 1930s through the 1950s. There are also some illustrative, iconographic materials, including albums, drawings, and artistic postcards, from the archives of security organs, particularly from the prerevolutionary Department of Police and the Security Service (*Okhrana*) Division.

Working Conditions: Researchers are accommodated in the working offices of the branch, or in the main museum, as needed.

Reference Facilities: A card catalogue in the GMPIR Division of Fonds covers the documentary materials held in the branch. Finding aids for the GMPIR holdings are in the process of being computerized.

Copying: Photocopies can be prepared.

FINDING AIDS — PUBLISHED — GENERAL:

Muzei SPb (1994), p. 127; *Muzei Leningrada* (1989), pp. 53–55; *Muzei Leningrada* (1982), pp. 22–23.

There is no published guide to the archival materials in the museum.

Gosudarstvennyi Sankt-Peterburgskii memorial'nyi muzei V. I. Lenina (Istoriko-memorial'nyi muzei "Smol'nyi")
[St. Petersburg State V. I. Lenin Memorial Museum (Smol'nyi Historico-Memorial Museum)]

Agency: Komitet po kul'ture Administratsii Sankt-Peterburga
[Committee on Culture of the Administration of St. Petersburg]

Address: 193060, St. Petersburg, pl. Proletarskoi diktatury, Smol'nyi, komn. 137
Telephone: 278-14-61
Transport: metro: Chernyshevskaia; bus: 14, 22, 26, 46, 134, 136, 137; trol.: 5, 7, 11, 15, 16, 18, 49; tram: 10, 12, 16, 32
Hours: by appointment

Director: Lidiia Alekseevna Dmitrieva (*tel.* 278-13-21)
Head of Division of Fonds: Nina Ivanovna Karpenko (*tel.* 234-16-11)

HISTORY:
Memorial'nyi muzei V. I. Lenina—Filial Tsentral'nogo muzeia V. I. Lenina
[V. I. Lenin Memorial Museum—Branch of the Central Museum of V. I. Lenin] (1937–1992)

The museum was reorganized in 1991 in the Smol'nyi Institute and includes under its administration four memorial apartments occupied by Vladimir Il'ich Lenin (Ul'ianov, 1870–1924) in St. Petersburg. The first predecessor of the present museum opened in the apartment in the Smol'nyi Institute where Lenin and Nadezhda Konstantinovna Krupskaia lived from October 1917 through March 1918, to which in 1974 was added the working office of Lenin. Before 1917 the building had been used for the Smol'nyi Institute, a school for daughters of the nobility. The Smol'nyi museum earlier constituted the Leningrad Branch of the Central Museum of V. I. Lenina (*Leningradskii filial Tsentral'nogo muzeia V. I. Lenina*) (1937–February, 1992), but was reorganized in 1991. In 1992 the present museum accessioned part of the fonds and the library of the former Leningrad Branch of the Central Lenin Museum.

Two branches under the museum in other Lenin apartments are now used for temporary exhibits:

(1) Apartment-Museum of the Elizarovs (*Muzei-kvartira Elizarovykh na ul. Shirokoi [Lenina]*), which had been a museum since 1927 associated with the family of Lenin's brother-in-law Mark T. Elizarov. (197136, St. Petersburg, ul. Shirokaia [Lenina], 52/9, kv. 24; tel. 235-37-78).

(2) Apartment-Museum of the Alliluevs (*Muzei-kvartira Alliluevykh*), opened as a museum in 1938, which was principally associated with the Communist activist Sergei Iakovlevich Alliluev, and where Lenin had stayed during 7–9 July 1917. (193144, St. Petersburg, ul. 10-ia Sovetskaia, 17, kv. 20; tel. 271-25-79).

HOLDINGS: over 5,500 units, late 19th c.–1992
documentary fond—158 units (1917–1992); negatives—ca. 4, 500; sound recordings—446; films—35

The general Division of Fonds of the museum includes some documentary materials accessioned from the former Leningrad Branch of the V. I. Lenin Central Museum, which include the archival materials and scientific and technical documentation from eleven Lenin memorial museums in

Leningrad. There are also memoirs and recollections of Lenin and his colleagues in the revolutionary movement, letters from revolutionaries and Communist Party veterans, films, photographs and sound recordings. The museum also holds documentation, including pictorial and photographic materials, relating to the Smol'nyi Institute for daughters of the nobility (*Vospitatel'noe obshchestvo blagorodnykh devits*), which had occupied the building before 1917.

Access: The fonds of the museum are in the process of being properly arranged and described, hence many of them are currently not available to researchers.

Reference Facilities: Reference facilities are currently being developed.

Library Facilities: The museum library (10,000 volumes) contains literature on Lenin and his published writings, including many rare editions. There are also audiovisual materials. There are thematic card catalogues on the life and work of V. I. Lenin.

Copying: There are no copying facilities.

FINDING AIDS — PUBLISHED — GENERAL:

Muzei SPb (1994), pp. 130–33; *Biblioteki SPb* (1993), p. 53; *Peterburg* (1992), p. 679; Myl'nikov (1970), p. 35.

There is no published guide to the documentary materials in the museum.

h-426. *Memorial'nye muzei V. I. Lenina: (Ocherki-putevoditeli po memorial'nym muzeiam V. I. Lenina v Leningrade i v Leningradskoi oblasti).* Compiled by A. Ia. Velikanova. Leningrad: Lenizdat, 1974. 360 p. (Lib: DLC; MH)

> The guide gives an idea of the holdings of several of the Lenin museums in St. Petersburg and Leningrad Oblast which have been closed down or reprofiled and whose fonds have been transferred to the V. I. Lenin Memorial Museum in Smol'nyi.

h-427. Pykhachev, L. N. "Komnata-muzei V. I. Lenina v Smol'nom: (K istorii sozdaniia pervykh memorial'nykh muzeev V. I. Lenina." In *Materialy nauchno-tekhnicheskoi konferentsii Leningradskogo elektrotekhnicheskogo instituta sviazi: Obshchestvennye nauki,* vol. 5, pp. 23–24. Leningrad, 1971.

Muzei istorii goroda Lomonosova
[Museum of the History of the Town of Lomonosov]

Agency: Otdel kul'tury administratsii g. Lomonosova
[Division of Culture of the Administration of the Town of Lomonosov]

Address: 189510, St. Petersburg, Lomonosov, ul. Eleninskaia, 25
Telephone: 422-39-47
Transport: suburban train from Baltic Station to Oranienbaum
Hours: MTu–F 9:00–13:00, 14:00–17:00

Head: Iuliia Valer'evna Kuchuk
Chief Curator: Valentin Andreevich Miuziev

HISTORY:

Lomonosovskii kraevedcheskii muzei
[Lomonosov Regional Studies Museum] (1972–1978)

The town of Oranienbaum, a city administrative district (*uezdnyi gorod*) within St. Petersburg Guberniia for periods after 1780, was important as the site of the imperial palace by the same name (see H–80). In 1948 the town was renamed in honor of M. V. Lomonosov. The museum was founded in 1972 as the Lomonosov Regional Studies Museum, but in 1974 became a branch of the Oblast Regional Studies Museum (*Oblastnoi kraevedcheskii muzei*). In 1978 it became a branch of the State Museum of the History of Leningrad (since 1991, St. Petersburg—H–65). In 1994 it became an independent museum under local administration. Although the Oranienbaum State Palace-Park Preserve (see H–80) reverted to its traditional name in 1993 (and the name of the railroad station was never changed), the town itself, and hence the museum, retains the name of Lomonosov.

HOLDINGS: ca. 27,000 units, 1850s–1990s

Within the Division of Fonds the museum holds documents on the history of the town of Lomonosov (Oranienbaum before 1948). Documentation relates to the building of the eighteenth- and nineteenth-century palaces and parks; the residence in Oranienbaum of prominent figures in the world of Russian science and culture (M. V. Lomonosov, M. P. Musorgskii, I. I. Shishkin, F. I. and I. F. Stravinskii, and others); the involvement of civilians and soldiers from the local garrison in the Oranienbaum Uprising during the February Revolution in 1917; and the events of the Civil War and the Second World War.

In the "Volost Chieftan" (*Volostnoi starshina*) fond (not yet properly arranged), there are documents relating to peasant government of the local uezd. The "Armorer Fond" (*fond oruzheinikov*) contains documents (late 19th–early 20th cc.) from the Officers' Infantry and Armory School (*Ofitserskaia strelkovaia i oruzheinaia shkola*), which was made famous by the work of such military engineers as N. M. Filatov, V. G. Fedorov, V. A. Degtiarev, and F. V. Tokarev.

Documents on the history of the Second World War, which include memoirs and recollections, letters, photographs and sound recordings have been put into two fonds entitled the "Memorial Book" (*Kniga pamiati*) and the "Council of Veterans of the Oranienbaum Bridgehead" (*Sovet veteranov Oranienbaumskogo platsdarma*—1941–1944).

The museum also holds the personal papers of the writer V. V. Bianki, the gunsmith N. M. Filatov, and the local historian A. I. Karkhu.

Access: Research access requires a letter in the name of the director of the museum indicating the subject and aim of the research.

Reference Facilities: There is a general descriptive and a reference card catalogue for the Division of Fonds.

FINDING AIDS — PUBLISHED — GENERAL:

Muzei SPb (1994), p. 118; *Muzei Leningrada* (1982), p. 33.

There is no published guide to the archival materials in the museum.

Kraevedcheskii muzei goroda Pushkina
[Regional Studies Museum of the Town of Pushkin]

Agency: Otdel kul'tury Administratsii g. Pushkina
[Division of Culture of the Administration of the Town of Pushkin]

Address: 189620, St. Petersburg, g. Pushkin, ul. Leont'evskaia, 28
Telephone: 466-55-10
Transport: suburban train from Vitebsk Station or metro: Kupchino + suburban train from Kupchino RR platform to Detskoe Selo (Tsarskoe Selo) + bus 382 (to stop "Gostinyi Dvor"); or metro: Moskovskaia + bus 287
Hours: M–ThSaSu 10:00–18:00

Head: Natal'ia Alekseevna Davydova (*tel.* 465-99-82)
Chief Curator: Nadezhda Aleksandrovna Kornilova

HISTORY:

Muzei istorii g. Pushkina
[Museum of the History of the Town of Pushkin] (1977–1996)

The museum was founded in 1977 as a Museum of History of the Town of Pushkin (Tsarskoe Selo before 1918, Detskoe Selo from 1918–1937). In 1986, it was moved into the building of the city administration, and it became a branch of the State Museum of the History of Leningrad—after 1991 of St. Petersburg (H–65). In the summer of 1996, it became an independent state museum and assumed its present name. Although the Tsarskoe Selo Palace-Park Museum-Preserve (see H–84) reverted to its traditional name in 1992 (and the name of the railroad station remained Detskoe Selo [Tsarskoe Selo]), as of the end of 1998, the town itself, and hence the museum, retains the name of Pushkin.

Access: For access to archival materials, an official application or personal letter is required addressed to the head of the museum, indicating the subject and aim of the research.

Library Facilities: There is a library (ca. 2,800 vols.) which contains reference material on the history and architecture of Pushkin, and which is open to researchers during the same hours as the archive.

Arkhiv
[Archive]

Telephone: 466-55-10
Hours: MWSu 10:00–15:00
Technical Worker: Nadezhda Aleksandrovna Kornilova

HOLDINGS: ca. 8,000 units, later 19th c.–1990s

manuscript fond—1,415 units; scientific archive—204 units; photographs—3,397; negatives—1,402; slides—535; postcards—292

The museum holds documentary and pictorial materials on the history of the town of Pushkin (Tsarskoe Selo). These include collections made by local historians, original documents and copies of documents from the late nineteenth and early twentieth centuries, photographs, and plans of the town and its environs.

There are photographic records of the building and consecration of the Imperial Fedorovsk Cathedral and of the village of Fedorovsk, and a huge collection of original drafts and plans by the architect V. N. Maksimov, who was closely associated with Tsarskoe Selo. There are a number of documentary and pictorial materials illustrating the history of the four famous schools in Tsarskoe Selo—the Emperor Nicholas Lyceum for Boys (*Nikolaevskaia muzhskaia gimnaziia*), the Empress Maria Lyceum for Girls (*Mariinskaia zhenskaia gimnaziia*), the Ecclesiastical Girls' School (*Zhenskoe uchilishche dukhovnogo vedomstva*), and the Levitskaia Private School (*Chastnaia shkola Levitskoi*).

There are photographs and personal recollections of Lenin's stay at Tsarskoe Selo and of the events of 1917 and subsequent years. There are also materials on the first radio station in Tsarskoe Selo, as well as manuscripts and photographs of A. B. Vasenko, one of the first Soviet stratisphere aviators. There are also photographs of poets and writers who lived in Tsarskoe Selo—O. D. Forsh, T. G. Gnedich, and V. Ia. Shishkov. Among other graphic materials are drawings by the artists Iu. Iu. and M. Iu. Klever.

There are documents relating to the history of Pushkin during the Second World War, which give details on the military units that took part in the defense and the liberation of the town. These include photographs and memoirs of the German occupation and a photograph album depicting the destruction inflicted on the town during the war. A number of documents show the postwar history of the town with emphasis on its restoration and its social and cultural life.

Working Conditions: Researchers are accommodated in working offices, where materials are available the same day they are ordered.

Reference Facilities: There are card catalogues and historical reports compiled by the museum staff on various aspects of the history of the town, including the history of streets, buildings, place-names, and personalia (prominent personages in the world of literature, arts, and science associated with Pushkin/Tsarskoe Selo). There is also a necropolis card catalogue of the graves in the cemeteries of Pushkin/Tsarskoe Selo and Pavlovsk, and the architectural monuments in those towns.

Copying: Photocopying facilities are available.

FINDING AIDS — PUBLISHED — GENERAL:

Muzei SPb (1994), p. 119; *Biblioteki SPb* (1993), p. 59.

There is no published guide to the archival materials in the museum.

❋⊷ H–71 ⊷❋

Rossiiskii etnograficheskii muzei (REM)
[Russian Ethnographic Museum]

Agency: Ministerstvo kul′tury RF (Minkul′tury Rossii)
[Ministry of Culture]

Address: 191011, St. Petersburg, ul. Inzhenernaia, 4/1
Telephone: 219-11-10, 210-35-13; *Fax:* (812) 315-85-02
Website: http://www.cape.nw.ru/ethnos/rem.htm
Transport: metro: Gostinyi Dvor, Nevskii prospekt; bus: 25; trol.: 1, 5, 7, 10, 22, 44
Hours: Tu–Su 10:00–17:00

Director: Igor′ Vasil′evich Dubov (*tel.* 311-86-22)
Deputy Director for Scientific Work: Natal′ia Moiseevna Kalashnikova (*tel.* 219-13-37)
Deputy Director for Commerce: Aleksandr Afanas′evich Mirin (*tel.* 210-46-27)
Chief Curator: Liudmila Borisovna Uritskaia (*tel.* 219-13-51)

HISTORY:
Russkii muzei Imperatora Aleksandra III—Etnograficheskii otdel (EO RM)
    [Emperor Alexander III Russian Museum—Ethnographic Division] (1901–1917)
Russkii muzei—Etnograficheskii otdel (EO RM)
    [Russian Museum—Ethnographic Division] (1917–1934)
Gosudarstvennyi etnograficheskii muzei (GEM)
    [State Ethnographic Museum] (1934–1948)
Gosudarstvennyi muzei etnografii narodov SSSR (GMEN SSSR)
    [State Museum of Ethnography of the Peoples of the USSR] (1948–1991)

The museum, founded in 1901 as the Ethnographic Division (*Etnograficheskii otdel*) of the Russian Museum, and opened to the public in 1923, ranks as one of the richest ethnographic museums in the world. It is housed in the building that was specially constructed for the Ethnographic Division in 1900–1911 by the architect V. F. Svin′in. In 1934 the division was reorganized as a separate museum and named the State Ethnographic Museum (GEM). In 1948 it acquired the collections of the State Museum of the Peoples of the USSR (*Gosudarstvennyi muzei narodov SSSR*) in Moscow, which had been closed down during the Second World War. The latter had formerly been the Central Museum of Ethnology (*Tsentral′nyi muzei narodovedeniia*), which had originally been founded in 1924 from the collections of the Ethnographic Division of the Rumiantsev Museum, among others. After the merger, the museum was renamed the State Ethnographic Museum of the Peoples of the USSR. In December 1991 it was added to the federal register of the most valuable monuments of the cultural heritage of the peoples of the Russian Federation. In 1992 the museum was renamed the Russian Ethnographic Museum (*Rossiiskii etnograficheskii muzei*), but, to be sure, it holds extensive collections relating to the culture, ethnography, and contemporary folk art of ethnic groups throughout the former USSR.

Access: Permission for research in the archives must be requested in an official letter stating the subject and aim of the research. In the case of foreign scholars, the letter should be addressed to, and permission is required from, the museum director; in the case of Russian (and CIS) nationals—from the chief curator. Fees are charged for research, with higher fees for foreigners. The staff of institutions that have academic cooperation agreements with the Russian Ethnographic Museum are entitled to work in the archives free of charge.

All processed archival fonds are currently open to researchers with the exception of the fond of the Tenishev Ethnographic Bureau (see h-432 and h-433). As of fall 1997 that fond is closed to outside scholars in connection with an ongoing publication project, although access is possible to the sections covering the gubernias of Iaroslavl, Kostroma, and Riazan. Permission for access to the library should be requested from the museum administration.

Library Facilities: The REM Scientific Library (ca. 105,000 vols.) was founded in 1901 under the Ethnographic Division of the Russian Museum. The library has collected books on ethnography, history, and folk art. The library includes the private book collections of Grand Duke George (Georgii) Mikhailovich, the Slavic literature and folklore scholar A. N. Pypin, and the ethnographers E. N. Studenetskaia and B. Z. Gamburg.

Arkhiv
[Archive]

Telephone: 219-16-58
Hours: TuW 10:00–13:00, 14:00–17:00
Head: Elena Ivanovna Rachkova

HOLDINGS: 15 fonds, ca. 17,000 units, 1873–1989 (1806, 1850s–1860s)
   drawings, prints—9,191 units; institutional fonds—6,514 units; personal papers—701 units

The archive holds fonds of institutions, societies, and private individuals who worked in the field of ethnography during the second half of the nineteenth and twentieth centuries. There are the administrative records of the Russian Ethnographic Museum itself and its various predecessors: the Ethnographic Division of the Russian Museum; the Central Museum of Ethnology; the State Museum of the Peoples of the USSR in Moscow; the Steering Committee of the First All-Russian Ethnographic Exhibition in Moscow; the Ethnographic Divisions of the Rumiantsev Museum, including the Dashkov collection of national costumes; and the Society of Friends of Natural Science, Anthropology, and Ethnography (*Obshchestvo liubitelei estestvoznaniia, antropologii i etnografii*) at Moscow University.

These materials include documentation on the history of the founding of the museums and the formation of collections; scientific writings and field studies by the museum staff; plans for work; reports on expeditions and assignments; journals and protocols of the academic, methodological, and restoration councils and the Fond Purchasing Commissions; clerical and financial documentation; and personnel records and personal files on the staff. The documents of the Jewish Section of the Ethnographic Division of the Russian Museum (1924–1941) have been preserved and include materials gathered on expeditions by the Section Head, I. M. Pul'ner. There are also documents from the Ethnographic Ensemble (*etnograficheskii ansambl'*) collected by B. Sal'mont, who studied the ethnography of the Buriat Mongols and popularized the science of ethnography.

The largest and most valuable of the fonds held by the museum is that of the Ethnographic Bureau of Prince V. N. Tenishev (*Etnograficheskoe biuro kn. V. N. Tenisheva*), with documents and records illustrating the social, economic, political and legal position and the way of life of the Russian peasantry at the end of the nineteenth century. Prince Tenishev drew up what he called an "Ethnographic Questionnaire on the Peasants of Central Russia" consisting of 500 questions, which he distributed to the rural intelligentsia between 1898 and 1900. The answers to these questions formed the basis of a sizeable archive (1,906 files), which his widow, M. K. Tenisheva, donated to the

Ethnographic Division of the Russian Museum in 1904. (Another part of the Tenishev fond is held in the sound recordings archive of the Institute of Russian Literature—IRLI RAN—E–28).

The personal fonds in the archive include the papers of the archeologists S. A. Teploukhov (mostly relating to archeological expeditions) and G. A. Bonch-Osmolovskii; the Slavic literature and folklore scholar A. N. Pypin (especially his bibliographic materials relating to Russian and foreign literature and folklore); and the ethnographers A. A. Makarenko, I. Peisak, E. N. Studenetskaia, B. Z. Gamburg, Z. P. Predtechenskaia, and A. S. Morozova. These include their scholarly works and supplementary materials, field diaries and reports of expeditions, inventories of finds and collections, sketches, photographs, other biographical and scientific documents, and correspondence.

The museum holds a small collection of 78 manuscript books (17th–19th cc.), some of which were collected by the museum staff on expeditions to the northern regions of Russia between 1928 and 1930. These include the illustrated *sinodik* (readings for the deceased) for the family of Ostrozhskii princes; two illuminated *tsvetniki* (edificatory text, or florilegium); "Tale of the Pskov-Pecherskii Monastery" (*Povest' o Pskovo-Pecherskom monastyre*); two short chronicles; the story of the conception and birth of Peter the Great and the journal of his foreign travels; a description of the coronation of Empress Elizabeth (Elizaveta Petrovna) in 1741; codices with collected writings of the Pomor'e Old Believers; and nineteenth-century codices of verses and songs.

The illustrative fond contains drawings, watercolors, and engravings in the traditional styles of the peoples of Russia and other countries.

Working Conditions: Researchers are accommodated in the working offices of the archive, where materials are delivered the same day they are ordered.

Reference Facilities: *Opisi* of processed fonds are available for readers. There is an annotated manuscript index to the Tenishev collection (prepared by A. G. Danilin).

Copying: Selected documents may be photocopied for illustrating scholarly publications.

Fototeka
[Photograph Archive]

Telephone: 219-16-24
Hours: W 10:00–13:00, 14:00–17:00
Head: Valeriia Borisovna Zolotareva

HOLDINGS: 175,747 units, 1965–1990s

The photograph collection includes pictures of people at work, various crafts and trades, home life, clothes, ornaments, and armaments. Many photographs portray religious ceremonies, festive celebrations, and customs of the peoples of Russia and neighboring countries from the mid-nineteenth through the twentieth century.

Reference Facilities: There are inventories of the collections, subject and alphabetic catalogues, and a catalogue of collectors (for staff use).

Copying: Copies of photographs can be prepared.

FINDING AIDS — PUBLISHED — GENERAL:

Muzei SPb (1994), pp. 51–52; *GAF Spravochnik* (1991), pp. 37–38; *Muzei Leningrada* (1989), pp. 95–98; *G&K Spravochnik* (1983), p. 272; *Muzei Leningrada* (1982), pp. 51–52; PKG *M&L* (1972), p. 344; Malyshev (1949), p. 456.

For coverage of the development of the ethnographic collections in this and other St. Petersburg museums, and related archival materials, see a-527–a-530.

h-430. *Gosudarstvennyi muzei etnografii narodov SSSR: [Al'bom].* Compiled by L. G. Lel'chuk and M. D. Perlina. Leningrad: "Aurora," 1989. 191 p. + plates. Introduction by S. A. Avizhanskaia. (Lib: MH)

> A brief guide, predominantly an album of color illustrations, with an introduction about the museum history and holdings (pp. 3–33).

h-430.1. *Museum of the Ethnography of the Peoples of the USSR.* Compiled by L. G. Lel'chuk and M. D. Perlina. Translated by A. Staros. Leningrad: Aurora Art Publishers, 1990. 191 p. + plates. Introduction by S. A. Avizhanskaia. (Lib: MH)

> An English translation of h-430.

h-430.2. *Gosudarstvennyi muzei etnografii narodov SSSR: Putevoditel'.* Compiled by E. A. Korsun. Leningrad: Lenizdat, 1980. 216 p. + 48 plates. (Lib: DLC; MH)

> An earlier tourist guide to the museum with introduction about the history and collections.

h-431. Dmitriev, V. A. "50 let Gosudarstvennogo muzeia etnografii narodov SSSR." *Sovetskaia etnografiia*, 1985, no. 2, pp. 146–48. (Lib: DLC; IU; MH)

FINDING AIDS — SPECIALIZED:

h-432. Nachinkin, N. "Materialy 'Etnograficheskogo biuro' V. N. Tenisheva." *Sovetskaia etnografiia*, 1955, no. 1, pp. 159–63. (Lib: DLC; IU; MH)

> A detailed description of the Tenishev collection. See also coverage of the Tenishev materials in S. A. Tokarev, *Istoriia russkoi etnografii (Dooktiabr'skii period)* (M.: "Nauka," 1966), pp. 403–406.

h-433. Firsov, B. M.; and Kiseleva, I. G. *Byt velikorusskikh krest'ian-zemlepashtsev: Opisanie materialov Etnograficheskogo biuro kniazia V. N. Tenisheva (na primere Vladimirskoi gubernii).* St. Petersburg: Izd-vo Evropeiskogo Doma, 1993. 471 p. (Lib: DLC; IU; MH)

> A publication of materials from the records of the Ethnographic Bureau of Prince Tenishev, covering Vladimir Guberniia. An extensive introduction provides references to previous studies and descriptive materials about the entire collection. An appendix (pp. 355–469) reprints the 1898 version of the V. N. Tenishev program, *Programma Etnograficheskikh svedenii o krest'ianakh tsentral'noi Rossii* (2d ed., Smolensk, 1898).

h-434. Belous, T. I. "Arkhiv V. N. Tenisheva: Nizhegorodskie materialy po traditsionnym obriadam russkikh krest'ian." In *Istoricheskaia nauka i arkhivy: Tezisy dokladov nauchno-prakticheskoi konferentsii, 19–20 oktiabria 1993 g,* edited by A. A. Kulakov et al., pp. 75–78. Nizhnii Novgorod: Izd-vo Volgo-Viatskogo kadrovogo tsentra, 1993. (Lib: DLC; IU; MH)

FINDING AIDS — SPECIALIZED — UNPUBLISHED:

h-435. "Katalog fotokollektsii muzeia po narodam Sibiri i Dal'nego Vostoka." Compiled by V. K. Taut. Typescript. Arkhiv REM, f. 2, op. 1, d. 1808.

> Describes REM photographic materials arranged by ethnic groups (Finno-Ugric, Turkic, etc.) with an index of the surnames of the collectors and the chronological time frame and subjects of their collections from prerevolutionary times to the early 1970s. Includes name and subject indexes with collection numbers and surnames of collectors and names of ethnic groups.

Gosudarstvennyi muzei istorii religii (GMIR)
[State Museum of the History of Religion]

Agency: Ministerstvo kul'tury RF (Minkul'tury Rossii)
[Ministry of Culture]

Address:	191186, St. Petersburg, Kazanskaia pl., 2
Telephone:	312-35-86; *Fax:* (812) 311-94-83
E-mail:	yan@relig-museum.ru
Website:	http://www.relig-museum.ru;
	http://www.bestrussia.com/net/muzei/muzrel/win.htm
Transport:	metro: Nevskii prospekt, Gostinyi Dvor
Hours:	MTuTh–Su 11:00–18:00

Director: Stanislav Alekseevich Kuchinskii (*tel.* 312-35-86)
Deputy Director for Scientific Work: Aleksandr Ivanovich Tafintsev (*tel.* 311-45-49)
Scientific Secretary: Ol'ga Semenovna Khizhniak (*tel.* 311-29-30)
Chief Curator: Irina Aleksandrovna Martynchuk (*tel.* 312-27-66)

HISTORY:

Muzei istorii religii AN SSSR (MIR)
  [Museum of the History of Religion AN SSSR] (1931–1954)
Muzei istorii religii i ateizma AN SSSR (MIRiA)
  [Museum of the History of Religion and Atheism AN SSSR] (1954–1961)
Gosudarstvennyi muzei istorii religii i ateizma (GMIRiA)
  [State Museum of the History of Religion and Atheism] (1961–1990)

The museum was founded in 1931 as the Museum of the History of Religion under the Academy of Sciences of the USSR, on the initiative of the ethnographer, V. G. Bogoraz-Tan, and was opened to the public in 1932. It occupies the Cathedral of the Mother of God of Kazan (*Sobor Kazanskoi Bozh'ei Materi*), built between 1801 and 1811 by the serf architect A. N. Voronikhin, which had been closed to religious services in 1928. Its holdings were augmented by collections from a number of museums that were shut down, including in 1938 materials from the State Antireligious Museum (*Gosudarstvennyi Antireligioznyi muzei*—1930–1937), which had been housed in the former Isaac Cathedral in Leningrad (H–86), and in 1947 from the Central Antireligious Museum in Moscow (*Tsentral'nyi antireligioznyi muzei*—1928–1946). The museum also acquired materials from various private collections and documents accumulated on expeditions. In 1961 the museum was transferred to the jurisdiction of the Ministry of Culture of the RSFSR. The present name of the museum dates from 1990. The museum is still housed in the Kazan Cathedral, one wing of which was reopened for religious services in 1992.

The Scientific Historical Archive and the current Fond of Photographs and Sound Recordings are both part of the Division of Fonds. The archive was organized in 1953 on the initiative of V. D. Bonch-Bruevich, the early Bolshevik intellectual who had previously organized the extensive archival holdings of the State Literary Museum in Moscow (see H–33) and who then directed the Museum of the History of Religion under the Academy of Sciences. Part of the documentation had previously been part of the museum exhibits fond, but also consisted of materials brought together from the various predecessor museums. Additional holdings were acquired in copy from TsGALI SSSR (now RGALI—B–7) in Moscow and some documents came from TsGIA SSSR (now RGIA—B–3), and from the Archive of the Academy of Sciences of the USSR in Leningrad (now PFA RAN—E–20). The Fond of Photographs and Sound Recordings was formed as a separate administrative entity in 1968.

Access: Permission for research in the archives and library must be obtained from the museum administration on the basis of an official letter indicating the subject and aim of research.

Working Conditions: Researchers are accommodated in working offices of the museum. Materials are delivered soon after they are ordered.

Library Facilities: The museum library (ca. 168,000 vols.) contains literature on theology, dogmatics, religious practices, the history of churches, religious propagation and atheism, history, archeology, ethnography, philosophy, sociology, literary criticism, and art. It has incunabula and early Russian printed books dating back to the sixteenth century, as well as secular and religious periodicals. There are books from the libraries of the Imperial Orthodox Palestine Society (*Imperatorskoe Pravoslavnoe Palestinskoe obshchestvo*), the Central Antireligious Museum in Moscow, the Kazan Cathedral, the Catholic Church of St. Catherine (*Ekaterininskii kostel*), the Synodal Library, and the Workers' Antireligious University (*Rabochii antireligioznyi universitet*). (Tel. 314-58-47).

Copying: Xerox facilities are available and photographic copies can be made of graphic materials.

Nauchno-istoricheskii arkhiv
[Scientific Historical Archive]

Telephone: 312-27-66
Hours: MTuThF 11:00–17:00 (closed—July and August)
Head: Irina Viktorovna Tarasova

HOLDINGS: 43 fonds, ca. 24,000 units, 15th c.–1970s
MS books—870 units (15th–20th cc.); archival collections—8 (16th–20th cc.); institutional fonds—7 (19th–20th cc.); personal fonds—28 (18th–20th cc.)

The archive holds records of several state institutions (including GMIR and its predecessors) and social organizations, a significant group of personal papers, and a several subject-oriented collections on the history of religion and antireligious movements.

The fonds of the State Museum of the History of Religion and the Central Antireligious Museum (constituting the administrative records of the museum itself and its predecessors) contain documentation on the scholarly, exhibition, and collection activities of the staff—including articles written by the museum staff, exhibition plans, work notes for lectures and excursions, and expedition reports. The fonds of the Central Council of the Union of Militant Atheists (*Tsentral'nyi sovet Soiuza voinstvuiushchikh bezbozhnikov*), the Moscow Vegetarian Society, the Combined Council of Conscientious Objector Communes and Groups (*Ob"edinennyi sovet obshchin i grupp po otkazu ot voinskoi povinnosti*), and other social organizations contain charters, minutes of meetings, other informational documentation, and personal files on group members, as well as files of legal proceedings against conscientious objectors.

There are editorial records of a number of journals and periodicals, including the "Bulletin of the Holy Synod" (*Vestnik Sviashchennogo Sinoda*), the "Voice of Tolstoi and Unity" (*Golos Tolstogo i Edinenie*), the "Holy Christian Molokanin" (*Dukhovnyi khristianin-molokanin*), and the "Atheist" (*Bezbozhnik*), which contain editorial files, correspondence with readers, and informational material. The fond of the V. G. Chertkov "Free Speech" (*Svobodnoe slovo*) Publishing House is of particular interest, containing as it does a collection of documentary records on the life of various sectarian groups and on instances of religious persecution in Russia during the late nineteenth and early twentieth centuries.

There are personal papers of such prominent Tolstoians as P. I. Biriukov, I. M. Tregubov, E. V. Molostova, M. S. Dudchenko, and F. A. Strakhov, which include personal documents, literary writings, correspondence and collections of documents on the history of religious movements. There are also the personal papers of the Dukhobor V. A. Makaseev, which include articles, diary notes, letters, and material on the life of the Dukhobors in Canada; of S. I. Bystrov, who made a study of the Old Believers; and of N. I. Subbotin, a professor at the Moscow Theological Academy and a church historian. There are the personal papers of a number of Soviet scholars who studied religion, including Professor S. G. Lozinskii (with works on the history of Catholicism, Protestantism, and Judaism in the Middle Ages); M. M. Sheinman (with his studies of the history of religion since the birth of Christ); the museum specialist A. A. Nevskii (materials on Orthodox iconography); the scholar of Buddhism M. I. Lavrov, who served as Russian consul in the Orient; and the Soviet government official and propagandist of atheism P. A. Krasikov. In the largest fond are the personal papers of the museum director, historian, and revolutionary V. D. Bonch-Bruevich, which include a large collection of documents on the history of sectarianism, orthodoxy, and free-thinking in late nineteenth to mid-twentieth century Russia, correspondence with religious activists, and a collection of photographs.

The rich collection of manuscript books (15th–20th cc.) includes apocryphal works (Jewish and early Christian literature not included in the Bible), lives of saints, liturgical texts, various religious compilations (*sborniki*) with edifying texts, choral manuscripts, legends and parables, annals and chronicles, polemics, spells or exorcisms, herbals, texts on astrology, and free-thinking and philosophical works in the Old Church Slavonic, Russian, and Latin languages. The oldest of the manuscripts are a late fifteenth-century Psalter and an inspirational compilation known as the *Izmaragd*. There are several manuscript *sinodiki* (prayers for the deceased) from the Solovetskii Monastery (17th c.). Russian materials include the collection of the Kostroma historian and literary specialist N. N. Vinogradov.

Materials relating to the Orthodox Church are not a major part of the holdings, since most Orthodox Church records are held in state archives. Nevertheless, the collection of "Materials on the History of the Orthodox Church" has scattered documents relating to the history of a number of parishes and monasteries with reference to their economic situation, and to relations between Church and State, trends within the Orthodox Church, and religious education; there are also some theological works and sermons. More important, original materials document other Christian sects, both in Russia and in foreign countries. The collection of "Materials on the History of Sectarianism in Russia" has documentation on the Old Believers, Baptists, Jehovah's Witnesses, and Tolstoians, among other groups, relating to their history, teachings, organization, and relations with civil authorities. The collection entitled "Materials on the History of Freemasonry in Russia" contains documents from individual lodges, descriptions of Masonic rituals and ceremonies, letters, and hermetic writings. Another significant collection comprises "Materials on the History of Atheism and Free-Thinking."

Graphic materials (held in the general fond of exhibits) include pictures of religious monuments and places of pilgrimage; portraits of priests; lithographs and chromolithographs on dogmatic subjects and on the iconography of different faiths; cheaply produced religious literature of a moralizing nature; anticlerical engravings; collections of antireligious posters, Old Believer drawings and posters (18th–19th cc.), especially from the collection of V. G. Druzhinin. There are also engravings by Russian masters, such as L. Bunin, I. S. Klauber, I. Rozonov, N. I. Utkin, A. G. Ukhtomskii, and A. F. Zubov; and well-known European artists.

The Oriental Fond includes a collection of greetings cards from China made by V. M. Alekseev in 1906 and 1907, and an album of the Taoist Pantheon consisting of 227 drawings from a collection made by M. I. Lavrov.

N.B. A large part of the administrative records of the museum itself for the years 1933–1976 is now held in TsGALI SPb (D–15, fond 195 [4039]).

Reference Facilities: The reference system of the archive is currently being further developed. There are *opisi* for the fonds that have already been processed.

Fotofonofond
[Fond of Photographs and Sound Recordings]

Telephone: 312-27-66
Hours: MTuThF 11:00–15:00
Curator: Tat'iana Mikhailovna Gel'fman

HOLDINGS: ca. 54,000 units, 1880–1990s
     photographs and negatives—52,420; sound recordings—341

The Photograph Archive holds documentary photographs on the history of religion and atheism from the late nineteenth to the early twentieth centuries. There is a large collection of photographs from the Imperial Orthodox Palestine Society, which includes pictures of churches, religious monuments belonging to various faiths, and places of religious pilgrimage in Russia and the Middle East. The collection also holds prints showing religious services and celebrations, portraits of priests, and ethnographic materials. The work of the noted St. Petersburg photographer, Karl (K. K.) Bulla, is well represented.

There are postrevolutionary documentary photographs on such themes as the work of the religious organizations; relations between Church and State; the history of the antireligious movement (which was comprised of clubs and associations, as well as the Congresses of the Union of Militant Atheists); and the holding of lay ceremonies and celebrations during the Soviet period. There are also the portraits of such noted propagandists of atheism as E. M. Iaroslavskii and A. A. Osipov. Apart from original prints and negatives, there are a large number of reproductions from literature on the history of religion, which are used for exhibition purposes, displays, and albums.

The Sound Recordings Archive contains recordings of ritual and other church music, including Orthodox liturgies, Old Believer choral works, Dukhobor prayers, Buddhist services, and Shaman (medicine-man) chanting. There are also recordings of speeches and reports by scholars and propagandists of atheism; lectures on iconography by A. A. Nevskii; and materials from scholarly conferences.

Reference Facilities: There is a subject card catalogue.

FINDING AIDS — PUBLISHED — GENERAL:

GAF Spravochnik (1991), pp. 113–16; *Muzei SPb* (1994), p. 107; *Peterburg* (1992), p. 242; *Biblioteki SPb* (1993), p. 54; *Muzei Leningrada* (1989), pp. 72–81; *G&K Spravochnik* (1983), pp. 272–74, 438; *Muzei Leningrada* (1982), pp. 38–39; PKG *M&L* (1972), p. 345; Sup. 1 (1976), p. 142; Myl'nikov (1970), p. 44.

There is no comprehensive published guide to the archival materials in the museum.

h-440. *Muzei istorii religii i ateizma: Putevoditel'.* Compiled by A. M. Leskov and
     Ia. I. Shurygin. Leningrad: Lenizdat, 1981. 144 p. + 16 plates. [Minkul't RSFSR; GMIRiA]
     (Lib: DLC; IU; MH)
          Describes the history of the museum and gives details about its exhibits.

h-441. *Muzei istorii religii i ateizma: Spravochnik-putevoditel'.* Compiled by N. P. Krasnikov
     and M. S. Butinova. Moscow/Leningrad: "Nauka," 1965. 195 p. [Minkul't RSFSR;
     GMIRiA] (Lib: MH)
          An earlier, slightly more detailed guide to the museum.

h-442. Shurygin, Ia. I. "Obzor fondov." *Ezhegodnik MIRA* 1 (1957): 459–64. (Lib: DLC; IU; MH)

> Emphasizes and lists artistic holdings, paintings, drawings, and sculpture in the museum collections, but makes only brief mention of archival materials. A second article by the same author (pp. 437–58) details the history of the Kazan Cathedral.

h-443. Snigireva, E. A. "K piatidesiatiletiiu muzeia. (Po materialam Rukopisnogo otdela Gosudarstvennogo muzeia istorii religii i ateizma)." In *Nauchno-ateisticheskie issledovaniia v muzeiakh: Sbornik nauchnykh trudov,* edited by I. Kh. Cherniak et al., [vol. 3], pp. 133–47. Leningrad: Izd-vo GMIRiA, 1986. [Minkul't RSFSR; GMIRiA] (Lib: DLC; IU; MH)

> Describes the founding of the museum and its development and work from 1932 to 1955. Includes information on collecting activities, the museum's holdings, library, and archives.

h-444. Diuzheva, G. N. "Iz opyta komplektovaniia fondov v GMIRiA na primere novykh postuplenii za 1979–1984 gody." In *Muzei v ateisticheskoi propagande: Sbornik [nauchnykh] trudov,* edited by R. F. Filippova et al., pp. 123–27. Leningrad: Izd. GMIRiA, 1985. [Minkul't RSFSR; GMIRiA] (Lib: DLC)

Scientific-Historical Archive

h-445. Mordasova, I. V. "Arkhiv Muzeia istorii religii i ateizma i ego ispol'zovanie v muzeinoi ekspozitsii." In *Vsesoiuznaia konferentsiia-seminar "Arkhivnye fondy khudozhestvennykh muzeev SSSR,"* vol. 1, pp. 168–71. Moscow, 1981.

> A brief survey of the archival holdings of the museum with reference to a number of specific fonds and the politico-ideological use of the materials for antireligious exhibits.

h-446. Emeliakh, L. I. "Starinnye rukopisnye knigi Muzeia istorii religii i ateizma AN SSSR." *TODRL* 13 (1957): 556–60. (Lib: DLC; IU; MH)

> A preliminary survey of 9 manuscript books (15th–18th cc.).

h-447. Gendrikov, V. B. "Kratkii putevoditel' po fondam lichnogo proiskhozhdeniia Rukopisnogo otdela Muzeia istorii religii i ateizma." In *Ateizm, religiia, sovremennost': Sbornik nauchnykh trudov,* pp. 212–23. Leningrad: "Nauka," 1973. (Lib: DLC; IU; MH)

> Lists the personal papers in the archive with mention of their main subject matter.

h-448. Emeliakh, L. I. "Arkhivnye istoriko-ateisticheskie dokumenty v ekspozitsiiakh muzeev." In *Muzei v ateisticheskoi propagande: Sbornik [nauchnykh] trudov,* edited by R. F. Filippova et al., pp. 30–38. Leningrad: Izd. GMIRiA, 1979. [Minkul't RSFSR; GMIRiA] (Lib: DLC; MH)

PhotoPhonoFond

h-449. Romanov, L. N. "Fonoteka Gosudarstvennogo muzeia istorii religii i ateizma." In *Muzei v ateisticheskoi propagande: Sbornik [nauchnykh] trudov,* edited by R. F. Filippova et al., pp. 88–100. Leningrad: Izd. GMIRiA, 1982. [Minkul't RSFSR; GMIRiA] (Lib: DLC)

> Characterizes the collections of sound recordings, and describes the main principles and purposes behind their accessioning.

Museum Series of Collected Articles

h-451. *Problemy formirovaniia i izucheniia muzeinykh kollektsii Gosudarstvennogo muzeia istorii religii: Sbornik nauchnykh trudov.* Edited by A. V. Khrshanovskii, A. V. Konovalov, et al. Leningrad: Izd. GMIR, 1990. 279 p. [Minkul't RSFSR; GMIR] (Lib: DLC; MH)

h-452. *Pravoslavie v Drevnei Rusi: Sbornik nauchnykh trudov.* Edited by L. I. Emeliakh, M. S. Butinova, et al. Leningrad: Izd. GMIRiA, 1989. 151 p. [Minkul't RSFSR; GMIRiA] (Lib: DLC; MH)

h-453. *Muzei v ateisticheskoi propagande: Sbornik [nauchnykh] trudov.* Edited by
R. F. Filippova, M. S. Butinova, et al. 10 vols. Leningrad: Izd. GMIRiA, 1979–1988.
[Minkul't RSFSR; GMIRiA] (Lib: DLC; MH[inc])

> Part of the museum's series of annual volumes of collected articles, including surveys of fonds and
> individual documents, with emphasis on the antireligious exhibits in the museum.

h-454. *Nauchno-ateisticheskie issledovaniia v muzeiakh: Sbornik nauchnykh trudov.* Edited
by E. A. Snigireva, M. S. Butinova, et al. 6 vols. Leningrad: Izd-vo GMIRiA, 1983–1988.
[Minkul't RSFSR; GMIRiA] (Lib: DLC; MH[inc])

> A series of volumes of collected articles issued by the museum includes articles on the history of the
> museum and surveys of its fonds, as well as other studies of atheism.

h-455. *Ezhegodnik muzeia istorii religii i ateizma. (Ezhegodnik MIRA)* Moscow/Leningrad,
1957–1964. 7 vols. [Minkul't RSFSR; GMIRiA] (Lib: DLC; IU; MH)

> A series of volumes of collected scholarly studies issued by the museum, emphasizing atheism, with
> regular bibliographies of literature on the subject.

FINDING AIDS — SPECIALIZED:

For coverage of Jewish-related holdings, see *Jewish Doc.* (1996), pp. 57.

Scientific-Historical Archive

h-457. Tarasova, Irina Viktorovna; and Klymasz, Robert Bogdan. "Doukhobor Materials in the
Collections of the Museum of Religious History in St. Petersburg." In *Spirit Wrestlers:
Centennial Papers in Honour of Canada's Doukhobors Heritage,* pp. 217–32. Hull,
Quebec: Canadian Museum of Civilization, 1995. "Mercury Series (Canadian Centre for
Folk Culture Studies)," vol. 67. (Lib: MH)

> A survey of the documents of the Dukhobors for the years 1862–1946. The original Russian text
> was prepared for publication, but has not yet appeared.

h-458. Tarasova, Irina Viktorovna. "Apokrify po spiskam XVIII–XIX vv. iz sobraniia GMIRiA."
In *Pravoslavie v Drevnei Rusi: Sbornik nauchnykh trudov,* edited by L. I. Emeliakh et al.,
pp. 67–73. Leningrad: Izd. GMIRiA, 1989. [Minkul't RSFSR; GMIRiA] (Lib: DLC; MH)

> A survey of the eighteenth- and nineteenth-century apocryphal works in the museum, with more
> detailed listing of some 30 manuscript apocryphal writings.

h-459. Shakhnovich, Mikhail Iosifovich. "Idei antichnogo ateizma v russkom rukopisnom
pamiatnike XVIII v. "Zertsalo bezbozhiia." (Iz kollektsii Gosudarstvennogo muzeia istorii
religii i ateizma)." In *Nauchno-ateisticheskie issledovaniia v muzeiakh: Sbornik nauchnykh
trudov,* edited by E. A. Snigireva et al., pp. 5–17. Leningrad: Izd-vo GMIRiA, 1986.
[Minkul't RSFSR; GMIRiA] (Lib: DLC; MH)

> A history of the acquisition, and a description and analysis of a manuscript codex of eighteenth-
> century atheistic writings.

h-460. Shakhnovich, Mikhail Iosifovich. "V. D. Bonch-Bruevich—issledovatel' religiozno-
obshchestvennykh dvizhenii v Rossii." *Ezhegodnik MIRA* 7 (1964): 293–300. (Lib: DLC; IU; MH)

> Discusses the antireligious studies and collections of Bonch-Bruevich, who directed the museum
> and contributed to its archival holdings.

h-461. Gol'dberg, Nikolai Moiseevich. "Pamiati starshego nauchnogo sotrudnika Muzeia
istorii religii i ateizma AN SSSR professora S. G. Lozinskogo." *Ezhegodnik MIRA* 1
(1957): 519–521. (Lib: DLC; IU; MH)

> Describes the work of the church historian and professor, S. G. Lozinskii, who was associated with
> the museum and whose personal papers are held in the archive.

Fond of Photographs and Sound Recordings

h-462. Diuzheva, G. N. " 'Palestinskaia' kollektsiia fotografii v sobranii GMIRiA." In *Muzei v ateisticheskoi propagande: Sbornik [nauchnykh] trudov*, edited by R. F. Filippova et al., pp. 121–23. Leningrad: Izd. GMIRiA, 1986. [Minkul't RSFSR; GMIRiA] (Lib: DLC)

> A brief survey of the documentary photographs of the Imperial Orthodox Palestine Society (9,347 units from 1858 to 1900) and a list of the main subject headings.

Graphic Collections

h-463. Chenskaia, G. A. "O lubochnykh kartinkakh v sobranii GMIRa." In *Problemy formirovaniia i izucheniia muzeinykh kollektsii Gosudarstvennogo muzeia istorii religii: Sbornik nauchnykh trudov*, edited by A. V. Khrshanovskii et al., pp. 81–95. Leningrad: Izd. GMIR, 1990. [Minkul't RSFSR; GMIR] (Lib: DLC)

> A description of nineteenth-century popular satirical cartoons (*lubok*) and Soviet posters from the 1920s done in the same style.

h-464. Stetskevich, M. S. "Istoriko-religiovedcheskii analiz serii angliiskikh graviur pervoi treti XIX v. iz sobraniia GMIRiA." In *Muzei v ateisticheskoi propagande: Sbornik [nauchnykh] trudov*, edited by R. F. Filippova et al., pp. 60–81. Leningrad: Izd. GMIRiA, 1988. [Minkul't RSFSR; GMIRiA] (Lib: DLC; MH)

> An outline description of 9 early nineteenth-century English etchings taken from the drawings of T. Shepherd and showing a number of London churches and their historical connections with the Church of England.

Oriental Collections

h-465. Sazykin, Aleksei Georgievich. "Kratkoe opisanie kollektsii mongol'skikh rukopisei i ksilografov, khraniashcheisia v Gosudarstvennom muzee istorii religii i ateizma." In *Muzei v ateisticheskoi propagande: Sbornik [nauchnykh] trudov*, edited by R. F. Filippova et al., pp. 101–12. Leningrad: Izd. GMIRiA, 1982. [Minkul't RSFSR; GMIRiA] (Lib: DLC)

> A general description of the collection and scholarly description of 21 manuscripts (early 19th–early 20th cc.).

h-466. Stetskevich, T. A. "Osnovnye vidy izobrazitel'nogo materiala po islamu v sobranii Muzeia istorii religii." In *Problemy formirovaniia i izucheniia muzeinykh kollektsii Gosudarstvennogo muzeia istorii religii: Sbornik nauchnykh trudov*, edited by A. V. Khrshanovskii et al., pp. 194–220. Leningrad: Izd. GMIR, 1990. [Minkul't RSFSR; GMIR] (Lib: DLC)

> An outline of the pictorial materials in the Islamic collection, which includes cheaply produced religious literature—lithographs and chromolithographs, drawings, engravings and photographs (mid-19th–early 20th cc.)

h-467. Garanin, I. P. "Kitaiskii blagozhelatel'nyi lubok iz kollektsii V. M. Alekseeva." *Ezhegodnik MIRA* 7 Moscow/Leningrad, (1957): 315–27. [Minkul't RSFSR; GMIRiA] (Lib: DLC; IU; MH)

> Describes the collection and includes a detailed catalogue of 13 popular wood-block prints.

h-468. Garanin, I. P. "Kitaiskii antikhristianskii lubok XIX v." *Ezhegodnik MIRA* 4 (1960): 403–26. (Lib: DLC; IU; MH)

> Describes materials in an album from the collection of V. M. Alekseev with a description of each of the 32 wood-block prints.

Military and Military History Museums

❉⤙ ⟊⟊ H–73 ⟊⤚❉

Voenno-istoricheskii muzei artillerii, inzhenernykh voisk i voisk sviazi (VIMAIViVS)
[Military History Museum of the Artillery, Corps of Engineers, and Signal Corps]

Agency: Ministerstvo oborony RF (Minoborony Rossii)
[Ministry of Defense]
Glavnoe raketno-artilleriiskoe upravlenie (GRAU)
[Chief Rocket-Artillery Directorate]

Address: 197046, St. Petersburg, Aleksandrovskii park (*formerly* park Lenina), 7
Telephone: 238-47-04, 232-20-57; *Fax:* (812) 238-47-04
Transport: metro: Gor'kovskaia; bus: 25, 46, 65, 134; tram: 2, 6, 26, 34, 63
Hours: W–Su 11:00–17:00

Chief: Valerii Mikhailovich Krylov (*tel.* 238-47-33; 232-20-57)
Deputy Chief: Aleksandr Nikolaevich Sautin
Scientific Secretary: Igor' Aleksandrovich Taubin (*tel.* 238-47-39)
Chief Curator: Aleksandr Nikolaevich Kulinskii (*tel.* 238-46-97)
Head of the Library: Elena Mikhailovna Kirkina (*tel.* 238-47-45)
Chief, Editorial Publication Division: Andron Nikolaevich Stepaniuk (*tel.* 238-47-16)

HISTORY:

Tseikhgauz Petropavlovskoi kreposti
[Storehouse of the Peter and Paul Fortress] (1703–1756)
Dostopamiatnyi zal Sankt-Peterburgskogo Arsenala
[Memorabilia Hall of the St. Petersburg Arsenal] (1756–1868)
Muzeum Nikolaevskoi inzhenernoi akademii i uchilishcha
[Museum of the Nicholas Engineering Academy and School] (1855–1917)
Artilleriiskii muzei
[Artillery Museum] (1868–1903)
Artilleriiskii istoricheskii muzei (AIM)
[Artillery History Museum] (1903–1963)
Voenno-istoriko-bytovoi muzei
[Military Historical Daily-Life Museum] (1918–1937)
Voenno-inzhenernyi istoricheskii muzei
[Military-Engineering History Museum] (1920–1946)
Tsentral'nyi istoricheskii voenno-inzhenernyi muzei
[Central Historical Museum of Military Engineering] (1946–1963)
Voenno-istoricheskii muzei artillerii i inzhenernykh voisk
[Military History Museum of the Artillery and Corps of Engineers] (1963–1965)
Voennyi muzei sviazi
[Military Museum of Communications] (1944–1965)

One of the richest military history museums in Russia, and certainly the richest in terms of its archival holdings, the museum began its history under Peter I in 1703 as the Store House in the

Peter and Paul Fortress, known by its German name "Tseikhgaus" (*Ger.* Zeichhaus), sometimes referred to as the Store House for Memorabilia and Curiosities, which was a collecting point for exhibits from the Artillery Corps, including foreign trophies. After 1756 it was known as the Repository for Memorabilia under the St. Petersburg Arsenal. In 1868 the collections were moved and installed in the building of the former Kronwerk (*Kronverk*) Arsenal (1850–1860, designed by the architect P. I. Tamanskii), adjoining the Peter and Paul Fortress, and the exhibits were renamed the Artillery Museum. Starting in 1903 it was known as the Artillery History Museum (AIM). In 1917 and 1918 the museum exhibits and archive were evacuated to Iaroslavl and returned in 1919. There were some losses from a fire in AIM in the 1930s.

In 1918, a separate Military Historical Daily-Life Museum was established, which in 1937 was consolidated with AIM. During World War II, the museum holdings were evacuated to Novosibirsk, and also suffered some losses en route.

The Historical Archive (documentary fond) and library were established in 1872, by the military historian N. E. Brandenburg, who then directed the museum. Brandenburg arranged the transfer to the museum of seventeenth- and eighteenth-century records from the archive of the Main Artillery Administration (*Glavnoe artilleriiskoe upravlenie*), which he described in published catalogues, and he also encouraged the acquisition of other materials including books for the library. As a result of subsequent accessions, the museum consolidated a major complex of records from various organs of artillery administration in Russia, beginning with the Gunnery (*Pushkarskii*) *prikaz* and extending through 1910. Currently these documentary materials comprise the Division of Fonds for the History of Artillery and the Signal Corps (First Division of Fonds).

The original collection of documents relating to the history of the Corps of Engineers (now the Second Division of Fonds) was begun in 1758, with the foundation of a museum for the consolidated artillery and engineering schools, which from 1855 was called the Museum of the Nicholas Engineering Academy and School (*Muzei Nikolaevskoi inzhenernoi akademii i uchilishcha*). After the Revolution it was known as the Military-Engineering History Museum (1920–1946), and later the Central Historical Museum of Military Engineering (1946–1963). In 1963 after that museum was consolidated with AIM, the combined museum was renamed the Military History Museum of the Artillery and the Corps of Engineers.

The museum received its present name in 1965 when the additional Division for the History of the Signal Corps was added on the basis of the Military Museum of Communications, which had been founded in 1944.

The graphic materials in the museum include displays acquired from the abolished Military Historical Daily-Life Museum, which in 1918 was organized in the process of transfer to state custody the holdings of prerevolutionary museums of various Army units. That museum also received the collection of General-Field Marshal Grand Duke Michael (Mikhail) Nikolaevich, materials from the Trophy Commission from World War I, the museums of the First and Second Cadet Corps, the museum of other military schools, productions from the M. B. Grekov Studio of Military Artists, and the graphic arts collection of the Military Museum of the Military Communication Academy.

Access: For access to the archival materials an official letter of application should be addressed to the chief of the museum, which must be endorsed with his authorization.

Working Conditions: Advance orders are necessary through the reading room (not more than 10 units in one order) for the First Division of Fonds. In other divisions researchers are accommodated in the working offices, where materials are available the day they are ordered.

Library Facilities: The museum library (ca. 95,000 vols.), which holds books on the history of military science, was founded in 1879. It includes books from the libraries of the Russian Historical Society, the Main Artillery Administration, the Michael Artillery Academy (*Mikhailovskaia artilleriiskaia akademiia*), and various prerevolutionary Russian military units. There are card catalogues of personal names, museum staff publications, rare editions, among others. (Tel. 238-47-45).

Copying: Photographs and xerox copies can be prepared, although documents from the First Division of Fonds may not be reproduced. Use of copies of documents for research, publishing, and exhibition purposes is subject to appropriate charges fixed in agreement with the administration.

Otdel fondov istorii artillerii i voisk sviazi (Pervyi otdel fondov)
[Division of Fonds for the History of the Artillery and Signal Corps (First Division of Fonds)]

Hours: Historical Archive—M–F 9:00–17:00 (by appointment)
Chief: Aleksandr Nikolaevich Sautin (*tel.* 238-47-36)
Scientific Specialist of the History Archive:
   Liliia Konstantinovna Makovskaia (*tel.* 238-46-42)

HOLDINGS: ca. 300,000 units, 1628–1990s
   documentary materials—238,489 units (215,802 units—in Historical Archive) (17th–20th cc.);
   technical drawings—8,430 units; graphic materials—23,255 units

The division (which includes the Historical Archive) holds documents on the history of Russian artillery from 1628 to the present day, which originated from the various offices of artillery administration in Russia. There include records of the seventeenth-century Gunnery (*Pushkarskii*) *prikaz*, the Artillery *prikaz*, the Main Artillery and Fortifications Chancellery (*Kantseliariia Glavnoi artillerii i fortifikatsii*), the Artillery Department (*Artilleriiskii departament*), the Headquarters of the Commander in Chief of the Artillery (*Shtab general-fel'dtseikhmeistera*), the Main Artillery Administration (GAU), with its various commissions, committees, and technical and military training schools. Materials on the history of the artillery for the years 1918–1940 are fragmentary. They include correspondence, technical journals, reports, and particularly technical drawings relating to the invention, improvement, and testing of new artillery and small arms.

   Apart from documentation originating from the artillery offices, the archive also contains some material that was once held in various regimental museums, as well as documents from the Imperial Russian Military History Society (*Imperatorskoe Russkoe voenno-istoricheskoe obshchestvo*), the Trophy Commission (*Trofeinaia komissiia*), and the archive of the former Military Museum of the Military Communications Academy (*Voennyi muzei Voennoi akademii sviazi*).

   There are the personal papers of military historians and archeologists, such as Lieutenant-General N. E. Brandenburg (1839–1903), who directed the museum starting in 1872, N. M. Pechenkin (1871–1918), and Major-General D. P. Strukov (1864–1920), who was secretary of the Military History Society, as well as a number of small fonds from such noted commanders as Generals of Infantry M. I. Dragomirov (1830–1905) and M. D. Skobelev (1843–1882), and Admiral F. F. Bellinsgauzen (Bellingshausen) (1778–1852), and from Russian and Soviet designers, such as Colonel-General V. G. Grabin (1900–1980) and Lieutenant-General V. G. Fedorov (1874–1966), who were both doctors of technical sciences.

   The museum possesses an extensive collection of photographs and graphic materials on the history of artillery, the engineer corps, and the signal corps. These include portraits of military commanders; drawings of battle scenes and military uniforms; technical drawings of firearms and side-arms, ammunition, and signalling equipment; and plans and drawings of plants, arsenals, and fortresses, covering a period from the eighteenth to the early twentieth centuries.

Reference Facilities: There is a complete list of fonds—"Spisok fondov Arkhiva VIMAIViVS" (59 prerevolutionary and 65 Soviet-period fonds) and a two-part register of *opisi*—"Kniga ucheta opisei Arkhiva VIMAIViVS." There are inventory *opisi*. Subject and name card catalogues include paragraphs from the 1957 guide, by origin and provenance of the materials, subject coverage of materials (1917–1956), and author files.

   Subject survey indexes include "Perechen' tematicheskikh ukazatelei arkhivnykh dokumentov Istoricheskogo arkhiva Artilleriiskogo istoricheskogo muzeia," consisting of 48 manuscript indexes, including ones on the history of Leningrad, textual drawings, great Russian commanders, men of the Russian artillery, Russian inventors, and M. V. Lomonosov, among others.

There are a number of thematic surveys of fonds. There are two unpublished catalogues, one covering documentation of military communications—"Katalog sredstv voennoi sviazi russkoi i sovetskoi armii" (1987), and one covering documentation from World War II—"Spravochnik po dokumentam Velikoi Otechestvennoi voiny 1941–1945" (1990).

A computerized database is being established for the division holdings.

Otdel fondov istorii inzhenernykh voisk (Vtoroi otdel fondov)
[Division of Fonds for the History of the Corps of Engineers (Second Division of Fonds)]

Telephone: 238-47-69
Hours: by appointment
Chief: Aleksei Alekseevich Denisenkov

HOLDINGS: ca. 23,000 units, 17th–20th cc.
documents of military units—ca. 2,500 units (1941–1945);
personal papers—2,800 units (18th–20th cc.); plans and drawings of fortresses—ca. 4,000 units (17th–20th cc.); photographs—ca. 1,500; artistic documents—ca. 10,000 units

The division holds materials on the history of military engineering and the Corps of Engineers, on types of equipment employed by the engineers, and on military operations from the seventeenth to the twentieth century. There is documentation relating to many fortresses, arsenals, and military factories, with documents, diagrams, plans and technical drawings showing fortifications and defense works in use in Russia during the eighteenth and nineteenth centuries.

There are personal papers of a number of prominent military engineers, technicians, and lecturers at the Nicholas Engineering Academy (from 1918—the V. V. Kuibyshev Military Engineering Academy [*Voenno-inzhenernaia akademiia im. V. V. Kuibysheva*]), including those of General K. A. Shil'der (Schilder) (1786–1854), the engineer and composer Major-General César Cui (Ts. A. Kiui) (1835–1918), Lieutenant-General K. I. Velichko (1856–1927), the professor and doctor of technical sciences, Lieutenant-General V. V. Iakovlev (1871–1945), Lieutenant-General D. M. Karbyshev (1880–1945), Colonel of the Engineers V. F. Shperk (1895–1978), Lieutenant-General and doctor of technical sciences S. A. Khmel'kov (1879–1945), and Major-General M. S. Ovchinnikov (1889–1963).

Among graphic materials there is an album of miniature watercolors entitled (in Russian) "A Collection of Plans of Fortresses on the Borders of the Russian Empire, Accompanied by Descriptions and Pointers Showing Permanent Gun Emplacements and the Deployment of Garrisons, with an Appended General Map and the Line Installations as of 1792," which was presented to Catherine the Great.

Reference Facilities: There is an unpublished catalogue of the engineering documentation, "Katalog inzhenerno-dokumental'nogo fonda russkoi armii" (1992), and reference card catalogues for documents relating to military operations of the Soviet Army engineering units (1989). A computerized database is being established for the division holdings.

Fototeka
[Photograph Archive]

Chief: Ivan Mikhailovich Portnov (*tel.* 238-46-35)

HOLDINGS: 215,000 units, mid-19th c.–1995
negatives and film footage—84,524 units (mid-19th c.–1994)

The Photograph Archive holds photographs and negatives showing artillery equipment, and engineering and signals technology employed from the sixteenth to the twentieth century. There are diagrams of military operations, portraits of prominent commanders, scholars, technicians, designers, and prominent historical personages. There are also reproductions of pictures and drawings on military themes, and prints of documents relating to the history of artillery and the engineer and signal corps.

Reference Facilities: There are subject and alphabetic catalogues for staff use.

FINDING AIDS — PUBLISHED — GENERAL:

Muzei SPb (1994), p. 163; *Biblioteki SPb* (1993), pp. 200–201; *Peterburg* (1992), p. 119; *Muzei Leningrada* (1989), pp. 110–16; G&K *Spravochnik* (1983), pp. 270–71; *Muzei Leningrada* (1982), pp. 46–48; PKG *M&L* (1972), pp. 350–51; Myl'nikov (1970), p. 33.

Historical Archive

h-470. *Putevoditel' po istoricheskomu arkhivu muzeia.* Compiled by A. P. Lebedianskaia, E. V. Rozenbetskaia, et al. Edited by I. P. Ermoshin. Leningrad, 1957. 235 p. (Lib: IU; MH) [IDC-R-10,932]

> A survey of materials in the archive dating from the seventeenth century to 1940, covering what is now part of the First Division of Fonds. See also the compiler's separate survey article, "Artilleriiskoe dokumental'noe nasledie v Istoricheskom arkhive Artilleriiskogo istoricheskogo muzeia," in [Leningradskii Dom uchenykh im. M. Gor'kogo, Voenno-istoricheskaia sektsiia], *Sbornik dokladov*, no. 1 (L., 1957), pp. 96–102.

General Guides to the Museum and its History

h-471. *Voenno-istoricheskii muzei artillerii, inzhenernykh voisk i voisk sviazi: Kratkii putevoditel'.* Compiled by V. N. Tiagunov, F. E. Pashko, M. A. Bogatenkov, et al. Edited by A. A. Sotnikov and A. A. Bumagin. 5th ed. Leningrad, 1966. 231 p. (Lib: IU; MH)

> EARLIER ED.: *Artilleriiskii istoricheskii muzei: Kratkii putevoditel'.* Edited by A. A. Bumagin. L., 1954. 82 p.

> A detailed tourist guide to the museum, but does not cover the archival materials. The earlier 1954 edition is much briefer.

h-472. Krylov, Valerii Mikhailovich. "Dlia pamiati na vechnuiu slavu." *Voenno-istoricheskii zhurnal*, 1998, no. 2, pp. 83–87. (Lib: DLC; MH)

> A brief report on the history of the museum with confirmation of its founding as the "Tseikhgaus" in 1703, and other details about the development of the museum and its holdings.

h-472.1. Chernov, I. "V Artilleriiskom istoricheskom muzee." 1960, no. 7, pp. 120–22. (Lib: DLC; MH)

> A brief report on the museum with mention of its archival holdings and publication activities.

h-473. Ermoshin, I. P. "Artilleriiskii istoricheskii muzei k 40-i godovshchine Vooruzhennykh Sil Sovetskogo Soiuza: (Istoriograficheskii ocherk)." *Sbornik issledovanii i materialov AIM* 2 (1958): 209–40.

h-474. Peshchanskii, Mikhail Aleksandrovich. *Artilleriiskii istoricheskii muzei: Kratkii istoricheskii ocherk s 1917 po 1927 gg.* Leningrad: Izd-vo AIM, 1927. 24 p.

h-475. Chugunov, I. P.; and Krylov, Valerii Mikhailovich. "Voenno-istoricheskii ordena Krasnoi Zvezdy muzei artillerii, inzhenernykh voisk i voisk sviazi." *Bezopasnost' i zhizn'*, 1995, no. 1, pp. 125–30; no. 2, pp. 179–81. (Lib: DLC)
A popular history of the museum during two centuries.

h-476. Strukov, Dmitrii P. *Putevoditel' po Artilleriiskomu istoricheskomu muzeiu.* St. Petersburg: Artilleriiskii muzei, 1912. 155 p. (Lib: DLC; MH)
The last guide published before 1917, with considerable detail about the holdings.

h-477. Brandenburg, Nikolai Efimovich. *Putevoditel' po S.-Peterburgskomu Artilleriiskomu istoricheskomu muzeiu. Otdel 1: Doistoricheskii.* St. Petersburg, 1902. [89] p.
The first published guide to the museum includes a survey of its exhibitions, part of which have since been transferred to other museums.

h-478. Brandenburg, Nikolai Efimovich. "Artilleriiskii muzei, ego proshedshee i nastoiashchee." *Artilleriiskii zhurnal*, 1876, no. 12, pp. 1355–56.

Library

h-479. Mazets, T. P. "Baza dlia nauchnoi raboty. (Biblioteka muzeia s 1876 g. do nashikh dnei)." *Sbornik issledovanii i materialov AIM* 5 (1990): 212–20.
A brief history of the library acquisitions and activities during the last century.

h-480. Sidorenko, E. G. "Biblioteka Artilleriiskogo istoricheskogo muzeia." *Artilleriiskii zhurnal*, 1954, no. 5, pp. 48–50. (Lib: IU; MH)
A brief history of the museum library, with a description of its holdings and activities.

Bibliography

h-481. Lebedianskaia, A. P. "Materialy dlia bibliografii Artilleriiskogo istoricheskogo muzeia RKKA i ego pamiatnikov." *Sbornik issledovanii i materialov AIM* 1 (1940): 270–77.
Includes references to descriptions and publications of archival materials (1835–1939).

Museum Series

h-482. *Sbornik issledovanii i materialov [Artilleriiskogo istoricheskogo muzeia Krasnoi Armii/ VIMAIViVS].* Moscow/Leningrad, 1940–. 8 vols. through 1997.
Vol. 1: ———. . . *Krasnoi Armii.* 1940; vols. 2–4: 1958–1959.
Vol. 5: *Sbornik issledovanii i materialov [VIMAIViVS].* 1990.
Vol. 6: *Sbornik issledovanii i materialov [VIMAIViVS].* SPb., 1993.
Vol. 7: *Sbornik issledovanii i materialov [VIMAIViVS].* 1996.
Vol. 8: *"Poveliteli ognia" (Posviashchaetsia 135-letiiu GRAU): Sbornik issledovanii i materialov [VIMAIViVS].* 1997.
A series of collected scholarly articles on military history predominantly based on materials in the museum. In addition to the articles listed below from earlier volumes, the fifth volume (1990) contains an article by S. V. Bazhen, "Perenesenie kollektsii voiskovykh muzeev v gosudarstvennye khranilishcha" (pp. 196–211), detailing the expansion of the collections after 1917.
Volume 7 includes an article by A. I. Gladkii, "Pervoe stoletie: Khronika primechatel'nykh sobytii v istorii muzeia," describing the museum's early development.

FINDING AIDS — SPECIALIZED:

Documentary Materials (Historical Archive)

h-483. *Katalog arkhivnykh dokumentov po Severnoi voine 1700–1721 gg.* Compiled by
E. V. Rozenbetskaia. Edited by I. P. Ermoshin et al. Leningrad, 1959. 433 p. [AIM]
(Lib: DLC; MH) [IDC-R-10,933]
> A detailed catalogue of the archival holdings relating to the Northern War covering the years
> 1700–1721.

h-484. *Arkhiv russkoi artillerii.* Vol. 1: *(1700–1718).* Compiled by D. Strukov. Edited by
N. Brandenburg. St. Petersburg: Tip. Artilleriiskogo zhurnala, 1889. 410 p. Only one
volume published. (Lib: DLC; IU; MH) [IDC-R-10,934]
> A detailed catalogue of holdings relating to the period 1700–1718, covering materials transferred to
> the museum from the archive of the Main Artillery Administration in 1873, among others.

h-484.1. Brandenburg, Nikolai Efimovich. *Materialy dlia istorii Artilleriiskago upravleniia v
Rossii: Prikaz artillerii (1701–1720 g.).* St. Petersburg: Tip. Artilleriiskago zhurnala, 1876.
v, 555 p. (Lib: MH)
> A detailed administrative history of the prikaz under Peter I, based on its records held by the museum
> with frequent citations to the relevant documents. Thirty-seven documentary appendices include key
> administrative regulations and descriptions of early munitions factories, among other subjects.

h-485. Chernukha, V. G. "Materialy arkhiva Artilleriiskogo istoricheskogo muzeia o voennykh
deistviiakh 1863 g. na Ukraine." In *K stoletiiu geroicheskoi bor'by 'Za nashu i vashu
svobodu': Sbornik statei i materialov o vosstanii 1863 g,* pp. 280–91. Moscow: "Nauka,"
1963. (Lib: DLC; IU; MH)
> Describes materials relating to the Polish rebellion of 1863 in the museum.

h-486. Prussak, A. V. "Obzor materialov Artilleriiskogo istoricheskogo muzeia po istorii
zavodov i remesel petrovskogo vremeni." *Sbornik issledovanii i materialov AIM* 1
(1940): 241–52.
> A detailed survey of materials on individual factories or workshops.

h-487. Lebedianskaia, A. P. " 'Report' 1757 o 'Dostopamiatnykh' orudiiakh v Orenburgskom
okruge (Iz materialov Arkhiva Artilleriiskogo istoricheskogo muzeia RKKA)." *Sbornik
issledovanii i materialov AIM* 1 (1940): 252–57.

h-488. Prussak, A. V. "Arkhiv Artilleriiskogo istoricheskogo muzeia kak istochnik po
izucheniiu Pugachevskogo dvizheniia." *Sbornik issledovanii i materialov AIM* 1
(1940): 263–69.

h-489. Makovskaia, Liliia Konstantinovna. "Arkhivnye dokumenty o kadetskikh korpusakh v
fondakh Voenno-istoricheskogo muzeia artillerii." *Bombardir*, 1995, no. 1, pp. 66–69.

Pictorial Materials

h-490. *Katalog proizvedenii izobrazitel'nogo iskusstva.* Book 2: *Risunki.* Edited by
A. A. Sotnikov. Leningrad, 1972. 757 p. "Katalogi Voenno-istoricheskogo muzeia
artillerii, inzhenernykh voisk i voisk sviazi."
> Describes a large part of the drawings and portraits held by the museum relating to Russian military
> history, from both prerevolutionary and Soviet periods. Organized thematically and chronologically,
> with name and geographic indexes.

Tsentral'nyi voenno-morskoi muzei (TsVMM)
[Central Naval Museum]

Agency: Ministerstvo oborony RF (Minoborony Rossii)
[Ministry of Defense]

Address:	199034, St. Petersburg, Birzhevaia pl., 4
Telephone:	328-25-01; 328-25-02 (inquiry office); *Fax:* (812) 328-27-01
E-mail:	museum@mail.admiral.ru
Website:	http://www.bestrussia.com/net/wmf/win.htm
Transport:	metro: Nevskii prospekt, Gostinyi Dvor, Vasileostrovskaia, Sportivnaia; trol.: 1, 7, 9, 10; bus: 10
Hours:	W–Su 10:30–17:30

Chief: Evgenii Nikolaevich Korchagin (*tel.* 328-27-01)
Scientific Secretary: Sergei Danilovich Klimovskii (*tel.* 328-27-02)
Chief of Division of Fonds: Kirill Alekseevich Tulin (*tel.* 328–24–02)

HISTORY:

Model'-kamora
　　[Model Chamber] (1709–1805)
Muzeum pri Admiralteiskom departamente
　　[Museum of the Admiralty Department] (1805–1817)
Morskoi muzeum
　　[Naval Museum] (1817–1827)
Model'-kamera
　　[Model Chamber] (1827–1867)
Morskoi muzei
　　[Naval Museum] (1867–1908)
Morskoi muzei im. Imperatora Petra Velikogo
　　[Emperor Peter the Great Naval Museum] (1908–1918)
Tsentral'nyi morskoi muzei Sovetskoi respubliki (TsMM)
　　[Central Naval Museum of the Soviet Republic] (1918–1923)
Morskoi muzei
　　[Naval Museum] (1923–1926)

The richest naval museum in the world began its history in 1709, when Peter the Great decided to build a "Model Chamber" for the purpose of storing technical drawings and models of all ships launched from his shipyards. In 1805 it was converted into a full-fledged museum attached to the Admiralty, and in 1817 named the Naval Museum. Over the years it began to acquire documents and items relating to the history of the Russian Fleet. In 1827, after the Decembrist Uprising, Emperor Nicholas I ordered the museum closed down (two of the Decembrists had worked in the museum), and parts of its collections were dispersed among other institutions or acquired by private individuals. Forty years later under a new emperor, the Naval Museum was revived and its exhibits and fonds created anew, and from 1908–1918 it bore the honorific name of Peter the Great.

After the October Revolution it became the Central Naval Museum of the Soviet Republic, and documents and exhibits from nationalized private collections and from the Hermitage and other museums were transferred to it. From 1923 to 1926 its name was changed back to its earlier form, and it came under the control of the People's Commissariat of the Navy. In 1926 it was given its present name—the Central Naval Museum. In 1939 it was moved into the historic building of the former Stock Exchange (*Fondovaia birzha*), which had been constructed in 1805–1810 on the design of the Swiss architect Jean-François Thomas de Thomon.

The museum currently has four branches:

(1) The Museum on the Cruiser "Aurora" (*Muzei na kreisere "Avrora"*), (197046, St. Petersburg, Petrogradskaia nab., tel. 230-84-40).

(2) The D–2 Submarine "Narodovolets" Museum (*Muzei "Podvodnaia lodka D–2 "Narodovolets"*) (199106, St. Petersburg, Vasil'evskii ostrov, Shkiperskii protok, 10; tel. 356-52-77).

(3) The Lifeline Museum (*Muzei "Doroga zhizni"*) (188675, Leningradskaia oblast', Vsevolozhskii raion, pos. Osinovets, st. "Ladozhskoe Ozero"; tel. [8-270] 69-466).

(4) The Kronstadt Fortress Museum (*Muzei "Kronshtadtskaia krepost'"*) (189610, Kronshtadt, Iakornaia pl., 1; *tel.* 236-47-13).

Access: Access to archival materials requires an official letter, stating the subject and purpose of the research, addressed to the museum chief.

Working Conditions: Fees are charged on an hourly basis for research for commercial purposes, but fees may be lowered or waived for academic research. All services by museum specialists are on a fee basis. Researchers are accommodated in the working premises, since there is no formal reading room. Files are normally delivered the day they are ordered.

Reference Facilities: In all the divisions there are official card catalogues (subject, chronological, and personal-name) inventory registers for staff use. A computerized database is currently being created covering the museum holdings.

Library Facilities: The museum library (ca. 15,000 vols.) holds literature on the history of the Navy, as well as maps and audiovisual materials.

Copying: Photographic and xerox copying facilities are available, although large-format technical drawings usually cannot be copied.

Sektor dokumentov i rukopisei
[Sector of Documents and Manuscripts]

Telephone: 328-24-02
Hours: WTh 9:30–16:00
Head: Elena Evgen'evna Galkina

HOLDINGS: 35,900 units, early 18th–20th cc.

The sector holds documents on the history of the Russian Fleet from the eighteenth to the twentieth centuries. They include original statutes, decrees, reports and other documentation issued by the naval agencies, together with documents relating to ships (logs and watch records); scientific writings written by seafarers, scholars, and shipbuilders; and biographical documents of admirals, officers, and seamen (including forms, autobiographies, charters, certificates, diaries, memoirs and recollections, and award attestations).

There are also the personal papers of the seafarer Iu. F. Lisianskii (1773–1837); the revolutionary P. P. Shmidt (1867–1906), and various Soviet commanders: Admiral L. M. Galler (1883–1950), Commander in Chief of the Baltic Fleet and Chief of Staff of the Navy; Admiral K. I. Dushenov (1895–1940), Commander in Chief of the Northern Fleet; Admiral P. I. Smirnov-Svetlovskii (1897–1943), Commander in Chief of the Volga and Dnieper Naval Flotillas; L. E. Berlin, Orientalist and organizer of the Volga-Kama Naval Flotilla; S. P. Lukashevich, Commissar for the North Sea Navy (1920) and author of the naval dictionary; and A. G. Golovko and Ts. L. Kunikov, who fought in the Second World War.

Sektor khraneniia fotografii i negativov
[Sector for Preserving Photographs and Negatives]

Telephone: 328-26-01
Hours: WTh 9:30–16:00
Curator: Larisa Ivanovna Bereznitskaia

HOLDINGS: over 180,000 units, late 1860s–1995

This sector holds documentary photographs on the history of the Russian Navy from the mid-nineteenth century to the present day. It contains photographs of the various stages of shipbuilding, as well as of naval campaigns and operations, round-the-world navigation, and geographic and scientific expeditions. There are photographs devoted to the revolutionary movement in the fleet and the latter's involvement in the Russian Revolution of 1905 and in the revolutions of February and October, 1917. The sector also holds material on naval operations during the Civil War and World War II, and on naval exercises, campaigns and maneuvres during the postwar years. There is a collection of the portraits of famous fleet commanders, shipbuilders, and sailors.

Sektor khraneniia chertezhei
[Sector for Preserving Technical Drawings]

Telephone: 328-26-01
Hours: WTh 9:30–16:00
Curator: Viacheslav Mikhailovich Zhezhel'

HOLDINGS: ca. 15,000 units, 1709–1990s

The fond holds original and copies of technical drawings of ships, models, dry-docks, and machinery used in shipbuilding and fleets in Russia from the eighteenth to the twentieth centuries. Among them are two student drawings of ships with the original autograph of Peter I (1709).

Sektor khraneniia proizvedenii izobrazitel'nogo iskusstva
[Sector for Preserving Works of Fine Arts]

Telephone: 328-26-01
Hours: WTh 9:30–16:00
Curator: Vera Borisovna Morozova

HOLDINGS: ca. 52,000 units, 18th c.–1900s

This sector holds pictorial materials on the history of the Russian fleet from the eighteenth through the twentieth century. These include drawings, watercolors, engravings, and lithographs done not only by famous artists, but also by seamen wishing to record the events of naval campaigns and operations. On exhibit are the watercolor drawings of A. Depal'do, a naval cadet, who painted the Black Sea Fleet under the command of F. F. Ushakov in its battles with the Turks on the Kerch Straits (1790) and at Cape Kaliakria (1791); the paintings of R. F. Frents, who depicted the events in Senate Square on December 14, 1825; and portraits by V. F. Timm, who painted the heroes of the Defense of Sebastopol (1854–1855).

Reference Facilities: A catalogue of the pictorial materials is being prepared for publication.

Sektor khraneniia modelei korablei i korabel'nykh priborov
[Sector for Preserving Model Ships and Naval Instruments]

Telephone: 328-24-02
Hours: ThF 9:30–16:00
Curator: Andrei Leonidovich Larionov

HOLDINGS: ca. 10 units, 1751–1807

This sector holds manuscripts and graphic documents on the history of shipbuilding in Russia (18th–20th cc.). Among its holdings are: a work by the geodesic specialist Petr Boi—"Rukovodstvo po morskim i voennym naukam" (1751); a manuscript of Iu. F. Lisianskii—"Opoznavatel'nye signaly" (1799); the navigation log of the sloop "Neva," under the command of Lt. Captain Iu. F. Lisianskii, during its round-the-world voyage (1803–1806); and the manuscript "Morskoi telegraf i signal'naia kniga" compiled by Vice-Admiral D. N. Seniavin during military operations of Russia against Turkey (1805–1807).

FINDING AIDS — PUBLISHED — GENERAL:

Muzei SPb (1994), pp. 168–71; *Biblioteki SPb* (1993), p. 200; *Peterburg* (1992), p. 653; *Muzei Leningrada* (1989), pp. 99–110; G&K *Spravochnik* (1983), p. 270; *Muzei Leningrada* (1982), pp. 40–46; PKG *M&L* (1972), p. 353; Myl'nikov (1970), p. 47.

There is no published guide to the archival materials in the museum. A catalogue of the pictorial materials in the Sector for Preserving Works of Fine Arts is being prepared for publication.

h-494. *Tsentral'nyi voenno-morskoi muzei: Putevoditel'.* Compiled by P. K. Azarov, M. A. Fateev, M. V. Konits, N. V. Moskvin, et al. Leningrad: Lenizdat, 1979. 215 p. (Lib: DLC)
A popular guide to the exhibits, which briefly recounts the history of the museum and its most interesting exhibits.

h-495. Kuleshov, I. M.; Kushnarev, E. G.; Marat, Kh. S., et al. *Tsentral'nyi Voenno-Morskoi muzei: Putevoditel'.* Leningrad: Lenizdat, 1968. 238 p. (Lib: MH)
A tourist guide to the museum exhibits.

h-496. Shapovalov, A. A.; and Larionov, A. A. "Tsentral'nyi Voenno-Morskoi muzei." *Voenno-istoricheskii zhurnal,* 1985, no. 7, pp. 93–96. (Lib: DLC; IU; MH)
A brief account of the history of the museum.

h-497. Ogorodnikov, S. F. *Model'-kamera, vposledstvii Morskoi muzei imeni Petra Velikogo: Istoricheskii ocherk, 1709–1909.* St. Petersburg, 1909. 96 p. (Lib: IU)

FINDING AIDS — SPECIALIZED:

h-498. *Zapiski muzeia.* Edited by I. M. Kuleshov, F. I. Demidov, et al. 3 vols. Leningrad, 1958–1968. [TsVMM]
Vol. 1: Edited by F. I. Demidov et al. L., 1958. 95 p.
Vol. 2: Edited by I. M. Kuleshov et al. L., 1960. 189 p. Vol. 3: L., 1968. 235 p.
The first volume has an historical survey on the establishment of the Kronstadt Fortress Museum and its holdings (pp. 9–91). The second volume, honoring the 250th anniversary of TsVMM, includes surveys of the history of the museum (pp. 7–12), the manuscript and documentary holdings (pp. 71–78), and the photographic holdings (pp. 104–15). The third volume describes posters from the early years of Soviet rule (pp. 207–20) and surveys documentary materials from RGAVMF (B–5) relating to the participation of sailors of the Baltic Fleet in the October Revolution in Petrograd (pp. 221–33).

Voenno-meditsinskii muzei (VMM)
[Military Medical Museum]

Agency: Ministerstvo oborony RF (Minoborony Rossii)
[Ministry of Defense]
Glavnoe voenno-meditsinskoe upravlenie (GVMU)
[Main Military Medical Department]

Address:	191180, St. Petersburg, Lazaretnyi per., 2
Telephone:	315-53-58; *Fax:* (812) 164-73-38; 310-20-25; *RdngRm:* 315-68-92
Transport:	metro: Pushkinskaia
Hours:	M–F 9:00–12:00, 13:00–17:00

Chief: Anatolii Andreevich Budko (*tel.* 315-67-28)
Deputy Chief for Scientific Research: Aleksei Alekseevich Arkhipenok (*tel.* 315-73-67)

HISTORY:

Muzei voenno-meditsinskoi sluzhby Krasnoi Armii
[Museum of the Military Medical Service of the Red Army] (II–IX.1943)
Voenno-meditsinskii muzei s nauchno-issledovatel'skimi otdelami po izucheniiu opyta voiny
[Military Medical Museum with Scientific Research Divisions for Study of the Experience of War]
(IX.1943–1948)
Voenno-meditsinskii muzei Vooruzhennykh Sil SSSR
[Military Medical Museum of the Armed Forces of the USSR] (1948–1953)

A museum-archive was organized within the medical services of the Red Army to provide for the scientific information and processing needs for medical records of wartime army medical brigades. The Military Medical Museum was first established in Moscow in February 1943 as the Museum of the Military Medical Service of the Red Army, and its first exhibits were opened in April in an evacuation hospital for the Western Front. Since October 1943, it has been called the Military Medical Museum, initially with separate research divisions to study wartime experience. It was transferred to Leningrad in 1945 and housed in a reconstructed building that had initially been used before 1917 as a military field hospital for the Semenov Regiment.

Opened to the public in 1951, the museum serves simultaneously as a scientific research center, a public museum for cultural enlightenment and military medical exhibits, and a reference center for medical records. The Archive of Military Medical Records is under the jurisdiction of the Military History Center of the Armed Forces under the General Staff (see *C–04).

The Scientific Library of the museum was started in Moscow in 1943 and transferred to Leningrad with the museum in 1945.

Access: Since 1982 the exhibition wing of the Military Medical Museum has been undergoing major renovation, but researchers can be accommodated and socio-legal and medical inquiries are being processed for veterans or members of the armed forces.

Permission to work with the archival materials must be obtained from the museum chief by a written request from a sponsoring organization, or a personal letter of application from private individuals, stating the theme and purpose of the intended research. Foreign researchers must obtain a letter from their sponsoring Russian organization.

Permission to consult specific documents and files in the Archive of Military Medical Records and in the Scientific Research Division of Fonds must be obtained from the museum chief or his deputy for scientific research work. Personal medical records of living individuals are legally subject to privacy considerations for 75 years after their creation.

All staff services to outside researchers are provided on a fee basis.

Copying: Photographic and xerox copies can be prepared for materials in all divisions.

Arkhiv voenno-meditsinskikh dokumentov
[Archive of Military Medical Records]

Telephone: 315-73-28
Hours: M–F 9:00–12:00, 13:00–17:00
Chief of Archive—Deputy Chief for Archival Work: Gennadii Aleksandrovich Dunin
(*tel.* 315-72-91)

HOLDINGS: ca. 8,300 fonds, ca. 57,000,006 units, 1939–1997

The Archive of Military Medical Records holds fonds with records of over 8,000 military units, institutions, and military medical administrative bodies starting with the period of military operations around the lake of Khasan (Hassan) in Manchuria (1938), the Khalkhin-Gol (Halhin-Gol) River on the Mongolian border (1939), and the Soviet-Finnish War (1939–1940). The largest documentation dates from the period of World War II (1939–1945). There are also records from postwar military engagements, such as the wars in Afghanistan, Tadzhikistan, Moldova (Pridnestrov'e), Northern Ossetia, and Chechnia, including service records and documentary reports of the sick and injured.

There are personnel files of medical service personnel from the Army and Navy, many of which also provide records of their earlier service careers in military medical institutions. These fonds also contain the medical histories of soldiers, officers, and non-commissioned officers, on the basis of which disability certificates were issued and other socio-legal inquiries are processed.

Working Conditions: Files should be ordered in advance in the reading room.

Reference Facilities: There are inventory registers and various card catalogues designated for staff use.

Nauchno-issledovatel'skii otdel sbora, nauchnoi obrabotki
i khraneniia muzeinykh fondov
[Scientific Research Division of Accession, Processing,
and Preservation of Museum Fonds]

Telephone: 315-69-48
Hours: M–F 9:00–12:00, 13:00–17:00
Chief: Vladimir Andreevich Egorov (*tel.* 315-69-48)

HOLDINGS: ca. 210,000 units, 1843–1990s (some documents 1792–1838)
personal papers—230 fonds; archival collections—ca. 25,000 units; photographs—ca. 110,000; films—30; graphics (drawings, watercolors, engravings)—ca. 1,700 units

Historical archival materials are held in the Scientific Research Division for Collection, Scientific Processing, and Preservation of Museum Fonds. Documentation in various collections, personal fonds, and audiovisual holdings pertains to the development of Russian military medicine from its beginnings to the present day, and show medical aid in practice both at the front and in the rear.

Documentary collections include eighteenth- and nineteenth-century medical textbooks, as well as a wide variety of other historic materials relating to military medicine.

There are 230 fonds with personal papers of army medical personnel (18th–19th cc.). These include fonds of such famous nineteenth- and twentieth-century doctors as N. I. Pirogov, S. P.

Botkin, G. I. Turner, V. A. Oppel', A. A. Vishnevskii, N. N. Burdenko, E. N. Pavlovskii, and L. A. Orbeli. Personal papers include medical studies and related materials (manuscripts of monographs and articles), biographical documents, correspondence, and memoirs.

The vast photographic holdings document work of the military medical services starting with the early twentieth century, but most of the photographs relate to the period of World War II. There is a special collection of pictures of statues, tombstones, and other memorials to military doctors throughout the former USSR.

Drawings retained are mostly those done at the front.

There are copies of films on the work of medical institutions and teaching hospitals, as well as the life and work of famous doctors.

Working Conditions: Researchers are accommodated in the staff working offices. Files should be ordered in advance.

Nauchnaia biblioteka
[Scientific Library]

Hours: M–F 9:00–12:00, 13:00–17:00
Head: Galina Konstantinovna Nesterenko (*tel.* 315-68-92)

HOLDINGS: ca. 2,300 units, 1940s–1990s
manuscripts—ca. 720 units (1946–1994); dissertations—ca. 1,500 units (1950–1981)

The Scientific Library (ca. 80,000 vols., including 4,500 pre-1917 imprints), in addition to published literature on medicine and especially military medicine, holds many unpublished works of the museum staff, including research work and surveys and catalogues of the manuscript collections in the museum. Of special note are the collected biographies of departmental heads in the Military Medical Academy (18th–20th cc.), prepared in the 1950s (14 vols.); the manuscript of V. I. Shestov's history of Russian military and naval medicine during the first half of the nineteenth century (6 vols., 1969); and some 50 unpublished bibliographic guides, compiled by A. V. Shabunin and others, to articles on the history of medicine published in periodical journals (19th–20th cc.). The library also retains dissertations defended at the Military Medical Academy and other institutions.

Working Conditions: Books and documentary materials are available in the reading room immediately after they have been ordered.

Reference Facilities: There are subject card catalogues on the history of military medicine, the history of medicine, typewritten works by museum staff, and personalia files of military doctors.

FINDING AIDS — PUBLISHED — GENERAL:

Muzei SPb (1994), p. 164; *Biblioteki SPb* (1993), p. 188; *Peterburg* (1992), p. 120; G&K *Spravochnik* (1983), p. 61; *Muzei Leningrada* (1982), p. 48–49.

h-499. Krutov, Valentin Sergeevich; and Troianovskaia, O. V. "AIPS v arkhive Voenno-meditsinskogo muzeia." *Otechestvennye arkhivy*, 1996, no. 5, pp. 103–105. (Lib: DLC; IU; MH)
A detailed account of the archive, predominantly from World War II.

h-500. Shabunin, A. V. *Voenno-meditsinskii muzei (1943–1993): Istoricheskii ocherk.* Edited by E. A. Nechaev. St. Petersburg: VMM MO RF, 1993. 160 p. [VMM] (Lib: DLC)
The first part covers the history of VMM, its precursors, its transfer from Moscow to Leningrad, and its development in the postwar decades; the second part describes the research, exhibition, and archival functions of the museum and how its holdings were collected. Includes a brief description of the

museum archives. Appendices give main dates in the VMM history, a chronological list of its directors and their deputies, and an alphabetical list of VMM staff who served for twenty or more years.

h-501. Varlamov, V. M. "Rozhdennyi v dni voiny." *Leningradskaia panorama*, 1986, no. 12, pp. 20–22. (Lib: DLC; IU; MH)

> A brief history of the establishment and organization of the museum, and the acquisition of holdings.

h-502. *Izdaniia Voenno-meditsinskogo muzeia: Bibliograficheskii spravochnik k 50-letiiu muzeia.* Compiled by A. V. Shabunin, I. V. Chernysheva, and G. K. Nesterenko. Edited by V. S. Krutov. St. Petersburg: VMM MO RF, 1992. 39 p. [VMM]

> A bibliography of VMM publications, arranged chronologically by years and alphabetically by authors within years. Includes a subject index.

World War II

h-503. *Lechebnye uchrezhdeniia Krasnoznamennogo Baltiiskogo flota v period Velikoi Otechestvennoi voiny 1941–1945 gg.: Spravochnik-ukazatel'.* Compiled by V. V. Fedotov, V. S. Stasevich, and V. V. Sosin. Edited by Iu. N. Vdovichenko and V. S. Krutov. Kaliningrad: Tip. gazety "Strazh Baltiki," 1994. 107 p. [Meditsinskaia sluzhba Baltiiskogo flota; VMM]

> A reference aid compiled from the VMM archives and other sources. Describes the institutions that were part of the medical services of the Baltic Fleet during World War II, with details about their organizational structure and changes during the course of the war, their initial locations at the outbreak of war and subsequent movements, and their medical evacuation work. Includes a geographic index.

h-504. *Voennye vrachi—uchastniki Velikoi Otechestvennoi voiny 1941–1945 gg.: Kratkii biograficheskii spravochnik.* Edited by V. S. Krutov and I. M. Chizh. 3 vols. St. Petersburg: VMM, 1995–1997. 203 p., 248 p., 148 p. [VMM] (Lib: DLC)

> A three-volume directory with short biographies of doctors in the military medical services (army and navy) during World War II, including those who provided medical care for the armed forces in front-line positions.

Personal Fonds

h-505. *Katalog personal'nykh fondov.* Compiled by G. S. Moroz. Edited by V. M. Varlamov. Leningrad: VMM MO SSSR, 1982. 132 p. [VMM]

> Describes the personal papers of 22 nineteenth- and twentieth-century military doctors (in alphabetical order)—with brief biographical data, data of the number of documents and their inclusive dates, and a brief annotation of each fond.

h-506. *Vospominaniia i dnevniki v fondakh muzeia: Katalog rukopisei.* Compiled by V. P. Gritskevich. Edited by N. V. Safonov, M. M. Kantorovich, et al. Leningrad: VMM MO RF, 1980. 310 p. [VMM] (Lib: IU)

> A catalogue of manuscript memoirs and diaries of 28 nineteenth- and twentieth-century doctors. Individual chapters are supplemented by published selections. Includes an index of names, as well as chronological and geographic indexes.

Pictorial (Graphic Art) Collections

h-507. *Katalog proizvedenii izobrazitel'nogo iskusstva (grafika).* Compiled by A. P. Voronina. Edited by F. A. Ivan'kovich. Leningrad: VMM MO SSSR, 1990. 134 p. [VMM MO SSSR] (Lib: DLC)

> A subject and chronological catalogue of the graphic works in the museum that are devoted to the work of military doctors from the Napoleonic War of 1812 to World War II and the postwar period. Includes alphabetic indexes of authors and personal names.

h-507A. *Pamiatniki voennym medikam: Spravochnik-katalog.* Compiled by V. A. Egorov and
G. I. Vinokurov. Edited by V. S. Krutov. St. Petersburg, 1995. 200 p. [VMM]
> A catalogue of monuments, both collective monuments, individual monuments, and tombstones
> honoring military doctors from the Napoleonic War of 1812 through World War II, located throughout
> the former USSR. Exact references are given to photographs (and in some cases related documentation)
> held in the museum. Includes identification of the doctors honored, and the sculptors or other artists
> who created the monuments. Geographic index.

FINDING AIDS — SPECIALIZED:

Specialized Biographical Directories

h-508. *Mediki—Geroi Sovetskogo Soiuza: Katalog.* Compiled by A. P. Voronina. Edited by
V. M. Varlamov. Leningrad: VMM MO SSSR, 1985. 139 p. [VMM MO SSSR]
> Information from the museum fonds on the life and work of military doctors who were named
> Heroes of the Soviet Union. The catalogue is arranged in alphabetical order of surnames.

h-509. *Voennye mediki—kavalery ordena Slavy trekh stepenei: Katalog.* Compiled by
M. M. Kantorovich. Edited by V. M. Varlamov. Leningrad: VMM MO SSSR, 1983. 35 p.
[VMM]
> A catalogue of documents, exhibits, and photographs arranged in alphabetical order by surnames.

h-510. *Sovetskie meditsinskie sestry, nagrazhdennye medal'iu Florens Naitingeil: Spravochnik
i katalog muzeinykh fondov.* Compiled by V. O. Aksinenko, A. A. Lopatenok, and
G. R. Nikolaev. Leningrad: VMM MO SSSR, 1989. 127 p. [VMM]
> Provides short biographies of Soviet nurses who were awarded the Florence Nightingale Medal
> from 1961 to 1987. Lists relevant archival documents and related museum exhibits.

Individual Personal Fonds

h-511. *Elanskii Nikolai Nikolaevich (1894–1964): Katalog personal'nogo fonda i
bibliograficheskii ukazatel'.* Compiled by A. P. Voronina and A. V. Shabunin. Edited by
V. S. Krutov. St. Petersburg: VMM MO RF, 1993. 64 p. [VMM]

h-511A. *Krotkov Fedor Grigor'evich (1896–1983): Katalog personal'nogo fonda i
bibliograficheskii ukazatel'.* Compiled by A. P. Voronina, V. S. Stasevich, S. V. Smolina,
and A. V. Shabunin. Edited by V. S. Krutov. St. Petersburg: VMM, 1995. 84 p.

h-512. *Kupriianov Petr Andreevich (1893–1963): Katalog personal'nogo fonda i
bibliograficheskii ukazatel'.* Compiled by A. P. Voronina and A. V. Shabunin. Edited by
A. F. Mefodovskii. St. Petersburg: VMM MO RF, 1992. 83 p. [VMM]

h-512A. *Oppel' Vladimir Andreevich (1872–1932): Katalog personal'nogo fonda i
bibliograficheskii ukazatel'.* Compiled by A. P. Voronina, N. M. Danilova, E. V. Zotova,
et al. Edited by V. S. Krutov. St. Petersburg: VMM, 1997. 96 p.

h-513. *Orbeli Leon Abragovich (1882–1958): Katalog personal'nogo fonda.* Compiled by
M. M. Kantorovich. Edited by N. V. Safonov. Leningrad: VMM MO SSSR, 1981. 41 p.
[VMM]

h-514. *Pavlovskii Evgenii Nikanorovich (1884–1965): Katalog personal'nogo fonda.*
Compiled by R. A. Kupchinskii. Edited by V. M. Varlamov. Leningrad: VMM MO SSSR,
1984. 63 p. [VMM]

h-514A. *Smirnov Efim Ivanovich (1904–1989): Katalog personal'nogo fonda i bibliograficheskii ukazatel'.* Compiled by A. P. Voronina and A. V. Shabunin. Edited by V. S. Krutov. St. Petersburg, 1994. 136 p.

h-515. *Solov'ev Zinovii Petrovich: Katalog personal'nogo fonda.* Compiled by A. P. Voronina. Edited by N. V. Safonov. Leningrad: VMM MO SSSR, 1976. 37 p. [TsVMU MO SSSR; VMM]

h-516. *Vishnevskii Aleksandr Aleksandrovich (1906–1975): Katalog personal'nogo fonda.* Compiled by M. Kh. Egorov and V. M. Varlamov. Leningrad: VMM MO SSSR, 1986. 42 p. [VMM]

Gosudarstvennyi memorial'nyi muzei oborony i blokady Leningrada (GMMOBL)
[State Memorial Museum of the Defense and Blockade of Leningrad]

Agency: Komitet po kul'ture Administratsii Sankt-Peterburga
[Committee on Culture of the Administration of St. Petersburg]

Address:	191028, St. Petersburg, Solianoi per., 9
Telephone:	273-76-47; *Fax:* (812) 275-84-82
Transport:	metro: Chernyshevskaia + bus 14, 46, 134 to "Ulitsa Furmanova"
Hours:	MTuTh–Su 10:00–17:00

Director: Anatolii Aleksandrovich Shishkin (*tel. / fax:* 275-84-82)

HISTORY:

Muzei oborony Leningrada
[Museum of the Defense of Leningrad] (1945–1952)

The predecessors of the museum were the various exhibitions that were held between 1941 and 1944 during the Seige (blockade and defense) of Leningrad. In 1945 materials from the exhibition "Heroic Defense of Leningrad" (*Geroicheskaia oborona Leningrada*), which had been held in 1944, formed the basis for the Museum of the Defense of Leningrad, which was officially opened in 1946. In 1949 the museum was closed to the public following the arrest of leading party officials in the city, in what became known as the Leningrad Affair, and repressive measures were taken against its directors. In 1952 the museum was closed down completely, and in 1953 its holdings were partially destroyed. What was left was transferred to a number of other museums: the Museum of the History of Leningrad (H–65), the Museum of the Great October Socialist Revolution (H–66), the Central Naval Museum (H–74), the Military History Museum of the Artillery, Corps of Engineers, and Signal Corps (H–73), and the State Russian Museum (H–89), among others. In 1989 the museum was revived—by decision of the Leningrad City Council—under the name of the State Memorial Museum of the Defense and Blockade of Leningrad.

Access: Access to archival materials requires an official letter addressed to the museum director stating the subject and aim of the research. For foreign researchers a letter from their Russian sponsoring institution is required.

Library Facilities: The library (ca. 15,000 vols.) collects literature on the subject matter of the museum, and includes the collections of L. V. Pokrovskii and the artist V. A. Ivanov.

Rukopisno-dokumental'nyi sektor
[Manuscript-Documentary Sector]

Telephone:	275-78-84
Hours:	by appointment
Curator:	Natal'ia Valentinovna Fedotova

HOLDINGS: 7,500 units, 1933–1990s

The Manuscript-Documentary Sector, which is part of the Division of Fonds (*Otdel fondov*), holds documents on the history of the defense and blockade of Leningrad. There are the memoirs and recollections of those who took part in the events, descriptions of military operations on the Leningrad Front, materials on the history of individual military units and partisan brigades, and the personal papers of those who lived in Leningrad during the blockade.

Working Conditions: Researchers are accommodated in the museum offices, where materials are delivered soon after they are ordered.

Reference Facilities: There are inventory *opisi* and catalogues.

Copying: There are no copying facilities.

FINDING AIDS — PUBLISHED — GENERAL:

Muzei SPb (1994), p. 122; *Biblioteki SPb* (1993), p. 59; *Peterburg* (1992), p. 401.

There is no published guide to the archival materials in the museum.

h-520. *Leningrad v bor'be mesiats za mesiatsem, 1941–1944.* Edited by A. R. Dzeniskevich. St. Petersburg: "Lans," 1994. 349 p. [Assotsiatsiia istorikov blokady i bitvy za Leningrad v gody Vtoroi mirovoi voiny; GMMOBL] (Lib: DLC)

h-521. Kutuzov, V. "Muzei oborony Leningrada." *Dialog,* 1988, no. 24, pp. 21–27.
Surveys the history of the organization and closure of the first Museum of the Defense of Leningrad (1946–1949), and its recent reestablishment.

Gosudarstvennyi memorial'nyi muzei A. V. Suvorova (GMM A. V. Suvorova)
[A. V. Suvorov State Memorial Museum]

Agency: Komitet po kul'ture Administratsii Sankt-Peterburga
[Committee on Culture of the Administration of St. Petersburg]

Address: 193015, St. Petersburg, ul. Saltykova-Shchedrina, 43
Telephone: 274-26-25; 279-39-14; *Fax:* (812) 274-28-50
Transport: metro: Chernyshevskaia; bus: 22, 46, 134; trol.: 15, 18, 49

Director: Aleksandr Ivanovich Kuz'min (*tel.* 274-26-28)
Chief Curator: Elena Alekseevna Vvedenskaia (*tel.* 274-26-82)

HISTORY:

Suvorovskii muzei pri Nikolaevskoi voennoi akademii
[Suvorov Museum under the Nicholas Military Academy] (1904–1918)
Gosudarstvennyi Voenno-istoricheskii muzei A. V. Suvorova
[A. V. Suvorov State Military History Museum] (1949–1991)

The museum was founded on the basis of an exhibition that was opened in 1900 at the Nicholas (Nikolaevskaia) Military Academy under the Army General Staff to mark the centennial of the death of the Russian military commander Aleksandr Vasil'evich Suvorov (1730–1800). Between 1901 and 1904 a special building, financed by public subscription, was constructed to house the new museum, which was opened in 1904 under the auspices of the Nicholas Academy. In 1918 the exhibits together with the Academy were evacuated to Ekaterinburg, and subsequently to Kazan, where they were captured by the White Army and taken to Vladivostok along with the Academy of the General Staff. In 1919 the museum building was turned over to the Petrograd Corps of Military Engineers, and the remaining property to the military section of the Division for Protection of Monuments of Art and Antiquity (*Otdel okhrany pamiatnikov isskustva i stariny*). In 1922 both the museum building and its property were assigned to the Division of Museums of the Petrograd Administration of Scientific Institutions (*Petrogradskoe upravlenie nauchnykh uchrezhdenii*) of the Academic Center under the People's Commissariat of Education.

In 1923 the property of the Nicholas Academy of the General Staff was transferred to the Military Academy of the Workers' and Peasants' Red Army (RKKA) in Moscow. Shortly afterwards the exhibits of the Suvorov Museum were returned to Petrograd, but the museum itself was not opened to the public. In 1925 its fonds were turned over to the Military Historical Daily-Life Museum (*Voennyi istoriko-bytovoi muzei*). In 1932 the building came under the control of the Lenin Military and Political Academy (*Voenno-politicheskaia akademiia im. Lenina*), and then it was used as a clubhouse for the Academy of Military Transport (*Voenno-transportnaia akademiia*). Later in the 1930s the building housed the Aircraft Museum (*Aeromuzei*), and in 1937 the exhibits of the Suvorov Museum were transferred to the Artillery History Museum (H–73). The building was damaged by a bomb in 1943, and was restored in 1950–1951, after which the museum was again opened to the public.

Access: Access to the archival materials requires an official letter addressed to the museum director, indicating the subject and aim of the research.

Library Facilities: The museum library was founded in 1904 and contains books on military history (20,000 vols.), including a number of rare imprints. It includes part of the collections of M. V. Leshkovskii and A. I. Liubimov. (Tel. 247-26-28).

Fond redkoi knigi, kinofotofononegateki, redkikh pechatnykh i rukopisnykh istochnikov
[Fond of Rare Books; Film, Photograph, Negative, and Sound Archives; and Rare Printed and Manuscript Sources]

Telephone: 274-26-31
Hours: by appointment
Curator: Konstantin L'vovich Koziurenok

HOLDINGS: 4,837 units, early 18th c.–1970s
basic fond—3,246 units (early 18th c.–1970s); auxiliary fond—1,591 units

The archival materials include documentation on the life and work of the eighteenth-century General and Supreme Commander (*Generalissimus*) of the Russian military forces, A. V. Suvorov, and the development of military science in Russia from the eighteenth to the twentieth century. The manuscripts are not assigned to a separate section, but included in the holdings of the rare books fond.

Among them are letters and documents relating to Suvorov and his relatives, including a number of Suvorov autographs, such as reports written or dictated by him regarding military operations, and letters to members of his family and relatives. There are a number of official awards and letters patent, including charters conferring upon him "the Key to Kobrin" and the titles of "Count of the Holy Roman Empire of the German Nation," and military rosters including his name in different military units in the course of his career. There are maps and diagrams of military campaigns and battles drawn by Suvorov himself. There are several journals and diaries of participants in the Swiss-Italian campaign of 1799, including General P. I. Bagration. There is a whole complex of documents relating to the Russian Army in the eighteenth and nineteenth centuries, as well as certificates of military decorations, and other materials relating to Suvorov's comrades-in-arms, P. I. Bagration, N. Griazev, and I. Grigorovich.

Among the personal papers of several of Suvorov's biographers or those who wrote about his military exploits, are those of Generals A. I. Mikhailovskii-Danilevskii, and A. F. Petrushevskii (among the most interesting archives in the museum), and military historian and astronomer V. P. Engel'gardt (Engelhardt) (including his correspondence with Petrushevskii). The papers of D. A. Miliutin include materials on the Russo-Austrian campaign in 1799 and drafts and fragments of his five-volume monograph on the Franco-Russian campaign in 1799 (published in St. Petersburg, 1852–1857). There are also papers of the military historian Colonel A. N. Orlov and the executor of Suvorov's estate, Count D. I. Khvostov.

Documentation on the history of the museum includes documents of the Suvorov Commission (1898–1904), which raised the public funding throughout the country for the building of the museum. There are some of the administrative records of the museum itself, along with archival materials, including pictorial and photographic materials.

Documents from the Soviet period relate to the military careers of the units and officers who were awarded the Order of Suvorov (founded in 1942) and to the partisan brigades bearing Suvorov's name. Among these are documents of N. I. Archakov, V. N. Kushnarenko, A. A. Novikov, V. Z. Romanovskii, and V. P. Sviridov. There is a special collection, "The Suvorov Legacy in the Soviet Armed Forces," with reference to a number of prominent Soviet military commanders.

Among pictorial materials are many portaits of Suvorov himself. There are photographs of Russian officers and military commanders as well as portraits of the Cavaliers of the Order of Suvorov.

Working Conditions: Researchers are accommodated in working premises, where materials are available the day they are ordered.

Reference Facilities: There are inventories and subject card catalogues, but manuscript materials are listed together with other materials in the general fond.

Copying: Xerox copies can be prepared.

FINDING AIDS — PUBLISHED — GENERAL:

Muzei SPb (1994), p. 165; *Biblioteki SPb* (1993), p. 201; *Peterburg* (1992), p. 600; *GAF Spravochnik* (1991), pp. 106–107; *Muzei Leningrada* (1989), pp. 116–19; *Muzei Leningrada* (1982), pp. 49–50; PKG *M&L* (1972), p. 352; Myl'nikov (1970), p. 32.

There is no published guide to the archival materials in the museum.

h-522. Meerovich, Grigorii Il'ich. *Muzei A. V. Suvorova: Istoriko-kraevedcheskii ocherk.* Leningrad: Lenizdat, 1981. 152 p. (Lib: DLC; MH)

h-523. Meerovich, Grigorii Il'ich. "Sobranie arkhivnykh dokumentov v Gosudarstvennom voenno-istoricheskom muzee A. V. Suvorova i ego ispol'zovanie v nauchno-issledovatel'skoi, ekspozitsionnoi i massovo-propagandistskoi rabote." In *Vsesoiuznaia konferentsiia-seminar "Arkhivnye fondy khudozhestvennykh muzeev SSSR,"* vol. 1, pp. 172–86. Moscow, 1981.

A brief survey of the archival materials in the museum relating to Suvorov, his biographers, and his military legacy.

h-524. Okhotnikov, I. V. *Muzei A. V. Suvorova.* Leningrad: Lenizdat, 1969. 83 p. "Turistu o Leningrade."

A short history of the museum and guide to the exhibits.

h-525. *Muzei A. V. Suvorova: Putevoditel'.* Compiled by A. M. Kuchumov and N. F. Kozhemiachenko. Leningrad: Lenizdat, 1954. 142 p. [Upravlenie kul'tury ispolkoma Leningradskogo gorodskogo soveta deputatov trudiashchikhsia]

Muzei istorii militsii Glavnogo upravleniia vnutrennikh del Sankt-Peterburga i Leningradskoi oblasti
[Museum of the History of the Militia of the Main Administration of Internal Affairs of St. Petersburg and Leningrad Oblast]

Agency: Ministerstvo vnutrennikh del RF (MVD Rossii)
[Ministry of Internal Affairs]
Glavnoe upravlenie vnutrennikh del Sankt-Peterburga i Leningradskoi oblasti
[Main Administration of Internal Affairs of St. Petersburg and the Leningrad Oblast]

Address:	193024, St. Petersburg, ul. Poltavskaia, 12, Dvorets kul'tury im. F. E. Dzerzhinskogo
Telephone:	277-78-25
Transport:	metro: ploshchad' Vosstaniia; trol.: 1, 14, 22; bus: 26
Hours:	M–F 9:30–18:15 (by appointment)

Chief: Valerii Pavlovich D'iachkov (*tel.* 279-42-33)
Deputy Chief: Viktor Vasil'evich Merkushev (*tel.* 277-78-25)
Head of Division of Fonds: Anatolii Ivanovich Khorev (*tel.* 277-78-25)

HISTORY:

Muzei Krasnoznamennoi Leningradskoi militsii GUVD Lenoblgorispolkomov
[Museum of the Red Banner Leningrad Militia of the Main Administration of Internal Affairs of the Leningrad City and Oblast Executive Committee] (1977–1992)

The Museum of the History of the Militia was founded in 1976 as a structural subdivision of the Main Administration for Internal Affairs of the Leningrad City and Oblast Executive Committee (*Lenoblgorispolkomy*)—since 1992 of St. Petersburg and Leningrad Oblast. It was opened to the public in 1977.

HOLDINGS: ca. 3,500 units, 1917–1990s
personal papers—ca. 600 units; negatives—2,719

In its Depository of Fonds (*Fondokhranilishche*) the museum holds documents and photographs relating to the history of the militia under the Main Administration of Internal Affairs in St. Petersburg and Leningrad Oblast. Documentation relates to such varied matters as criminal investigation, militia participation in military operations during the World War II, and the training of police dogs. There are administrative documentation and biographical materials on NKVD/ MVD veterans, including promotions and awards, letters, memoirs and recollections, photographs, among others. There are also documents (mainly photographs) on the history of the St. Petersburg police in the late nineteenth and early twentieth century.

Access: Access to work with archival materials requires a letter addressed to the museum chief stating the subject and purpose of the research.

Working Conditions: Researchers are accommodated in museum offices, where documents are delivered soon after they are ordered.

Reference Facilities: Opisi are available.

Library Facilities: There is a small specialized library containing literature on the profile of the museum, which is accessible to readers.

Copying: The museum has no facilities for photographic or xerox copying. Sponsoring organizations, however, may apply for researchers to use their own copying equipment, for which a charge is made.

FINDING AIDS — PUBLISHED — GENERAL:
Muzei SPb (1994), p. 136; *Peterburg* (1992), pp. 400–401.

There is no published guide to the archival materials in the museum.

h-526. *Muzei istorii Krasnoznamennoi Leningradskoi militsii: [Ekspozitsiia].* Leningrad: "Khudozhnik RSFSR," 1983. 31 p. [MVD SSSR; GUVD Lenoblgorispolkoma; Upravlenie politiko-vospitatel'noi raboty]
> A brief tourist pamphlet describing only the museum exhibits.

Historico-Architectural Museums and Palace Museum-Preserves

❦❧ H–79 ❧❦

Gosudarstvennyi dvortsovo-parkovyi muzei-zapovednik "Gatchina" (GMZ "Gatchina")
[Gatchina State Palace-Park Museum-Preserve]

Agency: Komitet po kul'ture Administratsii Sankt-Peterburga
[Committee on Culture of the Administration of St. Petersburg]

Address: 188350, Leningradskaia oblast', g. Gatchina, Ekaterinverderskii (*formerly* Krasnoarmeiskii) prosp., 1
Telephone: (812-71) 215-09; *Fax:* (812-71) 223-21; 216-88
Website: http://alexanderpalace.org/gatchina
Transport: suburban train from Baltic station
Hours: MW–F 10:00–16:00

Director: Nikolai Sergeevich Tret'iakov (*tel.* [812-71] 215-09)
Deputy Director for Scientific Work: Tat'iana Dmitrievna Kozlova (*tel.* [812-71] 138-23)
Chief Curator: Adelaida Sergeevna Elkina (*tel.* [812-71] 218-48, 136-81)
Curator, Fond of Graphics, Manuscripts, and Rare Books:
Valentina Vladimirovna Fedorova (*tel.* [812-71] 218-48)
Curator, Photograph and Negative Archive:
Irina Eduardovna Ryzhenko (*tel.* [812-71] 136-81)

HISTORY:

Gatchinskii khudozhestvenno-istoricheskii muzei
[Gatchina Art-Historical Museum] (1918–1930)
Gatchinskii dvorets-muzei i park
[Gatchina Palace-Museum and Park] (1930–1941)
Gosudarstvennyi Gatchinskii dvorets-muzei i park
[Gatchina State Palace-Museum and Park] (1985–1993)

Until 1716 Gatchina was a country house belonging to Natal'ia Alekseevna, the sister of Peter the Great. In 1734 it passed into the hands of the Kurakin family, and in the mid-1760s to Count G. G. Orlov, who began building a palace and park on the grounds, originally designed by Antonio Rinaldi and later transformed by Vincenzo Brenna. Catherine II bought the estate in 1783 and presented it to her heir, Pavel Petrovich (the future Emperor Paul I). In 1796 Paul I decided to transform his residence into a town. In the mid-nineteenth century the whole ensemble was rebuilt by R. I. Kuz'min.

After nationalization following the Revolution, the museum was founded in 1918 as the first Historical Daily-Life and Art Palace-Museum in the environs of Petrograd under the name of the Gatchina Art-Historical Museum. Some of the imperial furnishings and library were turned over to the Hermitage, and some, unfortunately, later went to the All-Union Antiquarian Company (*Vsesoiuznoe obshchestvo "Antikvariat"*) and were sold abroad.

In 1923 the town Gatchina was renamed Trotsk, and in 1929 Krasnogvardeisk, which it remained until 1944. The palace, however, retained the name of Gatchina. During the 1930s the museum was known as the Gatchina Palace-Museum. At the beginning of the war, in 1941 the contents of the Palace-Museum were moved to St. Isaac's Cathedral, while the more valuable exhibits were evacuated for safekeeping to Sarapul. Some of the exhibits and the remaining part of the library were removed by the Nazi invaders.

The palace, the pavilions, and the park were badly damaged during the Second World War. Some partial restoration work was done, but from 1950 to 1985 the palace was used for other purposes. As a result of wartime displacements and the fact that the palace was not immediately restored as a museum, many of the archival materials, together with the remaining exhibits, were scattered in different places.

Serious restoration work begun in the 1970s, and in 1985 a museum was reopened in the palace. Many of the exhibits and manuscript materials began to be returned from the State Hermitage, the Tsarskoe Selo Museum-Preserve, the museums of the Moscow Kremlin, and other places. However, a large part of the archival materials and library (including portions returned from abroad) remain in the Pavlovsk Palace-Museum, and many others are missing (including those sold abroad). The present name of the museum dates from 1993, and restoration continues.

N.B. Prerevolutionary records of the Gatchina Palace Administration and documents on the history of the architectural monuments at Gatchina are held in RGIA (B–3, fond 493). The administrative records of the museum from the Soviet period (1917–1931, 1934–1972) are held in TsGALI SPb (D–15, fond 309). Documentation on the fate of the palace during and after World War II can be found in the fond of the Central Repository for Museum Fonds of the Leningrad Suburban Palaces under the Cultural Administration of the Leningrad City Executive Committee (*Tsentral'noe khranilishche muzeinykh fondov Leningradskikh prigorodnykh dvortsov Upravleniia kul'tury Lengorispolkoma*) (TsGALI SPb, fond 387; 1943–1956).

HOLDINGS: ca. 4,000 units, 1749–1990s

manuscripts—346 units (1783–1895); watercolors and miniatures—309 units (18th c.); prints—459 units (18th–20th cc.); photographs and negatives—1,450 (19th–20th cc.); technical drawings—ca. 1,300 units (18th–20th cc.)

Archival materials are all considered part of the general Division of Fonds of the museum, although they are actually retained in the Fond of Manuscripts, the Fond of Watercolors and Drawings, the Fond of Technical Drawings, the Fond of Engravings, the Fond of Rare Books, the Fond of Photographs and Negatives, and the archive of the Scientific Division of the museum.

The Fond of Manuscripts contains documents from the Tower Cabinet (*Bashennyi kabinet*) of Paul I in the Gatchina Palace and part of the archive of the Gatchina Palace Administration (*Gatchinskoe dvortsovoe pravlenie*) (1783–1845, 1895). They include documentation on those serving in the palace military units and the palace guard, accounts of military maneuvres, descriptions of the estate, and documents relating to economic and property management. Among the manuscripts are "A Shoreline Inventory of the Gatchina Lakes" (*Beregovaia opis' Gatchinskikh ozer*) (1783), which contains an account of the estates owned by Count G. G. Orlov, and daily reports on construction of the palace and park during the years 1793–1795. There is also a fond with materials relating to Lieutenant-General M. M. Borozdin, a hero of the Napoleonic War of 1812, containing the family tree of the Borozdin family as well as letters and orders issued by Catherine II, Paul I, Maria Fedorovna, Alexander I, and Nicholas I.

The Fond of Watercolors and Drawings contains a late eighteenth-century "Atlas of the Gatchina Palace" (*Atlas Gatchinskomu dvortsu*), compiled by Admiral Count G. G. Kushelev for Paul I, and a travel album with drawings by the architect N. A. L'vov, which was compiled during his journey back and forth from St. Petersburg to the estate of Nikol'skoe near Torzhok (1789–1803).

The Fond of Technical Drawings contains draft plans for buildings erected in St. Petersburg and its suburbs (mid-18th–19th c.). They include plans for the facade and drafts for the interior decoration of the Winter Palace (including the Throne Room by Giacomo Quarenghi); draft designs for the banqueting tables in the Winter and Summer Palaces in St. Petersburg and the Kremlin Palace in Moscow done by Bartolomeo Francesco Rastrelli in the time of the Empress Elizabeth (Elizaveta Petrovna); and plans and facades for the palaces at Oranienbaum and Ropsha. There are also plans and copies of designs for town, palace, and park buildings at Gatchina (late 18th c.–late 19th c.), which have been signed by such architects as Vincenzo Brenna and A. M. Baikov (some of these bear the signature of approval of the Empress Maria Fedorovna), N. V. Dmitriev, and R. I. Kuz'min. There are also the draft plans for the St. Petersburg Synagogue (late 19th c.).

The Fond of Engravings contains the original works of a number of Russian nineteenth- and twentieth-century artists depicting full-dress military uniforms from the time of Paul I and Alexander I done in watercolors and gold.

Manuscript inventories of the palace furniture (1917–1925 and 1938–1940) have been preserved. The auxiliary fond has an album with photographs of Gatchina from the late nineteenth century, as well as pre- and postwar photographs and negatives of the palace and parks, the interior decoration, sculpture, and other exhibits in the museum collections. Recently the museum received as a gift from Elizabeth II, Queen of England, duplicates of photographs showing the visits of the last Russian emperors to Gatchina.

Access: A letter addressed to the director is required for access to archival materials in the museum, stating the purpose of research. There is an access fee, and if archival material is to be published, the conditions must be agreed upon with the administration.

Working Conditions: Researchers are accommodated in working offices of the Division of Fonds, where as a rule, materials are available soon after they are ordered.

Reference Facilities: There are card catalogues and inventories for staff use. A computerized database describing the archives is currently being compiled.

Library Facilities: An auxiliary library (4,300 volumes) was founded at the same time as the museum on the basis of book collections from the Gatchina Palace (started late 18th c.) containing the personal libraries of Paul I, Empress Maria Fedorovna, Alexander III, Grand Duke Michael (Mikhail) Aleksandrovich, and Nicholas II. The library contains books on history, military history, and art. (Tel. [8-271] 238-48)

Copying: There are no copying facilities in the museum. Copies, however, may be made for an additional charge, if researchers have their own equipment.

FINDING AIDS — PUBLISHED — GENERAL:

Muzei SPb (1994), p. 65; *Biblioteki SPb* (1993), p. 60; *Peterburg* (1992), p. 145; *GAF Spravochnik* (1991), p. 131; *Muzei Leningrada* (1982), pp. 94–96.

There is no published guide of the archival materials in the museum.

h-528. *Gatchina.* Compiled by A. S. Elkina (Iolkina) and N. S. Tretiakov (Tretyakov). 127 p. + plates. In: *Imperial Palaces in the Vicinity of St. Petersburg: Watercolours, Paintings and Engravings from the XVIIIth and XIXth Centuries* (4 vol. boxed set), edited by Emmanuel Ducamp. Paris: Alain de Gourcuff, 1992. (Lib: MH)

> An elaborate album of illustrations from prerevolutionary engravings and watercolors with an introductory essay and annotations in English. Includes indexes of artists and engravers.

h-529. Kiuchariants, Dzhul'etta Arturovna; and Raskin, Abram Grigor'evich. *Gatchina: Khudozhestvennye pamiatniki.* Leningrad: Lenizdat, 1990. 238 p. (Lib: DLC; IU; MH)

A popular account of the history of Gatchina and its palace and park ensemble based on a study of archival and literary sources.

h-530. Makarov, Vladimir Kuz'mich; and Petrov, Anatolii Nikolaevich. *Gatchina.* Leningrad: "Iskusstvo," 1974. 101 p. + 85 plates. Summary and list of illustrations in English, French, and German. (Lib: MH)

> An introductory history of the palace based on archival sources with references to available materials. Includes a brief bibliography and index of names.

h-531. Piriutko, Iurii Minaevich. *Gatchina: Khudozhestvennye pamiatniki goroda i okrestnostei.* 2d ed. Leningrad: Lenizdat, 1979. 143 p. + 46 plates. (Lib: MH)

> 1st ED.: L.: Lenizdat, 1975. 134 p. + 24 plates. (Lib: MH).

> A guide to places of interest in Gatchina and the surrounding region. Contains a detailed history of the park and palace ensemble and of the town of Gatchina.

h-532. Pomarnitskii, Andrei Valentinovich. *Gatchinskii dvorets-muzei i park: [Putevoditel'].* [Leningrad]: Lenizdat, 1939. 84 p.

> LATER VERSION: Balaeva, S. N.; and Pomarnitskii, Andrei Valentinovich. *Gatchina.* Moscow: "Iskusstvo," 1952. 86 p. + plates. "Pamiatniki russkoi khudozhestvennoi kul'tury." (Lib: MH).

> The exceedingly brief guide describes the prewar collections, parts of which were destroyed or lost during the war. The postwar 1952 publication includes some of the same illustrations and relates wartime losses, but it was prepared before the palace was restored as a museum.

h-532.1. *Gatchina pri Pavle Petroviche, Tsesareviche i Imperatore.* Compiled by S. Kaznakov, N. Lansere, G. Pine, A. Trubnikov, and P. Veiner. Edited by A. A. Alekseev. St. Peterburg: LIGA, 1995. 350 p. "Mramornaia seriia." (Lib: MH)

> A collection of well-illustrated and annotated essays reprinted from *Starye gody* (July–Sept. 1914), with bibliographical references and an introduction by the editor.

Gosudarstvennyi muzei-zapovednik "Oranienbaum" (GMZ "Oranienbaum")
[Oranienbaum State Museum-Preserve]

Agency: Komitet po kul'ture Administratsii Sankt-Peterburga
[Committee on Culture of the Administration of St. Petersburg]

Address:　　189510, St. Petersburg, Lomonosov, Dvortsovyi prosp.
　　　　　　　(*formerly* prosp. Iunogo Lenintsa), 48
Telephone:　422-47-96; *Fax:* (812) 423-16-18; 422-47-96
Transport:　suburban train from Baltic Station to Oranienbaum
Hours:　　　MW–F 11:00-17:00

Director: Valerii Vasil'evich Chel'tsov (*tel.* 423-16-25)
Deputy Director for Scientific Work: Liudmila Alekseevna Savonovich (*tel.* 423-47-96)
Chief Curator: Vera Sergeevna Liskova (*tel.* 422-37-53)

HISTORY:

Oranienbaumskie dvortsy i parki
　[Oranienbaum Palaces and Parks] (1918–1941)
Oranienbaumskie dvortsy-muzei i parki
　[Oranienbaum Palace-Museums and Parks] (1944–1948)
Dvortsy-muzei i parki g. Lomonosova
　[Lomonosov Palace-Museums and Parks] (1948–1984)
Gosudarstvennyi khudozhestvenno-arkhitekturnyi dvortsovo-parkovyi muzei-zapovednik v g. Lomonosove
　[State Art-Architectural Palace-Park Museum-Preserve in Lomonosov] (1984–1993)

The palace of Oranienbaum (the town was renamed Lomonosov in 1948 in honor of M. V. Lomonosov), originally belonged to Prince A. D. Menshikov, and was one of the finest Russian estates of the eighteenth century. The Great Palace was built in 1713–1725 by Giovanni Maria Fontana and Gottfried Schädel, but later rebuilt in the 1770s by Antonio Rinaldi. In 1723 Oranienbaum was taken over by the state and became an imperial residence (1743–1761—the summer residence of Grand Duke Peter [Piotr] Fedorovich, later Emperor Peter III; and after 1832— Grand Duke Michael [Mikhail] Pavlovich and his heirs), but from the end of the nineteenth century through 1917 it was owned by the Dukes of Mecklenburg-Strelitskii. From 1780 to 1796 and from 1802 to 1848 Oranienbaum was considered a city administrative district (*uezdnyi gorod*) within St. Petersburg Guberniia.

A museum was founded in August 1918 on the basis of the park and palace complex, which had been nationalized by the state under the Administration of the Oranienbaum Palaces and Parks. In 1927 Oranienbaum became a raion center in Leningrad Oblast, but from 1927 to 1939 and from 1941 to 1945 the museum was under the control of the Administration of the Peterhof Palace-Museums. During that period only the Chinese Palace was open to the public, since the main Oranienbaum Palace was territorially located in a frontier zone where special permission was required for entry. The so-called Oranienbaum Corridor did not fall under German occupation during World War II, and for this reason the palaces, museums, and parks were only partially damaged. Restoration work began in 1944, and in 1953 the Palace of Peter III was opened to the public. This was followed in 1959 by the opening of the Switchback Pavilion (*Katal'naia gorka*). After the war a number of the palaces and other buildings were used for various non-museum purposes, and consequently restoration work continues to the present. The Oranienbaum State Palace-Park Preserve reverted to its traditional name in 1993, but as of the end of 1998, the town itself retains the name of Lomonosov.

N.B. Prerevolutionary records of the Oranienbaum Palace Administration for the years 1796–1917 are held in RGIA (B–3, fond 492—2,472 units), which also includes the documents and records of the Oranienbaum Administrative Office under Peter III (1748–1796). The administrative records of the Oranienbaum museums for the years 1940–1974 are held in TsGALI SPb (D–15, fond 102). Documentation on the fate of palace during and after World War II can be found in the fond of the Central Repository for Museum Fonds of the Leningrad Suburban Palaces under the Cultural Administration of the Leningrad City Executive Committee (*Tsentral'noe khranilishche muzeinykh fondov Leningradskikh prigorodnykh dvortsov Upravleniia kul'tury Lengorispolkoma*) (TsGALI SPb, fond 387; 1943–1956).

For the Museum of the History of the Town of Lomonosov (Oranienbaum), which also holds materials relating to the palace museum-preserve, see H–69.

Access: Research access requires an official letter to the director of the museum-preserve, stating the subject and purpose of research. Foreign citizens are required to have a letter from their Russian sponsoring organization, which must be endorsed by the director.

Working Conditions: Researchers are accommodated in the museum offices, where materials are available the day they are ordered.

Reference Facilities: There are inventories for staff use and reference card catalogues.

Library Facilities: The book fond (ca. 2,200 vols.), which is administratively part of the Auxiliary Fond, contains art, historical and reference literature in Russian and a number of foreign languages (1920s–1990s), as well as a small number of prerevolutionary publications dating back to 1891.

Copying: The museum has no copying facilities.

Osnovnoi muzeinyi fond
[Basic Museum Fond]

Hours: by appointment
Chief Curator: Vera Sergeevna Livkova (*tel.* 422-37-53)
Curator of the Rare Book Fond: Ol'ga Vladimirovna Sidorenko

HOLDINGS: ca. 600 units, late 18th c.–1917
manuscripts—90 units (1796–1917); photographs—226 (early 19th–early 20th cc.); drafts—226 units (late 18th–late 19th cc.)

Within the Basic Museum Fond, the Rare Books Fond retains some files of the Oranienbaum Palace Administration (*Oranienbaumskoe dvortsovoe pravlenie*) (1796–1917, 90 files), including inventories of the palace and park buildings, construction and restoration plans, blueprints and technical drawings (late 18th c.–late 19th c.), and photographs (late 19th c.–early 20th c.). There are also draft plans for the Great Menshikov Palace at Oranienbaum, which was built by E. Preis and Oscar Gustav (O. E.) Paulson during the second half of the nineteenth century.

The Graphic Arts Fond contains folders with scaled projections of the palace and park ensemble done by the French topographic engineer Pierre-Antoine de Saint-Hilaire during the last quarter of the eighteenth century and technical drawings made by the architect Antonio Rinaldi in 1772.

Nauchno-vspomogatel'nyi fond nauchno-fondovogo otdela
[Scientific Auxiliary Fond of the Scientific Fonds Division]

Telephone: 422-37-53
Hours: MW–F 10:00–16:00
Head: Nadezhda Ivanovna Belogubtseva

HOLDINGS: ca. 15,000 units, 1928–1993

manuscripts—737 units (1928–1993); photographs—2,124 (1946–1992); drafts—2,425 (1946–1993); negatives—4,814 (1946–1993)

The Scientific Auxiliary Fond includes reports of the academic staff of the museum on the history of the building of the Oranienbaum ensemble and the restoration work done to the architectural monuments and their interiors. There are technical drawings, sketches, blueprints, estimates and other technical documentation on the restoration of the palaces and of individual works of art. There are also materials on the evacuation of museum exhibits during the war, postwar inventories, plans for exhibitions and displays, and other documentation on the work of the Oranienbaum museums.

The Photograph Archive (*fototeka*) contains a small number of photographs of the Dukes of Mecklenburg-Strelitskii, who owned the palaces in the late nineteenth century. There is an album with pictures of the town of Oranienbaum, as well as photographs of holiday resorts in Germany, Switzerland, Italy and other European countries taken at the turn of the century. The postrevolutionary period is represented by prints and negatives of architectural monuments, palace interiors, the park and outbuildings, and various ornamental *objets d'art.*

FINDING AIDS — PUBLISHED — GENERAL:

Muzei SPb (1994), p. 63; *Peterburg* (1992), pp. 353–54; *GAF Spravochnik* (1991), pp. 131–32; *Muzei Leningrada* (1989), pp. 202–207; *Muzei Leningrada* (1982), pp. 92–94.

There is no published guide to the archival materials in the museum-preserve.

h-533. Kiuchariants, Dzhul'etta Arturovna. *Khudozhestvennye pamiatniki goroda Lomonosova.* Leningrad: Lenizdat, 1985. 174 p. + 48 plates. (Lib: DLC; IU; MH)

> EARLIER ED.: L., 1980. 167 p. + 48 plates. (Lib: MH)

> This guide, based on extensive use of archival documentation, describes many of the architectural monuments of the museum-preserve and the town of Lomonosov. Includes bibliography of earlier literature.

h-534. Raskin, Abram Grigor'evich. *Gorod Lomonosov: Dvortsovo-parkovye ansambli XVIII veka.* 2d ed. Leningrad: "Iskusstvo," 1981. 136 p. Summaries in English, French, and German. (Lib: IU)

> 1st ED.: L., 1979. 136 p. + plates. (Lib: DLC; MH)

> An elaborate album of pictures with a detailed introduction regarding the palace-park ensemble (pp. 5–43). English, French, and German resumés. Includes bibliography of earlier guides and related literature.

Gosudarstvennyi muzei-zapovednik "Pavlovsk" (GMZ "Pavlovsk")

[Pavlovsk State Museum-Preserve]

Agency: Komitet po kul'ture Administratsii Sankt-Peterburga
[Committee on Culture of the Administration of St. Petersburg]

Address: 189623, St. Petersburg, Pavlovsk, ul. Revoliutsii, 20
Telephone: 470-21-55, 470-60-55; *Fax:* (812) 470-29-61
Website: http://www.bestrussia.com/net/pavlovsk/win.htm;
http://www.alexanderpalace.org/pavlovsk/menu.htm
Transport: suburban train from Vitebsk Station; or metro: Kupchino + suburban train from Kupchino RR platform to Pavlovsk + bus: 370, 383
Hours: M–ThSaSu 10:00–17:00 (research by appointment)

Director: Iurii Vital'evich Mudrov (*tel.* 470-21-55)
Chief Curator: Aleksei Nikolaevich Guzanov (*tel.* 470-63-25)
Curator, Painting and Graphic Fond: Nina Ivanovna Stadnichuk (*tel.* 470-60-55)
Curator, Photograph Fond: Ol'ga Ivanovna Lebedeva (*tel.* 470-60-55)

HISTORY:

Pavlovskii dvorets-muzei i park
[Pavlovsk Palace-Museum and Park] (1918–1941, 1945–1957)
Pavlovskii park i muzei khudozhestvennogo ubranstva russkikh dvortsov XVIII–XIX vv.
[Pavlovsk Park and Museum of the Decoration of Russian Eighteenth- and Nineteenth-Century Palaces] (1957–1983)
Gosudarstvennyi khudozhestvenno-arkhitekturnyi dvortsovo-parkovyi muzei-zapovednik v g. Pavlovske
[Pavlovsk State Art-Architectural Palace Museum-Preserve] (1983–1992)

In 1777 an estate was built in the village of Pavlovskoe for the Grand Duke Pavel Petrovich (who became Emperor Paul I in 1796). In 1793 the village was redesignated as the town of Pavlovsk, where over a period of fifty years a fine park and palace was built by the Scottish architect Charles Cameron, Vincenzo Brenna, A. N. Voronikhin and other architects, sculptors, and painters. The main palace was first erected in 1782–1784 from designs of Cameron, but was redesigned after a fire in 1803. The library was designed by Carlo (K. I.) Rossi. Until 1917 Pavlovsk remained one of the Russian imperial residences.

In 1918 the town of Pavlovsk was renamed Slutsk in honor of Vera (Bertha) Bronislavovna Slutskaia (1874–1917), who was killed fighting there during the Revolution. (The town kept that name until 1944, although the palace retained its traditional name of Pavlovsk). In the same year a museum was opened in the palace, which was frequently renamed as it came under the control of different authorities, principally the Pavlovsk Palace-Museum and Park Administration (*Upravlenie Pavlovskogo dvortsa-muzeia i parka*). Some of the imperial furnishings and many of the most valuable books from the library were turned over to the Hermitage, and some, unfortunately, went to the All-Union Antiquarian Company (*Vsesoiuznoe obshchestvo "Antikvariat"*), and were sold abroad. There was a major sale abroad from the library by Antikvariat in 1929, and additional withdrawals in 1932. By the beginning of World War II, only approximately one-third of the library remained.

When the Nazis invaded the USSR in 1941, the valuables from the palace-museum were removed to the St. Isaac's Cathedral Museum in Leningrad or buried in the ground. From September 1941 to January 1944, Pavlovsk was occupied by the Germans, and the palace buildings and the park suffered severe damage. A fire in the palace during the war resulted in the loss of a large number of books from the Rossi Library, although the manuscripts were removed in time. Most of the remaining books in the library were taken by the Nazis. Some were found in Kaliningrad in 1945, and others were returned from Austria by British authorities, but many are still missing from Pavlovsk. Some parts of the palace archive and part of the library were turned over to RGADA (B–2), RGIA (B–3), and TsGIA SPb (D–13).

After the war the Pavlovsk Museum became a central repository for valuables from the suburban palaces in Gatchina and Pushkin, the buildings of which were used for other purposes, and as a result, some library books and furnishings from those palaces remain in Pavlovsk. Restoration work on the palace began in 1944 and lasted until 1970, when it was reopened to the public. After the war many of the documents and museum exhibits were brought back from the various suburban palaces, particularly Gatchina and Pushkin (Tsarskoe Selo), as part of a general plan to return exhibits to their original locations. Restoration work on the parks continues to the present day. In 1983 the government passed a resolution giving Pavlovsk the status of a state preserve.

N.B. A large part of the prerevolutionary records of the Pavlovsk City Administration (fond 493; 21,656 units—1778–1918) and the Pavlovsk Town Council (*ratusha*) (fond 494; 113 units—1797–1811) are held in RGIA (B–3), which include considerable documentation about the palace. Most of the postrevolutionary administrative records of the Pavlovsk museum for the years 1935–1973 are held in TsGALI SPb (D–15, fond 310). Documentation on the fate of the palace during and after World War II can be found in the fond of the Central Repository for Museum Fonds of the Leningrad Suburban Palaces under the Cultural Administration of the Leningrad City Executive Committee (*Tsentral'noe khranilishche muzeinykh fondov Leningradskikh prigorodnykh dvortsov Upravleniia kul'tury Lengorispolkoma*) (TsGALI SPb, fond 387; 1943–1956).

HOLDINGS: ca. 36,000 units, 16th–20th cc.
   negatives—ca. 33,000 (1930s–1990s); photographs—1,439 (late 19th–early 20th cc., 1930s–1990s)

Archival materials are held for the most part within the Painting and Graphic Art Fond, which is administratively considered part of the basic museum holdings.

Manuscripts remaining from the imperial palace library (known as the Rossi Library), dating from the sixteenth through the nineteenth century, contain texts on religious and secular subjects and include some illuminated manuscripts. Most numerous among the early Russian manuscript books (16th–18th cc.) are apocryphal and liturgical texts: a Psalter; Gospels; the Books of the Apostles; the Apocalypse; choral manuscripts in both the early non-linear, neumatic notation and later linear notation; church calendars (*mesiatseslovy*); calendars of saints and religious festivals (*sviattsy*); collections of canons; anthems and hymns sung in praise of Russian holy men and icons of the Virgin; and a collection of the sermons of St. John Chrysostom, St. Cyril of Alexandria, and Lucidarius.

Included among the late seventeenth-century manuscripts are the "Debate on Religious Faith with Voldemar, Heir to the Throne of Denmark"; an essay entitled "On the Origins of the Ancient Slovenian People"; and a tale of how St. Cyril (Constantine) established the Slavonic alphabet. Seventeenth- and eighteenth-century pedagogic and scientific literature is represented by a cosmography and a collection of arithmetical problems. There are also nineteenth-century manuscript essays on the history of the Old Testament and the history of the Orthodox Church, as well as Church services and prayers.

Part of the collection relating to the imperial Romanov family includes textbooks and lesson books of Grand Duke Paul (Pavel Petrovich) and Grand Duchess Maria Fedorovna, and their correspondence with other members of the imperial family and with the Pavlovsk city administrator Karl Küchelbäcker (K. I. Kiukhel'beker) (1780s). There are some manuscript library catalogues and other documentation relating to the imperial family.

There are some additional documentary materials relating to the history of the palace and its owners, some of which were originally part of the Rossi Library. There are some documents relating to the Pavlovsk Town Administration (*Pavloskoe gorodovoe pravlenie*) during the late eighteenth and early nineteenth centuries. These include income and expenditure accounts, building estimates and estimates for decoration work on the Pavlovsk Palace, building accounts presented by the architect Vincenzo Brenna, records of furniture acquisitions by the palace, and property inventories from the palaces of Pavlovsk and Gatchina.

The Painting and Graphic Art Fond has numerous original works done by Russian and European graphic artists (drawings, watercolors, engravings) from the late eighteenth to the early twentieth century, most of which are landscape pictures of the suburbs of St. Petersburg. They include views of the parks at Pavlovsk, Gatchina, and Tsarskoe Selo by S. F. Shchedrin, A. E. Martynov, and O. A. Kiprenskii. There are also a number of original drawings (many of them signed) of the Empress Maria Fedorovna and her children and descendants, particularly Grand Duke Constantine (Konstantin) Romanov, who was a poet (*pseud.* K. R.) and president of the St. Petersburg Academy of Sciences.

The museum Photograph Archive (*Fototeka*) contains both interior and exterior views of the palace, the park, and the outbuildings. There are sets of photographs showing the restoration work done on the palace and the park from the 1930s to the present. There are also a few prerevolutionary photographic portraits of the imperial family.

Access: For access to archival materials, an official letter to the director is required, stating the subject and aim of the research.

Working Conditions: Researchers are accommodated in working areas of the museum. Materials are normally available the day they are ordered, but a prior appointment for research is required.

Library Facilities: A library (now ca. 12,000 volumes) was originally formed in 1782 on the basis of the 33 books in the travelling library of Catherine II (presented to her son Paul [Pavel Petrovich]) and grew to include books from the collections of Paul I and the Empress Maria Fedorovna, along with other members of the imperial family (by 1914 it included 20,895 volumes). Approximately two-thirds of the volumes were requisitioned in the late 1920s and early 1930s, many of which were sold abroad. Many of the remaining volumes were taken by the Nazis during the war. Only a very small part (some 1,200 volumes) of the imperial collection remained after the Second World War. In addition to the manuscripts mentioned above, the library includes books on history, philosophy, culture, and some cartographic materials. There is a manuscript catalogue of the main Pavlovsk Palace library (late 18th c.–1822). (See above regarding other manuscript books from the palace library.)

Copying: There are no copying facilities available.

FINDING AIDS — PUBLISHED — GENERAL:

Muzei SPb (1994), p. 61; *Biblioteki SPb* (1993), p. 58; *Peterburg* (1992), pp. 466–67; *GAF Spravochnik* (1991), p. 132; *Muzei Leningrada* (1989), pp. 196–202; *Muzei Leningrada* (1982), pp. 90–92.

There is no published guide of the archival materials in the museum-preserve.

h-535. *Pavlovsk.* Edited by Emmanuel Ducamp. 2 vols. Paris: Alain de Gourcuff, 1993.
(Lib: MH)
Vol. 1: *The Palace and the Park.* Compiled by M. A. Flit, A. N. Guzanov, L. V. Koval', Iu. V. Mudrov, et al. Photographs by Claudio Carpi. 254 p.
Vol. 2: *The Collections.* Compiled by A. V. Alekseeva, I. V. Alekseeva, E. V. Korolev, et al. Photographs by V. F. Dorokhov and V. A. Vorontsov. 223 p.

An elaborate, richly illustrated set of two albums with authoritative texts and illustrations of the park, the palace, and its collections. The second volume includes a section on the Rossi Library by I. V. Alekseeva (pp. 22–37), with an introductory essay about its development, prerevolutionary holdings, and their postrevolutionary fate, together with colored photographs of title pages, frontispieces, and illustrations from many of the volumes.

h-535.1. *Pavlovsk.* Compiled by Iu. V. Mudrov and V. A. Belanina. Edited by E. Ducamp. Paris: Alain de Gourcuff, 1992. 101 p. + plates. (Lib: MH) In: *Imperial Palaces in the Vicinity of St. Petersburg: Watercolours, Paintings and Engravings from the XVIIIth and XIXth Centuries* (4 vol. boxed set).

An elaborate album of illustrations from prerevolutionary engravings and watercolors with an introductory essay and annotations in English. Includes indexes of artists and engravers.

h-536. Nesin, Vadim Nikolaevich; and Sautkina, Galina Nikolaevna. *Pavlovsk imperatorskii i velikokniazheskii, 1777–1917.* St. Petersburg: Zhurnal "Neva," 1996. 288 p. + plates. (Lib: MH)

A popular illustrated, but unannotated, history honoring the bicentenial of the city of Pavlovsk. Includes a selected bibliography (pp. 286–87), but no archival references.

h-536.1. *Pavlovsk. Imperatorskii dvorets: Stranitsy istorii.* Compiled and edited by Iu. V. Mudrov. St. Petersburg: "Art Palas," Lenart, 1997. 381 p. Includes a facsimile of the 1903 edition *Pavlovskii dvorets: Khudozhestvennye sokrovishcha Rossii.* (Lib: MH)

A detailed, richly illustrated album presenting facsimile editions of several prerevolutionary accounts, including the pamphlet, "Materialy dlia opisaniia khudozhestvennykh sokrovishch Pavlovska" (SPb, 1903), based on a description by Empress Maria Fedorovna, with supplemental commentaries and photographs. Additional articles about the palace, its history, and holdings include one by A. Prakhov on the library—"Biblioteka Rossi" (pp. 343–46), listing many of the original holdings.

h-537. Massie, Suzanne. *Pavlovsk: The Life of a Russian Palace.* Boston: Little, Brown & Co., 1990. xx, 394 p. + 64 plates. (Lib: DLC; IU; MH) Paperback ed.: Blue Hill, ME: Heart Tree Press, 1990. xx, 394 p. + plates. A Russian translation is also available.

A detailed (but undocumented), popular history of Pavlovsk both before and after the Revolution. Traces the fate of the museum-preserve during World War II and details the subsequent restoration.

h-538. Zelenova, Anna Ivanovna. *Dvorets v Pavlovske.* 2d ed. Leningrad: Lenizdat, 1986. 95 p. + 16 plates (Lib: DLC; IU; MH)

1st ED.: L.: Lenizdat, 1978. 135 p. + plates. (Lib: MH)

An illustrated tourist guide to the palace with historical summary.

h-538.1. Kuchumov, Anatolii Mikhailovich. *Pavlovsk: Putevoditel'.* 4th ed. Leningrad: Lenizdat, 1980. 160 p. + 32 plates. (Lib: DLC; IU; MH)

1st ED.: L.: Lenizdat, 1972. 103 p.

A tourist guide to the palace-museum and the park, describing their history and the exhibits.

h-538.2. Kuchumov, Anatolii Mikhailovich. *Pavlovsk Palace and Park.* Translated by V. Travlinsky and J. Hine. Leningrad: Aurora Art Publishers, 1975. 443 p. + plates. (Lib: MH)

A large-format album, with introductory text, bibliography and index, and mostly colored illustrations.

h-538.3. Shvarts, Vsevolod Sergeevich. *Pavlovsk: Dvortsovo-parkovyi ansambl' XVIII-XIX vv.* Leningrad: "Iskusstvo," Leningradskoe otd-nie, 1980. 134 p. + plates. (Lib: DDO; MH) Summary and legends in English, French, and German.

A history and description of the palace and park (pp. 5–46), with bibliography (p. 47) and elaborate colored illustrations.

FINDING AIDS — SPECIALIZED:

h-539. Tolkacheva, G. A. "Drevnerusskie rukopisi Pavlovskogo dvortsa-muzeia." *TODRL* 25 (1970): 349–50. (Lib: DLC; IU; MH)

> A brief description of 42 Russian manuscript books (16th–19th cc.) from the palace library.

h-540. *Katalog vystavki knig iz Biblioteki Pavlovskogo dvortsa.* Compiled by I. V. Alekseeva. Sankt-Peterburg: BAN, 1994. 27 p. Introduction and text in Russian and French. (Lib: MH)

> An exhibition catalogue of 54 books (including several manuscripts) from the prerevolutionary Pavlovsk library, including 37 books that belonged to Empress Maria Feodorovna, 3 that belonged to Catherine II, and 15 to Paul I. See also Alekseeva's essay in h-535.

h-540.1. Firsov, G. "Biblioteka Rossi v Pavlovskom dvortse-muzee." *Al'manakh bibliofila* 6 (1979): 66–72. (Lib: DLC; IU; MH)

> Describes the Rossi Library, including manuscript books and its graphic collections, only part of which remain today in Pavlovsk. Part of the library was sold abroad after the Revolution, and the remaining part was looted by the Nazis during World War II. Many of the Nazi-looted books were returned to the USSR, but it is not possible to establish the exact losses or their present location.

h-541. Vitiazeva-Lebedeva, Vera Aleksandrovna. "Pavlovskii dvorets: K istorii stroitel'stva." In *Pamiatniki istorii i kul'tury Peterburga: Issledovaniia i materialy,* edited by A. V. Pozdnukhov, pp. 108–34. St. Petersburg: "Politekhnika," 1994. (Lib: DLC; MH)

> Draws heavily on the archival materials in Pavlovsk with significant description of some of the documents relating to the history of the palace.

Gosudarstvennyi muzei-zapovednik "Petergof" (GMZ "Petergof")
[Peterhof State Museum-Preserve]

Agency: Komitet po kul'ture Administratsii Sankt-Peterburga
[Committee on Culture of the Administration of St. Petersburg]

Address: 198903, St. Petersburg, Petergof, ul. Razvodnaia (*formerly* Kominterna), 2
Telephone: 427-74-25; *Fax:* (812) 427-93-30
Transport: suburban train from Baltic Station to Novyi Petergof; water transport (in summer) from Angliiskaia (*formerly* Krasnogo Flota) nab.
Hours: Tu–Su 10:30–17:00

General Director: Vadim Valentinovich Znamenov (*tel.* 427-93-30)
Deputy General Director for Preservation: Nina Valentinovna Vernova (*tel.* 427-54-53)
Chief Curator: Tamara Nikolaevna Nosovich (*tel.* 427-98-97)

HISTORY:

Petergofskii dvorets-muzei
    [Peterhof Palace-Museum] (1918–1930)
Petergofskie gosudarstvennye muzei i parki
    [Peterhof State Museums and Parks] (1930–1945)
Dvortsy, muzei i parki g. Petrodvortsa
    [Palaces, Museums, and Parks of Petrodvorets] (1945–XII.1983)
Gosudarstvennyi khudozhestvenno-arkhitekturnyi dvortsovo-parkovyi muzei-zapovednik v g. Petrodvortse
    [State Art-Architectural Palace-Park Museum-Preserve in Petrodvorets] (XII.1983–XII.1992)

Building was begun on the palace and parks of Peterhof (Rus. Petergof) in 1709 by order of Peter the Great. The nucleus of the complex is the elegant imperial residence, the Great Palace, first designed by the architect Jean-Baptiste-Alexandre Le Blond. Subsequently, the main palace was enlarged in 1746–1751 by Bartolomeo Francesco Rastrelli. Rastrelli was also involved in designs of the elaborate fountains and subsidiary palaces, some of which were designed by Johann Friedrich Braunstein, M. G. Zemtsov, and Niccolò Michetti, among other architects.

Nationalized after the Revolution, in 1918 Peterhof was organized as a palace-museum of historical daily-life and art. Frequently renamed during the Soviet period, during the 1930s it was principally known as the Peterhof State Museums and Parks. Many imperial treasures from the palace were confiscated at various points in the 1920s and 1930s, and unfortunately a large number were sold abroad. By 1941, only 11,700 books remained in the palace library. After the Nazi invasion in 1941, more than 8,000 exhibits and historical documentation were evacuated and some of the sculptures in the park were buried. From 1941 to 1944 Peterhof was occupied by the Germans and suffered extensive damage. The great palace was significantly destroyed as were many of the fountains. The Neptune fountain was looted by the Nazis and taken to Nuremberg, where it was found and returned by American forces after World War II. Restoration of the palace and park, renamed Petrodvorets in 1945, began immediately after the war, and by the 1960s was largely completed, although it was another decade before the Great Palace was reopened to tourists. Restoration work on some of the outbuildings in the parks still continues. The present name dates from 1992, when the Peterhof Museum-Preserve reverted to its traditional name.

N.B. The prerevolutionary archive of the Peterhof Palace Administration (*Petergofskoe dvortsovoe pravlenie*) was transferred in 1953 to RGIA (B–3, fond 490—1732–1918). The administrative records of the museum for the years 1918–1921 and 1944–1974 are housed in TsGALI SPb (D–15, fond 312). Documentation on the fate of the palace during and after World War II can be found in the fond of the Central Repository for Museum Fonds of the Leningrad Suburban Palaces under the Cultural Administration of the Leningrad City Executive Committee (*Tsentral'noe khranilishche muzeinykh fondov Leningradskikh prigorodnykh dvortsov Upravleniia kul'tury Lengorispolkoma*) (TsGALI SPb, fond 387; 1943–1956).

Access: For access to the museum fonds a letter to the director is required stating the subject and the purpose of the research.

Library Facilities: A library was opened in 1977 on the basis of the museum book fond (ca. 20,000 vols.), which contains literature on history and the history of art, as well as audiovisual materials. There are card catalogues of rare editions and a facts-and-figures file on the history and culture of St. Petersburg and its environs, and on Russian art.

Arkhiv
[Archive]

Hours: by appointment
Head: Tat'iana Anatol'evna Igumnova

HOLDINGS: 1 fond, 72,128 units, 18th–20th cc.
photographs—ca. 21,000 (1897–1990s)

The museum archive, administratively part of the Scientific Division (*Nauchnyi otdel*), holds materials on the history of Peterhof including inventories of the interior contents, albums, plans, and technical drawings made by the eighteenth- and nineteenth-century architects Niccolò Michetti, Bartolomeo Francesco Rastrelli, P. Neelov, V. I. Bazhenov, Friedrich von Wistinghausen, Nicholas Benois (N. L. Benua), Harald Julius Bosse, Joseph Charlemagne (I. I. Sharleman'), and A. I. Shtakenshneider (Stakenschneider). Also preserved are the detailed late eighteenth-century scaled perspective drawings by the French engineer Pierre-Antoine de Sainte-Hilaire.

The photograph (*fototeka*) and negative (*negateka*) archives contain individual photographs and photo albums showing views of the park and the fountains, the facades and interiors of the palaces, and the pavilions, some of which were taken before the revolution. There are also photographs of the paintings, graphics, sculptures and other *objets d'art* housed in the museum. There is a collection of photographs showing damage during World War II.

Working Conditions: Materials are available in the reading room the day they are ordered.

Reference Facilities: There are *opisi* in addition to inventories and card catalogues for staff use.

Copying: Xerox copies can be prepared.

FINDING AIDS — PUBLISHED — GENERAL:

GAF Spravochnik (1991), p. 132–33; *Muzei Leningrada* (1989), pp. 182–88; *Muzei Leningrada* (1982), pp. 83–86.

There is no published description of the archival materials in the museum.

h-542. *Putevoditel' po Petergofu/ Peterhof CD Guide.* Moscow: KomInfo, [1995]. CD-ROM for use with Windows.

A new multimedia CD-ROM tourist guide with text and sound in both English and Russian with digitized photographs of the parks, fountains, and palace interiors. In some places there are added film clips and sound commentary. Includes a brief history of the palace with commentary about major attractions and pop-up notes about some of the major architects and others associated with its development. A brief introduction and printed instructions accompany the CD-ROM.

h-542.1. *Peterhof.* Compiled by V. V. Znamenov and I. M. Gurevich (Gourievich). Edited by E. Ducamp. Paris: Alain de Gourcuff, 1992. 103 p. + plates. (Lib: MH) In: *Imperial Palaces in the Vicinity of St. Petersburg: Watercolours, Paintings and Engravings from the XVIIIth and XIXth Centuries* (4 vol. boxed set).

> An elaborate album of illustrations from prerevolutionary engravings and watercolors with an introductory essay and annotations in English. Includes indexes of artists and engravers.

h-543. Raskin, Abram Grigor'evich. *Petrodvorets: Dvortsy-muzei, parki, fontany.* 2d ed. Leningrad, 1988. 190 p. + plates. (Lib: DLC)

> 1st ED.: L.: Lenizdat, 1984. 191 p. + 16 plates.
>
> A popularized tourist guide indicating restoration work underway at the time.

h-543.1. *Petrodvorets (Peterhof): Palaces and Pavilions, Gardens and Parks, Fountains and Cascades, Sculptures.* Compiled by Abram G. Raskin. Leningrad: Aurora Art Publishers, 1978. 372 p. + 18 plates. (Lib: DDO; MH)

> A large-format album with an introductory essay on the history of the palace. Predominantly colored plates have brief annotations in English. Includes an extensive bibliography (pp. 368–72) and index of persons associated with the palace.

h-543.2. Gurevich, Il'ia Mikhailovich. *Petrodvorets.* Leningrad: "Khudozhnik RSFSR," 1976. 72 p. "Pamiatniki gorodov Rossii." (Lib: IU)

> A popular guide illustrated with photographs and giving brief details on the history of Petrodvorets and its best known monuments.

h-544. *Petergof: Al'manakh: Iz istorii dvortsov i kollektsii.* Edited by V. Gusarov and E. Spiridonov. St. Petersburg: Biograficheskii institut "Studia Biografika," 1992. 190 p. (Lib: DLC; MH)

h-545. Arkhipov, Nikolai Il'ich; and Raskin, Abram Grigor'evich. *Petrodvorets.* Moscow/Leningrad: "Iskusstvo," 1961. 331 p. + plates. (Lib: DDO; DLC; MH)

> A large-format album, the first two-thirds of which is a scholarly history of the palace ensemble with extensive references to archival sources.

h-546. I[zmailov], M[ikhail Mikhailovich]. *Putevoditel' po Petergofu/ Guide de Péterhof.* St. Petersburg: T-vo R. Golike i A. Vil'borg, 1909. 246 p. (Lib: DLC; IU; MH)

> The most authoritative prerevolutionary bilingual illustrated guide honoring the 200th anniversary of the palace, providing a detailed description of the palace complex as it was in the early twentieth century.

h-546.1. Ardikutsa, Vasilii Efimovich. *Petrodvorets: Putevoditel'.* 8th ed. Leningrad: Lenizdat, 1974. 192 p. (Lib: DLC; IU; MH)

> EARLIER ED.: *Fontany Petrodvortsa: Illiustrirovannyi putevoditel'.* [L.]: Lenizdat, 1972. 142 p. + 48 plates. (Lib: MH)
>
> A tourist guide to the palace ensemble.

Muzei sem'i Benua—
Filial Gosudarstvennogo muzeia-zapovednika "Petergof"

[Benois Family Museum—Branch of the Peterhof State Museum-Preserve]

Agency: Komitet po kul'ture Administratsii Sankt-Peterburga
[Committee on Culture of the Administration of St. Petersburg]

Address: 198903, St. Petersburg, g.
               Petergof, Dvortsovaia (*formerly* Sovetskaia) pl., 8
Telephone: 427-99-32; *Fax:* (812) 427-93-30
Transport: suburban train from Baltic Station to Novyi Petergof
Hours: MTu–F 10:00–17:00; archive: by appointment

Head: Nikolai Niikolaevich Krylov
Head of Archive: Irina Anatol'evna Zolotinkina

HISTORY:

The museum was founded in 1988 to honor Alexandre N. Benois (Aleksandr Nikolaevich Benua) (1870–1960), the Russian painter, art historian and critic, and his family (of French origin), who had been active in Peterhof (Rus. Petergof) before the Revolution. The initiative for its establishment came from the painter's son Nicolà Benois (Nikolai Aleksandrovich Benua) (1901–1988), chief set designer for the La Scala Theater in Milan, with the backing of the Ministry of Culture of the USSR, the Embassy of the USSR in France, the Consulate General of the USSR in Milan, the Rodina Society, and the directors of the Peterhof State Museum-Preserve. A substantial contribution to the founding of the museum was made by the family and relatives of A. N. Benois living in Russia and abroad, particularly his grandson, the architect P. A. Braslavskii, and the British director and actor Peter Ustinov.

HOLDINGS: 4 fonds, 2,137 units, 1698–1991

The archive contains documentary material on the Benois family, whose contribution to the arts in Russia and abroad has been considerable. The original collection consisted of the papers of Alexandre Benois (1870–1960), the Russian painter, art historian, and critic, who was one of the founding members of the World of Art (*Mir iskusstva*) association. The materials were donated to the museum by his descendants living in Paris. They comprise biographical documents and literary manuscripts including Benois' diary for the years 1916–1917; his correspondence on exhibitions and theater performances in Vienna, Paris, Milan, and other European cities (1926–1960); and portraits and group photographs of members of his family.

    The archives contain documents and other material from the private collection of E. B. Serebriakov (Russia), P. A. Braslavskii, and D. I. Vyshnegradskii (France), children's drawings from the Benois family presented by the State Russian Museum, and xerox copies of seventeenth- and eighteenth-century documents regarding Benois' French ancestors.

    There are also personal papers of Benois' son, Nicolà (Nikolai) Aleksandrovich Benois (1901–1988), the theater designer, and his brother, Leontii Nikolaevich Benois (1856–1928), the architect. There are documents from the archives of the Serebriakov family, including the personal papers of the Russian painter Z. E. Serebriakova (1884–1967), which include certificates of her birth, christening, and marriage, her diplomas, photographs of her paintings and graphics, and correspondence with her children.

The archives also contain business correspondence relating to the founding of the museum and the preparation of its exhibitions.

Access: For access to the archival materials, an official letter is required stating the subject and purpose of research which has been endorsed by the director of the Peterhof Museum-Preserve.

Working Conditions: Researchers are accommodated in working areas of the museum, where materials are available the day they are ordered.

Reference Facilities: The archive is being arranged into fonds and a reference system is being established. There are inventory *opisi* for fonds that have been processed and a computer database for the museum holdings.

Copying: Facilities are available for photographic and xerox copies.

FINDING AIDS — PUBLISHED — GENERAL:

Muzei Peterburga (1994), p. 58; *Peterburg* (1992), p. 401.

There is no guide or other published description of the archival holdings.

h-547. *Muzei sem'i Benua/ Benois Family Museum.* St. Petersburg: Vneshtorgizdat, 1992. 20 p. Parallel text in Russian and English. (Lib: MH)
> A brief tourist guide describing the museum exhibits.

Gosudarstvennyi khudozhestvenno-arkhitekturnyi dvortsovo-parkovyi muzei-zapovednik "Tsarskoe Selo" (GMZ "Tsarskoe Selo")
[Tsarskoe Selo State Art-Architectural Palace-Park Museum-Preserve]

Agency: Komitet po kul'ture Administratsii Sankt-Peterburga
[Committee on Culture of the Administration of St. Petersburg]

Address:	189620, St. Petersburg, g. Pushkin, ul. Sadovaia, 7
Telephone:	466-66-69; *Fax:* (812) 465-21-96; *RdngRm:* 470-55-71
Website:	http://www.alexanderpalace.org/catherinepalace/
Transport:	suburban train from Vitebsk Station or Kupchino RR platform (metro: Kupchino) to Detskoe Selo (Pushkin) + bus 371, 372; or metro: Moskovskaia + bus 287
Hours:	MW–F 10:00–17:00

General Director: Ivan Petrovich Sautov (*tel.* 466-66-69)
Deputy Director for Scientific Work and Chief Curator:
  Larisa Valentinovna Bardovskaia (*tel.* 465-20-17)
Curator of the Manuscript-Documentary Fond:
  Galina Dmitrievna Khodasevich (*tel.* 470-55-71)

HISTORY:
Tsarskosel'skie dvortsy
  [Tsarskoe Selo Palaces] (1917–1918)
Detskosel'skie dvortsy-muzei i parki
  [Detskoe Selo Palace-Museums and Parks] (1918–1938)
Dvortsy-muzei i parki g. Pushkina
  [Palace-Museums and Parks in Pushkin] (1938–1983)
Gosudarstvennyi khudozhestvenno-arkhitekturnyi dvortsovo-parkovyi muzei-zapovednik g. Pushkina
  [State Art-Architectural Palace-Park Museum-Preserve in Pushkin] (1983–1990)

The Tsarskoe Selo State Art-Architectural Palace-Park Museum-Preserve dates back to 1710, when the lands on which it is situated were given as a present by Peter the Great to his wife, the future Empress Catherine I. In 1725 it became one of the country residences of the imperial family. Over the next hundred years a number of palaces, pavilions, and other structures were built here to the design of such famous architects as Johann Friedrich Braunstein, A. V. Kvasov, S. I. Chevakinskii, Bartolomeo Francesco Rastrelli, Charles Cameron, Giacomo Quarenghi, and V. P. Stasov. The biggest are the Great Catherine Palace and the Alexander Palace. In 1808 the town of Tsarskoe Selo became the center of an administrative subdivision (*Tsarskosel'skii uezd*) of St. Petersburg Guberniia. In 1811 a lyceum was opened here, which Aleksandr Pushkin attended from 1811 to 1817.

After the Revolution, the town of Tsarskoe Selo was renamed Detskoe Selo in 1918, and following nationalization, the palace was opened as a museum of historical life and art under control of the Administration of the Detskoe Selo Artistic Properties (until 1922). Subsequently it was under the control of the Detskoe Selo Palace-Museum Administration and then, after 1928, the combined Administration of the Detskoe Selo and Pavlovsk Palace-Museums. Many of the imperial treasures and palace furnishings, along with books and manuscripts from the palace library, were confiscated. A number of them were turned over to the All-Union Antiquarian Company (*Vsesoiuznoe obshchestvo "Antikvariat"*) for sale abroad in the late 1920s and others were exported in the early 1930s. In 1937 the town of Detskoe Selo was renamed Pushkin to mark the centennial of the death of the poet Aleksandr Sergeevich Pushkin, and the name of the palace complex was changed accordingly.

During the Second World War the most valuable articles in the museum were evacuated, while the rest were buried. From 1941 to 1944 Pushkin was occupied by the Germans, and the palaces suffered extensive damage. They were plundered and their art treasures were removed (including the panels in the Amber Room of the Catherine Palace, which have still not been recovered). A large part of the library was shipped to Germany by the Nazis, but recovered in Austria by British forces and returned to the USSR; however, not all of the books have been returned to Tsarskoe Selo. Restoration work began after the war, and the first halls of the Great Palace were opened to the public in 1959. Today the main buildings of architectural interest have been restored, although restoration work is still continuing. The present name of the museum dates from 1992, when Palace-Park Museum-Preserve reverted to its traditional name, but as of the end of 1998, the town itself retains the name of Pushkin. In April 1997 the museum was added to the federal register of the most valuable monuments of the cultural heritage of the peoples of the Russian Federation.

N.B. The prerevolutionary records of the Tsarskoe Selo Palace Administration (*Tsarskosel'skoe dvortsovoe pravlenie*) (fond 487—1710–1919) and the Chancellery of the Chief Administrator of the Palace Administration and Town of Tsarskoe Selo (*Kantseliariia glavnoupravliaiushchego dvortsovymi pravleniiami i gorodom Tsarskoe Selo*) (fond 486—1817–1865) are held in RGIA (B–3). The earlier administrative archive of the museum (1917–1923, 1937–1981) is held in TsGALI SPb (D–15, fond 411). Documentation on the fate of palace during and after World War II can be found in the fond of the Central Repository for Museum Fonds of the Leningrad Suburban Palaces under the Cultural Administration of the Leningrad City Executive Committee (*Tsentral'noe khranilishche muzeinykh fondov Leningradskikh prigorodnykh dvortsov Upravleniia kul'tury Lengorispolkoma*) (TsGALI SPb, fond 387; 1943–1956).

For the Regional Studies Museum of the Town of Pushkin, which also holds materials relating to the palace museum-preserve, see H–70.

HOLDINGS: ca. 35,300 units, mid-18th c.–1995

manuscript-documentary fond—ca. 1,700 units (1945–1990s); photographs—30,000 (late 19th c.–1995); technical drawings—3,601 units (18th c.–1990s)

Archival materials, dispersed among different museum collections, are to be found in the Fond of Technical Drawings, the Manuscript-Documentary Fond, and the Photographic Documents Fond.

The Fond of Technical Drawings contains documents relating to the building and restoration of the Catherine Palace, the Alexander Palace, the Catherine Park, the Alexander Park, and the various pavilions in the parks. The drawings represent the work of a number of nineteenth- and early twentieth-century architects, including V. P. Stasov, the Gornostaev Brothers, K. A. Ton (Thon), A. G. Bakh, R. I. Bakh, and V. Vidov. There is also graphic documentation (drafts, architectural plans, and drawings) of contemporary restorers.

The Manuscript-Documentary Fond retains materials relating to the postwar restoration, as well as inventories of exhibits, historical information on the monuments, and other documentation.

The Photographic Documents Fond contains views of the town, the facades and interiors of the palaces, the park buildings, the monuments, and the town buildings, as well as pictures of the postwar restoration work. There are also a few photographs dating back to prerevolutionary times.

Access: A letter to the director is required for access to the archival materials and the library, stating the subject and purpose of research.

Working Conditions: Researchers are accommodated in working premises; materials are generally available the day they are ordered.

Reference Facilities: There are inventory *opisi* and official card catalogues for staff use (personal names and subjects), as well as other supplementary card catalogues.

Library Facilities: The palace library was dispersed and/or destroyed during World War II, although a large part of it was sold abroad earlier. The museum library (9,000 vols.) was formed in 1969 and contains books on the history of art and culture. There is a card catalogue of rare imprints.

Copying: Photographic and xerox copies can be prepared.

FINDING AIDS — PUBLISHED — GENERAL:

Muzei SPb (1994), p. 59; *Biblioteki SPb* (1993), p. 58; *Peterburg* (1992), pp. 528–30; *GAF Spravochnik* (1991), p. 133; *Muzei Leningrada* (1989), pp. 188–96; *Muzei Leningrada* (1982), pp. 87–90.

There is no published guide to the archival materials in the museum.

h-548. *Tsarskoe Selo.* Compiled by I. P. Sautov and L. V. Bardovskaia. 103 p. + plates. In: *Imperial Palaces in the Vicinity of St. Petersburg: Watercolours, Paintings and Engravings from the XVIIIth and XIXth Centuries*, edited by Emmanuel Ducamp. Paris: Alain de Gourcuff, 1992. (4 vol. boxed set). (Lib: MH)

> An elaborate album of illustrations from prerevolutionary engravings and watercolors with an introductory essay and annotations in English. Includes indexes of artists and engravers.

h-549. Lemus, Vera Vladimirovna; Emina, E. S.; Gladkova, E. S., et al. *Muzei i parki Pushkina.* 6th ed. Leningrad: Lenizdat, 1980. 128 p. (Lib: DLC)

> 3d ED.: Compiled by G. P. Balog, E. S. Gladkova, et al. L., 1969. 189 p. (Lib: MH)
>
> A popular guide to the history of the town, the palaces and park, and to exhibitions held at the museum-preserve.

h-549.1. *Dvortsy i parki goroda Pushkina: Litsei, Ekaterininskii dvorets, Kameronova galereia, Ekaterininskii park, Aleksandrovskii dvorets i park.* Edited by V. V. Lemus. Leningrad: "Avrora," 1986. 226 p. + 169 plates. Photographs by M. A. Velichko et al. (Lib: MH)

> EARLIER ED.: *Pushkin: Muzei i parki: Al'bom.* Compiled by V. V. Lemus. Leningrad: Lenizdat, 1980. 64 p. + plates. (Lib: DLC)
>
> A photograph album with brief details on the history of the museum, the palace, and the park.

h-549.2. *Pushkin: Palaces and Parks: The Lyceum, the Catherine Palace, the Cameron Thermae, the Catherine Park, the Alexander Palace and Park.* Compiled by V. V. Lemus. Translated by Boris Grudinko. Leningrad: "Avrora," 1984. 28 p. + 169 plates. Photographs by M. A. Velichko et al. (Lib: MH)

> A translation of an earlier edition of h-549.1.

h-550. Vil'chkovskii, Sergei Nikolaevich. *Tsarskoe Selo.* 2d ed. St. Petersburg: T-vo R. Golike i Vil'borg, 1911. 277 p. (Lib: DLC; IU; MH)

> REPRINT ED.: St. Petersburg: Titul, 1992 (with preface by A. A. Alekseev).
>
> 1st ED.: *Tsarskoe Selo: Putevoditel'*, 1910. 227 p. + plates. (Lib: MH)
>
> FRENCH ED.: *Tsarskoe Selo.* [Berlin-Schoneberg], Meisenbach Riffarth, 1912. 271 p. + plates. (Lib: MH)
>
> GERMAN ED.: Vil'chkovskii, Sergei Nikolaevich (Wiltschkowski, S.). *Zarskoje Selo.* Berlin, Meisenbach Riffarth, 1911. 301 p. + plates. (Lib: MH)
>
> A classic prerevolutionary illustrated guide with detailed history.

h-551. Petrov, Anatolii Nikolaevich. *Pushkin: Dvortsy i parki.* 2d ed. Leningrad: "Iskusstvo," 1969. 231 p. + plates. (Lib: DLC; IU; MH)

> A large-format album of black-and-white pictures. The first half of the volume provides a detailed history of the palace ensemble with extensive references to archival sources.

h-552. Gollerbakh, Erikh Fedorovich; and Losev, V. M. *Literatura o Detskom Sele.* Leningrad: Leningradskoe obshchestvo kollektsionerov, 1933. 66 p.

h-553. Benua, Aleksandr Nikolaevich (Benois, Alexandre). *Tsarskoe Selo v tsarstvovanie imperatritsy Elisavety Petrovny: Materialy dlia istorii iskusstva v Rossii v XVIII veke po glavneishim arkhitekturnym pamiatnikam.* [St. Petersburg]: Izd. tovarishchestva R. Golike i A. Vil'borg, 1910. 11 p., 264 p., xlv p. + 59 plates. (Lib: MH)

> An elaborate album with reproductions of the author's original watercolors, along with engravings and photographs of the palace and park. Documentary appendices include ground plans and inventories of the palace contents and many citations of original documentation, not all of which is still extant. The copy in the library of Harvard University is a presentation edition bound in red morocco, presumably from the palace library.

Letnii sad i dvorets-muzei Petra I
[Summer Garden and Palace-Museum of Peter I]

Agency: Komitet po kul'ture Administratsii Sankt-Peterburga
[Committee on Culture of the Administration of St. Petersburg]

Address:	191041, St. Petersburg, Letnii sad
Telephone:	312-77-15
Transport:	metro: Nevskii prospekt, Gostinyi Dvor
Hours:	M–F 10:00–17:00

Director: Galina Romanovna Bolotova (*tel.* 312-96-66)
Deputy Director for Scientific Work: Nataliia Dmitrievna Kareeva (*tel.* 312-77-15)
Chief Curator: Galina Aleksandrovna Khvostova (*tel.* 312-77-15)

HISTORY:

Letnii dvorets Petra I—Filial Istoriko-bytovogo otdela Gosudarstvennogo Russkogo muzeia
[Summer Palace of Peter I—Branch of the Historical Daily-Life Division of the State Russian Museum]
(1925–1934)

The Summer Palace of Peter I, an architectural monument of the Petrine period (designed by Domenico Trezzini and Andreas Schlüter, 1710–1714), was used for historical and art exhibitions at the turn of the twentieth century. After the October Revolution the Palace and the Summer Gardens were put under state protection. From 1923 to 1925 a so-called historical daily-life museum was housed in the halls of the palace, which from 1925 to 1934 was administratively a branch of the Historical Daily-Life Division of the State Russian Museum (H–89) and was used for exhibition purposes. In 1934 it became an independent historical daily-life memorial museum devoted to the times of Peter I. Its affiliated branch—the Little House of Peter I—became a museum in 1930. Following the German invasion in 1941 most of the exhibits were removed, but the Summer Palace suffered under artillery bombardment during the war. It was opened to the public again in 1947.

N.B. A large part of the museum records for the years 1939–1975 are held in TsGALI SPb (D–15, fond 339 [9560]).

HOLDINGS: ca. 26,000 units, early 18th c.–1990s

photocopies of archival documents—5,000 units; photographs—ca. 15,000 (early 20th c.–1990s); negatives—ca. 6,000 (early 20th c.–1990s); prints and engravings—432 units (early 18th–20th cc.); scientific-technical documentation—598 units (1941–1990s)

Archival materials in the museum are not held in a separate division, but rather are held as an administrative part of the Scientific Division.

The Main Fond (*Osnovnoi fond*) of the Summer Palace-Museum and the Little House of Peter I contains engravings and lithographs by Nicholas Larmessin, Adriaan Schoonebeeck, Maurice Baquoi, A. F. Zubov, and other artists (18th–20th cc.) who depicted the times of Peter the Great.

The Auxiliary Fond (*Nauchno-vspomogatel'nyi fond*) of the Scientific Division holds manuscript works of museum specialists, as well as a collection of copies and extracts relating to the museum from files in a number of state archives (18th–20th cc.; ca. 5,000 units). There are also photographs of the sculptures in the Summer Garden and the facades and interiors of the Summer Palace and the Little House of Peter I (20th c.).

The Technical Documentation Fond contains estimates, diagrams and technical drawings, architectural measurements, and administrative documents issued by the State Inspectorate for the Preservation of Monuments (1941–1990).

Access: Research access to the fonds requires a letter to the director, stating the subject and purpose of research.

Working Conditions: Researchers are accommodated in the museum offices, where materials are available the day they are ordered.

Reference Facilities: There is a subject catalogue of the negative archive, an inventory of the technical documentation, and a catalogue of scientific works by the museum staff.

Library Facilities: The book fond (ca. 1,500 vols.) contains literature on seventeenth- to twentieth-century history, and on Russian and European art during the period of Peter I.

Copying: There are no copying facilities available.

FINDING AIDS — PUBLISHED — GENERAL:

Muzei SPb (1994), pp. 51–53; *Biblioteki SPb* (1993), p. 59; *Peterburg* (1992), pp. 344–46; *Muzei Leningrada* (1989), pp. 81–84; *Muzei Leningrada* (1982), pp. 80–83; Myl'nikov (1970), p. 41.

There is no published guide to the archival materials in the museum.

h-555. Kuznetsova, Ol'ga Nikolaevna; and Borzin, Boris Fedorovich. *Letnii sad i Letnii dvorets Petra I.* Leningrad, 1988. 190 p. (Lib: DLC; IU; MH)

> EARLIER ED.: *Letnii sad, Letnii dvorets, Domik Petra I.* Compiled by O. N. Kuznetsova, A. K. Sementovskaia, Sh. I. Shteiman. 6th ed. Leningrad: Lenizdat, 1968. 95 p. (Lib: MH)

> > An illustrated tourist guide more detailed than earlier editions by Kuznetsova, with other authors.

h-556. Bolotova, Galina Romanovna. *Letnii sad.* 2d ed. Leningrad: "Khudozhnik RSFSR," 1988. 152 p. (Lib: DLC; MH)

h-556.1. *Leningrad House of Peter I: Summer Gardens and Palace of Peter I / Leningrad Domik Petra I: Letnii sad i Dvorets.* Edited by K. M. Egorova. Leningrad: "Aurora," 1975. 126 p. + plates. Introduction by K. M. Egorova. Text and captions in English and Russian. (Lib: MH)

> > A bilingual album with introductory text and extensive color photographs. Includes a bibliography and index of names.

Gosudarstvennyi muzei "Isaakievskii sobor" (GMIS)
[Isaac Cathedral State Museum]

Agency: Komitet po kul'ture Administratsii Sankt-Peterburga
[Committee on Culture of the Administration of St. Petersburg]

Address: 190000, St. Petersburg, Isaakievskaia pl., 1
Telephone: 315-97-32; 312-07-21; 315-57-69
Transport: metro: Nevskii prospekt, Gostinyi Dvor; trol.: 5, 22
Hours: MTuTh–Su 11:00–19:00

Director: Georgii Petrovich Butikov (*tel.* 210-92-06)
Deputy Director for Scientific Work: Viktor L'vovich Razuvalov (*tel.* 210-91-95)
Chief Curator, Division of Scientific Accession, Registrations, and Preservation of Museum Fonds: Mansur Shakirovich Dominov (*tel.* 315-57-68)

HISTORY:

Antireligioznyi muzei
    [Antireligious Museum] (1931–1937)
Gosudarstvennyi muzei-pamiatnik "Isaakievskii sobor"
    [Isaac Cathedral State Museum-Monument] (1937–1963)
Muzei "Isaakievskii sobor"—Filial Gosudarstvennogo muzeia istorii Leningrada
    [Isaac Cathedral Museum—Branch of the State Museum of the History of Leningrad] (1963–1969)
Istoriko-khudozhestvennyi muzei "Isaakievskii sobor"
    [Isaac Cathedral Historico-Art Museum] (1969–1975)
Khudozhestvennyi muzei "Isaakievskii sobor"
    [Isaac Cathedral Art Museum] (1975–1977)

The museum was founded in 1928 in what had been the main church of St. Petersburg—St. Isaac's Cathedral (*Sobor Isaakia Dalmatskogo*), which was built between 1818 and 1858 as designed by the French architect Auguste Ricard de Montferrand. In 1928 the religious community of the Cathedral was disbanded on the order of the People's Commissariat of Education and the building was placed under the control of the Main Administration for Scientific, Museums, and Scientific-Art Institutions (Glavnauka). In 1931 the State Antireligious Museum was opened to the public in the former cathedral, but it lasted only until 1937, when it was closed down and its holdings transferred to the Museum of the History of Religion under the Academy of Sciences (H–72) in the former Kazan Cathedral. In 1937 the museum changed its orientation to become a museum of history and art with the new name of the Isaac Cathedral State Museum-Monument (*Gosudarstvennyi muzei-pamiatnik "Isaakievskii sobor"*).

During the war the cellars and outbuildings of the cathedral were used as a repository for the museum holdings removed from the Leningrad suburban palaces. During the 1960s the museum was administered as a branch of the State Museum of the History of Leningrad (H–65). In 1969 it was given independent status, and since 1977 it has had its present name. Orthodox religious services were resumed in the cathedral in 1990.

The Isaac Cathedral Museum has two branches, neither of which has separate archival holdings:

(1) The Bleeding Saviour Museum-Monument (*Muzei-pamiatnik "Spas na krovi"*), which has been a branch since 1970, occupies the former Church of the Resurrection (*khram Voskreseniia Khristova*), which was built between 1883–1907 on the spot where Emperor

Alexander II was assassinated. (191011, St. Petersburg, nab. Kanala Griboedova, 2-a; tel. 210-92-01; 314-40-53).

(2) The Sampson Cathedral Museum-Monument (*Muzei-pamiatnik "Sampsonievskii sobor"*), which has been a branch since 1984, occupying the former Sampson Cathedral. The Cathedral is one of the oldest churches in St. Petersburg (1728–1740), built to honor the victory at Poltava under Peter I. (194156, Bol'shoi Sampsonievskii prosp., 41; tel. 542-33-77).

N.B. Most of the museum records for the years 1928–1950 and 1961 have been transferred to state archival custody and are now held in TsGALI SPb (D–15, fond 330 [9480]).

HOLDINGS: ca. 15,000 units, 1910–1990s
manuscript materials—ca. 500 units (1910–1990s); photographs and negatives—ca. 14,000 (1931–1990s)

Archival materials in the museum are not held in a separate division, but rather constitute part of the Division of Scientific Accession, Registration, and Preservation of Museum Fonds.

There is a special museum exhibition devoted to the main stages in the building of the cathedral, showing its interior and exterior decor and various restoration work—with copies of archival documents relating to the life and work of Auguste Ricard de Montferrand. There are lithographs with the architect's own drawings, including pictures of the other churches that preceeded the cathedral itself, as well as visual representations of the various periods of the cathedral's construction. There are also engravings, sketches, and watercolors illustrating the main events in the construction of the cathedral and showing the damage it suffered during the Second World War.

The museum archive contains documents on the restoration of the cathedral building itself and the two branches of the museum—the Bleeding Saviour Museum-Monument and the Sampson Cathedral Museum-Monument. The archives also hold engineering calculations for metal scaffolding (1912), plans, estimates, the reports of the technical commissions and technical inspection documents on the state of the building, expert findings, and estimates for the restoration of museum exhibits (1941–1983). There are also some materials involving the scientific activities of the museum—scholarly reports and methodological guidelines for excursions, among others. There are photographs documenting the restoration work and the architecture and ornamentation of all the monuments from 1931 to the 1980s.

Access: Access to the archival holdings requires a letter to the director, stating the subject and purpose of research.

Working Conditions: Researchers are accommodated in the museum offices, where materials are available the day they are ordered.

Reference Facilities: There are *opisi* for the museum archive.

Copying: There are no copying facilities available.

FINDING AIDS — PUBLISHED — GENERAL:

Muzei SPb (1994), pp. 40–44; *Peterburg* (1992), pp. 239–41; *GAF Spravochnik* (1991), pp. 126–27; *Muzei Leningrada* (1989), pp. 169–72; *Muzei Leningrada* (1982), pp. 66–68.

There is no guide to the archival materials in the museum.

h-557. Butikov, Georgii Petrovich. *Muzei "Isaakievskii sobor."* Leningrad: Lenizdat, 1991. 223 p. + 16 plates. (Lib: DLC)

2d ED.: Butikov, Georgii Petrovich; and Khvostova, Galina Aleksandrovna. *Isaakievskii sobor.* L.: Lenizdat, 1979. 176 p. + plates. (Lib: MH)

EARLIER ED.: *Gosudarstvennyi muzei-pamiatnik Isaakievskii sobor.* L.: Khudozhnik RSFSR, 1973. 70 p. "Ansambli Leningrada i prigorodov." (Lib: MH)

ENGLISH ED.: *St. Isaac's Cathedral, Leningrad.* Translated from the Russian by David and Judith Andrews. L.: Aurora Art Publishers, 1980. 163 p. (Lib: MH)

EARLIER ENGLISH ED.: L.: Aurora Art Publishers, 1974. 142 p. (Lib: MH).

A guide to the history and exhibits of the cathedral. Includes brief coverage of the two branches, biographical data on the architects and other artists involved, bibliography, and references to related archival services.

h-558. Razuvaev, V. L. "Ispol'zovanie nauchnogo arkhiva muzeia v izuchenii voprosov neravnomernykh osadok i deformatsii zdaniia Isaakievskogo sobora: Tezisy." In *Vsesoiuznaia konferentsiia-seminar "Arkhivnye fondy khudozhestvennykh muzeev SSSR,"* vol. 1, pp. 135–45. Moscow, 1981.

Provides a survey of documentation in the archive relating to the museum building.

Gosudarstvennyi muzei gorodskoi skul'ptury (GMGS)
[State Museum of Urban Sculpture]

Agency: Komitet po kul'ture Administratsii Sankt-Peterburga
[Committee on Culture of the Administration of St. Petersburg]

Address: 193167, St. Petersburg, Nevskii prospekt, 179/2, lit. A
Telephone: 277-17-16; 274-25-13; 274-26-35; *Fax:* (812) 274-25-79
Transport: metro: Ploshchad' Aleksandra Nevskogo
Hours: M–WF 9:00–17:00; Summer 11:00–19:00

Director: Vladimir Nikolaevich Timofeev (*tel.* 274-26-35)
Deputy Director for Scientific Work: Iurii Minaevich Piriutko (*tel.* 274-25-51)
Chief Curator: Vera Valentinovna Rytikova (*tel.* 274-25-13)
Head of Scientific Division: Rita Samuilovna Evseeva (*tel.* 277-35-07)

HISTORY:

Muzei-nekropol'
  [Necropolis-Museum] (1923–1932)
Muzei nadgrobnykh pamiatnikov
  [Museum of Tombstones] (1932–1936)
Leningradskii nekropol'
  [Leningrad Necropolis] (1936/1937–1939)
Muzei gorodskoi skul'ptury
  [Museum of Urban Sculpture] (1939–1969)

The first museum within the Alexander Nevskii Monastery (*Aleksandro-Nevskaia Lavra*) was founded in 1909 as the so-called Early Depository (*Drevlekhranilishche*), which lasted until 1918 and the early 1920s, when the Monastery was closed as a religious institution; its exhibits were transferred to the Russian Museum. A Necropolis-Museum (*Muzei-nekropol'*), was founded in 1923, when the cemeteries and burial vaults of the Monastery were taken over by the state. Renamed the Museum of Tombstones (*Muzei nadgrobnykh pamiatnikov*) in 1932, it was reorganized in 1936–1937 as the Leningrad Necropolis on the territory of the Alexander Nevskii Monastery. It then included the cemeteries of Lazarus (founded in 1716) and Tikhvinskoe (also known as the Necropolis of Masters of Art), the building of the Church of the Annunciation (*Tserkov' Blagoveshcheniia*) (1717–1722), the oldest in the Lavra, and part of the Volkovo Cemetery (founded in the 18th c.). The Lazarus Necropolis had earlier in the 1920s been included as part of the Museum of Old St. Petersburg.

In 1939 the museum was again reorganized as the Museum of Urban Sculpture, and all the historical cemeteries, monuments, and memorial plaques in the city came under its control. The necropolis was opened to visitors in 1947, and thereafter (1975), an exhibition of original autograph models for tombstones and memorial monuments in the cemetery and other city memorial sculpture was opened in the building of Church of the Annunciation.

The museum now has two branches:

(1) The Literary Bridges Necropolis-Museum (*Muzei-nekropol' "Literatorskie mostki"*), which, comprising a major part of the Volkovo Cemetery, came under the Leningrad Necropolis Museum in the 1930s. The museum opened an exhibit in the former Church of the Ascension (*Voznesenskaia tserkov'*) in 1955. (192007, St. Petersburg, ul. Rasstannaia, 30; tel. 166-23-83)

(2) The Narva Triumphal Arch Museum-Monument (*Muzei-pamiatnik "Narvskie triumfal'nye vorota"*), which was opened in 1987 with memorial exhibitions celebrating victory in the Patriotic War of 1812 against Napoleon and the subsequent European campaigns of the Russian Army. (198095, St. Petersburg, pl. Stachek; tel. 186-97-82).

N.B. Most of the records of the museum itself for the years 1939–1968 are held in TsGALI SPb (D–15, fond 405).

HOLDINGS: manuscript records—ca. 6,000 units (1930s–1990s);
photographs and negatives—ca. 40,000 (1930s–1990s)

The Scientific Division (*Nauchnyi otdel*) of the museum holds documents on the history of the building, preservation, and restoration of sculptural monuments, tombstones of cultural importance, and memorial plaques in St. Petersburg. Of special importance are registers that have been preserved for several cemeteries, including the comprehensive register of burials in the Alexander Nevskii Lavra—"Khronologicheskii spisok o pogrebennykh v Aleksandro-Nevskoi lavre, 1716–1916." There are also designs for tombstones and other monuments that were built during the Soviet period and for the successful entries in competitions to design monuments in Leningrad.

There are also graphic materials and documentation relating to the Siege of Leningrad. There are drawings, studies, and technical drawings by the architects A. N. Aruzhchev, A. I. Gegello, E. A. Levinson, and V. N. Tsaleporovskii, and the sculptors V. Ia. Bogoliubov, N. V. Dadykin, V. V. Isaev, and M. G. Manizer.

The photograph archive (*fototeka*) contains photographic prints and negatives of tombstones and other memorial and monumental sculpture, and of the historical and memorial plaques to be found in St. Petersburg.

Access: For research access, a letter of application is required to the director or chief curator.

Working Conditions: Researchers are accommodated in the museum offices, where materials are available the day they are ordered.

Reference Facilities: There are inventory registers for staff use and auxiliary card catalogues.

Copying: There are no copying facilities available.

Comment: A questionnaire about the archival holdings was not returned to Rosarkhiv.

FINDING AIDS — PUBLISHED — GENERAL:

Muzei SPb (1994), pp. 35–39; *Peterburg* (1992), pp. 399–400; *GAF Spravochnik* (1991), p. 124; *Muzei Leningrada* (1989), pp. 172–76; *Muzei Leningrada* (1982), pp. 68–73.

There is no published guide to the archival holdings in the museum.

h-559. Netunakhina, Galina Dmitrievna. *Muzei gorodskoi skul'ptury: Putevoditel'.* 3d ed. Leningrad: Lenizdat, 1981. 144 p. (Lib: MH)

2d ED. (with Nina Iliodorovna Udimova): *Muzei gorodskoi skul'ptury: Kratkii putevoditel'.* L., 1972. 183 p. "Turistu o Leningrade." (Lib: MH)

1st ED. (with Nina Iliodorovna Udimova): *Gorodskie pamiatniki. Nekropol' Aleksandro-Nevskoi lavry. Literaturnye mostki: [Kratkii putevoditel'].* L., 1963. 251 p. (Lib: MH)
A brief history and guide to the cemetery and museum exhibits.

h-560. *Istoricheskie kladbishcha Peterburga: Spravochnik-putevoditel'.* Compiled by A. V. Kobak and Iu. M. Piriutko. St. Petersburg: Izd-vo Chernysheva, 1993. 639 p. (Lib: DLC; IU; MH) (Also listed as a-575).
A very detailed guide based on extensive archival research covering cemeteries in St. Petersburg, many of which have been associated with the museum. See the lengthy historical chapter (pp. 8–60),

drawing on materials in the museum (along with other sources), and other introductory essays on architecture, epitaphs, and various styles of tombs. Guides to specific cemeteries that come under the museum include extensive coverage of Alexander Nevskii Lavra (pp. 130–61), and the branch Literary Bridges Necropolis-Museum, including the Volkovo Cemetery (pp. 315–54).

h-561. *Sobranie sovetskoi skul'ptury: Katalog.* Compiled by G. N. Shkoda. Leningrad: "Sovetskii khudozhnik," 1968. 112 p. [Upravlenie kul'tury Ispolkoma Lengorsoveta; Muzei gorodskoi skul'ptury] Preface by G. N. Shkoda.

   Includes an index of names (pp. 110–12).

Art Museums

❋⊶ H–88 ⊷❋

Gosudarstvennyi Ermitazh (GE)
[State Hermitage]

Agency: Ministerstvo kul'tury RF (Minkul'tury Rossii)
[Ministry of Culture]

Address: 191186, St. Petersburg, Dvortsovaia nab., 34–36
Telephone: 110-96-10; 110-96-04; 311-36-01 (foreign office);
Fax: (812) 311-90-09 (foreign office); 311-91-80; 110-96-57
E-mail: interface@hermitage.ru
Website: http://www.hermitage.ru
Transport: metro: Gostinyi Dvor, Nevskii prospekt; trol.: 1, 7, 9, 10
Hours: Tu–Su 10:30–18:00; F 10:30–15:00

Director: Mikhail Borisovich Piotrovskii (*tel.* 110-96-01)
Deputy Director for Scientific Work: Georgii Vadimovich Vilinbakhov (*tel.* 110-96-02)
Head of Division of Foreign Affairs:
   Natal'ia Vasil'evna Kolomiets (*tel.* 311–36–01; 110–96–45)
Scientific Secretary: Nina Pavlovna Lavrova (*tel.* 110–96–10)

HISTORY:
   Imperatorskii Ermitazh
   [Imperial Hermitage] (1764–1917)

The Hermitage, one of the largest museums in the world, was founded in 1764 as a repository for the works of art collected by Empress Catherine II in a separate building attached to the Winter Palace. From the eighteenth to the early twentieth century, purchases for the museum were made abroad and in Russia of many large private collections of paintings, engravings, drawings, *objets d'art*, coins, medals, books, and manuscripts. The museum was first opened to the public in 1852.

After the October Revolution it was given its present name. The museum holdings were considerably enlarged by nationalized art from the imperial suburban palaces; from several large private collections, such as those of the Stroganov, Iusupov, and Shuvalov families; from the museums of the Academy of Arts (H–90) and the Baron Stieglitz (Shtiglits) Museum of Industrial Arts (H–94); and from the State Museum Fond (*Gosudarstvennyi muzeinyi fond*), a collecting organ for nationalized treasures. With the enlargement of its collections the museum took over the entire Winter Palace, and the museum structure was reorganized. During the 1920s and 30s many of the valuable museum treasures were turned over to various export agencies, including the All-Union Antiquarian Company (*Vsesoiuznoe obshchestvo "Antikvariat"*), or the so-called Export Fund, for sale abroad at auction and to diplomats and foreign businessmen within the country for foreign currency. Many other treasures from the State Museum Fond were given to museums throughout the USSR, including the A. S. Pushkin Museum of Fine Arts in Moscow (H–26), and especially those in non-Russian union republics. During the Second World War, a large part of the collections

1068

was evacuated to Sverdlovsk, but some treasures were lost during the blockade of Leningrad. The museum acquired many "trophy" works of art from Germany and Eastern Europe in the immediate postwar years, including many that had been sequestered by the Nazis from private sources.

In December 1991 the State Hermitage was added to the federal register of the most valuable monuments of the cultural heritage of the peoples of the Russian Federation. Archival and other manuscript materials are found in many of the different divisions. Although drawings and some other graphic materials in its collections are usually classified among the visual arts, nonetheless, many graphic materials held by the museum are also of archival interest, and are accordingly mentioned at least in passing below.

The archive of the museum itself (now within the Division of Manuscripts and Documentary Fonds), preserving its own administrative, scientific, and research records, was begun in 1805. In 1928 agreement was reached with the Administration of Central Archives (*Tsentrarkhiv*) for the Hermitage archive to remain permanently under the control of the museum (although some postrevolutionary records through 1937 were transferred to TsGALI SPb, as noted below). The Photograph Archive was begun in 1919 on the basis of a collection of photographs held by the Picture Gallery (*Kartinnaia galereia*), which was part of the Combined Hermitage Library. In 1925 the Photograph Archive became a separate subdivision.

The Hermitage Library was founded in 1762 as the personal library of Empress Catherine II. In the 1860s and again after 1917, the majority of its manuscripts were transferred from the Hermitage and other imperial libraries to the Imperial Public Library, and now constitute the Hermitage Collection (*Ermitazhnoe sobranie*) in the Division of Manuscripts of the Russian National Library (RNB—G–15). A few of these manuscripts were subsequently returned to the Hermitage and are now held in the Cabinet of Rare Books (*Kabinet redkoi knigi*) and in other divisions of the museum. After the October Revolution the Hermitage Library acquired manuscript materials from the libraries of various imperial palaces and from a number of nationalized private collections in Petrograd, although some of these were then turned over to *Antiquariat* or sold abroad directly. Subsequently, there were new acquisitions from other sources. For example, in 1932 the library acquired some twenty Slavonic and Russian manuscripts from a Pomor'e Old Believer community. The manuscript materials were subsequently arranged as a separate fond within the Cabinet of Rare Books, which was opened in 1962 within what is now called the Central Scientific Library.

The Division of West European Art was founded in 1764, but its present name dates to 1930. The Sector for Drawings was organized in 1805, but in 1930 became part of the Division of Graphic Art, and since 1948, it has been part of the Division of Western European Art. The Engravings Section was founded in 1805–1806 as the Cabinet of Prints and Engravings (*Kabinet estampov*). In 1920 it became the Division of Engravings (*Otdelenie graviur*), and from 1930 to 1948 was part of the Division of Graphic Art.

The Division of the History of Russian Culture was established in 1941 on the basis of collections earlier held in the Historical Daily-Life Division (*Istoriko-bytovoi otdel*) of the State Russian Museum (H–89). Part of its Sector for Russian Culture in the First Third of the Eighteenth Century now occupies the A. D. Menshikov Palace (*Dvorets A. D. Menshikova*), constructed in 1710–1714 for Prince Aleksandr Danilovich Menshikov, the Governor-General of the city and Baltic lands under Peter I, (199164, St. Petersburg, Universitetskaia nab., 15; tel. 213-11-12; 213-80-01).

The Division of the History and Culture of the Orient was established in 1920 as the Medieval Islamic Section. In 1921 it was renamed the Caucasian, Iranian, and Central Asian Section, and in 1926 given its present name.

The Division of Numismatics developed out of the original coin collections acquired by Catherine II in 1771. Starting in 1786, it was known as the Mint Cabinet (*Mintskabinet*, from the German *Münzkabinett*), and from 1864, the Coins Section (*Monetnoe otdelenie*). Its present name dates from 1918.

Access: Permission for research work in the Archive and Photograph Archive, and in holdings in other museum divisions, requires an official letter stating the subject and purpose of the research, addressed to the Deputy Director for Scientific Work. Simultaneously researchers should submit a written application for a pass to enter the required division. Permission to work in the Cabinet of Rare Books Room must be obtained from the director of the Scientific Library on the basis of an official letter.

Otdel rukopisei i dokumental'nogo fonda (Arkhiv i Fotoarkhiv) (ORDF)
[Division of Manuscripts and Documentary Fond (Archive and Photograph Archive)]

Telephone: 110-96-46; *RdngRm:* 110-96-46
Hours: WTh 11:00–13:00, 14:00–16:00;
Photograph Archive: Tu–Th 11:00–13:00, 14:00–16:30
Head: Galina Ivanovna Kachalina
Head of Photo Archive: Valentina Fedorovna Marishkina (*tel.* 110-96-89)

HOLDINGS: 46 fonds, 32,917 units, 1767–1992
institutional fonds—5 (1767–1991); personal fonds—41 (1800–1982); negatives—65,257
(original 39,021, reproductions 26,236) (early 20th c.–1990s); positives—381 (early 20th c.–1950s)

The Hermitage Archive comprises the administrative records of one of the largest museums in the world from the time of its founding to the present day, and accordingly constitutes the basic source for its history and activities—its foundation; the provenance, acquisition, displacement, and transformation of its collections; its organization, exhibition, and restoration functions; and its scientific research, educational, and publication activities.

Of particular importance are the original manuscript inventories and catalogues of the private collections accessioned by the Hermitage (late 18th–early 20th cc.), most of which have been preserved, including the collections of Sir Robert Walpole, First Earl of Oxford (accessioned in 1767), D. P. Tatishchev (1846), and the Marquis of Campana (1861), together with those of the St. Petersburg and suburban residences of the imperial family—the Anichkov Palace, the Elagin Island Palace, the Summer Palace, the Tauride Palace, the palaces of Gatchina, Ropsha, Peterhof, and Tsarskoe Selo, and the Michael (*Mikhailovskii*) Castle. There are documents granting A. S. Pushkin access to the Voltaire library (1832) and relating to the manuscripts of Peter the Great (1858) held in the museum library. The fond entitled "The Libraries and Arsenals of His Imperial Majesty" (*Sobstvennye Ego Imperatorskogo Velichestva biblioteki i arsenaly*, 1825–1928) contains files on the acquisition of books, engravings, lithographs, and drawings for the imperial palace libraries. There are also catalogues and inventories of the armory, uniforms, and archeological monuments held in the Tsarskoe Selo Arsenal and the Arsenal of the Nicholas (*Nikolaevskii*) Palace, as well as correspondence relating to their display in exhibitions and their transfer to various museums.

The Fond of the Architect of the Winter Palace (1839–1890s) contains watercolors, lithographs, plans, and technical drawings of the rooms of the Winter Palace, and the buildings of the Hermitage and the Hermitage Theater. A separate fond has been formed for pictorial materials on the history of the Hermitage (1865–1993), which includes posters and tickets, as well as drawings by such Russian and Soviet artists as Alexandre Benois (Benua), S. P. Iaremich, E. K. Lipgardt, V. V. Miliutina, and G. S. Vereiskii, and I. A. Vsevolozhskii, all of whom are connected with the museum.

The archive holds materials from the Leningrad Division of Glavnauka of the People's Commissariat for Education (*Narkompros RSFSR*) (1917–1935). These include rulings, regulations, and circular letters of Glavnauka, together with orders, instructions, and documents regarding the accession of *objets d'art* from private individuals and institutions, the protection of church valuables, the transfer of *objets d'art* to other museums in Moscow, Leningrad and other cities, and files on the liquidation of the Museum Fond.

There are personal papers of various scholars and artists whose work was connected with the Hermitage. These include the papers of the historian and first museum director, S. A. Gedeonov; antiquarians Heinrich Karl Ernst Köhler and Oscar Waldhauer (O. F. Val'dgauer); Egyptologist B. A. Turaev; archeologists B. A. Latynin and A. P. Mantsevich; numismatists N. P. Bauer, R. R. Fasmer, A. K. Markov, O. F. Retovskii, and A. N. Zograf; artists and art specialists A. N. Benois, N. N. Ge, V. F. Levinson-Lessing, E. G. Lisenkov, D. A. Schmidt, and B. K. Veselovskii; and restoration specialist P. I. Kostrov.

The Photograph Archive retains photographic materials relating to the Hermitage, as well as an extensive collection of historical daguerrotypes and photographs acquired by the museum and others donated by various organizations during the 1920s and 1930s. Three fonds—originals, reproductions, and positive prints—reproduce and provide a complete permanent record of all the museum exhibits, including sculpture, paintings, and decorative or applied art; the facades and interiors of the museum buildings; architectural plans and projects; permanent and temporary exhibitions; the work of the museum divisions and the restoration workshops; and portraits of the museum staff. There are also photographs of the prerevolutionary collections of the Hermitage, the interiors of rooms of the imperial family in the Winter Palace, the evacuation of the collections during the First World War, the infirmary, the halls occupied by Provisional Government troops, and some unique shots taken of the rooms in the Winter Palace after the devastation of 26–27 October 1917. There is a large collection of reproductions illustrating the history of world art, including negatives and prints from the collections of the Baron Stieglitz (Shtiglits) Museum and the Imperial Carriage Museum (*Pridvorno-koniushennyi muzei*). The history of photography in Russia is well represented by the collections of such famous St. Petersburg photographers as Gibshman, Karl von Hahn (K. E. Gan), K. Kubesh, and F. L. Mikolaevskii (Nikolaevskii) (the official Hermitage photographer, 1890–1917), among others.

N.B. Part of the postrevolutionary records of the Hermitage were transferred to state archival custody and are now held in TsGALI SPb (D–15; fond 5; 1921–1937).

Working Conditions: Materials are delivered to the reading room soon after they are requested.

Reference Facilities: There are *opisi* for individual fonds in the Archive and the Photographic Archive, as well as subject and alphabetic card catalogues.

Copying: Photographic and xerox copies can be prepared.

Tsentral'naia nauchnaia biblioteka—Kabinet redkoi knigi (TsNB)
[Central Scientific Library—Cabinet of Rare Books]

Telephone: 219-86-79; 219-86-52
Hours: Tu–Sa 10:00–12:00, 13:00–17:00
Head: Evgeniia Ivanovna Makarova (*tel.* 110-96-79)
Head of the Cabinet of Rare Books: Kseniia Nikolaevna Griazeva (*tel.* 110-97-58)

HOLDINGS: 4 (collections) fonds, ca. 450 units, 12th c.–20th c.
  Slavonic-Rus' MS books—63 units (14th–19th cc.); Russian secular manuscripts—214 units
  (18th–20th cc.); foreign manuscripts—ca. 120 units (11th–19th cc.);
  charters, diplomas, patents—ca. 40 units (13th–20th cc.)

Most interesting in the Cabinet of Rare Books is the collection of Slavonic and Russian manuscripts and manuscript books (14th–19th cc.), including several on parchment. The earliest of these is a parchment copy of the Chronicle of George Amartol (Georgios Amartolos, late 14th–early 15th c.). There are also early tales and legends, a collected codex of Arkhangel'sk Deacon Lavrentii Ivanov, the spiritual *Tsvetnik* (Florilegium, or anthology of edifactory texts) of Hierodeacon Gerasim

1071

Belogradets, a late seventeenth-century illuminated manuscript of the Gospels, legends of the Icons of the Virgin, psalters, prayer-books, services for the Russian saints, calendars of saints and religious festivals (*sviattsy*), lives of saints, chronicles, codices of religious chants, a parchment folio with a miniature and the beginning of the Gospel According to St. Mark (from the library of Nicholas II), an illuminated "Book of the Seventh Heaven and the Creation of Adam and Eve" (*Kniga o sed'mi nebesakh, o sotvorenii Adama i Evy*) with inscriptions by F. I. Buslaev, a richly decorated *Torzhestvennik* (solemn orations apropos important events) with Pomor'e ornamentation, a redaction of the "Velikoe Zertsalo," tracts on popular medicine (*lechebniki*) and medicinal herbs (*travniki*), an illuminated list of noble ranks and titles—"*Tituliarnik*"—(ca. 1670s), and codices of imperial decrees.

There are also Russian secular manuscripts (18th–20th cc.), including albums and diaries, travel notes, and descriptions of palaces, galleries, towns and gubernias in Russia. Among the more prominent manuscripts are "The Core of Russian History" ("*Iadro rossiiskoi istorii*") by A. I. Mankiev; verses by M. V. Lomonosov, A. P. Sumarokov, and N. Leont'ev; a satire on the Masons; sixteen folios of commentary in the hand of Catherine II on a French manuscript on Russian history "Introduction à l'histoire générale de la Russie" by Gâbriel Senac de Meilhan; a manuscript decorated with watercolors of "The Russian Apothegm" (*Rossiiskii Apofegmat*), or "Notes from the Instructions (*Nakaz*) for the Commission for the New Code of Laws (*Novoe ulozhenie*)" of 1778; a memorandum dated 1781 on changes to be made in the uniform of the Guards of the Preobrazhenskii Regiment with illustrations done in gouache and signed by G. A. Potemkin; a muster roll of the same regiment done in watercolors with autographs of A. V. Suvorov; muster rolls for the Semenov Regiment and units of other guards from the period of Catherine II; and a notebook of V. A. Zhukovskii. Of considerable interest are the numerous volumes of the "Genealogical Notes" ("*Genealogicheskie zametki*") of Prince A. B. Lobanov-Rostovskii, which amount to a collection of unique historical data on Russian family trees. And no less interesting is the "Systematic Catalogue of His Imperial Majesty's Library," which belonged to Emperor Nicholas II.

There is a small collection of charters, diplomas, and letters patent, many of them richly ornamented on parchment, including a few bearing the signatures of General Burkhard Münnich (Minikh), Catherine II, and Nicholas I.

The collection of Western European manuscripts (11th–19th cc.), which contains predominantly lay writings in Latin, French, German, and Italian, is currently being reprocessed. Among them is one of the oldest and finest copies (11th c.) of Cicero's dialogue "On Friendship" (*De Amicitia*). There is also a catalogue of gems by A. Miliotti and an "Inventory of the Collection of Gems," which became part of Catherine the Great's collection, illustrated with drawings and written by the director of the Dresden Academy of Arts, Giovanni Battista Casanova.

Working Conditions: Only materials that have been processed and described are available for researchers in the reading room.

Reference Facilities: The four fonds of manuscripts are currently in various stages of arrangement and description.

Copying: Xerox copies can be prepared.

Otdel istorii russkoi kul'tury (OIRK)
[Division of the History of Russian Culture]

Hours: WTh 11:00–17:00
Head: Galina Nikolaevna Komelova (*tel.* 110-96-61)

HOLDINGS: ca. 85,000 units, 15th–20th cc.

> MS books—233 units (14th–19th cc.); photographs—ca. 40,000 units; drawings and watercolors—ca. 11,000 units; etchings—more than 40,000 units

The division holds Slavonic and Russian manuscript books, manuscripts, and documents (15th–18th cc.), acquired from urban churches or from private collectors. The F. A. Kalikin collection (purchased in 1948) contains, for example, a codex with tales and epistles of Maksim Grek (16th c.); the "Russian Grapes" (*"Vinograd rossiiskii"*) of S. Denisov (18th c.); a seventeenth-century land-survey register (*Kniga soshnogo i vytnogo pis'ma'*) with additional "Arithmetic" (*"Arifmetika"*); an Old Believer Pomor'e "Answers" (*Pomorskie otvety*) (1723); a sixteenth-century Prologue; and a large collected sixteenth- and seventeenth-century codex including tales, legends, lives of saints, and other compositions. Also of Pomor'e provenance is a richly ornamented sixteenth-century Books of the Apostles and an eighteenth-century book of canticles (*Stikhiry*).

From other collections the division has acquired several dozen scrolled registers (*stolbtsy*) (17th–18th cc.) containing household records, business transactions, extracts from census registers, petitions, letters patent, and charters (including the imperial charter issued to the merchant Ia. Stroganov in 1568); fifteenth- and sixteenth-century illuminated Gospels; a list of noble ranks and titles (*Tituliarnik*); a mid-seventeenth-century field church calendar (*Mesiatseslov*), once belonging to Colonel G. V. Vul'f (Wolff) of the Petrine Army; an illuminated manuscript of the Vision of St. Gregory (*Grigor'evo videnie*) (late 17th c.); an eighteenth-century Nomocanon (*Kormchaia*); an early nineteenth-century album of verses illustrated with watercolors; and a collection of eighteenth-century Old Believer manuscript religious codices (*sborniki*).

The collections of Russian Graphic Arts include drawings, watercolors, engravings, lithographs and plates illustrating the military uniforms of all the countries in the world. There is also a unique collection of portraits of the Decembrists and pictures of the places where they were held in confinement and sent into exile to Siberia. There are folders of the watercolors and drawings of O. A. Kiprenskii, G. G. Gagarin, and other masters of the Russian school.

The division also holds photographs and postcards showing the history, culture, religion, and art of the peoples of Russia.

Otdel zapadnoevropeiskogo iskusstva (OZEI)
[Division of Western European Art]

Hours: WTh 11:00–17:00
Head: Irina Nikolaevna Novosel'skaia (*tel.* 110-96-24)
Deputy Head: Tat'iana Kirillovna Kustodieva (*tel.* 110-97-13)
Head, Sector of Drawings: Irina Sergeevna Grigor'eva (*tel.* 110-96-97)
Acting Head, Sector of Engravings: Larisa Aleksandrovna Dukel'skaia (*tel.* 110-96-82)

HOLDINGS: ca. 528,000 units, 12th–20th cc.

> MS books and manuscripts—ca. 32 units; drawings—ca. 40,000 units; miniatures—over 2,100 units; engravings and lithographs—ca. 486,000 units

Archival and manuscript materials are found in several different sectors within the Division of Western European Art. The Sector for Drawings holds materials from a number of private collections, including those of Count Ludwig von Cobenzl (K. Kobentsl') (acquired in 1768), Count Heinrich

Brühl (G. Briul') (1769), P. P. Divov (1833), Luigi Grassi (1862), Prince A. B. Lobanov-Rostovskii (1897), Grand Duke Sergei Aleksandrovich (1911), E. A. Evreinova (1913), and S. P. Iaremich (1919); and those acquired after the Revolution (1925–1929) through the State Museum Fond from the nationalized collections of the Shuvalov, Iusupov, Stroganov, and Saxe-Altenburg families, among others. Important institutional collections include those from the Library of the St. Petersburg Academy of Sciences (the collection of Peter I), the Baron Stieglitz (Shtiglits) Library and Museum (1923–1927), the library and museums of the Academy of Arts (1924), the Winter Palace and its library, the State Russian Museum (1929–1930), and the abolished State Museum of Modern Western Art in Moscow (1934–1949). The drawings themselves are only mentioned in passing here, as most of them should be considered "art" rather than "archival" materials.

The Sector for Drawings has a number of manuscripts of Western European provenance (early 12th–19th cc.) in French, Italian, Dutch, German, Spanish, and Greek, including 22 illuminated with miniatures, and 2 with drawings. Most of these were transferred from the Hermitage Library and had been acquired from previously private collections, including the Library of the Baron Stieglitz Central School of Industrial Arts. These include, for example, an early twelfth-century Psalter, a "Hunting Book" of Gaston Phoebus, Count de Foix (late 14th c.), the "Principles of Government" of Diomedes Caraffa (1477), the "Roman de la Rose" (early 16th c.), and a manuscript copy of Leonardo da Vinci's "Treatise on Painting" (mid-1630s).

There are graphic works representative of all the Western European schools from the fifteenth to the twentieth centuries in various media, including drawings of architectural monuments and decoration, ornamental and applied art, landscapes and portraits. There are also collections of pastels and miniatures, technical architectural drafts amd drawings by European and Russian architects, and drawings done by theatrical decorators and designers. There are drawings by such architects as Auguste de Montferrand, A. N. Voronikhin, Jean-François Thomas de Thomon, and Giacomo Quarenghi. There are the watercolors of K. A. Ukhtomskii, E. P. Gau, and Luigi Premazzi, depicting the interiors of the imperial palace, among other subjects.

The Sector of Engravings includes Western European engravings, lithographs, and other types of prints acquired from many important Western European collections (15th–20th cc). They have not been retained as part of their originating collections, but are rather catalogued as individual folios, albums, and displays, featuring various genres and techniques. These range from a collection of English caricatures (late 18th–early 19th cc.) to albums of original engravings and prints, and reproductions from originals by many European masters.

Otdel istorii i kul'tury Vostoka (OIKV)
[Division of the History and Culture of the Orient]

Hours: WTh 11:00–17:00
Head: Anatolii Alekseevich Ivanov (*tel.* 110-96-83, 312-19-53)
Deputy Head: Tamara Ivanovna Zeimal' (*tel.* 110-97-47)
Chief Curator: Natal'ia Vladimirovna Venevtseva (*tel.* 110-97-56)

HOLDINGS: ca. 1,000 units, 5th–20th cc.

Manuscripts, graphic materials, and photographs are not arranged separately, but are rather intermingled with other parts of the division holdings.

The division holds manuscripts on folklore and religious subjects written on papyrus and parchment in Coptic, Greek, and Arabic, which came from the private collections of V. G. Bok, B. A. Turaev, and N. P. Likhachev. Among them are a papyrus with Arabic and Coptic inscriptions and a parchment folio representation of Christ-Emmanuel. There are some Arabic, Persian and Turkish manuscripts (12th–20th cc.), including a copy of the "Khamsek" of the Persian poet Nizami with miniatures from Herat (ancient Aria, in Northwest Afghanistan) prepared in 1431 for Sultan Shah-Rukh. There are more than 20 illuminated Armenian manuscripts (most received from the Lviv Historical Museum in 1924), including a Gospel, which was transcribed in 1200 and decorated with miniatures by Toros the Philosopher in Drazark (Cilician Armenia). Recently revealed among the Hermitage post-World War II trophy collections are 560 Pahlevi papyri and parchments from Middle Persia.

From the collection of the Baron Stieglitz Museum there are drawings of the mosaic panels on the Mausoleum of Shah-Zinda in Samarkand (1898–1904); architectural details from the Mausoleum of Gur-Emir drawn by P. P. Pokryshkin (1898); watercolor copies by Romberg of the murals at Afrasiaba (1913); folders of Oriental carpet designs compiled by the artist A. A. Bogoliubov; signed engravings of Arabic inscriptions from the collection of N. I. Veselovskii; Central Asian landscapes by V. A. Krachkovskaia; photographs of the ancient city of Pendzhikent taken by A. Iu. Iakubovskii (1947); and plans and photographs of the caves in the Buddhist Monastery of Kara-Tepe made in 1961 by an expedition headed by B. Ia. Stavisskii. The division also holds the archives of the art historian and Byzantine scholar, A. P. Smirnov (1889–1930).

Working Conditions: Researchers are accommodated in the working offices.

Reference Facilities: There are inventory registers and inventories as well as subject and alphabetic card catalogues.

Otdel numizmatiki (ON)
[Division of Numismatics]

Telephone: 110-96-29
Hours: WTh 11:00–16:00
Head: Vsevolod Mikhailovich Potin (*tel.* 312-19-80)
Head of the Library: Genrietta Iosifovna Ginzburg

HOLDINGS: ca. 100 units, 18th–20th cc.

The archive and library of the Division of Numismatics holds a number of manuscript scholarly catalogues of the numismatics collections of the Hermitage (18th–20th cc.) and of collections of other museums, institutions, and societies, as well as of the private collections acquired by the museum. These include a manuscript album entitled: "Drawings of Russian Medals and Interesting Coins Made for Triumphal Celebrations and for Joyful and Sorrowful Occasions" (early 18th c.) and the inventories (*Reviziia*) of the *Mintskabinet* and of the "Exceptional Valuables" (*dragotsennoe*) collection in the Kunstkammer (1768); manuscripts by two of Hermitage curators, A. I. Luzhkov (1780s) and G. Nigri, the latter containing a general survey of the *Mintskabinet* (1820s); and catalogues compiled by the curators, Heinrich Karl Ernst Köhler (ca. 1830), K. I. Sedzher (1838), and Marie-Felicité (M. I.) Brosset (1861).

There are also catalogues of the collections in the Numismatic Museum of the St. Petersburg Academy of Sciences (1836, 1854, 1894) and in the Academy of Arts (1923); catalogues of the private collections of General P. K. Sukhtelen (Suchtelen) (1823), A. Ia. Italinskii (1828), G. I. Lisenko (1830s), and the Pskov merchant F. M. Pliushkin (1925); and Jakob Reichel; O. F. Retovskii's collection of coins from the Trebizond Empire (1926); the collections of Hofmeister (Steward of the Household) G. P. Alekseev (1927), Count I. I. Tolstoi (1918), and N. P. Likhachev (1938); designs for the Constantine rouble (1825) which would have been issued had Alexander I's brother, Konstantin Pavlovich, not abdicated in favor of his younger brother, Nicholas I; inventories of the Kyiv Pechers′ka Lavra (Monastery of the Caves) treasure (1898); and an unfinished catalogue of Byzantine coins compiled by N. P. Bauer (1918–1919), among others. The division also holds bronze engraving plates for Oriental coins, designer's proofs, and lithographic plates of an unpublished volume of the transactions (*Zapiski*) of the Numismatic Division of the Russian Archeological Society (1919).

Working Conditions: There is a reading room in the library of the division, where materials are delivered soon after they are ordered.

Reference Facilities: There are inventories and register books along with alphabetic and subject card catalogues.

FINDING AIDS — PUBLISHED — GENERAL:

Muzei SPb (1994), pp. 19–22; *Biblioteki SPb* (1993), p. 60; *Peterburg* (1992), pp. 677–78; *GAF Spravochnik* (1991), pp. 38–40; *Muzei Leningrada* (1989), pp. 120–53; *Muzei Leningrada* (1982), pp. 56–61; PKG *M&L* (1972), p. 341; *Myl'nikov* (1970), p. 20; *Malyshev* (1949), pp. 455–56.

There is no comprehensive published guide to all of the manuscript and archival materials in the museum, nor are there published descriptions of many of the divisions, although there are recent guides to some sections of the Hermitage Archive.

General and Historical Surveys

h-565. *Great Art Treasures of the Hermitage Museum, St. Petersburg.* Edited by V. A. Suslov. 2 vols. London: Booth-Clibborn Editions; New York: Abrams, 1994. (Lib: DDO; DLC; MH)

Vol. 1: *Art of the Early Cultures, Classical Antiquities, Oriental Works of Art, Coins and Medals, Arms and Armour.* 692 p.

Vol. 2: *Western European Art, Russian Art and Culture.* 879 p.

An elaborate two-volume folio edition with colored illustrations from the Hermitage collections. Authoritative introductions characterize major divisions of the museum, exhibiting samples of the treasures of world art from paleolithic times to the twentieth century. Annotations include notes about provenance and sources of acquisition. Each volume has separate indexes and bibliography.

h-566. Voronikhina, Liudmila Nikolaevna. *Gosudarstvennyi Ermitazh.* 2d ed. Moscow: "Iskusstvo," 1992. 399 p.

1st ED.: L.: "Iskusstvo," 1983. 456 p. + plates. "Goroda i muzei mira." (Lib: DLC; MH).

A popular history of the foundation and development of the Hermitage collections, characterizing all divisions of the museum, with emphasis on monuments of world art from paleolithic times to the twentieth century. Includes bibliography (pp. 382–87).

h-567. *Ermitazh: Istoriia i sovremennost'.* Edited by V. A. Suslov. Moscow: "Iskusstvo," 1990. 367 p. (Lib: IU; MH)

A detailed history of the museum from its foundation to the present with a survey of the formation of its collections in different divisions, including information on the archival materials.

h-568. Piotrovskii, Boris Borisovich. *Ermitazh: Istoriia i kollektsii.* [Moscow]: "Iskusstvo," 1980. 215 p. (Lib: DLC; IU)

A history of the museum and the formation of its collections. Includes name and geographic indexes.

h-568.1. Piotrovskii, Boris Borisovich. *The Hermitage: Its History and Collections.* Edited by Patrick Creagh. Translated by L. N. Lezhneva. New York: Johnson Reprint Corp., Harcourt Brace Jovanovich, 1982. 215 p. + plates. (Lib: MH)

An English translation of h-568. Includes a bibliography.

h-569. *Ermitazh za 200 let (1764–1964): Istoriia i sostav kollektsii, rabota muzeia.* Edited by B. Piotrovskii. Moscow/Leningrad: "Sovetskii khudozhnik," 1966. 184 p. Introduction by B. B. Piotrovskii. (Lib: DLC; IU; MH)

h-570. Persianova, Ol'ga M. *Sokrovishchnitsa mirovogo iskusstva: Obzor kollektsii Ermitazha.* Edited by M. I. Artamonov. 3d ed. Leningrad: "Sovetskii khudozhnik," 1964. 156 p. (Lib: IU; MH)

 EARLIER ED.: *Ermitazh, sokrovishchnitsa mirovoi kul'tury i iskusstv.* L.: Izd-vo Gos. Ermitazha, 1960. 111 p. (Lib: MH).

h-571. Varshavskii, Sergei Petrovich; and Rest, Boris Isaakovich. *Ermitazh: Ocherki iz istorii Gosudarstvennogo Ermitazha, 1764–1938.* Edited by I. A. Orbeli. Moscow/Leningrad: "Iskusstvo," 1940. 256 p. (Lib: DDO; IU)

 EARLIER ED.: Leningrad: "Leningradskaia pravda," 1939. ii, 252 p. (Lib: MH).

 A history of the museum from the time of Catherine II to the 1930s.

h-572. Varshavskii, Sergei Petrovich; and Rest, Boris Isaakovich. *Riadom s Zimnim: [Iz istorii Gosudarstvennogo Ermitazha. Ermitazh pered Oktiabrem].* Leningrad: "Sovetskii khudozhnik," 1969. 152 p. (Lib: DLC; IU; MH)

 An historical and documentary account based on a wide range of archival sources covering the period from 1907–October 1917.

h-573. Varshavskii, Sergei Petrovich; and Rest, Boris Isaakovich. *Bilet na vsiu vechnost'.* 2d ed. Leningrad: Lenizdat, 1981. 496 p. (Lib: IU; MH)

 An historical and documentary account based on a wide range of archival sources covering the postrevolutionary history to the mid-1920s.

h-574. Varshavskii, Sergei Petrovich; and Rest, Boris Isaakovich. *Podvig Ermitazha: Dokumental'naia povest'.* 3d ed. Leningrad: Lenizdat, 1985. 174 p. "Biblioteka molodogo rabochego." (Lib: DLC; IU; MH)

 2d ED.: *Podvig Ermitazha: Gosudarstvennyi Ermitazh v gody Velikoi Otechestvennoi voiny.* L.: "Sovetskii khudozhnik," 1969. 192 p. (Lib: MH)

 1st ED.: L., 1965. 190 p. + 6 plates. (Lib: MH).

 Describes the efforts and activities of the staff to save the Hermitage collections during World War II.

h-574.1. Varshavskii, Sergei Petrovich; and Rest, Boris Isaakovich. *The Ordeal of the Hermitage: The Siege of Leningrad, 1941–1944.* Translated by Arthur Shkarovsky-Raffe. Leningrad: Aurora Art Publishers/ New York: Abrams, 1985. 270 p. + 34 plates. (Lib: MH)

 An elaborately illustrated, large-format English-language account (prepared for foreign consumption) of the Hermitage during the war, including evacuation, wartime damage, and postwar reconstruction. Includes many colored illustrations of the Hermitage buildings and present-day interiors with black-and-white pictures of wartime damage and evacuation efforts. Identical to h-574.2, except for the variant English title (also notes the original Russian title *Spasennyi dlia chelovechestva*). Some of the materials duplicate the coverage in h-574; but this edition differs significantly from that Russian version.

h-574.2. Varshavskii, Sergei Petrovich; and Rest, Boris Isaakovich. *Saved for Humanity: The Hermitage During the Siege of Leningrad, 1941–1944.* Translated by Arthur Shkarovsky-Raffe. Leningrad: Aurora Art Publishers, 1985. 270 p. + 34 plates. (Lib: MH)

 Identical to h-574.1 (with the original Russian title *Spasennyi dlia chelovechestva*), except for the variant title; issued directly by "Aurora" without collaboration with the New York publisher.

h-575. Zhil', F. A. *Muzei Imperatorskogo Ermitazha: Opisanie razlichnykh sobranii, sostavliaiushchikh muzei, s istoricheskim vvedeniem ob Ermitazhe imperatritsy Ekateriny II i o obrazovanii Muzeia Novogo Ermitazha.* St. Petersburg: Tip. Imp. AN, 1861. xxxiii, 409, [8] p. (Lib: DDO; DLC; IU)

 In addition to its coverage of other parts of the museum, includes a survey of the manuscript collections (pp. 25–117) and library (pp. 119–37) of the Imperial Hermitage, although most of the manuscripts described are now in the Hermitage Collection in the Manuscript Division of RNB (G–15).

Archive and Photographic Archive

h-576. *Arkhiv Gosudarstvennogo Ordena Lenina Ermitazha: Putevoditel'.* Compiled by
G. Kachalina and E. M. Iakovleva. Leningrad: GE, 1988. 40 p. (Lib: DLC)

> The first part of the guide is a survey of five fonds—the Hermitage Fond, the Imperial Libraries and Arsenal Fond, the Architect of the Winter Palace Fond, the State Museum Fond, and the Collection of Pictorial Materials, which contain documents from 1767 to the present.

h-577. *Lichnye arkhivnye fondy Gosudarstvennogo Ermitazha: Spravochnik.* Compiled by
G. Kachalina. St. Peterburg: GE, 1992. 28 p. + 16 plates. (Lib: DLC; IU; MH)

> A description of 21 personal fonds in the archives of the State Hermitage.

h-578. *Fotoarkhiv Gosudarstvennogo Ermitazha: Spravochnik-putevoditel'.* Compiled by
V. F. Marishkina. St. Petersburg: GE, 1992. 22 p. + 19 plates. (Lib: DLC; IU; MH)

> The first published guide to the Photographic Archive. Includes an article by the compiler on the history of photography in the Hermitage (pp. 8–21).

h-579. Miroliubova, G. A.; and Petrova, T. A. *Russkaia fotografiia, 1840–1910: Iz sobraniia Ermitazha.* Leningrad: GE, 1991. 55 p. (Lib: MH)

> An exhibition catalogue of Russian artistic and documentary photography from the Hermitage collections, with an index of photographers and firms (pp. 54–55).

h-580. Marishkina, Valentina Fedorovna. "Fotograf Imperatorskogo Ermitazha F. L. Mikolaevskii: (Lichnyi arkhiv)." In *Ermitazhnye chteniia pamiati B. B. Piotrovskogo: Tezisy dokladov,* edited by E. V. Zeimal', pp. 32–33. St. Petersburg, 1993. (Lib: DLC; MH)

> A survey of photographic materials of F. L. Mikolaevskii (Nikolaevskii), the initial "official" photographer of the Hermitage (1890–1917), part from the Ministry of the Imperial Court, but most purchased from his daughter E. F. Nikolaevskaia.

h-581. Marishkina, Valentina Fedorovna. "Gospital' v Zimnem dvortse." *Sovetskii muzei,* 1991, no. 6, pp. 52–56. (Lib: DLC; IU)

> A published survey of photographic materials relating to soldiers in the hospital of the Winter Palace, which was organized under the tutelage of the imperial family during World War I.

h-581A. "Card Catalog of the Library of the State Hermitage Museum, St. Petersburg." New York: Norman Ross Publishers, 1998–. 480 microfiche.

> A microfiche edition of the Hermitage Library catalogue, covering over 700,000 volumes in Russian and other languages, in several series, including rare books, periodicals, manuscripts, and museum catalogues.

h-582. *Biblioteka Ermitazha v imenakh i sobraniiakh: Katalog vystavki k Mezhdunarodnomu kollokviumu bibliofilov, 14–16 sentiabria 1994 g.* Compiled by G. Vilinbakhov et al. St. Petersburg: GE, 1994. 88 p. Introduction by E. I. Makarova. Parallel texts in Russian and French. (Lib: DLC; MH)

> Provides a summary history and survey of the collections.

h-583. Vol'tsenburg, Oskar Eduardovich. *Biblioteka Ermitazha: Kratkii istoricheskii ocherk.* Leningrad, 1940. 80 p. [GE] (Lib: DDO; MH)

> A history of the library of the Imperial State Hermitage and the fate of its collections.

h-584. Pavlova, Zhermena K. *Imperatorskaia biblioteka Ermitazha. 1762–1917.* [Tenafly, NJ]: Ermitazh, 1988. 213, [8] p. Added English title page: *The Hermitage Imperial Library, 1762–1917.* (Lib: DLC; IU; MH)

> A popularized account of the prerevolutionary Hermitage Library by a former curator with supplementary information on the fate of its collections after 1917. Includes considerable bibliography (pp. 203–13). See also the same author's essay in h-587.

h-585. Shcheglov, V. V. *Sobstvennye Ego Imperatorskogo Velichestva biblioteki i arsenaly: Kratkii istoricheskii ocherk. 1715–1915 gg.* Petrograd: Gosudarstvennaia tip., 1917. 169 p.
> An account by the chief librarian of the imperial libraries before the Revolution, containing much valuable information on the history and fate of the manuscript collections.

h-586. Budaragin, Vladimir Pavlovich. "Drevne-russkie rukopisi Kabineta redkoi knigi Nauchnoi biblioteki Ermitazha." *TODRL* 41 (1988): 420–23. (Lib: DLC; IU; MH)
> A brief survey of 60 early Russian manuscripts in the Cabinet of Rare Books.

h-587. Afiani, Vitalii Iur'evich. "Dokumental'nye sokrovishcha Ermitazha." *AE za 1989 god* (1990): 265–66. (Lib: DLC; IU; MH)

h-588. *Nauchnaia biblioteka Ermitazha.* Edited by A. I. Korobochko. Leningrad, 1975. "Trudy Gosudarstvennogo Ermitazha," vol. 16. (Lib: DLC; IU; MH)
> Includes a history of the book collection of Catherine II by Zh. K. Pavlova (pp. 6–32), including some manuscript materials, an analysis of a manuscript by the French art critic François Meil, "Salon de 1814" (pp. 61–65), a sixteenth-century "Stammbuch" (travel album) (pp. 66–72), and a catalogue of etchings by the engraver Basile Mathé (1856–1917) (pp. 133–60), along with other articles covering rare printed books in the library collection.

h-589. *Rossiia–Frantsiia. Vek Prosveshcheniia. Russko-frantsuzskie kul'turnye sviazi v XVIII stoletii: Katalog vystavki.* Edited by O. V. Mikats. Leningrad, 1987. 301 p. [Minkul't SSSR; GE]
> The catalogue contains published annotations to three manuscript books (nos. 146, 158, 180) in the Hermitage Library that were displayed at the exhibition.

h-590. Kostsova, Aleksandra Semenovna. " 'Tituliarnik' sobraniia Gosudarstvennogo Ermitazha." In *Russkaia kul'tura i iskusstvo,* edited by V. N. Vasil'ev et al., pp. 16–40. 1959. "Trudy Gosudarstvennogo Ermitazha," vol. 3. (Lib: DDO; MH)
> Analyzes the *Tituliarnik* held in the Hermitage Library in comparison with other well-known illuminated manuscripts of that type.

Division of Russian Culture

h-591. *Gosudarstvennyi Ermitazh: Putevoditeli po vystavkam: Arkhitektura Petrograda-Leningrada v pamiatnikakh izobrazitel'nogo iskusstva i arkhitekturnykh chertezhakh.* Compiled by L. V. Antonova and T. M. Sokolova. Edited by M. I. Artamonov. Moscow: "Iskusstvo," 1954. 68 p.
> A survey of the Russian architectural graphic materials (18th–19th cc.).

h-592. *Arkhitekturnaia grafika Rossii: Pervaia polovina XVIII v.: Nauchnyi katalog sobraniia Ermitazha.* Compiled by A. N. Voronikhina. Leningrad, 1981. 170 p. + 6 plates. (Lib: DLC; IU; MH)

h-593. Kostsova, Aleksandra Semenovna; and Kurochkina, N. *Drevnerusskie stennye rospisi v risunkakh nachala XX v. iz sobraniia Ermitazha: Katalog vremennoi vystavki.* Leningrad: GE, 1977. 6 p.

Oriental Division

h-594. Bank, Alisa Vladimirovna. *Vostochnye sobraniia Ermitazha. (Obshchaia kharakteristika, osnovnye linii issledovaniia)/ The Oriental Collections of the Hermitage Museum.* Leningrad: Izd-vo GE, 1960. 86 p. (XXV Mezhdunarodnyi kongress vostokovedov). (Lib: DLC; MH) Parallel text in Russian and English.
> A detailed survey of the history of the formation and activities of the museum in the Byzantine and Oriental fields. Includes bibliography (pp. 53–83).

h-595. Ernshtedt, Petr Viktorovich. *Koptskie teksty Gosudarstvennogo Ermitazha.* Moscow/ Leningrad: Izd-vo AN SSSR, 1959. 191 p. [AN SSSR; Otdelenie literatury i iazyka] (Lib: DDO; DLC; MH)

> A scholarly description of Coptic papyri (4th–10th cc.), with facsimiles of some texts.

Byzantine Collections

h-596. *Vizantinovedenie v Ermitazhe.* Edited by V. S. Shandrovskaia. Leningrad, 1991. 146 p. (K Mezhdunarodnomu kongressu vizantinistov, Moskva, 8–15 avgusta 1991 goda/ Published on the occasion of the 18th International Congress of Byzantine Studies, August 1991, Moscow. Parallel text in Russian and English). [GE] (Lib: DDO; MH)

> A detailed survey of Byzantine holdings in the Hermitage with well-annotated studies of the history of many of the major collections involved, including those from archeological expeditions and private collections such as those of N. P. Likhachev and A. P. Smirnov. Includes bibliography (pp. 120–43).

Division of Numismatics

h-597. *Numizmatika v Ermitazhe: Sbornik nauchnykh trudov.* Edited by V. M. Potin. Leningrad: Gos. Ermitazh, 1987. 191 p. (Lib: DDO; MH)

> A collection of articles celebrating the bicentennial of the Hermitage numismatics collections, including a history of the division (1787–1987) by the division head (pp. 3–9) and articles about several different collections, with references to available manuscript catalogues. Includes considerable bibliography.

Gosudarstvennyi Russkii muzei (GRM)
[State Russian Museum]

Agency: Ministerstvo kul'tury RF (Minkul'tury Rossii)
[Ministry of Culture]

Address: 191011, St. Petersburg, ul. Inzhenernaia, 4/2
Telephone: 219-16-15; *Fax:* (812) 314-41-53
E-mail: gusev@russ–museum.spb.su
Website: http://www.rusmuseum.ru
Transport: metro: Nevskii prospekt, Gostinyi Dvor
Hours: M 10:00–17:00; W–Su 10:00–18:00

Director: Vladimir Aleksandrovich Gusev (*tel.* 219-41-53)
Deputy Director for Scientific Work: Evgeniia Nikolaevna Petrova (*tel.* 314-41-45)
Deputy Director for Restoration, Registration, and Storage:
  Ivan Ivanovich Karlov (*tel.* 315-31-56)
Scientific Secretary: Liudmila Mikhailovna Kurenkova (*tel.* 315-64-36)

HISTORY:

Russkii muzei Imperatora Aleksandra III (RM)
  [Russian Museum of Emperor Alexander III] (1895–1917)
Russkii muzei (RM)
  [Russian Museum] (1917–1925)

The museum was founded in 1895 as an artistic, archeological, and cultural-historic collection under the name of the Russian Museum of Emperor Alexander III and opened to the public in 1898 in the [Grand Duke] Michael (*Mikhailovskii*) Palace, constructed in 1819–1825 by the architect Carlo Rossi for Alexander I's brother, Mikhail Pavlovich. Its collections were largely made up of paintings and early Russian *objets d'art* transferred from the Museum of the Academy of Arts and from imperial collections in the Hermitage and the palaces in Gatchina and Tsarskoe Selo, as well as from private collections bought by or donated to the museum. These latter included the collections of Prince A. B. Lobanov-Rostovskii, Prince G. G. Gagarin, Princess M. K. Tenisheva, and the historians and Byzantinists N. P. Kondakov (1909) and N. P. Likhachev (1913), among others. Before the 1917 Revolution the museum had divisions for arts, ethnography (founded in 1902), and historical daily-life (*istoriko-bytovoi*) (founded in 1913), as well as a memorial division devoted to the Emperor Alexander III. With the expansion of its holdings additional space was needed, and in 1912–1916, the neighboring Benois Corpus was constructed nearby, named after its architect L. N. Benois (Benua). The museum was nationalized in 1917, and since 1925 it has been known under its present name of the State Russian Museum.

The nationalization of art treasures and the redistribution of museum holdings after 1917 considerably enlarged the collections of the State Russian Museum. Some exhibition space was added to the museum when in 1925, the Summer Palace of Peter I (H–85), which had been turned into a museum in 1923, became a branch, specifically under the Historical Daily-Life Division. That division, however, was abolished in 1924, when the Summer Palace became a separate museum, and the remaining collections from Historical Daily-Life Division were transferred to the Hermitage, where since 1941 they formed the basis for its Division for the History of Russian Culture (see H–88). In the 1930s the Oriental and Byzantine art collections from the Russian Museum were likewise transferred to the Hermitage. Also during the 1920s and 30s, numerous items from the Russian Museum—mainly paintings and icons—were taken over by the State Museum Fond (*Gosudarsvennyi muzeinyi fond*), some for sale abroad, and others for transfer to museums throughout the RSFSR and especially to the non-Russian union republics. There were some direct transfers to other museums in Leningrad.

In 1934 the holdings of the entire Ethnographic Division of the Russian Museum were transferred to the State Ethnographic Museum, which is now the Russian Ethnographic Museum (REM—H–71). Balancing such losses from transfers, the Russian Museum collections were substantially increased in the 1920s, and again starting in the 1960s, thanks to museum-funded expeditions sent out, especially to northern regions of the Russian Federation, to gather materials that were in need of preservation, and that were of interest as potential exhibits to the museum. The State Russian Museum is currently the largest museum of Russian art in the country. In June 1992 it was added to the federal register of the most valuable monuments of the cultural history of the Russian Federation.

Archival materials, including manuscripts, are held in a number of museum divisions or sectors, or are classified as separate "fonds" within the rich and varied holdings of the museum. Drawings and graphic materials are usually classified among the visual arts, but many of the museum graphic holdings, and especially photographs and other audiovisual materials, nonetheless are also of an archival interest and are accordingly mentioned, at least in passing, below.

The Division of Manuscripts was begun in 1895, and now comprises a structural part of the museum itself. The Fond of Photographic Materials existed since 1898 as part of the Art Division, but was reorganized as the Photograph, Film, and Video Sector in 1990.

The Fond of Graphic Arts is based on donations made by Princess M. K. Tenisheva and Prince G. G. Gagarin, together with the nationalized collections of the imperial family and such nineteenth- and early twentieth-century collectors as M. P. Botkin, S. S. Botkin, V. N. Argutinskii-Dolgorukov, and E. E. Reitern. Various other graphic collections from museums that were closed down between 1920 and 1950 have also been turned over to the Russian Museum.

The Division of Soviet Graphic Arts was organized in 1979. In 1932 the collection of Soviet graphic arts was already organized as a separate fond, although it still formed part of the Division of Soviet Art. That division was endowed with a number of private collections formed by such collectors as A. P. Ostroumova-Lebedeva (1956), P. A. Shillingovskii (1947), and G. M. Levitin (1984). It was subsequently enriched by a collection of the works of P. N. Filonov presented to the museum by his sister, E. N. Glebova (1977), and in 1985 it received some 200 folios of contemporary graphic art from the Union of Artists of the USSR.

A repository for various exhibits relating to Russian ecclesiastical history and icon painting was opened in 1914 as part of the museum's Arts Division. After the Revolution this was made into the Division of Early Russian Art, but in 1972 it was divided into two separate parts, which now form the Division of Early Russian Painting and the Division of Early Russian Applied Art.

Three important palaces in St. Petersburg have recently been turned over to the Russian Museum and now form official branches:

(1) Michael (Engineering) Castle (*Mikhailovskii [Inzhenernyi] zamok*) was turned over to the Russian Museum in 1991. Built in 1797–1800 by the architect Vincenzo Brenna, it was briefly an imperial residence until Paul I was assassinated there in 1801. Subsequently, a large part of the building was occupied by the Main Engineering School, principally known as the Nicholas Engineering Academy (*Nikolaevskaia inzhenernaia akademiia*), the source of its second name. A national portrait gallery is now being developed there. The Photograph, Film, and Video Sector was moved to this building during 1997. (191011, St. Petersburg, ul. Sadovaia, 2; tel. 210-41-73).

(2) The Marble Palace (*Mramornyi dvorets*) was turned over to the Russian Museum in 1992. It was built in 1768–1785 by the architect Antonio Rinaldi for Count G. G. Orlov, but

subsequently was owned by the imperial family (from 1832 by Grand Duke Constantine [Konstantin] Nikolaevich). From 1937 until 1991, it housed the Leningrad Branch of the Central Museum of V. I. Lenin. (191065, St. Petersburg, ul. Millionnaia, 5/1; tel. 312-91-96).

(3) The Stroganov Palace (*Stroganovskii dvorets*) was turned over to the Russian Museum in 1991. Built in 1752–1754 by the architect Bartolomeo Rastrelli, in the eighteenth century it was owned by A. S. Stroganov, president of the Academy of Arts, and remained with the Stroganov family until 1917, housing one of the richest private art collections in Russia. (191186, St. Petersburg, Nevskii prosp., 17; tel. 311-82-38).

Access: Access by researchers to archival holdings in all divisions and the museum library requires an official letter from the researcher's sponsoring Russian institution to the director or deputy director for scientific work, stating the subject and the purpose of research.

Working Conditions: Researchers are accommodated in the various division offices as required, as there is no formal reading room in the museum. Materials are normally delivered immediately after they are ordered.

Library Facilities: The Scientific Library of the museum (135,000 volumes) contains literature on Russian art and includes the libraries of the Committee for Popularization of Art Publications (*Komitet populiarizatsii khudozhestvennykh izdanii*), the Trustees' Committee for Russian Iconography (*Komitet popechitel'stva o russkoi ikonopisi*), and the Baron Stieglitz School of Industrial Art (*Uchilishche tekhnicheskogo risovaniia barona Shtiglitsa*), as well as the private library collections of A. N. Benois (Benua), V. V. Lebedev, A. S. Suvorin, and many others. There are card catalogues for literature about the museum, exhibition catalogues, the private library of Alexandre Benois (A. N. Benua), "Rossica," for personalia (names of artists, sculptors, and architects), and for publications prepared by the museum staff. (Tel. 219-16-12).

Copying: Copying facilities are limited, but photographic and xerox copies can be made as well as colored slides with the permission of the museum administration. Photographic prints from negatives in the Photograph Sector can be ordered through the museum photographic laboratory.

Otdel rukopisei—Vedomstvennyi arkhiv
[Division of Manuscripts—Agency Archive]

Telephone: 219-16-79
Hours: WTh 10:00–13:00, 14:00–17:00
Head: Irina Pavlovna Lapina

HOLDINGS: 211 fonds, 20,995 units, 1721–1987

The Division of Manuscripts contains the archives of various art institutions and the personal papers of many painters and art specialists, relating to the history of Russian art from the eighteenth through the twentieth century.

The Agency Archive, which is a structural part of the Division of Manuscripts, holds the administrative records of the Russian Museum itself, along with those of its various predecessor components. Some museum records, however, such as those of the Division of Early Russian Painting and the Division of Early Russian Applied Arts, are kept within the individual divisions (see below).

Among other institutional records is documentation of the New Society of Painters (*Novoe obshchestvo khudozhnikov*), the Youth League (*Soiuz molodezhi*), and the Circle of Lovers of Fine Editions (*Kruzhok liubitelei iziashchnykh izdanii*), including files relating to their organizational activities and exhibitions. These include draft foundation charters, protocols of meetings, exhibition catalogues, letters written by painters whose work has been shown at exhibitions, and financial documents. There is also some documentation regarding the Academy of Arts (although most of the prerevolutionary Academy records are in RGIA, and those from the Soviet period remain in

RAKh). Among the earliest materials are some graduation testimonials and diplomas of V. L. Borovikovskii, M. I. Tankov, and F. I. Shubin, from the Academy of Arts; some documents relating to the architect Domenico Trezzini (1721–1722); and an early eighteenth-century manuscript medical compendium illustrated with drawings and engravings.

Among the many fonds of personal papers are those of such nineteenth- and twentieth-century painters as K. P. and A. P. Briullov, M. V. Dobuzhinskii, P. N. Filonov, I. N. Kramskoi, I. E. Repin, A. I. and K. A. Somov, K. S. Petrov-Vodkin, and M. A. Vrubel'. The papers of the artist A. N. Benois also reflect his work as art critic and historian. There are personal papers of the sculptors L. V. Shervud (Sherwood) and S. D. Er'zia and the art historians and collectors, N. N. Vrangel', V. T. Georgievskii, and A. V. Prakhov. There are the manuscripts of monographs, articles, reports, and lectures as well as drawings and sketches. The division also contains documents on organizational activity and public participation in such art movements as the *Peredvizhnyki,* or Association of Itinerant Art Exhibitions (*Tovarishchestvo peredvizhnykh khudozhestvennykh vystavok*) and the "World of Art" (*Mir iskusstva*). Personal documentation includes diaries, notebooks, memoirs, diplomas, correspondence, and photographs. The division also holds the personal papers of V. F. Eval'd (Ewald), who taught history to Grand Duke Alexander (Aleksandr) Aleksandrovich, later to become Emperor Alexander III.

The P. Ia. Dashkov Collection contains the original works of painters and architects, personal albums devoted to the life and work of a number of artists, and the manuscripts of articles, together with documents, letters, photographs and drawings by such artists as M. M. Antokol'skii, I. N. Kramskoi, Auguste Ricard de Montferrand, A. M. Opekushin, Bartolomeo Carlo Rastrelli, I. E. Repin, Domenico Trezzini, V. M. Vasnetsov, and V. V. Vereshchagin.

Reference Facilities: There are inventory *opisi* for most fonds, and a card catalogue of personalia.

Sektor foto-kino-videodokumentov
[Sector of Photographic, Film, and Video Documents]

Address: ul. Sadovaia, 2
Telephone: 219-16-70
Hours: W 10:00–13:00, 14:00–17:00
Head: Galina Aleksandrovna Polikarpova

HOLDINGS: ca. 250,000 units, 1860–1990s
  photographs—ca. 100,000; negatives—ca. 115,000; positives—ca. 19,000 units;
  photo albums—121 (3,386 pictures) (1860s–1990s); slides—1,240; films—1;
  postcards—ca. 50,000 units; pressclippings—1 collection (1860s–1960s)

This sector holds negatives, photographic prints (including original photographs), photograph albums, and color slides, illustrative of the pictorial and decorative arts of Russia, as well as bookplates and bindings, and that represent the history of Russian art from the 1850s to the 1990s. Some of the earliest materials include albums presented to the imperial family, collections of photos made in the late nineteenth and early twentieth centuries by those involved in the world of the arts and by private collectors like Prince G. G. Gagarin, Alexandre Benois (A. N. Benua), and V. V. Mashukov. There is also a collection of reproductions and printed graphics done in the late nineteenth and early twentieth centuries, and a collection of newspaper and magazine clippings on arts subjects (1860s–1960s).

Working Conditions: During 1997, the sector holdings were moved to the Michael (Engineering) Castle (*Mikhailovskii [Inzhenernyi] zamok*), and by 1998 were open in their new premises.

Reference Facilities: There are inventories according to different types of materials (negatives, prints, slides), and a card catalogue of authors and personalia.

Otdel risunka
[Division of Drawings]

Telephone: 219-16-07
Hours: W 10:00–17:30
Head: Gennadii Ivanovich Chugunov

HOLDINGS: ca. 70,000 units, 18th–20th cc.

One of the largest collections of Russian drawings in the country, the division encompasses individual drawings, sketches from albums, still-life and nature drawings, and the notebooks of numerous artists covering a period from the eighteenth through the twentieth century. Although most would be classified as art, rather than archives, they nonetheless deserve mention here.

Among the holdings are drawings by A. E. Egorov depicting genre scenes from St. Petersburg life; watercolors and drawings by O. A. Kiprenskii, K. P. Briullov, and S. F. Shchedrin; pencil portraits by I. N. Kramskoi and I. E. Repin; landscape sketches by I. I. Shishkin; watercolors by I. I. Levitan; study sketches for paintings by P. A. Fedotov; albums with views of towns on the Volga by the Chernetsov Brothers; and illustrations done by A. A. Agin and P. M. Boklevskii for the works of Russian nineteenth-century writers.

Reference Facilities: There are subject and alphabetic card catalogues, and inventories available for researchers.

Otdel graviury XVIII–nach. XX vv.
[Division of Engravings (18th–early 20th cc.)]

Telephone: 219-16-60
Hours: W 10:00–17:30
Head: Elena Fominichna Petinova

HOLDINGS: ca. 70,000 units, 18th c.–1917

Collections in this division embrace a wide range of prerevolutionary Russian prints and engravings. Dating from the eighteenth century, there are, for example, engravings that depict episodes during the Northern War and the building of Russia's new capital during the reign of Peter I. There is an album of engravings showing a plan and twelve views of the city based on drawings done by M. I. Makhaev (1753). There are portrait etchings done by E. P. Chemesov of famous personages of the eighteenth century, engravings by N. I. Utkin, engraved political caricatures by A. G. Venetsianov from the Patriotic War of 1812 against Napoleon, and lithographs done by P. M. Boklevskii illustrating the works of Russian nineteenth-century writers.

The graphic art collection covering the late nineteenth and early twentieth centuries includes works by Alexandre Benois (Benua), Léon Bakst (*pseud.* of L. S. Rozenberg), N. S. Goncharova, E. E. Lansere (Lanceray), V. V. Mate (Basile Mathe), V. A. Serov, and M. A. Vrubel'. There are also works by the poets as V. V. Maiakovskii, V. V. Khlebnikov, and A. E. Kruchenykh, among others.

The division also holds original copper plates dating from the eighteenth to the early twentieth century. These include the works of masters from the Chamber of Engravers (*Graviroval'naia palata*) of the St. Petersburg Academy of Sciences and the personal plates of V. V. Mate (Basile Mathe) and M. A. Dobrov.

Reference Facilities: There are subject and alphabetic card catalogues, and inventory registers for staff use.

Otdel sovetskoi grafiki
[Division of Soviet Graphic Arts]

Telephone: 219-16-69
Hours: W 10:00–17:30
Head: Natal'ia Mikhailovna Kozyreva

HOLDINGS: ca. 50,000 units, 1917–1994

The collection contains easel watercolors and drawings, book illustrations and designs (including originals, preparatory materials, studies, alternative versions, and models for books), magazine, newspaper, and applied graphics, theater graphics, posters, and all types of printed graphic design—xylographs (wood engravings), etchings, lithographs, line-engravings, and monotypes.

There are works of some of the greatest masters of the Russian *avant-garde*—K. S. Malevich, P. N. Filonov; drawings and watercolors by I. Ia. Bilibin, R. R. Fal'k, K. S. Petrov-Vodkin; engravings by A. P. Ostroumova-Lebedeva and V. A. Favorskii; lithographs by A. L. Kaplan and A. S. Vedernikov; as well as works created during the Siege of Leningrad by V. V. Zen'kovich, A. F. Pakhomov, and P. M. Kondrat'ev, along with others.

The collection reflects the main trends in Russian art of the latter part of the twentieth century. The so-called "Severe Style" of the 1960s is represented by the drawings and engravings of V. A. Vetrogonskii, A. A. Ushin, I. V. Golitsin, and G. F. Zakharov, among others. "Underground" graphics of the 1970s include, among others, the work of A. P. Belkin, G. S. Bogomolov, M. M. Shemiakin. The "Post-Modernism" of the 1980s and 1990s is represented by the production of V. A. Golubev, A. O. Florenskii, D. V. Shagin, and others; while art of the postwar decades also includes the work by artists of different generations and different schools, such as P. I. Basmanov, Z. P. Arshakuni, and N. E. Popov, and many more.

Reference Facilities: There is an alphabetic card catalogue and inventory registers for staff use.

Otdel drevnerusskoi zhivopisi (ODRZh)
[Division of Early Russian Painting]

Telephone: 219-16-66
Hours: W 10:00–17:00
Head: Tat'iana Borisovna Vilinbakhova

HOLDINGS: ca. 300 units, 1920s–1994 (some documents late 19th–early 20th cc.)

The fond of subsidiary materials includes graphic and printed tracings of icons dating from the late seventeenth to the early twentieth century, as used in the practical work of icon painters. There is a collection of tracings taken from fresco paintings in Kyiv, Novgorod, Pskov and other centers of medieval Rus'—the work of V. V. Suslov and student copyists from the Art Study Division of the Academy of Arts during the 1920s.

The division archive contains the diaries and working materials of a number of art restorers (1913–1930s), particularly I. Ia. Chelnokov and Ia. V. Sosin (ca. 20 units), reports of restoration inspections of the exhibits held in the Division of Early Russian Painting, plans and reports of the restoration studio for early Russian painting and needlework, the minutes and protocols of scholarly meetings held by the division (1930s–1970s), and texts of reports and catalogues compiled by the division staff (1930s–present).

The photograph archive contains the prints of icons in the process of restoration and prerevolutionary photographs of works of early Russian art. These include photographs by I. F. Barshchevskii, of material collected from expeditions to Arkhangel'sk, Leningrad, Novgorod, and

Pskov Oblasts and to the Karelian Autonomous Republic (1950s–1970s), along with the working materials for publications issued by the division and photographs of exhibits and museum exhibitions.

Reference Facilities: There are reference card catalogues of works of art in monasteries and private collections, and of the iconography of many works of art among the museum's holdings, with references to available published literature and archival sources.

Library Facilities: There is a library devoted to the history of early Russian and Byzantine art available to researchers, which contains the collections of two former heads of the division—Iu. N. Dmitriev and V. K. Laurina.

Otdel drevnerusskogo prikladnogo iskusstva (ODRPI)
[Division of Early Russian Applied Art]

Telephone: 219-16-66
Hours: W 10:00–17:00
Head: Izila Ivanovna Pleshanova

HOLDINGS: ca. 100 units, 1930s–1994

The division archive contains the reports of restoration work inspections carried out on the exhibits held in the division together with the texts of reports made by members of staff (including unpublished ones) and the manuscript catalogues of collections from the 1930s to the present.

Reference Facilities: There are reference card catalogues of works of art from the private collections of M. P. Botkin, V. V. Suslov, and others; card catalogues of acquisitions from the vestries of monasteries; and card catalogues of individual collections (needlework, valuable finds, etc.) with information on the sources of acquisition and references to literature and archival materials.

FINDING AIDS — PUBLISHED — GENERAL:

Muzei SPb (1994), pp. 23–28; *Biblioteki SPb* (1993), p. 73; *Peterburg* (1992), p. 553; *GAF Spravochnik* (1991), pp. 116–19; *Muzei Leningrada* (1989), pp. 153–69; *Muzei Leningrada* (1982), pp. 61–63; PKG M&L (1972), p. 340; Myl'nikov (1970), p. 37.

There is no published guide to the archival materials in the museum.

h-598. *The Russian Museum: A Centennial Celebration of a National Treasure. The State Russian Museum.* Compiled by V. A. Gusev (Vladimir Gusyev) and E. N. (Yevgenia) Petrova. Translated from the Russian by Kenneth MacInnes. St. Petersburg: Palace Editions; New York: Distributed by H. N. Abrams, 1998. 263 p. + plates. (Lib: MH-F)

    A lavishly illustrated album from the Russian Museum, with short essays in English on the history of the museum and its holdings from different periods in the history of Russian art.

h-598A. *Gosudarstvennyi Russkii muzei: Otchet, 1993–1997.* Compiled by E. N. Petrova et al. Edited by V. A. Gusev. St. Petersburg: Palace Editions, 1998. 96 p. + plates. Introduction by Vladimir A. Gusev. [GRM]

    The latest official report of the Russian Museum, with current data about the organization, exhibitions, conferences, publications (including exhibition catalogues), and other activities of the museum. Prepared in an elaborate illustrated edition with sample illustrations from the museum holdings.

h-599. *1000 Years of Russian Art: The State Russian Museum, Saint Petersburg.* Alameda, CA: Digital Collections, Inc., 1996. CD-ROM + user's guide (27 p.). Introduction by Vladimir A. Gusev. (Lib: MH-F)

> A sophisticated English-language CD-ROM guide and research aid. Includes floor plans and surveys of the different sections of the museum. A brief introduction by the director gives a history and characterization of the collections. Approximately 1,300 well-indexed images of paintings, sculptures, and other works of art (with an explanatory caption about each artist), grouped according to different periods and museum sections, can be searched under different access points, resorted as desired, and enlarged with zoom features.

h-600. *Gosudarstvennyi Russkii muzei. Iz istorii muzeia: Sbornik statei i publikatsii.* Compiled by I. N. Karasik and E. N. Petrova. St. Petersburg, 1995. 309 p. Introduction by Vladimir A. Gusev. [GRM]

> A collection of articles covering various aspects of the museum history, and the development of its several divisions. Includes an extensive bibliography of publications about the museum compiled by L. I. Vladimirova (pp. 291–97).

h-601. Alianskii, Iurii Lazarevich. *Rasskazy o Russkom muzee.* 3 ed. Leningrad: "Iskusstvo," 1987. 238 p. (Lib: DLC; IU; MH)

> 2d ED.: L.: Lenizdat, 1981. 247 p. + 25 plates. (Lib: DLC; MH)
>
> 1st ED.: *Rasskazy o Russkom muzee, a takzhe o starom Mikhailovskom dvortse i ego stroitele Rossi, o prevrashchenii dvortsa v muzei, o sud'bakh poloten i statui i drugie istorii iz biografii znamenitoi kollektsii.* L.: "Iskusstvo," 1964. 275 p. + plates. (Lib: MH).
>
> A popular account of the history of the museum, its acquisitions, and the scientific activities of the staff.

h-602. Petrov, Gennadii Fedorovich. *Idem po Russkomu muzeiu: Istoriko-iskusstvovedcheskii ocherk.* Leningrad: Lenizdat, 1982. 192 p. + 16 plates. "Biblioteka molodogo rabochego." (Lib: DLC; IU)

> Traces the history of the museum and acquisition of its collections, with emphasis on the structure and work of the museum during the Soviet period.

h-603. Lebedev, Georgii E. *Gosudarstvennyi Russkii muzei, 1895–1945.* Leningrad/Moscow: "Iskusstvo," 1946. 102 p. + 22 plates. (Lib: DLC; IU; MH)

> A brief history of the museum.

h-604. Baltun, Petr Kazimirovich. *Russkii muzei—evakuatsiia, blokada, vosstanovlenie: (Iz vospominanii muzeinogo rabotnika).* Edited by A. I. Savinova. Moscow: "Izobrazitel'noe iskusstvo," 1981. 129 p. (Lib: DLC; IU; MH) Introduction by A. K. Lebedev.

> Recounts the efforts of the museum staff to preserve the museum collections during World War II. Includes extracts from the diary of G. E. Lebedev kept during the Siege of Leningrad.

FINDING AIDS — SPECIALIZED:

Division of Drawings

h-605. Pushkarev, Vasilii Alekseevich. *Akvareli i risunki v Gosudarstvennom Russkom muzee, XVIII–nachalo XX vv. [Al'bom].* Moscow: "Izobrazitel'noe iskusstvo," 1982. 217 p. (Lib: DLC; IU; MH)

Division of Early Russian Painting

h-606. *Drevnerusskie freski: Kopii iz sobraniia Gosudarstvennogo Russkogo muzeia: Katalog.* Compiled by A. A. Mal'tseva. Leningrad: GRM, 1983. 16 p. Introduction by A. A. Mal'tseva.

Nauchno-issledovatel'skii muzei Rossiiskoi Akademii khudozhestv   (NIM RAKh)
[Scientific Research Museum of the Russian Academy of Arts]

Agency: Rossiiskaia Akademiia khudozhestv (RAKh)
[Russian Academy of Arts]

Address: 199034, St. Petersburg, Universitetskaia nab., 17
Telephone: 213-35-78; *Fax:* (812) 213-67-68
Transport: metro: Vasileostrovskaia, Sportivnaia; bus: 6, 7, 47; trol.: 10, 23
Hours: W–F 10:00–17:00

Director: Ekaterina Vasil'evna Grishina (*tel.* 213-61-69)
Deputy Director for Scientific Work: Veronika Troianovna Bogdan (*tel.* 213-64-96)
Chief Curator: Zhozefina Borisovna Rybakova (*tel.* 213-64-96)
Scientific Secretary: Irina Igorevna Ivanova (*tel.* 213-64-96)

HISTORY:

Muzei Imperatorskoi Akademii khudozhestv
   [Museum of the Imperial Academy of Arts] (1757–1917)
Muzei Akademii khudozhestv
   [Museum of the Academy of Arts] (1917–1918, V–VIII.1921)
Muzei Petrogradskikh gosudarstvennykh svobodnykh khudozhestvenno-uchebnykh masterskikh
   (Muzei PGSKhUM)
   [Museum of the Petrograd State Free Art Training Studios] (1918–1921)
Muzei Vysshikh khudozhestvenno-tekhnicheskikh masterskikh (Muzei VKhUTEMAS)
   [Museum of the Higher Technical Art Studios] (1921–1922)
Muzei khudozhestvenno-tekhnicheskogo instituta (Muzei VKhUTEIN)
   [Museum of the Higher Technical Art Institute] (1922–1930)
Muzei Instituta proletarskikh izobrazitel'nykh iskusstv (Muzei INPII)
   [Museum of the Institute of Proletarian Fine Arts] (1930–1932)
Muzei Leningradskogo instituta zhivopisi, skul'ptury i arkhitektury (Muzei LINZhAS)
   [Museum of the Leningrad Institute of Painting, Sculpture, and Architecture] (1932–1933)
Muzei Instituta zhivopisi, skul'ptury i arkhitektury VAKh (Muzei IZhSA VAKh)
   [Museum of the Institute of Painting, Sculpture, and Architecture
   of the All-Russian Academy of Arts] (1933–1944)
Muzei Instituta zhivopisi, skul'ptury i arkhitektury im. I. E. Repina VAKh (Muzei IZhSA VAKh)
   [Museum of the I. E. Repin Institute of Painting, Sculpture, and Architecture
   of the All-Russian Academy of Arts] (1944–1947)
Nauchno-issledovatel'skii muzei AKh SSSR (NIM AKh SSSR)
   [Scientific Research Museum of the Academy of Arts of the USSR] (1947–1991)

The oldest art museum in Russia, NIM RAKh was originally founded in 1757 at the same time as the Academy of Arts. It is still housed in its handsome original building on the Neva Embankment, erected in 1765–1788 from the plans of Jean-Baptiste Vallin de la Mothe by A. F. Kokorinov. By the beginning of the twentieth century the art and historical collections in the Imperial Academy of Arts included a Picture Gallery, the separate Count N. A. Kushelev-Bezborodko Picture Gallery, the Kraushold (V. E. Krauzol'd) Collection of Paintings, a Museum of Ancient and Western European Sculpture, a collection of architectural models of the Alhambra, early Roman monuments, and other Western architectural ensembles, a collection of architectural drawings, and a collection of medals and coins known as the Mint Cabinet (*Mintskabinet*; from the German *Münzkabinet*).

After the October Revolution the museum was abolished and part of its fonds were transferred to the Hermitage, the Russian Museum, and to a number of provincial museums. The remaining exhibits were used to form a museum that became part of the network of art workshops and studios and subsequently of the Higher Technical Art Institute, which in 1930 was reorganized as the Institute of Proletarian Fine Arts and then after 1933 as the Institute of Painting, Sculpture, and Architecture of the All-Russian Academy of Arts. After the formation of the Academy of Arts of the USSR in 1947, the museum was given the status of a research center. Together with other subdivisions of the Russian Academy of Arts, the museum (NIM RAKh) is now under the control of the Presidium of the Academy of Arts. Archival materials are held in several different divisions of the museum.

Separate exhibitions with related archival materials are housed in four divisions that were previously administered as museum branches (two have separate listings and the other two are described below):

(1) The I. I. Brodskii Apartment-Museum (*Muzei-kvartira I. I. Brodskogo*) (H–91).

(2) The Chistiakov House-Museum (*Dom-muzei P. P. Chistiakova*) (H–92).

(3) The Kuindzhi Apartment-Museum (*Muzei-kvartira A. I. Kuindzhi*) (see below) established in 1991, was opened in 1993 in the apartment (near the RAKh museum) where the well-known landscape painter and professor of the Academy of Arts, Arkhip Ivanovich Kuindzhi (1841–1910), lived from 1897 until his death in 1910.

(4) The Shevchenko Memorial Studio (*Memorial'naia masterskaia T. G. Shevchenko*) (see below) was opened as a branch in 1964 in the studio where the Ukrainian poet and artist Taras Shevchenko (1814–1861) lived and worked after his return from exile in 1858 until his death. It now constitutes a separate division of the museum expositions within the RAKh museum compound.

The I. E. Repin Penates Estate-Museum (*Muzei-usad'ba I. E. Repina "Penaty"*) remains a branch of the museum (H–93). The S. T. Konenkov Memorial Studio-Museum (*Memorial'nyi muzei-masterskaia S. T. Konenkova*) in Moscow is also a branch (H–156).

N.B. For more details about the history of the RAKh and descriptions of the RAKh Bibliographic Archive and the Photographic Reproduction Archive, see E–45; for the RAKh Scientific-Library, see G–18.

Access: For access to archival materials, an official personal letter of application to the director is required, stating the subject and aim of the research.

Working Conditions: Researchers are accommodated in the working offices of the museum, where materials are available the day they are ordered.

Reference Facilities: There are inventory registers for staff use and catalogues arranged according to author, subject, and genre.

Copying: Photocopies can be made through the RAKh photographic laboratory.

Otdel grafiki
[Division of Graphic Arts]

Telephone: 213-64-96
Hours: F 10:00–17:00
Head: Diliara Safaralieva

HOLDINGS: ca. 36,500 units, 16th–20th cc.

The Division of Graphic Arts has a considerable collection of engravings, drawings and lithographs, which have been acquired by the Academy of Arts over a period of two and a half centuries. Most of these would be considered works of visual art, although many of them are also of archival interest. The collection that was donated by Count I. I. Shuvalov, the founder and first chief director of the Academy of Arts in 1758, includes albums of sixteenth- to eighteenth-century European engravings and other graphics that once belonged to the Academy President, I. I. Betskoi.

Also included in the division are the works of E. P. Chemesov, N. I. Utkin, V. V. Mate (Basile Mathé), and A. P. Ostroumova-Lebedeva, among others, together with a large collection of eighteenth- and nineteenth-century Russian drawings. The division also contains the finest works of those who attended the Academy of Arts (18th–early 20th cc.), as well as works done by students of the I. E. Repin Institute of Painting, Sculpture and Architecture and the V. I. Surikov Institute of Arts in Moscow.

Otdel arkhitektury
[Division of Architecture]

Telephone: 213-64-96
Hours: F 10:00–17:00
Head: Valerii Konstantinovich Shuiskii

HOLDINGS: ca. 34,000 units, 18th–20th cc.

This division holds one of the largest collections of architectural graphics (18th–20th cc.) in Russia. There are drafts, plans, and technical drawings done by the students, teachers, academicians, and retired personnel of the Academy of Arts. The drawings and plans of Russian and European architectural monuments (some of which are no longer in existence) are not only of artistic, but also of historical and archeological interest. The collection contains examples of the draftsmanship of such architects as V. I. Bazhenov, I. A. Fomin, M. F. Kazakov, Carlo (K. I.) Rossi, V. A. Shchuko, A. V. Shchusev, V. V. Suslov, and A. N. Voronikhin, among others.

Fotonegateka
[Photograph and Negative Archive]

Telephone: 213-64-96
Hours: F 10:00–17:00
Head: Tat'iana Konstantinovna Kal'

HOLDINGS: photographs—ca. 78,000 (1850s–1990s)

The collection contains photographs and negatives of architecture, sculpture, and pictorial art that are held in the RAKh Scientific-Research Museum, as well as photographs documenting the history of the Academy of Arts.

Memorial'naia masterskaia T. G. Shevchenko
[T. H. Shevchenko Memorial Studio]

Telephone: 213-35-78
Hours: F 11:00–17:00
Head: Tat'iana Pavlovna Babal'iants

HOLDINGS: ca. 100 units, 19th c.

The T. H. (*Rus.* G.) Shevchenko Memorial Studio, an administrative division of the museum, retains and exhibits documents and other material relating to the life and work of the Ukrainian poet and national hero Taras Hryhorovych (*Rus.* Grigor'evich) Shevchenko (1814–1861), who lived and worked in the building of the Academy from 1858 until his death in 1861. Among photocopies is the page from the parish register recording his birth; the diploma he received on completing the Academy of Arts; the file prepared by the Third Department (*III Otdelenie*) on the Ukrainian-Slavonic Society (*Ukraino-slavianskoe obshchestvo*) and on the artist Shevchenko (1847); an extract from the minutes of the Academic Council of the Imperial Academy of Arts in remembrance of Shevchenko (1882); and group and individual photographs of some of his contemporaries, including N. G. Chernyshevskii, Marko Vovchok (*pseud.* of M. O. Vilins'ka-Markovych), A. G. Venetsianov, and M. Iu. Viel'gorskii. There are also etchings done by Shevchenko, such as "Virsavia" (from a picture by K. P. Briullov) and "The Parable of the Vineyard," among others.

N.B. Other archival materials relating to the Shevchenko exhibits are held in other RAKh divisions. See also the detailed catalogue of Shevchenko manuscripts (a-157), most of which are held in Ukraine.

Muzei-kvartira A. I. Kuindzhi
[A. I. Kuindzhi Apartment-Museum]

Address: 199034, St. Petersburg, Vasil'evskii ostrov, Birzhevoi prosp., 1/10
Telephone: 213-31-33; 213-45-88
Hours: by appointment
Transport: metro: Nevskii prospekt, Gostinyi Dvor, Vasileostrovskaia;
trol.: 1, 7, 9, 10; bus: 10
Head: Elena Ivanovna Prasolova

HOLDINGS: ca. 100 units, 19th–20th cc.

The Kuindzhi Apartment-Museum (now administered as a division of NIIM RAKh) exhibits documentation and memorabilia relating to the life and work of Arkhip Ivanovich Kuindzhi (1841–1910), the Russian landscape painter who was a professor at RAKh. There are photocopies of documents held in the Scientific Bibliographic Archive (see E–45) and other repositories, pictures of his studio at the Academy of Arts, and group and individual portraits of A. I. Kuindzhi and his contemporaries and students at the Academy of Arts. There is also some original graphic work done by Russian artists who were Kuindzhi's pupils—Nicholas Roerich (N. K. Rerikh), A. A. Rylov, and K. F. Bogaevskii, and also by members of the Kuindzhi Society of Artists—I. I. Brodskii and K. Ia. Kryzhitskii, among others.

N.B. Other archival documents relating to the Kuindzhi exhibits are held in other RAKh divisions.

Working Conditions: Although this division has recently been closed (1995–1996) for restoration, NIM RAKh can provide facilities for researchers.

FINDING AIDS — PUBLISHED — GENERAL:

Muzei SPb (1994), pp. 29–30; *Peterburg* (1992), p. 398; *Muzei Leningrada* (1982), pp. 64–65.

There is no published guide to the archival materials in the museum.

h-607. Grishina, Ekaterina Vasil'evna; and Litovchenko, E. N. *Nauchno-issledovatel'skii muzei Akademii khudozhestv SSSR: Al'bom.* Moscow: Izobrazitel'noe iskusstvo, 1989. 238 p. [AKh SSSR]

h-608. *Nauchno-issledovatel'skii muzei Akademii khudozhestv SSSR: Al'bom.* Compiled by T. E. Grave, E. N. Maslova, and L. Iablochkina. Moscow: Izobrazitel'noe iskusstvo, 1973. 117 p. [AKh SSSR] (Lib: MH)
> A richly illustrated album with a brief history of the museum.

h-609. *Akademiia khudozhestv SSSR. Nauchno-issledovatel'skii muzei: Al'bom reproduktsii.* Compiled by T. A. Petrova. Leningrad: Izogiz, 1959. 34 p.
> Includes a brief history of the museum and its holdings, but does not mention the manuscript materials.

h-610. Galich, L. F.; Maslova, Elizaveta Nikolaevna; Rokhlina, S. V., et al. *Russkaia i sovetskaia khudozhestvennaia shkola: Putevoditel'.* Leningrad/Moscow: "Sovetskii khudozhnik," 1965. 140 p. [AKh SSSR; NIM] (Lib: DLC; IU)
> Although basically an illustrated guide to the exhibits, provides considerable historical information.

h-611. *Russkaia arkhitektura XI–nachala XX vv.: Katalog otdela istorii russkoi arkhitektury.* Compiled by L. T. Pushnina and S. V. Rokhlina. Moscow: Izd-vo AKh SSSR, 1962. 117 p. + plates. [AKh SSSR; NIM] (Lib: DLC; MH)
> A scholarly catalogue of architectural plans and drawings held by the museum. More extensive than the 1965 pamphlet by L. T. Pushnina (h-612) and the briefer 1940 description of the division (h-613).

h-612. *Russkaia arkhitektura XI–nachala XX vekov: Putevoditel'.* Compiled by L. T. Pushnina. Leningrad/Moscow: "Sovetskii khudozhnik," 1965. [AKh SSSR; NIM]
> A catalogue of the exhibitions in the Division of Russian Architecture with mention of the documentary and graphics collections.

h-613. Smirnov, A. V.; and Grimm, G. *Muzei Akademii khudozhestv. (Arkhitekturnyi otdel): Kratkii ocherk.* Leningrad, 1940. 28 p. [VAKh]
> A catalogue of the exhibitions in the Division of Russian Architecture with mention of the documentary and graphics collections.

h-614. Sadkova, N. V. *Memorial'naia masterskaia T. G. Shevchenko: Putevoditel'.* Leningrad: "Khudozhnik RSFSR," 1970. 55 p. [AKh SSSR; NIM] (Lib: DLC; MH)
> A brief tourist pamphlet includes reference to manuscript materials; it lists original Shevchenko paintings, drawings, and watercolors held by the museum.

h-615. *Kuindzhi i ego ucheniki: Katalog vystavki.* Compiled by Z. V. Lukina. Edited by E. Grishina. Leningrad: "Iskusstvo," 1973. 56 p. + plates. Introduction by A. I. Roshchina. [AKh SSSR; NIM] (Lib: MH)
> A brief introduction (pp. 5–12) to an album of reproductions from an anniversary exhibition refers to the original art of Kuindzhi and his pupils, some of which remain in the Kuindzhi Apartment-Museum.

Muzei-kvartira I. I. Brodskogo—
Otdel Nauchno-issledovatel'skogo muzeia RAKh

[I. I. Brodskii Apartment-Museum—
Division of the Scientific Research Museum of RAKh]

Agency: Rossiiskaia Akademiia khudozhestv (RAKh)
[Russian Academy of Arts]

Address:	191011, St. Petersburg, pl. Iskusstv, 3, kv. 1
Telephone:	314-36-58
Transport:	metro: Nevskii prospekt, Gostinyi Dvor, Kanal Griboedova; bus: 7, 22, 25; trol.: 1, 5, 10, 44
Hours:	by appointment

Acting Head: Natal'ia Mikhailovna Balakina (*tel.* 213-64-96 [NIM RAKh])

HISTORY:

The museum was opened in 1949 in the apartment where the painter Isaak Izrailevich Brodskii (1884–1939), professor and director of the All-Russian Academy of Arts (1934–1939), lived and worked from 1924 to 1939. The museum is administered as a division of the RAKh Scientific Research Museum (H–90), as a memorial to the artist, who was one of the central figures on the Soviet art scene during the 1920s and 1930s.

HOLDINGS: 1,500 units, late 19th–20th cc.

The museum retains originals and copies of documents relating to I. I. Brodskii's life and work. These include his diploma on graduating from the Academy of Arts, messages of congratulation, decoration certificates, E. I. Brodskii's recollections of his father, letters, and other documentary material. There are individual and group photographs of Brodskii and various other prominent figures in the world of arts, like F. I. Chaliapin (Shaliapin), A. M. Gor'kii, S. A. Esenin (Yesenin), and I. E. Repin.

On exhibit in the museum is Brodskii's own art collection, which includes graphic works of Russian and Soviet artists in the late nineteenth and first half of the twentieth century. Represented here are such artists as I. E. Repin, B. M. Kustodiev, F. A. Maliavin, V. A. Serov, Alexandre Benois (A. N. Benua), K. A. Somov, M. V. Dobuzhinskii, V. E. Makovskii, and G. S. Vereiskii, among others.

Access: Research in the museum holdings requires the permission of the director's office of the RAKh Scientific Research Museum (H–90). A letter of application to the director should state the subject and aim of the research.

Working Conditions: Researchers are accommodated in the museum offices, where materials are available the day they are ordered.

Reference Facilities: There are staff inventory registers and auxiliary catalogues for staff use.

Copying: There are no copying facilities available in this museum, although copies can be ordered through RAKh.

FINDING AIDS — PUBLISHED — GENERAL:

Muzei SPb (1994), p. 31; *Peterburg* (1992), p. 100; *Muzei Leningrada* (1982), p. 65.

There is no published guide to the archival materials in the museum.

h-617. *Zhivopis', grafika, skul'ptura XVII–XX vv.: Muzei-kvartira I. I. Brodskogo: [Al'bom– katalog].* Compiled by I. N. Barsheva et al. Leningrad: "Iskusstvo," Leningradskoe otdelenie, 1989. 271 p. [AKh SSSR; NIM; Muzei-kvartira I. I. Brodskogo] (Lib: DLC; MH)
  A catalogue of Brodskii's art collection, which is held in the museum.

h-618. *Muzei-kvartira I. I. Brodskogo: Al'bom–katalog.* Compiled by O. P. Andreeva and I. N. Barsheva. Leningrad: "Izobrazitel'noe Iskusstvo," 1985. 174 p. [AKh SSSR; NIM; Muzei-kvartira I. I. Brodskogo] (Lib: MH)
  An album with 127 reproductions of Brodskii's own works and his art collection, with an introduction (pp. 5–16) about the museum and its holdings.

h-619. Brodskii, Iosif Anatol'evich. *Muzei-kvartira I. I. Brodskogo. Leningrad: Katalog.* Compiled by E. A. Pilonova and V. V. Lototskaia. Leningrad: "Khudozhnik RSFSR," 1958. 73 p. + 15 plates. [AKh SSSR; NIM] (Lib: DLC)

h-620. *Muzei-kvartira I. I. Brodskogo: Putevoditel'.* Compiled by Z. V. Lukina. Leningrad/ Moscow: "Sovetskii khudozhnik," 1969. 55 p. [RAKh SSSR; NIM] (Lib: IU)
  A brief tourist guide to the museum.

Dom-muzei P. P. Chistiakova—
Otdel Nauchno-issledovatel'skogo muzeia RAKh

[P. P. Chistiakov House-Museum—
Division of the Scientific Research Museum of RAKh]

Agency: Rossiiskaia Akademiia khudozhestv (RAKh)
[Russian Academy of Arts]

Address: 189620, St. Petersburg, g. Pushkin, Moskovskoe shosse, 23
Telephone: 470-77-12
Transport: suburban train from Vitebsk station or Kupchino RR platform
(metro: Kupchino) to Detskoe Selo (Pushkin)
Hours: WSa 10:00–17:00

Head: Elena Borisovna Churilova (*tel.* 470-70-85)

HISTORY:

The museum was opened in 1987 in the Chistiakov country house (*dacha*) in the town of Pushkin (before 1918, Tsarskoe Selo; 1918–1937, Detskoe Selo) that once belonged to painter and art teacher Pavel Petrovich Chistiakov (1832–1919), a professor of portrait and historical painting at the Imperial Academy of Arts.

The museum is now administered as a division (*otdel*) of the RAKh Scientific Research Museum (H–90).

N.B. The personal papers of P. P. Chistiakov are held in the Manuscript Sector of the State Russian Museum (H–89) and in the Manuscript Division of the Tret'iakov State Gallery (H–23). The papers of the Chistiakov Memorial Circle (*Kruzhok pamiati P. P. Chistiakova*) are to be found in the Scientific Bibliographic Archive (*Nauchno-bibliograficheskii arkhiv*) of RAKh (E–45).

HOLDINGS: ca. 550 units, 1840s–1980s
documents—35 units (1850s–1970s); photographs—ca. 100 (1870s–1980s);
graphics (drawings, watercolors)—ca. 400 units (1840s–1980s)

The documentary holdings of the museum constitute part of the Chistiakov family archive, previously held in the family by the painter's grandson, Ia. V. Durdin, and his niece, O. E. Meier-Chistiakova. They include documents relating to the biography of Chistiakov's father-in-law, E. E. Meier, and his niece, V. M. Baruzdina, documents on the building of his dacha, and diaries, among other papers.

Photographic holdings include portraits of P. P. Chistiakov, members of his family, his friends and pupils, including the writer O. D. Forsh, the musician and composer Iu. F. L'vova, the painter and poet M. A. Voloshin, and the painters V. E. Savinskii and V. M. Baruzdina. There are also photographs of places associated with Chistiakov's life and work, such as Krasnyi Kholm (Tver Guberniia), where the painter spent his childhood.

There are drawings by Chistiakov and his pupils, including the classwork of V. E. Savinskii (drawings, watercolors and albums of sketches) and albums of drawings done by Chistiakov's daughter, A. P. Chistiakova. There are also a number of pencil portraits of M. A. Vrubel' by E. O.

Kirienko-Voloshina (the mother of M. A. Voloshin); O. A. Vaksel', the actress, by V. M. Baruzdina; M. V. Nesterov by T. A. Mollot; and N. A. Bruni and V. M. Baruzdina by V. I. Savinskii.

Access: Research in the museum holdings requires the permission of the director's office of the RAKh Scientific Research Museum (H–90). A letter of application to the director should state the subject and aim of the research.

Working Conditions: Researchers are accommodated in the museum offices, where materials are available the day they are ordered.

Reference Facilities: There are inventories and catalogues for staff use.

Copying: There are no copying facilities available in this division.

FINDING AIDS — PUBLISHED — GENERAL:

Muzei SPb (1994), p. 33.

There is no published guide to the archival holdings in the museum.

h-621. Churilova, Elena Borisovna. *Dom-muzei P. P. Chistiakova: [g. Pushkin].* Leningrad: "Khudozhnik RSFSR," 1988. 15 p. [NIM RAKh]

h-622. Churilova, Elena Borisovna. "V masterskoi P. P. Chistiakova." *Sovetskii muzei,* 1988, no. 4, p. 15. (Lib: DLC; IU; MH)
    A history of the P. P. Chistiakov House-Museum.

FINDING AIDS — GENERAL — UNPUBLISHED:

h-623. Churilova, Elena Borisovna. "Dom-muzei P. P. Chistiakova v g. Pushkine: Putevoditel'." Edited by L. P. Ganicheva. Leningrad, 1989. 88 p. Typescript.
    This first guide to the museum remains unpublished.

Muzei-usad'ba I. E. Repina "Penaty"—
Filial Nauchno-issledovatel'skogo muzeia RAKh

[I. E. Repin Penates Estate Museum—
Branch of the Scientific Research Museum of RAKh]

Agency: Rossiiskaia Akademiia khudozhestv (RAKh)
[Russian Academy of Arts]

Address:	189648, Leningradskaia oblast', pos. Repino, Primorskoe shosse, 411
Telephone:	231-66-33; 213-64-96
Transport:	suburban train from Finland station or Udel'naia RR platform to Repino
Hours:	MW–F 11:00–17:00

Head of Branch: Liudmila Aleksandrovna Mishina

HISTORY:

The museum was opened in 1940 on the country estate of the Russian painter Il'ia Efimovich Repin (1844–1930) in the village of Kuokkala (now Repino), where Repin lived from 1903 to 1930. After his death Penates became the property of the Academy of Arts of the USSR. During the war the museum holdings were evacuated to Leningrad. In 1944 the buildings on the estate were destroyed by fire. In 1962 after reconstruction and restoration work, the museum was once again opened to the public. The museum is administered as a branch of the RAKh Scientific Research Museum (H–90).

HOLDINGS: 1,800 units, 19th–20th cc.

The museum retains copies of documents relating to I. E. Repin's life and work, his family, contemporaries and pupils, together with his original photographs and drawings. On display are photocopies of the painter's main works, original drawings, studies for paintings, watercolors, and posters, together with similar work done by his friends and pupils. There are copies of his correspondence with such people as I. N. Kramskoi, P. M. Tret'iakov, A. M. Gor'kii, and M. P. Musorgskii, among others. There are also the proofs of a book of memoirs written by Repin, entitled "The Past is Close" (*Dalekoe blizkoe*) with the author's corrections, messages of congratulation, clippings from newspapers and magazines about the painter, and individual and group photographs.

The museum is currently preparing microfilms of the manuscript material relating to Repin held in archives and by private individuals, and is also making a collection of photographic reproductions of his works.

Access: Research in the museum holdings requires the permission of the director's office of the RAKh Scientific Research Museum (H–90). A letter of application to the director should state the subject and aim of the research.

Reference Facilities: There are inventory registers for staff use and card catalogues.

Copying: There are no copying facilities available in this branch.

FINDING AIDS — PUBLISHED — GENERAL:

Muzei SPb (1994), p. 34; *Peterburg* (1992), p. 472; *Muzei Leningrada* (1989), pp. 176–79; *Muzei Leningrada* (1982), pp. 65–66.

There is no published guide to the archival holdings in the museum.

h-624. *"Penaty" : Muzei-usad'ba I. E. Repina: Putevoditel'.* Compiled by E. G. Levenfish, M. A. Karpenko, and E. V. Kirillina. Edited by E. G. Levenfish. 3d ed. Leningrad: Lenizdat, 1980. 96 p. + 32 plates. Summary in English and French. [AKh SSSR; NIM] (Lib: DLC; IU; MH)

    2d ED.: L., 1976. 88 p.

    EARLIER ED.: Compiled by N. A. Sadovyi. L.: Lenizdat, 1965. 40 p. (Lib: MH).

      Describes the history of the museum and its exhibits.

Muzei dekorativno-prikladnogo iskusstva Sankt-Peterburgskoi gosudarstvennoi khudozhestvenno-promyshlennoi akademii (Muzei DPI)
[Museum of Decorative and Applied Arts
of the St. Petersburg State Academy of Industrial Arts]

Agency: Ministerstvo obshchego i professional'nogo obrazovaniia RF
(Minobrazovannia Rossii)
[Ministry of General and Professional Education]

Address: 191028, St. Petersburg, Solianoi per., 13
Telephone: 273-38-04; 273-32-58 (Museum)
Transport: metro: Chernyshevskaia; trol.: 3, 8, 15, 19;
tram: 2, 12, 14, 19, 25, 32, 34, 54; bus: 14, 134
Hours: Tu–Sa 11:00–16:30 (by appointment)

Academy Rector: Aleksei Iur'evich Talashchuk
Museum Director: Aleksandr Igorevich Bartenev (*tel.* 273-32-58)
Chief Curator: Galina Alekseevna Vlasova
Curator of Graphic Fond: Tat'iana Vital'evna Shcherbina
Head of Library: Irina Nikolaevna Guseva (*tel.* 272-24-22)

HISTORY:
Muzei tsentral'nogo uchilishcha tekhnicheskogo risovaniia barona A. L. Shtiglitsa
[A. L. Stieglitz Museum of the Central School of Technical Drawing] (1878–1923)
Muzei Leningradskogo vysshego khudozhestvenno-promyshlennogo uchilishcha
[Museum of the Leningrad Higher School of Industrial Arts] (1945–1953)
Muzei Leningradskogo vysshego khudozhestvenno-promyshlennogo uchilishcha im. V. I. Mukhinoi
[Museum of the V. I. Mukhina Leningrad Higher School of Industrial Arts] (1953–1991)
Muzei Sankt-Peterburgskogo vysshego khudozhestvenno-promyshlennogo uchilishcha im. V. I. Mukhinoi
[Museum of the V. I. Mukhina St. Petersburg Higher School of Industrial Arts] (1991–XI. 1994)

The present museum owes its origin to the prerevolutionary Stieglitz Museum, established in 1878 as an adjunct to the Central School of Technical Drawing (later usually "Industrial Arts"), which had been founded by the wealthy financier and patron of the arts, Baron A. L. Stieglitz (Shtiglits) in 1876. Opened in 1879, the school trained artists in decorative and applied art and drawing teachers for secondary schools. The present building, designed by the school's first director, M. E. Mesmacher (Mesmakher), was constructed specially for the museum in 1885–1895, and was considered one of the finest museum buildings in Europe of the period. The museum opened to the public in 1896 with some 30,000 exhibits of Russian and European origin on display illustrating the development of various styles—one of the largest collections of decorative and applied art in Europe in the late nineteenth and early twentieth centuries. During the First World War the museum was closed down. After the October Revolution a large part of the collection was turned over to the Hermitage and other Petrograd museums, and the Stieglitz Museum continued to function only until 1923.

In 1945 the museum was reopened as an exhibition of the Leningrad School of Industrial Arts (Higher School after 1948) for the purposes of exhibiting the best work done by students and graduates. Some of the collections that had previously belonged to the prerevolutionary museum were returned by the State Hermitage. In 1952 the school was merged with the Moscow Institute of Decorative and Applied Arts, and the museum collections were considerably enlarged by exhibits transferred from the museum of the Moscow Institute. In 1953 it was renamed in honor of the Soviet sculptress Vera Ignat'evna Mukhina (1889–1953).

Its present name dates to 1994, when the Leningrad (St. Petersburg) Higher School was reorganized as the St. Petersburg State Academy of Industrial Arts. Currently the museum exhibits occupy only the ground floor, but the upper story is being renovated with plans for exhibits on the history and development of the school since its foundation in the nineteenth century.

N.B. The main archive of the museum, with documentation for the years 1936–1979, is held in TsGALI SPb (D–15). Most of the prerevolutionary holdings and documentation were dispersed.

HOLDINGS: ca. 7,000 (3,000—unarranged) units, late 19th–20th cc.

The Graphic Art Fond is currently undergoing reprocessing. Most of the collection consists of works done by students of the Stieglitz Central School of Technical Drawing. There are designers' originals, pressrun copies, and architectural plans and drawings done by Russian painters, sculptors, designers, and architects, as well as individual works by European masters, including copies, studies, and designs for mosaics, frescoes, paintings and sculptures. There are also designs for ornamental wood carving as used in the production of furniture or on larger architectural projects; designs for furniture and kitchenware; for jewelry and church utensils; for ceramics, tiles and glassware; and for fabrics, carpets, tapestries, and clothing.

Access: Access to the archival holdings requires an official letter addressed to the rector of the Academy or the museum director stating the subject and aim of the proposed research.

Working Conditions: Researchers are accommodated in the museum offices, where materials are available the day they are ordered.

Reference Facilities: There are *opisi* and a card catalogue. A new reference system for the Graphic Arts Fond is currently being prepared.

Library Facilities: The school library (ca. 140,000 vols.) was founded in 1879. Its prerevolutionary collections included many manuscript books, as well as valuable seventeenth- and eighteenth-century albums (many with miniatures) acquired at auctions in Western Europe. It acquired the libraries of P. E. Kornilov, V. P. Koz'menko, and I. A. Vaks. But most of the prerevolutionary holdings were subsequently dispersed, when the museum was closed down. The library now holds literature on the decorative and applied arts, as well as standard technical documentation. There is a card catalogue of illustrations. (Library tel.: 272-24-22).

Copying: Photocopies can be prepared.

FINDING AIDS — PUBLISHED — GENERAL:

Muzei SPb (1994), p. 45; *Biblioteki SPb* (1993), p. 72; *Peterburg* (1992), p. 139, 400; *Muzei Leningrada* (1982), p. 78; *Muzei vuzov* (1975), pp. 179–80.

h-625. *Muzei barona Shtiglitsa: Proshloe i nastoiashchee/ Baron Stieglitz Museum: The Past and the Present.* Compiled by G. E. Prokhorenko and G. A. Vlasova. Edited by E. N. Guseva. St. Petersburg: "Sezar," 1994. 200 p. "Zhemchuzhiny Peterburga." (Lib: IU; MH) Added English title page, preface, introduction, and captions.
> The first publication on the history of the school and museum founded by Baron A. L. Stieglitz, with elaborate colored illustrations. References are given to those parts of the prerevolutionary collection that are now held in the Hermitage. See also the brief chapter about some of the prerevolutionary holdings in h-596.

Literary Museums

❧ H–95 ❧

Vserossiiskii muzei A. S. Pushkina (VMP)
[All-Russian A. S. Pushkin Museum]

Agency: Ministerstvo kul'tury RF (Minkul'tury Rossii)
[Ministry of Culture]

Address: 191187, St. Petersburg, nab. Reki Moiki, 12
Telephone: 311-90-20, 312-19-62; *Fax:* (812) 311-38-01
E-mail: stepanov@infopro.spb.su
Website: http://www.pushkin.ru/spb/pushkin;
               http://www.bestrussia.com/net/pushkin/win.htm
Transport: metro: Nevskii prospekt, Gostinyi Dvor
Hours: M–F 11:00–17:00

Director: Sergei Mikhailovich Nekrasov (*tel.* 311-38-01)
Chief Curator: Tat'iana Georgievna Aleksandrova (*tel.* 315-98-04)

HISTORY:

Gosudarstvennyi muzei A. S. Pushkina
[State A. S. Pushkin Museum] (1938–1949)

The origin of the present museum dates to the end of 1925, when the apartment of Aleksandr Sergeevich Pushkin (1799–1837) on the Moika embankment (nab. Reki Moiki, 12) was given over to *Pushkinskii Dom* (Pushkin House—E–28). The apartment is in the house where the poet lived during the last four months of his life and where he died after a duel. It was used, starting in 1926, to house the so-called historico-literary life exhibits of the Literary Museum of Pushkinskii Dom.

In 1937 an All-Union Pushkin Exhibition was opened in Moscow in the State Historical Museum (GIM) to coincide with the centennial of the poet's death, and materials from Pushkinskii Dom and from other archives, museums, and libraries were exhibited there. At the same time a Pushkin Exhibition was opened in the Hermitage. In March 1938 the Council of People's Commissars decreed that all the materials from the Pushkin exhibitions should be used as the basis for a new State Pushkin Museum (*Gosudarstvennyi muzei A. S. Pushkina*) in Moscow. After the closure of the exhibition in GIM, the fonds of the new State Pushkin Museum were stored there, but due to lack of premises the new museum could not be opened to the public before the outbreak of war. During the war the museum fonds were evacuated to Tashkent, and after the war they were returned to Moscow and stored unpacked in the A. M. Gor'kii Institute of World Literature.

In 1947 the government decided that all the fonds of the museum should be transferred to Pushkin House (IRLI/PD) in Leningrad, which in 1948, on the instructions of the Presidium of the Academy of Sciences of the USSR, further accessioned a very rich collection of Pushkin manuscripts (2,000 units, including 500 autograph literary manuscripts of the poet). Other fonds of the Pushkin State Museum were transferred in the same year to the town of Pushkin, where the All-Union Pushkin Museum was staging an exhibition in the Alexander Palace (1949–1952). In 1954 the latter exhibition was moved to the Hermitage.

In 1953 all Pushkin materials held in the Institute of Russian Literature (apart from the manuscripts and the poet's library), together with the Pushkin apartment, the N. A. Nekrasov Apartment-Museum (H–96), and the Pushkin Preserve in the village of Mikhailovskoe were transferred to the authority of the Ministry of Culture of the USSR. In 1956 the All-Union Pushkin Museum came under the control of the Ministry of Culture of the RSFSR. The present name dates from 1991. In April 1997 the museum was added to the federal register of the most valuable monuments of the cultural heritage of the peoples of the Russian Federation.

Today the All-Russian Pushkin Museum is a complex of museums, which includes the Pushkin Literary Exhibition and four memorial museums that are administrated as branches:

(1) The A. S. Pushkin Apartment-Museum (*Muzei-kvartira A. S. Pushkina*), established in 1925 in the same building as the museum headquarters, which exhibits some of the original materials from the museum holdings (see below). (tel. 314-00-06)

(2) The Memorial Lyceum-Museum (*Memorial'nyi muzei-litsei*) in the town of Pushkin (Tsarskoe Selo, known as Detskoe Selo from 1918–1937, and Pushkin since 1937), established in 1949 in the former Tsarskoe Selo Lyceum, which Pushkin attended. (189620, St. Petersburg, g. Pushkin, ul. Sadovaia, 2; tel. 465-64-11).

(3) The A. S. Pushkin Dacha-Museum (*Muzei-dacha A. S. Pushkina*) in the town of Pushkin (Tsarskoe Selo), established in 1958. (189620, g. Pushkin, ul. Pushkinskaia, 2; tel. 476-69-90).

(4) The N. A. Nekrasov Apartment-Museum (*Muzei-kvartira N. A. Nekrasova*) (see H–96).

The State Pushkin Museum-Preserve (*Gosudarstvennyi muzei-zapovednik A. S. Pushkina*) in the village of Mikhailovskoe remains under separate administration, and exhibits some original Pushkin materials along with duplicates from his personal library. Founded in 1922, it came under the authority of the Main Administration for Scientific, Museum, and Academic Art Institutes (Glavnauka) under the People's Commissariat for Education of the RSFSR. It came under IRLI/PD (E–28) in 1934. (181388, Pskovskaia oblast', Pushkinskie gory, s. Mikhailovskoe; tel/fax (8-81146) 2-34-90; tel. 2-10-48).

When the All-Union Pushkin Museum was transferred from the Academy of Sciences of the USSR to the Ministry of Culture of the USSR in 1953, most of the manuscript materials with the exception of a number of exhibition documents, remained in the Institute of Russian Literature (IRLI/PD—E–28). Archival materials now held in the VMP Division of Fonds are principally those acquired by the museum since 1953.

HOLDINGS: ca. 2,000 units, 18th–20th cc.

personal fonds—21; archival collections—8 (late 18th–20th cc.)

Archival materials are held as part of the museum's larger Division of Fonds. The museum holds 21 personal fonds, connected in one way or another with the life of Aleksandr Sergeevich Pushkin, his ancestors, his relatives, his descendents, and his friends. These papers include the family archives of the Gannibal, the Goncharov, the Nashchokin, the Malinovskii, the Ivashev, the Khomutov, and the Rall' families. There are diaries, property-management records, and correspondence. Also held here are the personal papers of the Pushkin scholars M. A. and T. G. Tsiavlovskii and B. V. Tomashevskii.

The archival collections include lists of the works of such Russian writers as G. R. Derzhavin, K. F. Ryleev, A. S. Pushkin, V. A. Zhukovskii, A. S. Griboedov, and P. A. Viazemskii. There are domestic albums covering the years 1820 to 1860 and containing diary-type notes, verses, and drawings. The archives also have collections of letters and original manuscripts by such contemporaries of Pushkin as V. A. Zhukovskii, E. A. Baratynskii, I. I. Dmitriev, M. F. Orlov, and A. P. Kern. Then there are collections of domestic and property-management documents, which include petitions, deeds of purchase, orders for post-horses, leave of absence certificates, nobility charters, certificates of civil rank, military and civilian printed edicts, as well as collections of manuscript and printed musical scores. The museum also has a number of original works by numerous twentieth-century writers, poets, painters and critics, such as A. M. Gor'kii, V. V. Veresaev, and R. M. Glier, among others.

Access: Access to the archival holdings requires an official letter from the researcher's sponsoring institution or a personal letter of application addressed to the director of the museum stating the subject and aim of the proposed research.

Working Conditions: Researchers are accommodated in the working rooms of the Fonds Division, where materials are available the day they are ordered.

Reference Facilities: There are inventories of documents and a catalogue of personal names. The application of archival rules to the arrangement of documents was introduced in 1991.

Library Facilities: The Book Fond of the museum, which was founded in 1954 on the basis of books from Pushkinskii Dom, includes duplicates of books from Pushkin's personal library; part of the library of the Imperial Alexander Lyceum (transferred in the 1960s from the library of the Gor'kii State University in Sverdlovsk, and in 1985 from the Leningrad Branch of the Union of Writers of the USSR); books from the collections of N. I. Novikov and the Turgenev brothers; and the collections of L. V. Gubar, S. L. Markov, and V. A. Krylov. There are approximately 70,000 volumes of publications on Pushkin and his contemporaries. There is a card catalogue of Pushkiniana and a card catalogue for publications by the museum staff, as well as several facts-and-figures files.

Copying: Photographic and xerox copies can be prepared.

FINDING AIDS — PUBLISHED — GENERAL:

Muzei SPb (1994), pp. 82–87; *Biblioteki SPb* (1993), p. 70; *Peterburg* (1994), p. 530; *GAF Spravochnik* (1991), pp. 144–45; *Lit. muzei Leningrada* (1987), pp. [1–9]; *Muzei Leningrada* (1989), pp. 208–12, 217–20; *Muzei Leningrada* (1982), p. 99–100.

h-630. *Doma u Pushkina.* Edited by V. F. Shubin. St. Petersburg: "Arsis," 1994. 112 p. "ARS: Rossiiskii zhurnal iskusstv: Tematicheskii vyp.," vol. 1. (Lib: MH)

> A collection of articles about the museum including outline descriptions of some of the materials in the main and auxiliary fonds.

h-631. Popova, Nina Ivanovna. *Muzei-kvartira A. S. Pushkina.* Leningrad: Lenizdat, 1989. 23 p. + 19 plates. (Lib: DLC; IU; MH)

> EARLIER ED.: L., 1979. 78 p. + 8 plates. (Lib: MH)

h-631.1. Popova, Nina Ivanovna. *Muzei-kvartira A. S. Pushkina na Moike/ Pushkin Memorial Museum on the Moika Embankment.* Moscow: "Sovetskaia Rossiia," 1989. 127 p. Added title page and summary in English. (Lib: MH)

h-632. Popova, Nina Ivanovna. *Muzei-kvartira A. S. Pushkina.* Leningrad: "Khudozhnik RSFSR," 1980. 196 p. Text in English, French, German, and Russian. (Lib: DLC; IU; MH)

h-633. Minina, A. I. "Stranitsy istorii muzeia." In *Pushkiniana Vsesoiuznogo muzeia A. S. Pushkina: Sbornik nauchnykh statei,* edited by S. M. Nekrasov, pp. 3–11. Leningrad, 1988. [Minkul't RSFSR; VMP]

> Surveys the history of the museum from the founding of the Pushkin Library in 1879 and the opening of the Pushkin Exhibition in the Alexander Lyceum (1881) through the 1980s.

h-634. Popova, Nina Ivanovna. "Vchera i zavtra kvartiry na Moike, 12." *Sovetskii muzei,* 1983, no. 2, pp. 18–21. (Lib: DLC; IU; MH)

> Surveys the history of the Pushkin Apartment-Museum.

h-635. *Vsesoiuznyi muzei A. S. Pushkina: Katalog.* Compiled by A. Iu. Veis et al. Leningrad/ Moscow: "Iskusstvo," 1957. 327 p. + plates. (Lib: DLC; MH)

h-636. Granovskaia, Nina Ivanovna. *Vsesoiuznyi muzei A. S. Pushkina: Ocherk-putevoditel'.* Leningrad: Lenizdat, 1985. 208 p. + 48 plates. (Lib: IU; MH)

Memorial'nyi muzei-kvartira N. A. Nekrasova—
Filial Vserossiiskogo muzeia A. S. Pushkina

[N. A. Nekrasov Memorial Apartment-Museum—
Branch of the All-Russian A. S. Pushkin Museum]

Agency: Ministerstvo kul'tury RF (Minkul'tury Rossii)
[Ministry of Culture]

Address: 191104, St. Petersburg, Liteinyi prosp., 36, kv. 4
Telephone: 272-01-65
Website: http://www.pushkin.ru/nekrasov.html
Transport: metro: Vladimirskaia, Dostoevskaia, Maiakovskaia, Chernyshevskaia;
tram: 5, 12, 14, 28, 32, 34, 54; trol.: 3, 8, 19 (stop Liteinyi prospekt)
Hours: MWF–Su 11:00–17:00, Th 13:00–17:00; Fonds—by appointment

Head: Elena Iur'evna Glevenko (*tel.* 272-04-81)
Curator: Ol'ga Aleksandrovna Zamarenova (*tel.* 279-09-15)

HISTORY:

In 1938 the Presidium of the Leningrad City Soviet passed a resolution to organize a Nekrasov museum, but it was not opened before the outbreak of World War II. The museum was opened in 1946 to mark the 125th anniversary of the birth of the Russian poet, housed in the flat where Nikolai Alekseevich Nekrasov (1821–1877/1878) lived, together with I. I. Panaev and A. Ia. Panaeva, from 1857 until his death. Initially under the jurisdiction of the Institute of Russian Literature (IRLI), since 1953 the museum has been a branch of the All-Union (now All-Russian) A. S. Pushkin Museum (H–95), under the Ministry of Culture.

HOLDINGS: ca. 300 units, 1850s–1880s; 1917–1980s

The museum has a small collection of manuscript materials relating to Nekrasov and his contemporaries, which are retained as part of both the Main Fond and the Auxiliary Fond of museum holdings.

The Main Fond contains a number of documents relating to Nekrasov, including a copy of the poem "Korobeiniki," autographed visiting cards, the address given by the students of Khar'kiv University and the Veterinary Institute (1877), letters to N. V. Kholshevnikov and I. I. Panaev (1860s and 1870s), and photographs. Materials originating from other persons include letters written by M. E. Saltykov-Shchedrin, N. G. Chernyshevskii, and F. M. Dostoevskii; documents on the condition of serfs; a notebook of the writer A. A. Bogdanov (1874–1939); albums of drawings and verses (19th c.); and a letter to the museum by K. I. Chukovskii.

There are also documentary materials from the poet's friends and acquaintances, arranged into fonds. The Panaev family fond contains the manuscript "Secret Notes of Secretary of State Panaev" (1859), as well as letters from relatives and photographs. The fond of I. G. Zykov (1827–1889), who organized a school in the village of Abakumtsevo subsidized by Nekrasov, includes his recollections and letters from his daughter. The fond of V. I. Pyzin (1892–1983), who researched the Panaev family tree, consists of manuscript literary criticism, notes, letters, and materials relating to the Panaev family.

There are also personal papers of three Nekrasov scholars: Professor V. E. Evgen'ev-Maksimov (1883–1955), A. V. Popov (1881–1965), and S. A. Reiser (1905–1989). These include manuscripts of scholarly works, materials relating to Nekrasov and the staff of the journal *Sovremennik*, letters, memoirs, maps and photographs of places associated with Nekrasov, and portraits of the poet's contemporaries.

The Auxiliary Fond holds letters from artists and people who have donated items to the museum, together with original verses on Nekrasov by such twentieth-century poets as M. V. Isakovskii, R. A. Rozhdestvenskii, A. A. Surkov, and A. T. Tvardovskii.

Access: Access to the archival holdings requires an official letter from the researcher's sponsoring institution or a personal letter of application addressed to the director of the All-Russian Pushkin Museum (H–95), stating the subject and aim of the proposed research.

Working Conditions: Researchers are accommodated in the museum offices, where materials are available the day they are ordered.

Reference Facilities: There are catalogues of the main and auxiliary fonds, and an inventory of documents of personal papers.

Library Facilities: The Book Fond (ca. 2,000 vols.) contains literature on Nekrasov and his contemporaries, including books and rare editions. There are five books from the poet's own library (see h-639) with dedicatory inscriptions.

Copying: There are no facilities for copying documents.

FINDING AIDS — PUBLISHED — GENERAL:

Muzei SPb (1994), p. 88; *Biblioteki SPb* (1993), p. 70; *GAF Spravochnik* (1991), pp. 145–46; *Muzei Leningrada* (1989), p. 220–23; *Muzei Leningrada* (1982), p. 102; *Lit. muzei Leningrada* (1987), pp. [10–17]; Myl'nikov (1970), p. 45.

h-637. [Glevenko, Elena Iur'evna]. *Muzei-kvartira N. A. Nekrasova.* [Leningrad]: Vneshtorgizdat, 1990. 18 p. In English, Russian, German and French.
This advertising brochure gives brief information on the history of the museum and its exhibits.

h-637.1. Loman, Ol'ga Vladimirovna. *Muzei-kvartira N. A. Nekrasova.* 2d ed. Leningrad: Lenizdat, 1971. 68 p. "Turistu o Leningrade." (Lib: MH)
A tourist guide to the museum and its exhibits.

h-638. Pritsker, E. D. "Kak dom stal muzeem." *Leningradskaia panorama*, 1985, no. 9, pp. 20–22. (Lib: DLC; IU; MH)
A history of the Nekrasov Apartment-Museum.

FINDING AIDS — SPECIALIZED:

h-639. Glevenko, Elena Iur'evna. "Razyskivaetsia biblioteka." *V mire knig*, 1983, no. 10, pp. 51–52. (Lib: DLC; IU; MH)
Analyzes the history of the Nekrasov library, part of which perished on his estate, Karabikha (363 titles). The author has tried to establish the contents of that part of the poet's library that remained in St. Petersburg and to trace its subsequent fate. The museum currently has five books from this collection with dedicatory inscriptions.

Gosudarstvennyi literaturno-memorial'nyi muzei F. M. Dostoevskogo
[F. M. Dostoevskii State Literary Memorial Museum]

Agency: Komitet po kul'ture Administratsii Sankt-Peterburga
[Committee on Culture of the Administration of St. Petersburg]

Address: 191002, St. Petersburg, Kuznechnyi per., 5/2
Telephone: 112-03-07 (Museum Fonds); 311-40-31 (Scientific Division);
              Fax: (812) 311-18-04
E-mail: natalia@d-museum.spb.su
Website: http://www.dux.ru/win/spb/dostmus/muz1
Transport: metro: Vladimirskaia, Dostoevskaia
Hours: Tu–F 10:00–18:30

Director: Natal'ia Tuimibaevna Ashimbaeva (*tel.* 311-18-04)
Chief Curator: Nataliia Vasil'evna Pavlova (*tel.* 112-00-03)

HISTORY:

The museum was founded in 1968 on the initiative of G. M. Fridlender and other scholars at the Institute of Russian Literature (PD/ IRLI AN SSSR) with the support of A. A. Prokof'ev, the head of the Leningrad Branch of the Union of Writers. It was opened in 1971 in the apartment where the Russian writer Fedor Mikhailovich Dostoevskii (1821–1881), lived from 1878 until his death in 1881.

Earlier the museum had two branches, the Anna Akhmatova Museum in the Fontanka (Fountain) House (*Muzei Anny Akhmatovoi v Fontannom Dome*) (H–98) and the M. M. Zoshchenko Literary Memorial Museum (*Literaturno-memorial'nyi muzei M. M. Zoshchenko*) (H–100), both of which are now administered independently.

Archival materials are held in three different divisions of the museum.

Access: Access to the archival materials requires an official application stating the subject and purpose of research.

Working Conditions: Researchers are accommodated in the museum offices. Materials are available the day they are ordered.

Library Facilities: The Book Fond of the museum (22,000 vols.) was founded in 1971 and includes literature on the writer and his era; editions published during his lifetime; books with literary autographs by F. M. Dostoevskii, A. N. Maikov, and A. F. Koni; and rare books.

Copying: Copying may be done with the permission of the museum curator.

Fond rukopisei
[Fond of Manuscripts]

Telephone: 112–03–07
Hours: M–F 10:30–17:30
Curator: Rimma Romanovna Fatkhullina

HOLDINGS: 11 (5 unarranged) fonds, 1847–1972
general fond—329 units (1847–1972)

The Fond of Manuscripts contains documents originating with relatives of the writer and his contemporaries, as well as materials from the annual "Dostoevskii and World Culture" conferences that have been held in the museum since 1974. The papers of A. G. Dostoevskaia (Dostoevskii's second wife, *née* Snitkina) include her letters to relatives and other personal documents; a manuscript copy of a comedy written by Dostoevskii's brother, M. M. Dostoevskii, entitled "The Eldest Sister and the Youngest Sister" (*Starshaia i men'shaia*); and letters from the writer's grandson, A. F. Dostoevskii (1885–1968) on transferring the remains of his grandmother, A. G. Dostoevskaia, from Yalta to Leningrad.

The papers of the writer and journalist A. U. Poretskii (1819–1879) include letters written by A. P. and R. P. Norshtein and letters from Dostoevskii's doctor, S. D. Ianovskii, and his wife, A. I. Shubert, among others. There are also materials of the journal "Sunday Leisure" (*Voskresnyi dosug*), which Poretskii edited, including authors' manuscripts, letters to the editor, manuscript copies of verses by A. S. Pushkin, I. S. Nikitin, and other nineteenth-century poets, and one of the closest-to-the-original copies of Belinskii's famous letter to Gogol'.

The papers of E. A. Rykacheva, Dostoevskii's niece, contain her correspondence with relatives (1866–1899).

There are also scattered individual documents from various persons—for example, a letter from A. F. Koni (1921); verses of V. S. Solov'ev and his letters to the architect and painter, F. G. Berenshtam; and a letter from an unknown person about Dostoevskii's speech on Pushkin.

Reference Facilities: The main fond has been arranged and described and the auxiliary fond has been partially described.

Fond fotografii, afish, programm
[Fond of Photographs, Posters, and Programs]

Telephone: 112-03-07
Hours: by appointment
Curator: Natal'ia Vladimirovna Shvarts

HOLDINGS: general fond—ca. 1,400 units (mid-19th c.–1994)

The collection of documentary photographs includes original pictures of Dostoevskii (some signed by the writer) and members of his family: his first wife, M. D. Dostoevskaia (*née* Konstant); second wife, A. G. Dostoevskaia (*née* Snitkina); sisters V. M. Karepina, V. M. Ivanova, and A. M. Golenovskaia (*née* Sheviakova); brothers M. M. Dostoevskii and A. M. Dostoevskii; nieces, V. A. Savost'ianova and E. A. Rykacheva; son, F. F. Dostoevskii; and daughter, L. F. Dostoevskaia. There are also portraits of his contemporaries, like V. G. Belinskii, D. V. Grigorovich, N. A. Nekrasov, A. P. Filosofova, A. A. Shtakenshneider (Stakenschneider) and his sister, E. A. Shtakenshneider, A. F. Koni, A. N. Maikov, O. F. Miller, I. I. Panaev, Ia. P. Polonskii, M. G. Savina, V. S. Solov'ev, A. S. Suvorin, and Countess S. A. Tolstaia. There are also photographs of places connected with the life and work of the writer.

The collection entitled "Theater and Cinema" includes posters and programs for plays based on the plots of Dostoevskii's novels.

Reference Facilities: The main fond has been arranged and described and the auxiliary fond has been partially described.

Fond grafiki
[Fond of Graphic Arts]

Telephone: 112-03-07
Hours: by appointment
Curator: Marianna Isaakovna Brusovani

HOLDINGS: general fond—ca. 4,000 units (mid-19th c.–1990s)

The graphic art collection includes illustrations of the works of Dostoevskii and other works on the theme of "Dostoevskii's St. Petersburg." Of considerable interest are the illustrations by M. M. Shemiakin, E. I. Neizvestnyi, and Iu. Perevezentsev. There are also graphic plates by P. M. Boklevskii, I. I. Vaulin, and D. A. Shmarinov, among others.

Reference Facilities: There are inventory registers for staff use and alphabetical card catalogues.

FINDING AIDS — PUBLISHED — GENERAL:

Muzei SPb (1994), p. 90; *Biblioteki SPb* (1993), p. 70; *GAF Spravochnik* (1991), p. 152; *Muzei Leningrada* (1989), pp. 223–25; *Muzei Leningrada* (1982), pp. 102–04; *Lit. muzei Leningrada* (1987), pp. [18–26].

h-640. Bograd, Ganna L'vovna; Rybalko, Bela Nurievna; and Tustanovskaia, Evgeniia Mikhailovna. *Literaturno-memorial'nyi muzei F. M. Dostoevskogo.* Leningrad: Lenizdat, 1981. 104 p. (Lib: DLC; IU)

   A guide to the museum exhibits as they were then organized.

Muzei Anny Akhmatovoi v Fontannom Dome
[Anna Akhmatova Museum in the Fontanka (Fountain) House]

Agency: Komitet po kul'ture Administratsii Sankt-Peterburga
[Committee on Culture of the Administration of St. Petersburg]

Address:	191104, St. Petersburg, nab. Fontanki, 34 (entrance from Liteinyi per., 53)
Telephone:	272-40-80; 272-57-58; *Fax:* (812) 272-20-34
E-mail:	nina@anna-museum.spb.su; U.S. representative: veraigor@voicenet.com
Website:	http://www.voicenet.com/~veraigor/Museum/Achmatova/Achmatova.html;
	http://www.museum.ru/museum/akhmatova/fountain_house/
Transport:	metro: Nevskii prospekt, Gostinyi Dvor, Vladimirskaia, Dostoevskaia
Hours:	Tu–Sa 11:00–18:00 (research—by appointment)

Director: Nina Ivanovna Popova (*tel.* 272-18-11)
Chief Curator: Irina Petrovna Sizykh
Curator of the Manuscript Fonds: Elena L'vovna Kurnikova

HISTORY:

The museum was founded in 1989, in the garden wing of the Sheremetev Palace—also known as the Fontanka (Fountain) House (*Fontannyi Dom*). The house itself was built in 1750–1755, and the garden wing was erected in the 1840s. There, in a flat on the third floor, the beloved Silver Age poet, Anna Andreevna Akhmatova (*pseud.* of Gorenko) (1889–1966), lived from 1924–1941 and 1944–1952 with her second husband, Nikolai Nikolaevich Punin (1888–1953). Punin, one of the best-known Russian art critics and director of the Hermitage, was arrested in 1936, and again in 1949, after which he died in a prison camp. In addition to exhibits honoring Akhmatova, the museum also features an exhibit honoring N. N. Punin, preserving his working study. Initially a branch of the Dostoevskii Museum (H–97), the museum came under independent administration in 1990. During 1997 there was a temporary exhibition honoring the memory of the Nobel prize-winning poet Joseph Brodsky (Iosif Aleksandrovich Brodskii, 1940–1996), whom Akhmatova greatly admired, and who died in exile in New York City.

HOLDINGS: 10 fonds, 1,414 units, 1780s–1990s
original documents—902 units; xerox copies of documents—512 units; personal fonds—7

The Manuscript Fond within the museum's Division of Fonds retains some personal papers of a number of Silver Age poets. These include Anna Akhmatova, M. A. Kuzmin (1872–1936), and O. E. Mandel'shtam (1891–1938) and his family. There are also personal papers of the poet, translator, photographer, and collector, L. V. Gornung (1902–1993); the art historian and head of the Engravings Division of the State Hermitage, E. G. Lisenkov (1885–1954); the Polytechnical Institute lecturer (*dotsent*), M. V. Latmanizov (1905–1980), who was a great admirer of the works of Akhmatova; and the French literary historian and critic, Eliane Moch-Bickert (Mok-Biker).

The Akhmatova fond contains autograph literary manuscripts (some from the M. S. Lesman collection), her translations, biographical documents (including the honorary degree of Doctor of Literature, conferred by Oxford University in 1965), correspondence, and xerox copies of documents held in TsGALI SPb (D–15), the Manuscript Division of RNB (G–15), and in private archives.

Among materials in the M. A. Kuzmin papers are drawings made by Kuzmin, manuscripts of his poetry, and biographical documents acquired by the museum from the Moscow collector, M. V. Tolmachev. The Mandel'shtam family fond has, for example, a collection of letters written by N. Ia. Mandel'shtam to S. M. Gluskina, L. M. Gluskina, and I. D. Amusin, as well as documents relating to the poet's father, E. V. Mandel'shtam. There are a number of documents collected by Eliane Moch-Bickert (Mok-Biker), which relate to the Parisian period in the life and work of O. A. Glebova-Sudeikina, the heroine of Akhmatova's "Poem Without a Hero."

The museum also has a collection of autograph literary manuscripts, copies of literary works and other documents from such prominent figures in the world of Russian twentieth-century culture as I. A. Brodskii, B. L. Pasternak, and P. N. Luknitskii, among others.

Within the administrative records of the museum itself is documentation of the history of the museum, posters, programs for special evenings, and other documents. There is a separate fond of documents relating to the museum exhibits.

Access: Requests for research access require an official letter, indicating the subject and purpose of research.

Working Conditions: Researchers are accommodated in the museum offices, where materials are available the day they are ordered.

Reference Facilities: There are inventories and catalogues of the main and auxiliary museum fonds. There is a detailed catalogue of all the material in the Kuzmin and Akhmatova fonds. Work has begun on producing a computerized catalogue of the collection.

Library Facilities: The museum Book Fond (ca. 13,000 vols.), includes parts of the personal libraries of Akhmatova and I. A. Brodskii, and part of the library collection of M. S. Lesman. While specializing in publications by and about Silver Age writers, the library has also acquired many other books on literature and literary criticism.

Copying: Xerox copies can be prepared.

FINDING AIDS — PUBLISHED — GENERAL:

Muzei SPb (1994), p. 92; *Biblioteki SPb* (1993), p. 70; *Peterburg* (1992), p. 664.

There is no published guide to the archival and manuscript materials in the museum. For the 1989 catalogue of the Lesman library and manuscript collection, a part of which is now held in the museum, see a-143.

h-641. *Muzei Anny Akhmatovoi v Fontannom Dome.* Compiled by I. G. Kravtsova, E. V. Kuz'mina, N. I. Popova, and A. G. Terekhov. Leningrad: "Petropol'," 1991. 49 p. (Lib: DLC; IU; MH)

> A description of the exhibits in the museum, including documents, photographs, graphic materials, postcards, books, and other items.

Muzei-kvartira A. A. Bloka—Filial GMISPb
[A. A. Blok Apartment-Museum—
Branch of the State Museum of the History of St. Petersburg]

Agency: Komitet po kul'ture Administratsii Sankt-Peterburga
[Committee on Culture of the Administration of St. Petersburg]

Address:	190121, St. Petersburg, ul. Dekabristov, 57, kv. 21, 23
Telephone:	216-45-40; 113-86-27
Transport:	tram: 31, 33, 42; bus: 22 (to prosp. Maklina)
Hours:	MTu, Th–Sa 11:00–18:00

Director: Tat'iana Vasil'evna Pavlova (*tel.* 113-86-33)

HISTORY:

The museum was founded in 1980, to honor the centennial of the birth of the Russian poet Aleksandr Aleksandrovich Blok (1880–1921), and occupies the apartments where Blok lived from 1912 until his death on 7 August 1921. The museum is administered as a Branch of the State Museum of the History of St. Petersburg (GMISPb—H–65).

Some of the museum exhibits were assembled from personal effects and memorabilia that had earlier been deposited in the Literary Museum in Pushkinskii Dom. An important collection of Blok-related materials, including archival materials, were acquired from N. P. Il'in in 1977–1978. A few books, documents, and photographs are displayed in the museum itself, but most of the archival materials are retained as part of the A. A. Blok Fond in the State Museum of the History of St. Petersburg. Because of the disastrous physical condition of the premises where they are currently housed, they are closed to the public and negotiations are under way to transfer that collection to the museum itself.

N. B. Other major parts of the Blok papers are held in Pushkinskii Dom (E–28), the Russian State Library (G–1), and RGALI (B–7).

Access: Most of the archival materials that comprise the A. A. Blok Fond, which is considered part of the holdings of the Branch Museum, are currently retained on the main museum premises (GMISPb—H–65), but are unfortunately closed to the public for technical reasons.

Fond A. A. Bloka
[A. A. Blok Fond]

Address:	196046, St. Petersburg, Petropavlovskaia krepost', 3
Telephone:	238-46-08
Transport:	metro: Gor'kovskaia
Curator:	Natal'ia Ksenofontovna Tsendrovskaia

HOLDINGS: archival materials—ca. 2,000 units (late 19th c.–1920s); photographs—ca. 300
(late 19th c.–1920s)

The A. A. Blok Fond holds that part of the poet's papers that were acquired from N. P. Il'in, which contain some original manuscripts, including drafts of some of his poems. There is some of his correspondence with relatives, including his mother, A. A. Kublitskaia-Piottukh, his aunt S. A. Kublitskaia-Piottukh, and his uncle, F. A. Kublitskii-Piottukh; and with his contemporaries Iu. N. Verkhovskii, L. A. Del'mas, P. K. Labutin, and I. A. Rudomazina. Other documents relate to Blok's family and close friends, namely his wife, L. D. Mendeleeva-Blok, his mother, and his aunts M. A. Beketova and S. A. Kublitskaia-Piottukh.

Some literary autographs are preserved from Blok's literary contemporaries and friends: Iu. N. Verkhovskii, Z. N. Gippius, S. M. Gorodetskii, E. I. Ivanov and his family, F. K. Sologub (*pseud. of* F. K. Teternikov), A. N. Tolstoi, and G. I. Chulkov. There are also memoirs of his wife's students, and correspondence regarding the organization of the A. A. Blok Museum. Among photographic documents are portraits of the poet and pictures of family and friends autographed by A. A. Blok.

Working Conditions: As noted above, the Blok Fond is closed until appropriate premises can be found and arrangements made for their transfer.

Reference Facilities: There are inventory registers and a card catalogue of names.

FINDING AIDS — PUBLISHED — GENERAL:

Muzei SPb (1994), p. 95; *Lit. muzei Leningrada* (1987), pp. [27–32].

There is no published guide to the archival materials in the museum or the Blok Fond.

Literaturno-memorial'nyi muzei M. M. Zoshchenko
[M. M. Zoshchenko Literary-Memorial Museum]

Agency: Komitet po kul'ture Administratsii Sankt-Peterburga
[Committee on Culture of the Administration of St. Petersburg]

Address:	191186, St. Petersburg, ul. Malaia Koniushennaia, 4/2, kv. 119
Telephone:	311-78-19
Transport:	metro: Kanal Griboedova; trol.: 1, 5, 7, 10, 22, 44
Hours:	Tu–Sa 11:30–18:00

Director: Kirill Stanislavovich Kuz'min

HISTORY:

The museum was opened in 1992, on the initiative of city literary circles, in apartment 119, where the writer Mikhail Mikhailovich Zoshchenko (1895–1958) lived from 1934 until his death. Initially a branch of the Dostoevskii Museum (H–97), the museum became independent in 1993.

N.B. Other Zoshchenko papers are held in Pushkinskii Dom (IRLI/PD—E–28).

HOLDINGS:

The collections include several literary manuscripts and other documentary materials of M. M. Zoshchenko, and his personal library, which was presented to the museum by the Moscow literary critic Iu. V. Tomashevskii.

Comment: The Rosarkhiv questionnaire about the archival holdings was not returned.

FINDING AIDS — PUBLISHED — GENERAL:

Muzei SPb (1994), p. 96.

There is no published guide to the museum, nor description of the archival holdings.

Sankt-Peterburgskii muzei V. V. Nabokova
[St. Petersburg Museum of V. V. Nabokov]

Agency: Obshchestvo kul'turno-prosvetitel'nykh i blagotvoritel'nykh
ob"edinenii "Nabokovskii fond"
[Nabokov Fund Society of Cultural-Enlightenment and Charitable
Associations]

Address: 190000, St. Petersburg, ul. Bol'shaia Morskaia, 47
Telephone: 315-47-13; *Fax:* (812) 312-65-94
E-mail: fnab@comset.spb.ru
Transport: trol.: 5, 22, 44; bus: 3, 10, 22
Hours: M–F 11:00–17:00

Director: Vadim Petrovich Stark
Scientific Secretary: Irina Petrovna Dobrovol'skaia

HISTORY:

Postoiannaia vystavka "Istoriia doma Nabokovykh"
[History of the Nabokov House—Permanent Exhibition] (IV.1993–VI.1997)

The museum exhibits were opened in April 1993 on the initiative of the Nabokov Fund in the family home (dating from the 1740s), where the writer Vladimir Vladimirovich Nabokov (1899–1977) was born and lived until he was 18. In June 1997 its status was changed from a "Permanent Exhibition" to that of an actual museum.

N.B. The personal archive of Nabokov is retained in Montreux, Switzerland, by the writer's son Dmitrii, with whom the museum is in regular contact. Other Nabokov papers are held in the Houghton Library of Harvard University, Cambridge, MA, USA.

HOLDINGS: statistics not available.

The collections, still in a state of formation, already include photographs and works of art. Family albums of the Nabokovs and part of Nabokov's butterfly collection were donated to the new museum by Harvard University.

Comment: A questionnaire about the archival holdings was not received by Rosarkhiv.

FINDING AIDS — PUBLISHED — GENERAL:

Muzei SPb (1994), p. 97.

There is no published guide to the museum, nor description of the archival holdings.

Museums of Theater, Musical, and Circus Arts

❈⊷ H–102 ⊶❈

Sankt-Peterburgskii gosudarstvennyi muzei teatral'nogo i muzykal'nogo iskusstva (SPbGMTiMI)
[St. Petersburg State Museum of Theater and Musical Arts]

Agency: Komitet po kul'ture Administratsii Sankt-Peterburga
[Committee on Culture of the Administration of St. Petersburg]

Address: 191011, St. Petersburg, pl. Ostrovskogo, 6
Telephone: 311-21-95; *Fax:* (812) 314-77-46
Transport: metro: Gostinyi Dvor, Nevskii prospekt

Hours: MTh–Su 10:00–18:00; W 13:00–19:00
Director: Irina Viktorovna Evstigneeva (*tel.* 315-52-43)
Chief Curator: Ol'ga Sokratovna Kara-Demur (*tel.* 311-23-29)

HISTORY:
Muzei petrogradskikh gosudarstvennykh akademicheskikh teatrov (Muzei Akteatrov)
    [Museum of the Petrograd State Academic Theaters] (1918–1924)
Muzei leningradskikh gosudarstvennykh akademicheskikh teatrov (Muzei Lengosteatrov)
    [Museum of the Leningrad State Academic Theaters] (1924–1929)
Muzei leningradskikh gosudarstvennykh teatrov (Muzei Lengosteatrov)
    [Museum of the Leningrad State Theaters] (1929–1933)
Leningradskii gosudarstvennyi teatral'nyi muzei (LGTM)
    [Leningrad State Theater Museum] (1933–1980)
Leningradskii gosudarstvennyi muzei teatral'nogo i muzykal'nogo iskusstva (LGMTiMI)
    [Leningrad State Museum of Theater and Musical Arts] (1980–1991)

The museum of the Petrograd State Academic Theaters was founded in December 1918 (on the order of A. V. Lunacharskii), on the basis of materials from the Production Department (*Postanovochnaia chast'*) of the Administration of Imperial Theaters (*Direktsiia imperatorskikh teatrov*), including its archives and library as well as the former museum of the Imperial Alexandra (*Aleksandrinskii*) Theater. The exhibits were first opened to the public in 1922. Established in the building that previously housed the theater administration and theater school (constructed starting in 1818 as designed by Carlo [K. I.] Rossi), the museum took over a number of important private collections, which had been nationalized as part of the State Museum Fond, including those of the performers I. F. Gorbunov, A. E. Molchanov, V. V. Protopopov, and S. F. Svetlov, and the House-Museum of M. G. Savina. The name and formal administrative affiliation of the museum changed several times during the Soviet period, but its collections remained relatively stable. In 1934 the museum acquired part of the collections of the Music Library of the Administration of Imperial Theaters (see G–22). The current name of the museum dates from 1991.

    The museum has five branches, the archival collections of which are included in the fonds of the St. Petersburg State Museum of Theater and Musical Arts:

    (1) The Museum of Musical Instruments (*Muzei muzykal'nykh instrumentov*), originally founded on the initiative of Count Stakelberg (Shtakel'berg) in 1900, had a complicated history after the

Revolution. It was established in its present premises in 1940, in the building now occupied by the Russian Institute of the History of Art (E–46). Since 1984 it has been a branch of what is now SPbGMTiMI. (190000, St. Petersburg, Isaakievskaia pl., 5; tel. 314-53-94; 314-53-45).

(2) The N. A. Rimskii-Korsakov Memorial Apartment-Museum (*Memorial'nyi muzei-kvartira N. A. Rimskogo-Korsakova*) (H–103), which was opened in 1971.

(3) The Museum of the History of Russian Operatic Theater and the F. I. Chaliapin Memorial Apartment (*Muzei istorii russkogo opernogo teatra i memorial'naia kvartira F. I. Shaliapina*), first opened in 1975. It was substantially renovated and reopened in 1995 in the building of the former Perm School, where the well-known Russian opera singer Fedor Ivanovich Chaliapin (Shaliapin) (1873–1938) lived from 1914 until his emigration in 1922. Chaliapin's archive and personal possessions were preserved by his close friend and former owner of the apartment, I. G. Dvorishchin, and subsequently transferred to the museum. Some of the archival materials, rich in documentation on the history of Russian opera, are exhibited in addition to Chaliapin's collection of Russian art. (197022, St. Petersburg, ul. Graftio, 2/6; tel. 315-53-43, 312-23-96).

(4) The Samoilov Family Memorial Apartment-Museum (*Memorial'nyi muzei-kvartira Samoilovykh*), opened in 1994, is housed in the building where the Russian actor of the Imperial Alexandra Theater, Vasilii Vasil'evich Samoilov (1812–1887), lived with his family, many of whom followed his footsteps on the stage. The exhibits, including "The Samoilov Dynasty and Theater Life of Petersburg," are based on the rich personal fond of V. V. Samoilov, long held in SPbGMTiMI, together with the collection of his son. (191065, St. Petersburg, ul. Stremiannaia, 8; tel. 275-20-01/ext. 214).

(5) The Sheremetev House on Fontanka (*Fontannyi dom Sheremetevykh*), transferred to the State Museum of Theater and Music in 1990, ranks as a landmark of Russian architecture of the eighteenth century. The house where the Sheremetev family lived for 150 years was long a center of the musical life of Petersburg. It was nationalized together with its collections in 1918. During the 1920s it was used for the Museum of Early Life (*Muzei starogo byta*), which was part of the Historical Daily-Life Division of the Russian Museum, but it was subsequently used by various other organizations. (191186, St. Petersburg, nab. Reki Fontanki, 34; tel. 272-38-98).

Access: For access to the archival and library holdings, a letter is required from the researcher's sponsoring institution to the director of the museum, although a personal application may be acceptable.

Working Conditions: Researchers are accommodated in the museum offices, where materials are available the day they are ordered.

Reference Facilities: There are catalogues for staff use in the Divisions of Manuscripts and Documents, of Drawings, and of Prints and Engravings. There are catalogue registers for individual items in the repository, inventory registers of acquisitions, and "passport" registers for the most valuable materials.

Library Facilities: The museum Book Fond (ca. 15,000 vols.) includes part of the library of the Imperial Theaters, as well as the private book collections or parts thereof that once belonged to L. I. Zheverzheev, Iu. M. Iur'ev, A. E. Molchanov, and L. D. Blok, among others. The library holds literature on the theater and audiovisual materials. There are working files and card catalogues on theater personalia and theater productions, as well as facts-and-figures indexes on national and foreign theaters and theater buildings. A computer database is currently being established covering the holdings.

Copying: Xerox and photographic copies can be prepared.

Otdel rukopisei i dokumentov
[Division of Manuscripts and Documents]

Telephone: 311-35-43
Hours: Tu 11:00–18:00 (by appointment)
Head: Liudmila Petrovna Bastrakova

HOLDINGS: 80 fonds, ca. 20,000 units, 1725–1990s

The Division of Manuscripts and Documents holds predominantly manuscript materials on the history of the theater in Russia and other parts of the world. There is a considerable collection of manuscript materials relating to the activities of the major St. Petersburg theaters—the Imperial Alexandra (*Aleksandrinskii*), the Imperial Maria (*Mariinskii*), the Musorgskii Malyi Theater of Opera and Ballet (*Malyi teatr opery i baleta im. M. P. Musorgskogo*), the Tovstonogov Bolshoi Drama Theater (*Bol'shoi dramaticheskii teatr im. G. A. Tovstonogova*), and the Komissarzhevskaia Theater (*Teatr im. V. F. Komissarzhevskoi*). Among the documents, which span the eighteenth to the twentieth centuries, are official files of the Administration of Imperial Theaters; lists of repertory companies; scenarios for operas, ballets, operettas, and theater productions; company repertoires, draft programs, and play lists; notes and sketches made during rehearsals; and the personal papers of famous directors and performers.

Much of the collection is made up of documents pertaining to the life and work of the performers, directors, ballet-masters, and composers who worked in the drama and music theaters of St. Petersburg. Most prominent among these are the fonds of N. A. Bromlei and B. M. Sushkevich, A. Ia. Vaganova, T. M. Vecheslova, E. A. Korchagina-Aleksandrovskaia, O. A. Spesivtseva, F. I. Chaliapin (Shaliapin), D. D. Shostakovich, E. I. Time, and Iu. M. Iur'ev. There are also manuscripts of books, and articles, as well as notes, memoirs, and correspondence. There are individual original autograph documents of Gioacchino Rossini, Maria Taglioni, Marius Petipa, A. P. Chekhov, A. A. Blok, Maksim (A. M.) Gor'kii, V. V. Maiakovskii, V. I. Nemirovich-Danchenko, K. S. Stanislavskii, and S. M. Eisenstein (Eizenshtein), among many others.

Reference Facilities: Previous catalogues were made according to museum regulations—whereby materials were grouped by name, location, date, or subject matter—without respect to archival provenance, but in recent years the division has transferred to an archival system and has been rearranging materials into fonds according to their provenance. The division has working catalogues and card catalogues covering theater personalia, theater performances, as well as an index of facts and figures on Russian, Soviet, and foreign theater companies and theaters. A computer database is currently being established covering the fonds.

Otdel foto i reproduktsii
[Division of Photographs and Reproductions]

Telephone: 311-23-29
Hours: Tu 11:00–18:00
Head: Eiba Kaiatonovna Norkute

HOLDINGS: ca. 210,000 units, 19th–20th cc.

This division holds a collection of group and individual portraits of prominent Russian and foreign theater personalia, as well as photographs of scenes from opera, ballet, and theater performances. There are also materials on theater architecture—photographs documenting theater performances abroad; photograph albums; photo- and printed reproductions; newspapers clippings; negatives; documentary films, and other pictorial material on the theater.

The largest photographic collections came from the actresses M. G. Savina and V. F. Komissarzhevskaia, actor Iu. M. Iur'ev, ballerina A. P. Pavlova, and opera singer F. I. Chaliapin (Shaliapin). There is a unique collection of photographs of the first performance of Tchaikovsky's (Chaikovskii's) ballet, "Sleeping Beauty" (*Spiashchaia krasavitsa*) in the Mariinskii Theater.

There is also a collection of photograph albums, including those that belonged to the director and composer E. F. Napravnik, the singers L. V. Sobinov and M. A. Slavina, and ballet-master M. M. Fokin (Michel Fokine).

Otdel risunka
[Division of Drawings]

Telephone: 311-23-29
Hours: Tu 11:00–18:00
Head: Elena Mikhailovna Fedosova

HOLDINGS: ca. 25,000 units, 18th–20th cc.

This division contains hand-drawn portraits of Russian and foreign actors and actresses together with sketches of stage sets and performers made during performances, and other products of theater decorative art. The art of stage designing is represented here by the original work of Giuseppe Valeriani, Antonio Canoppi, Antonio and Carlo Bibiena-Galli, and Pietro Gottardo di Gonzaga for plays performed at the Mariinskii Theater during the eighteenth century, and a collection of studies by Alfred Roller for the first performance of Glinka's opera "Ruslan and Ludmilla." There are also original autograph albums of graphic works by Alfred Roller, M. A. Shishkov, F. I. Stravinskii, and M. M. Fokin (Michel Fokine).

The largest collection of materials from the late nineteenth and early twentieth centuries includes stage set designs by Léon Bakst (*pseud. of* L. S. Rozenberg), Alexandre Benois (A. N. Benua), K. A. Korovin, and S. Iu. Sudeikin, as well as those from the postrevolutionary period by N. P. Akimov, T. G. Bruni, and N. I. Al'tman, among others. Contemporary set designers are widely represented, together with theater caricatures and portraits of prominent figures in the theater world.

Otdel graviur i litografii
[Division of Prints and Engravings]

Telephone: 311-23-29
Hours: Tu 11:00–18:00
Head: Elena Igorevna Grushvitskaia

HOLDINGS: ca. 10,000 units, 18th–20th cc.

This division contains printed graphics including color and black-and-white portraits of theater personalities; costume designs; stage sets from plays; genre-painting; pictures of national festivities and customs; and illustrations of theater architecture in both Europe and Russia. The portraits include those of such prominent figures as ballerina A. I. Istomina and the Soviet actress A. O. Stepanova; directors K. A. Kavos and A. N. Verstovskii; and composers M. I. Glinka and P. I. Tchaikovsky (Chaikovskii), to name only a few. An album which once belonged to ballet-master M. M. Fokin (Michel Fokine) contains engravings of medieval dancing, fine arts, and objects of architectural interest. The V. V. Protopopov Collection contains graphic material on Russian folk festivities, scenes from operas and ballets, and costume designs.

Otdel afish i programm
[Division of Posters and Programs]

Telephone: 311-23-29
Hours: Tu 11:00–18:00
Head: Ninel' Semenovna Pliatskovskaia

HOLDINGS: ca. 60,000 units, 19th–20th cc.

The collection of posters and programs contains notices, handbills, play announcements, invitation cards, admission passes, visiting cards, and similar material relating to theater productions during the nineteenth and twentieth centuries. Daily programs have been preserved of the Bolshoi Theater season in St. Petersburg for the years 1840–1875.

Fonoteka
[Sound Recordings Archive]

Telephone: 310-50-08
Hours: W–F 11:00–18:00
Head: Liudmila Georgievna Mochalova

HOLDINGS: ca. 23,000 units, 1898–1990s

This division retains collections of grammophone records, tape recordings, and other sound recordings of the great Russian and foreign musicians and actors, and of symphonic works. Among the Russian names recorded here are A. M. Davydov, F. I. Chaliapin (Shaliapin), S. Ia. Lemeshev, A. V. Nezhdanova, M. P. Maksakova, and N. A. Obukhova. Foreign singers include Enrico Caruso, Maria Callas, and Nicolaus Gedda. The A. E. Pavlov Collection contains material on the history of the Russian and Soviet stage.

FINDING AIDS — PUBLISHED — GENERAL:

Muzei SPb (1994), pp. 69–74; *Biblioteki SPb* (1993), p. 80; *Peterburg* (1992), pp. 610, 612; *GAF Spravochnik* (1991), pp. 138–39; *Muzei Leningrada* (1989), pp. 226–27; *Muzei Leningrada* (1982), pp. 74–76; Myl'nikov (1970), pp. 38–39; PKG *M&L* (1972), p. 333; *Muzykal'nyi Leningrad* (1958), pp. 395–400.

There is no published guide to the archival holdings in the museum.

h-643. Kochetov, A. N. "Istoriia i osnovnye napravleniia deiatel'nosti Leningradskogo gosudarstvennogo teatral'nogo muzeia." In *Teatr i dramaturgiia,* vol. 1, pp. 434–41. Leningrad, 1959. "Trudy Nauchno-issedovatel'skogo instituta teatra, muzyki i kinematografii." (Lib: DLC; MH) [IDC-in R-10,927]

h-644. Uros, A. "Nachalo teatral'nogo muzeia." *Neva,* 1981, no. 9, pp. 198–200. (Lib: DLC; IU; MH)

> A brief history of the founding and work of the Museum of the Petrograd State Theaters between 1919 and 1921.

h-645. *Balet Peterburga-Petrograda-Leningrada: Iz fondov Leningradskogo gosudarstvennogo muzeia teatral'nogo i muzykal'nogo iskusstva.* Compiled and edited by N. I. Metelitsa. Leningrad, 1989. 62 p. [Minkul't RSFSR; LGMTiMI] (Lib: MH)

h-646. *L'art du ballet en Russie, 1738–1940.* Paris, 1991. 140 p.

> A catalogue of the exhibition on Russian ballet (18th–early 20th cc.) held at the Opéra de Paris Garnier with displays from the museum collections.

h-647. *100 Years of Russian Ballet, 1830–1930: An Exhibition from the Leningrad State Museum of Theater and Music.* New York: Eduard Nakhamkin Fine Arts, 1991. 51 p. (Lib: MH) With an introductory essay by Gennady Smakov.

> A catalogue of a New York exhibition on Russian ballet from the museum holdings.

Memorial′nyi muzei-kvartira N. A. Rimskogo-Korsakova— Filial Sankt-Peterburgskogo gosudarstvennogo muzeia teatral′nogo i muzykal′nogo iskusstva

[N. A. Rimskii-Korsakov Memorial Apartment-Museum—Branch of the St. Petersburg State Museum of Theater and Musical Arts]

Agency: Komitet po kul′ture Administratsii Sankt-Peterburga
[Committee on Culture of the Administration of St. Petersburg]

Address:	191002, St. Petersburg, Zagorodnyi prosp., 28
Telephone:	113-32-08
Transport:	metro: Vladimirskaia, Dostoevskaia; trol.: 3, 8, 15
Hours:	W–Su 10:00–18:00

Director: Larisa Ivanovna Chirkova (*tel.* 311-32-08)

HISTORY:

The museum was opened in 1971 as a branch of the Leningrad State Theater Museum—now SPbGMTiMI (H–102)—in the apartment where the composer Nikolai Andreevich Rimskii-Korsakov (1844–1908) lived with his family from 1893 until his death, and which was at the center of St. Petersburg musical and cultural life.

N.B. Other archival materials of and relating to N. A. Rimskii-Korsakov are held in the main collections of SPbGMTiMI (H–102), including other parts of the collections on which the exhibits in this branch are based.

The extensive Rimskii-Korsakov archival materials that were earlier held in the former special Museum-Archive of N. A. and A. N. Rimskii-Korsakov (*Muzei-arkhiv N. A. i A. N. Rimskikh-Korsakovykh*), which had been established in 1944 as part of the Scientific Research Institute of Theater and Music (NIITiM), were later combined with other archival holdings under the successor institute to form what is now the Cabinet of Manuscripts in RIII (E–46), which still retains a considerable part of the Rimskii-Korsakov papers.

Other personal papers and original music scores of N. A. Rimskii-Korsakov are held in the Manuscript Division of RNB (G–15) and in the Library of the St. Petersburg N. A. Rimskii-Korsakov State Conservatory (G–19).

Some original and copies of archival materials are held by the Rimskii-Korsakov House-Museum (*Dom-muzei N. A. Rimskogo-Korsakova*) in Tikhvin (187300, Leningradskaia oblast′, g. Tikhvin, ul. Rimskogo-Korsakova, 12; tel. 1-15-09).

HOLDINGS: complete statistics not available; mid-19th–early 20th cc.
photographs—ca. 100; drawings—13 units

The memorial exhibition devoted to N. A. Rimskii-Korsakov contains materials relating to both his work as a composer and biographical documents. There are original copies of his music scores, a draft of the composer's will, his service record, invitation cards, letters and telegrams, visiting cards, printed concert programs, calendars, individual and group photographs of prominent musicians, and collections of sound recordings of his musical works. The collection of original congratulatory cards and drawings include sketches and drawings by I. E. Repin, M. A. Vrubel', and K. A. Korovin.

Access: Research access requires an official letter identifying the researcher and indicating the subject and aim of the research.

Working Conditions: Researchers are accommodated in the museum offices, where materials are available the day they are ordered.

Reference Facilities: There are inventories of the exhibits, a card catalogue of the books and music scores in the library, and a card catalogue of the sound recordings.

Library Facilities: The reference library (ca. 500 vols.) contains, most significantly, the remaining part of Rimskii-Korsakov's own library, which has been augmented by additional literature on Russian music, audiovisual materials, and translations. There is a facts-and-figures file on N. A. Rimskii-Korsakov.

Copying: There are no copying facilities available in this branch.

FINDING AIDS — PUBLISHED — GENERAL:

Muzei SPb (1994), p. 74; *Biblioteki SPb* (1993), p. 80; *Muzei Leningrada* (1989), pp. 228–29; *Muzei Leningrada* (1982), p. 76.

There is no published guide to the archival holdings in the museum.

h-648. Rimskaia-Korsakova, Tat'iana Vladimirovna. *Muzei-kvartira N. A. Rimskogo-Korsakova v Leningrade: Kratkii ocherk-putevoditel'*. Leningrad: "Muzyka," 1976. 72 p. (Lib: MH)
   Provides a brief history of the memorial museum and describes its exhibits.

Muzei tsirkovogo iskusstva (MTsI)
[Museum of Circus Arts]

Agency: Sankt-Peterburgskii tsirk
[St. Petersburg Circus]

Address:	191011, St. Petersburg, nab. Reki Fontanki, 3
Telephone:	210-44-13; *Fax:* (812) 314-80-59
Transport:	metro: Nevskii prospekt, Gostinyi Dvor, Vladimirskaia, Dostoevskaia; tram: 12, 13, 14, 34; trol.: 3, 8, 15
Hours:	M–F 11:00–15:00 (by appointment)

Director: Natal'ia Georgievna Kuznetsova
Curator: Larisa Vasil'evna Smirnova

HISTORY:

Muzei tsirka i estrady
[Museum of the Circus and Musical Stage] (1928–1965)

The only museum devoted to the circus in Russia was opened in 1928 in the building of the Leningrad Circus. The original holdings came from the private collection of V. Ia. Andreev, a collector of items relating to the history of the theater, the musical stage, and the circus. From 1941 to 1945 the museum ceased to function. During the Siege of Leningrad the museum was hit by a bomb and many of the exhibits were destroyed. The museum was reopened in 1946 and was given its present name in 1965.

N.B. The archival records of the Leningrad Circus itself for the years 1933–1966 are held in TsGALI SPb (D–15, fond 273).

HOLDINGS: ca. 80,000 units, late 18th–20th cc.

institutional fonds—3; personal fonds—29; photographs and negatives—ca. 20,000; prints and drawings—ca. 7,000 units

The museum fonds document the history of the circus in Russia and abroad. The manuscript fond has a collection of scripts for clown acts, circus acts, feature acts, and other circus attractions. The museum retains the archive of A. N. Shirai, the manuscripts of writer A. A. Barten, and the personal papers of a number of circus performers. There is a card catalogue on the circus prepared by A. Ia. Shneer.

The museum is particularly rich in graphic materials (engravings, drawings, costume designs, and circus ring designs). There are also many posters, playbills, programs, and newspaper clippings, along with photographs and negatives.

Working Conditions: Researchers are accommodated in the museum offices, where materials are available the day they are ordered.

Reference Facilities: There are inventory registers of fonds and card catalogues. There are also auxiliary indexes of circus personalia (performers and workers), types of circus acts, scripts and scenarios, and photographs.

Library Facilities: The museum possesses about 6,000 volumes.

Copying: Photographic and xerox copies can be prepared.

FINDING AIDS — PUBLISHED — GENERAL:

Muzei SPb (1994), p. 76; *Biblioteki SPb* (1993), pp. 80–81; *Peterburg* (1992), p. 401.

There is no published guide to the archival holdings in the museum.

h-649. Weise, R. "50 Jahre Leningrader Zirkusmuseum." *Unterhaltungskunst*, 1979, no. 1, p. 28.

> A brief announcement of the 50th anniversary of the founding of the Circus Museum.

h-650. Medvedev, Matvei Naumovich. *Leningradskii tsirk*. Leningrad: Lenizdat, 1975. 144 p. + plates. Preface by O. Popov. (Lib: IU; MH)

> EARLIER ED.: L., 1965. 58 p. "Turistu o Leningrade." (Lib: MH).
> A survey history of the Leningrad circus with a separate chapter devoted to the collections of the museum. Includes bibliography.

Museums of Science and Medicine

⊱ H–105 ⊰

Muzei-arkhiv D. I. Mendeleeva pri Sankt-Peterburgskom gosudarstvennom universitete (MAM pri SPbGU)
[D. I. Mendeleev Museum and Archive at St. Petersburg State University]

Agency: Ministerstvo obshchego i professional'nogo obrazovaniia RF
(Minobrazovaniia Rossii)
[Ministry of General and Professional Education]

Address: 199034, St. Petersburg, Vasil'evskii ostrov,
Mendeleevskaia liniia, 2 (Universitetskaia nab., 7/9)
Telephone: 328-29-82; 328-97-44
Transport: metro: Vasileostrovskaia, Sportivnaia, Gostinyi Dvor, Nevskii prospekt;
trol.: 1, 7, 9, 10; bus: 6, 7, 10; tram: 31
Hours: M–F: 10:00–16:00

Director: Igor' Sergeevich Dmitriev (*tel.* 328-97-37)

HISTORY:
Kabinet D. I. Mendeleeva pri Imperatorskom Sankt-Peterburgskom universitete
[Cabinet of D. I. Mendeleev at the Imperial St. Petersburg University] (1911–1914)
Kabinet D. I. Mendeleeva pri Leningradskom gosudarstvennom universitete
[Cabinet of D. I. Mendeleev at Leningrad State University] (1924–1952)
Muzei i nauchnyi arkhiv D. I. Mendeleeva pri Leningradskom gosudarstvennom universitete
[D. I. Mendeleev Museum and Scientific Archive at Leningrad State University] (1952–1991)

The Mendeleev Memorial Cabinet was opened in 1911 in the university apartment which the eminent chemist Dmitrii Ivanovich Mendeleev (1834–1907) occupied from 1866 to 1890. Initiative for the museum came from Mendeleev's relatives, pupils, and colleagues—particularly A. E. Favorskii, V. E. Tishchenko, L. A. Chugaev, and V. N. Ipat'ev, who acquired the apartment from his widow, A. E. Mendeleeva, together with Mendeleev's library, part of his archive, and furnishings from his study. In 1928 another Mendeleev Museum (*Mendeleevskii muzei*) was organized under the All-Union Scientific Research Institute of Metrology and Standardization (VIMS—*Vsesoiuznyi nauchno-issledovatel'nyi institut metrologii i standardizatsii*), which included a large portion of Mendeleev's manuscript legacy.

In 1952, on the basis of a government resolution for the study of the scientific legacy of Mendeleev, Mendeleev's study at LGU was reorganized into a formal museum and centralized archive, and it received a number of documents from other archival repositories throughout the country, including those earlier held in the VIMS museum. In 1963 the separate D. I. Mendeleev Museum, which then existed under the Main Chamber of Weights and Measures (now the D. I. Mendeleev Institute of Metrology) was abolished, and the Museum-Archive received the holdings which had been used for exhibits there. Today the Museum-Archive has the richest collection of documents in Russia on the life and work of Mendeleev and remains under the auspices of St. Petersburg State University.

Access: A letter from the researcher's sponsoring institution is required stating the subject and purpose of research. In the case of foreign scholars, a letter from the researcher's sponsoring Russian institution is required, or a recommendation from an authoritative specialist.

Library Facilities: There is a working library of publications about D. I. Mendeleev, in addition to the personal library of Mendeleev, including many interesting marginalia.

Nauchnyi arkhiv D. I. Mendeleeva
[D. I. Mendeleev Scientific Archive]

Telephone: 328-29-82; 328-97-37
Hours: M–Th 11:00–17:00
Head: Nina Georgievna Karpilo

HOLDINGS: 4 fonds, ca. 50,000 units, 18th–20th cc.

The Scientific Archive retains Mendeleev's personal and scientific papers, along with those of members of his family and other relatives, as well as materials of biographers and others who have researched his work.

Mendeleev's vast manuscript legacy includes scientific studies and associated writings, working diaries and notebooks, biographical materials, and correspondence. Mendeleev's art collection consists of photographic reproductions of great paintings by Russian and foreign artists, while his library consists of some 20,000 books, brochures, offprints of articles, and newspaper clippings. Many of the books have his personal marginalia.

Fonds of Mendeleev's relatives include personal papers of the family of E. I. Kapustina (*née* Mendeleeva, 1816–1901), the scientist's elder sister; her children and relatives; the Smirnovs, including documents of Ia. I. Smirnov, a curator in the Hermitage and historian of Christian art and archeology; Mendeleev's first wife, F. N. Mendeleeva (*née* Leshcheva, 1828–1903) and his daughter from his first marriage, O. D. Trigorova (*née* Mendeleeva, 1868–1950); and Mendeleev's second wife, A. I. Mendeleeva (*née* Popova, 1860–1942) and her children, I. D. Mendeleev (1883–1936) and M. D. Mendeleeva (married name Kuz'mina, 1886–1952). These fonds include family correspondence, diaries, recollections of D. I. Mendeleev, correspondence relating to the publication of Mendeleev's manuscript legacy, and portraits of relatives and friends.

A separate fond has been assigned for documents originating from Mendeleev's students and colleagues, including B. P. Veinberg, V. I. Tishchenko, M. N. Mladentsev, and A. V. Skvortsov, and from contemporary researchers who have studied Mendeleev's life and work. There is also a collection of biographical materials relating to Mendeleev.

The museum has collected photocopies of documents relating to Mendeleev from other repositories in Russia and abroad.

Working Conditions: Researchers are accommodated in the museum offices, where materials are available the same day they are ordered.

Reference Facilities: There are inventory registers of the processed fonds, inventory catalogues of the main fonds, catalogues of correspondence by author, and inventory and subject catalogues of Mendeleev's personal library. There are also subsidiary working catalogues of Mendeleev's work.

Copying: There are no copying facilities available in the museum, but copies may be made through the university office or photographic laboratory.

FINDING AIDS — PUBLISHED — GENERAL:

Muzei SPb (1994), p. 197; *Biblioteki SPb* (1993), p. 83; *Muzei Leningrada* (1982), p. 118–20; *Muzei vuzov* (1975), pp. 40–42; PKG *M&L* (1972), p. 331; Myl'nikov (1970), p. 43.

h-655. Kerova, Liudmila Sergeevna; and Minaeva, Nadezhda Andreevna. *Muzei D. I. Mendeleeva: Putevoditel'.* Edited by R. B. Dobrotin. Leningrad: Izd-vo Leningradskogo un-ta, 1975. 39 p. + 12 plates. [LGU] Added title and summary in English: *D. I. Mendeleev Museum: A Guide-Book.*

h-655.1. *Muzei-arkhiv D. I. Mendeleeva: Putevoditel'.* Compiled by R. B. Dobrotin and I. N. Filimonova. 2d ed. Leningrad: Izd-vo LGU, 1969. 49 p. [LGU; MAM]
EARLIER ED.: Compiled by A. A. Makarenia. L.: Lenizdat, 1965. 44 p. "Turistu o Leningrade." (Lib: MH).
Includes brief mention of the archive and library.

h-656. *Arkhiv D. I. Mendeleeva.* [Vol. 1]: *Avtobiograficheskie materialy: Sbornik dokumentov.* Leningrad: Izd-vo LGU, 1951. 207 p. Preface by M. D. Mendeleev. [LGU; MAM] (Lib: DLC; IU) [IDC-R-10,925]
Lists many of the archival materials, including manuscripts of Mendeleev's writings and the volumes of his correspondence held in the museum. Includes a published edition of a short autobiographical essay from the archive.

h-657. *Pis'ma i telegrammy, adresovannye D. I. Mendeleevu: Bibliograficheskii ukazatel'.* Compiled by O. P. Kamenogradskaia, V. A. Tarasova, and T. V. Bashkirova. Edited by L. S. Kerova. Leningrad: BAN, 1984. 217 p. (Lib: IU; MH)

h-658. Dobrotin, Roman Borisovich; and Karpilo, Nina Georgievna. *Biblioteka D. I. Mendeleeva.* Leningrad: "Nauka," Leningradskoe otdelenie, 1980. 222 p. [AN SSSR; IIET] (Lib: DLC; IU; MH)

h-659. Makarenia, Aleksandr Aleksandrovich; and Filimonova, Irina Nikolaevna. *D. I. Mendeleev i Peterburgskii universitet.* Leningrad: Izd-vo LGU, 1969. 109 p. [LGU] (Lib: DLC; IU; MH)
Includes an appended essay about the memorial museum at LGU (pp. 98–108).

Tsentral'nyi nauchno-issledovatel'skii geologorazvedochnyi muzei im. akademika F. N. Chernysheva (TsNIGR muzei)

[F. N. Chernyshev Central Geological Survey Scientific Research Museum]

Agency: Ministerstvo prirodnykh resursov RF (MPR Rossii)
[Ministry of Natural Resources]

Address: 199026, St. Petersburg, Vasil'evskii ostrov, Srednii prospekt, 74
Telephone: 323-95-90; 328-92-48
Transport: metro: Vasileostrovskaia; tram: 11, 18, 40
Hours: M–F 10:00–17:00

Director: Anatolii Mikhailovich Karpunin (*tel.* 328-06-34)
Head, Sector of the Main Collection Fond:
       Svetlana Vasil'evna Rakhova (*tel.* 323-95-90)
Head, the Book Fond: Tat'iana Vasil'evna Peshina (*tel.* 328-92-48)

HISTORY:

Tsentral'nyi geologicheskii muzei (TsGM)
   [Central Geological Museum] (1930–1935)

The founding of the Geological Committee of Russia in St. Petersburg in 1882 marked the beginning of systematic geological studies in Russia. Its director was the eminent Russian geologist and paleontologist Feodosii Nikolaevich Chernyshev (1856–1914). In the following year the committee founded a library and began a collection of minerals, which eventually became a museum. A special building was constructed for the committee in 1914, and the museum occupied the second floor.

The museum remained a division of the Geological Committee until 1930, when it became the Central Geological Museum and was first opened to the public. In 1935 it was renamed the Central Geological Survey Scientific Research Museum with the honorific name of Chernyshev. Although administratively independent, the museum has remained closely associated with the Central Geological Survey Scientific Research Institute (*Tsentral'nyi nauchno-issledovatel'skii geologorazvedochnyi institut*—TsNIGRI) (1929–1939), which after 1939 was renamed the All-Union Geological Institute (*Vsesoiuznyi geologicheskii institut*—VSEGEI), and in 1992, the All-Russian Geological Institute. The museum shares the building with the All-Russian Geological Library, which was founded in 1882, together with the Geological Committee.

HOLDINGS: ca. 14,000 units, 1890–1990s

photographic portraits (scientific auxiliary fond)—ca. 400 units (1890–1990s)

The Manuscripts and Documents Fond within the museum's Sector of the Main Collection Fond (*Sektor osnovnogo kollektsionnogo fonda*) retains a variety of archival materials in the fields of geology and paleontology.

Of special note are the card catalogues covering 13,000 museum collections and detailed monographic paleontological catalogues covering more than 1,000,000 items. These catalogues provide information on the geological structure of the regions of Russia and the former Soviet republics, mineral deposits, collections of minerals, and the state of the country's mineral wealth.

The Scientific Auxiliary Fond holds individual and group photographic portraits of the famous members of the Geological Committee (1882–1929), the Central Geological Survey Scientific-Research Institute (1929–1939), and the subsequent All-Union Geological Institute (1939–1992). There are extensive geological survey maps, as well as other graphic materials on display panels such as those used for exhibitions of stones to illustrate and explain the items exhibited.

Access: Access to the archival materials requires an official letter of application addressed to the museum director stating the subject and purpose of research. Access is automatic for Russian citizens, but foreign researchers must obtain the special permission of the museum director.

Working Conditions: Researchers are accommodated in the working rooms of the sector, where materials are available the day they are ordered.

Reference Facilities: There are registration books, scientific catalogues and "passport data" descriptions of all collections and items, mainly for staff use; there are also card catalogues arranged numerically, regionally, and by author. Data on the fonds is currently being computerized.

Library Facilities: In addition to printed reference materials, the museum's Book Fond holds manuscript reports, explanatory notes intended for staff use, and guides to the museum exhibits. There are also catalogues of the monographic paleontological collections and to the mineral ores held in the museum. (Book Fond tel.: 328-92-48).

Since the museum shares a building with the All-Russian Geological Library (*Vserossiiskaia geologicheskaia biblioteka*), established together with the Geological Committee in 1882, researchers can avail themselves of that extensive library (ca. 1,000,000 volumes), which is exceedingly rich in geological and paleontological literature with many rare editions. (Library tel. 355-72-12).

Copying: Xerox copies can be prepared.

FINDING AIDS — PUBLISHED — GENERAL:

Muzei SPb (1994), p. 184; *Muzei Leningrada* (1982), p. 109.

There is no published description of the archival holdings in the museum.

h-660. *Geologicheskie issledovaniia Geolkoma–TsNIGRI–VSEGEI: Putevoditel' po ekspozitsii TsNIGR muzeia.* Compiled by I. N. Kurek and O. A. Sobolev. Edited by E. Baskov. Leningrad: VSEGEI, 1988. 88 p. [Mingeologii SSSR; VSEGEI; TsNIGR muzei]
> A history of geological research done by staff of the Geological Committee and the All-Union Geological Institute. Provides a brief description of the structure and holdings of the museum and of the All-Union Geological Library. Includes biographical data on prominent scholars in the field.

h-661. Varfolomeev, P. N. *Iz istorii Tsentral'nogo nauchno-issledovatel'skogo geologorazvedochnogo muzeia.* Leningrad: "Nedra," Leningradskoe otdelenie, 1975. 44 p. [Mingeologii SSSR; TsNIGR muzei]
> A history of the museum and its development during the Soviet period.

h-662. *Putevoditel' po TsNIGR muzeiu.* Compiled by P. N. Varfolomeev, T. E. Vul'f, and N. N. Lobasheva. Leningrad: "Nedra," 1974. 98 p. [Mingeologii SSSR; TsNIGR muzei]
> A short history of the organization of the museum, its structure, and activities.

h-663. *Katalog monograficheskikh paleontologicheskikh kollektsii, khraniashchikhsia v TsNIGR muzee.* Compiled by T. M. Mal'chevskaia and L. V. Romanovskaia. 2 vols. Leningrad: "Nedra," Leningradskoe otdelenie, 1966–1971. 176 p., 47 p. [Gos. geologicheskii komitet SSSR; TsNIGR muzei] (Lib: CRL; DLC; MH [vol. 1])

Muzei meteorologii Glavnoi geofizicheskoi observatorii im. A. I. Voeikova (Muzei GGO)

[Museum of Meteorology of the A. I. Voeikov Main Geophysical Observatory]

Agency: Federal'naia sluzhba Rossii po gidrometeorologii i monitoringu okruzhaiushchei sredy (Rosgidromet)
[Federal Service of Russia for Hydrometeorology and Monitoring Environmental Conditions]

Address: 194018, St. Petersburg, ul. Karbysheva, 7
Telephone: 247-43-90; 247-86-70
Transport: metro: Ploshchad' Muzhestva + tram 53, 61, 38
Hours: by appointment

Director of Observatory: Gennadii Ivanovich Prilipko (*tel.* 247-86-70)
Director of Observatory: Valentin Petrovich Meleshko

HISTORY:

Meteorologicheskii muzei Glavnoi fizicheskoi observatorii (Muzei GFO)
[Meteorological Museum of the Main Physical Observatory] (1849–1894, 1917–1924)
Meteorologicheskii muzei Nikolaevskoi glavnoi fizicheskoi observatorii
[Meteorological Museum of the Nicholas Main Physical Observatory] (1895–1917)
Meteorologicheskii muzei Glavnoi geofizicheskoi observatorii (Muzei GGO)
[Meteorological Museum of the Main Geophysical Observatory] (1924–1949)
Meteorologicheskii muzei Glavnoi geofizicheskoi observatorii im. A. I. Voeikova (Muzei GGO)
[Meteorological Museum of the A. I. Voeikov Main Geophysical Observatory] (1949–1990)

The Main Physical Observatory of the Corps of Mining Engineers (*Korpus gornykh inzhenerov*) was founded on the initiative of Academician Adolf Kupffer (A. Ia. Kupfer) in 1849 on the basis of the earlier Normal Observatory for Meteorological and Magnetic Observations (*Normal'naia observatoriia meteorologicheskikh i magnitnykh nabliudenii*). Plans were underway since 1849 for a meteorological museum, but they were never realized until the 1920s. In 1866 the observatory was transferred from the control of the Department of Mining to that of the Imperial Academy of Sciences, where it remained until 1918.

From 1921 to 1929 the Main Physical Observatory supervised all meteorological work in the country. In 1924 it was renamed the Main Geophysical Observatory, and in 1927 a Meterological Museum was officially opened (nab. Leitenanta Shmidta, 39), but changed its location several times. The exhibits were evacuated during the war and returned to Leningrad in 1944. The museum was reopened, but existed on voluntary contributions.

To mark its centennial in 1949, the observatory was given the honorific name of the founder of climatology in Russia, Aleksandr Ivanovich Voeikov (1842–1914). It continued as a central scientific research institution carrying out research on atmospheric physics. The museum holdings were enlarged with the collections of the Geophysics Museum, which had been closed down. In 1977 the Meteorological Museum was transferred to the building of the church of Simeon and Anna (built in 1731–1734), but since the building was returned to the Church in 1991, permanent exhibition premises are still being organized.

N.B. Materials relating to the correspondence and administration of the Observatory over the years 1840 to 1924 (fond 337) are held in the PFA RAN (E–20).

HOLDINGS: ca. 20,000 units, 1729–1988

The museum holds extensive historical documentation on the development of meteorology and on the Main Geophysical Observatory. These include manuscript reports from the Observatory's various departments; scientific works of associated scholars; logs recording meteorological observations. There are memorial addresses given on the occasion of the Observatory's jubilees and the personal documents of some of the staff meteorologists, including their awards and certificates (1885–1915).

There are extensive photographs, including pictures of the places where observations were made and of instruments and equipment, and photographs of the staff. There are also photograph albums from the State Meteorological Service (*Gosmeteosluzhba*) and from different stations and field locations.

Access: Researchers should call ahead to verify access possibilities. Currently the museum will only service inquiries on a fee-for-service basis, and researchers are not permitted access to documents. In recent years, the museum has been closed but plans to be reopened in the summer of 1999.

Reference Facilities: There are inventory registers and reference card catalogues for staff use.

Library Facilities: The Scientific-Technical Library (ca. 400,000 vols.) was founded in 1849. It holds literature on climatology, meteorology, aerology, atmospheric physics, and environmental protection, and has a number of rare editions, reports on research work, and manuscript dissertations. There are reference and subject card catalogues, and card catalogues of the research reports and the dissertations.

Copying: No copying facilities are available.

FINDING AIDS — PUBLISHED — GENERAL:

Muzei SPb (1994), p. 193; *Biblioteki SPb* (1993), p. 89; *Peterburg* (1992), p. 374.

There is no published description of the archival holdings in the museum.

h-664. Korovchenko, A. S. "Pervaia geofizicheskaia biblioteka Rossii." In *Knizhnoe delo v kul'turnoi i obshchestvennoi zhizni Leningrada*, pp. 8–14. Leningrad, 1984. (Lib: DLC; IU)
A history and survey of the work of the library of the Main Geophysical Observatory.

Muzei Arktiki i Antarktiki Arkticheskogo i antarkticheskogo nauchno-issledovatel'skogo instituta (MAA AANII)
[Museum of the Arctic and Antarctica of the Arctic and Antarctica Scientific Research Institute]

Agency: Federal'naia sluzhba Rossii po gidrometeorologii i monitoringu okruzhaiushchei sredy (Rosgidromet)
[Federal Service of Russia for Hydrometeorology and Monitoring Environmental Conditions]

Address: 191040, St. Petersburg, ul. Marata, 24-a
Telephone: 311-25-49; *Fax:* (812) 352-26-88
Transport: metro: Maiakovskaia, Vladimirskaia, Dostoevskaia; tram: 10, 16, 28, 39, 49
Hours: W–Su 10:00–17:00

Director: Nikolai Gavrilovich Iagodnitsyn (*tel.* 113-19-98)
Chief Curator: Vera Iakovlevna Dement'eva

HISTORY:
Muzei Arktiki
[Museum of the Arctic] (1930–1958)

The museum was founded in 1930 as the Museum of the Arctic, as a division of the All-Union Arctic Institute (*Vsesoiuznyi arkticheskii institut*) which had itself been founded in 1930 on the basis of the earlier Institute for Research on the Far North (*Institut po izucheniiu Severa*) (1925–1930). The museum was opened to the public in 1937 in the building of the former Nikol'skii (*Nikol'skaia*) Old Believer Church (constructed in 1838), which had been turned over to the museum in 1934. In 1958 it was renamed the Museum of the Arctic and Antarctica (*Muzei Arktiki i Antarktiki*).

The Manuscript and Documentary Fond was formed in 1934 on the basis of materials acquired on expeditions to the Arctic and Antarctica, from gifts presented by private individuals, and also from documentation transferred from the former Main Administration of the Hydrometeorological Service (*Glavnoe upravlenie gidrometsluzhby*) of the Council of Ministers of the USSR. There are also significant archival materials in the Photograph Fond and the Graphic Art Fond.

HOLDINGS: ca. 52,000 units, early 19th–20th cc. (some documents 1733)
documentary fond—4,470 units; positives—35,400 units; negatives—11,200 units; graphic materials—434 units

Documentary collections in the museum are devoted to the history of research and development in the polar regions of the Arctic and the Antarctica, and contain manuscripts in Russian, English, Norwegian, and Japanese. There are the manuscript journals (logs) and other documentation of scientific expeditions, the work of the polar stations, the discovery of new geographic features, and the opening of the Northern Sea Route. There are autograph documents, such as those of the Norwegian polar explorers Roald Amundsen and Fridtjof Nansen and the Russian scholars I. D. Papanin, E. T. Krenkel', and M. M. Somov. There are maps, scientific reports, expedition diaries, observation logs, photographs, and various other graphic and cartographic materials. A separate documentary complex records the ethnographic study of the tribes in the Russian Far North.

There are also personal papers of a number of polar researchers and ship captains.

Access: Access to the archival holdings requires an official letter addressed to the director stating the subject and aim of the proposed research.

Working Conditions: Researchers are accommodated in the museum offices, where materials are available the day they are ordered.

Reference Facilities: There are card catalogues to all the museum fonds, including the Manuscript and Documents Fond, the Photograph Fond, and the Graphic Arts Fond. A guide to the museum holdings is in the process of being published.

Library Facilities: The Book Fond of the museum (ca. 5,000 volumes) consists primarily of literature and cartographic materials on the Arctic and the Antarctica.

Copying: Photographic and xerox copies can be prepared.

FINDING AIDS — PUBLISHED — GENERAL:

Muzei SPb (1994), p. 182; *Biblioteki SPb* (1993), p. 93; *Peterburg* (1992), p. 64; *Muzei Leningrada* (1982), pp. 112–14; PKG *M&L* (1972), p. 346; Myl'nikov (1970), p. 42.

There is no published guide to the archival materials in the museum.

h-668. Strugatskii, Vladimir I. *K poliusam Zemli: Rasskazy iz Muzeia Arktiki i Antarktiki.* Leningrad: Lenizdat, 1984. 208 p. + 32 plates. (Lib: IU; MH)
> A popular account of research in the polar regions on the basis of the exhibits contained in the museum.

h-669. Gakkel', Iakov Iakovlevich. *Za chetvert' veka: Obzor deiatel'nosti Arkticheskogo instituta Glavsevmorputi za 25 let, 1920–1945.* Moscow/Leningrad: Glavsevmorput', 1945. 108 p. [Arkticheskii NII Glavnogo upravleniia Severnogo morskogo puti pri SNK SSSR] (Lib: DLC)

h-670. *XXV let nauchnoi deiatel'nosti Arkticheskogo instituta: 1920–1945: [Sbornik statei].* Edited by V. Kh. Buinitskii. Leningrad/Moscow: Glavsevmorput', 1945. 400 p. [Arkticheskii NII Glavnogo upravleniia Severnogo morskogo puti pri SNK SSSR]

Tsentral'nyi muzei pochvovedeniia im. V. V. Dokuchaeva (TsMP)

[V. V. Dokuchaev Central Museum of Pedology]

Agency: Rossiiskaia Akademiia sel'skokhoziaistvennykh nauk (RASKhN)
[Russian Academy of Agricultural Sciences]

Address:	199034, St. Petersburg, Birzhevoi prosp., 6
Telephone:	328-55-01, 328-54-02
Transport:	metro: Nevskii prospekt, Gostinyi Dvor, Vasileostrovskaia; trol.: 1, 7, 9, 10; bus: 10
Hours:	M–F 9:00–17:00

Director: Boris Fedorovich Aparin (*tel.* 328-56-02)
Head of Exhibition and Fonds: Larisa Viktorovna Zykina (*tel.* 328-56-02)

HISTORY:

Tsentral'nyi pedologicheskii muzei im. V. V. Dokuchaeva
[V. V. Dokuchaev Central Pedological Museum] (1904–1912)
Muzei Dokuchaevskogo pochvennogo komiteta
[Museum of the Dokuchaev Pedologic Committee] (1912–1925)
Muzei Pochvennogo instituta im. V. V. Dokuchaeva pri AN SSSR
[Museum of the V. V. Dokuchaev Pedological Institute] (1925–1946)
Tsentral'nyi muzei pochvovedeniia im. V. V. Dokuchaeva AN SSSR
[V. V. Dokuchaev Central Museum of Pedology] (1946–1961)
Tsentral'nyi muzei pochvovedeniia im. V. V. Dokuchaeva VASKhNIL
[V. V. Dokuchaev Central Museum of Pedology] (1961–1991)

The museum was founded in 1902 by Vasilii Vasil'evich Dokuchaev (1846–1903) to house his extensive collection of soil samples (started in 1880), which were subsequently expanded by his students and successors. The first and only museum of soil sciences in the world opened in 1904, the year after Dokuchaev's death, as the V. V. Dokuchaev Central Museum of Pedology, sponsored by the Free Economic Society (*Vol'noe ekonomicheskoe obshchestvo*). In 1912 the museum was transferred to the jurisdiction of the Dokuchaev Soil Committee.

In 1918 the museum was taken over by the Academy of Sciences of the USSR and in 1925 became part of the Dokuchaev Institute of Pedology. To mark the centennial of Dokuchaev's birth in 1946, the museum was made an independent institution under the Academy of Sciences and was renamed the V. V. Dokuchaev Central Museum of Pedology. In 1961 the museum was transferred to the jurisdiction of the V. I. Lenin All-Union Academy of Agricultural Sciences (VASKhNiL), which in 1992 was renamed the Russian Academy of Agricultural Sciences (RASKhN). The museum is currently housed in a former maritime warehouse of the Stock Exchange (constructed in 1826–1832) at the point of Vasilevskii Island.

HOLDINGS: ca. 5,000 units, late 19th c.–1990s

maps—ca. 250 units (late 19th c.–1990s);

Archival materials are found in a number of the different museum fonds, including the Manuscripts and Documents Fond, the Historical Fond, the Memorial Fond, the Cartographic Fond, and the

Fond of Photographic Documents. Most of the documentation relates to the development of pedology in Russia, the geography of soils, and soil use in agriculture, and to individual specialists in the field, including Dokuchaev.

There is a large collection of photographs taken by Dokuchaev, which has been augmented by his successors. The Cartographic Fond has a collection of maps dating back to the first soil maps of Russia made in the late nineteenth century.

Access: Access to the archival holdings requires an official letter addressed to the director stating the subject and aim of the proposed research.

Working Conditions: Researchers are accommodated in the museum lecture theater. Files are available the day they are ordered.

Reference Facilities: There are official staff catalogues of all of the museum holdings. The collections of historical documents are currently being rearranged. Work has begun on a computerized catalogue of the museum holdings.

Library Facilities: The museum library (ca. 27,000 vols.), founded in 1904, holds literature on pedology, geography, chemistry, and biology. It also has reports on staff research work and manuscript dissertations.

Copying: There are no copying facilities, but researchers are permitted to use their own equipment for copying purposes.

FINDING AIDS — PUBLISHED — GENERAL:

Muzei SPb (1994), p. 179; *Biblioteki SPb* (1993), p. 93; *Peterburg* (1992), p. 506; *Muzei Leningrada* (1982), p. 110.

h-671. *Tsentral'nyi muzei pochvovedeniia im. V. V. Dokuchaeva: [Prospekt-putevoditel'].* Compiled by V. K. Pestriakov, R. P. Dedenina, and V. A. Dolotov. Edited by N. N. Rozov. Moscow: "Nauka," 1974. 32 p. [X Mezhdunarodnyi kongress pochvovedov; TsMP]
     Provides a short history of the museum and survey of the exhibits.

h-672. *Tsentral'nyi muzei pochvovedeniia im. V. V. Dokuchaeva: Putevoditel'.* Edited by V. K. Pestriakov, T. V. Aristovskaia, V. V. Ponomarev, et al. Leningrad: "Kolos," Leningradskoe otdelenie, 1970. 125 p. [VASKhNIL; TsMP]
     Describes only the exhibits.

h-673. Butuzova, O. V. *Tsentral'nyi muzei pochvovedeniia im. V. V. Dokuchaeva: [Putevoditel'].* Leningrad: Lenizdat, 1969. 31 p. [TsMP] (Lib: DLC)
     A popular brochure.

Muzei gigieny Tsentra meditsinskoi profilaktiki g. Sankt-Peterburga
[Museum of Hygiene of the St. Petersburg Center for Preventive Medicine]

Agency: Komitet po zdravookhraneniiu Administratsii Sankt-Peterburga
[Committee on Public Health of the Administration of St. Petersburg]

Address: 191011, St. Petersburg, ul. Ital'ianskaia, 25
Telephone: 210-85-06
Transport: metro: Nevskii prospekt, Gostinyi Dvor; tram: 2, 5, 34;
trol.: 1, 5, 7, 10, 22, 44; bus: 7, 22
Hours: M–F 9:30–18:00

Chief: Galina Alekseevna Vladimirova (*tel.* 311-70-33)
Head of Museum: Alla Vasil'evna Dubovik (*tel.* 311-42-27)

HISTORY:
Muzei-vystavka zdravookhraneniia pri Gorzdravotdele
[Museum-Exhibition of Public Health under the City Health Department] (1918–1931)
Vystavka zdravookhraneniia Leningradskogo gorodskogo Doma sanitarnoi kul'tury
[Exhibition of Public Health of the Leningrad City House of Sanitation and Hygiene]
(1931–1932)
Muzei-vystavka zdravookhraneniia Leningradskogo gorodskogo Doma sanitarnogo prosveshcheniia
[Museum-Exhibition of Public Health of the Leningrad City House of Health Education]
(1932–1988)
Muzei-vystavka zdravookhraneniia Tsentra zdorov'ia g. Leningrada
[Museum-Exhibition of Public Health of the Leningrad Health Center] (1989–1991)
Muzei gigieny Tsentra zdorov'ia g. Sankt-Peterburga
[Museum of Hygiene of the St. Petersburg Health Center] (XI.1991–VIII.1993)

The Museum-Exhibition of Public Health was founded in 1918 for the purpose of public health education, and opened under the Petrograd City Health Department (Gorzdravotdel) in 1919, on the initiative of the People's Commissar for Public Health, N. A. Semashko. In 1931 the exhibitions came under the newly opened House of Sanitation and Hygiene, sponsored by the City Health Department. In 1932 they were reorganized as a permanent exhibition and, later that year, came under the renamed House of Health Education.

In 1989 the Leningrad Health Center was established, and the health education service was reorganized into the Service for Encouraging the Formation of a Healthy Way of Life. In 1991 the museum was renamed the Museum of Hygiene. In 1993 the Leningrad Health Center was renamed the St. Petersburg Center for Preventive Medicine and transferred to the direct jurisdiction of the Committee on Public Health of the St. Petersburg Mayor's Office. Since 1996 it has been under the Administration of St. Petersburg.

HOLDINGS: 20 (3 unarranged) fonds, 728 units, 1883–1979
manuscript documents—73 units; personal papers—256 units; photographs—129

The Museum of Hygiene holds scattered documentary collections with the personal papers of a number of medical researchers: Academicians V. I. Ioffe, M. D. Tushinskii, and N. V. Lazarev; the head of the Pharmacology Department at the Second Medical Institute, S. V. Anichkov, I. A. Vigdorchik, who was given a high award for his services to medicine; I. G. Fridliand, a professor of the State Institute for Qualification of Physicians (*Gosudarstvennyi institut usovershenstvovaniia vrachei*); G. I. Kopzon, the Chief Venereologist in Leningrad during the siege; Professor E. S. London of the Institute of Experimental Medicine; and the sculptor L. V. Shervud (Sherwood). Documents include the manuscripts of medical works on such subjects as epidemiology, immunology, occupational diseases, work hygiene, and medical evaluation of fitness for work. There are also documents relating to the life and work of medical scholars and doctors, which include letters of recommendation, diaries written during the Siege of Leningrad, and documentary photographs.

Access: For access to archival materials, a letter should be addressed to the chief of the Center for Preventive Medicine, stating the subject and purpose of the proposed research.

Working Conditions: Researchers are accommodated in the museum offices, where materials are available the day they are ordered.

Reference Facilities: There are official inventory registers and auxiliary card catalogues.

Library Facilities: The Medical Library of the Center for Preventive Medicine (ca. 150,000 vols.), founded in 1919 on the basis of the Library of Zemstvo Doctors (*Biblioteka zemskikh vrachei*), holds literature on medicine and public health. There are card catalogues including coverage of medical personalia.

Copying: There are no copying facilities available, but copies may be made, if researchers bring their own equipment.

FINDING AIDS — PUBLISHED — GENERAL:

Muzei SPb (1994), p. 203; *Biblioteki SPb* (1993), p. 188.

There is no guide to the archival materials in the museum.

h-674. *Muzei-vystavka zdravookhraneniia Leningradskogo gorodskogo Doma sanitarnogo prosveshcheniia: [Putevoditel']*. Compiled by Z. K. Snegireva. Moscow: "Moskovskaia pravda," 1965. 71 p. [In-t sanitarnogo prosveshcheniia Minzdrava SSSR; Leningradskii gorodskoi Dom sanitarnogo prosveshcheniia]
    PREVIOUS ED.: Edited by L. P. Zabolotskaia. Leningrad, 1959.
      A brief guide to the museum exhibits.

h-675. *Putevoditel' po Muzeiu zdravookhraneniia Leningradskogo oblzdravotdela.* Leningrad: Izd-vo Leningradskogo meditsinskogo zhurnala, 1928. 33 p. [Lektsionno-ekskursionnoe biuro K/o LOSPS; Sanprosvetbiuro Lenoblzdrava]
      The first printed guide to the museum.

Museums of Transportation and Communications

❧ H–111 ❧

Tsentral'nyi muzei zheleznodorozhnogo transporta (TsMZhT)
[Central Museum of Railroad Transport]

Agency: Sankt-Peterburgskii gosudarstvennyi universitet putei soobshcheniia
(PGUPS)
St. Petersburg State University of Transportation
Ministerstvo putei soobshcheniia RF (MPS Rossii)
[Ministry of Transportation]

Address: 190068, St. Petersburg, Sadovaia ul., 50
Telephone: 315-14-76; 168-80-05
Transport: metro: Sennaia ploshchad', Sadovaia; tram: 2, 5, 14, 54
Hours: M–Th 11:00–17:00

Director: Galina Petrovna Zakrevskaia
Head, Division of Fonds: Oleg Sergeevich Liutin

HISTORY:
Muzei Instituta Korpusa inzhenerov putei soobshcheniia
[Museum of the Institute of the Corps of Transportation Engineers] (1813–1864)
Muzei pri Institute inzhenerov putei soobshcheniia
[Museum of the Institute of Transportation Engineers] (1864–1877)
Muzei pri Institute inzhenerov putei soobshcheniia Imperatora Alexandra I
[Museum of the Emperor Alexander I Institute of Transportation Engineers]
(1877–1882, 1890–1910)
Muzei pri Vysshei akademii inzhenernogo dela
[Museum of the Higher Academy of Engineering] (1882–1890)
Muzei putei soobshcheniia Imperatora Nikolaia I
[Emperor Nicholas I Museum of Transportation] (1902–1910)
Muzei putei soobshcheniia
[Museum of Transportation] (1910–1932)
Muzei zheleznodorozhnogo transporta (MZhT)
[Museum of Railroad Transport] (1932–1987)
Tsentral'nyi muzei zheleznodorozhnogo transporta SSSR (TsMZhT)
[Central Museum of Railroad Transport of the USSR] (1987–1991)

The first museum of the history of technology and also the first museum devoted specifically to railroads in Russia was founded in 1813 as part of the Institute of the Corps of Transportation Engineers, but it was not open to the public until 1862. Initially under the Main Administration of Transportation and Public Buildings, it was later, the Ministry of Transportation (or literally, Means of Communication). In 1902 the museum was installed in the present building, which was specially constructed for the museum by the architect P. S. Kupinskii. In 1910 the museum was combined with, and its holdings were enlarged by, the collections from the previously separate

Emperor Nicholas I Museum of Transportation, which had been founded in 1902, and the building itself was enlarged accordingly. At that point it became known as the Museum of Transportation, and until 1917 was part of the Emperor Alexander I Institute of Transportation Engineers.

During the First World War and the Civil War the museum was closed. The Museum of Transportation was reopened in 1924 under the jurisdiction of the newly reorganized (initially in 1924, Petrograd) Leningrad Institute of Transportation Engineers (*Leningradskii institut inzhenerov putei soobshcheniia*—LIIPS). In 1932 appropriate parts of the museum holdings were removed for the creation of a separate Museum of Water Transportation (*Muzei vodnogo transporta*) and accordingly, the museum was renamed the Museum of Railroad Transportation. It was administratively subordinate to the also renamed Leningrad Institute of Railroad Transport Engineers (*Leningradskii institut inzhenerov zheleznodorozhnogo transporta*—LIIZhT), although in the mid-1930s it was administered as a separate entity under the People's Commissariat of Transportation (1933–1938).

During the Second World War the museum was evacuated to Novosibirsk, but the main part of the collections remained in Leningrad for the duration of the siege. After the war the museum returned to Leningrad and was reopened to the public in 1948. In 1949 LIIZhT was renamed in honor of the Soviet transportation engineer Vladimir Nikolaevich Obraztsov (1874–1949), and until 1987 the museum was administratively part of LIIZhT. In 1987 the museum became independent of LIIZhT and was administered separately under the jurisdiction of the Ministry of Railroad Transportation of the USSR (1987–1991). During that period it was named the Central Museum of Railroad Transport of the USSR.

In 1991, the Leningrad Institute became the St. Petersburg Institute of Railroad Transport Engineers, but in 1993, it was raised to the rank of a university and renamed the St. Petersburg State University of Transportation—PGUPS (*Sankt-Peterburgskii gosudarstvennyi universitet putei soobshcheniia*). At that time, the museum again became part of the University, which remains under the administrative auspices of the Ministry of Transportation of the Russian Federation.

N.B. Considerable related documentation on the history of LIIZhT and specialists connected with the Institute (now the St. Petersburg State University of Transportation—PGUPS) is held by the Scientific-Technical Library of the University (NTB PGUPS—G–24).

HOLDINGS: ca. 19,000 units, early 19th–20th cc.
documentary fond—ca. 5,500 units; photographs and negatives—ca. 11,000;
scientific-technical documents—ca. 100 units; prints, drawings—ca. 600 units;
photograph and sketching albums—ca. 1,000 units

The extensive archival materials held by the museum are arranged within the Division of Fonds (*Otdel fondov*) and are to be found in four subsidiary museum fonds—the Manuscripts and Documents Fond, the Library Fond, the Fond of Photographs and Negatives, and the Fond of Albums and Graphic Arts.

The Manuscripts and Documents Fond contains documentation on the history of LIIZhT (now a university—PGUPS) and its related activities, predominantly from the prerevolutionary period. These include, for example, an account of the journeys made by P. P. Mel'nikov to England, Scotland and Ireland in the years 1837 and 1838, imperial orders relating to the Tsarskoe Selo Railroad (1855–1857), sample railroad tickets dating back to 1881, administrative documentation from the People's Commissariat of Transportation and later Ministry of Railroads (including regulations and circular instructions and reports, 1935 to 1983), and collections of maps and plans of the railroads in the Russian Empire and in the USSR.

There is extensive documentation associated with specialists who were connected with the planning, construction, and exploitation of the railroad system throughout the country—scientific works, technical drawings and plans, diplomas, certificates and attestations, and patents for inventions, as well as congratulatory addresses and testimonials. There are documents of some of many famous designers and inventors, such as M. Ia. Gekkel', K. A. Shishkin, A. M. Brylev, and A. A. Kuskov.

The museum Book Fond (see also under Library Facilities) contains manuscript works on the history of the railroad engineering plants and workshops, and on the construction of individual railroad sections. Some of these bear explanatory notes and the calculations of well-known engineers.

The Fond of Photographs and Negatives retains pictures relating to the history of the railroads and railroad transportation. There are views of local and major railroad stations, rolling stock, and railroad construction, pictures illustrating the history of the Institute of Transportation Engineers, portraits of officials from state transportation agencies, government figures, and railroad specialists.

The Fond of Graphic Arts (*Fond izobrazitel'nogo iskusstva*) has some rare albums of watercolors, as well as engravings, lithographs, and drawings relating to railroad transportation.

Access: Access to the archival holdings requires an official letter from a sponsoring institution or a personal letter of application addressed to the director stating the subject and aim of the proposed research.

Working Conditions: Researchers are accommodated in the museum conference hall, where materials are available the day they are ordered.

Reference Facilities: Materials within all fonds are recorded in a subject card catalogue, and and there is a registration card catalogue of inventoried holdings. *Opisi* have been prepared for personal fonds, maps, and albums, and there is a catalogue of works of graphic arts.

Library Facilities: The museum library holdings (ca. 7,000 vols.) were started in the 1860s, and have been augmented by the personal libraries of a number of railroad specialists, including V. N. Obraztsov. In addition to the manuscript materials mentioned above, there is literature on the history and present state of railroad transportation, including many rare imprints of Russian, Soviet, and foreign origin. (Library tel. 315-14-76). Note also the nearby Scientific-Technical Library of the St. Petersburg State University of Transportation—TsNB PGUPS (G–24), with which the museum was earlier administratively affiliated.

Copying: Photocopies can be prepared.

FINDING AIDS — PUBLISHED — GENERAL:

Muzei SPb (1994), p. 187; *Nauchno-tekh. muzei* (1992), pp. 24–25; *Biblioteki SPb* (1993), pp. 170–71; *Peterburg* (1992), p. 208; *Muzei Leningrada* (1982), p. 115–17; PKG *M&L* (1972), p. 349; Myl'nikov (1970), p. 28.

There is no published description of the archival holdings in the museum.

h-680. *Putevoditel' po Muzeiu zheleznodorozhnogo transporta.* Leningrad: "Transport," 1971. 72 p. Resumé in English, German and French. [MPS SSSR; LIIZhT; MZhT]

Tsentral'nyi muzei Oktiabr'skoi zheleznoi dorogi (TsMOZhD)
[Central Museum of the October Railroad]

Agency: Ministerstvo putei soobshcheniia RF (MPS Rossii)
[Ministry of Transportation]
Upravlenie Oktiabr'skoi zheleznoi dorogi
[Administration of the October Railroad]

Address: 191025, St. Petersburg, Liteinyi prosp., 62
Telephone: 272-44-77, 279-34-32
Transport: metro: Vladimirskaia, Dostoevskaia, Maiakovskaia; trol.: 3, 8, 15, 19; tram: 28, 34
Hours: M–F 11:00–17:00; May–October: 12:00–17:00; fonds—by appointment

Director: Valentina Ivanovna Misailova (*tel.* 168-68-91)
Head, Division of Fonds: Tat'iana Mikhailovna Aleksandrovich (*tel.* 279–34–32)
Acting Chief Curator: Liudmila Vital'evna Lipatova

HISTORY:

Muzei Oktiabr'skoi zheleznoi dorogi
[Museum of the October Railroad] (1978–1980)

The museum was opened in 1978 as the Museum of the October Railroad, which connects the northwestern sections of the Russian rail network. Since 1980 the museum has been the coordinating center for twenty-five other railroad museums, and hence "central" was added to its official name.

HOLDINGS: 13,285 units, 1837–1995

manuscripts—101 units (1940s–1990s); documents—2,231 units (19th c.–1990s); photographs—2,688 units (late 19th c.–1990s); negatives—7,500 units (1940s–1990s); drawings—756 units (1940s–1990s)

Within the museum's Division of Fonds (*Otdel fondov*), archival materials are held in five subsidiary fonds: for manuscripts, documents, photographs, negatives, and graphic arts, almost all of them documenting the history of the October Railroad, the first mainline rail network in Russia.

The rail network comprised a number of lines: the Tsarskoe Selo Line, opened in 1837 as the first passenger line in the country; the St. Petersburg-Moscow Line (known as the Nicholas [*Nikolaevskaia*] Line, 1855–1923); the St. Petersburg-Warsaw Line (opened in 1853); the Peterhof Line (opened in 1857); the Oranienbaum Line (opened in the 1860s); and a number of other lines including the St. Petersburg-Baltic Line; the Irinovsk Line; the Primorsk-Sestroretsk Line; the Novgorod Line; the Moscow-Vindava-Rybinsk Line; the Finland Line; the Northwestern Line; the Murmansk Line; and part of the Kalinin Line.

There are documents relating to the planning, building, and utilization of the lines after they were opened, to the rolling stock, and to the work of such railroad engineers and designers as P. P. Mel'nikov, N. O. Kraft, N. I. Lipin, and D. I. Zhuravskii.

Access: Access to the archival holdings requires an official letter from the sponsoring institution or a personal letter of application addressed to the director stating the subject and aim of the proposed research.

Working Conditions: Researchers are accommodated in the museum offices, where materials are available the day they are ordered.

Reference Facilities: There is a main inventory register, a card catalogue for the manuscripts; and subject card catalogues.

Library Facilities: The museum library holdings (ca. 1,500 vols.), specialized in literature on the history of railroad transportation, include rare editions and some manuscript materials.

Copying: Photographic and xerox copies can be ordered.

FINDING AIDS — PUBLISHED — GENERAL:

Muzei SPb (1994), p. 188; *Biblioteki SPb* (1993), p. 171.

There is no published description of the archival holdings in the museum.

h-681. *Putevoditel' po Tsentral'nomu muzeiu Oktiabr'skoi zheleznoi dorogi.* Compiled by A. I. Avgusteniuk and V. Misailova. Edited by M. I. Voronin, P. F. Metel'kov, et al. Leningrad: Lenizdat, 1981. 149 p.
    A brief description of the museum exhibits.

Gosudarstvennyi muzei istorii aviatsii (GMIA)
[State Museum of the History of Aviation]

Agency: Komitet po kul'ture Administratsii Sankt-Peterburga
[Committee on Culture of the Administration of St. Petersburg]

Address: 199026, St. Petersburg, Shkiperskii protok, 21 (a/ia [box] 807)
Telephone: 355-61-62; *Fax:* (812) 113-58-96
Transport: metro: Primorskaia; trol.: 10; bus: 7

Director: Aleksandr Borisovich Solov'ev
Deputy Director for Scientific-Research Work: Arkadii Ivanovich Beliakov

HISTORY:

The museum was founded in March 1991 as the St. Petersburg State Museum of Aviation. The museum fonds are in the process of being arranged.

HOLDINGS: ca. 18,000 units, 1885–1990s

The museum has collected documentation on the history of Russian naval and polar aviation. There are documents on the life and work of A. F. Mozhaiskii, the inventor of the first Russian airplane. There are also documents on the first historical flights and the places where they took off from, were forced to land, or in some cases crashed. The museum also holds the design drawings of the first airplanes.

The film, photography and sound recordings library contains films, photographs, and sound recordings relating to the history of aviation with particular reference to St. Petersburg as the home of the first Russian manned flight. There is also material on the conquest of the air in the Russian Far North and over the Arctic Ocean, on the Soviet Air Force during the Second World War, and on the latest developments in aircraft technology.

Access: Access to the fonds requires a letter to the museum director stating the subject and purpose of research.

Working Conditions: Researchers are accommodated in the museum offices, where materials are available the day they are ordered.

Reference Facilities: There are inventory registers and card catalogues for staff use.

Library Facilities: The book fond contains literature on the history of avaition, following the profile of the museum.

Copying: No copying facilities are available.

FINDING AIDS — PUBLISHED — GENERAL:
Muzei SPb (1994), p. 190.

There is no published guide to the archival materials in the museum.

Tsentral'nyi muzei sviazi im. A. S. Popova (TsMS)
[A. S. Popov Central Museum of Communications]

Agency: Gosudarstvennyi komitet RF posviazi i informatsii
(Goskomsviazi Rossii)
[State Committee for Communications and Information]

Address:	190000, St. Petersburg, ul. Pochtamtskaia (*formerly* Soiuza Sviazi), 7
Telephone:	311-92-06
Transport:	metro: Nevskii prospekt, Gostinyi Dvor; trol.: 5, 14, 22
Hours:	Tu–Sa 10:00–17:00

Director: Natal'ia Nikolaevna Kuritsyna (*tel.* 315-48-73)

HISTORY:

Telegrafnyi muzei
  [Telegraph Museum] (1872–1884)
Pochtovo-telegrafnyi muzei
  [Postal and Telegraph Museum] (1884–1924)
Muzei narodnoi sviazi
  [Museum of People's Communications] (1924–1945)

The first postal and telegraph museum in Russia, and one of the richest of this type in the world, was founded in 1872 as the Telegraph Museum on the basis of an exhibition held at the Moscow Polytechnic Museum. It has been housed since 1924 in a building constructed in the late eighteenth century for Prince A. A. Bezborodko, which was taken over by the postal service in 1829. In 1945, to mark the 50th anniversary of the invention of radio, the museum was given the honorific name of the Russian physicist and inventor Aleksandr Stepanovich Popov (1859–1905). Earlier under the Ministry of Communications of the USSR, and then the State Committee for Communications and Information Development of the Russian Federation, it is now under the Ministry of Communications.

Access: As of 1999, the museum is closed for major renovation, but can still occasionally provide facilities for researchers. Researchers should present an official letter of application addressed to the director stating the subject and purpose of their research.

Library Facilities: The museum has a technical library (ca. 120,000 vols.), with a unique collection of literature on the development of electronics and communications, philately, and computer and measurement technology. There are card catalogues on the history of communications, prominent persons in the field of communications and philately.

Issledovatel'skii otdel dokumental'nykh fondov
[Research Division of Documentary Fonds]

Telephone: 311-92-06
Hours: by appointment
Head: Nadezhda Ivanovna Losich

HOLDINGS: 45 (1 unarranged) fonds, 3 collections , 50,185 units, 1762–1990s (some documents 1722) institutional fonds—5; personal papers—16 fonds; postage stamps—ca. 3,000,000 units

The museum holds a unique collection of historical documentation relating to postal, telegraph, telephone, radio, and television communications. There are fonds with records of a number of institutions, including the museum itself, personal papers, and documentary collections.

Documents on the history of the postal services in Russia include the high government decrees on postal agencies; reports of the Ministry of Internal Affairs; annual reports of postal agencies and the Main Postal Administration; circular letters of instruction and regulations from the Main Postal Administration; and documents on the early history of post roads, postage stamps, post offices, rural postal services (*zemskaia pochta*), and postal and telegraphic districts (*pochtovo-telegrafnye okrugi*). There are also examples of the various types of postal delivery, authorizations for post horses, postal regulations, and samples of notepaper.

Institutional fonds include records of the Nizhnii Novgorod Radio Laboratory, the Central Radio Laboratory, and the Institute of Radio Reception and Acoustics. The latter two fonds retain technical reports for the years 1918–1928, reports on specific subjects and on assignments abroad, staff files, memoirs of the staff, and a collection of glass negatives.

The records of the Central Communications Museum itself contain inventory registers, correspondence about acquisitions, the papers of the Academic Council (*Uchenyi sovet*), documents on the organization of exhibitions, and scholarly works written by the museum staff.

Personal fonds include archival materials of the main chief of the Postal Department, A. N. Golitsyn; P. L. Shilling, who invented the first electromagnetic apparatus (1832); Moritz Hermann Jacobi (B. S. Iakobi), who invented new types of telegraph machines (1840–1850); A. S. Popov, who invented radio (1895); and B. L. Rozing, who made the first television electronic-ray tube (1907). There are papers of various other inventors, including M. Freidenberg, O. Adamian, and B. Grabovskii; People's Commissar for Postal and Telegraph Services V. N. Podbel'skii; and a number of historians of technology, including B. A. Ostroumov, I. V. Brenev, V. A. Burliand, and A. V. Iarotskii. These contain correspondence relating to inventions, personal documents, biographical materials, and photographs.

Thematically arranged collections (fonds)—devoted to postal, telephone, telegraph, radio, television, and space communications—contain documents on the development of communications; biographical information on inventors; and technical data on communications equipment and on the building and operation of telephone exchanges, radio stations, and the television center in Leningrad.

There is also a collection of maps, which include maps of the Russian Empire, postal maps of various guberniias, and maps of postal and telegraph districts (*okrugi*). A collection of technical drawings contain views and facades of post offices in St. Petersburg and the Russian guberniias, city plans, and related materials. There are also collections of films, slides, microfilms, and other film and photographic documents related to the development of various branches of communications. The museum stamp collection (estimates range from 5 to 7 million items), which contains stamps from every country in the world, is one of the largest in Russia.

Working Conditions: Researchers are accommodated in the museum offices, where materials are available the day they are ordered.

Reference Facilities: There are *opisi* of fonds and card catalogues. There are also unpublished surveys of fonds.

Copying: There are no copying facilities available.

FINDING AIDS — PUBLISHED — GENERAL:

Nauchno-tekh. muzei (1992), pp. 36–37; *Muzei SPb* (1994), p. 186; *Biblioteki SPb* (1993), p. 110; *Peterburg* (1992), p. 565; *Muzei Leningrada* (1982), pp. 111–12; PKG *M&L* (1972), p. 347; Myl'nikov (1970), p. 49.

There is no comprehensive published guide to the archival materials in the museum, although many of them are well described in the publications below.

h-682. *Kollektsiia A. S. Popova: Katalog.* Compiled by Kh. A. Ioffe, N. N. Kuritsina, L. I. Zolotinkina, et al. St. Petersburg: TsMS, 1995. 142 p. (Also listed as a-150).

A catalogue of the exhibits in the fonds of the A. S. Popov Central Communications Museum. Also covers the A. S. Popov Memorial Museum-Laboratory at Kronstadt (H–116), the A. S. Popov Memorial Museum at the St. Petersburg State University of Electrical Engineering (H–115), and the Central Naval Museum (H–74). It gives an annotated list of documentary materials, including manuscripts of scientific works together with preparatory notes, biographical and scientific documents, and letters written by A. S. Popov (pp. 78–91). The appendix contains published letters (pp. 92–130), an index of names, and a bibliography of relevant literature.

h-683. *Materialy po istorii sviazi v Rossii XVII–nachala XX vv. [Pochta, telegraf, telefon, radio, televidenie]: Obzor dokumental'nykh materialov.* Compiled by F. I. Bunina et al. Edited by N. A. Mal'tseva. Leningrad: GAU, 1966. 335 p. [Minsviazi SSSR; TsMS; GAU pri SM SSSR; TsGIA SSSR; LGIA] (Lib: DLC; IU; MH) [IDC-R-10,735] (Also listed as a-387).

Includes detailed coverage of archival holdings in the museum, in addition to those held in RGIA (B–3) and TsGIA SPb (D–13).

h-684. *Katalog muzeinykh veshchei.* Compiled by S. V. Artiushina, N. I. Balas, V. V. Blozhis, et al. Moscow: "Sviaz'," 1976. 143 p. [Minsviazi SSSR; TsMS]

h-685. *[Putevoditel'].* Compiled by V. P. Bronevitskii, M. V. Vislenev, U. Z. Zinov'eva, et al. Leningrad: [Khudozhnik RSFSR], 1962. 235 p. [Minsviazi SSSR; TsMS]

A guide to the exhibitions on the history of communications in Russia. Contains a bibliography of 77 titles.

h-686. Fedorov, A. D. "Tsentral'nyi muzei sviazi im. A. S. Popova." *Vestnik sviazi,* 1953, no. 1, pp. 20–21. (Lib: DLC; MH)

FINDING AIDS — SPECIALIZED:

h-687. *Sovetskie pochtovye marki: Kratkoe opisanie sovetskikh pochtovykh marok, eksponiruemykh na vystavke v Tsentral'nom muzee sviazi im. A. S. Popova.* [Leningrad], [1958]. 80 p. + plates. [Minsviazi SSSR; TsMS]

Memorial'nyi muzei A. S. Popova
[A. S. Popov Memorial Museum]

Agency: Ministerstvo obshchego i professional'nogo obrazovaniia RF
(Minobrazovaniia Rossii)
[Ministry of General and Professional Education]
Sankt-Peterburgskii gosudarstvennyi elektrotekhnicheskii universitet (ETU)
[St. Petersburg State Electrotechnical University]

Address:	197376, St. Petersburg, ul. Professora Popova, 5
Telephone:	234-59-00, 234-03-94; *Fax:* (812) 346-27-58
E-mail:	root@post.etu.spb.ru; shaposhn@rectorat.etu.ru
Website:	http://www.eltech.ru/win/mus_kv.htm
	(university library): http://www.ruslan.ru:8001/spb/univer/univer_etu.html
Transport:	metro: Petrogradskaia; bus: 10, 71, 128; trol.: 31
Hours:	M–F 11:00–17:00

Director: Larisa Igorevna Zolotinkina (*tel.* 234-59-00)
University Rector: Oleg Vasil'evich Alekseev (*tel.* 234-44-65;
e-mail: puzanov@svr.etu.spu.ru)

HISTORY:

The A. S. Popov Memorial Museum was founded in 1948 under the auspices of the V. I. Ul'ianov-Lenin Leningrad Electrotechnical Institute (now St. Petersburg University). The Russian scientist and inventor of radio, Aleksandr Stepanovich Popov (1859–1905) was appointed Professor and head of the Department (*kafedra*) of Physics at the predecessor Electrotechnical Institute in 1901 and Director of the Institute in 1905. The Institute was raised to the status of University in 1993, and subsequently dropped the honorific name of Ul'ianov-Lenin.

The museum is located partly in the physicist's former laboratory and partly in the apartment (opened in 1967) where he lived from 1903 until his death in 1905, and administratively remains part of the University (see ETU—H–118). The museum has recently reopened following major renovations. A fiftieth-anniversary conference took place in 1998.

HOLDINGS: 12 fonds, ca. 20,000 units, 1859–1990s

The archival holdings of the museum contain original manuscript materials relating to the life and work of A. S. Popov, and his family and relatives, including documents in Russian, French, English and German. Among these the most interesting relate to his discovery of radio. There are sound recordings of events held to perpetuate the memory of the inventor with recordings of famous people speaking about him.

There are photographs and negatives recording the various stages of Popov's scientific work and his work as a teacher and public figure. There are also photographs taken by Popov himself, and portraits of his family and children. Among graphic materials are a number of drawings and watercolors done by A. S. Popova-Kapustina, R. A. Popova, A. A. Popov, and K. I. Rudakov.

There is also the manuscript of a collection of articles about faculty and students of the Leningrad Institute of Electrical Engineering who suffered political repression during the years 1930–1945.

Access: Research access to materials in the A. S. Popov Memorial Museum requires an official letter addressed to the rector of the University (ETU—H–118). Research in some of the materials may be subject to fees for those not associated with the University. The museum has been undergoing renovation, in preparation for its fifteith anniversary, but arrangements can be made to accommodate researchers.

Working Conditions: A renovated reading room is being opened to accommodate researchers.

Reference Facilities: There is an unpublished guide to the museum in Russian and English. There are inventory registers and a card catalogue for staff use.

Library Facilities: The nearby ETU Fundamental Library (over 1,100,000 vols.) holds literature on electrical engineering, electronics, automation, computer sciences, and the natural sciences, as well as manuscript dissertations defended at the Institute/University and normative-technical documentation. (Library address: ul. Prof. Popova, 5, korpus 1; tel.: 234-89-58; fax: [812] 346-27-58; e-mail: vsk@lib.etu.spb.ru; website: http://www.ruslan.ru:8001/spb/univer/univer_etu.html.) (See also under H–118)

Copying: There are no copying facilities available in the museum. Photographic and xerox copies can, however, be prepared through the appropriate services at the university (ETU).

FINDING AIDS — PUBLISHED — GENERAL:

Muzei SPb (1994), p. 200; *Peterburg* (1992), p. 505; *Muzei vuzov* (1975), pp. 89–90.

See the description of documents in the museum as listed in the general catalogue of archival materials regarding A. S. Popov (a-150/h-682).

Memorial'nyi muzei-laboratoriia izobretatelia radio A. S. Popova

[Memorial Museum-Laboratory of the Inventor of Radio A. S. Popov]

Agency: Ministerstvo oborony RF (Minoborony Rossii)
[Ministry of Defense]

Address:	189610, Leningradskaia oblast', g. Kronshtadt, ul. Makarovskaia (*formerly* Iiul'skaia), 1/3
Telephone:	236-47-66
Transport:	suburban train from Baltic Station to Oranienbaum, and then water transport (in summer); metro: Chernaia rechka + bus 510
Hours:	M–W, F–Su 10:00–17:00

Director: Iurii Ivanovich Spiridonov

HISTORY:

The first exhibition devoted to Aleksandr Stepanovich Popov (1859–1905), the inventor of radio, was organized in Kronstadt (*Rus.* Kronshtadt) soon after his death in 1906. The exhibition, based on the site where Popov had worked from 1883 to 1901, was founded on the initiative of Popov's friend and assistant, P. N. Rybkin, who became the first director of the museum. The Memorial Laboratory-Museum was founded in 1960. It contains the scientific instruments and equipment used by Popov in his experiments with radio, as well as documents, photographs, and negatives connected with the invention of radio.

HOLDINGS: ca. 1,000 units, 1890–1950s

The museum retains the personal papers (mainly scientific works) and radio equipment of Petr Nikolaevich Rybkin (1864–1948), who was a radio mechanic and A. S. Popov's assistant. For a period of some fifty years Rybkin trained radio operators—first in a mine-laying and detection class and then in the A. S. Popov School of Communications in Kronstadt. The manuscripts include Rybkin's unpublished memoirs and documents relating to the work of the mine-laying and detection class.

The museum also holds photographic prints and negatives (1890–1950) of mining officers' classes, specializing in mine-laying and detection, and of the signals training unit of the Baltic Fleet.

Access: Entry into Kronstadt requires a pass or an assignment order (*komandirovochnoe predpisanie*). Research access requires an official written application which must be appropriately endorsed by the Kronstadt Military Commandant, who has controlling authority over the museum.

Working Conditions: Researchers are accommodated in the museum offices. When requesting to see negatives, preliminary arrangements must be made by telephone with the museum director; other materials are available immediately.

Reference Facilities: There are inventory registers and an alphabetical card catalogue for staff use.

Library Facilities: There is an auxiliary book fond (ca. 1,000 vols.) containing specialized literature relating to the work and holdings of the museum, which is available to researchers.

Copying: There are no copying facilities available.

FINDING AIDS — PUBLISHED — GENERAL:

Muzei SPb (1994), p. 201.

There is no published description of the archival holdings in the museum. Some of the documents held in the museum are described in the general catalogue of archival materials relating to A. S. Popov (a-150/h-682).

Museums of Technological Universities

✱⊷ H–117 ⊷✱

Istoriko-tekhnicheskii muzei Sankt-Peterburgskogo gosudarstvennogo tekhnicheskogo universiteta (ITM SPbGTU)
[Historico-Technical Museum of St. Petersburg State Technical University]

Agency: Ministerstvo obshchego i professional'nogo obrazovaniia RF
(Minobrazovaniia Rossii)
[Ministry of General and Professional Education]

Address: 195251, St. Petersburg, ul. Politekhnicheskaia, 29
Telephone: 247-20-95; *Fax:* (812) 552-60-86
Website: *(university):* http://www.unilib.neva.ru/stu/home.html
Transport: metro: Politekhnicheskaia; bus: 69, 103; trol.: 4, 13, 21, 30, 34, 50
Hours: M–F 14:00–17:00

University Rector:
Iurii Sergeevich Vasil'ev (*tel.* 247-16-16; *e-mail:* president@citidel.stu.neva.ru)
Museum Director: Nina Pavlovna Gerbyleva (*tel.* 552-78-62)

HISTORY:

Istoriko-tekhnicheskii muzei Leningradskogo politekhnicheskogo instituta im. M. I. Kalinina
(Muzei LPI)
[Historico-Technical Museum of the M. I. Kalinin Leningrad Polytechic Institute] (1981–1990)
Istoriko-tekhnicheskii muzei Leningradskogo gosudarstvennogo tekhnicheskogo universiteta
(Muzei LGTU)
[Historico-Technical Museum of Leningrad State Polytechnic University] (1990–1991)

The Historico-Technical Museum of Leningrad Polytechnic Institute was established in 1981 on the basis of an exhibition on the history of the M. I. Kalinin Leningrad Polytechnic Institute (LPI), which had initially been organized in 1976. The museum acquired part of its present collections from the former M. A. Shatelen Museum of Electrical Engineering which, founded before World War I, remained active through the 1920s.

The present St. Petersburg State Technical University, now one of the most prestigious institutions of higher technical education in Russia, is a direct successor to the Polytechnic Institute that was established in St. Petersburg in 1899 and was opened in 1902 (*Sankt-Peterburgskii politekhnicheskii institut*). It was given the honorific name of Peter I in 1910.

After the October Revolution, in 1918, the institute was renamed the First Petrograd Polytechnic Institute (*Pervyi Petrogradskii politekhnicheskii institut*), and in 1923 renamed to honor the Bolshevik revolutionary leader Mikhail Ivanovich Kalinin—the M. I. Kalinin Petrograd (after 1924, Leningrad) First Polytechnic Institute—LPI (*Petrogradskii [Leningradskii] Pervyi politekhnicheskii institut im. M. I. Kalinina*). In 1930 several separate specialized institutes were organized on its basis, but in 1934 all were once again consolidated under the name of the Leningrad Industrial Institute (*Leningradskii industrial'nyi institut*). In 1940 the institute reverted to its previous name of the M. I. Kalinin Leningrad Polytechnic Institute (LPI). In 1990 its status was raised to that of a university and it was renamed Leningrad (since 1991, St. Petersburg) State Technical University. It subsequently dropped the honorific name of M. I. Kalinin.

N.B. The main archival records of the Polytechnic Institute for the prerevolutionary period are held in TsGIA SPb (D–13, fond 478—1899–1912), while records for the Soviet period are held in TsGA SPb (D–12) and TsGANTD SPb (D–17).

HOLDINGS: ca. 40,000 units, 1899–1990s

All of the museum holdings are organized into main and auxiliary fonds, both of which contain documentary materials, including graphic materials, photographs, and negatives on the history of SPbGTU. There are documents dating back to the late nineteenth century on the academic, organizational, and public work of the various faculties and departments. The most complete fonds are those of the Faculty of Mechanical Engineering, and the Departments of Metallurgy and Chemistry. The museum holds the original map of the State Commission for the Electrification of Russia (GOELRO).

Materials of personal origin include documents of and relating to instructors and graduates, and there are a number of fonds of individual scientists, scholars, and teachers—the electrical engineers M. A. Shatelen, M. V. Kravchenko, and A. M. Zalesskii; the physicists D. V. Skobel'tsyn, Iu. A. Krutkov, and D. N. Nasledov; the lighting engineer P. M. Tikhodeev; the hydraulic engineer M. D. Chertousov; the specialist in automation and telemechanics control M. P. Kostenko; and the metallurgist M. M. Karnaukhov, among others. There are some letters and manuscripts of the physicists A. F. Ioffe and P. L. Kapitsa.

There are also materials gathered for a collection of articles about faculty and students of the Leningrad Institute who suffered political oppression during the years 1930–1945.

Access: Research access to materials in the A. S. Popov Memorial Museum requires an official letter addressed to the rector of the University.

Research work in the museum holdings is on a fee basis. A letter of guarantee from the researcher's sponsoring institution should be addressed to the museum director stating the form and amount of payment. In the case of outside researchers, fees are also charged for use of the reading room in the Fundamental Library.

Working Conditions: Researchers are accommodated in the museum offices, where materials are available the day they are ordered.

Reference Facilities: There are inventories of the personal papers, acquisition registers for the main and auxiliary fonds, receipts for museum exhibits, a register of transfers of fonds, and a number of auxiliary card catalogues. But many of the reference facilities are only for staff use.

Library Facilities: What is now the Fundamental Library of SPbGTU was founded in 1903, soon after the Institute, and its holdings have developed with the Institute itself (now ca. 2,900,000 vols.). In addition to literature on science, technology, and industry, the library holds a vast quantity of literature on the humanities (philosophy, politics, economics and art). It retains a number of library collections from earlier institutes, such as the Institute of Industrial Transportation, the Institute of Electric Welding, and the Cabinet of Mathematical Statistics, as well as the memorial and personal libraries of the economist, poliltician, and philosopher, P. B. Struve; the prerevolutionary minister of finance S. Iu. Witte (Vitte); the historian, A. A. Kornilov; the economist, geographer and statistician, V. E. Den; and even a collection of numismatic publicaitons once belonging to Grand Duke George [Georgii] Mikhailovich. There are a number of prerevolutionary library collections from leading professors of the St. Petersburg Polytechnic Institute.

Many of the imprints dating from the sixteenth to the nineteenth centuries have ex libris and dedicatory inscriptions of well-known personages of science and culture. There are complete sets of the prerevolutionary Russian codes of laws and other official government publications, as well as complete runs of many prerevolutionary journals. There are dissertations defended at the Institute; reports on research, project, and design work; and various audiovisual materials.

There is a card catalogue on scholars of the Polytechnic Institute. An integrated electronic catalogue is being established, which will show all acquisitions since 1991. An information center, entitled "Institutions of Higher Education at Home and Abroad" (*Otechestvennaia i zarubezhnaia vysshaia shkola*) has a database covering some 8,000 entries on problems of education. (Library tel.: 552-75-59; fax: (812) 551-76-54; e-mail: libmaster@unilib.unilib.neva.ru; website: http://www.unilib.neva.ru/lib/home.html, and can also be reached through the "ruslan.ru" server).

Copying: Photographic and xerox copies can be ordered from the photographic laboratory and the copying office of the University.

FINDING AIDS — PUBLISHED — GENERAL:

Muzei SPb (1994), p. 206; *Biblioteki SPb* (1993), pp. 95–96; *Muzei vuzov* (1975), p. 85.

There is no published guide to the archival materials in the museum.

h-690. *Iz istorii Leningradskogo ordena Lenina politekhnicheskogo instituta, 1899–1989.* Leningrad, 1989. 87 p.
> Includes a chronological summary of major events in the history of the Institute from 1899.

h-691. *75 let Leningradskomu politekhnicheskomu institutu: [Sbornik statei].* Edited by K. P. Seleznev. Leningrad: LPI, 1974. 144 p. "Trudy Leningradskogo politekhnicheskogo instituta im. M.I. Kalinina," vol. 339. [Minvuz RSFSR; LPI]

h-692. *Istoriia instituta: [Sbornik statei].* Edited by V. V. Danilevskii, M. N. Potekhin, and V. S. Smirnov. Leningrad, 1957. 146 p. "Trudy Leningradskogo politekhnicheskogo instituta im. M. I. Kalinina," vol. 190. [Minvuz SSSR; LPI]

Muzei istorii Sankt-Peterburgskogo gosudarstvennogo elektrotekhnicheskogo universiteta (Muzei istorii ETU)

[Museum of the History of St. Petersburg State Electrotechnical University]

Agency: Ministerstvo obshchego i professional'nogo obrazovaniia RF
(Minobrazovaniia Rossii)
[Ministry of General and Professional Education]

Address: 197376, St. Petersburg, ul. Professora Popova, 5, korpus 3
Telephone: 234-46-51; 234-84-85
E-mail: shaposhn@rectorat.etu.ru; (university library): vsk@lib.etu.spb.ru
Website: http://www.eltech.ru/win/mus_hist.htm;
              (university library): http://www.ruslan.ru:8001/spb/univer/univer_etu.html
Transport: metro: Petrogradskaia; bus: 10, 71, 128; trol.: 31
Hours: M–Th 10:00–16:00

University Rector: Dmitrii Viktorovich Puzanov (*tel.* 234-44-65;
   e-mail: puzanov@svr.etu.spu.ru))
Museum Director: Liudmila Nikolaevna Nikolaeva (*tel.* 234-84-85)

HISTORY:

Muzei istorii Leningradskogo (after 1991, Sankt-Peterburgskogo) elektrotekhnicheskogo instituta
    im. V. I. Ul'ianova-Lenina (Muzei istorii LETI)
    [Museum of the History of V. I. Ul'ianov-Lenin Leningrad (after 1991, St. Peterburg)
    Electrotechnical Institute] (1986–IV.1993)
Muzei istorii Sankt-Peterburgskogo gosudarstvennogo elektrotekhnicheskogo universiteta
    im. V. I. Ul'ianova-Lenina (Muzei istorii ETU)
    [Museum of the History of V. I. Ulianov-Lenin St. Petersburg State Electrotechnical University]
    (IV.1993–)

The Museum of the History of St. Petersburg State Electrotechnical University (ETU, sometimes SPbGETU) was opened in 1986 to celebrate the centennial of the founding of what was then the V. I. Ul'ianov-Lenin Leningrad Electrotechnical Institute (LETI).

The Institute itself was originally founded in 1886 as the Technical School of the Postal and Telegraph Agencies. In 1891 it was reorganized as the imperial Alexander III Electrotechnical Institute (*Elektrotekhnicheskii institut im. Aleksandra III*) under the Ministry of Internal Affairs. In 1918 the Institute came under the control of the People's Commissariat of Education (Narkompros). From 1929 to 1930 the Leningrad Electrotechnical Institute (LETI) was under the authority of the People's Commissariat of Heavy Industry; from 1931 to 1935 it came under the People's Commissariat of Defense Industry; and from 1946 to 1952 it was controlled by the People's Commissariat (Ministry) of the Shipbuilding Industry. Starting in 1946 the Institute also came under the authority of the Ministry of Higher Education (Minvuz SSSR), now the Ministry of General and Professional Education of the Russian Federation. The Institute was raised to the status of university April 1993, and it subsequently dropped the honorific name of Ul'ianov-Lenin.

HOLDINGS: 9 fonds, ca. 10,000 units, 1893–1990s
MS books—4 units (1920s–1930s); photographs—2,092; negatives—273;
archival collections—4,197 units; auxiliary fond (photographs, etc.)—3,391 units

The museum of the history of the University (ETU) has collected archival documents and photographs relating to the development of the oldest electrical institute in Russia. There is also documentation on the life and work of its most famous scientists, scholars, faculty, and graduates, including A. S. Popov, A. I. Berg, G. O. Graftio, and I. G. Freiman, A. A. Smurov, and V. P. Vologdin.

Access: Research access to materials in the museum requires an official letter addressed to the rector of the University, stating the subject and aim of the research.

Working Conditions: Researchers are accommodated in the museum offices, where materials are available the day they are ordered.

Reference Facilities: There are 17 inventory registers and 7 auxiliary card catalogues.

Library Facilities: The nearby ETU Fundamental Library (over 1,100,000 vols.) holds literature on electrical engineering, electronics, automation, computer sciences, physical sciences, and technology, as well as manuscript dissertations defended at the Institute/University and normative-technical documentation. (Library address: ul. Prof. Popova, 5, korpus 1; tel.: 234-89-58; fax: [812] 346-27-58; e-mail: vsk@lib.etu.spb.ru; website: http://www.ruslan.ru:8001/spb/univer/univer_etu.html).

Copying: There are no copying facilities available in the museum. Photographic and xerox copies can, however, be made through the appropriate services at ETU.

FINDING AIDS — PUBLISHED — GENERAL:

Muzei SPb (1994), p. 149; *Biblioteki SPb* (1993), pp. 98–99; *Peterburg* (1992), pp. 675–76; *Muzei vuzov* (1975), p. 85.

There is no published description of the archival materials in the museum.

h-693. *LETI im. V. I. Ul'ianova (Lenina): K 100-letiiu so dnia osnovaniia: Sbornik statei.*
Edited by O. V. Alekseev. Moscow: "Radio i sviaz'," 1986. 271 p.
A collection of articles honoring the centennial of the Institute, which was also the occasion for the founding of the museum. Contains a bibliography of literature on LETI (pp. 258–69).

Muzei istorii Sankt-Peterburgskogo gosudarstvennogo tekhnologicheskogo universiteta rastitel'nykh polimerov (Muzei istorii SPbGTURP)

[Museum of the History of St. Petersburg State Technological University for Plant Polymers]

Agency: Ministerstvo obshchego i professional'nogo obrazovaniia RF
(Minobrazovaniia Rossii)
[Ministry of General and Professional Education]

Address: 198092, St. Petersburg, ul. Ivana Chernykh, 4
Telephone: 186-86-79; *Fax:* (812) 186-86-00
Transport: metro: Narvskaia; bus: 2, 35, 55, 73; trol.: 8, 20; tram: 31, 33, 34
Hours: MWF 15:00–17:30 (closed July and August)

University Rector: Otto Alekseevich Terent'ev (*tel.* 186-57-44)
Director of Museum: Boris Vital'evich Pekarskii (*tel.* 186-76-20)

HISTORY:

Muzei istorii Leningradskogo tekhnologicheskogo instituta tselliulozno-bumazhnoi promyshlennosti
(Muzei istorii LTITsBP)
[Museum of the History of the Leningrad Technological Institute of Pulp and Paper Manufacturing]
(1959–1992)
Muzei istorii Sankt-Peterburgskogo tekhnologicheskogo instituta tselliulozno-bumazhnoi promyshlennosti
(Muzei istorii SPbTI TsBP)
[Museum of the History of the St. Petersburg Institute of Pulp and Paper Manufacturing] (1992–1993)

The Museum of the History of the University (then the Institute) was founded in 1988.

The present St. Petersburg State Technological University for Plant Polymers is an outgrowth of the earlier Institute of Pulp and Paper Manufacturing. The original Institute was founded in 1931 as the V. M. Molotov All-Union Institute of Industrial Cooperation. It developed from the Moscow Institute of Cottage Crafts and Producers Cooperatives (*Moskovskii institut kustarnoi promyshlennosti i promyslovoi kooperatsii*) (founded in 1930) as part of the V. M. Molotov All-Union Industrial Cooperation Training Center (*Vsesoiuznyi uchebnyi kombinat promyshlennoi kooperatsii im. V. M. Molotova*). In 1938 the center was closed down and the Institute became an independent higher educational establishment. During the Second World War the Institute was evacuated to Kislovodsk, where from 1942 to 1943 it came under German occupation. Later it moved to Tashkent, where it functioned as the Tashkent Branch of the V. M. Molotov Leningrad Technological Institute. In 1945 the Institute returned to Leningrad, and in 1959 it was reorganized as the Leningrad Technological Institute of Pulp and Paper Manufacturing. Its present name dates from 1993, when its status was raised to that of a university.

HOLDINGS: ca. 2,600 units, 1931–1990s

manuscript documents—1,200 units (1945–1990s); photographs—1,430 (1945–1990s)

Documentary materials are held both in the Main and the Auxiliary Fonds of the museum. These comprise a small collection of original manuscript documents and photographs pertaining to the history of the University and its faculties and departments, together with material on the scholars who have worked there since the war, including information on their scientific research and theoretical work. However, original documentation on the work of the Institute for the years 1931–1945 has been lost, and there are now only copies of documents held in the state archives and the university archive.

Access: Research access to materials in the museum requires an official letter from the sponsoring organization addressed to the rector of the University, stating the subject and aim of the research.

Working Conditions: Researchers are accomodated in the exhibition room or in other museum premises.

Library Facilities: The SPbGTURP Scientific-Technological Library (ca. 740,000 vols.) was founded in 1925 as the library of the Technical College of Industrial Cooperation. It possesses the largest collection in the country of literature on cellulose and paper technology. It also retains reports on scientific-research and experimental design work, as well as dissertations defended at the University.

Copying: Photographic and xerox copies can be prepared.

FINDING AIDS — PUBLISHED — GENERAL:

Muzei SPb (1994), p. 152; *Biblioteki SPb* (1993), p. 156; *Peterburg* (1992), p. 616.

There is no published guide to the archival materials in the museum.

FINDING AIDS — GENERAL — UNPUBLISHED:

h-695. Pekarskii, Boris Vital'evich. "Muzei istorii Sankt-Peterburgskogo gosudarstvennogo universiteta rastitel'nykh polimerov: Putevoditel'." St. Petersburg, 1994. 51 p. Typescript.
Surveys the history of the University since its founding and describes the holdings and exhibits in the museum.

Muzei istorii Sankt-Peterburgskogo gosudarstvennogo universiteta tekhnologii i dizaina (Muzei istorii SPbGUTiD)
[Museum of the History of St. Petersburg State University
of Technology and Design]

Agency: Ministerstvo obshchego i professional'nogo obrazovaniia RF
(Minobrazovaniia Rossii)
[Ministry of General and Professional Education]

Address: 191065, St. Petersburg, ul. Bol'shaia Morskaia (*formerly* Gertsena), 18, auditoriia 215a
Telephone: 311-97-04; 315-16-83
Transport: metro: Nevskii prospekt, Gostinyi Dvor; trol.: 1, 5, 7, 10, 14, 22
Hours: M–F 10:00–17:00

University Rector: Viktor Egorovich Romanov (*tel.* 315-75-25)
Pro-Rector for Scientific Work: Vladimir Gennad'evich Tiranov (*tel.* 315-74-74)
Head of Museum: Valentina Vasil'evna Antoniuk (*tel.* 311-97-04)
Director of Library: Ol'ga Nikolaevna Terova (*tel.* 311-96–45)
Head of Library Reading Room: Larisa Vasil'evna Kovalevskaia (*tel.* 315-11-29)

HISTORY:
Muzei istorii Leningradskogo instituta tekstil'noi i legkoi promyshlennosti im. S. M. Kirova
(Muzei istorii LITLP)
[Museum of the History of S. M. Kirov Leningrad Institute of Textiles and Light Industry]
(1980–II.1992)
Muzei istorii Sankt-Peterburgskogo instituta tekstil'noi i legkoi promyshlennosti im. S. M. Kirova
(Muzei istorii SPbITLP)
[Museum of the History of S. M. Kirov St. Petersburg Institute of Textiles and Light Industry]
(II.1992–XII.1992)

The Museum of the History of Leningrad Institute of Textiles and Light Industry was founded in 1980—marking the 50th anniversary of the Institute—as a public museum attached to the Department of the History of the CPSU. In December 1981 it was made into an independent subdivision under the authority of the rector's office.

Its predecessor was founded in 1930 when the Faculty of Textiles of Leningrad Technological Institute was separated out—after the reorganization of its parent body—to become the Leningrad Textiles Institute. In 1935 the Institute was named after S. M. Kirov. In December, 1992 it was renamed the present St. Petersburg State University of Technology and Design, an outgrowth of what before December 1992 was the S. M. Kirov Leningrad Institute of Textiles and Light Industry (after February 1992, the St. Petersburg Institute of Textiles and Light Industry).

HOLDINGS: ca. 3,000 units, 1930–1990s
graphic sheets—ca. 200 units (1991–1995)

The museum holds documents on the history of the University, including the history of its faculties and departments, and materials on the scientific, pedagogic, and public work undertaken by the professors, lecturers, students, and outstanding graduates. These include photograph albums with pictures of academic study and student life, a collection of wall newspapers from all the faculties (1934–1962), a collection of graphic materials showing various design studies exhibited at international and Russian student designer competitions (1991–1995).

Access: Access to the archival holdings requires an official letter or a personal application addressed to the Pro-Rector for Scientific Work stating the subject and aim of the proposed research.

Working Conditions: Researchers work in the reading room of the main university library, where documents are available the day they are ordered.

Reference Facilities: There are inventories and thematic card catalogues.

Library Facilities: The main library of the University (ca. 520,000 vols.) was founded in 1930 and holds literature on light industry and decorative and applied art. It also has assessments of research and experimental design work, dissertations defended at the University, and a large collection of manuscript memoirs and recollections by students and lecturers. (Library tel.: 311-96-45).

Copying: Both photographic and xerox copies can be prepared.

FINDING AIDS — PUBLISHED — GENERAL:

Biblioteki SPb (1993), p. 147; *Peterburg* (1992), p. 612.

There is no published guide to the archival materials in the museum.

Factory Museums

✴⊹ ⊹✴ H–121 ⊹✴

Muzei istorii tekhniki Otkrytogo aktsionernogo obshchestva "Kirovskii zavod"
[Museum of the History of Technology of the Kirov Factory
Open Joint-Stock Company]

Agency: Otkrytoe aktsionernoe obshchestvo (OAO) "Kirovskii zavod"
[Kirov Factory Open Joint-Stock Company]

Address: 198188, St. Petersburg, prosp. Stachek, 72
Telephone: 184-22-33; *Fax:* (factory): (812) 252-04-16 (factory)
Transport: bus: 83, 111; trol.: 8, 20, 27, 37
Hours: M–F 10:00–16:00

Director: Pavel Sergeevich Gerasimov (*tel.* 183-88-41)

HISTORY:

The museum, devoted to the history of one of the oldest and largest factories in St. Petersburg, was established in 1962 and is located in the I. I. Gaza Palace of Culture and Technology (*Dvorets kul'tury i tekhniki im. I. I. Gazy*), where the factory wartime command operated during the Siege of Leningrad.

The initial predecessor of the factory was a cast-iron foundry established on Kotlin Island (near the Kronstadt [Kronshtadt] Fortress) in 1789, on the initiative of the Scottish industrialist, Charles Haskins (Gaskoin). The foundry was reestablished by decree of Emperor Paul I in St. Petersburg in 1801, and hence known as the St. Petersburg Cast Iron Foundry (*S.-Peterburgskii chugunoliteinyi zavod*). After N. I. Putilov purchased the foundry from the state treasury in 1868, it was known as the Putilov Factory. Under its new owner, it grew to become the largest metallurgical plant in prerevolutionary Russia.

From 1922 to 1934 known as the "Krasnyi Putilovets" Factory, it produced machine tools, tractors, and other metallurgical products. The factory was renamed to honor Leningrad Party leader Sergei Mironovich Kirov after his assassination in 1934. In subsequent decades the factory was known for its production of "Kirovets" tractors, the "Lenin" atomic icebreaker, and equipment for the merchant fleet. Later awarded the "Red Banner of Labor" and other awards, its official name was hence—*Kirovskii Ordena Lenina, Ordena Krasnogo Znameni, Ordena Trudovogo Krasnogo Znameni mashinostroitel'nyi i metallurgicheskii zavod im. S. M. Kirova*. Since privatization, it assumed its present name, although has retained the honorific name of Kirov.

HOLDINGS: statistics not available

The museum displays significant documents and photographs on the history of the factory, including those from the prerevolutionary period.

N.B. Remaining factory records (1860–1928) are held in TsGIA SPb (D–13, fonds 1309, 1418, and 1270). Additional postrevolutionary records are held in TsGA SPb (D–12).

Comment: A questionnaire about the archival holdings in the museum was not returned to Rosarkhiv.

FINDING AIDS — PUBLISHED — GENERAL:

Muzei SPb (1994), p. 155; *Biblioteki SPb* (1993), p. 120; *Peterburg* (1992), p. 264.

There is no published guide to the archival materials in the museum.

h-698. *Istoriia Kirovskogo (byv. Putilovskogo) metallurgicheskogo i mashinostroitel'nogo zavoda v Leningrade.*
    [Vol. 1]: Mitel'man, M.; Glebov, B.; and Ul'ianskii, A. G. *Istoriia Putilovskogo zavoda, 1789–1917.* Edited by V. A. Bystrianskii. 3d ed. Moscow: Izd-vo Sotsial'no-ekonomicheskoi literatury, 1961. 720 p. "Istoriia zavodov." (Lib: MH)
    2d ED. (condensed): Moscow/Leningrad: OGIZ/Gospolitizdat, 1941. 630 p. + plates [Leningradski insititut istorii VKP(b)] (Lib: MH)
    1st ED.: L., 1939. 756 p. (Lib: MH[mf])
    [Vol. 2]: Kostiuchenko, Stanislav Alekseevich; Khrenov, I.; and Fedorov, Iu. *Istoriia Kirovskogo zavoda, 1917–1945.* Moscow: "Mysl'," 1966. 702 p. "Istoriia zavodov." (Lib: MH).

> A detailed history of the factory since its founding in 1789. The second edition (1941) is somewhat condensed and popularized in comparison to the first. All editions repeat the detailed list of fonds (originally in 11 different archives) in which documentation was found; the 1961 edition updates the archival names, but retains the full list of fonds (pp. 716–18). The second volume has only abbreviated, Soviet-style citations in footnotes, but does not provide names of fonds or actual documents, as was done in the first volume.

Muzei istorii Gosudarstvennogo proizvodstvennogo ob"edineniia "Zavod im. M. I. Kalinina"

[Museum of the History of the M. I. Kalinin State Manufacturing Association]

Agency: Ministerstvo ekonomiki RF (Minekonomikii Rossii)
[Ministry of Economics]

Address: 199155, St. Petersburg, ul. Ural'skaia, 1
Telephone: 350-89-06, 350-87-04 (factory secretary); *Fax:* (factory): (812) 352-57-35
Transport: metro: Vasileostrovskaia; tram: 6; bus: 6, 41, 151
Hours: M–F 9:00–12:30, 13:30–17:00

Director: Mariia Dmitrievna Kashirina (*tel.* 350-89-06)
Chief Curator: Natal'ia Aleksandrovna Grigor'eva

HISTORY:

The museum was founded in 1975 to portray the history of the M. I. Kalinin Factory.

The factory itself was founded in 1869 as the St. Petersburg Ammunition Factory. In 1892, it was renamed the Petersburg Pipe and Instrument Factory (*Peterburgskii trubochnyi i instrumental'nyi zavod*), under the patronage of P. B. Baranovskii, although it also continued to produce ammunition. Known as the St. Petersburg (and subsequently Petrograd) Pipe Factory (*Peterburgskii trubochnyi zavod*) from 1900–1922, thereafter it took the name of Bolshevik revolutionary leader Mikhail Ivanovich Kalinin (1875–1946). During the late 1930s the factory produced machine tools as well as ammunition, and during the Second World War, it became famous for its production of rocket projectors.

HOLDINGS: ca. 10,000 units, late 19th c.–1990s

The main and subsidiary fonds hold photographs and documents on the history of the plant and on the work and public activity of the workers and the engineering and technical personnel, both before the October Revolution and during the Soviet period.

Access: Access to the museum is free, and documentation is available to bona fide researchers.

Working Conditions: Researchers are accommodated in the museum offices, where materials are available the day they are ordered.

Reference Facilities: There are official documents of receipt and transfer of materials, registers of acquisitions to the main and the subsidiary fonds, inventory card catalogues, and card catalogues of "honored Kalinin Plant workers," who have been awarded medals and decorations.

Library Facilities: The Scientific-Technical Library of the factory (ca. 70,000 vols.) was founded in 1929. It holds literature on engineering and radio electronics, as well as standard technical documentation. There are subject card catalogues.

Copying: Photographic and xerox copies may be prepared.

FINDING AIDS — PUBLISHED — GENERAL:

Biblioteki SPb (1993), p. 118.

There is no published guide to the archival materials in the museum.

Istoriko-proizvodstvennyi muzei Sankt-Peterburgskoi obuvnoi fabriki "Skorokhod"
[Historico-Manufacturing Museum of the St. Petersburg Skorokhod Shoe Factory]

Agency: Aktsionernoe obshchestvo otkrytogo tipa (AOOT) "Roslegprom"
[Roslegprom Open Joint-Stock Company]

Address: 196084, St. Petersburg, ul. Zastavskaia, 33
Telephone: 298-92-40; *Fax:* (812) 296-93-02
Transport: metro: Moskovskie vorota
Hours: museum closed; research by appointment

Director of the Factory: Nikolai Ivanovich Peregudov (*tel.* 298-35-32)
Acting Director of the Museum: Natal'ia Evgen'evna Romanova
Head of the Archive: Elena Anatol'evna Popova (*tel.* 298-92-91)

HISTORY:

Istoriko-proizvodstvennyi muzei Sankt-Peterburgskoi obuvnoi fabriki "Skorokhod" im. Ia. A. Kalinina
[Historico-Manufacturing Museum of the Ia. A. Kalinin St. Petersburg Skorokhod Shoe Factory]

The Historico-Manufacturing Museum of the Skorokhod Shoe Factory was founded in 1971.

The factory itself was founded in 1882 by a German joint-stock company, the Association of St. Petersburg Mechanized Shoe Manufacturers (*Tovarishchestvo Sankt-Peterburgskogo mekhanicheskogo proizvodstva obuvi*). In 1910 it was renamed the Skorokhod Association of St. Petersburg Mechanized Shoe Manufacturers (*Tovarishchestvo Sankt-Peterburgskogo mekhanicheskogo proizvodstva obuvi "Skorokhod"*) (*skorohod* is the Russian word for "footman" or "runner").

In 1918 the factory was nationalized and renamed the Skorokhod First State Shoe Factory (*Pervaia gosudarstvennaia obuvnaia fabrika "Skorokhod"*). In 1922 it was given the added honorific name of the Bolshevik worker in the Skorokhod Factory, Iakov Andreevich Kalinin (1980–1919), who became Chairman of the Factory Committee and Leader of the Bolshevik Party Branch and one of the organizers of the Red Guards. In 1962 the factory was consolidated with the Second Skorokhod factory and renamed the Ia. A. Kalinin "Skorokhod" Shoe Manufacturing Association (*Proizvodstvennoe obuvnoe ob"edinenie "Skorokhod" im. Ia. A. Kalinina*).

Foreign collaboration began in 1987, and in 1990 the Production Association was liquidated and then became part of a larger foreign economic, manufacturing and trade concern, Interlenprom. The factory dropped the name of Kalinin, and, since privatization, has been operated by the Roslegprom (the acronym for "Russian light industry") Open Joint-Stock Company. Unfortunately, the museum has not been maintained as it was during the Soviet period, and is now officially closed to visitors, although much of the documentation and exhibits remain intact.

N.B. The main extant part of the prerevolutionary factory records are held in TsGIA SPb (D–13, fond 1221—1,380 units, 1882–1918); records for the years 1918–1975 are held in TsGA SPb (D–12).

HOLDINGS: ca. 20,000 units, 1882–1990s
photographs and negatives—17,444 units (1890s to present)

Archival materials in the museum constitute documentation that has not been designated to be transferred for permanent retention in state archives, but that retains significant historic interest.

There are originals and copies of important documents, together with photographs and films concerning the history of the factory.

Among these are the memoirs of war and labor veterans; documentation on the activities of political and social organizations in the factory; personal documents of well-known production managers, engineers, and workers (including official identity cards, CPSU and Komsomol cards, entry permits, labor-record books, certificates of awards, documents of planning reports and inventions, diplomas and certificates); and materials relating to socialist emulation competitions. There is a special collection of documents relating to the wartime years (1941–1945).

There are films about the Skorokhod Factory. Photographs (starting in 1890) include negatives and prints of labor veterans; views of the factory buildings, production lines, installations, interiors of shop floors, divisions, and laboratories; pictures of equipment; materials relating to sporting events and collaborative patronage arrangements (*shefskaia pomoshch'*), among others.

The current archive of the factory holds documents for the years 1927–1989 relating to its work force (orders, personal data cards, personnel files, and personal accounts, etc). It also holds the main factory administrative records covering the basic activities of the enterprise for the years 1976 to 1990 (designated for permanent retention), which are scheduled to be transferred to TsGA SPb (D–12).

Access: Access to archival materials in the museum or the factory archive requires a letter addressed to the factory director, stating the subject and aim of the proposed research. As of fall 1998, the factory museum is not normally open to visitors, but special arrangements can be made for researchers.

Working Conditions: Researchers are accommodated in the museum offices, where materials are available the day they are ordered.

Reference Facilities: There are *opisi* of the materials which have been arranged and card catalogues of factory personnel files.

Library Facilities: The Scientific-Technical Library of the factory (ca. 100,000 vols.) was founded in 1924. It specializes in literature relating to shoe manufacturing.

Copying: Xerox copies can be prepared.

FINDING AIDS — PUBLISHED — GENERAL:

Muzei SPb (1994), p. 159; *Biblioteki SPb* (1993), p. 152; *Peterburg* (1992), p. 250, 577.

There is no published guide to the archival materials in the museum.

h-699. *Istoriia Leningradskoi Gosudarstvennoi obuvnoi fabriki "Skorokhod" im. Ia. Kalinina.* [Leningrad], 1969.

Istoricheskii muzei Aktsionernogo obshchestva otkrytogo tipa (AOOT) "Sevkabel'"

[Historical Museum of the Sevkabel' Open Joint-Stock Company]

Agency: Aktsionernoe obshchestvo otkrytogo tipa (AOOT) "Sevkabel'"
[Sevkabel' (Northern Cable) Open Joint-Stock Company]

Address: 199106, St. Petersburg, Vasil'evskii ostrov, Kozhevennaia liniia, 40
Telephone: (trade union secretary): 217-23-23; *Fax:* (812) 217-28-30 (factory)
Transport: metro: Primorskaia; trol.: 10; bus: 128, 151
Hours: M–Th (by appointment)

Director: Tamara Semenovna Tarasova (*tel.* local 118)
Trade-Union Committee Chairman: Iurii Iakovlevich Sipovich (*tel.* 217-23-23)

HISTORY:

Muzei istorii proizvodstvennogo ob"edineniia "Sevkabel'"
[Museum of History of the Sevkabel' Manufacturing Association] (1979–1993)

The Historical Museum of the Sevkabel' (Northern Cable) Company was founded in 1979 with public funding to mark the centennial of the opening of the original plant. Since 1986 the museum has been under the control of the factory Trade Union Committee.

The original plant was founded in 1879 by the St. Petersburg subsidiary of the German company Siemens and Galske Joint-Stock Company. It was nationalized and renamed after 1917. In 1975 the Northern Cable Plant (*Severnyi kabel'nyi zavod*) joined the Scientific-Research, Project Construction Design, and Technological Cable Institute (*Nauchno-issledovatel'skii, proektno-konstruktorskii i tekhnologicheskii kabel'nyi institut*) to form the Sevkabel' Production Group. Since 1993 Sevkabel' has been a public joint-stock company, specializing in electrical engineering.

N.B. The archives of the Siemens and Galske Joint-Stock Company of Russian Electrical Engineering Plants are held in TsGIA SPb (D–13, fond 1249, 1,390 units—1854–1918); factory records relating to the Sevkabel' Plant for the Soviet period are held in TsGA SPb (D–12).

HOLDINGS: 738 units, 1899–1990s

The museum holds a small collection of documents on the history of the plant starting from the prerevolutionary time of the predecessor Siemens and Galske Joint-Stock Company of Russian Electrical Engineering Plants. There are documents relating to such matters as worker involvement in the revolutionary movement; the work of CP and Komsomol organizations; defense work during the Siege of Leningrad; and the factory products and technical research. There are also materials on the best-known "hero" workers, particularly Aleksandr and Anna Kirillovna Zalomov, who were the inspiration for the main characters in Gor'kii's novel "Mother" (*Mat'*).

Access: Entry into the Sevkabel' Plant requires advance arrangements with the museum director for a pass. Hence a prior appointment should be arranged by telephone, following the delivery of a letter stating the subject and purpose of research.

Working Conditions: Researchers are accommodated in the museum offices, where materials are available the day they are ordered.

Reference Facilities: There are inventory registers for staff use.

Library Facilities: The Scientific-Technical Library (ca. 50,000 volumes) was founded in 1929. It holds literature on electrical engineering and economics. In addition to openly published literature, there is technical regulatory documentation, reports on scientific research and experimental design work, and manuscript dissertations. There are reference card catalogues. (Library tel.: 217-85-65).

Copying: Xerox copies can be made through the plant administration.

FINDING AIDS — PUBLISHED — GENERAL:

Muzei SPb (1994), p. 157; *Biblioteki SPb* (1993), p. 100; *Peterburg* (1992), p. 568.

There is no published guide to the archival materials in the museum.

h-700. Shitov, M. A. *Severnyi kabel'nyi: Istoriia Leningradskogo proizvodstvennogo ob"edineniia "Sevkabel'."* Leningrad: Lenizdat, 1979. 261 p.

> Published to mark the centennial of the factory, the volume—based partly on materials held in the museum—gives an account of factory history, particularly during the Soviet period.

Muzei istorii Aktsionernogo obshchestva "Izhorskii zavod"
[Museum of the History of the Izhora Factory Joint-Stock Company]

Agency: Aktsionernoe obshchestvo (AO) "Izhorskii zavod"
[Izhora Factory Joint-Stock Company]

Address: 189630, St. Petersburg, Kolpino, Sovetskii bul'var, 29; Dvorets kul'tury i tekhniki "Izhorskii" (entrance from the rear of no. 4)
Telephone: 481-85-84
Transport: metro: Zvezdnaia + bus 296 to Kolpino;
or Kolpino suburban train to "Izhorskii zavod"
Hours: M–F 9:00–17:00

Director: Galina Alekseevna Efimova (*tel.* 484-15-43)

HISTORY:

The museum, devoted to the historic Izhora Factory in the vicinity of St. Petersburg, was established in 1967.

The factory itself was founded in 1722 by order of Peter I, under the Admiralty *prikaz*, and was known as the Admiralty Izhora Factory, and later the Admiralty and Mechanical Factory (*Izhorskii admiralteiskii i mekhanicheskii zavod*). In 1803 it was reorganized for the production of heavy machinery and machine-tools, but continued also to produce naval vessels, and later armoured vehicles.

Nationalized after 1917, it was known in the interwar period and during World War II for its production of sheet metal, heavy machinery (including tanks), and heavy construction equipment. During the postwar period, among other things, it produced equipment and fittings for nuclear power stations. From 1948 through 1989 the factory bore the honorific name of A. A. Zhdanov. Since privatization, it has operated has been the Izhora Factory Joint-Stock Company.

HOLDINGS: statistics not available

The museum retains significant archival materials, consisting of documents, photographs, and other graphic materials on the history of the factory. These include diaries and memoirs of workers and plant foremen.

N.B. Remaining prerevolutionary factory records are held in TsGIA SPb (D–13). Postrevolutionary records are held in TsGA SPb (D–12).

Comment: A questionnaire about the archival holdings in the museum was not returned to Rosarkhiv.

FINDING AIDS — PUBLISHED — GENERAL:

Peterburg (1992), p. 231.

There is no published description of the archival materials in the museum.

h-701. Pozdtakov, O. A. *Izhortsy: Kratkii ocherk istorii Izhorskogo Ordena Lenina i Ordena Trudovogo Krasnogo Znameni zavoda im. A. A. Zhdanova (1722–1960).* Leningrad: Lenizdat, 1960. 300 p. + plates.

Provides an account of factory history.

h-702. Zav'ialov, Sergei Ivanovich. *Izhorskii zavod.* Vol. 1. Leningrad, 1976. 366 p. + plates. "Istoriia fabrik i zavodov." (Lib: MH)

1st ED.: *Istoriia Izhorskogo zavoda.* Vol. 1. Edited by M. P. Baklaikin, B. P. Pozern, and G. S. Zaidel'. M.: "Istoriia zavodov", 1934. 410 p.

Vol. 2: Kutuzov, Evgenii Vasil'evich; Efimova, Galina Alekseevna; Irklei, Aleksandr Samoilovich. *Izhorskii zavod.* Leningrad, 1974. 381 p. "Istoriia fabrik i zavodov." (Lib: MH)

*Efimova, G. A., Tiutenkov, A. G. *Izhorskii zavod.* Vol. 3. Leningrad, 1988.

Provides a detailed, although undocumented, history of the factory—based on archival documents, including some materials held in the museum. The first edition of the first volume prepared in the 1930s includes detailed descriptions of the documentation from the factory records used in preparation of each chapter, before they were transferred to state archival custody.

Sankt-Peterburgskii gosudarstvennyi muzei khleba

[St. Petersburg State Bread Museum]

Agency: Komitet po kul'ture Administratsii Sankt-Peterburga
[Committee on Culture of the Administration of St. Petersburg]

Address:	191040, St. Petersburg, Ligovskii prosp., 73
Telephone:	164-11-10; *Fax:* (812) 164-13-59
Website:	http://www:museum.ru/bread/; http://www.bakery.spb.ru
Transport:	metro: Ligovskii prospekt; Ploshchad' Vosstaniia;
	tram: 10, 25, 44, 49; trol.: 42
Hours:	M–F 10:00–17:00 (research—by appointment)

Director: Marina Dmitrievna Iakoleva
Chief Curator: Liubov' Iur'evna Berezovskaia

HISTORY:

Muzei istorii khlebopecheniia (MIKh)
[Museum of the History of Bread-Baking] (1988–1993)

The unique Museum of the History of Bread-Baking (MIKh) was opened to the public in 1988, under the auspices of the Ministry of Bread Products of the RSFSR (*Ministerstvo khleboproduktov RSFSR*). From 1991 until July of 1993 it was under the administrative jurisdiction of the Petersburg Bread Territorial Manufacturing Association (*Territorial'noe proizvodstvennoe ob"edinenie "Petrokhleb"*). In 1993 it was granted the status of a "state" museum, and is now under the Committee on Culture of the Administration of St. Petersburg.

HOLDINGS: ca. 5,000 units, 1794–1990s

The museum holds historical, ethnographic, and technological documents on the history of bread-baking and the production of other cereal products.

Access: Research access requires a passport or other identification card.

Working Conditions: Researchers are accommodated in the museum offices, where materials are available the day they are ordered.

Reference Facilities: There are inventory registers and inventory card catalogues for staff use. Descriptive data on the museum holdings are currently being computerized.

Library Facilities: The Book Fond (ca. 2,000 vols.) holds literature on the ethnography of eating habits throughout the world and the history of bread-baking in Russia, including recipes for bakery products. There is a facts-and-figures card catalogue.

Copying: Xerox copies can be prepared.

FINDING AIDS — PUBLISHED — GENERAL:

Muzei SPb (1994), p. 139; *Biblioteki SPb* (1993), p. 153.

There is no published guide to the archival materials in the museum.

Additional Museums with Archival Holdings

Information about the following museums has become available since the 1997 Russian version of the Moscow-St. Petersburg directory appeared and since the latest Rosarkhiv questionnaires and follow-up inquiries were processed. Most of these listings are incomplete, and inadequately verified for integration into Part H of the directory itself. In many cases, the institutions were established—or acquired significant archival materials—relatively recently and hence did not appear in earlier directories. In other cases, they had not responded to questionnaires, and information about their archival holdings was not otherwise available. Rather than omit them entirely, we present preliminary listings here. Although it was not feasible to visit each museum, many of them have kindly responded to telephone inquiries, but not all could not be canvassed. More complete listings based on questionnaires specifically oriented to archival holdings and available reference facilities for researchers are planned for an expanded version of the ArcheoBiblioBase datafiles.

Coverage of these museums has benefited particularly from the newly published directory of Moscow museums, *Vse muzei Moskvy* (1997) (a-94), the electronic data from "Muzei Rossii/ Museums of Russia" (1996–) available on the Internet (a-90), and several other recent specialized directories, all of which are listed above in Part A–4. References to published listings in such directories are cited in all cases, as explained in the Procedural Introduction.

Moscow

Historical Museums

⸻ H–150 ⸻

Vystavochnyi zal "Muzei Izmailovo"/
Muzei Rossiiskoi imperatorskoi familii
[Izmailovo Museum Exhibition Hall/ Museum of the Russian Imperial Family]

Address: 105023, Moscow, pl. Zhuravleva, ul. Malaia Semenovskaia, 1
Telephone: 963-89-95
Transport: metro: Elektrozavodskaia; trol.: 22, 32; bus: 36
Hours: M–F 11:00–18:00

HISTORY:

The museum was founded as the Izmailovo Exhibition Hall in 1992 on the basis of the Pervomaiskii Raion Regional Studies Museum. In 1995 the Exhibition Hall was consolidated with the Memorial Museum of the Russian Imperial Family, which had been founded in 1994. It occupies the premises of the Nosov House, which was constructed in 1880 for the wealthy textile merchant Vasilii Dmitrievich Nosov, who was associated by marriage with a number of other prominent Moscow families.

HOLDINGS:

The museum has brought together an extensive collection of exhibits, especially relating to the imperial family, including original documents, photographs, portraits, graphic materials, books, and numismatic collections, among others. An important collection of materials donated by the family of Grand Duke Vladimir Kirillovich Romanov includes documents, photographs, and personal memorabilia. The museum has collected additional photographs, documentation, and other personal effects of the imperial family.

Library Facilities: The museum has a large collection of books and reference materials on the history of Moscow.

FINDING AIDS — PUBLISHED — GENERAL:

Muzei Moskvy (1997), pp. 76–78.

Muzei "Dom na naberezhnoi"
["House on the Embankment" Museum]

Address: 103073, Moscow, ul. Serafimovicha, 2, pod"ezd 1
Telephone: 231-38-92
Transport: metro: Polianka; Borovitskaia; trol.: 33, 1, 8; bus: 6
Hours: W 17:00–20:00; Sa 14:00–17:00

HISTORY:

The museum opened in 1989 in the so-called "House on the Embankment," sometimes known as "Government House," where many well-known government and cultural figures lived. The building was made famous by the novel of the same name by Iurii V. Trifonov, who grew up in that large complex built during the years 1927–1931 (on the plans of the architect B. M. Iofan). Because many of its notorious inhabitants were subsequently repressed during the Stalin epoch, it became known as the "Brotherly Grave (*Bratskaia Mogila*)."

HOLDINGS:

The museum has collected many personal effects and memorabilia of its former inhabitants, including documents, books, and photographs.

FINDING AIDS — PUBLISHED — GENERAL:

Muzei Moskvy (1997), p. 72.

Muzei rossiiskikh metsenatov i blagotvoritelei
[Museum of Russian Patrons and Philanthropists]

Agency: Independent social organization

Address: 117049, Moscow, ul. Donskaia, 9
Telephone: 237-53-49; *Fax:* (095) 956-31-05
Website: http://moscow.lvl.ru/culture/museum/metsen/metsen.html
Transport: metro: Oktiabr'skaia
Hours: M–F 13:00–18:00

Director: Mariia Anatol'evna Veselova
Chief Curaror: Lev Nikolaevich Krasnopevtsev

HISTORY:

The museum was established in 1992 in the house where the late nineteenth-century Moscow philanthropist I. G. Prostiakov opened a special school, and which later housed an international organization for Russian famine relief.

HOLDINGS:

The museum has been collecting documentary materials and memorabilia relating to philanthropy in Russia and to individual wealthy Russian philanthropists, such as the Bakhrushin, Guchkov, Sytin, Tret'iakov, and Shekhtel' families.

FINDING AIDS — PUBLISHED — GENERAL:

Muzei Moskvy (1997), pp. 73–74.

Tsentr muzeinykh initsiativ "Kuntsevo"
[Kuntsevo Center for Museum Initiatives]

Agency: Regional social organization

Address:	121357, Moscow, proezd Zagorskogo, 23
Telephone:	444-03-66
Transport:	metro: Kuntsevskaia + bus 190, 610, 612, 45; Kievskaia + bus 157, 505
Hours:	M–Su 10:00–19:00

Director: Valentina Vasil'evna Kutia
Chief Curaror: Larisa Anatol'evna Bogatova

HISTORY:

Kuntsevskii kraevedcheskii muzei [Kuntsevo Regional Studies Museum] (1963–1989)
Muzei-klub "Kuntsevo" [Kuntsevo Museum-Club] (1989–1996)

The Kuntsevo Regional Studies Museum was established in 1963 in a building that was originally constructed in the late nineteenth century as a dacha for a wealthy banker in the village of Zhukovka. Initially the Regional Studies Museum collected materials relating to archeology, nineteenth-century life, and World War II. The museum was reorganized in 1989 as the Kuntsevo Museum Club, and became associated with the Russian Association of UNESCO clubs. Its present name dates from 1996.

HOLDINGS:

The museum retains documents dating from the beginning of the nineteenth century to the present. Emphasis is on local documentation, including personal papers of well-known individuals associated with the village of Kuntsevo. There are also significant documentary holdings relating to World War II.

Working Conditions: A special room is available for researchers.

Reference Facilities: There are card catalogues for all of the documentary materials. A computer database is being started.

FINDING AIDS — PUBLISHED — GENERAL:

Muzei Moskvy (1997), pp. 74–76.

Dom-muzei Ia. V. Briusa
[Jacob Bruce House-Museum]

Address: Moskovskaia oblast', Shchelkovskii raion, sanatorii "Monino"
Telephone: (095) 971-37-18
Transport: suburban train from Iaroslavl Station to Monino + bus 32
(stop "Sanatorii 'Monino'")
Hours: WSu 10:00–14:00

HISTORY:

The recently established museum honors Jacob Bruce (Iakov Vilimovich Brius) (1669–1735), a decendent of the kings of Scotland, who was one of the foreign advisors of Peter I and took Russian citizenship. Under Peter I, he was a senator and president of the Mining and Manufacturing Collegium. The museum is housed on an early Moscow-region estate, Glinka, which was prominent in the eighteenth century, but which never belonged to Bruce himself.

N.B. The personal library of Jacob Bruce is now held in BAN (G–16), where a scholarly catalogue was issued in 1989 (see g-309).

HOLDINGS:

The museum has gathered copies of archival documents relating to Bruce and the epoch of the reforms of Peter I. Exhibits present considerable information about the history of the Russian Army, artillery, and Navy during the late seventeenth and early eighteenth century.

Historico-Architectural Museums and Museum-Preserves

✳— H–155 —✳

Gosudarstvennyi istoriko-arkhitekturnyi i prirodno-landshaftnyi muzei-zapovednik "Tsaritsyno"
[Tsaritsyno State Historico-Architectural
and Natural-Landscape Museum-Preserve]

Agency: Ministerstvo kul'tury RF (Minkul'tury Rossii)
[Ministry of Culture]

Address: 115569, Moscow, ul. Dol'skaia, 1
Telephone: 321-07-43; *Fax:* (095) 321-07-43
Transport: metro: Orekhovo, Tsaritsyno
Hours: W–F 11:00–18:00; SaSu 10:00–18:00;
October–April: W–F 11:00–16:00; SaSu 10:00–16:00

Director: Vsevolod Ivanovich Anikovich (*tel.* 321-63-66)
Scientific Secretary: Valentina Petrovna Mashkova
Chief Curaror: Liudmila Grigor'evna Kleiman

HISTORY:

The Tsaritsyno State Historico-Architectural and Natural-Landscape Museum-Preserve has existed as a museum for only a little over ten years in the park and architectural ensemble purchased in 1775 by Empress Catherine II from the Kantemir family. At the end of the sixteenth century under the name of Chernaia griaz (Black Mud), there had been a country estate for Boris Godunov's sister Irina Godunova, wife of Tsar Feodor I, but the main buildings were destroyed during the Polish invasion of 1612. Later the village of Bogoroditskoe was inherited by the Golitsyn family, but Peter I presented it to Dmitri Kantemir of Moldavia. After Catherine II purchased the property, the palace and gardens were reconstructed as a suburban summer Moscow residence for the empress. The main palace ensemble erected in 1789–1782 on plans of the architect V. I. Bazhenov displeased the empress, and it was subsequently reconstructed on plans of the architect M. F. Kazakov. After the Revolution, a museum was established on the estate, but it was closed down in 1932.

Collecting materials for a reconstructed museum in Tsaritsyno started in the 1960s under the Ministry of Culture, but it was only in the mid-1980s that the museum was formally reestablished with the intention that it would house a state museum of decorative and applied arts of the peoples of the USSR. Since the mid-1980s the museum collections have been extensively expanded. Restoration of the main palace ensemble began in the early 1990s, with the opening of one of the buildings in 1994. It was given the status of a "museum-preserve" in 1993 and considered a monument of history and culture of federal significance.

Although most important are its collections of contemporary decorative and applied arts, including porcelain, as well as folk art collections, there are some archival materials of interest.

Arkhiv i Biblioteka
[Archive and Library]

Head: Georgii Sergeevich Piggot (*tel.* 393-05-86)

HOLDINGS: ca. 2,500 units, 1836–present

The archive and library of the museum retain documentation and related reference materials pertaining to the history of the Tsaritsyno imperial residence, its reconstruction, and to the collections of decorative and applied arts that have been gathered in the present museum.

FINDING AIDS — PUBLISHED — GENERAL:

Muzei Moskvy (1997), pp. 179–83.

h-752. *Tsaritsyno.* Compiled by T. E. Berdnikova, O. V. Dokuchaeva, et al. Edited by V. E. Sokolov et al. Moscow, 1996. 64 p. [Sovet po izucheniiu i okhrane kul'turnogo i prirodnogo naslediia pri Prezidiume RAN] (Lib: MH)
> A brief tourist pamphlet with details about history and natural setting.

h-753. Sergeev, Igor' Nikolaevich. *Tsaritsyno. Stranitsy istorii: [Putevoditel'].* Moscow, 1993. 250 p. + plates. Includes English preface. (Lib: MH)
> A popular history of the estate with illustrations, historical plan, a list of architects involved, and bibliography.

h-754. Mineeva, Klavdiia Ivanovna. *Tsaritsyno: Dvortsovo-parkovyi ansambl'.* Moscow: "Iskusstvo," 1988. 133 p. + plates. Includes English resumés and captions. (Lib: MH-F)
> A beautifully illustrated history of the estate with reproductions of its buildings and various historical plans.

Art Museums

·— H–156 *—·*

Memorial'nyi muzei-masterskaia S. T. Konenkova— Filial Nauchno-issledovatel'skogo muzeia Rossiiskoi Akademii khudozhestv (NIM RAKh)
[S. T. Konenkov Memorial Studio-Museum— Branch of the Scientific Research Museum of the Russian Academy of Arts]

Agency: Rossiiskaia Akademiia khudozhestv (RAKh)
[Russian Academy of Arts]

Address: 103009, Moscow, ul. Tverskaia, 17
Telephone: 229-44-72; 229-61-39
Website: http://moscow.lvl.ru/culture/museum/konenkov/konen.html
Transport: metro: Pushkinskaia, Tverskaia, Chekhovskaia
Hours: W–Su 11:00–19:00

Director: Tat'iana Ivanovna Krauts (*tel.* 229-61-39)
Chief Curaror: Svetlana Leonidovna Bobrova

HISTORY:

The museum was established in 1974 honoring the centennial of the birth of the Russian sculptor and graphic artist Sergei Timofeevich Konenkov (1874–1971), in the house where he spent the last third of his life, after he received special permission to return from emigration in the United States (1923–1945). It is administered as a branch of the Scientific Research Museum of the Russian Academy of Arts in St. Petersburg (H–90).

HOLDINGS:

In addition to sculpture and personal memorabilia, the museum retains original autographs and other documents, as well as unique negatives and photographs of the sculptor and his work.

FINDING AIDS — PUBLISHED — GENERAL:

Muzei Moskvy (1997), pp. 103–07.

Muzei im. N. K. Rerikha
[N. K. Roerich Museum]

Agency: Mezhdunarodnyi tsentr Rerikhov
[International Roerich Center]

Address:	121019, Moscow, Malyi Znamenskii per., 3/5
Telephone:	203-79-88
Transport:	metro: Kropotkinskaia, Borovitskaia
Hours:	TuThSa 11:00–19:00

HISTORY:

The museum was founded in 1991, under the auspices of the International Roerich (Rerikh) Center, and opened to the public in February 1993, honoring the Russian artist, archeologist, and philosopher Nikolai Konstantinovich Roerich (Rerikh) (1874–1947) and his family. Roerich, a graduate of the Russian Academy of Arts, was one of the initiators of the World of Art (*Mir iskusstva*) movement, before he left Russia. He lived with his family in India starting in the 1920s, and also spent considerable time in emigration in the United States. The museum is now located in the elegant columned eighteenth-century mansion in the Lopukhin estate within the Belyi gorod (White City) region of Moscow.

Although the name of the museum honors N. K. Roerich, it also includes materials relating to his wife, Elena Ivanovna Roerich (Rerikh) (1879–1955), who was interested in philosophy, culture, and art of Europe and Asia, and their sons. The elder son, Iurii Nikolaevich (1902–1960), was a prominent Oriental scholar. The younger, Sviatoslav Nikolaevich (1904–1993), also an artist, was one of the initiators of the museum and arranged the transfer of his father's paintings from India in 1989. The museum was opened to the public in 1993, soon after the death of Sviatoslav Roerich.

N.B. Additional papers of N. K. Roerich are now held in RGALI (B–7—fond 2408) and in the State Tret'iakov Gallery (H–23—fond 44). There is also a special collection and memorial cabinet exhibit for Roerich in the State Museum of the Orient (H–29). A memorial cabinet was established for his son Iurii Nikolaevich in the library of the Institute of Oriental Studies (E–4), after it acquired his rich collections relating to Tibet and Indian studies. Also of note is the Nicholas Roerich Museum located in New York City (address: 319 West 107th Street, New York, NY 10025; tel: 212-864-7752; fax: 212-864-7704; e-mail: director@roerich.org; website: http://www.roerich.org).

HOLDINGS:

Of particular importance in terms of archives, many of Roerich's papers, personal library, and memorabilia have been brought together by the museum, including those that have been returned from India with his paintings.

Library Facilities: The library of the International Roerich Center (*Biblioteka Mezhdunarodnogo tsentra Rerikhov*), first organized in 1990, has been expanding its collections relating to cultural history, philosophy, theosophy, religion, folklore, and Oriental studies. (Library tel.: 203-88-22; website: http://www.openweb.ru/windows/mcr).

FINDING AIDS — PUBLISHED — GENERAL:

Muzei Moskvy (1997), pp. 117–20.

Moskovskii gosudarstvennyi muzei Vadima Sidura
[Vadim Sidur Moscow State Museum]

Agency: Komitet po kul'ture Pravitel'stva Moskvy
[Committee on Culture of the Government of Moscow]

Address: 111394, Moscow, ul. Novogireevskaia, 37, stroenie 2
Telephone: 918-51-81; *Fax:* (095) 918-56-33
E-mail: mvs@glasnet.ru
Website: http://www.glasnet.ru/ m̄vs
Transport: metro: Perovo
Hours: W–Su 12:00–19:00

Director: Mikhail Vadimovich Sidur (*tel.* 918-51-82)
Chief Curaror: Galina Artemovna Sidur

HISTORY:

Muzei Vadima Sidura [Vadim Sidur Museum] (1989-1995)

The Museum of Vadim Sidur was established in July 1989 in the Perovo Exhibition Hall, where exhibits of the work of the repressed Soviet Russian sculptor and graphic artist Vadim Abramovich Sidur (1924–1986) first opened in Moscow in 1987 in the face of great political opposition. The museum was raised to the status of a state museum by decree of Moscow Mayor Yurii M. Luzhkov in 1995. The museum honoring Sidur has collected significant materials relating to the artist and to unofficial art in the Soviet Union during the 1950s through 1980s.

HOLDINGS:

Of particular importance in terms of archives, the museum has collected considerable documentation and memorabilia relating to Sidur, including some from abroad. There are some copies of documents confiscated by the KGB that have been transferred to the museum from the FSB archive. The museum also holds the personal papers of several other unofficial artists, including A. S. Slepyshev and Iu. N. Larin.

FINDING AIDS — PUBLISHED — GENERAL:

Muzei Moskvy (1997), pp. 121–22.

Muzei narodnoi grafiki
[Museum of Folk Graphic Arts]

Agency: Komitet po kul'ture Pravitel'stva Moskvy
[Committee on Culture of the Government of Moscow]

Address: 103045, Moscow, Malyi Golovin per., 10
Telephone: 208-51-82
Website: http://.moscow.lvl.ru/culture/museum/narodg/narodg.html
Transport: metro: Sukharevskaia, Turgenevskaia, Chistye prudy
Hours: Tu–F 10:00–18:00

Director: Viktor Petrovich Penzin
Deputy Director: Lollii Petrovich Zamoiskii
Chief Curaror: Elena Ivanovna Tatukova

HISTORY:

The museum was established in 1992 on the initiative of folk artist Viktor Petrovich Penzin with the support of the Committee on Culture of the Moscow City Government. Most of the exhibits came from Penzin's own historical collection.

HOLDINGS: ca. 6,000 units, late XVII s.–to present

The museum retains an exceptionally rich collection of Russian *lubok*, the popular folk wood-block prints, which for exhibit purposes have been arranged in an historical context starting with the eighteenth century. Among its earliest holdings is the Bible illustrated by V. Koren' (1692–1696). Exhibits and other graphic holdings within the museum fonds, include the work of late eighteeenth- and early nineteenth century artists I. I. Terebenev and A. G. Venetsianov; early twentieth-century *lubok* of K. S. Malevich, A. V. Lentulov, D. S. Moor (*pseud. of* D. S. Orlov), and G. I. Narbut, among others; *lubok* from the 1930s of V. Kulikov and B. M. Kustodiev; as well as more contemporary *lubok* and other graphic materials in the tradition of popular folk arts.

FINDING AIDS — PUBLISHED — GENERAL:

Muzei Moskvy (1997), pp. 110–11.

Literary and Bibliophile Museums

❋⊰ H–160 ⊱❋

Moskovskii gosudarstvennyi muzei S. A. Esenina
[S. A. Esenin Moscow State Museum]

Agency: Komitet po kul'ture Pravitel'stva Moskvy
[Committee on Culture of the Government of Moscow]

Address: 113054, Moscow, Bol'shoi Strochenovskii per., 24, stroenie 2
Telephone: 958-16-74; 954-97-64; *Fax:* 958-16-74
Transport: metro: Serpukhovskaia
Hours: M–Sa 10:00–18:00

Director: Svetlana Nikolaevna Shetrakova
Chief Curator: Svetlana Petrovna Esenina

HISTORY:

The museum honoring the Russian poet Sergei Aleksandrovich Esenin (sometimes Yesenin in English) (1895–1925), opened in 1995 to mark the centennial of his birth, in the house where Esenin lived from 1911 to 1918. It received official state status in 1996.

N.B. Some Esenin papers are held in RGALI (B–7—fond 190), while most other Esenin personal effects are held in the Konstantinovo Memorial House-Museum in Riazan Oblast.

HOLDINGS:

The museum has already gathered a small collection of original documentary and audiovisual materials, including photographs and memorabilia, and is actively acquiring additional sources.

FINDING AIDS — PUBLISHED — GENERAL:

Muzei Moskvy (1997), pp. 222–23.

Kul'turnyi tsentr "Dom-muzei Mariny Tsvetaevoi"
[Marina Tsvetaeva House-Museum Cultural Center]

Agency: Komitet po kul'ture Pravitel'stva Moskvy
[Committee on Culture of the Government of Moscow]

Address:	121069, Moscow, Borisoglebskii per., 6
Telephone:	202-35-43
Website:	http://moscow.lvl.ru/culture/museum/tsvet/tsvet.html
Transport:	metro: Arbatskaia; Smolenskaia; trol.: 2
Hours:	Tu–Su 12:00–17:00

Director: Esfir' Semenovna Krasovskaia
Chief Curator: Dmitrii Anatol'evich Beliaev (*tel.* 203-53-69)

HISTORY:

The museum was opened in 1992 in the house in the Arbat district, where the poetess Marina Ivanovna Tsvetaeva (1892–1941) lived during the years 1914–1922, before her emigration. The museum started under the auspices of the Russian International Cultural Fond, but it has since been registered under the Government of Moscow.

There are several other memorial museums honoring Tsvetaeva in the Moscow region, for which visits and research can be arranged through the Tsvetaeva Center.

HOLDINGS:

In addition to personal effects and memorabilia, the museum has already collected some original documentation, including letters to and from Tsvetaeva, as well as part of her library with autographs and marginalia.

Working Conditions: A reading room is available for researchers.

Reference Facilities: There are card catalogues for all of the documentary materials. A computer database is being started.

Library Facilities: The museum library has developed an extensive collection of publications by and relating to Tsvetaeva, her family, and literary circle (tel. 203-59-97).

FINDING AIDS — PUBLISHED — GENERAL:

Muzei Moskvy (1997), pp. 230–31.

Moskovskii literaturnyi muzei-tsentr K. G. Paustovskogo
[K. G. Paustovskii Moscow Literary Museum Center]

Agency: Komitet po kul'ture Pravitel'stva Moskvy
[Committee on Culture of the Government of Moscow]

Address: 109472, Moscow, Kuz'minki-Zarech'e, Kuz'minskii park, 17
Telephone: 172-77-91
Transport: metro: Riazanskii prospekt + bus 29; Tekstil'shchiki, Vykhino + trol. 38
Hours: WSaSu 14:00–17:00

Director: Il'ia Il'ich Komarov
Deputy Director: Aleksei Aleksandrovich Kirilenko

HISTORY:

Narodnyi shkol'nyi muzei K. G. Paustovskogo
[K. G. Paustovskii People's School Museum] (1975–1982)
Narodnyi muzei K. G. Paustovskogo
[K. G. Paustovskii People's Museum] (1982–1987)
Literaturnyi muzei-tsentr K. G. Paustovskogo
[K. G. Paustovskii Literary Museum-Center] (1987–1994)

The K. G. Paustovskii Moscow Literary Museum Center began its existence as a school museum in 1975. In 1982 it was reorganized as a "People's Museum," and was thereafter housed in the so-called "Grey Dacha"—a monument of wooden architecture of the eighteenth century, which was part of a former Golitsyn family estate, which unfortunately had been rather hastily reconstructed. The museum received government status in 1987 and was renamed the K. G. Paustovskii Literary Museum Center, with exhibits honoring the Russian writer Konstantin Georgievich Paustovskii (1892–1968). Its present name dates from August 1994. Since August 1997 the museum is located on the territory of the Kuz'minki-Liublino Nature and Historico-Recreational Complex.

N.B. A fond for papers of K. G. Paustovskii has been established in RGALI (B–7), but contains only a few incoming and outgoing letters.

HOLDINGS:

The museum has gathered a collection of Paustovskii manuscripts, rare photographs, and memorabilia, including books with dedicatory autographs.

FINDING AIDS — PUBLISHED — GENERAL:

Muzei Moskvy (1997), p. 229.

Muzei-kvartira I. D. Sytina
[I. D. Sytin Apartment-Museum]

Agency: Obshchestvo knigoliubov [Moscow Bibliophile Society]
Independent social organization

Address:	103009, Moscow, ul. Tverskaia, 12, kv. 274
Telephone:	229-07-75
Transport:	metro: Tverskaia, Chekhovskaia, Pushkinskaia
Hours:	M–Sa 12:00–19:00

Director: Natal'ia Nikitichna Aleshina
Chief Curator: Neliia Borisovna Putilovskaia

HISTORY:

The Sytin Apartment-Museum honors the Moscow publisher, Ivan Dmitrievich Sytin (1851–1934), housed in the apartment where Sytin lived the last seven years of his life. It was transferred by Sytin's heirs to the Moscow Bibliophile Society (*Obshchestvo knigoliubov*) in 1986, together with significant archival materials and bibliophile collections. The museum exhibits reflect the history of Sytin's activities in publishing and popular enlightenment, which started in 1876. With the emergence of the publishing house "Posrednik" in the 1880s, Sytin developed the largest popular literary publishing operation in Russia, which continued into the 1920s.

HOLDINGS:

The museum retains Sytin's family archive, memorabilia, bibliophile collections, and editions published under Sytin's auspices.

Working Conditions: A reading room is available for researchers.

Reference Facilities: There are card catalogues for all of the documentary materials.

FINDING AIDS — PUBLISHED — GENERAL:

Muzei Moskvy (1997), pp. 235–36.

Muzei ekslibrisa
[Ex Libris Museum]

Agency: Mezhdunarodnoe soobshchestvo knigoliubov
[International Society of Bibliophiles]

Address: 103031, Moscow, ul. Pushechnaia, 7/5
Telephone: 928-29-98
Transport: metro: Kuznetskii most, Lubianka
Hours: M–F 10:00–17:00

Director: Vladimir Vasil'evich Loburev
Chief Curator: Lidiia Vasil'evna Chumachenko

HISTORY:

The unique Ex Libris Museum, the only museum devoted to bookplates in Russia, was established in 1991 on the basis of several important bibliophile collections.

HOLDINGS:

Its holdings include over 26,000 Russian and 20,000 foreign ex libris and related bibliophile exhibits from 34 different countries.

Working Conditions: A reading room is available for researchers.

Reference Facilities: A card catalogue is being compiled.

FINDING AIDS — PUBLISHED — GENERAL:

Muzei Moskvy (1997), p. 130.

Theater Museums

✦— H–165 —✦

Muzei Gosudarstvennogo akademicheskogo Bol'shogo teatra (Muzei GABT)

[Museum of the State Academic Bol'shoi Theater]

Address: 103009, Moscow, Okhotnyi riad, 8/2
Telephone: 292-00-25
Transport: metro: Okhotnyi Riad, Teatral'naia, Ploshchad' Revoliutsii
Hours: Tu–F (summer: M–F) 10:00–18:00
          (research: by appointment—WF 15:00–18:00)

Director: Valerii Il'ich Zarubin (*tel.* 292-00-25)

HISTORY:

The museum was established in 1920. For the purpose of its exhibits and productions of the theater, the museum has retained considerable archival materials relating to the history of the Bolshoi Theater during the nineteenth and twentieth centuries. Most of the archive of the theater and personal papers of performers have been transferred to state archives and other specialized theater museums or libraries. A few of the exhibits are open to the public during theater performances.

N.B. A large part of the archive of the Bol'shoi Theater for the period starting in 1917 has been transferred to RGALI (B–7, fond 648). Descriptions of those holdings can be found in the published guides to TsGALI (now RGALI).

HOLDINGS: (19th–20th cc.)

manuscripts—over 2,000; theater decorations—ca. 11,000; portraits—500; posters and programs—over 80,000; photographs—2,000; negatives—over 60,000; sound recordings (records)—1,500

The Manuscript Division retains some theater documentation. Other divisions with materials of archival interest are the Division of Portraits—with many portaits of performing artists; the Division of Posters and Programs; the Division of Theater Costumes—which retains many original costumes as well as costume designs; the Division of Photographs—with over 2,000 autographed photographs of theater performers and a large negative archive (over 60,000); and the Division of Sound Recordings—which retains only phonograph records—from the first recording of F. I. Chaliapin (Shaliapin) to the present. Although individual collections and personal papers are usually transferred to other museums or archives, if they do happen to be presented to the Bol'shoi Theater, they are distributed among the appropriate divisions of the museum.

Access: Research arrangements must be made in advance with the director, on the basis of an official letter from the researcher's sponsoring institution.

Reference Facilities: Each division has a separate card catalogue covering its holdings.

Muzei Gosudarstvennogo akademicheskogo Malogo teatra
[Museum of the State Academic Malyi Theater]

Address: 103009, Moscow, Teatral'naia (*formerly* Sverdlova) pl., 1/6
Telephone: 921-85-48; *Fax:* (095) 921-03-50
Transport: metro: Okhotnyi Riad, Teatral'naia, Ploshchad' Revoliutsii
Hours: M-F 11:00-17:00 (by appointment)

Director of the theater: Viktor Ivanovich Korshunov
Director of the Museum: Nina Ivanovna Sorokina (*tel.* 921-85-48)

HISTORY:

Established in 1926, the exhibits were first opened as a museum in 1927. Since 1991, although some exhibitions are presented in the foyer during theater performances, the museum is not registered officially as a public museum and is not open for excursions.

N.B. Most of the archive of the Malyi Theater has been transferred to RGALI (B–7, fond 649). Part of the Malyi Theater documentation and special collections formed the basis for the Central Theater Library (established in the early 1920s), which is now the Russian State Library for the Arts (G–6), and other parts of their theater collections have been transferred to the Bakhrushin Museum (H–42).

HOLDINGS:

No significant part of the theater archives (1920s–1990s) remain in the theater itself, and there are no manuscript collections. The theater does retain theater graphic materials, most especially a collection of stage and costume designs used for their productions. They also have a fond of photographs and negatives, and a comprehensive collection of theater programs, posters, and reviews of their productions. Of particular interest is the book collection of the Russian actor A. I. Iuzhin (*ca.* 40,000 vols.), which includes promptbooks along with other theater-related literature.

Access: Research arrangements must be made in advance and require special permission of the director, on the basis of an official letter from the researcher's sponsoring institution.

Reference Facilities: There are special card catalogues for each of the fonds or separate collections, and also a card catalogue for directors, actors, and theater designers.

Museums of Science and Agriculture

⟪ H–167 ⟫

Memorial'nyi muzei-kvartira K. A. Timiriazeva
[K. A. Timiriazev Memorial Apartment-Museum]

Agency: Sel'skokhoziaistvennaia akademiia im. K. A. Timiriazeva
(MSKhA)—Moskovskaia
[K. A. Timiriazev Moscow Academy of Agriculture]

Address: 103009, Moscow, Romanov per., 2, kv. 29
Telephone: 202-80-64
Transport: metro: Arbatskaia, Biblioteka im. Lenina
Hours: Tu–Sa 10:00–16:00

HISTORY:

The Memorial Aparment-Museum, honoring the biologist, agronomist, and science professor Kliment Arkad'evich Timiriazev (1843–1920), opened in 1942, as a branch of the Timiriazev Museum of Biology, in the apartment where Timiriazev lived from 1899 until his death in 1920. In 1946 the museum was transferred to the jurisdiction of the Academy of Agriculture, and in 1958 underwent significant renovation. The museum features five rooms of exhibits regarding his scientific activities, including his library and working study.

HOLDINGS:

The museum retains Timiriazev's scientific archive, library, photographs, and other memorabilia. Of particular importance is Timiriazev's library (*ca.* 6,000 vols.), including some books with dedicatory autographs and marginalia. Timiriazev's archive (12,000 units) includes manuscripts, scientific and personal correspondence, notebooks, and honorary diplomas, among other documents. The photograph archive (2,500 units) includes scientific photospectograms, artistic landscape photographs by Timiriazev and his son, A. K. Timiriazev, as well as photographs of the scholar and his family.

FINDING AIDS — PUBLISHED — GENERAL:

Muzei Moskvy (1997), p. 250; *Pamiatniki nauki i tekhniki v muzeiakh* 2 (1996).

Gosudarstvennyi muzei zhivotnovodstva im. E. F. Liskuna
[E. F. Liskun State Museum of Animal Husbandry]

Agency: Moskovskaia Sel'skokhoziaistvennaia akademiia im.
K. A. Timiriazeva (MSKhA)
[K. A. Timiriazev Museum Academy of Agriculture]

Address: 127550, Moscow, ul. Timiriazevskaia, 48
Telephone: 976-38-70
Transport: metro: Voikovskaia + tram 27; Timiriazevskaia + bus 87;
Dinamo + bus 22, 112
Hours: M–F 10:00–16:00

Director: Valerii Sergeevich Sysoev
Senior Scientific Associate: Alevtina Pavlovna Goremykina

HISTORY:

The Liskun State Museum of Animal Husbandry, bearing the honorific name of the zoologist, agronomist, and reknown Russian scholar of animal husbandry, Efim Fedotovich Liskun (1873–1958), was established in 1950 under the K. A. Timiriazev Moscow Academy of Agriculture in the area of the former Petrovsko-Razumovskoe estate. It occupies a house constructed in the eighteenth century for Count N. G. Razumovskii, President of the Petersburg Academy of Sciences. The museum presents extensive exhibits relating to the history of livestock management and animal husbandry starting from the eighteenth century.

HOLDINGS: documentary materials—ca.10,000 units (18th–20th cc.)

The museum retains a significant collection of documentary materials (ca. 10,000 items) about agrarian practices and technology relating to wildlife, livestock management, and animal husbandry. Most of the collection had been initially brought together by E. F. Liskun in the late nineteenth and early twentieth century from his expeditions throughout the Russian Empire and abroad. There are many original archival documents, photographs, engravings, and other graphic materials. Published materials represent the writings of many Russian specialists in the field. The museum includes a Liskun memorial cabinet, which includes a reconstruction of Liskun's study, together with exhibits of documentary materials, photographs, and memorabilia, as well as Liskun's personal library.

Access: Despite major renovation of the museum starting in 1997, researchers are being accommodated. Access to documentation is by official letter from the researcher's sponsoring organization addressed to the director of the museum.

Working Conditions: Researchers are accommodated in working offices.

FINDING AIDS — PUBLISHED — GENERAL:

Muzei Moskvy (1997), pp. 289–291.

Museums of Transportation and Communications

— H–169 *—*

Narodnyi muzei Moskovskogo metropolitena
[People's Museum of the Moscow Metropolitan (Subway)]

Agency: Moskovskii metropoliten
[Moscow Metropolitan Subway]

Address:	119048, Moscow, Khamovnicheskii val, 36
Telephone:	222-73-09
Website:	http://www.metro.ru
Transport:	metro: Sportivnaia
Hours:	M 11:00–18:00; Tu–F 9:00–16:00

Director: Valentin Alekseevich Bolotov (*tel.* 222-78-33)

HISTORY:

The museum, devoted to the development of the Moscow underground metropolitan transport system, was opened to the public in 1967 and occupies the second and third floors of the metro station "Sportivnaia."

N.B. Archival records of the Moscow metro designated for permanent preservation have been transferred to TsMAM (D–1).

HOLDINGS:

The museum has brought together significant documentation, including photographs and other graphic materials, relating to the history of the Moscow metro. It retains extensive collections relating to the history of Moscow public transportation; the architecture, planning, and construction of the metro; and the metro during World War II.

Working Conditions: Researchers are accommodated in working offices.

FINDING AIDS — PUBLISHED — GENERAL:

Muzei Moskvy (1997), p. 295.

h-755. Kamenev, Vladimir Nikolaevich. "Narodnyi muzei Moskovskogo metropolitena." In *Pamiatniki nauki i tekhniki: 1986,* pp. 233–40. Moscow: "Nauka," 1987.
Provides a history and short survey of the museum holdings.

Muzei vody
[Museum of Waterworks]

Agency: Moskovskoe gosudarstvennoe predpriiatie "Mosvodokanal"
[Mosvodokanal Moscow State Enterprise]

Address: 109440, Moscow, Sarinskii pr., 13
Telephone: 276-92-13
Transport: metro: Proletarskaia
Hours: MWTh 10:00–17:00

HISTORY:

The museum, organized in 1993 under the auspices of the Moscow State Enterprise "Mosvodokanal," is located on the site of the former main pumping station for Moscow canalization (1898).

HOLDINGS:

The museum has brought together significant original documentation regarding the development of the Moscow canal system and water works, including manuscripts, technical plans and drawings, photographs, and published materials, dating back to the early nineteenth century.

FINDING AIDS — PUBLISHED — GENERAL:

Muzei Moskvy (1997), pp. 288–89.

Muzei istorii russkoi pochty
[Museum of the History of the Russian Postal Service]

Agency: Gosudarsvennyi komitet RF po sviazi i informatsii
(Goskomsviazi Rossii)
[State Committee for Communications and Information]
Proizvodstvennoe ob″edinenie "Mospochtamt"
[Mospochtamt Production Association]

Address:	101000, Moscow, ul. Miasnitskaia, 26
Telephone:	923-82-41; 924-65-97
Transport:	metro: Chistye prudy, Turgenevskaia

HISTORY:

The museum was founded in 1987 in the building of one of the central Moscow post offices (built in 1850).

HOLDINGS:

The museum has brought together significant original documentation regarding the development of the Russian postal, telegraph, and radio service, including early photographs and a large collection of stamps and postcards.

FINDING AIDS — PUBLISHED — GENERAL:

Nauchno-tekhn. muzei (1992), p. 30.

✵ H–172 ✵

Uchebno-geodezicheskii muzei
("Zolotye komnaty I. I. Demidova")
Moskovskogo gosudarstvennogo universiteta geodezii i
kartografii (Muzei MIIGAiK)
[Geodesic Educational Museum (I. I. Demidov Golden Rooms)
of Moscow State University for Geodesy and Cartography]

Agency: Moskovskii gosudarstvennyi universitet geodezii i kartografii (MIIGAiK)
[Moscow State University of Geodesy and Cartography]

Address: 103064, Moscow, Gorokhovskii per., 4
Telephone: 267-45-33
Transport: metro: Kurskaia, Chistye prudy; Kitai-gorod + trol. 25, 45;
Baumanskaia + trol. 45

Director: Inessa Borisova Poliantseva (*tel.* 267-45-33)
Chief Curator: Tat'iana Vladimirovna Iliushina

HISTORY:

Uchebno-geodezicheskii muzei Moskovskogo instituta inzhenerov geodezii, aerofotos"emki i kartografii
(MIIGAiK) [Geodesic Educational Museum of the Moscow Institute of Geodesic, Aerial-Photography,
and Cartographic Engineers] (1980–1993)

The museum was founded in 1980 under the Kafedra (Department) of Geodesy of what was then the
Moscow Institute of Geodesic, Aerial-Photography, and Cartographic Engineers—MIIGAiK
(*Moskovskii institut inzhenerov geodezii, aerofotos"emki i kartografii*). It is now part of the successor
Moscow State University of Geodesy and Cartography—MIIGAiK (despite the changed status, the
acronym remains the same). The museum was founded on the basis of an earlier museum of
geodesic instruments which had been established in 1842, under the Constantine Land-Survey
Institute (opened in 1779). It is housed in the palatial city home of the Demidov family, a late
eighteenth-century architectural monument, which housed the Land-Survey Institute before the
Revolution—the name of the museum accordingly bears the family name.

N.B. Some of the records of the Institute, including scientific-technical documentation are now held by
the Central Archive Scientific-Technical Documentation of Moscow—TsANTDM (D–5, fond 36).

HOLDINGS:

In addition to the collection of astronomical and geodesic instruments and other technical exhibits,
the museum has brought together original documentary materials regarding the development of
cartography, geodesy, and survey engineering. There is considerable documentation on the history
of the Institute itself and its prerevolutionary predecessor. There are many unique early maps and
atlases, including a unique 1843 Russian manuscript atlas, rare engravings, albums, and photographs,
as well as rare early printed books.

FINDING AIDS — PUBLISHED — GENERAL:

Nauchno-tekhn. muzei (1992), p. 45; *Pamiatniki nauki i tekhniki v muzeiakh* 2 (1996).

Narodnyi muzei istorii Rossiiskogo khimiko-tekhnologicheskogo universiteta im. D. I. Mendeleeva (Muzei RKhTU)
[People's Museum of the History of the D. I. Mendeleev
Russian University of Chemical Technology]

Agency: Rossiiskii khimiko-tekhnologicheskii universitet
im. D. I. Mendeleeva
[D. I. Mendeleev Russian University of Chemical Technology]

Address: 123290, Moscow, 1-i Prichal'nyi proezd, 6
Telephone: 259-26-80; *Fax:* (university): (095) 200-42-04
E-mail: (university): rector@inhti.msk.su
Transport: metro: Polezhaevskaia
Hours: by appointment

Director: Serafim Serafimovich Aralov (*tel.* 259-26-80; 259-33-17)

HISTORY:

Muzei istorii instituta i istorii khimicheskikh tekhnologii Moskovskogo khimiko-tekhnologicheskogo instituta
im. D. I. Mendeleeva
[Museum of the History of the Institute and History of Chemical Technology of the
D. I. Mendeleev Moscow Chemical Technological Institute]

The museum was founded in 1985 on the basis of private collections and materials collected by what was then the D. I. Mendeleev Moscow Institute of Chemical Technology. It was then known as the Museum of the History of the Institute and of Chemical Technology. Subsequently, the Institute was reorganized as a university with "Russian" added to its name, and the name of the museum changed accordingly.

HOLDINGS:

The museum has brought together manuscript and graphic materials, as well as a large photographic collection relating to the development of chemical technology with various applications and the history of the Institute. In addition to providing exhibits for the museum, the collections serve as the basis of scientific research studies in the history of chemical technology.

FINDING AIDS — PUBLISHED — GENERAL:

Nauchno-tekhn. muzei (1992), p. 46.

Muzei tsentra podgotovki kosmonavtov im. Iu. A. Gagarina (Muzei TsPK)

[Museum of the Iu. A. Gagarin Cosmonauts Training Center]

Agency: Rossiiskii gosudarstvennyi nauchno-issledovatel'skii ispytatel'nyi tsentr
podgotovki kosmonavtov im. Iu. A. Gagarina
[Iu. A. Gagarin Russian State Scientific Research and
Testing Center for Training Cosmonauts]
Ministerstvo oborony RF/ Rossiiskoe kosmicheskoe agentstvo (RKA)
[Ministry of Defense/ Russian Space Agency]

Address: 141160, Moskovskaia oblast', Zvezdnyi gorodok, Muzei TsPK
Telephone: 526-38-17; *Fax:* (095) 526-26-12
Website: http://howe.iki.rssi.ru/GCTC

Director of TsPK: Lt. General Petr Il'ich Klimuk
Director of Museum: Ivan Kolotov

HISTORY:

The museum was founded in 1967 in Zvezdnyi gorodok (Star City) in Moscow Oblast (about 50 km. from Moscow), on the initiative of the world's first cosmonaut Iu. A. Gagarin. The Gagarin Cosmonaut Training Center itself was renamed in 1995 the Iu. A. Gagarin Russian State Scientific Research and Testing Center for Training Cosmonauts under the Ministry of Defense and the Russian Space Agency.

HOLDINGS:

The museum has brought together rich collections for its extensive exhibits, including original documentation, photographs, and other audiovisual materials relating to space exploration, cosmonaut training, and work in space. The Iu. A. Gagarin Memorial Cabinet includes a reconstruction of Gagarin's working study, together with exhibits of documentary materials, photographs, and memorabilia.

FINDING AIDS — PUBLISHED — GENERAL:

Nauchno-tekhn. muzei (1992), pp. 32–33.

Nauchno-memorial'nyi muzei N. E. Zhukovskogo
[N. E. Zhukovskii Scientific-Memorial Museum]

Agency: Federal'naia aviatsionnaia sluzhba Rossii (FAS Rossii)
[Federal Aviation Service]
Tsentral'nyi aero-gidrodinamicheskii institut im. N. E. Zhukovskogo (TsAGI)
[N. E. Zhukovskii Central Institute of Aero-Hydrodynamics]

Address:	107005, Moscow, ul. Radio, 17
Telephone:	237-50-54; 261-69-60; 263-45-58
Transport:	metro: Krasnye vorota + trol. 24
Hours:	M–F 10:00–18:00

HISTORY:

The museum was opened in 1956 under the auspices of N. E. Zhukovskii Central Institute of Aero-Hydrodynamics, having been established in 1947 to honor the centennial of the birth of the Russian aerodynamic specialist, Nikolai Egorovich Zhukovskii (1847–1921). Zhukovskii, one of the founders of the Kuchino Aero-Hydrodynamics Institute in 1904, was particularly important in the development of Russian aviation. Subsequently he helped establish, and was the first director of, the Central Institute of Aero-Hydrodynamics, which now bears his name.

The museum has two branches:
(1) The N. E. Zhukovskii House-Museum (*Dom-muzei N. E. Zhukovskogo*).
(2) The S. A. Chaplygin Apartment-Museum (*Muzei-kvartira S. A. Chaplygina*), honoring the aerodynamics engineer Sergei Alekseevich Chaplygin (1869–1942), who worked with Zhukovskii and jointly organized the Central Institute of Aero-Hydrodynamics.

HOLDINGS:

In addition to its technical exhibits, the museum retains significant original documentation. There is also an extensive collection of photographs, negatives, and motion pictures relating to the history of aviation. The museum has some of Zhukovskii's papers, including correspondence, books, and other memorabilia. There are also some archival materials relating to scientific and technological developments (1927–1936) collected by S. P. Korolev, which were donated to the N. E. Zhukovskii House-Museum by his wife (see H–60).

FINDING AIDS — PUBLISHED — GENERAL:

Nauchno-tekhn. muzei (1992), p. 26–27; *Pamiatniki nauki i tekhniki v muzeiakh* 1 (1992).

Factory Museums

❧ H–176 ❧

Muzei Moskovskogo aktsionernogo obshchestva otkrytogo tipa "Slava" (Vtoroi chasovoi zavod) (MAOOT "Slava")
[Museum of the Slava Moscow Open Joint-Stock Company (Second Clock Factory)]

Agency: Moskovskoe aktsionernoe obshchestvo otkrytogo tipa "Slava"
(Vtoroi chasovoi zavod)
[Slava Moscow Open Joint-Stock Company
(Second Clock Factory)]

Address: 125040, Moscow, Leningradskii prosp., 8
Telephone: 257-03-32, factory: 257-00-36
Transport: metro: Belorusskaia
Hours: M–F 9:00–14:00

Director: Tamara Mikhailovna Lepeshkina (*tel.* 257-03-32)

HISTORY:

Muzei trudovoi slavy Vtorogo moskovskogo chasovogo zavoda
[Museum to the Glory of Labor of the Second Moscow Clock Factory] (1967–1990)
Muzei Moskovskogo proizvodstvennogo ob"edineniia "Vtoroi chasovoi zavod"
(Muzei MPO "Vtoroi chasovoi zavod")
[Museum of the Second Clock Factory Moscow Production Association] (1990–1992)

The Museum to the Glory of Labor was founded in 1967 to portray the history of the Second Clock Factory.

The factory itself was founded in 1924 as the Moscow Electromechanical Factory and later known as the Second Clock Factory. Privatized in 1992, the enterprise is now known as the Slava Moscow Open Joint-Stock Company (Second Clock Factory).

HOLDINGS:

In addition to its extensive collection of over 3,500 watches, the museum has significant documentary sources relating to the history of the factory since 1924, including an extensive collection of photographs and motion pictures.

Library Facilities: The museum has a library of related literature.

FINDING AIDS — PUBLISHED — GENERAL:

Nauchno-tekhn. muzei (1992), p. 56.

Muzei Zavoda schetno-analiticheskikh mashin im. V. D. Kalmykova

[Museum of the V. D. Kalmykov Calculator Factory]

Agency: Otkrytoe aktsionernoe obshchestvo "Moskovskii zavod schetno-analiticheskikh mashin im. V. D. Kalmykova" (OAO "AO SAM")
[V. D. Kalmykov Moscow Calculator Factory Open Joint-Stock Company]
Ministerstvo ekonomiki RF
[Ministry of Economics]

Address: 107006, Moscow, ul. Nizhniaia Krasnosel'skaia, 35
Telephone: 263-81-72, factory: 261-93-48
Transport: metro: Krasnosel'skaia
Hours: M–W 9:00–16:00

Head of Museum: Irina Vasil'evna Murashova (*tel.* 263-81-72)

HISTORY:

The museum was founded in 1975 in celebration of the sesquicentennial of one of the largest factories in the country producing calculators and similar technology. The factory itself was founded in 1923, and from 1931 until 1994, it was known as the V. D. Kalmykov Calculator Factory (*Zavod shchetno-analiticheskikh mashin im. V. D. Kalmykova*). In 1994 it was privatized as a joint-stock company, known as the V. D. Kalmykov Moscow Calculator Factory Open Joint-Stock Company (Otkrytoe *Aktsionernoe obshchestvo "Moskovskii zavod schetno-analiticheskikh mashin im. V. D. Kalmykova*—AOOT "AO SAM"). Reorganized again in 1996, the factory remains under the Ministry of Economics.

HOLDINGS:

The museum has significant documents, memoirs, graphic materials, and other materials relating to the history of the factory (1923–1985), including an extensive collection of photographs and motion pictures.

Library Facilities: The museum has a library of related literature.

FINDING AIDS — PUBLISHED — GENERAL:

Nauchno-tekhn. muzei (1992), p. 57.

Muzei Aktsionernogo obshchestva "Moskvich"
(Muzei AO "Moskvich")
[Museum of the Moskvich Joint-Stock Company]

Agency: Aktsionernoe obshchestvo "Moskvich"
[Moskvich Joint-Stock Company]

Address: 109316, Moscow, Volgogradskii prosp., 42
Telephone: 911-72-70; (factory): 911-09-91, 911-25-54
Transport: metro: Tekstil'shchiki; bus: 30, 161, 193, 291
Hours: M–F 9:00–17:00 (by appointment)

Director: Viktor Sergeevich Voronov (*tel.* 911-72-70)

HISTORY:

Muzei Avtomobil'nogo zavoda im. Leninskogo komsomola (Muzei AZLK)
[Museum of the Lenin Komsomol Automobile Factory] (1980–1994)

The museum was founded in 1980 on the basis of an informal public museum, in honor of the 50th anniversary of one of the major Moscow automobile factories that now produces Moskvich automobiles. The museum is housed in a special building constructed for the purpose of exhibition and scientific research work on the subject of the history of automobile construction and related subjects.

A factory existed in the same location immediately prior to the Revolution, but the automobile factory itself was started in 1930, known first as the Moscow Auto Construction Factory (*Moskovskii avtosborochnyi zavod*), and then as the State Communist Youth International Auto Construction Factory in Moscow (*Gosudarstvennyi avtosborochnyi zavod im. Kommunisticheskogo internatsionala molodezhi v Moskve*). In 1939 it was renamed the Moscow Communist Youth International Automobile Factory (*Moskovskii avtomobil'nyi zavod im. Kommunisticheskogo internatsionala molodezhi*). During the war the factory was evacuated to Sverdlovsk, and in its place in Moscow was a center for repairing tanks. In 1945 it was reestablished as the Moscow Factory for Economy-Size Automobiles (*Moskovskii zavod malolitrazhnykh avtomobilei*—MZMA) and in 1968 took the name of the Komsomol—AZLK (*Avtomobil'nyi zavod im. Leninskogo komsomola*), by which it was known until 1994. It then became the Moskvich Stock Company (*Aktsionernoe obshchestvo [AO] "Moskvich"*).

N.B. Some of the records of the factory, including scientific-technical documentation on the construction of some models of the Moskvich are now held by the Central Archive Scientific-Technical Documentation of Moscow—TsANTDM (D–5, fond 40, 1946–1958).

HOLDINGS:

The museum has significant original documentary and graphic sources relating to the history of the factory (1932 to present), including letters, memoirs, technical drawings, photographs, and films.

FINDING AIDS — PUBLISHED — GENERAL:

Nauchno-tekhn. muzei (1992), p. 59.

Muzei trudovoi i revoliutsionnoi slavy Moskovskogo radiozavoda "Temp" (Muzei MRZ "Temp")
[Museum to the Glory of Labor and Revolution
of the Moscow Temp Radio Factory]

Agency: Gosudarstvennoe predpriiatie firma Moskovskii radiozavod "Temp"
[State Enterprise Firm Temp Moscow Radio Factory]

Address: 113054, Moscow, ul. Bakhrushina, 7/1
Telephone: (factory): 953-33-27, 951-92-14, 953-02-76
Transport: metro: Paveletskaia

Director: Natal'ia Vasil'evna Dudoladova (*tel.* 951-14-11)

HISTORY:

The museum was founded in 1974 on the basis of a public museum, honoring the operation of the radio factory for seventy years.

The factory was founded in 1918 as the First State Electro-Technical Factory (*Pervyi gosudarstvennyi elektrotekhnicheskii zavod*). In 1925 it was renamed the Moscow Electro-Mechanical Factory—Moselektrik (*Moskovskii elektromekhanicheskii zavod*). The factory was taken over by the Ministry of Defense in 1932, and renamed Factory no. 203 in the name of the Georgian revolutionary leader Sergo (*pseud.* of Grigorii Konstantinovich) Ordzhonikidze (*Zavod 203 im. G. K. Ordzhonikidze*); while it kept that honorific name, its numbers were changed several times up to 1965. It was awarded the First Order of Lenin in 1931, and the second in 1945. In 1965 it was renamed the Moscow Dual Order of Lenin Radio Factory (*Moskovskii dvazhdy ordena Lenina radiozavod*), and in 1972—the Moscow Temp Radio Factory (*Moskovskii dvazhdy ordena Lenina radiozavod "Temp"*). Remaining under the Ministry of Economics, the factory was again renamed in 1998—the Moscow Temp Radio Factory State Enterprise—MRZ "Temp" (*Gosudarstvennoe predpriiatie firma Moskovskii dvazhdy ordena Lenina radiozavod "Temp"*).

HOLDINGS:

The museum has collected original documentary and photographic sources relating to the history of the factory, including materials relating to workers' participation in the revolutionary movement.

FINDING AIDS — PUBLISHED — GENERAL:

Nauchno-tekhn. muzei (1992), p. 60.

h-760. Gendin, G. S. *Istoriia Moskovskogo radiozavoda.* Moscow: "Radio i sviaz'," 1990. 160 p. + photographs.

Narodnyi muzei istorii Metallurgicheskogo zavoda "Serp i Molot"

[People's Museum of the History of the Hammer and Sickle Metallurgical Plant]

Agency: Aktsionernoe obshchestvo "Metallurgicheskii zavod 'Serp i Molot'"
[Hammer and Sickle Metallurgical Plant Stock Company]

Address: 109033, Moscow, Zolotorozhskii val, 11 (Tamozhennyi pr., 12)
Telephone: 278-45-00; 278-73-70; 278-90-00 (ext. 3318)
Transport: metro: Ploshchad' Il'icha
Hours: M–Sa 9:00–16:00 (by appointment)

HISTORY:

The museum was founded in 1966 to portray the history of one of the first and largest metallurgical plants in Russia.

The factory itself was founded as the Moscow Metallurgical Plant Society (*Tovarishchestvo Moskovskogo metallurgicheskogo zavoda*) in 1883 by the French manufacturer Jules Goujon, and hence bore the name of his company (*Obshchestvo "Guzhon i Ko"*); it was frequently popularly known simply as the Goujon Plant. Nationalized after the Revolution, it was familiarly known as the former Goujon Plant (*byvshii Guzhonovskii zavod*), but in 1922 it took the official name of the Hammer and Sickle Large Moscow Metallurgical Plant (*Moskovskii bol'shoi metallurgicheskii zavod "Serp i molot"*). The plant was recently privatized.

N.B. Some of the records of the plant, including scientific-technical documentation, are now held by the Central Archive of Scientific-Technical Documentation of Moscow—TsANTDM (D–5, fond 12, 1883–1929).

HOLDINGS:

The museum has a particularly rich collection of documentation regarding the plant, starting with its foundation in 1883. There are significant prerevolutionary materials, with some building plans, manufacturing designs, papers of factory directors, photographs, and other graphic materials.

Muzei istorii Aviatsionnogo kompleksa im. S. V. Il'iushina
[Museum of the History of the S. V. Il'iushin Aviation Complex]

Agency: Otkrytoe aktsionernoe obshchestvo
"Aviatsionnyi kompleks im. S. V. Il'iushina"
[Ilyiushin Aviation Complex Open Joint-Stock Company]

Address: 125190, Moscow, Leningradskii prosp., 45 G
Telephone: 943-84-41; *Fax:* (095) 212-21-32
Website: http://www.infoart.ru/avia/company/il/index.htm
Transport: metro: Aeroport; trol.: 12, 70; tram: 23
Hours: M–F 10:00–17:00 (by appointment)

Aviation Complex General Director: Vladimir Il'ich Zhdanov
Museum Director: Marina Sergeevna Ivanova

HISTORY:

The museum was founded in 1979 on the basis of the memorial cabinet (office) of the aeronautics engineer and designer, Sergei Vladimirovich Il'iushin (sometimes Ilyiushin in English) (1894–1977), which is preserved in its original state. The museum is located in the Experimental Design Office building of the firm, where original planes are preserved, along with a giant diorama representing aerial developments during World War II. The museum portrays the history of the most important airplane factories of the Soviet Union and now of the Russian Federation, along with a memorial tribute to Il'iushin and other individuals associated with the development of the "Il" aircraft.

HOLDINGS:

The museum has a rich collection of documentation regarding the history of the Il'iushin Aviation Complex, including factory records, original airplane designs, photographs, and other graphic materials. There are many models of "Il" planes and those produced by other Soviet factories. Additional documentation and printed sources relate to the development of worldwide aviation and aeronautic engineering. There are some personal papers and memorabilia of Il'iushin, along with those of the associated aeronautic engineer G. V. Novozhilov and the test-pilot V. K. Kokkinaki. Films and videocasettes are preserved regarding S. V. Il'iushin and the aircraft factory.

Access: Limited access to the museum for organized groups is possible on the basis of an advance formal, sealed institutional petition to the General Director of the Il'iushin Aviation Complex, which must be endorsed by the General Director. A similar formal application is required for researchers who may want to acquire copies of documents or photographs.

Copying: Copies of documents and photographs can be ordered at commercial rates by formal written request.

Additional Museums with Archival Holdings

St. Petersburg

Literary Museums

❧ H–200 ❧

Munitsipal'nyi muzei "Anna Akhmatova. Serebrianyi vek"
[Municipal Museum of Anna Akhmatova and the Silver Age]

Address: 198096, St. Petersburg, prosp. Stachek, 67, kv. 4
Telephone: 185-04-42
Transport: metro: Avtovo
Hours: M–Sa 10:00–18:00

Director: Valentina Andreevna Bilichenko

HISTORY:

The museum, honoring the Russian poetess Anna Andreevna Akhmatova (1888–1966), was initially founded in 1980 under the sponsorship of the Baltic Factory Shipyard (see H–204), but in 1993 was officially recognized as a municipal museum.

HOLDINGS:

The museum, initially based on the personal collection of the director, has brought together considerable memorabilia and documentation relating to Akhmatova, her first husband, Russian poet Nikolai Stepanovich Gumilev (1996–1921), and their son, the well-known historian-Orientalist, Lev Nikolaevich Gumilev (1912–1992). There are some books from their libraries with autographs and marginalia, as well as additional documentation relating to the Silver Age.

FINDING AIDS — PUBLISHED — GENERAL:

Muzei SPb (1994), p. 94.

"A muzy ne molchali..."
["But the Muses Were Not Silent..."]

Address:	190121, St. Petersburg, Rabochii per., 4/6
Telephone:	114-00-51; 114-08-81
Transport:	bus: 22; tram: 14, 31, 33, 54
Hours:	M–F 9:00–17:00

Director: Evgenii Alekseevich Lind (*tel.* 114-57-83)

HISTORY:

The museum was opened in 1968, celebrating the arts during the Siege (Blockade) of Leningrad during World War II—with an antiwar orientation, and has received donations and/or materials for temporary exhibits from many artists and intellectuals.

HOLDINGS:

The museum has gathered significant original materials regarding the performing and visual arts during the Blockade, although some of its exhibits have been received only on temporary loan.

FINDING AIDS — PUBLISHED — GENERAL:

Muzei SPb (1994), p. 124.

❋⊷ H–202 ⊷❋

Muzei istorii Sankt-Peterburgskogo gosudarstvennogo Tekhnologicheskogo instituta (Tekhnicheskogo universiteta) (Muzei istorii SPbTI)

[Museum of the History of the St. Petersburg State Technological Institute (Technical University)]

Agency: Sankt-Peterburgskii gosudarstvennyi Tekhnologicheskii institut (Tekhnicheskii universitet) (SPbTI)
[St. Petersburg State Technological Institute (Technical University)]

Address: 198013, St. Petersburg, Moskovskii prosp., 26
Telephone: 259-48-56
Transport: metro: Tekhnologicheskii institut; tram: 28, 34; trol.: 3, 8, 15, 17
Hours: M–F 9:00–17:00

Director: Sofiia Ivanovna Kudoiarova (*tel.* 259-48-56)

HISTORY:

The museum was founded in 1836, at the same time as the Institute itself, but in 1936, it was closed down and most of its extensive exhibits were transferred to other museums, including the Museum of Railroad Transport (H–111). A museum for the history of the Institute, which then bore the name of the Leningrad City Council—Lensovet State Technological Institute (LTI)—was opened again in 1950. In 1993, the Institute was designated the status of a university, which is now reflected as part of its official name (although its acronym remains the same—SPbTI).

HOLDINGS:

Along with other exhibits, the museum has brought together original documentation, including graphic and photographic materials, portraying the history of the Institute since its establishment during the reign of Nicholas I.

FINDING AIDS — PUBLISHED — GENERAL:

Muzei SPb (1994), p. 150.

Factory Museums

❊❊ H–203 ❊❊

Muzei "Rossiiskie bumazhnye den'gi" fabriki "Goznak"
[Goznak Factory Museum of Russian Paper Money]

Agency: Sankt-peterburgskaia bumazhnaia fabrika "Goznak"
[Goznak St. Petersburg Paper Factory]

Address:	198103, St. Petersburg, nab. Fontanki, 144A
Telephone:	292-92-64; factory office: 316-92-64; *Fax:* (812) 251-46-46 (factory)
Transport:	tram: 1, 16, 28, 29; trol.: 3
Hours:	by appointment

Director: Sofiia Veniaminovna Smirnova (*tel.* 316-92-64)

HISTORY:

The museum, founded in 1989, is located in the administrative building of the factory.

The factory itself dates from 1818, when it was founded as the official government agency for printing paper money and other official paper (*Ekspeditsiia zagotovleniia gosudarstvennykh bumag*). Before 1917, it operated as a commercial enterprise under the control of Augustin de Betancourt (Béthencourt; A. A. Betankur), the well-known architect and civil engineer in Russian service. In addition to paper money, the factory (or paper mill and mint) produced postage stamps and fine editions of books and albums.

Nationalized after the Revolution, in 1922 it was known as "Krasnyi Gosznakovets," and later, by 1930, as "Gosznak." It is now known officially as the Goznak St. Petersburg Paper Factory (*Sankt-peterburgskaia bumazhnaia fabrika "Goznak"*).

HOLDINGS:

The museum has brought together a significant collection of original documentation and graphic materials relating to the production of paper money, as well as other aspects of the paper industry in Russia.

FINDING AIDS — PUBLISHED — GENERAL:

Muzei SPb (1994), p. 158; *Peterburg* (1992), p. 103.

h-770. *Istoriia Leningradskoi bumazhnoi fabriki Goznaka.* Compiled by M. A. Shcherbakov and N. A. Zegzhda. Edited by V. A. Efanov et al. Leningrad: Lenizdat, 1988. 206 p. + plates. "Istoriia fabrik i zavodov." (Lib: DLC; MH)
     A popular history of the factory without documentation or bibliography.

Muzei aktsionernogo obshchestva "Baltiiskii zavod"
[Museum of the Baltic Factory Joint-Stock Company]

Address:	199026, St. Petersburg, Vasil'evskii ostrov, Kosaia liniia, 13
Telephone:	217-95-01; factory (Kosaia liniia, 16): 217-45-76, 217-02-02;
Fax:	(812) 217-12-27 (factory)
Transport:	bus: 7, 42, 128, 151, 152; tram: 18, 37; trol.: 10, 23
Hours:	M–Th 9:00–16:30; F 9:00–15:30 (by appointment)

HISTORY:

The museum was established in 1980, as an internal factory museum, to present the history of one of the major Russian shipbuilding enterprises.

The factory itself was founded in 1856/1857 as the Baltic Shipbuilding and Mechanical Plant under the proprietorship of the British industrialists Kapper and MacPherson. After 1873 it was known as the Anglo-Russian Baltic Shipbuilding and Mechanical Association (*Anglo-russkoe Baltiiskoe sudostroitel'noe i mekhanicheskoe obshchestvo*). The shipyard produced the cruiser "Aurora" of revolutionary fame and the battleships "Suvorov," "Rossiia," and "Borodino."

Nationalized after the Revolution, the factory was renamed in honor of the Georgian revolutionary leader Sergo (*pseud.* of Grigorii Konstantinovich) Ordzhonikidze. It was known for the production of submarines and, starting in the 1970s, atomic submarines.

HOLDINGS:

The museum has a significant collection of original documentation, including photographs and other graphic materials, relating to the history of the shipyard.

FINDING AIDS — PUBLISHED — GENERAL:

Muzei SPb (1994), p. 157; *Peterburg* (1992), p. 75.

h-775. Kuznetsov, K. A.; Livshits, L. Z.; and Pliasunov, V. I. *Baltiiskii sudostroitel'nyi, 1856–1917: Ocherk istorii Baltiiskogo sudostroitel'nogo zavoda im. Sergo Ordzhonikidze.* Leningrad: "Sudostroenie," 1970. 559 p.

> Provides a history of the shipbuilding plant, with documentary appendixes (pp. 523–44) and bibliography (pp. 550–57).

Muzei pri aktsionernom obshchestve
"Lomonosovskii farforovyi zavod"
[Museum of the Lomonosov Porcelain Factory Joint-Stock Company]

Address: 193171, St. Petersburg, prosp. Obukhovskoi Oborony, 151
Telephone: 560-83-00; *Fax:* (812) 560-82-11 (factory)
Transport: metro: Lomonosovskaia
Hours: M–F 8:30–17:30

Director: Natal'ia Sergeevna Petrova

HISTORY:

The museum was founded in 1844 under the Imperial Porcelain Factory, which since 1925 was known as the Leningrad M. V. Lomonosov Porcelain Factory.

The factory itself was founded in 1744 as the Porcelain Manufacture (*Portselinovaia manufaktura*), the first in Russia and one of the first in Europe. In 1765 it was renamed the Imperial Porcelain Factory (*Imperatorskii farforovyi zavod*).

Nationalized after the Revolution it was reorganized as the State Porcelain Factory in 1923, and in 1925 took the name of Lomonosov. According to an October 1998 newspaper report, the factory was sold to an as-yet-undeclared foreign buyer, which, it is to be hoped, will not affect the museum, factory archive, and its rich graphic collections.

HOLDINGS:

In addition to rich collections of its decorative porcelain products themselves, the museum has many graphic materials, representing designs by well-known architects, sculptors, and artists, includings V. V. Kandinskii, K. S. Malevich, Jean-Dominique Rachette (Zh. D. Rashett), S. S. Pimenov, A. N. Voronikhin, Carlo Rossi, K. A. Somov, and S. V. Chekhonin, among others.

FINDING AIDS — PUBLISHED — GENERAL:

Muzei SPb (1994), p. 46; *Peterburg* (1992), p. 636.

h-778. Lansere, Alla Konstantinovna. *Russkii farfor: Iskusstvo pervogo v Rossii farforovogo zavoda/ Russian porcelain: The art of the first Russian porcelain works.* Leningrad: "Khudozhnik RSFSR," 1968. 270 p. + plates. Added titles in German and French; text also in English, German and French. (Lib: MH-F)

h-779. *Russkii khudozhestvennyi farfor: Sbornik statei o Gosudarstvennom farforovom zavode.* Edited by E. F. Gollerbakh and M. B. Farmakovskii. Leningrad, 1924. 165 p.+ plates. (Lib: MH-F)

> An illustrated collection of articles on the history of the factory, including one about the history of the museum since its foundation in 1844 (pp. 115–29). Includes extensive bibliography (pp. 160–62) and short French resumés and captions.

h-780. "Farfornyi zavod im. M. V. Lomonosova." *Voprosy istorii estestvoznaniia i tekhniki,* 1962, no. 12, pp. 238–39. (Lib: DLC; IU; MH)

Muzei proizvodstvennogo ob"edineniia "Arsenal" im. M. V. Frunze

[Museum of M. V. Frunze Arsenal Production Association]

Address: 195009, St. Petersburg, ul. Komsomola, 1/3
Telephone: 542-28-46; *Fax:* (812) 512-26-15 (factory)
Transport: bus: 136, 137; tram: 6, 14, 19, 23, 30, 38, 51; trol.: 3, 8, 12, 19, 38, 43
Hours: M–F 9:00–16:00 (by appoinment)

Director: Petr Aleksandrovich Tirin

HISTORY:

The museum was founded in 1970, representing the history of one of the earliest industrial enterprises in Russia.

The factory itself was founded by an imperial *ukaz* of Peter I in 1711, as *Liteinyi dvor*, for the production of cannons and other artillery. An exhibition hall was organized as the Memorabilia Hall, especially for exhibits of a military nature, which later came under the Kronwerk Arsenal as part of the Artillery Museum, as it was then known (see H–73).

After the Revolution, the industrial enterprise continued and was known as the Red Arsenal Mechanical Factory (*Mekhanicheskii zavod Krasnyi Arsenal*) and later the Arsenal Machine Tools Factory (*Mashinostroitel'nyi zavod Arsenal*), which took the honorific name of the Bolshevik military leader Mikhail Vasil'evich Frunze (1885–1925). In 1970, with the support of the Artillery History Museum, the present armaments and machine tools factory opened its own museum, which is now housed in the building of the former St. Petersburg Arsenal.

HOLDINGS:

The museum has brought together a significant collection of documentation (both original and copies), as well as photographs, engravings, and other graphic materials, relating to the long and illustrious history of the armaments factory.

FINDING AIDS — PUBLISHED — GENERAL:

Muzei SPb (1994), p. 156; *Peterburg* (1992), p. 65.

Appendix 1

Selected List of Laws and Other Regulatory Acts Relating to Archives (August 1991–March 1999)

The following list has been compiled during the past few years in connection with the ongoing ArcheoBiblioBase project and study of archival development in Russia. It makes no pretense to be comprehensive. Rather, emphasis is on laws and decrees relating to archival developments discussed in the foregoing directory and in the related Grimsted essay (**a-706**).

According to post-August 1991 legislative and executive usage, normative acts have been issued predominantly in the following categories, all of which have the effect of law:

A federal law (*zakon*), is passed by both houses of parliament and takes effect when signed by the President.

A directive (*postanovlenie*) is issued by a federal executive organ, such as an executive organ of the Government (*Pravitel'stvo*) or legislative body, or before 1993 by the Council of Ministers or the Presidium of the Supreme Soviet, and also has the effect of law.

A presidential decree (*ukaz*) also has the effect of law and takes effect when signed by the President.

A presidential directive (*rasporiazhenie*), abbreviated "rp" after the number, sometimes translated as regulation—usually is employed for lower-level acts, and does not require confirmation.

A regulation or order (*polozhenie*) may be issued by any government executive agency, but has the authority of law only when confirmed (*utverzhdeno*) by a presidential decree (*ukaz*) or by other legislative or executive action.

Citations are, to the extent possible, to the official versions of laws and other acts as published in the successive federal registers. A few laws, that should have gone to press just before the October Days in 1993, such as the law "On State Secrets" (**L-21**), were officially published only in *Rossiiskaia gazeta*. Likewise, several 1991 normative acts relating to archives listed here were never included in the official printed registers of federal laws. Because of inadequate periodical indexes, including for *Rossiiskaia gazeta*, references to all published versions are not systematically provided.

After an initial draft of this list was completed, the compiler acquired copies of the in-house typescript annual lists of normative acts relating to archival affairs compiled and continuously updated by the Rosarkhiv Central Scientific Library (see below). The Rosarkhiv lists, which have not been published nor widely circulated, are based only on official, openly published federal registers. Comparison with those lists has yielded references to a few additional acts. However, the present list does not include many of the other references listed by the Rosarkhiv Library, such as those relating to matters of budget, federal employees, the appointment of individual archival directors, or other arrangements for individual archives, and the like, which were in fact confirmed by an official federal directive or presidential decree. At the end of 1997, the Rosarkhiv Library became administratively part of the State Archive of the Russian Federation (GA RF), but work on the lists continued. Due to the budgetary crisis, that library at first was unable to subscribe to the federal register issues, and then has recently suffered delays in receipt of the federal register. Nevertheless, compilation continues, and librarians there have kindly given the compilers access to their ongoing files.

For obvious reasons it is not possible to include decrees or other directives that have been issued with a "classified" status. Such is the case, for example, with the presidential decree of late August or early September 1995 calling for declassification of the records of the Soviet Military Administration in Germany (SVAG), and likewise the corresponding earlier August 1992 presidential decree declaring SVAG records closed to research.

The compilers are grateful to a number of friends and colleagues for suggestions and additions to the list, and further suggestions will be gratefully appreciated. The rubrics assigned below remain preliminary, and there may be some overlap among categories. Since almost all of the acts listed have the effect of law, a distinction within rubrics is not made among the different types of legal acts involved. The 1996 article by A. N. Artizov on the subject of archival laws (a-699) suggests a somewhat different organization and includes important references to legal acts adopted by local regions (sub"ekty) of the Russian Federation.

Organization and Stucture of Federal Executive Agencies

We have not listed all of the laws and regulations for the reorganization and renaming of many federal executive agencies, particularly those involving only one or two individual agencies. The following major changes should be noted however:

The presidential decree of 14 August 1996, "O strukture federal'nykh organov ispolnitel'noi vlasti": Ukaz Prezidenta Rossiiskoi Federatsii ot 14 avgusta 1996, no. 1177 (Sobranie zakonodatel'stva RF, 1996, no. 34, st. 4082) brought a number of important changes to agencies included in this directory. In a few cases, and specifically the federal security services, names reverted to their older form as a result of a follow-up decree, "Voprosy federal'nykh organov ispolnitel'noi vlasti": Ukaz Prezidenta Rossiiskoi Federatsii ot 6 sentiabria 1996, no. 1326 (Sobranie zakonodatel'stva RF, 1996, no. 37 [9 September], st. 4264).

Other major structural changes of federal executive agencies occurred in 1998, the first as a presidential decree issued on 30 April—"O strukture federal'nykh organov ispolnitel'noi vlasti": Ukaz Prezidenta Rossiiskoi Federatsii ot 30 aprelia 1998, no. 483 (Sobranie zakonodatel'stva RF, 1998, no. 18, st. 2020). The latest structure is that outlined in the presidential decree of 22 September 1998—"O strukture federal'nykh organov ispolnitel'noi vlasti": Ukaz Prezidenta Rossiiskoi Federatsii ot 22 sentiabria 1998, no. 1142 (Sobranie zakonodatel'stva RF, 1998, no. 39 [29 September], st. 4886).

* * * * *

Bibliography of Legal Acts Relating to Archives

"Opublikovannye dokumenty, obespechivaiushchie pravovuiu osnovu deiatel'nosti arkhivnykh uchrezhdenii Rossii: Bibliograficheskii ukazatel'." Moscow, 1994–. Typescript. [Rosarkhiv; Nauchnaia biblioteka federal'nykh arkhivov].

Pt .1: "——(1991–1993 gg)." M., 1994. 10 p.

Pt. 2: "——(1994 g.)." M., 1995. 7 p.

Pt. 3: "——(1995 g.)." M., 1996. 8 p.

Pt. 4: "——(1996 g.)." M., 1997. 10 p.

Pt. 5: "——(1997 g.)." M., 1998. 12 p.

Pt. 6: "Dokumenty, obespechivaiushchie pravovuiu osnovu deiatel'nosti arkhivnykh uchrezhdenii Rossii: Biulleten' [1998 g.]." M., 1999. 28p.

A chronological listing of federal laws, decrees, and regulations relating to archives prepared by the staff of the Rosarkhiv central library, since 1997, part of GA RF.

1. Basic Laws and Decrees Regulating Archival Affairs

L-1. "O partiinykh arkhivakh": Ukaz Prezidenta RSFSR ot 24 avgusta 1991 g., no. 83. *Vedomosti S"ezda narodnykh deputatov RSFSR i Verkhovnogo Soveta RSFSR*, 1991, no. 35 (29 August), st. 1157.

Published in *Otechestvennye arkhivy*, 1992, no. 1, p. 3.

L-2. "Ob arkhivakh Komiteta gosudarstvennoi bezopasnosti SSSR": Ukaz Prezidenta RSFSR ot 24 avgusta 1991 g., no. 84. *Vedomosti S"ezda narodnykh deputatov RSFSR i Verkhovnogo Soveta RSFSR*, 1991, no. 35 (29 August), st. 1156.

Published in *Otechestvennye arkhivy*, 1992, no. 1, p. 3.

L-3. "O razvitii arkhivnogo dela v RSFSR": Postanovlenie Sovete Ministrov RSFSR ot 12 oktiabria 1991 g., no. 531. Published in *Otechestvennye arkhivy*, 1992, no. 1, p. 4.

Provides for the abolition of Glavarkhiv SSSR and names Roskomarkhiv as its successor agency. Otherwise not published in the official collection of laws.

L-4. "O Rossiiskom tsentre khraneniia i izucheniia dokumentov noveishei istorii i Tsentre khraneniia sovremennoi dokumentatsii": Postanovlenie SM RSFSR ot 12 oktiabria 1991 g., no. 532. Published in *Otechestvennye arkhivy*, 1992, no. 1, p. 4.

Establishes two new archives on the basis of the former CPSU central archives. Otherwise not published in the official collection of laws. The supplemental lists of nationalized CPSU documentation were not included in that published version.

L-5. "Ob obrazovanii komissii po organizatsii peredachi-priema arkhivov KPSS i KGB SSSR na gosudarstvennoe khranenie i ikh ispol'zovaniiu": Postanovlenie Prezidiuma Verkhovnogo Soveta RSFSR ot 14 oktiabria 1991 g. *Vedomosti S"ezda narodnykh deputatov RSFSR i Verkhovnogo Soveta RSFSR*, 1991, no. 47 (21 November), st. 1592.

See the Resolution (*Reshenie*) of this Commission relating to KGB archives presented to the Supreme Council over the signature of Commission Chairman, D. A. Volkogonov, in February 1992, published in *Karta* (Riazan), no. 1 (1993): 6–7. (see c-36).

L-6. "O vremennom poriadke dostupa k arkhivnym dokumentam i pravilakh ikh ispol'zovaniia": Postanovlenie Verkhovnogo Soveta RF ot 19 iiunia 1992 g., no. 3088–I. *Vedomosti S"ezda narodnykh deputatov RF i Verkhovnogo Soveta RF*, 1992, no. 28 (16 July), st. 1620. MODIFICATION: See L-18.

Initially issued as "Prikaz Roskomarkhiva," no. 161 (14 July 1992). Reprinted in brochure form by Rosarkhiv. Published in *Otechestvennye arkhivy*, 1992, no. 5, p. 3 and in *Informatsionnyi biulleten'* [Roskomarkhiva], 1992, no. 1, pp. 19–20. A copy is included as an appendix to *Archives in Russia 1993*. An English translation appears in an article by P. K. Grimsted, "New Decree on Russian Archives," in *AAASS Newsletter* 32:5 (November 1992): 3–5.

L-7. "Polozhenie o Komitete po delam arkhivov pri Pravitel'stve RF i seti federal'nykh gosudarstvennykh arkhivov i tsentrov khraneniia dokumentatsii": Confirmation: Postanovlenie Pravitel'stva RF ot 24 iiunia 1992 g., no. 430. Published in *Otechestvennye archivy, 1992, no. 4, p. 3.*

SUPPLEMENT 1: "Polozhenie o Komitete po delam arkhivov pri Pravitel'stve RF."
SUPPLEMENT 2: "Set' federal'nykh gosudarstvennykh arkhivov i tsentrov khraneniia dokumentatsii."
MODIFICATION: "O sozdanii Rossiiskogo gosudarstvennogo arkhiva nauchno-tekhnicheskoi dokumentatsii": Postanovlenie Pravitel'stva RF ot 9 iiunia 1995 g., no. 575. *Sobranie zakonodatel'stva RF*, 1995, no. 25, st. 2395.
MODIFICATION: See **L-19**.

Also published in *Informatsionnyi biulleten'* [Roskomarkhiva], 1992, no. 1, pp. 5–17. The 1995 modification provides for the consolidation of two of the archives listed.

1215

L-8 "Soglashenie o pravopreemstve v otnoshenii gosudarstvennykh arkhivov byvshego Soiuza SSR": Confirmation: Rasporiazhenie Prezidenta RF ot 6 iiulia 1992 g., no. 343–rp. *Vedomosti S"ezda narodnykh deputatov RF i Verkhovnogo Soveta RF*, 1992, no. 28 (16 July), st. 1673.
> Published in *Vestnik arkhivista*, 1992, no. 4 (10), pp. 3–5.

L-9. "Osnovy zakonodatel'stva Rossiiskoi Federatsii o kul'ture": Zakon RF ot 9 oktiabria 1992 g., no. 3612–I. *Vedomosti S"ezda narodnykh deputatov RF i Verkhovnogo Soveta RF*, 1992, no. 46 (19 November), st. 2615.
> Published in *Rossiiskaia gazeta*, no. 248 (17 November 1992), p. 5.
>
> Regulates cultural materials that constitute the Russian cultural heritage, including archival materials, providing for open access, use, and state preservation.

L-10. "Polozhenie o Gosudarstvennoi arkhivnoi sluzhbe Rossii": Confirmation: Postanovlenie Pravitel'stva RF ot 22 dekabria 1992 g., no. 1006. *Sobranie aktov Prezidenta i Pravitel'stva RF*, 1993, no. 4 (25 January), st. 303.
> Published in *Otechestvennye arkhivy*, 1993, no. 2, pp. 3–7.
>
> The new regulation for Rosarkhiv, served to implement the 30 September 1992 reorganization of executive organs that provided for the reorganization of Roskomarkhiv as Rosarkhiv—Ukaz Prezidenta RF, no. 1148 ot 30 sentiabria 1992—*Vedomosti S"ezda narodnykh deputatov RF i Verkhovnogo Soveta RF*, 1992, no. 41 (16 October), st. 2278.

L-11. "O poriadke vedomstvennogo khraneniia dokumentov i organizatsii ikh v deloproizvodstve": Postanovlenie Soveta Ministrov—Pravitel'stva RF ot 3 marta 1993 g., no. 191. *Sobranie aktov Prezidenta i Pravitel'stva RF*, 1993, no. 10 (8 March), st. 850.
> Published in *Otechestvennye arkhivy*, 1993, no. 3, pp. 3–4.

L-12. "Ob Arkhivnom fonde Rossiiskoi Federatsii i arkhivakh": Osnovy zakonodatel'stva RF ot 7 iiulia 1993 g., no. 5341–I. *Vedomosti S"ezda narodnykh deputatov RF i Verkhovnogo Soveta RF*, 1993, no. 33 (19 August), st. 1311.
> Published in *Rossiiskaia gazeta*, no. 156 (14 August 1993), p. 5. Reprinted in brochure form by Rosarkhiv. A copy of the new law is printed in *Novaia i noveishaia istoriia*, 1993, no. 6, pp. 3–11. An analysis follows by V. P. Kozlov (pp. 12–15).
>
> A draft projected revision for the 1993 law was published in *Otechestvennye arkhivy*, 1998, no. 6, pp. 21–33: "Proekt Federal'nogo zakona 'O vnesenii izmenenii i dopolnenii v Osnovy zakonodatel'stva Rossiiskoi Federatsii ob Arkhivnom fonde Rossiiskoi Federatsii i arkhivakh'," but as of mid-1999 had not yet been enacted.

L-13. "O realizatsii gosudarstvennoi politiki v arkhivnom dele": Postanovlenie Soveta Ministrov—Pravitel'stva RF ot 23 avgusta 1993 g., no. 838. *Sobranie aktov Prezidenta i Pravitel'stva RF*, 1993, no. 35 (30 August), st. 3342.

L-14. "Polozhenie ob Arkhivnom fonde Rossiiskoi Federatsii" and "Polozhenie o Gosudarstvennoi arkhivnoi sluzhbe Rossii": Confirmation: Ukaz Prezidenta RF ot 17 marta 1994 g., no. 552. *Sobranie aktov Prezidenta i Pravitel'stva RF*, 1994, no. 12 (21 March), st. 878.
> Published in *Otechestvennye arkhivy*, 1994, no. 3, pp. 3–12, and in *Rossiiskaia gazeta* (1 April 1994), p. 4. See the 1994 amendments in L-15.

> MODIFICATION: (1996) "O vnesenii izmenenii v Polozhenie ob Arkhivnom fonde Rossiiskoi Federatsii, utverzhdennoe Ukazom Prezidenta Rossiiskoi Federatsii ot 17 marta 1994 g. no. 552": Confirmation: Ukaz Prezidenta RF ot 1 aprelia 1996 g., no. 460. *Sobranie zakonodatel'stva RF*, 1996, no. 15 (8 April), st. 1575.
>> Published in *Informatsionnyi biulleten'* [Rosarkhiva], no. 14 (1996), p. 2.
>>
>> Amends the 1994 regulation (§8) providing for the long-term retention of archives by two additional KGB successor agencies—the Federal Border Service (*Federal'naia pogranichnaia sluzhba RF*) and the Federal Agency for Government Communications and Information—FAPSI (*Federal'noe agentstvo pravitel'stvennoi sviazi i informatsii*) under the President of the Russian Federation.

MODIFICATION: (1998) "O vnesenii izmenenii v Ukaz Prezidenta Rossiiskoi Federatsii ot 17 marta 1994 g. no. 552 "Ob utverzhdenii Polozheniia ob Arkhivnom fonde Rossiiskoi Federatsii i Polozheniia o Gosudarstvennoi arkhivnoi sluzhbe Rossii" i v Polozhenie ob Arkhivnom fonde Rossiiskoi Federatsii": Ukaz Prezidenta RF ot 1 dekabria 1998 g., no. 1447. *Sobranie zakonodatel'stva RF*, 1998, no. 49 (7 December), st. 6007.

L-15. "Polozhenie o Federal'noi arkhivnoi sluzhbe Rossii": Confirmation: Postanovlenie Pravitel'stva RF ot 28 dekabria 1998 g., no. 1562. *Sobranie zakonodatel'stva RF*, 1999, no. 1 (4 January), st. 203.

> Published in *Otechestvennye arkhivy*, 1999, no. 1, pp. 3–8, and in *Rossiiskaia gazeta*, no. 26 (11 February 1999), p. 4.

L-16. "O Muzeinom fonde Rossiiskoi Federatsii i muzeiakh v Rossiiskoi Federatsii": Federal'nyi zakon ot 26 maia 1996 g., no. 54–FZ. *Sobranie zakonodatel'stva RF*, 1996, no. 22 (27 May), st. 2591.

> Published in *Rossiiskaia gazeta*, no. 104 (4 June 1996), p. 4, together with a commentary by Anna Kolupaeva, an expert from the Administration of Museums in the Ministry of Culture, in the form of an interview with journalist Tat'iana Kharlamova.

L-17. "Polozheniia o Muzeinom fonde Rossiiskoi Federatsii, o Gosudarstvennom kataloge Muzeinogo fonda Rossiiskoi Federatsii, o litsenzirovanii deiatel'nosti muzeev v Rossiiskoi Federatsii": Confirmation: Postanovlenie Pravitel'stva RF ot 12 fevralia 1998 g., no. 179. *Sobranie zakonodatel'stva RF*, 1998, no. 8 (23 February), st. 949.

L-18. "Pravila raboty pol'zovatelei v chital'nykh zalakh gosudarstvennykh arkhivov Rossiiskoi Federatsii": Prikaz Rosarkhiva ot 6 iiulia 1998 g., no. 51. Zaregistrirovano v Miniuste RF 16 dekabria 1998, no. 1660. Published in *Rossiiskaia gazeta*, no. 247 (29 December), p. 6.

> Reprinted in brochure form by Rosarkhiv. An English translation is included as Appendix 3 in the present directory (pp. 0000–00). A copy appears on the ABB website http://www.iish.nl/~abb.

L-19. "O federal'nykh gosudarstvennykh arkhivakh": Confirmation: Postanovlenie Pravitel'stva RF ot 15 marta 1999 g., no. 283. *Sobranie zakonodatel'stva RF*, 1999, no. 12 (22 March), st. 1485.

> Published in *Rossiiskaia gazeta*, no. 247 (29 December 1998), p. 6. Published in *Otechestvennye arkhivy*, 1999, no. 3, pp. 3–4.

2. Basic Laws and Decrees Regulating Access and Use of Archives: State Secrets, Commercial Secrets, and Declassification

The official texts of most federal laws and regulations in this category through 1997 have been reprinted in the journal *Zakon: Zhurnal dlia delovykh liudei*, no. 2 (February 1998) (Lib: DLC; MH-L), issued as a supplement to the newspaper *Izvestiia*.

a. Laws and Decrees Regarding State Secrets

L-20. "O zashchite gosudarstvennykh sekretov Rossiiskoi Federatsii": Ukaz Prezidenta RF ot 14 ianvaria 1992 g., no. 20. *Vedomosti S"ezda narodnykh deputatov RSFSR i Verkhovnogo Soveta RSFSR*, 1992, no. 4 (23 January), st. 166.

L-21. "O gosudarstvennoi taine": Zakon RF ot 21 iiulia 1993 g., no. 5485–I. "O poriadke vvedeniia v deistvie Zakona Rossiiskoi Federatsii 'O gosudarstvennoi taine,' no. 5486–I ot 21 iiulia 1993 g." Published in *Rossiiskaia gazeta*, no. 182 (21 September 1993), pp. 5–6.

MODIFICATION: "O vnesenii izmenenii i dopolnenii v Zakon Rossiiskoi Federatsii 'O gosudarstvennoi taine' [i tekst Zakona Rossiiskoi Federatsii 'O gosudarstvennoi taine' ot 21 iiulia 1993 g. no. 5486–I]": Federal'nyi zakon ot 6 oktiabria 1997 g., no. 131–FZ. *Sobranie zakonodatel'stva RF*, 1997, no. 41 (13 October), st. 4673 (includes the text of the original 1993 law).

> Although a published version of the law did not appear in the official registers of government laws in 1993, it was published with the 1997 modification. The law and modification are also published in *Zakon*, no. 2, pp. 9–20.

AMENDMENT: "Voprosy zashchity gosudarstvennoi tainy": Ukaz Prezidenta RF ot 30 marta 1994 g., no. 614. *Sobranie aktov Prezidenta i Pravitel'stva RF*, 1994, no. 13 (28 March), st. 1050.

> Provides for the temporary authority of the State Technical Commission until the Interagency Commission for Determining State Secrets is established (See L-24).

L-22. "Perechen' dolzhnostnykh lits organov gosudarstvennoi vlasti, nadeliaemykh polnomochiiami po otneseniiu svedenii k gosudarstvennoi taine": Confirmation: Rasporiazhenie Prezidenta RF ot 11 fevralia 1994 g. *Sobranie aktov Prezidenta i Pravitel'stva RF*, 1994, no. 7 (14 February), st. 506.

MODIFICATION: "Perechen' dolzhnostnykh lits organov gosudarstvennoi vlasti, nadeliaemykh polnomochiiami po otneseniiu svedenii k gosudarstvennoi taine": Confirmation: Rasporiazhenie Prezidenta RF ot 30 maia 1997 g., no. 226–rp. *Sobranie zakonodatel'stva RF*, 1997, no. 22 (2 June), st. 2573.

> The modification is published in *Zakon*, no. 2, p. 30.

L-23. "Pravila otneseniia svedenii, sostavliaiushchikh gosudarstvennuiu tainu, k razlichnym stepeniam sekretnosti": Confirmation: Postanovleniie Pravitel'stva RF ot 4 sentiabria 1995 g., no. 870. *Sobranie zakonodatel'stva RF*, 1995, no. 37 (11 September), st. 3619.

> Published in *Rossiiskaia gazeta*, no. 179 (14 September 1995), p. 3; *Zakon*, no. 2, pp. 34–35.

L-24. "O Mezhvedomstvennoi komissii po zashchite gosudarstvennoi tainy": Ukaz Prezidenta RF ot 8 noiabria 1995 g., no. 1108. *Sobranie zakonodatel'stva RF*, 1995, no. 46 (13 November), st. 4418.

> Published in *Rossiiskaia gazeta*, no. 224 (18 November 1995), p 6. Establishes the Interagency Commission for Determining State Secrets, which had been called for by the July 1993 law, but not previously established. See the later decree providing for the members of the Commission and its functions (L-26).

L-25. "Perechen' svedenii, otnesennykh k gosudarstvennoi taine": Confirmation: Ukaz Prezidenta RF ot 30 noiabria 1995 g., no. 1203. *Sobranie zakonodatel'stva RF*, 1995, no. 49 (4 December), st. 4775.

MODIFICATION: "Perechen' svedenii, otnesennykh k gosudarstvennoi taine": Confirmation: Ukaz Prezidenta RF ot 24 ianvaria 1998 g., no. 61. *Sobranie zakonodatel'stva RF*, 1998, no. 5 (2 February), st. 561.

> Published in *Rossiiskaia gazeta*, no. 246 (27 December 1995), p. 5; *Zakon*, no. 2, pp. 20–26. A more detailed secret supplemental version was also issued in accordance with the earlier 1993 law itself (L-21).

L-26. "Voprosy Mezhvedomstvennoi komissii po zashchite gosudarstvennoi tainy": Ukaz Prezidenta RF ot 20 ianvaria 1996 g., no. 71.

"Polozhenie o Mezhvedomstvennoi komissii po zashchite gosudarstvennoi tainy";
"Struktura Mezhvedomstvennoi komissii po zashchite gosudarstvennoi tainy";
"Sostav Mezhvedomstvennoi komissii po zashchite gosudarstvennoi tainy": Confirmation: Ukaz Prezidenta RF ot 20 ianvaria 1996 g., no. 71. *Sobranie zakonodatel'stva RF*, 1996, no. 4 (22 January), st. 268.

MODIFICATION: "O nekotorykh voprosakh Mezhvedomstvennoi komissii po zashchite gosudarstvennoi tainy": Ukaz Prezidenta RF ot 14 iiunia 1997 g., no. 594. *Sobranie zakonodatel'stva RF*, 1997, no. 25 (23 June), st. 2899.

Provides for the composition and function of the "Interagency Commission for Determining State Secrets," established in November 1995 (see L-24), and also annuls the temporary authority of the State Technical Commission as provided for in the March 1994 decree amending the law "On State Secrets" (L-21).

> Published in *Zakon*, no. 2, pp. 27–30.

L-27. "O Gosudarstvennoi programme obespecheniia zashchity gosudarstvennoi tainy v Rossiiskoi Federatsii na 1996–1997 gg.": Ukaz Prezidenta RF ot 9 marta 1996 g., no. 346. *Sobranie zakonodatel'stva RF*, 1996, no. 12 (20 March), st. 1057.

L-28. "Instruktsiia o poriadke dopuska dolzhnostnykh lits i grazhdan Rossiiskoi Federatsii k gosudarstvennoi taine": Confirmation: Postanovlenie Pravitel'stva RF ot 28 oktiabria 1995 g., no. 1050.

> Published in *Zakon*, no. 2, pp. 36–45.

L-29. "Polozhenie o poriadke dopuska lits, imeiushchikh dvoinoe grazhdanstvo, lits bez grazhdanstva, a takzhe lits iz chisla inostrannykh grazhdan, emigrantov i reemigrantov k gosudarstvennoi taine": Confirmation: Postanovlenie Pravitel'stva RF ot 22 avgusta 1998 g., no. 1003. *Sobranie zakonodatel'stva RF*, 1998, no. 35 (1 September), st. 4407.

b. Regulations Governing Commercial Secrets

L-30. "O perechne svedenii, kotorye ne mogut sostavliat' kommercheskuiu tainu": Postanovlenie Pravitel'stva RSFSR ot 5 dekabria 1991 g., no. 35. *Sobranie Postanovlenii Pravitel'stva RF*, 1992, no. 1–2, st. 7.

c. Declassification of Soviet-Period Archives

L-31. ["Ob obrazovanii Komissii po rassekrechivaniiu dokumentov, sozdannykh KPSS"]: Rasporiazhenie Prezidenta RF ot 22 sentiabria 1994 g., no. 489–rp." *Sobranie zakonodatel'stva RF,* 1994, no. 22 (26 September), st. 2498.

> Published in *Rossiiskaia gazeta*, no. 185 (27 September 1994), p. 4. An English translation and analysis by Mark Kramer appears in *CWIHP Bulletin* 4 (Fall 1994): 89. Published in *Otechestvennye arkhivy*, 1995, no. 1, pp. 3–4, followed by a commentary by V. P. Kozlov (pp. 4–5).

L-32. "Ob ustanovlenii poriadka rassekrechivaniia i prodleniia srokov zasekrechivaniia arkhivnykh dokumentov Pravitel'stva SSSR": Postanovlenie Pravitel'stva RF ot 20 fevralia 1995 g., no. 170. *Sobranie zakonodatel'stva RF*, 1995, no. 9 (27 February), st. 762.

> Published in *Rossiiskaia gazeta*, no. 44 (1 March 1995), p. 16. An English translation is published in *Social History and Russia* (IISH, Amsterdam), no. 1 (April 1995): 6–7 (with incorrect dates cited).

d. Laws and Decrees Relating to Human Rights, Rehabilitation, and the Politically Repressed (and Related Archives)

L-33. "O reabilitatsii zhertv politicheskikh repressii": Zakon RSFSR ot 18 oktiabria 1991 g. *Vedomosti S"ezda narodnykh deputatov RSFSR i Verkhovnogo Soveta RSFSR*, 1991, no. 44 (31 October), st. 1428.

> See also the enabling directive, "O poriadke vvedeniia v deistvie Zakona RSFSR 'O reabilitatsii zhertv politicheskikh repressii' ": Postanovlenie Verkhovnogo Soveta RSFSR ot 18 oktiabria 1991 g., no. 531. *Vedomosti S"ezda narodnykh deputatov RSFSR i Verkhovnogo Soveta RSFSR*, 1991, no. 44 (13 October), st. 1429.
>
> MODIFICATIONS: See L-37.

L-34. "O komissiiakh po reabilitatsii zhertv politicheskikh repressii": Postanovlenie Prezidiuma Verkhovnogo Soveta RSFSR ot 16 dekabria 1991 g., no. 2046–I. *Vedomosti S"ezda narodnykh deputatov RSFSR i Verkhovnogo Soveta RSFSR*, 1992, no. 1 (2 January), st. 13.

A further confirming directive (*postanovlenie*) was issued by the Presidium of the Supreme Council, 30 March 1992 g., no. 2610–I, *Vedomosti S"ezda*, 1992, no. 17, st. 901.

An additional confirming directive (*postanovlenie*) and the appointment of a chairman of the Commission was issued by the Presidium of the Supreme Council, 26 October 1992 g., no. 3753/I–I, *Vedomosti S"ezda*, 1992, no. 45, st. 2582.

L-35. "O sniatii ogranichitel'nykh grifov s zakonodatel'nykh i inykh aktov, sluzhivshikh osnovaniem dlia massovykh repressii i posiagatel'stv na prava cheloveka": Ukaz Prezidenta RF ot 23 iiunia 1992 g., no. 658. *Vedomosti S"ezda narodnykh deputatov RF i Verkhovnogo Soveta RF*, 1992, no. 26 (2 July), st. 1510.

L-36. "Ob obrazovanii Komissii pri Prezidente Rossiiskoi Federatsii po reabilitatsii zhertv politicheskikh repressii'": Ukaz Prezidenta RF ot 2 dekabria 1992 g., no. 1509. *Vedomosti S"ezda narodnykh deputatov RF i Verkhovnogo Soveta RF*, 1992, no. 49 (10 December), st. 2944.

L-37. "O vnesenii izmenenii i dopolnenii v Zakon RSFSR 'O reabilitatsii zhertv politicheskikh repressii'": Zakon RF ot 22 dekabria 1992 g., no. 4185–I. *Vedomosti S"ezda narodnykh deputatov RF i Verkhovnogo Soveta RF*, 1993, no. 1 (7 January), st. 21.

————: Federal'nyi zakon ot 4 noiabria 1995 g., no. 166–FZ. *Sobranie zakonodatel'stva RF*, 1995, no. 45 (6 November), st. 4242.

Amendments for the 18 October 1991 law (L-33).

L-38. "O vosstanovlenii zakonnykh prav rossiiskikh grazhdan—byvshikh sovetskikh voennoplennykh i grazhdanskikh lits, repatriirovannykh v period Velikoi Otechestvennoi voiny i v poslevoennyi period": Ukaz Prezidenta RF ot 24 ianvaria 1995 g., no. 63. *Sobranie zakonodatel'stva RF*, 1995, no. 5 (30 January), st. 394.

e. Laws and Directives Relating to Information Resources

L-39. "Ob informatsii, informatizatsii i zashchite informatsii": Federal'nyi zakon ot 20 fevralia 1995 g., no. 24–FZ. *Sobranie zakonodatel'stva RF*, 1995, no. 8 (20 February), st. 609.

Published in *Rossiiskaia gazeta*, no. 39 (22 February 1995), pp. 15–16. Article 13, paragraphs 1 and 2, give organs of state authority the right to restrict access "to information resources pertaining to the activities of their organs," which could be interpreted to give federal agencies full discretion over their own archives. See the comments to this effect by Mark Kramer in *CWIHP Bulletin* 5 (Fall 1995): 77.

L-40. "Ob uchastii v mezhdunarodnom informatsionnom obmene": Federal'nyi zakon ot 4 iiulia 1996 g., no. 85–FZ. *Sobranie zakonodatel'stva RF*, 1996, no. 28 (8 July), st. 3347.

Following a letter of inquiry from Rosarkhiv about the difficulties of applicability of this law to archival affairs, legislative authorities assured Rosarkhiv that an amended version of the law would be prepared in the fall of 1996, but as of mid-1999, a new law or amendments had not been passed.

L-41. "Polozhenie o litsenzirovanii deiatel'nosti po mezhdunarodnomu informatsionnomu obmenu": Confirmation: Postanovlenie Pravitel'stva RF ot 3 iiunia 1998 g., no. 564. *Sobranie zakonodatel'stva RF*, 1998, no. 23 (13 July), st. 2559.

f. Documentation Relating to Atomic Weapons

L-42. "O podgotovke i izdanii ofitsial'nogo sbornika arkhivnykh dokumentov po istorii sozdaniia iadernogo oruzhiia v SSSR": Ukaz Prezidenta RF ot 17 fevralia 1995 g., no. 160. *Sobranie zakonodatel'stva RF*, 1995, no. 8 (20 February), st. 658.

Published in *Rossiiskaia gazeta*, no. 44 (1 March 1995), p. 14. An English translation by David Russel Stone appears in *CWIHP* 5 (Spring 1995): 57.

> See also the directive, "Sbornik arkhivnykh dokumentov," on the implementation of the February 1995 decree and appointing a commission for declassification (24 May 1995), no. 728–r, signed by Prime Minister Viktor Chernomyrdin, published in *Rossiiskaia gazeta*, 7 June 1995, p. 5; an English translation by Mark Kramer is published in *CWIHP* 6/7 (Winter 1995/1996): 266–71.

3. Laws and Directives Regulating Archives/Records of Specific Federal Agencies

a. Archive of the President RF

L-43. "Ob Arkhive Prezidenta Rossiiskoi Federatsii": Ukaz Prezidenta RF ot 31 dekabria 1991 g., no. 338. *Vedomosti S"ezda narodnykh deputatov RSFSR i Verkhovnogo Soveta RSFSR*, 1992, no. 3 (16 January), st. 95.

> Published in *Vestnik AP RF*, no. 1, in *Istochnik*, 1995, no. 1, p. 116, together with three other secret documents issued earlier by Soviet President Gorbachev, about the organization of AP RF. The archive, including the records from the archive of the Politburo, was officially transferred from the control of the President of the USSR to the President of the RSFSR by the secret directive, "O peredache arkhiva Prezidenta SSSR v arkhiv Prezidenta RSFSR": Rasporiazhenie Prezidenta SSSR, 23 December 1991, no. 3152–rp (ibid., p. 115).

L-44. "Voprosy Arkhiva Prezidenta Rossiiskoi Federatsii": Rasporiazhenie Prezidenta RF ot 17 fevralia 1992 g., no. 56–rp. *Vedomosti S"ezda narodnykh deputatov RF i Verkhovnogo Soveta RF*, 1992, no. 9 (27 February), st. 432.

L-45. "Polozhenie ob Arkhive Prezidenta Rossiiskoi Federatsii: Sostav dokumentov Arkhiva Prezidenta Rossiiskoi Federatsii": Confirmation: Rasporiazhenie Prezidenta RF ot 25 marta 1994 g., no. 151–rp. *Sobranie aktov Prezidenta i Pravitel'stva RF*, 1994, no. 13 (28 March), st. 1019.

> Provides for the permanent retention of holdings in AP RF, including the historical part, to a much more restrictive extent than in previous decrees.

L-46. "O merakh po sovershenstvovaniiu struktury Administratsii Prezidenta Rossiiskoi Federatsii": Ukaz Prezidenta RF ot 12 fevralia 1998 g., no. 162. *Sobranie zakonodatel'stva RF*, 1998, no. 7 (16 February), st. 827

> Abolishes AP RF as previously organized, placing the archival functions and holdings under a different agency structure within the Administration of the President (see C–1).

L-47. "Polozhenie ob Upravlenii informatsionnogo i dokumentatsionnogo obespecheniia Prezidenta Rossiiskoi Federatsii": Confirmation: Ukaz Prezidenta RF ot 15 aprelia 1998 g., no. 377. *Sobranie zakonodatel'stva RF*, 1998, no. 16 (20 April), st. 1831.

> Regulates the archival functions within the newly reorganized Administration for Information and Documentary Support of the President.

b. Security and Intelligence Service Records (Former KGB)
   See also L-2 and L-5

L-48. "Ob operativno-rozysknoi deiatel'nosti": Zakon RF ot 29 aprelia 1992 g., no. 2506–I. *Vedomosti S"ezda narodnykh deputatov RF i Verkhovnogo Soveta RF*, 1992, no. 17 (23 April), st. 892.

> MODIFICATION: See L-53.
>> Amendments to the law are recorded in *Vedomosti S"ezda*, 1992, no. 33, st. 1912.
>> A paragraph in the law places all information about agents and their informants of the KGB and its predecessors (without time limitation) in the category of "state secrets," thus limiting the categories of KGB documentation that can be declassified. A copy of the law with accompanying analysis was issued as a separate brochure: *Zakon ob operativno-rozysknoi deiatel'nosti* (M.: Iuridicheskaia literatura, 1994).

L-49. "O vneshnei razvedke": Zakon RF ot 8 iiulia 1992 g., no. 3245–I. *Vedomosti S"ezda narodnykh deputatov RF i Verkhovnogo Soveta RF*, 1992, no. 32 (13 August), st. 1869.

> See the later regulation passed in December 1995 and signed into law January 1996 (L-55).

L-50. "O federal'nykh organakh pravitel'stvennoi sviazi i informatsii": Zakon RF ot 19 fevralia 1993 g., no. 4524–I. *Vedomosti S"ezda narodnykh deputatov RF i Verkhovnogo Soveta RF*, 1993, no. 12 (25 March), st. 423.

> Regulates the Government Communications Service and related organs, which have taken over functions of counterespionage and ciphered communications, previously handled by the KGB. Establishes the regulation (art. 18, para. 3) that records of the organs are to be kept by the agency itself, but that those of "scientific-historical value" are eventually to be transferred to federal archives.

L-51. "O sroke dostupa k arkhivnym dokumentam, otnosiashchimsia k sfere deiatel'nosti vneshnei razvedki": Postanovlenie Verkhovnogo Soveta RF ot 23 iiulia 1993 g., no. 5505–I. *Vedomosti S"ezda narodnykh deputatov RF i Verkhovnogo Soveta RF*, 1993, no. 34 (26 August), st. 1397.

> Establishes a 50-year ruling from the date of creation during which period documents relating to foreign intelligence activities are to be closed.

L-52. "Ob organakh Federal'noi sluzhby bezopasnosti v Rossiiskoi Federatsii." Federal'nyi zakon ot 3 aprelia 1995 g., no. 40–FZ. *Sobranie zakonodatel'stva RF*, 1995, no. 15 (10 April), st. 1269.

> Article 7 deals specifically with the FSB archives, essentially giving the agency the right to retain and protect its own records, and establishes the inviolability of documents revealing methods and agents with no time limit, although there is a provision for documentation "of historical and scientific value" to be transferred to federal archives.

L-53. "Ob operativno-rozysknoi deiatel'nosti": Federal'nyi zakon ot 12 avgusta 1995 g., no. 144–FZ. *Sobranie zakonodatel'stva RF*, 1995, no. 33 (14 August), st. 3349.

MODIFICATION: "O vnesenii izmenenii i dopolnenii v Federal'nyi zakon 'Ob operativno-rozysknoi deiatel'nosti'": Federal'nyi zakon ot 5 ianvaria 1999 g., no. 6–FZ. *Sobranie zakonodatel'stva RF*, 1999, no. 2 (11 January), st. 233.

> Revises and amends the 1992 law (L-48). A paragraph in the law places all information about current agents and their informants of the FSB and its predecessors in the category of "confidential," in a slightly modified form from the earlier 1992 version, but still requiring written permission for access.

L-54. "Polozhenie o Federal'noi sluzhbe bezopasnosti Rossiiskoi Federatsii." Confirmation: Ukaz Prezidenta RF ot 6 iiulia 1998 g., no. 806. *Sobranie zakonodatel'stva RF*, 1998, no. 28 (13 July), st. 3320.

> Deals with the structure and functions of the RSB, but does not regulate archival functions nor does it add any related clarification regarding potential declassification and access or archival preservation.

L-55. "O vneshnei razvedke": Federal'nyi zakon ot 10 ianvaria 1996 g., no 5–FZ. *Sobranie zakonodatel'stva RF*, 1996, no. 3 (15 January), st. 143.

> Published in *Rossiiskaia gazeta*, no. 9 (17 January 1996), pp. 4–5. Passed by the Duma on 8 December 1995 as a general law covering foreign intelligence agencies. In addition to the SVR, the law also covers the Chief Intelligence Directorate (GRU), the Federal Communications and Information Service, and the foreign-intelligence section of the FSB. Article 7 deals specifically with the right of each of these agencies to retain and protect their own agency archives (similar to L-52), although provides for documentation "of historical and scientific value" to be transferred to federal archives.

L-56. "O gosudarstvennoi okhrane": Federal'nyi zakon ot 27 maia 1996 g., no. 57–FZ. *Sobranie zakonodatel'stva RF*, 1996, no. 22 (27 May 1996), st. 2594.

> Published in *Rossiiskaia gazeta*, no. 106 (6 June 1996), pp. 4–5. A general law pertaining to all security and intelligence agencies, including the armed forces. Article 17 provides for the retention of their own archives by the agencies involved, but also specifies that materials of "historical and scientific value are to be declassified and transferred to archives under Rosarkhiv."

L-57. "Polozhenie o mezhvedomstvennykh komissiiakh Soveta Bezopasnosti Rossiiskoi Federatsii": [Polozhenie o Mezhvedomstvennoi komissii Soveta Bezopasnosti Rossiiskoi Federatsii po informatsionnoi bezopasnosti]: Confirmation: Ukaz Prezidenta RF ot 19 sentiabria 1997 g., no. 1037. *Sobranie zakonodatel'stva RF*, 1997, no. 39 (29 September), st. 4527.

c. Ministry of Foreign Affairs

L-58. "O Ministerstve inostrannykh del Rossiiskoi Federatsii": Ukaz Prezidenta RF ot 14 marta 1995 g., no. 271. *Sobranie zakonodatel'stva RF*, 1995, no. 12 (20 March), st. 1033.

> Article 5 gives MID the right to retain its archives permanently.

d. State Radio-Television and Motion Picture Archives
See also L-72 regarding deposit copies.

L-59. "O Gosudarstvennom fonde kinofil'mov Rossiiskoi Federatsii": Postanovlenie Pravitel'stva RF ot 30 dekabria 1994 g., no. 1457. *Sobranie zakonodatel'stva RF*, 1995, no. 2 (9 January), st. 155.

L-60. "O Gosudarstvennom fonde televizionnykh i radioprogramm Rossiiskoi Federatsii": Postanovlenie Pravitel'stva RF ot 13 dekabria 1995 g., no. 1232. *Sobranie zakonodatel'stva RF*, 1995, no. 51 (18 December), st. 5073.

> See also the earlier provisions for Gosteleradiofond (C–17) in the presidential decree, "O sovershenstvovanii gosudarstvennogo upravleniia v sfere massovoi informatsii": Ukaz Prezidenta RF ot 20 dekabria 1993 g., no. 2255. *Sobranie aktov Prezidenta i Pravitel'stva RF*, 1993, no. 52 (27 December), st. 5067.

L-61. "O Gosudarstvennoi podderzhke kinematografii Rossiiskoi Federatsii": Federal'nyi zakon ot 22 avgusta 1996 g., no. 126–FZ. *Sobranie zakonodatel'stva RF*, 1996, no. 35 (16 August), st. 4136.

> Provides for the retention of archival copies of feature films (in C–16) and newsreels (in B–11), with appropriate copyright provisions.

L-62. "Ustav Gosudarstvennogo fonda kinofil'mov Rossiiskoi Federatsii": Confirmation: Postanovlenie Pravitel'stva RF ot 2 aprelia 1997 g., no. 370. *Sobranie zakonodatel'stva RF*, 1997, no. 14 (7 April), st. 1634.

> Replaces the provisions of L-59.

4. Provisions for Accession and Preservation of Specific Agency or Types of Agency Records

a. Documentation of the Supreme Soviet and Other Agencies, Including Mass Media

L-63. "O sokhranenii istoricheskikh dokumentov, sviazannykh s deiatel'nost'iu byvshego Verkhovnogo Soveta Rossiiskoi Federatsii, a takzhe nekotorykh sredstv massovoi informatsii i obshchestvennykh organizatsii": Rasporiazhenie Prezidenta RF ot 22 oktiabria 1993 g., no. 700–rp. *Sobranie aktov Prezidenta i Pravitel'stva RF*, 1993, no. 43 (25 October), st. 4091.

> Calls for the preservation of documentation of the Supreme Soviet that had been retained in the Russian White House, following the October 1993 suppression of the Supreme Soviet and the armed clashes in Moscow that followed.

L-64. "O prieme dokumentov redaktsii gazet *Pravda* i *Sovetskaia Rossiia*": Rasporiazhenie Soveta Ministrov–Pravitel'stva RF ot 14 oktiabria 1993 g., no. 1846–r. *Sobranie aktov Prezidenta i Pravitel'stva RF*, 1993, no. 43 (25 October), st. 4161.

b. Scientific-Technical Documentation

L-65. "O prodlenii ogranichitel'nogo khraneniia arkhivnykh dokumentov, soderzhashchikh svedeniia po razrabotkam v oblasti atomnoi nauki i tekhniki": Postanovlenie Prezidiuma Verkhovnogo Soveta RF ot 21 dekabria 1992 g., no. 4140–I. *Vedomosti S"ezda narodnykh deputatov RF i Verkhovnogo Soveta RF*, 1993, no. 1 (7 January), st. 39.

> Specifically relates to extended preservation of documentation relating to the development of atomic energy.

L-66. Polozhenie o gosudarstvennoi sisteme nauchno-tekhnicheskoi informatsii: Confirmation: Postanovlenie Pravitel'stva RF ot 24 iiulia 1997 g., no. 950. *Sobranie zakonodatel'stva RF*, 1997, no. 31 (4 August), st. 3696.

> Calls for the preservation of scientific-technical documentation in appropriate archives (such as B–9, C–12–C–15) and libraries.

c. Records of Vital Statistics (ZAGS)

L-67. "Ob aktakh grazhdanskogo sostoianiia": Federal'nyi zakon ot 15 noiabria 1997, no. 143–FZ. *Sobranie zakonodatel'stva RF*, 1997, no. 47 (24 November), st. 5340.

d. Personnel Records

L-68. "Ob obespechenii sokhrannosti dokumentov po lichnomu sostavu vysvobozhdaemykh rabotnikov v resul'tate obrazovaniia, reorganizatsii i likvidatsii iuridicheskikh lits": Rasporiazhenie Pravitel'stva RF ot 21 marta 1994 g., no. 358–r. *Sobranie aktov Prezidenta i Pravitel'stva RF*, 1994, no. 13 (28 March), st. 1048.

5. Laws and Decrees Regarding Copyright and Licensing Use of Archival Documents and Archival Deposit Copies

L-69. "Vremennye polozheniia o poriadke zakliucheniia litsenzionnykh dogovorov na ispol'zovanie dokumentov gosarkhivov i tsentrov dokumentatsii RF v kommercheskikh tseliakh." Moscow: Rosarkhiv, 1993.

> Published in *Otechestvennye arkhivy*, 1993, no. 2, p. 112.
>
> The temporary regulation was adopted in the Rosarkhiv Collegium 10 February 1993 and printed for in-house circulation. Since it was not confirmed by higher government action, it does not appear

as an official law or regulation. As of mid-1999, regulation is no longer in force, but a new one has not been issued, hence Rosarkhiv does not have the right to issues licenses for commercial use of documentation.

L-70. "Ob avtorskom prave i smezhnykh pravakh: Zakon RF ot 9 iiulia 1993 g., no. 5351–I. *Vedomosti S"ezda narodnykh deputatov RF i Verkhovnogo Soveta RF*, 1993, no. 32 (12 August), st. 1242.

L-71. "O gosudarstvennoi politike v oblasti okhrany avtorskogo prava i smezhnykh prav: Ukaz Prezidenta RF ot 7 oktiabria 1993 g., no. 1607. *Sobranie aktov Prezidenta i Pravitel'stva RF*, 1993, no. 41 (11 October), st. 3920.

L-72. "Ob obiazatel'nom ekzempliare dokumentov": Federal'nyi zakon ot 29 dekabria 1994 g., no. 77–FZ. *Sobranie zakonodatel'stva RF,* 1995, no. 1 (2 January), st. 1.
> Provides for an archival deposit copy of all films produced in Russia in Gosfil'mofond and Gosteleradiofond, as well as an archival copy of published books and journals in the All-Russian Book Chamber.

L-73. "Polozhenie o litsenzirovanii deiatel'nosti po obsledovaniiu sostoianiia arkhivnykh fondov, ekspertize, opisaniiu, konservatsii i restavratsii arkhivnykh dokumentov": Postanovlenie Pravitel'stva RF ot 24 iiulia 1995 g., no. 747. *Sobranie zakonodatel'stva RF*, 1995, no. 31 (31 July), st. 3134.
> Published in *Otechestvennye arkhivy*, 1995, no. 5, p. 3–6.

6. Regulations Relating to Restitution and Transfer Abroad of Archives and Other Cultural Treasures

a. Export and Import of Cultural Treasures

L-74. "O vyvoze i vvoze kul'turnykh tsennostei": Zakon RF ot 15 aprelia 1993 g., no. 4804–I." *Vedomosti S"ezda narodnykh deputatov RF i Verkhovnogo Soveta RF*, 1993, no. 20 (20 May), st. 718.
> Regulates the transfer of cultural treasures to and from abroad and prohibits the export of designated cultural treasures.

b. Displaced Cultural Treasures as a Result of World War II

L-75. "O moratorii na vozvrashchenie kul'turnykh tsennostei, peremeshchennykh v gody Velikoi Otechestvennoi voiny": Postanovlenie Gosudarstvennoi Dumy Federal'nogo sobraniia RF ot 21 aprelia 1995 g., no. 725–I GD. *Sobranie zakonodatel'stva RF*, 1995, no. 19 (8 May), st. 1721.
> Establishes a moratorium on restitution of foreign cultural treasures brought to Russia after World War II until the adoption of appropriate Russian legislation regulating the matter.

L-76. "Ob obmene arkhivnykh dokumentov Kniazheskogo doma Likhtenshtein, peremeshchennykh posle okonchaniia Vtoroi mirovoi voiny na territoriiu Rossii, na arkhivnye dokumenty o rassledovanii obstoiatel'stv gibeli Nikolaia II i chlenov ego sem'i (arkhiv N. A. Sokolova)": Postanovlenie Gosudarstvennoi Dumy Federal'nogo sobraniia RF ot 13 iiunia 1996 g., no. 465–II GD. *Sobranie zakonodatel'stva RF*, 1996, no. 26 (24 June), st. 3043.

L-77. "O vozvrate Germanskoi Storone mikrofil'mov dokumentov TsK SEPG": Rasporiazhenie Prezidenta RF ot 16 aprelia 1997 g., no. 133–rp. *Sobranie zakonodatel'stva RF*, 1997, no. 16 (21 April), st. 1891.

L-78. ["O peredache Federativnoi Respublike Germaniia na osnove vzaimnosti arkhivnykh materialov, otnosiashchikhsia k V. Ratenau"]: Rasporiazhenie Prezidenta RF ot 16 aprelia 1997 g., no. 134–rp. *Sobranie zakonodatel'stva RF*, 1997, no. 16 (21 April), st. 1892.

L-79. ["O poriadke i usloviiakh peredachi Germanskoi Storone mikrofil'mov dokumentov TsK SEPG"]: Rasporiazhenie Pravitel'stva RF ot 16 iiunia 1997 g., no. 834–r. *Sobranie zakonodatel'stva RF* 1997, no. 26 (30 June), st. 3102.

L-80. "O kul'turnykh tsennostiakh, peremeshchennykh v Soiuz SSR v rezul'tate Vtoroi mirovoi voiny i nakhodiashchikhsia na territorii Rossiiskoi Federatsii": Federal'nyi zakon ot 15 aprelia 1998 g., no. 64–FZ. *Sobranie zakonodatel'stva RF*, 1998, no. 16 (20 April), st. 1799.

L-81. "Ob obmene arkhivnykh dokumentov Frantsuzskoi Respubliki, peremeshchennykh na territoriiu Rossiiskoi Federatsii v rezul'tate Vtoroi mirovoi voiny, na arkhivnye dokumenty rossiiskogo proiskhozhdeniia, nakhodiashchiesia na territorii Frantsuzskoi Respubliki": Postanovlenie Gosudarstvennoi Dumy Federal'nogo sobraniia RF ot 22 maia 1998 g., no. 2504–II GD. *Sobranie zakonodatel'stva RF*, 1998, no. 24 (15 June), st. 2662.

L-82. "O peredache Velikobritanii peremeshchennykh na territoriiu Rossiiskoi Federatsii v rezul'tate Vtoroi mirovoi voiny lichnykh dokumentov i dokumentov, udostoveriaiushchikh lichnost' voennosluzhashchikh Britanskogo ekspeditsionnogo korpusa": Postanovlenie Gosudarstvennoi Dumy Federal'nogo sobraniia RF ot 16 sentiabria 1998 g., no. 2973–II GD. *Sobranie zakonodatel'stva RF*, 1998, no. 39 (29 September), st. 4862.

7. Decrees and Orders Relating to the Federal Register of Monuments of the Russian Cultural Heritage

L-83. "Ob osobo tsennykh ob"ektakh natsional'nogo naslediia Rossii": Ukaz Prezidenta RF ot 18 dekabria 1991 g., no. 294." *Vedomosti S"ezda narodnykh deputatov RSFSR i Verkhovnogo Soveta RSFSR*, 1991, no. 52 (26 December), st. 1891.

L-84. "Ob osobo tsennykh ob"ektakh kul'turnogo naslediia narodov Rossiiskoi Federatsii": Ukaz Prezidenta RF ot 30 noiabria 1992 g., no. 1487. *Vedomosti S"ezda narodnykh deputatov RF i Verkhovnogo Soveta RF*, 1992, no. 49, st. 2936.

L-85. "Polozhenie o Gosudarstvennom ekspertnom sovete pri Prezidente Rossiiskoi Federatsii po osobo tsennym ob"ektam kul'turnogo naslediia narodov Rossiiskoi Federatsii": Confirmation: Ukaz Prezidenta RF ot 28 marta 1993 g., no. 410. *Sobranie aktov Prezidenta i Pravitel'stva RF*, 1992, no. 23 (11 June), st. 1961.

L-86. "O vkliuchenii otdel'nykh ob"ektov v Gosudarstvennyi svod osobo tsennykh ob"ektov kul'turnogo naslediia narodov Rossiiskoi Federatsii": Ukaz Prezidenta RF ot 6 noiabria 1993 g., no. 1847. *Sobranie aktov Prezidenta i Pravitel'stva RF*, 1993, no. 45 (8 November), st. 4334.
   Published in *Otechestvennye arkhivy*, 1993, no. 6, p. 16.

L-87. "Polozhenie o Gosudarstvennom svode osobo tsennykh ob"ektov kul'turnogo naslediia narodov Rossiiskoi Federatsii": Postanovlenie Pravitel'stva RF ot 6 oktiabria 1994 g., no. 1143. *Sobranie zakonodatel'stva RF*, 1994, no. 25 (11 June), st. 2710.

L-88. "O vkliuchenii otdel'nykh ob"ektov v Gosudarstvennyi svod osobo tsennykh ob"ektov kul'turnogo naslediia narodov Rossiiskoi Federatsii": Ukaz Prezidenta RF ot 24 ianvaria 1995 g., no. 64. *Sobranie zakonodatel'stva RF*, 1995, no. 5 (30 January), st. 395.
   Published in *Otechestvennye arkhivy*, 1995, no. 2, p. 3.

L-88. "O vkliuchenii otdel'nykh ob"ektov v Gosudarstvennyi svod osobo tsennykh ob"ektov kul'turnogo naslediia narodov Rossiiskoi Federatsii": Ukaz Presidenta RF ot 2 aprelia 1997 g., no. 275. *Sobranie zakonodatel'stva RF*, 1997, no. 14 (7 April), st. 1606.

L-89. "O vkliuchenii otdel'nykh ob"ektov v Gosudarstvennyi svod osobo tsennykh ob"ektov kul'turnogo naslediia narodov Rossiiskoi Federatsii": Ukaz Presidenta RF ot 15 ianvaria 1998 g., no. 30. *Sobranie zakonodatel'stva RF*, 1998, no. 3 (19 January), st. 315.

Appendix 2

Glossary of Russian Terms
for Archival and Manuscript Research

The brief glossary below is a selective guide to Russian archival terminology, emphasizing those terms that occur most often in the present directory. Given the extensive coverage of manuscript collections, including Slavonic manuscript books, a few terms frequently found in the names and/or descriptions of early manuscripts, including Orthodox liturgical books, are also included.

For more extensive, but nonetheless brief coverage of the most important Russian (Soviet) archival terms and their meanings, see the recent *Kratkii slovar' arkhivnoi terminologii* (Moscow/Leningrad: GAU, VNIIDAD, MGIAI, 1968; [IDC-R-9886]) to which the present glossary is much indebted. A more extensive glossary appeared in 1982, but with shorter definitions: *Slovar' sovremennoi arkhivnoi terminologii sotsialisticheskikh stran*, vol. 1, compiled by A. S. Malitikov, K. I. Rudel'son et al. (Moscow: Glavarkhiv/VNIIDAD, 1982). While it provides equivalents in the languages of the Communist bloc outside the USSR, no equivalents are given for the languages of the non-Russian Soviet republics.

The 1984 dictionary issued by the International Council on Archives provides brief French and English definitions of Western archival terminology with equivalents in several languages: *Dictionary of Archive Terminology: Dictionnaire de terminologie archivistique. English and French, With Equivalents in Dutch, German Italian, Russian and Spanish*, compiled by Frank B. Evans, François-J. Himly, and Peter Walne, edited by Peter Walne (Munich: K. G. Saur, 1984). Although Russian-language translations are furnished, Russian archival terms are not defined in the context of Russian/Soviet usage, and hence the equivalents given do not always reflect Russian practice. A similar problem will be encountered in the new edition of the ICA glossary nearing completion, as was apparent in the committee hearings during the ICA Congress in Beijing (September 1996); while the new edition will provide Russian definitions for Russian terms, there are as yet no provisions for translation of the defnitions in other languages.

For extensive treatment of Russian historical terms in English, see the *Dictionary of Russian Historical Terms from the Eleventh Century to 1917*, compiled by Sergei G. Pushkarev, and edited by George Vernadsky and Ralph T. Fisher, Jr. (New Haven, 1970); unfortunately, it is now out-of-print. Only a small number of such terms are included below, in particular, those not likely to be found in standard Russian-English dictionaries, and those with special meanings in Russian/Soviet archival literature.

Some of the definitions and descriptions of types of early Orthodox Church liturgical books have been adapted from the very helpful "Glossary" in *Lev Krevza's A Defense of Church Unity and Zaxarija Kopystens'kyj's Palinodia* , Part 2: *Sources* (Cambridge, MA: Harvard Ukrainian Research Institute, 1995; "Harvard Library of Early Ukrainian Literature," English Translations, vol. III, pt. 2), and from other religious handbooks.

For further discussion of some terms involved in Russian archival arrangement and reference publications, see Chapter 2 in Grimsted, *A Handbook for Archival Research in the USSR* (Washington, DC: Kennan Institute for Advanced Russian Studies and the International Research & Exchanges Board, 1989), and some of the Soviet archival textbooks cited there.

akt (pl. *akty*): official document, act. The formal official record of a deed or transaction, originating from state, ecclesiastic, or private sources. There is considerable scholarly dispute about the exact categories of documents that should be designated as *akty*. In prerevolutionary Russia the term usually refers to documents prepared according to established formulae or juridical norms, such as treaties, contracts, deeds, or the like.

akt grazhdanskogo sostoianiia: record of civil status (i.e. civil registry document). (1) An official document or certificate drawn from records of vital statistics. (2) Registry records of civil status, formed according to published formulae for recording a birth, death, marriage, divorce, change of name, adoption, etc. Throughout the Soviet Union, and continuing in the Russian Federation, such records are maintained by special registry offices—*Otdel zapisi aktov grazhdanskogo sostoianiia* (ZAGS).

aktovaia kniga: register book. A volume in which official decisions or resolutions of juridical or civic authorities were entered, or copies of official outgoing documents from a specific office. Most commonly used with reference to record books of pre–nineteenth-century courts and other local administrative offices in western areas of the Russian Empire that had been part of the Grand Duchy of Lithuania and (after 1569) the Polish-Lithuanian Commonwealth.

arkheografiia: archeography. (1) The scholarly work of collecting, identifying, cataloging, describing, and publishing manuscripts or other historical sources; traditionally used with reference to medieval manuscript books or other early historical documents, e.g., in connection with the work of the Archeographic Commission (from 1834) or archeographic expeditions. (2) The methodology of the publication of historical sources; used in Soviet archive literature and now retained in post-Soviet usage with reference to official documentary publication programs. Although the term "archeography" is rarely used in Western literature, it merits retention as appropriate to the post-Soviet Russian context. It is defined in Webster's unabridged dictionary as (from the Greek) "The systematic analysis of antiquities." For a recent discussion of the evolution of archeography, see a-709–a-709.1.

arkhiv: archive(s). (Note: Although the word is usually used in the plural in English, in this volume, because a distinction between singular and plural is often necessary, the Russian (and German) use of the singular form has been observed.) (1) A special institution devoted to the care, permanent storage, and public reference use of official non-current records and other documentary materials. In addition to the storage of *official* state records, but in Soviet and now Russian archives also serve as collecting agencies which house business, church, and private records, personal papers, films, manuscript collections, and miscellaneous documentary collections as well. (See *kollektsiia*.) (2) The preserved records of an institution, organization, or family, produced in the course of its normal function, business, or activities. In this sense the term is often used synonymously with *fond* (see below), or in English "records." It may contain printed as well as manuscript materials. The term is also used in Russia for personal and family papers, as well as those from private institutional sources. (3) An area within the creating agency where the non-current records are temporarily stored. In prerevolutionary usage, when records tended to remain in the custody of their creating agencies, the term referred to that part of the institution devoted to the retention of records. (4) A temporary storage center, usually *vedomstvennyi arkhiv* (see below).

arkhivnoe delo: archival affairs; archivistics (German, *Archivwesen*) (1) Matters pertaining to archives, their development, administration, and holdings. (2) Sometimes used with reference to a single file, synonymously with *delo*.

arkhivnaia spravka: an official report or attestation produced on the basis of archival documentation.

arkhivovedenie: archival affairs, archival science (German, *Archivwissenschaft*). Generally used in the sense of a special discipline devoted to the study of archival theory and practice, and of the organization, administration, and history of archival institutions.

Arkhivnyi fond Rossiiskoi Federatsii: Archival Fond of the Russian Federation. A legal concept that embraces all archival materials in Federal, state regional, and private archives in the Russian Federation, including those held in libraries, museums, and institutions of the Russian Academy of Sciences, the Russian Academy of Arts, and other institutions. By law (see L-14 and the Introduction by V. P. Kozlov), the Archival Fond RF is divided into "State" and "Non-State" parts, covering respectively those materials in state archives or other agencies, and those in non-governmental custody. (See also the variant use of *fond*.)

avtograf: autograph. (1) An original document. (2) A manuscript written by the hand of the author. (3) A signed document the special value of which is based on the authenticity of the signature or autograph it bears. (4) The actual signature of an individual, and/or the author of a document.

Chasoslov, Chasoslovets: Book of Hours, Horologion. A liturgical book for church readers and cantors, containing both the unchangeable parts of the daily cycle and changeable (but repeatable) parts of the weekly and yearly cycle. Also includes a Menologion (see *Mesiatseslov*) with rubrics, hymns, and readings for saints' days (i.e. feasts for different saints).

chernovik: draft. The initial, rough, or early version of a manuscript or document, as opposed to its final form; may be used with reference to a typewritten or handwritten text (see *kontsept*).

chertezh: (1) draft, plan. An initial outline of a document or a sketch for an architectural or engineering plan, as opposed to the final version (compare *chernovik*). (2) tracing. A traced copy of a map, engineering or architectural plan, or other document.

delo (pl. *dela*): dossier, file. (1) A group of documents in a folder or file unit relating to the same transaction, or brought together to retain information about a person or corporate entity. (2) A basic classification unit within archives constituting the smallest thematic unit-division within a fond referring to a single item of business. Russian state archives now officially use the term *edinitsa khraneniia* (see below). (3) A major type of *edinitsa khraneniia* (see below); although in cases where a *delo* consists of several different files or documents, each of these may be assigned a separate number as an *edinitsa khraneniia*.

delo fonda: the administrative file for a specific fond, containing usually officially registered information about its history and formation.

deloproizvodstvo: (1) recordkeeping practices. The collective chancellery or recordkeeping functions of a government office or agency. The process of keeping or producing documentation or records in the context of a specific office, usually by a governmental administrative function. Sometimes refers collectively to the records produced by a specific office or official function with emphasis on their form/formulae of production. (2) records management. The selection, care, and management of records produced by a given office or agency, particularly with regard to their eventual archival disposition.

diplomatika: diplomatics. An auxiliary historical discipline devoted to the analysis of documents in terms of their customary format or the formal elements present in their texts. These vary in different areas or periods, and are thus of importance for determining the date, origin, and authenticity of texts.

dokument: (1) document, record. Any official document or historical source with recorded information, i.e. an historical, literary, or other source, produced in the course of or reflecting the function, business, or activity of an individual or an institutional office (in the plural, the equivalent to the American usage of records). (2) A single manuscript item, or official record, usually other than a letter. In Russian usage includes not only an official communication of a specific form, but also electronic record, photograph, sound recording, or a pictorial representation produced on any medium. (3) document. An official written instrument or act, especially with reference to an official pre-nineteenth-century (usually medieval document, such as a charter (see *gramota*) or treaty, prepared according to established formulae or juridical norms, and often prepared on parchment with an official seal. In this sense, often used synonymously with *akt* (2) (see above).

dokumentovedenie: A discipline devoted to the official production of documents or documentary records as a result of the normal function, business, or activity of an individual institution or office. More often used with reference to the production of contemporary official documentation, or records management, rather than those from earlier historical period. (See also *deloproizvodstvo*.)

drevlekhranilishche: repository of antiquities. From early ecclesiastical usage, that portion of a library or monastery where early books and documents were stored.

edinitsa khraneniia (abbr. *ed. khr.*): storage unit. The smallest physical unit division within a fond bearing a separate item number. It may consist of an individual manuscript or group of related documents, a film, or a bound volume of documents. In the case of many state textual records, such a unit coincides with an individual *delo* (see above) and is referred to as such.

ekspertiza; *ekspertiza tsennosti dokumental'nykh materialov*: appraisal. The systematic survey of files or documents within a given fond, with the aim of determining those that should or should not be kept for permanent preservation.

faksimile: facsimile. An exact copy which reproduces the physical features of the original, although not necessarily in the same size. Traditionally an exact copy made by hand, but now generally a photographic reproduction of the original.

fastsikula: facsicle. (1) A separate section bearing some common physical or subject characteristics within a collected bound manuscript book. (2) A separate segment of a continuous composition written and/or published in fragments.

filigran': watermark (see *vodianoi znak*).

filigranovedenie, filigranografiia: filigranology. The scientific study of watermarks (*vodianye znaki* or *filigrani*), usually with the object of dating or authenticating texts written or printed on paper from the fourteenth century onwards.

fil'moteka: a film library. (1) A systematic collection of motion pictures. (2) The area in which motion picture films are stored in an archive.

fond or *arkhivnyi fond*: fond. (Note: The term "fond" has been anglicized in this book, because it has no precise English equivalent.) The basic organizational grouping within all Russian (Soviet) repositories; broadly corresponds to, but should be distinguished from, the "record group" or "archive group" of American and British terminology. Individual archival fonds comprise the records, or the complex of documentary materials, of an institution or organization, or of one of its major structural divisions, produced in the exercise of its institutional functions or activities. The concept is also used with reference to the natural accumulation of papers of an individual or family (i.e., *lichnyi fond*, or *famil'nyi fond*). Since all documents or manuscripts in archives and other repositories are now divided into fonds and assigned fond numbers, a number of earlier documentary or manuscript collections are also classified as fonds, and maintained intact as such, although these are clearly "collections" (see *kollektsiia*) rather than naturally accumulated records. According to Russian (Soviet) practice, an archival fond should remain undivided in a single repository (see *printsip proiskhozhdeniia; provenientsprintsip* [German, provenienzprinzip]); in many cases, however, when parts of institutional records or family papers have through the years been subdivided or broken up, they are usually not reintegrated, although an attempt is often made to secure microfilms or other reproductions of the dispersed sections. (See also the variant use of the term in *Arkhivnyi fond Rossiiskoi Federatsii*.)

fond lichnogo proiskhozhdeniia: personal papers. An archival fond containing documents that were produced by (or originated with) an individual as opposed to an office or institution.

fonoteka: sound recording (or audio) library. (1) A systematic collection of sound recordings. (2) The area in which phonograph records or other types of sound recordings are stored in an archive or other institution.

formuliarnyi spisok (pl. *formuliarnye spiski*): biographic questionnaire, personnel record. In prerevolutionary usage, an official questionnaire in specific format to be completed by an individual within the bureaucracy at various points of his career, with biographic data and record of previous service. The Russian equivalent of a curriculum vitae.

fototeka: photographic library. (1) A systematic collection of photographs. (2) The area in which photographs are stored in an archive or other institution.

gosudarstvennyi arkhiv (gosarkhiv): state archive. An official public archive, usually for records appraised for permanent retention. During the Soviet period used for archives administered by the State Archival Administration (Glavarkhiv)—in contradistinction to Communist Party archives. In post-Soviet Russia refers to an official archive open to the public, as opposed to (1) an agency archive, or the archives that form part of a specific government agency; or (2) an archive established by a non-governmental agency.

Gosudarstvennyi arkhivnyi fond (GAF): State Archival Fond. A collective legal concept for all archival materials that are considered the property of the state, as used during the Soviet regime.

gramota (pl. *gramoty*): diploma, charter, official document. (1) An official charter, deed, or other type of conveyance. An official written document prepared according to established formulae or juridical norms. Rarely used for post-eighteenth-century documents, except those on parchment with official seals. (2) More broadly, or loosely, especially in nineteenth-century usage, any written document, particularly one dating from the period of Muscovite Russia. (See the Pushkarev historical dictionary for definitions of many types of *gramoty* used in Muscovite Russia.)

grif: a mark of classification on a document (secret, top secret, confidential, or the like).

inkunabul, or *inkunabula* (pl. *inkunabuly*) : incunabulum, incunable, *pl.* incunabula. A book printed before 1501. Sometimes loosely applied to early printed books of the immediate post-incunable period, but see *paleotip(y)* for imprints from 1501–1550.

irmologion: hermologion. A liturgical book listing the initial lines (incipits) of chants selected from different parts of the Orthodox liturgy (namely from the *Oktoikh, Triod'*, and *Mineia*). Since such books were used by the clergy rather than the choir, they normally do not include musical notation.

1233

istochnikovedenie: The study of the nature, classification, availability, and use of historical sources. In Russian usage often classified as a separate ancilliary historical discipline. Many of the studies published under this rubric are of considerable importance for scholars using unpublished archival materials, but the term covers studies of published documents and of other types of historical sources as well.

kadastr: cadastre, cadaster. An official list—in a bound register or on separate sheets—enumerating plots of land used in apportioning taxes. Usually includes reference to the types of land and/or to the number of households occupying the plots.

Kanonnik: A book of canticles presented in their specific, appropriate order in the Orthodox liturgy. Since such books were used by the choir or cantors, they normally contain musical notation.

kartoteka: card catalogue.

kartochnaia opis': An inventory (see *opis'*) prepared in the form of a card catalogue, in which each *edinitsa khraneniia* is recorded on index cards.

katalog: catalog(ue). A comprehensive enumeration (published, in manuscript, or in card form) of individual items in a collection or fond or on a specialized subject, etc., as distinct from a more generalized *putevoditel'* or *obzor*. Used more often for manuscript or documentary collections in distinction to an *opis'* [inventory] for archival fonds, although the terms are used interchangeably in some manuscript repositories. When a catalogue of a manuscript collection includes more detailed scholarly description, it is usually termed an *opisanie* (see below). When the term is used in state archives it usually implies a card catalogue.

khranilishche, or *arkhivokhranilishche*: (1) stacks, or archival stacks. That portion of the archive in which records are actually stored. (2) depository, repository, storage facility. An institution, or part thereof, where archival materials or manuscript collections are retained.

kniga postuplenii: acquisitions register, accession register. A registration book for accessions by the archive.

kollektsiia, arkhivnaia kollektsiia, or *kollektsiia dokumental'nykh materialov*: collection, archival collection, or collection of documentary materials. An artificially assembled group of individual documents, dossiers, or other units. The items may have been assembled by theme or type, geographical or chronological origin, or merely by the individual or institution that brought them together. The term *kollektsiia* can be used with reference to a group of medieval or Oriental manuscript books, but such a collection more traditionally bears the name *sobranie* (see below). A *kollektsiia* is thus technically distinguished from a fond (see *fond* above), but for convenience collections are now usually assigned fond numbers, and are often loosely referred to as fonds.

kontsept: draft. (now antiquated; today usually *chernovik*.) The original or preliminary version of a document, usually in the handwriting of the author, as opposed to the later official copy in the hand of a scribe. The term is usually used with reference to official texts before the advent of typing, although it can also be used with reference to literary manuscripts or other preliminary drafts, as opposed to a later version. (See also *chernovik*.)

konvoliut: convolute; collection. A group of manuscripts or other documents of miscellaneous origin bound together in a single volume. Usually used with reference to early manuscripts, but also may be applied to any volume comprising several disparate parts such as a bound group of pamphlets. The Russian term *sbornik* (see below) is often used instead of this more technical Western term.

Kormchaia: See *Nomokanon (Kormchaia)*.

kratkii spravochnik: short handbook. A specific type of finding aid which includes less detail than does an archival *putevoditel'* or *spravochnik* (see below). For an archive, it would usually provide a brief description of the holdings and some of the most important fonds, and possibly a list of the numbers and names of fonds.

laminatsiia: lamination. The process of bonding or permanently uniting superimposed layers of paper, plastic, or other materials, usually for the purposes of preservation of damaged or permanently important documents or manuscripts.

lichnyi fond: personal fond. Personal papers of a private individual.

list (abbr. *l.* pl. *ll*): folio, leaf, sheet. A leaf of a manuscript book or bound volume of documents, or an individual sheet within a file folder or dossier. Individual folios within an *edinitsa khraneniia* are usually numbered consecutively on the recto if they do not carry an original numeration. The verso or overleaf second page is cited as the *oborotnaia storona* (abbr. *ob.*). To be distinguished from *stranitsa*, or page.

list ispol'zovaniia: A record sheet inserted in every archival storage unit in Russian (Soviet) state archives, on which a reader must record his or her name and the use to be making of the materials.

litsevaia rukopis': illuminated manuscript. An early manuscript adorned with illuminations.

makulatura: documentary materials considered of no scientific value that has been designated to be destroyed or recycled as waste paper.

manuskript: manuscript. The use of the Latin term is rare in Soviet archival practice, and is used only in the context of an early medieval text, especially a manuscript book. (See *rukopis'* below).

Mesiatseslov: Menologion. A calendar of Orthodox saints from September to August, sometimes containing short lives of the saints listed.

metricheskaia kniga: metricular (matricular) book, parish register. A register maintained locally by parish clergy to record birth, marriage, confirmation, and death of individual parishioners. A standardized format was adopted by the Orthodox Church in the Russian Empire in the eighteenth century.

metrika: metrica, matricula. (1) A register book recording state acts, and also outgoing charters or other documents issued by the chancellery, especially used in early Poland and Lithuania. (2) The records of royal chancelleries in prepartition Poland and Lithuania, such as the Lithuanian Metrica and the Crown Metrica. (3) An act of civil status, i.e., an extract from a *metricheskaia kniga* (see above), usually made for official purpose, as the equivalent of a birth, marriage, or death certificate.

Mineia: Menaion. An Orthodox liturgical book for a given month, divided according to days and providing the services for the commemoration of appropriate saints. A *Minei mesiachny* (Monthly Menanion) would be a collection of 12 *Mineia* for every month of the year.

miniatiura: miniature. The illustrations or illuminations in a medieval manuscript or book.

nauchno-spravochnyi apparat (NSA): reference facilities or system; literally, scientific reference apparatus. The term is used for the reference facilities of archives and manuscript repositories, comprising the complex of published and unpublished finding aids, such as *opisi*, bound or card catalogues, and other reference materials.

nauchno-tekhnicheskaia dokumentatsiia: scientific-technical documentation. A generic name for technical and scientitic-research documentation relating to technology, engineering, manufacturing, construction, transportation, and the like, usually including a high percentage of graphic and technical materials. In Soviet, and now in Russian, practice, such materials are usually kept in special divisions and, in some instances, special archives.

Nomokanon (Kormchaia): Nomocanon. A compilation of canon law, usually including additional general information about ecumenical and other important Orthodox Church councils.

oborot (oborotnaia storona) (abbr. *ob.*): verso. The left-hand (or overleaf) page of a bound volume or the second page of an individual sheet or document.

obzor: survey. A general published description of archival materials usually with reference to a specified theme or group of documents, as opposed to a more detailed and systematic *opis'* or *katalog*. Usually described as an *obzor fonda* when the coverage is limited to the materials in a specific fond, or as an *obzor dokumental'nykh materialov* when the coverage includes materials on a special subject from a number of different fonds.

Oktoikh ("osmoglasnik"). A liturgical book containing texts of the Orthodox liturgy (*Stikhiry* and *Kanony*) for each day of the week, with musical notation for eight voices.

opis': inventory, file list. The basic finding aid or shelf list for an archival fond or documentary collection. Describes consecutively the physical and/or structural nature of each storage unit (*edinitsa khraneniia*) within a fond and the number of individual items or folios contained therein, together with their basic substantive elements such as date, author, and functional origin. The term *opis'* may also be used for a published inventory or catalogue taking for its basis the original *opis'* of the fond or parts thereof; it implies the coverage by number, usually accompanied by a brief description, of the individual items within the fond, and hence is to be differentiated from the more generalized survey found in an archival *putevoditel'*. For some types of collections or descriptive purposes, the term *opis'* is used interchangeably with *katalog* or *opisanie* (compare these entries); these latter terms are more traditionally used with reference to manuscript collections. (See also *opisanie*, *katalog*, and the "Procedural Introduction.")

opisanie: descriptive catalogue, description. The exact technical connotation of the term has varied in different periods and in different institutions; because the word has the general meaning "description" in Russian, it is sometimes used loosely to connote only a very generalized, *obzor* type of description. Usually, however, it is employed with reference to a detailed description of the individual units in a manuscript or documentary collection or (more rarely) of an archival fond. A published *opisanie* may often be limited to materials on a special subject, or of a special type, or to the analytical description of a single manuscript or small group of documents. In some manuscript repositories the term is used interchangeably with *katalog* or with *opis'*, but when a distinction is implied, an *opisanie* usually means a more detailed scholarly description of individual manuscripts (such as medieval manuscript books or literary manuscripts), including precise reference to their physical form, characteristics, and basic content. (See also *opis'* and *katalog*, and the "Procedural Introduction.")

osobaia papka: special file. The highest classified status of documents during the Soviet regime, particularly used for high-level CPSU and security service documentation. Special top-secret documents relating to a particular matter were enclosed in a special closed, and usually sealed and numbered, folder with highly limited access.

paleografiia: paleography. The study of handwriting and of the representation of different written letters of the alphabet in different periods and locations. Considered one of the ancillary historical disciplines, paleography is particularly important to the dating, decipherment, and internal criticism of medieval handwritten texts and inscriptions.

paleotip(y): An early printed book with an imprint from 1501 to 1551. (See *inkunabul* for pre-1500 imprints.)

palimpsest: palimpsest. An early manuscript, written on parchment, which had earlier been used one or more times for another text.

pechat' (Latin: *sigillum*): seal. (1) A device bearing a distinctive design created in order to impart an impression in relief to authenticate a document. Originally used upon wax or clay or other soft, tenacious substance, later (as a stamp) directly on parchment or paper itself. (2) An impression made by such a device in wax, wafer, or similar substance, and hence also the piece of wax, etc., bearing the impression. In early usage, for official documents (see *gramota*, *privilegiia*), the substance bearing the impression was attached to the document by ribbon, or cord, etc. Later the impression was made in a substance which was in turn impressed directly in the paper or parchment. More recently, the wax substance was replaced by ink, gold or silver leaf, or the like. Initially used in lieu of a signature, the seal became a mark of authentication of an official document, and is still often used in conjunction with a signature, and today in official cases with an official ink stamp, impressive device, or the like. (3) Such a device or impression used to ensure the privacy of a communication or packet, the wax being affixed at a point or points of closure in such a way as to prevent opening without evidence of breaking the wax or similar substance.

perechen': list, inventory, schedule. An archival finding aid usually involving only a brief summary listing of fonds, or a simple, unannotated list, as opposed to the more detailed "guide" (*putevoditel'*). In some instances, the term is also used for a type of inventory (*opis'*) with an item-, or folder-level listing of the contents of a fond or collection.

pergament: parchment. (1) The skin of a sheep or goat specially prepared for writing on, used before paper became widely available. Earlier used both for manuscript books and documents, later normally used for official documents, such as diplomas or charters. (2) A document on parchment.

podlinnik: original. (1) An authentic signed copy of an official document. (2) A manuscript in the hand of the author (see *avtograf*).

Poluustav: Semitypikon. (1) An Orthodox liturgical book similar to the Horologion (*Chasoslov*—see above) for church readers and cantors, containing both the unchangeable parts of the daily cycle and changeable (but repeatable) parts of the weekly and yearly cycle. Also includes a the *Ustav* (*Tipik*, or *Tipikon*—see below) with instructions for the order of services for every day of the year. (2) (lower cased) A type of early writing (and hence used with reference to the document or manuscript produced), succeeding *ustav*, characterized by small, irregular, and some raised letters, not joined or linked together.

protokol: protocol, minutes, aide-memoir. The officially agreed-upon, approved account or minutes of a meeting, often consisting only of the resolutions taken on given issues and omitting discussion and/or alternative opinions.

printsip proiskhozhdeniia (provenientsprintsip): provenance (German, *Provenienzprinzip*). Principle of organization of archival records whereby materials are preserved in the order in which they were produced or received by their creating agency or according to their original internal arrangement. As an extension of this principle, archivists use the French term *respect des fonds*, to indicate that archival fonds should be retained without interfering with the original recordkeeping system and without subdividing materials from a single source (see *fond*).

1237

putevoditel': guide. A type of archival finding aid published by Russian (Soviet) repositories that gives systematic coverage of the contents of a single archive or major section thereof. Usually organized according to the major subdivisions of the given archive, the *putevoditel'* provides a brief annotated description of the major, and usually a list of the minor, fonds with precise data about their institutional origin, size, dates, and major contents. Although it may list various subdivisions and specific units within the fonds, it does not give item numbers-and hence does not replace an inventory or *opis'* from the point of view of the researcher. Many post-Soviet Russian *putevoditeli* are now also providing a breakdown of *opisi* within individual fonds.

razriad: section, division, category. (1) A division in some prerevolutionary archives into which documentary materials were arranged for classification and cataloguing purposes. Often, *razriady* were established without respect to the fond, institutional origin or creating agency, or original internal arrangement of the documents. (2) In some institutions as a holdover from repositories of prerevolutionary origin the term is used as a synonym for *kollektsiia* in the case of collections of documents from varied sources brought together on a geographical or subject basis. (3) Since in Muscovite Russia the term was associated with military categories or divisions for the purpose of military administration, and the *Razriadnyi prikaz* constituted the central bureau of military affairs, *razriady* or *razriadnye knigi* were also used to designate register books for official military and civil administrative appointments and service records. During the same period, *dvortsovye razriady* were registers of court officials.

rezoliutsiia: a handwritten order or comment written on a document, usually by the person to whom it was addressed, indicating further use or directions regarding the contents of the document. (See also *viza*.)

rossyp': fragmentary, unarranged documents, or fragmentary folios of documents that have not been arranged in files or defined storage units.

rukopis': manuscript. (1) A document written by hand. (2) A manuscript written in the hand of the author, as in the original draft of a literary or musical composition; an autograph (see above). (3) An early manuscript book, rarely referred to by the Latin derivative *manuskript*. (4) The handwritten or typewritten (sometimes *mashinopis'*) text from which the published version is prepared.

sbornik: collection, compilation, convolute. A group of texts of miscellaneous origin, bound or otherwise kept together. With reference to early manuscripts, used in the sense of a compilation or convolute (sometimes russified *konvoliut*), i.e., a bound volume containing documents of disparate origins, as opposed to a single continuous text (see *konvoliut*). Also used in the case of published collections of texts of miscellaneous origin or authorship in a single volume or group of volumes, such as a volume of articles by different authorship.

skrepa: (1) The signature of a scribe or secretary (of the eighteenth and early nineteenth centuries) or of a *d'iak* (fifteenth through seventeenth centuries) attesting to the authenticity of the text and form of an official document. Before the eighteenth century such a signature would be endorsed in each sheet of a series of documents or a *stolbets* (see below), attesting in addition its proper order in relation to others. (2) In contemporary usage, a paper clip.

Sinodik: An Orthodox liturgical book of prayers and readings for the deceased.

sobranie: collection. A group of manuscripts or documents brought together and assembled artificially by an individual or institution, usually from diverse sources or points of origin. Often used as a synonym for *kollektsiia* (see above), except that the term *sobranie* is used more frequently with reference to collections of medieval or Oriental manuscripts, and is almost invariably used when Slavic manuscript books are in question. Distinguished from *sbornik* (see above).

sprava: The signature of a responsible official on the verso of the last sheet of an important document authenticating the correctness of the final text; mostly used prior to the eighteenth century.

spravochnik: directory, handbook. A specific type of finding aid of a more general nature than a *putevoditel'* (see above). Generally used as a summary locater for many different institutions, with only brief description of their holdings and/or other data.

sstav: A single sheet of a *stolbets*, or the point at which two sheets are glued together.

Stikhiry: A book of Orthodox Church canticles for special holidays or feasts.

stolbets (stolp): A roll or register used in Muscovite *prikazy* formed by gluing together individual documents from a single section of a bureau or office. In the nineteenth century a number of the extant *stolbets* from some of the *prikazy* were cut apart and bound together in volumes to provide for easier archival storage.

stolpik: A relatively small *stolbets* (see above) usually containing documents relating to a more limited matter, which were not affixed to the general *stolbets* of the bureau in question.

sviattsy: calendar of saints and religious festivals.

Tipik (tipikon): see *Ustav*.

Tituliarnik: a volume with charts or lists of noble ranks and titles.

Torzhestvennik: a volume with solemn orations apropos important events.

Triod', Tripesnets: Triodion. An Orthodox liturgical book for the periods of movable feast when an incomplete canon is sung, namely only three (or four) odes, in addition to the complete canons of the immovable feasts. (See also *Tsvetnik*.)

Triod' tsvetnaia: Floral Triodion. An Orthodox liturgical book containing a continuation of the Lenten Triodion for the period from Easter Sunday to the first Sunday after Pentecost (All Saints' Sunday).

Tsvetnik: Florilegium. An anthology or compilation of edificatory texts and/or allegories.

ukazatel': index, register. A detailed listing of the contents of a fond or a group of archival holdings, usually organized alphabetically or by subject. Usually used with a descriptive adjective indicating the type of index involved. Sometimes used in the sense of a detailed, item-by-item inventory or register, as a Slavic-origin equivalent for the Latin-origin term *registr* (4).

Ustav (Tipik, or Tipikon): (1) A book of instructions on the order of Orthodox services for every day of the year. (2) A book of juridical instructions, regulations, or laws, such as the official founding regulations for a specific institution or organization. (3) (lower cased) A type of early writing (and hence used with reference to the document or manuscript produced), characterized by large, square, and heavily impressed individual letters, not joined or linked together.

vedomstvennyi arkhiv: temporary archive. A record-storage center to which various non-current institutional records from neighboring areas are transferred for description and appraisal, or for temporary storage before those destined for permanent preservation are transferred to permanent state archives.

viza: endorsement. An endorsement or annotation, written by hand and signed, usually at the top of a document, indicating the consent of the addressee to the request or instruction presented in the official letter or document. May include an additional instruction for implementation or forwarding to another individual or office. (see also *rezoliutsiia*.)

vnutrenniaia opis': internal register, internal *opis'*. A register of documents within a particular file that is included within the file or bound volume itself.

vodianoi znak: watermark. A design impressed in paper in the course of its manufacture and visible when the paper is held up to light. Sometimes referred to as *filigran'*.

vspomogatel'nye istoricheskie distsipliny: ancillary (*sometimes* auxiliary) historical disciplines. Scholarly disciplines often associated with the analysis of archival sources or manuscript materials, such as diplomatics, watermark analysis, metrology, paleography, sphragistics, chronology, and the like.

vypiska: extract, notes. A copied extract or notes from a textual document.

Appendix 3

Regulations for Work of Users in Reading Rooms of the State Archives of The Russian Federation *

1. General Provisions

1.1. The current Regulations have been formulated in accordance with the Constitution of the Russian Federation, the "Basic Legislation of the Russian Federation on the Archival Fond of the Russian Federation and Archives" of 7 July 1993 (no. 5341-1) [**L-12**], the federal law "On Information, Informatization, and the Protection of Information" of 20 February 1995 (no. 24-FZ) [**L-39**], and the "Regulation on the Archival Fond of the Russian Federation" and "Regulation on the State Archival Service of Russia," confirmed by the decree of the President of the Russian Federation of 17 March 1994 (no. 552) [**L-14**].

1.2. The Regulations establish rules for users' work with open (i.e. declassified) documents in reading rooms (viewing rooms, rooms for listening to sound documents, etc.)[1] of the state archives and centers for the preservation of documents of the Russian Federation.[2]

1.3. The working rules, obligations of archival employees for service to users in the reading rooms, and their responsibilities are determined by laws and regulations of the Russian Federation, and by the legal regulations of the Federal Archival Service of Russia.

1.4. All users have equal rights of access to documents in archives.

1.5. Fees are not charged for using reading rooms and documents.

1.6. Paid services are offered to users by archives according to established rates.

1.7. On the basis of the present Regulations each archive should produce a document setting forth the rules for the use of archival materials in their reading rooms, taking into consideration the specific character of their content and the particularities of the operation of their archives. The aforementioned documents must not contradict the present Regulations.

1.8. The working routine of reading rooms is to be established by the administration of individual archives.

2. Instructions for Admittance of Users to Archival Reading Rooms

2.1. Users are admitted to reading rooms on the basis of a personal letter of application. Users conducting research in accordance with official work plans of scholarly institutions or fulfilling institutional work orders should supply appropriate letters from their sponsoring organizations.

2.2. Personal applications or letters should include the family name, first name, and patronymic of the user, position, scholarly rank, and highest educational degree, and the topic and chronological dates of their research.

2.3. Permission for work in the reading room is given by the archival administration for the period necessary for the user, usually one year from the date of authorization. Questions of needed extension should be resolved with the archival administration or reading room staff.

2.4. All users should familiarize themselves with the present Regulations and fill out a standard application form (appendix # 1).

2.5. Reading room passes are issued upon the presentation of an official identification document by users.

---

* "Pravila raboty pol'zovatelei v chital'nykh zalakh gosudarstvennykh arkhivov Rossiiskoi Federatsii": Prikaz Rosarkhiva," no. 51 (6 July 1998), Registered with the Ministry of Justice RF, 16 December 1998, no. 1660; published in *Rossiiskaia gazeta*, no. 247 (29 December 1998), p. 6, and in *Otechestvennye arkhivy*, 1999, no. 3.

[1] *Hereafter*—reading rooms.

[2] *Hereafter*—archive, archives.

3. Rights, Duties, and Responsibilities of Users

3.1. Archival reference materials (*opisi*, catalogues, surveys), files and documents, including positive copies of motion pictures, photographic documents (in the form of positive prints or control copies on cards of archival photograph catalogues), and sound documents related to the user's research topic, as well as technical equipment for work with microform copies and with audiovisual and machine readable documents, should be available for users.

3.2 Users working in reading rooms of archives have a right:

3.2.1. To receive information about the working arrangements of reading rooms, services performed by archives through reading rooms, and the rules and conditions of availability of these services.

3.2.2. To receive consultations with archival specialists about the composition and content of documents relating to their subject of research, and about reference materials available in the archives.

3.2.3. To receive information, including in written form, about the reason for refusal (delay) to issue files (documents), existing restrictions on delivery and copying of documents related to their research topic, and the length of time during which such restrictions will apply.

3.2.4. To appeal a refusal of delivery of archival documents or reference materials on their research topic in accordance with current laws and regulations.

In order to settle contested questions users may appeal to the administration of the archive, to agencies regulating archival services for regional Subjects of the Russian Federation, to the Federal Archival Service of Russia (Rosarkhiv), and to judicial institutions of the Russian Federation, according to established procedures.

3.2.5. To use published and manuscript materials from the holdings of scientific reference libraries and reference-information facilities.

3.2.6. To order or prepare themselves copies of archival documents on the subject of their research, and to take notes on files, documents, and archival reference materials charged out to them.

3.2.7. Within technical capacities, and with the special permission of the archival administration, to use personal technical equipment (personal computers, tape recorders, dictaphones) or to rent archival technical equipment in the archive. The use of technical equipment is permitted if it does not interfere with the work of other users.[3]

3.2.8. To bring into a reading room, by agreement with the head of the reading room (staff person), typed or printed texts and page proofs of scholarly work. A special pass should be issued for such materials.
Handwritten materials belonging to users can be taken in and out without a pass.

3.3. Users may be accompanied by interpreters and assistants.

3.4. Users are obliged to:

3.4.1. Observe the present "Regulations for Work [of Users] in Reading Rooms of Archives of the Russian Federation."

3.4.2. Sign in the reading room register of researchers on each visit.

3.4.3. Fill in the sheets of usage (*listy ispol'zovaniia*) within all perused files, indicating the date of use, last name and initials (legibly), and nature of work performed on the file (perusal of documents, taking notes, etc.).

3.4.4. After finishing work on every visit, return any *opisi*, files (storage units), and published editions to the reading room staff person.

3.4.5. Observe technical requirements for using equipment and film during work with microforms or documents on special or electronic media.

3.4.6. Observe the reading room working routine, and keep quiet and order during working hours.

---

[3] Use of technical equipment containing scanning devices (except in cases described in the paragraph 5.8 of the current Regulations) is not permitted.

3.4.7. Furnish the required reference to the source for any archival information received that may be cited or published, i.e. indicate the name of the archive containing the documents and their reference data (fond, *opis'*, file [or storage unit], and folio numbers), in accordance with the Law of the Russian Federation "On Information, Informatization and the Protection of Information" (ch.12, sec.2).

3.5. Users should present to the archive a bibliographic reference or a copy of any publication prepared on the basis of documents in the archive.

3.6. Questions raised about the theft or damage of archival documents by users shall be settled according to the current laws and regulations.

3.7. Users who have committed acts that cause material loss to an archive bear responsibility according to procedures established by current laws and regulations.

4. Instructions for Delivery of Files, Documents, Microforms, and Published Material, and for Provision of Reference Facilities

4.1. Files and other materials are delivered to users on the basis of completed order forms.

Files and other materials are issued to the user with the user's signature on the order form for every unit of the material issued.[4]

4.2. 5 *opisi*, 10–20 files, or 10–20 units of film documents and sound documents with recorded time of no more then 3 hours, may be issued at one time. The administration of archives may establish other norms for charging out files and documents, considering the specific content of documents.

4.3. Time limits for delivery of *opisi*, files, documents and other materials are established by the administration of archives, but should not exceed 3 working days from the day they are ordered.

Reference works and other printed editions, and copies of *opisi* that are kept in the reading room, are available to users on the day of order.

4.4. *Opisi* and other archival reference aids can be issued for up to 5 days; unbound and especially valuable documents—for up to 5 days; unique documents, with the permission of archival administration—for one day; file units, microforms, and printed editions—for one month.

Extension of the time limit for keeping and using *opisi*, files, documents, and other materials in reading rooms should be arranged with the staff of reading rooms (except in the case of unique documents). Extension of the time limit for using unique and especially valuable documents is to be determined by the archival administration, with a new order form to be filled out as necessary. Time limits for a repeated delivery are to be established by the archival administration.

4.5. When [microform] copies for use (*fondy pol'zovaniia*) are available, original documents are not usually issued to the reading room.

Original documents may be issued to users in exceptional cases, with the permission of the archival administration, in consideration of specific circumstances (for instance, the necessity to examine the particularities of a document's external appearance, malfunctioning technical equipment for work with microforms, poor quality of copies, a user's medical condition preventing work with microforms, or other circumstances).

4.6. Film, photographic, and sound documents are issued to users only in the form of copies.

4.7. In order to ensure the continuing preservation of archival documents, it is not permitted:

4.7.1. To enter reading room in overcoats, or to bring in briefcases, sport and utility bags (size more then 200x300 millimeters), plastic sacks, and umbrellas.

Smoking, or the consumption of food and drink is permitted only in specially designated areas.

4.7.2. To take files out of the reading room, to transfer files to a third person, to leave open files unprotected from sun and electric light for an extended period of time, to write or trace with a sheet of paper placed on top of documents, to bend corners of folios, to copy documents using tracing paper, to place files within alien objects, to move folios within unbound files or from one file into another.

---

[4] The present rule also applies for issuing and use of materials from archival reference libraries.

4.7.3. While working with archival documents, to use glue, scotch-tape, markers, white-out for typewriters, carbon paper, ink pens, or scissors and other cutting instruments.

4.8. It is prohibited to enter changes in the text of documents, or to make notes, corrections, and underlining on documents or file folders.

4.9. Upon receiving *opisi*, files, and other materials, users should verify their condition and state of preservation in the presence of reading room staff.

If a user finds any damage or defects in files, documents, and microforms, a missing folio within a file, or incorrect foliation, he should inform the reading room staff.

4.10. **Delivery of files and documents may be refused or delayed in the case of:**

—their poor physical condition;

—restrictions on the use of documents, established in accordance with laws and regulations of the Russian Federation or by the creator of the fond (record group) upon transfer of the documents to the archive for permanent preservation;

—necessity for the archival staff to work with the documents (reference work, thematic processing of fonds, preparation of informational reports to official inquiries by state agencies, preparation of documentary publications, preparation of preservation copies or copies for use, conducting inspection, appraisal, or inventory of documents, restoration work or copying of documents, declassification processing, etc.);

—loan of files and documents for temporary use by other institutions;

—display of the materials ordered on exhibition;

—their issuance to another user.

Files (records or documents) that have not been technically processed (arranged and described in *opisi*) are not issued to the reading room.

5. Copying and Issuance of Copies of Archival Documents Ordered by Users

5.1. Xerox copies, microform copies, photographic prints, and positive copies of film and photographic documents can be made upon the request of users, subject to the technical capacities of archives and the physical condition of the documents. The quality of copies prepared is ensured by the archives.

5.2. Orders for copying should be formulated by users on special order forms and transmitted to the reading room staff. Precise archival indentification [(fond, *opis'*, file unit, folios, etc.)] should be indicated in the request.

When a large number of copies is requested, archival administration may require that an attached summary list of documents to be copied is appended to the order form.

5.3. Copying of documents from the "Non-State Part" of the Archival Fond of the Russian Federation, as well as of documents from personal fonds, is conducted according to the terms established by the creators of the fonds [i.e. creating agencies of records or papers] or their legal successors (heirs), who transferred the documents for permanent or depository retention in the archive.

In the absence of copying restrictions established on transfer of the records, they may be copied according to regular procedures.

5.4. Copying of documents that are subject to copyright (*avtorskoe pravo*), including documents of a creative nature and audiovisual documents, is performed in accordance with the law of the Russian Federation "On Copyright and Related Rights" [L-70].

5.5. The volume, time limit, and types of copies that can be prepared are regulated by the administration of the archive, in accordance with technical capacities and the physical condition of the documents.

5.6. The copying of a fond or collection in its entirety can be done only with the permission of the archival administration.

Orders for copying documents are not accepted if the copying could cause physical damage to the documents, or if the documents are in poor physical condition.

Requests for copying unique documents, or documents from files requiring rebinding or restoration, must be approved by the archival administration in each specific instance.

5.7. The copying of unpublished *opisi*, catalogues, card files, databases, and other archival reference materials in their entirety on the request of users is not permitted. The permissible volume of copying should be decided with the archival administration in each specific instance.

5.8. In exceptional cases, given a lack of technical capacities in the archive, copying with the use of technical equipment belonging to users may be allowed.

Copying with the user's technical equipment, including scanners, photographic- and video-cameras, etc., may be done only with the permission of the archival administration within their premises and under the supervision of the reading room staff.

Archives are not responsible for the quality of copies of documents made with technical equipment belonging to users.

5.9. Upon approval of the archival administration, users may be permitted on their own (independently) to copy pictorial and graphic materials, maps, plans, and technical drawings or to invite a specialist to do so (a draftsman, photographer, artist). In such cases, the copying must be performed within the premises of the archive and under the staff supervision in observation of rules for ensuring the safety of the documents.

5.10. Copies of documents are issued to users or their authorized representatives upon their signature, or they may be sent to an indicated address.

5.11. Copies of partially declassified documents, prepared by archives upon request of users, with the exclusion from the text of the classified parts, are issued according to general procedures.

5.12. A special pass, signed by a responsible official, should be issued authorizing the removal of copies from the archive.

Appendix # 1

To the Regulations for the Work of Users in Reading Rooms
of State Archives of the Russian Federation.

Name of the state archive

USER REGISTRATION FORM

Last name _____

Name _____ Patronymic _____

Place of work (study) and position _____

_____

_____

Organization sending the user, its address _____

_____

Education _____

Academic degree, title _____

Subject and chronological framework of research _____

_____

_____

Permanent address _____

_____

Telephone (home) _____ (work) _____

Series and No. of Identification Document _____

_____

I am familiar with the Regulations for work of users in reading rooms of state archives of the Russian Federation and agree to observe them.

Date _____   _____(Signature)

ORDER OF THE FEDERAL ARCHIVAL SERVICE OF RUSSIA
6 July 1998, no. 51, Moscow
Registered in the Ministry of Justice (Miniust) RF on 16 December 1998, registration no.1660

On approval of the Regulations for Work of Users in Reading Rooms of State Archives of the Russian Federation

In order to improve the work of state archives and centers for the preservation of documentation of the Russian Federation in protecting the constitutional rights of citizens to information, [and the work] of organizations serving users in reading rooms in accordance with the current conditions of their operation

I order:

1. The approval of the appended "Regulations for Work of Users in Reading Rooms of State Archives of the Russian Federation."

2. That the administrations of archival institutions of the Rosarkhiv system are to bring their current documents regulating the organization of work of users in reading rooms into conformity with these approved Regulations.

   That the directors of federal state archives and centers for the preservation of documentation should present for the approval of Rosarkhiv their documents regulating the organization of work of users in reading rooms, revised in accordance with these approved Regulations.

3. Not to use on the territory of the Russian Federation the "Regulations for work of researchers in reading rooms of state archives of the USSR," approved by the order of Glavarkhiv of the USSR on 29 September 1989 (no. 64).

4. That control of the implementation of the current Order be delegated to the Department for the Use of Archival Documents (T. F. Pavlova).

Chairman of Rosarkhiv
V. KOZLOV

Index/Correlation Table
of Abbreviations and Acronyms
for Previous and Present Repositories

This index lists acronyms and other abbreviations for all of the previous names and current names listed in the present directory, followed by the complete Russian-language name and an English translation in brackets, as found in the text itself. In the case of previous names, correlation is provided with a "See" reference to the present acronym, name of the repository, and English-language translation in brackets. Current repository numbers are shown in boldface type. In a few cases, more than one cross-reference is cited; this occurs, for example, where holdings from a single earlier archive have been transferred to two different current ones, or when there is (or was) a second listing for the institution (such as a Leningrad/St. Petersburg branch). When the same acronym is retained for several different variant names at different times, the variant names are also cited (numbered in chronological order), but the acronyms are not repeated. When the same acronym is still used for a post-1991 repository, the latest name is preceded with a "See" and the current number appears in bold. Note that in many instances, "SSSR" [USSR] was used with acronyms of all-union insitutions, to distinguish from similar institutions in the union republics or different regions, but it is retained here only when most common, or when deemed necessary in the present context. Normally, "AN SSSR" or "RAN" is also not repeated here with acronyms of Academy institutes.

For additional abbreviations and acronyms, not involving the current and previous names of repositories, see the list of "Abbreviations and Acronyms" at the beginning of Volume 1, pp. lxv–lxxviii.

AAN—Arkhiv Akademii nauk SSSR [Archive of the Academy of Sciences of the USSR]. *See* ARAN—Arkhiv Rossiiskoi Akademii nauk [Archive of the Russian Academy of Sciences], **E–1**, *and* PFA RAN—Sankt-Peterburgskii filial Arkhiva Rossiiskoi Akademii nauk [St. Petersburg Branch of the Archive of the Russian Academy of Sciences], **E–20**

AGA—Akademiia grazhdanskoi aviatsii [Academy of Civil Aviation], **E–59**

AIM—Artilleriiskii istoricheskii muzei [Artillery History Museum]. *See* VIMAIViVS—Voenno-istoricheskii muzei artillerii, inzhenernykh voisk i voisk sviazi [Military History Museum of the Artillery, Corps of Engineers, and Signal Corps], **H–73**

AK/AK RAN—Arkheograficheskaia komissiia Narkomprosa RSFSR/RAN [Archeographic Commission of the People's Commissariat of Education]. *See* SPbF IRI—Sankt-Peterburgskii filial Instituta rossiiskoi istorii RAN [St. Petersburg Branch of the Institute of Russian History], **E–24**

AKA—Arkhiv Krasnoi Armii [Archive of the Red Army]. *See* RGVA—Rossiiskii gosudarstvennyi voennyi arkhiv [Russian State Military Archive], **B–8**

AKh SSSR—Akademiia khudozhestv SSSR [Academy of Arts of the USSR]. *See* RAKh—Rossiiskaia Akademiia khudozhestv [Russian Academy of Arts], **E–45**; NB RAKh—Nauchnaia biblioteka Rossiiskoi Akademii khudozhestv [Scientific Library of the Russian Academy of Arts], **G–18**; *and* NIM RAKh—Nauchno-issledovatel'skii muzei Rossiiskoi Akademii khudozhestv [Scientific Research Museum of the Russian Academy of Arts], **H–90, H–91—H–93, H–156**

AMN SSSR—Akademiia meditsinskikh nauk SSSR [Academy of Medical Sciences of the USSR]. *See* RAMN—Rossiiskaia akademiia meditsinskikh nauk [Russian Academy of Medical Sciences], **E–40**, *and* NIIEM—Nauchno-issledovatel'skii institut eksperimental'noi meditsiny RAMN [Scientific Research Institute of Experimental Medicine of the Russian Academy of Medical Sciences], **E–47**

AMO SSSR—Arkhiv Ministerstva oborony SSSR [Archive of the Ministry of Defense of the USSR]. *See* TsAMO—Tsentral'nyi arkhiv Ministerstva oborony RF [Central Archive of the Ministry of Defense], **C–4**

AMVS SSSR—Arkhiv Ministerstva Vooruzhennykh Sil SSSR [Archive of the Ministry of the Armed Forces of the USSR]. *See* TsAMO—Tsentral'nyi arkhiv Ministerstva oborony RF [Central Archive of the Ministry of Defense], **C–4**

AO Lengorispolkoma—Arkhivnyi otdel Ispolkoma Leningradskogo gorodskogo Soveta deputatov trudiashchikhsia [Archival Division of the Leningrad City Executive Committee of the Council of Workers' Deputies]. *See* AU SPbiLO—Arkhivnoe upravlenie Sankt-Peterburga i Leningradskoi oblasti [Archival Administration of St. Petersburg and Leningrad Oblast], **D–012**

AO "Moskvich"—Muzei. *See* Muzei AO "Moskvich"

AO UVD LO—Arkhivnyi otdel Upravleniia vnutrennikh del Leningradskoi oblasti [Archival Division of the Leningrad Oblast Administration of Internal Affairs]. *See* AU SPbiLO—Arkhivnoe upravlenie Sankt-Peterburga i Leningradskoi oblasti [Archival Administration of St. Petersburg and Leningrad Oblast], **D–012**

AOR—Arkhiv Oktiabr'skoi revoliutsii [Archive of the October Revolution]. *See* GA RF—Gosudarstvennyi arkhiv Rossiiskoi Federatsii [State Archive of the Russian Federation], **B–1**

AORLO—Arkhiv Oktiabr'skoi revoliutsii Leningradskoi oblasti [Archive of the October Revolution of Leningrad Oblast]. *See* TsGA SPb—Tsentral'nyi gosudarstvennyi arkhiv Sankt-Peterburga [Central State Archive of St. Petersburg], **D–12**

AORMO—Arkhiv Oktiabr'skoi revoliutsii Moskovskoi oblasti [State Archive of the October Revolution of Moscow Oblast]. *See* TsGAMO—Tsentral'nyi gosudarstvennyi arkhiv Moskovskoi oblasti [Central State Archive of Moscow Oblast], **D–8**

AP RF—Arkhiv Prezidenta Rossiiskoi Federatsii [Archive of the President of the Russian Federation], **C–1**

APN—Akademiia pedagogicheskikh nauk RSFSR/SSSR. *See* RAO—Rossiiskaia akademiia obrazovaniia [Russian Academy of Education], **E–42**

ARAN—Arkhiv Rossiiskoi Akademii nauk [Archive of the Russian Academy of Sciences], **E–1**

Arkhiv GUPVI—Arkhiv Glavnogo upravleniia po delam voennoplennykh i internirovannykh MVD SSSR [Archive of the Main Administration for Affairs of Prisoners of War and Internees]. *See former* TsKhIDK—Tsentr khraneniia istoriko-dokumental'nykh kollektsii [Center for Preservation of Historico-Documentary Collections], **B–8A** (now part of RGVA, **B–8**)

Arkhiv INO—Arkhiv Inostrannogo otdela VChK/GPU/OGPU/GUGB [Archive of the Foreign Division VChK/GPU/OGPU/GUGB]. *See* Arkhiv SVR Rossii—Operativnyi arkhiv Sluzhby vneshnei razvedki RF [Operational Archive of the Foreign Intelligence Service], **C–7**

Arkhiv Istparta—Arkhiv Komissii dlia sobiraniia i izucheniia materialov Oktiabr'skoi revoliutsii i istorii Rossiiskoi kommunisticheskoi partii TsK VKP[b] [Archive of the Commission to Collect and Study Materials on the October Revolution and History of the Russian Communist Party of the CC RCP(b)]. *See* RGASPI—Rossiiskii gosudarstvennyi arkhiv sotsial'no-politicheskoi istorii [Russian State Archive of Socio-Political History], **B–12**

Arkhiv KGIOP—Nauchno-metodicheskii informatsionno-izdatel'skii sektor (vedomstvennyi arkhiv) Komiteta po gosudarstvennomu kontroliu, ispol'zovaniiu i okhrane pamiatnikov istorii i kultury Sankt-Peterburga [Scientific-Methodological Information-Publication Sector (Agency Archive) of the Committee for State Control, Use, and Preservation of Monuments of History and Culture of St. Petersburg], **D–21**

Arkhiv Kominterna—Arkhiv III [Kommunisticheskogo] Internatsionala [Archive of the Third (Communist) International]. *See* RGASPI—Rossiiskii gosudarstvennyi arkhiv sotsial'no-politicheskoi istorii [Russian State Archive of Socio-Political History], **B–12**

Arkhiv Minatoma—Otraslevoi otdel fondov Ministerstva RF po atomnoi energii [Branch Division of Fonds of the Ministry of Atomic Energy], **C–10**

Arkhiv PGU—Arkhiv Pervogo glavnogo upravleniia KGB SSSR [Archive of the First Chief Directorate of the KGB USSR]. *See* Arkhiv SVR Rossii—Operativnyi arkhiv Sluzhby vneshnei razvedki RF [Operational Archive of the Foreign Intelligence Service], **C–7**

Arkhiv PU—Arkhiv Pervogo upravleniia NKVD/MVD SSSR [Archive of the First Directorate NKVD/MVD SSSR]. *See* Arkhiv SVR Rossii—Operativnyi arkhiv Sluzhby vneshnei razvedki RF [Operational Archive of the Foreign Intelligence Service], **C–7**

Arkhiv RGTRK "Ostankino"—Arkhiv Rossiiskoi gosudarstvennoi teleradiokompanii "Ostankino" [Archive of the Ostankino Russian State Television and Radio Company], **C–19**

Arkhiv SVR Rossii—Operativnyi arkhiv Sluzhby vneshnei razvedki RF [Operational Archive of the Foreign Intelligence Service], **C–7**

Arkhiv UFSB Moskvy—Arkhiv Upravleniia Federal'noi sluzhby bezopasnosti po g. Moskve i Moskovskoi oblasti [Archive of the Administration of the Federal Security Service for Moscow and Moscow Oblast], **D–9**

Arkhiv UFSB SPb—Arkhiv Upravleniia Federal'noi sluzhby bezopasnosti po Sankt-Peterburgu i Leningradskoi oblasti [Archive of the Administration of the Federal Security Service for St. Petersburg and Leningrad Oblast], **D–19**

Arkhiv VGU—Gosudarstvennyi geodezicheskii arkhiv Vysshego geodezicheskogo upravleniia pri VSNKh SSSR [State Geodesic Archive of the High Geodesic Administration under the VSNKh SSSR]. *See* TsKGF—Tsentral'nyi kartografo-geodezicheskii fond [Central Cartographic-Geodesic Fond], **C–14**

Arkhiv ZAGS MO—Arkhiv Upravleniia zapisi aktov grazhdanskogo sostoianiia Administratsii Moskovskoi oblasti [Archive of the Administration for Registration of Vital Statistics of the Administration of Moscow Oblast], **D–11**

Arkhiv ZAGS Moskvy—Ob"edinennyi arkhiv Upravleniia zapisi aktov grazhdanskogo sostoianiia Pravitel'stva Moskvy [Consolidated Archive of the Administration for Registration of Vital Statistics of the Government of Moscow], **D–10**

Arkhiv ZAGS SPb—Gorodskoi i oblastnoi arkhiv zapisei aktov grazhdanskogo sostoianiia Sankt-Peterburga [City and Oblast Archive for Registration of Vital Statistics of St. Petersburg], **D–20**

Arkhiv-ROA—Obshchestvennyi nauchno-issledovatel'skii tsentr "Arkhiv-ROA" [Social Scientific Research Center—Archive of the Russian Liberation Army], **F–10**

ASPbM—Arkhiv Sankt-Peterburgskoi Mitropolii [Archive of the St. Petersburg Metropolitanate], **F–20**

AU Lenoblgorispolkomov—Arkhivnoe upravlenie Leningradskogo oblastnogo i gorodskogo ispolnitel'nykh komitetov [Archival Administration of the Leningrad Oblast and City Executive Committee]. *See* AU SPbiLO—Arkhivnoe upravlenie Sankt-Peterburga i Leningradskoi oblasti [Archival Administration of St. Petersburg and Leningrad Oblast], **D–012**

AU Mosgorispolkoma—Arkhivnoe upravlenie Mosgorispolkoma [Archival Administration of the Moscow City Executive Committee]. *See* Mosgorarkhiv—Moskovskoe gorodskoe ob"edinenie arkhivov [Moscow Consolidated Municipal Archives], **D–01**

AU Mosoblispolkoma—Arkhivnoe upravlenie Mosoblispolkoma [Archival Administration of the Moscow Oblast Executive Committee]. *See* Mosoblkomarkhiv—Komitet po delam arkhivov Administratsii Moskovskoi oblasti [Committee for Archival Affairs of the Administration of Moscow Oblast], **D–08**

AU SPbiLO—Arkhivnoe upravlenie Sankt-Peterburga i Leningradskoi oblasti [Archival Administration of St. Petersburg and Leningrad Oblast], **D-012**

AVM SSSR—Arkhiv Voennogo ministerstva SSSR [Archive of the Military Ministry of the USSR]. *See* TsAMO—Tsentral'nyi arkhiv Ministerstva oborony RF [Central Archive of the Ministry of Defense], **C–4**

AVP RF—Arkhiv vneshnei politiki Rossiiskoi Federatsii [Archive of Foreign Policy of the Russian Federation], **C–2**

AVP SSSR—Arkhiv vneshnei politiki SSSR [Archive of Foreign Policy of the USSR]. *See* AVP RF—Arkhiv vneshnei politiki Rossiiskoi Federatsii [Archive of Foreign Policy of the Russian Federation], **C–2**

AVPR—Arkhiv vneshnei politiki Rossii [Archive of Foreign Policy of Russsia]. *See* AVPRI— Arkhiv vneshnei politiki Rossiiskoi Imperii [Archive of Foreign Policy of the Russian Empire], **C–3**

AVPRI—Arkhiv vneshnei politiki Rossiiskoi Imperii [Archive of Foreign Policy of the Russian Empire], **C–3**

AZLK—Muzei. *See* Muzei AZLK

BAN (1)—Biblioteka Akademii nauk SSSR [Library of the Academy of Sciences of the USSR]. *See* (2)—Biblioteka Akademii nauk Rossii [Library of the Russian Academy of Sciences], **G–16**

Biblioteka Doma aktera—Biblioteka Dvortsa rabotnikov iskusstv im. K. S. Stanislavskogo [Library of the K. S. Stanislavskii Palace for Workers in the Arts]. *See* Biblioteka SPbO STD RF—Biblioteka Sankt-Peterburgskogo otdeleniia Soiuza teatral'nykh deiatelei RF [Library of St. Petersburg Division of the Union of Theater Workers], **G–23**

Biblioteka IAKh—Biblioteka Imperatorskoi Akademii khudozhestv [Library of the Imperial Academy of Arts]. *See* NB RAKh—Nauchnaia biblioteka Rossiiskoi Akademii khudozhestv [Scientific Library of the Russian Academy of Arts], **G–18**

Biblioteka INPII—Biblioteka Instituta proletarskikh izobrazitel'nykh iskusstv [Library of the Institute of Proletarian Fine Arts] *See* NB RAKh—Nauchnaia biblioteka Rossiiskoi Akademii khudozhestv [Scientific Library of the Russian Academy of Arts], **G–18**

Biblioteka LDA—Biblioteka Leningradskoi Dukhovnoi Akademii [Library of Leningrad Theological Academy]. *See* Biblioteka SPbDAiS—Biblioteka Sankt-Peterburgskoi Pravoslavnoi Dukhovnoi Akademii i Seminarii [Library of the St. Petersburg Orthodox Theological Academy and Seminary], **G–26**

Biblioteka LIIZhT (1)—Biblioteka Leningradskogo instituta inzhenerov zheleznodorozhnogo transporta [Library of the Leningrad Institute of Railroad Transport Engineers]

(2)—Biblioteka Leningradskogo instituta inzhenerov zheleznodorozhnogo transporta im. Ia. E. Rudzutaka [Library of the Ia. E. Rudzutak Leningrad Institute of Railroad Transport Engineers]

(3)—Biblioteka Leningradskogo instituta inzhenerov zheleznodorozhnogo transporta im. akad. V. N. Obraztsova [Library of the V. N. Obraztsov Leningrad Institute of Railroad Transport Engineers]. *See* NTB PGUPS—Nauchno-tekhnicheskaia biblioteka Sankt-Peterburgskogo gosudarstvennogo universiteta putei soobshcheniia [Scientific-Technical Library of the St. Petersburg State University of Transportation], **G–24**

Biblioteka LINZhAS—Biblioteka Leningradskogo instituta zhivopisi, skul'ptury i arkhitektury [Library of the Leningrad Institute of Painting, Sculpture, and Architecture]. *See* NB RAKh—Nauchnaia biblioteka Rossiiskoi Akademii khudozhestv [Scientific Library of the Russian Academy of Arts], **G–18**

Biblioteka LO VTO—Biblioteka Leningradskogo otdeleniia Vserossiiskogo teatral'nogo obshchestva [Library of the Leningrad Division of the All-Russian Theater Society]. *See* Biblioteka SPbO STD RF—Biblioteka Sankt-Peterburgskogo otdeleniia Soiuza teatral'nykh deiatelei RF [Library of St. Petersburg Division of the Union of Theater Workers], **G–23**

Biblioteka MGIAI—Biblioteka Moskovskogo gosudarstvennogo istoriko-arkhivnogo instituta [Library of the Moscow State Historico-Archival Institute]. *See* Biblioteka RGGU— Biblioteka Rossiiskogo gosudarstvennogo gumanitarnogo universiteta [Library of the Russian State University for the Humanities], **G–5**

Biblioteka MGU—Biblioteka Moskovskogo gosudarstvennogo universiteta [Library of Moscow State University]. *See* NB MGU—Nauchnaia biblioteka im. A. M. Gor'kogo Moskovskogo gosudarstvennogo universiteta im. M. V. Lomonosova [A. M. Gor'kii Scientific Library of M. V. Lomonosov Moscow State University], **G–2**

Biblioteka PIIPS—Biblioteka Petrogradskogo (Leningradskogo) instituta inzhenerov putei soobshcheniia [Library of the Petrograd (Leningrad) Institute of Transportation Engineers]. *See* NTB PGUPS—Nauchno-tekhnicheskaia biblioteka Sankt-Peterburgskogo gosudarstvennogo universiteta putei soobshcheniia [Scientific-Technical Library of the St. Petersburg State University of Transportation], **G–24**

Biblioteka PIIT—Biblioteka Peterburgskogo instituta inzhenerov zheleznodorozhnogo transporta [Library of the St. Petersburg Institute of Railroad Transport Engineers]. *See* NTB PGUPS—Nauchno-tekhnicheskaia biblioteka Sankt-Peterburgskogo gosudarstvennogo universiteta putei soobshcheniia [Scientific-Technical Library of the St. Petersburg State University of Transportation], **G–24**

Biblioteka RGGU—Biblioteka Rossiiskogo gosudarstvennogo gumanitarnogo universiteta [Library of the Russian State University for the Humanities], **G–5**

Biblioteka RMO—Biblioteka Russkogo muzykal'nogo obshchestva [Library of the Russian Music Society]. *See* NMB SPbGK—Nauchno-muzykal'naia biblioteka Sankt-Peterburgskoi gosudarstvennoi konservatorii im. N. A. Rimskogo-Korsakova [Scientific Music Library of the N. A. Rimskii-Korsakov St. Petersburg State Conservatory], **G–19**

Biblioteka RTO (1)—Biblioteka Moskovskogo teatral'no-statisticheskogo biuro Russkogo Teatral'nogo obshchestva [Library of the Moscow Theater-Statistical Office of the Russian Theater Society]

(2)—Teatral'naia biblioteka Russkogo teatral'nogo obshchestva [Theater Library of the Russian Theater Society]

(3)—Nauchnaia teatral'naia biblioteka Russkogo teatral'nogo obshchestva [Scientific Theater Library of the Russian Theater Society]. *See* TsNB STD RF—Tsentral'naia nauchnaia biblioteka Soiuza teatral'nykh deiatelei RF [Central Scientific Library of the Union of Theater Workers], **G–8**

Biblioteka SPbDA—Biblioteka Sankt-Peterburgskoi Dukhovnoi Akademii [Library of St. Petersburg Theological Academy]. *See* Biblioteka SPbDAiS—Biblioteka Sankt-Peterburgskoi Pravoslavnoi Dukhovnoi Akademii i Seminarii [Library of the St. Petersburg Orthodox Theological Academy and Seminary], **G–26**

Biblioteka SPbDAiS—Biblioteka Sankt-Peterburgskoi Pravoslavnoi Dukhovnoi Akademii i Seminarii [Library of the St. Petersburg Orthodox Theological Academy and Seminary], **G–26**

Biblioteka SPbO STD RF—Biblioteka Sankt-Peterburgskogo otdeleniia Soiuza teatral'nykh deiatelei RF [Library of the St. Petersburg Division of the Union of Theater Workers], **G–23**

Biblioteka VKhUTEINa—Biblioteka Vysshego khudozhestvenno-tekhnicheskogo instituta [Library of the Higher Technical Art Institute]. *See* NB RAKh—Nauchnaia biblioteka Rossiiskoi Akademii khudozhestv [Scientific Library of the Russian Academy of Arts], **G–18**

Biblioteka VKhUTEMAS—Biblioteka Vysshikh khudozhestvenno-tekhnicheskikh masterskikh [Library of the Technical Art Studios]. *See* NB RAKh—Nauchnaia biblioteka Rossiiskoi Akademii khudozhestv [Scientific Library of the Russian Academy of Arts], **G–18**

Biblioteka VMedA (1)—Fundamental'naia biblioteka Voenno-meditsinskoi akademii im. S. M. Kirova [Fundamental Library of the S. M. Kirov Military Medical Academy].
    See (2)—Biblioteka VMedA—Fundamental'naia biblioteka Voenno-meditsinskoi akademii [Fundamental Library of the Military Medical Academy], **G–25**
Biblioteka VPSh—Biblioteka Vysshei partiinoi shkoly pri TsK KPSS [Library of the Higher Party School under the CC CPSU]. *See* Biblioteka RGGU—Biblioteka Rossiiskogo gosudarstvennogo gumanitarnogo universiteta [Library of the Russian State University for the Humanities], **G–5**
Biblioteka VTO—Nauchnaia biblioteka Vserossiiskogo teatral'nogo obshchestva [Scientific Library of the All-Russian Theater Society]. *See* TsNB STD RF—Tsentral'naia nauchnaia biblioteka Soiuza teatral'nykh deiatelei RF [Central Scientific Library of the Union of Theater Workers], **G–8**
BIN (1)—Botanicheskii institut AN SSSR [Botanical Institute]
    (2)—Botanicheskii institut im. V. L. Komarova AN SSSR [V. L. Komarov Botanical Institute]. *See*
    (3)—Botanicheskii institut im. V. L. Komarova RAN [V. L. Komarov Botanical Institute], **E–33**
BMM—Gosudarstvennaia biblioteka-muzei Maiakovskogo [Maiakovskii State Library-Museum]. *See* GMM—Gosudarstvennyi muzei V. V. Maiakovskogo [V. V. Maiakovskii State Museum], **H–36**

DAPVKhO—Dom aviatsii, protivovozdushnoi i khimicheskoi oborony im. M. V. Frunze [M. V. Frunze House of Aviation, Anti-Aircraft, and Chemical Defense]. *See* TsDAiK—Tsentral'nyi Dom aviatsii i kosmonavtiki [Central House of Aviation and Space Exploration], **H–58**
Dom aktera—Biblioteka. *See* Biblioteka Doma aktera
DPI—Muzei. *See* Muzei DPI

EO RM (1)—Russkii muzei Imperatora Aleksandra III—Etnograficheskii otdel [Emperor Alexander III Russian Museum—Ethnographic Division]
    (2)—EO RM—Russkii muzei—Etnograficheskii otdel [Russian Museum— Ethnographic Division]. *See* REM—Rossiiskii etnograficheskii muzei [Russian Ethnographic Museum], **H–71**
ETU—Muzei istorii. *See* Muzei istorii ETU

FSB Rossii. *See* TsA FSB Rossii
FSK RF. *See* TsA FSK RF
FTG GMISPb—Fond tirazhirovannoi grafiki, Istoriko-kul'turnyi muzei-zapovednik "Petropavlovskaia krepost'"—Gosudarstvennyi muzei istorii Sankt-Peterburga [Fond of Printed Graphic Art, Peter-Paul Fortress Historico-Cultural Museum-Preserve—State Museum of the History of St. Petersburg], **H–65**
FTI (1)—Fiziko-tekhnicheskii institut AN SSSR [Physico-Technical Institute].
    (2)—Fiziko-tekhnicheskii institut im. A. F. Ioffe AN SSSR [A. F. Ioffe Physico-Technical Institute].
    See (3)—Fiziko-tekhnicheskii institut im. A. F. Ioffe RAN [A. F. Ioffe Physico-Technical Institute], **E–29**
FTO GRI—Fiziko-tekhnicheskii otdel Gosudarstvennogo rentgenologicheskogo instituta [Physico-Technical Division of the State Institute of Radiology]. *See* FTI—Fiziko-tekhnicheskii institut im. A. F. Ioffe RAN [A. F. Ioffe Physico-Technical Institute], **E–29**

FTS-TV "Rossiia"—Federal'naia teleradioveshchatel'naia sluzhba "Rossiia" [Rossiia Federal Television and Radio Broadcasting Service]. *See* OAO TRK "Peterburg"—Otkrytoe aktsionernoe obshchestvo "Teleradiokompaniia 'Peterburg'" [Petersburg Television and Radio Broadcasting Open Joint-Stock Company], **F–15**

GA RF—Gosudarstvennyi arkhiv Rossiiskoi Federatsii [State Archive of the Russian Federation], **B–1**

GA RSFSR—Gosudarstvennyi arkhiv RSFSR [State Archive of the RSFSR]. *See* GA RF—Gosudarstvennyi arkhiv Rossiiskoi Federatsii [State Archive of the Russian Federation], **B–1**

GABT—Muzei. *See* Muzei GABT

GAFKE—Gosudarstvennyi arkhiv feodal'no-krepostnicheskoi epokhi [State Archive of the Feudal-Serfdom Epoch]. *See* RGADA—Rossiiskii gosudarstvennyi arkhiv drevnikh aktov [Russian State Archive of Early Acts], **B–2**

GAIMK—Gosudarstvennaia Akademiia istorii material'noi kul'tury [State Academy of the History of Material Culture]. *See* IA—Institut arkheologii RAN [Institute of Archeology], **E–3**, *and* IIMK—Institut istorii material'noi kul'tury RAN [Institute of the History of Material Culture], **E–22**

GAIS—Gosudarstvennaia Akademiia iskusstvoznaniia [State Academy of Art Studies]. *See* RIII—Rossiiskii institut istorii iskusstv [Russian Institute of the History of Art], **E–46**

GALOV—Gosudarstvennyi arkhiv Leningradskoi oblasti v g. Vyborge [State Archive of Leningrad Oblast in Vyborg]. *See* LOGAV—Leningradskii oblastnoi gosudarstvennyi arkhiv v g. Vyborge [Leningrad Oblast State Archive in Vyborg], **D–18**

GAMID—Sankt-Peterburgskii Glavnyi arkhiv Ministerstva inostrannykh del [Main Archive of the Ministry of Foreign Affairs]. *See* AVPRI—Arkhiv vneshnei politiki Rossiiskoi Imperii [Archive of Foreign Policy of the Russian Empire], **C–3**

GAMO—Gosudarstvennyi arkhiv Moskovskoi oblasti [State Archive of Moscow Oblast]. *See* TsGAMO—Tsentral'nyi gosudarstvennyi arkhiv Moskovskoi oblasti [Central State Archive of Moscow Oblast], **D–8**

GANTD Leningrada—Gosudarstvennyi arkhiv nauchno-tekhnicheskoi dokumentatsii Leningrada [State Archive of Scientific-Technical Documentation of Leningrad]. *See* TsGANTD SPb—Tsentral'nyi gosudarstvennyi arkhiv nauchno-tekhnicheskoi dokumentatsii Sankt-Peterburga [Central State Archive of Scientific-Technical Documentation of St. Petersburg], **D–17**

GAORSS LO/GAOR LO—Gosudarstvennyi arkhiv Oktiabr'skoi revolutsii i sotsialisticheskogo stroitel'stva Leningradskoi oblasti [State Archive of the October Revolution and Socialist Construction of Leningrad Oblast]. *See* TsGA SPb—Tsentral'nyi gosudarstvennyi arkhiv Sankt-Peterburga [Central State Archive of St. Petersburg], **D–12**

GAORSS LO–Filial—Filial Leningradskogo gosudarstvennogo arkhiva Oktiabr'skoi revoliutsii i sotsialisticheskogo stroitel'stva v Vyborge [Branch of the Central State Archive of the October Revolution and Socialist Construction in Vyborg]. *See* LOGAV—Leningradskii oblastnoi gosudarstvennyi arkhiv v g. Vyborge [Leningrad Oblast State Archive in Vyborg], **D–18**

GAORSS LO–Fotootdel—Fotootdel Gosudarstvennogo arkhiva Oktiabr'skoi revoliutsii i sotsialisticheskogo stroitel'stva Leningradskoi oblasti [Photograph Division of the State Archive of the October Revolution and Socialist Development of Leningrad Oblast] , **D–16**. *See* TsGAKFFD SPb—Tsentral'nyi gosudarstvennyi arkhiv kinofotofonodokumentov Sankt-Peterburga (Central State Archive of Documentary Films, Photographs, and Sound Recordings of St. Petersburg), **D–16**

GAORSS MO/GAOR MO—Gosudarstvennyi arkhiv Oktiabr'skoi revoliutsii i
sotsialisticheskogo stroitel'stva Moskovskoi oblasti [State Archive of the October
Revolution and Socialist Construction of Moscow Oblast]. *See* TsMAM—Tsentral'nyi
munitsipal'nyi arkhiv Moskvy [Central Municipal Archive of Moscow], **D–1,** *and*
TsGAMO—Tsentral'nyi gosudarstvennyi arkhiv Moskovskoi oblasti [Central State Archive
of Moscow Oblast], **D–8**

GAP RKP—Gosudarstvennyi arkhiv pechati, Rossiiskaia knizhnaia palata [State Archive of
Publications, Russian Book Chamber], **C–18**

Gatchina. *See* GMZ "Gatchina"

GAU MVD SSSR—Glavnoe arkhivnoe upravlenie MVD SSSR [Main Archival Administration of
the Ministry of Internal Affairs of the USSR]. *See* Rosarkhiv—Federal'naia arkhivnaia
sluzhba Rossii [Federal Archival Service of Russia], **B–0**

GAU NKVD SSSR—Glavnoe arkhivnoe upravlenie NKVD SSSR [Main Archival Administration
of the People's Commissariat of Internal Affairs of the USSR]. *See* Rosarkhiv—Federal'naia
arkhivnaia sluzhba Rossii [Federal Archival Service of Russia], **B–0**

GAU pri SM RSFSR/Glavarkhiv RSFSR—Glavnoe arkhivnoe upravlenie pri Sovete Ministrov
RSFSR [Main Archival Administration under the Council of Ministers of the RSFSR].
See Rosarkhiv—Federal'naia arkhivnaia sluzhba Rossii [Federal Archival Service of Russia],
B–0

GAU pri SM SSSR/Glavarkhiv SSSR—Glavnoe arkhivnoe upravlenie pri Sovete Ministrov
SSSR [Main Archival Administration under the Council of Ministers of the USSR].
See Rosarkhiv—Federal'naia arkhivnaia sluzhba Rossii [Federal Archival Service of
Russia], **B–0**

GAVP—Gosudarstvennyi arkhiv vneshnei politiki [State Archive of Foreign Policy].
See AVPRI—Arkhiv vneshnei politiki Rossiiskoi Imperii [Archive of Foreign Policy of the
Russian Empire], **C–3**

GBL—Gosudarstvennaia biblioteka SSSR im. V. I. Lenina [V. I. Lenin State Library].
See RGB—Rossiiskaia gosudarstvennaia biblioteka [Russian State Library], **G–1**

GBMT—Gosudarstvennyi biologicheskii muzei im. K. A. Timiriazeva [K. A. Timiriazev State
Biological Museum], **H–52**

GDM—Gosudarstvennyi Darvinovskii muzei [State Darwin Museum], **H–53**

GE—Gosudarstvennyi Ermitazh [State Hermitage], **H–88**

GEM—Gosudarstvennyi etnograficheskii muzei [State Ethnographic Museum]. *See* REM—
Rossiiskii etnograficheskii muzei [Russian Ethnographic Museum], **H–71**

GEOKhI—Institut geokhimii i analiticheskoi khimii im. V. I. Vernadskogo RAN [V. I.
Vernadskii Institute of Geochemistry and Analytical Chemistry], **E–17**

Geospravbiuro GK—Geodezicheskoe spravochnoe biuro Geodezicheskogo komiteta VSNKh
SSSR [Geodesic Reference Bureau of the Geodesic Committee VSNKh SSSR]. *See* TsKGF—
Tsentral'nyi kartografo-geodezicheskii fond [Central Cartographic-Geodesic Fond], **C–14**

GFF/Gosfil'mofond—Gosudarstvennyi fond kinofil'mov RF [State Fond of Motion Pictures], **C–16**

GFTI—Gosudarstvennyi fiziko-tekhnicheskii institut [State Physico-Technical Institute].
See FTI—Fiziko-tekhnicheskii institut im. A. F. Ioffe RAN [A. F. Ioffe Physico-Technical
Institute], **E–29**

GFTRI—Gosudarstvennyi fiziko-tekhnicheskii rentgenologicheskii institut [State Physico-
Technical Institute of Radiology]. *See* FTI—Fiziko-tekhnicheskii institut im. A. F. Ioffe
RAN [A. F. Ioffe Physico-Technical Institute], **E–29**

GFO—Muzei. *See* Muzei GFO *and* Muzei GGO

GGK—Tsentral'noe Geospravbiuro. *See* Tsentral'noe Geospravbiuro GGK

GGO—Glavnaia geofizicheskaia observatoriia [Main Geophysical Observatory]. *See* Gosfond—Gosudarstvennyi fond dannykh o sostoianii prirodnoi sredy [State Fond of Data on Environmental Conditions], **C–13**, *and* Muzei GGO—Meteorologicheskii muzei Glavnoi geofizicheskoi observatorii [Meteorological Museum of the Main Geophysical Observatory]. **H–107**

GIALO—Gosudarstvennyi istoricheskii arkhiv Leningradskoi oblasti [State Historical Archive of Leningrad Oblast]. *See* TsGIA SPb—Tsentral'nyi gosudarstvennyi istoricheskii arkhiv Sankt-Peterburga [Central State Historical Archive of St. Petersburg], **D–13**

GIAMO—Gosudarstvennyi istoricheskii arkhiv Moskovskoi oblasti [State Historical Archive of Moscow Oblast]. *See* TsIAM—Tsentral'nyi istoricheskii arkhiv Moskvy [Central Historical Archive of Moscow], **D–2**

Gidrometfond—Gosudarstvennyi fond gidrometeorologicheskikh materialov [State Fond of Hydrometeorological Materials]. *See* Gosfond—Gosudarstvennyi fond dannykh o sostoianii prirodnoi sredy [State Fond of Data on Environmental Conditions], **C–13**

GIFK—Gosudarstvennyi institut fizicheskoi kul'tury im. P. F. Lesgafta [P. F. Lesgaft State Institute of Physical Education]. *See* SPbGAFK—Sankt-Peterburgskaia gosudarstvennaia akademiia fizicheskoi kul'tury im. P. F. Lesgafta [P. F. Lesgaft St. Petersburg State Academy of Physical Culture], **E–60**

GIII—Gosudarstvennyi institut istorii iskusstv [State Institute of the History of Art]. *See* RIII—Rossiiskii institut istorii iskusstv [Russian Institute of the History of Art], **E–46**

GIM—Gosudarstvennyi Istoricheskii muzei [State Historical Museum], **H–1**. *See also* OR/RO GIM—Otdel rukopisei i staropechatnykh knig, Gosudarstvennyi Istoricheskii muzei [Division of Manuscripts and Early Printed Books, State Historical Museum], **H–1**

GIMZ—Gosudarstvennyi institut meditsinskikh znanii [State Institute of Medical Knowledge]. *See* SPbGSGMI—Sankt-Peterburgskii gosudarstvennyi sanitarno-gigienicheskii meditsinskii institut [St. Petersburg State Sanitary-Hygiene Medical Institute], **E–58**

GIOP GlavAPU—Gosudarstvennaia inspektsiia po okhrane pamiatnikov Leningrada Glavnogo arkhitekturno-planirovochnogo upravleniia Leningradskogo gorodskogo soveta deputatov trudiashchikhsia—Nauchno-arkhitekturnyi kabinet [State Inspection for the Preservation of Monuments of Leningrad of the Leningrad Main Architectural-Planning Administration of the Leningrad City Soviet of Workers' Deputies—Scientific Architectural Office]. *See* Arkhiv KGIOP—Nauchno-metodicheskii informatsionno-izdatel'skii sektor (vedomstvennyi arkhiv) Komiteta po gosudarstvennomu kontroliu, ispol'zovaniiu i okhrane pamiatnikov istorii i kul'tury Sankt-Peterburga [Scientific-Methodological Information-Publication Sector (Agency Archive) of the Committee for State Control, Use, and Preservation of Monuments of History and Culture of St. Petersburg], **D–21**

GKP—Gosudarstvennaia tsentral'naia knizhnaia palata RSFSR [State Central Book Chamber]. *See* RKP—Rossiiskaia knizhnaia palata [Russian Book Chamber], **C–18**

Glavarkhiv pri Narkomprose RSFSR—Glavnoe upravlenie arkhivnym delom pri Narkomprose RSFSR [Main Administration for Archival Affairs under the People's Commissariat of Education RSFSR]. *See* Rosarkhiv—Federal'naia arkhivnaia sluzhba Rossii [Federal Archival Service of Russia], **B–0**

Glavarkhiv RSFSR/GAU pri SM RSFSR—Glavnoe arkhivnoe upravlenie pri Sovete Ministrov RSFSR [Main Archival Administration under the Council of Ministers of the RSFSR]. *See* Rosarkhiv—Federal'naia arkhivnaia sluzhba Rossii [Federal Archival Service of Russia], **B–0**

Glavarkhiv SSSR/GAU pri SM SSSR—Glavnoe arkhivnoe upravlenie pri Sovete Ministrov SSSR [Main Archival Administration under the Council of Ministers of the USSR]. *See* Rosarkhiv—Federal'naia arkhivnaia sluzhba Rossii [Federal Archival Service of Russia], **B–0**

GLM—Gosudarstvennyi literaturnyi muzei [State Literary Museum], **H–33**

GM—GTsPO—Gosudarstvennyi muzei—gumanitarnyi tsentr "Preodolenie" im. N. A. Ostrovskogo [N. A. Ostrovskii State Museum—Humanitarian Center "Overcoming"], **H–37**

GMDT—Gosudarstvennyi muzei detskikh teatrov [State Museum of Children's Theaters], **H–44**

GMEN SSSR—Gosudarstvennyi muzei etnografii narodov SSSR [State Museum of Ethnography of the Peoples of the USSR]. *See* REM—Rossiiskii etnograficheskii muzei [Russian Ethnographic Museum], **H–71**

GMGS—Gosudarstvennyi muzei gorodskoi skul'ptury [State Museum of Urban Sculpture], **H–87**

GMIA—Gosudarstvennyi muzei istorii aviatsii [State Museum of the History of Aviation], **H–113**

GMII—Gosudarstvennyi muzei izobrazitel'nykh iskusstv im. A. S. Pushkina [A. S. Pushkin State Museum of Fine Arts], **H–26**

GMIL—Gosudarstvennyi muzei istorii Leningrada [State Museum of the History of Leningrad]. *See* GMISPb—Istoriko-kul'turnyi muzei-zapovednik "Petropavlovskaia krepost'"—Gosudarstvennyi muzei istorii Sankt-Peterburga [Peter-Paul Fortress Historico-Cultural Museum-Preserve—State Museum of the History of St. Petersburg], **H–65**

GMINV—Gosudarstvennyi muzei iskusstva narodov Vostoka [State Museum of the Art of Peoples of the Orient]. *See* GMV—Gosudarstvennyi muzei Vostoka [State Museum of the Orient], **H–29**

GMIR—Gosudarstvennyi muzei istorii religii [State Museum of the History of Religion], **H–72**

GMIRiA—Gosudarstvennyi muzei istorii religii i ateizma [State Museum of the History of Religion and Atheism]. *See* GMIR—Gosudarstvennyi muzei istorii religii [State Museum of the History of Religion], **H–72**

GMIS—Gosudasrstvennyi muzei "Isaakievskii sobor" [Isaac Cathedral State Museum], **H–86**

GMISPb—Istoriko-kul'turnyi muzei-zapovednik "Petropavlovskaia krepost'"—Gosudarstvennyi muzei istorii Sankt-Peterburga [Peter-Paul Fortress Historico-Cultural Museum-Preserve—State Museum of the History of St. Petersburg], **H–65**

GMK i "Usad'ba Kuskovo XVIII veka"—Gosudarstvennyi muzei keramiki i "Usad'ba Kuskovo XVIII veka" [State Museum of Ceramics and the Kuskovo Estate of the Eighteenth Century], **H–21**

GMM—Gosudarstvennyi muzei V. V. Maiakovskogo [V. V. Maiakovskii State Museum], **H–36**

GMM A. V. Suvorova—Gosudarstvennyi memorial'nyi muzei A. V. Suvorova [A. V. Suvorov State Memorial Museum], **H–77**

GMMOBL—Gosudarstvennyi memorial'nyi muzei oborony i blokady Leningrada [State Memorial Museum of the Defense and Blockade of Leningrad], **H–76**

GMNII—Gosudarstvennyi muzykal'nyi nauchno-issledovatel'skii institut [State Scientific Research Institute of Music]. *See* RIII—Rossiiskii institut istorii iskusstv [Russian Institute of the History of Art], **E–46**

GMOM—Gosudarstvennyi muzei oborony Moskvy [State Museum of the Defense of Moscow], **H–9**

GMP—Gosudarstvennyi muzei A. S. Pushkina [A. S. Pushkin State Museum], **H–34**

GMPIR—Gosudarstvennyi muzei politicheskoi istorii Rossii [State Museum of the Political History of Russia], **H–66**

GMR SSSR—Gosudarstvennyi muzei revoliutsii SSSR [State Museum of Revolution of the USSR]. *See* GTsMSIR—Gosudarstvennyi tsentral'nyi muzei sovremennoi istorii Rossii [State Central Museum of the Contemporary History of Russia], **H–4**

GMT—Gosudarstvennyi muzei L. N. Tolstogo [L. N. Tolstoi State Museum], **H–35**

GMV—Gosudarstvennyi muzei Vostoka [State Museum of the Orient], **H–29**

GMVOSR—Gosudarstvennyi muzei Velikoi Oktiabr'skoi sotsialisticheskoi revoliutsii—Filial Tsentral'nogo muzeia revoliutsii SSSR [State Museum of the Great October Socialist

Revolution—Branch of the Central Museum of Revolution of the USSR]. *See* GMPIR—Gosudarstvennyi muzei politicheskoi istorii Rossii [State Museum of the Political History of Russia], **H–66**

GMZ "Gatchina"—Gosudarstvennyi dvortsovo-parkovyi muzei-zapovednik "Gatchina" [Gatchina State Palace-Park Museum-Preserve], **H–79**

GMZ "Oranienbaum"—Gosudarstvennyi muzei-zapovednik "Oranienbaum" [Oranienbaum State Museum-Preserve], **H–80**

GMZ "Pavlovsk"—Gosudarstvennyi muzei-zapovednik "Pavlovsk" [Pavlovsk State Museum-Preserve], **H–81**

GMZ "Petergof"—Gosudarstvennyi muzei-zapovednik "Petergof" [Peterhof State Museum-Preserve], **H–82**

GMZ "Tsarskoe Selo"—Gosudarstvennyi khudozhestvenno-arkhitekturnyi dvortsovo-parkovyi muzei-zapovednik "Tsarskoe Selo" [Tsarskoe Selo State Art-Architectural Palace-Park Museum-Preserve], **H–84**

GNIIS—Gosudarstvennyi nauchno-issledovatel'skii institut iskusstvoznaniia [State Scientific Research Institute of Art Studies]. *See* RIII—Rossiiskii institut istorii iskusstv [Russian Institute of the History of Art], **E–46**

GNIITiM—Gosudarstvennyi nauchno-issledovatel'skii institut teatra i muzyki [State Scientific Research Institute of Theater and Music]. *See* RIII—Rossiiskii institut istorii iskusstv [Russian Institute of the History of Art], **E–46**

GNIMA—Gosudarstvennyi nauchno-issledovatel'skii muzei arkhitektury im. A. V. Shchuseva [A. V. Shchusev State Scientific Research Museum of Architecture], **H–28**

GOPB—Gosudarstvennaia obshchestvenno-politicheskaia biblioteka [State Socio-Political Library]. *See under* RGASPI, **B–12**

GO SSSR—Geograficheskoe obshchestvo SSSR [Geographic Society of the USSR]. *See* RGO—Russkoe geograficheskoe obshchestvo [Russian Geographic Society], **E–26**

"Gorokhovaia, 2"—Muzei "Gorokhovaia, 2"—Filial Gosudarstvennogo muzeia politicheskoi istorii Rossii ["Gorokhovaia, 2" Museum—Branch of the State Museum of the Political History of Russia], **H–67**

Gosarkhiv—Gosudarstvennyi arkhiv Rossiiskoi imperii [State Archive of the Russian Empire]. *See* RGADA—Rossiiskii gosudarstvennyi arkhiv drevnikh aktov [Russian State Archive of Early Acts], **B–2**

Gosfil'mofond—Vsesoiuznyi gosudarstvennyi fond kinofil'mov [All-Union State Fond of Motion Pictures]. *See* Gosfil'mofond Rossii/GFF—Gosudarstvennyi fond kinofil'mov RF [State Fond of Motion Pictures], **C–16**

Gosfond—Gosudarstvennyi fond dannykh o sostoianii prirodnoi sredy [State Fond of Data on Environmental Conditions], **C–13**

Gosteleradiofond—Gosudarstvennyi fond televizionnykh i radioprogramm [State Fond of Television and Radio Programs], **C–17**

GPB—Gosudarstvennaia Publichnaia biblioteka im. M. E. Saltykova-Shchedrina [M. E. Saltykov-Shchedrin State Public Library]. *See* RNB—Rossiiskaia natsional'naia biblioteka [Russian National Library], **G–15**

GPIB—Gosudarstvennaia publichnaia istoricheskaia biblioteka Rossii [State Public Historical Library], **G–3**

GPIB RSFSR—Gosudarstvennaia publichnaia istoricheskaia biblioteka RSFSR [State Public Historical Library of the RSFSR]. *See* GPIB—Gosudarstvennaia publichnaia istoricheskaia biblioteka Rossii [State Public Historical Library of Russia], **G–3**

GPM—Gosudarstvennyi Politekhnicheskii muzei [State Polytechnic Museum], **H–57**

GRDB—Gosudarstvennaia respublikanskaia detskaia biblioteka RSFSR [State Republican Children's Library of the RSFSR]. *See* RGDB—Rossiiskaia gosudarstvennaia detskaia biblioteka [Russian State Children's Library], **G–9**

GRDBR—Gosudarstvennaia respublikanskaia detskaia biblioteka Rossii [Russian State Republican Children's Library]. *See* RGDB—Rossiiskaia gosudarstvennaia detskaia biblioteka [Russian State Children's Library], **G–9**

GRM—Gosudarstvennyi Russkii muzei [State Russian Museum], **H–89**

GTG—Gosudarstvennaia Tret'iakovskaia galereia [State Tret'iakov Gallery], **H–23**

GTRK "Peterburg–5 kanal"—Gosudarstvennaia televizionnaia radioveshchatel'naia kompaniia "Peterburg–5 kanal" [Petersburg 5th Channel State Television and Radio Broadcasting Company]. *See* OAO TRK "Peterburg"—Otkrytoe aktsionernoe obshchestvo "Teleradiokompaniia 'Peterburg'" [Petersburg Television and Radio Broadcasting Open Joint-Stock Company], **F–15**

GTsMMK—Gosudarstvennyi tsentral'nyi muzei muzykal'noi kul'tury im. M. I. Glinki [M. I. Glinka State Central Museum of Musical Culture], **H–45.** *See also* Filial GTsMMK—Muzei-kvartira A. B. Gol'denveizera—Filial Gosudarstvennogo tsentral'nogo muzeia muzykal'noi kul'tury im. M. I. Glinki [A. B. Gol'denveizer Apartment-Museum—Branch of M. I. Glinka State Central Museum of Musical Culture], **H–47**

GTsMSIR—Gosudarstvennyi tsentral'nyi muzei sovremennoi istorii Rossii [State Central Museum of the Contemporary History of Russia], **H–4**

GTsTB—Gosudarstvennaia tsentral'naia teatral'naia biblioteka [State Central Theater Library]. *See* RGBI—Rossiiskaia gosudarstvennaia biblioteka po iskusstvu [Russian State Library for the Arts], **G–6**

GTsTM—Gosudarstvennyi tsentral'nyi teatral'nyi muzei im. A. A. Bakhrushina [A. A. Bakhrushin State Central Theater Museum], **H–42**

GUGF—Glavnoe upravlenie geologicheskikh fondov [Main Administration of Geological Fonds]. *See* Rosgeolfond—Gosudarstvennoe geologicheskoe predpriiatie "Rossiiskii federal'nyi geologicheskii fond" [Russian Federal Geological Fond State Geological Enterprise], **C–12**

GUPVI. *See* Arkhiv GUPVI

IA (1)—Institut arkheologii AN SSSR [Institute of Archeology]. *See* (2)—IA—Institut arkheologii RAN [Institute of Archeology], **E–3,** *and now also* IIMK—Institut istorii material'noi kul'tury RAN [Institute of the History of Material Culture], **E–22**

IAAE—Institut antropologii, arkheologii i etnografii AN SSSR [Institute of Anthropology, Archeology, and Ethnography]. *See* IEA—Institut etnologii i antropologii im. N. N. Miklukho-Maklaia RAN [N. N. Miklukho-Maklai Institute of Ethnology and Anthropology], **E–7,** *and* Kunstkamera/MAE—Muzei antropologii i etnografii im. Petra Velikogo RAN [Peter the Great Museum of Anthropology and Ethnography (Kunstkammer)], **E–25**

IAE (1)—Institut antropologii i etnografii AN SSSR [Institute of Anthropology and Ethnography].
      See (2)—IEA—Institut etnologii i antropologii im. N. N. Miklukho-Maklaia RAN [N. N. Miklukho-Maklai Institute of Ethnology and Anthropology], **E–7,** *and* Kunstkamera/MAE—Muzei antropologii i etnografii im. Petra Velikogo RAN [Museum of Anthropology and Ethnography of Peter the Great (Kunstkammer)], **E–25**

IAE—Institut atomnoi energii im. I. V. Kurchatova [I. V. Kurchatov Institute of Atomic Energy]. *See* RNTs KI—Rossiiskii nauchnyi tsentr "Kurchatovskii institut" [Kurchatov Institute Russian Scientific Center], **E–41**

IAI AN SSSR—Istoriko-arkheograficheskii institut AN SSSR [Historico-Archeographic Institute]. *See* SPbF IRI—Sankt-Peterburgskii filial Instituta rossiiskoi istorii RAN [St. Petersburg Branch of the Institute of Russian History], **E–24**

IAI RGGU—Istoriko-arkhivnyi institut Rossiiskogo gosudarstvennogo gumanitarnogo universiteta [Historico-Archival Institute of the Russian State University for the Humanities], **E–52**

IAK—Imperatorskaia Arkheograficheskaia komissiia [Imperial Archeographic Commission]. *See* SPbF IRI—Sankt-Peterburgskii filial Instituta rossiiskoi istorii RAN [St. Petersburg Branch of the Institute of Russian History], **E–24**

IAK—Imperatorskaia Arkheologicheskaia komissiia [Imperial Archeological Commission]. *See* IIMK—Institut istorii material'noi kul'tury RAN [Institute of the History of Material Culture], **E–22**

IAKh—Imperatorskaia Akademiia khudozhestv [Imperial Academy of Arts]. *See* RAKh—Rossiiskaia Akademiia khudozhestv [Russian Academy of Arts], **E–45**. *See also* NB RAKh—Nauchnaia biblioteka Rossiiskoi Akademii khudozhestv [Scientific Library of the Russian Academy of Arts], **G–18**, *and* NIM RAKh—Nauchno-issledovatel'skii muzei Rossiiskoi Akademii khudozhestv [Scientific Research Museum of the Russian Academy of Arts], **H–90, H–91—H–93, H–156**

IDD MID—Istoriko-dokumental'nyi departament Ministerstva inostrannykh del RF [Historico-Documentary Department of the Ministry of Foreign Affairs], **C–02**

IDU MID RF—Istoriko-dokumental'noe upravlenie MID RF [Historico-Documentary Administration of the Ministry of Foreign Affairs]. *See* IDD MID—Istoriko-dokumental'nyi departament Ministerstva inostrannykh del RF [Historico-Documentary Department of the Ministry of Foreign Affairs], **C–02**

IDU MID SSSR—Istoriko-diplomaticheskoe upravlenie MID SSSR [Historico-Diplomatic Administration of the Ministry of Foreign Affairs of the USSR]. *See* IDD MID—Istoriko-dokumental'nyi departament Ministerstva inostrannykh del RF [Historico-Documentary Department of the Ministry of Foreign Affairs], **C–02**

IE (1)—Institut etnografii AN SSSR [Institute of Ethnography];
(2)—Institut etnografii im. N. N. Miklukho-Maklaia AN SSSR [N. N. Miklukho-Maklai Institute of Ethnography]. *See* IEA—Institut etnologii i antropologii im. N. N. Miklukho-Maklaia RAN [N. N. Miklukho-Maklai Institute of Ethnology and Anthropology], **E–7**, *and* Kunstkamera/MAE—Muzei antropologii i etnografii im. Petra Velikogo RAN [Peter the Great Museum of Anthropology and Ethnography (Kunstkammer)], **E–25**

IEA—Institut etnologii i antropologii im. N. N. Miklukho-Maklaia RAN [N. N. Miklukho-Maklai Institute of Ethnology and Anthropology], **E–7**

IEM AMN SSSR—Institut eksperimental'noi meditsiny Akademii meditsinskikh nauk SSSR [Institute of Experimental Medicine of the Academy of Medical Sciences of the USSR]. *See* NIIEM—Nauchno-issledovatel'skii institut eksperimental'noi meditsiny RAMN [Scientific Research Institute of Experimental Medicine of the Russian Academy of Medical Sciences], **E–47**

IF—Institut fiziologii im. I. P. Pavlova RAN [I. P. Pavlov Institute of Physiology], **E–32**

IFP (1)—Institut fizicheskikh problem [Institute of Physics Problems]
(2)—Institut fizicheskikh problem im. S. I. Vavilova [S. I. Vavilov Institute of Physics Problems].
See (3)—Institut fizicheskikh problem im. P. L. Kapitsy RAN [P. L. Kapitsa Institute of Physics Problems], **E–12**

IGP—Institut gosudarstva i prava RAN [Institute of State and Law], **E–6**

IGPAN—Institut gosudarstva i prava AN SSSR [Institute of State and Law]. *See* IGP—Institut gosudarstva i prava RAN [Institute of State and Law], **E–6**

II—Institut istorii AN SSSR [Institute of History]. *See* IRI—Institut rossiiskoi istorii RAN [Institute of Russian History], **E–5**, *and* SPbF IRI—Sankt-Peterburgskii filial Instituta rossiiskoi istorii RAN [St. Petersburg Branch of the Institute of Russian History], **E–24**

II SSSR—Institut istorii SSSR AN SSSR [Institute of History of the USSR]. *See* IRI—Institut rossiiskoi istorii RAN [Institute of Russian History], **E–5**, *and* SPbF IRI—Sankt-Peterburgskii filial Instituta rossiiskoi istorii RAN [St. Petersburg Branch of the Institute of Russian History], **E–24**

IIaM—Institut iazyka i myshleniia AN SSSR [Institute of Language and Thought]. *See* IRIa—Institut russkogo iazyka im. V. V. Vinogradova RAN [V. V. Vinogradov Institute of the Russian Language], **E–10**

IIET (1)—Institut istorii estestvoznaniia i tekhniki AN SSSR [Institute of the History of Natural Science and Technology].

> *See* (2)—Institut istorii estestvoznaniia i tekhniki im. S. I. Vavilova RAN [S. I. Vavilov Institute of the History of Natural Science and Technology], **E–2**. *See also* SPbF IIET—Sankt-Peterburgskii filial Instituta istorii estestvoznaniia i tekhniki im. S. I. Vavilova RAN [St. Petersburg Branch of the S. I. Vavilov Institute of the History of Natural Science and Technology], **E–21**

III—Institut istorii iskusstv [Institute of the History of Art]. *See* RIII—Rossiiskii institut istorii iskusstv [Russian Institute of the History of Art], **E–46**

IIMK—Institut istorii material'noi kul'tury im. N. Ia. Marra AN SSSR [N. Ia. Marr Institute of the History of Material Culture]. *See* IA—Institut arkheologii RAN [Institute of Archeology], **E–3**, *and* IIMK—Institut istorii material'noi kul'tury RAN [Institute of the History of Material Culture], **E–22**

IIMK—Institut istorii material'noi kul'tury RAN [Institute of the History of Material Culture], **E–22**

IINiT—Institut istorii nauki i tekhniki AN SSSR [Institute of the History of Science and Technology]. *See* IIET—Institut istorii estestvoznaniia i tekhniki im. S. I. Vavilova RAN [S. I. Vavilov Institute of the History of Natural Science and Technology], **E–2**, *and* SPbF IIET—Sankt-Peterburgskii filial Instituta istorii estestvoznaniia i tekhniki im. S. I. Vavilova RAN [St. Petersburg Branch of the S. I. Vavilov Institute of the History of Natural Science and Technology], **E–21**

IKAN—Institut kristallografii im. A. V. Shubnikova RAN [A. V. Shubnikov Institute of Crystallography], **E–13**

IML—TsPA . *See* TsPA IML

IMLI (1)—Institut mirovoi literatury im. M. Gor'kogo AN SSSR [A. M. Gor'kii Institute of World Literature].

> *See* (2)—Institut mirovoi literatury im. A. M. Gor'kogo RAN [A. M. Gor'kii Institute of World Literature], **E–9**

INA—Institut narodov Azii AN SSSR [Institute of the Peoples of Asia]. *See* IV—Institut vostokovedeniia RAN [Institute of Oriental Studies], **E–4**, *and* SPbF IV—Sankt-Peterburgskii filial Instituta vostokovedeniia RAN [St. Petersburg Branch of the Institute of Oriental Studies], **E–23**

INEOS—Institut elementoorganicheskikh soedinenii im. A. N. Nesmeianova RAN [A. N. Nesmeianov Institute of Elementary Organic Compounds], **E–16**

INKhS—Institut neftekhimicheskogo sinteza im. A. V. Topchieva RAN [A. V. Topchiev Institute of Petrochemical Synthesis], **E–14**

INO—Arkhiv. *See* Arkhiv INO

INPII. *See* Muzei INPII *and see also* Biblioteka INPII

IOGEN—Institut obshchei genetiki im. N. I. Vavilova RAN [N. I. Vavilov Institute of General Genetics], **E–18**

IOKh—Institut organicheskoi khimii im N. D. Zelinskogo RAN [N. D. Zelinskii Institute of Organic Chemistry], **E–15**

IP—Institut psikhologii RAN [Institute of Psychology], **E–8**

IPAN—Institut psikhologii AN SSSR [Institute of Psychology]. *See* IP—Institut psikhologii RAN [Institute of Psychology], **E–8**

IPB—Imperatorskaia Publichnaia biblioteka [Imperial Public Library]. *See* RNB—Rossiiskaia natsional'naia biblioteka [Russian National Library], **G–15**

IPIN—Institut po izucheniiu narodov SSSR [Institute for the Study of the Peoples of the USSR]. *See* Kunstkamera/MAE—Muzei antropologii i etnografii im. Petra Velikogo RAN [Peter the Great Museum of Anthropology and Ethnography (Kunstkammer)], **E–25**, *and* Institut russkoi literatury (Pushkinskii Dom) RAN [Institute of Russian Literature (Pushkin House)], **E–28**

IPM—Institut prikladnoi matematiki im. M. V. Keldysha RAN [M. V. Keldysh Institute of Applied Mathematics], **E–11**

IRI—Institut rossiiskoi istorii RAN [Institute of Russian History], **E–5**

IRIa (1)—Institut russkogo iazyka RAN [Institute of the Russian Language].
    See (2)—Institut russkogo iazyka im. V. V. Vinogradova RAN [V. V. Vinogradov Institute of the Russian Language], **E–10**

IRIaz—Institut russkogo iazyka AN SSSR [Institute of the Russian Language]. *See* IRIa— Institut russkogo iazyka im. V. V. Vinogradova RAN [V. V. Vinogradov Institute of the Russian Language], **E–10**

IRLI/PD (1)—Institut russkoi literatury AN SSSR [Institute of Russian Literature].
    See (2)—Institut russkoi literatury (Pushkinskii Dom) RAN [Institute of Russian Literature (Pushkin House)], **E–28**

IS—Institut sotsiologii RAN. *See* SPbF IS—Sankt-Peterburgskii filial Instituta sotsiologii RAN [St. Petersburg Branch of the Institute of Sociology], **E–27**

ISS—Institut sovetskogo stroitel'stva [Institute of Soviet Construction]. *See* IGP—Institut gosudarstva i prava RAN [Institute of State and Law], **E–6**

Istpart—Komissia po sobiraniiu i izucheniiu materialov po istorii Oktiabr'skoi revoliutsii pri Narkomprose RSFSR [Commission to Collect and Study Materrials for the History of the October Revolution under Narkompos RSFSR. *See* Tsentral'nyi arkhiv obshchestvennykh dvizhenii Moskvy (TsAODM) [Central Archive of Social Movements of Moscow], **D–3** *and* Rossiiskii gosudarstvennyi arkhiv sotsial'no-politicheskoi istorii (RGASPI) [Russian State Archive of Socio-Political History], **B–12**

ITM SPbGTU—Istoriko-tekhnicheskii muzei Sankt-Peterburgskogo gosudarstvennogo tekhnicheskogo universiteta [Historico-Technical Museum of St. Petersburg State Technical University], **H–117**

IV—Institut vostokovedeniia RAN [Institute of Oriental Studies], **E–4**

IVAN/ IV AN SSSR—Institut vostokovedeniia AN SSSR [Institute of Oriental Studies]. *See* IV— Institut vostokovedeniia RAN [Institute of Oriental Studies], **E–4**, *and* SPbF IV—Sankt-Peterburgskii filial Instituta vostokovedeniia RAN [St. Petersburg Branch of the Institute of Oriental Studies], **E–23**

IZhSA VAKh—Muzei. *See* Muzei IZhSA VAKh

KGB SSSR. *See* TsA KGB SSSR

KGIOP—Arkhiv. *See* Arkhiv KGIOP

Kinosev—Petrogradskii oblastnoi kinematograficheskii komitet Soiuza Severnykh kommun [Petrograd Oblast Cinematographic Committee of the Union of Northern Communes]. *See* Lenfil'm—Kinostudiia "Lenfil'm" [Lenfil'm Studio], **C–24**

KIZ—Komissiia po istorii znanii Rossiiskoi AN [Commission on the History of Knowledge of the Russian Academy of Sciences]. *See* SPbF IIET—Sankt-Peterburgskii filial Instituta istorii estestvoznaniia i tekhniki im. S. I. Vavilova RAN [St. Petersburg Branch of the S. I. Vavilov Institute of the History of Natural Science and Technology], **E–21**

Kolomenskoe—Muzei-zapovednik. *See* Muzei-zapovednik "Kolomenskoe"

Komintern. *See* Arkhiv Kominterna

Komissiia "Russkaia nauka"—Komissiia po izdaniiu sbornika "Russkaia nauka" Rossiiskoi AN [Commission to Publish a "Russian Science" Collection of the Russian Academy of Sciences (Russian Science Commission)]. *See* SPbF IIET—Sankt-Peterburgskii filial Instituta istorii estestvoznaniia i tekhniki im. S. I. Vavilova RAN [St. Petersburg Branch of the S. I. Vavilov Institute of the History of Natural Science and Technology], **E–21**

Kunstkamera/MAE—Muzei antropologii i etnografii im. Petra Velikogo RAN [Peter the Great Museum of Anthropology and Ethnography (Kunstkammer)], **E–25**

LAFOKI (1)—Laboratoriia nauchno-prikladnoi fotografii i kinematografii AN SSSR/RAN [Laboratory of Scientific-Applied Photography and Cinematography (Moscow and Leningrad/St. Petersburg)], **E–19, E–34**

    (2)—Laboratoriia nauchno-prikladnoi fotografii, kinematografii i televideniia RAN [Laboratory of Scientific-Applied Photography, Cinematography, and Television (Moscow)], **E–19**

LChIE—Leningradskaia chast' Instituta etnografii im. N. N. Miklukho-Maklaia AN SSSR [Leningrad Section of the N. N. Miklukho-Maklai Institute of Ethnography]. *See* Kunstkamera/MAE—Muzei antropologii i etnografii im. Petra Velikogo RAN [Peter the Great Museum of Anthropology and Ethnography (Kunstkammer)], **E–25**

LDA—Biblioteka. *See* Biblioteka LDA

Lenfil'm—Kinostudiia "Lenfil'm" [Lenfil'm Studio], **C–24**

Lengosteatr—Muzei. *See* Muzei Lengosteatrov

Leningradkino—Leningradskii kinokhudozhestvennyi trest [Leningrad Cinema Arts Trust]. *See* Lenfil'm—Kinostudiia "Lenfil'm" [Lenfil'm Studio], **C–24**

Lennauchfil'm (1)—Leningradskaia kinostudiia nauchno-populiarnykh fil'mov [Leningrad Film Studio for Documentary Films].

    See (2) —Lennauchfil'm—Sankt-Peterburgskaia kinostudiia nauchno-populiarnykh fil'mov "Lennauchfil'm" [St. Petersburg Studio for Documentary Films—Lennauchfilm], **C–25**

LEPA—Leningradskoe otdelenie Edinogo partiinogo arkhiva [Leningrad Division of the Unified Party Archive]. *See* TsGAIPD SPb—Tsentral'nyi gosudarstvennyi arkhiv istoriko-politicheskikh dokumentov Sankt-Peterburga [Central State Archive of Historico-Political Documents of St. Petersburg], **D–14**

LETI—Muzei istorii. *See* Muzei istorii LETI *and see also* Muzei istorii ETU

LF LAFOKI—Leningradskii filial Laboratorii nauchno-prikladnoi fotografii i kinematografii AN SSSR [Leningrad Branch of the Laboratory of Scientific-Applied Photography and Cinematography]. *See* LAFOKI—Laboratoriia nauchno-prikladnoi fotografii i kinematografii RAN [Laboratory of Scientific-Applied Photography and Cinematography], **E–34**

LF VIEM—Leningradskii filial Vsesoiuznogo instituta eksperimental'noi meditsiny im. A. M. Gor'kogo [Leningrad Branch of the A. M. Gor'kii All-Union Institute of Experimental Medicine]. *See* NIIEM—Nauchno-issledovatel'skii institut eksperimental'noi meditsiny RAMN [Scientific Research Institute of Experimental Medicine of the Russian Academy of Medical Sciences], **E–47**

1264

LFTI—Leningradskii fiziko-tekhnicheskii institut [Leningrad Physico-Technical Institute]. *See* FTI—Fiziko-tekhnicheskii institut im. A. F. Ioffe RAN [A. F. Ioffe Physico-Technical Institute], **E–29**

LFZ—Muzei. *See* Muzei LFZ

LGAKFFD—Leningradskii gosudarstvennyi arkhiv kinofotofonodokumentov [Leningrad State Archive of Documentary Films, Photographs, and Sound Recordings]. *See* TsGAKFFD SPb—Tsentral'nyi gosudarstvennyi arkhiv kinofotofonodokumentov Sankt-Peterburga [Central State Archive of Documentary Films, Photographs, and Sound Recordings of St. Petersburg], **D–16**

LGALI—Leningradskii gosudarstvennyi arkhiv literatury i iskusstva [Leningrad State Archive of Literature and Art]. *See* TsGALI SPb—Tsentral'nyi gosudarstvennyi arkhiv literatury i iskusstva Sankt-Peterburga [Central State Archive of Literature and Art of St. Petersburg], **D–15**

LGANTD—Leningradskii gosudarstvennyi arkhiv nauchno-tekhnicheskoi dokumentatsii [Leningrad State Archive of Scientific-Technical Documentation]. *See* TsGANTD SPb—Tsentral'nyi gosudarstvennyi arkhiv nauchno-tekhnicheskoi dokumentatsii Sankt-Peterburga [Central State Archive of Scientific-Technical Documentation of St. Petersburg], **D–17**

LGAORSS—Leningradskii gosudarstvennyi arkhiv Oktiabr'skoi revoliutsii i sotsialisticheskogo stroitel'stva [Leningrad State Archive of the October Revolution and Socialist Construction]. *See* TsGA SPb—Tsentral'nyi gosudarstvennyi arkhiv Sankt-Peterburga [Central State Archive of St. Petersburg], **D–12**

LGIA—Leningradskii gosudarstvennyi istoricheskii arkhiv [Leningrad State Historical Archive]. *See* TsGIA SPb—Tsentral'nyi gosudarstvennyi istoricheskii arkhiv Sankt-Peterburga [Central State Historical Archive of St. Petersburg], **D–13**

LGK—Leningradskaia gosudarstvennaia konservatoriia im. N. A. Rimskogo-Korsakova [N. A. Rimskii-Korsakov Leningrad State Conservatory]. *See* NMB SPbGK—Nauchno-muzykal'naia biblioteka Sankt-Peterburgskoi gosudarstvennoi konservatorii im. N. A. Rimskogo-Korsakova [Scientific Music Library of the N. A. Rimskii-Korsakov St. Petersburg State Conservatory], **G–19**

LGMTiMI—Leningradskii gosudarstvennyi muzei teatral'nogo i muzykal'nogo iskusstva [Leningrad State Museum of Theater and Musical Arts]. *See* SPbGMTiMI—Sankt-Peterburgskii gosudarstvennyi muzei teatral'nogo i muzykal'nogo iskusstva [St. Petersburg State Museum of Theater and Musical Arts], **H–102**

LGITMiK NIO—*See* NIO LGITMiK

LGPI—Leningradskii gosudarstvennyi pedagogicheskii institut im. A. I. Gertsena [A. I. Herzen (Gertsen) Leningrad State Pedagogical Institute]. *See* RGPU—Rossiiskii gosudarstvennyi pedagogicheskii universitet im. A. I. Gertsena [A. I. Herzen (Gertsen) Russian State Pedagogical University], **E–56**

LGTB—Leningradskaia gosudarstvennaia teatral'naia biblioteka im. A. V. Lunacharskogo [A. V. Lunacharskii Leningrad State Theater Library]. *See* SPbGTB—Sankt-Peterburgskaia teatral'naia biblioteka [St. Petersburg State Theater Library], **G–21**

LGTM—Leningradskii gosudarstvennyi teatral'nyi muzei [Leningrad State Theater Museum]. *See* SPbGMTiMI—Sankt-Peterburgskii gosudarstvennyi muzei teatral'nogo i muzykal'nogo iskusstva [St. Petersburg State Museum of Theater and Musical Arts], **H–102**

LGTU—Muzei. *See* Muzei LGTU

LGU (1)—Leningradskii gosudarstvennyi universitet [Leningrad State University] (2)—Leningradskii gosudarstvennyi universitet im. A. S. Bubnova [A. S. Bubnov Leningrad State University] (3)—Leningradskii gosudarstvennyi universitet im. A. A. Zhdanova [A. A. Zhdanov Leningrad State University]. *See* SPbGU—Sankt-Peterburgskii gosudarstvennyi universitet [St. Petersburg State University], **E–55**, *and* NB SPbGU—Nauchnaia biblioteka im. M. Gor'kogo Sankt-Peterburgskogo gosudarstvennogo universiteta [M. Gor'kii Scientific Library of St. Petersburg State University], **G–17**

LIIKKh—Leningradskii institut inzhenerov kommunal'nogo khoziaistva [Leningrad Institute of Communal Facilities Engineers]. *See* SPbGASU—Sankt-Peterburgskii gosudarstvennyi arkhitekturno-stroitel'nyi universitet [St. Petersburg State University of Architecture and Civil Engineering], **E–57**

LIIKS—Leningradskii institut inzhenerov kommunal'nogo stroitel'stva [Leningrad Institute of Communal Construction Engineers]. *See* SPbGASU—Sankt-Peterburgskii gosudarstvennyi arkhitekturno-stroitel'nyi universitet [St. Petersburg State University of Architecture and Civil Engineering], **E–57**

LIIZhT—Biblioteka. *See* Biblioteka LIIZhT and TsMZhT

LIKS—Leningradskii institut kommunal'nogo stroitel'stva [Leningrad Institute of Communal Construction]. *See* SPbGASU—Sankt-Peterburgskii gosudarstvennyi arkhitekturno-stroitel'nyi universitet [St. Petersburg State University of Architecture and Civil Engineering], **E–57**

LINZhAS. *See* Muzei LINZhAS *and see also* Biblioteka LINZhAS

LIP AN—Laboratoriia izmeritel'nykh priborov AN SSSR [Laboratory of Measuring Instruments]. *See* RNTs KI—Rossiiskii nauchnyi tsentr "Kurchatovskii institut" [Kurchatov Institute Russian Scientific Center], **E–41**

LISI—Leningradskii inzhenerno-stroitel'nyi institut [Leningrad Institute of Engineering and Construction]. *See* SPbGASU—Sankt-Peterburgskii gosudarstvennyi arkhitekturno-stroitel'nyi universitet [St. Petersburg State University of Architecture and Civil Engineering], **E–57**

LITLP—Muzei istorii. *See* Muzei istorii LITLP

LKTR—Komitet po televideniiu i radioveshchaniiu Lenoblgorispolkomov [Committee for Television and Radio Broadcasting of the Leningrad Oblast and City Executive Committee]. *See* OAO TRK "Peterburg"—Otkrytoe aktsionernoe obshchestvo "Teleradiokompaniia 'Peterburg'" [Petersburg Television and Radio Broadcasting Open Joint-Stock Company], **F–15**

LO AAN—Leningradskoe otdelenie Arkhiva Akademii nauk SSSR [Leningrad Division of the Archive of the Academy of Sciences of the USSR]. *See* PFA RAN—Sankt-Peterburgskii filial Arkhiva Rossiiskoi Akademii nauk [St. Petersburg Branch of the Archive of the Russian Academy of Sciences], **E–20**

LO IIET—Leningradskoe otdelenie (*after* 1975, Leningradskii otdel) Instituta istorii estestvoznaniia i tekhniki AN SSSR [Leningrad Division of the Institute of the History of Natural Science and Technology]. *See* SPbF IIET—Sankt-Peterburgskii filial Instituta istorii estestvoznaniia i tekhniki im. S. I. Vavilova RAN [St. Petersburg Branch of the S. I. Vavilov Institute of the History of Natural Science and Technology], **E–21**

LO IIMK—Leningradskoe otdelenie Instituta istorii material'noi kul'tury AN SSSR [Leningrad Division of the Institute of the History of Material Culture]. *See* IIMK—Institut istorii material'noi kul'tury RAN [Institute of the History of Material Culture], **E–22**

LO LAFOKI—Leningradskoe otdelenie Laboratorii nauchno-prikladnoi fotografii i kinematografii AN SSSR [Leningrad Division of the Laboratory of Applied Photography and Cinematography]. *See* LAFOKI—Laboratoriia nauchno-prikladnoi fotografii i kinematografii RAN [Laboratory of Scientific-Applied Photography and Cinematography], **E–34**

LO TsPA—Leningradskoe otdelenie Tsentral'nogo partiinogo arkhiva [Leningrad Division of the Central Party Archive]. *See* TsGAIPD SPb—Tsentral'nyi gosudarstvennyi arkhiv istoriko-politicheskikh dokumentov Sankt-Peterburga [Central State Archive of Historico-Political Records of St. Petersburg], **D–14**

LO VTO—Biblioteka. *See* Biblioteka LO VTO

LOAOR—Leningradskii oblastnoi arkhiv Oktiabr'skoi revoliutsii [Leningrad Oblast Archive of the October Revolution]. *See* TsGA SPb—Tsentral'nyi gosudarstvennyi arkhiv Sankt-Peterburga [Central State Archive of St. Petersburg], **D–12**

LOGAIS—Leningradskoe otdelenie Gosudarstvennoi Akademii iskusstvoznaniia [Leningrad Division of the State Academy of Art Studies]. *See* RIII—Rossiiskii institut istorii iskusstv [Russian Institute of the History of Art], **E–46**

LOGAV—Leningradskii oblastnoi gosudarstvennyi arkhiv v g. Vyborge [Leningrad Oblast State Archive in Vyborg], **D–18**

LOGIA—Leningradskii oblastnoi gosudarstvennyi istoricheskii arkhiv [Leningrad Oblast State Historical Archive]. *See* TsGIA SPb—Tsentral'nyi gosudarstvennyi istoricheskii arkhiv Sankt-Peterburga [Central State Historical Archive of St. Petersburg], **D–13**

LOIA—Leningradskoe otdelenie Instituta arkheologii AN SSSR [Leningrad Division of the Institute of Archeology AN SSSR]. *See* IIMK—Institut istorii material'noi kul'tury RAN [Institute of the History of Material Culture], **E–22**

LOIE—Leningradskoe otdelenie Instituta etnografii im. N. N. Miklukho-Maklaia AN SSSR [Leningrad Division of the N. N. Miklukho-Maklai Institute of Ethnography]. *See* Kunstkamera/MAE—Muzei antropologii i etnografii im. Petra Velikogo RAN [Peter the Great Museum of Anthropology and Ethnography (Kunstkammer)], **E–25**

LO IVAN/LOIV, *See* LOIV/LO IVAN

LOII—Leningradskoe otdelenie Instituta istorii AN SSSR [Leningrad Division of the Institute of History]. *See* SPbF IRI—Sankt-Peterburgskii filial Instituta rossiiskoi istorii RAN [St. Petersburg Branch of the Institute of Russian History], **E–24**

LOII SSSR—Leningradskoe otdelenie Instituta istorii SSSR AN SSSR [Leningrad Division of the Institute of History of the USSR]. *See* SPbF IRI—Sankt-Peterburgskii filial Instituta rossiiskoi istorii RAN [St. Petersburg Branch of the Institute of Russian History], **E–24**

LOINA—Leningradskoe otdelenie Instituta narodov Azii AN SSSR [Leningrad Division of the Institute of the Peoples of Asia]. *See* SPbF IV—Sankt-Peterburgskii filial Instituta vostokovedeniia RAN [St. Petersburg Branch of the Institute of Oriental Studies], **E–23**

LOIV/LOIV AN—Leningradskoe otdelenie Instituta vostokovedeniia AN SSSR [Leningrad Division of the Institute of Oriental Studies]. *See* SPbF IV—Sankt-Peterburgskii filial Instituta vostokovedeniia RAN [St. Petersburg Branch of the Institute of Oriental Studies], **E–23**

LOSPS—Leningradskii oblastnoi sovet professional'nykh soiuzov [Leningrad Oblast Council of Trade Unions]. *See* Ob"edinennyi arkhiv SPbFP—Ob"edinennyi arkhiv Sankt-Peterburgskoi (Leningradskoi) federatsii profsoiuzov [Consolidated Archive of the St. Petersburg (Leningrad) Federation of Trade Unions], **F–14**

LOTsIA—Leningradskoe otdelenie Tsentral'nogo istoricheskogo arkhiva [Leningrad Division of the Central Historical Archive]. *See* RGIA—Rossiiskii gosudarstvennyi istoricheskii arkhiv [Russian State Historical Archive], **B–3**

LPI. *See* Muzei LPI, *and* ITM LPI

LSGMI—Leningradskii sanitarno-gigienicheskii meditsinskii institut [Leningrad Sanitary-Hygiene Medical Institute]. *See* SPbGSGMI—Sankt-Peterburgskii gosudarstvennyi sanitarno-gigienicheskii meditsinskii institut [St. Petersburg State Sanitary-Hygiene Medical Institute], **E–58**

LTITsBP—Muzei istorii. *See* Muzei istorii LTITsBP

LVIA—Leningradskii voenno-istoricheskii arkhiv [Leningrad Military History Archive]. *See* RGVIA—Rossiiskii gosudarstvennyi voenno-istoricheskii arkhiv [Russian State Military History Archive], **B–4**

MAA AANII—Muzei Arktiki i Antarktiki Arkticheskogo i antarkticheskogo nauchno-issledovatel'skogo instituta [Museum of the Arctic and Antarctica of the Arctic and Antarctica Scientific Research Institute], **H–108**

MAE—Muzei antropologii i etnografii im. Petra Velikogo Rossiiskoi AN [*after* 1925, AN SSSR] [Peter the Great Museum of Anthropology and Ethnography of the Russian Academy of Sciences (*after* 1925, of the USSR)]. *See* Kunstkamera/MAE—Muzei antropologii i etnografii im. Petra Velikogo RAN [Peter the Great Museum of Anthropology and Ethnography (Kunstkammer)], **E–25**

MAKID—Moskovskii arkhiv kollegii inostrannykh del [Moscow Archive of the Collegium of Foreign Affairs] (*later* MGAMID). *See* RGADA—Rossiiskii gosudarstvennyi arkhiv drevnikh aktov [Russian State Archive of Early Acts], **B–2**, *and* AVPRI—Arkhiv vneshnei politiki Rossiiskoi Imperii [Archive of Foreign Policy of the Russian Empire], **C–3**

MAM pri SPbGU—Muzei-arkhiv D. I. Mendeleeva pri Sankt-Peterburgskom gosudarstvennom universitete [D. I. Mendeleev Museum and Archive at St. Petersburg State University], **H–105**

MAMIu—Moskovskii arkhiv Ministerstva iustitsii [Moscow Archive of the Ministry of Justice]. *See* RGADA—Rossiiskii gosudarstvennyi arkhiv drevnikh aktov [Russian State Archive of Early Acts], **B–2**

MAOOT "Slava"—Muzei Moskovskogo aktsionernogo obshchestva otkrytogo tipa "Slava" (Vtoroi chasovoi zavod) [Museum of the Slava Moscow Open Joint-Stock Company (Second Clock Factory)], **H–176**

MB RF. *See* TsA MB RF

MB SPbF—Muzykal'naia biblioteka Sankt-Peterburgskoi filarmonii im. D. D. Shostakovicha [Music Library of the D. D. Shostakovich St. Petersburg Philharmonic], **G–20**

M-BIO—Arkhiv Moskovskogo obshchestvennogo biuro informatsionnogo obmena [Archive of the Moscow Social Bureau of Information Exchange], **F–4**

MDA—Moskovskaia Dukhovnaia Akademiia [Moscow Theological Academy], **G–11**

Memorial. *See* NIPTs "Memorial" *and* NITs "Memorial" SPb

MGAMID—Moskovskii glavnyi arkhiv Ministerstva inostrannykh del [Moscow Main Archive of the Ministry of Foreign Affairs]. *See* RGADA—Rossiiskii gosudarstvennyi arkhiv drevnikh aktov [Russian State Archive of Early Acts], **B–2**, *and* AVPRI—Arkhiv vneshnei politiki Rossiiskoi Imperii [Archive of Foreign Policy of the Russian Empire], **C–3**

MGIAI—Moskovskii gosudarstvennyi istoriko-arkhivnyi institut [Moscow State Historico-Archival Institute]. *See* IAI RGGU—Istoriko-arkhivnyi institut Rossiiskogo gosudarstvennogo gumanitarnogo universiteta [Historico-Archival Institute of the Russian State University for the Humanities], **E–52**, *and* Biblioteka RGGU—Biblioteka Rossiiskogo gosudarstvennogo gumanitarnogo universiteta [Library of the Russian State University for the Humanities], **G–5**

MGK—Moskovskaia gosudarstvennaia konservatoriia im. P. I. Chaikovskogo [P. I. Tchaikovsky Moscow State Conservatory], **E–53**. *See also* NMB MGK—Nauchnaia muzykal'naia biblioteka im. S. I. Taneeva Moskovskoi gosudarstvennoi konservatorii im. P. I. Chaikovskogo [S. I. Taneev Scientific Music Library of the P. I. Tchaikovsky Moscow State Conservatory], **G–7**

MGPI—Moskovskii gosudarstvennyi pedagogicheskii institut im. V. I. Lenina [V. I. Lenin Moscow State Pedagogical Institute]. *See* MPGU—Moskovskii pedagogicheskii gosudarstvennyi universitet [Moscow State Pedagogical University], **E–51**

MGU—Moskovskii gosudarstvennyi universitet im. M. V. Lomonosova [M. V. Lomonosov Moscow State University], **E–50**. *See also* Arkhiv MGU [Archive of M. V. Lomonosov Moscow State University], **E–50**, *and* NB MGU—Nauchnaia biblioteka im. A. M. Gor'kogo Moskovskogo gosudarstvennogo universiteta im. M. V. Lomonosova [A. M. Gor'kii Scientific Library of M. V. Lomonosov Moscow State University], **G–2**

MID. *See* IDD MID, *and* IDU MID RF, *and* IDU MID SSSR

MIGM—Muzei istorii g. Moskvy [Museum of the History of the City of Moscow], **H–5**

MIIGAiK—Muzei. *See* Muzei MIIGAiK

Minatom—Arkhiv. *See* Arkhiv Minatoma

Minatomenergoprom—Arkhiv. *See* Arkhiv Minatoma

MIR—Muzei istorii religii AN SSSR [Museum of the History of Religion AN SSSR]. *See* GMIR—
   Gosudarstvennyi muzei istorii religii [State Museum of the History of Religion], **H–72**

MIRiA—Muzei istorii religii i ateizma AN SSSR [Museum of the History of Religion and
   Atheism AN SSSR]. *See* GMIR—Gosudarstvennyi muzei istorii religii [State Museum of the
   History of Religion], **H–72**

MIRM—Muzei istorii i rekonstruktsii Moskvy [Museum of the History and Reconstruction of
   Moscow]. *See* MIGM—Muzei istorii g. Moskvy [Museum of the History of the City of
   Moscow], **H–5**

MKhAT—Muzei. *See* Muzei MKhAT

MMG—Muzei-masterskaia skul'ptora A. S. Golubkinoi—Filial Gosudarstvennoi Tret'iakovskoi
   galerei [Studio-Museum of the Sculptress A. S. Golubkina—Branch of the State Tret'iakov
   Gallery], **H–24**

MMK—Memorial'nyi muzei kosmonavtiki [Memorial Museum of Space Exploration], **H–59**

MMNA—Memorial'nyi muzei nemetskikh antifashistov v g. Krasnogorske [Memorial Museum
   of German Anti-Fascists in Krasnogorsk], **H–10**

Mosfil'm—Kinokontsern "Mosfil'm" [Mosfil'm Motion Picture Company], **C–20**

Mosgorarkhiv—Moskovskoe gorodskoe ob"edinenie arkhivov [Moscow Consolidated
   Municipal Archives], **D–01**

Mosoblkomarkhiv—Komitet po delam arkhivov Administratsii Moskovskoi oblasti [Committee
   for Archival Affairs of the Administration of Moscow Oblast], **D–08**

MGA—Partiinyi arkhiv Instituta istorii partii moskovskogo [oblastnogo] komiteta i
   Moskovskogo gorodskogo komiteta VKP(b)/KPSS [Party Archive of the Institute of Party
   History of the Moscow (Oblast) Committee and Moscow City Committee of the All-Russian
   CP/CPSU] See TsAODM—Tsentral'nyui arkhiv obshchestvennykh dvizhenii Moskvy
   [Central Archive of Social Movements of Moscow], **D–3**

MPGU—Moskovskii pedagogicheskii gosudarstvennyi universitet [Moscow State Pedagogical
   University], **E–51**

MPO "Vtoroi chasovoi zavod"—Muzei. *See* Muzei MPO "Vtoroi chasovoi zavod"

MPR Rossii. *See* Rosgeolfond—Gosudarstvennoe geologicheskoe predpriiatie "Rossiiskii
   federal'nyi geologicheskii fond" [Russian Federal Geological Fond State Geological
   Enterprise], **C–12**

MR—Muzei revoliutsii [Museum of Revolution]. *See* GTsMSIR—Gosudarstvennyi tsentral'nyi
   muzei sovremennoi istorii Rossii [State Central Museum of the Contemporary History of
   Russia], **H–4**

MRZ "Temp"—Muzei. *See* Muzei MRZ "Temp"

MSKhA—Moskovskaia sel'skokhoziaistvennaia akademiia im. K. A. Timiriazeva [K. A.
   Timiriazev Moscow Academy of Agriculture]. *See museums under the Academy,* **H–56, H–
   167, H–168**

MSPS [Arkhiv]—Arkhiv Mezhdunarodnogo sodruzhestva pisatel'skikh soiuzov [Archive of the
   International Association of Writers' Unions], **F–2**

MTsI—Muzei tsirkovogo iskusstva [Museum of Circus Arts], **H–104**

Muzei Akteatrov—Muzei petrogradskikh gosudarstvennykh akademicheskikh teatrov [Museum
   of the Petrograd State Academic Theaters]. *See* SPbGMTiMI—Sankt-Peterburgskii
   gosudarstvennyi muzei teatral'nogo i muzykal'nogo iskusstva [St. Petersburg State Museum
   of Theater and Musical Arts], **H–102**

Muzei AO "Moskvich"—Muzei Aktsionernogo obshchestva "Moskvich" [Museum of the Moskvich Joint-Stock Company], **H–178**

Muzei AZLK—Muzei Avtomobil'nogo zavoda im. Leninskogo komsomola [Museum of the Lenin Komsomol Automobile Factory]. *See* Muzei AO "Moskvich"—Muzei Aktsionernogo obshchestva "Moskvich" [Museum of the Moskvich Joint-Stock Company], **H–178**

Muzei DPI—Muzei dekorativno-prikladnogo iskusstva Sankt-Peterburgskoi gosudarstvennoi khudozhestvenno-promyshlennoi akademii [Museum of Decorative and Applied Art of the St. Petersburg State Academy of Industrial Arts], **H–94**

Muzei GABT—Muzei Gosudarstvennogo akademicheskogo Bol'shogo teatra [Museum of the State Academic Bol'shoi Theater], **H–165**

Muzei GFO—Meteorologicheskii muzei Glavnoi fizicheskoi observatorii [Meteorological Museum of the Main Physical Observatory]. *See* Muzei GGO—Muzei meteorologii Glavnoi geofizicheskoi observatorii im. A. I. Voeikova [Museum of Meteorology of the A. I. Voeikov Main Geophysical Observatory], **H–107**

Muzei GGO (1)—Meteorologicheskii muzei Glavnoi geofizicheskoi observatorii [Meteorological Museum of the Main Geophysical Observatory]. *See* (2)—Muzei meteorologii Glavnoi geofizicheskoi observatorii im. A. I. Voeikova [Museum of Meteorology of the A. I. Voeikov Main Geophysical Observatory], **H–107**

Muzei INPII—Muzei Instituta proletarskikh izobrazitel'nykh iskusstv [Museum of the Institute of Proletarian Fine Arts]. *See* NIM RAKh—Nauchno-issledovatel'skii muzei Rossiiskoi Akademii khudozhestv [Scientific Research Museum of the Russian Academy of Arts], **H–90**

Muzei istorii ETU—Muzei istorii Sankt-Peterburgskogo gosudarstvennogo elektrotekhnicheskogo universiteta [Museum of the History of the St. Petersburg State Electrotechnical University], **H–118**

Muzei istorii LETI—Muzei istorii Leningradskogo/Sankt-Peterburgskogo elektrotekhnicheskogo instituta V. I. Ulianova-Lenina [Museum of the History of the V. I. Ulianov-Lenin Leningrad/ St. Petersburg State Electrotechnical Institute]. *See* Muzei istorii ETU—Muzei istorii Sankt-Peterburgskogo gosudarstvennogo elektrotekhnicheskogo universiteta [Museum of the History of the St. Petersburg State Electrotechnical University], **H–118**

Muzei istorii LITLP—Muzei istorii Leningradskogo instituta tekstil'noi i legkoi promyshlennosti im. S. M. Kirova [Museum of the History of S. M. Kirov Leningrad Institute of Textiles and Light Industry]. *See* Muzei istorii SPbGUTiD—Muzei istorii Sankt-Peterburgskogo gosudarstvennogo universiteta tekhnologii i dizaina [Museum of the History of St. Petersburg State University of Technology and Design], **H–120**

Muzei istorii LTITsBP—Muzei istorii Leningradskogo tekhnologicheskogo instituta tselliulozno-bumazhnoi promyshlennosti [Museum of the History of the Leningrad Technological Institute of Pulp and Paper Manufacturing]. *See* Muzei istorii SPbGTURP— Muzei istorii Sankt-Peterburgskogo gosudarstvennogo tekhnologicheskogo universiteta rastitel'nykh polimerov [Museum of the History of St. Petersburg State Technological University for Plant Polymers], **H–119**

Muzei istorii SPbETU. *See* Muzei istorii ETU

Muzei istorii SPbGK—Muzei istorii Sankt-Peterburgskoi gosudarstvennoi konservatorii im. N. A. Rimskogo-Korsakova [Museum of the History of the N. A. Rimskii-Korsakov St. Petersburg Conservatory]. *See under* NMB SPbGK—Nauchno-muzykal'naia biblioteka Sankt-Peterburgskoi gosudarstvennoi konservatorii im. N. A. Rimskogo-Korsakova [Scientific Music Library of the N. A. Rimskii-Korsakov St. Petersburg State Conservatory], **G–19**

Muzei istorii SPbGTURP—Muzei istorii Sankt-Peterburgskogo gosudarstvennogo tekhnologicheskogo universiteta rastitel'nykh polimerov [Museum of the History of St. Petersburg State Technological University for Plant Polymers], **H–119**

Muzei istorii SPbGUTiD—Muzei istorii Sankt-Peterburgskogo gosudarstvennogo universiteta tekhnologii i dizaina [Museum of the History of St. Petersburg State University of Technology and Design], **H–120**

Muzei istorii SPbITLP—Muzei istorii Sankt-Peterburgskogo instituta tekstil'noi i legkoi promyshlennosti im. S. M. Kirova [Museum of the History of S. M. Kirov St. Petersburg Institute of Textiles and Light Industry]. *See* Muzei istorii SPbGUTiD—Muzei istorii Sankt-Peterburgskogo gosudarstvennogo universiteta tekhnologii i dizaina [Museum of the History of St. Petersburg State University of Technology and Design], **H–120**

Muzei istorii SPbTI—Muzei istorii Sankt-Peterburgskogo gosudarstvennogo Tekhnologicheskogo instituta (Tekhnicheskogo universiteta) [Museum of the History of the St. Petersburg State Technological Institute (Technical University)], **H–202**

Muzei istorii SPbTI TsBP—Muzei istorii Sankt-Peterburgskogo tekhnologicheskogo instituta tselliulozno-bumazhnoi promyshlennosti [Museum of the History of the St. Petersburg Institute of Pulp and Paper Manufacturing]. *See* Muzei istorii SPbGTURP—Muzei istorii Sankt-Peterburgskogo gosudarstvennogo tekhnologicheskogo universiteta rastitel'nykh polimerov [Museum of the History of St. Petersburg State Technological University for Plant Polymers], **H–119**

Muzei IZhSA VAKh—Muzei Instituta zhivopisi, skul'ptury i arkhitektury im. I. E. Repina VAKh [Museum of the I. E. Repin Institute of Painting, Sculpture, and Architecture of the All-Russian Academy of Arts]. *See* NIM RAKh—Nauchno-issledovatel'skii muzei Rossiiskoi Akademii khudozhestv [Scientific Research Museum of the Russian Academy of Arts], **H–90**

Muzei Lengosteatrov (1)—Muzei leningradskikh gosudarstvennykh teatrov [Museum of the Leningrad State Theaters] (2)—Muzei leningradskikh gosudarstvennykh akademicheskikh teatrov [Museum of the Leningrad State Academic Theaters]. *See* SPbGMTiMI—Sankt-Peterburgskii gosudarstvennyi muzei teatral'nogo i muzykal'nogo iskusstva [St. Petersburg State Museum of Theater and Musical Arts], **H–102**

Muzei LFZ—Muzei pri aktsionernom obshchestve "Lomonosovskii farforovyi zavod" [Museum of the Lomonosov Porcelain Factory Joint-Stock Company], **H–205**

Muzei LGTU—Istoriko-tekhnicheskii muzei Leningradskogo gosudarstvennogo tekhnicheskogo universiteta [Historico-Technical Museum of Leningrad State Polytechnic University]. *See* ITM SPbGTU—Istoriko-tekhnicheskii muzei Sankt-Peterburgskogo gosudarstvennogo tekhnicheskogo universiteta [Historico-Technical Museum of St. Petersburg State Technical University], **H–117**

Muzei LINZhAS—Muzei Leningradskogo instituta zhivopisi, skul'ptury i arkhitektury [Museum of the Leningrad Institute of Painting, Sculpture, and Architecture]. *See* NIM RAKh—Nauchno-issledovatel'skii muzei Rossiiskoi Akademii khudozhestv [Scientific Research Museum of the Russian Academy of Arts], **H–90**

Muzei LPI—Istoriko-tekhnicheskii muzei Leningradskogo politekhnicheskogo instituta im. M. I. Kalinina [Historico-Technical Museum of M. I. Kalinin Leningrad Polytechic Institute]. *See* ITM SPbGTU-Istoriko-tekhnicheskii muzei Sankt-Peterburgskogo gosudarstvennogo tekhnicheskogo universiteta [Historico-Technical Museum of St. Petersburg State Technical University], **H–117**

Muzei MIIGAiK (1)—Uchebno-geodezicheskii muzei Moskovskogo instituta inzhenerov geodezii, aerofotos"emki i kartografii [Geodesic Educational Museum of the Moscow Institute for Geodesic, Aerial-Photography, and Cartographic Engineers]. *See* (2)— Uchebno-geodezicheskii muzei ("Zolotye komnaty I. I. Demidova") Moskovskogo gosudarstvennogo universiteta geodezii i kartografii [Geodesic Educational Museum (Golden Rooms of I. I. Demidov) of Moscow State University of Geodesy and Cartography], **H–172**

Muzei MKhAT (1)—Muzei Moskovskogo Khudozhestvennogo Akademicheskogo teatra im.
A. M. Gor'kogo [Museum of the A. M. Gorkii Moscow Academic Art Theater]. *See*
(2)—Muzei MKhAT—Muzei Moskovskogo Khudozhestvennogo Akademicheskogo teatra
[Museum of the Moscow Academic Art Theater], **H–43**

Muzei MPO "Vtoroi chasovoi zavod"—Muzei Moskovskogo proizvodstvennogo ob"edineniia
"Vtoroi chasovoi zavod" [Museum of the Second Clock Factory Moscow Production
Association]. *See* MAOOT "Slava"—Muzei Moskovskogo aktsionernogo obshchestva
otkrytogo tipa "Slava" (Vtoroi chasovoi zavod) [Museum of the Slava Moscow Open Joint-
Stock Company (Second Clock Factory)], **H–176**

Muzei MRZ "Temp"—Muzei trudovoi i revoliutsionnoi slavy Moskovskogo radiozavoda
"Temp" [Museum to the Glory of Labor and Revolution of the Moscow Temp Radio
Factory], **H–179**

Muzei PGSKhUM—Muzei Petrogradskikh gosudarstvennykh svobodnykh khudozhestvenno-
uchebnykh masterskikh [Museum of the Petrograd State Free Art-Training Studios]. *See*
NIM RAKh—Nauchno-issledovatel'skii muzei Rossiiskoi Akademii khudozhestv
[Scientific Research Museum of the Russian Academy of Arts], **H–90**

Muzei RKhTU—Narodnyi muzei istorii Rossiiskogo khimiko-tekhnologicheskogo universiteta
im. D. I. Mendeleeva [People's Museum of the History of D. I. Mendeleev Russian
University of Chemical Technology], **H–173**

Muzei TsPK—Muzei Tsentra podgotovki kosmonavtov im. Iu. A. Gagarina [Museum of the
Iu. A. Gagarin Cosmonaut Training Center], **H–174**

Muzei VKhUTEIN—Muzei khudozhestvenno-tekhnicheskogo instituta [Museum of the Higher
Technical Art Institute]. *See* NIM RAKh—Nauchno-issledovatel'skii muzei Rossiiskoi
Akademii khudozhestv [Scientific Research Museum of the Russian Academy of Arts], **H–
90**

Muzei VKhUTEMAS—Muzei Vysshikh khudozhestvenno-tekhnicheskikh masterskikh
[Museum of the Higher Technical Art Studios]. *See* NIM RAKh—Nauchno-issledovatel'skii
muzei Rossiiskoi Akademii khudozhestv [Scientific Research Museum of the Russian
Academy of Arts], **H–90**

Muzei VVS—Muzei Voenno-vozdushnykh sil [Museum of the Military Air Force], **H–7**

Muzei-zapovednik "Kolomenskoe"—Gosudarstvennyi khudozhestvennyi istoriko-
arkhitekturnyi i prirodno-landshaftnyi muzei-zapovednik "Kolomenskoe" [Kolomenskoe
State Art Historico-Architectural and Natural Landscape Museum-Preserve], **H–20**

MVD Rossii. *See* TsA MVD Rossii

MVD SSSR. *See* TsA MVD Rossii

MVZhK—Moskovskie vysshie zhenskie kursy prof. V. I. Ger'e [Moscow Higher Courses for
Women of Prof. V. I. Ger'e]. *See* MPGU—Moskovskii pedagogicheskii gosudarstvennyi
universitet [Moscow State Pedagogical University], **E–51**

MZhT—Muzei zheleznodorozhnogo transporta [Museum of Railroad Transport]. *See*
TsMZhT—Tsentral'nyi muzei zheleznodorozhnogo transporta [Central Museum of Railroad
Transport], **H–111**

NB AKh SSSR—Nauchnaia biblioteka Akademii khudozhestv SSSR [Scientific Library of the
Academy of Arts of the USSR]. *See* NB RAKh—Nauchnaia biblioteka Rossiiskoi Akademii
khudozhestv [Scientific Library of the Russian Academy of Arts], **G–18**

NB LGU—Nauchnaia biblioteka im. M. Gor'kogo Leningradskogo gosudarstvennogo
universiteta im. A. A. Zhdanova (*earlier* im. A. S. Bubnova) [M. Gor'kii Research Library of
A. A. Zhdanov (*earlier* A. S. Bubnov) Leningrad State University]. *See* NB SPbGU—
Nauchnaia biblioteka im. M. Gor'kogo Sankt-Peterburgskogo gosudarstvennogo
universiteta [M. Gor'kii Scientific Library of St. Petersburg State University], **G–17**

NB MGU—Nauchnaia biblioteka im. A. M. Gor'kogo Moskovskogo gosudarstvennogo universiteta im. M. V. Lomonosova [A. M. Gor'kii Scientific Library of M. V. Lomonosov Moscow State University], **G-2**

NB RAKh—Nauchnaia biblioteka Rossiiskoi Akademii khudozhestv [Scientific Library of the Russian Academy of Arts], **G-18**

NB SPbGU—Nauchnaia biblioteka im. M. Gor'kogo Sankt-Peterburgskogo gosudarstvennogo universiteta [M. Gor'kii Scientific Library of St. Petersburg State University], **G-17**

NB VAKh—Nauchnaia biblioteka Vserossiiskoi Akademii khudozhestv [Scientific Library of the All-Russian Academy of Arts]. *See* NB RAKh—Nauchnaia biblioteka Rossiiskoi Akademii khudozhestv [Scientific Library of the Russian Academy of Arts], **G-18**

NBA RAKh—Nauchno-bibliograficheskii arkhiv Rossiiskoi Akademii khudozhestv [Scientific Bibliographic Archive of the Russian Academy of Arts], **E-45**

NBA RKP—Nauchno-bibliograficheskii arkhiv, Rossiiskaia knizhnaia palata [Scientific Bibliographic Archive of the Russian Book Chamber], **C-18**

NIIEM—Nauchno-issledovatel'skii institut eksperimental'noi meditsiny RAMN [Scientific Research Institute of Experimental Medicine of the Russian Academy of Medical Sciences], **E-47**

NIIOP APN SSSR—Nauchno-issledovatel'skii institut obshchei pedagogiki Akademii pedagogicheskikh nauk SSSR [Scientific Research Institute of General Pedagogy of the Academy of Pedagogical Sciences of the USSR]. *See* NIITP i MIO RAO—Nauchno-issledovatel'skii institut teoreticheskoi pedagogiki i mezhdunarodnykh issledovannii v obrazovanii RAO [Scientific Research Institute of Theoretical Pedagogy and International Research in Education], **E-42**

NIITP i MIO RAO—Nauchno-issledovatel'skii institut teoreticheskoi pedagogiki i mezhdunarodnykh issledovannii v obrazovanii [Scientific Research Institute of Theoretical Pedagogy and International Research in Education], **E-42**

NIM AKh SSSR—Nauchno-issledovatel'skii muzei AKh SSSR [Scientific Research Museum of the Academy of Arts of the USSR]. *See* NIM RAKh—Nauchno-issledovatel'skii muzei Rossiiskoi Akademii khudozhestv [Scientific Research Museum of the Russian Academy of Arts], **H-90**

NIM RAKh—Nauchno-issledovatel'skii muzei Rossiiskoi Akademii khudozhestv [Scientific Research Museum of the Russian Academy of Arts], **H-90, H-91—H-93, H-156**

NIO LGITMiK—Leningradskii gosudarstvennyi institut teatra, muzyki i kinematografii im. N. K. Cherkasova—Nauchno-issledovatel'skii otdel [N. K. Cherkasov Leningrad State Institute of Theater, Music, and Cinematography—Scientific Research Division]. *See* RIII— Rossiiskii institut istorii iskusstv [Russian Institute of the History of Art], **E-46**

NIOR BAN—Nauchno-issledovatel'skii otdel rukopisei, Biblioteka Rossiiskoi Akademii nauk [Scientific Research Division of Manuscripts, Library of the Russian Academy of Sciences], **G-16**

NIPTs "Memorial"—Nauchno-informatsionnyi i prosvetitel'skii tsentr "Memorial" [Memorial Scientific Information and Enlightenment Center], **F-5**

NITs "Memorial" SPb—Nauchno-informatsionnyi tsentr "Memorial" v Sankt-Peterburge [Memorial Scientific Information Center of St. Petersburg], **F-17**

NITsKD SSSR—Nauchno-issledovatel'skii tsentr kosmicheskoi dokumentatsii SSSR [Scientific Research Center for Space Documentation of the USSR]. *See* RGANTD—Rossiiskii gosudarstvennyi arkhiv nauchno-tekhnicheskoi dokumentatsii [Russian State Archive of Scientific-Technical Documentation], **B-9**

NITsTD SSSR—Nauchno-issledovatel'skii tsentr tekhnicheskoi dokumentatsii SSSR [Scientific Research Center for Technical Documentation of the USSR]. *See* RGANTD—Rossiiskii gosudarstvennyi arkhiv nauchno-tekhnicheskoi dokumentatsii [Russian State Archive of Scientific-Technical Documentation], **B-9**

NKID—Obshchii arkhiv. *See* Obshchii arkhiv NKID

NMB LGK—Nauchno-muzykal'naia biblioteka Leningradskoi gosudarstvennoi konservatorii im. N. A. Rimskogo-Korsakova [Scientific Music Library of the N. A. Rimskii-Korsakov Leningrad State Conservatory]. *See* NMB SPbGK—Nauchno-muzykal'naia biblioteka Sankt-Peterburgskoi gosudarstvennoi konservatorii im. N. A. Rimskogo-Korsakova [Scientific Music Library of the N. A. Rimskii-Korsakov St. Petersburg State Conservatory], **G–19**

NMB MGK (1)—Nauchnaia muzykal'naia biblioteka Moskovskoi gosudarstvennoi konservatorii [Scientific Music Library of the Moscow State Conservatory]. *See* (2)—Nauchnaia muzykal'naia biblioteka im. S. I. Taneeva Moskovskoi gosudarstvennoi konservatorii im. P. I. Chaikovskogo [S. I. Taneev Scientific Music Library of the P. I. Tchaikovsky Moscow State Conservatory], **G–7**

NMB SPbGK—Nauchno-muzykal'naia biblioteka Sankt-Peterburgskoi gosudarstvennoi konservatorii im. N. A. Rimskogo-Korsakova [Scientific Music Library of the N. A. Rimskii-Korsakov St. Petersburg State Conservatory], **G–19**

NTB PGUPS—Nauchno-tekhnicheskaia biblioteka Sankt-Peterburgskogo gosudarstvennogo universiteta putei soobshcheniia [Scientific-Technical Library of the St. Petersburg State University of Transportation], **G–24**

OAO TRK "Peterburg"—Otkrytoe aktsionernoe obshchestvo "Teleradiokompaniia 'Peterburg'" [Petersburg Television and Radio Broadcasting Open Joint-Stock Company], **F–15**

Ob"edinennyi arkhiv SPbFP—Ob"edinennyi arkhiv Sankt-Peterburgskoi (Leningradskoi) federatsii profsoiuzov [Consolidated Archive of the St. Petersburg (Leningrad) Federation of Trade Unions], **F–14**

Obshchii arkhiv NKID—Obshchii arkhiv Narkomata inostrannykh del RSFSR-SSSR [General Archive of the People's Commissariat of Foreign Affairs]. *See* AVP RF—Arkhiv vneshnei politiki Rossiiskoi Federatsii [Archive of Foreign Policy of the Russian Federation], **C–2**

ODRPI GRM—Otdel drevnerusskogo prikladnogo iskusstva, Gosudarstvennyi Russkii muzei [Division of Early Russian Applied Art, State Russian Museum], **H–89**

ODRZh GRM—Otdel drevnerusskoi zhivopisi, Gosudarstvennyi Russkii muzei [Division of Early Russian Paintings, State Russian Museum], **H–89**

OGIM—Ob"edinenie "Gosudarstvennyi Istoricheskii muzei" [Consolidated State Historical Museum]. *See* GIM—Gosudarstvennyi Istoricheskii muzei [State Historical Museum], **H–1**

OIKV GE—Otdel istorii i kul'tury Vostoka, Gosudarstvennyi Ermitazh [Division of the History and Culture of the Orient, State Hermitage], **H–88**

OIRK GE—Otdel istorii russkoi kul'tury, Gosudarstvennyi Ermitazh [Division of the History of Russian Culture, State Hermitage], **H–88**

ON GE—Otdel numizmatiki, Gosudarstvennyi Ermitazh [Division of Numismatics, State Hermitage], **H–88**

ONIZ RNB—Otdel notnykh izdanii i zvukozapisei, Rossiiskaia natsional'naia biblioteka [Division of Music Scores and Sound Recordings, Russian National Library], **G–15**

OPI GIM—Otdel pis'mennykh istochnikov, Gosudarstvennyi Istoricheskii muzei [Division of Written Sources, State Historical Museum], **H–1**

OR BAN—Otdel rukopisei, Biblioteka Akademii nauk [Division of Manuscripts of the Library of the Academy of Sciences]. *See* NIOR BAN—Nauchno-issledovatel'skii otdel rukopisei, Biblioteka Akademii nauk Rossii [Scientific Research Division of Manuscripts of the Library of the Russian Academy of Sciences], **G–16**

OR GLM—Otdel rukopisnykh fondov, Gosudarstvennyi literaturnyi muzei [Division of Manuscript Fonds, State Literary Museum], **H–33**

OR GTG—Otdel rukopisei, Gosudarstvennaia Tret'iakovskaia galereia [Division of Manuscripts, State Tret'iakov Gallery], **H–23**

OR IMLI—Otdel rukopisei i khudozhestvennoi illiustratsii, Institut mirovoi literatury im. A. M. Gor'kogo RAN [Division of Manuscripts and Artistic Illustrations, A. M. Gor'kii Institute of World Literature], **E–9**

OR RGB—Otdel rukopisei, Rossiiskaia gosudarstvennaia biblioteka [Division of Manuscripts, Russian State Library], **G–1**

OR RNB—Otdel rukopisei, Rossiiskaia natsional'naia biblioteka [Division of Manuscripts, Russian National Library], **G–15**

OR/RO GIM—Otdel rukopisei i staropechatnykh knig, Gosudarstvennyi Istoricheskii muzei [Division of Manuscripts and Early Printed Books, State Historical Museum], **H–1**

Oranienbaum. *See* GMZ "Oranienbaum"

ORDF GE—Otdel rukopisei i dokumental'nogo fonda (Arkhiv i Fotoarkhiv), Gosudarstvennyi Ermitazh [Division of Manuscripts and Documentary Fond (Archive and Photograph Archive), State Hermitage], **H–88**

ORKiR NB MGU—Otdel redkikh knig i rukopisei, Nauchnaia biblioteka im. A. M. Gor'kogo Moskovskogo gosudarstvennogo universiteta im. M. V. Lomonosova [Division of Rare Books and Manuscripts, A. M. Gor'kii Scientific Library of M. V. Lomonosov Moscow State University], **G–2**

ORKR NB SPbGU—Otdel redkikh knig i rukopisei, Nauchnaia biblioteka im. M. Gor'kogo Sankt-Peterburgskogo gosudarstvennogo universiteta [Division of Rare Books and Manuscripts, M. Gor'kii Scientific Library of St. Petersburg State University], **G–17**

ORRKK/OR BAN—Otdel rukopisei, redkoi knigi i kartografii, Biblioteka Rossiiskoi Akademii nauk [Division of Manuscripts, Rare Books, and Cartography of the Library of the Russian Academy of Sciences]. *See* NIOR BAN—Nauchno-issledovatel'skii otdel rukopisei, Biblioteka Rossiiskoi Akademii nauk [Scientific Research Division of Manuscripts of the Library of the Russian Academy of Sciences], **G–16**

ORRK Biblioteka VMedA—Otdel rukopisei i redkoi knigi, Fundamental'naia biblioteka Voenno-meditsinskoi akademii [Division of Manuscripts and Rare Books, Fundamental Library of the Military Medical Academy], **G–25**

OZEI GE—Otdel zapadnoevropeiskogo iskusstva, Gosudarstvennyi Ermitazh [Division of Western European Art, State Hermitage], **H–88**

PA Istpart Lenobkoma KPSS—Partiinnyi arkhiv Instituta istorii partii Lenobkoma KPSS [Party Archive of the Institute of Party History of the Leningrad Oblast Committee of the CPSU]. *See* TsGAIPD SPb—Tsentral'nyi gosudarstvennyi arkhiv istoriko-politicheskikh dokumentov Sankt-Peterburga [Central State Archive of Historico-Political Records of St. Petersburg], **D–14**

PA Istparta MGK i MK KPSS—Partiinnyi arkhiv Instituta istorii partii MGK i MK KPSS [Party Archive of the Institute of Party History of the Moscow City Committee and the Moscow (Oblast) Committee of the CPSU]. *See* TsAODM—Tsentral'nyi arkhiv obshchestvennykh dvizhenii Moskvy [Central State Archive of Social Movements of Moscow], **D–3**

PA Istparta MGK i MK VKP(b)—Partiinyi arkhiv pri Institute istorii partii MGK i MK VKP(b) [Party Archive under the Institute of Party History of the Moscow City Committee and Moscow (Oblast) Committee of the All-Russian CP]. *See* TsAODM—Tsentral'nyi arkhiv obshchestvennykh dvizhenii Moskvy [Central Archive of Social Movements of Moscow], **D–3**

PA Lenobgorkom VKP[b]—Partiinyi arkhiv Leningradskogo obkoma i gorkoma VKP(b) [Party Archive of the Leningrad Oblast and City Committees of the All-Russian CP]. *See* TsGAIPD SPb—Tsentral'nyi gosudarstvennyi arkhiv istoriko-politicheskikh dokumentov Sankt-Peterburga [Central State Archive of Historico-Political Records of St. Petersburg], **D–14**

PA Lenobkom VKP[b]—Partiinyi arkhiv Leningradskogo obkoma VKP(b) [Party Archive of the Leningrad Oblast Committee of the All-Russian Communist Party]. *See* TsGAIPD SPb—Tsentral'nyi gosudarstvennyi arkhiv istoriko-politicheskikh dokumentov Sankt-Peterburga [Central State Archive of Historico-Political Records of St. Petersburg], **D–14**

Pavlovsk. *See* GMZ "Pavlovsk"

PD/IRLI (1)—Pushkinskii Dom AN SSSR [Pushkin House]/ Institut russkoi literatury (Pushkinskii Dom) AN SSSR.

    See (2) PD/IRLI RAN—Pushkinskii Dom RAN [Pushkin House]/ Institut russkoi literatury (Pushkinskii Dom) RAN [Institute of Russian Literature (Pushkin House)], **E–28**

Peterburg-5 kanal. *See* GTRK "Peterburg-5 kanal"

Petergof. *See* GMZ "Petergof"

PEU—Peterburgskii Evreiskii universitet [St. Petersburg Jewish University]. *See* Institut issledovanii evreiskoi diaspory Peterburgskogo Evreiskogo universiteta [Institute of Research on the Jewish Diaspora of St. Petersburg Jewish University], **F–21**

PFA RAN—Sankt-Peterburgskii filial Arkhiva Rossiiskoi Akademii nauk [St. Petersburg Branch of the Archive of the Russian Academy of Sciences], **E–20**

PGI—Petrogradskii gosudarstvennyi institut im. A. I. Gertsena [A. I. Herzen Petrograd State Institute]. *See* RGPU—Rossiiskii gosudarstvennyi pedagogicheskii universitet im. A. I. Gertsena [A. I. Herzen Russian State Pedagogical University], **E–56**

PGSKhUM—Muzei. *See* Muzei PGSKhUM

PGSPS—Petrogradskii (Leningradskii) gubernskii sovet profsoiuzov [Petrograd (Leningrad) Guberniia Council of Trade Unions]. *See* Ob"edinennyi arkhiv SPbFP—Ob"edinennyi arkhiv Sankt-Peterburgskoi (Leningradskoi) federatsii profsoiuzov [Consolidated Archive of the St. Petersburg (Leningrad) Federation of Trade Unions], **F–14**

PGU—Pedagogicheskii gosudarstvennyi universitet im. V. I. Lenina [V. I. Lenin State Pedagogical University]. *See* MPGU—Moskovskii pedagogicheskii gosudarstvennyi universitet [Moscow State Pedagogical University], **E–51**

PGUPS. *See* Muzei PGUPS *and* NTB PGUPS

PIAK AN SSSR—Postoiannaia istoriko-arkheograficheskaia komissiia AN SSSR [Permanent Historico-Archeographic Commission]. *See* SPbF IRI—Sankt-Peterburgskii filial Instituta rossiiskoi istorii RAN [St. Petersburg Branch of the Institute of Russian History], **E–24**

PIIaF—Peterburgskii institut iadernoi fiziki im. B. P. Konstantinova RAN [(B. P. Konstantinov) Petersburg Institute of Nuclear Physics], **E–30**

PIIPS—Biblioteka. *See* Biblioteka PIIPS

PIIT—Biblioteka. *See* Biblioteka PIIT

POFKO—Petrogradskii okruzhnoi fotokinootdel [Petrograd Okrug Photo-Cinematographic Division]. *See* Lenfil'm—Kinostudiia "Lenfil'm" [Lenfil'm Studio], **C–24**

PPI. *See* 3-ii PPI—Tretii Petrogradskii pedagogicheskii institut [Third Petrograd Pedagogical Institute]

PU—Arkhiv. *See* Arkhiv PU

RAIMK—Rossiiskaia Akademiia istorii material'noi kul'tury [Russian Academy of the History of Material Culture]. *See* IA—Institut arkheologii RAN [Institute of Archeology], **E–3**, *and* IIMK—Institut istorii material'noi kul'tury RAN [Institute of the History of Material Culture], **E–22**

RAKh—Rossiiskaia Akademiia khudozhestv [Russian Academy of Arts], **E–45**.

    See also NB RAKh—Nauchnaia biblioteka Rossiiskoi Akademii khudozhestv [Scientific Library of the Russian Academy of Arts], **G–18**, *and* NIM RAKh—Nauchno-issledovatel'skii muzei Rossiiskoi Akademii khudozhestv [Scientific Research Museum of the Russian Academy of Arts], **H–90, H–91—H–93, H–156**

RAMN—Rossiiskaia akademiia meditsinskikh nauk [Russian Academy of Medical Sciences], **E–40**. *See also* NIIEM—Nauchno-issledovatel'skii institut eksperimental'noi meditsiny RAMN [Scientific Research Institute of Experimental Medicine of the Russian Academy of Medical Sciences], **E–47**

RAN—Rossiiskaia Akademiia nauk [Russian Academy of Sciences]. *See* ARAN—Arkhiv Rossiiskoi Akademii nauk [Archive of the Russian Academy of Sciences], **E–1** *and* PFA RAN—Sankt-Peterburgskii filial Arkhiva Rossiiskoi Akademii nauk [St. Petersburg Branch of the Archive of the Russian Academy of Sciences], **E–20**

RAO—Rossiiskaia Akademiia obrazovaniia [Russian Academy of Education]. *See* NIITP i MIO RAO—Nauchno-issledovatel'skii institut teoreticheskoi pedagogiki i mezhdunarodnykh issledovannii v obrazovanii RAO [Scientific Research Institute of Theoretical Pedagogy and International Research in Education], **E–42**

RASKhN—Rossiiskaia Akademiia sel'skokhoziaistvennykh nauk [Russian Academy of Agricultural Sciences]. See museum under the Academy, **H–109**

RDF GMISPb—Rukopisno-dokumental'nyi fond, Istoriko-kul'turnyi muzei-zapovednik "Petropavlovskaia krepost'"—Gosudarstvennyi muzei istorii Sankt-Peterburga [Manuscript-Documentary Fond, Peter-Paul Fortress Historico-Cultural Museum-Preserve—State Museum of the History of St. Petersburg], **H–65**

REM—Rossiiskii etnograficheskii muzei [Russian Ethnographic Museum], **H–71**

RGADA—Rossiiskii gosudarstvennyi arkhiv drevnikh aktov [Russian State Archive of Early Acts], **B–2**

RGAE—Rossiiskii gosudarstvennyi arkhiv ekonomiki [Russian State Archive of the Economy], **B–6**

RGAFD—Rossiiskii gosudarstvennyi arkhiv fonodokumentov [Russian State Archive of Sound Recordings], **B–10**

RGAK—Rossiiskaia gosudarstvennaia arkheologicheskaia komissiia [Russian State Archeological Commission]. *See* IA—Institut arkheologii RAN [Institute of Archeology], **E–3**, *and* IIMK—Institut istorii material'noi kul'tury RAN [Institute of the History of Material Culture], **E–22**

RGAKFD—Rossiiskii gosudarstvennyi arkhiv kinofotodokumentov [Russian State Archive of Documentary Films and Photographs], **B–11**

RGALI—Rossiiskii gosudarstvennyi arkhiv literatury i iskusstva [Russian State Archive of Literature and Art], **B–7**

RGANI—Rossiiskii gosudarstvennyi arkhiv noveishei istorii [Russian State Archive of Contemporary History], **B–13**

RGANTD—Rossiiskii gosudarstvennyi arkhiv nauchno-tekhnicheskoi dokumentatsii [Russian State Archive of Scientific-Technical Documentation], **B–9**

RGASPI—Rossiiskii gosudarstvennyi arkhiv sotsial'no-politicheskoi istorii [Russian State Archive of Socio-Political History], **B–12**. *See also* former TsKhDMO, **B–12A**

RGAVMF—Rossiiskii gosudarstvennyi arkhiv Voenno-Morskogo Flota [Russian State Archive of the Navy], **B–5**

RGB—Rossiiskaia gosudarstvennaia biblioteka [Russian State Library], **G–1**

RGBI—Rossiiskaia gosudarstvennaia biblioteka po iskusstvu [Russian State Library for the Arts], **G–6**

RGDB—Rossiiskaia gosudarstvennaia detskaia biblioteka [Russian State Children's Library], **G–9**

RGGU—Rossiiskii gosudarstvennyi gumanitarnyi universitet [Russian State University for the Humanities]. *See* Biblioteka RGGU—Biblioteka Rossiiskogo gosudarstvennogo gumanitarnogo universiteta [Library of the Russian State University for the Humanities], **G–5**, *and* IAI RGGU—Istoriko-arkhivnyi institut Rossiiskogo gosudarstvennogo gumanitarnogo universiteta [Historico-Archival Institute of the Russian State University for the Humanities], **E–52**

RGIA—Rossiiskii gosudarstvennyi istoricheskii arkhiv [Russian State Historical Archive], **B–3**

RGNTA—Rossiiskii gosudarstvennyi nauchno-tekhnicheskii arkhiv [Russian State Scientific-Technical Archive]. *See* RGANTD—Rossiiskii gosudarstvennyi arkhiv nauchno-tekhnicheskoi dokumentatsii [Russian State Archive of Scientific-Technical Documentation], **B–9**

RGO—Russkoe geograficheskoe obshchestvo [Russian Geographic Society], **E–26**

RGPU—Rossiiskii gosudarstvennyi pedagogicheskii universitet im. A. I. Gertsena [A. I. Herzen Russian State Pedagogical University], **E–56**

RGTRK "Ostankino"—Rossiiskaia gosudarstvennaia teleradiokompaniia "Ostankino" [Ostankino Russian State Television and Radio Company]. *See* Arkhiv RGTRK "Ostankino"—Arkhiv Rossiiskoi gosudarstvennoi teleradiokompanii "Ostankino" [Archive of the Ostankino Russian State Television and Radio Company], **C–19**

RGTRK "Peterburg"—Rossiiskaia gosudarstvennaia teleradiokompaniia "Peterburg" [Petersburg Russian State Company for Television and Radio Broadcasting]. *See* OAO TRK "Peterburg"—Otkrytoe aktsionernoe obshchestvo "Teleradiokompaniia 'Peterburg'" [Petersburg Television and Radio Broadcasting Open Joint-Stock Company], **F–15**

RGVA—Rossiiskii gosudarstvennyi voennyi arkhiv [Russian State Military Archive], **B–8.** *See also former* TsKhIDK, **B–8A**

RGVIA—Rossiiskii gosudarstvennyi voenno-istoricheskii arkhiv [Russian State Military History Archive], **B–4**

RIII—Rossiiskii institut istorii iskusstv [Russian Institute of the History of Art], **E–46**

RKhTU—Muzei. *See* Muzei RKhTU

RKP—Rossiiskaia knizhnaia palata [Russian Book Chamber], **C–18**

RM (1)—Russkii muzei Imperatora Aleksandra III [Russian Museum of Emperor Alexander III] (2)—Russkii muzei [Russian Museum]. *See* GRM—Gosudarstvennyi Russkii muzei [State Russian Museum], **H–89**

RMO—Russkoe muzykal'noe obshchestvo [Russian Music Society]. *See* Biblioteka RMO

RNB—Rossiiskaia natsional'naia biblioteka [Russian National Library], **G–15**

RNITsKD—Rossiiskii nauchno-issledovatel'skii tsentr kosmicheskoi dokumentatsii [Russian Scientific Research Center for Space Documentation]. *See* RGANTD—Rossiiskii gosudarstvennyi arkhiv nauchno-tekhnicheskoi dokumentatsii [Russian State Archive of Scientific-Technical Documentation], **B–9**

RNTs KI—Rossiiskii nauchnyi tsentr "Kurchatovskii institut" [Kurchatov Institute Russian Scientific Center], **E–41**

RO GIM/GIM RO—*See* OR/RO GIM

RO TsNB STD RF—Rukopisnyi otdel, Tsentral'naia nauchnaia biblioteka Soiuza teatral'nykh deiatelei RF [Manuscript Division, Central Scientific Library of the Union of Theater Workers], **G–8**

ROA—Russkaia osvoboditel'naia armiia [Russian Liberation Army]. *See* Arkhiv-ROA

Rosarkhiv (1)—Gosudarstvennaia arkhivnaia sluzhba Rossii [State Archival Service of Russia]. *See* (2) Rosarkhiv—Federal'naia arkhivnaia sluzhba Rossii [Federal Archival Service of Russia], **B–0**

Rosgeolfond—Gosudarstvennoe geologicheskoe predpriiatie "Rossiiskii federal'nyi geologicheskii fond" [Russian Federal Geological Fond State Geological Enterprise], **C–12**

Rosgidromet—Federal'naia sluzhba Rossii po gidrometeorologii i monitoringu okruzhaiushchei sredy [Federal Service of Russia for Hydrometeorology and Monitoring Environmental Conditions]. *See* Gosfond, **C–13**

Roskomarkhiv (1)—Komitet po delam arkhivov pri Sovete Ministrov RSFSR [Committee for Archival Affairs under the Council of Ministers of the RSFSR]

(2)—Komitet po delam arkhivov pri Pravitel'stve Rossiiskoi Federatsii [Committee for Archival Affairs under the Government of the Russian Federation]. *See* Rosarkhiv—Federal'naia arkhivnaia sluzhba Rossii [Federal Archival Service of Russia], **B–0**

RPB (1)—Rossiiskaia Publichnaia biblioteka [Russian Public Library]

(2)—Rossiiskaia Publichnaia biblioteka im. M. E. Saltykova-Shchedrina [M. E. Saltykov-Shchedrin Russian Public Library]. *See* RNB—Rossiiskaia natsional'naia biblioteka [Russian National Library], **G–15**

RTO—Russkoe teatral'noe obshchestvo [Russian Theater Society]. *See* Biblioteka RTO

RTsKhIDNI—Rossiiskii tsentr khraneniia i izucheniia dokumentov noveishei istorii [Russian Center for Preservation and Study of Records of Modern History]. *See* RGASPI—Rossiiskii gosudarstvennyi arkhiv sotsial'no-politicheskoi istorii [Russian State Archive of Socio-Political History], **B–12**

Sevzapkino—Severo-zapadnoe oblastnoe fotokinoupravlenie [Northwest Regional Photo-Cinematographic Administration]. *See* Lenfil'm—Kinostudiia "Lenfil'm" [Lenfil'm Studio], **C–24**

Soiuzgeolfond—Ob"edinenie "Vsesoiuznyi geologicheskii fond" [Consolidated All-Union Geological Fond]. *See* Rosgeolfond—Gosudarstvennoe geologicheskoe predpriiatie "Rossiiskii federal'nyi geologicheskii fond" [Russian Federal Geological Fond State Geological Enterprise], **C–12**

Sovkino—Leningradskaia fabrika "Sovkino" [Sovkino Leningrad Factory]. *See* Lenfil'm—Kinostudiia "Lenfil'm" [Lenfil'm Studio], **C–24**

SP SSSR—Soiuz pisatelei SSSR [Union of Writers of the USSR]. *See* MSPS—Arkhiv Mezhdunarodnogo Sodruzhestva pisatel'skikh soiuzov [Archive of the International Association of Writers' Unions], **F–2**

SPb AK SPbF IS—Sankt-Peterburgskii Arkhiv-kollektsiia netraditsionnykh periodicheskikh izdanii i dokumentov obshchestvennykh dvizhenii, Sankt-Peterburgskii filial Instituta sotsiologii RAN [St. Petersburg Archive-Collection of Nontraditional Periodicals and Documents of Social Movements, St. Petersburg Branch of the Institute of Sociology], **E–27**

SPbDA—Biblioteka. *See* Biblioteka SPbDA

SPbDAiS—Biblioteka. *See* Biblioteka SPbDAiS

SPbETU—Muzei istorii. *See* Muzei istorii ETU

SPbF IEA—Sankt-Peterburgskii filial Instituta etnologii i antropologii im. N. N. Miklukho-Maklaia AN SSSR/RAN [St. Petersburg Branch of the N. N. Miklukho-Maklai Institute of Ethnology and Anthropology]. *See* Kunstkamera/MAE—Muzei antropologii i etnografii im. Petra Velikogo RAN [Peter the Great Museum of Anthropology and Ethnography (Kunstkammer)], **E–25**

SPbF IIET—Sankt-Peterburgskii filial Instituta istorii estestvoznaniia i tekhniki im. S. I. Vavilova RAN [St. Petersburg Branch of the S. I. Vavilov Institute of the History of Natural Science and Technology], **E–21**

SPbF IRI—Sankt-Peterburgskii filial Instituta rossiiskoi istorii RAN [St. Petersburg Branch of the Institute of Russian History], **E–24**

SPbF IS—Sankt-Peterburgskii filial Instituta sotsiologii RAN [St. Petersburg Branch of the Institute of Sociology], **E–27**

SPbF IV—Sankt-Peterburgskii filial Instituta vostokovedeniia RAN [St. Petersburg Branch of the Institute of Oriental Studies], **E–23**

SPbFP—Ob"edinennyi arkhiv. *See* Ob"edinennyi arkhiv SPbFP

SPbGAFK—Sankt-Peterburgskaia gosudarstvennaia akademiia fizicheskoi kul'tury im. P. F. Lesgafta [P. F. Lesgaft St. Petersburg State Academy of Physical Culture], **E–60**

SPbGASU—Sankt-Peterburgskii gosudarstvennyi arkhitekturno-stroitel'nyi universitet [St. Petersburg State University of Architecture and Civil Engineering], **E–57**

SPbGETU. *See* Muzei istorii ETU

SPbGK—Sankt-Peterburgskaia gosudarstvennaia konservatoriia im. N. A. Rimskogo-Korsakova. *See* NMB SPbGK—Nauchno-muzykal'naia biblioteka SPbGK [Scientific Music Library of the N. A. Rimskii-Korsakov St. Petersburg State Conservatory], **G–19**, *and* Muzei istorii SPbGK [Museum of the History of the N. A. Rimskii-Korsakov St. Petersburg State Conservatory], **G–19**

SPbGKTR—Sankt-Peterburgskii gosudarstvennyi komitet po televideniiu i radioveshchaniiu [St. Petersburg State Committee for Television and Radio Broadcasting]. *See* OAO TRK "Peterburg"—Otkrytoe aktsionernoe obshchestvo "Teleradiokompaniia 'Peterburg'" [Petersburg Television and Radio Broadcasting Open Joint-Stock Company], **F–15**

SPbGMTiMI—Sankt-Peterburgskii gosudarstvennyi muzei teatral'nogo i muzykal'nogo iskusstva [St. Petersburg State Museum of Theater and Music], **H–102**

SPbGSGMI—Sankt-Peterburgskii gosudarstvennyi sanitarno-gigienicheskii meditsinskii institut [St. Petersburg State Sanitary-Hygiene Medical Institute], **E–58**

SPbGTB—(1) Sankt-Peterburgskaia gosudarstvennaia teatral'naia biblioteka im. A. V. Lunacharskogo [A. V. Lunacharskii St. Petersburg State Theater Library].

 See (2)—Sankt-Peterburgskaia gosudarstvennaia teatral'naia biblioteka [St. Petersburg State Theater Library], **G–21**

SPbGTU. *See* ITM SPbGTU

SPbGTURP—Muzei istorii. *See* Muzei istorii SPbGTURP

SPbGU—Sankt-Peterburgskii gosudarstvennyi universitet [St. Petersburg State University], **E–55**, *and* NB SPbGU—Nauchnaia biblioteka im. M. Gor'kogo Sankt-Peterburgskogo gosudarstvennogo universiteta [M. Gor'kii Scientific Library of St. Petersburg State University], **G–17**. *See also* MAM pri SPbGU—Muzei-arkhiv D. I. Mendeleeva pri Sankt-Peterburgskom gosudarstvennom universitete [D. I. Mendeleev Museum and Archive at St. Petersburg State University], **H–105**

SPbGUTiD—Muzei istorii. *See* Muzei istorii SPbGUTiD

SPbISI—Sankt-Peterburgskii inzhenerno-stroitel'nyi institut [St. Petersburg Institute of Engineering and Construction]. *See* SPbGASU—Sankt-Peterburgskii gosudarstvennyi arkhitekturno-stroitel'nyi universitet [St. Petersburg State University of Architecture and Civil Engineering], **E–57**

SPbITLP—Muzei istorii. *See* Muzei istorii SPbITLP

SPbO STD RF—Biblioteka. *See* Biblioteka SPbO STD RF

SPbTI—Muzei istorii. *See* Muzei istorii SPbTI

SPbTI TsBP—Muzei istorii. *See* Muzei istorii SPbTI TsBP

STD—Soiuz teatral'nykh deiatelei RF [Union of Theater Workers]. *See* TsNB STD and Biblioteka SPbO STD

SVR Rossii—Arkhiv. *See* Arkhiv SVR Rossii

Teleradiofond/Gosteleradiofond—Vsesoiuznyi fond televizionnykh i radioprogramm [All-Union Fond of Television and Radio Programs]. *See* Gosteleradiofond—Gosudarstvennyi fond televizionnykh i radioprogramm [State Fond of Television and Radio Programs], **C–17**

3-ii PPI (1)—Tretii Petrogradskii pedagogicheskii institut [Third Petrograd Pedagogical Institute] (2)—Tretii Petrogradskii pedagogicheskii institut im. A. I. Gertsena [A. I. Herzen (Gertsen) Third Petrograd Pedagogical Institute]. *See* RGPU—Rossiiskii gosudarstvennyi pedagogicheskii universitet im. A. I. Gertsena [A. I. Herzen (Gertsen) Russian State Pedagogical University], **E–56**

TsA FSB Rossii—Tsentral'nyi arkhiv Federal'noi sluzhby bezopasnosti RF [Central Archive of the Federal Security Service], **C–6**

TsA FSK RF—Tsentral'nyi arkhiv Federal'noi sluzhby kontrrazvedki RF [Central Archive of the Federal Counter-Intelligence Service]. *See* TsA FSB Rossii—Tsentral'nyi arkhiv Federal'noi sluzhby bezopasnosti RF [Central Archive of the Federal Security Service], **C–6**

TsA KGB SSSR—Tsentral'nyi arkhiv Komiteta gosudarstvennoi bezopasnosti SSSR [Central Archive of the KGB]. *See* TsA FSB Rossii—Tsentral'nyi arkhiv Federal'noi sluzhby bezopasnosti RF [Central Archive of the Federal Security Service], **C–6**

TsA MB RF—Tsentral'nyi arkhiv Ministerstva bezopasnosti RF [Central Archive of the Ministry of Security]. *See* TsA FSB Rossii—Tsentral'nyi arkhiv Federal'noi sluzhby bezopasnosti RF [Central Archive of the Federal Security Service], **C–6**

TsA MVD Rossii—Tsentral'nyi arkhiv (Tretii otdel) Ministerstva vnutrennikh del RF [Central Archive (Third Division) of the Ministry of Internal Affairs], **C–8**

TsA MVD SSSR—Tsentral'nyi arkhiv Ministerstva vnutrennikh del SSSR [Central Archive of the Ministry of Internal Affairs of the USSR]. *See* TsA MVD Rossii—Tsentral'nyi arkhiv (Tretii otdel) Ministerstva vnutrennikh del RF [Central Archive (Third Division) of the Ministry of Internal Affairs], **C–8**

TsA VKP i FNPR—Tsentral'nyi arkhiv Vseobshchei konfederatsii profsoiuzov i Federatsii nezavisimykh profsoiuzov Rossii [Central Archive of the General Confederation of Trade Unions and the Federation of Independent Trade Unions of Russia], **F–1**

TsA VLKSM—Tsentral'nyi arkhiv Vsesoiuznogo Leninskogo kommunisticheskogo soiuza molodezhi [Central Archive of the All-Union Communist Youth League]. *See former* TsKhDMO—Tsentr khraneniia dokumentov molodezhnykh organizatsii [Center for Preservation of Records of Youth Organizations], **B–12A** (now part of RGASPI, **B–12**)

TsA VTsSPS—Tsentral'nyi arkhiv Vsesoiuznogo tsentral'nogo soveta professional'nykh soiuzov [Central Archive of the All-Union Central Council of Trade Unions]. *See* TsA VKP i FNPR—Tsentral'nyi arkhiv Vseobshchei konfederatsii profsoiuzov i Federatsii nezavisimykh profsoiuzov Rossii [Central Archive of the General Confederation of Trade Unions and the Federation of Independent Trade Unions of Russia], **F–1**

TsA VTsSPS i TsKPS—Tsentral'nyi arkhiv Vsesoiuznogo tsentral'nogo soveta professional'nykh soiuzov i Tsentral'nogo komiteta professional'nykh soiuzov [Central Archive of the All-Union Central Council of Trade Unions and the Central Committee of Trade Unions]. *See* TsA VKP i FNPR—Tsentral'nyi arkhiv Vseobshchei konfederatsii profsoiuzov i Federatsii nezavisimykh profsoiuzov Rossii [Central Archive of the General Confederation of Trade Unions and the Federation of Independent Trade Unions of Russia], **F–1**

TsADKM—Tsentral'nyi arkhiv dokumental'nykh kollektsykh Moskvy [Central Archive of Documentary Collections of Moscow], **D–7**

TsAKFD RSFSR—Tsentral'nyi arkhiv kinofotodokumentov RSFSR [Central Archive of Documentary Films and Photographs of the RSFSR]. *See* RGAKFD—Rossiiskii gosudarstvennyi arkhiv kinofotodokumentov [Russian State Archive of Documentary Films and Photographs], **B–11**

TsAI IAI RGGU—Tsentr arkhivnykh issledovanii, Istoriko-arkhivnyi institut Rossiiskogo gosudarstvennogo gumanitarnogo universiteta [Center for Archival Research, Historico-Archival Institute of the Russian State University for the Humanities], **E–52**

TsAKA—Tsentral'nyi arkhiv Krasnoi Armii [Central Archive of the Red Army]. *See* RGVA—Rossiiskii gosudarstvennyi voennyi arkhiv [Russian State Military Archive], **B–8**

TsALIM—Tsentral'nyi arkhiv literatury i iskusstva Moskvy [Central Archive of Literature and Art of Moscow], **D–6**

TsAMO—Tsentral'nyi arkhiv Ministerstva oborony RF [Central Archive of the Ministry of Defense], **C–4**

TsAMO SSSR—Tsentral'nyi arkhiv Ministerstva oborony SSSR [Central Archive of the Ministry of Defense of the USSR]. *See* TsAMO—Tsentral'nyi arkhiv Ministerstva oborony RF [Central Archive of the Ministry of Defense], **C–4**

TsANTDM—Tsentral'nyi arkhiv nauchno-tekhnicheskoi dokumentatsii Moskvy [Central Archive of Scientific-Technical Documentation of Moscow], **D–5**

TsAODM—Tsentral'nyi arkhiv obshchestvennykh dvizhenii Moskvy [Central Archive of Social Movements of Moscow], **D–3**

TsAOR—Tsentral'nyi arkhiv Oktiabr'skoi revoliutsii [Central Archive of the October Revolution]. *See* GA RF—Gosudarstvennyi arkhiv Rossiiskoi Federatsii [State Archive of the Russian Federation], **B–1**

TsAPD (1)—Tsentral'nyi arkhiv profdvizhenniia [Central Archive of the Trade-Union Movement] (2)—Tsentral'nyi arkhiv profdvizheniia i organizatsii truda [Central Archive of the Trade-Union Movement and Labor Organizations]. *See* TsA VKP i FNPR—Tsentral'nyi arkhiv Vseobshchei konfederatsii profsoiuzov i Federatsii nezavisimykh profsoiuzov Rossii [Central Archive of the General Confederation of Trade Unions and the Federation of Independent Trade Unions of Russia], **F–1,** *and* Gosudarstvennyi arkhiv Rossiiskoi Federatsii [State Archive of the Russian Federation], **B–1**

Tsarskoe Selo. *See* GMZ "Tsarskoe Selo"

TsAU RSFSR—Tsentral'noe arkhivnoe upravlenie RSFSR [Central Archival Adminisration of the RSFSR]. *See* Rosarkhiv—Federal'naia arkhivnaia sluzhba Rossii [Federal Archival Service of Russia], **B–0**

TsAU SSSR—Tsentral'noe arkhivnoe upravlenie Soiuza SSR [Central Archival Administration of the USSR]. *See* Rosarkhiv—Federal'naia arkhivnaia sluzhba Rossii [Federal Archival Service of Russia], **B–0**

TsAVV—Tsentral'nyi arkhiv vnutrennikh voisk MVD RF [Central Archive of Internal Troops], **C–9**

TsBKGI GUKSK—Tsentral'noe biuro kartografo-geodezicheskoi isuchennosti Glavnogo upravleniia gosudarstvennoi s"emki i kartografii NKVD SSSR [Central Bureau for Cartographic-Geodesic Investigations of the Main Administration for State Survey and Cartography of the NKVD]. *See* TsKGF—Tsentral'nyi kartografo-geodezicheskii fond [Central Cartographic-Geodesic Fond], **C–14**

TsBPS—Tsentral'noe biuro profsoiuzov [Central Bureau of Trade Unions]. *See* Ob"edinennyi arkhiv SPbFP—Ob"edinennyi arkhiv Sankt-Peterburgskoi (Leningradskoi) federatsii profsoiuzov [Consolidated Archive of the St. Petersburg (Leningrad) Federation of Trade Unions], **F–14**

TsBRD—Tsentral'naia biblioteka russkoi dramy pri Gosudarstvennom akademicheskom teatre dramy im. A. S. Pushkina [Central Library of Russian Drama of the A. S. Pushkin State Academic Theater of Drama]. *See* SPbGTB—Sankt-Peterburgskaia teatral'naia biblioteka [St. Petersburg State Theater Library], **G–21**

TsDAiK—Tsentral'nyi Dom aviatsii i kosmonavtiki [Central House of Aviation and Space Exploration], **H–58**

TsDAPVKhO—Tsentral'nyi Dom aviatsii, protivovozdushnoi i khimicheskoi oborony im. M. V. Frunze [M. V. Frunze Central House of Aviation, Anti-Aircraft, and Chemical Defense]. *See* TsDAiK—Tsentral'nyi Dom aviatsii i kosmonavtiki [Central House of Aviation and Space Exploration], **H–58**

TsDNA—Tsentr dokumentatsii "Narodnyi arkhiv" [People's Archive Documentation Center], **F–3**

Tsentral'noe Geospravbiuro GGK—Tsentral'noe geodezicheskoe spravochnoe biuro Glavnogo Geodezicheskogo komiteta VSNKh SSSR [Central Geodesic Reference Bureau of the Main Geodesic Committee of the VSNKh SSSR]. *See* TsKGF—Tsentral'nyi kartografo-geodezicheskii fond [Central Cartographic-Geodesic Fond], **C–14**

Tsentrarkhiv—Upravlenie Tsentral'nym arkhivom pri VTsIK RSFSR [Administration of the Central Archive under the All-Russian Central Executive Committee RSFSR]. *See* Rosarkhiv— Federal'naia arkhivnaia sluzhba Rossii [Federal Archival Service of Russia], **B–0**

TsFFKA SSSR—Tsentral'nyi fotofonokinoarkhiv SSSR [Central Photo, Sound, and Film Archive of the USSR]. *See* RGAFD—Rossiiskii gosudarstvennyi arkhiv fonodokumentov [Russian State Archive of Sound Recordings], **B–10**; *and* RGAKFD—Rossiiskii gosudarstvennyi arkhiv kinofotodokumentov [Russian State Archive of Documentary Films and Photographs], **B–11**

TsFL—Tsentral'naia fotolaboratoriia AN SSSR [Central Photographic Laboratory]. *See* LAFOKI—Laboratoriia nauchno-prikladnoi fotografii, kinematografii i televideniia RAN [Laboratory of Scientific-Applied Photography, Cinematography, and Television], **E–19**, *and* LAFOKI—Laboratoriia nauchno-prikladnoi fotografii i kinematografii RAN [Laboratory of Scientific-Applied Photography and Cinematography], **E–34**

TsGA g. Moskvy—Tsentral'nyi gosudarstvennyi arkhiv g. Moskvy [Central State Archive of the City of Moscow]. *See* TsMAM—Tsentral'nyi munitsipal'nyi arkhiv Moskvy [Central Municipal Archive of Moscow], **D–1**; TsIAM—Tsentral'nyi istoricheskii arkhiv Moskvy [Central Historical Archive of Moscow], **D–2**; *and* TsMADSN—Tsentral'nyi moskovskii arkhiv dokumentov na spetsial'nykh nositeliakh [Central Moscow Archive for Documents on Special Media], **D–4**

TsGA g. Moskvy—Tsentral'nyi gosudarstvennyi arkhiv g. Moskvy—Kinofotofono otdel [Central State Archive of the City of Moscow—Audiovisual Division]. *See* TsMADSN— Tsentral'nyi moskovskii arkhiv dokumentov na spetsial'nykh nositeliakh [Central Moscow Archive for Documents on Special Media], **D–4**

TsGA KF SSR–Filial—Filial Tsentral'nogo gosudarstvennogo arkhiva Karelo-Finskoi SSR [Branch of the Central State Archive of the Karelian-Finnish SSR]. *See* LOGAV— Leningradskii oblastnoi gosudarstvennyi arkhiv v g. Vyborge [Leningrad Oblast State Archive in Vyborg], **D–18**

TsGA RSFSR—Tsentral'nyi gosudarstvennyi arkhiv RSFSR [Central State Archive of the RSFSR]. *See* GA RF—Gosudarstvennyi arkhiv Rossiiskoi Federatsii [State Archive of the Russian Federation], **B–1**

TsGA SPb—Tsentral'nyi gosudarstvennyi arkhiv Sankt-Peterburga [Central State Archive of St. Petersburg], **D–12**

TsGADA—Tsentral'nyi gosudarstvennyi arkhiv drevnikh aktov SSSR [Central State Archive of Early Acts of the USSR]. *See* RGADA—Rossiiskii gosudarstvennyi arkhiv drevnikh aktov [Russian State Archive of Early Acts], **B–2**

TsGAIPD SPb—Tsentral'nyi gosudarstvennyi arkhiv istoriko-politicheskikh dokumentov Sankt-Peterburga [Central State Archive of Historico-Political Documents of St. Petersburg], **D–14**

TsGAKA—Tsentral'nyi gosudarstvennyi arkhiv Krasnoi Armii [Central State Archive of the Red Army]. *See* RGVA—Rossiiskii gosudarstvennyi voennyi arkhiv [Russian State Military Archive], **B–8**

TsGAKFD SSSR—Tsentral'nyi gosudarstvennyi arkhiv kinofotodokumentov SSSR [Central State Archive of Documentary Films and Photographs of the USSR]. *See* RGAKFD— Rossiiskii gosudarstvennyi arkhiv kinofotodokumentov [Russian State Archive of Documentary Films and Photographs], **B–11**

TsGAKFFD Leningrada—Tsentral'nyi gosudarstvennyi arkhiv kinofotofonodokumentov Leningrada [Central State Archive of Documentary Films, Photographs, and Sound Recordings of Leningrad]. *See* TsGAKFFD SPb—Tsentral'nyi gosudarstvennyi arkhiv kinofotofonodokumentov Sankt-Peterburga [Central State Archive of Documentary Films, Photographs, and Sound Recordings of St. Petersburg], **D–16**

TsGAKFFD g. Moskvy—Tsentral'nyi gosudarstvennyi arkhiv kinofotofonodokumentov g. Moskvy [Central State Archive of Documentary Films, Photographs, and Sound Recordings of the City of Moscow]. *See* TsMADSN—Tsentral'nyi moskovskii arkhiv dokumentov na spetsial'nykh nositeliakh [Central Moscow Archive for Documents on Special Media], **D–4**

TsGAKFFD RSFSR—Tsentral'nyi gosudarstvennyi arkhiv kinofotofonodokumentov RSFSR [Central State Archive of Documentary Films, Photographs, and Sound Recordings of the RSFSR]. *See* RGAFD—Rossiiskii gosudarstvennyi arkhiv fonodokumentov [Russian State Archive of Sound Recordings], **B–10** *and* RGAKFD—Rossiiskii gosudarstvennyi arkhiv kinofotodokumentov [Russian State Archive of Documentary Films and Photographs], **B–11**

TsGAKFFD SPb—Tsentral'nyi gosudarstvennyi arkhiv kinofotofonodokumentov Sankt-Peterburga [Central State Archive of Documentary Films, Photographs, and Sound Recordings of St. Petersburg], **D–16**

TsGAKFFD SSSR—Tsentral'nyi gosudarstvennyi arkhiv kino foto fonodokumentov SSSR [Central State Archive of Documentary Films, Photographs, and Sound Recordings of the USSR]. *See* RGAFD—Rossiiskii gosudarstvennyi arkhiv fonodokumentov [Russian State Archive of Sound Recordings], **B–10**, *and* RGAKFD—Rossiiskii gosudarstvennyi arkhiv kinofotodokumentov [Russian State Archive of Documentary Films and Photographs], **B–11**

TsGALI Leningrada—Tsentral'nyi gosudarstvennyi arkhiv literatury i iskusstva Leningrada [Central State Archive of Literature and Art of Leningrad]. *See* TsGALI SPb—Tsentral'nyi gosudarstvennyi arkhiv literatury i iskusstva Sankt-Peterburga [Central State Archive of Literature and Art of St. Petersburg], **D–15**

TsGALI SPb—Tsentral'nyi gosudarstvennyi arkhiv literatury i iskusstva Sankt-Peterburga [Central State Archive of Literature and Art of St. Petersburg], **D–15**

TsGALI SSSR—Tsentral'nyi gosudarstvennyi arkhiv literatury i iskusstva SSSR [Central State Archive of Literature and Art of the USSR]. *See* RGALI—Rossiiskii gosudarstvennyi arkhiv literatury i iskusstva [Russian State Archive of Literature and Art], **B–7**

TsGAMO—Tsentral'nyi gosudarstvennyi arkhiv Moskovskoi oblasti [Central State Archive of Moscow Oblast], **D–8**

TsGANKh SSSR—Tsentral'nyi gosudarstvennyi arkhiv narodnogo khoziaistva SSSR [Central State Archive of the National Economy of the USSR]. *See* RGAE—Rossiiskii gosudarstvennyi arkhiv ekonomiki [Russian State Archive of the Economy], **B–6**

TsGANTD Leningrada—Tsentral'nyi gosudarstvennyi arkhiv nauchno-tekhnicheskoi dokumentatsii Leningrada [Central State Archive of Scientific-Technical Documentation of Leningrad]. *See* TsGANTD SPb—Tsentral'nyi gosudarstvennyi arkhiv nauchno-tekhnicheskoi dokumentatsii Sankt-Peterburga [Central State Archive of Scientific-Technical Documentation of St. Petersburg], **D–17**

TsGANTD SPb—Tsentral'nyi gosudarstvennyi arkhiv nauchno-tekhnicheskoi dokumentatsii Sankt-Peterburga [Central State Archive of Scientific-Technical Documentation of St. Petersburg], **D–17**

TsGANTD SSSR—Tsentral'nyi gosudarstvennyi arkhiv nauchno-tekhnicheskoi dokumentatsii SSSR [Central State Archive of Scientific-Technical Documentation of the USSR]. *See* RGANTD—Rossiiskii gosudarstvennyi arkhiv nauchno-tekhnicheskoi dokumentatsii [Russian State Archive of Scientific-Technical Documentation], **B–9**

TsGAODM—Tsentral'nyi gosudarstvennyi arkhiv obshchestvennykh dvizhenii g. Moskvy [Central State Archive of Social Movements of Moskow]. *See* TsAODM—Tsentral'nyi arkhiv obshchestvennykh dvizhenii Moskvy [Central Archive of Social Movements of Moscow], **D–3**

TsGAOR—Tsentral'nyi gosudarstvennyi arkhiv Oktiabr'skoi revoliutsii [Central State Archive of the October Revolution]. *See* GA RF—Gosudarstvennyi arkhiv Rossiiskoi Federatsii [State Archive of the Russian Federation], **B–1**

TsGAOR Leningrada—Tsentral'nyi gosudarstvennyi arkhiv Oktiabr'skoi revoliutsii i sotsialisticheskogo stroitel'stva Leningrada [Central State Archive of the October Revolution and Socialist Construction of Leningrad]. *See* TsGA SPb—Tsentral'nyi gosudarstvennyi arkhiv Sankt-Peterburga [Central State Archive of St. Petersburg], **D–12**

TsGAOR SSSR—Tsentral'nyi gosudarstvennyi arkhiv Oktiabr'skoi revoliutsii, vysshikh organov gosudarstvennoi vlasti i organov gosudarstvennogo upravleniia SSSR [Central State Archive of the October Revolution, Supreme Organs of State Power, and Organs of State Administration of the USSR]. *See* GA RF—Gosudarstvennyi arkhiv Rossiiskoi Federatsii [State Archive of the Russian Federation], **B–1**

TsGAORiSS SSSR/TsGAOR SSSR—Tsentral'nyi gosudarstvennyi arkhiv Oktiabr'skoi revoliutsii i sotsialisticheskogo stroitel'stva SSSR [Central State Archive of the October Revolution and Socialist Construction of the USSR]. *See* GA RF—Gosudarstvennyi arkhiv Rossiiskoi Federatsii [State Archive of the Russian Federation], **B–1**

TsGAORSS g. Moskvy—Tsentral'nyi gosudarstvennyi arkhiv Oktiabr'skoi revoliutsii i sotsialisticheskogo stroitel'stva g. Moskvy [Central State Archive of the October Revolution and Socialist Construction of the City of Moscow]. *See* TsMAM—Tsentral'nyi munitsipal'nyi arkhiv Moskvy [Central Municipal Archive of Moscow], **D–1**

TsGASA—Tsentral'nyi gosudarstvennyi arkhiv Sovetskoi Armii [Central State Archive of the Soviet Army]. *See* RGVA—Rossiiskii gosudarstvennyi voennyi arkhiv [Russian State Military Archive], **B–8**

TsGAVMF SSSR—Tsentral'nyi gosudarstvennyi arkhiv Voenno-Morskogo Flota SSSR [Central State Archive of the Navy of the USSR]. *See* RGAVMF—Rossiiskii gosudarstvennyi arkhiv Voenno-Morskogo Flota [Russian State Archive of the Navy], **B–5**

TsGAZ SSSR—Tsentral'nyi gosudarstvennyi arkhiv zvukozapisei SSSR [Central State Archive of Sound Recordings of the USSR]. *See* RGAFD—Rossiiskii gosudarstvennyi arkhiv fonodokumentov [Russian State Archive of Sound Recordings], **B–10**

TsGF Rosgeolfond—Tsentral'noe geologicheskoe fondokhranilishche, Gosudarstvennoe geologicheskoe predpriiatie "Rossiiskii federal'nyi geologicheskii fond" [Central Geological Fond Depository, Russian Federal Geological Fond State Geological Enterprise], **C–12**

TsGFSTU—Tsentral'nyi gosudarstvennyi fond standartov i tekhnicheskikh uslovii [Central State Fond for Standards and Technical Specifications], **C–15**

TsGIA g. Moskvy—Tsentral'nyi gosudarstvennyi istoricheskii arkhiv g. Moskvy [Central State Historical Archive of the City of Moscow]. *See* TsIAM—Tsentral'nyi istoricheskii arkhiv Moskvy [Central Historical Archive of Moscow], **D–2**

TsGIA Leningrada—Tsentral'nyi gosudarstvennyi istoricheskii arkhiv Leningrada [Central State Historical Archive of Leningrad]. *See* TsGIA SPb—Tsentral'nyi gosudarstvennyi istoricheskii arkhiv Sankt-Peterburga [Central State Historical Archive of St. Petersburg], **D–13**

TsGIA SPb—Tsentral'nyi gosudarstvennyi istoricheskii arkhiv Sankt-Peterburga [Central State Historical Archive of St. Petersburg], **D–13**

TsGIA SSSR—Tsentral'nyi gosudarstvennyi istoricheskii arkhiv SSSR [Central State Historical Archive of the USSR]. *See* RGIA—Rossiiskii gosudarstvennyi istoricheskii arkhiv [Russian State Historical Archive], **B–3**

TsGIAL—Tsentral'nyi gosudarstvennyi istoricheskii arkhiv v Leningrade [Central State Historical Archive in Leningrad]. *See* RGIA—Rossiiskii gosudarstvennyi istoricheskii arkhiv [Russian State Historical Archive], **B–3**

TsGIAM—Tsentral'nyi gosudarstvennyi istoricheskii arkhiv v g. Moskve [Central State Historical Archive in Moscow]. *See* GA RF—Gosudarstvennyi arkhiv Rossiiskoi Federatsii [State Archive of the Russian Federation], **B–1**

TsGLA SSSR—Tsentral'nyi gosudarstvennyi literaturnyi arkhiv [Central State Literary Archive]. *See* RGALI—Rossiiskii gosudarstvennyi arkhiv literatury i iskusstva [Russian State Archive of Literature and Art], **B–7**

TsGM—Tsentral'nyi geologicheskii muzei [Central Geological Museum]. *See* TsNIGR Muzei—Tsentral'nyi nauchno-issledovatel'skii geologorazvedochnyi muzei im. akademika F. N. Chernysheva [F. N. Chernyshev Central Geological Survey Scientific Research Museum], **H–106**

TsGOA SSSR—Tsentral'nyi gosudarstvennyi (Osobyi) arkhiv SSSR [Central State (Special) Archive of the USSR]. *See former* TsKhIDK—Tsentr khraneniia istoriko-dokumental'nykh kollektsii [Center for Preservation of Historico-Documentary Collections], **B–8A** (now part of RGVA, **B–8**)

TsGVIA SSSR—Tsentral'nyi gosudarstvennyi voenno-istoricheskii arkhiv SSSR [Central State Military History Archive of the USSR]. *See* RGVIA—Rossiiskii gosudarstvennyi voenno-istoricheskii arkhiv [Russian State Military History Archive], **B–4**

TsIAM—Tsentral'nyi istoricheskii arkhiv Moskvy [Central Historical Archive of Moscow], **D–2**

TsKGF—Tsentral'nyi kartografo-geodezicheskii fond [Central Cartographic-Geodesic Fond], **C–14**

TsKGF UGGN GUGK SSSR—Tsentral'nyi kartografo-geodezicheskii fond Upravleniia gosudarstvennogo geodezicheskogo nadzora Glavnogo upravleniia geodezii i kartografii pri SNK-SM SSSR [Central Cartographic-Geodesic Fond of the Main Geodesic and Cartographic Administration]. *See* TsKGF—Tsentral'nyi kartografo-geodezicheskii fond [Central Cartographic-Geodesic Fond], **C–14**

TsKhDMO—Tsentr khraneniia dokumentov molodezhnykh organizatsii [Center for Preservation of Records of Youth Organizations]. *See former* TsKhDMO, **B–12A** (now part of RGASPI, **B–12**)

TsKhIDK—Tsentr khraneniia istoriko-dokumental'nykh kollektsii [Center for Preservation of Historico-Documentary Collections]. *See former* TsKhIDK, **B–8A** (now part of RGVA, **B–8**)

TsKhSD—Tsentr khraneniia sovremennoi dokumentatsii [Center for Preservation of Contemporary Documentation]. *See* RGANI—Rossiiskii gosudarstvennyi arkhiv noveishei istorii [Russian State Archive of Contemporary History], **B–13**

TsMADSN—Tsentral'nyi moskovskii arkhiv dokumentov na spetsial'nykh nositeliakh [Central Moscow Archive for Documents on Special Media], **D–4**

TsMAM—Tsentral'nyi munitsipal'nyi arkhiv Moskvy [Central Municipal Archive of Moscow], **D–1**

TsMiAR—Tsentral'nyi muzei drevnerusskoi kul'tury i iskusstva im. Andreia Rubleva [Andrei Rublev Central Museum of Early Russian Culture and Art], **H–27**

TsMM—Tsentral'nyi morskoi muzei Sovetskoi respubliki [Central Naval Museum of the Soviet Republic]. *See* TsVMM—Tsentral'nyi voenno-morskoi muzei [Central Naval Museum], **H–74**

TsMOZhD—Tsentral'nyi muzei Oktiabr'skoi zheleznoi dorogi [Central Museum of the October Railroad], **H–112**

TsMP—Tsentral'nyi muzei pochvovedeniia im. V. V. Dokuchaeva [V. V. Dokuchaev Central Museum of Pedology], **H–109**

TsMR SSSR—Tsentral'nyi muzei revoliutsii SSSR [Central Museum of Revolution of the USSR]. *See* GTsMSIR—Gosudarstvennyi tsentral'nyi muzei sovremennoi istorii Rossii [State Central Museum of the Contemporary History of Russia], **H–4**

TsMS—Tsentral'nyi muzei sviazi im. A. S. Popova [A. S. Popov Central Museum of Communications], **H–114**

TsMVS—Tsentral'nyi muzei Vooruzhennykh Sil [Central Museum of the Armed Forces], **H–6**

TsMVS SSSR—Tsentral'nyi muzei Vooruzhennykh Sil SSSR [Central Museum of the Armed Forces of the USSR]. *See* TsMVS—Tsentral'nyi muzei Vooruzhennykh Sil [Central Museum of the Armed Forces], **H–6**

TsMZhT (1)—Tsentral'nyi muzei zheleznodorozhnogo transporta SSSR [Central Museum of Railroad Transport of the USSR]. *See* (2)—Tsentral'nyi muzei zheleznodorozhnogo transporta [Central Museum of Railroad Transport], **H–111**

TsNB GE—Tsentral'naia nauchnaia biblioteka—Kabinet redkoi knigi, Gosudarstvennyi Ermitazh—GE [Central Scientific Library—Cabinet of Rare Books, State Hermitage], **H–88**

TsNB STD (1)—Tsentral'naia nauchnaia biblioteka Soiuza teatral'nykh deiatelei RSFSR [Central Scientific Library of the Union of Theater Workers of the RSFSR].
 See (2)—Tsentral'naia nauchnaia biblioteka Soiuza teatral'nykh deiatelei RF [Central Scientific Library of the Union of Theater Workers], **G–8**

TsNB VTO—Tsentral'naia nauchnaia biblioteka Vserossiiskogo teatral'nogo obshchestva [Central Scientific Library of the All-Russian Theater Society]. *See* TsNB STD—Tsentral'naia nauchnaia biblioteka Soiuza teatral'nykh deiatelei RF [Central Scientific Library of the Union of Theater Workers], **G–8**

TsNIGR Muzei—Tsentral'nyi nauchno-issledovatel'skii geologorazvedochnyi muzei im. akademika F. N. Chernysheva [F. N. Chernyshev Central Geological Survey Scientific Research Museum], **H–106**

TsNIT MGU—Gruppa "Tsentr vizual'noi antropologii" Tsentra novykh informatsionnykh technologii, Moskovskii gosudarstvennyi universitet [Center of the Visual Anthropology Group of the Center for New Information Technology, Moscow State University], **E–50**

TsPA IMELS—Tsentral'nyi partiinyi arkhiv Instituta Marksa, Engel'sa, Lenina, Stalina pri TsK KPSS [Central Party Archive of the Institute of Marx, Engels, Lenin, and Stalin under the CC CPSU]. *See* RGASPI—Rossiiskii gosudarstvennyi arkhiv sotsial'no-politicheskoi istorii [Russian State Archive of Socio-Political History], **B–12**

TsPA IML—Tsentral'nyi partiinyi arkhiv Instituta Marksa, Engel'sa, Lenina/ Institut Marksizma-Leninizma pri TsK VKP[b]–KPSS [Central Party Archive of the Marx, Engels, Lenin Institute/ Institute of Marxism-Leninism under the CC CPSU]. *See* RGASPI—Rossiiskii gosudarstvennyi arkhiv sotsial'no-politicheskoi istorii [Russian State Archive of Socio-Political History], **B–12**

TsPA IML pri TsK KPSS—Tsentral'nyi partiinyi arkhiv Instituta marksizma-leninizma pri TsK KPSS [Central Party Archive of the Institute of Marxism-Leninism under the CC CPSU]. *See* RGASPI—Rossiiskii gosudarstvennyi arkhiv sotsial'no-politicheskoi istorii [Russian State Archive of Socio-Political History], **B–12**

TsPA ITIS—Tsentral'nyi partiinyi arkhiv Instituta teorii i istorii sotsializma TsK KPSS [Central Party Archive of the Institute of the Theory and History of Socialism under the CC CPSU]. *See* RGASPI—Rossiiskii gosudarstvennyi arkhiv sotsial'no-politicheskoi istorii [Russian State Archive of Socio-Political History], **B–12**

TsPB—Tsentral'naia Politekhnicheskaia biblioteka [Central Polytechnic Library]. *See under* GPM—Gosudarstvennyi Politekhnicheskii muzei [State Polytechnic Museum], **H–57**

TsPK—Muzei. *See* Muzei TsPK

TsVIA—Tsentral'nyi voenno-istoricheskii arkhiv [Central Military History Archive]. *See* RGVIA—Rossiiskii gosudarstvennyi voenno-istoricheskii arkhiv [Russian State Military History Archive], **B–4**

TsVMA—Tsentral'nyi voenno-morskoi arkhiv [Central Naval Archive], **C–5**

TsVMM—Tsentral'nyi voenno-morskoi muzei [Central Naval Museum], **H–74**

UFSB Moskvy—Arkhiv. *See* Arkhiv UFSB Moskvy

UFSB SPb—Arkhiv. *See* Arkhiv UFSB SPb

UGIOP—Arkhiv—Ob"edinennyi vedomstvennyi arkhiv Upravleniia Gosudarstvennoi inspektsii po okhrane pamiatnikov istorii i kul'tury [Consolidated Agency Archive of the Administration of the State Inspection for the Preservation of Monuments of History and

Culture]. *See* Arkhiv KGIOP—Nauchno-metodicheskii informatsionno-izdatel'skii sektor (vedomstvennyi arkhiv) Komiteta po gosudarstvennomu kontroliu, ispol'zovaniiu i okhrane pamiatnikov istorii i kul'tury Sankt-Petersburga [Scientific-Methodological Information-Publication Sector (Agency Archive) of the Committee for State Control, Use, and Preservation of Monuments of History and Culture of St. Petersburg], **D–21**

Upravlenie ZAGS—Upravlenie zapisi aktov grazhdanskogo sostoianiia Ministerstva iustitsii RF [Administration for Registration of Vital Statistics of the Ministry of Justice], **C–011**. *See also* Arkhiv ZAGS MO, Arkhiv ZAGS Moskvy, *and* Arkhiv ZAGS SPb

VAKh—Vserossiiskaia Akademiia khudozhestv [All-Russian Academy of Arts]. *See* RAKh—Rossiiskaia Akademiia khudozhestv [Russian Academy of Arts], **E–45**; NB RAKh—Nauchnaia biblioteka Rossiiskoi Akademii khudozhestv [Scientific Library of the Russian Academy of Arts], **G–18**; *and* NIM RAKh—Nauchno-issledovatel'skii muzei Rossiiskoi Akademii khudozhestv [Scientific Research Museum of the Russian Academy of Arts], **H–90, H–91—H–93, H–156**

VAU GA—Vysshee aviatsionnoe uchilishche grazhdanskoi aviatsii [Higher Aviation School of Civil Aviation]. *See* AGA—Akademiia grazhdanskoi aviatsii [Academy of Civil Aviation], **E–59**

VAU GVF—Vysshee aviatsionnoe uchilishche Grazhdanskogo vozdushnogo flota [Higher Aviation School of the Civil Air Fleet]. *See* AGA—Akademiia grazhdanskoi aviatsii [Academy of Civil Aviation], **E–59**

VGBIL (1)—Vsesoiuznaia gosudarstvennaia biblioteka inostrannoi literatury [All-Union State Library for Foreign Literature]

(2)—Vsesoiuznaia gosudarstvennaia biblioteka inostrannoi literatury im. M. I. Rudomino [M. I. Rudomino All-Union State Library for Foreign Literature].

See (3)—Vserossiiskaia gosudarstvennaia biblioteka inostrannoi literatury im. M. I. Rudomino [M. I. Rudomino All-Russian State Library for Foreign Literature], **G–4**

VGF—Vsesoiuznyi geologicheskii fond [All-Union Geological Fond]. *See* Rosgeolfond—Gosudarstvennoe geologicheskoe predpriiatie "Rossiiskii federal'nyi geologicheskii fond" [Russian Federal Geological Fond State Geological Enterprise], **C–12**

VGO—Vsesoiuznoe geograficheskoe obshchestvo [All-Union Geographic Society]. *See* RGO—Russkoe geograficheskoe obshchestvo [Russian Geographic Society], **E–26**

VGSB—Vsesoiuznoe geodezicheskoe spravochnoe biuro [All-Union Geodesic Reference Bureau]. *See* TsKGF—Tsentral'nyi kartografo-geodezicheskii fond [Central Cartographic-Geodesic Fond], **C–14**

VGU—Arkhiv. *See* Arkhiv VGU

VKP i FNPR. *See* TsA VKP i FNPR

VIA—Voenno-istoricheskii arkhiv [Military History Archive]. *See* RGVIA—Rossiiskii gosudarstvennyi voenno-istoricheskii arkhiv [Russian State Military History Archive], **B–4**

VIEM—Vsesoiuznyi institut eksperimental'noi meditsiny [All-Union Institute of Experimental Medicine]. *See* NIIEM—Nauchno-issledovatel'skii institut eksperimental'noi meditsiny RAMN [Scientific Research Institute of Experimental Medicine of the Russian Academy of Medical Sciences], **E–47**

VIMAIViVS—Voenno-istoricheskii muzei artillerii, inzhenernykh voisk i voisk sviazi [Military History Museum of the Artillery, Corps of Engineers, and Signal Corps], **H–73**

VKhUTEIN—Biblioteka *and* Muzei. *See* Biblioteka VKhUTEINa *and* Muzei VKhUTEIN

VKhUTEMAS—Biblioteka *and* Muzei. *See* Biblioteka VKhUTEMAS *and* Muzei VKhUTEMAS

VKP—Vsesoiuznaia knizhnaia palata [All-Union Book Chamber]. *See* RKP—Rossiiskaia knizhnaia palata [Russian Book Chamber], **C–18**

VLKSM. *See* TsA VLKSM

VMedA (1)—Voenno-meditsinskaia akademiia im. S. M. Kirova [S. M. Kirov Military Medical Academy].
  See (2)—Voenno-meditsinskaia akademiia [Military Medical Academy] *and* Biblioteka VMedA—Fundamental'naia biblioteka Voenno-meditsinskoi akademii [Fundamental Library of the Military Medical Academy], **G–25**
VMM—Voenno-meditsinskii muzei [Military Medical Museum], **H–75**
VMP—Vserossiiskii muzei A. S. Pushkina [All-Russian A. S. Pushkin Museum], **H–95**
VNIII—Vserossiiskii nauchno-issledovatel'skii institut iskusstvoznaniia [All-Russian Scientific Research Institute of Art Studies]. *See* RIII—Rossiiskii institut istorii iskusstv [Russian Institute of the History of Art], **E–46**
VPSh—Biblioteka. *See* Biblioteka VPSh
2-oi LMI—Vtoroi Leningradskii meditsinskii institut [Second Leningrad Medical Institute].
  See SPbGSGMI—Sankt-Peterburgskii gosudarstvennyi sanitarno-gigienicheskii meditsinskii institut [St. Petersburg State Sanitary-Hygiene Medical Institute], **E–58**
2-oi MGU—Vtoroi Moskovskii gosudarstvennyi universitet [Second Moscow State University].
  See MPGU—Moskovskii pedagogicheskii gosudarstvennyi universitet [Moscow State Pedagogical University], **E–51**
VTO—Vserossiiskoe teatral'noe obshchestvo [All-Russian Theater Society]. *See* TsNB STD—Tsentral'naia nauchnaia biblioteka Soiuza teatral'nykh deiatelei RF [Central Scientific Library of the Union of Theater Workers], **G–8**, *and* Biblioteka SPbO STD RF—Biblioteka Sankt-Peterburgskogo otdeleniia Soiuza teatral'nykh deiatelei RF [Library of St. Petersburg Division of the Union of Theater Workers], **G–23**
VTsDNA—Vsesoiuznyi Tsentr dokumentatsii "Narodnyi arkhiv" [People's Archive All-Union Documentation Center]. *See* TsDNA—Tsentr dokumentatsii "Narodnyi arkhiv" [People's Archive Documentation Center], **F–3**
VTsIK RSFSR—Upravlenie Tsentral'nym arkhivom [Administration of the Central Archive under the All-Russian Central Executive Committee RSFSR]. *See* Tsentrarkhiv
VTsSPS—Vsesoiuznyi tsentral'nyi sovet professional'nykh soiuzov [All-Union Central Council of Trade Unions]. *See* TsA VTsSPS, *now* TsA VKP i FNPR—Tsentral'nyi arkhiv Vseobshchei konfederatsii profsoiuzov i Federatsii nezavisimykh profsoiuzov Rossii [Central Archive of the General Confederation of Trade Unions and the Federation of Independent Trade Unions of Russia], **F–1**
VTsSPS i TsKPS. *See* TsA VTsSPS i TsKPS
VUA—Voenno-uchenyi arkhiv Glavnogo shtaba [Military Science Archive of the General Staff]. *See* RGVIA—Rossiiskii gosudarstvennyi voenno-istoricheskii arkhiv [Russian State Military History Archive], **B–4**
VVS—Voenno-vozdushnye sily [Military Air Force]. *See* Muzei VVS

ZAGS—Zapis' aktov grazhdanskogo sostoianiia [Registration of Vital Statistics].
  See Upravlenie ZAGS, Arkhiv ZAGS MO, Arkhiv ZAGS Moskvy, *and* Arkhiv ZAGS SPb
ZIN (1)—Zoologicheskii institut AN SSSR [Zoological Institute].
  See (2)—Zoologicheskii institut RAN [Zoological Institute], **E–31**

Author Index

This index includes the names of all authors, compilers, and/or editors listed in the general bibliography and in the bibliographic entries under individual repositories (lowercased entries). An "a" following the entry denotes an author mentioned in the annotation. This index does not include names listed in introductory sections or textual passages. References throughout are to bibliographic code numbers, found in the left-hand margin at the start of each entry, rather than to page numbers. Citations of names use the native-language spelling for the basic author entry, unless an alternate preferred form is indicated. Alternate forms are cross-referenced unless they would appear as a contingent entry. Full first names and patronymics have been added to the extent possible, on the basis of library catalogues and other sources, even though they are not always cited on the title page, colophon, or elsewhere in the publication itself.

1299

Index of Personal Names

This index references names of individuals or families cited in the directory with the repository number (with upper-cased part designation) for those that appear in the text and/or the number (with lower-cased part designation) of the appropriate bibliographic entry. To the extent possible we have tried to identify the individual named, but that has not been possible in some cases, when such information was not available on the questionnaires furnished by the repositories or in reference literature available to the compilers.

Because most Russian sources and the Russian ABB files cite only initials for first names and patronymics, no attempt has been made to provide full names here. However, in the case of names of foreigners, whenever possible we identify the country of origin and provide the full name in the spelling of the original language (along with the Library of Congress transliteration from Russian). This is very difficult and at times even controversial, since many foreigners living and working in Russia adopted Russian nationality and Russian forms of their names with assigned patronymics (especially if they were baptized in the Orthodox Church). Nevertheless, it is useful to have both spellings. Because Russian renders foreign names phonetically rather than letter by letter (for example, "Gan" or "Gun" for Hahn), names retransliterated from the Cyrillic may be virtually unrecognizable.

Normally, for consistency's sake, and because we are dealing with archival materials in Russia that researchers may want to order there, we have used "systematic" LC transliteration for Russian personal names, including the Russian endings "ii" and "ov," rather than the "y" or "ff" forms often encountered in the West, especially for popular Russian writers or composers (Rimskii-Korsakov, rather than Rimsky-Korsakov or Rimsky-Korsakoff; Tolstoi, rather than Tolstoy; L. D. Trotskii, rather than Leon Trotsky). Accordingly, we have not followed the American-library standard of the Name Authority File (NAF) of the Library of Congress, which designates selective "y" endings to well-known figures, which in our text would result in Peter Illych Tchaikovsky for the composer, but "Chaikovskii" for his father and brother! To aid recognition by non-Russian-speakers, however, we are using the form "Tchaikovsky" as the main entry, as well as familiar forms of Russian names used in the West for individuals such as Alexandre Benois (A. N. Benua), César Cui (Ts. A. Kiui), Sergei Eisenstein (S. M. Eizenshtein), A. I. Herzen (Gertsen), and V. I. Meyerhold (Meierkhol'd); forms used in emigration, such as Fedor Chaliapin (F. I. Shaliapin) and Nicholas Roerich (N. K. Rerikh); and anglicized first names for Russian sovereigns and members of the imperial family. Although Yeltsin is spelled in English with the familiar initial "Y," rather than Eltsin, the LC spelling of S. A. Esenin (with a cross-reference for Yesenin) is used for the poet. While the NAF has not been checked systematically, we have frequently added parenthetical references to familiar Western forms and, where the entry would not be adjacent in alphabetical order, we have often cross-referenced NAF or other Western forms. Although pseudonyms are cited where known, they are not usually cross-referenced (unless there are citations to other members of the same family), unless the individual's real name is widely known or used in print.

Since the emphasis in this volume is on archival materials, references to related documentation or personal papers held in a given repository are given primacy in entries under each individual name; hence subentries do not always appear in alphabetical order. While this index may help to locate materials in some lesser-known collections, researchers should be warned that it does not constitute a locator index for personal or family papers in Moscow and St. Petersburg repositories. Often in our characterization of the holdings of a given repository, only a few examples of personal papers are cited, particularly in large archives where we list only a handful out of the hundreds held there. New guides to many individual archives provide more comprehensive listings, and many other specialized reference tools cited in Part A will help. However, until the three-volume Soviet-period directory of personal papers (a-114) is updated and expanded, researchers should not expect to locate personal papers easily in all repositories.

Alianskii, S. M. (publisher), papers, H–41, h-295, h-296

Alikhanov, A. I. (physicist), papers, E–29

Alliluev, S. A. (communist leader), papers, B–12

Alliluev, S. Ia. (revolutionary, friend of V. I. Lenin), family apartment-museum, H–68

Al'pert, M. (news photographer), photograph collection, B–11

Al'tman, N. I. (artist), theater designs, H–102

Amartol, George (Georgios Amartolos), 14th–15th c. chronicle, G–16, H–88

Amfilokhii (P. I. Sergievskii), Archimandrite (archeographer, Slavicist), manuscript collection, G–15

Amundsen, Roald (Norwegian polar explorer), documents, H–108

Amusin, I. D., correspondence with N. Ia. Mandel'shtam, H–98

Anastasevich, V. G. (historian, archeographer), papers, E–24

Anders, G. E. (music librarian), music library collection, G–19

Andreas, Saint (archbishop of Crete), manuscripts, G–18, G–26

Andreev, A. A. (Soviet CP official), papers, B–12, H–4

Andreev, L. N. (writer): papers, B–7, E–28; film footage, B–11; photographs, D–16

Andreev, N. N. (physicist), papers, D–17

Andreev, V. Ia., theater and circus collection, H–104

Andreevskii, L. G. (photographer), photographs, H–65

Andrianova-Peretts, V. P. (philologist), papers, E–28

Andronikov, I. L. (writer, literary scholar), films, c-100.1

Andronov, I. K. (scientist, methodologist), iconographic materials, E–2

Andropov, Iu. V. (Soviet CP leader): papers, C–1; and KGB archives, C–6

Anichkov, N. N. (physician), papers, E–47

Anichkov, S. V. (pharmacologist), papers, H–110

Anikst, A. A. (theater critic, translator, literary historian), theater library collection, G–8

Anin, M. I. (artist, art historian), collection on Borodino panorama painter, H–11

Anisfel'd (Anisfeldt), B. I. (artist), drawings, G–21

Anninskii, S. A. (historian), papers, e-148

Anokhin, P. K. (physician), papers, E–40

Antokol'skii, M. M. (sculptor), papers, H–19, H–89

Antonii (Mel'nikov), Metropolitan, archive, F–20

Antonin (A. I. Kapustin), Archimandrite, Oriental manuscript collection, G–15

Antonov, A. I., General, papers, C–4

Antonov, O. K. (aeronautical engineer, designer), papers, B–9, b-233

Antonov-Ovseenko, V. A. (Soviet CP official), papers, B–1, B–8, b-26

Antropov, N. P., 1812 war documents, H–11

Apraksin family (gentry landowners), archive, G–1

Aragon, Louis (French writer), papers, E–9

Araia, Francesco (Italian composer), manuscript music scores, G–19, G–22

Arakcheev, A. A., General (military minister), papers, B–4, E–24, G–15, H–1

Aranovich, S. D. (film director), films, C–24

Arapov, B. A. (composer), papers, D–15

Arbor, Rolle (Romanian Doctor), battleship "Potemkin" photographs, H–4

Archakov, N. I. (military officer), papers, H–77

Archimedes (Greek mathematician and inventor), manuscript, G–16

Ardens, N. N. (literary critic), papers, H–35

Aref'ev, M. S. (Soviet regional official), papers, b-26

Arenskii, A. S. (composer), papers, E–28, G–7, H–48

Areskin (Erskine), Robert (physician), library collection, G–16

Argunov, F. S. (serf architect), H–21

Argutinskii-Dolgorukov, V. N., Count, General, graphic art collection, H–89

Arifi, Mahmud (15th-c. Persian poet), manuscript, H–29

Arinkin, M. I. (physician), papers, G–25

Arkharov family (gentry landowners), papers, E–24

Arkhipova, I. K. (singer), films, c-156

Armand, I. (Elizaveta) F. (revolutionary), papers, B–12

Arsen'ev, V. S. (gentry landowner, government official), manuscript collection, G–1

Arshakuni, O. K. (architect), drawings, D–21

Arshakuni, Z. P. (artist), graphic art, H–89

Artem'ev, A. I. (statistician, historian, geographer), manuscript collection, G–15

Artem'ev-Khlyzov family (Pomor'e peasants), archive, H–5, h-86

Artsimovich, L. A. (nuclear physicist), papers, E–29, E–41

Aruzhchev, A. N. (architect), architectural drawings, H–87

Astrakova, T. A. (architect), manuscript collection, H–33, h-268

Astyrev, N. M. (revolutionary), papers, H–65

Atasheva, R. M. (Eisenstein's wife), and museum of cinema, H–50

Augustine, Saint (Church father, philosopher), manuscript, G–15

Avenarius, G. A. (film critic), papers, C–16

Averbakh, I. A. (film director), films, C–24

Averchenko, A. T. (writer), papers, B–7

Avtokratov, V. N. (historian), papers, b-22

Avvakum Petrovich, Protopope, manuscripts, B–2, E–28, G–16

Axelrod, P. B. *See* Aksel'rod (Axelrod), P. B.

Azanchevskii, M. P. (musicologist, composer), music collection, G–19

Azar'in, Simon (Church writer), manuscripts, h-175

Azarov, V. B. (writer), papers, H–65

Azernikova, E. V. (theater critic, historian), theater library collection, G–8

Babadzhanian, A. A. (composer), papers, H–45

Babel', I. E. (writer), papers, E–9, G–1

Babeuf, Gracchus (*pseud. of* François Noël) (French socialist), papers, B–12

Babir, N. I. (photographer), photographs, H–32

Babushkin, M. S. (aviator), papers, B–6

Bach, Carl Philipp Emanuel (German composer), autographs, G–19

Bach, Johann Sebastian (German composer), music scores, E–28, E–46

Baer, Karl Ernst von (K. M. Ber) (Estonian scholar, zoologist): papers and documentary collection, E–20; library collection, E–31, G–16
——and establishment of RGO, E–26

Bagants, Friedrich Heinrich (F. G.) (artist): drawings, H–65; watercolors, E–22

Bagramian, I. Kh., Marshal, autographed books, H–16

Bagration, P. I., General, papers, B–4, H–77

Bagritskii (*pseud. of* Dziubin), E. G. (poet), papers, E–9

Baikov, A. M. (architect), architectural drawings, H–79

Bakh, A. G. (architect), architectural drawings, H–84

Bakh, A. N. (biochemist, revolutionary), papers, B–9, b-233

Bakh, R. I. (architect, sculptor), architectural drawings, H–84

Bakhmet'ev, A. N. (*Hofmeister*, Moscow Educational District administrator), papers, D–2

Bakhrushin, A. A. (industrialist, civic leader, theater historian, GTsTM founder), theater collection, H–42, h-301

Bakhrushin, A. P. (industrialist, amateur historian), historical collection, G–3, H–1

Bakhrushin, Iu. A. (ballet historian), papers and theater collection, H–42

Bakhrushin family (merchants, industrialists, philanthropists), papers, H–5, H–42, H–152

Bakhtin, V. S. (ethnographer), folklore collection, E–28

Bakst, Léon (*pseud. of* L. S. Rozenberg) (artist, stage designer): papers, H–42; theater graphics, G–21, H–89, H–102

Bakunin, M. N. (revolutionary, anarchism theorist), papers, B–12

Bakunin family (St. Petersburg and Tver gentry landowners), papers, B–1

Bakushanskii, A. V. (art historian), papers, H–23

Bal'mont, K. D. (poet), autographs, G–4, H–49

Balakirev, M. A. (composer): papers and music scores, G–19, g-204, H–45, h-319; recordings, H–45

Balandin, A. A. (chemist), papers, b-233

Balanin, D. V. (military commander), papers, G–15

Balashov family (proprietors of mines and estates), papers, E–24

Balug'ianskii, M. A. (Petersburg University rector), papers, E–55

Balukhatyi, S. D. (literary historian), papers, E–28

Balzac, Honoré de (French writer), literary autographs, E–28, G–15

Bantysh-Kamenskii, D. N. (historian, archeographer): papers, E–24; documentary collection, E–28
——and MGAMID archive, b-57, c-25

Baquoi, Maurice (artist), engravings, H–85

Baranovskii, E. I. (lawyer, government official), papers, G–3

Baranzin, E. V. (revolutionary), archive, H–4

Baratynskii, E. A. (poet): papers, H–39, H–47, H–95; portraits, H–34

Barbusse, Henri (French writer), papers, E–9, E–28, h-267

Barclay de Tolly (Barklai de Tolli), M. B., General, Field Marshal, papers, B–4, b-131

Bard, A. (artist), drawings, H–36

Bardin, I. P. (chemist, engineer), papers, b-233.1

Barents, Willem (Dutch navigator), 16th-c. map, H–1

Bariatinskii, A. I., General, Field Marshal (bibliophile): manuscript collection, H–1; library G–3

Bariatinskii family (princes, gentry landowners), archive, G–1

Barkan, D. D. (scientist, engineer), papers, B–9

Barma (16th-c. architect), and St. Basil's Cathedral, H–3

Barshchevskii, I. F. (photographer), photographs, G–18, H–28, H–89, h-243

Barskov, Ia. D. (historian, publisher), papers, G–1

Barsov, E. V. (folklorist), manuscript collection, H–1

Barsukov, N. P. (historian, archeographer), papers and family papers, H–22

Barten, A. A. (writer), manuscripts, H–104

Bartol'd, V. V. (Wilhelm Barthold) (Orientalist): papers, E–20; library, E–23; photograph collection, E–23

Bartolomei, I. A. (numismatist), papers, E–24

Baruzdina, V. M. (artist), drawings and photographs, H–92

Basil (Basilius) (the Great), Saint (Church father), manuscript, H–27

B–3, H–17, H–28, H–82, H–90; and Tsaritsyno
Estate, H–155

Bebel, August (German socialist), papers, B–12

Becher, Johannes (German writer), papers, E–9

Bede (Baeda), Saint (the Venerable) (British historian, theologian), manuscript, G–15

Bedniakov, I. I., memoirs, and A. S. Golubkina, H–24

Bednyi, Dem′ian (*pseud. of* E. A. Pridvorov) (poet): papers, E–9; library, H–33, h-271

Beethoven, Ludwig van (German composer): manuscript music scores, G–22, H–45, h-320; autographs, G–19; television films, c-115.1

Beketova, M. A. (translator, biographer of A. Blok), documents, H–99

Bekhterev, V. M. (neuropathologist, psychologist, physiologist), papers, D–13

Bekhtereva, N. P. (physiologist), papers, E–47

Bekker, R. R., library, E–46

Beleliubskii, N. A. (civil engineer, bridge designer): papers, B–9, G–24; library, G–24

Belen′kii, A. I. (news photographer), photograph collection, F–16

Belen′kii, M. S. (Hebraist), papers, F–21

Belgarde, Counts Heinrich and August von (Austrian aristocrats), trophy archive, B–8A

Beliaev, A. R. (writer), papers, D–15

Beliaev, I. (script writer), films, c-107.19

Beliaev, M. P. (music publisher), publishing house papers, H–45

Beliaev, S. V. (architect), archive, E–45

Beliaev, V. V. (artist), archive, E–45

Belinskii, A. A. (film director), films, c-107.20

Belinskii (Belinsky), V. G. (literary critic, revolutionary democrat): papers, E–28, e-212, G–15, g-32, g-183, H–33, H–97; photographs, H–97

Belkin, A. P. (artist), graphic art, H–89

Belli, V. A. (naval officer), papers, B–5

Bellinsgauzen (Bellingshausen), F. F., Admiral (polar explorer), papers, B–5, H–73

Belogradets, Gerasim, Hierodeacon (Ierodiakon), religious manuscript, H–88

Belogrud, A. E. (architect), archive, E–45

E–20, G–17; library, G–26

Benkendorf family (landed gentry, diplomats, military leaders), papers, B–1

Benois (Benua), Albert N. (artist), drawings, H–65

Benois, Alexandre (A. N. Benua) (artist, art historian): papers, H–42, H–83, H–89; drawings, G–6, G–21, H–65, H–88, H–89, H–91, H–102; watercolors, h-553; photograph collection, H–89; library, H–89

Benois (Benua), L. N. (artist, architect), H–89; papers, E–45, H–83

Benois, Nicola (N. A.Benua) (Italian theater designer), papers, H–83

Benois, Nicholas (N. L. Benua) (architect): papers, G–15; architectural drawings, g-213, H–82

Benois (Benua) family (artists, architects, cultural historians): papers and drawings, H–83; memorial museum, H–83, h-547

Ber, K. M. *See* Baer, Karl Ernst von (K. M. Ber)

Béranger, Pierre Jean de (French poet), autographs, E–28

Berberova, N. N. (writer), papers, F–9

Berchich, Ivan (Dalmatian Slavicist), manuscript collection, G–15

Berdiaev, N. A. (religious philosopher), papers, F–9

Beregovskii, M. Ia. (music critic), papers, E–46

Berenshtam, F. G. (architect, artist), letters, H–97

Berestov, V. D. (writer), autographed books, G–9

Beretti, A. V. and V. I. (architects), papers, G–24

Bereznikov family (landowners), papers, H–1

Berezovs′kyi, M. S. (Ukrainian composer), manuscript music scores, H–45

Berg, A. I. (radioelectronics engineer, physicist), documents, H–118

Berg, L. S. (geographer, ichthyologist), papers, E–20, E–26

Berggol′ts, O. F. (poetess), speeches, D–15

Bergamasco, Charles (Karl) (photographer), photographs, H–65

Beriia (Beria), L. P. (CP leader, security chief): special files addressed to, catalogue, B–1, b-16; nuclear committee chair, C–10

Brodskii, I. I. (artist): papers, E–45, H–91; drawings, H–90; memorial museum, H–90, H–91, h-617–h-620

Brodsky, Joseph. *See* Brodskii, I. A. (Joseph Brodsky)

Brokar, G. I. *See* Brocart, Henri (G. I. Brokar)

Bromlei, Iu. V. (historian, ethnographer), papers, G–5

Bromlei, N. A. (theater historian), papers, H–102

Bronnikov, F. A. (architect), papers, H–28

Brosset, Marie-Felicité (M. I.) (Orientalist): papers, E–23; numismatic catalogue, H–88

Bruce, Jacob Daniel (Ia. V. Brius) (Russified Scottish diplomat, military commander, scholar): library, G–16, g-309; memorial museum, H–154

Brühl (Briul'), Heinrich von, Count (Saxon statesman), graphic arts collection, H–88

Bruni, N. A. (artist), portraits, H–92

Bruni, T. G. (artist), drawings, H–102

Brylev, A. M. (engineer, designer), papers, H–111

Bryullov. *See* Briullov

Budberg family (barons, Baltic landed gentry), manuscripts, g-310

Budde, E. F. (linguist), manuscript collection, E–28

Bugaeva, K. N. (wife of Andrei Belyi), papers, H–34

Bukharin, N. I. (Soviet CP leader, statesman): papers, B–12, b-251, C–1, c-4; as IINiT director, E–2, E–21

Bulgak, Ia. (photographer), photographs, H–32

Bulgakov, M. A. (writer), papers, B–7, E–28, G–1, H–43, H–33

Bulgakov, S. N. (religious philosopher, economist), papers, F–9

Bulgakov, V. F. (bibliographer), papers, E–28, H–35

Bulich, S. K. (music critic), library, E–46

Bulla, A. K. (photographer), photographs, D–21, d-44, H–65

Bulla, Karl (K. K.) (German photographer), photographs, D–21, d-44, H–65, H–72

Bulla, V. K. (photographer), photographs, D–16, d-44, H–4, H–65

Bulychev, K. (writer), autographed books, G–9

Bunin, I. A. (writer): papers, B–7, E–9, e-212, F–8, F–9, G–6; papers, survey, a-133

Bunin, L. (artist), engravings, H–72

Buonarotti, Filippo Michele (Italian-born French revolutionary), papers, B–12

Burdenko, N. N. (surgeon), papers, E–40, H–75

Burenin, N. E. (photographer, revolutionary): papers, H–66; photograph collection, E–9

Bur'ianov, A. F. (social-democrat), papers, G–15

Burliand, V. A. (historian of technology), papers, H–114

Burliuk, D. D. (artist): papers, H–26; manuscripts, H–36

Burov, K., book dust-cover collection, G–1

Burylichev, P. G. (Moscow Oblast administrator), papers, D–8

Buryshkin, P. A. (industrialist), papers, H–1

Buslaev, F. I. (philologist, art historian): papers, E–10, G–2, H–33; papers, survey, a-134; Slavic manuscript collection, G–15; inscriptions, H–88; library, G–2, g-74

Butkevich, R. A. (follower of L. N. Tolstoi), papers, H–35

Butkov, P. G. (historian), documentary collection, E–28

Butlerov, A. M. (chemist), papers, E–20

Butmi, V. A. (art historian), papers, D–21

Butovich, Ia. I. (horse breeder), manuscripts, H–56

Buturlin family (landed gentry), estate and family papers, E–24

Buturlin, D. P. (military historian), papers, B–4

Bychkov, A. F. (historian, library director), manuscript collection, g-169

Bykov, G. V. (historian of chemistry), papers, E–2

Bykov, K. M. (physiologist), papers, E–47

Byron, George (British poet): autographs, E–28; portraits, H–34

Bystrov, S. I. (religion historian), papers, H–72

Callas, Maria (Greek opera singer), recordings, H–102

Callot, Jacques (French artist), graphic art, G–15

Calogerà, Angelo (abbot), correspondence catalogue, g-234

Cameron, Charles (Scottish architect), H–81, H–84; drawings, G–24

Campana, Giampietro Marquis of (Italian noble, art collector), art collection, catalogue, H–88

Camporesi, Francesco (F. I.) (Italian artist), engravings, H–18

Canoppi, Antonio (Italian theater designer), drawings, H–102

Caraffa, Diomedes (Italian writer), manuscript, H–88

Carter, James (U.S. President), correspondence with Brezhnev, a–369

Caruso, Enrico (Italian opera singer): autographs, G–21; recordings, H–102

Casanova, Giovanni Battista (Dresden Academy of Arts director), gem collection inventory, H–88

Catherine I, Empress (of Russia), and Tsarskoe Selo, H–84

Catherine II (the Great), Empress (of Russia): records, B–2, E–24; documents, G–1, G–15, H–11, H–73, H–79, H–88, H–155; library, G–15, H–81, H–88, h-540, h-588; gem collection, H–88; numismatic collection, H–88
—— and Gatchina, H–79; and the Hermitage, g-175, H–88, h-571, h-575; and the Imperial

Public Library, G–15; and Tsaritsyno, H–155; and Tsarskoe Selo, H–84; and Pavlovsk, h-540

Catullus, Gaius Valerius (Roman poet), manuscript, E–24

Chaadaev, P. Ia. (philosopher, writer), papers, B–7

Chagall, Marc (artist), papers, H–26

Chagin, P. I. (poet), papers, H–36

Chaianov, A. V. (economist), papers, B–6

Chaikovskii (Tchaikovsky), M. I. (playwright), papers, H–48

Chaikovskii (Tchaikovsky), P. I. *See* Tchaikovsky, P. I. (Chaikovskii , P. I.)

Chaliapin, Feodor (F. I. Shaliapin) (opera singer): papers, F–8, G–21, H–42, H–46, H–102; photographs, D–16, H–42, H–45, H–91, H–102; portraits, G–19; recordings, H–45, H–102, H–165; memorial museum, H–45, H–102, h-330

Chapaev, V. I. (Civil War hero), papers, H–6

Chaplygin, S. A. (aerodynamics engineer), memorial museum, H–175

Chapygin, A. P. (writer), papers, E–9

Charlemagne, Joseph (I. I. Sharleman') (Russian architect), architectural drawings, H–65, H–82

Charles XII, King (of Sweden), autographs, G–15

Châteaubriand, François René de (French writer, statesman), literary autographs, E–28

Cheboksarov, N. N. (ethnographer), papers, E–7

Chebyshev, P. L. (mathematician), papers, E–1

Cheever, John (American writer), recordings, G–4

Chegodaev, A. D. (art historian), papers, H–26

Chekhonin, S. V. (artist), drawings, H–205

Chekhov, A. P. (writer): papers, B–7, E–46, G–1, G–6, G–21, H–33, H–40, H–42, h-310, H–102; papers, catalogues,
b-173, e-212, g-33, g-34; promptbooks, G–21; photographs, H–35, h-310; films, c-100.2; memorial museum, H–33, H–40, h-265

Chekhov, M. A. (actor, theater director): papers, G–8; photographs, H–47

Chekhov, N. P. (brother of A. P. Chekhov), drawings, H–40

Chekhov, N. V. (educator), papers, E–42

Chekhov, S. M. (nephew of A. P. Chekhov), drawings, H–40

Chekhova, M. P. (sister of A. P. Chekhov), drawings, H–40

Chelnokov, I. Ia. (art restorer, museum curator), papers, H–89

Chemesov, E. P. (artist), engravings, E–25, G–18, H–89, H–90

Cherkasov, N. K. (actor), papers and recordings, G–23, F–15

Cherkasskii, A. M., Prince (statesman), documentary collection, H–21

Chernenko, K. U. (Soviet CP leader), papers, C–1

Chernetsov, G. G. and N. G. (artists): papers, E–45; drawings, H–89

Chernetsov, V. N. (archeologist), photograph collection, E–3

Cherniakhovskii, I. D., General, papers, H–6

Chernigovskii, V. N. (physiologist), papers, E–47

Chernomorskii, S. I. (bolshevik revolutionary), and Moscow CP archive, D–3

Chernyshev, F. N. (geologist, paleontologist): papers, E–20; mineral and paleontological collection, H–106

Chernyshev, V. I. (linguist), papers, E–10

Chernyshevskii (Chernyshevsky), N. G. (literary critic, radical publicist): papers, b-174, e-234, H–96, h-267; autographs, H–33; photographs, H–90

Chertkov, A. D. (historian, archeologist): Slavic manuscript collection, H–1, h-32; library, G–3

Chertkov, G. I., General, library, B–3

Chertkov, V. G. (publicist, publisher): papers, H–24, H–35, H–72; photographs, H–35

Chertousov, M. D. (hydraulic engineer), papers, H–117

Chertov, G. (news photographer), photograph collection, H–65

Cherubini, Luigi (Italian composer), papers, E–46, G–19

Cheskii, I. V. (artist), engravings, G–18

Chevakinskii, S. I. (architect), H–84

Chichagov, D. N. (architect), H–1

Chicherin, G. V. (statesman, diplomat), diplomatic records, C–2

Chichibabin, A. E. (chemist), papers, E–20

Ching dynasty, Chinese manuscripts, g-254

Chingis-khan. *See* Genghis Khan (Chingis-khan)

Chistiakov, Iu. E. (archeologist), archeological reports, H–26

Chistiakov, P. P. (artist): papers, E–45, H–89, H–90; family archive, H–92; memorial museum, H–90, H–92, h-621–h-623

Chistiakova, A. P. (artist), drawings, H–92

Chistovich, Ia. A. (hygienist, forensic physician, medical historian), papers, G-25

Chizhov family (industrialists), archive, G–1

Chopin, F. F. (Polish pianist, composer), films, c-115.18A

Chou Ying (Chinese painter), drawings, H–29

Chrysostom, Saint John (Church father), sermons, H–81

Chub. *See* Mikhail (Chub), Archbishop

Chugaev, L. A. (chemist), and Mendeleev archive, H–105

Chukov. *See* Grigorii (Chukov), Metropolitan

Chukovskii, K. I. (*pseud. of* N. V. Korneichukov) (writer): papers, G–1, H–96; memorial museum, H–33

Chulkov, G. I. (writer, literary historian), papers, H–24, H–99

Chulkov, N. P. (archivist, historian of Moscow), papers, H–5, h-87

Chuloshnikov, A. P. (historian), documentary collection, E–5

Chuprov, A. I. (economist, publicist), papers, D–2

Churakov, N. G., graphic arts collection, G–15

Cicero, Marcus Tullius (Roman philosopher, orator), manuscripts, G–15, G–16, H–88

Cluseret, Gustave-Paul (French socialist), papers, B–12

Cobenzl (Kobentsl'), Ludwig, Count von (Austrian diplomat), art collection, H–88

Colarossi, Filippo (artist, architect), and A. S. Golubkina museum, H–24

Collins, Wilkie (British writer), literary autographs, E–28

Constantine (Konstantin) Konstantinovich (*pseud.* K. R.), Grand Duke (of Russia): papers, E–28; drawings, H–81

Constantine (Konstantin) Nikolaevich, Grand Duke (of Russia): naval records, B–5 ; and Marble Palace, H–89

Constantine (Konstantin) Pavlovich, Grand Duke (of Russia): military records, b-131; Constantine ruble design, H–88

Cooper, James Fenimore (American writer), literary autographs, E–28

Copernicus, Nicolaus (Polish astronomer), autographs, G–1

Cotogni, Antonio (Italian composer), portraits, G–19

Cromwell, Oliver (English general, statesman), autographs, E–24

Cui, César (Ts. A. Kiui) (composer, military engineer); papers, G–15, G–19, G–22, H–73

Curie, Pierre and Marie (*née* Sklodovska) (physical chemists), photographs, E–2

Cusack, Dymphna (Australian writer), recordings, G–4

Cyprianus, Saint (bishop of Carthage), manuscript, G–26

Cyril (Kirill) (Constantine), Saint (Apostle of the Slavs), tale of the Slavonic alphabet, H–81

Cyril (Kirill) Vladimirovich, Grand Duke (of Russia), library, B–5

Cyril of Alexandria, Saint, Archbishop (Roman Catholic ecclesiastic), sermons, H–81

Cyril of Turov (Turau). *See* Kirill Turovskii (Cyril of Turov [Turau]), Saint

d'Alembert, Jean Le Rond. *See* Alembert, Jean Le Rond d'

Dadykin, N. V. (sculptor), drawings, H–87

Daguerre, Louis-Jacques-Mandé (French physicist, painter, inventor), correspondence, e-39

Dal' (Dahl), V. I. (writer, linguist), *lubok* collection, G–15

Damame-Demartrais, Michel-François (French artist), drawings, H–28

Daneliia, G. N. (film director), film studio, C–20

Daniil Zatochnik (12–13th c. religious writer), manuscripts, E–28

Danilin, N. M. (conductor, conservatory professor), papers, h-323

Dansker, O. L. (theater historian), manuscript, E–46

Dante Alighieri (Italian poet): manuscripts, e-137; portraits, H–34

Dargomyzhskii, A. S. (composer): manuscript music scores, G–19, G–22; recordings, H–45

Darwin, Charles (naturalist), letters, H–53

Dashkov, P. Ia. (bibliographer, historical collector): manuscript collection, E–28; art and manuscript collection, H–89; engravings collection, H–1

Datsario, Giuseppe. *See* Daziaro (Datsiaro), Giuseppe

Davis, Angela (American human-rights activist), recordings, G–4

Davydov, A. M. (singer), recordings, H–102

Davydov, D. V., General (poet), manuscripts, H–34

Davydov, K. Iu. (violist, conductor), portraits, G–19

Davydov, V. L. (Tchaikovsky's nephew), personal and family papers, H–48

Davydovskii, I. V. (physician), papers, E–40

Daziaro (Datsario), Giuseppe (lithographic publisher), albums, G–1, H–65, h-280

Debussy, Claude (French composer), recordings, H–45

Degtiarev, S. A. (composer), music scores, G–19

Degtiarev, V. A. (military engineer), H–69

Deich (Deych), G. M. (archivist), collection of Jewish-related documents, a-535

Deich, L. G. (revolutionary), papers, G–15

Delabart, Gérard (French artist), graphic art, G–1, H–28, H–65

Delektorskaia, L. N. (secretary of Henri Matisse), papers, H–26

Delescluze, Louis-Charles (French socialist), papers, B–12

Delibes, Léo (French composer), manuscripts, G–22

Del'mas, L. A. (singer), papers, H–99

Demidov, A. (Peterburg Conservatory official), music collection, G–19

Dudchenko, M. S. (follower of L. N. Tolstoi), papers, H–72

Dudin, M. A. (poet), papers, D–15

Dunaev, B. I. (photographer), photographs, H–28

Dunaevskii, I. O. (composer), films, c-115.4

Durand, André (French artist), engravings, G–1

Durdin, Ia. V. (grandson of P. P. Chistiakov), papers, H–92

Dürer, Albrecht (German artist), drawings, G–15

Dürkoop, Rudolf (Dutch photographer), photographs, H–32

Durova, N. Iu. (circus trainer), autographed books, G–9

Dushenov, K. I. (naval commander), papers, H–74

Duthier, J. de (Diut'e Zh.) (French Secretary of State), archive, b-77

Duze (Duze-Checchi), Eleonora (Italian actress), letters, G–21

Dvorishchin, I. G. (Chaliapin apartment owner), and Chaliapin archive, H–102

Dybenko, P. E. (revolutionary, military commander), papers, B–8

Dzerzhinskii (Dzierżyński), F. E. (revolutionary, Cheka-GPU chief): papers, B–12, b-278, C–6, C–7, H–4, H–15; memorial museum, H–67

Dzhivelegov, A. K. (theater critic, historian), theater library collection, G–8

Efimenko, P. P. (archeologist), papers, E–22

Efimov, G. V. (historian), papers, D–12

Efimov, I. E. (artist), papers, H–24

Efimov, I. S. (artist, sculptor), letters, H–24

Efremov, I. V. (folklorist), early sound collection, E–28

Efremov, O. N. (actor, theater director), films, c-107.3

Efremov, P. A. (bibliographer, literary scholar), literary collection, E–28

Egor'ev, V. E. (naval commander), papers, B–5

Egor'ev-Svarichevskii family, papers, H–5

Egorov, A. E. (artist), drawings, H–89

Egorov, E. E. (merchant), manuscript collection, G–1

Egorov, V. E. (artist), film graphic art, H–50

Ehrenburg, I. G. See Erenburg (Ehrenburg), I. G.

Eisenstein, Sergei (S. M. Eizenshtein) (film director): papers, B–7, C–16; autographs, H–102; memorial museum, H–50

Ekster, Aleksandra (*pseud. of* A. A. Grigorovich) (graphic artist, theater designer), drawings, H–42, h-304

El' Lissitsky. See Lissitsky, El' (*pseud. of* Lazar M. Lisitskii)

Elagin family (Novgorod landowners), papers, G–15

Elanskii, N. N. (medical officer), papers, h-511

Elenkin, A. A. (botanist), manuscripts, E–33

Eleonskaia, E. N. (folklorist), papers, H–33

Eliasberg, K. I. (conductor): library, G–20; recordings, F–15

El'iash, Nikolai I. (theater critic, historian), theater library collection, G–8

Eliseev, A. (artist); autographed books, G–9

Elizabeth (Elizaveta Petrovna), Empress (of Russia): Coronation, H–71; and Tsarskoe Selo, h-553

Elizabeth (Elizaveta Alekseevna), Grand Duchess/ Empress (of Russia, wife of Alexander I), music collection, E–46

Elizabeth II, Queen (of England), gift of imperial photographs, H–79

Elizarov, M. T. (revolutionary): family memorial museum, H–68; and Lenin Museum, H–68

Elizaveta Alekseevna, Grand Duchess/Empress. *See* Elizabeth (Elizaveta) Alekseevna, Grand Duchess/ Empress (of Russia, wife of Alexander I).

Elizaveta Petrovna, Empress (of Russia). *See* Elizabeth (Elizaveta) Petrovna, Empress (of Russia)

El'tsin, B. N. *See* Yeltsin (Eltsin), B. N.

El'tsin, S. V. (conservatory professor), music collection, G–22

Enei, E. E. (artist), film graphic art, H–50

Engel'gardt, L. N. (writer), library, H–39

Engel'gardt (Engelhardt), V. P. (military historian, astronomer), papers, H–77

Engel'gardt family, and Tiutchev Muranovo Estate Museum, H–39

Engelhardt, V. P. *See* Engel'gardt (Engelhardt), V. P.

Engels, Friedrich (German socialist): manuscripts, B–12; museum of, a-112, B–12, b-278

Ensh, G. A. *See* Jenšs, J. (G. A. Ensh)

Epifanii (monk, old believer), manuscripts, E–28

Epinay, Louise Florence Petronille Tardieu d'Esclaves, Marquise d' (French 18th-c. writer), Voltaire's letters to, g-263

Er'zia (*pseud. of* Nefedov), S. D. (sculptor), papers, H–89

Erdeli, K. A. (musician), recordings, H–45

Erdman, B. R. (artist), stage design sketches, G–6

Eremin, Iu. P. (photographer), photographs, H–32

Erenburg (Ehrenburg), I. G. (writer, public figure), photographs, B–11

Erfurt, Hugo (German photographer), photographs, H–32

Ermler, F. M. (film director): papers, D–15; film studio, C–24

Ermolov, A. P., General, papers, B–4

Ermolova, M. N. (actress): papers, H–42; letters, G–21; memorial museum, H–42

Ern, V. F. (religious philosopher), papers, H–24

Ershov, M. I. (film director), films, C–24

1335

Golubinskii, E. E. (Church historian), library, G–5

Golubkina, A. S. (sculptress), memorial museum, H–24, h-200, h-201

Golubov, S. N., library, H–34

Goncharov, I. A. (writer): papers, B–7, e-212, e-213, G–15, g-189; drawings, E–28

Goncharov family (landowners, industrialists), papers, B–2, H–34, H–95

Goncharov, V. V. (assistant of I. V. Kurchatov), films, H–54

Goncharova, N. S. (artist): memorial museum, H–23, drawings, H–36, H–89

Gonzaga, Pietro di Gottardo (Italian graphic artist, theater designer): papers, H–42; graphic art, G–21, H–102

Gorbachev, M. S. (CP leader, president of the USSR): papers, C–1, c-3; and AP RF, C–1

Gorbunov, I. F. (actor), theater collection, H–102

Gorbunov-Posadov, M. I. (engineer, metrologist), papers, B–9

Gorchakov, A. M. (diplomat, foreign minister), papers, B–1

Gordeev, N. V. (art critic), papers, H–17

Gordlevskii, V. A. (turkologist), library and memorial cabinet, E–4

Goren, A. I. (architect), H–66

Gor'kii, Maksim (A. M.; Maksim or Maxim Gorky) (pseud. of A. M. Peshkov) (writer): archive and family papers, E–9; papers, descriptions, E–9, e-21–e-25, e-228, H–33, H–66, H–93, H–95, H–102; censor's copies and promptbooks, G–21; personal library, E–9; library catalogue, e-29; graphic art, B–11, D–16, E–9, e-26, e-27, E–28, H–91; photographs, catalogue, e-28; memorial museum, E–9, e-26–e-29

—— and workers' movement, a-340

Gornostaev brothers (architects), architectural drawings, H–84

Gornung, L. V. (poet, translator, photographer), papers, H–98

Gorodetskii, S. M. (poet), papers, H–33, H–36, H–99

Gorskii, A. A. (ballet-master), papers, H–42

Gorskii, A. D. (historian), memorial volume, a-753

Got'e, Iu. V. (historian), papers, E–1

Goujon, Jules (French industrialist), and factory museum, H–180

Gounod, Charles (French composer), autographs, G–19

Grabar', I. E. (artist, art historian), papers, H–23, h-43

Grabin, V. G., General (military engineer, designer), papers, H–73

Grabovskii, B. (inventor), papers, H–114

Graftio, G. O. (electrical engineer, physicist), papers, D–17, H–65, H–118

Granin, D. A. (writer), papers, D–15

Granovskii, T. N. (historian): papers, G–1, G–2, g-78, H–1; library, g-80

Grassi, Luigi (Italian art collector), drawings collection, H–88

Grebnev, V. P. (photographer), photograph collection, G–1, H–1

Grechko, A. A., Marshal (defense minister): papers, B–8, C–1; autographed books, H–16

Gregory I (the Great), Saint (Church father, pope), manuscripts, G–16

Gregory of Sinai (Gregorius Sinaita), Saint, Metropolitan, manuscripts, G–26

Greig, A. S. and S. K., Admirals, papers, B–5, G–15

Grek, Maksim. See Maximus the Greek, Saint (Maksim Grek, Michael Trivolis)

Grekov, M. B. (artist): papers, b-178, h-97; studio collection, H–73

Griazev, N. (military officer), and Suvorov museum, H–77

Griaznov, M. P. (archeologist), papers, E–22

Griboedov, A. S. (writer, diplomat): papers, E–28, G–2, H–34, H–42, H–95; censor's copies and promptbooks, G–21; portraits, H–34

Grieg, Edvard (Norwegian composer), recordings, H–45

Grigor'ev, A. (architect), H–34

Grigor'ev, A. A. and A. K., and V. A. (photographers), photograph collection, D–21

Grigor'ev, A. V. (artist), collection of biographic data on artists, H–23

Grigor'ev, V. V. (Mongolian specialist), papers, B–3, E–23

Grigorii (Chukov), Metropolitan, papers, F–20

Grigorii Sinait. See Gregory of Sinai

Grigorovich, D. V. (writer), photographs, H–97

Grigorovich, I. (military officer), and Suvorov museum, H–77

Grigorovich, V. I. (Slavicist), family, manuscript collection, G–1

Grimm, D. I. and G. D. (educators), papers, E–45

Grimm, E. D. (historian), library, E–56

Grimm, G. G. (architect, historian of architecture), library, G–18

Grin, A. (pseud. of A. S. Grinevskii) (writer), papers, B–7

Grinberg, A. P. and G. A. (physicists), papers, E–29

Grinkova, N. P. (literary scholar), papers, E–56

Grits, T. S. (army newspaper editor), Moscow Defense documents, H–9

Gross, E. F. (physicist), papers, E–29

Grot, Ia. K. (literary historian), papers, E–10, E–20, E–28

Grum-Grzhimailo, G. E. (geographer, zoologist), papers, E–26

Il'in, A. A. (historian, cartographer, numismatist), papers, E–26

Il'in, N. P., collection relating to A. A. Blok, H–99

Il'inskii, I. V. (actor), films, c-107.6

Il'iushin, S. V. (aeronautic engineer, aircraft designer): papers, B–9, b-233, H–181; memorial museum, H–181

Ilovaiskii, D. I. (historian), papers, H–1

Imshenetskii, N. I., WWII prison song collection, E–28

Inokhodtsev, P. B. (astronomy professor), library, G–17

Inostrantsev, A. A. (geologist), papers, E–55

Inostrantsev, K. A. (Arabist, historian), E–23

Ioann of Kronshtadt (Kronstadt) (I. I. Sergiev), Father (Archpriest [Protoierei]), papers, D–13

Ioasaf (Skripitsin), Metropolitan, H–3; manuscripts, H–18

Iofan, B. M. (architect), H–151

Ioffe (Joffé), A. F. (physicist): papers, D–17, E–20, E–29, H–117; recordings, F–15; family photographs, E–29

Ioffe (Joffé), V. I. (physician), papers, H–110

Iokhel'son, V. I. (ethnographer), folklore collection, E–28

Iolshin, N. M. (military leader), papers, h-5.2

Iordanskii, N. N. (psychologist, educator), papers, E–42

Iosif Volotskii (Joseph of Volotsk) (I. Sanin) (hegumen), B–2

Ipat'ev, V. N. (chemist): papers, b-233; and Mendeleev archive, H–105

Ippolitov-Ivanov, M. M. (composer), papers, H–45

Isaev, V. V. (sculptor), drawings, H–87

Isakovskii, M. V. (poet), manuscripts, H–33, H–96

Istomina, A. I. (ballerina), portraits, H–102

Italinskii, A. Ia., numismatic collection, H–88

Iudenich, N. N., General, military records, B–8

Iudin, S. S. (surgeon), medical library collection, E–40

Iunatov, A. A. (botanist), manuscripts, E–33

Iuon, K. F. (artist), papers, H–23

Iur'ev, Iu. M. (actor), papers, library, and photographs, H–102

Iurgenson, P. I. (publisher), publishing house papers, H–45

Iurovskii, A. N. (engineer), papers, B–6

Iusupov (Yusupov) family (gentry landowners, statesmen): papers, B–2; art collection, H–88

Iusupova (née Naryshkina), Z. I., Princess, papers, E–28

Iutkevich, S. I. (film director), film studio, C–24

Iuzhin, A. I. (actor): papers, B–7; recordings, E–28; theater book collection, H–166

Ivan III, Tsar of Russia, *Sudebnik* (judicial codex), B–2

Ivan IV (the Terrible), Tsar of Russia: *Sudebnik* (judicial codex), B–2, G–17; manuscripts, E–28; library, a-646; monastic letter to, G–26

Ivanov, A. I. (Byzantinist), papers, G–26

Ivanov, B. E. (writer), papers, D–7

Ivanov, E. I. (poet), and his family, literary autographs, H–99

Ivanov, Lavrentii. *See* Lavrentii Ivanov

Ivanov, V. A. (artist), papers, G–17; library, H–76

Ivanov, V. I. (poet), dedicatory autographs, H–49

Ivanov, Viacheslav V. (cultural historian), films, E–50

Ivanov, Vsevolod V. (writer), papers, G–1

Ivashentseva, G. A. (physician), papers, D–12

Ivashev family (gentry landowners), archive, H–95

Ivasheva, V. V. (literary scholar), papers, G–4

Iversen, Iu. G. (Jules-Gotlieb) (numismatist), papers, B–3

Jaba, August (A. D. Zhaba) (Russian consul in Erzurum [Erzerum], Turkey), Kurdish manuscript collection, e-101, g-253

Jacobi, Moritz Herrmann (B. S. Iakobi) (inventor), papers, H–114

Jami (15-c. Persian poet), manuscript, H–29

Jenšs, J. (Ensh, G. A.) (historian, watermark specialist), watermark collection, G–16

Joffé, A. F. *See* Ioffe (Joffé), A. F.

Joffé, V. I. *See* Ioffe (Joffé), V. I.

Joseph of Volotsk. *See* Iosif Volotskii (Joseph of Volotsk) (I. Sanin)

Josephus Flavius (Jewish historian), Latin manuscript, G–1

Joullien, Marc-Antoine (French publicist and political figure), papers, B–12

Justinian I, Emperor (of Byzantium), legal codex, g-345

Kabalevskii, D. B. (composer), papers, H–45

Kablukov family (gentry landowners, government officials), papers, E–24

Kachalov (*pseud. of* Shverubovich), V. I. (actor): papers, H–43; photographs, H–46; recordings, D–4

Kaden, N. N. (botanist), photograph collection, H–52

Kadol', O. (artist), engravings, G–1

Kafengauz, L. B. (engineer), papers, B–6

Kaganovich, L. M. (Soviet CP leader), papers, B–12, b-296, C–1

Kalachov, N. V. (archeographer), papers, B–3

Kalaidovich, K. F. (historian), papers, G–15

Kalikin, F. A., Slavic manuscript collection, a-181, E–28, H–88

Kalinin, M. I. (Bolshevik, Soviet government leader): papers, B–12, H–4; microfilmed papers, b-294; CP memoirs collection, D–14; memorial museum, H–4
——home and GMPIR, H–66

Kamenev (*pseud. of* Rozenfel'd), L. B. (Soviet CP leader), papers, B–12, b-251

Khizhinskii, L. S. (architect), drawings, D–21

Khlebnikov, A. V. (photographer), photographs, H–32

Khlebnikov, V. V. (poet): manuscripts, G–15, H–36; drawings, H–89

Khlebnikova, N. V., correspondence with A. S. Golubkina, H–24

Khlopkin, N. S., papers, H–54

Khludov, A. I. (merchant, manufacturer), manuscript collection, H–1, h-31

Khvoiko, V. V. (archeologist), archeological photographs, E–22

Khmel'kov, S. A., General, papers, H–73

Khmyrov, M. D. (regional studies specialist), manuscript collection, G–3, g-104

Khodasevich, V. F. (poet), manuscripts, F–8

Khodasevich, V. N. (artist), stage design sketches, G–6

Khodotov, N. N. (actor), theater library and manuscript collection, G–21

Khokhlov, I. S. (Moscow Oblast administrator), papers, D–8

Kholshevnikov, N. V., correspondence with N. A. Nekrasov, H–96

Khomiakov, A. S. (writer, philosopher, Slavophile): papers, H–1; dissertation on, G–26

Khomutov family (gentry landowners, Pushkin associates), archive, H–95

Khrushchev, N. S. (Soviet CP leader): papers, C–1; photographs, D–4; recordings, B–10; MVD "special files" addressed to, catalogue, b-15

Khrushchev-Seleznev family, H–34

Khvoiko, V. V. (archaelogist), photograph collection, E–22

Khvol'son, D. A. (Orientalist, Hebraist), papers, E–23, e-45

Khvostov, D. I., Count (writer, publisher, statesman), papers and family archive, E–28, H–77

Khvostov, N. B. (poet), papers and family archive, E–28

Kikoin, I. K. (physicist): papers, E–41, H–54; documents relating to Kurchatov, H–54

Kiprenskii, O. A. (artist), drawings, H–81, H–88, H–89

Kireevskii family (gentry landowners), papers, E–10

Kirienko-Voloshina, E. O. (mother of M. A. Voloshin), drawings, H–92

Kirill (Gundiaev), Metropoliltan of Kaliningrad and Smolensk (earlier Archbishop), papers, F–20

Kirill, Saint. See Cyril (Kirill) (Constantine)

Kirill Turovskii (Cyril of Turov [Turau]), Saint (writer, preacher), tale of, G–26

Kirill Vladimirovich, Grand Duke (of Russia). See Cyril (Kirill) Vladimirovich, Grand Duke (of Russia)

Kirov (pseud. of Kostrikov), S. M. (Soviet CP leader): papers, B–12; microfilmed papers, b-294; photographs, H–6; CP memoirs collection, D–14; memorial museum, H–65, h-408

Kiselev, P. D., General (statesman), papers, G–1

Kiselev, S. V. (archeologist), papers, E–3

Kitaev, A. A. (photographer), photographs, H–65

Kitaigorodskaia, G. (linguist, educator), films, E–50

Kiui, Ts. A. See Cui, César (Ts. A. Kiui)

Kiukhel'beker, K. I. See Küchelbecker, Karl (K. I. Kiukhel'beker)

Kiuner, N. V. (ethnographer), papers, E–25

Kizevetter, A. A. (Russian historian, political activist), papers, G–8

Klauber, I. S. (artist), engravings, H–72

Klein, R. I. (architect), papers, H–26

Klein, V. K. (art historian), papers, H–17

Klements, D. A. (anthropologist, ethnographer), photograph collection, E–23

Klepikov, P. V. (photographer), photographs, H–32

Klepikov, S. A. (watermark specialist), watermark collection, G–16

Klever, M. Iu. and Iu. Iu. (artists), drawings, H–70

Kligman, M. M. (documentary film director), films, C–25

Klimkovskii, N. N. (mining engineer), papers, G–17

Klimov, Iu. M. (documentary film director), films, C–25

Klinchin, P.M. (theater historian), manuscript, E–46

Kliuchevskii, V. O. (historian): papers, E–1, E–5, G–1, G–3, g-9; documentary collection, E–24

Klucis, Gustav (Klutsis, G. G.) (Latvian photographer), photographs, H–36

Klushantsev, P. V. (documentary film director), films, C–25

Kniazev, A. G. (military commander), papers, H–16

Kniazev, F. S. (poet), documentary collection, E–28

Knipper-Chekhova, O. L. (actress, wife of A. P. Chekhov), papers, H–43

Kobeko, P. P. (physicist), papers, E–29

Kobentsl', K. See Cobenzl (Kobentsl'), Ludwig, Count von

Kobozev, I. S. (news photographer), photographs, B–11

Kobzarev, Iu. B. (physicist), papers, E–29

Kochin, N. I. (writer), papers, D–7

Kochubei family (landowners), archive, B–3

Koehne, Berngard (B. V. Kene) (numismatist, genealogist), papers, B–3

Kogan, L. B. (violinist), films, c-115.7

Köhler, Heinrich Karl Ernst (E. G.) (historian, archeologist), papers, H–88

Kokhius, V. and P., 1812 war documents, H–12

Kokkinaki, V. K. (test piolot), papers, H–181

Kokorinov, A. F. (architect), H–90

Kokovtsov, P. K. (Orientalist), papers, E–23, e-45

Kolbasin, D. Ia. and E. Ia. (literary scholars), papers, G–2

Penzin, V. P. (folk artist), historical *lubok* collection, H–159

Peresvetov, R. T. (historian), papers, D–7

Peretts, V. N. (Slavicist): manuscript collection, E–28; seminar library manuscript catalogue, g-342

Pereverzev, D. S., papers, H–54

Perevezentsev, Iu. (artist), drawings, H–97

Perscheid, Nicolas (German photographer), photographs, H–32

Peshekhonov, A. V. (economist, publicist), manuscripts, G–15

Peshkov, A. M. *See* Gor'kii, Maksim (A. M.; Maksim *or* Maxim Gorky) (*pseud. of* A. M. Peshkov)

Peshkov, M. A. (son of Maksim Gor'kii), photographs, E–9

Peshkova, E. P. (wife of Maksim Gor'kii), papers, E–9

Peter I (the Great), Emperor (of Russia): chancellery records, B–2; military records, B–4; naval records, B–5, H–65, H–74; manuscripts and documents, E–24, E–28, G–2, G–15, g-176, g-308, H–1, h-38A, H–65, H–74, H–88; manuscripts and documents, surveys and catalogues, b-59, e-142; library and manuscript collection, G–16, g-291, g-297; medical records, G–25; portraits, G–15; history of, H–71;
———and Admiralty Izhora Factory, H–125; and Apothecary Garden, E–33, e-245; and armaments factory, H–206; and higher education, E–55; and Kunstkammer, E–25; and Peterhof, H–82; and Summer Palace, H–85, h-555, h-556.1; and Tsarskoe Selo, H–84

Peter II, Emperor (of Russia), medical reports, G–25

Peter III, Emperor (of Russia), and Oranienbaum Palace, H–80

Peter of Alexandria (10th c. Byzantinist), Greek chronicle, G–2

Petipa, Marius (M. I.) (French-Russian choreographer, ballet-master): papers, B–7; autographs, H–102

Petrarch (Francesco Petrarca) (Italian poet), manuscript, G–16

Petrianov-Sokolov, I. V. (chemist), papers, survey, b-233

Petrov, A. L. (historian, Slavicist), manuscript collection, G–16

Petrov, A. P. (composer), manuscript music scores, F–15

Petrov, P. P. (chemical engineer, GPM director), H–57

Petrov-Vodkin, K. S. (artist): papers, B–7, H–89; drawings, H–89

Petrovskii, A. A. (electrical engineer), paper, H–57

Petrovskii, A. S., engravings collection, G–1, g-44

Petrushevich (Petrushevych), A. S. (Ukrainian priest, historian, ethnographer), manuscript collection, G–16

Petrushevskii, A. F., General (military historian), papers, H–77

Petrushevskii, D. M. (historian), library, E–56

Petrushevskii, G. K. (zoologist), E–31

Petrushevych, A. S. *See* Petrushevich (Petrushevych), A. S.

Philaret. *See* Filaret (Philaret) (V. M. Drozdov), Metropolitan of Moscow and Kolomenskoe

Picasso, Pablo (Spanish artist), papers, H–26

Pieck, Wilhelm (German socialist), anti-Nazi documents, H–10

Pikhoia, R. G. (historian, Rosarkhiv chairman), archival reports, a-691, a-692

Piksanov, N. K. (literary scholar), papers, E–28

Pimenov, S. S. (artist), graphic art, H–205

Pinchuk, V. B. (sculptor), archive, E–45

Pinkevich, A. P. (educator), papers, E–56

Piotrovskii, B. B. (Orientalist, Hermitage director), recordings, F–15

Piranesi, Francesco (Italian architect, engraver), engravings collection, description, g-354

Piranesi, Giambattista (Italian architect): architectural drawings, H–65; engravings, E–57, G–15, G–18; engraivings collection, description, g-354

Pirogov, N. I. (surgeon, educator), papers, G–25, H–75

Pisarev, D. I. (publicist, literary critic), manuscripts, catalogue, e-235

Pisemskii, A. F. (writer), papers, B–7

Pivovarov, V. A. (merchant), manuscript collection, G–17

Platon (P. G. Levshin), Metropolitan (Church historian), papers, G–1

Platonov, K. K. (psychologist), papers, E–8

Platonov, S. F. (historian, archivist): papers, G–15, g-195; police investigatory files, D–19, d-52

Plehve, V. K. *See* Pleve (Plehve), V. K.

Plekhanov, G. V. (revolutionary, art and literary critic, publicist): papers, B–12, H–49, H–66; archive and library (Plekhanov House), G–15

Plekhanov, I. E., Colonel, papers, D–7

Plekhanov, P. V. (radio journalist), recordings, B–10

Pletnev, P. A. (literary critic, poet, publisher), papers, E–28

Pletneva, S. A. (archeologist), papers, E–3

Pleve (Plehve), V. K. (interior minister), papers, G–15

Pliatskovskii, M. S. (composer), children's music recordings, G–9

Pliatt, R. Ia. (actor), films, c-107.13

Pliny the Elder (Gaius Plinius Secundus) (Roman scholar), manuscript copy, G–16

Plisetskaia, M. M. (ballerina), films, c-115.14

Pliushar, A. A. *See* Pluchart, Adolph (A. A. Pliushar)

Solov'ev, Z. P. (public health official), papers, h-515

Solov'ev-Sedoi, V. P. (composer): papers, D–15; manuscript music scores, F–15

Solzhenitsyn, A. I. (writer): foundation documentation, F–5; and Russia Abroad library, F–9

Somov, A. I. (art historian), papers, H–89

Somov, K. A. (artist), papers, H–89; graphic art, H–42, H–91, H–205

Somov, M. M. (oceanologist, polar explorer), documents, H–108

Somov family (18th-c. merchants, officials), papers, E–24

Sophia (Sof'ia) Alekseevna, Princess (Tsarevna), illuminated Gospel copied by, E–28; and the *Strel'tsy,* Museum of, H–2

Sorge, Friedrich-Albert (German revolutionary, socialist), documentary collection, B–12

Sorge, Richard (intelligence officer), documents, H–10

Sorokin, Pitirim (P. A.) (SR, social philosopher, publicist), papers, e-236

Soroko-Rosinskii, V. N. (educator), papers, E–56

Sosin, Ia. V. (art restorer), papers, H–89

Spasskii, P. N. *See* Fotii (P. N. Spasskii), Archimandrite

Spegal'skii, Iu. P. (archeologist), papers, E–22

Speranskii. *See* Mikhail (Speranskii), Archpriest

Speranskii, A. D. (physiopathologist), papers, E–47

Speranskii, M. N. (literary historian), papers, E–10

Speranskii, M. M., Count (statesman), papers, G–15, g-198

Speranskii, S. B. (architect), papers, D–17

Sperantova, V. A. (actress), papers, H–44

Spesivtseva, O. A. (ballerina), papers, H–102

Spirin, I. T. (polar aviator), papers, B–6

Spitsyn, A. A. (Slavicist, archeologist), papers and photograph collection, E–22

Spontini, Gasparo (Italian composer), autographs, G–19

Sreznevskii, I. I. (Slavicist): papers, G–15; manuscript collection, G–16

Sreznevskii, V. I. (son of Sreznevskii, I. I.), manuscript collection, G–16

Stackelberg (Shtakel'berg), Counts, and Museum of Musical Instruments, H–102

Stakenschneider, A. A. *See* Shtakenshneider (Stakenschneider), A. A.

Stakenschneider, A. I. *See* Shtakenshneider (Stakenschneider), A. I.

Stakhovich, M. A. (publicist), music collection, G–7

Stalin (*pseud. of* Dzhugashvili), I. V.: Politburo records, B–12, b-264, C–1; military records, B–8; papers, B–12, b-251, C–1, c-6; NKVD/MVD "special files" addressed to, catalogue, b-13; sources for nuclear development under, a-385, a-386

Stanislavskii, A. L. (historian); memorial essays, a-308

Stanislavskii (*pseud. of* Alekseev), K. S. (theater director, actor): papers, G–8, H–42, H–43, H–102; photographs, G–6, H–46, H–47; memorial museum, H–43

Stannevich, E. I. (writer), marginalia, a-448

Starosel'skaia-Nikitina, O. A. (historian of physics), papers, E–2

Starov, I. E. (architect), drawings, G–15

Stasiulevich, M. M. (publisher), archive, E–28

Stasov, V. P. (architect), architectural drawings, B–3, E–57, H–1, H–17, H–84

Stasov, V. V. (music and art critic): papers, G–15, G–24, g-206, H–23; library, G–19; music manuscript collection, g-207

Stavisskii, B. Ia. (archeologist, Orientalist), photographs, H–88

Steblin-Kamenskii, M. I. (historian), papers, e-148

Stefan, Kh. F. (botanist), library, E–33

Steklov, V. A. (mathematician), documentary collection, E–20

Stepanova, A. O. (actress), portraits, H–102

Stieglitz (Shtiglits, Stiglits), A. L., Baron (banker, patron of the arts): art collection, H–88, h-625; library, H–89, H–94

——and Museum of Industrial Art, H–94, h-625

Stolypin, P. A. (statesman, Council of Ministers president), papers, B–3

Stone, Irving (American writer), recordings, G–4

Storozhenko, G. V. (educator), papers, D–8

Strakhov, F. A. (L. N. Tolstoi follower), papers, H–72

Strakhov, N. N. (philosopher, publicist, literary critic), book collection, G–17

Strannoliubskii, A. N. (educator), papers, G–17

Strauss, Johann (Austrian composer), autographs, E–46

Stravinskii, F. I. (singer): library, G–19; graphic art, H–102

——and Oranienbaum, H–69

Stravinskii, I. F. (Igor Stravinsky) (composer, conductor): recordings, H–45; and Oranienbaum, H–69

Strekalov, V. V. (photographer), collection of negatives, E–45

Stroev, P. M. (historian, Slavicist), manuscript collection, E–24, G–15

Stroganov, manuscript collection, g-220

Stroganov, A. S., Count (Academy of Arts president): art collection, H–89; library, G–18; ——and Stroganov Palace, H–89

Stroganov, Ia. (merchant), imperial charter, H–88

Stroganov, P. A., Count, collection, b-77

Stroganov, S. G., Count (Archeological Commission chair): papers, E–22; manuscript collection, G–16

Tatarinov, A. A. (missionary in China), papers, G–25

Tatishchev, D. P. (diplomat): papers, G–15; art collection catalogue, H–88

Tatishchev, Iu. V. (genealogist, museum curator), papers, E–24

Tatishchev, S. S. (historian), papers, B–3

Tatishchev, V. N. (historian): papers, H–1; manuscript collection, G–16; bibliography on, a-158; and chronicle studies, a-864

Tauber, V. I. (artist), children's music recordings, G–9

Tchaikovsky (Chaikovskii), M. I. (playwright), papers, H–48

Tchaikovsky, Peter I. (P. I. Chaikovskii): papers, B–7, E–46, G–7, G–19, G–22, H–23, H–45, H–48, H–102; papers, catalogues, a-135, b-172, h-322, h-338; family papers, H–48; portraits, D–16, H–102; films, catalogue, c-117; recordings, c-153, E–28; memorial museum (Klin), H–48, h-335–h-339

Tenin, B. M. (actor): library, G–8; papers and memorial apartment, G–8

Tenishev, V. N., Prince (landowner, ethnographer), Ethnographic Bureau collection, H–71, h-432–h-434

Tenisheva, M. K., Princess (wife of V. N. Tenishev, patron of the arts), H–71; graphic arts collection, H–89

Teploukhov, S. A. (archeologist), papers, H–71

Teplov, B. N. (psychologist), E–8

Terebenev, I. I. (artist), *lubok*, H–159

Terent'ev, L. N. (ethnographer), papers, E–7

Ternov, B. N. (museum director), papers, H–26

Thackeray, William (British writer), literary autographs, E–28

Thälmann, Ernst (German socialist), anti-Nazi documents, H–10

Thomon, Jean-François Thomas de (French architect), H–74; architectural drawings, G–24, H–88

Tikhanov, P. N. (bibliophile), manuscript collection, G–15

Tikhodeev, P. M. (lighting engineer), papers, H–117

Tikhomirov, M. N. (historian), chronicle studies, a-864

Tikhon (Belavin, V.), Patriarch, documents, F–12

Tikhonov, N. S. (writer, public figure), speeches, D–15

Tikhonravov, N. S. (literary scholar, archeographer), family manuscript collection, G–1

Tillo, A. A. (geodesist, cartographer), papers and library, E–26

Time, E. I. (actress), papers, D–15, G–21, H–102

Timiriazev, A. K. (son of K. A. Timiriazev), photographs by, H–167

Timiriazev, K. A. (biologist, agronomist): papers and memorial museum, H–167; Biological Museum named after, H–52

Timm, V. F. (artist), drawings, H–74

Timofeev, N. (composer, musician theorist), music collection, F–15

Timofeev-Resovskii, N. V. (biologist, geneticist), papers, E–1

Tischendorf, Konstantin (Constantin) von (archeographer), manuscript collection, G–15, g-215

Tishchenko, V. E. (chemist): papers, E–20, H–105; and Mendeleev archive, H–105

Tissé, Eduard (cameraman), films, B–11

Titov, A. A. (archeographer, Slavicist), manuscript collection, G–15

Tiuneev, V. A. (archivist), a-693

Tiutchev, F. I. (poet): papers, G–1, H–47; library, H–39; family papers, H–39; early editions, E–9

Tizengauzen (Tissenhausen), V. G. (archeologist, Orientalist), papers, E–22, E–23

Tobuzin family (gentry landowners), estate documentation, E–24

Todorovskii, A. I., General, papers, E–5

Tokarev, F. V. (military engineer): papers, b-233; documents, H–69

Tokmakov, L. (artist), autographed books, G–9

Tolbukhin, F. I., Marshal, papers, H–6

Tolmachev, M. V. (Moscow collector), and M. A. Kuzmin papers, H–98

Tolstaia, S. A. (*née* Bers) (wife of L. N. Tolstoi): papers, H–35; photographs, H–97

Tolstaia-Esenina, S. A. (granddaughter of L. N. Tolstoi), papers, H–35

Tolstaia-Popova, A. I. (granddaughter of L. N. Tolstoi), papers, H–35

Tolstikov, V. P. (archeologist), archeological reports, H–26

Tolstoi, A. N. (Alexei Tolstoy) (writer): autographs, E–9, H–99; memorial museum, H–33

Tolstoi, F. A. (senator, bibliographer), manuscript collection, G–15, G–16, g-307

Tolstoi, I. I., Count (archeologist, Academy of Arts president), numismatic collection, H–88

Tolstoi, I. L. (son of L. N. Tolstoi), papers, H–35

Tolstoi, L. L. (son of L. N. Tolstoi), papers, H–35, h-288

Tolstoi, L. N. (Leo Tolstoy), Count (writer): papers, B–7, G–21, H–33, H–35, H–47; papers, descriptions and catalogues, a-159, b-189, h-281–h-289; family papers, H–35, h-287; graphic art, D–16, E–28, e-213, H–35; recordings, E–28; films, B–11, c-100.14; documentation on followers of, H–35, H–72; library, H–35; memorial museum and archive, H–35; manuscripts relating to, g-200

Tolstoi, P. P., Count (military officer), papers, E–24

Turgenev, A. I. (historian, archeographer, Decembrist), papers, H–1

Turgenev, I. S. (writer): papers, B–7, E–28, G–1, G–2, G–15, G–21, H–33; papers, surveys and descriptions, b-187, b-189.1, e-212, e-213, g-41, g-75, g-201, h-267; drawings, E–28; photographs, H–35; films, c-100.15; early editions, E–9

Turgenev, N. I. (economist, Decembrist): papers, H–1; autographs, H–33

Turgenev family, library, G–2, H–95

Turgeneva, A. A. (wife of Andrei Belyi), papers, H–34

Turkovskii, S. Ia. (sculptor), archive, E–45

Turovskii, Kirill. *See* Kirill Turovskii

Turner, G. I. (physician), papers, G–25, H–75

Tushinskii, M. D. (physician), papers, H–110

Tvardovskii, A. T. (poet, *Novyi Mir* editor): manuscripts, H–96; films, c-100.13

Tverskoi, L. M. (sculptor), archive, E–45

Twain, Mark (*pseud.* of Samuel L. Clemens) (American writer), autographs, E–28

Tynianov, Iu. N. (literary scholar, writer), papers, B–7

Uglov, F. G. (surgeon), papers, D–17

Ukhtomskii, A. A. (physiologist), papers, E–20

Ukhtomskii, A. G. (artist, engraver), engravings, H–72

Ukhtomskii, A. V., 1905 Revolution documents, H–4

Ukhtomskii, D. V. (architect), architectural drawings, H–17

Ukhtomskii, E. E. (ethnographer), book collection, E–25

Ukhtomskii, K. A. (artist), watercolors, H–88

Ul'ianinskii, D. V. (bibliographer), library catalogue, a-847

Ul'ianinskii, N. Iu., newspaper clippings collection, G–1

Ul'ianov, M. (actor), recordings, c-132

Ul'ianov, N. P. (artist), drawings, H–49

Ul'ianov, V. I. *See* Lenin (*pseud. of* Ul'ianov), V. I.

Ulanova, G. S. (ballerina), films, c-115.23

Undol'skii, V. M. (bibliographer), manuscript collection, G–1, g-19

Ureklian, L. A., theater graphics collection, G–6

Urusov, A. I. (literary scholar), archive, a-605

Ushakov, F. F., Admiral, paintings of, H–74

Ushakov, N. I. (photographer), photographs, H–28

Ushin, A. A. (artist), graphic art, H–89

Ushinskii, K. D. (educator), family photograph collection, E–56

Uskov, N. V. (physician), papers, E–47

Usman Efendi (Orientalist, philologist), library, E–4

Uspenskii, A. I. (historian, ethnographer), library, G–26

Uspenskii, D. I. (historian, ethnographer), papers, H–17, h-165

Uspenskii, E. N. (writer), autographed books, G–9

Uspenskii, K. A. *See* Porfirii (K. A. Uspenskii), Archimandrite

Uspenskii, M. I. (historian, ethnographer): manuscript collection, G–16; library, G–26

Uspenskii, V. M. (Orientalist, diplomat), Oriental manuscript collection, G–17

Ustinov, N. (artist), autographed books, G–9

Ustinov, Peter (British actor, director), Benois family documents, H–83

Utamaro, Kitagawa (Japanese artist, engraver), engravings, H–29

Utesov, L. O. (singer, musician), films, c-115.24

Utkin, B. (news photographer), photographs, H–65

Utkin, N. I. (artist, engraver), engravings, G–18, H–72, H–89, H–90

Utkin, V. P. (artist), film graphic art, H–50

Uvarov, A. S., Count (archeologist, historian, GIM founder): Slavic manuscript collection, H–1, h-27–h-30; library, G–3

Vaganova, A. Ia. (ballerina, educator), papers, H–102

Vagner, V. A. (biologist), photograph collection, H–53

Vail', G. M. (news correspondent), photograph collection, H–6

Vakhrameev (Vakhromeev), I. A. (Iaroslavl merchant, bookseller, historical document collector), manuscript collection, H–1, h-26

Vakhtangov, E. B. (theater director), papers, H–42

Vaksel', O. A. (actress), portraits, H–92

Vaks, I. A., art library collection, H–94

Vaksel', P. L. (music critic), manuscript collection, G–15

Val'dgauer, O. F. *See* Waldhauer, Oscar

Val'kov family (Pinega peasants), library, E–28

Valeriani, Giuseppe (Italian stage designer), stage designs, H–102

Valk, S. N. (historian): papers, E–24, e-147; memorial essays, a-313

Vallin de la Mothe, Jean-Baptiste (French architect), H–90

Vannikov, B. L. (minister of armaments), papers, H–54

Varlamov, A. E. (composer), music scores, G–19

Vasenko, A. B. (aeronautic engineer), documents and photographs, H–70

Vasil'chikov family (landed gentry, military commanders, government officials), archive, B–3

Vasil'ev, A. I. (18th-c. physician), and medical library, G–25

Vasil'ev, A. I. (historian), papers, E–24, e-148

Vasil'ev, A.V. (architect), drawings, D–21

Vasil'ev, B. D. (architect), papers, D–17

Vasil'ev, L. L. (linguist), papers, E–10

Vasil'ev, N. M. (Moscow Oblast administrator), papers, D–8

Vasil'ev, N. V. (revolutionary, socialist), papers, G–15

Vasil'ev, P. V. (actor), papers, h-303

Vasil'ev, V. I. (photographer), MGU photographs, F–3

Vasil'ev, V. P. (Orientalist, Sinologist), manuscript collection and Chinese maps, G–17

Vasilenko, S. N. (composer), papers, H–45

Vasilevich, G. M. (ethnographer), papers, E–25

Vasilevskii, A. M., Marshal, autographed books, H–16

Vasilii III, Grand Prince of Muscovy, and Novodevichii Monastery, H–2

Vasilii (K. Krivoshin), Archbishop of Brussels, library, G–26

Vasilii Velikii. See Basil (Basilius), Saint (the Great)

Vasnetsov, A. M. (artist): papers, H–23, h-43; theater program designs, H–42; memorial museum, H–5, H–23

Vasnetsov, V. M. (artist): papers, B–7, H–19, H–23, H–25, H–89; papers, survey, b-188; family papers, H–25; memorial museum, H–5, H–23, H–25, h-205

Vatagin, V. A. (artist), drawings, H–52

Vatsetis, I. I. (military commander), papers, B–8

Vatsuro, V. E. (theater historian), manuscript, E–46

Vaulin, I. I. (artist), graphic plates, H–97

Vavilov, N. I. (botanist, geneticist): papers, D–17, E–18, E–20, E–26; memorial museum, E-18

Vavilov, S. I. (physicist, Academy of Sciences president): papers, D–17, E–1; Institute of Physics Problems named after, E–12

Vdovenko, B. E. (news correspondent), photograph collection, H–6

Veber family (historians), papers, H–5

Vecheslova, T. M. (ballerina), papers, H–102

Vedernikov, A. S. (artist), lithographs, H–89

Veinberg, B. P. (chemist), papers, H–105

Veksler, V. I. (physicist, mathematician), papers, survey, b-213

Vel'iaminov-Zernov family (landowners), estate documentation, E–24

Velichko, K. I. (military engineer), papers, H–73

Velichko, V. V. (writer), library, g-80

Veligonova, E. F., Odessa defense photograph collection, H–16

Venetsianov, A. G. (artist): engraved cariacatures, H–89; *lubok*, H–159; photographs, H–90

Venevitinov, D. V. (poet, literary critic), portraits, H–34

Venevitinov family (landowners, statesmen, cultural leaders), archive, G–1

Vengerov, S. A. (literary historian): papers, C–18, E–28; library, E–28

Vengerov, V. Ia. (film director), films, C–24

Venck, Karl Friedrich Christian. *See* Wenck (Venck), Karl Friedrich Christian

Verdi, Giuseppe (Italian composer), autographs, E–46, G–1

Vereiskii, G. S. (artist): papers, G–15; library, G–18; graphic art, G–18, H–88, H–91

Veresaev (*pseud. of* Smidovich), V. V. (physician, writer), manuscripts, G–6, H–95

Vereshchagin, A. P. (artist), papers, H–11

Vereshchagin, V. V. (artist), papers, H–89

Verkhovskii, Iu. N. (poet, literary scholar), correspondence with A. Blok, H–99

Verkhovskii, V. N. (chemist, educator), papers, E–56

Vermorel, Auguste Jean-Marie (French socialist), papers, B–12

Vernadskii, V. I. (bio-geochemist, philosopher of science): papers, D–17, E–1, E–17; library, E–2; memorial museum, E–17

——Commission on the History of Science, E–21

Verstovskii, A. N. (composer, director): manuscript music scores, G–7, G–22; portraits, H–102

Vertinskii, A. N. (singer, musician), recordings, B–10

Vertov, Dziga (*pseud. of* D. A. Kaufman) (film director): papers, C–16; films, B–11

Veselago, F. F. (naval historian), papers, G–2

Veselovski, A. N. (literary historian): manuscripts, e-212; documentary collection, E–28

Veselovskii, B. K. (art historian), papers, H–88

Veselovskii, I. N. (historian of mathematics and mechanics), papers, E–2

Veselovskii, N. I. (Orientalist): papers, E–22; collection, H–88

Veselovskii, S. B. (historian): papers, E–1; historical documentary collection, E–24; genealogical studies, a-556

Vesnin brothers (architects): papers, H–28; architectural drawings, h-240

Vetrogonskii, V. A. (artist), engravings, G–18, H–89

Vezenberg (Wesenberg) (photographer), photographs, H–65

Viardo, Pauline (French singer, musician), documents, E–46

Viazemskii, P. A., Prince (poet): papers, H–34, H–95; Pushkin autograph, G–22

Viazemskii, S. M., SPb historical collection, D–15

Viazemskii family, Princes (landowners, government officials, cultural leaders), archive, B–7

Vidov, V. (architect), architectural drawings, H–84

Viel'gorskii, M. Iu. (composer): papers, E–28, G–19; photographs, H–90

Zakharov, G. F. (artist), graphic art, H–89

Zakharov, N. N. (art historian), papers, H–17

Zakharov, P. I. (Orientalist), Oriental manuscript collection, G–17

Zaleman, K. G. (philologist, Orientalist), g-338, g-340

Zalesskii, A. M. (electrical engineer), papers, H–117

Zalka, Mate (*pseud. of* Bela Frankl) (Hungarian writer), papers, H–37

Zalmanov, A. S. (physician), papers, G–25

Zalomov, Aleksandr and Anna Kirillovna, "hero" workers, H–124

Załuski (Zalusskii) brothers, Counts (Polish noble landowners, bishops, statesmen): library collection, G–15; manuscript collection, g-222, g-223, g-237, g-239

Zamiatin, E. I. (writer), papers, E–9, g-159

Zamiatin, S. N. (archeologist), papers, E–22, E–25

Zamoiskii, P. I. (writer), papers, E–9

Zankov, L. V. (psychologist), papers, E–42

Zasulich, V. I. (revolutionary): papers, G–15; microfilmed papers, b-294

Zavadovskii, B. M. (biologist), papers, H–52

Zavalishin, D. I. (Decembrist, memoirist), papers, H–1

Zavarov, A. I. (architect), papers, survey, b-213

Zavarzin, A. A. (hystologist, embryologist), papers, E–47

Zavoiskii, E. K. (nuclear physicist), papers, H–54

Zavoloko, I. N., collection, E–28

Zdekauer, N. F. (physician), papers, G–25

Zdobnov, N. V. (bibliographer), papers, C–18

Zel'dovich, Ia. B. (physicist), papers, H–54

Zelikin, S., films, c-107.19

Zelinskii, N. D. (chemist): papers, b-213, E–1, E–15; library, E–15; memorial museum, E–15

Zemenkov, B. S. (historian of Moscow), papers, H–5

Zemliachka (*pseud. of* Samoilova), R. S. (revolutionary), papers, H–4

Zemtsov, M. G. (architect), and Peterhof palaces, H–82

Zen'kovich, V. V. (artist), graphic art, H–89

Zernov, N. M. (religious philosopher), papers and photographs, G–4

Zetkin, Clara (German socialist), papers, B–12

Zhaba, A. D. *See* Jaba, August

Zharov, M. I. (actor), films, c-107.18

Zhdanov, A. A. (Soviet CP leader): papers, B–12; microfilmed papers, b-294; CP memoirs collection, D–14

Zhdanov, I. N. (literary historian), manuscript collection, G–16

Zhdanov, V. A. (literary scholar), papers, H–35

Zhebelev, S. A. (historian, archeologist), library, E–24

Zheliabuzhskii, Iu. A. (photographer), photograph collection, E–9

Zherebov, L. P. (educator), papers, B–9

Zheverzheev, L. I. (art historian), library, H–102

Zhiliardi, D. I. *See* Gilardi, Domenico (Zhiliardi, D. I.)

Zhirinovskii, V. V. (politician), LDPR documentation, photographs, D–4, F–3

Zhirmunskii, V. M. (philologist), folklore collection, E–28

Zholtovskii, I. V. (architect), architectural drawings, H–28

Zhukov, G. K., Marshal: papers, B–8, C–1, H–6; audiovisual sources, D–4

Zhukov, P. F. (government official, bibliophile), book collection, G–17, g-344

Zhukov, P. S. (photographer): photographs, D–16; photographs, survey, d-45

Zhukovskii, N. E. (aerodynamics engineer, designer), papers, memorial museum, H–175

Zhukovskii, V. A. (poet): papers, E–28, G–1, H–34, H–47, H–88, H–95; drawings, E–28

Zhuravlev, D. N. (actor), films, c-100.16

Zhuravlev family (industrialists), papers, H–1

Zhuravskii, D. I. (engineer, designer), papers, H–112

Zhurbin, A. B. (composer), children's song recordings, G–9

Ziloti, A. I. (pianist, composer), papers and library, E–46

Zimin, A. A. (historian), memorial essays, a-303

Zimmerman, Iu. G. (publisher), publishing house papers, H–45

Zinchenko, I. K., manuscript collection, G–15

Zinov'ev (*pseud. of* Radomysl'skii), G. E. (revolutionary, CP leader), papers, B–12, b-26, b-251, C–1

Zivert, L. L. (photographer), photograph collection, H–65

Zlinchenko, K. P. (revolutionary, literary critic), papers, b-26

Zograf, A. N. (numismatist), papers, H–88

Zola, Émile (French writer), autographs, E–28

Zolotarev, Karp (early Rus' painter), documentary film, H–27

Zonaras, Ioann (Byzantium historian), chronicle manuscripts, G–16

Zoshchenko, M. M. (writer): papers, E–28, H–100; memorial museum, H–97, H–100

Zubalov, I. K., ceramic collection, H–21

Zubkov, I. M. (photographer), photographs, H–65

Zubov, A. F. (artist, engraver), engravings, H–72, H–85

Zubov, P. A., Count, General (governor), papers, H–1

Zubov, V. A., Count, General-in-Chief, papers, H–1

Zubov, V. P., Count (landowner, friend of A. S. Pushkin), library, E–46

Zui, Iona, Deacon, manuscript, H–18

Zurov, L. (secretary of I. A. Bunin), archive, F–9

Zykov, I. G. (populist educator), papers, H–96

Subject Index

The index that follows combines entries for geographic place names, administrative-territorial divisions, names of agencies, institutions, and organizations, as well as major subject entries. Names of individual persons appear only if they are part of an official institutional name or organization (i.e. an institution named after or "in honor of" an individual—*imeni* in Russian), but otherwise they will be found in the separate index of personal names. Papers or manuscripts of named individuals will appear in that name index (see pp. 1321). Alphabetization follows a word-by-word principle.

Archival repositories are usually cited under the key word of their name, but many that have no subject-oriented key word and that are familiarly known by their acronym (especially the major federal archives under Rosarkhiv) are listed under their current acronym, or at least cross-referenced accordingly. Repository numbers in boldface indicate principal entries for current repositories describing their holdings.

Cross-references are provided for alternate forms of names or citations, but in some cases, where it is shorter to repeat one or two numbered entries than to cross-reference the entire name, and for the convenience of users, they will be repeated. When the subsidiary reference is to a current repository, often the main repository number is repeated in the cross-reference, but subentries will be found only under the full entry.

Subentries are generally arranged in alphabetical order, except when a logical ordering principle supersedes. For example, under repository entries, general coverage—usually under the entry "holdings" or "history and holdings"—and "guides and surveys" precede the alphabetical sequence. Under subject or geographic categories, entries for "bibliographies," "directories," or similar general reference aids precede the alphabetical sequence. Where applicable, chronological breakdowns, usually under the heading "*by period*," precede other alphabetized subentries. Sometimes other hierarchical entries take precedence over strict alphabetical order, for example, major bodies of holdings or records from a particular agency usually precede more specialized subentries.

Specialized references provided within general large subject categories should be seen as samples, rather than an exhaustive coverage of holdings in all repositories, and are usually given only if they are specifically referenced in the account of "holdings" within the given repository.

While efforts have been made to include references to all previous repository names, as a space-saving expedient, contingent institutional names closely resembling one another, and with references only to the same current repository number, have been combined, and full names are not always given here. Readers should refer to the acronym correlation table for a complete listing of previous names and acronyms with cross-references to their present institutional form. Usually subentries such as "history," "holdings," and "bibliographies" are provided only for current repositories.

References are to the numbered repository entries (preceded by a capital letter indicating the part of the volume in which they are located) rather than to pages. Bibliographic entries for reference aids appear with lower-case letters (corresponding to the lettered volume parts) preceding their numbers.

butterfly collection, Nabokov Museum, H–101
Byloe (journal), editorial records, H–33
Byzantine sources
  bibliography, catalogues, and surveys, a-180, a-210–a-219
  Moscow holdings, B–2, G–1, G–2, H–1
  personal papers of Byzantinists, a-123, G–17, G–26
  SPb holdings
    GRM, H–89
    Hermitage, H–88, h-594, h-596
    IIMK, E–22
    libraries, G–15—G–18
    PFA RAN, E–20
  See also Greek manuscripts
Byzantine Studies Commission, records, E–20

Cabinet of Ministers (USSR), records, B–1, C–1
  Archival Administration (Glavarkhiv) under, B–0
Cable, Northern (Sevkabel'), Historical Museum, documentary holdings, H–124, h-700
Cadet Corps, museums, materials from, H–73, h-489
Cadet Party, records, G–15
  V. I. Vernadskii documents, E–17
Cairo Geniza manuscripts, G–15, g-250
Calculator Factory, V. D. Kalmykov, Museum, H–177
Canada, sources relating to
  documents from, E–24
  Dukhobor sources, H–72, h-457
  folklore materials, E–28
canal construction, sources relating to, G–24
  Moscow, H–170
  See also transportation, sources relating to
Cancer Biochemistry, Laboratory of (RAMN), records, E–40
Capella, M. I. Glinka, records, D–15
Capella and Orchestra, Imperial Court, music manuscripts, E–46, g-209
Cappadocia, manuscripts from, H–26
captured records, trophy archives from former TsKhIDK, B–8A, b-211–b-218. *See also* trophy archives, books, and mansucripts, WWII
caricatures, political, B–12; English drawings, H–88
Carpatho-Ruthenian manuscripts, g-241
Carpenter's Workshop, Abramtsevo, documentation, H–19
Carriage Museum, Imperial
  photographs, H–88
  transfers to Hermitage, H–88
Carter-Brezhnev Project, Cold War sources, a-369
Cartographic and Geodesic Engineers, Moscow Institute of, Museum, H–172
Cartographic and Geodesic Investigations, Central Bureau (TsBKGI GUKSK), C–14

cartographic materials
  bibliographies and surveys, a-583–a-599, a-843, a-849, C–18
  borderlands, C–3, H–15
  Central Asia, E–21
  Far East, h-44, G–1, G–17
  geological, C–12, H–55, H–106, H–109
  GOELRO, H–117
  library collections, C–18, G–1, G–2, G–15, G–16, G–24, g-291, g-313
  linguistic/dialectological, E–10
  military, B–4, B–8, C–4, H–6, H–9, H–12, H–73, H–77
  Moscow region, D–8, H–5, H–9, h-45
    Kremlin buildings, H–17
  museum collections
    GIM, H–1, h-7, h-8, h-44
    GMII, H–26, h-222
    GNIMA, H–28, h-243
    Muzei MIIGAiK, H–172
    Nekrasov associations, H–96
    Pavlovsk, H–81
  naval, a-585, B–5, b-152, C–5, H–74
  polar research, H–108
  pre-1917, B–3, E–5, G–1, G–3, G–15, H–1
    AVPRI holdings, C–3
  RAN collections
    ARAN, E–1
    BAN, G–16, g-291, g-313
    IRLI/PD expedition maps, E–28
    Kunstkamera/ MAE, E–25
    PFA RAN, E–20
    RGO, E–26
  Siberia, e-99, h-44
  SPb/Leningrad Oblast, D–13, D–17, D–18, D–21, H–65
  transport and communications, G–24, H–111, H–114
  TsKGF, C–14
  See also geography, sources relating to; Land-Survey Archive
Cartographic Service of the Navy, Central, Archive of, B–5
Cartographic-Geodesic Fond, Central (TsKGF), history and holdings, **C–14**
  Division of Geodesic Fonds, **C–14**
Cartography, Division of, State Historical Museum (GIM), **H–1**, h-7, h-8, h-44
Cartography and Geodesy, Institute/Moscow State University of, Museum, **H–172**
Caspian Sea, Russian naval records, B–5
Catherine II, "Cabinet" (office) records, B–2
Catholic Church of St. Catherine, library and materials from, H–72

cosmonauts, materials relating to, B–9, H–4, H–7,
    H–58—H–60, H–174
  photographs and documentary films, B–11
  See also space exploration, sources relating to;
    space museums
Cosmonauts, Iu. A. Gagarin Russian State Scientific
  Research and Testing Center for Training
  documentation, H–58
  Museum (Muzei TsPK), **H–174**
Cossack records, RGVIA, b-130
Cossack Troops, Main Administration for, records,
  B–4
costume designs, theater. *See* theater, sources relating to
Council of Ministers (pre-1917), records, B–3;
  publications, b-114
Council of Ministers (USSR/RSFSR)
  records, B–1
  General Division (USSR) records, C–1
  Main Administration of Geodesy and
    Cartography, TsKGF, C–14
  Main Archival Administration of (GAU/
    Glavarkhiv), under, B–0
  religious cults, b-21
  security/intelligence records, C–6, C–7
  State Committee for Cinematography (Goskino)
    under, C–16
Council of People's Commissars (SNK/Sovnarkom
  RSFSR/SSSR)
  records, B–1, B–12
  institutes under, E–47
  Northern Oblast, records, D–12
  regulations of, C–18
Counterintelligence (military), Directorate of
  (SMERSH), records, C–7
Counterintelligence Service, Federal (FSK, *now*
  FSB), Central Archive (TsA FSB RF), C–6;
  archival materials from, H–28
Courland, Duchy of, sources relating to
  diplomatic materials (pre-1800), b-57, c-20
  library and manuscript collection, G–16, g-298
Court (Imperial) Archive, records, B–2, b-51–b-53
Court (Imperial) Chancellery, Main, records, B–2
court (Imperial), estate records, B–2, B–3
  photographs, B–11
Court, Imperial, Ministry of, records, B–3
  Moscow Division, General Archive, B–2
Court Orchestra (Imperial), Library, G–20
court (legal) records. *See* legal records
CPSU/CP, All-Russian. *See* Communist Party of the
  Soviet Union (CPSU)
Cracow Union of Assistance for Political Prisoners,
  records, b-278
Credit Society, Moscow City, records, D–2

Crimea, sources relating to
  archeological records, E–3, E–22
  A. P. Chekhov Museum, G–1
  folklore materials, E–22, E–28
  manuscripts from Simferopol, G–1
  photographs, E–3, H–1
  Swedish relations documentation , e-141
Crimean (Simferopol) Pedagogical Institute, Slavic
  manuscripts, G–1
Crimean Tatars, *samizdat*, microfiche collection, a-421.4
Crimean War, sources relating to, G–15, H–74
  naval documentation, B–5
  photographs, B–11
Criminal Affairs, Special Chancellery records, B–3
Criminal Division, Ministry of Justice, records, B–1
Croatia, folklore materials, E–28
Crown (Polish) Metrica, b-60–b-61, b-63, b-65
Crystallography, A. V. Shubnikov Institute of
  (IKAN) (AN SSSR/RAN), archival holdings,
  E–13
  N. V. Belov Memorial Cabinet-Museum, **E–13**
Cuba, sources relating to
  revolutionary documentation, H–4, h-69
  1962 crisis, a-371
  technical documentation, B–9, D–17
Cultural Fund, Russian, Archive-Library of,
  holdings, **F–8**, f-10–f-12.2
  Russian émigré records, f-11–f-12.1
Cultural Relations Abroad, All-Union Society for
  (VOKS), records, B–1
  photographs, B–11, H–4
Cultural Treasures, Commission for Control of
  Export Abroad, records, D–15
Culture, Committee on, Administration of St.
  Petersburg
  library under, G–21
  museums under, H–65, H–68, H–76, H–77,
    H–79—H–87, H–97—H–100, H–102, H–103,
    H–113, H–126
Culture, Committee on, Moscow Government,
  library-fond under, F–9
  museums under, H–5, H–9, H–11, H–20—H–22,
    H–30, H–34, H–36—H–38, H–49,
    H–52, H–53, H–59, H–60, H–158—H–162
Culture, Committee on, Moscow Oblast, museums
  under, H–39—H–41, H–48
Culture, M. Gor'kii Palace of, photographs, D–4
Culture, and Life, Archive of the National Economy,
  B–0
Culture, Main Administration for, Executive
  Committee, records
  Leningrad, D–15
  Moscow D–6

North Sea
    British-Soviet naval operations, records, C–5
    Navy, documentation, H–74
Northern Fleet, documentation, B–5, b-143, C–5, H–74
Northern (Leningrad) Front. *See* Leningrad Blockade
    (WWII); World War II, sources relating to
Northern Oblast, records, D–12
    Provisional Government, records, B–1
    Union of Communes of, records, D–12
Northern Russia (Far North)
    Arctic research materials, H–108, H–113
    folklore materials, E–28
    railroad documentation, H–113
Northern War (1700–1721), sources relating to,
    G–15, h-483
    engravings, H–89
    naval documentation, B–5
Northwestern Railroad, sources relating to, H–112
Norway, sources relating to
    polar research documentation, H–108
    trophy archives (WW2) from, b-213
Nöteborg (Swedish). *See* Shlissel'burg
Novaia Ladoga, naval yard, records, B–5
Novgorod
    early archives and manuscripts, a-196, a-327,
        B–2, b-74, E–24, E–28, E–56, G–15
    birchbark charters, H–1, h-34–h-35
    cartographic materials, a-596
    chronicle sources, G–16, H–1
    church records, E–24
    church restoration records, E–22, H–89
    construction records, G–24
    graphic materials, D–21
"Novgorod Chronicle," First, Fourth, manuscript, H–1
Novgorod Guberniia
    archival commission, bibliography, a-838
    cartographic materials, a-596, a-597
    Lutheran parish registers, b-112
Novgorod Oblast, ZAGS records, D–20
Novgorod Railroad, sources relating to, H–112
Novodevichii Monastery (Convent) Museum (under
    GIM), history and holdings, **H–2**, h-49–h-51
    cemetery records, H–2, h-51
    library and manuscript collection, H–1, H–2
Novoe vremia (journal), editorial records, G–15
Novo-Lipetsk Metallurgical Combine, films, B–11, C–5
Novorossiia, demographic documentation, a-572
Novorossiisk, naval base, records, C–5
Novosibirsk
    historical photographs, H–1
    wartime evacuation to, H–73, H–111
Novosibirsk Young Audience Theater, records, H–44
Novospasskii Monastery, manuscript collection, h-18

Novosti Press Agency (APN/RIA)
    records, B–1, B–9
    photographs, C–17
Novovoronezh, atomic power station,
    documentation, E–41
Novyi mir (journal), editorial records, E–9
nuclear energy. *See* atomic energy, sources relating to
nuclear physics. *See* physics, sources relating to, nuclear
Nuclear Physics, (B. P. Konstantinov) Petersburg
    Institute of (PIIaF RAN—*earlier* LIIaFAN
    SSSR), archival holdings, **E–30**
Numismatic Society, Moscow, records, H–1
numismatics, sources relating to, B–3
    museum collections, H–1, H–90, H–117, H–150
    Numismatics Division of, State Hermitage, H–88,
        h-597
    Orientalia collections, E–23
    RAN holdings, E–22, E–24, E–26
Nuremberg, International Tribunal, records, B–1,
    C–2

oblast archives
    KGB records, D–9, D–19
    Leningrad/SPb, D–012, D–18
    history, D–13, D–18, d-30
    Moscow, D–08, D–8
    ZAGS archive, D–11, D–20
    See also individual archives
Obninsk (Kaluzhskaia Oblast), State Fond of Data on
    Environmental Conditions (Gosfond), **C–13**
Obraztsov, V. N., Leningrad Institute of Railroad
    Transport Engineers, Library (Biblioteka LIIZhT,
    now NTB PGUPS), G–24, g-370–g-372
Obvodnoi kanal (journal), F–5
Occupied Eastern Territories, Nazi Ministry for,
    records, B–8A
oceanography, sources relating to, E–1, E–26
    scientific-technical documentation, D–17
October Days (1993), sources relating to, g-106
October Railroad, records, D–12
    Central Museum of (TsMOZhD), archival
        holdings, **H–112**, h-681
    trade-union records, F–14
October Revolution, sources relating to, B–1, B–12,
    H–1, H–4, H–66
    bibliography and surveys, a-268, a-364, h-61, h-67
    films and photographs, B–11, b-258, H–5, H–66,
        H–88, h-420–h-422
        TV films, c-92, c-94, c-95
    handbills, catalogues, h-76, h-76.1, h-423
    military documentation, B–8
    Military-Revolutionary Committees (VRK),
        records, B–1

Paris
- Benois family papers from, H–83
- diplomatic documentation (pre-1917), C–3
- Russian ballet exhibit, h-646
  - ballet photographs, G–8
- Russian émigré literary materials from, F–9
- Turgenev Library records, B–1
- *See also* France, sources relating to

Paris Commune, sources relating to, B–12, G–15; newspapers and leaflets, G–15, g-265

Paris Garnier, Opéra de, Russian ballet exhibit, h-646

parish registers, b-112, C–011, H–22, H–72
- surveys and source studies, a-547, a-549, a-552A, a-552B, a-559, a-560
- German, a-539, b-112
- Kremlin churches, H–17
- microfilmed records, a-559, a-560
- Moscow/ Moscow Oblast, D–2, D–8, D–10, D–11
  - Kolomenskoe and D'iakovo region, H–20
- SPb, D–13
  - card catalogues, D–13
  - TsGA transfers, D–20
  - TsGIA SPb transfers, D–20
- *See also* genealogy, sources relating to; ZAGS, archives

Partiinaia zhizn' (journal), editorial records, D–3

partisan movement (WWII), documentation, B–8, H–6, H–8, H–65
- Leningrad Headquarters, D–14
- Leningrad Oblast, H–76
- Minsk and Polessia Oblasts, H–4

Party Archive, Central, of the Institute of Marx, Engels, Lenin, and Stalin (TsPA IMELS), B–12

Party Archive, Unified, Leningrad Division (LEPA), D–14

Party Archive of the Institute of Party History of the Leningrad Oblast Committee of the CPSU [*earlier* VKP(b)] (LPA), D–14

Party Archive of the Institute of Party History of the Moscow City Committee, and the Moscow (Oblast) Committee of the CPSU [*earlier* VKP(b)] (MPA), D–3

Party archives. *See* Communist Party of the Soviet Union (CPSU), archives and records, *and individual archives*

Pashkov Palace, and GBL/RGB, manuscript collections, G–1

Pashto manuscripts, E–23, e-107

Pasternak, B. L., House-Museum, and GLM, H–33

patent documentation, B–9, b-233

Patent Library, Technical, All-Union/ Russian State, records, B–9

Pathé Brothers, cinema society, films, B–11

Patriarchate (Russian Orthodox Church), Moscow, Archive, F–12

Moscow Theological Academy (MDA) under, **G–11**, g-137–g-139

St. Petersburg Eparchial Administration of
- Archive of the SPb Metropolitanate, **F–20**
- Library of the SPb Theological Academy, **G–26**

sound recordings collection, B–10

Synodal Library under, **G–10**

See also Orthodox Church (Russian), sources relating to

Patriarchial Library. *See* Synodal Library of the Moscow Patriarchate, **G–10**

Patriarchial Palace, archive, H–17

Patriotic War (1812). *See* Napoleonic Wars

Patriotic War of 1812, Museum of, in Borodino Station, H–12

Patriotic War, Great. *See* World War II (Great Patriotic War), sources relating to

Patriotic War, Great (World War II), Central Museum (1941–1945), history and holdings, **H–8**

Patrons and Philanthropists, Russian, Museum of, holdings, **H–152**

Paul I, Emperor, Cabinet (office) of, records, B–2

Paustovskii, K. G., (Moscow) Literary Museum Center, holdings, **H–162**

Pavlov, I. P., Institute of Evolutionary Physiology and Pathology of Nervous Functions, E–32

Pavlov, I. P., Museum Laboratory, and NIIEM Museum, E–47

Pavlov, I. P., Physiological Institute/ Institute of Physiology (IF AN SSSR/RAN), archival holdings, **E–32**
- Pavlov Memorial Apartment-Museum, **E–32**
- Pavlovo branch, E–32

Pavlov, I. P., Physiological Society, records, E–1

Pavlovsk Palace-Museum/ State Museum-Preserve, archival and library holdings, **H–81**, h-535–h-541
- architectural drawings, H–22
- documentary collection, D–13
- Gatchina holdings from, H–79
- restoration films, D–21

Pavlovsk Railway Station Orchestra, music collection, G–20

Pavlovsk Town Administration, records, H–81

Pavlovskii Posad Worsted Mill, post-1917, records, D–8

Peace, International Association of Funds for/ Soviet Fund for, "Sud'ba" World War II database, H–8

Peace, Soviet Committee for Defense of, documentation, B–1, H–7

Peasant Affairs, Main Committee on, records, B–3

Peasant Affairs, St. Petersburg Guberniia Administration, records, D–13

Writers' Council, Moscow, archive, H–33
writers' societies, records, D–15, E–9, E–28, G–1,
    G–6, G–15, H–33, H–95, h-269. *See also*
    literature, Russian, sources relating to; *and*
    individual societies
writers' unions, records, B–7, D–15, E–9, F–2. *See*
    also literature, Russian, sources relating to
Writers' Unions, International Association of
    (MSPS), Archive, F–2
Written Texts, Early, Society of Friends of,
    manuscripts from, G–15

xylographs (wood-block prints)
    Chinese, E–23, e-85, e-88, G–1, G–15, g-255,
        H–72, h-467, h-468
    Japanese, E–23, e-99
    Mongolian, e-104–e-106, h-465
    Oriental, E–23, e-103, e-114, e-115, G–17

Yale University Press, Russian documentary series,
    a-877
Yalta
    A. P. Chekhov Museum, G–1, H–97
    film studio photographs, H–50
Yalta Conference, documentation, C–2
Yasenevo. *See* Iasenevo
Yasnaya Poliana (Tula Oblast), Tolstoi Estate
    Museum, H–35
    photographs, H–47
Yiddish manuscripts, E–23
    Yiddish drama, SPb collection, G–21
YIVO (New York City), Archive, E–52
    Project Judaica, archival database, a-531–a-533.1
YMCA-Press (Paris), Russian émigré materials
    from, F–9
Young Audience Theaters, records, H–44
youth festivals, records, B–12A
Youth International, Communist (KIM), records,
    B–12
Youth League (*Soiuz molodezhi*), records in GRM,
    H–89
Youth League, All-Union Communist (Komsomol).
    See Komsomol (All-Union Leninist
    Communist Youth League) (VLKSM)
Youth Organizations, Center for Preservation of
    Records of (TsKhDMO). *See* Socio-Political
    History, Russian State Archive of (RGASPI—
    earlier RTsKhIDNI/TsPA), holdings from
    former TsKhDMO (Komsomol), **B–12A**
Youth Organizations of the USSR, Committee for
    Affairs of, records, B–12A
Youth Theater of the Lithuanian SSR, State, records,
    H–44

Yugoslavia, sources relating to, e-212, H–4
    literary manuscripts, e-212
    trophy archives from, B–1, B–7, C–3

Zachat'evskii Monastery (Convent), documentation,
    H–2
Zagorsk. *See* Sergiev Posad (*Soviet-period name*
    Zagorsk)
Zagorsk (Sergiev Posad) Historico-Art Museum-
    Preserve, H–18, h-169–h-175
ZAGS (Registration of Vital Statistics), archives,
    C–011, c-50–c-53
    Moscow, **D–10**, **D–11**
    St. Petersburg, **D–20**
Zakharkovo (village), materials relating to, H–22
Zaporizhian Sich, "Koshevoi" archive, E–24
Zaraisk, TsGAMO Branch, D–08, D–8
Zaraisk *uezd*, archival materials from, D–8
Zariad'e (Moscow raion), archeological expedition
    films, E–3
Zariad'e (Romanov Boyars Home), museum under
    GIM, H–1
Zelinskii, N. D., Institute of Organic Chemistry
    (IOKh AN SSSR/RAN), holdings, **E–15**
    records, E–1
    Zelinskii Memorial Cabinet-Museum, **E–15**
Zemlia ("Land") (journal), editorial records, H–33
Zemlia sovetskaia (journal), editorial records,
    E–28
"Zhanr" Film Studio, history, C–20
Zhdanov, A. A., Leningrad State University (LGU),
    E–55, G–17, H–105
Zhirinovskii, V. V., Liberal-Democratic Party of,
    documentary materials, F–3
    photographs, D–4
Zhostovo Factory of Decorative Designs, post-1917
    records, D–8
Zhuk, S. Ia., All–Union Scientific Research,
    Planning and Prospecting Institute for
    Hydrotechnical Construction (Gidroproekt),
    records, B–9
Zhukovka (village, Moscow Oblast), and Kuntsevo
    Regional Studies Museum, H–153
Zhukovskii, N. E., Air Force Engineering Academy,
    documentation, H–58
Zhukovskii, N. E., Scientific-Memorial Museum,
    H–175
    sound recordings collection, B–10
    Zhukovskii House-Museum branch, **H–175**
        S. P. Korolev papers, H–60
ZIL Automobile Factory, records, D–1
    photographs, D–4
Ziloti, A. I., Orchestra, music collection, G–20

Patricia Kennedy Grimsted is a Research Associate of the Ukrainian Research Institute at Harvard University and an Honourary Fellow of the International Institute of Social History in Amsterdam. Trained as a historian (PhD University of California–Berkeley), Dr. Grimsted is a foremost authority on Soviet and Russian archives. She is the author of a series of reference directories of archives in Moscow and Leningrad (1972 and 1976), the Baltic countries and Belorussia (1981), and Ukraine and Moldavia (1988); a handbook for researchers in the USSR (1989); and specialized monographs and other works on archival and historical topics. Together with her Russian colleagues, she compiled and edited the preliminary 1992–1993 English-language directories and the 1997 Russian-language directory that are the foundation for the present work, all prepared from the ArcheoBiblioBase system maintained under the auspices of the Federal Archival Service of Russia (Rosarkhiv) in Moscow.